To Joe
Happy 50th
Love Mom

The Complete Armchair Book of

BASEBALL

The Complete
Armchair Book of
BASEBALL

AN ALL-STAR LINEUP CELEBRATES AMERICA'S NATIONAL PASTIME

Introductions by A. Bartlett Giamatti & Peter V. Ueberroth
Edited by John Thorn
Illustrations by James Stevenson & Bernie Fuchs

GALAHAD BOOKS
NEW YORK

First Galahad Books edition published in 1997.

Galahad Books
A division of BBS Publishing Corporation
386 Park Avenue South
New York, NY 10016

Galahad Books is a registered trademark of BBS Publishing Corporation.

Published by arrangement with Scribner, an imprint of Simon & Schuster, Inc.

Library of Congress Catalog Card Number: 97-73430

ISBN: 1-57866-004-1

Printed in the United States of America.

CONTENTS

THE ARMCHAIR
BOOK OF BASEBALL

Edited by John Thorn
Illustrations by James Stevenson

Foreword by Peter V. Ueberroth

To my parents, Richard and Victoria

CONTENTS

Foreword

The game of baseball, born in a simpler time, has endured social upheavals, quantum technological leaps, geographical expansion, and world wars. It continues to flourish, grow, and maintain its grip on the spirit and hopes of Americans.

It is a game full of paradoxes: as old as the horse and buggy, yet as modern as the Concorde; as slow as a sweltering summer afternoon, yet as swift as a thunderbolt; as simple as a hand-held calculator, yet as complex as calculus.

How has this game managed to bridge time and space? How does one explain America's fascination with its tradition and voluminous statistics? Baseball is a realm of fairness and order where imagery, mysticism, and alchemy in the confines of the baseball diamond tickle the little boy or girl in all of us. Though it appears to be detached from the real world in many respects, it often reflects the best and worst of our society.

Baseball doesn't exist in a vacuum. Some of its darkest days have made the biggest headlines. There was the Black Sox scandal in 1919, the beanball death of Ray Chapman in 1920, the poignant courage of Lou Gehrig, the banning of black athletes for decades, the untimely death of Roberto Clemente, and a myriad of players arrested and suspended for drug-related offenses.

But mainly, baseball is about heroes. Try to convince a diehard fan that the Baby Ruth candy bar was named after Ruth Cleveland, President Grover Cleveland's daughter, and not Babe Ruth. Almost every American—man, woman, or child—has a baseball hero—from Christy Mathewson to Sandy Koufax —depending on the era. In the age of television, who will ever forget Hank Aaron rounding the bases for the seven hundred and fifteenth time or Reggie Jackson shining as Mr. October? Who hasn't counted along with Pete Rose as he closed in on Ty Cobb's all-time record number of hits?

One of the most enjoyable moments I've had in the game came when I brought Mickey Mantle and Willie Mays back to the baseball family. They are two heroes of my generation and it was an honor to welcome them home.

From *Damn Yankees* to *The Natural*, the magic of baseball is elusive and impossible to explain. Perhaps this is one reason that it has captured the hearts of Americans for generations, that the country's greatest writers have turned on their creative juices to try to unlock its secrets. Like a magnet, baseball draws out the imaginations of all it touches.

Here, in *The Armchair Book Of Baseball*, several of our greatest novelists, political writers, poets, satirists, and sports reporters take us around the playing fields and behind the scenes with wonderful stories and anecdotes about America's pastime. They write how baseball is essentially good. As a fan, I admire their abilities and thank them for putting their thoughts on paper for all who care about the sport to share.

But as commissioner of Major League Baseball, I am more than a fan. I am responsible to all the spectators as well as to the players, owners, managers, coaches, and ticket takers for keeping the game vibrant. This isn't always easy. What makes the task easier and ultimately worthwhile is reading recollections, views, and stories such as those that follow.

Whether in a backyard, in an airport, on a train, or in the venerable armchair, reading this book will recreate the passion that makes baseball America's game. This book can be read and enjoyed by both adults and youngsters and passed from one generation to the next—much as the game itself is. It's part of the tradition baseball inspires.

Peter V. Ueberroth
June, 1985

Introduction

Baseball is the writer's game. From the Elysian Fields of Hoboken to the green fields of the mind, the grand old game and the printed word were made for each other. The game's primal team, the 1842 Knickerbockers, were named in tribute to Washington Irving, who as Diedrich Knickerbocker borrowed a folk tale from Europe and molded it into "Rip Van Winkle"—much as America took the English game of rounders and made it over as baseball. (Irving's 1820 story opens with some lines by a fellow named Cartwright; occultists may make of that what they will.) No other sport plays upon the heart and mind so subtly, with so delightful a blend of the simple and the complex—like a magician's stunt or a phrase well-turned. It is a classically beautiful game, its appeal more form than color; yet the color deepens in retrospect, both in the memory and in print, so that thinking about baseball provides a pleasure quite different from that had by watching it.

The way we think about baseball, and the way writers depict it, has changed in the past twenty years or so. Fans are not as fanatic nor writers as florid: the "gee whiz" style pretty much went out with Kilroy, and the hard-boiled, sardonic stance that followed seems now a self-caricature. Rice, Runyon, Gallico, Cannon—these were giants in their day, but in some measure because the general level of baseball writing was so poor: the styles they pioneered were risky, and lesser scriveners trying their hands at it were guilty of some truly wretched excesses. The terrain of recent baseball literature may not display the lofty peaks of the Golden Age, but the overall level is assuredly higher. This phenomenon happens to parallel one that has been observed in baseball (see the discussion in this volume by Stephen Jay Gould).

The Armchair Book of Baseball celebrates the writer's game, principally of the past two decades, a period that began with pundits anointing professional football as the new national pastime and closed with baseball at unprecedented heights of popularity. These years brought significant new events—divisional play, artificial turf, the designated hitter, free agency; new luminaries—Rose, Seaver, Jackson, Schmidt, Steinbrenner; and new trends—statistical analysis, revisionist history, tell-all memoirs. And best of all for the reader, the past two decades have brought an outpouring of good, fresh baseball writing—so much, in fact, that I could more easily have gathered a book three times this size with no diminution of quality.

The general principles of selection were two: to bring together the best writing that, when collected, would present a panoramic view of today's game and how it got to be that way and to include no more than one piece by any writer (otherwise, what reason could there be not to reprint the complete opus of Lee Allen?). An additional consideration was to avoid pieces that had been anthologized elsewhere, notably in Charles Einstein's splendid *Fireside Book of Baseball*, a three-volume series begun in 1956.

I wish to thank artist James Stevenson; Maron Waxman and Marta Goldstein of Scribners; designer Alan Benjamin; and as usual, friend and collaborator David Reuther. For bibliographic help and courtesy beyond the call, I am grateful to Tom Heitz of the National Baseball Library in Cooperstown; a special tip of the cap as well to Myron Smith, whose outstanding bibliography of baseball I was fortunate to examine in manuscript. And for leads to offbeat baseball pieces, my colleagues in the Society for American Baseball Research—principally, Dan Hotaling, Fred Ivor-Campbell, Charlie Owen, and Lyle Spatz; also, Marty Appel, Bob Barnett, Merritt Clifton, Frederick C. Collingnon, Jr., Steven G. Cotton, Bill Felber, Barry Gifford, Tom Granahan, John R. Husman, Jack Kavanagh, Bob Koltermann, Dan Schlossberg, James K. Skipper, Jr., Jim Smith, Ray Welsh.

JOHN THORN
Saugerties, New York

The alliterative title of this first piece plays upon that of a Conan Doyle story, *A Study in Scarlet*, which introduced a certain detective with extraordinary powers of deduction. Appropriate, in that Lee Allen was the Sherlock Holmes of baseball—the finder of lost players, connoisseur of curious facts, debunker of well-entrenched myths, and until his death in 1969 the Historian of the Baseball Hall of Fame. His demographic files and unparalleled knowledge of the game were essential resources in the creation of *The Baseball Encyclopedia*. Besides, he was a writer of warmth and charm, as this chapter from *The Hot Stove League* (1955) attests.

LEE ALLEN

A Study in Suet

During the nation's great depression, when attendance dwindled and even major-league teams faced an uncertain future, life was particularly burdensome for the two clubs in Philadelphia. Shibe Park, the home of the Athletics, and Baker Bowl, the shabby nesting place of the Phillies, were seldom filled to capacity. One dreary afternoon, Dave Driscoll, business manager of the Dodgers, was walking in Philadelphia and chanced to pass Baker Bowl. The Phillies were on the road, but in spite of that a pathetic vendor of peanuts was hawking his wares before an imaginary crowd near the entrance to the bleachers.

"There won't be a crowd here today," Driscoll told him. "Why don't you go to Shibe Park?"

"I've been to Shibe Park," the vendor replied. "There's nobody there either."

It was this situation that helped explain a remark made at the time by Joe McCarthy, the great manager of the Yankees. McCarthy had a pitcher at New York by the name of Walter Brown, a mammoth right-hander. Although possessed of a great number of physical assets, Brown was used sparingly. When he did work, it was usually in Philadelphia against the Athletics.

"Why is it you pitch Brown only in Philadelphia?" McCarthy was asked one day.

"It's the only way I know to fill Shibe Park," Joe quipped.

McCarthy's reasoning was impeccable, for Walter, at 265 pounds, was the heaviest player who had ever appeared on the major-league scene. Strangely, he owed his start to one of the lightest men the game has ever known, Rabbit Maranville. During the season of 1925, Maranville managed the Cubs for about a month, and it was at that time that Brown, a sandlotter who had been pitching around Brockton, Massachusetts, reported to him. Walter was so heavy that he found traveling uncomfortable, but he was to do plenty of it during his career. The trail that began in Chicago led to Sarasota, New Orleans, Cleveland, Omaha, Oklahoma City, New York, Jersey City, Newark, Cincinnati, and New York again before he wound up his career in 1941. He is now the proprietor of a sporting goods store at Freeport, Long Island.

The peculiar thing about Brown's weight was that he put on 68 of his 265 pounds during a single winter. He belonged to Cleveland at the time and weighed only 197 at the close of the 1927 season. But after an operation for the removal of his tonsils, he shot up to 265, and despite working out five hours a day at the YMCA gymnasium, he was never able to shed the excess suet.

But Brown was no clown. He pitched big-league ball for twelve years and won more games than he lost. He was also a particular favorite at Newark, where he won twenty and lost six in 1934 and led the International League in earned-run percentage. Hy Goldberg of the Newark *Evening News* was asked one day what sort of stuff Brown threw. "He throws a fastball, curve, and the biggest shadow in baseball," Goldberg sallied.

Players as fat as Brown usually delight the galleries. When a player can overcome the handicap of excess weight, it is usually because he has other assets that more than make up for his bulk. Cy Young, winner of more games than any pitcher in major-league history, reached his greatest peak of popularity toward the end of his career, when a bulging paunch made it almost impossible for him to field bunts. Ernie Lombardi, who sometimes weighed close to 240, was the most popular performer that Cincinnati ever had.

Bob Fothergill was another of the game's famed fatties who attained a tremendous degree of popularity. A stroke cut him down at the age of thirty-nine in 1938, but he is still recalled with sweet nostalgia in Detroit, where the fans worshipped him and where he simply pulverized the ball from 1922 through 1929.

Waite Hoyt, one of the finest of Yankee pitchers and now a Cincinnati broadcaster, still shudders whenever he thinks about pitching to Fothergill and his mates. "It was awful," Hoyt has frequently said. "The Yankees would go into Detroit for a series in August and find that the entire Tiger outfield would be hitting nearly .400. Ty Cobb and Harry Heilmann were bad enough, but in some ways Fothergill was the most frightening of all. He was murder!"

Fothergill weighed about 235 pounds when he was in shape, but he was surprisingly light on his feet. Once, thinking he had been thrown at by George Earnshaw of the Athletics, he smashed a majestic home run and then climaxed his tour of the bases with a somersault that saw him land on home plate with both feet.

His full name was Robert Roy Fothergill, and he carried a handsome suitcase around the American League that had his initials, R.R.F., in big letters. When asked what they stood for, he would always reply, "For Runs Responsible For."

Fothergill really belonged in a previous age. He was one of the last of those rare spirits who appeared to play for the fun of it, and he seemed able to extract the fullest amount of pleasure from life. After the game, you could find him with a thick porterhouse steak and a seidel of beer, and he would chuckle to himself and mumble out of the side of his mouth, "Imagine getting paid for a life like this!"

Finally, Detroit sold him to the White Sox, but before leaving the team he made fifty-one separate bets with friends that he would get a safe hit the first time up in his new uniform. Several days later all fifty-one received identical telegrams: "Pay up. I singled to left."

Frank (Shanty) Hogan was a catcher whose dietary requirements startled John McGraw, led to frequent finings, and were responsible for some of the game's most repeated stories. Hogan weighed about 240 when in his best form, and it is probable that at certain times he weighed almost as much as Walter Brown. This would be difficult to prove for, unlike Brown and Fothergill, Hogan was reluctant to get on the scales. Chief Bender, the veteran scout of the Athletics, recalls that when he was a coach for the Giants in 1931, Hogan bet four or five players five dollars each that he would weigh 230 or less when the season began, but that when the campaign did start, they could not induce him to settle the argument.

Hogan may have been fat, but he had plenty of courage. One day, after being hit on the jawbone by a fastball from the hand of Guy Bush of the Cubs, he trotted to first base without even rubbing his chin.

Still another leading heavyweight was Garland Buckeye, a big bird from Heron Lake, Minnesota, who had trials with the Senators, Indians, and Giants for a decade starting in 1918. Buckeye was a southpaw pitcher, and his weight was officially listed at 238. He was also a good batter, but was far too portly to be used at any other position. His weight put him on the defensive, and he used to say, "I'm not fat really. Now just feel that leg. You can see I'm just big-boned." Buckeye did his last professional pitching at Milwaukee. One day he attempted to field a bunt, fell on his stomach, and was helped to his feet by two infielders. That was enough to teach him it was time to quit the game. . . .

The first player to quit the game because of being overweight was Ned

Williamson of the Chicago White Stockings, considered the greatest third baseman who ever lived, and a fine shortstop as well, at the time of his death. Williamson was a member of a band of players that toured the world following the season of 1888, and in a game at Paris, France, he was injured in a strange manner, cutting his knee on a rock that lay on the field while sliding into third. The enforced idleness following his injury caused him to gain an enormous amount of weight, and he was never able to regain his old form, abandoning the game after the season of 1890. He then became a victim of dropsy and died at Hot Springs, Arkansas, where he had gone for treatment, March 3, 1894.

When Babe Ruth started spraying home runs around American League lawns in 1919 and finished with twenty-nine for the season, writers were hard put to discover whose record he had surpassed. At first it was believed that John (Buck) Freeman of Washington had set the mark at twenty-five in 1899, but then Ernest J. Lanigan, one of the game's foremost authorities, made it known that Williamson had hit twenty-seven for the White Stockings in 1884.

Actually, Williamson's home run record is somewhat tainted. Prior to 1884, all fair balls hit over the short fences at Chicago were ruled two-base hits. The rule was changed that winter, and the result was something of a joke. The 1884 National League schedule called for only fifty-six contests in each park, and the White Stockings connected for 131 home runs in their home games and their opponents for sixty-one more. When Williamson socked three over the beckoning barrier in right in the second game on Decoration Day, he became the first major leaguer to account for that many in the same game. Of his twenty-seven homers, only two were smashed out on the road, both at Buffalo.

Williamson and Ruth were alike in many ways. Ned was childless but, like Ruth, genuinely devoted to children. He always carried candy and pennies for them, and when his funeral was held at his home in Chicago, the house was jammed with hundreds of urchins who looked as if their hearts would break.

Players who have attracted attention because they were underweight have been much more rare than those who had to struggle to get the pounds off. One of the first was Frederick (Bones) Ely, a shortstop who lasted from 1884 to 1902. Ely's nickname is self-explanatory, and when he batted he presented such a delicate picture that fans were afraid a pitched ball might splinter him.

Most of the extremely light players attained prominence in the nineteenth century. William (Candy) Cummings, now immortalized at Cooperstown because he is believed to have discovered the curveball, actually weighed only 120 in his prime. Dave Birdsall, with Boston of the old National Association, was the lightest catcher at 126 pounds. Bobby Mitchell, who became the major leagues' first southpaw when he joined Cincinnati in 1877, weighed in at 135.

Mitchell's catcher, George Miller, weighed only 150, and when they joined the Reds from a team at Springfield, Ohio, that year, they were known as the Pony Battery.

Bill Veeck's midget, Eddie Gaedel, of course, was the lightest player of all time. It seems unlikely that any professional of the future will weigh less than his 65 pounds.

There are other physical characteristics, aside from weight, that have made certain players stand out. Slowness of foot, small feet, bowleggedness, baldness, and the wearing of glasses or mustache have often marked players for ridicule.

The smallest feet in major-league history were the property of Art Herring, a pitcher who spent most of his career with the Tigers and Dodgers. He wore a size three shoe. Myril Hoag, an outfielder with the Yankees, also had a peculiar pair of feet, wearing a size four shoe on one tootsy and a four and one-half on the other.

Lave Cross, a catcher and third baseman who played in the majors for twenty-one years, mostly with the Philadelphia teams, was the most bowlegged player of all time, although, in this department Honus Wagner was not far behind.

Most players of today do not affect mustaches, and when they do, they wear trim, businesslike ones. The last mustache of the handlebar variety adorned the lip of Silent John Titus, outfielder of the Phillies from 1903 to 1912. After returning to his home at St. Clair, Pennsylvania, as a young man following the Spanish–American War, Titus grew his mustache, along with friends who were members of the St. Clair Athletic Club, as a group project. When he joined the Phillies, he retained it, and it made him recognizable on the field in the days when players were not numbered.

Titus also invariably draped a toothpick in his mouth, both at bat and in the field, claiming it kept chewing tobacco off his teeth. Rival pitchers always tried to knock it out of his mouth, but none succeeded, although Albert (Lefty) Leifield of the Pirates came closest, knocking off his cap one day. Titus always kept the toothpick at the side of his mouth until he decided to take a swing at the ball, and then he moved it in toward the center. Pitchers eventually discovered this mannerism and forced him to hit at bad pitches whenever they saw the toothpick change position, and began to whittle down his batting average.

Full beards, of course, have disappeared from American faces, and except on the chins of eccentrics have not been seen for years. In his excellent book, *Lost Men of American History*, Stewart Holbrook has traced the history of beards and mustaches in the United States, pointing out that not a single signer of the Declaration of Independence wore one, but that they came into favor about 1860. In baseball, there was an old belief that hair on the face was an aid to eyesight, and though players were ashamed to wear glasses, they raised mustaches instead. The last player in the majors to wear a full beard on the field was Jack Remsen, an outfielder with Brooklyn who last played in 1884. Clark Griffith, owner of the Washington Senators, signed a bearded pitcher, Allen Benson, in 1934, but that was mostly a stunt, and Benson, a House of David alumnus, disappeared after working in only two games.

Bald players have long been grateful for the custom of wearing caps. Tony Rensa, a catcher with the Tigers and Phillies in 1930, was so sensitive about his bald pate that he fastened his cap to his head with great wads of chewing gum. Every time he threw off his mask to chase a high foul, his cap remained on his head, and he was spared the indignity of titters from the crowd.

Jimmy Ring, who pitched for the Phillies when Art Fletcher managed the team, always refused to work in the opening game of the season, and Fletcher believed it was because he would have to bare his head when "The Star-Spangled Banner" was played. It seems that early in his career Ring was warming up to pitch an opener when the band began to blare, and there was nothing for him to do but expose his head of skin. Fletcher claimed that he found the remarks from the stands so embarrassing that he vowed never again to pitch an opening game. Fortunately for Jimmy, he did his pitching in the days before World War II. Since that time, the national anthem has been standard procedure at most parks, not only for the opener but every day.

By general consent the *New Yorker* essayist is in a league all his own, having retired the trophy with his third winning collection of writings on baseball: *Late Innings*, in which this splendid piece appears. The time is May 1981, the battleground is Yale Field, and the antagonist lancers are Ron Darling of the Elis and Frank Viola of St. John's; the chorus features the author and Joe Wood, ninety-one years old. In 1912, known as Smokey Joe, Wood had gone 34–5 for the Red Sox, with three more wins in the World Series—including the finale, over Christy Mathewson in extra innings. History may be a seamless web, in Bruce Catton's phrase, but on this day the juncture of past, present, and future was inspiringly clear.

ROGER ANGELL

The Web of the Game

JUNE 1981

An afternoon in mid-May, and we are waiting for the game to begin. We are in shadow, and the sunlit field before us is a thick, springy green—an old diamond, beautifully kept up. The grass continues beyond the low chain-link fence that encloses the outfield, extending itself on the right-field side into a rougher, featureless sward that terminates in a low line of distant trees, still showing a pale, early-summer green. We are almost in the country. Our seats are in the seventh row of the grandstand, on the home side of the diamond, about halfway between third base and home plate. The seats themselves are more comforting to spirit than to body, being a surviving variant example of the pure late-Doric Polo Grounds mode: the backs made of a continuous running row of wood slats, divided off by pairs of narrow cast-iron arms, within which are slatted let-down seats, grown arthritic with rust and countless layers of gray paint. The rows are stacked so closely upon each other (one discovers) that a happening on the field of sufficient interest to warrant a rise or half-rise to one's feet is often made more memorable by a sharp crack to the kneecaps delivered by the backs of the seats just forward; in time, one finds that a dandruff of gray paint flakes from the same source has fallen on one's lap and scorecard. None of this matters, for this view and these stands and this park—it is Yale Field, in New Haven—are renowned for their felicity. The grandstand is a low, penumbrous steel-post shed that holds the infield in a pleasant horseshoe-curved embrace. The back wall of the grandstand, behind the uppermost row of seats, is broken by an arcade of open arches, admitting a soft back light that silhouettes the upper audience and also discloses an overhead bonework of struts and beams supporting the roof—the pigeonland of all the ballparks of our youth. The game we are waiting for—Yale vs. St. John's University—is a considerable event, for it is part of the National Collegiate Athletic Association's Northeast regional tournament, the winner of which will qualify for a berth at the national collegiate championships in Omaha in June, the World Series of college baseball. Another pair of teams, Maine and Central Michigan—the Black Bears and the Chippewas—have just finished their game here, the first of a doubleheader. Maine won it, 10–2, but the ultimate winner will not be picked here for three more days, when the four teams will have completed a difficult double-elimination tournament. Good, hard competition, but the stands at Yale Field are half empty today. Call them half full, because everyone on hand—some twenty-five hundred fans—must know something about the quality of the teams here, or at least enough to qualify either as a partisan or as an expert, which would explain the hum of talk and expectation that runs through the grandstand even while the Yale team, in pinstriped home whites, is still taking infield practice.

I am seated in a little sector of senior New Haven men—Townies rather than Old Elis. One of them a couple of rows in front of me says, "They used to fill this place in the old days, before there was all the baseball on TV."

His neighbor, a small man in a tweed cap, says, "The biggest crowd I ever saw in here—the biggest ever, I bet—was for a high-school game. Shelton and Naugatuck, about twenty years ago."

An old gent with a cane, seated just to my left, says, "They filled it up that day the Yankees came here, with Ruth and Gehrig and the rest of them. An exhibition game."

A fan just beyond the old gentleman—a good-looking man in his sixties, with an open, friendly face, a large smile, and a thick stand of gray hair—leans toward my neighbor and says, "When *was* that game, Joe? 1930? 1932?"

"Oh, I can't remember," the old man says. "Somewhere in there. My youngest son was mascot for the Yankees that day, so I could figure it out, I suppose." He is not much interested. His eyes are on the field. "Say, look at these fellows throw!" he says. "Did you see that outfielder peg in the ball?"

"That was the day Babe Ruth said this was about the best-looking ballpark he'd ever ever seen," the man beyond says. "You remember that."

"I can remember long before this park was built," the old man says. "It was already the Yale ballfield when I got here, but they put in these stands later—Who is this shortstop? He's a hefty-looking bird."

"How many Yale games do you think you've seen, Joe?" the smiling man asks.

"Oh, I couldn't begin to count them. But I haven't seen a Yale team play in—I don't know how long. Not for years. These fellows today, they play in the Cape Cod League in the summers. They let the freshmen play here now, too. They recruit them more, I suppose. They're athletes—you can see that."

The Yale team finishes its warm-up ritual, and St. John's—light-gray uniforms with scarlet cap bills and scarlet socks—replaces it on the field.

"St. John's has always had a good club," the old man tells me. "Even back when my sons were playing ball, it was a good ball team. But not as good as this one. Oh, my! Did you see this catcher throw down to second? Did you see that! I bet you in all the years I was here I didn't have twenty fellows who could throw."

"Your sons played here?" I ask him. "For Yale?"

"My son Joe was captain in '41," he says. "He was a pitcher. He pitched against my son Steve here one day. Steve was pitching for Colgate, and my other son, Bob—my youngest—was on the same Colgate team. A good little left-handed first baseman."

I am about to ask how that game turned out, but the old man has taken out a small gold pocket watch, with a hunting case, which he snaps open. Three-fourteen. "Can't they get this *started*?" he says impatiently.

I say something admiring about the watch, and he hands it to me carefully. "I've had that watch for sixty-eight years," he says. "I always carried it in my vest pocket, back when we wore vests."

The little watch has a considerable heft to it: a weight of authority. I turn it over and find an inscription on the back. It is in script and a bit worn, but I can still make it out:

PRESENTED TO JOE WOOD
BY HIS FRIEND A. E. SMITH
IN APPRECIATION OF HIS SPLENDID
PITCHING WHICH BROUGHT THE
WORLD'S CHAMPIONSHIP
TO BOSTON IN 1912.

"Who was A. E. Smith, Mr. Wood?" I ask.
"He was a manufacturer."
I know the rest. Joe Wood, the old gentleman on my left, was the baseball

coach at Yale for twenty years—from 1923 to 1942. Before that, he was a sometime outfielder for the Cleveland Indians, who batted .366 in 1921. Before *that*, he was a celebrated right-handed pitcher for the Boston Red Sox—Smokey Joe Wood, who won thirty-four games for the Bosox in 1912, when he finished up with a record of 34–5, pitching ten shutouts and sixteen consecutive victories along the way. In the World Series that fall—one of the two or three finest ever played—he won three of the four games he pitched, including the famous finale: the game of Hooper's catch and Snodgrass's muff and Tris Speaker's killing tenth-inning single. Next to Walter Johnson, Smokey Joe Wood was the most famous fastballer of his era. Still is, no doubt, in the minds of the few surviving fans who saw him at his best. He is ninety-one years old.

None of this, I should explain—neither my presence at the game nor my companions in the stands—was an accident. I had been a fervent admirer of Smokey Joe Wood ever since I read his account of his baseball beginnings and his subsequent career in Lawrence Ritter's *The Glory of Their Times*, a cherished, classic volume of oral history of the early days of the pastime. Mr. Wood was in his seventies when that book was published, in 1966, and I was startled and pleased a few weeks ago when I ran across an article by Joan Whaley, in *Baseball Digest*, which informed me that he was still hale and still talking baseball in stimulating fashion. He was living with a married daughter in New Haven, and my first impulse was to jump in my car and drive up to press a call. But something held me back; it did not seem quite right to present myself uninvited at his door, even as a pilgrim. Then Ron Darling and Frank Viola gave me my chance. Darling, who was a junior at Yale this past year, is the best pitcher ever to take the mound for the Blue. He is better than Johnny Broaca, who went on to pitch for the Yankees and the Indians for five seasons in the mid-1930s; he is better than Frank Quinn, who compiled a 1.57 career earned-run average at Yale in 1946, '47, and '48. (He is also a better all-around ballplayer than George Bush, who played first base and captained the Elis in 1948, and then somehow drifted off into politics instead of baseball.) Darling, a right-handed fastball thrower, won eleven games and lost two as a sophomore, with an earned-run average of 1.31, and this year he was 9–3 and 2.42, with eighty-nine strikeouts in his ninety-three innings of work—the finest college pitcher in the Northeast, according to major-league scouts, with the possible exception of Frank Viola, a junior left-handed curveball ace at St. John's, who was undefeated this year, 9–0, and had a neat earned-run average of 1.00. St. John's, a Catholic university in Queens, is almost a baseball powerhouse—not quite in the same class, perhaps, as such perennial national champions or challengers as Arizona, Arizona State, Texas, and Southern California, whose teams play Sun Belt schedules of close to sixty games, but good enough to have gone as the Northeast's representative to the national tournament in

Omaha in 1980, where Viola defeated the eventual winner, Arizona, in the first round. St. John's, by the way, does not recruit high-school stars from faraway states, as do most of these rival college powers; all but one player on this year's thirty-three-man Redmen squad grew up and went to school in New York City or in nearby suburbs. This 1981 St. John's team ran off an awesome 31–2 record, capturing the Eastern College Metro (Greater New York, that is) elimination, while Yale, winning its last nine games in a row, concluded its regular season with a record of 24–12–1, which was good enough to win its first Eastern Intercollegiate League championship since 1956. (That tie in Yale's record was a game against the University of Central Florida, played during the Elis' spring-training tour in March, and was called because of darkness after seven innings, with the score tied at 21–21. Darling did not pitch that day.) The two teams, along with Central Michigan (Mid-America Conference) and Maine (New England Conference), qualified for the tournament at New Haven, and the luck of the draw pitted Yale (and Darling) against St. John's (and Viola) in the second game of the opening doubleheader. Perfect. Darling, by the way, had indicated that he might be willing to turn professional this summer if he were to be picked in an early round of the annual amateur draft conducted by the major leagues in mid-June, and Viola had been talked about as a potential big-leaguer ever since his freshman year, so their matchup suddenly became an obligatory reunion for every front-rank baseball scout east of the Ohio River. (About fifty of them turned up, with their speed-guns and clipboards, and their glowing reports of the game, I learned later, altered the draft priorities of several clubs.)

Perfect, but who would get in touch with Mr. Wood and persuade him to come out to Yale Field with me for the game? Why, Dick Lee would—Dick Lee, *of course.* Richard C. Lee (he was the smiling man sitting just beyond Smokey Joe in our row) is a former Democratic mayor of New Haven, an extremely popular (eight consecutive terms, sixteen years in office), innovative officeholder who, among other things, presided over the widely admired urban renewal of his city during the 1960s and, before that, thought up and pushed through the first Operation Head Start program (for minority-group preschoolers) in the country. Dick Lee knows everybody in New Haven, including Smokey Joe Wood and several friends of mine there, one of whom provided me with his telephone number. I called Lee at his office (he is assistant to the chairman of the Union Trust Company, in New Haven) and proposed our party. "Wonderful!" he cried at once. "You have come to the right man. I'll bring Joe. Count on me!" Even over the telephone, I could see him smiling.

Dick Lee did not play baseball for Yale, but the nature of his partisanship became clear in the very early moments of the Yale–St. John's game. "Yay!" he shouted in a stentorian baritone as Ron Darling set down three St. John's batters in order in the first. "Yay, Ron *baby*!" he boomed out as Darling dismissed three more batters in the second, fanning the last two. "Now *c'mon*, Yale! Let's get something started, gang! Yay!" Lee had told me that he pitched for some lesser-known New Haven teams—the Dixwell Community House sandlot team and the Jewish Home for Children nine (the Utopians), among others—while he was growing up in the ivyless Newhallville neighborhood. Some years later, having passed up college altogether, he went to work for Yale as its public-relations officer. By the time he became mayor, in 1953, the university was his own—another precinct to be worried about and looked after. A born politician, he appears to draw on some inner deep-water reservoir of concern that enables him to preside effortlessly and affectionately over each encounter of his day; he was the host at our game, and at intervals he primed Joe Wood with questions about his baseball past, which he seemed to know almost by heart.

"Yes, that's right, I did play for the Bloomer Girls a few games," Mr. Wood said in response to one such cue. "I was about sixteen, and I was pitching for our town team in Ness City, Kansas. The Bloomer Girls were a barnstorming team, but they used to pick up a few young local fellows on the sly to play along with them if they needed to fill out their lineup. I was one of those. I never wore a wig, though—I wouldn't have done that. I guess I looked young enough to pass for a girl anyway. Bill Stern, the old radio broadcaster, must have used that story about forty times, but he always got it wrong about the wig."

There was a yell around us, and an instantly ensuing groan, as Yale's big freshman catcher, Tony Paterno, leading off the bottom of the second, lined sharply to the St. John's shortstop, who made a fine play on the ball. Joe Wood peered intently out at the field through his thickish horn-rimmed spectacles. He shook his head a little. "You know, I can't hardly follow the damned ball now," he said. "It's better for me if I'm someplace where I can get up high behind the plate. I was up to Fenway Park for two games last year, and they let me sit in the press box there at that beautiful park. I could see it all from there. The grounds keeper has got that field just like a living room."

I asked him if he still rooted for the Red Sox.

"Oh, yes," he said. "All my life. A couple of years ago, when they had that big lead in the middle of the summer, they asked me if I'd come up and throw out the first ball at one of their World Series games or playoff games. But then they dropped out of it, of course. Now it looks like it'll never happen."

He spoke in a quiet, almost measured tone, but there was no tinge of disappointment or self-pity in it. It was the voice of age. He was wearing a blue windbreaker over a buttoned-up plaid shirt, made formal with a small dark-red bow tie. There was a brown straw hat on his bald head. The years had imparted a delicate thinness to the skin on his cheeks and neck, but his face had a determined look to it, with a strong chin and a broad, unsmiling mouth. Watching him, I recalled one of the pictures in *The Glory of Their Times*—a team photograph taken in 1906, in which he is sitting cross-legged down in front of a row of men in baggy baseball pants and lace-up, collared baseball shirts with "NESS CITY" across the front in block letters. The men are standing in attitudes of cheerful assurance with their arms folded, and their mushy little baseball gloves are hanging from their belts. Joe Wood, the smallest player in the picture, is wearing a dark warm-up shirt, with the sleeves rolled halfway up his forearms, and his striped baseball cap is pushed back a little, revealing a part in the middle of his hair. There is an intent, unsmiling look on his boyish face—the same grave demeanor you can spot in a subsequent photograph, taken in 1912, in which he is standing beside his Red Sox manager, Jake Stahl, and wearing a heavy woollen three-button suit, a stiff collar, a narrow necktie with a stickpin, and a stylish black porkpie hat pulled low over his handsome, famous face: Smokey Joe Wood at twenty-two. (The moniker, by the way, was given him by Paul Shannon, a sportswriter for the Boston *Post*; before that, he was sometimes called Ozone Wood—"ozone" for the air cleaved by the hapless batters who faced him.) The young man in the photographs and the old man beside me at the ballpark had the same broad, sloping shoulders, but there was nothing burly or physically imposing about him then or now.

"What kind of a pitcher were you, Mr. Wood?" I asked him.

"I had a curve and a fastball," he said. "That's all. I didn't even have brains enough to slow up on the batters. The fastball had a hop on it. You had to be *fast* to have that happen to the ball."

I said that I vividly recalled Sandy Koufax's fastball, which sometimes seemed to jump so violently as it crossed the plate that his catcher had to shoot up his mitt to intercept it.

"Mine didn't go up that far. Just enough for them to miss it." He half turned to me as he said this, and gave me a little glance and an infinitesimal smile. A twinkle. "I don't know where my speed came from," he went on. "I wasn't any bigger or stronger-looking then than I am now. I always could throw hard, and once I saw I was able to get batters out, I figured I was crazy enough to play ball for a living. My father was a criminal lawyer in Kansas, and before that out in Ouray, Colorado, where I first played ball, and my brother went to law school and got a degree, but I didn't even graduate from high school. I ate and slept baseball all my life.''

The flow of recollection from Joe Wood was perhaps not as smooth and rivery as I have suggested here. For one thing, he spoke slowly and with care—not unlike the way he walked to the grandstand at Yale Field from the parking lot beyond left field, making his way along the grass firmly enough but looking where he was going, too, and helping himself a bit with his cane. Nothing infirm about him, but nothing hurrying or sprightly, either. For another, the game was well in progress by now, and its principals and sudden events kept interrupting our colloquy. Ron Darling, a poised, impressive figure on the mound, alternated his popping fastballs with just enough down-breaking sliders and an occasional curveball to keep the St. John's batters unhappy. Everything was thrown with heat—his strikeout pitch is a Seaver-high fastball, but his slider, which slides at the last possible instant, is an even deadlier weapon—but without any signs of strain or anxiety. He threw over the top, smoothly driving his front (left) shoulder at the batter in picture-book style, and by the third or fourth inning he had imposed his will and his pace on the game. He was rolling. He is a dark-haired, olive-skinned young man (he lives in Millbury, Massachusetts, near Worcester, but he was born in Hawaii; his mother is Chinese–Hawaiian by birth) with long, powerful legs, but his pitcherlike proportions tend to conceal, rather than emphasize, his 6 feet 2 inches and 195 pounds. He also swings the bat well enough (.331 this year) to play right field for Yale when he isn't pitching; in our game he was the designated hitter as well as the pitcher for the Elis.

"That's a nice build for a pitcher, isn't it?" Joe Wood murmured during the St. John's fifth. Almost as he spoke, Darling executed a twisting dive to his right to snaffle a hard-hit grounder up the middle by Brian Miller, the St. John's shortstop, and threw him out at first. (Hey-*hey*!" Dick Lee cried. "Yay, Ronnie!") "*And* he's an athlete out there," Wood added. "The scouts like that, you know. Oh, this fellow's a lot better than Broaca ever was."

Frank Viola, for his part, was as imperturbable as Darling on the mound, if not quite as awesome. A lanky, sharp-shouldered lefty, he threw an assortment of speeds and spins, mostly sinkers and down-darting sliders, that had the Yale batters swinging from their shoe tops and, for the most part, hammering the ball into the dirt. He had the stuff and poise of a veteran relief pitcher, and the St. John's infield—especially Brian Miller and a stubby, ebullient second baseman named Steve Scafa—performed behind him with the swift, almost haughty confidence that imparts an elegance and calm and sense of ease to baseball at its best. It was a scoreless game after five, and a beauty.

"What was the score of that game you beat Walter Johnson in, in your big year?" Dick Lee asked our guest between innings.

We all knew the answer, I think. In September of 1912, Walter Johnson came to Fenway Park (it was brand-new that year) with the Senators and pitched against young Joe Wood, who then had a string of thirteen consecutive victories to his credit. That summer, Johnson had established a league record of sixteen straight wins, so the matchup was not merely an overflow, sellout affair but perhaps the most anticipated, most discussed nonchampionship game in the American League up to that time.

"We won it, 1–0," Joe Wood said quietly, "but it wasn't his fault I beat him that day. If he'd had the team behind him that I did, he'd have set every kind of record in baseball. You have to remember that Walter Johnson played for a second-division team almost all through his career. All those years, and he had to work from the bottom every time he pitched."

"Were you faster than he was?" I asked.

"Oh, I don't think there was ever anybody faster than Walter," he murmured.

"But Johnson said just the opposite!" Dick Lee cried. "He said no one was faster than *you*."

"He was just that kind of fellow, to say something like that," Wood said. "That was just like the man. Walter Johnson was a great big sort of a pitcher, with hands that came clear down to his knees. Why, the way he threw the ball, the only reason anybody ever got even a foul off him was because everybody in the league knew he'd never come inside to a batter. Walter Johnson was a prince of men—a gentleman first, last, and always."

It came to me that this was the first time I had ever heard anybody use the phrase "a prince of men" in a nonsatiric fashion. In any case, the Johnson–Wood argument did not really need settling, then or now. Smokey Joe went on to tie Johnson with sixteen straight victories that season—an American League record, subsequently tied by Lefty Grove and Schoolboy Rowe. (Over in the National League that year, Rube Marquard won *nineteen* straight for the Giants—a single-season mark first set by Tim Keefe of the Giants in 1888 and untouched as yet by anyone else.) Johnson and Wood pretty well divided up the A.L. mound honors that summer, when Johnson won thirty-two games and lost twelve, posting the best earned-run average (1.39) and the most strike-outs (303), while Wood won the most games and established the best winning percentage with his 34–5 mark (not including his three World Series wins, of course).

These last figures are firmly emplaced in the baseball crannies of my mind, and in the minds of most students of the game, because, it turned out, they represent the autumn of Joe Wood's pitching career as well as its first full flowering. Early in the spring of 1913, he was injured in a fielding play, and he was never near to being the same pitcher again. One of the game's sad speculations over the years has been what Joe Wood's status in the pantheon of great pitchers would be if he had remained sound. I did not need any reminder of his accident, but I had been given one just the same when Dick Lee introduced me to him, shortly before the game. We had stopped to pick up Mr. Wood at his small, red-shuttered white house on Marvel Road, and when he came down the concrete path to join us I got out of Lee's Cadillac to shake the hand that once shook the baseball world.

"Mr. Wood," I said, "this is a great honor."

"Ow—*ow!*" he cried, cringing before me and attempting to extricate his paw.

"Oh, oh . . . I'm *terribly* sorry," I said, appalled. "Is it—is this because of your fall off the roof?" Three years ago, at the age of eighty-eight, he had fallen off a ladder while investigating a leak, and had cracked several ribs.

"Hell, no!" he said indignantly. "This is the arm I threw out in 1913!"

I felt awful. I had touched history—and almost brought it to its knees.

Now, at the game, he told me how it all happened. "I can't remember now if it was on the road or at Fenway Park," he said. "Anyway, it was against Detroit. There was a swinging bunt down the line, and I went to field it and slipped on the wet grass and went down and landed on my hand. I broke it right here." He pointed to a spot just below his wrist, on the back of his freckled, slightly gnarled right hand. "It's what they call a subperiosteal fracture. They put it in a cast, and I had to sit out a while. Well, this was in 1913, right after we'd won the championship, and every team was out to get us, of course. So as soon as the cast came off, the manager would come up to me every now and then and want to know how soon I was going to get back to pitching. Well, maybe I got back to it too soon and maybe I didn't, but the arm never felt right again. The shoulder went bad. I still went on pitching, but the fastball had lost that hop. I never threw a day after that when I wasn't in pain. Most of the time, I'd pitch and then it would hurt so bad that I wasn't able to raise my hand again for days afterward. So I was about a halftime pitcher after that. You have to understand that in those days if you didn't work you didn't get paid. Now they lay out as long as they need to and get a shot of that cortisone. But we had to play, ready or not. I was a married man, just starting a family, and in order to get my check I had to be in there. So I pitched."

He pitched less, but not much less well. In 1915, he was 15–5 for the Red Sox, with an earned-run average of 1.49, which was the best in the league. But the pain was so persistent that he sat out the entire 1916 season, on his farm, near Shohola, Pennsylvania, hoping that the rest would restore his arm. It did not. He pitched in eight more games after that—all of them for the Cleveland Indians, to whom he was sold in 1917—but he never won again.

"Did you become a different kind of pitcher after you hurt your arm?" I asked. "More off-speed stuff, I mean?"

"No, I still pitched the fastball."

"But all that pain—"

"I tried not to think about that." He gave me the same small smile and bright glance. "I just loved to be out there," he said. "It was as simple as that."

Our afternoon slid by in a distraction of baseball and memory, and I almost felt myself at some dreamlike doubleheader involving the then and the now— the semi-anonymous strong young men waging their close, marvelous game on the sunlit green field before us while bygone players and heroes of baseball history—long gone now, most of them—replayed their vivid, famous innings for me in the words and recollections of my companion. Yale kept putting men aboard against Viola and failing to move them along; Rich Diana, the husky center fielder (he is also an All-Ivy League halfback), whacked a long double to left but then died on second—the sixth stranded Eli base runner in five innings. Darling appeared to be struggling a little, walking two successive batters in the sixth, but he saved himself with a whirling pickoff to second base—a timed play brilliantly completed by his shortstop, Bob Brooke—and then struck out St. John's big first baseman, Karl Komyathy, for the last out. St. John's had yet to manage a hit against him.

In the home half of the sixth, Yale put its leadoff batter aboard with a single but could not bunt him along. Joe Wood was distressed. "I could teach these fellows to bunt in one minute," he said. "Nobody can't hardly bunt anymore. You've got to get your weight more forward than he did, so you're not reaching for the ball. And he should have his right hand higher up on the bat."

The inning ended, and we reversed directions once again. "Ty Cobb was the greatest bat-handler you ever saw," Wood said. "He used to go out to the ballpark early in the morning with a pitcher and work on hitting the ball to all fields, over and over. He batted that strange way, with his fists apart, you know, but he could have hit just as well no matter how he held it. He just knew what to do with a bat in hand. And base running—why, I saw him get on base and steal second, steal third, and then steal home. *The* best. A lot of fellows in my time shortened up on the bat when they had to—that's what the St. John's boys should try against this good pitcher. Next to Cobb, Shoeless Joe Jackson was the best left-handed hitter I ever saw, and he was always down at the end of the bat until there were two strikes on him. Then he'd shorten up a little, to give himself a better chance."

Dick Lee said, "That's what you've been telling Charlie Polka, isn't it, Joe?"

"Yes, sir, and it's helped him," Wood said. "He's tried it, and now he knows that all you have to do is make contact and the ball will fly a long way."

Both men saw my look of bewilderment, and they laughed together.

"Charlie Polka is a Litte League player," Dick Lee explained. "He's about eleven years old."

"He lives right across the street from me," Wood said. "He plays for the 500 Blake team—that's named for a restaurant here in town. I've got him shortened up on the bat, and now he's a hitter. Charlie Polka is a natural."

"Is that how you batted?" I asked.

"Not at first," he said. "But after I went over to Cleveland in 1917 to join my old roommate, Tris Speaker, I started to play the outfield, and I began to take up on the bat, because I knew I'd have to hit a little better if I was going to make the team. I never was any wonder at the plate, but I was good enough to last six more years, playing with Spoke."

Tris Speaker (Wood had called him by his old nickname, Spoke) was the Joe DiMaggio or Willie Mays of the first two decades of this century—the nonpareil center fielder of his day. "He had a beautiful left-handed arm," Joe Wood said. "He always played very shallow in center—you could do that in those days, because of the dead ball. I saw him make a lot of plays to second base from there—pick up what looked like a clean single and fire the ball to second in time to force the base runner coming down from first. Or he could throw the ball behind a runner and pick him off that way. And just as fine a man as he was a ballplayer. He was a Southern gentleman—well, he was from Hubbard, Texas. Back in the early days, when we were living together on the beach at Winthrop during the season, out beyond Revere, Spoke would sometimes cook up a mess of fried chicken in the evening. He'd cook, and then I'd do the dishes."

Listening to this, I sensed the web of baseball about me. Tris Speaker had driven in the tying run in the tenth inning of the last game of the 1912 World Series, at Fenway Park, after Fred Merkle and Chief Meyers, of the Giants, had let his easy foul pop fall untouched between them. A moment or two later, Joe Wood had won his third game of the Series and the Red Sox were champions. My father saw that game—he was at Harvard Law School at the time, and got a ticket somehow—and he told me about it many times. He was terrifically excited to be there, but I think my mother must have relished the famous victory even more. She grew up in Boston and was a true Red Sox fan, even though young women didn't go to many games then. My father grew up in Cleveland, so he was an Indians rooter, of course. In 1915, my parents got married and went to live in Cleveland, where my father began to practice law. Tris Speaker was traded to the Indians in 1916—a terrible shock to Red Sox fans—and Joe Wood came out of his brief retirement to join him on the club a year later. My parents' first child, my older sister, was born in Cleveland late in 1916, and the next year my father went off to Europe—off to the war. My mother once told me that in the summer afternoons of 1917 she would often push a baby carriage past League Park, the Indians' home field, out on Linwood Avenue, which was a block or two away from my parents' house. Sometimes there was a game going on, and if she heard a roar of pleasure from the fans inside she would tell herself that probably Tris Speaker had just done something special. She was lonely in Cleveland, she told me, and it made her feel good to know that Tris Speaker was there in the same town with her. "Tris Speaker and I were traded to Cleveland in the same year," she said.

A yell and an explosion of cheering brought me back to Yale Field. We were in the top of the seventh, and the Yale second baseman and captain, Gerry Harrington, had just leaped high to snatch down a burning line drive—the force of it almost knocked him over backward in midair. Then he flipped the ball to second to double off a St. John's base runner and end the inning. "These fellows came to *play*!" Dick Lee said.

Most no-hitters produce at least one such heaven-sent gift somewhere along the line, and I began to believe that Ron Darling, who was still untouched on the mound, might be pitching the game of his young life. I turned to ask Mr. Wood how many no-hitters he recalled—he had seen Mathewson and Marquard and Babe Ruth (Ruth, the pitcher, that is) and Coveleski and the rest of them, after all—but he seemed transfixed by something on the field. "Look at *that*!" he said, in a harsh, disbelieving way. "This Yale coach has his own coaches out there on the lines, by God! They're professionals—not just players, the way I always had it when I was here. The coach has his own coaches . . . I never knew that."

"Did you have special coaches when you were coming up with the Red Sox?" I said, hoping to change his mood. "A pitching coach, I mean, or a batting coach?"

He didn't catch the question, and I repeated it.

"No, no," he said, a little impatiently. "We talked about the other players and the pitchers among ourselves in those days. We players. We didn't need anybody to help us."

He was staring straight ahead at the field. I thought he looked a bit chilly. It was well past five o'clock now, and a skim of clouds had covered the sun.

Dick Lee stole a glance at him, too. "Hey, Joe, doesn't this Darling remind you a little of Carl Hubbell on the mound?" he said in a cheerful, distracting sort of voice. "The way he picks up his front leg, I mean. You remember how Hubbell would go way up on the stretch and then drop his hands down by his ankles before he threw the ball?"

"Hubbell?" Joe Wood said. He shook his head, making an effort. "Well, to me this pitcher's a little like that fellow Eckersley," he said slowly. "The way he moves forward there."

He was right. Ron Darling had exactly the same float and glide that the Red Sox' Dennis Eckersley conveys when he is pitching well.

"How do today's players compare with the men you played with, Mr. Wood?" I asked.

"I'd rather not answer that question," he said. He had taken out his watch again. He studied it and then tucked it away carefully, and then he glanced over at me, perhaps wondering if he had been impolite. "That Pete Rose plays hard," he added. "Him and a few more. I don't *like* Pete Rose, exactly, but he looks like he plays the game the way we did. He'd play for the fun of it if he had to."

He resumed his study of the field, and now and then I saw him stare again at the heavyset Yale third-base coach on our side of the diamond. Scoreless games make for a long day at the ballpark, and Joe Wood's day had probably been longer than ours. More than once, I had seen him struggle to his feet to catch some exciting play or moment on the field, only to have it end before he was quite up. Then he would sit down again, leaning on his cane while he lowered himself. I had more questions for Mr. Wood, but now I tried to put them out of my mind. Earlier in the afternoon, he had remarked that several old Yale players had dropped in at his house before the game to say hello and to talk about the old days. "People come by and see me all the time," he had said. "People I don't even know, from as far away as Colorado. Why, I had a fellow come in all the way from Canada the other day, who just wanted to talk about the old days. They all want that, somehow. It's gone on too long."

It had gone on for him, I realized, for as long as most lifetimes. He had played ball for fourteen years, all told, and people had been asking him to talk about it for nearly sixty years. For him, the last juice and sweetness must have been squeezed out of these ancient games years ago, but he was still expected to respond to our amateur expertise, our insatiable vicariousness. Old men are patronized in much the same fashion as athletes; because we take pride in them, we expect their intimacy in return. I had intruded after all.

We were in the eighth now . . . and then in the ninth. Still no score, and each new batter, each pitch was greeted with clappings and deepening cries of encouragement and anxiety from the stands and the players alike. The close-packed rows hummed with ceaseless, nervous sounds of conversation and speculation—and impatience for the dénouement, and a fear of it, too. All around me in our section I could see the same look of resignation and boredom and pleasure that now showed on my own face, I knew—the look of longtime fans who understand that one can never leave a very long close game, no matter how much inconvenience and exasperation it imposes on us. The difficulty of baseball is imperious.

"Yay! Yay!" Dick Lee cried when Yale left fielder Joe Dufek led off the eighth with a single. "Now come *on*, you guys! I gotta get home for dinner." But the next Yale batter bunted into a force play at second, and the chance was gone. "Well, all right—for *breakfast!*" Lee said, slumping back in his seat.

The two pitchers held us—each as intent and calm and purposeful as the other. Ron Darling, never deviating from the purity of his stylish body-lean and leg-crook and his riding, down-thrusting delivery, poured fastballs through the diminishing daylight. He looked as fast as ever now, or faster, and in both the ninth and the tenth he dismissed the side in order and with four more strikeouts. Viola was dominant in his own fashion, also setting down the Yale hitters one, two, three in the ninth and tenth, with a handful of pitches. His rhythm—the constant variety of speeds and location on his pitches—had the enemy batters leaning and swaying with his motion, and, as antistrophe, was almost as exciting to watch as Darling's flair and flame. With two out in the top of the eleventh, a St. John's batter nudged a soft little roller up the first-base line—such an easy, waiting, schoolboy sort of chance that the Yale first baseman, O'Connor, allowed the ball to carom off his mitt: a miserable little butchery, except that the second baseman, seeing his pitcher sprinting for the bag, now snatched up the ball and flipped it toward him almost despairingly. Darling took the toss while diving full-length at the bag and, rolling in the dirt, beat the runner by a hair.

"Oh, my!" said Joe Wood. "Oh, my, oh, my!"

Then in the bottom of the inning Yale suddenly loaded the bases—a hit, a walk, another walk (Viola was just missing the corners now)—and we all came to our feet, yelling and pleading. The tilted stands and the low roof deepened the cheers and sent them rolling across the field. There were two out, and the Yale batter, Dan Costello, swung at the first pitch and bounced it gently to short, for a force that ended the rally. Somehow, I think, we knew that we had seen Yale's last chance.

"I would have taken that pitch," I said, entering the out in my scorecard. "To keep the pressure on him."

"I don't know," Joe Wood said at once. "He's just walked two. You might get the cripple on the first pitch and then see nothing but hooks. Hit away."

He was back in the game.

Steve Scafa, leading off the twelfth, got a little piece of Darling's first pitch on the handle of his bat, and the ball looped softly over the shortstop's head and into left: a hit. The loudspeakers told us that Ron Darling's eleven innings of no-hit pitching had set a new N.C.A.A. tournament record. Everyone at Yale Field stood up—the St. John's players, too, coming off their bench and out onto the field—and applauded Darling's masterpiece. We were scarcely seated again before Scafa stole second as the Yale catcher, Paterno, bobbled

the pitch. Scafa, who is blurrily quick, had stolen thirty-five bases during the season. Now he stole third as well. With one out and runners at the corners (the other St. John's man had reached first on an error), Darling ran the count to three-and-two and fanned the next batter—his fifteenth strikeout of the game. Two out. Darling sighed and stared in, and then stepped off the mound while the St. John's coach put in a pinch-runner at first—who took off for second on the very next pitch. Paterno fired the ball quickly this time, and Darling, staggering off the mound with his follow-through, did not cut it off. Scafa came 10 feet down the third-base line and stopped there, while the pinch-runner suddenly jammed on the brakes, stranding himself between first and second: a play, clearly—an inserted crisis. The Yale second baseman glanced twice at Scafa, freezing him, and then made a little run at the hung-up base runner to his left and threw to first. With that, Scafa instantly broke for the plate. Lured by the vision of the third out just a few feet away from him on the base path, the Yale first baseman hesitated, fractionally and fatally, before he spun and threw home, where Scafa slid past the tag and came up, leaping and clapping, into the arms of his teammates. That was the game. Darling struck out his last man, but a new St. John's pitcher, a right-handed fireballer named Eric Stampfl, walked on and blew the Elis away in their half.

"Well, that's a shame," Joe Wood said, getting up for the last time. It was close to six-thirty, but he looked fine now. "If that man scores before the third out, it counts, you know," he said. "That's why it worked. I never saw a better-played game anyplace—college or big-league. That's a swell ballgame."

Several things happened afterward. Neither Yale nor St. John's qualified for the college World Series, it turned out; the University of Maine defeated St. John's in the final game of the playoffs at New Haven (neither Viola nor Darling was sufficiently recovered from his ordeal to pitch again) and made the trip to Omaha, where it, too, was eliminated. Arizona State won the national title. On June 9th, Ron Darling was selected by the Texas Rangers at the major-league amateur-player draft in New York. He was the ninth player in the country to be chosen. Frank Viola, the thirty-seventh pick, went to the Minnesota Twins. (The Seattle Mariners, who had the first pick this year, had been ready to take Darling, which would have made him the coveted No. 1 selection in the draft, but the club backed off at the last moment because of Darling's considerable salary demands. As it was, he signed with the Rangers for a hundred-thousand-dollar bonus.) On June 12th, the major-league players unanimously struck the twenty-six big-league teams. The strike has brought major-league ball to a halt, and no one can predict when play will resume. Because of this sudden silence, the St. John's–Yale struggle has become the best and most vivid game of the year for me, so far. It may stay that way even after the strike ends. "I think that game will always be on my mind," Ron Darling said after it was over. I feel the same way. I think I will remember it all my life. So will Joe Wood. Somebody will probably tell Ron Darling that Smokey Joe Wood was at the game that afternoon and saw him pitch eleven scoreless no-hit innings against St. John's, and someday—perhaps years from now, when he, too, may possibly be a celebrated major-league strikeout artist—it may occur to him that his heartbreaking 0–1 loss in May 1981 and Walter Johnson's 0–1 loss at Fenway Park in September 1912 are now woven together into the fabric of baseball. Pitch by pitch, inning by inning, Ron Darling had made that happen. He stitched us together.

Kafka would laugh out loud. This classic assault on sense and syntax is generally associated with Abbott and Costello, who, having performed it in the 1945 film *Naughty Nineties*, are presumed to have written it. They didn't. Who did? Naturally. When Bud and Lou first formed a team in 1937, each was an experienced vaudeville comic. A key ingredient of their enormous success in the 1940s and 1950s was a file of some 2,000 stock routines from the burlesque stage, including "Who's on First?" The version transcribed below was presented to the Baseball Hall of Fame in 1956.

ANONYMOUS

Who's on First?

ABBOTT: You know, strange as it may seem, they give ball players nowadays very peculiar names. . . . Now, on the Cooperstown team we have Who's on first, What's on second, I Don't Know is on third—

COSTELLO: That's what I want to find out. I want you to tell me the names of the fellows on the Cooperstown team.

ABBOTT: I'm telling you. Who's on first, What's on second, I Don't Know is on third.

COSTELLO: You know the fellows' names?

ABBOTT: Yes.

COSTELLO: Well, then, who's playin' first?

ABBOTT: Yes.

COSTELLO: I mean the fellow's name on first base.

ABBOTT: Who.

COSTELLO: The fellow's name on first base for Cooperstown.

ABBOTT: Who.

COSTELLO: The guy on first base.

ABBOTT: Who is on first base.

COSTELLO: Well, what are you asking me for?

ABBOTT: I'm not asking you—I'm telling you. Who is on first.

COSTELLO: I'm asking you—who's on first?

ABBOTT: That's the man's name.

COSTELLO: That's who's name?

ABBOTT: Yes.

COSTELLO: Well, go ahead, tell me!

ABBOTT: Who.

COSTELLO: The guy on first.

ABBOTT: Who.

COSTELLO: The first baseman.

ABBOTT: Who is on first.

COSTELLO: Have you got a first baseman on first?

ABBOTT: Certainly.

COSTELLO: Well, all I'm trying to find out is what's the guy's name on first base.

ABBOTT: Oh, no, no, What is on second base.

COSTELLO: I'm not asking you who's on second.

ABBOTT: Who's on first.

COSTELLO: That's what I'm trying to find out.

ABBOTT: Well, don't change the players around.

COSTELLO: I'm not changing anybody.

ABBOTT: Now, take it easy.

COSTELLO: What's the guy's name on first base?

ABBOTT: What's the guy's name on second base.

COSTELLO: I'm not askin' ya who's on second.

ABBOTT: Who's on first.

COSTELLO: I don't know.

ABBOTT: He's on third. We're not talking about him.

COSTELLO: How could I get on third base?

ABBOTT: You mentioned his name.

COSTELLO: If I mentioned the third baseman's name, who did I say is playing third?

ABBOTT: No, Who's playing first.

COSTELLO: Stay offa first, will you?

ABBOTT: Please. Now what is it you want to know?

COSTELLO: What is the fellow's name on third base?

ABBOTT: What is the fellow's name on second base.

COSTELLO: I'm not askin' ya who's on second.

ABBOTT: Who's on first.

COSTELLO: I don't know.
ABBOTT & COSTELLO: Third base.

COSTELLO: (*Makes noises*) You got an outfield?
ABBOTT: Oh, sure.
COSTELLO: Cooperstown has got a good outfield?
ABBOTT: Oh, absolutely.
COSTELLO: The left fielder's name?
ABBOTT: Why.
COSTELLO: I don't know, I just thought I'd ask.
ABBOTT: Well, I just thought I'd tell you.
COSTELLO: Then tell me who's playing left field.
ABBOTT: Who's playing first.
COSTELLO: Stay out of the infield.
ABBOTT: Don't mention any names out here.
COSTELLO: I want to know what's the fellow's name in left field.
ABBOTT: What is on second.
COSTELLO: I'm not asking you who's on second.
ABBOTT: Who is on first.
COSTELLO: I don't know.
ABBOTT & COSTELLO: Third base.
COSTELLO: (*Makes noises*)
ABBOTT: Now take it easy, man.
COSTELLO: And the left fielder's name?
ABBOTT: Why.
COSTELLO: Because.
ABBOTT.: Oh, he's center field.
COSTELLO: Wait a minute. You got a pitcher on the team?
ABBOTT: Wouldn't this be a fine team without a pitcher.
COSTELLO: I don't know. Tell me the pitcher's name.
ABBOTT: Tomorrow.
COSTELLO: You don't want to tell me today?
ABBOTT: I'm telling you, man.
COSTELLO: Then go ahead.
ABBOTT: Tomorrow.
COSTELLO: What time?
ABBOTT: What time what?
COSTELLO: What time tomorrow are you gonna tell me who's pitching?
ABBOTT: Now listen, Who is not pitching. Who is on—
COSTELLO: I'll break your arm if you say who's on first.
ABBOTT: Then why come up here and ask?

COSTELLO: I want to know what's the pitcher's name.

ABBOTT: What's on second.

COSTELLO: I don't know.

ABBOTT & COSTELLO: Third base.

COSTELLO: Ya gotta catcher?

ABBOTT: Yes.

COSTELLO: The catcher's name.

ABBOTT: Today.

COSTELLO: Today. And Tomorrow's pitching.

ABBOTT: Now you've got it.

COSTELLO: That's all. Cooperstown got a couple of days on their team. That's all.

ABBOTT: Well, I can't help that.

COSTELLO: (*Makes noises*)

ABBOTT: All right. What do you want me to do?

COSTELLO: Gotta catcher?

ABBOTT: Yes.

COSTELLO: I'm a good catcher too, you know.

ABBOTT: I know that.

COSTELLO: I would like to play for the Cooperstown team.

ABBOTT: Well, I might arrange that.

COSTELLO: I would like to catch. Now, I'm being a good catcher, Tomorrow's pitching on the team and I'm catching.

ABBOTT: Yes.

COSTELLO: Tomorrow throws the ball and the guy up bunts the ball.

ABBOTT: Yes.

COSTELLO: Now, when he bunts the ball—me being a good catcher—I want to throw the guy out at first base, so I pick up the ball and throw it to who?

ABBOTT: Now, that's the first thing you've said right.

COSTELLO: (*shouts*) I don't even know what I'm talking about.

ABBOTT: Well, that's all you have to do.

COSTELLO: Is throw it to first base.

ABBOTT: Yes.

COSTELLO: Now, who's got it?

ABBOTT: Naturally.

COSTELLO: Who has it?

ABBOTT: Naturally.

COSTELLO: Naturally.

ABBOTT: Naturally.

COSTELLO: I throw the ball to Naturally.

ABBOTT: You throw it to Who.

COSTELLO: Naturally.

ABBOTT: Naturally. Well, say it that way.

COSTELLO: That's what I'm saying.

ABBOTT: Now don't get excited. Now don't get excited.

COSTELLO: I throw the ball to first base.

ABBOTT: Then Who gets it.

COSTELLO: He better get it.

ABBOTT: That's it. All right now, don't get excited. Take it easy.

COSTELLO: Hmmmmmph.

ABBOTT: Hmmmmmph.

COSTELLO: Now, I throw the ball to first base, whoever it is grabs the ball, so the guy runs to second.

ABBOTT: Uh-huh.

COSTELLO: Who picks up the ball and throws it to What. What throws it to I Don't Know. I Don't Know throws it back to Tomorrow—a triple play.

ABBOTT: Yeah. It could be.

COSTELLO: Another guy gets up and it's a long fly ball to center. Why? I don't know. And I don't care.

ABBOTT: What was that?

COSTELLO: I said, 'I don't care.'

ABBOTT: Oh, that's our shortstop.

Old Anon, that most prolific and versatile of authors, is the only one to appear twice in this volume. Before composing "Who's on First?" he was a staffer for *The New York Times*, wherein this grand description of a rather ordinary game appeared on April 26, 1912. They don't write 'em like this any more—mixing the rhythms of Broadway and ancient Greece—and more's the pity. "Here's one that will bring the weeps," indeed: not for a ballgame lost but for a style of baseball writing that, because of its excesses in the 1920s, was not mourned upon its passing. Today's reporter views his efforts as secondary to the game and its players, an attitude that is commendably modest but tends to produce bland, "just-the-facts-ma'am" coverage of the incidents of the game, embellished only by banal quotes about hanging curveballs and "seeing the ball good." The nameless scribe who gladdened the hearts of *Times* readers back in 1912 reminds one of Rice and Runyon and, in spots, of another nameless scribe to whom history has given the name Homer.

ANONYMOUS

Yankees Toss Game Away in Thirteenth

Here's one that will bring the weeps.

The Yankees and the Athletics were tied in the thirteenth inning at 4–4. Rube Oldring jarred Ford's damp hurl to the center lawn for a single. Ford's next moist fling slipped and went wild, Oldring racing to second, and then to third. Gabby Street recovered the unruly ball, made a desperate heave to Coleman at third base, and the ball traveled on to left field, Oldring coming home with the run which won the game. Score, 5–4.

Play on, professor—a little more of that funeral march.

Some 3,500 persons, mostly men, sat through to the bitter end, and everyone got cold smoked beef when he walked into the Missus for dinner at 7:30 last evening. That wasn't all they got.

This is the conversation, husband speaking: "Say, Mrs. Wife, you ought to have seen that pitching duel between Bender and Ford. The Yanks tied it up in the sixth, and after that both flingers were airtight."

Mrs. Wife now talking: "Say, you, what do you think this is—an all-night lunch? Why don't you board up at the ballpark? You'll find something to eat at the 'Ham-And' place around the corner."

It was a ball game worth missing your dinner for. The Yankees showed more fight and vim than in any game this season. For a long time they refused to be whipped, and their chances were just as good as the world's champions until they cracked in the thirteenth inning and began to toss the ball all over the lot. Wolverton's men had several excellent chances to win the game, but they lacked the final punch.

The Yankees are in pretty bad shape, and had to rely on green recruits to fill the gaps made by the hospital patients. The whole outfield is now disabled, Hartzell being yesterday's victim, while Cree and Walter are still recuperating.

In the second inning, Daniels in center and Hartzell in right both chased after Bender's high fly. The players came together with an awful bump, and Hartzell stretched out on the grass, unconscious. A gash was cut in his chin, and he was carried to the clubhouse. Benny Kauff took his place, and was all hot sand and ginger in the game. Kauff made two fine hits and ran the bases fast, scoring two of the Yankee runs.

It was a toss-up between Bender and Ford. Both pitched great after the sixth inning, getting stronger as they went along. It was the first big game the big Chippewa Indian has pitched since the World Series last fall, and he looks as if he were good for a couple more World Series. Ford was back to his best form and, with men on the bases, was very effective. Ragged support behind him aided the Athletics in their run harvest.

Philadelphia activity started in the second. Murphy was safe when Martin threw wild to Chase at first. McInnis beat out a bunt to Ford, and Barry sacrificed the pair up a notch. Then, who comes along but Ira Thomas, who wallops a "pippin" to deep center for a zwei hassocks, scoring Murphy and McInnis. The Yanks got one in that stanza, when Kauff ripped a single to center, went down to second on Zinn's out, and scored on Gardner's hit to the middle patch.

In the fourth, Barry did a brazen piece of business. Murphy singled, went to second on McInnis's out and to third on a passed ball. Barry's roller went to Coleman, and Murphy was nailed while skipping up and down the third-base line, Barry racing around to third, while half a dozen Yankees riveted their attention on Murphy. As Ford was pitching to Thomas, Barry started down the third-base line like a runaway colt.

The mammoth nerve of him! The grand larceny was committed with all the Yankees looking on with their baby-blue eyes wide open. Barry slid in safe, while the Yankees continued the nap. Get out the alarm clock.

In the fifth, Oldring was safe on a rap which skinned Gardner's shins, and he scored on Collins's double to right. In the same inning, the Yankees began to rush up from behind. Gardner singled and Street strolled. Ford sacrificed them along a base, and they both tore home on Daniels's safe smash to center.

Sixth inning—Yanks at bat, two out. Benny Kauff banged out a safety to right and went to second when Murphy juggled the ball. Kauff scored on Zinn's single to center. The score is tied. Nifty, what?

Ford and Bender both closed up like morning glories in the sun. At nine innings, not a run in sight. Tenth inning, the same thing. In the eleventh inning, Collins walked on Ford's only pass of the day, and got to third on two outs. He stuck there as if planted in glue.

The Yankees should have won in the twelfth inning. Young Martin, the new shortstopper whom Wolverton has just recalled from Rochester, poled a high-powered three-bagger to the darkest corner of right field. He had plenty of time to make the circuit, but was held at third base because of poor coaching. It was a burning shame that such a healthy smash could go to seed, but Martin was tagged coming in on Zinn's grounder.

Then followed the fitful thirteenth, when the strong-armed pegs of Ford and Street permitted Oldring to breeze home with the hurrah tally.

Employees of the New York Yankees know that the boss's door is always open: it revolves. Managers, coaches, p.r. men, secretaries, and of course players—all are advised to keep their bags packed. Yet George M. Steinbrenner III—the man Red Smith referred to simply as "George III"—is not hard of heart, only of head, as were his various spiritual ancestors and contemporary peers. The impetuous/domineering style of ownership was patented by Chris Von Der Ahe, owner of the champion St. Louis Browns of the 1880s, and refined by such men as the Giants' Andrew Freedman and the Indians' Bill Veeck. And if Yankee fans think George is overinvolved with the on-field operations of the team, let them recall that Braves' owner Ted Turner once managed the team from the dugout—in uniform!—and Oakland's Charlie Finley once tried to bribe Vida Blue to change his given name to "True."

RUSSELL BAKER

Love Me, Love My Bear

I have never been able to fire anybody and, as a result, promotions have always passed me by. This is why I sought out George Steinbrenner, the owner of the New York Yankees and probably the most successful firer in the annals of unemployment.

Naturally, I had expected to meet an ogre, and, so, was delighted by the charm with which he received my proposal. I began by confessing that it was unusual. "Mr. Steinbrenner," I explained, "I want to study firing and I want to study under the best man in the field. Will you help me learn?"

Instead of the tirade I anticipated, these words produced a strange silence during which his eyes moistened and he struggled to hold back emotion. At length he said, "The best. . . . Nobody's ever said anything like that about me before."

"Oh, you have a good heart, Mr. Steinbrenner. I can see that. I know you'll help me, sir." He dabbed at his eyes with a handkerchief.

"I haven't been all torn up inside like this since the time they took away my teddy bear," he said, picking up the phone and asking his receptionist to step in.

"Yes, Mr. Steinbrenner?" said the receptionist.

"You're fired," he said.

"May I ask why?"

"For letting in people who remind me of the time they took my teddy bear away. I can't run a baseball team while I'm wondering whatever happened to that dear old teddy bear of mine."

When the receptionist had gone, I expressed admiration for the ease and rapidity with which he had conducted the firing. "Why, the receptionist didn't even call you a brute or an ingrate," I said.

"She didn't dare," said Mr. Steinbrenner. "If she had, she would have blown her chances of managing the Yankees."

I couldn't believe that, after firing her from a receptionist's job, he would hire her back to manage the team.

"Why not?" he asked. "At the rate I fire managers, I can't afford to be picky. Which reminds me—"

He dialed the phone. "I'm calling a sportswriter pal," he whispered. Then: "This is George, Sol. . . . Yeah, terrible about that last road trip. I've got it from the horse's mouth the Yankees are looking for a new manager. . . . Don't quote me."

He hung up. I felt radiant with hero worship. Mr. Steinbrenner was not only going to fire the manager; he was letting me know how he did it. "That will be headlines in the paper tomorrow," I said.

"You bet your sweet patootie," he said. "It'll put the Yankees back on page one, stir up the fans, get the old turnstiles clicking faster. When you fire somebody, son, fire with a purpose. It's good for the box office."

"You're the greatest, Mr. Steinbrenner."

"Now don't go getting me all choked up again," he said.

I saw this was the moment to push my case. "If it's not asking too much," I said, "could I come in some day and fire somebody for you while you watched me to make sure I'm doing it right?"

He rose from his desk and embraced me. "I like you, kid. You could be good, really good," he said. "I'm putting you on the payroll as junior assistant in charge of minor firings. Be in here tomorrow morning early and I'll let you fire a couple of peanut vendors."

I was too overcome to trust my voice, so I merely nodded, sniffled, and moved to the door.

"Before you go," he said.

"Yes."

"About this manager I've got to fire—do you know who's managing the Yankees this week?"

Not wanting to blow my big chance by revealing that I didn't follow baseball, I gave him the name of the only baseball manager I could remember. "It's Earl Weaver," I said.

As I left, he had Weaver on the telephone. "Earl, baby," he was saying, "you're through. Drop by the cashier's window and pick up your paycheck. . . ."

I reported early next morning to fire peanut vendors. Mr. Steinbrenner led in the first, then stood behind me to observe my technique. The peanut vendor was a small, cuddly fellow with plump, round cheeks and a great deal of hair.

"Vendor," I snarled, and then paused.

"Yes sir. Bag of peanuts, sir?"

"What are you waiting for?" asked Mr. Steinbrenner. "Give him the ax."

"I can't," I said.

"Can't! Why not?"

"He reminds me of my dear old teddy bear," I said.

I heard Mr. Steinbrenner snuffle and suppress a sob behind me. Then: "Nobody can talk about teddy bears around me and get away with it," he said in a voice hoarse with sorrow. "You're fired."

I was leaving the Stadium when a guard said Mr. Steinbrenner wanted me on the phone. "Give me your phone number, kid," he said. "I'm going to need some new managers next spring."

This article by the fifteen-year major-league veteran appeared not in *The Sporting News* or the Sunday sports section, but in the September 1941 issue of the *Atlantic Monthly*. Then again, the writer was not your ordinary ballplayer: He was a *summa cum laude* graduate of Princeton, master of a dozen languages (in none of which, it was observed, could he hit), and, it was revealed after his death in 1972, a master spy in both Japan and Occupied Europe. Ironically, the intellectual who could describe the catcher as "the Cerberus of baseball" himself wielded the tools of ignorance, and in 1924 he was the object of that famous scouting-report barbarism, "Good field, no hit."

MOE BERG

Pitchers and Catchers

I

Baseball men agree with the philosopher that perfection—which means a pennant to them—is attainable only through a proper combination of opposites. A team equally strong in attack and in defense, well-proportioned as a unit, with, of course, those intangibles, morale, enthusiasm, and direction—that is the story of success in baseball. Good fielding and pitching, without hitting, or vice versa, is like Ben Franklin's half a pair of scissors—ineffectual. Lopsided pennant failures are strewn throughout the record books. Twenty-game winners or .400 hitters do not ensure victory. *Ne quid nimis*. Ty Cobb, baseball genius, helped win pennants early in his career, but from 1909 through 1926, his last year at Detroit, he and his formidable array of hitters failed—they never found the right combination. Ed Walsh, the great White Sox spitball pitcher, in 1908 won forty or practically half of his club's games, to this day an individual pitching record, but alone he couldn't offset his own "hitless wonders." Walter Johnson the swift, with over 400 victories, waited almost twenty years before his clubmates at Washington helped him to a championship. Every pennant winner must be endowed both at the plate and in the field. Even Babe

Ruth's bat, when it loomed largest, couldn't obscure the Yankees' high-caliber pitching and their tight defense in key spots.

With all the importance that hitting has assumed since the Babe and home runs became synonymous, I note that Connie Mack, major-league manager for almost half a century, household name for strategy wherever the game is played, still gives pitching top rating in baseball.

A Walter Johnson, a Lefty Grove, a Bob Feller, cannon-ball pitchers, come along once in a generation. By sheer, blinding speed they overpower the hitter. Johnson shut out the opposition in 113 games, more than the average pitcher wins in his major-league lifetime. Bob Feller continues this speed-ball tradition. We accept these men as pitching geniuses, with the mere explanation that, thanks to their strong arms, their pitches are comparatively untouchable. When Walter Johnson pitched, the hitter looked for a fastball and got it; he looked— but it didn't do him much good. Clark Griffith, then manager of the Washington Club, jestingly threatened Walter with a fine any time he threw a curve. "Griff" knew that no variation in the speed king's type of pitch was necessary. But what of the other pitchers who are not so talented?

Many times a pitcher without apparent stuff wins, whereas his opponent, with what seems to be a great assortment, is knocked out of the box in an early inning. The answer, I believe, lies in the bare statement, "Bat meets ball"; any other inference may lead us into the danger of overcomplication. The player himself takes his ability for granted and passes off his success or lack of it with "You do or you don't." Call it the law of averages.

Luck, as well as skill, decides a game. The pitcher tries to minimize the element of luck. Between the knees and shoulders of the hitter, over a plate just 17 inches wide, lies the target of the pitcher, who throws from a rectangular rubber slab on a mound 60 feet, 6 inches distant. The pitcher has to throw into this area with enough on the ball to get the hitter out—that is his intention. Control, natural or acquired, is a prerequisite of any successful pitcher: he must have direction, not only to be effective, but to exist.

Because of this enforced concentration of pitches, perhaps the game's most interesting drama unfolds within the limited space of the ball-and-strike zone. The pitcher toes the mound; action comes with the motion, delivery, and split-second flight of the ball to the catcher. With every move the pitcher is trying to fool the hitter, using his stuff, his skill and wiles, his tricks and cunning, all his art to win.

Well-known to ballplayers is the two-o'clock hitter who breaks down fences in batting practice. There is no pressure; the practice pitcher throws ball after ball with the same motion, the same delivery and speed. If the practice pitcher varies his windup or delivery, the hitters don't like it—not in batting practice— and they show their dislike by sarcastically conceding victory by a big score to the batting practice pitcher and demanding another. This is an interesting phenomenon. The hitter, in practice, is adjusting himself to clocklike regularity of speed, constant and consistent. He is concentrating on his timing. He has to coordinate his vision and his swing. This coordination the opposing pitcher wants to upset from the moment he steps on the rubber and the game begins. The very duration of the stance itself, the windup and motion, and the form of delivery are all calculated to break the hitter's equilibrium. Before winding up, the pitcher may hesitate, outstaring the notoriously anxious hitter in order to disturb him. Ted Lyons, of the Chicago White Sox, master student of a hitter's habits, brings his arms over his head now once, now twice, three or more times, his eyes intent on every move of the hitter, slowing up or quickening the pace of his windup and motion in varying degrees before he delivers the pitch. Cy Young, winner of most games in baseball history—he won 511—had four different pitching motions, turning his back on the hitter to hide the ball before he pitched. Fred Marberry, the great Washington relief pitcher, increased his effectiveness by throwing his free, nonpivot foot as well as the ball at the hitter to distract him.

In 1884, when Connie Mack broke in as a catcher for Meriden, Charlie Radbourn—who won sixty games for Providence—could have cuffed, scraped, scratched, fingernailed, applied resin, emery, or any other foreign substance to, or spit on the two balls the teams started and finished the game with. "Home-Run" Baker, who hit two balls out of the park in the 1911 World Series to win his nickname—and never more than twelve in a full season—characterizes a defensive era in the game. During the last war, it was impossible to get some of the nine foreign ingredients that enter into the manufacture of our baseball. To make up for the lack of the superior foreign yarn, our machines were adjusted to wind the domestic product tighter. In 1919, when the war was over, the foreign yarn was again available, but the same machines were used. The improved technique, the foreign ingredients, Babe Ruth and bat, conspired to revolutionize baseball. It seems prophetic, with due respect to the Babe, that our great American national game, so native and representative, could have been so completely refashioned by happenings on the other side of the world.

II

The importance of the bat has been stressed to such an extent that, since 1920, foreign substances have been barred to the pitcher, and the spitball outlawed. The resin bag, the sole concession, is used on the hands only to counteract perspiration. The cover of the ball, in two sections, is sewed together with stitches, slightly raised, in one long seam; today's pitcher, after experimentation and experience, takes whatever advantage he can of its surface to make his various pitches more effective by gripping the ball across or along two rows of stitches, or along one row or on the smooth surface. The pitcher is always working with a shiny new ball. A game today will consume as many as eight dozen balls instead of the two roughed and battered ones which were the limit in 1884.

With the freak pitch outlawed and the accent put on hitting in the modern game, the pitcher has to be resourceful to win. He throws fast-, slow-, and breaking balls, all with variations. He is fortunate if his fastball hops or sinks, slides or sails, because, if straight as a string or too true, it is ineffective. The ball has to do something at the last moment. The curve must break sharply and not hang. To add to his repertory of balls that break, the pitcher may develop a knuckle ball (fingers applied to the seam, knuckled against, instead of gripping the ball), a forkball (the first two fingers forking the ball), or a screwball (held approximately the same as an orthodox fastball or curveball but released with a twist of the wrist the reverse of a curve). The knuckle and forkballs flutter through the air, wavering, veering, or taking a sudden lurch, without revolving like the other pitches; they are the modern counterpart of the spitball, a dry spitter.

The pitcher studies the hitter's stance, position at the plate, and swing, to establish the level of his natural batting stroke and to detect any possible weakness. Each hitter has his own individual style. The pitcher scouts his form and notes whether he holds the bat on the end or chokes it, is a free swinger or a chop hitter. He bears in mind whether the hitter crowds, or stands away from, the plate, in front of or behind it, erect or crouched over it. Whether he straddles his legs or strides forward to hit, whether he lunges with his body or takes a quick cut with wrist and arm only, whether he pulls a ball, hits late or through the box—all these things are telltale and reveal a hitter's liking for a certain pitch, high or low, in or out, fast, curve, or slow.

To fool the hitter—there's the rub. With an assortment at his disposal, a pitcher tries to adapt the delivery, as well as the pitch, to the hitter's weakness. Pitchers may have distinct forms of delivery and work differently on a given hitter; a pitcher throws overhand, three-quarter overhand (which is about midway between overhand and sidearm), side arm, or underhand. A crossfire is an emphasized sidearm pitch thrown against the forward foot as the body leans to the same side as the pitching arm at the time of the motion and delivery. Not the least important part of the delivery is the body follow-through to get more stuff on the pitch and to take pressure off the arm. Having determined the hitter's weakness, the pitcher can throw to spots—for example, "high neck in," low outside, or letter high. But he never forgets that, with all his equipment, he is trying to throw the hitter off his timing—probably the best way to fool him, to get him out. Without varying his motion, he throws a change-of-pace fastball or curveball, pulls the string on his fastball, slows up, takes a little off or adds a little to his fast-ball.

Just as there are speed kings, so there are hitters without an apparent weakness. They have unusual vision, power, and great ability to coordinate these in the highest degree. They are the ranking, top hitters who hit everything in the strike zone well—perhaps one type of pitch less well than another. To these hitters the pitcher throws his best pitch and leaves the result to the law of averages. Joe DiMaggio straddles in a spread-eagle stance with his feet wide apart and bat already cocked. He advances his forward foot only a matter of inches, so that, with little stride, he doesn't move his head, keeping his eyes steadily on the ball. He concentrates on the pitch; his weight equally distributed on both feet, he has perfect wrist action and power to drive the ball for distance. Mel Ott, on the other hand, lifts the front foot high just as the pitcher delivers the ball; he is not caught off balance or out of position, because he sets the foot down only after he has seen what type of pitch is coming. With DiMaggio's stance one must have good wrist action and power. With Ott's, there is a danger of taking a long step forward before one knows what is coming. But Mel does not commit himself.

Rogers Hornsby, one of the game's greatest right-hand hitters, invariably took his position in the far rear corner of the batter's box, stepped into the pitch, and hit to all fields equally well. Ty Cobb was always a step ahead of the pitcher. He must have been because he led the American League in hitting every year but one in the thirteen-year period 1907–19. He outstudied the pitcher and took as many positions in the batter's box as he thought necessary to counteract the type of motion and pitch he was likely to get. He adapted his stance to the pitcher who was then on the mound; for Red Faber, whose spitball broke sharply down, Cobb stood in front of the plate; for a curveball left-hander, Ty took a stance behind the plate in order to hit the curve after it broke, because, as Ty said, he could see it break and get hold of it the better. For Lefty O'Doul, one of the greatest teachers of hitting in the game, there are no outside pitches. Lefty stands close to the plate; his bat more than covers it; he is a natural right-field pull hitter. Babe Ruth, because of his tremendous, unequaled home-run power, and his ability to hit equally well all sorts of pitches with a liberal stride and a free swing, and consistently farther than any other player, has demonstrated that he had the greatest coordination and power of any hitter ever known. Ted Williams, of the Boston Red Sox, the only current .400 hitter in the game, completely loose and relaxed, has keen enough eyes never to offer at a bad pitch; he has good wrist and arm action, leverage, and power. Jimmie Foxx, next to Babe Ruth as a home-run hitter, steps into a ball, using his tremendous wrists and forearms for his powerful, long and line drives. These hitters do not lunge with the body; the front hip gives way for the swing, and the body follows through.

III

The game is carried back and forth between the pitcher and the hitter. The hitter notices what and where the pitchers are throwing. If the pitcher is getting him out consistently, for example, on a curve outside, the hitter changes his mode of attack. Adaptability is the hallmark of the big-league hitter. Joe Cronin, playing manager of the Red Sox, has changed in his brilliant career from a fastball, left-field pull hitter to a curveball and a right-field hitter, to and fro through the whole cycle and back again, according to where the pitchers are throwing. He has no apparent weakness, hits to all fields, and is one of the greatest "clutch" hitters in the game. *Plus ça change, plus c'est la même chose.*

Like Walter Johnson, Lefty Grove was a fastball pitcher, and the hitters knew it. The hitters looked for this pitch; Lefty did not try to fool them by throwing anything else, but most of them were fooled, not by the type of pitch, but by his terrific speed. With two strikes on the hitter, Lefty did throw his curve at times, and that, too, led almost invariably to a strikeout. In 1935, Lefty had recovered from his first serious sore arm of the year before. Wear and tear, and the grind of many seasons, had taken their toll. Now he had changed his tactics, and was pitching curves and fastballs, one or the other. His control was practically perfect. On a day in that year in Washington, Heinie Manush, a great hitter, was at bat with two men on the bases. The game was at stake; the count was three balls and two strikes. Heinie stood there, confident, looking for Lefty's fastball. "Well," thought Heinie, "it might be a curve." Lefty was throwing the curve more and more now, but the chances with the count of

three-and-two were that Lefty would throw his fastball with everything he had on it. Fast or curve—he couldn't throw anything else; he had nothing else to throw. Heinie broke his back striking out on the next pitch, the first forkball Grove ever threw. For over a year, on the sidelines, in the bullpen, between pitching starts, Lefty had practiced and perfected this pitch before he threw it, and he waited for a crucial spot to use it. Lefty had realized his limitations. The hitters were getting to his fastballs and curveballs more than they used to. He wanted to add to his pitching equipment; he felt he had to. Heinie Manush anticipated, looked for, guessed a fastball, possibly a curve, but Lefty fooled him with his new pitch, a forkball.

Here was the perfect setup for outguessing a hitter. Lefty Grove's development of a third pitch, the forkball, is the greatest example in our time of complete successful change in technique by one pitcher. When a speed-ball pitcher loses his fast one, he has to compensate for such loss by adding to his pitching equipment. Lefty both perfected his control and added a forkball. Carl Hubbell's screwball, practically unhittable at first, made his fastball and curve effective. Lefty Gomez, reaching that point in his career where he had to add to his fastball and curveball, developed and threw his first knuckle ball this year. Grove, Gomez, and Hubbell, three outstanding left-handers—Grove and Gomez adding a forkball and a knuckle ball respectively to their fastballs and curveballs when their speed was waning, Hubbell developing a screwball early in his career to make it his best pitch and to become one of the game's foremost southpaws—so you have the build-up of great pitchers.

At first, the superspeed of Grove obviated the necessity of pitching brains. But, when his speed began to fade, Lefty turned to his head. With his almost perfect control and the addition of his forkball, Lefty now fools the hitter with his cunning. With Montaigne, we conceive of Socrates in place of Alexander, of brain for brawn, wit for whip. And this brings us to a fascinating part of the pitcher–hitter drama: Does a hitter guess? Does a pitcher try to outguess him? When the pitching process is no longer mechanical, how much of it is psychological? When the speed of a Johnson or a Grove is fading or gone, can the pitcher outguess the hitter?

IV

We know that the pitcher studies the strength and weakness of every hitter and that the hitter notes every variety of pitch in the pitcher's repertory; that the big-league hitter is resourceful, and quick to meet every new circumstance. Does he anticipate what the pitcher is going to throw? He can regulate his next pitch arbitrarily by the very last-second flick of the wrist. There is no set pattern for the order of pitches. Possible combinations are so many that a formula of probability cannot be established. He may repeat the fastball or curveball indefinitely, or pitch them alternately; there is no mathematical certainty what the pitch will be. There is no harmony in the pattern of a pitcher's pitches. And no human being has the power of divination.

But does this prevent a hitter from guessing? Does he merely hit what he sees if he can? Is it possible for a hitter to stand at the plate and use merely his vision, without trying to figure out what the pitcher might throw? The hitter bases his anticipation on the repertory of the pitcher, taking into account the score of the game, what the pitcher threw him the last time at bat, whether he hit that pitch or not, how many men are on base, and the present count on him. The guess is more than psychic, for there is some basis for it, some precedent for the next move; what is past is prologue.

The few extraordinary hitters whose exceptional vision and power to co-ordinate must be the basis for their talent can afford to be oblivious of anything but the flight of the ball. Hughie Duffy, who has the highest batting average in baseball history (he hit .438 in 1894), or Rogers Hornsby, another great-right-hand hitter, may even deny that he did anything but hit what he saw. But variety usually makes a hitter think. When Ty Cobb changed his stance at the plate to hit the pitcher then facing him, he anticipated not only a certain type of motion but also the pitch that followed it. He studied past performance. Joe DiMaggio hit a home run to break Willie Keeler's consecutive-games hitting record of forty-four, standing since 1897, and has since carried the record to fifty-six games. In hitting the home run off Dick Newsome, Red Sox pitcher, who has been very successful this year because of a good assortment of pitches, Joe explains: "I hit a fastball; I knew he would come to that and was waiting for it; he had pitched knucklers, curves, and sinkers." Jimmie Foxx looks for a particular pitch when facing a pitcher—for example, a curveball against a notorious curveball pitcher—and watches any other pitch go by. But when he has two strikes he cancels all thought of what the pitcher might throw; he then hits what he sees. Jimmie knows that if he looks for a certain pitch and guesses wrong, with two strikes on him, he will be handcuffed at the plate watching the pitch go by. Hank Greenberg, full of imagination, has guessed right most of the time—he hit fifty-eight home runs one year.

Just as Lefty Grove perfected control of his not-so-speedy fastball and curve, and added the forkball to give him variety, so even the outstanding hitters have to change their mode of attack later when their vision and reactions are not quite so sharp as they used to be.

V

The catcher squatting behind the hitter undoubtedly has the coign of vantage in the ballpark; all the action takes place before him. Nothing is outside his view except the balls-and-strikes umpire behind him—which is at times no hardship. The receiver has a good pair of hands, shifts his feet gracefully for inside or outside pitches, and bends his knees, not his back, in an easy, rhythmic motion, as he stretches his arms to catch the ball below his belt. The catcher has to be able to cock his arm from any position, throw fast and accurately to the bases, field bunts like an infielder, and catch foul flies like an outfielder. He must be adept at catching a ball from any angle, and almost simultaneously tagging a runner at home plate. The catcher is the Cerberus of baseball.

These physical qualifications are only a part of a catcher's equipment. He signals the pitcher what to throw, and this implies superior baseball brains on his part. But a pitcher can put a veto on a catcher's judgment by shaking him off and waiting for another sign. The game cannot go on until he pitches. Every fan has seen a pitcher do this—like the judge who kept shaking his head from time to time while counsel was arguing; the lawyer finally turned to the jury and said, "Gentlemen, you might imagine that the shaking of his head by His Honor implied a difference of opinion, but you will notice if you remain here long enough that when His Honor shakes his head there is nothing in it." (Judges, if you are reading, please consider this *obiter*.) One would believe that a no-hit, no-run game, the acme of perfection, the goal of a pitcher, would satisfy even the most exacting battery mate. Yet, at the beginning of the seventh inning of a game under those conditions, "Sarge" Connally, White Sox pitcher, said to his catcher, "Let's mix 'em up; why don't you call for my knuckler?" "Sarge" was probably bored with his own infallibility. He lost the no-hitter and the game on an error.

Of course, no player monopolizes the brains on a ball club. The catcher gives the signals only because he is in a better position than the pitcher to hide them. In a squatting position, the catcher hides the simple finger, fist, or finger-wiggle signs between his legs, complicating them somewhat with different combinations only when a runner on second base in direct line of vision with the signals may look in, perhaps solve them, and flash back another signal to the hitter.

Signal stealing is possible in many ways. The most prevalent self-betrayals are made by the pitcher and catcher themselves. Such detection requires the closest observation. A catcher, after having given the signal, gets set for the pitch; in doing so he may unintentionally, unconsciously, make a slight move— for example, to the right, in order to be in a better position to catch a right-hander's curveball. But more often it is the pitcher who reveals something either to the coaches on the base lines or—what is more telling—to the hitter standing in the batter's box.

The pitcher will betray himself if he makes two distinct motions for two different pitches—as, for example, a sidearm delivery for the curve and over-hand for the fast ball. A pitcher may also betray himself in his windup by raising his arms higher for the fastball than for the curve. In some cases, his eyes are more intent on the plate for one pitch than for another. Usually the curve is more difficult to control. If a pitcher has to make facial distortions, they should be the same for one pitch as for another.

A pitcher covers up the ball with his glove as he fixes it, to escape detection. Otherwise, he may reveal that he is holding the ball tighter for a curve than for a fastball, or even gripping the stitches differently for one than for the other. Eddie Collins, all-time star second baseman, was probably the greatest spy on the field or at bat in the history of the game. He was a master at "getting" the pitch for himself somewhere in the pitcher's manipulation of the ball or in his motion. This ability in no small part helped make him the great performer that he was.

Ballplayers would rather detect these idiosyncrasies for themselves, as they stand awaiting the pitch, than get a signal from the coach. The coach, on detecting something, gives a sign to the hitter either silently by some move—for instance, touching his chest—or by word of mouth—"Come on," for a curve. But this is dangerous unless the coach detects the pitches with 100 percent accuracy. There must be no doubt. Many times, in baseball, a club knows every pitch thrown and still loses. The hitter may be too anxious if he actually knows what is coming, or a doubt might upset him. And there is always the danger of a pitcher's suspecting that he is "tipping" himself off. He then deals in a bit of counterespionage by making more emphatic to the opposition his revealing mannerism to encourage them, only to cross them up at a crucial time.

The whole club plays as a unit to win. The signs that the pitcher and catcher agree on reflect the collective ideas, the judgment of all the players on how to get the opposition out. Preventing runs from scoring is as important as making them. The players know how the pitcher intends to throw to each opponent. They review their strategy before game time, as a result of which they know how the battery is going to work, and they play accordingly. The shortstop and second baseman see the catcher's signs and get the jump on the ball; sometimes they flash it by prearranged signal to the other players who are not in a position to see it. The outfielders can then lean a little, but only after the ball is actually released.

He is a poor catcher who doesn't know at least as well as the pitcher what a hitter likes or doesn't like, to which field he hits, what he did the last time, what he is likely to do this time at bat. The catcher is an on-the-spot witness, in a position to watch the hitter at firsthand. He has to make quick decisions, bearing in mind the score, the inning, the number of men on the bases, and other factors.

VI

Pitchers and catchers are mutually helpful. It is encouraging to a pitcher when a catcher calls for the ball he wants to throw and corroborates his judgment.

The pitcher very seldom shakes a catcher off because they are thinking alike in a given situation. By working together they know each other's system. Pitchers help catchers as much as catchers do pitchers. One appreciative catcher gives due credit to spitballer Red Faber, knuckle-baller Ted Lyons, and fastballer Tommy Thomas, all of the Chicago White Sox, for teaching him, as he caught them, much about catching and working with pitchers. Bill Dickey, great Yankee catcher, will readily admit that Herb Pennock taught him battery technique merely by catching a master and noting how he mixed up his pitches. Ray Schalk, Chicago White Sox, and Steve O'Neill, Cleveland Indians, were two of the greatest receivers and all-round workmen behind the plate in baseball history. Gabby Hartnett and Mickey Cochrane stood out as hitters as well as catchers, Mickey being probably the greatest inspirational catcher of our time.

The catcher works in harmony with the pitcher and dovetails his own judgment with the pitcher's stuff. He finds out quickly the pitcher's best ball and calls for it in the spots where it would be most effective. He knows whether a hitter is in a slump or dangerous enough to walk intentionally. He tries to keep the pitcher ahead of the hitter. If he succeeds, the pitcher is in a more advantageous position to work on the hitter with his assortment of pitches. But if the pitcher is in a hole—a two-and-nothing, three-and-one, or three-and-two count—he knows that the hitter is ready to hit. The next pitch may decide the ball game. The pitcher tries not to pitch a "cripple"—that is, tries not to give the hitter the ball he hits best. But it is also dangerous to overrefine. Taking the physical as well as the psychological factors into consideration, the pitcher must at times give even the best hitter his best pitch under the circumstances. He pitches hard, lets the law of averages do its work, and never second-guesses himself. The pitcher throws a fastball through the heart of the plate, and the hitter, surprised, may even take it. The obvious pitch may be the most strategic one.

The pitcher may throw overhand to take full advantage of the white shirts in the bleacher background. Breaking balls are more effective when thrown against the resistance of the wind. In the latter part of a day, when shadows are cast in a stadium ballpark, the pitcher may change his tactics by throwing more fastballs than he did earlier in the game.

The players are not interested in the score, but merely in how many runs are necessary to tie and to win. They take nothing for granted in baseball. The idea is to win. The game's the thing.

The University of Southern California baseball program, headed by coach Ron Dedeaux, has been highly successful in NCAA play and as a feeder of top-level talent to the major leagues. Fred Lynn, Don Buford, Ron Fairly, Steve Kemp, Dave Kingman, Roy Smalley, Rich Dauer—all are USC products. And Trojan pitchers include Tom Seaver, Bill Lee, Steve Busby, and Jim Barr—yet none of them won as many collegiate games as Bruce Gardner. The All-American Baseball Player of the Year in 1960, Gardner wanted more than anything to pitch in the big leagues. The dream died, and with it the dreamer.

IRA BERKOW and

MURRAY OLDERMAN

An American Tragedy

Los Angeles Police Department
Death Report: File #71-045 104
Date/Time deceased discovered: June 7, 1971. 0900 hours
Interviewing officers: Det. Richard Ortiz, Det. George Kellenberger

Officers notified of possible suicide at Bovard Athletic Field (baseball field), University of Southern California campus.

Officers observed deceased lying on his stomach on the grass. Deceased was in an open area of the baseball field approx. 18 ft. n/w of the pitcher's mound. Both hands were partially under the face and neck, with the left hand clutching a Smith & Wesson .38 spcl. rev., 3″ barrel.

The deceased had a gunshot wound to the left temple with an exit wound in the right temple. The body was rigid. The bullet that passed thru the head could not be located.

Next to the body, officers found a laminated plaque with the deceased's name on it, naming him as All-American Baseball Player of the Year for 1960. Under the right portion of the body clutched in the right hand was a laminated plaque of a B.S. degree from Univ. of So. Calif. issued to Bruce Clark Gardner.

Approx. 3 ft. from body toward pitcher's mound was full-page typewritten statement taped to smooth wood board and resembling the laminated plaques. The note indicated possible suicide. It was unaddressed and unsigned.

At six o'clock that morning, Bruce Cameron, a USC caretaker, had seen a body lying prone on the baseball infield, but he didn't approach it. He thought it was a student sleeping off a drunk. A couple of hours later, he and Mitharu Yamasaki, another campus caretaker, came closer. At Heritage Hall, where the USC athletic offices are housed, Virgil Lubberden, who often got to work early, saw them through a window. Jess Hill, then director of athletics, told his assistant to see what was going on.

"He was sprawled out, face down," Lubberden recalled. "I didn't realize at first it was Bruce. It was just unbelievable when I found out who it was."

At the Glasband–Willen Mortuary on Santa Monica Boulevard in Los Angeles, the crowd of mourners was so huge—about 500—that nearly half of them had to stand outside during the funeral service for Gardner.

Marty Biegel, the basketball coach at Fairfax High School, which Gardner had attended, delivered the eulogy with tears in his eyes. "Why? Dear God, explain to us why a thirty-two-year-old man like Bruce, so young, who had so much to give to so many, takes his life."

Bruce Clark Gardner won more games—forty—than any pitcher in USC history, including Tom Seaver, Bill Lee, Jim Barr, and Steve Busby. Before he ever pitched in a varsity game, he was offered a $66,500 bonus by the Chicago White Sox. He was handsome, intelligent, sensitive, and articulate. In junior high and high school, he was president of the student body. He was a talented pianist and entertainer. Nearly everyone who knew him came away feeling better for it.

Ron Mix, an All-American football player at USC and an All-Pro with the San Diego Chargers, knew Gardner well in college. "Bruce was a guy who seemingly had everything that God could bestow on one person," remembered Mix, now an attorney. "He was very bright—one of the top students in our class. He was a first-rate, decent person. If you could design your own life, what you'd like to be, you'd come up with a Bruce Gardner."

And yet, one June night nine years ago, Bruce Gardner, with most of his life left to live, walked out to the pitcher's mound at Bovard Field and put a bullet through his head.

In retrospect, it really ended for Gardner seven years earlier when he was released by Salem (Oregon) of the Northwest League. In 1960, fresh out of USC, he had signed a modest bonus contract of $12,000 with the Los Angeles Dodgers. The next year in the minors he won twenty games. Then he hurt his arm. By 1964, his professional baseball career was over. At twenty-five, Bruce Gardner, who had been brilliantly successful all his young life, considered himself a failure.

He returned home to Los Angeles, his lifelong dream of making the major leagues shattered—a dream he once had every reason to believe would become reality. Now lost, confused, his future unclear, Gardner began to feel frustration and bitterness.

Until now, Gardner's lengthy suicide note was never made public. Nor were the contents of his four thick, meticulously kept scrapbooks—15 × 13 art-form black Naugahyde-covered books with twenty-ring acetate pages—which he started to keep at seventeen.

At first, the scrapbooks tell a love story between Gardner and life. There are numerous photos of his parents, of young Betty Fegen, a pretty, twenty-five-year-old blond when she met Joe Gardner, and dark-haired, round-faced Joe ("robust, singing, smiling, friendly," wrote Gardner).

Betty and Joe married in 1937. Joe worked in an automotive parts store, and later started his own gas station. Gardner was born October 30, 1938. Baby pictures and photos of Gardner with his parents—he resembled his father—dominate the early pages. Happy childhood, happy family.

And then, suddenly, a funeral notice: "In memory of Joseph J. Gardner." Under it, Gardner wrote: "March 3, 1941, my father, Joe Gardner, died of strep throat, probably complicated by his own rheumatic fever as a boy"—and, ironically—"his death just preceded the use of penicillin."

Gardner included in his scrapbooks a poem—"The love and heart of my father"—composed when Gardner was nine:

When he had a heart
When he had a soul
God had to take my
Father to his goal

I dreamed of him too
and when I was
two years old he
had to go to his
goal. And after seven years
I saw his grave.

My father was
very kind and he
loved everybody that
was good and he said,
Never do anything that
you will be sorry for,
and his last words were

God bless you, and I
hope he did.

This is the end
of my story.
So, so long.

Despite his father's death, his boyhood seemed full and joyous—Cub Scouts, Halloween costumes, singing in a synagogue choir. And, at ten, he began to write about what would be the love and consuming passion of his life: baseball.

October, 1948: "Today was Halloween," he wrote. "I went trick or treating. I also thought about baseball. I made believe that I was the second Babe Ruth. When *The Babe Ruth Story* came to a local theater, I went in at two and came out after midnight. I sat through the main feature twice just to watch the Babe three times."

And later: "I had seen someone in school with a Marty Marion glove and I thought it was the greatest. I remember pulling my mother by the arm to the sporting goods store. No one was ever more willing to drop everything to play baseball than I was."

And at twelve, in 1950: "Ever since I have been playing baseball, it has been my ambition to one day be in the big leagues."

He was becoming a standout sandlot pitcher, as well as a model student. He wrote original poems, won "posture" contests, represented his school in city-wide oratorical contests, and was elected president of the student body of Bancroft Junior High in 1953.

"The election would be decided by the candidates' speeches," Gardner wrote. "I was last. This helped make the difference, because their weaknesses built up the dramatic strength of my speech. The scuffling during their speeches turned to silence during mine. I could feel the riveted attention to the last sentence. I won."

He also played the piano—at least partially out of a sense of commitment as the only child of a widowed mother. "After my dad's death, her life became a sacrifice," Gardner captioned one photo of his mother, who was working as a secretary at Temple Israel. "She went without things for herself so that I could have a baseball glove, piano lessons, braces on my teeth and a million other things. May I die on the spot if I try to forget it."

And he added: "I can't imagine how much different it would have been for mother if dad had lived."

When Gardner was about ten, Samuel Fegen, Betty's father, came to live with them in their two-floor, three-bedroom apartment in the primarily Jewish Fairfax district of Los Angeles. An orthodox Jew born in Russia who achieved

prosperity through real estate investments in the U.S., Fegen was a strict man who would get up every morning at four, tuck his fringed prayer shawl into his black pants, and walk to the synagogue to pray.

Under his grandfather's influence, Gardner was bar-mitzvahed, an occasion he describes glowingly. But this is the last mention of religion in the scrapbooks.

Meanwhile, there was growing tension in the home. "The grandpa was always accusing Bruce of stealing, of doing something wrong," recalled Barry Martin Biales, who would become one of Gardner's best friends, the executor of his estate and, ultimately, the owner of his scrapbooks. "Bruce would get upset, being accused of things he never did. And his mother, she was very frugal. There was a lock on the telephone. It was like a twilight zone in that house."

Not surprisingly, Gardner sought support outside the home—usually in the form of father figures. He found several, invariably baseball coaches—Bob Malcolm, his junior high school coach; Frank Shaffer, his coach at Fairfax High; and Tony Longo, father of his friend, Mike Longo, and coach of Gardner's American Legion team. "I practically raised Bruce," Tony Longo would say later. In the summers, Gardner's friends had a routine: meet at school, go to the beach, play baseball at a local park. But Gardner would skip the beach to wait for Longo to take him to play baseball.

Gardner's devotion to baseball was paying dividends. He gained a reputation as a left-handed pitching star in sandlot, American Legion, and high-school ball. Large crowds watched and cheered him.

Although he did not have a blazing fastball, he did have pinpoint control. And his concentration was intense. Art Harris, a boyhood friend and teammate, recalled: "There was always the sense of Bruce being a loner. When he was pitching, he seemed like a stranger in a crowd."

Something Gardner especially liked, he wrote, "was to pitch quickly, to force the action by pouring strikes past the hitter." He put himself on a strenuous running program, and he felt this gave him unmatched endurance and the capacity to work quickly. Friends remembered him running up the steps of the Fairfax bleachers in 90-degree heat in a sweat suit. "I honestly believe I ran more than any athlete in the history of Fairfax," he wrote.

In high school, Gardner was an honor student (he would finish seventy-sixth in a class of 403 in a school with a high academic reputation), student body president, honorary Mayor of Los Angeles for a day, and a piano player and singer who entertained at school assemblies.

Larry Wein, a neighbor and later a high school coach, remembered one incident. "Every kid grows up looking for a hero. In my case, it was Bruce Gardner. In fact, he was a hero for a lot of kids. I lived across the street from Fairfax, and I remember one time I was out on the track, running with my father. Bruce came over and asked if he could work out with us. That blew my mind. I mean, my hero was asking if he could work with us."

Gardner's high school career was a stream of successes. He made the varsity at sixteen, was 11–2 as a junior, and 18–1 in his senior year, leading his team into the city finals.

Major-league scouts came to his games. One was Harold (Lefty) Phillips of the Dodgers, considered a highly astute judge of baseball talent (he later managed the California Angels). Some time after Gardner's senior year in high school, Phillips filed the following confidential scouting report: "Has good stuff for eighteen-year-old but might be as good now as he ever will be. Real intelligent boy—might be too smart, know-it-all type. With a little more pitching and knowledge and experience should go into AA or at best AAA."

The Dodgers were anxious to sign him, even sending Larry Sherry—a former Fairfax High School pitching star and then a minor leaguer in the Dodger farm system—to persuade Gardner. But Gardner had already turned down an offer from the Pittsburgh Pirates of $4,000, and the Dodgers' offer had not been enough to keep him from college. On the advice of high school coach Shaffer and his mother, he had opted for an athletic grant-in-aid to USC.

A primary reason for attending USC, only 10 miles from his home, was Rod Dedeaux, the finest college baseball coach in the country. Dedeaux's sales pitch—that he'd work to get Gardner a bonus later and that a college education was worth $100,000—made sense to Betty Gardner. She was part of a tradition that found solace and power in learning. Sports, at best, were harmless diversions; at worst, a waste of time.

Gardner, in his desire to attach himself to an older man, sensed Dedeaux would fill the void. A graying, paunchy ex-ballplayer, he had become a wealthy trucking magnate in L.A. But, like Gardner, Dedeaux loved baseball first. That accounted for his USC salary—$1 a year. He pursued the job with fervor: "I have one set of rules—do everything absolutely right." With his devotion to discipline and a methodical approach to all things, Gardner seemed a perfect match for Dedeaux.

The freshman team at USC was coached by Joe Curi, which was fine for Gardner. "Curi loved me because I didn't complain and I was always ready," he wrote. "I was 10–0 for the season and held the USC varsity to a 0–0 tie. I was USC's freshman athlete of the year over my teammate Ron Fairly and shotputter Dave Davis. I was quickly becoming the best unsigned prospect in the United States."

This, it seemed, was likely to change quickly. Bob Pease, Gardner's manager on a sandlot team and a bird dog for the White Sox, recommended him to Hollis Thurston, Chicago's top scout on the West Coast. Gardner, accompanied by Tony Longo, was flown to Chicago for a tryout.

Gardner threw to a catcher in the bullpen at Comiskey Park. The big leagues. For twenty minutes, Thurston, Longo, manager Al Lopez, general manager John Rigney and farm director Glen Miller watched the 6-foot-1-inch, 185-pound southpaw.

Then Thurston turned to Longo and said, "We'll take him." He mentioned a big bonus figure. Longo said, "You'll have to talk to his mother." Gardner was only eighteen, and needed his mother's consent to sign.

The big number was $66,500, enormous in 1957. Gardner rushed home to tell his mother the news. Betty Gardner was not moved.

"Bruce came over to my house to talk with my father, who he was very close to," said Biales. "He looked sad. He told us about the offer, and said his mother wouldn't let him sign. My father said, 'Are you kidding? That kind of money doesn't come along every day.' Bruce said he had pleaded with his mother. I remember him saying, 'I was in tears. I asked her to, please, just sign it. I can go to school in the off-season. I'm ready now.' "

Longo couldn't believe it. But he understood. "Bruce was a good boy, the kind of kid you want for your own. He had fights with his mother, but who hasn't? When it was done, he listened to her. It's not like today. When a parent told you to do something, you did it."

Apparently, Mrs. Gardner was influenced greatly by Dedeaux, who emphasized the value of a college education—and that Gardner would get an even better deal after he graduated as a star. "I didn't approve of his signing, because I felt he needed security for the future. I wanted to help him become a success and make a lot of money. The trouble, I suppose, was that he felt I was interfering with his goal." (Betty Gardner remembers her son fondly—"he was magic, a wonderful, adorable person"—but finds it too painful to say much more about him now.)

Several of Gardner's USC teammates would leave school after signing major-league contracts, including Ron Fairly and Len Gabrielson. But Gardner, the dutiful son, stayed and, on the surface, seemed happy. "I don't know of anyone who enjoyed college more than Bruce," said Dedeaux.

Star athlete, excellent student, popular with the coeds, handsome. Gardner tried out for a bit part in the campus play, *Damn Yankees*. He won the lead— playing Joe Hardy, the man who loved baseball more than anything else in life—and was a hit. He had never sung or danced on stage before.

On the field, Gardner made All-League in each of his three varsity years. In his last two (27–4), he made All-NCAA District 8, and, in his final year, he was All-American. In 1960, he was named Player of the Year after leading the Trojans to the final game of the College World Series (USC lost).

And he liked and respected Dedeaux. Don Buford, a USC teammate and later a major leaguer: "Most of the guys who played for Rod felt the same way about him. Playing for Rod was, in some ways, like playing for a major-league man-ager, he was that good. But most of us looked on him as more than a coach. We relied on his judgment, even in personal matters. Bruce and I were only children. Both our fathers died when we were young, and we were both raised by our mothers. We didn't talk about it much, but, in some ways, it created a bond between us."

Dedeaux remembered Gardner as a friend. "One of the finest boys we ever had. There was never a more cooperative guy in any way."

In 1958, the season after not being allowed to accept the White Sox bonus, Gardner wasn't satisfied with his performance. He wrote: "I had my first poor year. I won almost all my games—13–1, with a 2.62 ERA—because we scored so many runs. But I lost a good deal off my fastball, probably because of losing so much weight." (Gardner had dropped 15 pounds to 170.)

There is a photo of Gardner, customary smile on his face, with three other USC pitchers. Next to the photo, he wrote in his scrapbook: "I look happy on the outside, but I'm thinking, 'What am I doing here? I should be in professional ball now, establishing my credentials.' "

He also wrote about leaving the practice field terribly upset. "I was running away. But who to? My grandfather? My mother? Rod Dedeaux?"

On May 21, 1958, Phillips amended his scouting file on Gardner: "Poor rotation on curve and hangs lots of breaking balls. Poor deception on change-up. His stuff is inconsistent. Poor pitching rhythm. Question his mental setup, don't believe he will stay with the game if the going gets tough. He has gone backward."

During Gardner's senior year, his grandfather died, which caused some family problems. His grandfather's will had been changed shortly before his death, leaving everything to Betty Gardner and nothing to his other daughter and three sons. (Two cousins estimated the inheritance at more than $100,000, although Mrs. Gardner wouldn't confirm the figure.)

"Bruce went to see his aunt and uncle," recalled Biales, "and they didn't want him in the house. 'Go tell your mother to give us the thousands she took,' they told him.

" 'Why blame me?' he said.

" 'We don't want you showing up anymore,' they said."

This disturbed Gardner, who had a great sense of family. Growing up without a father, he had clung to his relatives. But as he was hurt, so he would turn around and exhibit kindness to others. "He'd be at a party," Biales said, "and he'd see a wallflower, a plain girl sitting off by herself. 'That's unfair,' he'd say. 'She's not having a good time.' And he'd ask her to dance."

After Gardner's senior year, Phillips upgraded the scouting report: "Tall, rawboned, long arms, good agility. Best fastball tails away high and outside. Sharp-breaking curve. Should be signed for somewhere in the amount of the first-year draft price." Translation: a bonus of $12,000, to be paid out in three $4,000 installments. Gardner agreed; Phillips signed him.

Gardner was smiling in newspaper photos of the signing, but he later wrote: "I cried that night. I had thrown away three baseball seasons. I had thrown away a very important amount of money. And though I had a college degree, I couldn't see its importance. I was older, and there was something wrong with my arm. It took me a long time to warm up the last few games at USC."

The severity of his arm problem was never spelled out, but the arm was strong enough for him to enter professional baseball at the highest level of the minor leagues, the Dodgers' AAA team in Montreal in the International League.

Oddly enough, however, by major-league standards he was less of a prospect than after his freshman year. At eighteen, he didn't have the outstanding fastball. But he might have developed one. At twenty-one, he didn't have that fastball, and he never would.

Dedeaux thought it was a good deal anyway. "If he had signed after his freshman year," said the USC coach, "he would never have been sent to a AAA team. He'd have started much lower in the minors."

Perhaps. But the White Sox might have taken special care of him, bringing him along properly to protect their investment.

Montreal was a rude awakening. "He goes to Montreal," said Biales, "which is like forty-two games behind, and they had all these greasy old ballplayers. Bruce is knocking on hotel doors, 'Hello, this is Bruce Gardner reporting.'

" 'Get the hell out of here, you punk kid. I got a broad in here.' He had to sleep in the lobby. You know, they broke him in at Montreal. He had been a virgin. The guys said, 'Hey, we got to take care of this kid.' So they took him out and got him laid.

"Some people wonder if he was a homosexual, and couldn't face that fact in his macho sports world. If he was, I never knew it. He loved women, loved their bodies. He had a lot of affairs as he got older."

To the hardened veterans of pro ball, Gardner must have seemed vulnerable. Clean-cut, seemingly naive, a musician, college kid. There were few collegians in pro baseball then, and only a few had degrees, as Gardner did. Many players had not finished high school. Some veteran managers had not even attended high school.

Gardner wrote to Dedeaux: "Boy, what a difference. Pro ball isn't the glamorous life everybody thinks it is."

Johnny Werhas, a USC teammate who later played for the Angels and the Dodgers, felt that a lot of baseball people simply didn't understand Gardner. "They thought he was an oddball. But I tell you, he was way ahead of his time. He was eating health foods way before the fad. He went to chiropractors before anyone else. Once he removed all the hair on his left arm, as an experiment, to cut down wind resistance. People laughed, but years later swimmers like Mark Spitz and other athletes were doing the same thing." He also stood on his head doing yoga in the dugout. He said it brought more blood to his pitching arm.

After some undistinguished appearances at Montreal, where his record was 0–1, he reported for his first spring training at Dodgertown in Vero Beach, Florida, in 1961. The facilities were first-rate, but the caliber of baseball minds did not impress Gardner. "I can't believe these people", Gardner told Biales. "The only smart guy I met there was Walter O'Malley." O'Malley owned the Dodgers and once gave Gardner $100 for playing his favorite song on the lounge piano.

That first spring, Gardner still had not gotten over a case of mononucleosis. "Mononucle-what?" said one of the coaches. "Get out there and run. When I was your age, Gardner, I never had this mono-stuff you're talking about." Gardner's response? "Go tell Roy Campanella when you were his age, you never got in an auto accident." Campanella, the great Dodger catcher, was paralyzed for life after an auto mishap.

Gardner, who was supposed to be assigned to Greenville in AA classification, was sent instead to Reno of the California League. Class C. "What a waste,"

Gardner told a friend. "I'll probably win forty games. I should be pitching AAA ball."

Gardner was 20–4 at Reno. In his Dodger scouting report, Reno manager Roy Smalley described Gardner: "Excellent attitude, exceptional aptitude. Improving steadily, has endurance, good fielder, hits well, mentally tough. Has a chance to make majors." Smalley did not mention Gardner's occasional habit of standing on his head in the dugout, sometimes while the National Anthem was being played.

The official 1962 program of the Dodgers lists a handful of players with exceptional promise on their minor-league clubs. One was Gardner: "Former Trojan Bruce Gardner topped the California League in four departments. His 20–4 record gave him top victory total, and best percentage (.833). He also pitched most complete games, eighteen, and was the ERA leader with 2.82."

After the season ended, Gardner went to Fort Ord, California, to fulfill a military obligation. He was to serve six months and be out in time for spring training. But the Cold War escalated into the Berlin Crisis, active duty rosters were frozen, and Gardner injured his arm on maneuvers—possibly one time when he fell off a truck. Finally released in July, he was assigned to Spokane, a AAA team in the Pacific Coast League.

At the time, his mother was staying with one of Gardner's paternal aunts in Oakland. She begged him to take her along to Spokane. He didn't want to, but he couldn't stand to see her cry. So he piled everything he had in the world—including his mother—into his car and took off. He met the team on the road in Seattle and sent his mother on in the loaded car to Spokane to find an apartment.

Gardner had made $600 a month in Reno. He expected a minimum raise to $800 and thought he would probably get $1,000. He received a new contract for $700. And that wasn't the worst of it. "I came into Spokane at seven in the morning—and there my mother was in the car packed to overflowing and no place to go," he wrote. Apparently, only two places met Betty Gardner's standards of frugality. "One was a dingy basement apartment. The other was a *fucked* up, dilapidated Chinese hotel. I put my hand over my forehead and eyes and just sat still. I gave up. We took the Chinese hotel. I went to sleep on an empty, unmade cot and later got up and went to the ballpark like a POW. This was early August, 1962, and around this time Marilyn Monroe committed suicide. And this idea for the first time entered and cemented itself in my mind." It was also the first time Gardner had used any profanity in his writings.

He finished 1–5 in Spokane. There were hysterical shouting matches with his mother in which Gardner dredged up old hurts about not signing the big bonus contract. He was suffering, his arm hurt, and he was failing as a pitcher.

"I didn't sleep nights," he wrote. "Instead, I took piano lessons in Spokane. After each game I would go to the studio and beat the piano until morning. I even smoked cigarettes for the first time. Then I could go back to the Chinese hotel and sleep all day on that shitty cot."

Spokane manager Preston Gomez's succinct report on Gardner: "Says arm hurts. So have to wait for him to get better before make determination."

There is still vagueness about the origins of his arm problem. But it was clear the snap in his pitches was diminishing. So was his confidence as he prepared for another season. He wrote: "In spring training, Tommy Lasorda didn't even say hello. [The year before, Lasorda had held Gardner up as an example of how to throw the difficult 'drop' curve.] It's a game of survival of the fittest. A twenty-game winner fits. A one-game winner doesn't. My pitching was forced. I had trouble getting anything on the ball."

During his years in the minors, there is no mention of his father in the scrapbooks. Two photographs put in about this time are noteworthy, though. One shows Gardner's father in a dark suit, buttoned up, smiling, with his arm around a friend. In the photo directly below, taken more recently, Gardner is posed and dressed identically—with his arm around the son of his father's friend.

In 1963, he was assigned to Salem (Oregon) in Class A, pitched poorly, and was sent to Great Falls (Montana) in the Pioneer League. His last night in Salem was spent with a girl named Jo. "It was the most beautiful time I'd ever had. In the morning she brought her baby over (from a previous marriage), made breakfast. I dreamed of life as it should be, packed everything I owned again into the car and traveled to Great Falls."

There, getting by on guile, he was 10–4 with a 4.07 ERA. And the dream of a major-league career persisted. That December he sent Christmas cards with a picture of himself in a Dodger uniform.

Betty Gardner still worried about her son. Early in 1964, she wrote to Fresco Thompson, vice-president of personnel for the Dodgers:

May I introduce myself? I am Bruce Gardner's mother. Confidentially, I am concerned about my son. Could you give me any information about his future with the Dodgers? How fast is his ability as a pitcher? How is he progressing, etc.?

I am very proud of my son and eager to help him make good. He is very ambitious and loves baseball very much. I wonder if there is anything I can do to help him achieve his aspirations.

P.S. Of course, I would not want Bruce to know that I am writing to you as he may think I am being too forward.

Thompson responded:

You are, undoubtedly, aware that Bruce began his professional career by winning 20 and losing 4 in 1961. For some reason, he has been unable to recapture the form which he showed in 1961.

At spring training in 1962, he indulged in self-diagnosis and self-treatment of real and imaginary ills. On two occasions, I personally went to his room to see why he had not reported for practice. Each time I found him in bed with what he had diagnosed as a respiratory condition. He was treating himself despite the fact that we had a full time Doctor and Registered Nurse on the premises at all times.

He then began visiting chiropractors in Vero Beach and elsewhere for soreness in his arm. Mrs. Gardner, in all my baseball experience, I have never heard of one of these bone-poppers curing a baseball player of anything.

Baseball is a difficult and demanding taskmaster. One must, during the baseball season, apply himself solely and diligently to becoming a ballplayer. This I do not think Bruce does at all times. With most youngsters in the Dodger Organization, baseball is the end. With Bruce, this is not so; baseball is a means to an end. What that end is no amount of probing and delving has uncovered.

Gardner discovered these letters in 1968 and put them in his scrapbooks. He wrote: "Boy, oh boy. Some of the things she says in that letter sure hurt. 'Proud of my son and eager to help him make good.' How come we never discussed this? She didn't seem proud in 1957. It's a little late now.

"But Fresco's answers are as ridiculous as my mother's questions. 'How fast is his pitching ability?' Her main question was 'etc.' That's Jewish for 'I don't know what I'm interested in asking so you tell me.'

"So he tells her that I was sick in 1962. Since I was actually sick during 1961, that's also the year I had my successful season. He forgets I was in the Army in 1962. Then I suppose he convinced my mother I wasn't really dedicated. Fresco had a real talent for: thinking, over-eating, over-drinking and using the word 'taskmaster'."

Gardner's last training camp was in 1964 at Vero Beach. "Bruce was the hardest working guy I ever saw," said Jimmy Campanis, his catcher that final season. "He would run and run and run." But he broke an ankle practicing slides and wasn't ready to pitch again until early summer, when he reported to Salem. A rule of thumb among major-league teams is three years to rise in the minors. Salem was Gardner's last chance.

"Good kid," recalled his last manager, Stan Wasiak. "Hard worker, high-class boy. But sometimes I got the feeling he thought he was above me, in intellectual status."

At the ballpark, Gardner struggled to a 2–2 record in nineteen appearances, finished none of his three starts, and had an earned-run average of 5.40. An old USC teammate, Marcel Lachemann, played in the same league that year and thought Gardner pitched "almost like an amateur. It was sad watching it." He was nearly twenty-six years old, a faded prospect.

"I was up in the press box late one night after a game," remembered Bob Schwartz, sports news editor of Salem's morning newspaper, the *Oregon Statesman*. "I saw Bruce on the field, fully dressed. He was standing on the mound. I'm sure he didn't know I was there. He smoothed the rubber with his foot, then walked around the mound. I went back to work. When I had finished, he was gone."

In a confidential Dodger report, a scout wrote: "Has no future." Gardner concurred. "My arm could only take an inning," he wrote. "Damaged by now." But he felt bitterness toward the Dodger organization: "Too many kinds of people that can't be decent unless you're leading the bandwagon."

From the scrapbooks: "Notice of Official Release. September 30, 1964. You are officially notified of the non-disposition of your contract. You are released unconditionally. Fresco Thompson."

Gardner now faced the classic dilemma of the former pro athlete, the one-time star: What do you do when the cheers stop, when the lifelong dream collapses? Whom could he blame? Whom could he strike back at? He was not a violent person. He never even threw at a hitter. He remembered when Marilyn Monroe committed suicide, how he felt. One day, about a month after he was released, Gardner went to Vernon, a small town near Los Angeles, and bought a .38 Smith & Wesson blue-steel pistol in a pawn shop.

He told Biales: "I went home to plan to shoot myself, but the phone rang and got my mind off it."

Biales was stunned. "Are you serious?"

"Yeah," said Gardner. "Everything's so low. The baseball's over and there's nothing left for me."

On June 4, 1965, Betty Gardner, now having frequent shouting matches with her son, again wrote to Fresco Thompson:

My son seems so unhappy at the end result of his baseball career.

I hate to see him so unhappy. It is partially due to a scout making a high offer one day and reneging the next day, that has caused Bruce to be this way.

I think perhaps if he could in any way work with baseball (which has been his dream since he was 10 years old) that he would not now be so depressed. Do you think there is any phase of the game he could fit into?

Thompson replied two weeks later:

I am indeed sorry that Bruce appears to be so unhappy due to the fact that he is now out of baseball.

I must say that Bruce has absolutely no one to blame but himself for his present predicament. We gave Bruce every opportunity to take full advantage of his God-given baseball talents. He appeared, however, to have many other things on his mind.

I regret that I cannot advise you of some other phase of the game in which he might fit. Professional baseball is an exacting taskmaster and in order to succeed, a full-time effort is required.

Gardner wrote: "Now my career is over. Eight years late and now my mother is concerned. My mother's philosophy is to get concerned when it's too late. But create the predicament by not using reason beforehand. She says a scout reneged. I guess because I didn't sign. He didn't renege. She shouted, 'No,' at me. I'm afraid the shadows of Rod Dedeaux in the wings made her unable to move in any direction.

"Quit bothering the wrong man [Fresco Thompson], mother! Looking back, I don't see what I could have done differently except to quit baseball earlier. My life was taken away."

Outwardly, Gardner seemed to adjust. He was a real-estate salesman, then sold mutual funds. He dressed nattily and flashed jewelry. In 1968, he won a trip to Bermuda and the next year was awarded another trip—to Puerto Vallerta, Mexico—for his sales success.

There he fell in love with a "beautiful, intelligent and charming girl" from Vancouver named Donna. He wrote a song about her the first day he met her, "with the sound of xylophone and mariachi in my mind."

> . . . there wasn't anything such as tomorrow
> They would wine and dine and laugh,
> And the day just seemed like half;
> She was the essence of his life—
> such a madonna.
> But when it came time to leave,
> How his soul would ache and grieve;
> It tore his heart to have to say, Mañana Donna, mañana Donna,
> It's so hard to be apart,
> For you have entered in my heart,
> Life is too short to want to say,
> mañana Donna . . .

He visited her in Canada but soon concluded, "Her enthusiasm didn't equal mine."

There were other girls—exotic Latins he met in some of the strip joints in which he played the piano—and for a time there was a serious liaison with a slim blond named Pat. But they all faded, too. He complained he could never get the girl he wanted.

In 1970, his mutual funds career collapsed because of a slump in the market. Friends and relatives who had invested with him lost money—and he felt real guilt about it. He trained to become a bank manager for a savings company, but he was let go after four months. He was told he didn't have the background for the position.

"In the last two weeks of 1970, I became very despondent and thought of ending my life, which hasn't been a rare thought for me for over a decade now," he wrote.

His cousin, Paul Fegen, remembered Gardner's disillusionment with life "because he couldn't make of himself what everyone else thought he should have. He was disappointed that he couldn't make money, because in school he was always the hero. He was like an aging actor who no longer could get parts. With Bruce, it happened suddenly."

Gardner still maintained an interest in baseball, and often went to games at Dodger Stadium with Biales. He would sit high behind home plate, watch the pitcher intently, and say, "That should be me out there." Periodically, he visited the Dodger clubhouse to look up old teammates who had made it— Campanis, Lefebvre, Werhas, Fairly. "I didn't sense any bitterness or envy in him," said Werhas. "He seemed happy for me."

So to the world at large, Gardner maintained a smile. And he still went out of his way to extend a kindness. In December of 1970, he organized a surprise party for the managers of his apartment building, Arthur and Virginia Searles. He wrote a letter to the apartment building owner, Mr. Meltzer, describing the good job they did. The Searleses framed the letter.

"But do you know what else Bruce did?" Virginia Searles would later ask rhetorically. "He deliberately sent the invitation to Mr. Meltzer a day late, so he wouldn't be there. Mr. Meltzer wasn't the friendly type, and Bruce felt he didn't appreciate us as much as he should. When Mr. Meltzer called me, he said, 'I would have come to the party but I got the letter a day late.' All of us in the building thought it was a wonderful joke."

To earn a steady living, Gardner took a job as a physical education and health teacher at Dorsey High School in southwest Los Angeles. It's a predominantly black school, with a small percentage of Oriental students. Gardner also coached the junior varsity baseball team to a 13–2 record, winning a championship for the first time in the school's history.

The star of the jayvee squad was Vassie Gardner, no relation. Vassie Gardner is black. He was a pitcher; he is now an outfielder with Chattanooga of the Southern League.

"Mr. Gardner reminded me of the coach on the TV program, *White Shadow*— only he was years ahead of it, and he was for real," said Vassie Gardner. "We were mainly a black team, and it was hard for me to believe a white guy would really care for me. He thought I had the potential to make the major leagues. But I was running loose on the streets. He'd call my house to make sure I was all right. Once he asked me to move in with him. He'd kind of adopt me.

"Guys used to joke around, say Mr. Gardner's funny. A faggot. Because of the way he walked. Real straight. But he wasn't effeminate. He scared the hell out of me when he got mad.

"One day, I was late for practice. He told me to take a lap around the field. I told him I wasn't going to do it. Oh, did he get angry. So I said, 'Well, I better run a lap.' About halfway, I ducked behind a backstop on the other side of the field. As soon as I stopped, I felt someone grab me from behind. It was Mr. Gardner; he'd been running behind me. He wrestled me to the ground. He was strong. And he began hitting me in the stomach. Playfully, not really hurting me. 'I'm tired of your bullshit,' he told me. 'You're going to start doing things right, and you're going to get your ass out here and become a ballplayer.'

"He talked about his career. Something messed it up, a bad arm. He was my man. I wish he was still living. It happened too fast; I was just getting to know him."

Ironically, at the same time he was having this kind of impact on his players, Gardner was telling friends and relatives how he hadn't found anything worth doing, how useless he felt. And aimless.

Jim Lefebvre, his teammate at Salem and then with the Dodgers, saw him sitting alone in the box seats in Dodger Stadium one day in 1971. "I went over to him and asked him how he was doing. He said, 'Oh, okay.' I asked him what he was up to, and he told he was coaching junior high school. I asked how he liked it. He said, 'It's not what I want to be doing.' His eyes had a vacant quality. He seemed alone, inside himself."

On the first Thursday in June of 1971, his boyhood buddy, Art Harris, saw Gardner at Dodger Stadium at the city high-school-baseball championship game. "Good," Art thought to himself, "he's with some other people." Harris was sensitive to Gardner's loneliness. Then Harris spotted Dedeaux and Casey Stengel, a close friend of Dedeaux, walking down the aisle together. "Bruce turned around and saw Dedeaux," Harris said. "Rod gave him the usual, 'Hi, Tiger.' Bruce's face turned as white as a gym towel. Looking back, I know now that he was already planning to kill himself."

Bruce Gardner, sensitive and dedicated, wasn't trained to handle failure. When Al Campanis, the Dodgers' vice-president for personnel (and father of

Gardner's teammate, Jimmy), was asked what he remembered most about Gardner, he said:

"He didn't win."

On Friday afternoon, June 4, 1971, Vassie Gardner was playing basketball in the Dorsey gym and turned to see his coach staring at him. "He was just standing and watching me," he said. "I never saw that stare before. I guess he knew he was going to go away."

Gardner stayed in all of Saturday and Saturday night. He fastidiously arranged his bookshelves. In his bedroom, there was a neat pile of *Playboy* magazines, which would later shock one of his aunts. His clothes in the closet were hung meticulously in sections—pants, suits, coats. Stacks of record albums neatly flanked his stereo. The blond wood furniture was dusted. The seascape oil painting on the wall behind the stereo was perfectly straight. The lid of the piano was pulled down over the keys.

On Sunday, Virginia Searles saw Gardner neatly folding his wash in the laundry room. She said, "Good morning, Bruce." He said, "Good morning." That was it. She knew Gardner was a private person, though friendly. If he didn't want to say anything more, that was fine.

That was the last time anyone saw Bruce Gardner alive.

At 11:30, Arthur Searles made his nightly security check around the building. He noticed that Gardner's Buick LeSabre was parked in an odd place. The driveway had eighteen individual carports on each side, with Gardner's spot designated No. 1, his apartment number. He always parked it there. Perfectly. This night, the car was parked on the incline at the end of the driveway. Since Searles saw no light in Gardner's apartment, he decided not to knock. Gardner—"such a thoughtful neighbor"—would take care of the problem the next day.

At that moment, Gardner was probably lying in bed in the dark. Apparently, he had made the decision at least as far back as Friday. Ken Bailey, the tennis coach, had seen Gardner grading books for his four gym classes. Bailey thought it was odd. School didn't close for two weeks.

Sometime after midnight, it is presumed, Gardner rose from his bed and began his final preparations:

The chronology is uncertain, but he probably sat down at his Remington manual typewriter to type his suicide note. He poured himself a shot of Scotch. He kept the liquor for guests, because he never drank. But in times of distress, he would often do something out of character—like the time in Spokane when an argument with his mother drove him to his first cigarette. As he typed up two copies of the suicide note—and a will, which he left in the roller—he drank some more. (He would eventually consume the equivalent of four highballs, according to the coroner's report.) The will gave most of his $3,000 estate to Biales. He left $1 to his mother.

Gardner then placed one copy of the suicide note into the last page of his scrapbook, and carefully taped the other note onto a wooden board.

He washed his glass and returned the bottle of Scotch to the cabinet.

He shaved, brushed his dark brown curly hair—cut short because he didn't like the way it kinked.

He put on a tan sport shirt with thin collar, a black sweater, blue-striped slacks, and black loafers. Then he slipped into a brown corduroy jacket with leather buttons.

He gathered the three plaques he would carry with him: the baseball All-American certificate, his USC diploma, the suicide note.

From the back of his top drawer in the bedroom, he removed the pistol and put it in his jacket pocket.

Before leaving, he made his bed. A detective would say later that the apartment was so tidy it looked as if Gardner had been expecting guests.

He picked up the plaques, closed the lights, walked outside, and double-locked the door. It was cool in Los Angeles for a June morning, 57 degrees. He buttoned his jacket. It was about three A.M.

He put the three plaques in the car, and backed out onto Cattaraugus Avenue.

The route he usually took was through a quiet neighborhood of small, single-story homes to the Santa Monica Freeway. The divided concrete strip is invariably quiet at that hour. On the left are the lights of Beverly Hills and the Hollywood hills. Two of his closest cousins, Paul Fegen and Arlene Rosenthal, were asleep in large homes in the high section—the kind of luxurious homes Gardner never had. He drove past the Fairfax Avenue turnoff, exit to the neighborhood in which he was the big star. He drove past La Brea, the exit he would normally take to Dorsey High School. The exits rolled by—Crenshaw, Arlington, Normandy, and finally Vermont and the turnoff to USC. He almost certainly clicked the right-turn signal. He was a careful driver, never got a ticket, followed all the rules of the road.

At Jefferson Boulevard, he would turn left, then right on McClintock to the USC campus. The security guardhouse, built on a small island at the entrance, was empty. He turned into 34th Street and parked halfway down the block. Bovard Field was only 300 yards away. It was quiet.

Gardner got out of the car with his three plaques, the gun in his pocket. He walked past Founders Hall, then through the slightly dewy hedge to the baseball field. The gate was locked. He climbed over the wooden fence, probably at its lowest point—along left field—where it was 7 feet high.

The moon was three nights short of full, and it cast a bright light, creating shadows on the field. Gardner walked across the moist grass to the pitcher's mound, surrounded by empty stands which were once filled with fans cheering for him. He placed the suicide note on the grass at the edge of the circle. He walked a few feet more and lay down, halfway to second base. He lay straight. When they found him, he wouldn't be crumpled and awkward. His right elbow cradled the All-American plaque and his degree. With his pitching hand, he removed the pistol from his jacket pocket, then raised it to his temple.

Only the typewritten note nearby would be left to explain.

Let my blood be the pathetic proof to those who have heard Rod Dedeaux say that a college education is worth $100,000 more in a man's lifetime. Because it is so deceitfully true. The man who starts at $800 a month versus the one who starts at $600 a month will wind up, after forty years, with $100,000 more.

And isn't that enough reason to shatter the hopes and dreams of an eighteen-year-old boy who has the opportunity to sign into professional baseball with offers high in five figures?

To keep him in college, don't let him believe that he could do anything with that kind of money but squander it. Don't ask what it is the boy wants to accomplish. Because he might tell you that he would like to go into professional baseball, especially in light of the fact that many who know baseball have regarded him very highly. And that it's his love.

Then don't look too carefully at the facts. Don't think that a good student—president of Bancroft Junior High and Fairfax High—with the determination of a winning miler, captain and three-year cross-country runner, and the excellence of an All-City pitcher, could possibly have the wherewithal to make decisions concerning his own life.

Since he is too young to sign for himself, scare his mother. It's even easier, because his father passed away when the son was three. Let the mother feel that her boy will be wandering skid row if he leaves college. So that when he begs her to let him sign, she has nothing but shouts of "no." Do all these things carefully, Rod Dedeaux, and you will have an All-American. And his mother will get her vicarious college degree. Don't let any of his advantages get in the way of your National Championship.

He'll have graduated before your half-truths become the realities of his place in the world. And then he'll wonder where is the magic in the education you don't seek, and why so much energy is compulsively wasted in containing his bitterness and moving one foot in front of the other to get to each day's meaningless job. Where his $800 a month won't buy the home he's never had, meet the friends he's never entertained, nor call the mother he never wants to see. To what direction have the fragments of his broken heart discarded his ability to give and receive love?

But given another thirty-two years—in retirement he'll be able to look back with that overpowering joyful knowledge that some people in their work-a-day world jobs didn't earn the $100,000 more that he did in his. And that's when he'll hug his diploma and die of unhappiness. But somehow I don't need to wait anymore for that day. I reached it years and years ago.

I saw no value in my college education. I saw life going downhill every day and it shaped my attitude toward everything and everybody. Everything and every feeling that

I visualized with my earned and rightful start in baseball was the focal point of continuous failure. No pride of accomplishment, no money, no home, no sense of fulfillment, no leverage, no attraction. A bitter past, blocking any accomplishment of a future except age.

I brought it to a halt tonight at thirty-two.

The 1980s have wrought a queasy new turn on the alumni reunion: a curdled-fantasy baseball camp for the old-boy set, complete with now-rotund heroes of yore. Was Dorian Gray ever on a baseball card? Or Ricardo Montalban? Never mind—only a determined spoilsport would find this frolic a downer. Boys of winter, play on.

ROY BLOUNT, JR.

We All Had a Ball

I have a T-shirt and two sweat shirts that say "I PLAYED BASEBALL AGAINST THE 1969 CUBS." This intro lets me get on with the rest of the story. "Hello, my name is Blat, Blong, Bough—whatever, it doesn't matter—and the very fact that Ferguson Jenkins was playing me deep enough to catch a ball hit 350 feet tells you something" is how I usually begin.

"Excuse me?" people reply.

"I hit a ball 350 feet," I say.

"Where?"

"Pulled it dead to left. It was caught—over the shoulder, but still, he must have been playing me pretty deep—by Ferguson Jenkins. He was in left at the time. You know how guys over thirty-five are; they like to live out their fantasies, and Jenkins probably always wanted to rob a sportswriter of extra bases. Earlier in camp, he called me—just a minute, I think I have the exact wording somewhere . . . here it is: 'A good hitter.' O.K., you *could* say that's the kind of thing he might say to his nephew, but still. . . ."

"No, I mean where, like in, what park?"

"Scottsdale Stadium. Arizona. Which was strangely appropriate, because. . . ."

"Oh. Thin air."

Thin air. I may have to get another T-shirt that says "I HIT A BASEBALL 350 FEET AND WHY IS IT THAT EVERYONE'S REACTION IS 'THIN AIR'?" The whole trouble with my baseball career, and my life, is that my T-shirts have to have too many words on them.

My game shirt, the authentic Chicago away uniform shirt I was wearing when I hit the ball 350 feet, has only one word on it: "CUBS." The All-Star Baseball School's weeklong camp last month for men over thirty-five, which culminated with a game against some of the '69 Cubs, was the closest I will come to fitting myself into that word, that one round patch.

How close was that?

What? Who are *you* with?

This was an oft fantasized experience you had, right? So this is your oft fantasized interview.

About time.

You weren't satisfied with your press coverage at the camp?

No. *Time* magazine unaccountably attributed my 350-foot shot to Art Lessel, a sixty-three-year-old pilot.

Yeah, but what about the thin air?

I'll tell you about thin air. Thin air is when Randy Hundley, who was one of the former Cubs I played against, pops a ball incalculably high into what we call the Big Arizona Sky. Being camped under a fly in Arizona is like looking over the side of a boat after a camera you just dropped into Lake Michigan. And I'll tell you something else about thin air. Thin air is when I, the third baseman, fresh from the triumph of hitting a ball 350 feet, find myself in the position of having to come to grips with a pop-up that resembles the average person's concept of a pop-up about as much as Ralph Sampson resembles your gym teacher.

In other words, a tough chance.

But that's not all. To try to catch it, I have to drift toward the same spot where, in 1970, I had my darkest day as a sportswriter, when Leo Durocher— who managed the Cubs then and was managing them again in this game— branded me as the anti-Cub right there in front of the whole team. Anyway, I miss it.

Really? The pop-up? Why do you miss it?

I don't miss it now. I missed it then. And three days later it's on national TV. At least my friends and I think that's me we see, though I find out much later it's some other guy missing a different pop-up. But by then, the damage to my psyche and reputation had been done.

What were you called? You and the other sixty-two men over thirty-five who, for $2,195 each, lived out a boyhood dream by working out with major leaguers?

"Campers." I would have liked "prospects" better. By the way, two or three guys under thirty-five slipped in. Can you imagine how far I would have hit the ball if I'd been their age? I'm forty-one! True, I never hit a ball that far when I *was* under thirty-five. That was the longest ball I ever hit in my life. And maybe the last. What a way to go out! But what if I'm getting better? What if I have yet to come into my oft fantasized-own? Baseball! You just won't let go! I might say, however, that it was never my boyhood dream to miss a pop-up in front of thousands of people.

The All-Star School, which is operated by Hundley and Chicago entrepreneur Allan Goldin, usually instructs kids, right?

Yes, we were the historic first middle-aged campers. And we seem to have struck a chord. Every television network was all over us. Another Cub camp, also in Scottsdale, is planned for April, and a company called Baseball Fantasies Fulfilled has announced an April camp in Tempe featuring old Dodgers.

How did the Cub camp work?

Very well. We had the Scottsdale facilities that the Cubs formerly used for spring training, and we were drilled in fundamentals by '69 Cubs Hundley, Jenkins, Billy Williams, Ron Santo, Ernie Banks, Glenn Beckert, Jim Hickman, Rich Nye, Ken Rudolph and Gene Oliver, and by slightly later-vintage Cubs José Cardenal and Steve Stone. The old Cubs also played with us in intrasquad games. Nobody wanted to look like a jerk in front of them. Take away the Cubs and the camp would have degenerated into middle-aged doctors, lawyers, brokers, and businessmen rolling around on the ground fighting over whose bat it was. There should be Cubs at the U.N.

And on the last day of camp, in Scottsdale Stadium—where the fences are all deeper than 350 feet—before around 4,200 fans and a host of media folks who don't really care about the longest ball a person ever hit in his entire life, the old Cubs beat us 23–6.

Does that mean you were seventeen runs short of being as good as a team of major leaguers, one of whom, Jenkins, is still active, and, incidentally, is 6 feet 5 inches and is the guy who caught your soaring drive over his shoulder?

It's hard to say. I do know that I came within about 15 inches of catching what you would call a major-league pop-up. I remember thinking to myself, while drifting over toward the spot in foul territory where I first met Durocher in 1970, "Oh, well, God, I guess . . . mine." Privately, I hoped that Jimmy Stuart, a commodities trader in Chicago who won the plaque for Most Aggressive Camper, would hustle pushily over from shortstop and call me off of it, and I would've given him a look of annoyance and let him have it. But he didn't.

I looked up at that thing. And what struck me was, "This pop-up doesn't care who I am." Also, the sun was in my eyes. "The sun is in my eyes," I thought. "And I *still* don't know what made Durocher say what he said in

1970. And anyway, what in the hell am I supposed to do with this thing? I'm a writer. I'm forty-one years old. And I was never all that good when I was twenty-one. And it's not even really spring yet. The pop-ups are ahead of the third basemen. And . . ."

And you missed it. . . . Could you give us an idea of what a typical day in camp was like?

Thank you for changing the subject. First of all, we take a bus from our hotel to the '69 Cubs' spring workout fields (now used by the Giants) on Hayden Road, where we enter a dressing room and don big-league uniforms. Right? Most of us would have been willing to die at that point. All right, my pants were too big. But if angels offered me a golden robe, would I say, "Only if you've got it in a 44 long"? And the old Cubs are sitting around telling stories about Durocher, their manager in '69 (as well as '70, when I met him), and how hard he was on nonregulars, whom he referred to as "the rest of you bleep." There was the time Lee Thomas went up to pinch-hit and Durocher sat on the bench saying, "Look at that bleep bleep bleep. He can't run, he can't hit, I don't know why the bleep bleep bleep I got him. Look at him! He's going to pop up." And sure enough, Thomas popped up. Durocher swore for several minutes, then turned to Ted Savage and told him to pinch-hit next. "Why should I go up there," said Savage, "and subject myself to abuse?"

Would you say you were subjected to big-league baseball without the abuse?

Well, to some extent. In all candor, I would have to say that this was where the $2,195 came in. Half of that may have been for overhead and the other half for not having Durocher come in until the end of the week. But there was some abuse, after all. There were all those reporters. And aerobics.

Aerobics were led by Susie Warren, who is what you might call lithe. And she made us campers do terrible things with our bodies, to music. Cardenal would accompany us, using a bat as a baton and crying *"No más! No más!"* Otherwise, the Cubs grunted and groaned with the rest of us. I have found it possible to live a normal life without reflecting upon the fact that I have hamstrings. I did not find this possible while performing aerobics.

Hamstrings a-twang, we would leave Susie and take on the easier part of the day: playing hardball. We would divide into five squads and rotate from field to field and Cub to Cub. Williams showed me that I'd been holding a bat wrong all my life. You're supposed to hold it up in the forward, or fingers, part of the hand, not back up against the pad. Because when—or if—you hit a ball thrown at big-league batting-practice speed with the bat held back up against your pad, your right pad, if you bat right-handed, turns various shades of blue. This subject arose when I asked Williams why I had developed indigo hand.

It was Santo who explained why I'd developed it on my left hand, too. That was because I've been holding the glove wrong all my life. You're supposed to hold it so that the ball always hits in the webbing, he said. This was a piece of advice I was unable to use. I feel I'm doing well when I catch a ball with any part of the leather. Playing third base, I also developed indigo shoulder, chest, and thigh.

Hickman and Jenkins also explained to me that I'd been holding the ball wrong all my life. If you hold it along the seams, it veers. This is what Jenkins usually does, because as a pitcher he usually wants it to veer. This is what Hickman never did, because as a fielder he didn't want it to. This is what I, as a fielder, have often done down through the veers.

There are a great many intangibles in baseball, aren't there?

Yes, and I wonder whether I will ever get a feel for them.

What else would you do on a typical day of training, after finding out that you've always been holding everything wrong?

Go back to the dressing room. Sit around sweaty. Take a shower with a member of the Hall of Fame, Banks, who's saying, "There is a vast reservoir of potential in all of us waiting to be tapped!" Stiffen up. Walk out toward the bus like somebody who just got off a horse. Yet feel *primed*. Feel *bodily*.

And go back to the hotel and sit in the whirlpool with the Cubs. Santo tells about the time Rogers Hornsby went through the Cubs' minor-league camps checking out all the hitters. Hornsby called a bunch of them together in some bleachers and went down the rows. The first guy was black. "You better go back to shining shoes," Hornsby said, "because you can't hit." And he said more or less the same thing to one prospect after another. Santo and Williams were sitting together. "If he says that to me," Santo said to Williams, "I'm going to cry." And Hornsby came to Williams. "You," Hornsby said, "can hit in the big leagues right now." And he said the same thing to Santo.

Later, Santo was up in the bigs, in the All-Star Game. "And there are McCovey and Aaron and Mays, and Ron Santo, and some photographer is taking a picture of us together!" Santo says, beaming. We beam with him. Not only campers but also Cubs are returned to their youth.

Would you say that rejuvenation was a theme of the camp?

Yes. But also fading. The '69 Cubs, you know, were the team that blew the National League East title to the Miracle Mets. The Cubs looked as if they were going to run away with it. Until September. On the first day of camp, Hundley gave Stone, who was to be our coach in the big Friday game against the Cubs, a chance to address us. "Just stay close to them till Thursday," Stone advised. "These are the '69 Cubs. They fade."

I asked Banks how he knew when it was time to retire. "You lose your quickness," he said. "And you hear whispers. Rumors. 'He used to make that play.' 'He used to hit that pitch.' Or maybe they don't say anything, but you can see it when they look at you. You can see it in their eyes."

That sounded like what I had been going through since I was twelve. In my last Little League season I was pretty good, but since then it has been only flashes. Moments. Inklings of what it feels like to be a player.

Did you have any of those inklings with the Cubs?

I had so many inklings, I may never sort them out. "You look like you've played some ball," Hundley told me, and to give you some idea how that made me feel, here's a story. A reporter at the camp overheard some of the Cubs saying that Ken Schwab, a fifty-five year-old Illinois grain-farm owner, looked pretty good. After asking another camper to point out Schwab, the reporter went up to another person he thought had been indicated and said, "Hey, the Cubs are saying you look pretty good." The guy nearly fainted. "My lifelong dream!" he cried. "You can't imagine what this means to me. For a big-league player to say, 'Irvin Singletary looks pretty good!' " (I have changed his name.) Here's how I felt: 1) "I have played some ball! I *have* played some ball. I must have! All those years, some of the time, anyway, that was actually *ball* I was playing!" And 2) *"Me?"*

Then, too, there were simpler moments. Grounder hit at me, bing-bing-tapocketta, it's in my glove, I'm up with it smoothly, throwing, zip, it's over to the first baseman chest high, a couple of murmurs among the campers: "Got an arm."

"Don't throw too hard too soon," Santo tells me. And the next day he asks me, "How's your hose?"

It wouldn't have sounded much sweeter if it had been Jessica Lange asking.
How was your hose?
My hose was there, all right. My hose wasn't dead.
You sound surprised.
The irony of all this is that before the opportunity to play with the Cubs arose, I had planned to retire from organized ball. I had given Willie Stargell, who is my age, the chance to hang it up first. I didn't want to steal any of his thunder. This spring I was going to make a simple announcement.

There had been certain telltale signs. For instance, when the slo-pitch softball team that you think you belong to fails to inform you that the season is under way, you begin to wonder. That happened two seasons ago. Then, too, I had doubts about my hose.

The one thing I've had in baseball was an arm from third base. Aside from a tendency to hit, at best, singles to right and on defense to stare off into space, I've been, since Little League, a classic third baseman: too slow to run or to hide. And when the ball bounced off some part of my body, I could pick it up and make that throw. If my hose wasn't out of sorts.

Also, I could never hit slo-pitch softball pitching, which was the only kind I seemed likely to face again. I don't like a pitch that goes way up in the air. When I go to bed at night and either pitch or bat myself to sleep, I see curves, sliders, screwballs, and hummers. I can't hit pitching that I never see in my dreams.
You were going to confine yourself to fandom, then?
No, I thought I might go on as a sort of pitcher in the rye. Throwing batting practice to the young. You groove the ball to somebody, and he or she hits it on the nose and you both feel good. And so do people watching. It's like a comedy act. And it's interesting, because you can fail at it. In Scottsdale I threw BP to Santo, and I pressed too hard and didn't get the ball where he or I wanted it, and he kept popping it up. I got the feeling he was pressing, too, trying to hit pitches he should've laid off so I wouldn't feel bad. I pressed harder. It was like strained conversation. I wonder whether something like that wasn't going on between the '69 Cubs in the stretch, when they let each other down.
Do you have much experience throwing batting practice?
Ah. At the highest level of serious competition I reached, high school, that was my forte. Somebody once told me he'd run into my old high school coach, Ray Thurmond, who remembered me as a pitcher. I was, of course, a third baseman, but it was at throwing batting practice that I shone. I wore a hole in my right high-school baseball shoe throwing BP without a pitcher's toe. Those are the spikes I wore against the Cubs.
The shoes of a congenial player, a giving player.

Many people might prefer that their old coach remember them the way Durocher remembers Eddie Stanky, as one of those "scratching, hungry, diving ballplayers who come to kill you."

That's the kind of player I wanted to be. Scrappy. I remember the only time I ever broke up a double play. I was playing intramural softball, in college. Hit the second baseman just right, flipped him up into the air. Didn't hurt him, though. I actually think he enjoyed it, too. This is a terrible thing for someone who pretends to understand serious ball to say, but my deepest desire in sports isn't to win but to share a good time. Maybe that's why Durocher seemed outraged at the very sight of me, that day in 1970.

This was the incident that occurred over in foul territory near the third-base dugout, where you missed the pop-up?

I wish you wouldn't keep harping on that pop-up. To me, if I *catch* a pop-up that goes as high as the Washington Monument, that's news. Or if I hit a ball 350 feet. But to my critics and friends, the idea of me camped not quite under a pop-up, and tilting slightly to the left, and tilting slightly farther to the left, and then the ball coming down well beyond my grasp—that's their idea of something worthy of comment. What people usually say to me now, if I'm unable to start the conversation off on the right note, is, "I hear that you missed a pop-up."

I'm sorry. There are so many other things I wanted to ask you. Like, how did you prepare for the Cubs?

For the first time in my life, I worked out. I hate to work out. You have an angel on one shoulder saying "Go, go, go" and a devil on the other saying "Stop, stop, stop," and there you are in between, bored to death with the whole argument and wallowing in sheer, but not pleasant, kinesthesia.

I like to play ball. A ball takes you out of yourself. Of course, if you miss a ball, you snap back into yourself pretty quick, but then you have a lot to talk over with yourself. Even while you are out of yourself, you can be narrating semiconsciously. "He can still hit," you can be saying, referring to yourself in the third person. "Ball was in on him but he got that bat head out in front. . . ." The main reason I cover sports is so I can keep the vocabulary of my semiconscious narration up-to-date.

Now looming ahead of me was a shot at living that narration. I was there to write about it, sure, but it meant a lot more to me than that. So, do you know what I did? I lifted weights. Not only do I not like lifting weights, I deplore it. However, a person doesn't get many chances later on in life to whang a well-pitched baseball or to snag a well-hit one. A person doesn't want to come back from such a chance to report to his family, "I was overpowered."

My son has 10-pound dumbbells lying around the house. I started pumping them and swinging them and going through throwing and batting motions with them, and I didn't stop even when my daughter would collapse—her prerogative—in helpless laughter. I also split two cords of firewood down to the biggest pile of kindling in Massachusetts.

When you first encountered the wily hardball in Arizona, how did you feel?

Overpowered.

A hardball is a thing that, when you have not seen one with steam on it in many years, is upon you before you know it. And in the field I was lost in the complexity of hops. Grounders were like logarithms. Also, I didn't seem to hinge in the same places I used to. And my throwing was so zipless the first day that it moved me to compose a blues song:

> I used to have a rifle,
> I used to have a gun.
> Lord, Lord.
> I used to have a rifle,
> I used to have a gun.
> Now that ball floats over
> Like a cinnamon bun.

But you said your hose wasn't dead.

Several things happened. One is that our trainer, Harry Jordan, manipulated my arm and discovered that the tendon over the funny bone had popped out. At least that's what he claimed. He popped it back in. I've never heard of anyone being plagued by funny-bone-tendon problems before, but I know that as he worked, Harry made terrific deep crunching noises in his throat that served to keep some of the faint-hearted campers out of the training room altogether, so I'm willing to believe that Jordan was a funnybonologist.

Another thing that kept me going early in camp was my chewing. I was chewing good. I talked chewing on a knowledgeable basis with Jenkins, who bites right into an open can of snuff with his lower front teeth. I could chew with the big boys. I even chewed during aerobics. This helped.

Also, nobody was yelling at anybody. The spirit of Durocher wasn't in the camp. I don't respond to being yelled at. It distracts me from yelling at myself.

Then, too, I had all of my clichés working.

I thought sportswriters are supposed to eschew clichés.

Sportswriters, yes. Ballplayers use them to hone their concentration.

I was being interviewed by a TV crew. Most campers were interviewed so many times that they eventually stopped calling their wives to tell them to turn on the VCR.

"Are you feeling the pressure?" I was asked.

"Nah," I lied. "When the bell rings, the juices will flow."

And I spat. Television likes visual touches. If you want to get a statement heard and seen all across the land, remember to spit right after making it.

Then, all of a sudden, I picked up a ball the way the first caveman picked up the first good fist-sized rock. And I felt my hose start to fill with water again. I felt leaner, stronger, springier, *glad* to have hamstrings. The downside of this was that my pants became even baggier. But I wore a psychic T-shirt that said "PLAYING MYSELF INTO SHAPE."

And then you went on a tear, right?

No. Then I reached my nadir. I thought I had reached my nadir years ago, several times, but in the very first intrasquad game I hit another new low.

Because I let the guys down. "We are here," Banks had announced one day behind the batting cage, "to ameliorate the classic polarization of the self-motivated individual and the ideology of the group."

Excuse me. Did Banks say things like that often?

Banks said things that came from the Big Arizona Sky. When someone asked him whether he felt he had come along too soon, before the days of astronomical baseball salaries, he said, "No. Wish I'd been born sooner. With the philosophers. Days of Plato, and Socrates, and Alexander Graham Bell." When I asked him what would be a thrill for him, comparable to the thrill we campers were getting, he said, "To sing in the Metropolitan Opera."

What Banks most often said was, "*Veez*-ualize yourself hitting a home run!"

"Ernie," said a camper, "I thought we were just supposed to meet the ball, and it would take care of itself."

"No," he said. "It won't. It will not take care of itself. You have to see yourself inside the ball when it is in the pitcher's hand, and you're thinking, 'Time to take a long ride.' "

But don't change the subject. I'm ready to discuss my nadir.

You have a lot of heart as an interviewee, you know that?

Yes, but in the first intrasquad game, I made several plays of the kind that kill infield chatter. Here I was feeling, "Give me Jimmy Stuart and Bob Margolin and Bill Mitchell and Dennis Albano and Wally Pecs (best ballplayer's name in camp) and Dennis Ferrazzano and Tim Tyers and Scott Mermel and George Altemose and Dave Schultz and Steve Heiferman and the Arnold, Crawford, and Patti brothers, and I could take on anybody in the world." And what do I do in the first intrasquad game? I drop a line drive hit right at me. A third basemen who can't catch a line drive at his sternum is as dependable as a frog that can't balance on a lily pad. And I let an easy grounder go under my glove. That's like letting a baby's head bob around. And Margolin, who in real life runs a vanity press but is no one's vanity catcher, whips a throw down to nip a guy stealing third, but I don't dig it out of the dirt. In Arizona a lot of thin air can get between a person and the ball—and between a person and his mates, even if they don't yell at you.

And the first time at bat, I dribble into a double play. The next time, Stone is pitching. "Can you hit a curveball?" he asks me.

"No," I say.

He throws me a curveball.

And you miss it!

No. Worse. I take it on the inside corner. And this is what I hear, from Oliver on the other bench: "That's a hanger, Roy." I've just taken a hanging curveball for a strike! What Stone has done is throw me a curve that I could hit. And I took it! That's like Jack Benny giving you a straight line and you saying, "Oh. Excuse me. I wasn't listening."

Like I say, nobody yelled at us campers, but every now and then one of the big-leaguers would give us a quiet, chastening line, like, "Got to have that one," or, "That's where we need you, big man." The social fabric. The ideology of the group.

The next pitch from Stone isn't a hanger. Not a curve. It's down the pipe. And I go after it. "All right!" I think.

The ball intersects with my bat about three inches from my hands. It pops weakly to the catcher. I feel as if I've reached out for a proffered ice-cream cone and found it in my armpit. "Well," I think, "I am losing my mind."

That was your nadir!

Yes. It didn't help that I had margarita tongue from the night before.

Ah, I've always wondered about the big-league night life. What did you do that night!

For one thing, talked to Cardenal about creekus.

What are creekus!

"You know, creekus," Cardenal said. "Little things." He made sawing motions with his arms like a cricket producing sounds. "One time in Chicago I come to the park with my eyes swollen shut. 'Cause I couldn't sleep. 'Cause creekus was in my room all night. So I can't play. And Mike Royko in the paper, ohhh, he got on me.

"And last night in my room? Creekus again. I find seven of them behind the toilet. I kill them all. I go back to bed. I hear more creekus. I turn the light back on. I find five creekus behind the television. I call the desk. 'You got to send the exterminator!' If Royko had been there! I could have shown him creekus!"

But, you came back from that nadir, right!

Let me put it this way. The next evening I'm in the coffee shop. I eat a well-earned sandwich. I sign the check. And there's a place on the check for "comments." So I write, "I went three-for-five today." There not being much room, I didn't bother to add, "and fielded flawlessly."

What turned you around!

After my nadir, I talked to Stone. He told me about his Cy Young season with Baltimore in 1980, after which he had nothing left. "I threw over 60 percent breaking balls," he said. "I knew it would ruin my arm, but I was winning fifteen games in a row. One year of twenty-five and seven is worth five of fifteen and fifteen." Before a game, he said, he would take a Percodan if he felt he would need it in addition to the four aspirin he would routinely take every three innings. And he kept breaking off those hooks.

"Well," I sighed, "your straight one was too tough for me."

"No, that was my forkball," he said.

"Oh!" I said. My heart leapt. "What does it do?"

"Drops off like a spitball and moves in on you. Nobody can hit it."

No wonder you didn't hit it.

Precisely. Not only that, but I'd had a real major-league experience. I'd popped up a forkball. The next day, when we played our next intrasquad game, I was ready.

Would you like to tell us about it?

Single to right off Dr. Harry Soloway, the Chicago shrink who became nationally famous by telling the *Today* show that he wasn't giving any more interviews because the last reporter he talked to called him "the most inept ballplayer I have ever seen, man or boy." Except for his fame, a single to right off Dr. Harry Soloway is not an enduring achievement, but a solid single is a solid single. Then, off Cardenal, I ground out and single up the middle. Then, off Beckert, I fly to left. I'm pulling the ball!

A portent. For the 350 . . .

Although I don't realize it at the time. But now we get down to the last inning. Bases loaded. Beckert, who has been moving painfully and saying, "Now I remember why I retired," wants to get the game over. He's working in and out on me. This feels like actual baseball! Three and two. Comes in with a high, tight fastball. Too close to take. I foul it back. This is probably a thrill for Beckert, too: a second baseman getting a chance to work on a hitter. He delivers a funny-looking pitch on the outside corner.

And what do you do with it?

Rip it. On a line. But not a straight line. More satisfying than that. A line like a scimitar blade. Over the first baseman's head, and it *bites* the ground three feet fair. It goes blisteringly on its way, and I say to it, "Burn!"

A double. And such a double! I am most of the way to third when I see the runner ahead of me running toward me. Fortunately, he's heading back toward third, not second. He has become conservative and decided he can't score. But this is such a double that I am able to turn around and go 70 feet back into second standing up. I have hit the equivalent of a triple and a half.

That must have been a thrill.

I'll tell you the thrill. The thrill is what Beckert exclaims.

What does Beckert exclaim?

Beckert exclaims, "How did you hit that pitch?" He turns to Jenkins, who's umpiring. "Slider right on the outside corner!" he says. "And I had him set up!"

"I was looking for it," I reply.

"That's right!" says Jenkins. "That's a good hitter."

Wow! You were looking for it?

No. I lied. The truth was I had found my strength as a hitter. Which turned out to be very similar to my strength as a defensive back in football—which is that I am too slow to take a fake. My strength as a hitter, I now realize, is that I haven't got sense enough to be set up. Why do you think a person becomes a writer? It's because he can never figure anything out until afterward. In baseball down through the years I've often been trying, during the seventh inning, to figure out what happened in the fifth. And what happened was that I wasn't paying attention because I was wondering what I did wrong in the third. And what I did wrong in the third was boot one because I was thinking, "I've got to concentrate with every fiber of my being. Hmm, interesting phrase. I wonder what all the fibers of my being in concert would look like? A nice wool shirt?" Oh, those rare great moments in sports when my mind isn't working and my body is!

Another thing I do in this game is throw four guys out with my hose. My mind is a blank then, too.

Did you talk your triple and a half over with Beckert and Jenkins later?

No, not exactly. But I will say this. In my time I'd exchanged various glances with ballplayers. And a major-league manager once mistook me for a member of the Hall of Fame. That was when I called Billy Martin on the phone, and hearing my voice, he cried, "Mick? Mick? Is it the Mick?" He thought I was Mickey Mantle. When he realized I wasn't, we were both very disappointed.

But I had never exchanged a glance with a ballplayer that contained any hint that I, too, was a part of the actual ballplaying experience. One time, a Venezuelan sportscaster, Juan Vené, and I told Manny Sanguillen, when he was catching for the Pirates, that we had played baseball on opposing press teams.

"Softball?" asked Sanguillen.

"No, hardball."

Sanguillen was one of the most gracious ballplayers I've ever met. But Sanguillen shook his head and said, "You guys!"

That evening in Scottsdale after the second intrasquad game, I exchanged glances with Beckert and Jenkins that, to me—and I am talking in terms of diamond experience now—contained a hint of "us guys."

Tell me. This is another thing I have always wondered about. Do you ballplayers put your pants on one leg at a time, like everybody else?

I can only speak for myself. The answer in my case is: not always. After that intrasquad game, I got tired putting one leg on, stopped for a while and worked on the other one.

But you were ready for the big game the next day in Scottsdale Stadium?

Did I tell you I hit a ball 350 feet?

In passing, but tell me more about it.

I have always gotten on well with veterinarians. Rich Nye, who won twenty-six games in the big leagues, is now a veterinarian. If I didn't live so far from Des Plaines, Illinois, I'd send my dogs to him. Nye threw me a good pitch to hit.

Every camper got one at bat in the big game. By the time I got up, in the ninth or tenth of many innings, it had become clear that a few winded old Cubs are better than wave after fresh wave of old brokers, law professors, and salesmen. The crowd was diminished and restive.

"Representing *Sports Illustrated*," blared the loudspeaker, "Ray" and a mis-pronunciation of my last name. I strode to the plate and realized I didn't have on a helmet. I ran back and got one. I strode to the plate and realized that the flap covered the wrong ear. I ran back and got a left-eared one. Fan reaction indicated a doubting of my expertise. I dug in.

"Coming right down the middle," said Rudolph, who was catching.

All you selfless, unrecognized batting-practice pitchers out there, Keep it up! Your service will be repaid. Someday a veterinarian will lay one in there for you. In practice, Nye had shown me his real 80-mile-per-hour fastball, which I nearly hit. This one was a notch slower. Later he said he wished he'd thrown it harder; I would have cleared the fence. But I'll take my 350 feet, and the sound of a crowd that came to scoff and stayed to eat its heart out.

Anything else you'd like to say?

Yeah. I got my longest hit ever against a team managed by Leo Durocher.

Did I tell you about the first time I met Leo? It was in Scottsdale Stadium in the spring of 1970 that I, a cub reporter, innocently introduced myself to him. And he, standing outside the third-base dugout, pointed his finger at me and began to address, at the top of his lungs, the players who, a few months before, had been the '69 Cubs: "I want everybody to hear this! I'm not talking to this guy! I'm not saying a word!"

Just before he disappeared under the stands, he turned and added, "And he knows why!"

I didn't then and don't now. But it got to me. I loved baseball, and Durocher went all the way back through Willie Mays and Coogan's Bluff and the Gas-house Gang to Ruth. I couldn't shake the feeling that there must be something about me that didn't fit into the national pastime.

Did you ever run into Durocher again?

Not until camp week thirteen years later. At the banquet after the big game, he took the occasion to make an emotional talk. He confessed why the '69 Cubs folded: "They didn't give me 100 percent."

What a thing to say at this point! Would the man never let up?

"They gave me 140 percent." Ah. The Cubs had pressed. Durocher was conceding that he'd chewed on them too hard.

He also apologized publicly for embarrassing Santo nastily in a celebrated 1971 clubhouse meeting. After the banquet, Durocher and Santo embraced.

Durocher didn't apologize to me. He glared at me once but with no hint of recognition. He had relieved me, however, of one burden. I still don't know

---

ROY ALTON BLOUNT JR.
Name pronounced Blunt.

Born Oct. 4, 1941, at Indianapolis, Ind.
Height, depends. Weight, depends.
Throws and bats righthanded.
Hobby—Raising mixed-breed dogs.
Attended Vanderbilt University, Nashville, Tenn., and
Harvard University, Cambridge, Mass.

Year Club	League	Pos.	B.A.
1951—Tigers†	Little	OF	.063
1952—Tigers	Little	OF	.179
1953—Tigers	Little	3B	.320
1954—‡ .	(Did not play)		
1955—Pels	Babe Ruth	3B	.213
1956—Pels	Babe Ruth	3B	.265
1956—Decatur High B-Team ...	Region 4-AA	3B	.213
1957—Decatur High B-Team ...	Region 4-AAA	3B	.270
1958—Decatur High Varsity § .	Region 4-AAA	3B	.000
1959—Decatur High Varsity x .	Region 4-AAA	3B-1B	.000
1960–70— ‡	(Did not play)		
1971—Sports Illustrated vs. NY Press		C	.500
in Yankee Stadium, one game			
1972—NY Press vs. Venezuelan Press		3B	.400
in Venezuela, three games y			
1973—NY Press vs. Venezuelan Press		2B	.500
in Yankee Stadium, one game z			
1974— ‡	(Did not play)		
1983—All-Star Campers vs. each other		3B	.375
and '69 Cubs, three games a			—

Totals (In major league stadium or uniform) .... .409
      (Not in major league stadium or uniform) ... .201

† Nearly everyone else was bigger.
‡ On temporary inactive list.
§ Not very many at bats.
x Hardly any at bats.
y Wore New York Yankee and Met uniforms.
z Wore Yankee uniform.
a Wore Chicago Cub uniform. (Got to keep it. For $80.)

what made me anathema, but I do know it wasn't my fault that the Cubs didn't win in '69.

"Winning the pennant that year might have been anticlimactic for the kind of love we had on that team," said emcee Gene Oliver from the podium. However that may be, in 1969 Durocher seems, oddly enough, to have forged a team that couldn't win but did learn how to share a good time.

So you have no complaints?

No complaints? No complaints? What madman built a stadium whose fences are nowhere shorter than 355 feet?

Let me quote to the you the testimony of Steve Stone, and also of longtime Chicago baseball writer Richard Dozer, now of *The Phoenix Gazette*, who was as much of an official scorer as we had: "The ball is out in Fenway."

But . . . the air in Fenway isn't thin.

Yeah, and Hundley's pop-up doesn't go nearly so high, and I catch it and toss it over to Leo.

Reggie is large, he contains multitudes. If he sings a song of himself, who is to gainsay? Unfortunately, in recent years has come a horde of detractors who delight in his outfield misplays, his off-field mishaps, and his decline at the bat (his 1983 average of .194, while exceeding his self-proclaimed I.Q. of 160, fell short of his weight). And yet Reggie remains confident, if somewhat subdued. As Ol' Diz said, if you can do it, it ain't braggin' . . . and Mr. October has done it. Does Reggie go to Cooperstown? Does Frankie go to Hollywood? Of course; the question surely was answered long ago. Thomas Boswell is one of the game's most thoughtful writers; this essay originally appeared in his *Washington Post* column and was later collected in *How Life Imitates the World Series.*

THOMAS BOSWELL

Mr. October

Mark Twain said that politicians, old buildings, and prostitutes become respectable with age. Reggie Jackson would like to make it a foursome.

It isn't easy for a hurricane to become its own calm eye, but the former Buck Tater Man is trying. After years of straining to be the straw that stirs the drink, it has dawned on Jackson that, perhaps, he is the drink that is getting stirred.

When you go to the movies and get sued, when you walk to your car and get accused of battering a child, when you sit in your car and somebody walks up and points a revolver at your nose from six-inch range, it makes you wonder who's getting stirred. When your house burns down, it makes you wonder who's in control. When you foul off a sacrifice bunt and get suspended for insubordination, when you jog in from the outfield and your manager is waiting in the dugout to punch you, or when you step in a hole and disable yourself for a month, it makes you wonder about your luck, about your approach to things.

All this, and much more, has happened since Jackson came to the New York Yankees in 1977. From clubhouse fights, to an IRS-audit brouhaha, to banner headlines screaming, GUNMAN FIRES AT REGGIE ON MANHATTAN STREET, Jackson has never lacked for somber subjects to mull in his idle, thoughtful hours.

Slowly, he has changed. And is still changing. Like any fine protagonist in fiction, Jackson alters, grows, learns, regresses, doubles back, stakes out new ground before our eyes.

Jackson has not outlined his new position—his new image, as he perhaps unwisely chooses to call it—in any single way, but rather in a dozen ways. "I must take off my black hat . . . I have to control my tongue . . . I have to substantiate my thoughts rather than just raise hell . . . You have to sell yourself and politic a little in this life . . . I have to stop getting into things too deep . . . I don't want to offend . . . It's good to feel wanted and respected . . . Part of the trouble with Billy [Martin] was that I misunderstood his wants."

These snippets of conciliation, these bons mots of a once-burned, twice-shy man, are extracts from Jackson's conversation—all said within fifteen minutes. If the New York Yankee slugger suddenly has to go on the disabled list, no one should have to ask why. It'll be a slipped disc; this is a man spending a lot of time bending over backward. Jackson seems to be a man in the midst of a long, gradual, yet uneasy personal transition. His locker in the New York clubhouse is in the corner, almost hidden, as though he were an animal gone to earth. If Jackson now feels most comfortable with his back protected by a wall, he has good reason.

From his first day in pinstripes, Jackson was baseball's King Midas of fame, its Hester Prynne of sluggers with a dollar sign on his chest. Everything he touched turned to instant celebrity. Since Aesop, men have been warned to be careful when they make a wish. It just might come true. Jackson asked the free-agent genie for millions of dollars, a candy bar named after him, and a Yankee uniform.

And, brother, did he get it!

A passion for fame, for a lasting place in folklore, is perhaps the most easily comprehended, and the most easily excused, of vanities. Yet Jackson, who hit more homers than any man in baseball during the first fourteen full years of his career (424 from 1968 through 1981), is seldom judged generously. Few exceptional athletes have had to hear the words "fraud" and "phony" applied to themselves so often, even by teammates.

"Reggie is an average player," said Baltimore's average pitcher Jim Palmer after Jackson left Baltimore.

"Reggie Jackson has never done anything in his life that was not for effect. He's a total phony," said pitcher Bill Lee, perhaps proving the adage that we say of others those things that apply best to ourselves.

"Reggie is a charlatan, but a charlatan with credentials," said pitcher Don Sutton. "He cons people and sells himself, but he produces."

After the greatest slugging World Series in history in '77, what was Jackson's reward? His manager, Martin, platooned him against southpaws, batted him

seventh, and put a slew-footed catcher in his right-field position. What other star was ever treated so preposterously, yet remained so relatively silent? "I never pay any attention to anything Reggie says anyway," said Martin, while still Yankee skipper. "Why should I? His teammates don't."

Jackson's basic difficulty, one that may take him years to solve, is that, like politicians and poets on a grander scale, Jackson does not live a life in the conventional, everyday sense. He manufactures a legend, a personal history, with himself and his exploits at the center. Jackson's sin is that he has always been uniquely bad at hiding this conscious myth-making process. Baseball elects its heroes for life by bleacher plebiscite, not by self-appointment. The old game has never forgiven Jackson for proclaiming himself a "superstar"— the one-word title of his autobiography—before his public and peers had time to come to the same conclusion.

The irony, of course, is that with each year, with each new accomplishment, it becomes more obvious that Jackson is, and always has been, everything he claimed. The most elementary Jackson statistic—his glory in a nutshell—is that in those mere fourteen seasons he has been the cleanup hitter and offensive leader on nine division champions and five world champions. That alone, without a single personal stat, ought to be enough for Cooperstown.

Even when Jackson knows that his feats should speak for themselves, even when he knows that humility is the right card to play, he has always tipped his hand. He can mix hokum and genuine insight, subtle phrasing and pathetic bombast like no other star. Few men match his knack for having a good idea, then mopping the floor with it. If Jackson discussed the Bill of Rights long enough, he'd make you want to repeal it.

Yet this marathon philosophizer is the soul of pith. Who else in baseball says, "It was an insurance homer; that's why I hit it halfway to the Prudential Building," or "I hit it so far my eyes weren't good enough to see it land. That one had some voltage." Of all the athletes in all American sports, perhaps none has so much fun making phrases, or gets himself in so much trouble doing it. Jackson's epigrams—"hitting against Nolan Ryan is like eating soup with a fork"—are a mixture of image-laden Baptist preaching and a college-educated mind. The cruelest epithet that trails Jackson through the years is Mickey Rivers's taunt: "Reginald Martinez Jackson—white man's first name, Spanish middle name, and a black man's last name. No wonder you don't know who the hell you are." The truth is that, consciously or not, Jackson has chosen to meld and blend all the strains in his background, all the cultural lineages that he can draw upon from ghetto to campus to Park Avenue, and contain them in one personality. The result is often a brilliant blend of street-wise cynicism, tangy language, and the genuine worldliness of a man who has read some good books and seen a lot of great places.

It is impossible for such a man not to put a high value on his own opinions. No one ever mastered the tricks of the limelight game better than Jackson—the places to be, the times to be there, the expression to have on your face, if you want the microphones, the notepads, and the cameras to gather.

"I know how to answer questions," says Jackson. "I know how to tell the truth, but not hurt too many feelings . . . I can recognize a colorful quote . . . I don't think ballplayers understand the trouble they could save themselves if they paid attention to how to give an interview . . . I am aware that I sell myself and promote myself. Sometimes you do or say something for effect. But the real reason I have a good press is that I treat interviewers like people. In other words, I treat them the way I am not treated."

Of all Jackson's traits, the one which is most resented is his off-hand ability to steal headlines. In a prosaic locker room, he stands out like a walking poem. The most difficult task for Jackson as he matures will probably be the need to muzzle himself, renouncing the great pleasure he takes in ruminating. Already, it seems, he no longer seeks attention in the little ways that rankle other players. When he is not sedulously avoiding the media line of fire, he is driving the wordsmiths away with kindness, channeling the conversation to dull baseball labor topics or the like.

It may be Jackson's misfortune that the new Reggie, when he is eventually noticed, will be mistaken for a Madison Avenue concoction by a man who, after selling candy bars, jeans, VWs, and cologne, can certainly take care of repackaging and selling himself. It is probably more accurate that Jackson is simply showing the flip side of himself that has always been there, that has always been the best side of him, but also the least noticed.

"I didn't really know what I was getting into when I came to New York. I never guessed how tough this town was," he says. "It's a city that loves visiting celebrities and treats them great. Makes you want to come here. If they see you two days a year, you're royalty. If they see you every day, you're a bum."

How dramatically tunes change. When Jackson came to New York, former teammate Ken Holtzman predicted, "He'll love it. Reggie just soaks up attention. His desire for fame may be insatiable." Even Jackson, the spring after his three-homer Series game in '77, said, "You can't get too much of a good thing; I don't understand that idea. I wanted to come to the Yankees. I wanted to hit five home runs in a World Series. I've earned everything I've got. It's been hectic, sure. It's been hard. But it's been a pleasure."

However, like Midas, Jackson has had second thoughts about his good New York fortune. It is bitterly ironic that Jackson should have found Apple fans so hard to satisfy. Within big-league dugouts, Jackson is categorized as a player best appreciated by those who see him every day. But it takes an eye.

"Reggie's not a difficult player to manage, 'cause he's what you call a 'hard' player," says Baltimore's Earl Weaver. "He hustles, runs everything out, hates to embarrass himself. He'll take a guy out on the double play, or run into a wall, making a sliding catch. His whole career he's missed games because of 'hustle' injuries.

"Most important, he can reach a special level of concentration in the key situations that win games—just like Frank Robinson. And, kinda like Frank, when the score's 9–2 either way, his concentration lapses and he gives away at bats or makes a meaningless error. That may hurt his batting average or his fielding average, but it don't hurt his team none," said Weaver.

"Reggie's a curious person and he's a person who likes to be shown the respect he's earned. He'll ask you why you made a certain move that involved him, which is unusual, 'cause most players don't give a damn. You explain it. You teach him somethin' maybe he didn't know. He nods. He appreciates it."

Jackson is delighted with this synopsis of The Care and Feeding of Reggie as seen by The Certified Genius. "I loved playing for Earl Weaver [in '76]," said Jackson. "Now I could play for the little Weave. That man will chew you out, read you the riot act down to the ground, and then forget all about it."

Jackson's most endearing trait, but one that few people see, is that he respects anyone who will challenge him, force him to defend his position cogently, cut through the bluster. "Earl's right, he's right," says Jackson. "I give away at bats, I'm careless. Last night, I wasn't 'in' the game until the sixth inning. The cold weather distracted me . . . took my mind off business. Maybe that's an area where I can improve as I get older."

Like anyone with a true talent, Jackson searches for people who can spot his genuine flaws. Changing, improving as he ages, achieving a middle ground where all sides of his nature are put in perspective are now priorities for Jackson. One step in that direction was the short tenure of Dick Howser as Yankee manager. "Dick shows a lot of respect for me, makes me feel wanted," said Jackson, who, at thirty-four under Howser, had his best season since he was twenty-three. "He knows people, tries to understand them," adds Jackson, who, like the gifted child in class, is a devil when he must demand attention, but an angel when he gets it. "I'd go out of my way not to offend Howser because I think he's a fair man."

About the unfairnesses of the past, Jackson has learned to remain mute: every time he has talked, he has lost. "I don't think Billy is gone for good. I think he'll be back as manager of the Yankees. I can't explain why. I just think so," says Jackson with the same reverse-English assurance as the golfer who roots for his putts by yelling, "Don't go in the hole . . . don't you dare go in the hole!"

Of the other fellow in the old Yankee vicious triangle, Jackson says, "I have to realize that Steinbrenner's never been late with a paycheck. A professional athlete has to accept responsibilities. I've always understood that, but I thought it applied to staying in shape, bearing down every game. I understand now that it also means controlling your tongue, not being too disparagingly critical of the owner.

"Maybe I'm just seeing the other side—the side of the people who run things. I represent companies [in commercials] and accept their money, so I have a responsibility to project an image, to come across as a person who substantiates his thoughts, not as some guy who's blowing off again."

No project could be more difficult or against-the-grain for Jackson than this reining-in process. Just look at him. He wears his uniform like a star—tight, muscles bulging, top button of shirt open. He runs distinctively, bent forward, a picture of barely controlled power. He seems to carry a stage with him everywhere. It is as difficult for him not to mention his alleged 160 IQ as it is hard for him to remember not to flash his wallet full of $100 bills. And, everywhere, he runs into those who want to prick his balloon, like Rivers the day he cackled, "Reggie says he's got an IQ of 160. Out of what? A thousand?"

Even if Jackson's intelligence quotient doesn't test out a little above Mozart's and a tad below Voltaire's, Jackson has always wanted to run in the intellectual fast lane, or at least, somewhere near it. He loves the big words and the complicated issues, wants very much—perhaps too much—to have an opinion on all the topics he thinks a smart man should have one on. He can't resist a pretentious subject any more than he can lay off the fastball in his wheelhouse—even if it's a ball. So he'll always strike out plenty.

Most ballplayers, most people probably, would be inflamed if anyone wrote such things about them. Jackson once walked up to me with a story I had written. He pointed to the paragraph just above this one—word-for-word the same—and, shaking his head, said, "So true," then walked away.

It's not easy being a man who is embarrassed by short home runs.

For Jackson, the struggle continues to be all things. He wants to be compassionate, simple, religious. But he wears gold chains and owns a fleet of kingly cars. He loves being his team's player representative. No star warms more genuinely to the "noblesse oblige" of losing money in a strike since it benefits other marginal players who really need a union. The anomaly of being a millionaire labor spokesman is just his style.

It is not a rare psychological bent to want to be both the cop and the robber, the oppressed and the oppressor, the hero and the villain, the object of love as well as hate, the loner who is also the leader. But it is wearisome, this always swinging for the parking lot, always changing costumes and masks so that every role in the play can be yours. It is so much easier to be undisciplined, to fly in all directions at once, to satisfy all the different appetites and personalities in one half-forged mind. But even for such a man, the time comes when he must choose among all the characters in the cast of his soul.

The campaign for quiet respectability and calm affection shown aging future Hall of Famers has already begun. "I want very much to be in the Hall of Fame. I'd kind of like to wait until the room is empty at night and go in once to look at the plaque. I worry some that I've made enemies, that I have a reputation that might hurt my chances. I think 500 homers and 1,500 RBIs would prevent that."

What distinguishes the great player, the man in the Hall?

"The pride," says Jackson, "that makes a player believe that he's better than the rest."

Reggie Jackson says these words like a boy bringing home a drawing from school, one that has "A-plus" written in the corner. Perhaps he really doesn't mean to boast. What he wants, and still so seldom gets, is a measured, unhysterical response. Neither the rabid cheers nor boos that are supposed to be his fuel, but rather a friendly, honest appraisal that indeed his hard work has been found worthy.

Ball Four is to my mind the best baseball book ever written principally by a player; only Cap Anson's *A Ball Player's Career* comes close. Len Shecter (represented solo later in this volume) was the shaping force behind Bouton's words, but the words are recognizably Bouton's—this is not a ghosted job. The tempest that followed publication in 1970 left Bouton a pariah of the baseball world, shunned by players and management alike; even today he is invited to no old-timers' games. What was obscured amid all the controversy surrounding the book was Bouton's remarkable comeback. A twenty-one-game winner as a fastball pitcher for the Yankees of 1963, he hurt his arm and won only nine games in his last four years in New York. With his career seemingly finished, he hooked on with the expansion Seattle Pilots as a knuckle-balling reliever and appeared in seventy-three games in 1969. Even more remarkable, after dropping out of the majors after a weak 1970 season, he bobbed up again eight years later, starting and winning a game for the Atlanta Braves. Here, the memorable conclusion to *Ball Four*.

JIM BOUTON

The Grip

In the winter I always find myself remembering more good things than bad. And in many ways 1969 was a great season. I began it as a minor leaguer trying a new style and a new pitch and finished as a genuine gold-plated, guaranteed-not-to-tarnish major leaguer again. My seventy-three appearances for Seattle and Houston were fifth in the majors, and my two wins, three losses, and two saves say something—although I'm not sure what.

The pettiness and stupidity were exasperating, sometimes damaging. And it's going to be a long winter before I can enjoy having had my shoes nailed to the clubhouse floor. New levels of noncommunication were reached. Still, there were rewards. There were enough laughs in the bullpen and in the back of the bus to make me eager for a new season. I met a lot of people I'll feel warmly toward for the rest of my life. Observing and recording my experiences for this book taught me a great deal not only about others but about myself. (I'm not sure I liked everything I learned, but learning is often a painful experience.)

I lucked out with five great roommates: Gary Bell, Bob Lasko, Mike Marshall, Steve Hovley, and Norm Miller. I went the whole season without an injury. I traveled the country in both leagues. And I saw the look in my son Mike's face when I came back from a road trip and he turned his big eyes up at me and said shyly, "Hey Dad, you're Jim Bouton, aren't you?"

I enjoyed living in the Great Northwest for most of a season, and I'm sad that Seattle didn't keep its franchise. A city that seems to care more for its art museums than its ballpark can't be all bad.

The team will play in Milwaukee next season, and it will be a new team in every respect. Even before the franchise could be shifted, Marvin Milkes, operating on the theory that when you make a mistake you make a change, made a lot of changes. Joe Schultz was fired and signed on as coach in Kansas City, moving in considerably below Lou Piniella in the team's pecking order. Piniella, groomed for oblivion in the first weeks of spring training with Seattle, became Rookie of the Year in Kansas City, hitting .282. Sal Maglie, Ron Plaza, Eddie O'Brien, and Frank Crosetti were also fired. As this is written only Crosetti has hooked on—with Minnesota.

Fred Talbot, Diego Segui, Ray Oyler, George Brunet, Don Mincher, and Ron Clark were all traded to Oakland for some warm bodies. Dooley Womack was released, Merritt Ranew was sent to the minors, and Mike Marshall, sold to Houston, will be back with me this spring. Gary Bell, released by the White Sox, was signed by Hawaii. Hope he can handle *mai tais*.

Houston traded Curt Blefary to the Yankees for Joe Pepitone and we will have all spring to practice Joe's pickoff sign. Wade Blasingame was sent to the minors. Ted Williams of the MFL was Manager of the Year and the Fat Kid won Most Valuable Player.

I did not win Comeback of the Year, but I went to a local sports banquet the other night and took a bow from the audience. As I watched the trophies being handed out, my mind wandered and I saw myself being called up to the dais and accepting the Fireman of the Year award for 1970.

And then I thought of Jim O'Toole, and I felt both strange and sad. When I took the cab to the airport in Cincinnati I got into a conversation with the driver, and he said he'd played ball that summer against Jim O'Toole. He said O'Toole was pitching for the Ross Eversoles in the Kentucky Industrial League. He said O'Toole is all washed up. He doesn't have his fastball anymore, but his control seems better than when he was with Cincinnati. I had to laugh at that. O'Toole won't be trying to sneak one over the corner on Willie Mays in the Kentucky Industrial League.

Jim O'Toole and I started out even in the spring. He wound up with the Ross Eversoles and I with a new lease on life. And as I daydreamed of being Fireman of the Year in 1970, I wondered what the dreams of Jim O'Toole are like these days. Then I thought, would I do that? When it's over for me, would I be hanging on with the Ross Eversoles? I went down deep and the answer I came up with was yes.

Yes, I would. You see, you spend a good piece of your life gripping a baseball, and in the end it turns out that it was the other way around all the time.

The fashion in fans has changed, and so has the fashion in sportswriters. Both are cooler now. The hard-boiled, epigrammatic style of Cannon that was admired by Hemingway has fallen from favor. Nobody asked me, but . . . the great ones come back, and Cannon will. This, from the collection *Who Struck John?*

JIMMY CANNON

Gallery of Buffs

The baseball enthusiast, according to the standard image drama by editorial page and sports department cartoonists, is a fat man with a belly in his lap. The artists of journalism give him an insipid smile, put a hot dog in one hand and a bottle of soda pop in the other, and illuminate his pudgy features with ecstasy. The collar is crumpled by sweat and the shirt is unbuttoned at the throat. Usually, there is a damp handkerchief tied around his neck as a substitute for a scarf. Constant association with the species led me to make notes on various types I have encountered in ballparks.

The Gourmet: There is a pile of cracked shells on either thigh, and his coat lapels are covered with shreds of the nut. He usually picks the crisis in the ballgame to stand up and shake himself clean. The guy sitting next to him spends the next couple of innings trying to get the stuff out of his eyes.

The Dugout Spy: What occurs on the ballfield doesn't interest him; he ignores the action to concentrate on the players on the bench. He stares into the dugout, making snide remarks about the manager and the substitutes.

The Coach Hater: This fan loathes all coaches. The coach stands with his back to the stands, and the coach hater spends nine innings abusing him. He leaves the park for a failure unless the coach turns around to glare at him.

The Switcher: The switcher comes into the park to root for a team, but the score influences his affection. As soon as the club of his choice gets behind, he ridicules them.

The Brooder: If the shortstop kicks a ball on opening day, he bellows: "There goes the pennant!" He shouts this at every player who makes an error in every game he attends. The standing of the clubs doesn't motivate him. He yells it at Pittsburgh and the Yankees.

The Regretful Assessor: If a ball falls safely in the outfield, he smiles with a cruel contentment and says: "DiMaggio would of got it."

The Haberdasher: He behaves as though he were judging the ten best dressed men. Why, he wants to know, doesn't a big-league ballplayer pull up his pants? He doesn't know why players play in dirty uniforms and wonders why they don't change between innings.

The Fan Club: The fan club is interested in only one player. He talks constantly about his idol even when he is not involved in the play. He heckles all the other players but begs for fairness if his hero is not regarded with respectful noise by the neighbors.

The Coat Holder: The coat holder proclaims himself a ballplayer's closest friend. He may be a waiter in a lunch wagon where the athlete once had a cup of coffee. He might run an elevator in which the ballplayer took a ride. But he tells everyone what a great guy the player is and how close they are. The coat holder never brags of friendship with an obscure player. It is always the star.

The Brute: The brute beseeches the pitcher to hit the batter between the eyes. It is his contention that a pitcher who doesn't try to decapitate a hitter is yellow.

The Slider: The slider ducks through the special cops as soon as the game is over and slides into the nearest base.

The Actor: The actor doesn't glance at the game but watches the television camera. As soon as he thinks it is turned on him, he stands up and waves.

The Cynic: The cynic suspects every move a team makes. If there is a series of errors or a lot of hits, he turns to the guy alongside of him and asks: "You think they want to win?" If the fellow replies yes, the cynic says something like this: "Baseball is a business like everything else. What's good for the gate is good for baseball."

The Watchman: He is only concerned with the pitchers. If they step off the rubber or fake a guy back to a base, he shouts: "Balk!" There are more of these than any other kind.

The Optimist: Nothing is important if the other team does it. No matter what the score is, he has one comment. He bawls, "You lucky bum!"

The Poet: Over and over again, from the first to the last inning, he rumbles, "Well, well," no matter what happens.

This is an excerpt from the brilliant, scary novel *The Universal Baseball Association, Inc.: J. Henry Waugh, Prop.* It is a baseball book that is not about baseball, as could be said of Malamud's *The Natural* or Roth's *The Great American Novel*. Then again, Coover could well believe that baseball is not about baseball. J. Henry Waugh is a man obsessed with a table game he has invented: he may hold the dice, but the outcome of each roll of the bones brings genuine surprise and delight. Here, Pioneers' pitching phenom Damon Rutherford, son of the immortal Brock Rutherford, is one out shy of perfection against the rival Haymakers.

ROBERT COOVER

JHWH

Of course, it was just the occasion for the storybook spoiler. Yes, too obvious. Perfect game, two down in the ninth, and a pinch hitter scratches out a history-shriveling single. How many times it had already happened! The epochal event reduced to a commonplace by something or someone even less than commonplace, a mediocrity, a blooper worth forgetting, a utility ballplayer never worth much and out of the league a year later. All the No-Hit Nealys that Sandy sang about . . .

> No-Hit Nealy, somethin' in his eye,
> When they pitched low, he swung high,
> Hadn't had a hit in ninety-nine years,
> And then they sent him out agin
>   The Pi-yo-neers!

Henry turned water on to wash, then hesitated. Not that he felt superstitious about it exactly, but he saw Damon Rutherford standing there on the mound, hands not on the rosin bag, not in the armpits, not squeezing the ball, just at his side—dry, strong, patient—and he felt as though washing his hands might somehow spoil Damon's pitch. From the bathroom door, he could see the kitchen table. His Association lay there in ordered stacks of paper. The dice sat there, three ivory cubes, heedless of history yet makers of it, still proclaiming Abernathy's strikeout. Damon Rutherford waited there. Henry held his breath, walked straight to the table, picked up the dice, and tossed them down.

Hard John Horvath took a cut at Rutherford's second pitch, a letter-high inside curve, pulled it down the third-base line: Hatrack Hines took it backhanded, paused one mighty spellbinding moment—then fired across the diamond to Goodman James, and Horvath was out.

The game was over.

Giddily, Henry returned to the bathroom and washed his hands. He stared down at his wet hands, thinking: he did it! And then, at the top of his voice, *"WA-HOO!"* he bellowed, and went leaping back into the kitchen, feeling like he could damn well take off and soar if he had anyplace to go. *"HOO-HAH!"*

And the fans blew the roof off. They leaped the wall, slid down the dugout roofs, overran the cops, flooded in from the outfield bleachers, threw hats and scorecards into the air. Rooney hustled his Haymakers to the showers, but couldn't stop the Pioneer fans from lifting poor Horvath to their shoulders. There was a fight and Hard John bloodied a couple noses, but nobody even bothered to swing back at him. An old lady blew him kisses. Partly to keep Rutherford from getting mobbed and partly just because they couldn't stop themselves, his Pioneer teammates got to him first, had him on their own shoulders before the frenzied hometown rooters could close in and tear him apart out of sheer love. From above, it looked like a great roiling whirlpool with Damon afloat in the vortex—but then York popped up like a cork, and then Patterson and Hines, and finally the manager Barney Bancroft, lifted up by fans too delirious even to know for sure anymore what it was they were celebrating, and the whirlpool uncoiled and surged toward the Pioneer locker rooms.

"Ah!" said Henry, and: *"Ah!"*

And even bobbingly afloat there on those rocky shoulders, there in that knock-and-tumble flood of fans, in a wild world that had literally, for the moment, blown its top, Damon Rutherford preserved his incredible equanimity, hands at his knees except for an occasional wave, face lit with pleasure at what he'd done, but in no way distorted with the excitement of it all: tall, right, and true. People screamed for the ball. Royce Ingram, whose shoulder was one of those he rode on, handed it up to him. Women shrieked, arms supplicating. He smiled at them, but tossed the ball out to a small boy standing at the crowd's edge.

Henry opened the refrigerator, reached for the last can of beer, then glanced at his watch: almost midnight—changed his mind. He peered out at the space between his kitchen window and the street lamp: lot of moisture in the air still, but hard to tell if it was falling or rising. He'd brooded over it, coming home from work: that piled-up mid-autumn feeling, pregnant with the vague threat of confusion and emptiness—but this boy had cut clean through it, let light and health in, and you don't go to bed on an event like this! Henry reknotted his tie, put on hat and raincoat, hooked his umbrella over one arm, and went out to get a drink. He glanced back at the kitchen table once more before pulling the door to, saw the dice there, grinned at them, for once adjuncts to grandeur, then hustled down the stairs like a happy Pioneer headed for the showers. He stepped quickly through the disembodied street-lamp glow at the bottom, and whirling his umbrella like a drum major's baton, marched springily up the street to Pete's, the neighborhood bar.

> N-o-O-O-o Hit Nealy!
> Won his fame
> Spoilin' Birdie Deaton's
> Per-her-fect game!

The night above was dark yet the streets were luminous; wet, they shimmered with what occasional light there was from street lamps, passing cars, phone booths, all-night neon signs. There was fog and his own breath was visible, yet nearby objects glittered with a heightened clarity. He smiled at the shiny newness of things springing up beside him on his night walk. At a distance, car head lamps were haloed and taillights burned fuzzily, yet the lit sign in the darkened window he was passing, "DIVINEFORM FOUNDATIONS: TWO-WAY STRETCH," shone fiercely, hard-edged and vivid as a vision.

The corner drugstore was still open. A scrawny curly-headed kid, cigarette butt dangling under his fuzzy upper lip, played the pinball machine that stood by the window. Henry paused to watch. The machine was rigged like a baseball game, though the scores were unrealistic. Henry had played the machine himself often and once, during a blue season, had even played off an entire-all-UBA pinball tourney on it. Ballplayers, lit from inside, scampered around the basepaths, as the kid put english on the balls with his hips and elbows. A painted pitcher, in eternal windup, kicked high, while below, a painted batter in a half-crouch moved motionlessly toward the plate. Two girls in the upper corners, legs apart and skirts hiked up their thighs, cheered the runners on with silent wide-open mouths. The kid was really racking them up: seven free games showing already. Lights flashed, runners ran. Eight. Nine. "THE GREAT AMERICAN GAME," it said across the top, between the gleaming girls. Well, it was. American baseball, by luck, trial, and error, and since the famous playing rules council of 1889, had struck on an almost perfect balance between offense and defense, and it was that balance, in fact, that and the accountability—the beauty of the records system which found a place to keep forever each least action—that had led Henry to baseball as his final great project.

The kid twisted, tensed, relaxed, hunched over, reared, slapped the machine with a pelvic thrust; up to seventeen free games and the score on the lighted panel looked more like that of a cricket match than a baseball game. Henry moved on. To be sure, he'd only got through one UBA pinball tourney and had never been tempted to set up another. Simple-minded, finally, and not surprisingly a simple-minded ballplayer, Jaybird Wall, had won it. In spite of all the flashing lights, it was—like those two frozen open-mouthed girls and the batter forever approaching the plate, the imperturbable pitcher forever reared back—a static game, utterly lacking the movement, grace, and complexity of real baseball. When he'd finally decided to settle on his own baseball game, Henry had spent the better part of two months just working with the problem of odds and equilibrium points in an effort to approximate that complexity. Two dice had not done it. He'd tried three, each a different color, and the 216 different combinations had provided the complexity, all right, but he'd nearly gone blind trying to sort the colors on each throw. Finally, he'd compromised, keeping the three dice, but all white, reducing the total number of combinations to 56, though of course the odds were still based on 216. To restore—and, in fact, to intensify—the complexity of the multicolored method, he'd allowed triple ones and sixes—1–1–1 and 6–6–6—to trigger the more spectacular events, by referring the following dice throw to what he called his Stress Chart, also a three-dice chart, but far more dramatic in nature than the basic ones. Two successive throws of triple ones and sixes were exceedingly rare—only about three times in every two entire seasons of play on the average—but when it happened, the next throw was referred, finally, to the Chart of Extraordinary Occurrences, where just about anything from fistfights to fixed ball games could happen. These two charts were what gave the game its special quality, making it much more than just a series of hits and walks and outs. Besides these, he also had special strategy charts for hit-and-run plays, attempted stolen bases, sacrifice bunts, and squeeze plays, still others for deciding the ages of rookies when they came up, for providing details of injuries and errors, and for determining who, each year, must die.

A neon beer advertisement and windows lit dimly through red curtains were all that marked Pete's place. Steady clientele, no doubt profitable in a small way, generally quiet, mostly country-and-western or else old hit-parade tunes on the jukebox, a girl or two drifting by from time to time, fair prices. Henry brought his gyrating umbrella under control, left the wet world behind, and pushed in.

"Evening, Mr. Waugh," said the bartender.

"Evening, Jake."

Not Jake, of course, it was Pete himself, but it was a long-standing gag, born of a slip of the tongue. Pete was medium-sized, slope-shouldered, had bartender's bags beneath his eyes and a splendid bald dome, spoke with a kind of hushed irony that seemed to give a dry double meaning to everything he said— in short, was the spitting image of Jake Bradley, one of Henry's ballplayers, a Pastimer second baseman whom Henry always supposed now to be running a bar somewhere near the Pastime Club's ballpark, and one night, years ago, in the middle of a free-swinging pennant scramble, Henry had called Pete "Jake" by mistake. He'd kept it up ever since; it was a kind of signal to Pete that he was in a good mood and wanted something better than beer or bar whiskey. He sometimes wondered if anybody ever walked into Jake's bar and called him Pete by mistake. Henry took the middle one of three empty barstools. Jake— Pete—lifted a bottle of VSOP, raised his eyebrows, and Henry nodded. Right on the button.

The bar was nearly empty, not surprising; Tuesday, a working night, only six or seven customers, faces all familiar, mostly old-timers on relief. Pete's cats scrubbed and stalked, sulked and slept. A neighborhood B-girl named Hettie, old friend of Henry's, put money in the jukebox—old-time country love songs. Nostalgia was the main vice here. Pete toweled dust from a snifter, poured a finger of cognac into it. "How's the work going, Mr. Waugh?" he asked.

"Couldn't go better," Henry said and smiled. Jake always asked the right questions.

Jake smiled broadly, creasing his full cheeks, nodded as though to say he understood, pate flashing in the amber light. And it was the right night to call him Jake, after all: Jake Bradley was also from the Brock Rutherford era, must have come up about the same time. Was he calling it that now? The Brock Rutherford Era? He never had before. Funny. Damon was not only creating the future, he was doing something to the past, too. Jake dusted the shelf before

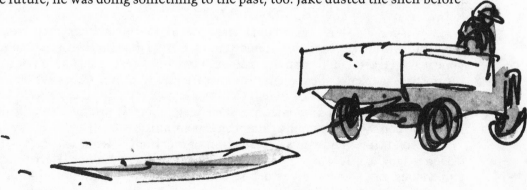

putting the cognac bottle back. He was once the middle man in five double plays executed in one game, still the Association record.

Hettie, catching Henry's mood apparently, came over to kid with him and he bought her a drink. A couple molars missing and flesh folds ruining the once-fine shape of her jaw, but there was still something compelling about the electronic bleat her stockings emitted when she hopped up on a barstool and crossed her legs, and that punctuation-wink she used to let a man know he was in with her, getting the true and untarnished word. Henry hadn't gone with her in years, not since before he set up his Association, but she often figured obliquely in the Book and conversations with her often got reproduced there under one guise or another. "Been gettin' any hits lately?" she asked, and winked over her tumbler of whiskey. They often used baseball idiom, she no doubt supposing he was one of those ballpark zealots who went crazy every season during the World Series and got written up as a character—the perennial krank—in the newspapers, and Henry never told her otherwise. Since she herself knew nothing at all about the sport, though, he often talked about his Association as though it were the major leagues. It gave him a kind of pleasure to talk about it with someone, even if she did think he was talking about something else.

"Been getting a lot," he said, "but probably not enough." She laughed loudly, exhibiting the gaps in her teeth. "And how about you, Hettie, been scoring a lot of runs?"

"I been scorin', boy, but I ain't got the runs!" she said, and whooped again. Old gag. The other customers turned their way and smiled.

Henry waited for her to settle down, commune with her drink once more, then he said, "Listen, Hettie, think what a wonderful rare thing it is to do something, no matter how small a thing, with absolute unqualified utterly unsurpassable *perfection!*"

"What makes you think it's so rare?" she asked with a wink, and switching top knee, issued the old signal. "You ain't pitched to me in a long time, you know."

He grinned. "No, but think of it, Hettie, to do a thing so perfectly that, even if the damn world lasted forever, nobody could ever do it better, because you had done it as well as it could possibly be done." He paused, let the cognac fumes bite his nostrils to excuse the foolish tears threatening to film his eyes over. "In a way, you know, it's even sad somehow, because, well, it's done, and all you can hope for after is to do it a second time." Of course, there were other things to do, the record book was, above all, a catalogue of possibilities...

"A second time! Did you say *perfection* or *erection?*" Hettie asked.

Henry laughed. It was no use. And anyway it didn't matter. He felt just stupendous, not so exultant as before, but still full of joy, and now a kind of heady aromatic peace seemed to be sweeping over him: ecstasy—yes, he laughed to himself, that was the only goddamn word for it. It was good. He bought another round, asked Pete: "How is it you stay in such good shape, Jake?"

"I don't know, Mr. Waugh. Must be the good Christian hours I keep."

And then, when the barkeep had left them, it was Hettie who suddenly turned serious. "I don't know what it is about you tonight, Henry," she said, "but you've got me kinda hot." And she switched top knee again: call from the deep.

Henry smiled, slowly whirling the snifter through minute cycles, warming the tawny dram in the palm of his hand. It was a temptation, to be sure, but he was afraid Hettie would spoil it for him, dissipate the joy and dull this glow, take the glory out of it. It was something he could share with no one without losing it altogether. Too bad. "It's just that nobody's bought you two straight drinks in a long time, Hettie," he said.

"Aw," she grumbled and frowned at her glass, hurt by that and so cooled off a little. To make up for it, he ordered her a third drink. He'd had enough, time to get back, had to make it to work in the morning, old Zifferblatt had been giving him a hard time for weeks now and just looking for a chance to raise hell about something, but Pete poured him one on the house. Not every day you pitched perfect games and got VSOP on the house. "Thanks, Jake," he said.

"Henry, hon', gimme some money to put in the jukebox."

Coins on the bar: he slid them her way. Stared into his snifter, saw himself there in the brown puddle, or anyway his eye.

> It was down in Jake's old barroom
> Behind the Patsies' park;
> Jake was settin' 'em up as usual
> And the night was agittin' dark.
> At the bar stood ole Verne Mackenzie,
> And his eyes was bloodshot red . . .

"The Day They Fired Verne Mackenzie": Sandy Shaw's great ballad. Dead now, Verne. First of the game's superstars, starting shortstop on Abe Flint's Excelsiors back in Year I, first of the Hall of Famers. But he got older and stopped hitting, and Flint, nice a guy as he was, had to let him go. And they all knew how Verne felt, even the young guys playing now who never knew him, because sooner or later it would be the same for them. Hettie leaned against him, head on his shoulder, humming the jukebox melodies to herself. He felt good, having her there like that. He sipped his brandy and grew slowly melancholy, *pleasantly* melancholy. He saw Brock the Great reeling boisterously down the street, arm in arm with Willie O'Leary and Frosty Young, those wonderful guys—and who should they meet up with but sleepy-eyed Mose Stanford and Gabe Burdette and crazy rubber-legged Jaybird Wall. Yes, and they were singing, singing the *old* songs, "Pitchin', Catchin', Swingin' " and "The Happy Days of Youth," and oh! it was happiness! and goddamn it! it was fellowship! and boys oh boys! it was significance! "Let's go to Jake's!" they cried, they laughed, and off they went!

"Where?" Hettie mumbled. She was pretty far along. So was he. Didn't realize he had been talking out loud. Glanced self-consciously at Pete, but Pete hadn't moved: he was a patient pillar in the middle of the bar, ankles and arms crossed, face in shadows, only the dome lit up. Maybe he was asleep. There was only one other customer, an old-timer, still in the bar. The neon light outside was probably off.

"To my place," he said, not sure it was himself talking. Could he take her up there? She leaned away from his shoulder, tried to wink, couldn't quite pull it off, instead studied him quizzically as though wondering if he really meant it. "Hettie," he whispered, staring hard at her, so she'd know he wasn't kidding and that she'd better not spoil it, "how would you like to sleep with . . . Damon Rutherford?"

She blinked, squinted skeptically, but he could see she was still pretty excited and she'd moved her hand up his pantleg to the seam. "Who's he?"

"Me." He didn't smile, just looked straight at her, and he saw her eyes widen, maybe even a little fear came into them, but certainly awe was there, and fascination, and hope, and her hand, discovering he could do it, yes, he could do it, gave a squeeze like Witness York always gave his bat for luck before he swung, and she switched knees: *wheep!* So he paid Jake, and together—he standing tall and self-assured, Hettie shiveringly clasped in his embrace—they walked out. As he'd foreseen, the neon light was out; it was dark. He felt exceedingly wise.

"What are you, Henry?" Hettie asked softly as they walked under the glowing nimbus of a mist-wrapped street lamp. His raincoat had a slit in the lining behind the pocket, and this she reached through to slip her hand into his coin pocket.

"Now, or when we get to my place?"

"Now."

"An accountant."

"But the baseball? . . ." And again she took hold and squeezed like Witness York, but now her hand was full of coins as well, and they wrapped the bat like a suit of mail.

"I'm an auditor for a baseball association."

"I didn't know they had auditors, too," she said. Was she really listening for once? They were in the dark now, next street lamp was nearly a block away, in front of Diskin's. She was trying to get her other hand on the bat, gal can't take a healthy swing without a decent grip, after all, but she couldn't get both hands through the slit.

"Oh, yes. I keep financial ledgers for each club, showing cash receipts and disbursements, which depend mainly on such things as team success, the buying and selling of ballplayers, improvement of the stadiums, player contracts, things like that." Hettie Irden stood at the plate, first woman ballplayer in league history, tightening and relaxing her grip on the bat, smiling around the spaces of her missing molars in that unforgettable way of hers, kidding with the catcher, laughing that gay timeless laugh that sounded like the clash of small coins, tugging maybe at her crotch in a parody of all male ballplayers the world over, and maybe she wasn't the best hitter in the Association, but the Association was glad to have her. She made them all laugh and forget for a moment that they were dying men. "And a running journalization of the activity, posting of it all into permanent record books, and I help them with basic problems of burden distribution, remarshaling of assets, graphing fluctuations. Politics, too. Elections. Team captains. Club presidents. And every four years, the Association elects a Chancellor, and I have to keep an eye on that."

"Gee, Henry, I didn't realize! . . ." She was looking up at him, and as they approached the street lamp, he could see something in her eyes he hadn't seen there before. He was glad to see it had come to pass, that she recognized—but it wouldn't do when they got to bed, she'd have to forget then.

"There are box scores to be audited, trial balances of averages along the way, seasonal inventories, rewards and punishments to be meted out, life histories to be overseen." He took a grip on her behind. "People die, you know."

"Yes," she said, and that seemed to excite her, for she squeezed a little harder.

"Usually, they die old, already long since retired, but they can die young, even as ballplayers. Or in accidents during the winter season. Last year a young fellow, just thirty, had a bad season and got sent back to the minors. They say his manager rode him too hard." Pappy Rooney. Wouldn't let go of the kid. "Sensitive boy who took it too much to heart. On the way, he drove his car off a cliff."

"Oh!" she gasped and squeezed. As though afraid now to let go. "On purpose?"

"I don't know. I think so. And if a pitcher throws two straight triple ones or sixes and brings on an Extraordinary Occurrence, a third set of ones is a beanball that kills the batter, while triple sixes again is a line drive that kills the pitcher."

"Oh, how awful!" He didn't tell her neither had ever happened. "But what are triple sixes, Henry?"

"A kind of pitch. Here we are."

Even climbing the stairs to his place, she didn't want to release her grip, but the stairway was too narrow and they kept jamming up. So she took her hand out and went first. From his squat behind the box, the catcher watched her loosening up, kidded her that she'd never get a walk because they could never get two balls on her. Over her shoulder, she grinned down upon him, a gap-tooth grin that was still somehow beautiful. Anyhow, she said, I *am* an Extraordinary Occurrence, and on that chart there's no place for mere passes! The catcher laughed, reached up and patted her rear. "You said it!" he admitted, letting his hand glide down her thigh, then whistle up her stocking underneath the skirt. "An Extraordinary Occurrence!"

She hopped two steps giddily, thighs slapping together. "Henry! I'm ticklish!"

He unlocked the door to his apartment, switched on a night light in the hall, leaving the kitchen and Association in protective darkness, and led her toward the bedroom.

"We're at your place," she said huskily when they'd got in there, and squeezed up against him. "Who are you now?" That she remembered! She was wonderful!

"The greatest pitcher in the history of baseball," he whispered. "Call me . . . Damon."

"Damon," she whispered, unbuckling his pants, pulling his shirt out. And "Damon," she sighed, stroking his back, unzipping his fly, sending his pants earthward with a rattle of buckles and coins. And "Damon!" she greeted, grabbing—and that girl, with one swing, he knew then, could bang a pitch clean out of the park. *"Play ball!"* cried the umpire. And the catcher, stripped of mask and guard, revealed as the pitcher Damon Rutherford, whipped the uniform off the first lady ballplayer in Association history, and then, helping and hindering all at once, pushing and pulling, they ran the bases, pounded into first, slid into second heels high, somersaulted over third, shot home standing up, then into the box once more, swing away, and run them all again, and "Damon!" she cried, and "Damon!"

Has there ever been a better baseball biography than *Babe?* No, not even Creamer's admirable *Stengel*. The subtitle of *Babe* is "The Legend Comes to Life"; here the life ends, heartbreakingly, although the legend will live always. Today, fifty years after Ruth played his last major-league game, no one has come along to challenge his position as the game's greatest player. Roger Maris and Henry Aaron have surpassed his home-run records, but Ruth remains the nonpareil, an American hero more implausible than Paul Bunyan and more beloved than any but Lincoln.

ROBERT W. CREAMER

"Joe, I'm Gone"

Colonel Ruppert died in January 1939. Ruth visited him in the hospital as he lay dying and was touched when Ruppert, who had never called him anything but Ruth, whispered, "Babe, Babe." Gehrig was dying, and at the Lou Gehrig Day ceremonies at Yankee Stadium on July 4th, Babe ended their long antagonism by impulsively putting his arm around Gehrig and hugging him.

Time was closing in. Playing golf with Ben Curry at Leewood, Ruth said, "I feel terrible," and lay down on the grass near the sixteenth tee. "His face was almost blue," Curry recalled. A car was brought out and Ruth was driven to the clubhouse, where he lay down on a bench and asked for a glass of water. A doctor had been called, and Curry was afraid to let him have anything before the doctor got there. He put a sip of water in a glass and gave it to him. Ruth said, "Damn it, give me a glass of water," and began to lift himself. He was given a full glass of water and drank all of it and drank another. After the doctor checked him out, he rested for a while and that night felt fine.

But it was apparently a mild heart attack, and a year or so later he had another. Late in 1941, he was invited to appear in *Pride of the Yankees*, a movie about Gehrig. His weight was nearly 270, and he dieted strenuously in order to be down to presentable size when work on the film began early in

1942. He lost 40 pounds in a few months and became edgy and irritable. He had a minor but frightening auto accident in December that depressed him terribly, an odd thing for a man who had been in so many accidents. He caught a bad cold, and early in the New Year, suffering from the cold and nervous exhaustion, he was taken from his apartment on a stretcher and sent to the hospital. He recovered quickly and was off hunting for a few days before going to California for the movie.

In Hollywood he worked hard on the Lou Gehrig movie and did a fine natural job of acting, even to the point of putting his fist through a Pullman car window in a pennant celebration scene. But the stringent working schedule demanded by the film combined with his own normally late hours did not mesh well. He caught another cold and it developed into pneumonia. Again he was hospitalized and for a day or so was reported to be near death. But he was out of the hospital in two weeks, and by the end of April, with the movie finished, was home in New York, healthy and playing golf.

During World War II, he did work for the Red Cross, bought $100,000 worth of war bonds, made appropriate comments about Hitler and Mussolini and the Japanese, voted against Franklin Roosevelt, and appeared frequently at benefits. He played a series of three golf matches with Ty Cobb for war charities, losing the first, winning the second, and losing the third. In August 1942, he appeared at a benefit affair in Yankee Stadium, where he batted against Walter Johnson. It was his first time in the Stadium as a player since 1934, and he was as excited as a kid about it, making sure his uniform was clean and pressed, his spiked shoes shined. Johnson threw seven pitches before Ruth lifted a high fly into the stands in right. The ball curved foul, but Ruth, always a showman, accepted it as a home run and ran around the bases while the crowd cheered. In May 1943, he was in uniform again for a game between two teams from the armed forces, both studded with professional players. Babe pinch-hit and walked. A couple of months later he managed a servicemen's team in another benefit at Yankee Stadium and put himself in as a pinch hitter against Johnny Sain. He hit one long foul and then walked. A pinch runner came out from the dugout, but Ruth waved him off. The next man singled and Ruth moved to second, but he pulled up lame and puffing. He accepted the pinch runner then and half walked, half jogged off the field. It was his last appearance in a formal game.

He was in the hospital toward the end of the war for a cartilage operation on his knee. After the war he let his hope of managing come alive again. The Ruppert estate sold the Yankees to a syndicate headed by MacPhail, and Barrow was no longer running the team. Ruth phoned MacPhail and asked him for the job of managing the Yankees' Newark farm club. It was an embarrassing retreat from his long-held position that he was a big leaguer who did not have to go back to the minors as an apprentice, but he was being realistic. MacPhail said he would get back to him. There was no answer for a few weeks and then a letter came.

"That's bad news," Ruth said. "When it's good news, they telephone."

MacPhail did not want Ruth and told him so in a polite, circuitous note that ended with a plea for Babe to become involved in a sandlot baseball program sponsored by the city of New York. That was the final humiliation. He went back to golf, bowling, and hunting.

In May 1946, when Jorge Pascual was trying to build up the Mexican League by enticing American major leaguers with offers of huge salaries, Ruth spent two weeks in Mexico City as Pascual's guest. He was called El Rey Jonronero in the Mexican newspapers. Now past fifty, he said quite plainly that he doubted he would sign any sort of a contract with Pascual, but he had a fine time anyway. He went to a bullfight, played golf, got sunburned, saw a few ballgames, swung at a couple of pitches in batting practice. He met fifty-eight-year-old Armando Marsans, a Cuban who had been an American League outfielder thirty years earlier when Ruth was still a pitcher. "You remember me?" asked Marsans, and Ruth's face lit up. "Sure I do," he said, and he did. Not the name, but the man. Marsans was managing in one of the games Ruth saw, and when he refused to take a pitcher out of a game despite a rally by the other

team, Ruth approved. "That's right," he called out. "Let him stay in there."

Because of the major leagues' antipathy for Pascual and the Mexican League, Ruth was asked if anyone tried to persuade him not to visit Mexico. "No," Babe said, "nobody asked me not to come. But that doesn't make any difference. I go where I please anyway."

Several months later Ruth began to complain of extreme pain over his left eye. He thought it was a sinus headache, but it hurt so much that in November he entered French Hospital in New York for a thorough examination. Not much attention was paid—he had been in and out of hospitals so often—but this time it was deadly serious. He had a malignant growth in the left side of his neck, in such a position that it nearly encircled the left carotid artery. When he was operated on, nerves had to be severed and the artery tied off, which adversely affected the left side of his head, including his larynx. Most of the cancerous growth was removed but some could not be, and he was given radiation treatment to control it.

The disease and its treatment debilitated him. He could not eat and had to be fed intravenously. He was in French Hospital for three months and lost 80 pounds. When he was discharged in February 1947, he went to Florida to rest in the sun. He regained enough strength to play golf a few times and go fishing, but the seriousness of his condition was evident in his appearance. In March, A. B. (Happy) Chandler, the new commissioner of baseball (Judge Landis died in 1944), declared that Sunday, April 27, would be Babe Ruth Day in the major leagues. Ceremonies were held in all the parks, but the most significant was in Yankee Stadium.

Ruth returned to New York in time to be at the Stadium for his day. He wore his familiar camel's hair overcoat and camel's hair cap, but he was thin, his color a bad yellowish tan, his voice a disheartening croak. Almost 60,000 people were in the Stadium. There was the usual plethora of speeches, including one from a thirteen-year-old who represented boys' baseball. Ruth spoke too, bending forward slightly from the hips to bring his mouth close to the microphone. His speech was extemporaneous.

"Thank you very much, ladies and gentlemen," he began, the awful voice sounding even harsher as it came from the loudspeakers. "You know how bad my voice sounds. Well, it feels just as bad. You know, this baseball game of ours comes up from the youth. That means the boys. And after you've been a boy, and grow up to know how to play ball, then you come to the boys you see representing themselves today in our national pastime. The only real game in the world, I think, is baseball. As a rule, some people think if you give them a football or a baseball or something like that, naturally, they're athletes right away. But you can't do that in baseball. You've got to start from way down, at the bottom, when you're six or seven years old. You can't wait until you're fifteen or sixteen. You've got to let it grow up with you, and if you're successful and you try hard enough, you're bound to come out on top, just like these boys have come to the top now.

"There's been so many lovely things said about me, I'm glad I had the opportunity to thank everybody. Thank you."

He smiled and waved to the crowd and walked slowly to the Yankee dugout.

The unexcised part of the tumor continued to grow, and Ruth was in extreme discomfort through the spring of 1947. He did not know what was wrong with him, and no one told him. Considine said, "Those who knew him best, Mel Lowenstein and Paul Carey, and Claire, believed that if he knew he had terminal cancer, it would destroy him. He'd go right out the window." For a time Ruth thought his teeth were infected, and he would wince with pain and mutter, "These damn teeth."

He was in constant pain that had to be relieved with morphine. He tried to work with Considine on his autobiography, but when he could not recall something he was trying to remember, he would break off the conversation and say, "Let's get the hell out of here and go hit a few." They would get into Ruth's Lincoln Continental and drive to the butcher shop on Ninth Avenue. Instead of ordering a steak to take to the golf course, Ruth would buy chopped meat, since he could not chew. In the shop he would pick up a cleaver and playfully threaten the butchers. "I'm going to chop your goddamned heads off," he'd say, to their evident delight. A girl, a nurse, would usually meet him in the butcher shop and ride out to the golf course, where she would walk around with them while they played. Sometimes at the club he felt so bad he would have only a soft-boiled egg, and he had trouble swallowing that. One day he looked at the egg in his misery and said, "To think of the steaks." For a time he continued to play eighteen holes, but as he grew weaker his games grew shorter. One day he teed up his ball, swung well, and hit the ball cleanly. It carried straight down the fairway, but for only about 90 yards. Ruth stood on the tee watching it and cried, cursing through the tears.

By June 1947 the pain had become so bad that his doctors decided to treat the cancer with an experimental new drug, a synthetic relative of folic acid, part of the vitamin B complex. Treatment began on June 29, and Ruth showed such remarkable improvement that in September a paper on his case was read at an International Cancer Congress meeting in St. Louis. He began to travel around the country doing promotional work on American Legion baseball for the Ford Motor Company. He also had Lowenstein draw up papers creating The Babe Ruth Foundation, which was designed to help underprivileged children. Late in September, MacPhail put on another Babe Ruth Day at Yankee Stadium to raise funds for the Ruth Foundation, and Babe was there to watch an old-timers' game played by Ty Cobb and Tris Speaker and others. He had hoped to be strong enough to be able to pitch an inning, but he was not.

His dramatic improvement was apparently only a temporary remission of the cancer, and he continued painfully ill. When Ruth was in Cincinnati for the Ford people, Waite Hoyt and his wife visited him in his hotel. Claire met them at the door and brought them into the living room of the suite where Ruth was sitting on a couch, his head down, nodding from the sedatives he was taking. On the table in front of him was a bottle of beer, which, Hoyt said, he drank for food. Babe lifted his head wearily.

"I'm glad to see you," he whispered.

They talked for a while, but he appeared so exhausted that Hoyt decided he and his wife should leave.

"We'd better go, Jidge."

Ruth nodded. "I am kind of tired," he said.

The Hoyts stood up to go, but Ruth whispered, "Wait a minute." Painfully, he got to his feet and went into the kitchen. From the refrigerator he took a small vase with an orchid in it and brought it back to the living room.

"Here," he said to Mrs. Hoyt. "I never gave you anything."

On Sunday, June 13, 1948, the Yankees celebrated the twenty-fifth anniversary of Yankee Stadium, and Ruth was invited to be there along with other members of the 1923 Yankees. Sick as he was, he was delighted with the idea. The Yankees held a banquet for all the old players at Ruppert's brewery the night before the game, but Ruth was not well enough to attend that. There was concern that he might not be at the Stadium either on Sunday because it was a dank, rainy day. But he came. The other old Yankees were already in the locker room when he arrived.

"Here he is now," one of them said in a low voice, and Ruth came in slowly, helped by Paul Carey and Frank Dulaney, his male nurse. His face split into a grin, a shriveled caricature of the beaming one he used to have, and in his croaking voice he spoke to his old teammates, calling most of them by their nicknames. Dulaney helped him take off his street clothes and put on his uniform. The old teammates stayed away until he had his uniform on, and so did the photographers. Then they began to take pictures, with Ruth posing willingly. The old Yankees were gathered together for a group photograph. Ruth, stooped, smiling, stood in the middle of the back row. Joe Dugan, standing half behind him, had a hand on his shoulder, and so did Wally Pipp.

The old-timers began to go out onto the field, and Ruth, accompanied by Dulaney and Carey, followed slowly down the runway to the dugout. It was early, and Ruth paused in the runway, a topcoat slung over his shoulders to keep off the chill. "I think you'd better wait inside," said Dulaney. "It's too damp here." Ruth was led back to the clubhouse and stayed there until it was nearly time for him to appear on the field. Then he came down the runway again and into the dugout, where room was made for him on the bench. Mel Harder, a Cleveland coach who had pitched against Ruth, came over to say hello.

Ruth said hoarsely, "You remember when I got five-for-five off you in Cleveland and they booed me?"

Harder smiled.

"Line drives," Ruth croaked, "all to left field. And they booed the shit out of me."

All the other old-timers had been introduced, the applause from the big crowd rising and falling as each name was called. It was time for Ruth. He got to his feet, letting the topcoat fall from his shoulders, and took a bat to use as a cane. He looked up at the photographers massed in front of the dugout. His name rang out over the public address system, the roar of the crowd began and, as W. C. Heinz wrote, "He walked out into the cauldron of sound he must have known better than any other man."

He walked slowly, and he was smaller than Babe Ruth should have been. He paused for the photographers, leaning on the bat, looking up at the crowded tiers of people. Near home plate he was met by Ed Barrow, a month past his eightieth birthday, who hugged him. At the microphone Ruth spoke briefly, saying how proud he was to have hit the first home run in the Stadium and how good it was to see his old teammates. When the ceremonies were over and the other old players trotted out to their positions for a two-inning game, Ruth left the field at Yankee Stadium for the last time. He was helped down into the dug-out and back along the runway to the clubhouse. The topcoat was put over his shoulders again, and he kept it on in the clubhouse. He felt chilly. The glow of the excitement was wearing off. Dugan, who played only one inning of the old-timers' game, came into the clubhouse.

"Hiya, Babe," Dugan said, sitting down next to him.

"Hello, Joe."

"Can you use a drink?"

"Just a beer."

A small bar had been set up in a corner of the locker room, and Dugan got a drink for himself and a beer for Ruth and brought them back. They sat there a while, sipping their drinks.

"How are things, Jidge?" Dugan asked.

"Joe, I'm gone," Ruth said. "I'm gone, Joe."

He started to cry, and Dugan did too.

A week or so later, Ruth was in the hospital again. He did not want to go, and when it was time to leave for the hospital he refused to get out of bed. Frank Dulaney said, "He was in terrible pain. I tried to cajole him, but he shook his head. He wouldn't get up. I sat on the side of his bed and talked to him. I said, 'If you were my father, I'd make you go.' He got up then."

As Dulaney helped him up the steps of Memorial Hospital, Ruth said, "Isn't this hospital for cancer?" Dulaney answered, "Cancer and *allied* diseases." Ruth grunted.

He never was told he had cancer, but he certainly knew it, at least toward the end. When Jim Peterson took Connie Mack to visit him, Ruth said, "Hello, Mr. Mack. The termites have got me."

Ruth was ambulatory in the hospital, and when he felt strong enough he would go out for a drive. Early in July, he paid his last visit to Baltimore, flying down for a charity game. It was rained out, but he had a chance to talk to Roger Pippen, who had been with him in Fayetteville in 1914. Back in his hospital room he watched baseball on television, a relatively new phenomenon, and was pleased by visits and mail. He received hundreds of letters every day. A few would be read to him and he would rasp his reaction. May Singhi Breen, a onetime radio star who, with her husband, the songwriter Peter DeRose, was close to Claire and Babe, took on the job of seeing to it that all the mail was answered. Many contained requests for autographs, and on days he felt well Ruth would ask for "my cards." These were postcards with his photograph, and he would sign a hundred or so at a time to keep a supply on hand. President Truman phoned him, and Betty Grable, whom he had met and liked in Hollywood, sent him a bottle of pine-scented cologne. He wanted the cologne in his bath water each day and sometimes he would grunt to Dulaney, "Toss a little around the room, Frank."

The last rites of the Catholic Church were administered on July 21, but Ruth rallied again after that. He left the hospital on the evening of July 26 to attend the premiere of *The Babe Ruth Story*. He was very uncomfortable watching the film and left well before it was over. He seemed content back in the hospital, and he never left it again. "All my obligations are over," he said. "I'm going to rest now. I'm going to take it easy."

In August, his condition steadily deteriorated. Claire stayed in a room across the hall, usually attended by a friend or by Julia or Dorothy. Few visitors were admitted, but Ruth, even though he was unable to say much, relished the visits. Paul Carey phoned Ford Frick one day and told him Babe would like to see him. Frick said the hospital was like a three-ring circus, with reporters and photographers waiting, and the deathwatch across the hall. He spoke to Claire for a moment and then went into the room.

"It was a terrible moment. Ruth was so thin it was unbelievable. He had been such a big man, and his arms were just skinny little bones and his face was so haggard. When I came in he lifted his eyes toward me and raised his right arm a little, only about three or four inches off the bed, and then it fell back again. I went over to the bed and I said, 'Babe, Paul Carey said you wanted to see me.' And Ruth said, in that terrible voice, 'Ford, I always wanted to see you.' It was just a polite thing to say. I stayed a few minutes and left and I spoke to Claire again across the hall and then I went home and the next day he was dead."

What is a muffin game? It is an 1860s travesty of baseball perpetrated by inept, out-of-shape, middle-aged supporters of an amateur club's first nine. A muffin muffed—he could not catch, or throw, or hit—but he could enjoy himself, and he certainly could entertain others. In the days when baseball was new, it was common to stage a muffin match after the regular contest had concluded. The delightful account below by one "Q. K. Philander Doesticks" appeared in *The Hartford Courant* of October 10, 1866, and may describe the "Great Muffin Game" held four months earlier between Hartford and Waterbury. By the way, the Pitchman is a pitcher, the Catchman a catcher, and the players are termed "monkeys" because of their gaudy uniforms.

Q. K. PHILANDER DOESTICKS

A Muffin Game

I squared myself, raised my big stick, and told the Pitchman to pitch in. He did so. The first ball came like a cannon shot, but I dodged it neatly. The next one hit me plump in the breast. I dropped the stick and asked him what he did that for. Cap told me to pick up the stick again and try to hit the ball. Did so. When I saw the ball coming, I poked my stick at it, but didn't hit it. The truth was I wasn't prepared to have it come so fast. Told the Pitchman to give me a fair ball, an easy one; then all the fellows laughed. Then I got mad—punched the stick at the next ball—didn't hit it; punched again—all the fellows yelled "Run, run—run you muffin! Run you diabolical fool, run! Run, I tell you!—" About this time I started to run; didn't look which way I went; ran into the Catchman, who stood behind me; bowled him over on his head. "Not that way—run, run," everybody yelled again. Changed my course; tumbled over the Umpire, and tangled my legs in his chair. Veered about, and dashed furiously against our Captain and caught a dim vision of his heels in the air, as I started on a new course, and backed into a sturdy policeman. Then tumbled over one of the base bags; some fellows yelled to "Stop!", others, "Run, run!" Started once more; dashed into a crowd of spectators and upset about a dozen; then pitched into the game keepers; finally ran into the fence, and fell all in a heap into a frog hole. When I was picked up, everything was spinning around the sky and the ballground was all mixed up; the policeman seemed to be floating in the air, and all the monkeys to be whirling round at a terrific rate among the clouds; while the spectators, the bases, the bags, the officers, the wagons, the clubhouse, the trees, bushes, and frog pond seemed to be joining in a frantic jig on the double quick, only ten times faster than any double quick ever executed. When I came to my senses, found everybody shrieking with laughter, and calling me "the dashedest muffin that ever held a club." My nose was bleeding, my elbows skinned, my hair full of burdocks, and my monkey clothes covered with mud and frog-spawn. Cap came over and soon as he could stop laughing long enough to speak, he said, "Well, of all the dashed muffins I ever saw, you are the dashedest!" I didn't wait for any more compliments, but went home.

For this ripping yarn I am indebted to my friend Fred Ivor-Campbell of Providence, who read it in that city's *Sunday Journal* in 1979 and fortunately saved it. Before being picked up by the Associated Press, Bill Doyle's deft profile appeared in the Holyoke *Transcript-Telegram*.

BILL DOYLE

Ticket Taker Talks Technique

Every Holyoke Millers player hopes to make the major leagues someday, and the team's head ticker taker has the same aspiration.

"My dream is to be a big-league ticket taker," admits Bill Kane of 38 Kane Rd.

Kane, a science teacher at Holyoke High School in the off-season, is in his rookie year as a Mackenzie Field ticket taker. He says he has worked hard to improve his ticket-tearing skills to get a chance to rip in the big leagues.

"I can rip from either side," said the 6 foot, 160 pounder, who claims only one thing has prevented him from making the jump to the majors.

"I have no experience with turnstiles whatsoever, and I think that's what's holding me back," he said.

Millers' general manager Tom Kayser thinks the rookie has plenty of potential. "He's got the style and he's got the personality, but he's a little weak in ticket tearing speed," Kayser noted. "His hand—eye coordination is off."

While Kane dreams of ripping in the majors, he doesn't have stars in his eyes.

"If I'm not there by the time I'm thirty, I'll have to reassess my future," said Kane, who will turn thirty in October. "I'm not getting any younger. When you get to be thirty, you have to realize you may never tear a ticket in the bigs."

Tearing tickets isn't easy, but Kane has it down to a science. One of the trickiest ticket tears is a multiple ticket rip.

"We just call it 'multiple' in the business," said Kane.

A multiple occurs when a ticket taker is handed more than one ticket to tear at the same time. "You must fold the tickets together and give them one quick rip," said Kane.

The only thing trickier than a multiple ticket rip is a double multiple rip. A double multiple rip is ripping two stacks of two or more tickets at once.

But, there's more to being a ticket taker than ripping. After ripping the ticket in half, a ticket taker must make sure he gives the rain check back to the fan and places the other half in the ticket box. Early in the season, Kane often became confused and gave the wrong half back to the fan.

Kane said he practices his ticket tearing by "tearing up the *Transcript* at home, but only after I read it."

Part of the job is being pleasant to incoming fans. Kane said he greets the fans with one of two phrases as he rips their tickets—"Enjoy the game" or "Don't kick the dirt."

Kane said he has wanted to be a minor-league ticket taker since he attended a game at the now-demolished Pynchon Park in Springfield as a boy.

"I idolized the ticket taker there," said Kane. "He was incredibly fast and sure-handed. And, he was tall."

Kane got his chance at ripping professional tickets after a one-year stint tearing for Holyoke Trade High School basketball games in 1976.

Kane's father, Ed, is also a ticket taker at Miller games. Ed has been shipped to the back gate while Bill rips at the busier Beech Street entrance. "They've decided to go with youth," said Kane.

Kane thinks ticket tearing just may run in the family's blood.

"My two-year-old son Chris tears up a lot of stuff at home," said Kane. "He might have what it takes."

Ticket takers have to stay relaxed during a game.

"I do stretching exercises because I don't want to run the risk of pulling a finger," he said.

Kane has managed to avoid injury so far this season, but admits he shares every ticket taker's fear—hangnails.

If Kane doesn't get his shot in the big leagues, he could settle for ripping tickets at movie theaters. But it wouldn't be the same.

"This is the American pastime," he said.

Open *The Baseball Encyclopedia* to the register of all the 13,000-odd men who have played even a minute of major-league baseball; first among these is Henry Aaron. He is also first in career home runs, and this is the one that put him over the top: Number 715. Aaron's previous homer, the one that tied the Babe, had come amid a swirl of controversy: Braves' management had considered benching him for the opening series in Cincinnati to insure maximum hometown promotional punch, but Commissioner Bowie Kuhn ordered the Braves to play Aaron, who diplomatically socked only the one homer on enemy soil.

JOSEPH DURSO

Aaron Hits 715th, Passes Babe Ruth

ATLANTA, April 8—Henry Aaron ended the great chase tonight and passed Babe Ruth as the leading home run hitter in baseball history when he hit No. 715 before a national television audience and 53,775 persons in Atlanta Stadium.

The forty-year-old outfielder for the Atlanta Braves broke the record on his second time at bat, but on his first swing of a clamorous evening. It was a soaring drive in the fourth inning off Al Downing of the Los Angeles Dodgers and it cleared the fence in left-center field, 385 feet from home plate.

Skyrockets arched over the jammed stadium in the rain as the man from Mobile trotted around the bases for the 715th time in a career that began a quarter of a century ago with the Indianapolis Clowns in the old Negro leagues.

It was 9:07 o'clock, thirty years after Ruth had hit his 714th on his first swing of the bat in the opening game of the season.

The history-making home run carried into the Atlanta bullpen, where a relief pitcher named Tom House made a dazzling one-handed catch against the auxiliary scoreboard. He clutched it against the boards, far below the grandstand seats, where the customers in "Home Run Alley" were massed, waiting to retrieve a cowhide ball that in recent days had been valued as high as $25,000 on the auction market.

So Aaron not only ended the great home run derby, but also ended the controversy that surrounded it. His employers had wanted him to hit No. 715 in Atlanta, and had even benched him on alien soil in Cincinnati.

The commissioner of baseball, Bowie Kuhn, ordered the Braves to start their star yesterday or face "serious penalties." And tonight the dispute and the marathon finally came home to Atlanta in a razzle-dazzle evening.

The stadium was packed with its largest crowd since the Braves left Milwaukee and brought major-league baseball to the Deep South nine years ago. Pearl Bailey sang the National Anthem; the Jonesboro High School band marched; balloons and fireworks filled the overcast sky before the game; Aaron's life was dramatized on a huge color map of the United States painted across the outfield grass, and Bad Henry was serenaded by the Atlanta Boy Choir, which now includes girls.

The commissioner was missing, pleading that a "previous commitment" required his presence tomorrow in Cleveland, and his emissary was roundly booed when he mentioned Kuhn's name. But Governor Jimmy Carter was there, along with Mayor Maynard Jackson, Sammy Davis, Jr., and broadcasters and writers from as far away as Japan, South America, and Britain.

To many Atlantans, it was the city's festive premiere of *Gone With the Wind* during the 1930s, when Babe Ruth was still the hero of the New York Yankees and the titan of professional sports. All that was needed to complete the evening was home run No. 715, and Aaron supplied that.

The first time he batted, leading off the second inning, Aaron never got the bat off his shoulder. Downing, a one-time pitcher for the Yankees, wearing number 44, threw a ball and called strike and then three more balls. Aaron, wearing his own number 44, took first base while the crowd hooted and booed because their hometown hero had been walked.

A few moments later, Henry scored on a double by Dusty Baker and an error in left field, and even made a little history doing that.

It was the 2,063rd time he had crossed home plate in his twenty-year career in the majors, breaking the National League record held by Willie Mays and placing Aaron behind Ty Cobb and Ruth, both American Leaguers.

Then came the fourth inning, with the Dodgers leading by 3–1 and the rain falling, with colored umbrellas raised in the stands and the crowd roaring every time Aaron appeared. Darrell Evans led off for Atlanta with a grounder behind second base that the shortstop, Bill Russell, juggled long enough for an error. And up came Henry for the eighth time this season and the second this evening.

Downing pitched ball one inside, and Aaron watched impassively. Then came the second pitch, and this time Henry took his first cut of the night. The ball rose high toward left-center as the crowd came to its feet shouting, and as it dropped over the inside fence separating the outfield from the bullpen area, the skyrockets were fired and the scoreboard lights flashed in 6-foot numerals: "715."

Aaron, head slightly bowed and elbows turned out, slowly circled the bases as the uproar grew. At second base he received a handshake from Dave Lopes of the Dodgers, and between second and third from Russell.

By now two young men from the seats had joined Aaron, but did not interfere with his 360-foot trip around the bases and into the record books.

As he neared home plate, the rest of the Atlanta team had already massed beyond it as a welcoming delegation. But Aaron's sixty-five-year-old father, Herbert Aaron, Sr., had jumped out of the family's special field-level box and outraced everybody to the man who had broken Babe Ruth's record.

By then the entire Atlanta bullpen corps had started to race in to join the fun, with House leading them, the ball gripped tightly in his hand. He delivered it to Aaron, who was besieged on the grass about 20 feet in front of the field boxes near the Braves' dugout.

Besides the ball, Henry received a plaque from the owner of the team, Bill Bartholomay; congratulations from Monte Irvin, the emissary from Commissioner Kuhn, and a howling, standing ovation from the crowd.

The game was interrupted for eleven minutes during all the commotion, after which the Braves got back to work and went on to win their second straight, this time by 7–4. The Dodgers, apparently shaken by history, made six errors and lost their first game after three straight victories.

"It was a fastball, right down the middle of the upper part of the plate," Downing said later. "I was trying to get it down to him, but I didn't and he hit it good—as he would."

"When he first hit it, I didn't think it might be going. But like a great hitter, when he picks his pitch, chances are he's going to hit it pretty good."

Afterward the Braves locked their clubhouse for a time so that they could toast Aaron in champagne. Then the new home run king reflected on his feat and on some intimations that he had not been "trying" to break the record in Cincinnati.

"I have never gone out on a ballfield and given less than my level best," he said. "When I hit it tonight, all I thought about was that I wanted to touch all the bases."

When is a homer that is not a homer a homer? When George Brett hit it off Goose Gossage in the ninth inning of a game played on July 24, 1983. Remember? The two-out, two-run homer sent the Royals into the lead 5–4—but only momentarily, for when the Yankees called Brett's bat to the attention of umpire Tim McClelland, he ruled that the pine tar was unacceptably high, invalidated the homer, and declared Brett out and the game over. Kansas City protested, and four days later American League President Lee MacPhail reversed the umpires' ruling: he restored the homer and the Royals' lead, and ordered that the bottom of the ninth inning be completed on an open date in the schedule, since the Royals and Yanks had concluded their seasonal animosities. On August 18, little more than a thousand fans came to witness the anticlimactic end of the game. This is one of "Glenn Eichler's All-Star Magic Tips" from *National Lampoon*.

GLENN EICHLER

George Brett's Vanished and Restored Homer

WHAT THE AUDIENCE SEES: In what appears to be a smooth, single movement, you hit a game-winning home run. The audience, enchanted, applauds—but wait! After some patter between the opposing team and the umpires, the run vanishes and you lose the game! The clapping dies out—only to double in strength when the run and the win mysteriously reappear.

HOW IT'S DONE: This is a particularly satisfying effect in that no sleight is necessary, and what the audience perceives as a magician's "gimmick" later turns out to be a clever bit of misdirection. Before your presentation, coat two-thirds of your bat with a funny-looking foreign substance (I recommend Louis Tannen's Magician Pine Tar #3). This is the "excuse" the umpire needs to vanish the home run. On closer inspection, both the audience and the league president will realize that the substance could not affect your hitting—and as they do, the run will suddenly rematerialize! A sophisticated electronic scoreboard that "goes wacky" during the trick will only heighten the hilarity!

EFFECT: The professional magician knows that some not necessarily "artful" tricks should be included in his repertoire for the sake of "flashiness." This effect can be particularly useful toward the end of a boring season, and doubles in its impressiveness if used against a team of overpaid shitheads.

CAVEATS: The main problem with this effect is in gauging how quickly to restore the home run; if you wait too long, the first part of the trick may be forgotten by the audience. I suggest that during the interval between the vanish and the restoration, you keep interest alive by cursing at reporters, physically attacking opposing players, and featuring your bat in overnight-courier ads.

These sardonic, gritty lines were published in Robert Fitzgerald's 1943 volume of poetry titled, eerily, *In the Rose of Time*. The fly ball that was made into a triple—maybe Cobb would have caught it in time, as in time Rose would catch him.

ROBERT FITZGERALD

Cobb Would Have Caught It

In sunburnt parks where Sundays lie,
Or the wide wastes beyond the cities,
Teams in gray deploy through sunlight.

Talk it up, boys, a little practice.

Coming in stubby and fast, the baseman
Gathers a grounder in fat green grass,
Picks it stinging and clipped as wit
Into the leather: a swinging step
Wings it deadeye down to first.
Smack. Oh, attaboy, attyoldboy.

Catcher reverses his cap, pulls down
Sweaty casque, and squats in the dust:
Pitcher rubs a new ball on his pants,
Chewing, puts a jet behind him;
Nods past batter, taking his time.

Batter settles, tugs at his cap:
A spinning ball: step and swing to it,

Caught like a cheek before it ducks
By shivery hickory: socko, baby:
Cleats dig into the dust. Outfielder,
On his way, looking over shoulder,
Makes it a triple. A long peg home.

Innings and afternoons. Fly lost in sunset.
Throwing arm gone bad. There's your old ballgame.
Cool reek of the field. Reek of companions.

Is the reserve clause legal? That was the question confronting Curt Flood in 1970 when he wrote this article for *Sport*, and it is the question he went on to confront unsuccessfully in the courts. On June 19, 1971, after two losses in lower courts, the star center fielder suffered a 5–3 defeat in the Supreme Court in his attempt to overturn the ninety-year-old clause. By refusing a trade from the Cardinals to the Phillies he gave up the 1970 season, and with it his $100,000 salary; relinquished any hope of a career in baseball management; and cut short, at age thirty-two, a career that might have earned him a place in the Hall of Fame. Financial need compelled him to return to baseball with the Washington Senators in early 1971, but his skills and concentration had faded; after only thirteen games he left for good. Players now commonly make a million dollars a year and in some cases more than twice that, but few could even name their benefactor—their emancipator. If ballplayers are free men today, they have Curt Flood to thank.

CURT FLOOD

Why I Am Challenging Baseball

This winter, on a warm and bright day in San Juan, Puerto Rico, I walked into a meeting at the Americana Hotel. Seated in the room, waiting to listen to me, were the player representatives of the big-league clubs—people like Reggie Jackson, Tom Haller, Jim Bunning, Tim McCarver, Joe Torre, Bob Clemente, Dal Maxvill. There were twenty-six ballplayers in all, the executive board of the Major League Baseball Players Association. Now I was going to try to tell them why I planned to challenge baseball's reserve clause in a case that could revolutionize the structure of baseball and stop twenty-four millionaire owners from playing God with thousands of ballplayers' lives.

I knew what I was risking. I might well not play the 1970 season. I might lose a salary of $90,000 a year—and maybe triple that, because I might never play a game of baseball again. I am only thirty-two and last year I hit .285 for the Cardinals, but I was aware that if I challenged the reserve clause in the courts, I could be blacklisted by every big-league team.

Yet I felt I had to accept the risks and I had come here to Puerto Rico to ask for the players' help and support. For twenty minutes I spoke to the players. I told them why I thought the reserve clause was bad for the players, for you—the fans—and for the game.

People later told me it was an emotional speech, and I guess it was. I said things that had been building up inside my chest for thirteen years, ever since a day in a ballpark in Maracaibo, Venezuela, when a nineteen-year-old ballplayer got a telegram that told him he had been traded.

At the time—1957—I belonged to the Cincinnati Reds. I hadn't wanted to come to Venezuela to play winter ball. But after two good years in the Reds' minor-league system, I'd been told I had the best chance of making the big club if I could learn to play third base.

So, the dutiful ballplayer, I went to a strange country to field groundballs off my chest. And there, sitting on a stool in the clubhouse, I got a long telegram from the Reds telling me I had been traded to the St. Louis Cardinals.

I stared at the telegram for maybe a half hour. I was shocked by the suddenness of the trade and uncertain now about myself, wondering: What do you have to do to make it in baseball? I had put two good years back to back. I had done everything they had asked. Now this.

I'd always known it wasn't going to be easy for me to make the big leagues. I was 5 feet 9 inches, 150 pounds, and black, and naturally you have doubts. Now I had to start with a strange new organization. It was like leaving a family you had grown up with and moving in with a family you had never met. I felt I was starting all over again in baseball, very much alone, insecure, and in a word, scared.

Later, when the numbness wore off, there was disappointment. I had grown up with Frank Robinson, played with him on Oakland streets when I was six years old. I'd run on those same streets with Vada Pinson when I was nine. Robinson and I were in the same outfield one year at McClymonds High School, then Pinson and I played together. Now Frank was the Reds' regular right fielder. Coming up the minor-league ladder was Vada Pinson and I was right behind him. Nothing would have thrilled me more than to have played alongside my old hometown buddies, Frank Robinson and Vada Pinson.

Someone playing God had dictated otherwise, and now I was the property of the Cardinals. Again the dutiful ballplayer, I reported to the Cardinals in the spring of 1958 and I won a job that year, a job I kept for twelve years. They were good and happy years for me, and my salary climbed close to the $100,000 mark, the highest any ballplayer who wasn't a pitcher or a home run hitter ever had received in baseball.

They were also good and happy years for the Cardinals and their owner, Mr. Gussie Busch. In three of five years—from 1964 to 1968—the Cardinals were National League champions and twice world champions.

But all during my years as a Cardinal I saw things happening that reminded me of that afternoon in the Maracaibo clubhouse when I'd felt for the first time the blunt impact of the reserve clause on my life. The reserve clause involves more than the trading and selling of human beings like sheep or cattle or, if you will, slaves. (I've been asked how a $90,000-a-year ballplayer can be a slave; I've answered that even a well-paid slave is still a slave.) As much as the trading and selling bothered me, what also made me see the inside were off-shoots of the reserve-clause situation that demean a man's dignity and strike directly at his rights as a human being.

There are a number of things that many fans and some ballplayers do not understand about the reserve clause. First of all, there is no reserve clause as such in a baseball player's contract. What there are, rather, are a multiplicity of provisions that chain a ballplayer to a club for life or until his contract is sold to another club. "If you don't play for me," a general manager can tell a ballplayer, "you don't play for anybody."

Many players first comprehend what the so-called reserve clause is all about when they come into the general manager's office to negotiate a raise.

"I had a good year," the ballplayer says. "I'd like a $5,000 raise."

"Well and good," says the general manager. "But we are not going to pay you that much money. And if you don't like it, you can quit playing baseball and find some other way of making a living."

The words are rarely that pointed or direct, but the implication is clear when a player is bargaining for more money: he must take the owner's last offer or not play at all. In that kind of a situation the ballplayer is obviously a second-class citizen. He knows it, and the baseball establishment knows it, and he is treated accordingly: with a paternal pat on the head when he stays in line, with the back of the hand when he doesn't. I know of no other employee in America today who is treated in such a degrading manner.

I never had to look beyond the Cardinal clubhouse, or my own locker, to see how the reserve clause degraded us all. One Sunday afternoon in a game against New York, I tried to break up a double play. The Mets' little shortstop, Bud Harrelson, tried to get out of my way, but he landed on my leg with his spikes. He cut a ten-inch wound from my knee to my thigh. They patched me up and I finished the game.

After the game, they put stitches on the wound and gave me an antitetanus shot. The shot knocked me loopy and all night long I was nauseous and dizzy, the leg stiff and painful. I finally got to sleep at six in the morning.

I knew that the Cardinals had scheduled a banquet for noon the next day and all the players were supposed to be there. But since the Cardinals knew how sick I'd been in the clubhouse, I was sure I wasn't expected to attend.

I got up about two in the afternoon and arrived at the park at around 3:30 or so. I found a note in my locker to see the general manager.

When I walked into his office, he said, "Missing that banquet will cost you $250."

"You don't understand," I said. I had already undressed to my shorts, and I showed him the stitched-up leg.

"No excuses," he said.

I paid the $250. I should not have had to put up with something like that, no man should. But because of the reserve clause, I could not say, "I quit," and still remain in baseball.

There was a time Bob Howsam, then our general manager, chewed out one of the players in the newspapers, claiming the player wasn't hustling. Every man on the club knew that the player hustled. If that player could have said, "I don't have to take this; I am a man and I am going somewhere else," you know damn well that Howsam would not have criticized him in public. But because the ballplayer was owned by one man—and one man only—he had to take it.

In the spring of 1969, every ballplayer on the Cardinals had to take it. The owner, Gussie Busch, invited his board of directors and all of the press to hear him chew us out in our clubhouse. On that day, millions of Americans learned in the newspapers that we had been publicly bawled out by our boss for being fat calves asking for too much money, that we were angering fans by not giving them autographs and annoying the press by refusing to be interviewed.

Certainly it is a boss's right to chew out his employees. But in public? I have about thirty employees working for me in my various businesses in St. Louis and I wouldn't think of dressing down one in front of another. But we had to listen silently and accept this public scolding of grown men, because we wouldn't say, "I quit," and walk away.

On that spring day, Gussie Busch spoke to a team that had come within one game of winning two straight world championships. I am convinced that the

1969 Cardinals placed on the field the nine best ballplayers in the world when Bob Gibson was pitching. But on that day last spring, Mr. Busch destroyed the intangible this team had—its unity and its feeling of pride in being a part of the Cardinal organization. We never got over that.

By the late summer of 1969, I was sure the Cardinals were going to trade me. I recalled what I had promised myself after I had been traded at nineteen—that I would never permit myself to be traded again.

I had spent twelve years in St. Louis. I had made my home there, built up my name and a thriving photographic and art business. Last year, Curt Flood's Art and Photo Studio photographed 83,000 St. Louis pupils for pictures to be used in school yearbooks. We plan to set up other Curt Flood Studios with franchise agreements. I also own a photo-finishing plant as well as real estate in St. Louis. It would make no sense to endanger those businesses by leaving St. Louis to spend six months playing baseball in a faraway city.

Near the end of the season I thought: If they trade me, I will quit. I thought at the time I had no other recourse, even though I had often talked about the reserve clause and how unfair it was. Why couldn't a ballplayer, say after ten years of service, be declared a free agent? He would likely sell himself for the next year to the team he had played for the year before, because he'd want to play in a city where he was making a name for himself. But if the salary and working conditions weren't right, he could do what any truck driver, lawyer, artist or workman can do—quit and go to work for someone else.

In my conversations with other players about the clause, I had said, "The reserve clause is either constitutional or unconstitutional. I never heard of anything that is half-constitutional."

Ninety-nine percent of the ballplayers I talked to agreed something should be done about the clause. But many had been so impressed by the owners' propaganda—that the reserve clause is the "backbone" of baseball—that they were afraid what would happen if it were ruled unconstitutional.

"Maybe we'd be cutting our own throats," I heard ballplayers say. "Maybe the game would be ruined."

You can't blame a guy who is making $50,000 a year for worrying that his job might suddenly disappear.

My answer to those ballplayers was this: Don't believe the owners' propaganda. "The reserve clause," I said, "exists for two reasons. One, to cut down the money the ballplayers get; and two, to give a feeling of power to men who like to play God over other people's lives."

In the back of my noggin, I believe, there was always the feeling that one day I would be the one to test the reserve clause. At thirty-two—and I may be inflating my ego here—I think I have the capabilities, the resources, and the integrity to challenge the clause in the courts without giving in to pressure.

During the closing days of the 1969 season, though, it was not in my conscious mind to test the clause. I guess I was too concerned wondering where I was going to be traded and what I was going to say if I was traded—whether I really had the courage to say, "I quit."

I got the news about the trade one afternoon by phone. I have known Bing Devine, the Cardinal general manager, for much of thirteen years, and he has been good to me and I think I have made a few dollars for him. He didn't call. One of the lower-echelon people in his office called and, with a voice that sounded like a tape-recording, he told me I had been traded to Philadelphia along with Tim McCarver, Joe Hoerner, and Byron Browne for Richie Allen, Cookie Rojas, and Jerry Johnson.

The next day I received a scrap of paper in the mail. It was from the Cardinals and it read: "Dear Mr. Flood: You have been Sold/ Traded/ Released/ Optioned."

Only the "Traded" box hadn't been blocked out, meaning I had been traded. That scrap was my official notice from the Cardinals telling me I was gone. Somehow, I thought, after twelve years of playing as best as I could for this club, someone might have written a note saying thanks and goodbye.

I phoned Bing Devine and told him I didn't want to leave St. Louis. Later I met with John Quinn of the Phillies and I explained to him that I had nothing against Philadelphia, but I had put twelve years of my life in St. Louis and I couldn't just yank up those twelve years and walk away.

I went off to Copenhagen, a place I dearly love, for a three-week vacation, still not knowing what I should do: quit, or take the $90,000 and try to keep my business in St. Louis while playing in Philadelphia.

When I returned to St. Louis I went to see my good friend and lawyer, Allan Zerman, in his office. We talked for a while and finally I said, "I have no other alternatives—it's either quit or go to Philadelphia."

Allan said quietly, "There is one other alternative."

Right away I knew what he meant. We talked about it, each of us getting more excited. I called Marvin Miller, the executive director of the Baseball Players Association. I flew to New York and told him I was thinking about testing the reserve clause in the courts.

Right from the start Marvin tried to discourage me. "If you go ahead with this," he told me, "forget any ideas you have about ever being the first black manager. Or even a coach or a scout—forget it." He talked about blacklisting and how long the legal proceedings could take—two or more years—and how much the legal fees would cost. He reminded me that even with a good case, I might lose. He emphasized how much I could lose in salary—maybe $200,000 or more.

He told me to mull over my decision. As Marvin said later, he was playing devil's advocate so he could be sure I understood how immense a task I was facing in taking on the baseball establishment. He also wanted to be sure I was sincere.

Allan and I thought about it for about a week. Sitting one night in a St. Louis restaurant, we added up all the pros and cons for the last time, looked at each other, and decided our decision was go.

At Marvin Miller's invitation I flew to Puerto Rico to speak to the executive board of the Players Association, asking for their help. After telling them much of what I have told you—how the reserve clause demeans every player as a man and cheats him as an employee—I answered questions.

Some of the players, I knew, were understandably skeptical about my motives. In the past, other players have used this facade—an attack on the reserve clause—to get money out of the owners in salary or as an out-of-court settlement.

One of the players, I've forgotten who, asked me, "If after you start this suit, someone comes knocking at your door and offers you a million dollars to withdraw the suit, what will you do?"

I looked at the man and I said, "I can't be bought."

Perhaps that convinced them. Anyway, after I had left the room, the twenty-six players voted unanimously to support me publicly, to help pay my legal expenses, and to help me get the best available counsel. A few days later, Marvin Miller contacted former Supreme Court Justice Arthur Goldberg, who, after studying the matter and meeting with me, agreed to represent me.

I flew home from Puerto Rico proud I had the backing of the players. I hope I will have the backing of the fans. I think my fight can help them to see better baseball. Right now we play 162 games and every ballplayer knows that is too many. Too often we plod onto the field, tired men going through the motions, while Joe Fan who has paid $5 for his seat thinks he is seeing big-league baseball. He isn't. He is being cheated. The ballplayers know it and the owners know it too.

Each year the Cardinals make a St. Louis–San Francisco–Houston–Los Angeles swing. We would be up and down in the air like yo-yos. When we got to Los Angeles, we'd be exhausted. Some of us checked how all the teams who made that swing had done, over a two-year period, in the first game of their series with the Dodgers. Over two years the opposition had scored an average of *less than two runs.*

Do you think it is accidental that Dodger owner Walter O'Malley plays a big hand in drawing up the National League schedule?

If we win this fight over the reserve clause, O'Malley and the other owners are going to have to let the players have a voice in drawing up the schedules. We will be a stronger position to demand a shorter schedule that doesn't cheat the fan.

Are we right in challenging the legality of the reserve clause? Let me answer you this way. Suppose you are an accountant. One day your boss says to you, "Joe, we are moving you to the other coast. Now don't worry. We'll pay your expenses, you'll get the same salary you're getting here, and maybe more."

"But I don't want to go 3,000 miles away from my family and friends," you say. "I don't want to tear up roots."

"Of course you can quit and get another job," your boss says. "But we've got this reserve clause in your contract, you know. You can't work ever again as an accountant if you quit working for us."

"But accounting is the only business I know," you say.

"Sorry," says your boss.

What would you do? As an accountant and as a man? You know what I am doing. Maybe now you can understand why I feel I have to do it—as a ballplayer and as a man.

A picture may be worth a thousand words, but these few words convey what a thousand pictures cannot—the *feel* of the game. From *The Orb Weaver*, issued in 1953.

ROBERT FRANCIS

The Base Stealer

Poised between going on and back, pulled
Both ways taut like a tightrope-walker,
Fingertips pointing the opposites,
Now bouncing tiptoe like a dropped ball
Or a kid skipping rope, come on, come on,
Running a scattering of steps sidewise,
How he teeters, skitters, tingles, teases,
Taunts them, hovers like an ecstatic bird,
He's only flirting, crowd him, crowd him,
Delicate, delicate, delicate, delicate—now!

This piece was written in the heat of one of the greatest pennant races ever, by one of the game's brightest, freshest reporters. Coming into this crucial four-game series at Fenway, where they had lost to the Yankees only twice in two years, the Red Sox were clinging to a four-game lead with twenty-four left to play. On July 19, they had enjoyed a fourteen-game margin, but then the Yanks fired Billy Martin, brought in Bob Lemon, and went on a tear that reduced the Boston lead to six games by the end of the month. There things stood until September, when the Boston Massacre marked the point at which the teams crossed paths; by mid-September the Red Sox were 3½ games out and presumed dead. However, they then displayed enormous heart, winning twelve of their final fourteen to storm into a final-day tie for the division lead. And then, to a Boston steeped in the sorrows of yesteryear, came Bucky Dent.

PETER GAMMONS

The Boston Massacre

The man had on a gray Brooks Brothers suit, which made him look for all the world as if he were Harvard '44, and he was leaning over the railing of the box next to the Red Sox dugout. "Zimmer!" he screamed, but Don Zimmer just stared dead ahead. The score at that point in last Friday night's game was 13–0 in favor of the Yankees and except to change pitchers a few times the Red Sox manager hadn't moved in three hours. He had stared as Mickey Rivers stood on third just two pitches into the game. He had stared as, for the second straight night, a Yankee batter got his third hit before Boston's ninth hitter, Butch Hobson, even got to the plate. He had stared as the Red Sox made seven errors. And now he stared as the man kept screaming his name.

"I've been a Red Sox fan for twenty years," the man hollered. "A diehard Red Sox fan. I've put up with a lot of heartaches. But this time you've really done it. This time my heart's been broken for good." Finally Zimmer looked up, just as security guards hauled the man away.

From Eastport to Block Island, New Englanders were screaming mad. Only a couple of weeks before, the Red Sox had been baseball's one sure thing, but now Fenway Park was like St. Petersburg in the last days of Czar Nicholas. Back in July, when Billy Martin still sat in the Yankee manager's office and

New York was in the process of falling fourteen games behind the Sox, Reggie Jackson had said, "Not even Affirmed can catch them." But by late last Sunday afternoon, when the 1978 version of the Boston Massacre concluded with New York's fourth win in a row over the Red Sox, the Yankees had caught them. And the Yanks had gained a tie for first in the American League East in such awesome fashion—winning sixteen of their last eighteen, including the lopsided victories that comprised the Massacre—that Saturday night a New Yorker named Dick Waterman walked into a Cambridge bar, announced, "For the first time a first-place team has been mathematically eliminated," and held up a sign that read: NY 35–49–4, BOS 5–16–11. Those figures were the combined line score of last weekend's first three games. The disparity between those sets of numbers, as much as the losses themselves, was what so deeply depressed Red Sox fans. "It's 1929 all over again," mourned Robert Crane, treasurer of the Commonwealth of Massachusetts.

The Red Sox and Yankees began their two-city, seven-game, eleven-day showdown in Boston last Thursday—it will continue with three games this weekend in New York—and it quickly became apparent that this confrontation would be quite different from their six-game shoot-out in late June and early July. On that occasion the Red Sox had beaten the Yanks four times and opened up a lead that appeared insurmountable. Back then the Yankees had so few healthy bodies that Catcher Thurman Munson was trying to become a right fielder, and one day a minor league pitcher named Paul Semall drove from West Haven, Connecticut, to Boston to throw batting practice. Had the New York brass liked the way he threw, Semall would have stayed with the Yankees and become a starter. By midnight, Semall was driving back to West Haven, and soon thereafter injuries became so rife among New York pitchers that reserve first baseman Jim Spencer was warming up in the bullpen.

Rivers, the center fielder and key to the Yankee offense, had a broken wrist. Both members of the double-play combination, Willie Randolph and Bucky Dent, were injured and out of the lineup. To complete the up-the-middle collapse, Munson was playing—sometimes behind the plate and sometimes in right—with a bad leg, and the pitching staff had been reduced to *Gong Show* contestants. Paul Semall got gonged. Dave Rajsish got gonged. Larry McCall got gonged. Catfish Hunter, Ed Figueroa, Dick Tidrow, Ken Clay, Andy Messersmith, and Don Gullett were all hurt or soon to be injured. Only the brilliant Ron Guidry stayed healthy. Almost singlehandedly he kept the bottom from falling out during July and early August.

Then, as the regulars gradually began getting back into the lineup, the blow-up between owner George Steinbrenner and Martin occurred. Martin resigned on July 24, and the next day Bob Lemon, who had recently been canned by the White Sox, took over. "The season starts today," Lemon told the Yankees.

"Go have some fun." Considering the disarray in New York during the preceding year and a half, that seemed a bit much to ask. So was catching Boston. No American League team had ever changed managers in midseason and won a championship. "Under Lemon we became a completely different team," says Spencer. "If Martin were still here, we wouldn't be," snaps one player. "We'd have quit. Rivers and Jackson couldn't play for him. But Lemon gave us a fresh spirit. We kept playing. We looked up, and Boston was right in front of us." The fact that a suddenly revived Hunter had won six straight, that Figueroa had regained health and happiness, that Tidrow had again become hale and that rookie right hander Jim Beattie had returned from the minors with his self-confidence restored didn't hurt.

And while the Yankees arrived in Boston 30–13 under Lemon and 35–14 since July 17—the night they fell fourteen games behind—the Red Sox had been stumbling. They were 25–24 since July 17. Their thirty-nine-year-old leader, Carl Yastrzemski, had suffered back and shoulder ailments in mid-July, and then he pulled ligaments in his right wrist that left him taped up and in and out of the lineup. He had hit three homers in two months. Second baseman Jerry Remy fractured a bone in his left wrist on August 25 and had not appeared in the lineup thereafter.

Catcher Carlton Fisk had been playing with a cracked rib, which he said made him feel as if "someone is sticking a sword in my side" every time he threw. Third baseman Butch Hobson has cartilage and ligament damage in both knees and bone chips in his right elbow. The chips are so painful that one night he had to run off the field during infield practice; his elbow had locked up on him. When New York came to town, he had a major-league-leading thirty-eight errors, most of them the result of bad throws made with his bad arm. Right fielder Dwight Evans had been beaned on August 29 and was experiencing dizziness whenever he ran. Reliever Bill Campbell, who had thirty-one saves and thirteen wins in 1977, had suffered from elbow and shoulder soreness all season.

The injuries tended to dampen Boston's already erratic, one-dimensional offense, which relies too heavily on power hitting even when everyone is healthy. They also ruined the Sox defense, which had been the facet of play most responsible for giving the Red Sox a ten-game lead over their nearest challenger, Milwaukee, on July 8. No wonder the pitching went sour, with Mike Torrez going 4–4 since the All-Star Game, Luis Tiant 3–7 since June 24, and Bill Lee 0–7 since July 15. And as Boston awaited its confrontation with the Yankees, it lost three out of five to Toronto and Oakland and two of three in Baltimore. The Sox' only lift came in Wednesday's 2–0 win over the Orioles. Tiant pitched a two-hitter that night, and Yaz, his wrist looking like a mummy's, hit a two-run homer. It was one of only two hits the Sox got off Dennis Martinez.

As play began Thursday night at Fenway Park, the Red Sox lead had dwindled to four games with twenty-four to play. "We'll be happy with a split," Lemon said. By 9:05 P.M. Friday—during the third inning of Game 2—Lemon turned to pitching coach-scout Clyde King and said, "Now I'll only be happy with three out of four." Right about then *The Washington Post*'s Tom Boswell was writing his lead: *"Ibid,* for details, see yesterday's paper." The details were downright embarrassing to the Red Sox.

The embarrassments had begun with a Hobson error in the first inning Thursday. Then a Munson single. And a Jackson single. Zap, the Yankees had two unearned runs. After giving up four straight singles to start the second inning, Torrez went to the showers. Munson had three hits—and the Yankees seven runs—before Hobson got his first at bat in the bottom of the third. After the seventh inning, someone in the press box looked up at the New York line on the scoreboard—2–3–2–5–0–1–0—and dialed the number. It was disconnected. When the game ended, the Yankees had twenty-one hits and a 15–3 victory.

New York's joy was tempered by two injuries. Hunter left the game with a pulled groin muscle in the fourth, too soon to get the victory, though the Yanks were leading 12–0. "The bullpen phone rang and six of us fought to answer it," said Clay, who won the phone call and the game. Hunter, it turned out, would probably miss only one start. In the sixth inning, Munson was beaned by Dick Drago. Though dizzy, Munson said he would be behind the plate Friday. "He smells blood," Jackson said.

The next night, the Yankees not only drained Boston's blood but also its dignity. Rivers hit rookie right hander Jim Wright's first pitch past first baseman George Scott into right field. On the second pitch, he stole second and cruised on into third as Fisk's throw bounced away from shortstop Rick Burleson. Wright had thrown two pitches, and Rivers was peering at him from third base. Wright went on to get four outs, one more than Torrez had; he was relieved after allowing four runs. His replacement, Tom Burgmeier, immediately gave up a single and walk before surrendering a mighty home run by Jackson.

Beattie, who in his Fenway appearance in June had been knocked out in the third inning and optioned to Tacoma in the sixth, retired eighteen in a row in one stretch, while the Red Sox self-destructed in the field. Evans, who had not dropped a fly in his first five and three-quarters years in the majors, dropped his second one of the week and had to leave the game. "I can't look up or down without getting dizzy," he said. Fisk had two throws bounce away for errors. Rivers hit a routine ground ball to Scott in the third and beat Scott to the bag, making him three-for-three before Hobson ever got up. The game ended with a 13–2 score and the seven Red Sox errors.

"I can't believe what I've been seeing," said King, who has watched about forty Red Sox games this season. "I could understand if an expansion team fell apart like that, but Boston's got the best record in baseball. It can't go on." On Saturday afternoon, Guidry took his 20–2 record to the mound. It went on.

This was to be the showdown of the aces. Dennis Eckersley, 16–6, was 9–0 in Fenway and had not been knocked out before the fifth inning all season. He had beaten the Yankees three times in a twelve-day stretch earlier in the year. When he blew a third strike past Jackson to end the bottom of the first, he had done what Torrez and Wright had not been able to do—shut the Yankees out in the first inning.

"It looked like it was going to be a 1–0 game, what with the wind whipping in and Eckersley looking like he'd put us back together," said Zimmer. After Burleson led off Boston's first with a single, Fred Lynn bunted. Guidry, who could have cut down Burleson at second, hesitated and ended up throwing to first. Then Dent bobbled Jim Rice's grounder in the hole for an infield single. Two on. But Guidry busted fastballs in on the hands of Yastrzemski and Fisk, getting them out on a weak grounder and called third strike, respectively. Despite leadoff walks in the next two Boston at bats, the Sox hitters were finished for the day. Rice's grounder would be their second and last hit of the afternoon.

Yastrzemski seemed to lift his catatonic team in the fourth with a twisting, leaping catch on the dead run that he turned into a double play. But three batters later, with two on and two out, all that Yaz and Eckersley had done to heighten Boston's morale unraveled when Lou Piniella sliced a pop fly into the gale in right center.

"It must have blown a hundred feet across, like a Frisbee coming back," says Eckersley. Lynn came in a few steps but he had no chance. Burleson made chase from shortstop, Scott took off from first. The ball was out of reach of both. Rice, who was playing near the warning track in right, could not get there. Frank Duffy, the second baseman, did, but when he turned and looked up into the sun he lost sight of the ball. It landed in front of him. It was 1–0. After an intentional walk to Graig Nettles, Dent dunked a two-strike pitch into left for two more runs. "That broke my back," said Eckersley. By the time the inning had ended, Eckersley was gone. There had been another walk, an error, a wild pitch, and a passed ball. Seven runs had scored. "This is the first time I've seen a first-place team chasing a second-place team," said NBC's Tony Kubek.

Guidry had not only become the second left-hander to pitch a complete game against the Red Sox in Fenway all season, but also was the first lefty to shut them out at home since 1974. "Pitchers are afraid to pitch inside here," he said. "But that's where you've got to."

The victory brought Guidry's record to 21–2, his earned-run average to 1.77, and his strikeouts to 220; it also brought the New York staff's ERA to 2.07 over the last twenty-six games. "They must be cheating," said Lynn. "Those aren't the same Yankees we saw before. I think George Steinbrenner used his clone money. I think those were Yankee clones out there from teams of the past."

"These guys are—I hope you understand how I use the word—nasty," said Jackson. "This is a pro's game, and this team is loaded with professionals. Tough guys. Nasty."

"This is two years in a row we've finished like this, so it must say something about the team's character," Tidrow said. Before Lemon took over, the only times the word "character" was used in the Yankee clubhouse it was invariably followed by the word "assassination."

With the 7–0 loss figured in, the Red Sox had lost eight out of ten. In those games they had committed twenty-four errors good for twenty unearned runs. Twice pop-ups to shallow right had dropped, leading to two losses and ten earned runs.

Tiant had been the only starting pitcher to win. Evans, Scott, Hobson, and Jack Brohamer, who most of the time were the bottom four in the batting order, were twelve for 123—or .098. "How can a team get thirty-something games over .500 in July and then in September see its pitching, hitting, and fielding all fall apart at the same time?" wondered Fisk.

After being bombarded in the first three games, all that the Red Sox could come up with in their effort to prevent the Yankees from gaining a first-place tie on Sunday was rookie lefthander Bobby Sprowl. In June, while the Sox were

beating the Yankees, Sprowl was pitching for the Bristol Red Sox against the West Haven Yankees.

Clearly he was not ready for their New York namesakes. He began by walking Rivers and Willie Randolph, lasted only two-thirds of an inning, and was charged with three runs. The most damaging blow came after Sprowl gave way to reliever Bob Stanley, who promptly yielded a single to Nettles that drove in two runners whom Sprowl had allowed to reach base. The Yankees would build a 6–0 bulge before coasting to an eighteen-hit, 7–4 victory. Suddenly, New York not only had a psychological edge on the Red Sox, but it also had pulled even with them in the standings.

"It's never easy to win a pennant," said Yastrzemski. "We've got three weeks to play. We've got three games in Yankee Stadium next weekend. Anything can happen." He stared into his locker. Anything already had.

Andrew Marvell wrote three centuries ago in "The Garden" (not alluding to the out-field): "The Mind, that Ocean where each kind / Does streight its own resemblance find; / Yet it creates, transcending these, / Far other Worlds, and other Seas; / Anni-hilating all that's made / To a green thought in a green Shade." Green is the eternal color—the color of spring, the color of hope, and the color of baseball. Yale's president and ardent fan wrote this loving essay in 1977.

A. BARTLETT GIAMATTI

The Green Fields
of the Mind

It breaks your heart. It is designed to break your heart. The game begins in the spring, when everything else begins again, and it blossoms in the summer, filling the afternoons and evenings, and then as soon as the chill rains come, it stops and leaves you to face the fall alone. You count on it, rely on it to buffer the passage of time, to keep the memory of sunshine and high skies alive, and then just when the days are all twilight, when you need it most, it stops. Today, October 2, a Sunday of rain and broken branches and leaf-clogged drains and slick streets, it stopped, and summer was gone.

Somehow, the summer seemed to slip by faster this time. Maybe it wasn't this summer, but all the summers that, in this my fortieth summer, slipped by so fast. There comes a time when every summer will have something of autumn about it. Whatever the reason, it seemed to me that I was investing more and more in baseball, making the game do more of the work that keeps time fat and slow and lazy. I was counting on the game's deep patterns, three strikes, three outs, three times three innings, and its deepest impulse, to go out and back, to leave and to return home, to set the order of the day and to organize the daylight. I wrote a few things this last summer, this summer that did not last, nothing grand but some things, and yet that work was just camouflage. The real activity was done with the radio—not the all-seeing, all-falsifying television—and was the playing of the game in the only place it will last, the enclosed, green field of the mind. There, in that warm, bright place, what the old poet called Mutability does not so quickly come.

But out here on Sunday, October 2, where it rains all day, Dame Mutability never loses. She was in the crowd at Fenway yesterday, a gray day full of bluster and contradiction, when the Red Sox came up in the last of the ninth trailing Baltimore 8–5, while the Yankees, rain-delayed against Detroit, only needing to win one or have Boston lose one to win it all, sat in New York washing down cold cuts with beer and watching the Boston game. Boston had won two, the Yankees had lost two, and suddenly it seemed as if the whole season might go to the last day, or beyond, except here was Boston losing 8–5, while New York sat in its family room and put its feet up. Lynn, both ankles hurting now as they had in July, hits a single down the right-field line. The crowd stirs. It is on its feet. Hobson, third baseman, former Bear Bryant quarterback, strong, quiet, over 100 RBIs, goes for three breaking balls and is out. The goddess smiles and encourages her agent, a canny journeyman named Nelson Briles.

Now comes a pinch hitter, Bernie Carbo, one-time Rookie of the Year, erratic, quick, a shade too handsome, so laid back he is always, in his soul, stretched out in the tall grass, one arm under his head, watching the clouds and laughing; now he looks over some low stuff unworthy of him and then, uncoiling, sends one out, straight on a right line, over the center-field wall, no cheap Fenway shot, but all of it, the physics as elegant as the arc the ball describes.

New England is on its feet, roaring. The summer will not pass. Roaring, they recall the evening, late and cold, in 1975, the sixth game of the World Series, perhaps the greatest baseball game played in the last fifty years, when Carbo, loose and easy, had uncoiled to tie the game that Fisk would win. It is 8–7, one out, and school will never start, rain will never come, sun will warm the back of your neck forever. Now Bailey, picked up from the National League recently, big arms, heavy gut, experienced, new to the league and the club; he fouls off two and then, checking, tentative, a big man off balance, he pops a soft liner to the first baseman. It is suddenly darker and later, and the announcer doing the game coast to coast, a New Yorker who works for a New York television station, sounds relieved. His little world, well-lit, hot-combed, split-second-timed, had no capacity to absorb this much gritty, grainy, contrary reality.

Cox swings a bat, stretches his long arms, bends his back, the rookie from Pawtucket, who broke in two weeks earlier with a record six straight hits, the kid drafted ahead of Fred Lynn, rangy, smooth, cool. The count runs two-and-two, Briles is cagey, nothing too good, and Cox swings, the ball beginning toward the mound and then, in a jaunty, wayward dance, skipping past Briles, feinting to the right, skimming the last of the grass, finding the dirt, moving now like some small, purposeful marine creature negotiating the green deep, easily avoiding the jagged rock of second base, traveling steady and straight now out into the dark, silent recesses of center field.

The aisles are jammed, the place is on its feet, the wrappers, the programs, the Coke cups and peanut shells, the detritus of an afternoon; the anxieties, the things that have to be done tomorrow, the regrets about yesterday, the accumulation of a summer: all forgotten, while hope, the anchor, bites and takes hold where a moment before it seemed we would be swept out with the tide. Rice is up, Rice whom Aaron had said was the only one he'd seen with the ability to break his records, Rice the best clutch hitter on the club, with the best slugging percentage in the league, Rice, so quick and strong he once checked his swing halfway through and snapped the bat in two, Rice the Hammer of God sent to scourge the Yankees, the sound was overwhelming, fathers pounded their sons on the back, cars pulled off the road, households froze, New England exulted in its blessedness, and roared its thanks for all good things, for Rice and for a summer stretching halfway through October. Briles threw, Rice swung, and it was over. One pitch, a fly to center, and it stopped. Summer died in New England and like rain sliding off a roof, the crowd slipped out of Fenway, quickly, with only a steady murmur of concern for the drive ahead remaining of the roar. Mutability had turned the seasons and translated hope to memory once again. And once again, she had used baseball, our best invention to stay change, to bring change on. That is why it breaks my heart, that game—not because in New York they could win because Boston lost; in that, there is a rough justice, and a reminder to the Yankees of how slight and fragile are the circumstances that exalt one group of human beings over another. It breaks my heart because it was meant to foster in me again the illusion that there was something abiding, some pattern and some impulse that could come together to make a reality that would resist the corrosion; and because after it had fostered again that most hungered-for illusion, the game was meant to stop, and betray precisely what it promised.

Of course, there are those who learn after the first few times. They grow out of sports. And there are others who were born with the wisdom to know that nothing lasts. These are the truly tough among us, the ones who can live without illusion, or without even the hope of illusion. I am not that grown-up or up-to-date. I am a simpler creature, tied to more primitive patterns and cycles. I need to think something lasts forever, and it might as well be that state of being that is a game; it might as well be that, in a green field, in the sun.

Here the noted paleontologist observes biology at play on the fields of Eden: time and change mark baseball after all. Are baseball players better than ever? Or did giants walk the earth in the good old days, never since equaled? No question provokes more angry words around the hot stove or at meetings of the Society for American Baseball Research—it approaches sacrilege to suggest that Ruth and Gehrig batted largely against patsies or that Cy Young would not have won 511 games against modern opponents. Sabermetricians (those dedicated to the coldly logical and statistical analysis of the game) have employed various methods of comparing the old-time player to the current model, none altogether satisfying. Gould's argument is different from but parallel to those of analysts Richard Cramer and Dallas Adams. They find a steady rise throughout baseball's history in the skill of the average player, thus making it ever more difficult to exceed the norm by the stupendous margins achieved by such batters as Ruth and Cobb or such pitchers as Radbourn and Johnson.

STEPHEN JAY GOULD

The Extinction of the .400 Hitter

I wish to propose a new kind of explanation for the oldest chestnut of the hot stove league—the most widely discussed trend in the history of baseball statistics: the extinction of the .400 hitter. Baseball aficionados wallow in statistics, a sensible obsession that outsiders grasp with difficulty and ridicule often. The reasons are not hard to fathom. In baseball, each essential action is a contest between two individuals—batter and pitcher, or batter and fielder—thus creating an arena of truly individual achievement within a team sport.

The abstraction of individual achievement in other sports makes comparatively little sense. Goals scored in basketball or yards gained in football depend on the indissoluble intricacy of team play; a home run is you against him. Moreover, baseball has been played under a set of rules and conditions sufficiently constant during our century to make comparisons meaningful, yet sufficiently different in detail to provide endless grist for debate (the "dead ball" of 1900–20 versus the "lively ball" of later years, the introduction of night games and relief pitchers, the changing and irregular sizes of ball parks, nature's own versus Astroturf).

No subject has inspired more argument than the decline and disappearance of the .400 hitter—or, more generally, the drop in league-leading batting averages during our century. Since we wallow in nostalgia and have a lugubrious tendency to compare the present unfavorably with a past "golden era," this trend acquires all the more fascination because it carries moral implications linked metaphorically with junk foods, nuclear bombs, and eroding environments as signs of the decline of Western civilization.

Between 1901 and 1930, league-leading averages of .400 or better were common enough (nine out of thirty years) and achieved by several players (Lajoie, Cobb, Jackson, Sisler, Heilmann, Hornsby, and Terry), and averages over .380 scarcely merited extended commentary. Yet the bounty dried up abruptly thereafter. In 1930, Bill Terry hit .401 to become the last .400 hitter in National League; and Ted Williams's .406 in 1941 marked the last pinnacle for the American League. Since Williams, the greatest hitter I ever saw, attained this goal—in the year of my birth—only three men have hit higher than .380 in a single season: Williams again in 1957 (.388, at age thirty-nine, with my vote for the greatest batting accomplishment of our era), Rod Carew (.388 in 1977), and George Brett (.390 in 1980). Where have all the hitters gone?

Two kinds of explanation have been offered. The first, naive and moral, simply acknowledges with a sigh that there were giants in the earth in those days. Something in us needs to castigate the present in the light of an unrealistically rosy past. In researching the history of misconduct, I discovered that every generation (at least since the mid-nineteenth century) has imagined itself engulfed in a crime wave. Each age has also witnessed a shocking decline in sportsmanship. Similarly, senior citizens of the hot stove league, and younger fans as well (for nostalgia seems to have its greatest emotional impact on those too young to know a past reality directly), tend to argue that the .400 hitters of old simply cared more and tried harder. Well, Ty Cobb may have been a paragon of intensity and a bastard to boot, and Pete Rose may be a gentleman by comparison, but today's play is anything but lackadaisical. Say what you will, monetary rewards in the millions do inspire single-minded effort.

The second kind of explanation views people as much of a muchness over time and attributes the downward trend in league-leading batting to changes in the game and its styles of play. Most often cited are improvements in pitching and fielding, and more grueling schedules that shave off the edge of excellence.

Another explanation in this second category invokes the numerology of baseball. Every statistics maven knows that following the introduction of the lively ball in the early 1920s (and Babe Ruth's mayhem upon it), batting averages soared in general and remained high for twenty years. League averages for all players (averaged by decade) rose into the .280s in both leagues during the 1920s and remained in the .270s during the 1930s, but never topped .260 in any other decade of our century. Naturally, if league averages rose so substantially, we should not be surprised that the best hitters also improved their scores.

Still, this simple factor cannot explain the phenomenon entirely. No one hit .400 in either league during 1931–40, even though league averages stood twenty points above their values for the first two decades of our century, when fancy hitting remained in vogue. A comparison of these first two decades with recent times is especially revealing. Consider, for example, the American League during 1911–20 (league average of .259) and 1951–60 (league average of .257). Between 1911 and 1920, averages above .400 were recorded during three years, and the leading average dipped below .380 only twice (Cobb's .368 and .369 in 1914 and 1915). This pattern of high averages was not just Ty Cobb's personal show. In 1912 Cobb hit .410, while the ill-fated Shoeless Joe Jackson recorded .395, Tris Speaker .383, the thirty-seven-year-old Nap Lajoie .368, and Eddie Collins .348. By comparison, during 1951–60, only three league-leading averages exceeded Eddie Collins's fifth-place .348 (Mantle's .353 in 1956, Kuenn's .353 in 1959, and Williams's .388, already discussed, in 1957). And the 1950s was no decade of slouches, what with the likes of Mantle, Williams, Minoso, and Kaline. A general decline in league-leading averages throughout the century cannot be explained by an inflation of general averages during two middle decades. We are left with a puzzle. As with most persistent puzzles, what we probably need is a new *kind* of explanation, not merely a recycling and refinement of old arguments.

I am a paleontologist by trade. We students of life's history spend most of our time worrying about long-term trends. Has life gotten more complex through time? Do more species of animals live now than 200 million years ago? Several years ago, it occurred to me that we suffer from a subtle but powerful bias in our approach to the explanation of trends. Extremes fascinate us (the biggest, the smallest, the oldest), and we tend to concentrate on them alone, divorced from the systems that include them as unusual values. In explaining extremes, we abstract them from larger systems and assume that their trends have self-generated reasons: if the biggest become bigger through time, some powerful advantage must attach to increasing size.

But if we consider extremes as the limiting values of larger systems, a very different kind of explanation often applies. If the *amount of variation* within a system changes (for whatever reason), then extreme values may increase (if total variation grows) or decrease (if total variation declines) without any special reason rooted in the intrinsic character or meaning of the extreme value itself. In other words, *trends in extremes* may result from systematic changes in amounts of variation. Reasons for changes in variation are often rather different from proposed (and often spurious) reasons for changes in extremes considered as independent from their systems.

Let me illustrate this unfamiliar concept with an example from my own profession. A characteristic pattern in the history of most marine invertebrates is called "early experimentation and later standardization." When a new body plan first arises, evolution seems to try out all manner of twists, turns, and variations upon it. A few work well, but most don't. Eventually, only a few survive. Echinoderms now come in five basic varieties (two kinds of starfish, sea urchins, sea cucumbers, and crinoids—an unfamiliar group, loosely resembling many-armed starfish on a stalk). But when echinoderms first evolved, they burst forth in an astonishing array of more than twenty basic groups, including some coiled like a spiral and others so bilaterally symmetrical that a few paleontologists have mistaken them for the ancestors of fish. Likewise, mollusks now exist as snails, clams, cephalopods (octopuses and their kin), and two or three other rare and unfamiliar groups. But they sported ten to fifteen other fundamental variations early in their history.

This trend to a shaving and elimination of extremes is pervasive in nature. When systems first arise, they probe all the limits of possibility. Many variations don't work; the best solutions are found, and variation diminishes. As systems regularize, their variation decreases.

From this perspective, it occurred to me that we might be looking at the problem of .400 hitting the wrong way round. League-leading averages are extreme values within systems of variation. Perhaps their decrease through time simply records the standardization that affects so many systems as they stabilize. When baseball was young, styles of play had not become sufficiently regular to foil the antics of the very best. Wee Willie Keeler could "hit 'em where they ain't" (and compile a .432 average in 1897) because fielders didn't yet know where they should be. Slowly, players moved toward optimal methods of positioning, fielding, pitching, and batting—and variation inevitably declined. The best now met an opposition too finely honed to its own perfection to permit the extremes of achievement that characterized a more casual age. We cannot explain the decrease of high averages merely by arguing that managers invented relief pitching, while pitchers invented the slider—conventional explanations based on trends affecting high hitting considered as an independent phenomenon. Rather, the entire game sharpened its standards and narrowed its ranges of tolerance.

Thus I present my hypothesis: the disappearance of the .400 hitter is largely the result of a more general phenomenon—a decrease in the variation of batting averages as the game standardized its methods of play—and not an intrinsically driven trend warranting a special explanation in itself.

To test such a hypothesis, we need to examine changes through time in the difference between league-leading batting averages and the general average for all batters. This difference must decrease if I am right. But since my hypothesis concerns an entire system of variation, then, somewhat paradoxically, we must also examine differences between *lowest* batting averages and the general average. Variation must decrease at both ends—that is, within the entire system. Both highest and lowest batting averages must converge toward the general league average.

I therefore reached for my trusty *Baseball Encyclopedia*, that *vade mecum* for all serious fans (though, at more than 2,000 pages, you can scarcely tote it with you). The encyclopedia reports league averages for each year and lists the five highest averages for players with enough official times at bat. Since high extremes fascinate us while low values are merely embarrassing, no listing of the lowest averages appears, and you have to make your way laboriously through the entire roster of players. For lowest averages, I found (for each league in each year) the five bottom scores for players with at least 300 at bats. Then, for each year, I compared the league average with the average of the five highest and five lowest scores for regular players. Finally, I averaged these yearly values decade by decade.

In the accompanying chart, I present the results for both leagues combined— a clear confirmation of my hypothesis, since both highest and lowest averages approach the league average through time.

Our decrease toward the mean for high averages seems to occur as three plateaus, with only limited variation within each plateau. During the nineteenth century (National League only; the American League was founded in 1901), the mean difference between highest average and league average was 91 points (range of 87 to 95, by decade). From 1901 to 1930, it dipped to 81 (range

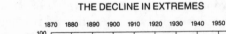

THE DECLINE IN EXTREMES

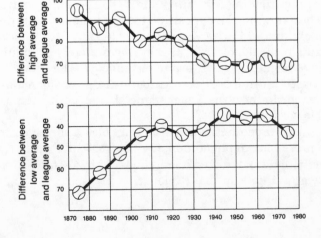

of only 80 to 83), while for five decades since 1931, it has averaged 69 (with a range of only 67 to 70). These three plateaus correspond to three marked eras of high hitting. The first includes the runaway averages of the 1890s, when Hugh Duffy reached .438 (in 1894) and all five leading players topped .400 in the same year. The second plateau includes all the lower scores of .400 batters in our century, with the exception of Ted Williams (Hornsby was tops at .424 in 1924). The third plateau records the extinction of .400 hitting.

Lowest averages show the same pattern of decreasing difference from the league average, with a precipitous decline by decade from 71 to 54 points during the nineteenth century, and two plateaus thereafter (from the mid-forties early in the century to the mid-thirties later on), followed by the one exception to my pattern—a fallback to the forties during the 1970s.

Nineteenth-century values must be taken with a grain of salt, since rules of play were so different then. During the 1870s, for example, schedules varied from sixty-five to eighty-five games per season. With short seasons and fewer at bats, variation must increase, just as, in our own day, averages in June and July span a greater range than final-season averages, several hundred at bats later. (For these short seasons, I used two at bats per game as my criterion for inclusion in statistics for low averages.) Still, by the 1890s, schedules had lengthened to 130–150 games per season, and comparisons to our own century become more meaningful.

I was rather surprised—and I promise readers that I am not rationalizing after the fact but acting on a prediction I made before I started calculating—that the pattern of decrease did not yield more exceptions during our last two decades, because baseball has experienced a profound destabilization of the sort that calculations should reflect. After half a century of stable play with eight geographically stationary teams per league, the system finally broke in response to easier transportation and greater access to almighty dollars. Franchises began to move, and my beloved Dodgers and Giants abandoned New York in 1958. Then, in the early 1960s, both leagues expanded to ten teams, and in 1969 to twelve teams in two divisions.

These expansions should have caused a reversal in patterns of decrease between extreme batting averages and league averages. Many less than adequate players became regulars and pulled low averages down (Marvelous Marv Throneberry is still reaping the benefits in Lite beer ads). League averages also declined, partly as a result of the same influx, and bottomed out in 1968 at .230 in the American League. (This lamentable trend was reversed by fiat in 1969 when the pitching mound was lowered and the strike zone diminished to give batters a better chance.) This lowering of league averages should also have increased the distance between high hitters and the league average. Thus I was surprised that an increase in the distance between league and lowest

averages during the 1970s was the only result I could detect of this major destabilization.

As a nonplaying nonprofessional, I cannot pinpoint the changes that have caused the game to stabilize and the range of batting averages to decrease over time. But I can suggest the sorts of factors that will be important. Traditional explanations that view the decline of high averages as an intrinsic trend must emphasize explicit inventions and innovations that discourage hitting—the introduction of relief pitching and more night games, for example. I do not deny that these factors have important effects, but if the decline has also been caused, as I propose, by a general decrease in variation of batting averages, then we must look to other kinds of influences.

We must concentrate on increasing precision, regularity and standardization of play—and we must search for the ways that managers and players have discovered to remove the edge that the truly excellent once enjoyed. Baseball has become a science (in the vernacular sense of repetitious precision in execution). Outfielders practice for hours to hit the cutoff man. Positioning of fielders changes by the inning and man. Double plays are executed like awesome clockwork. Every pitch and swing is charted, and elaborate books are kept on the habits and personal weaknesses of each hitter. The "play" in play is gone.

When the world's tall ships graced our bicentennial in 1976, many of us lamented their lost beauty and cited Masefield's sorrow that we would never "see such ships as those again." I harbor opposite feelings about the disappearance of .400 hitting. Giants have not ceded to mere mortals. I'll bet anything that Carew could match Keeler. Rather, the boundaries of baseball have been drawn in and its edges smoothed. The game has achieved a grace and precision of execution that has, as one effect, eliminated the extreme achievements of early years. A game unmatched for style and detail has simply become more balanced and beautiful.

In this lonely land of ours, where the beacon of individuality has guided us from the onset of nationhood, baseball has become the tie that binds. Where religion, family, class, even ideology unite people of other lands, here baseball is the lingua franca: it connects males across the barriers of class or age, as Donald Hall notes, and in its arcane ways lies the immigrant's sure path to becoming American. But what baseball does is apart from what it is, and like music or art, it is a thing of beauty for its own sake. This beautiful piece was published in the *National Review* in 1981.

DONALD HALL

Baseball and the Meaning of Life

Professor McCormick's suggestion is surely farfetched. Although dark-suited umpires may remind him of warlocks, although the pitcher's motion mimics dubious rituals, we must resist the suggestion that baseball retains elements of the Old Religion. We may admit the existence of Seasonal Parallels without lending credence to his speculations on the shape of home plate.

For baseball dies into the October ground as leaves fall obscuring basepath and pitcher's mound, littering empty dugouts and bullpens, flitting like spooked grounders over second base into the stiffening outfield grass. November rain expunges lime-powder foul lines from Centerville's Little League Park to Yankee Stadium, from Yakima to Bangor, from Key West to Iron Mountain. Soon in the north a colder powder, no less white, freezes diamond and foul territory together into an egalitarian alabaster plain below the cold green ranks of box, grandstand, and bleacher. The old game waits under the white; deeper than frozen grass, down at the frostline it waits. . . .

To return when the birds return. It starts to wake in the South, where it had never quite stopped, where winter is a doze of hibernation interrupted by sleepy, staggering, momentary wakenings, like bears or skunks in a northern thaw. The game wakes gradually, gathering vigor to itself as the days lengthen late in February and grow warmer; old muscles grow limber, young arms throw strong and wild, legs pivot and leap, bodies hurtle into bright bases *safe*. . . . Clogged vein-systems, in veteran oaks and left-fielders both, unstop themselves, putting forth leaves and line drives in Florida's March. Migrating north with the swallows, baseball and the grass's first green enter Cleveland, Kansas City, Boston.

Silly he may be, but on the whole we sympathize with Professor McCormick's imaginative anthropology (*The Bat and the Wand*. A. Doubleday. 60'6". Cooperstown. No date). At least we share the intuition that connects baseball with the meaning of life.

April baseball is tentative, exploratory, daring and timid together, poking a quivering finger into the risen year. May strengthens, sure-footed now, turning night into bright green day, springing with young manhood's energy and vanity toward the twilights of high summer. In June, the animal-plant, full-leaved and muscled with maturity, invites us to settle secure for a season.

We arrive at the ballpark early. The ballplayers have been here for hours, for BP and pepper and shagging outfield flies, as coaches with fungoes bang balls at the shins of shortstops, or raise cans of corn to the shallow outfield, or strike line drives off outfield walls and corners. We arrive and settle with scorecards and Cracker Jack and peanuts and Schlitz and hot dogs. There is a rasp in our voices, there is glory in our infant hearts, there is mustard on our T-shirts.

Soon the tunnel disgorges three young men in bright suits carrying gloves, then two more, then six. "Play catch?" one says to another. They sort themselves by twos, throwing baseballs hard at each other without effort, drawing ruler-straight lines like chalk-stripes between them. The soft pock of caught balls sounds in attentive ears.

The bullpen squad—a coach, a catcher, two longmen, two or three shortmen—ambles with fabulous unconcern, chewing as slowly as prize Holsteins, down the foul lines toward their condominium in right field. The ninth inning's fastballing superstar ace-reliefman is not among them, but back in the trainer's room lying flat on his back, reading *Swann's Way* or *Looney Tunes*, waiting to trot his urgent trot from dugout to bullpen at the start of the eighth, the game 1–1, the one-man cavalry alerted to threat of ambush at the mountain pass.

Anticipating cavalry, the organist assaults the score of "The Star-Spangled Banner," which we attempt to sing because of the fierce joy that fills us and threatens to choke our throats unless we loosen this joyful noise. Then we chew the song's ending, and lean forward to watch the young men assume the field in their vain uniforms, to hear "Play ball!" to allow the game's dance to receive our beings into its rhythms for two hours or three.

Ah, the game! The game!

But what of the meaning of life . . .

Baseball connects American males with each other, not only through bleacher friendships and neighbor loyalties, not only through barroom fights, but most importantly through generations. When you are small you may not discuss politics or union dues or profit margins with your father's cigar-smoking friends when your father has gone out for a six-pack; but you may discuss baseball. It is all you have in common, because your father's friend does not wish to discuss the Assistant Principal or Alice Bisbee Morgan. About the season's moment you know as much as he does; both of you may shake your heads over Lefty's wildness or the rookie who was called out last Saturday when he tried to steal home with two out in the ninth inning down by one.

And you learn your first lessons of the rainbow arc all living makes, but that baseball exaggerates. For when you are in sixth grade, the rook has fuzz on his face and throws to the wrong base; before you leave junior high school, he is a seasoned regular, his body filled out, his jowl rippled with tobacco; when you graduate from high school he is a grizzled veteran—even if you are not certain what grizzled means. In a few years, the green shoot becomes the withered stalk, and you learn the hill all beings travel by.

So Carl Yastrzemski enters his forty-second year. So Wilver Stargell's bones are stiff. While George Brett climbs the glorious mountain of his prime, all gut and muscle, his brother Ken watches with admiration and irony from the shadows of his quick sundown, who started the All-Star Game for the National League in 1974, his record thirteen and two, the lithe left arm bending sliders to catch the black—unbeatable, impervious, in his high stride hitting home runs from the ninth position. His brother George played AAA that year. That year somebody asked Ken Brett, "Why don't you play outfield when you're not pitching?" "Because they do not have that much money in Pittsburgh."

In 1980, Ken was released by the Dodgers, later signed on with George's KC as a long man in the bullpen. This year or next he will begin to make The Adjustment, as the players call it, when he leaves forever the game he doubtless began at the age of seven or eight. The light grows pale on the older players but never dwindles entirely away. . . . I remember Edd Roush, batting champion of 1917, ancient and glorious at an Old-timers' Game in 1975. Smokey Joe Wood, amazing fastballer of the 1912 Red Sox, signed autographs in Boston at a collectors' convention in 1980.

Let it be. Players age, and baseball changes, as veterans slide off by way of jets to Japan instead of buses to Spokane. Baseball changes, and we wish it never to change. Yet we know that inside the ball, be it horsehide or cowhide, the universe remains unaltered. Even if the moguls, twenty years from now, manage to move the game indoors and schedule twelve months a year, the seasons will remain implicit, like the lives of the players. Grow-lites do not legislate winter away. If the whole sport emigrates to Japan, baseball will remain a Zen garden.

For surely, as Professor McCormick fails to remind us, baseball sets off the meaning of life precisely because it is pure of meaning. As the ripples in the sand, in the Kyoto garden, organize and formalize the dust which is dust, so the diamonds and rituals of baseball create an elegant, trivial, enchanted grid on which our suffering, shapeless, sinful day leans for the momentary grace of order.

The lure for students of baseball history is the illusion that all that has ever happened is known or can be discovered. Witness Art Hill's interest in such a ballplaying cipher as Joe Cobb or W. P. Kinsella's in Moonlight Graham, a one-inning defensive replacement in 1905 whom he made a central figure in his novel *Shoeless Joe*. *The Baseball Encyclopedia* is more than a reference work: it is an ever-expanding Book of Life, for statistics are the vital part of baseball, the only tangible and imperishable remains of games played yesterday or a hundred years ago.

ART HILL

A Stroll Through
The Baseball Encyclopedia

John Paciorek, as every serious collector of baseball curiosa knows, is major-league baseball's leading lifetime hitter. No one ever hit for a higher average over an entire career. His career, which was all over before he reached his nineteenth birthday, consisted of one game for Houston in 1963, and it was quite remarkable as far as it went. He had three hits in three times at bat, walked twice, scored four runs and batted in three.

There are many other hitters with lifetime averages of 1.000, but most of them had only one time at bat. Among batters who never made an out, Paciorek's three for three is tops.

I have, as you can guess, been browsing through the record book, an utterly fascinating accumulation of baseball facts, ranging from the awe-inspiring to the ineffably trivial. Listed here is every man who ever played in a major-league game. Here is Ty Cobb, with his 4,191 hits and .367 lifetime batting average (both "unbreakable" records), right below Joe Cobb, who has no batting average at all. Consider Joe Cobb. The books tells us that he was born in Hudson, Pennsylvania, January 24, 1895, and died December 24, 1947; that he batted and threw right-handed; that he was 5 feet 9 inches tall and weighed 170 pounds, and that his last name was originally Serafin. All this for a man who appeared in one game for Detroit in 1918, apparently going to the plate once and getting a base on balls. In the matter of vital statistics, we know more about Joe Cobb than we do about Shakespeare. Shakespeare never played big-league baseball, so we know not whether he batted left or right (although some readers of the sonnets have pegged him as a switch hitter).

I marvel at the scope of these great baseball record books which have appeared in the past ten years or so, products of the computer age. They have conferred immortality of a sort on men whose names were lost to history for fifty years or more. And of each of them, however slender his record, it can be said, "He was a good ballplayer." If he hadn't been, he never would have been offered a big-league uniform, even for a day.

For me, the big books are also an exercise in nostalgia, recalling names I had forgotten countless years ago. But surely their most intriguing feature, to any genuine baseball zealot, is the small glimpses they offer of the lives of otherwise unknown performers, and the puzzling questions they often raise.

Take Bill Bergen, for example. There is a mystery surrounding him that may never be solved. He was no one-day player; quite the contrary. He came into the major leagues in 1901, when he was already twenty-eight years old, and managed to stick around for eleven years, although he hit over .200 just once. His lifetime batting average was a limp .170. The question is: why? Why was this incredibly bad hitter allowed to go to bat 3,116 times in major-league ball games? He was a catcher, and the assumption is that he must have been an awfully good one. My own theory is that his father owned the Brooklyn ball club, with which he spent most of his career.

Bergen, incidentally, was a teammate of three interesting players at Cincinnati in 1902, all of whom achieved fame (or something) with other teams. Harry Steinfeldt became the forgotten third baseman in the Chicago Cubs' infield immortalized in Franklin P. Adams's "Tinker to Evers to Chance." Sam Crawford was a twenty-two-year-old outfielder who hit .333 and then went on to Detroit, where he stayed for fifteen years, made the Hall of Fame, and collected the amazing lifetime total of 312 triples. No one but Cobb (Ty, not Joe), with 297, has ever come close to that figure, and he had almost 2,000 more at-bats than Sam.

The most remarkable player on that 1902 Cincinnati team, however, was Dummy Hoy, then forty years old and winding up a career that had begun in 1888. William Ellsworth (Dummy) Hoy was a deaf-mute who stood only 5 feet 4, but he had a lifetime batting average of .291, plus 607 stolen bases. He also was responsible for a small revolution in baseball tactics. The visual signals which are used by all teams were originally devised by Hoy's manager so he could communicate his wishes to him. Dummy Hoy died in 1961, just five months short of his 100th birthday. My father, as a very small boy, saw him play, I think. At least, he used to talk about him as if he had. Apparently, in those days, no one thought the name by which he was always identified at all demeaning.

Think about this. In 1906 the Chicago White Sox, the famous Hitless Wonders, were last in the league in hits, total bases, and team batting average. They produced a fraction over seven hits per game and had a grand total of six home runs! They also won the pennant and beat the Cubs in the World Series. The following year, they hit only five home runs, and in 1908 they achieved the seemingly impossible. In that year, playing 156 games, the White Sox hit three home runs (and still lost the pennant by just a game and a half). I feel reasonably sure this is the single-season record for futility in the power department.

Just as there are many batters with perfect batting averages, there are any number of pitchers in the book with won-lost records of 1.000—that is, they won at least one game and never lost one. The vast majority of them have 1–0 records, but there are more than a half dozen with 3–0 marks. The leader in this category is one Ben Shields, who must have been one of the luckiest pitchers ever to play the game. He won three games for the New York Yankees in 1925, kicked around the majors and minors for six years before resurfacing with the Philadelphia Phillies in 1931, where he won one game, despite giving up nine hits and seven walks in five innings of pitching. Over his career, he pitched a total of forty-one innings, during which he allowed fifty-five hits and twenty-seven walks and had an earned-run average of 8.34. But he was never charged with a loss. He is the only 4–0 pitcher in baseball history. (There have doubtless been several rookie pitchers with temporary 4–0 records, but they didn't know when to quit. Neither, apparently, did Ben Shields until it was forced upon him. But he got away with it.)

There is no mystery about Ben Shields. Plainly, the baseball gods favored him with one of their unpredictable smiles. And he hung around long enough to prove he wasn't good enough, perfect record notwithstanding. But what about the others, the dozens of 1.000 hitters and 1.000 pitchers (plus all the pitchers with 0.00 ERAs)? What happened to them? Their records are, I realize, deceptive, but still . . . when a man has fulfilled his obligation to perfection, why is he not then given another chance? Pure logic would dictate that there shouldn't be any 1.000 hitters or pitchers in the book. And yet there are too many to count. I wonder about them all.

There are, incidentally, only three pitchers in the book with "perfect perfect" records: won 1, lost 0, ERA 0.00. They are Nellie Rees (Washington, 1918), Paul Jaeckel (Cubs, '64), and Nestor Chavez (San Francisco, '67). The best of them was Jaeckel, who gave up only four hits in an eight-inning career. Where did he go? He is today only thirty-seven years old, and the Cubs might well consider giving him another chance.

But wait, here's a surprising development. There are, it's true, only three double-perfect pitchers *in the book*. But here's one who's not in the book. You'll remember him, though, if you're a baseball fan. The book I am using explains in the introductory notes that "men who were primarily non-pitchers are included in the pitcher register only if they pitched in five or more games." Rocky Colavito, he of the powerful biceps, 374 home runs and 1,159 RBI's, was beyond question a non-pitcher—primarily. But he pitched three innings of relief for Cleveland in 1958 and, ten years later, three more for the Yankees. In the latter game, he got the win over Detroit (and the Tigers went on to win the World Series that year). In all, Rocky pitched six innings, gave up only one hit, had an ERA of 0.00, won one and lost none. He was not only a "perfect perfect" pitcher, but the best of the lot. You might never have known that if I weren't an inveterate reader of small print.

One of the captivating features of the record book is the players' nicknames, especially those from the early part of the century. I am, first of all, stunned by the amount of research it must have taken to dig them up. No computer, it would seem, can be programmed to do that kind of work. But it is the names themselves, regardless of how they were uncovered, that stir the imagination. What do they mean?

No one would ask that question about such famous nicknames as those of Ty Cobb, who was called "the Georgia Peach," or Frank (Home Run) Baker. Cobb was from Georgia and was a peach of a player, and Baker earned his title by hitting two home runs in the 1911 World Series and banging out an average of seven per year over a career that spanned the great transition in baseball. (Baker broke in in 1908, the year the Chicago White Sox hit three home runs, and he was a teammate of Babe Ruth's in 1921 when the Babe hit fifty-nine.) But how, for example, did Dave Altizer of Pearl, Illinois, become known as "Filipino"? And why was little Arlie Latham, who played for six teams in three different leagues before the turn of the century, called "the Freshest Man on Earth"? (In 1909, evidently still fresh after a ten-year absence, Arlie Latham made a farewell appearance with the New York Giants at the age of forty-nine, and stayed long enough to steal his 791st base. It should be noted, however, that stolen bases before 1900 cannot be compared with twentieth-century steals since they were awarded on an entirely different basis.)

Names like Whitey, Hoss, Brickyard, Dapper Dan, and Big Bill are easily enough understood, and we can imagine how Benny (Earache) Meyer earned his designation. We can guess why Dirty Jack Doyle played for twelve different teams in seventeen years, too. Since he won 203 games, Al Orth (1895–1909) probably didn't mind being called "the Curveless Wonder," but what did Bill Lattimore do in his four-game stay with the 1908 Cleveland club to earn the title "Slothful Bill"? And how, in God's name, did Hub Perdue of the Boston Braves and St. Louis Cardinals (1911–15) come to be called "the Gallatin Squash"?

In the area of literary nicknames, there have been a number of "King" Lears and at least one "King" Lehr. More surprising, though, is Hal Janvrin, who played for several teams between 1911 and '22 and was called "Childe Harold." (Literary allusions are not common in baseball, but an interesting one comes along now and then. In recent years it has become fairly general to say of a poor infielder that he plays like the Ancient Mariner. That is, "he stoppeth one of three.")

Blue Sleeve Harper, Trolley Line Butler, Peaceful Valley Denzer, Dauntless Dave Danforth, Snooze Goulait, Buttermilk Tommy Dowd, Little All Right Ritchey, Sea Lion Hall. There's a story in every one of those names—undoubtedly in many cases a painfully dull one, but that's the chance you take. (Sea Lion Hall's baptismal name, incidentally, was Carlos Clolo. Figure that out.)

Finally, you may be interested to know that from 1908 to 1911, Albert Schweitzer (probably not the same one) played for the St. Louis Browns. His nickname was "Cheese."

Incredible but true. And how history might have altered if Fidel had gone on to become a New York Yanqui, or a Washington Senator, or even a Cincinnati Red.

DON HOAK with MYRON COPE

The Day I Batted Against Castro

Cuba was an American baseball player's paradise when I played there in the winter of 1950–51. Later, as a major-league third baseman, I became one of the better-paid ballplayers, but I was just an $800-a-month minor leaguer when I went to Cuba.

There the Cienfuegos club paid me $1,000 a month plus $350 a month for expenses. I had a cottage apartment at the elegant Club Nautico on the beach near Havana. The rent, thanks to a reduced rate obtained by the owner of our team, was $150. The $150 included:

(a) A spacious living room with floor-to-ceiling windows; two bedrooms; two baths; a screened patio in the rear; a dazzling flower garden out front.

(b) A fine old Cuban lady named Eeta, who did my housekeeping and cooking. (I had to pay her bus fare.)

(c) A guard to watch over my apartment.

Late at night, after the baseball games were over, I fished off the coral reefs for yellowtails and eels. By day, I went scuba diving for lobster or napped on the beach or walked across the road to the golf course to shoot a round. Cuba was the best place in the world to play baseball.

But even in those days, the students at the University of Havana were politically restless. At the Havana ballpark they'd frequently interrupt our games by staging demonstrations on the field.

They would pour down from the stands and parade across the field carrying banners. They would set off firecrackers and blow horns and shout slogans for ten or fifteen minutes and then go back to their seats. The dictator, Fulgencio Batista, tolerated them, perhaps because he did not consider them a serious threat to his power. His police allowed them to spend their energies. As a matter of fact, Batista himself sometimes witnessed the demonstrations, for he attended many games. Surrounded by bodyguards, he would sit through the commotion with arms folded across his chest and just a trace of a smile at the corner of his lips.

Another regular customer at the park was Fidel Castro. He had just received his law degree from the university, but he remained a well-known and flamboyant leader of the students. As a baseball fan, he belonged in the nut category.

I knew Castro's face well and I suspected he was something of a wild man because of the company he kept. He often came to the park with a man named Pedro Formanthael, who played right field for the Marianao club. Pedro was about forty but an excellent ballplayer. He stood no more than 5 feet 10 but was built very solidly and could hit with power. He wore a great mustache and had a temper that was just as black. He always carried a pistol a foot long, and I wondered how he fit it into his jacket. Anyhow, he and Castro were great pals.

Our Cienfuegos club was playing Pedro Formanthael's team in the Havana park the night I came face to face with Castro.

It was approximately the fifth inning, as I recall, when the firecrackers went off. Up went the banners. The horns blared, and down from the stands came the students—perhaps 300 of them. As fate would have it, I had just stepped into the batter's box when all hell broke loose. "Here we go again," I thought as I stepped out of the box to await order.

But on this night the demonstration took an unexpected turn.

Castro marched straight out to the mound and seized a glove and ball from the Marianao pitcher, a tall Cuban whose name I can't recall. The pitcher shrugged and walked off the field.

Castro then toed the rubber, and as he did so his appearance on the mound was so ridiculous that I cannot forget a single detail of it. He wore no glasses then, but he did have a beard—a funny little beard at the point of his chin that he obviously had taken great care to groom. He was tall and rather skinny.

He wore a long-sleeved white shirt—a type of shirt many Cubans favored. It had pleats like a formal dress shirt and a square bottom which was worn outside the trousers. Castro also wore tight black slacks and black suede shoes with pointed toes. His footwear was almost dandy, and as I see pictures of today's Castro in army fatigues and combat boots I am amused by the contrast.

However, I don't suppose a guy in black suede shoes would stand very well at the head of a people's revolution.

Anyhow, Castro put on the glove and ordered the Marianao catcher—a Cuban veteran named Mike Guerra, who had played for the Washington Senators and Philadelphia Athletics—to catch his repertoire. Castro wound up with a great windmill flourish, whirling his pitching arm overhead about six times. Obviously he considered himself an ace hurler, as the sportswriters say. Left-handers as a breed are eccentric, but Castro, a right-hander, looked kookier than any southpaw I have known.

I figured, "Let him have his fun," and watched him throw half a dozen pitches. The crowd was in an uproar. The students, ranged along the foul lines, were dancing with glee.

Suddenly Castro stopped throwing, glared at me, and barked the Spanish equivalent of "Batter up!"

I looked at the umpire but he only shrugged. "What the hell," I said, and stepped into the batter's box. I was not particularly anxious to defy Castro and his mob, because I knew the Latin temper to be an explosive force. Also, Castro's gunslinging buddy, Pedro Formanthael, was throwing me dirty looks from right field.

Castro gave me the hipper-dipper windup and cut loose with a curve. Actually, it was a pretty fair curve. It had a sharp inside break to it—and it came within an inch of breaking my head.

"Ball one!" said the umpire. Castro marched forward a few paces from the mound and stared daggers at him. The students expressed considerable displeasure. The umpire suggested to me that I had better start swinging or he would be compelled to call me out on strikes.

But I glanced at those students on the foul line and thought, "If I swing hard I'm liable to line a foul down there and kill somebody." I had to think fast because Castro, his floppy shirt billowing in the evening breeze, was already into his windup—a *super* hipper-dipper windup this time. I thought he would take off for the moon.

Finally he cut loose with a fastball—a good fastball, a regular bullet.

It came at me in the vicinity of the shins. Fortunately, I was a pretty fair bat handler, so I came around on the pitch with a short golf stroke and lofted a pop-foul over the heads of the students on the third-base line. I figured the best thing to do was to tap soft fouls into the stands.

Castro's third pitch was another fastball. He really zinged it. It scorched its way straight for my eyeballs. I leaned away, gave my bat a quick lurch, and managed another pop-foul into the stands.

Castro had two strikes on me and he was stomping pompously around the mound as though he had just conquered Washington, D.C.

At that point, however, a new factor entered the picture. The Hoak temper.

I've got a wee trace of Comanche blood, you see, and I imagine I have a temper that can match any Latin's from Havana to Lima. To me, baseball is war. In 1956 I played winter ball in the Dominican Republic, where I pleased the fans by hitting .394 and sliding into bases like a maniac. I am known there, even to this day, as Crazy Horse. When I played for Pittsburgh, a broadcaster there named me The Tiger. Mind you, I don't care to fight Castro and 300 Cubans under any circumstances, but if I have a bat in my hands I know I won't be the only guy to get hurt.

So I turned to the umpire and announced, "I've got a major-league career and big money and good times ahead of me, and I am not going to stand here and let some silly punk in a pleated shirt throw at my skull. Now just get that idiot out of the game."

Here, still another factor entered the picture. The *umpire's* temper.

His name was Miastri and he was a fine umpire. He was such a firebrand that when he threw a player out of a game he often fined him on the spot, and when he fined a guy he would turn around and look up to the press box and announce the amount of the fine with vigorous hand signals. And now he had decided he, too, had had a bellyful of Castro.

He marched over to the *policía*, who were lazily enjoying the fun from the grandstands, and ordered them in no uncertain terms to clear the field. Down they came from the stands, riot clubs brandished at shoulder level.

A knot of cops moved briskly on pitcher Castro. Briefly, he made a show of standing his ground, but the cops shoved him off the mound. He shuffled meekly toward the third-base grandstands, like an impudent boy who has been cuffed by the teacher and sent to stand in the corner.

My final memory of him is one that somehow strikes me funny to this day. As he crossed the third-base line I happened to look at his shoes. He had dust on his black suede shoes.

Looking back, I think that with a little work on his control, Fidel Castro would have made a better pitcher than a prime minister.

A fabulous character recalls a fabled time in sport and sportswriting, especially that inexhaustible fount of hilarious stories, the Bambino. Richards Vidmer covered the Yanks and covered up for them, too—that was the code until Jim Brosnan lifted the veil in *The Long Season* (1960) and Jim Bouton vaporized it a decade later. The passage below is a portion of the chapter devoted to Vidmer in Jerome Holtzman's wonderful oral history of American sportswriting, *No Cheering in the Press Box* (1974).

JEROME HOLTZMAN

Richards Vidmer
Remembers

Richards Vidmer was not the garden variety sportswriter. Unlike many of his colleagues, he was an outstanding athlete: He played baseball at the minor-league level (under the name Widmeyer, to protect his college eligibility), and football at George Washington College; and he later coached football at St. John's University in Washington, D.C. He was also an accomplished equestrian and a scratch golfer. During his second marriage, to the daughter of a Borneo rajah, he broke the boredom of a life of ease by working as a golf pro. Not surprisingly, he was closer to the athletes than most of his peers and admitted, "I didn't hang around with the writers. The ballplayers were my friends."

Mr. Vidmer was the inspiration for the book Young Man of Manhattan, *a romantic novel about a playboy sportswriter. He more or less stumbled into newspaper work, starting on the Washington (D.C.) Herald, and is best remembered for his work in New York, first as a baseball writer for the* Times *and then at the* Herald Tribune, *where he succeeded the famous Bill McGeehan and wrote a column titled "Down in Front." "The thing that saved my life in the newspaper business," explained Mr. Vidmer, "was that I never had any desire to have a drink until five o'clock, until after my work was done. Then, I could catch up with anybody."*

The son of a highly decorated brigadier general who fought at San Juan Hill, Mr. Vidmer lived on army posts on four continents. For several years he was a mascot of the football teams at West Point, when Eisenhower, Patton, and Mark Clark were cadets. Mr. Vidmer survived an air collision during World War I, as a pilot, and during World War II was in intelligence, principally under assignment to General Eisenhower's headquarters. He now lives in Orlando, Florida, with his third wife, and is still dashingly handsome at the age of seventy-five.

Hell, I should have been dead twenty years ago. If I'd known I was going to live so long I would have taken better care of myself. I was careless, reckless. I've done things—well, I must have been crazy. Like one time in Philadelphia. I was on the twelfth floor in a hotel, in a corner room, and there was somebody I wanted to see in the next room—another guy. I'd been drinking. Instead of going around the corner and walking in through the door, I climbed out my window and crawled from one ledge to the other. Now, how stupid can you be?

I was what you might call either a playboy or a rounder. I suppose I was more of a playboy. I wasn't much of a rounder. I mean, I didn't get drunk and wind up in alleys or things like that, if that's what a rounder is. A playboy is a guy who takes life as it comes, has a good time, and enjoys himself. I've certainly enjoyed my life.

I was raised in the army. People ask me where I come from. Hell, I don't come from anywhere. I didn't have a home town. I've lived all over the world— Japan, Philippines, Iowa, Vermont, Texas. My father was a career officer. He wound up a general—in the cavalry. He was a captain during the time I was growing up. Whenever he went out on maneuvers or something like that, why, I'd go out with the troops.

He was the adjutant at West Point in 1912–13–14, when I was a brat around twelve years old. I was the mascot of the Army football team and the bat boy for the baseball team. They took me along on their trips. I had a card, had it for years, "Admit Bearer to Army Team Wherever It May Be."

One of my favorite conversation pieces is a magazine that I've got around here which West Point puts out three or four times a year, a rather ornate thing. Someone sent me this copy which was devoted primarily to Eisenhower. Ike played on the football team, and there's a picture of him with some of the other players. My favorite thing is to say, "Now find me." They search around looking at the players. They can't find me. But I'm the little fellow standing right next to Ike.

The fellows at West Point when I was up there, the cadets at that time, were big generals in the second war. Eisenhower, Bradley, Gerhardt, Aaker, Mark Clark. Hell, I knew Patton all through his life, more or less. And, of course, I served in both wars. Air Force. I was in an air collision during the first war. Miracle that I came out alive.

I was a sportswriter for thirty years, between the wars. I guess I was a romantic guy in those days. Everybody who comes around asks me if it was true that I married a rajah's daughter. It's true. She was the daughter of the Rajah of Sarawak. It's the northern portion of Borneo and embraces an area larger than England, Scotland, and Wales put together. The rajah owned the whole thing, and it was a very rich country.

There was this book, *Young Man of Manhattan*. It came out in the late 1920s, '27 or '28. It was written by Katharine Brush. She wrote seven or eight books. Some of what she wrote was racy stuff in those days, but it'd be tame today. She was a girl friend of mine. She built the book on me, what she knew of my character. It was a successful book. They made a movie out of it. Preston Foster played the male lead.

But it was all fictionalized, of course. Toby McLean was the hero of the book. He's a sportswriter—a playboy, always having a good time, but never getting down to real business. He's going with this girl, and she's always after him to write a book. "Write a book! Write a book!" And he procrastinates and tells her, "Okay, okay! Someday! Someday!" It's during Prohibition, of course, and he gets some bad liquor and goes blind. Then, while he's blind, he writes a book, dictating it all to her, and when it's published she puts the book into his hands, a very tender scene. And of course the book's a great success. Kay Brush was wonderful. Oh, she could write like hell.

The other sportswriters got a big kick out of it. Some people still call me Toby to this day.

I'll tell you the kind of writer I was. One day this editor called me—this was in New York, when I was doing the sports column for the *Herald Tribune*. He was from one of those highbrow magazines. What's the name of it? *The Atlantic Weekly?* No, *The Atlantic Monthly*, that's it. He said would I write a piece about Joe DiMaggio, and I said, "What kind of piece?"

He said, "Anything you want to do. We just want you to write a piece about Joe DiMaggio."

I said, "How much for how much?"

He said, "Well, three hundred dollars for twenty-five hundred or three thousand words."

"Sure, I'll do it. When do you want it?"

They didn't need it until the twenty-eighth of the month. This was about the third of the month. "Sure," I said. "No problem."

Of course, you know me. I could have sat down and written it then. But I just put it off. By God, the twenty-eighth arrives and he calls me up and says, "You know, we haven't gotten that piece from you yet."

"Hey, you haven't? Now wait a minute, I sent that up there yesterday by messenger. Wait! I'll see if it's gone." I let the phone hang there for a minute or two. Then I said, "No, it's still here where I left it. It hasn't gone out yet."

You know, I sat down and wrote that thing—three thousand words. Never even read copy on it. Got a messenger and set it up there, and the next day he called me up. I thought, "Oh, oh, here comes the rewriting."

I said, "Did you get the piece all right?"

"Oh, yes, we've got it. Just exactly what we wanted. Exactly."

I remember Bill Corum—he was an old friend of mine. We'd been on the copy desk together, when we were young fellows. Bill once said, "When you sit down and write something in a hurry, it's good. But when you sit down and labor over it, it stinks."

One time—this was when I was married to my first wife—I had been in Pittsburgh and had gotten back home late. I was asleep. She woke me up about eleven o'clock and said, "We've got to be down at so-and-so's at noon because there's a buffet luncheon and cocktails."

I thought, "Oh, Jesus," but I said, "All right" and we went. It was a good party. Bankers and brokers, and everybody having a lot of drinks and a good time. I never wrote on Sundays for Monday's paper. All of a sudden, it's about five o'clock, and I said, "This isn't Sunday. It's Armistice Day. It's Monday. I've got to write a column!"

So I blew out of there, jumped on the train to the city. On the way in I thought, "What the hell can I write that won't take much time?" I decided I'd write some Armistice Day poetry. So I kind of got it in my head, and when I got up there I knocked it out on a typewriter. It didn't fill a column, but did fill this much and it was something different. Very serious. Of course, I'm drunker than hell.

Son of a bitch, if Alexander Woollcott doesn't call me the next day wanting to know if he could put it on the air.

I don't know if you feel this way, but when you get through writing a column, do you think, "Jesus, that's good"? I wasn't that way. Almost every time I did a column, I said, "Well, Jesus, I'll write a better one tomorrow. That's the best I can do today." I always said that. But every day it was the same thing. I always thought I'd do better tomorrow.

But once in a while I'd write a column and I'd say, "Jesus, there's a dinger." Yet the ones that I felt stunk, I'd get a hundred letters, sometimes, saying that was a great column, and the ones I thought were great, I'd never hear a word. I was a bad judge, I guess.

I wasn't a good reporter. I always figured you could read a box score and know what happened. I still do. When I'd write a ballgame, I'd write about some particular thing, not: "In the first inning Gehrig singled to right, in the second inning Meusel tripled to center, and in the third inning so-and-so grounded into a double play." The hell with that.

Oh, I'd bring it all in—who won and the important plays—but I used to start my stories with some angle—like, well, there was the day the Yankees had the bases filled with two outs in the ninth inning and they sent Mike Gazella to pinch-hit. An awfully nice guy. Went to Lafayette. And he stood up there and got a base on balls to force in the winning run. So I started off, "He also serves who only stands and waits."

I played a lot of golf. I played every morning on the road. As a result, I was generally late to the ballgames. I'd get to the press box in the third inning and ask someone to fill me in. One time, in St. Louis, I got there pretty late in the game, maybe the fifth or sixth inning, and I asked Will Wedge—he was the baseball man at the *Sun*—if anything special had happened.

"Oh," he says, "Babe hit another home run," which was routine in those days. But he said they had broadcast on the loudspeaker that they wanted the ball back.

I said, "What for? Was it especially long or something?"

Wedge didn't know, but he said a little Italian kid had retrieved the ball and had given it to the Babe. Wedge gave me the kid's name.

Then I remember that Babe and Claire—that was his wife—and I had been to a movie a couple of nights before, and Babe happened to say, "Well, the next one I hit will be my five hundredth."

Now, you know what a big to-do there is today when a guy hits five hundred home runs. Writers and photographers follow him around for weeks. But Babe had just mentioned it casually. I was probably the only writer who knew it was his five hundredth.

So I sat down and wrote how Babe had hit this home run and this little kid in the alley, an Italian kid, had chased the ball, and how he'd been trying to get a ball all these years but he never got one because the bigger kids had always beaten him to it. Finally, he gets a ball, his big moment, and a cop comes up and says to the kid, "Come with me."

The kid's scared.

He says, "I ain't done nuthin', I ain't done nuthin'."

And the cop says, "Babe Ruth wants to see you."

Now the kid knows he's in trouble.

So they bring him into the Yankee dugout and Babe Ruth gives him five bucks and a brand-new ball.

That was my story for the next day, not the fact that the Yankees won 18–

4 or 9–1, or something like that. What the hell, you can see that in the box score. Hell, I'd have it moving. I'd have some drama in it, or romance, or some damn thing. Not like they do it today.

But don't get the wrong impression. I wasn't a big scoop artist. Christ, no! That's why I had so many friends. I never could see blowing the whistle on somebody just for a big headline, a one-day sensation. I'll give you an example.

The day Lou Gehrig took himself out of the lineup and went up to the Mayo Clinic, I wasn't traveling with the Yankees. I was writing a column then, and the Yankees were on the road when Lou took himself out. When the club came home I went into the clubhouse and said, "What the hell's the matter with you, Lou? When you going to get back in the lineup?" I was always kidding with him.

He said, "Wait a minute," and called this fellow over. It was his doctor. He said to the doctor, "Talk to him." And the doctor looked at Lou and Lou said, "Go ahead, tell him anything you want. He's my pal." And Lou walks away.

I asked the doctor, "What's the matter with Lou?"

The doctor told me he's got a creeping paralysis. Nobody knows what causes it. If they knew, they could cure it, or at least stop it.

"What are his chances?"

"Well," the doctor says, "there has been much progress made in paralysis these last few years because of President Roosevelt. We hope we'll discover the cause and cure it in time."

"Suppose you don't?"

"Well, I'd say two years is the limit."

I'm the only writer who knows what's the matter with Lou. But I didn't write it. And why the hell should I? The public has to be informed, my ass! None of the public's damned business as long as he plays ball or doesn't play. That's the way I felt and that's why Lou told the doctor he could level with me. Lou knew damn well I wasn't going to rush into print for the sake of a headline.

Then, maybe two weeks later, Jimmy Powers found out and he spreads it all over the *News*—saying how all of Lou's teammates are afraid to sit next to him in the dugout, and so on, which was a God damn lie. But it was sensational, all right.

I was always reticent about writing anything that was going to hurt somebody, and of course, I would never write anything told to me in confidence. I only read excerpts of the Bouton book. I thought it was damned interesting and amusing—and true. I had seen the same thing, or similar things, thirty years before. Sure, ballplayers are like that. All athletes are like that. For God's sake, all men are like that. But I just don't see where a public figure's private life is anybody's business.

Hell, I could have written a story every day on the Babe. But I never wrote

about his personal life, not if it would hurt him. Babe couldn't say no to certain things. Hot dogs was the least of 'em. There were other things that were worse. Hell, sometimes I thought it was one long line, a procession.

I remember once we were coming north, at the end of spring training. We used to barnstorm and stop at all the little towns. We traveled on the train. Babe and some of the other ballplayers and myself, we'd play bridge between the exhibition games, in the morning before they had to go to the ballpark, and then after the ballgame until the train left, generally about eleven o'clock that night. In those days they used to start games at one o'clock, or one-thirty. We'd be through by three, and we'd go back to the hotel to Babe's room and start playing bridge, and surer than hell the phone would ring. I'd always answer it.

"Is Babe Ruth there?"

And I'd say, "No, he's not here right now. This is his secretary. Can I tell him who called?"

"This is Mildred. Tell him Mildred called."

And I'd say, "Mildred"—and the Babe would shake his head, meaning no. Get rid of her.

I'd say, "I'm sorry, he's not here right now, but I'll tell him that you called."

Well, before I could finish, Babe would be across the room, grab the phone, and say, "Hello, babe, c'mon up."

He couldn't say no.

Up she'd come and interrupt the bridge game for ten minutes or so. They'd go in the other room. Pretty soon they'd come out and the girl would leave. Babe would say, "So long, kid," or something like that. Then he'd sit down and we'd continue our bridge game. That's all. That was it. While he was absent we'd sit and talk, wait for him.

One evening in Philadelphia I was in the dining room and Babe had me paged. I went to the phone and Babe said, "What are you doing tonight?"

I said, "Nothing in particular."

And he said, "Come up about nine o'clock, will ya?"

I didn't know what he wanted, but I went up there at nine o'clock. Babe was in his dressing gown. There was some whiskey and ice, soda and whatnot on the table. Babe always had a suite. We had two or three drinks and chatted away about a lot of crap. He talked about Joe McCarthy. Babe had ambitions to be a manager and he never liked McCarthy. He always said McCarthy was a dumb Irishman who didn't know anything. After about a half hour of this I saw a shadow at the door in the other room, the bedroom, and I said, "Say, Claire isn't down with you, is she?"

He says, "No, she didn't come down this trip."

So I says, "Have you got a doll in there?"

And he said, "Yeah."

"Jesus, Babe, why didn't you tell me? I've been sitting here chewing the fat with you, and all the time you've got a doll in there."

"No, no," he says. "That's why I wanted you to come up. I thought I'd need a rest."

Oh, sure, that sort of thing is funny, but I didn't think it would add anything to the public image of the Babe. The public already had a good picture of him.

If you weren't around in those times, I don't think you could appreciate what a figure the Babe was. He was bigger than the president. One time, coming north, we stopped at a little town in Illinois, a whistle stop. It was about ten o'clock at night and raining like hell. The train stopped for ten minutes to get water, or something. It couldn't have been a town of more than 5,000 people, and by God, there were 4,000 of them down there standing in the rain, just waiting to see the Babe.

Babe and I and two other guys were playing bridge. Babe was sitting next to the window. A woman with a little baby in her arms came up and started peering in at the Babe. She was rather good looking. Babe looked at her and went on playing bridge. Then he looked at her again and finally he leaned out and said, "Better get away from here, lady. I'll put one in the other arm. . . ."

"Discerning the De Facto Standards of the Hall of Fame," read the subhead when this piece appeared in *The 1980 Baseball Abstract*. At that time a self-published, typewritten book, it began to pierce the fog of myth and misunderstanding with which baseball brahmins robed themselves. The 1980 effort attracted a few hundred devoted readers; today *The Bill James Baseball Abstract* is commercially published and claims a readership well in excess of 100,000. It is not too much to say that James has revolutionized the way fans think about the game and the way professionals write about it. This essay, like a modern dictionary, is not prescriptive but descriptive—it does not attempt to weigh the justice of the Cooperstown election system but simply to determine what the implied standards are and how prospective candidates stack up against them.

BILL JAMES

What Does It Take?

I used to write a lot about the Hall of Fame. I wrote about how they could design more equitable election systems. I wrote about why the different boards inevitably used different standards. I wrote about the statistical illusions that tend to reinforce the Senile Ballplayers Committee in their inevitable belief that the Boys I played with were the best ever. Nobody paid any attention. I made up charts that demonstrated the New York bias in the Hall of Fame's composition. No New Yorkers called to resign. Eventually I gave it up. I dislike howling into the wind.

What never ceases to amaze me is the hold that this unremarkable institution has on the imagination of baseball fans. You go to a meeting of the Society for American Baseball Research, and every third word is Cooperstown. Every separate interest group scratches at the base of this one pedestal. The Committee on the Negro Leagues wants to get more old-time blacks into the Hall of Fame. The Committee on Stat Analysis wants to establish standards for election to the Hall of Fame. The Committee on the Minor Leagues feels unfulfilled until there exists a minor-league Hall of Fame. And everybody and his fourteen-year-old son wants to collar me and explain why Ross Barnes, Arky Vaughan, Johnny Mize, and Bob Elliott belong in the Hall of Fame. I get sick of hearing about it. The Negro Leagues are fascinating, stat analysis will obviously hold my interest. The minor leagues are a delicious memory, and even Ross Barnes might be interesting if you knew something about him. Why must all of these topics be submerged into a never-ending argument about who belongs in the Hall of Fame?

Men without voices rattle their cups, I suppose. And so, for three *Abstracts*, I have said hardly a word about the Hall of Fame—admirable restraint, I think, if I must say so myself. But it is a major subject of stat analysis, and one can't avoid it forever. The notion floats around that one can detect patterns among the random selections of the various committees, and in that way discern some sort of general standards for Hall of Fame selection. What I propose to do here is to try to get those standards down on paper, to make them add, and in that way to bring some hard evidence out about what it is that will make a record stand out when the memory of the man has cooled.

Understand, I am not in the least talking about what Hall of Fame standards *should be*. I am talking about what they *are*. De Facto standards, inferred from a study of who has made it and who hasn't. If we can build a prediction formula that will take the records of Enos Slaughter, Chick Hafey, Gil Hodges, and Ralph Kiner and tell us that from that group Hafey and Kiner are the Hall of Famers, then we will have, it seems to me, that much better of an understanding of what it takes to become a Hall of Famer. That understanding we can then apply to the records of contemporary players.

In some ways the system which results is far from being logical. The Hall of Fame prediction system (HOFPS) awards 8 points for each season that an outfielder hits .300, only 3 points for each season that he drives in 100 runs. As a statement of the relative value of hitting .300 and driving in 100 runs, this is asinine. But it is also what works. The fact is that Indian Bob Johnson, Del Ennis, Bob Elliott, and Gil Hodges, who have around thirty 100-RBI seasons among them, are *not* in the Hall of Fame, while a bunch of singles hitters who have had about the same number of .320 seasons are.

So then, the prediction system. Actually, I have two prediction systems, one for pitchers, one for outfielders. Both require 100 points. There are no partial or percentage qualifications; 100 points and you're in, 99 and you're out. I don't have anything for infielders or catchers; somebody who has the time is encouraged to try to develop something. Anyway, here's what I have:

Pitchers
1. Count 3 points for each season of fifteen or more wins.
2. Count 10 points for each season of twenty wins.
   a. 20–20 seasons (that is, seasons with both twenty wins and twenty losses) should be counted as fifteen-victory seasons.

b. Seasons are not to be counted in more than one win category—that is, twenty-victory seasons are not to be double-counted with the fifteen-victory seasons, nor thirty-victory seasons as also twenty-victory seasons.

3. Count thirty-win seasons at 1 point per win recorded.

4. Career wins are not counted before 150. After 150, count 1 point per three wins until 235. For example, count 1 point for 153–155 career wins, 11 points of 183–185. Count 1 point for each win above 235.

5. Count 2 points for each World Series *start*.

6. Count 3 points for each World Series *win*.

   a. Total points awarded for World Series performance are not to exceed 30.

7. Count 5 points for each season leading the league in ERA.

8. Count 5 points for each season leading the league in strikeouts.

9. Count 1 point for each .010 the pitcher's career won-lost percentage is above .500.

There are thirty-six pitchers from this century (not counting the Negro Leagues) who are in the Hall of Fame. There are thirty-five pitchers from this century who would be predicted to be in the Hall of Fame. There are thirty-three pitchers who are on both lists, thus the HOFPS makes three or five errors, depending on how you figure it. The two pitchers who are not in although they have 100 qualification points are Carl Mays, who has been informally blacklisted because he threw the pitch that killed Ray Chapman, and Hal Newhouser, whose records are (rightfully) discounted because they were posted with the aid of a war.

The three pitchers who are in although they lack 100 qualification points are Addie Joss, Pop Haines, and Rube Marquard, who are in for reasons that I will be kind enough not to speculate on. I will add that not only do these pitchers not have 100 points, they're not close, either. These, unless I missed somebody, are the only five pitchers from this century for whom the system fails to make a correct In/Out decision.

Obviously, the first set of numbers that I tried did not draw that line there. At a glance it is not really obvious why Rube Waddell (184–141) is in the Hall of Fame but Lon Warneke (193–121) is not, or why Jack Chesbro (199–127) is in but Ed Reulbach (185–104) is not. Among the most pronounced patterns in the taste of Hall of Fame voters is that they are much impressed by pitchers who were starters on championship teams, thus the points awarded for World Series performance (the same is true among other players.) But the key element in most cases is twenty-victory seasons. Well, you've got a choice: you can get in by winning twenty games every year, or you can get there by winning 235 or more total.

Among active pitchers and recently retired pitchers, totals of note include:

Pitcher (W–L)	Points Under Rule Number:									Total	In/Out
	1	2	3	4	5	6	7	8	9		
Gomez (189–102)	9	40	0	13	14	16	10	15	14	131	In
Lemon (207–128)	6	70	0	19	8	6	0	5	11	125	In
Chesbro (199–127)	6	40	41	14*	0	0	0	0	11	112	In
Rixey (266–251)	12	40	41	59	0	0	0	0	1	112	In
Walsh (194–130)	9	30	39	14	4	6	10	10	9	131	In
Dean (150–83)	3	30	30	0	8	6	0	20	14	111	In
Hoyt (237–182)	8	20	0	30	22	8	5	0	6	109	In
Pennock (241–162)	18	20	0	34	10	15	0	0	9	106	In
Waddell (184–141)	12	30	0	12*	0	0	10	35	6	105	In
Lyons (260–230)	9	30	9	55	0	0	5	0	3	102	In
Bender (210–128)	18	20	0	20	20	10	0	0	12	100	In
Derringer (223–212)	12	40	0	24	14	6	0	0	1	97	Out
Reynolds (182–107)	18	10	0	10	18	12	5	10	13	96	Out
Drysdale (209–166)	15	20	0	19	12	9	0	15	5	95	Out
Bridges (194–138)	6	30	0	14	10	12	0	10	8	94	Out
Shawkey (198–150)	12	40	0	16	10	3	5	0	6	92	Out
Coombs (158–110)	0	20	30	2	12	15	0	0	9	88	Out
Walters (198–160)	12	30	0	16	6	6	10	5	5	90	Out
Cicotte (210–148)	9	30	0	20	10	6	5	0	8	88	Out
Warneke (193–121)	15	30	0	14	6	6	5	0	11	87	Out
Ferrell (193–128)	3	60	0	14	0	0	0	0	10	87	Out
Bunning (224–184)	21	10	0	24	0	0	0	15	4	84	Out
Burdette (203–144)	18	20	0	17	12	12	5	0	8	92	Out
Reulbach (185–104)	12	30	0	11	10	6	0	0	14	83	Out

But also:

	1	2	3	4	5	6	7	8	9	Total	In/Out
Mays (208–126)	6	50	0	19	14	9	0	0	12	110	Out
Newhouser (207–150)	9	40	0	19	6	6	10	10	8	108	Out
Marquard (204–179)	6	30	0	18	16	6	0	5	3	84	In
Haines (210–158)	5	30	0	20	8	9	0	0	7	79	In
Joss (160–97)	6	40	0	3	0	0	10	0	12	71	In

*Does not include pre-1900 accomplishments.

It is appropriate for those two to tie for the top spot. I was going to apologize for Luis Tiant's being shown as still needing a couple of points (6 wins would do it), because I thought he was an obvious in, but then I read that Bill Mead

| Pitcher (W–L) | Points Under Rule Number: | | | | | | | | | Total |
	1	2	3	4	5	6	7	8	9	
Seaver	18	50	0	28	8	3	25	15	13	160
Palmer	6	80	0	25	16	9	10	0	14	160
Gibson	15	50	0	44	18	12	5	5	9	158
Perry	24	50	0	72	0	0	0	0	6	152
Jenkins	9	70	0	40	0	0	0	5	7	131
Marichal	9	60	0	36	2	0	5	0	13	129
Hunter	6	50	0	24	18	15	5	0	7	125
Kaat	15	30	0	57	6	3	0	0	4	115
Carlton	15	40	0	25	2	0	5	10	8	105
Tiant	6	40	0	22	6	6	10	0	8	98
Lolich	18	20	0	22	6	9	0	5	3	83
Sutton	24	10	0	22	12	6	0	0	6	80
Niekro, P.	21	20	0	22	0	0	5	5	3	76
Ryan	12	20	0	5	0	0	0	35	1	73
Blue	9	30	0	2	10	0	5	0	8	64
Guidry	6	10	0	0	4	6	10	0	25	61
John	6	20	0	14	6	3	0	0	7	56
Richard	9	10	0	0	0	0	5	10	9	43

of SABR wrote an article in which he rated Tiant as a dark horse. I don't know how in the world he figured that. The contrast between his seat-of-the-pants analysis and the prediction formula is interesting; he has Ferguson Jenkins, with seven twenty-victory seasons and 247 career wins, in the same class with Mickey Lolich, in "more than even chance." Jenkins may have to wait a few years, like Robin Roberts, but he will obviously go, while Lolich is very unlikely to make it unless Hall of Fame standards drop markedly.

It should be noted that while Vida Blue (64 points) and Ron Guidry (61 points) look about even, this is not really true. Twenty-five of Guidry's points are "soft" points, which could be lost unless he is able to maintain a .756 lifetime won-lost percentage, which no one ever has. If he goes 12–12 in 1980, he will end the year with 55 points, six less than he has now. Blue, on the other hand, has crossed the magic "150" line above which career victory totals begin to help you, so if he goes 12–12 he will wind up the year with 67 points. If both were to go 21–10 and lead their leagues in ERA, Guidry would advance to 74 points, but Blue would leap to 87.

The system for outfielders delivers about the same degree of accuracy. Somehow I have misplaced my count of the number of outfielders from this century who are in the Hall of Fame, but it is about the same, somewhere around thirty. The system for outfielders makes, again, five errors. One of those, on Shoeless Joe Jackson, has nothing to do with statistics. Another, Richie Ashburn, probably will be changed within a few years; Ashburn is fully qualified and will eventually go. Two other players are figured as qualified but not in; both of them, interestingly enough, are players with impressive records, but records which are completely dwarfed by the company they keep. The names are Bobby Veach and Bob Meusel. One cannot think of Veach and Meusel without thinking about Crawford and Cobb and Ruth and Gehrig, and when you think about records like that, Veach and Meusel don't look so good. But they are, in fact, better than the records of many Hall of Famers. The fifth error is Harry Hooper, in for his defensive reputation, but far from being qualified as a hitter. And, again, I may have missed somebody:

Outfielders

1. Award 8 points for each season of hitting .300, 100 or more games, up to a limit of 60 points.
2. Award 15 points if the player has a lifetime batting average of .315 or better in 1,000 games.
3. Award 3 points per 100-RBI season.
4. Award 8 points per 200-hit season.
5. a. Award 4 points for each season leading the league in stolen bases.
   b. Award 5 points for each season leading in RBIs.
   c. Award 8 for leading in home runs.
   d. Award 12 for leading in batting.
6. Count 1 point per World Series Game Played, up to a limit of eighteen.
7. Add 10 points if the player has 3,000 career hits.
8. Add 10 points if the player has 400 career home runs.

There are 100 more players who just miss, but that's enough. I will leave the computation of the errors and the active outfielders for your idle moments, or mine. Perhaps in future *Abstracts* a list of the active players who are charting a Hall of Fame progression will be a regular feature. That, however, would require frequent updating of the system so as to continue to minimize errors. I have no idea how well the outfielder's system would adapt to other positions; I would guess very well at first and fairly well at third and second, but not very well at short and catcher. I haven't tried it.

Finally, I will offer my opinion with regard to the recurrent proposal that fixed statistical guidelines for Hall of Fame selection should be established. Explicit criteria, it is argued, would do two things: it would end the erosion

Player	Points awarded under rule number:											Total	In/Out
	1	2	3	4	5a	5b	5c	5d	6	7	8		
Wheat	60	15	6	24	0	0	0	12	12	0	0	129	In
Wilson	40	0	18	8	0	10	32	0	12	0	0	120	In
Snider	56	0	18	0	0	5	8	0	18	0	10	115	In
Manush	60	0	6	32	0	0	0	12	5	0	0	115	In
Combs	56	15	0	24	0	0	0	0	18	0	0	113	In
Waner, L.	60	15	0	32	0	0	0	0	4	0	0	111	In
Averill	60	15	15	16	0	0	0	0	3	0	0	109	In
Youngs	56	15	3	16	0	0	0	0	18	0	0	108	In
Roush	60	15	0	0	0	0	0	24	8	0	0	107	In
Kaline	60	0	9	8	0	0	0	12	7	10	0	106	In
Kiner	24	0	18	0	0	5	56	0	0	0	0	103	In
Carey	48	0	0	8	40	0	0	0	7	0	0	103	In
Hafey	48	15	9	0	0	0	0	12	18	0	0	102	In
Meusel, I.	48	0	12	16	0	5	0	0	18	0	0	99	Out
Walker, D.	60	0	6	0	0	0	8	12	12	0	0	98	Out
Slaughter	60	0	9	0	0	0	8	0	18	0	0	95	Out
Williams, K.	60	15	6	0	0	5	8	0	0	0	0	94	Out
Cramer	60	0	0	24	0	0	0	0	9	0	0	93	Out
Kuenn	60	0	0	16	0	0	0	12	4	0	0	92	Out

of standards that has already brought into the Hall too many second-rate stars, and it would end the "injustices" of players like Freddie Lindstrom and Pop Haines being inducted while obviously better players wait outside.

In my opinion, this is not the way. Justice? One cannot do an injustice to a bunch of numbers. One can deal unfairly with a man, with a memory perhaps, but not with lines of statistics. Such injustices as there are here have nothing to do with statistics, and will not be prevented by establishing statistical reference points.

The declining quality of Hall of Fame inductees, not to mention the fact that an increasing percentage of them are dead and forgotten, is caused by two things: 1) the system of multiple review boards, in which one takes up again the players who have already been passed over by the others, creates an inevitable downward spiral, as the decisions of the latter reflect back on the standards of the former. 2) More importantly, fair judgments are prevented by favoritism, by passions, by PR campaigns and personal loyalties—all of the things which create the vortex of controversy which is both the strength and the liability of the institution. So long as people carry every grand and petty cause that they stumble over to bang on the door of Cooperstown, that door will continue to be battered. If you would save the institution, then consider in your judgments not only what is good for your favorite player, but what is good for the Hall itself.

But there is an even better reason not to have statistical standards, which is that there is no way in the world to evolve a set of standards which is as comprehensive, as complex, as fair, or as open to improvement as is human judgment. I have spent all of my life, sad as it may sound, learning to understand baseball records. If I couldn't make up standards which are fair and comprehensive, who could? And I don't feel that I could. There are simply too many things in the game of baseball which are not measured, are poorly measured, are still in the process of being measured. You could state that Mark Belanger over his career has won as many games by his glove as Joe DiMaggio did by his bat, and while we might not agree, there is no way in hell that anybody could prove you wrong. Statistical analysis is simply one more way of understanding the game of baseball. It is not our place to stand in judgment of the others.

The Boys of Summer is a warm, evocative book that has stood the test of time. Although some of the Brooklyn Dodgers have not—"the boys of summer in their ruin," from Dylan Thomas's verse—Carl Erskine assuredly has. The Dodgers of our boyhood grew old, a disquieting fact; better, we may have thought, to preserve them in our memories as they were, frozen in a baseball-card pose, so that we too might stay young forever. Roger Kahn showed us that heroes grown frail, retired from the fray, remain men . . . and in other, greater arenas, still heroes.

ROGER KAHN

Carl and Jimmy

The Erskines' den extends square and compact from the living room. The walls are busy with plaques and books. "Would you like to drink the present you brought?" Carl asked. It was after dinner. He went to a cabinet under a bookcase and produced three scrapbooks, bound in brown tooled leather. "Some old fellow kept these. We didn't know anything about them until I came back here to live.

"I was looking beyond baseball, beyond a lot of things, and I enrolled in Anderson College as a thirty-two-year-old freshman." Erskine tells stories with a sense of detail. "All right," he said. "Monday morning. Eight-o'clock class. The start of freshman English. I get to the building. I got these gray hairs. It's two minutes to eight when I walk in, a little scared. All of a sudden the room gets quiet." Erskine grinned. "They thought I was the professor.

"I got in about sixty-five credits before Dad died and for a lot of reasons I had to quit. Heck, I wasn't only a thirty-two-year-old freshman. I became a thirty-six-year-old dropout."

Betty went for a Coke and a drink, and the ceremony of scrapbooks began. "Here's one of yours," Erskine said. "How does it read?" He had opened to the World Series strikeout story:

A crowd of 35,270 fans, largest ever to squeeze and elbow its way into Ebbets Field for a series contest, came to see a game the Dodgers had to win. They saw much more. They saw a game of tension, inescapable and mounting tension, a game that offered one climax after another, each more grinding than the one before, a game that will be remembered with the finest.

"John Mize," Erskine said, "was some hitter. But he had a pretty good mouth, too. All afternoon I could hear him yelling at the Yankee hitters. 'What are you doing, being suckers for a miserable bush curve?' Then he's pinch-hitting in the ninth and I get two strikes. Wham. John Mize's becomes the strikeout that breaks the record."

"On a miserable bush curve?"

"A sweet out."

"Here's the Scotch," Betty said. "And a Coke for you, Carl."

"But I wasn't out of it," Erskine said. He was sitting forward on a plush chair, his face furrowed with thought. "After Mize, I had to pitch to Irv Noren. I walked him. All right. Now here comes Joe Collins. I forget the record. All I can think is that the right-field wall is 297 feet away and Collins is a strong left-handed hitter who has struck out four times. Baseball is that way. One swing of the bat. He hits the homer. He scores two runs. He goes from goat to hero. He wins it all. Collins had the power and I'm thinking, 'Oh brother, he can turn this whole thing around for himself.'

"That's in my head. What I didn't know is over on the Yankee bench Mize and the others have been kidding Collins. They tell him the World Series goat record is five strikeouts. One more and his name goes into the book forever.

"He goes to the plate entirely defensive. He's choking up six inches on the bat. He's using it like a fly swatter.

"I get two strikes on him real fast. Still, I have this fear of the short porch in right. The last pitch I throw is a curve and it's a dandy. It snaps off and it's about ankle-high. So help me, he swings straight down. He beats it into the ground and gets enough of the ball to nub it back to me. I get my record. Think of the two minds. It ends with me scared to death of the long ball and Collins scared to death of striking out. He doesn't get to hit the long ball and I don't get to strike him out." Erskine grinned and refilled our glasses.

"A great thing about our family comes ten years later. It's 1963. Sandy Koufax goes out and strikes out fifteen Yankees. We're living here then, but we see it on television. And one of the boys, looking real blue, says, 'Don't feel sad, Dad. You still hold the record for *right-handers*.'

"All of the kids give pleasure, in different ways, the older boys, Susan, Jimmy. It's hard for some to understand that Jimmy is fun. Heck, we had an Olympics for all the retarded kids of Madison County and Jimmy won a big event."

"What event was that, Carl?"

"Ballbounce. He bounced a basketball twenty-one times."

Erskine sipped at his Coke. "You wonder, of course. You look for guilt. When was he conceived? Was somebody overtired? Did you really want him? A few months along in pregnancy Betty got a virus and ran 103. Did that affect Jim? Whose fault is it? We've talked to scientists and doctors and you know what mongolism is? A kind of genetic accident. There's an extra chromosome there that can come from mother or father and no one has any idea why, except that illness or being tired doesn't seem to have anything to do with it. You establish that, a man and his wife, and go on from there. You're not alone. Jimmy isn't alone. There are three thousand retarded children just here in Madison County, and when we came back to live here, there wasn't any place for them. I'm on a committee. We've set up schools. We're making beginnings."

Easy in his den, sitting against his louvered bookcases, the son of the Middle Border let his mind range. "The Erskines are Scots. It would have been my

great-great-great-grandfather who settled in Virginia, and then moved on to Boone County, Indiana. That's sixty miles west. I remembered my Scottish background once in the Ebbets Field clubhouse when a lady wrote me a letter. She lived in Scotland and had seen my picture in a magazine. I must be Scottish and a relative of hers. I looked just like her Uncle Willie."

"Willie Erskine?"

"Or something."

"How do Presbyterian Scots become Indiana Baptists?"

"Easy. The Baptists take anybody."

He got up and brought in a dish of nuts and picked up his story. "When my father was very small—Dad, if he were living, would be eighty-six years old—near the end of the nineteenth century, the Erskines left Boone County and moved here. Anderson was a center of glass-blowing, and there was a natural-gas industry. My family had swampy farmland in Boone County they'd gotten for twenty-five cents an acre. Now it's been drained, and it's really valuable. But there are Scots and there are Scots. My family sold the land for twenty-six cents an acre, or maybe twenty-four.

"The auto industry came to Anderson long ago and General Motors tied in with an electrical company called Remy Brothers. And that was Delco Remy, spark plugs and electrical systems. There are seventeen local plants. There's no one who's been here any time who hasn't worked part of his life—a year, a month, a week—for Delco Remy.

"My Dad was real interested in baseball, and I guess I had the most promise of his three boys. At night at the side of the house, there'd be four or five congregated for catch. It got to be quite a thing for these older people to play burnout with me. You know. Step closer and closer, keep throwing harder and harder. I'd hang in and end up with a bruised hand. At nine, I was pitching from sixty feet.

"It was Dad who showed me a curve. First he taught what *he* had: the old barnyard roundhouse. You threw it sidearm and it broke flat. No break at all, except sideways. When I was eleven, Dad bought a book on pitching. We're in the living room. Dad has the pitching book in his left hand, held open with a thumb, and he has a baseball in his right hand. He's reading, and very engrossed. The arm is carried back. The wrist is cocked. At this position you come forward with a snap and a spin of the fingers. He goes through the motion, staring at the book. He releases the baseball. The ball goes through the doorway to the dining room and into a big china cupboard with a glass front. It breaks the glass. It breaks the dishes. We stand there. Dishes keep falling out. My mother comes in." Erskine's eyebrows rose in merriment. "Maybe a year afterward my father said that was the best break he ever got on a curve."

It was the sort of boyhood Booth Tarkington memorialized with a romantic

Saturday Evening Post glow, but Erskine is an existential man. "I guess there wasn't any money," he said. "I needed a mastoid operation and for a long time I'd keep bringing laundry to the doctor's house. My mother was paying the surgeon by taking in his wash.

"Around 1930 there was a lynching thirty miles north in a town called Marion. The day after it happened, Dad drove me up and showed me where it was. Two Negroes had been taken out of the jail and hung in the jailyard. The bark was skinned off the tree where they were hung. I can still see that naked branch. There had been a scramble. People had made off with things as souvenirs. But there was a piece of rope. I saw a lynching rope before I was ten." His soft voice carried controlled horror.

"One Negro boy grew up in my neighborhood, Johnny Wilson. We played grade-school basketball together; he made all-state in high school and went on to the Globetrotters. He's a high-school coach today. Jumpin' Johnny Wilson ate maybe as many meals at my home as he did in his own. With a background like that, the Robinson experience simply was no problem. It was really beautiful in a way.

"Somewhere Jack said he appreciated help from some white teammates in establishing himself, but to me it goes the opposite. It's 1948. The Dodgers want me from Fort Worth. I'm twenty-one and scared. I don't know anybody on the big club. I cut their names from the newspapers when I was a kid. The team is in Pittsburgh. I walk into the Forbes Field dressing room carrying my duffel bag. Just inside the door Jackie Robinson comes over, sticks out his hand, and says, 'After I hit against you in spring training, I knew you'd be up here. I didn't know when, but I knew it would happen. Welcome.' "

Erskine's face lit. "Man," he said, "I'd have been grateful if anyone had said 'Hello.' And to get this not from just *any* ballplayer but from Jackie Robinson. I pitched that day and won in relief.

"Whenever Jack came to the mound, he always gave me the feeling he knew I could do the job. He just wanted to reassure me. Whatever words he used, the effect was: *There's no question about it. We know you can do it. Here's the ball. Get it done.* Times when I wasn't sure I could do it myself, he seemed to be.

"Now here's what bothers me. He wins a game. We go to the next town. We're all on the train, a team. But leaving the station, he doesn't ride on the team bus. He has to go off by himself. He can't stay in the same hotel. But I didn't do anything about it. Why? Why didn't I say, 'Something's wrong here. I'm not going to let this happen. Wherever he's going, I'm going with him.'

"I never did. I sat like everybody else, and I thought, 'Good. He's getting a chance to play major-league ball. Isn't that great?' And that's as far as I was at that time.

"Now I hear people putting him down. Black people. To Stokely Carmichael and Rap Brown, he's a period piece. When I hear that, I feel sorry for *them*. Carmichael and Brown can never understand what Robinson did. How hard it was. What a great victory.

"But he can understand them. He was a young black man once, and mad and hurt. He knows *their* feeling, and their ignorance must hurt him more."

In the little Indiana den, it is the old story of the father and the son, a startling sunburst over autumn haze, expressed by a father whose own son is robbed of expression.

Anderson, Indiana, site of the annual Church of God Camp Meeting, thirty thousand strong gathered within and about Anderson College's Styrofoam-domed amphitheater, dubbed "The Turtle" by undergraduates, is a community that takes pride in its parks. "There are thirty-eight in all," said Carl Erskine, the morning go-getter. He had risen early, driven Jimmy to school at the Methodist church on Jackson Street, phoned the insurance brokerage in which he is a partner, and stopped off at the First National Bank of Anderson, of which he is vice-president.

"I thought I'd show you a little of the town," he said at 10:30. "Then we can pick up Jimmy after class and the three of us can go to the Y." We crossed Dwight D. Eisenhower Memorial Bridge, fording the White River, and leading downtown. The old masonry structures of Anderson are yielding prominence. "That new one with the glass front is the bank. Next to it is the San Francisco Restaurant. This isn't San Francisco, or New York, but it isn't all that sleepy either. Now we'll head out toward the college."

A large library, donated by Charles E. Wilson of General Motors, stands near the Turtle. "I do a little radio sports show from here once a week, and I coach baseball," Erskine said.

"How do you move around?"

"You mean the limp? It's more embarrassing than anything else. When I was through with ball, I began to develop pains in my left hip, the hip you land on when you throw right-handed. The pains got worse and worse. My arm hurt every day for ten years, but *this* was agony. Finally I went to a local man, and he said I'd damaged a bone in the socket and the thing to do was to ease up. No running. No handball. I love handball. All right, I'm thirty-nine years and through, because the kicker is that he tells me if I do ease up, I only put off the wheelchair a few years. Whatever, a wheelchair is just ahead.

"When I was pitching and I had the constant arm pain, I went to Johns Hopkins and a famous surgeon said something was gone for good and I should pitch sidearm. But the only way I could get velocity and a good break was to come straight over. Saying pitch sidearm was really telling me don't pitch. I kept pitching overhand and it kept hurting, but I got a dozen years in the big leagues.

"This wasn't pitching. This was walking. I flew to the Mayo Clinic, and one of the surgeons there had worked out a procedure for rotating the bone in the hip socket. He said I could keep the pain and look all right. Or he could operate and stop the pain and leave me a limp." Erskine smiled as an irony stirred. "All the time I had bad pain, nobody knew. Now that I have the limp people keep coming up and asking if my leg hurts. With that limp they figure it must hurt bad and"—a thin, swift smile—"it's painless."

As we reached the Jackson Street Methodist church, boys and girls straggled out a doorway. The class for retarded children was letting out. One boy's head shook from side to side, flapping straight straw hair. A girl of eleven squinted through thick glasses. Someone was snorting. Jimmy Erskine saw his father and broke from the flagstone walk.

"Hello, Jim. Want to go swimming? Want to swim?"

"Ihmin," Jimmy Erskine said. "Ihmin." He jumped up and down with excitement.

A few blocks off, at the YMCA, Erskine put on gym clothes and dressed Jimmy. Carl and I shot baskets for twenty minutes. Erskine took one-hand set shots, as Indiana schoolboys did in 1945. Jimmy found a ball and bounced it. He bounced it three times, four times, five times. When he bounced it longer, he shouted with joy. Carl played a round of handball, his limp suddenly more noticeable. Jimmy sat next to me watching. "Hosh-uh," he said, and climbed into my lap. "Ihmin, Hosh-uh. Ihmin."

There were only three of us in the Y pool, warm, green, and redolent of chlorine. Carl swam with a smooth crawl. Jimmy splashed about, making little cries. "Swim, Jimmy," Carl said. "Show how you can swim."

Jim fell onto his stomach, thrashed his arms and floated for three strokes. Then he jerked over to his back and showed a wide grin.

"Attaboy, Jim."

"Hosh-uh," Jimmy said.

"Watch him jump in," Carl said. "Jump, Jim. Show us how you can jump into the water."

The little boy hurried to a ladder. His foot slipped at the lowest rung. Carl put a strong hand to Jim's right buttock and pushed. Jim stood by the side of the pool, took two deep breaths and jumped into a kind of dive. He struck the water hard, chest first.

"Good goin', Jim," Carl said.

Another grin split Jimmy Erskine's face. Praise delights him. He waded toward the ladder and, climbing for a second time, held a support with his left hand. Then to show his father that he knew how to learn, he placed his right hand on his own buttock. What Jimmy Erskine had learned, from his father's boost, was that one leaves a pool with a hand placed on a buttock.

After leisurely dinner at the San Francisco Restaurant, Carl asked, back in his small, warm den, if I remembered the World Series of 1952. The sun of October flooded my memory and I saw again the blue crystal sky and the three-colored playing field and shrill, excited people thronging to Yankee Stadium, and my father's walk, lurching with expectancy.

"I had first-class stuff," Erskine said. "Not much pain. The curve is sharp. We go into the fifth inning ahead four runs. Do you happen to remember the date? It was October 5. That was my fifth wedding anniversary. My control slips. A walk. Some hits. Mize rips one. I'm behind, 5–4. And here comes Dressen.

"I'm thinking, 'Oh, no. I got good stuff.' I look at Dressen coming closer and I think. The numbers are against me. October fifth. My *fifth* wedding anniversary. The *fifth* inning. I've given the Yankees *five* runs. Five must be my unlucky number.

"Charlie says to give him the ball. You weren't allowed to talk when he came out. He was afraid you might argue him into leaving you in, and you had to wait on the mound for the next pitcher, so's you could wish him good luck. Now Charlie has the ball. I'm through. The fives have done me in. Suddenly Dressen says, 'Isn't this your anniversary? Are you gonna take Betty out and celebrate tonight?'

"I can't believe it. There's seventy thousand people watching, as many as in all Anderson now, and he's asking what I'm doing that night. I tell him yes, I was planning to take Betty someplace quiet.

" 'Well,' Dressen says, 'then see if you can get this game over before it gets dark.' He hands me back the ball. I get the next nineteen in a row. We win in eleven. I took Betty out to dinner and we celebrated the first Series game I ever won."

"What do you think," I said, "your life would have been if you hadn't been a pitcher?"

"I don't know. It's like asking what my life would be without Jimmy. Poorer. Different. Who knows how?"

. . .Wooden shutters stand open behind Erskine's chair. Memories have poured, but night claws at the window. "Old Campy," Erskine says. Nine hundred miles away, Roy Campanella is sitting in a motorized wheelchair, with shriveled arms and withered stumps for legs.

"The worst thing I can imagine is what happened to Campy," Erskine said. He gazed at the ceiling. "Real intimacy develops between catcher and pitcher.

You work 120 pitches together every few days, after a while you think like one man.

"All right. Campy is hurt over the winter of 1957–58. That's the same winter the team moves to California. We start out playing in a football field, the Coliseum, with left real close, a China wall. You know how Campy used to hit high flies to left; as soon as I see the China wall, I think, 'Son of a buck, if Campy was well, he'd break Ruth's record, popping flies over that dinky screen.'

"We start badly. We get to Philadelphia. I'm supposed to pitch. It rains. Campy was born in Philadelphia. Whatever, I start thinking about him with his broken spine and I don't tell anybody anything, but I go to the station in the rain and take a train to New York. I find a cab and go to University Hospital. They say I can't see him. I persist. At last, okay.

"Now I'm the first person not family to visit, the first man who's come from the team.

"I get to his room. I'm still thinking of the short fence and Ruth's record. I open the door and there's a shrunken body strapped in a frame. I stand a long time staring. He looks back. He doesn't see just me. He sees the team. He starts to cry. I cry myself. He cries for ten minutes, but he's the one who recovers first. 'Ersk,' Campy says, 'you're player representative. Get better major medical for the guys. This cost me. Eight thousand dollars for just the first two days.'

"I say, 'Sure, Campy.'

" 'Ersk,' he says, 'you know what I'm going to do tomorrow? I'm working with weights and I'm going to lift five pounds.'

"I go there thinking of him breaking Babe Ruth's record, he's thinking of lifting five pounds. But he's enthusiastic. He starts to sound like the old Campy. He wants to know when I'm going to pitch. He's got some kind of setup where they turn the frame and he can watch TV. I'm going the next day in Philly if it doesn't rain, and he gets real excited. They'll be televising that one back to New York. 'I'll be watching, Ersk,' he says. 'Make it a good one.'

"I get out of there. By this time I'm pitchin' with a broken arm, but this one I got to win. I got to win it—I don't care if it sounds like a corny movie—for Roy.

"The next day I go out with my broken wing. I pitch a no-hitter for five innings. I end up with a two-hitter. I win it for Campy. That was the last complete game I ever pitched in the major leagues.

"I could look back and say I should have pitched a few more years. My arm doesn't hurt now. The game looks easy on television. But in 1959 I walked into the office of Buzzy Bavasi and told him I'd had enough. I was thirty-two years old and my arm was 110. It ached every day. Some of the time I could barely reach the plate. Buzzy said he'd put me on the voluntary retired list, and he went out to get his secretary to draw up the papers.

"I thought, *This is it.*' And all of a sudden in Buzzy's office in Los Angeles I'm seeing myself in the Kenmore Hotel room with Branch Rickey thirteen years before. I can see it clear as my hand. I can see my Navy bell-bottoms. I see Rickey puffing smoke. I see the way Dad looked. I hear the sound of Rickey's voice. That's the beginning. And here, I think, in Buzzy's office is the end.

"I say to myself, '*Wait!* I don't want this to end. Shouldn't I go for one more start?' And then I say, 'No. I don't want one more start. I've given myself every opportunity. At thirty-two, after 335 games, I'm worn-out.'

"I say to myself, 'Remember the way you feel. Burn this in your mind. *Strong!* Five years from now when you're back in Indiana and you start saying, the way all old ballplayers start saying, I could play another year, conjure up this feeling you have now.' "

"Have you had to do that, Carl?" I said.

"Only about five hundred times."

Erskine turned out the lights. He went upstairs and looked into Jimmy's room. The little boy breathed noisily in sleep.

No. And there never was one like John Kieran, either. He began as a sportswriter with the *New York Times* in 1916 and in 1927 inaugurated that paper's first signed column, "Sports of the Times," later home to Arthur Daley and Red Smith. In 1938 he became an electronic "personality" as a panelist on the popular *Information Please* radio program. By the mid-1940s his interests had turned from bats and balls to birds and flowers; not long thereafter his *Natural History of New York City* (1953) won for him the prestigious Burroughs Medal. This column appeared the day after Ruth hit his sixtieth.

JOHN KIERAN

Was There Ever a Guy Like Ruth?

New York, Oct. 2, 1927—Some four months ago or more there was printed in this column a versified query: "Was there ever a guy like Ruth?" From time to time Yankee rooters suggested the reprinting of the query, and now that Babe Ruth has answered it, a recital of the old question may be in order. Here it is:

A Query.

You may sing your song of the good old days till the phantom cows come
    home;
You may dig up glorious deeds of yore from many a dusty tome;
You may rise to tell of Rube Waddell and the way he buzzed them through,
And top it all with the great fastball that Rusie's rooters knew.
You may rant of Brouthers, Keefe, and Ward and half a dozen more;
You may quote by rote from the record book in a way that I deplore;
You may rave, I say, till the break of day, but the truth remains the truth:
From "One Old Cat" to the last "At Bat," was there ever a guy like Ruth?
He can start and go, he can catch and throw, he can field with the very
    best.

He's the Prince of Ash and the King of Crash, and that's not an idle jest.
He can hit that ball o'er the garden wall, high up and far away,
Beyond the aftermost picket lines where the fleet-foot fielders stray.
He's the Bogey Man of the pitching clan and he clubs 'em soon and late;
He has manned his guns and hit home runs from here to the Golden
    Gate;
With vim and verve he has walloped the curve from Texas to Duluth,
Which is no small task, and I beg to ask: Was there ever a guy like Ruth?

As a matter of fact, there was never even a good imitation of the Playboy of Baseball. What this big, good-natured, uproarious lad has done is little short of a miracle of sport. There is a common axiom: They never come back. But Babe Ruth came back twice. Just like him. He would.

It takes quite a bit of remembering to recall that the great home run hitter was once the best left-handed pitcher in baseball. When he was a member of the Boston Red Sox team, he set a record of pitching twenty-nine scoreless innings in World Series competition.

Then he started to slip and everybody said the usual thing: "Good-bye Forever!" (copyright by Tosti).

Babe gathered in all the "Good-byes" and said: "Hello, everybody! I'm a heavy-hitting outfielder."

And he was. He set a league record of twenty-nine home runs in 1919 and then he came to New York and took the cover off the siege gun.

That was Ruth's first comeback. A mild one. Others had done that, and the Babe yearned to be distinguished even from a chosen few. He wanted to be the One and Only. He nearly knocked the American League apart with fifty-four home runs in 1920, and in 1921 he set the record at fifty-nine circuit clouts for the season.

"It will stay there forever," prophesied the conservatives.

For five years the record was safe enough. In his bland and childlike way the Babe fell afoul of disciplinary and dietary laws, with the result that he was barred from the diamond for lengthy stretches on orders from Judge Landis, Miller Huggins, and the Ruth family physician.

He set the record of fifty-nine home runs when he was twenty-seven years old. In the following years he failed to come within hailing distance of his high-water mark, and once again everybody said: "Good-bye Forever!" (copyright by Tosti).

The Babe's answer was, "Say au revoir, but not good-bye!" And G. Herman Ruth was as right as rain. It was "au revoir" for five seasons, and in the sixth season the big boy came back with a bang!

Supposedly "over the hill," slipping down the steps of Time, stumbling toward the discard, six years past his peak, Babe Ruth stepped out and hung up a new home run record at which all the sport world may stand and wonder. What Dempsey couldn't do with his fists, Ruth has done with his bat. He came back.

Put it in the book in letters of gold. It will be a long time before anyone else betters that home-run mark, and a still longer time before any aging athlete makes such a gallant and glorious charge over the comeback trail.

And in Conclusion.

You may rise and sing till the rafters ring that sad and sorrowful strain:
"They strive and fail—it's the old, old tale; they never come back again."
Yes, it's in the dope, when they hit the slope they're off for the shadowed
  vale,
But the great, big Bam with the circuit slam came back on the uphill
  trail;
Came back with cheers from the drifted years where the best of them go
  down;
Came back once more with a record score to wear a brighter crown.
My voice may be loud above the crowd and my words just a bit uncouth,
But I'll stand and shout till the last man's out: There was never a guy
  like Ruth!

This is the opening chapter to *Shoeless Joe*, the powerfully imagined, lyrical, thrilling first novel by a professor at the University of Calgary who each summer tours the United States in his beat-up Datsun, visiting ballparks. What explains the hold of Joe Jackson on the imaginations of those who never saw him play? Why do we continue to hear of groups petitioning to get Jackson off baseball's blacklist and into the Hall of Fame? Why, despite considerable evidence that he accepted money to do less than his best in the 1919 World Series, is he still regarded as baseball's amalgam of Candide, Sacco, and Vanzetti? Perhaps because he was illiterate, perhaps because he hit .375 to lead all batters in that Series *anyway*, perhaps because he was a rube in the den of city slickers. Beats me. If I had to make a case for one of the eight Black Sox, I'd make it for Buck Weaver.

W. P. KINSELLA

Shoeless Joe Jackson Comes to Iowa

My father said he saw him years later playing in a tenth-rate commercial league in a textile town in Carolina, wearing shoes and an assumed name.

"He'd put on fifty pounds and the spring was gone from his step in the outfield, but he could still hit. Oh, how that man could hit. No one has ever been able to hit like Shoeless Joe."

Three years ago at dusk on a spring evening, when the sky was a robin's-egg blue and the wind as soft as a day-old chick, I was sitting on the verandah of my farm home in eastern Iowa when a voice very clearly said to me, "If you build it, he will come."

The voice was that of a ballpark announcer. As he spoke, I instantly envisioned the finished product I knew I was being asked to conceive. I could see the dark, squarish speakers, like ancient sailors' hats, attached to aluminum-painted light standards that glowed down into a baseball field, my present position being directly behind home plate.

In reality, all anyone else could see out there in front of me was a tattered lawn of mostly dandelions and quack grass that petered out at the edge of a cornfield perhaps fifty yards from the house.

Anyone else was my wife Annie, my daughter Karin, a corn-colored collie named Carmeletia Pope, and a cinnamon and white guinea pig named Junior who ate spaghetti and sang each time the fridge door opened. Karin and the dog were not quite two years old.

"If you build it, he will come," the announcer repeated in scratchy Middle American, as if his voice had been recorded on an old 78-r.p.m. record.

A three-hour lecture or a 500-page guide book could not have given me clearer directions: Dimensions of ballparks jumped over and around me like fleas, cost figures for light standards and floodlights whirled around my head like the moths that dusted against the porch light above me.

That was all the instruction I ever received: two announcements and a vision of a baseball field. I sat on the verandah until the satiny dark was complete. A few curdly clouds striped the moon, and it became so silent I could hear my eyes blink.

Our house is one of those massive old farm homes, square as a biscuit box with a sagging verandah on three sides. The floor of the verandah slopes so that marbles, baseballs, tennis balls, and ball bearings all accumulate in a corner like a herd of cattle clustered with their backs to a storm. On the north verandah is a wooden porch swing where Annie and I sit on humid August nights, sip lemonade from teary glasses, and dream.

When I finally went to bed, and after Annie inched into my arms in that way she has, like a cat that you suddenly find sound asleep in your lap, I told her about the voice and I told her that I knew what it wanted me to do.

"Oh love," she said, "if it makes you happy you should do it," and she found my lips with hers. I shivered involuntarily as her tongue touched mine.

Annie: She has never once called me crazy. Just before I started the first landscape work, as I stood looking out at the lawn and the cornfield, wondering how it could look so different in daylight, considering the notion of accepting it all as a dream and abandoning it, Annie appeared at my side and her arm circled my waist. She leaned against me and looked up, cocking her head like one of the red squirrels that scamper along the power lines from the highway to the house. "Do it, love," she said as I looked down at her, that slip of a girl with hair the color of cayenne pepper and at least a million freckles on her face and arms, that girl who lives in blue jeans and T-shirts and at twenty-four could still pass for sixteen.

I thought back to when I first knew her. I came to Iowa to study. She was the child of my landlady. I heard her one afternoon outside my window as she told her girl friends. "When I grow up I'm going to marry . . ." and she named me. The others were going to be nurses, teachers, pilots, or movie stars, but Annie chose me as her occupation. Eight years later we were married. I chose willingly, lovingly, to stay in Iowa. Eventually I rented this farm, then bought it, operating it one inch from bankruptcy. I don't seem meant to farm, but I want to be close to this precious land, for Annie and me to be able to say, "This is ours."

Now I stand ready to cut into the cornfield, to chisel away a piece of our livelihood to use as dream currency, and Annie says, "Oh, love, if it makes you happy you should do it." I carry her words in the back of my mind, stored the way a maiden aunt might wrap a brooch, a remembrance of a long-lost love. I understand how hard that was for her to say and how it got harder as the project advanced. How she must have told her family not to ask me about the baseball field I was building, because they stared at me dumb-eyed, a row of silent, thickset peasants with red faces. Not an imagination among them except to forecast the wrath of God that will fall on the heads of pagans such as I.

"If you build it, he will come."

He, of course, was Shoeless Joe Jackson.

> Joseph Jefferson (Shoeless Joe) Jackson
> Born: Brandon Mills, South Carolina, July 16, 1887
> Died: Greenville, South Carolina, December 5, 1951

In April 1945, Ty Cobb picked Shoeless Joe as the best left fielder of all time. A famous sportswriter once called Joe's glove "the place where triples go to die." He never learned to read or write. He created legends with a bat and a glove.

Was it really a voice I heard? Or was it perhaps something inside me making a statement that I did not hear with my ears but with my heart? Why should I want to follow this command? But as I ask, I already know the answer. I count the loves in my life: Annie, Karin, Iowa, Baseball. The great god Baseball.

My birthstone is a diamond. When asked, I say my astrological sign is hit and run, which draws a lot of blank stares here in Iowa where 50,000 people go to see the University of Iowa Hawkeyes football team while 500 regulars, including me, watch the baseball team perform.

My father, I've been told, talked baseball statistics to my mother's belly while waiting for me to be born.

My father: born, Glen Ullin, North Dakota, April 14, 1896. Another diamond birthstone. Never saw a professional baseball game until 1919 when he came back from World War I where he had been gassed at Passchendaele. He settled in Chicago, inhabited a room above a bar across from Comiskey Park, and quickly learned to live and die with the White Sox. Died a little when, as prohibitive favorites, they lost the 1919 World Series to Cincinnati, died a lot the next summer when eight members of the team were accused of throwing that World Series.

Before I knew what baseball was, I knew of Connie Mack, John McGraw, Grover Cleveland Alexander, Ty Cobb, Babe Ruth, Tris Speaker, Tinker-to-Evers-to-Chance, and, of course, Shoeless Joe Jackson. My father loved under-dogs, cheered for the Brooklyn Dodgers and the hapless St. Louis Browns, loathed the Yankees—an inherited trait, I believe—and insisted that Shoeless Joe was innocent, a victim of big business and crooked gamblers.

That first night, immediately after the voice and the vision, I did nothing except sip my lemonade a little faster and rattle the ice cubes in my glass. The vision of the baseball park lingered—swimming, swaying, seeming to be made of red steam, though perhaps it was only the sunset. And there was a vision within the vision: one of Shoeless Joe Jackson playing left field. Shoeless Joe Jackson who last played major-league baseball in 1920 and was suspended for life, along with seven of his compatriots, by Commissioner Kenesaw Mountain Landis, for his part in throwing the 1919 World Series.

Instead of nursery rhymes, I was raised on the story of the Black Sox Scandal, and instead of Tom Thumb or Rumpelstiltskin, I grew up hearing of the eight disgraced ballplayers: Weaver, Cicotte, Risberg, Felsch, Gandil, Williams, McMullin, and, always, Shoeless Joe Jackson.

"He hit .375 against the Reds in the 1919 World Series and played errorless ball," my father would say, scratching his head in wonder. "Twelve hits in an eight-game series. And *they* suspended *him*," Father would cry. Shoeless Joe became a symbol of the tyranny of the powerful over the powerless. The name Kenesaw Mountain Landis became synonymous with the Devil.

Building a baseball field is more work than you might imagine. I laid out a whole field, but it was there in spirit only. It was really only left field that concerned me. Home plate was made from pieces of cracked two-by-four embedded in the earth. The pitcher's rubber rocked like a cradle when I stood on it. The bases were stray blocks of wood, unanchored. There was no backstop or grandstand, only one shaky bleacher beyond the left-field wall. There was a left-field wall, but only about 50 feet of it, 12 feet high, stained dark green and braced from the rear. And the left-field grass. My intuition told me that it was the grass that was important. It took me three seasons to hone that grass to its proper texture, to its proper color. I made trips to Minneapolis and one or two other cities where the stadiums still have natural-grass infields and outfields. I would arrive hours before a game and watch the grounds keepers groom the field like a prize animal, then stay after the game when in the cool of the night the same groundsmen appeared with hoses, hoes, and rakes, and patched the grasses like medics attending to wounded soldiers.

I pretended to be building a Little League ballfield and asked their secrets and sometimes was told. I took interest in the total operation; they wouldn't understand if I told them I was building only a left field.

Three seasons I've spent seeding, watering, fussing, praying, coddling that field like a sick child. Now it glows parrot-green, cool as mint, soft as moss, lying there like a cashmere blanket. I've begun watching it in the evenings, sitting on the rickety bleacher just beyond the fence. A bleacher I constructed for an audience of one.

My father played some baseball, Class B teams in Florida and California. I found his statistics in a dusty minor-league record book. In Florida he played for a team called the Angels and, according to his records, was a better-than-average catcher. He claimed to have visited all forty-eight states and every major-league ballpark before, at forty, he married and settled down in Montana, a two-day drive from the nearest major-league team. I tried to play, but ground balls bounced off my chest and fly balls dropped between my hands. I might have been a fair designated hitter, but the rule was too late in coming.

There is the story of the urchin who, tugging at Shoeless Joe Jackson's sleeve as he emerged from a Chicago courthouse, said, "Say it ain't so, Joe."

Jackson's reply reportedly was, "I'm afraid it is, kid."

When he comes, I won't put him on the spot by asking. The less said the better. It is likely that he did accept money from gamblers. But throw the Series? Never! Shoeless Joe Jackson led both teams in hitting in that 1919 Series. It was the circumstances. The circumstances. The players were paid peasant salaries while the owners became rich. The infamous Ten Day Clause, which voided contracts, could end any player's career without compensation, pension, or even a ticket home.

The second spring, on a toothachy May evening, a covering of black clouds lumbered off westward like ghosts of buffalo, and the sky became the cold color of a silver coin. The forecast was for frost.

The left-field grass was like green angora, soft as a baby's cheek. In my mind I could see it dull and crisp, bleached by frost, and my chest tightened.

But I used a trick a grounds keeper in Minneapolis had taught me, saying he learned it from grape farmers in California. I carried out a hose, and, making the spray so fine it was scarcely more than fog, I sprayed the soft, shaggy spring grass all that chilled night. My hands ached and my face became wet and cold, but, as I watched, the spray froze on the grass, enclosing each blade in a gossamer-crystal coating of ice. A covering that served like a coat of armor to dispel the real frost that was set like a weasel upon killing in the night. I seemed to stand taller than ever before as the sun rose, turning the ice to eye-dazzling droplets, each a prism, making the field an orgy of rainbows.

Annie and Karin were at breakfast when I came in, the bacon and coffee smells and their laughter pulling me like a magnet.

"Did it work, love?" Annie asked, and I knew she knew by the look on my face that it had. And Karin, clapping her hands and complaining of how cold my face was when she kissed me, loved every second of it.

"And how did he get a name like Shoeless Joe?" I would ask my father, knowing the story full well but wanting to hear it again. And no matter how many times I heard it, I would still picture a lithe ballplayer, his great bare feet white as baseballs sinking into the outfield grass as he sprinted for a line drive. Then, after the catch, his toes gripping the grass like claws, he would brace and throw to the infield.

"It wasn't the least bit romantic," my dad would say. "When he was still in the minor leagues he bought a new pair of spikes and they hurt his feet. About the sixth inning he took them off and played the outfield in just his socks. The other players kidded him, called him Shoeless Joe, and the name stuck for all time."

It was hard for me to imagine that a sore-footed young outfielder taking off his shoes one afternoon not long after the turn of the century could generate a legend.

I came to Iowa to study, one of the thousands of faceless students who pass through large universities, but I fell in love with the state. Fell in love with the land, the people, the sky, the cornfields, and Annie. Couldn't find work in my field, took what I could get. For years, I bathed each morning, frosted my cheeks with Aqua Velva, donned a three-piece suit and snap-brim hat, and, feeling like Superman emerging from a telephone booth, set forth to save the world from a lack of life insurance. I loathed the job so much that I did it quickly, urgently, almost violently. It was Annie who got me to rent the farm. It was Annie who got me to buy it. I operate it the way a child fits together his first puzzle—awkwardly, slowly, but, when a piece slips into the proper slot, with pride and relief and joy.

I built the field and waited, and waited, and waited.

"It will happen, honey," Annie would say when I stood shaking my head at my folly. People looked at me. I must have had a nickname in town. But I could feel the magic building like a gathering storm. It felt as if small animals were scurrying through my veins. I knew it was going to happen soon.

One night I watch Annie looking out the window. She is soft as a butterfly, Annie is, with an evil grin and a tongue that travels at the speed of light. Her jeans are painted to her body, and her pointy little nipples poke at the front of a black T-shirt that has the single word RAH! emblazoned in waspish yellow capitals. Her red hair is short and curly. She has the green eyes of a cat.

Annie understands, though it is me she understands and not always what is happening. She attends ballgames with me and squeezes my arm when there's a hit, but her heart isn't in it and she would just as soon be at home.

She loses interest if the score isn't close, or the weather's not warm, or the pace isn't fast enough. To me it is baseball, and that is all that matters. It is the game that's important—the tension, the strategy, the ballet of the fielders, the angle of the bat.

"There's someone on your lawn," Annie says to me, staring out into the orange-tinted dusk. "I can't see him clearly, but I can tell someone is there." She was quite right, at least about it being *my* lawn, although it is not in the strictest sense of the word a lawn; it is a *left field.*

I have been more restless than usual this night. I have sensed the magic drawing closer, hovering somewhere out in the night like a zeppelin, silky and silent, floating like the moon until the time is right.

Annie peeks through the drapes. "There *is* a man out there; I can see his silhouette. He's wearing a baseball uniform, an old-fashioned one."

"It's Shoeless Joe Jackson," I say. My heart sounds like someone flicking a balloon with his index finger.

"Oh," she says. Annie stays very calm in emergencies. She Band-Aids bleeding fingers and toes, and patches the plumbing with gum and good wishes. Staying calm makes her able to live with me. The French have the right words for Annie—she has a good heart.

"Is he the Jackson on TV? The one you yell 'Drop it, Jackson' at?"

Annie's sense of baseball history is not highly developed.

"No, that's Reggie. This is Shoeless Joe Jackson. He hasn't played major-league baseball since 1920."

"Well, Ray, aren't you going to go out and chase him off your lawn, or something?"

Yes. What am I going to do? I wish someone else understood. Perhaps my daughter will. She has an evil grin and bewitching eyes and loves to climb into my lap and watch television baseball with me. There is a magic about her.

"I think I'll go upstairs and read for a while," Annie says. "Why don't you invite Shoeless Jack in for coffee?" I feel the greatest tenderness toward her then, something akin to the rush of love I felt the first time I held my daughter in my arms. Annie senses that magic is about to happen. She knows she is not part of it. My impulse is to pull her to me as she walks by, the denim of her thighs making a tiny music. But I don't. She will be waiting for me.

As I step out onto the verandah, I can hear the steady drone of the crowd, like bees humming on a white afternoon, and the voices of the vendors, like crows cawing.

A ground mist, like wisps of gauze, snakes in slow circular motions just above the grass.

"The grass is soft as a child's breath," I say to the moonlight. On the porch wall I find the switch, and the single battery of floodlights I have erected behind the left-field fence sputters to life. "I've tended it like I would my own baby. It has been powdered and lotioned and loved. It is ready."

Moonlight butters the whole Iowa night. Clover and corn smells are thick as syrup. I experience a tingling like the tiniest of electric wires touching the back of my neck, sending warm sensations through me. Then, as the lights flare, a scar against the blue-black sky, I see Shoeless Joe Jackson standing out in left field. His feet spread wide, body bent forward from the waist, hands on hips, he waits. I hear the sharp crack of the bat, and Shoeless Joe drifts effortlessly a few steps to his left, raises his right hand to signal for the ball, camps under it for a second or two, catches it, at the same time transferring it to his throwing hand, and fires it to the infield.

I make my way to left field, walking in the darkness far outside the third-base line, behind where the third-base stands would be. I climb up on the wobbly bleacher behind the fence. I can look right down on Shoeless Joe. He fields a single on one hop and pegs the ball to third.

"How does it play?" I holler down.

"The ball bounces true," he replies.

"I know." I am smiling with pride, and my heart thumps mightily against my ribs. "I've hit a thousand line drives and as many grounders. It's true as a felt-top table."

"It is," says Shoeless Joe. "It is true."

I lean back and watch the game. From where I sit the scene is as complete as in any of the major-league baseball parks I have ever visited: the two teams, the stands, the fans, the lights, the vendors, the scoreboard. The only difference is that I sit alone in the left-field bleacher and the only player who seems to have substance is Shoeless Joe Jackson. When Joe's team is at bat, the left fielder below me is transparent, as if he were made of vapor. He performs mechanically but seems not to have facial features. We do not converse.

A great amphitheater of grandstand looms dark against the sky, the park is surrounded by decks of floodlights making it brighter than day, the crowd buzzes, the vendors hawk their wares, and I cannot keep the promise I made myself not to ask Shoeless Joe Jackson about his suspension and what it means to him.

While the pitcher warms up for the third inning we talk.

"It must have been . . . It must have been like . . ." but I can't find the words.

"Like having a part of me amputated, slick and smooth and painless." Joe looks up at me and his dark eyes seem about to burst with the pain of it. "A friend of mine used to tell about the war, how him and a buddy was running across a field when a piece of shrapnel took his friend's head off, and how the friend ran, headless, for several strides before he fell. I'm told that old men wake in the night and scratch itchy legs that have been dust for fifty years.

That was me. Years and years later, I'd wake in the night with the smell of the ballpark in my nose and the cool of the grass on my feet. The thrill of the grass . . .''

How I wish my father could be here with me. If he'd lasted just a few months longer, he could have watched our grainy black-and-white TV as Bill Mazeroski homered in the bottom of the ninth to beat the Yankees 10–9. We would have joined hands and danced around the kitchen like madmen. ''The Yankees lose so seldom you have to celebrate every single time,'' he used to say. We were always going to go to a major-league baseball game, he and I. But the time was never right, the money always needed for something else. One of the last days of his life, late in the night while I sat with him because the pain wouldn't let him sleep, the radio picked up a static-y station broadcasting a White Sox game. We hunched over the radio and cheered them on, but they lost. Dad told the story of the Black Sox Scandal for the last time. Told of seeing two of those World Series games, told of the way Shoeless Joe Jackson hit, told the dimensions of Comiskey Park, and how, during the series, the mobsters in striped suits sat in the box seats with their colorful women, watching the game and perhaps making plans to go out later and kill a rival.

''You must go,'' Dad said. ''I've been in all the major-league parks. I want you to do it, too. The summers belong to somebody else now, have for a long time.'' I nodded agreement.

''Hell, you know what I mean,'' he said, shaking his head. I did indeed.

''I loved the game,'' Shoeless Joe went on. ''I'd have played for food money. I'd have played free and worked for food. It was the game, the parks, the smells, the sounds. Have you ever held a bat or a baseball to your face? The varnish, the leather. And it was the crowd, the excitement of them rising as one when the ball was hit deep. The sound was like a chorus. Then there was the chug-a-lug of the tin lizzies in the parking lots, and the hotels with their brass spittoons in the lobbies and brass beds in the rooms. It makes me tingle all over like a kid on his way to his first doubleheader, just to talk about it."

The year after Annie and I were married, the year we first rented this farm, I dug Annie's garden for her; dug it by hand, stepping a spade into the soft black soil, ruining my salesman's hands. After I finished, it rained, an Iowa spring rain as soft as spray from a warm hose. The clods of earth I had dug seemed to melt until the garden leveled out, looking like a patch of black ocean. It was near noon on a gentle Sunday when I walked out to that garden. The soil was soft and my shoes disappeared as I plodded until I was near the center. There I knelt, the soil cool on my knees. I looked up at the low gray sky; the rain had stopped and the only sound was the surrounding trees dripping fragrantly. Suddenly I thrust my hands wrist-deep into the snuffy-black earth. The air was pure. All around me the clean smell of earth and water. Keeping my hands buried I stirred the earth with my fingers and I knew I loved Iowa as much as a man could love a piece of earth.

When I came back to the house Annie stopped me at the door, made me wait on the verandah and then hosed me down as if I were a door with too many handprints on it, while I tried to explain my epiphany. It is very difficult to describe an experience of religious significance while you are being sprayed with a garden hose by a laughing, loving woman.

"What happened to the sun?" Shoeless Joe says to me, waving his hand toward the banks of floodlights that surround the park.

"Only stadium in the big leagues that doesn't have them is Wrigley Field," I say. "The owners found that more people could attend night games. They even play the World Series at night now."

Joe purses his lips, considering.

"It's harder to see the ball, especially at the plate."

"When there are breaks, they usually go against the ballplayers, right? But I notice you're three-for-three so far," I add, looking down at his uniform, the only identifying marks a large *S* with an *O* in the top crook, an *X* in the bottom, and an American flag with forty-eight stars on his left sleeve near the elbow.

Joe grins. "I'd play for the Devil's own team just for the touch of a baseball. Hell, I'd play in the dark if I had to."

I want to ask about that day in December 1951. If he'd lived another few years things might have been different. There was a move afoot to have his record cleared, but it died with him. I wanted to ask, but my instinct told me not to. There are things it is better not to know.

It is one of those nights when the sky is close enough to touch, so close that looking up is like seeing my own eyes reflected in the rain barrel. I sit in the bleacher just outside the left-field fence. I clutch in my hand a hot dog with mustard, onions, and green relish. The voice of the crowd roars in my ears. Chords of "The Star-Spangled Banner" and "Take Me Out to the Ballgame" float across the field. A Coke bottle is propped against my thigh, squat, greenish, the ice-cream-haired elf grinning conspiratorially from the cap.

Below me in left field, Shoeless Joe Jackson glides over the plush velvet grass, silent as a jungle cat. He prowls and paces, crouches ready to spring as, nearly 300 feet away, the ball is pitched. At the sound of the bat he wafts in whatever direction is required, as if he were on ball bearings.

Then the intrusive sound of a slamming screen door reaches me, and I blink and start. I recognize it as the sound of the door to my house, and, looking into the distance, I can see a shape that I know is my daughter, toddling down the back steps. Perhaps the lights or the crowd have awakened her and she has somehow eluded Annie. I judge the distance to the steps. I am just to the inside of the foul pole, which is exactly 330 feet from home plate. I tense. Karin will surely be drawn to the lights and the emerald dazzle of the infield. If she touches anything, I fear it will all disappear, perhaps forever. Then, as if she senses my discomfort, she stumbles away from the lights, walking in the ragged fringe of darkness well outside the third-base line. She trails a blanket behind her, one tiny fist rubbing a sleepy eye. She is barefoot and wears a white flannelette nightgown covered in an explosion of daisies.

She climbs up the bleacher, alternating a knee and a foot on each step, and crawls into my lap silently, like a kitten. I hold her close and wrap the blanket around her feet. The play goes on; her innocence has not disturbed the balance. "What is it?" she says shyly, her eyes indicating she means all that she sees.

"Just watch the left fielder," I say. "He'll tell you all you ever need to know about a baseball game. Watch his feet as the pitcher accepts the sign and gets ready to pitch. A good left fielder knows what pitch is coming, and he can tell from the angle of the bat where the ball is going to be hit, and if he's good, how hard."

I look down at Karin. She cocks one green eye at me, wrinkling her nose, then snuggles into my chest, the index finger of her right hand tracing tiny circles around her nose.

The crack of the bat is sharp as the yelp of a kicked cur. Shoeless Joe whirls, takes five loping strides directly toward us, turns again, reaches up, and the ball smacks into the glove. The final batter dawdles in the on-deck circle.

"Can I come back again?" Joe asks.

"I built this left field for you. It's yours anytime you want to use it. They play 162 games a season now."

"There are others," he says. "If you were to finish the infield, why, old Chick Gandil could play first base, and we'd have the Swede at shortstop and Buck Weaver at third." I can feel his excitement rising. "We could stick McMullin in at second, and Eddie Cicotte and Lefty Williams would like to pitch again. Do you think you could finish center field? It would mean a lot to Happy Felsch."

"Consider it done," I say, hardly thinking of the time, the money, the back-breaking labor it would entail. "Consider it done," I say again, then stop suddenly as an idea creeps into my brain like a runner inching off first base.

"I know a catcher," I say. "He never made the majors, but in his prime he was good. Really good. Played Class B ball in Florida and California . . ."

"We could give him a try," says Shoeless Joe. "You give us a place to play and we'll look at your catcher."

I swear the stars have moved in close enough to eavesdrop as I sit in this single rickety bleacher that I built with my unskilled hands, looking down at Shoeless Joe Jackson. A breath of clover travels on the summer wind. Behind me, just yards away, brook water plashes softly in the darkness, a frog shrills, fireflies dazzle the night like red pepper. A petal falls.

"God, what an outfield," he says. "What a left field." He looks up at me and I look down at him. "This must be heaven," he says.

"No. It's Iowa," I reply automatically. But then I feel the night rubbing softly against my face like cherry blossoms; look at the sleeping girl-child in my arms, her small hand curled around one of my fingers; think of the fierce warmth of the woman waiting for me in the house; inhale the fresh-cut grass smell that seems locked in the air like permanent incense; and listen to the drone of the crowd, as below me Shoeless Joe Jackson tenses, watching the angle of the distant bat for a clue as to where the ball will be hit.

"I think you're right, Joe," I say, but softly enough not to disturb his con-centration.

Is Ring Lardner a big-leaguer or a busher? This question dominated a 1985 literary convocation observing the centennial of his birth, as it has preoccupied Lardner's critics for generations. In 1925 Virginia Woolf (no baseball fan) wrote of *You Know Me Al*: "... he writes the best prose that has come our way. ... With extraordinary ease and aptitude, with the quickest strokes, the surest touch, the sharpest insight, he lets Jack Keefe the baseball player cut out his own outline, fill in his own depths, until the figure of the foolish, boastful, innocent athlete lives before us." F. Scott Fitzgerald, on the other hand, deplored Lardner's subject matter: "However deeply Ring might cut into it, his cake had exactly the diameter of Frank Chance's diamond. Here was his artistic problem. ..." Take your choice: a deep cut into a cupcake or a thumbprint in the icing of a seven-layer job—the diamond of Frank Chance or a diamond as big as the Ritz. Here, busher Jack Keefe, having made the Chicago White Sox ca. 1914, fills in friend Al. Enjoy.

RING LARDNER

A Busher's Letters Home

St. Joe, Missouri, April 7.

FRIEND AL: It rained yesterday so I worked to-day instead and St. Joe done well to get three hits. They couldn't of scored if we had played all week. I give a couple of passes but I catched a guy flatfooted off of first base and I come up with a couple of bunts and throwed guys out. When the game was over Callahan says That's the way I like to see you work. You looked better to-day than you looked on the whole trip. Just once you wound up with a man on but otherwise you was all O.K. So I guess my job is cinched Al and I won't have to go to New York or St. Louis. I would rather be in Chi anyway because it is near home. I wouldn't care though if they traded me to Detroit. I hear from Violet right along and she says she can't hardly wait till I come to Detroit. She says she is strong for the Tigers but she will pull for me when I work against them. She is nuts over me and I guess she has saw lots of guys to.

I sent her a stickpin from Oklahoma City but I can't spend no more dough on her till after our first payday the fifteenth of the month. I had thirty bucks on me when I left home and I only got about ten left including the five spot I won in the poker game. I have to tip the waiters about thirty cents a day and

I seen about twenty picture shows on the coast beside getting my cloths pressed a couple of times.

We leave here to-morrow night and arrive in Chi the next morning. The second club joins us there and then that night we go to Cleveland to open up. I asked one of the reporters if he knowed who was going to pitch the opening game and he says it would be Scott or Walsh but I guess he don't know much about it.

These reporters travel all round the country with the team all season and send in telegrams about the game every night. I ain't seen no Chi papers so I don't know what they been saying about me. But I should worry eh Al? Some of them are pretty nice fellows and some of them got the swell head. They hang round with the old fellows and play poker most of the time.

Will write you from Cleveland. You will see in the paper if I pitch the opening game.

Your old pal, JACK

Cleveland, Ohio, April 10.

OLD FRIEND AL: Well Al we are all set to open the season this afternoon. I have just ate breakfast and I am sitting in the lobby of the hotel. I eat at a little lunch counter about a block from here and I saved seventy cents on breakfast. You see Al they give us a dollar a meal and if we don't want to spend that much all right. Our rooms at the hotel are paid for.

The Cleveland papers says Walsh or Scott will work for us this afternoon. I asked Callahan if there was any chance of me getting into the first game and he says I hope not. I don't know what he meant but he may surprise these reporters and let me pitch. I will beat them Al. Lajoie and Jackson is supposed to be great batters but the bigger they are the harder they fall.

The second team joined us yesterday in Chi and we practiced a little. Poor Allen was left in Chi last night with four others of the recruit pitchers. Looks pretty good for me eh Al? I only seen Gleason for a few minutes on the train last night. He says, Well you ain't took off much weight. You're hog fat. I says Oh I ain't fat. I didn't need to take off no weight. He says One good thing about it the club don't have to engage no birth for you because you spend all your time in the dining car. We kidded along like that a while and then the trainer rubbed my arm and I went to bed. Well Al I just got time to have my suit pressed before noon.

Yours truly, JACK

Cleveland, Ohio, April 11.

FRIEND AL: Well Al I suppose you know by this time that I did not pitch and that we got licked. Scott was in there and he didn't have nothing. When they had us beat four to one in the eight inning Callahan told me to go out and warm up and he put a batter in for Scott in our ninth. But Cleveland didn't have to play their ninth so I got no chance to work. But looks like he means to start me in one of the games here. We got three more to play. Maybe I will pitch this afternoon. I got a postcard from Violet. She says Beat them Naps. I will give them a battle Al if I get a chance.

Glad to hear you boys have fixed it up to come to Chi during the Detroit serious. I will ask Callahan when he is going to pitch me and let you know. Thanks Al for the papers.

Your friend, JACK

St. Louis, Missouri, April 15.

FRIEND AL: Well Al I guess I showed them. I only worked one inning but I guess them Browns is glad I wasn't in there no longer than that. They had us beat seven to one in the sixth and Callahan pulls Benz out. I honestly felt sorry for him but he didn't have nothing, not a thing. They was hitting him so hard I thought they would score a hundred runs. A right-hander name Bumgardner was pitching for them and he didn't look to have nothing either but we ain't got much of a batting team Al. I could hit better than some of them regulars. Anyway Callahan called Benz to the bench and sent for me. I was down in the corner warming up with Kuhn. I wasn't warmed up good but you know I got the nerve Al and I run right out there like I meant business. There was a man on second and nobody out when I come in. I didn't know who was up there but I found out afterward it was Shotten. He's the center fielder. I was cold and I walked him. Then I got warmed up good and I made Johnston look like a boob. I give him three fastballs and he let two of them go by and missed the other one. I would of handed him a spitter but Schalk kept signing for fast ones and he knows more about them batters than me. Anyway I whiffed Johnston. Then up come Williams and I tried to make him hit at a couple of bad ones. I was in the hole with two balls and nothing and come right across the heart with my fast one. I wish you could of saw the hop on it. Williams hit it right straight up and Lord was camped under it. Then up come Pratt the best hitter on their club. You know what I done to him don't you Al? I give him one spitter and another he didn't strike at that was a ball. Then I come back with two fast ones and Mister Pratt was a dead baby. And you notice they didn't steal no bases.

In our half of the seventh inning Weaver and Schalk got on and I was going up there with a stick when Callahan calls me back and sends Easterly up. I don't know what kind of managing you call that. I hit good on the training trip and he must of knew they had no chance to score off me in the innings they had left while they were liable to murder his other pitchers. I come back to the bench pretty hot and I says You're making a mistake. He says If Comiskey had wanted you to manage this team he would of hired you.

Then Easterly pops out and I says Now I guess you're sorry you didn't let me hit. That sent him right up in the air and he bawled me awful. Honest Al I would of cracked him right in the jaw if we hadn't been right out where everybody could of saw us. Well he sent Cicotte in to finish and they didn't score no more and we didn't either.

I road down in the car with Gleason. He says Boy you shouldn't ought to talk like that to Cal. Some day he will lose his temper and bust you one. I says He won't never bust me. I says He didn't have no right to talk like that to me. Gleason says I suppose you think he's going to laugh and smile when we lost four out of the first five games. He says Wait till to-night and then go up to him and let him know you are sorry you sassed him. I says I didn't sass him and I ain't sorry.

So after supper I seen Callahan sitting in the lobby and I went over and sit down by him. I says When are you going to let me work? He says I wouldn't never let you work only my pitchers are all shot to pieces. Then I told him about you boys coming up from Bedford to watch me during the Detroit serious and he says Well I will start you in the second game against Detroit. He says But I wouldn't if I had any pitchers. He says A girl could get out there and pitch better than some of them have been doing.

So you see Al I am going to pitch on the nineteenth. I hope you guys can be up there and I will show you something. I know I can beat them Tigers and I will have to do it even if they are Violet's team.

I notice that New York and Boston got trimmed to-day so I suppose they wish Comiskey would ask for waivers on me. No chance Al.

Your old pal, JACK

P. S.—We play eleven games in Chi and then go to Detroit. So I will see the little girl on the twenty-ninth.

Oh you Violet.

Chicago, Illinois, April 19.

DEAR OLD PAL: Well Al it's just as well you couldn't come. They beat me and I am writing you this so you will know the truth about the game and not get a bum steer from what you read in the papers.

I had a sore arm when I was warming up and Callahan should never ought to of sent me in there. And Schalk kept signing for my fastball, and I kept giving it to him because I thought he ought to know something about the batters. Weaver and Lord and all of them kept kicking them round the infield and Collins and Bodie couldn't catch nothing.

Callahan ought never to of left me in there when he seen how sore my arm was. Why, I couldn't of threw hard enough to break a pain of glass my arm was so sore.

They sure did run wild on the bases. Cobb stole four and Bush and Crawford and Veach about two apiece. Schalk didn't even make a peg half the time. I guess he was trying to throw me down.

The score was sixteen to two when Callahan finally took me out in the eighth and I don't know how many more they got. I kept telling him to take me out when I seen how bad I was but he wouldn't do it. They started bunting in the fifth and Lord and Chase just stood there and didn't give me no help at all.

I was all O.K. till I had the first two men out in the first inning. Then Crawford come up. I wanted to give him a spitter but Schalk signs me for the fast one and I give it to him. The ball didn't hop much and Crawford happened to catch it just right. At that Collins ought to of catched the ball. Crawford made three bases and up come Cobb. It was the first time I ever seen him. He hollered at me right off the reel. He says You better walk me you busher. I says I will walk you back to the bench. Schalk signs for a spitter and I gives it to him and Cobb misses it.

Then instead of signing for another one Schalk asks for a fast one and I shook my head no but he signed for it again and yells Put something on it. So I throwed a fast one and Cobb hits it right over second base. I don't know what Weaver was doing but he never made a move for the ball. Crawford scored and Cobb was on first base. First thing I knowed he had stole second while I held the ball. Callahan yells Wake up out there and I says Why don't your catcher tell me when they are going to steal. Schalk says Get in there and pitch and shut your mouth. Then I got mad and walked Veach and Moriarty but before I walked Moriarty Cobb and Veach pulled a double steal on Schalk. Gainor lifts a fly and Lord drops it and two more come in. Then Stanage walks and I whiffs their pitcher.

I come in to the bench and Callahan says Are your friends from Bedford up here? I was pretty sore and I says Why don't you get a catcher? He says We don't need no catcher when you're pitching because you can't get nothing past their bats. Then he says You better leave your uniform in here when you go out next inning or Cobb will steal it off your back. I says My arm is sore. He says Use your other one and you'll do just as good.

Gleason says Who do you want to warm up? Callahan says Nobody. He says

Cobb is going to lead the league in batting and basestealing anyway so we might as well give him a good start. I was mad enough to punch his jaw but the boys winked at me not to do nothing.

Well I got some support in the next inning and nobody got on. Between innings I says Well I guess I look better now don't I? Callahan says Yes but you wouldn't look so good if Collins hadn't jumped up on the fence and catched that one off Crawford. That's all the encouragement I got Al.

Cobb come up again to start the third and when Schalk signs for a fast one I shakes my head. Then Schalk says All right pitch anything you want to. I pitched a spitter and Cobb bunts it right at me. I would of threw him out a block but I stubbed my toe in a rough place and fell down. This is the roughest ground I ever seen Al. Veach bunts and for a wonder Lord throws him out. Cobb goes to second and honest Al I forgot all about him being there and first thing I knowed he had stole third. Then Moriarty hits a fly ball to Bodie and Cobb scores though Bodie ought to of threw him out twenty feet.

They batted all round in the fourth inning and scored four or five more. Crawford got the luckiest three-base hit I ever see. He popped one way up in the air and the wind blowed it against the fence. The wind is something fierce here Al. At that Collins ought to of got under it.

I was looking at the bench all the time expecting Callahan to call me in but he kept hollering Go on and pitch. Your friends wants to see you pitch.

Well Al I don't know how they got the rest of their runs but they had more luck than any team I ever seen. And all the time Jennings was on the coaching line yelling like a Indian. Some day Al I'm going to punch his jaw.

After Veach had hit one in the eight Callahan calls me to the bench and says You're through for the day. I says It's about time you found out my arm was sore. He says I ain't worrying about your arm but I'm afraid some of our outfielders will run their legs off and some of them poor infielders will get killed. He says The reporters just sent me a message saying they had run out of paper. Then he says I wish some of the other clubs had pitchers like you so we could hit once in a while. He says Go in the clubhouse and get your arm rubbed off. That's the only way I can get Jennings sore he says.

Well Al that's about all there was to it. It will take two or three stamps to send this but I want you to know the truth about it. The way my arm was I ought never to of went in there.

Yours truly, Jack

The author of *Blue Highways*, from which this snip of a story is taken, traveled the small towns and back roads of America (the blue lines on the road map), recording what he saw and heard. This uncharacteristically cogent barroom banter took place in Bagley, North Dakota. By the way, the Cease Funeral Home ranks right up there with New York City's Terminal Delicatessen (by the bus station), but still several notches below my local Sans Souci Funeral Parlor.

WILLIAM LEAST HEAT MOON

Beans

With a bag of blueberry tarts, I went up Main to a tin-sided, false-front tavern called Michel's, just down the street from the Cease Funeral Home. The interior was log siding and yellowed knotty pine. In the backroom the Junior Chamber of Commerce talked about potatoes, pulpwood, dairy products, and somebody's broken fishing rod. I sat at the bar. Behind me a pronghorn antelope head hung on the wall, and beside it a televised baseball game cast a cool light like a phosphorescent fungus. "Hear that?" a dwindled man asked. He was from the time when boys drew "Kilroy-Was-Here" faces on alley fences. "Did you hear the announcer?"

"I wasn't listening."

"He said 'velocity'."

"Velocity?"

"He's talking about a fastball. A minute ago he said a runner had 'good acceleration.' This is a baseball game, not a NASA shot. And another thing: I haven't heard anybody mention a 'Texas leaguer' in years."

"It's a 'bloop double' now, I think."

"And the 'banjo hitter'—where's he? And what happened to the 'slow ball'?"

"It's a 'change-up.'"

The man got me interested in the game. We watched and drank Grain Belt. He had taught high-school civics in Minneapolis for thirty-two years, but his dream had been to become a sports announcer. "They put a radar gun on the kid's fastball a few minutes ago," he said. "Ninety-three point four miles per hour. That's how they tell you speed now. They don't try to show it to you: 'smoke,' 'hummer,' 'the high hard one.' I miss the old clichés. They had life. Who wants to hit a fastball with a decimal point when he can tie into somebody's 'heat'? And that's another thing: nobody 'tattoos' or 'blisters' the ball anymore. These TV boys are ruining a good game because they think if you can see it they're free to sit back and psychoanalyze the team. Ask and I'll tell you what I think of it."

"What do you think of it?"

"Beans. And that's another thing too."

"Beans?"

"Names. Used to be players named Butterbean and Big Potato, Little Potato. Big Poison, Little Poison, Dizzy and Daffy. Icehouse, Shoeless Joe, Suitcase, The Lip. Now we've got the likes of Rickie and Richie and Reggie. With names like that, I think I'm watching a third-grade scrub team."

The announcer said the pitcher had "good location."

"Great God in hemock! He means 'nibble the corners.' But which of these throwing clowns nibbles corners? They're obsessed with speed. Satchel Paige—there's a name for you—old Satch could fire the pill a hundred and five miles an hour. He didn't throw it that fast very often because he couldn't make the ball cut up at that speed. And, sure as spitting, his pitching arm lasted just about his whole life."

The man took a long smacking pull on his Grain Belt. "Damn shame," he said. "There's a word for what television's turned this game into."

"What's the word?"

"Beans," he said. "Nothing but beans and hot air."

If Ring Lardner hated what the lively ball did to his game (see the final piece in this collection), imagine his horror at the billiard-baseball played today, especially in Seattle's Kingdome and the Minneapolis Metrodome. The first artificial turf appeared, as everyone knows, in Houston's Astrodome. What few recall, however, is that the Astros of 1965—their first season in the new domed stadium—played on God's own sod, nourished by God's own sunlight shining through the transparent dome. However, experience with day games revealed that outfielders could not track fly balls in the glare. Painting the dome solved that problem but killed the grass, thus "paving" the way for Monsanto's Astroturf in 1966. Eugene J. McCarthy—poet, politician, and baseball player—wrote this article for *The New Republic* of November 22, 1982.

EUGENE J. McCARTHY

Baseball? Boingball.

At the opening of the 1978 baseball season, I wrote optimistically . . . of the future of the game, . . . noting that despite the introduction of the livelier ball, despite the use of aluminum and plastic bats below the level of the major leagues, and despite Charlie Finley and Bowie Kuhn, the game seemed to be thriving. But after watching several games in the new Minneapolis Metrodome, and watching as much of the recent World Series between the Cardinals of St. Louis and the Brewers of Milwaukee as I could stand, I have begun to wonder whether the integrity of the game, and the validity of its statistics, can survive in an era of domed stadiums and the artificial turf they contain.

Actually, the domes would be all right if one could play in them on something other than artificial turf. It is the turf that changes the game. Even to call it artificial turf is to offend against language. In their natural state baseball diamonds were never said to be turfed. As one moved up the scale of baseball, one went from the sandlot, to the diamond with dirt infield and grass outfield, and finally to the diamond with grass infield, grass outfield, and dirt basepaths. There was no such thing as "turf," whether natural or counterfeit. In any case, the covering called "artificial turf" is not turf of any kind. It is not even a carpet or rug, but some kind of plastic conglomerate, possibly suitable for tennis, which, it seems, can be played on almost any surface: clay, grass, plastic, wood, rubber, cement, or ground glass.

I began to have doubts about the future of the game one night as I listened to a broadcast from the Minneapolis Metrodome. The Twins were not doing very well, not just that night but in season play. I had read that the owner and manager of the team had explained the poor play by saying that the team had been built up in anticipation of playing on grass in the old outdoor park, and that the team was not tailored to the conditions under which the dome game was being played—mostly the size and shape of the enclosure and the quality of the playing surface (plus a few minor adjustments such as learning how to catch balls that had hit loudspeakers or support cables). Yet as I listened to the broadcast, I was puzzled by the announcers' comments. They would say things like, "This is a pitchers' duel, a tight one. It's the bottom of the third inning, it's tied at five and five, each team has ten hits, but neither one has hit a home run." Or they would say, "It's a long fly. The outfielder is running in on it." Or, "The shortstop has just made a great leaping catch of a ground ball on the third hop."

When I saw my first game in the new facility, my confusion cleared up but my doubts deepened. Outfielders did indeed run in on long flies, hoping to catch the ball on the second or third rebound bounce rather than have it go over their heads on the first bounce off the turf after rebounding from the wall. Yet outfielders seldom charged a short fly, or even a "Texas Leaguer," but most often turned tail and raced for the wall, looking back over their shoulders for the first hop as the ball returned from the stratosphere.

The infield game was something else. Nothing normal about it. There were easy two-hop plays, and occasionally a ball might bounce three times in the infield, on a deep play, before it was handled. There were few good plays by traditional standards. Mostly it was brilliant grabs, errors, base hits through the infield, and base hits *within* the infield, especially from balls that hit resilient turf somewhere between home plate and the pitcher's mound and then sprang twenty or thirty feet into the air—the runner making it to first base while the infielder waited patiently for the ball to descend.

And then came this year's World Series. The games played in Milwaukee were played on grass. But in St. Louis, in an open stadium, in a city that has good annual rainfall, where grass grows well, and where the team owner, Gus Busch, could afford a good grounds keeper, the games were played on "the carpet." There were two wholly different kinds of game played, depending on the covering. The victor was not the Cardinals, but the turf. Ground balls that under normal circumstances could have been caught slithered through the infield for hits. Hits that should have been singles at most rolled to the wall for doubles and triples. High bouncers, hit by St. Louis batters schooled, by report, to hit down on the ball, sailed over the pitcher's head. The turf was so bad that it actually played better in the rain.

So much for the game. Bad enough. But more serious, in the long run, is the effect on the statistics.

It is obvious that if the statistics that have been kept for over a hundred years, giving stability and continuity to the game of baseball, are to have any objective historical relevance, new scoring principles and methods will have to be introduced to reflect the differences between games played on artificial turf and those played on grass. Hits, errors, earned runs, extra base hits—everything is of a different order. Certainly all of the basic statistics should be separated—batting, fielding, pitching. Those made on grass could be incorporated into the established record books, those made on turf kept separate. Balls that hit the ground within an arc, drawn and marked on the field at, say, thirty feet from home plate, and that are caught before they touch the ground to bounce a second time, could be treated as though they were simple fly balls. Two short outfielders might be introduced, allowed to move within a limited range, as some soccer players are restricted, and permitted to catch or stop only ground balls. I anticipate that unless rules are changed or the turf banned or improved, we may enter an era in which the positions of shortstop and second base, formerly occupied by quick, small men, such as Rizzuto, Lazzeri, Crosetti, Fox, and others of modest stature, will be filled by men who are seven feet tall, with long arms and great leaping abilities. Reach, not movement, will become the important attribute. Announcers, instead of saying of an infielder that he has great lateral movement, will say he has great vertical movement. And instead of praising outfielders who, like Willie Mays, could "go back and get them," we will revere outfielders for their ability to play the angles, the rebounds, the caroms.

The alternative is to turn off the television broadcasts of baseball games, as I did during the Series, and to amuse oneself playing Atari baseball, which Billy Martin likes, or the rival Intellivision, which George Plimpton says is better.

When the Philadelphia Phillies squared off against the Kansas City Royals in the World Series of 1980, they were the only one of the original sixteen major-league franchises never to have won a championship. James Michener, who had seen his hapless Phils come up empty for six decades, learned of their victory in midair, en route to Bangkok; thereupon he dashed off this nimble paean to the Phillies, claimants at last to their own World Sillies.

JAMES MICHENER

Lines Composed in Exaltation over the North Atlantic

When they launched their quest in the play-offs, the Phillies, always a team of infinite class, asked the city's revered musician, Eugene Ormandy, to throw out the ball for the first game, and a local scribbler to start the second.

Ormandy won his game, I lost mine, proving that the piccolo is mightier than the Smith-Corona. The flawless artistry displayed by the Phils in the series was due in large part to this graceful beginning.

While flying to Bangkok during the World Series, I was prompted to scribble a verse on hearing the pilot announce, "The Phillies won."

> Crash the cymbals, blare the trumpets,
> Wreathe their noble brows with laurel.
> Heap the festive board with crumpets
> And with decorations floral.
> They deserve the fairest lilies—
> Who? The Phillies.

Through the long dark years they stumbled
Scarred with deep humiliations
But our cheering never crumbled
And we kept our expectations.

Yes, we loved them for their sillies—
Who? The Phillies.

Triple plays that did not triple,
Strikeouts with the bases loaded.
Pitchers serving up the cripple,
All our hopes again exploded.
Are they not a bunch of dillies?
Who? The Phillies.

Far behind in early innings,
Doomed to tragedy eternal,
They turn losses into winnings
Through some holy fire internal.
They give enemies the willies—
Who? The Phillies.

Bang the drum and toot the oboes,
Dance until the earth has shaken.
Cheer, for our beloved hoboes
Have at last brought home the bacon.

Garland them with timeless lilies!
Although they are a bunch of dillies
Who give honest men the willies.
We still love them for their sillies—
Hail, The Phillies.

No, not exactly, though the legend here is uncommonly close to the mark. Jim Murray of the *Los Angeles Times*, by acclamation the dean of baseball columnists, wrote this in 1972. Has Babe Herman been ill-used by the press? Perhaps . . . but no more so than Yogi Berra. Let me tell you this one: the Dodgers went into the ninth inning at Forbes Field with a 2–1 lead over Pittsburgh. The Pirates put two men on base with two out, but then, as Pie Traynor looped a routine liner to center, their rally seemed to have fallen short. Herman charged the ball, fell on his face, and saw the ball whiz by as the winning runs crossed the plate. The crestfallen Dodgers trudged off the field in defeat. Manager Wilbert Robinson, ever the kindhearted soul, put his arm around Herman. "What happened, Babe?" he inquired tenderly. *"When?"* was Herman's reply. And if that story's not strictly true, well, it ought to be.

JIM MURRAY

Did Babe Herman Triple into a Triple Play?

History, Henry Ford said, is bunk. Or did he?

Did George Washington really throw a dollar across the Rappahannock? Was that midnight rider really Paul Revere? Or two guys from Springfield? Did Shakespeare really write those plays? Think Patrick Henry really said, "Give me liberty or give me death"? Or did he say, "Lemme outta here, you guys are nuts!"

It's the same in sports. Did Babe Ruth really call his shot in the World Series? Did Willie Keeler really say, "Hit 'em where they ain't"?

Men usually become legends posthumously. Nothing promotes the growth of a legend like the demise of anyone who might contradict it.

Which is why I sought out Babe Herman at the Dodgers' Old-timers' luncheon one day last season. Mention the name "Babe Herman" in any gathering of baseball fans and the smiles immediately come to the corners of the mouth. The old joke is revived, of the guy hollering down from the grandstand to the street, "The Dodgers have three men on base!" And the question comes up from the pedestrian below, "Which base?"

Babe Herman's life was a series of fly balls bouncing off his cap, sliding into occupied bases, passing base runners with his head down, starting to trot in from the outfield with only the *second* out with the bases loaded, right? The Flatbush Follies, right? The "Daffiness Boys." The Daffy of the Daffy Dodgers. The guy who came into the league a big-eared rookie in 1926 and left it still a big-eared rookie nineteen years later.

One of the most famous paragraphs in baseball literature was the one the late John Lardner wrote: "Floyd Caves Herman never tripled into a triple play, but he once doubled into a double play, which is the next best thing." Or, "Floyd Caves Herman did not always catch fly balls on the top of his head, but he could do it in a pinch."

Unfortunately, Babe Herman slides into this occupied base, too. "Now, I'll tell you the truth of that," he said doggedly the other day. "In the first place, they said I 'tripled into a triple play,' but there was one out so how could I do that? Also, they forget I hit in the winning run in that game. Now, here is what happened: DeBerry [Brooklyn catcher] was on third, Dazzy Vance [Brooklyn pitcher] was on second, and Chick Fewster [second baseman] was on first. We were playing the Braves and George Mogridge hung a curve, and I hit it four feet from the top of the wall in right. DeBerry scores to put us ahead 3–2, which we stayed in the top of the ninth. Vance runs halfway to third, then he runs around third, then he starts to run back. Fewster is on third, so he starts back to second.

"Now, I got the throw beat, and I slide into second. Safe. Right? So, now, somebody hollers to Jimmy Cooney, the shortstop, and he throws home. Al Spohrer chases Vance back to third. Now, I go to third on the rundown and, naturally, I slide into third. Safe. Right. Now, I was called out for passing Fewster, but Vance is on third and it's his bag by the rules. Spohrer begins tagging everybody—but I am already out. It's like sentencing a dead man. Now, there are only two out, but Fewster wanders out to right field to get his glove and Doc Gautreau, the Braves' second baseman, chases him and tags him out.

"You see, there never were three men on third exactly. See how everything gets mixed up?

"Now, the fielding was another thing they got all mixed up. Here I was playing first base all those years and, one day, Bizzy Bissonette gets sick and can't play right field. So I say, 'Hell, I'll play it.' You see, it was this awful sun field out there, the toughest sun field in the league, and, the sunset, which came through the opening of the roof there, made it worse. So, we didn't have flip glasses in those days and, when it got dark enough, the sky was murder, and when the ball was hit up, there was this black spot you had to pick out of the sun. What? Oh, the black spot was the ball and you can see sometimes how you could camp under the wrong spot."

Like, the Babe sometimes found himself waiting for a mosquito to come down and while waiting he would feel this Thunk! on the back of his head.

As you can see from the foregoing, covering Babe Herman wasn't the simple historical endeavor that the Thirty Years' War was and, given the limitations of the medium, I would stack Lardner's history with Toynbee's any old day. After all, not many guys come up with the bases loaded and one out and drive home one run and three runners to third base. Somebody probably should have said simply, "Herman then doubled to right to load the base."

The idea of a designated hitter may have been bandied about on the Elysian Fields of Hoboken or during the 1890s, when a "courtesy runner" was permitted to take the base for an ailing batter without necessitating that batter's removal from the game (isn't "courtesy hitter" a cuter appellation than "designated hitter"?). However, the idea is at least as old as the 1920s, when John McGraw was asked his opinion of it and replied that one might as well "go all the way and let a club play nine defensive players in the field and then have nine sluggers do all the hitting." Messrs. Okrent and Ringolsby can't both be right. No matter that Bowie Kuhn, in his Solomonic wisdom, permitted the leagues to split the baseball baby in two in 1973. No matter that a poll of all fandom, as Peter Ueberroth has contemplated, would figure to be similarly divided. Either the designated hitter is good baseball or it isn't. The two camps are well represented below.

DANIEL OKRENT and

TRACY RINGOLSBY

Ban the DH . . . Save the DH

Daniel Okrent writes:
Nineteen seventy-three was a momentous year in baseball. Roberto Clemente died on his relief mission to Nicaragua. Henry Aaron took his home run total to the Ruthian precipice, hitting number 713. For the first time in the game's history, total attendance passed 30 million. Salary arbitration was instituted. The Oakland A's won the second of three straight world championships.

Yet all these events were dwarfed by an occurrence of such immense proportion, of such stunningly negative effect, that the year can be remembered for nothing else. As 1861 saw the Union rent in two; as 1914 plunged the world into pain and horror, as 1929 marked the end of prosperity, the onset of a decade's gloom—as all these watershed years stand out for the world, so must 1973 stand out for baseball.

For it was the year of the plague: the introduction into the game's rules of the designated hitter.

WHAT HAPPENED TO MY GAME?

There is nothing that can be said on behalf of the designated hitter rule. The case against it is clear and uncorrupted. It has done nothing to enrich the game, and it has done so much to sully its immortal symmetry that it should not be allowed to remain in force one day longer.

Spreading swiftly throughout baseball, a metastasizing monstrosity, the DH has become so pervasive that the National League is the *only* baseball league in the Western world—professional or amateur, adult or child, male or female— that requires the pitcher to bat. As such, it is the only league in the Western world that truly plays *baseball*, and not some adulterated form of the game. In the NL (and in Japan's Central League, the one other redoubt of the classical game), teams run risks each time they allow a pitcher to bat. Managers hold their breath as great sluggers, consigned to left field or first base, gather beneath pop flies. Front office personnel work into the night every spring, trying to balance a lineup while knowing no one can be hidden within its folds.

National League teams, and the brand of baseball they play, also happen to embody the fundamental tenet that underlies the game and gives it its texture: that every talent carries with it a concomitant price. Did Mark Belanger's glove justify his bat? In saying yes, Earl Weaver each season took a risk. Does Hal McRae's bat disguise his glove and his arm? We will never know. Hal McRae does not play baseball. Hal McRae hits.

AN IMPROPER BALANCE

With the Nationals playing the traditional game and the American League a mutant version, we find the two leagues diverging in a sport whose beauty rests in comparisons. They are, in effect, playing two different games—not subtly different, as is the case with the National Football League's two con- ferences, but as dissimilar as the NFL game is from the one played in the Canadian Football League. The World Series, that true symbol of baseball's interaction, is now merely an awkward test, forcing one team to alter the way it has excelled over 162 games. Simple matters like comparative salaries and statistics now must carry an asterisk. Is a National League pitcher of particular skills worth more than a comparable American Leaguer because he must bat? Or, if this left fielder is a worse-than-average fielder, is the DH (who never makes an error, or never throws to the wrong base) worth *more?*

Consider as well the managers that this rule has wrought. Only ten years after the introduction of the DH, there are managers like the White Sox's Tony La Russa who have never run a game—in the majors, minors, or winter ball— in which the pitchers batted. Soon enough we will meet managers who have never *played* in such a game, at any level, from Little League on up. Will the time come when an American League manager will panic in a no-DH World

Series? It's already happened—to the Yankees' Bob Lemon when he hit for Tommy John in 1981. Will the time come when a manager will be confined to American League jobs because of the narrowness of his experience? It is virtually inevitable.

It is not enough, however, to base one's arguments on imbalance between the leagues or on the awkwardness of different playing rules in alternate World Series or on the potential effect of the DH on the permanent class of baseball managers. Obviously, it would be easier to install the DH in the National League rule book than to excise it from the rules of hundreds of other leagues. But expediency is not our goal. Let us examine the designated hitter on its merits.

I noted before that there is nothing at all that can be said to justify the DH rule. Lest you think my ears have been closed to the dissimulating cries of its proponents, I will attempt to dismiss each argument they use:

1. *"It brings more offense into the game."*

Let us leave unsaid whether offense alone is a virtue (show me someone who categorically prefers high-scoring games to pitchers' contests and I'll show you a San Diego Charger). In 1982, there were 18.11 hits per American League game, 17.57 per National League game. That's .54 hits per game difference—only .27 *per team* per game. Go to two baseball games. Soak up the sun. Enjoy the action. Drink a few beers. Then tell me whether one more hit—*one hit*—in those two games would have made them more or less enjoyable for you.

Tell me, as well, whether the ecstasy produced by that hit compares to the anxiety wrought when there's a man on second in the ninth inning of a tie game and a single is lined to left—to Don Baylor and his popcorn arm. Tell me whether Philadelphians still weep over Manny Mota's drive to the wall in

the third game of the 1977 playoffs, a drive that anyone but Greg Luzinski would have caught. Tell me, finally, whether our appreciation of baseball is enhanced or diminished by the pain of Luzinski's failure, the prospect of Baylor's challenge—by the subtlety of defense—as much as by the fireworks of offense.

2. *"It enables a team to use popular players who might otherwise not earn a place in the everyday lineup."*

Designated hitters who saw action in the second week of May included these immortals: Jorge Orta, John Wockenfuss, Ron Jackson, Dave Edler, Mickey Hatcher, and Johnny Grubb. Surely this rule was not invented to provide employment opportunities for Ron Jackson, who over his seven major league seasons has posted a .266 batting average and forty-eight home runs. Come to think of it, perhaps it was: the first DH in history was the mild and inoffensive Ron Blomberg of the Yankees.

Except for the occasional Baylor or McRae, the charismatic Reggie, or the freakish Luzinski, designated hitters are by and large fairly unexceptional hitters. The great athletes, the game's nonpareils, are fielders as well as hitters, and as such are the ones who genuinely bring fans to the park: Mike Schmidt, Gary Carter, Eddie Murray, Robin Yount—all Gold Gloves, platinum bats, and the most popular players in their cities.

3. *"It extends the careers of the biggest stars."*

Last April 24, just before his back began to act up yet again, forty-three-year-old Carl Yastrzemski was the DH for the Red Sox. That same day, for the Phillies, forty-two-year-old Pete Rose played right field, thirty-nine-year-old Bill Robinson played third, and forty-year-old Tony Perez—released by Boston because, apparently, he was too old and infirm even to DH—played first base, keeping alive his streak of playing in every Philadelphia game this season.

Perez is playing in 1983 because he deserves to play, not because he has been granted a senior citizen's discount pass. To his credit, when Willie Stargell's skills deteriorated to the level of Carl Yastrzemski's, he retired. If we want to watch our old heroes, let's watch them on Old-timers' Day. It is not cold-hearted to prefer that heroes still be able to play heroically.

4. *"It allows pitchers more complete games."*

Undeniable. However, it would serve us well to ask what the price of those complete games might be. The lamed Oakland pitchers whom Billy Martin threw to the wolves in 1980 would probably be pretty forthright about this. Catfish Hunter averaged 235 innings per year before the DH came along; in the four years following its introduction he averaged 300—and saw his career crumble prematurely at age thirty-three. Three straight American League Cy Young Award winners—Steve Stone, Rollie Fingers and Pete Vuckovich—have seriously damaged their arms, perhaps irreparably, from overwork. The DH even creates strain for relievers. A Rich Gossage brought in to pitch the top of the eighth won't be removed for a pinch hitter in the bottom of the inning; under the sign of the designated hitter, the one-inning specialist starts going two or three. Over the course of a season, this can cripple a man who might appear three or four times a week.

5. *"It spares us the boredom, and the embarrassment, of watching pitchers hit."*

Is a pitcher's at bat necessarily boring? In my experience, when there's less than two out, a man on first and the pitcher at bat, something strange happens in the ballpark. Everybody knows that the pitcher will bunt—and the knowing focuses our attention. The park grows quiet, fans concentrate on the field, infielders charge the plate. The moment freezes. The bunt is, on its face, an exciting play; it is all the more so when the act is foreordained but the outcome is not.

Even if we concede that watching a pitcher hit is boring, this argument ill serves the most remarkable of baseball's athletes, namely those who can hit and pitch. Today the best hitting pitchers include Steve Carlton, Mike Krukow, and Tim Lollar; that they aren't bad pitchers either is very much to the point. They are better pitchers—they win more games—because they are good hitters. The best hitting pitchers a generation or two ago included Warren Spahn, Bob Lemon, Bob Gibson, Don Newcombe, and Don Drysdale (who occasionally even batted seventh or eighth in the order during his career). Those are three Hall of Famers, and two who've reached the Hall's doorstep. It isn't a coincidence.

6. *"Innovation vitalizes the game."*

The most specious argument of all, usually offered by football types or others who are fearful for the innate quality of the product *they* offer. Want more offense? Let's move first base 3 feet closer to home. Defense is boring? Let's tie the shortstop's shoelaces together. Stars are big draws? Bring back Whitey Ford and let him pitch from 40 feet. Change for its own sake in any endeavor is a questionable virtue; in baseball, where the lines of logic and continuity run back to the last major rule changes instituted in the late 1890s, it is specifically counterproductive.

There are some who say that the rule change that brought about the DH is partly responsible for the upsurge in baseball attendance over the past several years. If the DH is a help at the gate, why did the average National League club outdraw the average American League club by 150,000 fans last season? By 36,000 in strike-ridden 1981 and by nearly 200,000 in 1980?

I HAVE A DREAM

Proponents of the DH have never satisfactorily answered the sturdiest criticism of the institution—that it eliminates a manager's most fundamental, and most second-guessable, strategic dilemma, namely when to remove a pitcher. Why do they ignore this?

Could it be that the many strategic choices that fall solely upon National League managers do not appeal to these people? Do they not second-guess a manager who has left in a faltering pitcher because he leads off the next inning? Did that manager blow it by leaving him in, when he was fully aware that he had lost his best stuff—simply hoping that he could last the inning? Or should he have lifted that pitcher at the risk of having one of his relievers wasted on one batter, only to be removed in the bottom half of the inning in search of more runs. In this situation, the complexities that rest before a National League manager are just beginning. Once a manager has removed his relief pitcher for a pinch hitter, must he then remove another man—possibly one of his best defensive players, but a weak bat—so that he can hide his next pitcher in the batting order? And what of the sacrifice? If the manager's late-inning reliever is a good bunter, should a spot be found for him to bat in the next inning? Could the manager then move runners into scoring position and still keep this valuable reliever in the game?

Perhaps strategic choices, the subtle balance of a particular game, the dramatic content of the pitcher-batter confrontation—baseball's distinguishing characteristics—do not appeal to those in favor of the designated hitter.

Now, I don't mean to say that the American League general managers who continue to support the DH don't appreciate baseball; these gentlemen have built organizational strategies around developing (or retaining) purely offensive talents, and their work would be wasted if the DH were abolished now. But it is undeniable that, in their cases, necessity has mothered a bastard invention, a short-sighted view of the game that sacrifices its integrity for the sake of a silly and corrupting rule. It is worse when one considers that a rule specifically intended to be an experiment managed to become institutionalized by default. Within moments of the DH's tentative introduction back in 1973, as the pitchers who batted disappeared from the schools and colleges and minor-league systems, it too easily became a terrifying prospect to suddenly force them to bat once again. The experiment had become, to the American League, a strategic straitjacket. Having created Frankenstein, they were incapable of killing him.

I said at the outset that each day of the DH's continued existence was mortally wounding. Yet the DH cannot be easily obliterated without injuring a number of innocent parties. Thus, in the interest of those young pitchers who have not touched a bat since Little League (if then), and in acknowledgment of career choices made by professionals who no longer play defense, let the designated hitter rule live—for a period of time.

What baseball needs to do is declare that, effective opening day of 1988, the DH is dead. Watching the date approach, high schools will begin to revert to the classical nine-man lineup. Teams in the lower minors will begin to have their pitchers bat again, to train them for that approaching day when they will have no choice.

Young players like the White Sox's Ron Kittle will no longer arrive in the majors and be expected to learn a fielding position on the job, our fan dollars providing them with a tuition grant as they commit aggravated assault on simple fly balls. And the five-year waiting period will allow those once-great players now on the edge of decline to end their careers in the spotlight—not in the sideshow glare of that sad and distorted institution, the designated hitter.

Tracy Ringolsby writes:

Did you ever wonder why the National League is the only form of organized baseball—other than the Central League of Japan—that has not accepted the designated hitter? Well, wonder no more. It's stubbornness, plain and simple. After all, imagine what it would do to the ego of those National League owners to admit the junior circuit was right.

As every true baseball fan knows, the DH adds intrigue to the course of a game. It forces a manager to handle every decision separately and with solid rationale. Mostly, though, it serves its stated purpose—increased offense.

Let's get the statistics out of the way first. The DH has been in effect for ten years, and during that time it has undeniably helped perk up the production in the American League. Consider that during that decade, DHs have combined for a .259 batting average and produced 18,145 runs. National League pitchers, meanwhile, have hit .153 and produced less than a third as many runs (5,237). And if you're looking for home runs, the American League averaged one every thirty-seven at bats in 1982—thanks in part to one every twenty-nine times a DH came to bat—while the National League averaged a homer once every fifty-one trips.

So why all the fuss? Let's look at the arguments that are used to degrade the rule: it creates too much wear and tear on a pitcher's arm. It takes away from a manager's decision-making abilities. And, the most irritating of all, it's just not the way the game was meant to be played. Hogwash and more hogwash.

In the first two years of the DH, there was a modern-day high of American League pitchers who worked 250 innings or more (twenty-two in 1973 and twenty-three in 1974). But by the summer of 1982 that number had dropped to five, three less than the National League, which has two fewer teams.

Consider, too, that the percentage of complete games by American League pitchers has also declined during the DH decade. In the four years prior to the DH, American League pitchers completed 24.4 percent of their games. With the advent of the DH, that figure jumped to 31.6 in 1973 and to 33.5 by 1974. But it has dropped since then, hitting a recent-day low of 19.6 in 1982.

Sure, there have been a number of top American League pitchers to be sidelined by sore arms in recent years. But instead of classifying this malady as DH burnout, it could be more logically described as breaking ball burnout. The American League has the old ballparks, and old ballparks mean headaches for pitchers and pleasing nuances for hitters. As a result, American League pitchers tend to finesse their way to success. They can't rear back and fire fastballs, like their National League counterparts, fully aware that they have spacious pastures inside the fences where deep fly balls can be run down.

Those who claim that the DH limits managerial decision-making couldn't be further from the truth. In fact, it creates more pressures than ever when it comes to handling pitchers. An example: In the late innings of a National League ballgame, if a club is down a run and a man gets on base, the manager pinch hits for the pitcher. There are no questions asked; it's the move he has to make. Another example of brilliant National League managerial strategy: a pitcher is struggling in the middle of an inning, but he's due to lead off when his team comes to bat. So the manager stays with the hurler, forcing him to make pressure pitches that can really ruin an arm. He gives up the key hit, but the manager is not second-guessed. He was simply sparing the expense of using an extra pitcher by milking an extra out from one who had already lost his best stuff.

When a manager makes a pitching change in the American League, he has to be of firm conviction that he's bringing in a pitcher who can do the job better than the one he's replacing. Managing with the DH puts a premium on being able to handle pitchers. "You have to have the ability as a manager to say, 'This guy has had it,' and then take him out," says Baltimore pitching coach Ray Miller. "You have to have sound judgment of pitchers and what they are doing over the course of a game." In other words, you have to make pitching changes in the American League because you need to make a change, not because you need a run.

"You have to know the characteristics of your pitcher's stuff," adds St. Louis manager Whitey Herzog, who has managed both with the DH (in Kansas City) and without. "He might be rolling along and throwing a great game, but you can't get lulled to sleep by that. You have to be ready to make the move when he starts to lose something."

One of the refinements of managing with the DH that has developed over the last decade is the realization of the versatility it presents a manager in constructing a batting order.

By removing the pitcher from the line-up, a manager can blend the strengths of a nine-man hitting rotation. One of the outgrowths of this has been the "double-leadoff-man" theory, which simply means that it is as important to have speed at the bottom of the order as it is to have it at the top.

Before he had Willie Wilson to get things going in Kansas City, Herzog used to bat George Brett and Hal McRae one-two in his lineup. His speed men, Fred Patek and Frank White, hit eight and nine. By having Brett and McRae, his best hitters, lead off, he could get them more at bats, and after the first time around, he had them coming up right behind his fastest runners. "You only have a leadoff hitter the first time in the American League," Herzog says. "And your first hitter is never batting after a pitcher."

The DH continues to demand more strategy throughout the course of a game. How much soul-searching does it take for a manager to call for a sacrifice bunt when his pitcher comes to the plate with a runner on first? It's automatic, and worse, it's a defensive action to an offensive part of the game.

The one time true strategy does come into play in the National League is in the late innings of a tight game, when the manager pinch-hits for the hurler. That's when he must decide if he's going to make a double change, so that he can move the pitcher to a less important spot in the lineup. But with the DH that strategy is at work from the first inning on. What a pitcher-free lineup does is force a manager to consider all his options: do nothing, sacrifice, steal, or hit-and-run.

"It starts with your number six hitter," Herzog explains. "If he gets on base, you hit-and-run with your seventh hitter. Say he grounds out and moves the runner to second. If you've got a pitcher in the lineup, they'll pass your number eight hitter and go right to the pitcher. With the DH though, they've got to pitch to your hitters. It opens up a lot of things for you throughout your lineup."

It will open up more things once the American League managers are able to put a more complete offensive player in that role. Instead of following the pattern of using older players who are just hanging on as their DH, teams will eventually have to follow the lead of the Hal McRaes and Don Baylors. They are players who can contribute in many ways offensively. They don't clog up an offensive production line of which a DH is the foreman.

Isn't it time for those National League diehards to realize the pettiness of their arguments against the DH on "purist" grounds. It's so ironic for them to complain, when they believe in a league that has become the bastion of antiseptic ballparks and artificial playing surfaces.

Sure Abner Doubleday didn't include the DH in his rules. But don't tell me that Doubleday was thinking of double-knits, floodlights, television, and ersatz grass back when he decided that the bases should be 90 feet apart.

"Most people who talk about the sacrilege of the DH are National League owners whose teams play on artificial surfaces," Miller argues. "You talk about changing the game; I think any record that is set on artificial grass should have an asterisk next to it. Anyone who says the DH destroys the sanctity of the game, and plays on artificial grass is being sacrilegious himself, and a hypocrite." Now, all in favor say aye.

Of the making of lists there is no end. The impulse is irresistible, so why resist? Right.
My ten favorite team names (six of them are major-league!): the Hunkidoris, Tip-Tops,
Quicksteps, Skeeters, Innocents, Intrepids, Canaries, Orphans, Black Jokes, and Pearls.
Or how about thirteen major leaguers better known in other lines of work: Johnny
Berardino (actor), Frank Olin (industrialist), Arlie Pond (doctor), Byron Houck (cine-
matographer), Chuck Connors (actor), Sam Crane (sportswriter), Billy Sunday (evan-
gelist), Vinegar Bend Mizell (congressman), Ted Lewis (university president), Al Lawson
(aviator), John Tener (Pennsylvania governor), Fred Brown (U.S. senator), Joe Garagiola
(announcer). Or twenty-two . . . AARGH!

PHIL PEPE and

ZANDER HOLLANDER

Name Calling

"Mr. President, as the nation's No. 1 baseball fan, would you be willing to
name your all-time baseball team?"

When President Nixon not only said he would, but did, and made the sports
pages of just about every newspaper in the country with his selections, that
was an open invitation for everybody to get into the act.

In the interest of fair play, it seems only right that others be given equal
time.

What follows are the teams politicians, statespeople, and other celebrities
might have chosen if they had the time, the inclination, and the opportunity.
The selections are hypothetical, but the players chosen are real people who
actually played in the major leagues.

LEONID BREZHNEV

First base—Lefty O'Doul
Second base—Red Schoendienst
Third base—Red Rolfe
Shortstop—Pinky May

Outfield—Eric (The Red) Tipton
Outfield—Red Murray
Outfield—Lou (The Mad Russian) Novikoff
Catcher—Red Dooin
Pitcher—Lefty Gomez

DON VITO CORLEONE

First base—Joe Pepitone
Second base—Tony Lazzeri
Third base—Joe Torre
Shortstop—Phil Rizzuto
Outfield—Joe DiMaggio
Outfield—Rocky Colavito
Outfield—Carl Furillo
Catcher—Yogi Berra
Pitcher—Sal Maglie

FRANK BUCK

First base—Snake Deal
Second base—Nellie Fox
Third base—Possum Whitted
Shortstop—Rabbit Maranville
Outfield—Mule Haas
Outfield—Ox Eckhardt
Outfield—Goat Anderson
Catcher—Doggie Miller
Pitcher—Old Hoss Radbourn

e. e. cummings

first base—r. c. stevens
second base—a. j. mc coy
third base—i. i. mathison
shortstop—j. c. hartman
outfield—g. g. walker
outfield—j. w. porter
outfield—r. e. hildebrand
catcher—j. c. martin
pitcher—w. a. kearns

GOLDA MEIR

First base—Ron Blomberg
Second base—Rod Carew
Third base—Al Rosen
Shortstop—Eddie Feinberg
Outfield—Hank Greenberg
Outfield—Goody Rosen
Outfield—Cal Abrams
Catcher—Joe Ginsberg
Pitcher—Sandy Koufax

GOV. ALFRED E. SMITH

First base—Willie Smith
Second base—George Smith
Third base—Charlie Smith
Shortstop—Billy Smith
Outfield—Al Smith
Outfield—Reggie Smith
Outfield—Elmer Smith
Catcher—Hal Smith
Pitcher—Al Smith

JACK JONES

First base—Nippy Jones
Second base—Dalton Jones
Third base—Willie (Puddinhead) Jones
Shortstop—Cobe Jones
Outfield—Cleon Jones
Outfield—Ruppert Jones
Outfield—Fielder Jones
Catcher—Bill Jones
Pitcher—Randy Jones

LYNDON JOHNSON

First base—Deron Johnson
Second base—Don Johnson
Third base—Billy Johnson
Shortstop—Bob Johnson
Outfield—Alex Johnson

Outfield—Lou Johnson
Outfield—Indian Bob Johnson
Catcher—Cliff Johnson
Pitcher—Walter Johnson

SWEET GEORGIA BROWN

First base—Ike Brown
Second base—Jimmy Brown
Third base—Bobby Brown
Shortstop—Larry Brown
Outfield—Ollie Brown
Outfield—Bobby Brown
Outfield—Gates Brown
Catcher—Dick Brown
Pitcher—Mordecai (Three Finger) Brown

BETTY FRIEDAN

First base—Mary Calhoun
Second base—Sadie Houck
Third base—She Donahue
Shortstop—Lena Blackburne
Outfield—Gail Henley
Outfield—Baby Doll Jacobson
Outfield—Estel Crabtree
Catcher—Bubbles Hargrave
Pitcher—Lil Stoner

JAMES BEARD

First base—Juice Latham
Second base—Peaches Graham
Third base—Pie Traynor
Shortstop—Chico Salmon
Outfield—Soupy Campbell
Outfield—Peanuts Lowrey
Outfield—Oyster Burns
Catcher—Pickles Dillhoefer
Pitcher—Noodles Hahn

J. P. MORGAN

First base—Norm Cash
Second base—Don Money
Third base—Milton Stock
Shortstop—Ernie Banks
Outfield—Art Ruble
Outfield—Elmer Pence
Outfield—Bobby Bonds
Catcher—Gene Green
Pitcher—Jim Grant

NORMAN VINCENT PEALE

First base—Earl Grace
Second base—Johnny Priest
Third base—Frank Bishop
Shortstop—Angel Hermoso
Outfield—Dave Pope
Outfield—Hi Church
Outfield—Maurice Archdeacon

Catcher—Mickey Devine
Pitcher—Howie Nunn

JOHN COLEMAN

First base—Sunny Jim Bottomley
Second base—Nippy Jones
Third base—Gene Freese
Shortstop—Stormy Weatherly
Outfield—Hurricane Hazle
Outfield—Curt Flood
Outfield—Icicle Reeder
Catcher—Sun Daly
Pitcher—Windy McCall

JIMMY THE GREEK

First base—Frank Chance
Second base—Lucky Jack Lohrke
Third base—Charlie Deal
Shortstop—John Gamble
Outfield—Curt Welch
Outfield—Trick McSorley
Outfield—Ace Parker
Catcher—Candy LaChance
Pitcher—Shufflin' Phil Douglas

JOHN JAMES AUDUBON

First base—Andy Swan
Second base—Johnny Peacock
Third base—Jiggs Parrott
Shortstop—Chicken Stanley
Outfield—Ducky Medwick
Outfield—Goose Goslin
Outfield—Bill Eagle
Catcher—Birdie Tebbetts
Pitcher—Robin Roberts

FOSTER BROOKS

First base—Sherry Robertson
Second base—Mickey Finn

Third base—Billy Lush
Shortstop—Bobby Wine
Outfield—Jigger Statz
Outfield—Brandy Davis
Outfield—Half Pint Rye
Catcher—George Gibson
Pitcher—John Boozer

RAND-MCNALLY

First base—Frank Brazill
Second base—Chile Gomez
Third base—Frenchy Bordagaray
Shortstop—Sal Madrid
Outfield—Germany Schaefer
Outfield—Dutch Holland
Outfield—Clyde Milan
Catcher—Dick West
Pitcher—Vinegar Bend Mizell

QUEEN ELIZABETH

First base—Duke Carmel
Second base—Royal Shaw
Third base—Count Campau
Shortstop—John Knight
Outfield—Prince Oana
Outfield—Bris Lord
Outfield—Mel Queen
Catcher—Earl Averill
Pitcher—Clyde King

Just weeks before Jackie Robinson went to spring training in 1947 with the Brooklyn Dodgers, preparing to enter into the major leagues, the giant of Negro League baseball died. Josh, the black Babe Ruth—or was Babe the white Josh Gibson?—never got the chance to display his talents on a national stage. What might have been—not only for him, but for Cool Papa Bell, Oscar Charleston, Rube Foster, Pop Lloyd, Martin Dihigo, Judy Johnson, Buck Leonard, even the Satchel Paige and Monte Irvin of their primes? We will never know, but at least these men won eventual induction into the Baseball Hall of Fame, in no small measure because of the groundbreaking study of which this forms a chapter, *Only the Ball Was White*.

ROBERT PETERSON

Josh

There is a catcher that any big-league club would like to buy for $200,000. His name is Gibson . . . he can do everything. He hits the ball a mile. And he catches so easy he might as well be in a rocking chair. Throws like a rifle. Bill Dickey isn't as good a catcher. Too bad this Gibson is a colored fellow.
—Walter Johnson

There is a story that one day during the 1930s the Pittsburgh Crawfords were playing at Forbes Field in Pittsburgh when their young catcher, Josh Gibson, hit the ball so high and far that no one saw it come down. After scanning the sky carefully for a few minutes, the umpire deliberated and ruled it a home run. The next day the Crawfords were playing in Philadelphia when suddenly a ball dropped out of the heavens and was caught by the startled center fielder on the opposing club. The umpire made the only possible ruling. Pointing to Gibson he shouted, "Yer out—yesterday in Pittsburgh!"

Gibson fans of those years might concede that there was an element of exaggeration in the story, but not much. Josh Gibson was not merely a home run hitter; he was *the* home run hitter. He was the black Babe Ruth, and like the Babe a legend in his own time whose prodigious power was celebrated in fact and fancy. But while it is relatively easy to separate fact from fancy in Ruth's legend, Gibson's suffers from the paucity of certified records about the quantity and quality of his home run production. Old-timers credit Gibson with eighty-nine home runs in one season and seventy-five in another; many of them, of course, were hit against semipro competition.

Whatever the truth of these claims, a strong case can be made for the proposition that Josh Gibson, a right-hand batter, had more power than the great Babe. The clincher in the argument is the generally accepted fact that Gibson hit the longest home run ever struck in Yankee Stadium, Ruth's home for twelve seasons.

Baseball's bible, *The Sporting News* [June 3, 1967], credits Gibson with a drive in a Negro league game that hit just two feet from the top of the stadium wall circling the bleachers in center field, about 580 feet from home plate. It was estimated that had the drive been two feet higher it would have sailed out of the park and traveled some 700 feet!

Some old Negro league players say that Gibson's longest shot in Yankee Stadium struck the rear wall of the bullpen in left field, about 500 feet from the plate. But Jack Marshall, of the Chicago American Giants, recalls an epic blast by Gibson that went *out* of the stadium—the only fair ball ever hit out of the Yankees' park.

In 1934, Josh Gibson hit a ball off of Slim Jones in Yankee Stadium in a four-team doubleheader that we had there—the Philadelphia Stars played the Crawfords in the second game; we had played the Black Yankees in the first game. They say a ball has never been hit out of Yankee Stadium. Well, that is a lie! Josh hit the ball over that triple deck next to the bullpen in left field. Over and out! I never will forget that, because we were getting ready to leave because we were going down to Hightstown, New Jersey, to play a night game and we were standing in the aisle when that boy hit this ball!

Both Ruth and Gibson played before the era of the tape-measure home run, when every long hit is carefully computed, almost to the inch. None of Ruth's towering smashes was ever officially measured, but the best guess of his longest is 550 feet. Only one of Gibson's home runs was ever measured. He was with the Homestead Grays in Monessen, Pennsylvania, one day in the late 1930s when he hit a homer of such impressive dimensions that the mayor ordered the game stopped and a tape measure applied. The result: 512 feet.

Unlike Babe Ruth, whose swing was awesome and whose body wound up like a pretzel when he missed the ball, Gibson's power was generated with little apparent effort. Judy Johnson, who was Gibson's first manager, said:

> It was just a treat to watch him hit the ball. There was no effort at all. You see these guys now get up there in the box and they dig and scratch around before they're ready. Gibson would just walk up there, and he would always turn his left sleeve.

And when Gibson raised his front foot, the infielders began edging backward onto the grass. If he met the pitch squarely and it came to them on one hop, they knew the ball would be in their glove before Gibson could drop his bat.

Josh Gibson was born December 21, 1911, in Buena Vista, Georgia, a village not far from Atlanta. His father scratched a bare living from a patch of ground outside the village. Josh, the first child of Mark and Nancy Gibson, was named Joshua after his grandfather.

At intervals of three years, two other children were born to the Gibsons: Jerry, who would follow Josh into professional baseball as a pitcher with the Cincinnati Tigers, and Annie. By 1923 the Gibson youngsters were growing up, and it became clear to Mark that if they were to have better opportunities than he had had he must join the swelling migration of black men to the North. And so, late that year, he went to Pittsburgh, where he had relatives, to find work. He quickly got a job as a laborer for Carnegie-Illinois Steel, which was later absorbed by U.S. Steel. In early 1924, Mark sent for his family. Josh was twelve years old when the Gibsons settled down in Pleasant Valley, a Negro enclave in Pittsburgh's North Side.

While equal opportunity was only a pleasant dream for a Negro boy in Pittsburgh, still, the change from the oppressive atmosphere of a southern small town was welcomed. "The greatest gift Dad gave me," Gibson said later, "was to get me out of the South."

Baseball was new to the migrant from Georgia, but he was soon the first one chosen for sandlot pickup games when he began demonstrating a talent for hitting the ball. He was always looking for a ballgame, to play or to watch, and he thought nothing of strapping on rollerskates and skating six miles downriver to Bellevue to see a game.

The young Josh did not care especially for football or basketball, the other neighborhood sports, but swimming caught his interest and as a teenager he brought home a number of medals from the city playground pools. At sixteen he was on his first uniformed baseball club—the Gimbels A.C., an all-Negro amateur team playing in Pittsburgh. He was already a catcher, as he would be throughout his career, except for an occasional game in the outfield.

His education was over. Josh had gone through fifth grade in the Negro school in Buena Vista and continued in elementary school in Pittsburgh. He dropped out after the completing the ninth grade in Allegheny Pre-Vocational School, where he learned the rudiments of the electrician's trade. He immediately went to work as an apprentice in a plant that manufactured air brakes. But by this time it was clear that Gibson's vocation would be baseball. He was nearing his full size of 6 feet 1 inch and 215 pounds. He had a moon-round, trusting face, a friendly disposition, and the body of a dark Greek god. His broad shoulders sloped down to tremendous arms, thick with muscle, and his barrel chest tapered in the athlete's classic mold to a deceptively slim-looking waist. Like his arms, Gibson's legs were heavily muscled.

For a Pittsburgh Negro boy who loved baseball, his goal would have to be the Homestead Grays. He could envy the Pirates' heroes of his youth—the Waners, Lloyd and Paul, and Pie Traynor and Burleigh Grimes and Rabbit Maranville—but he could not hope to step into their shoes. The next best thing was the Homestead Grays, who had started twenty years before in the steel town a few miles upriver and were beginning to emerge as a national Negro baseball power. They had Smoky Joe Williams and Johnny Beckwith and Sam Streeter and Vic Harris and Martin Dihigo—names that meant nothing to the typical Pirate fan but that loomed large in Negro baseball.

In 1929 and 1930, when the Grays were strengthening their position as one of the best Negro ballclubs in the country, Josh Gibson was catching for the Crawford Colored Giants of Pittsburgh. This was a semipro club that Josh had had a hand in organizing around a city recreation building in Pittsburgh's Hill District. The Crawfords (not to be confused with Gus Greenlee's powerhouse, which was formed in 1931) played other semipro clubs in and around Pittsburgh for a few dollars a game. No admission was charged for their games, and the collection rarely brought in more than fifty dollars, although crowds of 5,000, attracted by the growing awareness of Gibson's power at the plate, were not uncommon.

The Grays, naturally, soon heard of the big, raw slugger. Judy Johnson, who managed Homestead in 1930, said:

> I had never seen him play but we had heard so much about him. Every time you'd look in the paper you'd see where he hit a ball 400 feet, 500 feet. So the fans started wondering why the Homestead Grays didn't pick him up. But we had two catchers. Buck Ewing was the regular catcher, and Vic Harris, an outfielder, used to catch if we were playing a doubleheader.

In late July, the Kansas City Monarchs, Negro National League champions of 1929, came to Pittsburgh for a series with the Grays, bringing along their new portable lighting system. On July 25, the Grays and Monarchs were battling under these uncertain lights in Forbes Field. Johnson remembers:

Joe Williams was pitching that night and we didn't know anything about lights. We'd never played under 'em before, and we couldn't use the regular catcher's signals, because if he put his hand down you couldn't see it. So we used the glove straight up for a fastball and the glove down—that was supposed to be the curve.

Some way Joe Williams and the catcher got crossed up. The catcher was expecting the curve and Joe threw the fastball and caught him right there, and split the finger. Well, my other catcher was Vic Harris and he was playing the outfield and wouldn't catch. So Josh was sitting in the grandstand, and I asked the Grays' owner, Cum Posey, to get him to finish the game. So Cum asked Josh would he catch, and Josh said, "Yeah, oh yeah!" We had to hold the game up until he went into the clubhouse and got a uniform. And that's what started him out with the Homestead Grays.

Gibson got no hits that night, but he made no errors, either, and that was strange, for he was still a raw-boned eighteen-year-old and clumsy with the mitt. For the rest of that season, Johnson said, "Josh would catch batting practice and then catch the game, he was so anxious to learn. He wasn't much of a catcher then, but he came along fast."

Despite his shortcomings as a catcher, Gibson became an instant regular on the Grays, although he was often used in the outfield during his first year in top competition. His bat simply had to be in the lineup somewhere.

There remains a wide division of opinion among ballplayers who played with and against Gibson during his prime as to his skill as a catcher. Many maintain that he became a good receiver, but never a great one. They hold that he never learned to catch foul pop-ups, that his arm was adequate, but no more than that, and that as a receiver he was not in the same class with Bruce Petway, who threw out Ty Cobb twice trying to steal second in a series in Cuba in the winter of 1910, or Biz Mackey, whose career began in 1920 and spanned thirty years on top clubs, or Frank Duncan, Kansas City Monarchs catcher of the 1920s.

Walter Johnson's description of Gibson as a rocking-chair catcher with a rifle arm suggests otherwise. Joining Walter Johnson in his opinion that Josh was a superior catcher is Roy Campanella, who was beginning his career in professional baseball with the Baltimore Elite Giants in 1937, about the time Gibson reached his peak. Campanella said that Gibson was a graceful, effortless receiver with a strong, accurate arm. He was, said Campy, "not only the greatest catcher but the greatest ballplayer I ever saw."

The middle ground between these extreme opinions is held by Jimmie

Crutchfield, an outfielder who was a teammate of Gibson on the Pittsburgh Crawfords from 1932 through 1936:

> I can remember when he couldn't catch this building if you threw it at him. He was only behind the plate because of his hitting. And I watched him develop into a very good defensive catcher. He was never given enough credit for his ability as a catcher. They couldn't deny that he was a great hitter, but they could deny that he was a great catcher. But I know!

In 1931, Josh Gibson was an established star on the Homestead Grays. He was credited with seventy-five home runs that years as the Grays barnstormed around Pennsylvania, West Virginia, Ohio, and into the southern reaches of New York State, feeding the growing legend about the young black catcher who could hit the ball a country mile. The next year he was lured to the Pittsburgh Crawfords by the free-spending Gus Greenlee to form with Satchel Paige perhaps the greatest battery in baseball history. Gibson stayed with Greenlee's Crawfords for five summers, his fame growing with each Brobdingnagian clout. In 1934 his record was sixty-nine home runs and in the other years his homer production, although not recorded, was from all accounts similarly Ruthian. Or perhaps Gibsonian.

As Greenlee's dream of a baseball dynasty soured, Gibson jumped back to the Grays near the end of the 1936 season. In 1937 he was listed on the Crawfords' spring roster, but by mid-March he was described as a holdout. John L. Clark, Greenlee's publicity man, wrote in the *Pittsburgh Courier* that Greenlee and Rufus (Sonnyman) Jackson, Grays' co-owner, were discussing a trade in which Gibson and Judy Johnson (who had been the Crawfords' third baseman since 1932) would go to the Grays for catcher Pepper Bassett and any infielder, plus $2,500. Here is a measure of Negro baseball's finances. The game's greatest slugger—who was also the paramount drawing card (always excepting Satchel Paige)—and Negro baseball's most accomplished third baseman were to be traded for two journeymen players and $2,500.

That the story was in part a ploy to bring Gibson to terms is evident from Clark's faint praise of the slugger. He said that Gibson was an asset to any club, "but not the kind of asset that more colorful and less capable players might be. With all this ability, he has not developed that 'it' which pulls the cash customers through the turnstiles—although he has been publicized as much as Satchel Paige." Gibson's lack of color, plus a rumor that he had an offer to manage an unnamed club at a higher salary than Greenlee would offer, made it likely that a trade would be made, Clark wrote. Gibson did not come to terms with Greenlee and a trade went through: Gibson and Johnson for

Pepper Bassett and Henry Spearman. No money changed hands. Johnson did not report to the Grays.

And so Josh Gibson returned to the Homestead Grays, his first team. Spring training had hardly begun when he heard the siren call of the dollar to be made with Satchel Paige in the Dominican Republic. He heeded the call. The *Pittsburgh Courier* reported, most improbably, that Gibson had gone to Trujillo-land with the consent of the Grays. In any event, he stayed only until July, returning in time to help the Grays win their first Negro National League championship.

For the next two years, Gibson's big bat was the piledriving punch on the strongest club in Negro baseball. Boasting Buck Leonard, Sam Bankhead, Vic Harris, and other sluggers in addition to Josh, the Grays dominated the league and toyed with their foes on the barnstorming trail. It was such a powerful and well-balanced team that it could survive the loss of Gibson and continue its mastery over the NNL in the 1940 and 1941 seasons after Gibson had jumped to the Mexican League. He earned $6,000 a season with Veracruz, according to the *Courier*, $2,000 more than he was paid by the Grays. If Cum Posey and Sonnyman Jackson had looked on with favor when he had gone to the Dominican Republic in 1937, they were not pleased by his contract-jumping in later years. They won a court judgment against Gibson for $10,000 and laid claim to his Pittsburgh home. But when he signed with the Grays for 1942, all was forgiven and they dropped the suit. Josh Gibson was at the height of his fame and near the peak of his incredible power, envied but popular with other Negro professional ballplayers, and the toast of Pittsburgh's black community. There was nowhere to go but down, and the slide would soon begin.

He had come into big-time Negro baseball twelve years before as a rookie of uncommon rawness, a young man so shy and retiring that when he visited in another player's home he spent the evening looking at his shoes. Now he was self-assured, the main attraction at any party, and he had developed a fondness for the bottle. Gibson's drinking never reached the point where he failed to show up for ballgames—or to hit with power—but in his final five seasons he was occasionally suspended for a few days for "failing to observe training rules," in Cum Posey's delicate phrase.

Another, more ominous, portent of the dark days ahead appeared when he began suffering from recurring headaches. On Jan. 1, 1943, he blacked out, lapsing into a coma that lasted all day and hospitalized him for about ten days. The diagnosis was a brain tumor. Doctors at Pittsburgh's St. Francis Hospital wanted to operate, but he would not permit it, according to his sister, Mrs. Annie Mahaffey. "He figured that if they operated, he'd be like a vegetable."

Gibson's knees, too, were giving him trouble, apparently the result of cartilage damage, and he was slowing to a snail's pace compared with his former speed. In his heyday, Gibson, despite his size, had been one of the fastest runners on the Grays. Yet, even while his troubles were pyramiding, Gibson was still the symbol of power. In 1944 he led the Negro National League in homers with six while batting .338 in 39 league games. The next year he was again home-run champion with eight and boasted a league-leading .393 average in 44 games. As a matter of course, he was chosen as the East's catcher in the East-West all-star games in 1944 and 1946. He missed the 1945 all-star game because it was played during one of his periodic suspensions for violating training rules.

Josh Gibson had played baseball the year-round every year from 1933 through 1945, spending the winter seasons in Puerto Rico, Cuba, Mexico, and Venezuela. His greatest thrill, he said, had been winning the batting title and the most-valuable-player award in the Puerto Rican League in 1941. (He was without doubt the most valuable player in the Negro National League for several seasons, but no MVP award was ever given in the NNL.)

Now, in the winter of 1946, his headaches and blackouts were increasing in frequency and severity, and for the first time since 1933 he stayed home in Pittsburgh. Outwardly, he remained a cheerful, easy-going giant, gregarious and friendly, and only his increasing attachment to liquor betrayed his concern about his illness. "He never got drunk so that he was staggering or anything like that," Mrs. Mahaffey recalled, "but still it worried you, because he wasn't really a drinking man."

On the evening of Jan. 20, 1947, Josh came home and told his mother that he felt sick. He said that he believed he was going to have a stroke. Mrs. Gibson said, "Shush, Josh, you're not going to have no stroke," but she sent him to bed. The family gathered around his bedside and waited for a doctor while Josh

laughed and talked. Then he sent his brother Jerry to the homes of friends to collect his scattered trophies and his radio and bring them home. "So Jerry came back about ten-thirty," Mrs. Mahaffey said, "and we were all laughing and talking, and then he had a stroke. He just got through laughing and then he raised up in bed and went to talk, but you couldn't understand what he was saying. Then he lay back down and died right off."

There are those who believe his death was caused by his disappointment at being denied the opportunity to play in the big leagues. Ted Page, an outfielder who was Gibson's teammate on the Crawfords, said, "Josh knew he was major-league quality. We would go to a major-league game if we had a day off. He was never the kind of a guy to say, 'I'm the great Josh Gibson,' but if he saw a player make a mistake he would say what should have been done, or he might say, 'I would have been expecting that.' "

Page said that Gibson never complained about the hard lot of the Negro professional.

> He wouldn't have traded his life for anything. One weekend, I remember, we played a twilight game at Forbes Field in Pittsburgh. Afterward we jumped in two cars and drove the 600 miles to St. Louis for a 2 P.M. game the next day. And the next day we drove 350 miles to Kansas City for a doubleheader. It was 110 in the shade, but he loved it. That night Josh and I were sitting on the back porch of the hotel and we saw a kid ballgame and we went and joined it. That's the kind of guy he was.

By the standards of Negro baseball, Gibson was well-paid for such labors. During the boom of the early 1940s, he was, next to Satchel Paige, the highest-salaried performer in the game, earning about $6,000 from the Homestead Grays for a five-month season and adding perhaps $3,000 in winter baseball. (A journeyman black player made about $1,250 for the summer and considerably less during the winter, if he played at all.) While Gibson's salary was higher than that of the average major-leaguer during this period, it was nowhere near that of white stars of his stature like Joe DiMaggio, Hank Greenberg, and Ted Williams.

Like them, he hit for a high average as well as for distance. Only for the last three years of his career are official records available, but they show him among the batting leaders in the Negro National League and suggest that in his prime he would have boasted a batting average not far below .400 against strong pitching.

As John L. Clark noted during Gibson's salary wrangle with the Crawfords in 1937, he was "colorless" in the same sense that Joe DiMaggio was. It was the colorlessness of perfection, the ability to do the difficult effortlessly. He loved the game and he played to win, but his performance excited only admiration and awe while Satchel Paige, with equally memorable though different skills, added to them a talent for showmanship. The result was that while hundreds went to the ballgame to see Gibson, thousands went to watch Paige.

Gibson died the year after Jackie Robinson had broken organized baseball's color line at Montreal and only months before Robinson would become the first Negro in the major leagues since Fleet and Weldy Walker in 1884. Gibson himself had had two tantalizing nibbles that suggested he might become the first to cross the line. In 1939, Wendell Smith of the *Courier* reported that Bill Benswanger, president of the Pittsburgh Pirates, had promised a trial for Josh and Buck Leonard, the Grays' slugging first baseman. Smith said Cum Posey had agreed to sell his two stars but Benswanger changed his mind. Benswanger's version was different. He said Cum Posey asked him not to sign Gibson because then other Negro stars would be taken and the Negro National League would be wrecked. In any case, no tryout was held.

A few years later, when the Homestead Grays were playing in Griffith Stadium regularly, Gibson and Leonard were called up to the Washington Senators' offices by Clark Griffith, the owner. "He talked to us about Negro baseball and about the trouble there would be if he took us into the big leagues," Leonard said. "But he never did make us an offer."

Griffith must have been sorely tempted to sign the two black men. His Senators were usually mired deep in the American League's second division, and when they were on the road he could look out of his office and watch Gibson and Leonard busting the fences in his park. In one game in 1943, Gibson hit three home runs there, one of them landing two feet from the top of the left-center-field bleachers, 485 feet from the plate. For the season, he belted eleven home runs to left field, the deep field in Griffith Stadium, playing there only once or twice a week, reportedly more than were hit to left in all American League action in that ballpark.

That Josh Gibson would have been one of baseball's superstars if the color line had been lowered earlier is beyond dispute. It is likely that he would have posed the most serious threat ever to Babe Ruth's lifetime record of 714 home runs in the major leagues.

Gibson did achieve a considerable measure of fame, parochial as it was, as the greatest hitter in Negro baseball. After Satchel Paige, his was easily the most famous name among black players. He is remembered with admiration, affection, and even wonder by old teammates and opponents alike, no small legacy for any man. Since Josh Gibson was not a man to pine for what might have been, perhaps the most fitting epitaph that could be devised was pronounced by Ted Page: "He was a big, overgrown kid who was glad for the chance he had. He loved his life."

Sam Rice retired in 1934 after batting .293, the *lowest* mark of his twenty-year career. He was only thirteen hits shy of 3,000, but in the days before recordmania, no one much cared—2,987 hits seemed a perfectly fine total. What folks did care about was the answer to baseball's great mystery: Did Sam Rice catch that ball in Game Three of the 1925 World Series, or did he not? Umpire Cy Rigler said he did, and that settled the ballgame but not the argument: Sam wasn't saying. He kept on not saying till the day he died, nearly half a century after the incident took place. And then . . .

SHIRLEY POVICH

A Voice from the Grave

Sam Rice's forty-nine-year secret has ended, with his own testimony from beyond the grave that he did, indeed, catch that long, homer-bound drive Earl Smith hit in the 1925 World Series between the Washington Senators and Pittsburgh Pirates.

The truth about the most disputed play in the seventy-one years of World Series history surfaced in a newly found testament written by Rice in 1965, "to be opened after my death."

The Washington outfielder died at eighty-four on October 13, 1974, having steadfastly refused to say unqualifiedly that he had made the catch on October 10, 1925, in Game Three of the Series. He long ago, however, had hinted he would put it in writing for the archives of the Baseball Hall of Fame.

Rice's document turned up the other day, but not at Cooperstown, New York, where Hall of Fame officials had combed the files for more than two weeks and were ready to dismiss reports of a Rice letter as unconfirmed rumor.

It surfaced in downtown New York City, at 30 Wall Street, where Paul S. Kerr, president of the Hall of Fame, has his office. Kerr, to whom the letter had been committed by Rice, was unaware that a search for the letter was under way.

Kerr made a ceremony of disclosing the contents of the letter left by Rice. Before witnesses, and as though ready to read a will, he slit open the envelope and recited its contents.

On that October Saturday almost fifty years ago, President and Mrs. Calvin Coolidge and 36,493 others jam-packed Griffith Stadium. Boy manager Bucky Harris made a defensive move that was prescient, after right fielder Joe (Moon) Harris singled home the run that gave the Senators their 4–3 lead in the seventh.

In the eighth, Harris replaced the slow moving Joe Harris as his right fielder, moved Sam Rice to that spot from center, and called in Earl McNeely as his center fielder.

Rice's speed (at thirty-five he may have still been the fastest man on the team) paid off for the Senators.

It took him into the path of Smith's swat into deep right center and he got a glove on it as man and ball crashed over the 3-foot fence into the seats. Rice and his trophy, or nontrophy, disappeared into the laps of the bleacher fans.

It was at least ten seconds before Rice disengaged himself to show the umpires a baseball in his glove.

In his letter, Rice described all the circumstances in the eighth inning of the game in which catcher Smith came to bat for Pittsburgh: "the ball was a line drive headed for the bleachers towards right center . . . I jumped as high as I could and back handed . . . but my feet hit the barrier . . . and I toppled . . . into the first row of bleachers . . . at no time did I lose possession of the ball."

Such was not the view of the Pirates, who protested loudly that Washington fans in the bleachers had replaced in Rice's glove the ball he had dropped. A score of Pittsburgh supporters in the bleachers offered affidavits that Rice did not hold the ball. The Senators won the game, 4–3, but lost the Series, four games to three.

For the remainder of his life, Rice helped to make mystery of the catch by refusing to make any comment except, "The umpire called him out, didn't he?" For the rest of his years, Rice's was the sardonic smile across the face of the baseball world.

It was at one of the annual, private dinners of members of the Baseball Hall of Fame at Cooperstown that Rice told fellow honorees that he had written his version of the catch, to be opened after his death.

Bill McKechnie, the Pirates' manager in 1925, was one of those to whom Rice confided in 1965 that he had written down his version of the catch. In a postscript, Rice wrote, "I approached McKechnie and said, 'What do you think will be in the letter.' His answer was, 'Sam, there was never any doubt in my mind but what you caught the ball.' "

McKechnie's agreement in 1965 that Rice had made the catch off Smith did not square with his opinion of the play on that October day in 1925.

According to *The Washington Post* account of the game, McKechnie was furious at the decision of umpire Cy Rigler in calling Smith out, and demanded that the other umpires overrule him. Like the other Pirates, McKechnie insisted that Rice had dropped the ball when he fell over the fence.

McKechnie, it was also reported in the *Post*, later took his protest to the box seat of Commissioner Kenesaw Mountain Landis, without success. Landis pointed out it was a judgment play that could not be appealed to him.

Rice's secret letter originally was supposed to go into his file at Cooperstown, but Hall of Fame officials have indicated that because of the public interest in it, it could have its own special display case.

The letter deposited by Rice with Kerr was actually inspired by the late Lee Allen, historian of the Hall of Fame. Allen refused to be content with Rice's evasion when questioned on the subject of the catch.

At each of Rice's visits to Cooperstown, Allen prodded Rice to make public his version of the disputed catch for the Cooperstown records.

When Rice refused to tell his secret, Allen pleaded, "You could at least leave us some kind of document to be opened after your death." It was this suggestion that Rice accepted.

Allen's death preceded Rice's, leaving many officials at Cooperstown unaware of the existence of the letter and fouling the search for it.

Rice was inducted into the Hall of Fame in 1963 by the special Old Timers' Committee, in recognition of his .322 lifetime batting average, his fame as a base stealer, and twenty years of consistent stardom in the American League.

He was more than the fielding star of the 1925 Series. His twelve hits led both teams at bat.

Over his twenty years in the American League, nineteen with Washington and one with Cleveland, Rice batted as high as .350 and .349, and was as great a threat on the bases as at bat. His sixty-three steals led the league in a year when Ty Cobb still was in his prime.

Rice was having a big year at bat in 1932 until late in the season, when his average slumped to a modest, for him, .323. Of course, he might have been tiring a bit near the season's end; he would be forty-one on his next birthday.

Barely 5 feet 10 and a mere 160 pounds, Rice was no overpowering figure in the batter's box. But he was the very model of a big-league hitter drawing a bead on a pitcher with malevolence aforethought.

An episode in Cleveland one year gave evidence of Rice's ability to manage his bat. A Cleveland pitcher, angered by a Washington home run, took a shot at the next batter, Rice, who was forced to hit the dirt. Dusting himself off,

Rice on the next pitch aimed a line drive and got him on the knee. Cleveland needed a new pitcher.

Later in the same game, another pitcher took a shot at Rice out of team loyalty, or some such. One pitch later, he was out of the game; Rice got him on the shin.

TESTIMONY OF SAM RICE: 'I HAD A DEATH GRIP ON IT'

Monday, July 26, 1965

It was a cold and windy day, the right field bleachers were crowded with people in overcoats and wrapped in blankets, the ball was a line drive headed for the bleachers towards right center. I turned slightly to my right and had the ball in view all the way, going at top speed and about 15 feet from bleachers jumped as high as I could and back handed and the ball hit the center of pocket in glove (I had a death grip on it). I hit the ground about five feet from a barrier about four feet high in front of bleachers with all my brakes on but couldn't stop so I tried to jump it to land in the crowd but my feet hit the barrier about a foot from top and I toppled over on my stomach into first row of bleachers, I hit my Adam's apple on something which sort of knocked me out for a few seconds but (Earl) McNeely arrived about that time and grabbed me by the shirt and pulled me out, I remember trotting back towards the infield still carrying the ball for about halfway and then tossed it towards the pitcher's mound. (How I have wished many times I had kept it.) At no time did I lose possession of the ball.

—Sam Rice

Most anyone's list of the five best baseball books ever written will include *The Glory of Their Times*, Larry Ritter's history of the early days of baseball as told by the men who played it. Indeed, such men as Red Barber and Stephen Jay Gould have called it the single greatest of all baseball books. I hasten to agree. The piece below has a curious history: it is a part of *The Glory of Their Times* and yet will not be found in that book. To interview the players, Ritter traveled some 75,000 miles in the early 1960s. His fascinating interview with former pitcher Marty McHale was taped in 1963 but inexplicably languished in the files of the Baseball Hall of Fame until 1982, when it became the centerpiece of the debut issue of a new baseball review, *The National Pastime*.

LAWRENCE S. RITTER

Ladies and Gentlemen, Presenting Marty McHale

Damon Runyon once wrote a story about me, saying this fellow McHale, who is not the greatest ballplayer that ever lived, is probably the most *versatile* man who ever took up the game. This was in the 1920s, after I had left baseball. So Johnny Kieran of *The New York Times* asked Babe Ruth about it, knowing he and I had been on the Red Sox together. Johnny said, "Marty played in the big leagues, he played football in college, he was on the track team, he was on the stage, he wrote for the Wheeler Syndicate and the *Sun*, he was in the Air Service"—and so forth. He went on listing my accomplishments until the Babe interrupted to say, "Well, I don't know about all those things, but he was the best goddamn singer I ever heard!"

You see, I sang in vaudeville for twelve years, a high baritone tenor—an "Irish Thrush," they called it then, and *Variety* called me "The Baseball Caruso." But even before vaudeville, before baseball even, I used to work in a lot of shows around Boston and made trips down to Wakefield, Winchester—minstrel shows, usually—and sometimes these little two-act sketches.

So when I joined the Boston club, a bunch of us—Buck O'Brien, Hughie Bradley, Larry Gardner, and myself—formed the Red Sox Quartette. After a while Gardner gave it up and a fellow named Bill Lyons stepped in. This Lyons was no ballplayer, but Boston signed him to a contract anyway, just to make the name of the act look proper. We were together three years, and when we broke up I was just as well satisfied because it was quite an ordeal keeping the boys on schedule. They just couldn't get used to that buzzer that tells you you're on next. They'd be a couple of minutes late and think nothing of it, but you can't *do* that in vaudeville, you know—you're *on*.

I did a single for about another three years, which was not very good—just good enough so that they paid for it—and then Mike Donlin and I got together. Now, you may not remember Mike, but he was—well, he was the Babe Ruth of his day. "Turkey Mike," they called him, because when he'd make a terrific catch or something he'd do a kind of turkey step and take his cap off and throw it up like a ham, a real ham; but he was a great one, he could live up to that stuff in the field or at the bat. His widow gave me some of his souvenirs: a gold bat and ball that were given to him as the most valuable player in 1905, some cuff links, and a couple of gold cups, one from the Giants and the other from the Reds. He hit over .350 for both of them.

Mike and I were together for five years, doing a double-entendre act called "Right Off the Bat"—not too much singing, Mike would only go through the motions—and we played the Keith-Orpheum circuit: twice in one year we were booked into the Palace in New York, and that was when it was the Palace, not the way it is now! They had nothing but the big headliners. When Mike left for Hollywood, I went back to doing a single. He made a bunch of pictures out there, and that's where he died.

Which did I like better, baseball or vaudeville? Well, I'd call it about 50–50. The vaudeville was more difficult, the traveling. Sure, you had to travel a lot in baseball, but you always had somebody taking care of your trunk, and your tickets and everything; all you had to do was get your slip, hop onto the train, and go to bed. When you got to the hotel your trunk was there. In vaudeville you had to watch your own stuff. I used to say to Mike, you're the best valet I know, because he was always on time with the tickets and had our baggage checks and everything all taken care of, right on the button all the time.

Of course, Mike and I wouldn't have been such an attraction if it hadn't been for baseball, so maybe I ought to tell you how I came to sign with the Red Sox in 1910. First of all, Boston was almost my hometown—I grew up in Stoneham, that's nine miles out, and if you took a trolley car and changed two or three times, you could get to the ballpark. Which I'd done only once—I only saw one big-league game before I played in one, and Cy Young pitched it; I wasn't really a Red Sox fan. But here comes the second reason for my signing: they gave me a *big* bonus. How big? Two thousand dollars, and back then that was money!

You see, that year for Maine University I had thrown three consecutive no-hitters, and the scouts were all over. I had a bid from Detroit, one from Pittsburgh, one from the Giants, and another from the Braves. And there was sort of a veiled offer from Cincinnati, which is an interesting story.

This Cincinnati situation, Clark Griffith was down there managing, and when I reported to the Red Sox, which was in June, following the end of the college term, his club was playing the Braves, over at Braves Field across the tracks from the Huntington Avenue park. Now, the Red Sox were on the road when I and some other college boys reported. We had signed, but the Red Sox didn't want us with them right away: they had to make room for us, they could only have so many players. So I remember that Griffith came over to the Red Sox park one morning to watch the boys work out. The clubhouse man told us we were all being watched—like you'd watch horses, you know, working out each morning, and he said if we wanted to stay with the club, better take it easy and not put too much on the ball and so on. See, the club usually asks waivers on the newcomers immediately upon reporting to see if anybody else is interested in them, and if so they can withdraw the waivers after a certain time.

I remember very definitely—I went out there and I was pitching to the hitters and I put everything I had on the ball, because after looking over that bunch of Red Sox pitchers I could see there was not much chance for a young collegian to crack that lineup.

At any rate, Griffith must have put in some claim, you see, because two days later I was on my way to Chicago to join the Red Sox. They had withdrawn the waivers. I joined them in Chicago and we went from there to Cleveland. I remember my pal Tris Speaker hurt his finger in Chicago and he was out for a few days, and Fordham's Chris Mahoney, who was an outfielder, a pitcher, and a good hitter, took his place.

He and I weren't the only college boys on that team, you know: Bill Carrigan, Jake Stahl, Larry Gardner, Duffy Lewis, Harry Hooper . . . even Speaker went to—not the University of Texas, but Texas Polyclinic, Polytechnic or something of that kind out there; only went for two years, but he went. And Ray Collins and Hughie Bradley, too. Buck O'Brien, he came the next year, he said, "I got a degree, I got a B.S. from Brockton." He said B.S. stood for boots and shoes, meaning that he worked in a factory.

Now, on this day in Cleveland we had Chris Mahoney playing right field, Harry Hooper moved over to center, and Duffy Lewis stayed in left, and Patsy Donovan put me in to pitch my first game in the big leagues against Joe Jackson and those Cleveland boys.

I wasn't what you'd call sloppily relaxed, but I wasn't particularly nervous, either. You see, I was one of the most egotistical guys that God ever put on this earth: I felt that I could beat anybody. I struck out ten of those Naps, including Jackson. The first time he was up, I had Joe two strikes, no balls, and I did something that the average big-league pitcher would never do. Instead of trying to fool him with a pitch, I stuck the next one right through there and caught him flat-footed. He never dreamed I'd do that.

So the next time up there the same thing happened. He hit a foul, then took a strike, and then Red Kleinow, an old head who was catching me, came out for a conference. He said, "What do you want to pitch him, a curveball?" And I said, "No, I'm going to stick another fast one right through there."

He said, "He'll murder it." Well—he did! Joe hit a ball that was like a shot out of a rifle against the right-field wall. Harry Hooper retrieved it in *left* center!

Yes, I had ten strikeouts, but I lost the ballgame. It was one of those sun-field things: a fellow named Hohnhurst was playing first base for Cleveland and, with a man on first, he hit a long fly to left-center field. Harry Hooper, who was in center this day, was dead certain on fly balls, but when Speaker was out there, as Harry said afterwards, he used to let Speaker take everything within range. Harry said he and Duffy Lewis didn't exactly get their signals crossed, but they were not sure as to who was going to take the ball.

Finally Duffy went for it, and just as he made his pitch for the ball the sun hit him right between the eyes and he didn't get his hands on the thing and the run, of course, scored, and Hohnhurst, the fellow who hit the ball—he got himself to second base. Ted Easterly got a single on top of that, and anyway, the score ended up 4–3. That was it.

I was supposed to be a spitball pitcher, but I had a better overhand curve, what they called a drop curve—you'd get that overspin on it and that ball would break much better than a spitter. I had what they call a medium-good fastball, not overpowering but good enough, and if you took something off your curve and your spitter, your fastball looked a lot better. For my slow one, the change-up as they call it now, I tried a knuckler but never could get any results with it, so I stole Eddie Karger's slow-breaking downer. He and I used to take two fingers off the ball and throw it with the same motion as we used for the fastball.

They still have those fellows today that throw spitters, but it doesn't make much difference—because even when the spitter was legal in my day, in both leagues you couldn't pick six good spitball pitchers. You'd take a fellow like Ed Walsh with the White Sox, the two Coveleskis, Burleigh Grimes, and the left-handed spitter in the National League, who has since lost both legs, Clarence Mitchell.

Now, Clarence was a good spitball pitcher, but Walsh was the best. He worked harder at it, had a better break, had better control of it, and he pitched in more ballgames than any pitcher in either league over a period of years.

Eddie Cicotte, he was with us in Boston, you know, he was going with a spitter for a while. He used to throw that emery ball, too, and then he developed what we call the "shine" ball. He used to have paraffin on different parts of his trousers, which was not legal, and he would just go over all the stitches with that paraffin, making the other part of the ball rougher. It was just like the emery situation, but in reverse, and an emery ball is one of the most dangerous, not like the spitter, which can be controlled. But Cicotte's main pitch was the knuckle ball, and he used that to such an extent that we called him Knuckles.

Joe Wood was with the Red Sox when I joined them, too. Now, there was a fellow who could do nearly everything well. He was a great ballplayer, not just a pitcher, he was a good outfielder, he was a good hitter, he was a good baseman, he would run like blazes, he used to work real hard before a ballgame, he was just a good all-around ballplayer and a great pitcher. And he was a fine pool player, too, and billiards. He could play any kind of a card game and well; also he was a good golfer. I think that he could have done nearly everything. If he were playing football, he'd be a good quarterback.

Joey was a natural—and talking about egotistical people, there's a guy who had terrific confidence, terrific. Without being too fresh, he was very cocky, you know. He just had "the old confidence."

I wasn't with Boston the year they won the World's Championship and Joey won those thirty-four games and then three more against the Giants, but I was at the Series and wrote a story about that final game. I saw the Snodgrass muff—he was careless, and that happens. But right after that he made a gorgeous running catch.

Earlier in that game Harry Hooper made the best catch I ever saw. I hear from Harry twice a year or so; he lives in California, and he's got plenty of the world's goods. Harry made this catch—he had his back to the ball—and from the bench it looked like he caught it backhanded, over his shoulder. After I sent my story to him, he wrote to me. "I thought it was a very good catch, too," he said, "but you were wrong in your perspective. When I ran for that ball, I ran with my back toward it and you guys with your craning necks were so excited about it, when I ran into the low fence"—you see, the bleachers came up from a low fence in Fenway—"the fence turned me around halfway to the right and I caught the ball in my bare right hand." Imagine!

In 1913 I joined the Yankees—they weren't called the Highlanders any more—and then three years later I went back to the Red Sox. Bill Carrigan, who was the Boston manager then, said, "Now that you're seasoned enough you can come back and pitch for a *big-league* team." The Yankees in those days were a terrible ballclub. In 1914 I lost sixteen games and won only seven, with an earned-run average under three. I got no runs. I would be beaten one to nothing, two to nothing, three to one, scores like that. You were never ahead of anybody. You can't win without runs. Take this fellow who's pitching for the Mets, Roger Craig, what did he lose—twenty-two, something like that? What did he win—five? One to nothing, two to nothing, terrible.

When I got to New York, Frank Chance was the manager, a great guy. He had a reputation as a really tough egg, but if you went out there and worked and hustled and showed him that you were interested in what you were doing, he would certainly be in your corner, to the extent that he would try and get you more money come contract time.

I have a watch, one of these little "wafer" watches, that Chance gave me in 1914 after I guess about the first month. I had won a couple of games for him, one of them was the opening game against the World Champion A's, and one day, just as a gesture, he said, he gave me this watch.

Frank and I were such good friends that late in 1914, when we were playing a series in Washington, after dinner, one evening he said let's take a little walk. So we went out to a park across from the hotel and sat down. "I'm going to quit," he said. "I can't stand this being manager, can't stand being the manager of this ballclub."

He said, "We're not going to get anyplace. I've got a good pitching staff"— and he did have a good pitching staff—"but you fellows are just batting your heads against the wall every time you go out there, no runs." The owners wouldn't get him any players, see, and he said, "I just can't take it—I'm going to quit."

He had already talked it over with the front office in New York, and one of

the reasons he took me out to the park was that he had told them which men he thought they should keep, and I happened to be one of three pitchers along with Slim Caldwell and Ray Fisher, and he said I know that you'll be working in vaudeville next winter and I would advise you to get yourself a two- or three-year contract, if you can, before you leave New York on your tour, which was very good advice—which advice I didn't take. I was too smart—you know how it is, very smart—so Mike Donlin and I went out on the Orpheum circuit that winter after opening at the Palace.

So Mike, before we left New York, he said, you better go over to the Yankee office and get yourself signed in before we leave for Chicago. He said, you never can tell what's going to happen. I, being very, very smart, I said, "No, I'll be worth more money to them in the spring than I am now after the publicity we will get in vaudeville this winter."

But I was wrong, because during the winter, while we were in Minneapolis at the Orpheum theater, Devery and Farrell sold the team to Ruppert and Huston. I'm quite sure I could have made a deal with Frank Farrell for a two- or three-year contract before leaving, but as I say I wasn't very smart.

When we got back east, Bill Donovan (that's Bill, not Patsy) had been appointed manager of the Yankees, and he was not in favor of anybody having a long-term contract. I didn't even last out the year with him.

It seemed every time I pitched against Washington I had Walter Johnson as an opponent, or Jim Shaw, either one. Griffith, he used to . . . I don't know . . . I had an idea he didn't pitch them against Caldwell. It seemed that every time Slim pitched, the team would get him three or four runs—though he didn't need them, he was a great pitcher.

Was Johnson as great a pitcher as they say? Let me tell you, he was *greater* than they say. He was with one of the worst ballclubs imaginable, not quite as bad as the old Yankees but almost as bad.

When I got out of the Air Service, after the War—you see, I quit baseball on the Fourth of July, I think, in 1917 and went into the Air Service—when I came out I went to work for the New York *Evening Sun*. I wrote articles, and the *Sun* used to run them every Saturday. The Wheeler Syndicate used to sell them to—wherever they could sell them, Boston, Philadelphia, Newark, anywhere they could, you know, and I used to get five, two, four, eight dollars apiece for them, and one of the stories that I wrote was about Walter Johnson.

I wrote one about Joey, too, and about Cicotte, and Mathewson, oh, so many of them. In the story about Johnson, I wondered what would have happened if he had been pitching for the Giants, who could get him five or six runs nearly every time he started, and I'm wondering if he'd *ever* lose a ballgame. I found out from Joe Vila, who was the sports editor for the Sun, that Matty didn't care very much for that.

Matty was a very good friend of Mike's, and so was McGraw, who was my sponsor into the Lambs Club. He was a Jekyll and Hyde character. Off the field he was very affable, but the minute he'd get in uniform, he was one of the toughest guys you'd ever want to know. Mike used to tell me a lot of inside information, which of course helped me when I was writing these stories.

Do you know about the movie Speaker and I made? In 1917, just before I went into the Service, we produced a motion picture of the big stars in both major leagues. We had $80,000 worth of bookings for the picture, and then they declared baseball during the War not essential, so all the bookings were canceled. We sold the rights to the YMCA to use it in the camps all over Europe, in the ships going over and back, and in the camps here.

After the War was over I showed the film to my friend Roxy, God rest him, and he took the thing over and showed it at the Rivoli and the Rialto and down to Fifth Avenue, and then I happened to come into Wall Street to work as a stockbroker—in 1920 I started my own firm, which I still run today—and I forgot all about the film.

It was put in the morgue some place up at the Rialto or the Rivoli, and the YMCA lost their prints somewhere over in France, but I had left in the tins some cuts and out-takes of the shots of—well, Speaker, Hooper, Ruth, Wood, Matty, and Johnson and all, and I still have them. I showed the clips only about two years ago at the Pathé projection room one day and they still look pretty good.

The game's a lot different today from what it was when I played. The biggest change—and the worst one, in my opinion—is the home run. Now, let's first talk of the fellow going up to the plate. Seventy-five percent of the time he goes up there with the thought of hitting the ball out of the ballpark, and it's not too difficult to do, because they have moved the ballpark in on him. Now, in right field and center field and left field, you've got stands. They used to have a bleacher, way out, in the old days, but the only home run you'd get would be if you hit it between the fielders. "In grounds," they'd call it, a home run in grounds: if a ball got in between those fielders and if you had any speed, they wouldn't be able to throw you out. Today, if you hit a good long fly it's in one of these short stands.

In the old days they juiced up the ball some, but when they talk about the dead ball—there *never* was any dead ball that I can remember. I've got a couple of scars on my chin to prove it. I saw Joe Jackson hit a ball over the top of the Polo Grounds in right field—*over the top of it*—off one of our pitchers, and I have never seen or heard of anyone hitting it over since, and that was around 1914–15, in there.

Today's ball is livelier, no doubt of that. They are using an Australian wool now in winding the core of the ball. In the old days they used wool but not one that is as elastic as this wool. The bats are whippier, too. But the principal reason for all these homers is the concentration of the hitter on trying to hit the ball out of the park.

The fielding today? Well, any of these boys in the big leagues today could field in any league at any time. I think the better equipment has more to do with the spectacular play. You take this here third baseman up with the Yankees—Clete Boyer—he's terrific, just terrific. Larry Gardner, who played third on the Boston team with me, he was a great third baseman, and he had that "trolley-wire throw" to first, but Larry was not as agile as Boyer. I think Boyer is a little quicker. But, if you want a fellow to compare with Boyer, take Buck Weaver of that Black Sox team. He would field with Boyer any day, and throw with him, and he was a better hitter. He would be my all-time third baseman.

Players of my day, give them the good equipment, and they would be just as good or better. Now, you take a fellow like Wagner—I don't mean the Wagner we had with the Red Sox, but the Pirates' Wagner, Honus Wagner, who came to see us in Pittsburgh at the theater, and he took up the whole dressing room with that big can of his. There was one of the most awkward-looking humans you ever saw, but he made the plays, without the shovel glove. And Speaker—could a big glove have made him any better?

As an outfielder, Speaker was in a class by himself. He would play so close to the infield that he'd get in on rundown plays! Then the next man perhaps would hit a long fly into center field and he would be on his bicycle with his back to the ball—not backing away, he'd turn and run—and you'd think he had a radar or a magnet or something because just at the proper time he'd turn his head and catch the ball over his shoulder.

Those fellows, Speaker, Lewis, and Hooper, they used to practice throwing, something that you don't see anymore. Those fellows would have a cap down near the catcher and they'd see who would come closest to the cap when they'd throw from the outfield. They all had marvelous arms. Nobody would run on them, and I think that most of the people who ever saw them play would say there was no trio that could compare with them.

Mike and I, in our act, we used to do a number called, "When You're a Long, Long Way From Home." In it I used to do a recitation, and the last two lines were, "When you're on third base alone, you're still a long, long way from home." It was serious, about life being like a game of baseball. Times have changed—a boy can't peek through a knothole in a concrete fence—but that's still true.

In the year Marty McHale spoke with Ritter, a rookie named Rose broke in with the Cincinnati Reds. He played second base then—rather well, too, though he didn't *look* like a second baseman. When he moved to left field, and right field, and third base, and finally first base, he wrestled those positions to the mat as well, never stylishly but always efficiently. At the bat he conjured up no visions of DiMaggio's dignity or Williams's fluidity or Mantle's power, but he chugged along until one day he woke up to find himself within striking distance of the Everest of batting records: Ty Cobb's 4,191 hits. Pete Rose has played the game with the vigor and drive of Cobb, though without his repellent ferocity. A throwback to the values of the dead ball era, a proud anachronism, Rose has played baseball with a unique vision that has, over two decades' time, been accompanied by an engaging voice. Here, *Quotations from Chairman Pete*, or, *The Little Red Book*.

PETE ROSE

La Vie en Rose

On awards: "I have gathered together a whole heap of trophies. The only award I've never won and don't ever want to win is the Comeback of the Year Award."

On sliding headfirst: "Sliding headfirst is the safest way to get to the next base, I think. And the fastest. You don't lose your momentum. . . . And there is one more important reason that I slide headfirst. It gets my picture in the newspaper."

On being a manager: "The manager of a team is like a stagecoach. He can't move unless he has the horses."

On happiness: "Making good money and having fun doing it at the same time is almost like having a license to steal. But there is the old saying that money can't buy happiness. If it could, I would buy myself four hits every game."

On self-control: "Everyone has seen a batter strike out. This grown man throws his bat and then kicks his helmet. Why did he take it out on the helmet and the bat? He was the one who couldn't hit the ball. If you want to do something to show you are angry, go beat your own head against the wall. You are the one who struck out."

On road games: "I like to play on the road. I usually get an extra time at bat out of a road game. The visiting team always seems to hit in the ninth inning. When you are at home and are leading in the game, you lose the possible at bat in the last of the ninth."

On team loyalty: "Sparky [Anderson] used to say that you don't win any games by staying in the clubhouse. I agree with him, so I have never been late. I have never missed batting practice. I've never missed a bus. I've never missed an airplane. But I do get sick once in a while."

On tough pitchers: "When people ask me, 'Who was the toughest pitcher you ever faced?', I have to say that there has never been a pitcher who over-impressed me. That's not meant to be a bragging statement. It's just that I get up for good pitchers."

On celebrations: "I don't drink. And if you don't drink, you don't celebrate very well. The real celebration comes only when the champagne flows after you win the World Series."

On having a street named for him in Cincinnati: "They should have named an alley after me for the way I acted in high school."

On New York Mets fans: "I enjoy Shea Stadium. But the fans are something else. I look upon each game there as an experience. I get to go to a zoo and don't have to pay admission."

On emotion: "It doesn't take much to get me up for baseball. Once the National Anthem plays, I get chills; I even know the words to it now."

On Ty Cobb: "I doubt that his lifetime .367 batting average would hold up in modern-day baseball. If Ty Cobb came up in 1963 like I did, he'd have a batting average of about .320."

To Carlton Fisk, in the tenth inning of Game Six of the 1975 Series: "This is some kind of game, isn't it?"

On winning: "Somebody's gotta win and somebody's gotta lose—and I believe in letting the other guy lose."

On speed: "I'm not a great runner. I'm no Joe Morgan, but I'm not bad for a white guy."

On fame: "I always say, the only time you gotta worry about getting booed is when you're wearing a white uniform. And I've never been booed wearing a white uniform."

On his love of the game: "I'd walk through hell in a gasoline suit to keep playing baseball."

Baseball is the great repository of national myths—commonly held beliefs that may or may not be "true," in baseball or in American life: fair play (sportsmanship), the rule of law (objective arbitration of disputes), equal opportunity (each side has its innings), the brotherhood of man (bleacher demographics), and so on. Baseball also provides contests and contestants of epic scale: the oft-told tales rise to the realm of myth, from which heights they nurture life and literature. This essay was published on the *New York Times* Op-Ed page on Opening Day, 1973.

PHILIP ROTH

My Baseball Years

In one of his essays George Orwell writes that, though he was not very good at the game, he had a long hopeless love affair with cricket until he was sixteen. My relations with baseball were similar. Between the ages of nine and thirteen, I must have put in a forty-hour week during the snowless months over at the neighborhood playfield—softball, hardball, and stickball pick-up games—while simultaneously holding down a full-time job as a pupil at the local grammar school. As I remember it, news of two of the most cataclysmic public events of my childhood—the death of President Roosevelt and the bombing of Hiroshima—reached me while I was out playing ball. My performance was uniformly erratic; generally okay for those easygoing pick-up games, but invariably lacking the calm and the expertise that the naturals displayed in stiff competition. My taste, and my talent, such as it was, was for the flashy, whiz-bang catch rather than the towering fly; running and leaping I loved, all the do-or-die stuff—somehow I lost confidence waiting and waiting for the ball lofted right at me to descend. I could never make the high-school team, yet I remember that, in one of the two years I vainly (in both senses of the word) tried out, I did a good enough imitation of a baseball player's *style* to be able to fool (or amuse) the coach right down to the day he cut the last of the dreamers from the squad and gave out the uniforms.

Though my disappointment was keen, my misfortune did not necessitate a change in plans for the future. Playing baseball was not what the Jewish boys of our lower-middle-class neighborhood were expected to do in later life for a living. Had I been cut from the high school itself, *then* there would have been hell to pay in my house, and much confusion and shame in me. As it was, my family took my chagrin in stride and lost no more faith in me than I actually did in myself. They probably would have been shocked if I had made the team.

Maybe I would have been too. Surely it would have put me on a somewhat different footing with this game that I loved with all my heart, not simply for the fun of playing it (fun was secondary, really), but for the mythic and aesthetic dimension that it gave to an American boy's life—particularly to one whose grandparents could hardly speak English. For someone whose roots in America were strong but only inches deep, and who had no experience, such as a Catholic child might, of an awesome hierarchy that was real and felt, baseball was a kind of secular church that reached into every class and region of the nation and bound millions upon millions of us together in common concerns, loyalties, rituals, enthusiasms, and antagonisms. Baseball made me understand what patriotism was about, at its best.

Not that Hitler, the Bataan Death March, the battle for the Solomons, and the Normandy invasion didn't make of me and my contemporaries what may well have been the most patriotic generation of schoolchildren in American history (and the most willingly and successfully propagandized). But the war we entered when I was eight had thrust the country into what seemed to a child—and not only to a child—a struggle to the death between Good and Evil. Fraught with perilous, unthinkable possibilities, it inevitably nourished a patriotism grounded in moral virtue and bloody-minded hate, the patriotism that fixes a bayonet to a Bible. It seems to me that through baseball I was put in touch with a more humane and tender brand of patriotism, lyrical rather than martial or righteous in spirit, and without the reek of saintly zeal, a patriotism that could not so easily be sloganized, or contained in a high-sounding formula to which you had to pledge something vague but all-encompassing called your "allegiance."

To sing the National Anthem in the school auditorium every week, even during the worst of the war years, generally left me cold. The enthusiastic lady teacher waved her arms in the air and we obliged with the words: "See! Light! Proof! Night! There!" But nothing stirred within, strident as we might be—in the end, just another school exercise. It was different, however, on Sundays out at Ruppert Stadium, a green wedge of pasture miraculously walled in among the factories, warehouses, and truck depots of industrial Newark. It would, in fact, have seemed to me an emotional thrill forsaken if, before the Newark Bears took on the hated enemy from across the marshes, the Jersey City Giants, we hadn't first to rise to our feet (my father, my brother, and I—along with our inimical countrymen, the city's Germans, Italians, Irish, Poles, and, out in the Africa of the bleachers, Newark's Negroes) to celebrate the America that had given to this unharmonious mob a game so grand and beautiful.

Just as I first learned the names of the great institutions of higher learning by trafficking in football pools for a neighborhood bookmaker rather than from our high school's college adviser, so my feel for the American landscape came less from what I learned in the classroom about Lewis and Clark than from following the major-league clubs on their road trips and reading about the minor leagues in the back pages of *The Sporting News.* The size of the continent got through to you finally when you had to stay up to 10:30 P.M. in New Jersey to hear via radio "ticker-tape" Cardinal pitcher Mort Cooper throw the first strike of the night to Brooklyn shortstop Pee Wee Reese out in "steamy" Sportsman's Park in St. Louis, Missouri. And however much we might be told by teacher about the stockyards and the Haymarket riot, Chicago only began to exist for me as a real place, and to matter in American history, when I became fearful (as a Dodger fan) of the bat of Phil Cavarretta, first baseman for the Chicago Cubs.

Not until I got to college and was introduced to literature did I find anything with a comparable emotional atmosphere and aesthetic appeal. I don't mean to suggest that it was a simple exchange, one passion for another. Between first discovering the Newark Bears and the Brooklyn Dodgers at seven or eight and first looking into Conrad's *Lord Jim* at age eighteen, I had done some growing up. I am only saying that my discovery of literature, and fiction particularly, and the "love affair"—to some degree hopeless, but still earnest—that has ensued, derives in part from this childhood infatuation with baseball. Or, more accurately perhaps, baseball—with its lore and legends, its cultural power, its seasonal associations, its native authenticity, its simple rules and transparent strategies, its longueurs and thrills, its spaciousness, its suspensefulness, its heroics, its nuances, its lingo, its "characters," its peculiarly hypnotic tedium, its mythic transformation of the immediate—was the literature of my boyhood.

Baseball, as played in the big leagues, was something completely outside my own life that could nonetheless move me to ecstasy and to tears; like fiction it could excite the imagination and hold the attention as much with minutiae as with high drama. Mel Ott's cocked leg striding into the ball, Jackie Robinson's pigeon-toed shuffle as he moved out to second base, each was to be as deeply affecting over the years as that night—"inconceivable," "inscrutable," as any night Conrad's Marlow might struggle to comprehend—the night that

Dodger wild man, Rex Barney (who never lived up to "our" expectations, who should have been "our" Koufax), not only went the distance without walking in half a dozen runs, but, of all things, threw a no-hitter. A thrilling mystery, marvelously enriched by the fact that a light rain had fallen during the early evening, and Barney, figuring the game was going to be postponed, had eaten a hot dog just before being told to take the mound.

This detail was passed on to us by Red Barber, the Dodger radio sportscaster of the forties, a respectful, mild Southerner with a subtle rural tanginess to his vocabulary and a soft country-parson tone to his voice. For the adventures of "dem bums" of Brooklyn—a region then the very symbol of urban wackiness and tumult—to be narrated from Red Barber's highly alien but loving perspective constituted a genuine triumph of what my English professors would later teach me to call "point of view." James himself might have admired the implicit cultural ironies and the splendid possibilities for oblique moral and social commentary. And as for the detail about Rex Barney eating his hot dog, it was irresistible, joining as it did the spectacular to the mundane, and furnishing an adolescent boy with a glimpse of an unexpectedly ordinary, even humdrum, side to male heroism.

Of course, in time, neither the flavor and suggestiveness of Red Barber's narration nor "epiphanies" as resonant with meaning as Rex Barney's pregame hot dog could continue to satisfy a developing literary appetite; nonetheless, it was just this that helped to sustain me until I was ready to begin to respond to the great inventors of narrative detail and masters of narrative voice and perspective like James, Conrad, Dostoevsky, and Bellow.

"Baseball-American," Ring Lardner called it in his 1921 contribution to H. L. Mencken's *The American Language*. Purists then deplored the incursion of ballfield patois into the native speech, but they were way off base. How pale a thing American English would be without *bonehead, rhubarb, rain check, pinch hitter, change-up, hit-and-run, rabbit ears*, and such. William Safire's lexicographic home run was written during the baseball strike of 1981, when the players took their ball and went home. (The previous strikes alluded to in the opening words took place in 1972 and 1912; correctly, William Safire does not count the season-long rebellion of 1890, in which the players formed their own league.)

WILLIAM SAFIRE

Out of Left Field

Because baseball's third strike has so impoverished the daily reading of the nation's national-pastime junkies, here is a survey from the Hot Stove League of the effect of baseball on the American language.

When a professor of atmospheric science predicted that recent changes in the sun's activity foretold a dry spell of several years in the Northeast, another expert—Robert Harnack, a meteorologist at Rutgers—called that forecast "completely out of left field."

Where in the heavens or on earth is "left field"? How did that area on the baseball field become the metaphoric epitome of far-outedness? To come "*from out of* left field" is to be rooted in the ridiculous, crackbrained, farfetched; to "*be* out *in* left field" is, according to *American Speech* magazine in 1961, to be "disoriented, out of contact with reality."

When asked for the derivation, members of the Abner Doubleday Lodge of the Lexicographic Irregulars lobbed in these ideas:

"In the older, less symmetrical baseball stadia," writes Robert J. Wilson, Jr., of Riverside, Connecticut, "left field was usually 'deeper' than right, and thus coming from left field was coming in from a 'far-out' region."

Our ambassador to the European office of the United Nations, Gerald Helman, writes from Geneva: "Right field was thought of as the most difficult to play because it was the 'sun field,' and required the fielder to have a strong arm for the long throw to third. As a consequence, the good hitting, poor fielding players were put in left. . . . Because of the defensive inadequacies of left fielders, you could expect almost anything to happen when the ball was hit to them."

On the other hand: "The power of a batter in baseball or softball is to his/her 'pull,' or opposite field," posits Thomas Carter of Dayton. "Since some 90 percent of the population is right-handed, this means that many more long hits can be expected to left field. Therefore, the left fielder will usually play farther back than the other outfielders. This then leads to the linking of 'left field' to a person, thing, or idea that is far out." Could be.

"Left field is about as far as one can get from the desirable seats," suggests Morton Brodsky of Lancaster, Pennsylvania. "The home team's bench is generally, if not always, along the first-base line. This makes the preference for hometown fans (1) from home plate to first base, (2) from home plate to third base, (3) right field, (4) left field. Of course, modern stadia have seating all the way around, but I think that 'out in left field' originated in the days when there was nothing out there but a fence."

"Imagine some right-hander of yesteryear (a preponderance of pioneer pitchers were right-handed)," says Jerry Oster of New York City, "with a big sidearm delivery such that the ball, especially to a right-handed batter, seemed to come out of left field."

Since the earliest citation of the phrase appeared in *American Speech*, I queried the editor of that publication, John Algeo, who is one of the heavy hitters in the big league of linguistics today. He assumed it had at least a pseudobaseball origin and appeared early in psychiatric slang; then he tossed himself a fat pitch: "The explanation that the left field was far off from the home base overlooks the fact that the right field is equally far from the home base and the center field is even farther. Why then left field instead of right field or center field?"

Professor Algeo took a hefty cut: "My guess (and it is no more than a guess) is that the expression is a metaphor referring to a baseball field, but was never actually a baseball term. Probably it was coined by someone who watched baseball but was not a player or real aficionado.

"To be in the *outfield* is to be far out. However, the expression *out in the outfield* is uneuphonious, redundant, and too general; it doesn't make a snappy remark. *Center* and *right* both have highly positive connotations that conflict with the sense of isolation that the term was wanted for. . . . *Center* suggests all the virtues of moderation and the golden mean. *Right* suggests correctness, dexterity, and so on (we don't have to go into the political associations). *Left* is certainly the best word for associations—lefties are a minority, they are sinister (etymologically at least) and (at least by pun) they get left behind."

Mr. Algeo concurs with Irregular Carter's observation that balls hit to left field are usually hit harder, causing the fielder to play deeper: "Since the left fielder is farther removed from the center of action in the infield, his position becomes a metaphor for isolation."

In addition, consider the flakiness factor: "Center field would not be appropriate," agrees David Zinman, science editor for *Newsday*, after checking with Stan Isaacs, who used to write a sports column called "Out of Left Field," "because it is the mainstream of the outfield. 'Right' field denotes correctness. . . . On the other hand, 'left' field has overtones of radicalism in politics. Also, left-handers, particularly pitchers, are often thought of as slightly different, sometimes screwy or dizzy individuals."

Like Lucy in the comic strip "Peanuts," Mrs. Melvin Golub of Dunkirk, Maryland, disagrees with everybody; it is her experience that "one rarely hits to left field. The outfielder has little to do; hence, he is lonely. . . . When our company plays softball, my son sends me out to play left field so I can't get into too much trouble." Such an iconoclastic view flies in the face of all statistics about where most hard-hit balls go, and is truly out of left field.

Ballpark Figure

First up, we have just seen how baseball is a rich source for metaphors. How many other expressions owe their origin to the game that started as "rounders" in England, became "the New York game" in the 1840s, and was spread across the United States by the New York and New Jersey regiments during the Civil War? I don't have even a ballpark figure.

Ballpark figure, however, stems from *ball grounds* and *ball fields* in the mid-nineteenth century, to *baseball park* in the 1890s, to *in the ballpark* around 1960.

"That's the windup," says lexicographer Stuart Flexner, who intends to demolish the Abner Doubleday myth in his next book. "Now here's the pitch: Our Random House dictionary citation files show the term first started out as *in the ballpark* (1962), as when talking about figures, estimates, etc., with 'I hope that's in the ballpark.' Then, in 1968, we first recorded *ballpark figure* from *The Seattle Times*."

Evidently the ballpark was used as a microcosm: To be *in the ballpark* (even if out in left field) was to be "in this world," just as to be *out of the ballpark* meant to be "totally out of play." Thus, an estimate—or "guesstimate"—that was adjudged within the range of reasonableness was *in the ballpark*, and a number of that sort recently became a *ballpark figure*.

Baseball terms were given wide circulation by the newspaper *baseball col-*

umn (1869), a creation of *The Brooklyn Union*. "Such columns," reports Flexner, "grew into the popular *sporting column, sporting page,* and *sporting section* (created primarily for baseball fans) in the 1890s, then became known as the *sports page* or *sports section* in the 1920s."

Other baseball metaphors and their debut dates: *to keep one's eye on the ball,* 1907; *to be off base* (disrespectful, wrong), 1912, which was also the year that introduced *to have something on the ball; right off the bat,* 1916; *go to bat for* (to support or defend), 1928; *to play ball with* (cooperate), 1930; *to be in there pitching* and *to take a rain check,* also the thirties. (The first rain check Flexner has was issued in St. Louis in 1884; if you have an earlier one, send it to him. They'll never replay that game.)

We've come to the final inning. Time to head for the dugout.

This is how it was when boys' baseball was still a game, before Little League came along. The passage below is from the 1975 novel *Pride of the Bimbos;* its author is John Sayles, also a film director and screenwriter whose credits include *Return of the Secaucus Seven* and *The Brother from Another Planet.* In 1981 he wrote, "I never thought about being a writer as I grew up; a writer wasn't something to *be.* An outfielder was something to be. Most of what I know about style I learned from Roberto Clemente." The Brooklyn Bimbos of Birmingham, Alabama, are a five-man barnstorming team that plays county fairs in the South. Denzel, the prime actor here, is the nine-year-old son of player Lewis Crawford and travels with the team.

JOHN SAYLES

Pick-up Game

Denzel wandered toward them with his glove under his arm. A few were in the outfield, crowding under liners and pop-ups that a tall boy threw them. "I got it!" they called in unison, "Mine, mine!" Off to one side a dark, barrel-chested kid was playing pepper with a boy who had a bandage over his eye. The rest milled around, joking, tossing gloves and hats in the air, fighting over the remaining bat to take practice swings. They all seemed to know each other.

Denzel squatted next to a thin boy who sat on his glove at the fringe of the action, watching expectantly. He was the only one there smaller than Denzel.

"Gonna be a game?"

"Uh-huh." The thin boy looked up at him, surprised.

"They got regular teams?"

"Nope. They pick sides."

Denzel nodded.

"Hope I get to play," said the thin boy. "When the teams don't come out even I got to sit," he said, "every single time."

He waited for a word of support but Denzel just grunted and moved several feet away. *Might think we come together.*

The ones on what seemed to be the field hacked around a little longer until a movement to start a game began. "Let's go," someone said. "Get this show on the road."

"Somebody be captains."

"Somebody choose up."

Gradually they wandered in and formed a loose group around a piece of packing crate broken roughly in the shape of a home plate. They urged each other to get organized and shrugged their indifference over who would be the captains.

"C'mon, we don't have all day."

"Somebody just choose."

"Big kids against the little kids!" said a fat boy in glasses and they all laughed.

"Good guys against the bad guys!"

"Winners against the losers!"

"The men against the mice!"

"Okay," said the dark, barrel-chested kid, "Whynt we just have the same captains as yesterday?"

"Yeah, but not the same teams."

"Too lopsided."

"That was a slaughter."

"We got scobbed."

"Do it then," said the fat boy, "Bake and the Badger."

"Yeah, shoot for first pick."

"Let's go, choose up."

There was a sudden movement, everybody spreading in a semicircle around two of the boys, jostling not to be behind anyone, the thin boy hopping up and running to join them. Denzel got up slowly and walked to the rear of them. No sense getting all hot and bothered. No big thing. He drifted through hips and shoulders, quietly, till he stood in view of the captains.

They were shooting fingers, best four out of seven, like the World Series. The barrel-chested boy was one of the captains, the one they called the Badger, and the tall boy who had been throwing flies was the other.

Denzel slipped his glove on. It was an oversized Ted Kluszewski model his daddy had handed down to him. Each of the fingers seemed thick as his wrist and there was no web to speak of and no padding in the pocket. Orange and gunky.

The tall boy won on the last shoot and the Badger scowled.

"Alley Oop!" Bake called without even looking.

"Haw-*raaat!*" A wiry kid with arms that hung to his knees trotted out from their midst and stood by Bake. "We got it now, can't lose. Can not *lose!*"

"Purdy!" The Badger barked it like an order and a solid-looking red-haired kid marched out and took his place.

The two first picks began to whisper and nudge at their captains.

"Vernon," whispered the wiry boy, "get Vernon."

"Vernon."

Vernon came to join them, and he and Alley Oop slapped each other's backs at being together.

"Royce," whispered the big redhead. "They get Royce we've had it."

"Royce," said the Badger, and Royce was welcomed into the fold.

"Psssst!" called the fat boy with the glasses to Alley Oop and Vernon. "Have him pick me. You guys need a third sacker."

"Ernie," they said, on their toes leaning over each of Bake's shoulders, "Ernierniernie!"

"Okay, Ernie," he said, and Ernie waddled out with his glove perched on top of his head.

"Gahs looked like you needed some help," he told them. "Never fear, Ernie is here!"

The captains began to take more time in their picking. They considered and consulted and looked down the line before calling out a name. The Badger pounded quick, steady socks into the pocket of his glove while beside him Purdy slowly flapped the jaws of his first-baseman's mitt. Soon there were more that had been chosen than that hadn't. The ones who were picked frisked and giggled behind their captains while the others who hadn't were statues on display. "You," the captains said now, still weighing abilities but unenthusiastic. Finally they just pointed. The Badger walked along the straggling line of left-overs like a general reviewing troops, stood in front of his next man and jerked his thumb back over his shoulder. When there was only one spot left for even teams Denzel and the thin boy were left standing. It was the Badger's pick.

Denzel stood at ease, eyes blank. It grew quiet. He felt the others checking him over and he smelled something. Topps bubble gum, the kind that came with baseball cards. He snuck a glance at the thin boy. His eyes were wide, fixed on the Badger, pleading. He had a round little puff of a catcher's mitt that looked like a red pincushion. There was no sign of a baseball ever having landed in it, no dent of a pocket.

Denzel felt the Badger considering him for a moment, eyes dipping to the thick-fingered old-timer's glove, but then he turned and gave a slight, exasperated nod to the thin boy. "We got him."

Before Denzel could get out of the way Bake's team streamed past him onto the field.

"First base!" they cried, "Dibs on shortstop!" Trotting around him as if he were a tree, looking through the space where he stood. "Bake?" they whined, "Lemme take left huh? I always get stuck at catcher or somethin." Denzel kept his face blank and tried to work the thing back down into his throat. They all knew each other, didn't know whether he was any good or not. No big thing.

He drifted off to the side, considered going back to the van, then sat beyond the third-base line to watch. As if that was what he had come to do in the first place. Nice day to watch a ballgame. He decided he would root for Bake's side.

"Me first," said the Badger, pointing with the bat handle, "you second, you third. Purdy you clean up. Fifth, sixth, semeightnon." They had full teams so Denzel couldn't offer to be all-time catcher and dive for foul tips. You didn't get to bat but it kept you busy and you could show them you could catch. Denzel kept his glove on.

He could tell he was better than a lot of them before they even started and some of the others when the end of the orders got up. The pitching was overhand but not fast. There was a rock that stuck out of the ground for first base and some cardboard that kept blowing so they had to put sod clumps on it for second and somebody's T-shirt for third. Bake played shortstop and was good and seemed a little older than the others. The one called Purdy, the big red-headed one, fell to his knees after he struck out. Everybody had backed way up for him. Alley Oop made a nice one-handed catch in center. Whenever there was a close play at a base, Badger would run over and there would be a long argument and he would win. The thin boy had to be backed up at catcher by the batting team so it wouldn't take forever to chase the pitches that went through. The innings went a long time even when there weren't a lot of runs because the pitchers were trying tricky stuff and couldn't get it close. Denzel followed the action carefully, keeping track of the strikes and outs and runs scored, seeing who they backed up for and who they moved in for, who couldn't catch, who couldn't throw, keeping a book on them the way his daddy and Pogo had taught him he should. When fat Ernie did something funny he laughed a little along with the rest of them. Once somebody hit a grounder too far off to the left for the third baseman or left fielder to bother chasing. "Little help!" they called, and Denzel scrambled after it. He backhanded it moving away, turned and whipped it hard into the pitcher. No one seemed to notice. He sat back down and the game started up again.

The Badger's side got ahead by three and stayed there, the two teams trading one or two runs each inning. They joked and argued with each other while waiting to bat. They practiced slides and catches in stop-action slow-motion and pretended to be TV commentators, holding imaginary microphones and interviewing themselves. They kept up a baseball chatter.

"*Hum*babe!" said the team in the field, "Chuckeratinthere*iss*gahcantit*iss*gahcatit! *Hum*babe! *N*osticknostickchuckeratinthere—"

"*Lets*go!" said the team at bat, "*Biginninbig*inninwegottateamwegotta-team*bang*itonoutthere! *Letsgolets* go!"

Late in the fifth inning a mother's voice wailed over the babble from a distance.

"Jonathaaaan!"

There was a brief pause, the players looking at each other accusingly, seeing who would confess to being Jonathan.

"Jonathan Phelps you get in here!"

The thin boy with the catcher's mitt mumbled something, looking for a moment as if he were going to cry, then ran off toward the camp.

Denzel squatted and slipped his glove on again. He wore it with his two middle fingers out, not for style but so he could make it flex a little. He waited.

The tall boy, Bake, walked in a circle at shortstop with his glove on his hip, looking around. "Hey kid!"

Who me? Denzel raised his eyebrows and looked to Bake.

"You play catcher for them."

Denzel began to rise but the Badger ran out onto the field. "Whoa na! No deal. I'm not takin him. Got enough easy outs awriddy. Will play thout a catcher, you gahs just back up the plate and will have to send somuddy in to cover if there's a play there."

Denzell squatted again and looked to Bake.

"Got to have even teams," he said. "I got easy outs too. If you only got eight that means your big hitters get up more."

"I'm not takin him, that's all there is to it." The Badger never looked to Denzel. "We don't need a catcher that bad. Not gonna get stuck with some little fairy."

Bake sighed. "Okay. He'll catch for us and you can have what's his name. Hewitt."

The Badger thought a minute, scowling, then agreed. Hewitt tossed his glove off and was congratulated on being traded to the winning side.

"Okay," said Bake, "you go catch. You're up ninth."

Denzel hustled behind the plate and the game started up. There was no catcher's gear, so though it was hardball he stood and one-hopped the pitches. He didn't let anything get by him to the kid who was backing him up. He threw the ball carefully to the pitcher. There were no foul tips. Badger got on and got to third with two out. Bake called time. He sent the right fielder in to cover the play at the plate and Denzel out to right.

The one called Royce was up. Denzel had booked him as strictly a pull-hitter. He played medium depth and shaded toward center. The first baseman turned and yelled at him.

"What you doing there? Move over. Get back. This gah can cream it!"

He did what the first baseman said but began to cheat in and over with the delivery.

The second pitch was in on the fists but Royce swung and blooped a high one toward short right. Denzel froze still.

"Drop it!" they screamed.

"Choke!"

"Yiyiyiyiyi!"

"I got it!" yelled somebody close just as Denzel reached up and took it stinging smack in the pocket using both hands the way his daddy had told him and then he was crashed over from the side.

He held on to the ball. Alley Oop helped him to his feet and mumbled that he was sorry, he didn't know that he really had it. The Badger stomped down on home plate so hard it split in half.

"Look what I found!" somebody called.

"Whudja step in, kid?"

"Beginner's luck."

Denzel's team trotted in for its at bats. While they waited for the others to get in their positions Bake came up beside him.

"That mitt looks like you stole it out of a display window in the Hall of Fame," he said, and Denzel decided to smile. "Nice catch."

The first man up flied out to left and then Ernie stepped in. Ernie had made the last out of the inning before.

"Hold it! Hold it rat there!" Badger stormed in toward the plate. "Don't pull any of that stuff, who's up? Ninth man aint it? The new kid?"

"We changed the batting order," said Ernie. "You can do that when you make a substitution. The new kid bats in my spot and I bat where Hewitt was."

"Uhn-uh. No dice."

"That's the rules."

"Ernie," said Bake, stepping in and taking the bat from him, "let the kid have his ups. See what he can do."

Bake handed the bat to Denzel and the Badger stalked back into the field. It was a big, thick-handled bat, a Harmon Killebrew 34. Denzel liked the looks of the other one that was lying to the side but decided he'd stay with what he was given.

The Badger's team all moved in close to him. The center fielder was only a few yards behind second base.

"Tryn get a piece of it," said Ernie behind him, "just don't whiff, kid."

"Easyouteasyouteasyout!" came the chatter.

Denzel didn't choke up on the big bat. See what he can do.

The first four pitches were wide or too high. He let them pass.

"C'mon, let's go!"

"Wastin time."

"Swing at it."

"Let him hit," said the Badger. "Not goin anywheres."

The next one was way outside and he watched it.

"Come *awn!*" moaned the Badger, "s'rat *o*ver!"

"Whattaya want kid?"

"New batter, new batter!"

"Start calling strikes!"

"Egg in your beer?"

"See what he can do."

The pitcher shook his head impatiently and threw the next one high and inside. Denzel stepped back and tomahawked a shot down the line well over the left fielder's head.

"Attaboy! Go! Go!"

"Dig, baby, all the way!"

"Keep comin, bring it on!"

By the time the left fielder flagged it down and got it in Denzel was standing up with a triple.

"Way to hit! Way to hit, buddy."

"Sure you don't want him, Badger?"

"Foul ball," said the Badger. He was standing very still with his glove on his hip. "Take it over."

This time Bake and half his team ran out to argue. The Badger turned away and wouldn't listen to them.

"Get outa here," they said. "That was fair by a mile. You gotta be blind."

He wouldn't listen. "Foul ball."

"Get *off* it," they said, "you must be crazy."

Denzel sat on the base to wait it out. The third baseman sat on his glove beside him and said nice hit. The Badger began to argue, stomping around, his face turning red, finally throwing his glove down and saying he quit.

"Okay," said Bake, "have it your way."

"Nope." The Badger sulked off but not too far. "If you gonna cheat I don't want nothin to do with it."

"Don't *be* that way, Badger, dammit."

"Hell with you."

"Okay," said Bake, looking over to Denzel and shrugging for understanding, "we'll take it over."

Denzel lined the first pitch off the pitcher's knee and into right for a single. Three straight hits followed him and he crossed the plate with the tying run. The first baseman made an error and then the Badger let one through his legs and the game broke open.

Denzel sat back with the rest of the guys. They wrestled with each other and did knuckle-punches to the shoulder.

They compared talent with a professional eye.

"Royce is pretty fast."

"Not as fast as Alley Oop."

"Nobody's that fast."

"Alley Oop can *peel*."

"But Royce is a better hitter."

"Maybe for distance but not for average."

"Nobody can hit it far as Purdy."

"If he connects."

"Yeah, he always tries to kill the ball. You got to just meet it."

"But if he ever connects that thing is gonna sail."

"Kiss it goodbye."

"Going, going, *gone!*"

Denzel sat back among them without talking, but following their talk closely, putting it all in his book. Alley Oop scored and asked Bake to figure his average for him, and Bake drew the numbers in the dust with a stick till he came up with .625. That was some kind of average, everybody agreed. They batted through the order and Denzel got another single up the middle and died at second. It was getting late so they decided it would be last ups for Badger's team. The Badger was eight runs down and had given up.

Bake left Denzel in right for the last inning but nothing came his way. Purdy went down swinging for the last out and they split up. Bake and the Badger left together, laughing, but not before Bake asked Denzel his name and said see you tomorrow.

Denzel didn't tell him that he'd be gone tomorrow. That they'd have to go back to Jonathan Phelps.

Poor General Doubleday. Through no fault of his own, he is remembered chiefly today for the great game he did not start (and never professed to—all such claims were made on his behalf posthumously) and scarcely at all for the great conflict he did start (the Civil War, inasmuch as he aimed the first shot fired in defense of Fort Sumter). His ghost will find no rest in Dr. Seymour's definitive examination of our national pastime's origins. This article, contributed to the *New-York Historical Society Quarterly* in 1956, was based upon the research done for his doctoral dissertation, the first devoted to baseball. His two-volume scholarly history, *Baseball: The Early Years* and *Baseball: The Golden Age*, inspired a burst of first-rate baseball books by the academy, from Jules Tygiel, Steven Riess, and David Voigt, among others. Lest you suspect that Dr. Seymour learned his baseball in an ivory tower, let me report that he was born in Brooklyn, served as batboy for the Dodgers in 1925–27, coached semipro ballclubs, and scouted for the Red Sox.

HAROLD SEYMOUR, Ph.D.

How Baseball Began

Baseball in the United States is both a sport and a business. It is also an important social institution in our complex American society. Recognized as the "national game," it has become a symbol of America in much the same way that the Olympic Games are associated with Greece or cricket with England. Baseball even has a mythology of its own. Part of that myth enshrines its origin. Traditionally, baseball is accepted as a home-grown product; but actually it is no more indigenous to the United States than the automobile or the idea of mass production in factories. The fact that baseball, too, had its inception abroad bolsters a truth frequently overlooked or ignored—that most inventions, ideas, and institutions seldom are the work of one individual in one country.

The myth concerning the origin of baseball began to take shape in the spring of 1889 at famous Delmonico's in New York City, where some 300 people, including such public figures as Mark Twain and Chauncey M. Depew, gathered to fete the squad of professional baseball players, headed by Albert G. Spalding, just returned from their world tour. Organized baseball had just approached the end of a decade of financial success and increasing popularity in America; and Spalding, then president of the Chicago Club and also head of a thriving sporting goods business, had felt the time opportune for spreading the gospel of the American national game abroad. He therefore had headed a band of professionals, consisting of his own club and a picked group of all-stars from the rest of the National League, on a globe-circling exhibition trip that included stops at Honolulu, Australia, and the Pyramids, and a game in England with the Prince of Wales among the spectators.

At the banquet, one of the speakers, Abraham G. Mills, fourth president[1] of the National League, perhaps made overexuberant by the occasion, said he wanted it distinctly understood that "patriotism and research" had established that the game of baseball was American in origin. His audience greeted this pronouncement with enthusiastic cries of "No rounders!" Thus, according to the New York *Clipper*, the English claim that America's national game was a descendant of the English game of rounders was "forever squelched."

The "research" to which Mills referred is somewhat obscure. Perhaps he had in mind the assertions of John Montgomery Ward, a prominent player and lawyer, who had stated unequivocally the previous year that baseball did not spring from rounders but was a product of the "genius of the American Boy."

But this question as to the birthplace of the game had become a subject of controversy only recently. Prior to the decade of the eighties, rounders had been generally accepted as the ancestor of baseball. However, after the Civil War, organized teams had attained importance, and baseball evolved from a simple, primitive game into a popular show business. It had gained prestige not unmixed with American pride in having a "national game." Consequently, its devotees found it increasingly difficult to countenance the notion that their favorite sport was of foreign origin. Pride and patriotism required that the game be native, unsullied by English ancestry—even if the rounders theory could be disproved by no stronger weapons than shouting and incantation.

Nevertheless, the rounders idea somehow was not to be "forever squelched." The doctrine persisted, although without clinching evidence. The issue was unresolved for years until brought to focus in an article that appeared in *Spalding's Guide for 1903*, written by the first great baseball sportswriter, the "Father

---

[1] Mills was not the third president, as generally claimed. After the death of William A. Hulbert, the League's second president, in 1882, A. J. Soden of the Boston Club succeeded to the office for a brief interval preceding the administration of Mills. *Spalding's Official Base Ball Guide for 1883* (New York: 1883), 97. (Published annually 1877–1939 under various titles, but hereinafter referred to as *Spalding's Guide.*)

of Baseball" and the leading advocate of the rounders argument, Henry Chadwick. He had always pleaded rounders, claiming that he had played the game in England as a boy, and that early American "town ball" was very similar to it. Two conspicuous features common to both games, Chadwick pointed out, were the use of four posts for base stations and putting runners out by throwing the ball at them—"soaking" or "plugging," as it was called.

Thus challenged, Spalding, the champion of the American theory,[2] suggested settling the question once and for all. A blue-ribbon commission was appointed consisting of seven men of "high repute and undoubted knowledge of Base Ball" and including two United States senators. The committee itself supplied the window-dressing while A. G. Mills, the chairman, did what actual work was done. After collecting testimony over a period of three years, consisting of recollections but no solid documentary evidence, Mills wrote and presented a report, dated December 30, 1907, to the effect that (1) baseball originated in the United States, and (2) the first method of playing it "according to the best evidence obtainable to date" was devised by General Abner Doubleday at Cooperstown, New York, in 1839.

The remarkable part of the report was the dragooning of Doubleday and Cooperstown on the sole basis of the recollections of one Abner Graves, one-time citizen of Cooperstown. His statement was recorded in a press release issued by the commission before its final report, which was entitled "The Origin of Baseball." Graves described a game of town ball in progress between pupils of Otsego Academy and Green's Select School when

... Doubleday then improved Town Ball, to limit the number of players, as many were hurt in collisions. From twenty to fifty boys took part in the game I have described. He also designed the game to be played by definite teams or sides. Doubleday called the game Base Ball, for there were four bases in it. Three were places where the runner could rest free from being put out, provided he kept his foot on the flat stone base. The pitcher stood in a six foot ring. The ball had a rubber center overwound with yarn to a size somewhat larger than the present sphere, and was covered with leather or buckskin. Anyone getting the ball was entitled to throw it at a runner between bases, and put him out by hitting him with it.[3]

[2] Significantly, Spalding contradicted his own assertions in his *Guide for 1878*, 5, where he stated that Englishmen who watched Americans playing baseball "accused them of playing rounders" and were not far out of the way since "the game unquestionably thus originated."

[3] "Statement of Abner Graves, Mining Engineer of Denver, Colorado, April 3, 1905," in the Abner Doubleday Papers, Cooperstown, New York.

Thus it was that a decision laid down by what has been called "an oecumenical council of baseball hierarchs"[4] became the basis of an American myth that persisted and continues to live down through the years. The average "fan" who knew or cared anything at all about the beginnings of the game he watched was under the impression that an inspired, spontaneous act by Abner Doubleday created it.[5]

Yet it is by no means certain that he ever was in Cooperstown. He was born in Ballston Spa, New York, and attended school at Auburn. If he did enroll at Green's Select School at Cooperstown, he certainly was not a schoolboy there in 1839, as Abner Graves claimed, since he had matriculated at West Point the previous autumn. It may well be that Doubleday had played ball with Graves and others; but if he had any significant or unusual connection with the game it is not revealed in local histories or in Doubleday's writings.[6] It

---

[4] Rollin L. Hartt, "The National Game," *Baseball Magazine, II* (Boston: August 1909), 42. The hand-picked commission was made up almost entirely of men who were, at one time or other, very prominent in organized baseball, including the two senators. They were Abraham G. Mills, Nicholas E. Young, Alfred J. Reach, George Wright, James E. Sullivan, Arthur P. Gorman, and Morgan G. Bulkeley.

[5] The tale found its way into print also. See for example Ralph Birdsall, *The Story of Cooperstown* (New York: 1917), 224, wherein the writer states that the "solemn form of procedure" (of the commission) "placed the matter beyond doubt." Louis C. Jones, in *Cooperstown* (New York: 1949), 60–61, equivocates, saying that recent historical evidence "appears to be uncontrovertible"; yet he continues to maintain that Graves's testimony "stands unimpaired." Writers' Program of the Iowa W.P.A., "Baseball! The Story of Iowa's Early Innings," *Annals of Iowa,* XXII (Des Moines: April 1941), 626, credited Doubleday and praised the "initiative" that later made him a business leader.

Even the *Dictionary of American Biography* (New York: 1944), V, 391, states that Doubleday "created baseball." The *Encyclopaedia Britannica* (Chicago: 1948), III, 1661, the *Encyclopedia Americana* (New York: 1948), III, 302, and *Collier's Encyclopedia* (New York: 1949), III, 214, have accepted the new evidence. *Compton's Pictured Encyclopedia* (Chicago: 1948), II, 53, takes a middle ground. More recently, Hy Turkin and S. C. Thompson, *The Official Encyclopedia of Baseball* (New York: 1951), 375, concede that most unbiased probers have been forced to acknowledge the claims of recent historical research. Nevertheless, these authors, along with baseball officials, continue to propagandize Cooperstown as a baseball "shrine"; and, since Cooperstown is irrevocably associated with Abner Doubleday, this is an indirect means of perpetuating the myth.

[6] *Chancellorsville and Gettysburg* (New York: 1882); *Gettysburg Made Plain; A Succinct Account of the Campaign and Battles, with the Aid of One Diagram and Twenty-nine Maps* (New York: 1909); *Reminiscences of Forts Sumter and Moultrie in 1860–'61* (New York: 1876). Doubleday, in recalling his boyhood, makes no mention of interest in baseball:

"You ask for some information as to how I passed my youth. I was brought up in a book store and early imbibed a taste for reading. I was fond of poetry and art and much interested in mathematical studies. In my outdoor sports I was addicted to topographical work and even as a boy amused myself by making maps of the country around my father's residence which was in Auburn Cayuga Co N.Y. [*sic*]" Abner Doubleday to Dear Sir [?], November 20, 1887, Doubleday Papers, Cooperstown, New York.

should be noted, too, that Abraham G. Mills had known Doubleday for years, dating from their association as soldiers in the Civil War; yet Mills never mentioned anything about Doubleday's alleged contribution to baseball prior to the publication of the Graves statement. For instance, why did Mills not take the obvious opportunity to proclaim Doubleday's supposed role while addressing that glittering company at Delmonico's on the origin of baseball?

The climax in the perpetuation of the Doubleday story came with the approach of 1939 when the major leagues made elaborate preparations to commemorate the "centennial" of the game. Large and impressive plans were formed for appropriate ceremonies at Cooperstown—and indeed carried out. A Baseball Hall of Fame was dedicated, a pageant portraying the historical highlights of the sport was presented, and an all-star contest between teams composed of baseball's all-time great players was played. All this was accompanied by the usual publicity build-up and fanfare.

The United States Government lent its seal of approval when the Post Office authorized a special baseball stamp marking the event. However, it did so not because of Doubleday, whose claims admittedly were "questionable," but because the date was "universally recognized in sport circles as marking the centennial"—a rather nice point. Doubleday's picture was cautiously omitted, and a sandlot scene substituted as the central motif with a house, barn, church, and school in the background.

Less fortunate, or perhaps more gullible, was a legislative committee of the State of New York charged with studying the situation. This committee held a public hearing at Cooperstown, August 7, 1937, at which representatives of the local chamber of commerce and of the local committee dealing with the problem appeared. According to the official report of the State legislature, "It was put in evidence that Cooperstown, New York, is the birthplace of baseball . . ." and the State committee recommended "that a centennial be properly celebrated at Cooperstown, New York, on the home site of the first game, the inauguration of baseball being the proud heritage of New York."

The committee went on to advocate that the event be "advertised and publicized in the pamphlets of the Conservation Department of the State of New York, and by road signs erected under its supervision. . . ." Finally, it was urged that the State of New York "appropriate . . . Ten Thousand ($10,000) . . . to be used in advertising and generally furthering the baseball . . . celebration."[7]

[7] *State of New York, Report of Joint Legislative Committee to Study the Situation Concerning the Inaugural Baseball Game and the Growth of the Sport.* Legislative Document 73 (Albany: 1938). Evidently the Congress of the United States, too, has fallen prey to this story. In its 1951 investigation, it concluded that baseball "is a game of American origin." "Organized Baseball; Report of the Subcommittee on the Study of Monopoly Power of the Committee on the Judiciary," *House Report*, No. 2002, p. 228, 82d Congress, 2d Session (Washington: 1952).

So it was that the Doubleday myth was crystallized and enshrined in concrete form by organized baseball. Actually, the entire edifice, which had always rested upon the flimsy foundation of an elderly man's memory of events sixty-eight years after they supposedly occurred, was constructed and sanctioned in the face of timely and unimpeachable evidence, published in the midst of centennial preparations, that Abner Doubleday had had little or nothing to do with the birth of the game; but rather, that it had sprung from rounders.[8] Adding to the difficulty, Bruce Cartwright reiterated an earlier claim that evidence in his possession showed his forebear, Alexander Cartwright, to have been the founder of baseball. Although embarrassed and chagrined, baseball officials, having already committed themselves, especially financially, to Doubleday, proceeded according to plan, while sports columnists either pointed out the discrepancy or got around it as gracefully as possible.[9]

Broadly speaking, no single person invented baseball. The game was the result of an evolutionary process over a long period of years. It is known that the ball was used from earliest civilization; and the evidence is overwhelming that it was familiar as far back as ancient Egypt and adjacent lands where the ball represented the idea of fertility.[10] And of course the Greeks were thoroughly familiar with ball play. It would be difficult to present a stronger argument for ball games than that to be found in Galen's treatise, entitled "Exercise with the Small Ball." E. Norman Gardiner, classical scholar, paraphrases this document as follows:

> The best of all exercises . . . are those which combine bodily exertion with mental recreation, such as hunting and ball-play. But ball-play has this advantage over hunting that its cheapness puts it within reach of the very poorest, while even the busiest man can find time to do it. Moreover, it can be practised with any degree of violence or moderation, at all times and in all conditions. It exercises every part of the body, legs, hands, and eyesight alike, and at the same time gives

[8] Robert W. Henderson, "Baseball and Rounders," *New York Public Library Bulletin*, XLIII (New York: April, 1939), 303–314. Aside from Henry Chadwick's protests, the first substantial debunking of the Doubleday myth was provided by Will Irwin, "Baseball: (I) Before the Professionals Came," *Collier's*, XLIII (May 8, 1909), 12.

[9] For example, the New York *Sun*, June 10, 1939, admitted the hoax, but said baseball as an American institution required a legend, so the public would therefore go ahead and take part in the "innocuous conspiracy." Fred Lieb, sportswriter, assigned to prepare a feature article on the centennial, admits he faked the story although he knew of the discrepancies in the Cooperstown myth. Frederick G. Lieb, *The Baseball Story* (New York: 1950), 15.

[10] John A. Krout, *Annals of American Sport, Pageant of America Series*, XV (New Haven: 1929), 114. Also Henderson, *Ball, Bat and Bishop*, 19. The Russians also claim that baseball originated from one of their ancient village games called lapta. *New York Times*, September 16, 1952, quoted a Soviet magazine, *Smena*: "It is well known that in Russian villages they played lapta, of which beizbol is an imitation. It was played in Russian villages when the United States was not even marked on the maps."

pleasure to the mind. In contrast with athletic exercises, which make men slow or produce one-sided development, ball-play produces strength and activity, and therefore trains all those qualities which are most valuable for a soldier. Finally, it is free from dangers. . . .[11]

To ascertain who invented baseball would be equivalent to trying to locate the discoverer of fire. But we are here concerned with what has direct bearing on the development of baseball in America, and there is sufficient evidence to indicate that various simple bat-and-ball games were indulged in by the settlers from the first. For example, the Dutch of New Netherland played "stool ball," thought to be the forerunner of cricket. Even in Puritan New England the play spirit was not as dead as commonly supposed. Ballplaying there was sufficently prominent to be forbidden by Governor Bradford of Plymouth.

Possibly the first record of an American baseball game is that mentioned in the journal of George Ewing, a Revolutionary soldier, who tells of playing a game of "base," April 7, 1778, at Valley Forge. Early familiarity with a game called baseball is understandable, for as early as 1744 John Newbery published in London *A Little Pretty Pocket-Book*, containing a rhymed description of "base-ball" along with a small picture illustrating the game.[12] Newbery, a farmer's son, accountant, patent-medicine dealer, and printer, not only was one of the first publishers of children's books, but also tried to please children as well as to improve them—a new and good idea for that time. This, like other children's books that followed it, was extremely popular and widely known—evidence that a game called baseball was familiar to English boys. The book was republished in New York in 1762, in Philadelphia in 1786, and again at Worcester, Massachusetts, in 1787. Therefore a ball game called baseball was familiar to Americans much before 1839, the year in which Doubleday is credited with christening the game with that name.

The link between baseball and the English game of rounders is no less strong. A compilation of children's games by William Clarke called *The Boy's Own Book: A Complete Encyclopedia of All the Diversions, Athletic, Scientific and Recreative* appeared in London in 1828. A number of editions was published, but the important one is the third, which appeared in 1829. It had a description of the game of rounders.[13] That same year, 1829, the first American edition

[11] E. Norman Gardiner, *Greek Athletic Sports and Festivals* (London: 1910), 187–188.

[12] Much of this portion of the discussion, including the relationship between baseball and rounders, is based upon Henderson, "Baseball and Rounders," 303–314, who published his evidence after the preparations for the Cooperstown ceremonies had been inaugurated.

[13] The game was known variously in England by the names base-ball, feeder, and rounders. The latter name came to be the most commonly used. The first London edition of *The Boy's Own Book* omits rounders. A copy of the second edition has not been located. Copies of the first and third London editions are in the Cleveland Public Library.

of the volume, likewise containing the rules for rounders, was printed. From this source we learn that rounders, a favorite game of western England, was played on a field on which were placed four stones or posts from 12 to 20 yards apart in a diamond-shaped pattern. The number of contestants was not specified; those on hand merely divided into two equal groups. The "out" side scattered about the field more or less haphazardly without taking up set positions, except for the "pecker" or "feeder" (pitcher), who gently tossed the ball a short distance to the "striker" (batter) from a fixed position also marked by a stone or post. The striker, if successful in meeting the ball, ran the bases clockwise as far as he could progress, depending upon the circumstances. Outs were registered when the striker did any of the following: (1) missed three swings (three-strikes rule), (2) hit the ball behind his position (one foul out), (3) had his batted ball caught, or (4) was struck by a thrown ball while attempting to negotiate the bases. The "in" side continued until each of its members had been put out, when the side that had been in the field had its innings.

So much for the game of rounders as such. The great significance of these rules is that five years after they were published in the United States they were reprinted by a Boston company which, in a book entitled *The Book of Sports*, by Robin Carver, reproduced them practically verbatim, changing only the title from "Rounders" to "Base, or Goal Ball" because, as he said, those were "the names generally adopted in our country."[14] By means of this minor alteration English rounders became American baseball.

Again in 1835 a Providence, Rhode Island, firm published *The Boys and Girls Book of Sports*, which likewise contained the rules for rounders as they appeared in *The Boy's Own Book* of 1829, merely substituting the heading "Base, or Goal Ball." Furthermore, in 1839 yet another sporting book appeared, *The Boy's Book of Sports: A Description of the Exercises and Pastimes of Youth*, published in New Haven. Instead of merely copying previously published rules on baseball, it tried to revise and clarify those already known. In doing so, it introduced for the first time the provision that the bases, laid out to form a "diamond," be run in counterclockwise fashion.

In the late eighteenth and early nineteenth centuries many references to ball games having been played are to be found, particularly in diaries and memoirs. Some of these were written at the time, but many are memories of older men recalling boyhood days and are therefore not as reliable as the contemporary accounts. Nor is it always certain which game of ball was played. Nevertheless

[14] Henderson dramatized the similarity by placing the texts of the same rules from each book in parallel columns in "Baseball and Rounders," 307; Henderson, *Ball, Bat and Bishop*, 154–157.

the evidence is that simple ball games were well known and played in the settled communities along the seaboard, especially in New York and the New England States. Certainly by the first decades of the nineteenth century, ball games were a common sight on the village greens and vacant fields or pastures as well as on college campuses.

So popular was ball in Worcester in 1816 that it was prohibited in the streets; and according to Thurlow Weed, people in Rochester, New York, busy and industrious as they were, found time for recreation. There, in 1825, a baseball club of fifty members, ages eighteen to forty, met every afternoon during the ball season to play on their eight to ten acres of ground. Weed even lists the best players, among whom were some of the leading citizens. In his journal written in 1835, Cyrus Parker Bradley, born in 1818, admits he never got over his boyhood love of playing and often was told "how ridiculous it was to come from the society of antiquarians and politicians and play ball with boys of six. But it is natural to me, infected by their mood, by my early life." The mass of boys indulged in playing "goal" in Bangor, Maine, according to Albert Ware Paine in his journal of 1836, recorded when he was twenty-three years old. And in Rhode Island ball play was performed even on Sunday.

A diary entry by a Princeton student in 1786 alludes to playing "baste ball" on the campus: "A fine day, play baste ball in the campus but am beaten for I miss both catching and striking the ball." At first, however, colleges discouraged students in the practice of ball playing. At least Princeton did, passing laws in 1787 against ball games on the ground that such were "low and unbecoming gentlemen" and constituted "great danger to the health by sudden and alternate heats and colds and as it tends by accidents . . . to disfiguring and maiming those who are engaged in it. . . ." Gradually it was found that student disorder and mischief decreased when surplus energy was worked off in games. At Bowdoin in 1824, ball games were initiated by the authorities themselves as a method of reducing sickness. The recommendation was well

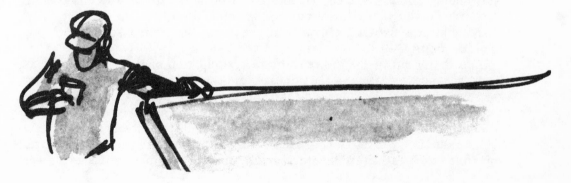

received and proved beneficial if we can take the word of Henry Wadsworth Longfellow, then a student. He wrote that ball playing

> . . . communicated such an impulse to our limbs and joints, that there is nothing now heard of, in our leisure hours, but ball, ball, ball. I cannot prophesy with any degree of accuracy concerning the continuance of this rage for play, but the effect is good, since there has been a thoroughgoing reformation from inactivity and torpitude.

Williams Latham, a student at Brown from 1823 to 1827, discussed his ball-playing experience there, explaining that sports were still unorganized; and that while ball games took place at Brown he did not enjoy them as much as he had at Bridgewater because only six or seven played on a side; hence much time was wasted running after the ball. He also complained of the pitching style because they "did throw so fair ball, They are affraid [sic] the fellow will hit it with his bat-stick." Likewise, at Harvard, where he finished in 1829, Oliver Wendell Holmes played ball. The same was true of George F. Hoar, who played various ball games during his boyhood in the 1830s and, after he entered Harvard in 1842, continued to engage in "the old-fashioned game of base." Hoar specified that chief among the games he played as a boy were four-old-cat, three-old-cat, two-old-cat, and base, games which, as he pointed out, were not very scientific.

These various ball games had common characteristics. They were all simple, some more so than others. All appealed to the same elementary satisfaction derived from projecting one's power by swatting and throwing an object hard and for distance, or the excitement of the race to arrive safely on the base ahead of the ball. The simplest of these early games was barn ball, limited to two players and requiring the smooth side of a building with some level ground in front of it. One boy threw the ball vigorously against the wall; the other, having taken his position about a dozen feet from the wall, struck at the rebounding ball with his bat. Upon connecting he ran to the wall and tried to return before his opponent recovered the ball and hit him with it. Naturally, they took turns, switching about after the batter was retired, so that each boy had his innings.

Apparently out of the desire to make participation of more boys possible, more advanced variations—the games of "old-cat"—were improvised. The simplest version of these, "one-old-cat," was derived from the old English game of "Tip Cat," wherein a wooden "cat," like a spindle, was placed on the ground, then tipped in the air and struck with a stick. "Old-cat" merely substituted a ball for the stick. "One-old-cat" had a batter, pitcher, and two bases. The batter hit from one base, ran to the other, and returned if possible until the ball was caught either on the fly or on one bounce. The number of lads could be increased by playing "two-, three-, or four-old-cat," which simply meant adding to the number of bases and batsmen. As the number of players increased, the opportunity and necessity for more team play presented itself.

For yet larger numbers of players, the game variously called "town-ball," "round-ball"—and later "Massachusetts ball" (to distinguish it from "the New York game")—were devised. These were the Americanized versions of English rounders and were played by large groups ranging anywhere from twelve to twenty or more on a side. Regulations varied, since there were no uniform rules; hence each community had its own particular variations—just as present-day sandlot players generally add their own touches to the official rules. One side batted around until each of its players was put out; then the other aggregation had its turn.

The frontier, however, did not nourish sport. The immediate battle to subdue the wilderness was too pressing to permit leisure for games. Labor and work, because they were essential, were glorified. The tendency, therefore, was to combine them with play whenever possible. Necessary work and needed sport frequently were synonymous. Barn-raisings or corn-huskings, required tasks, were converted into festive frolics as well. Likewise hunting and fishing were work; but the thrill of sport was not entirely absent. Such pure "sport" as was practiced on the frontier was rugged, boisterous, and even brutal, like wrestling and eye-gouging. Only when communities became more settled, enjoyed a degree of leisure, and cleared fields or village commons, did ball playing sprout and flourish; and even then sport was impeded by a lingering puritanism that frowned upon frivolity or pleasure.

In New England the belief remained that "play is folly rather than wisdom in a child; and he will soonest be an adult who puts on the adult's gravity," according to a well-known pedagogue of that section. He candidly relates how, because of his own youthful training in this belief, he made a practice, when a teacher, of cheating the pupils of as much time as possible from the fifteen minutes allotted to them at noon for sports. He continues apologetically: "I had not learned so fully as I have since done, that sports are as indispensable to the health of both the bodies and minds of children as their food, their drink, or their sleep. . . ."

Travelers noted the legal restrictions upon amusements; and one remarked upon the "hard precocity" of American youths who entered college at the age of fourteen and left at seventeen with degrees to commence business careers, with no interval to attain either gracefulness or health—"Athletic games and the bolder field sports being unknown." Enjoyment was associated with guilt— as illustrated by the Yankee who said he was "going to town, probably git [sic] good and drunk, and Lord how I'll hate it!" This attitude only slowly disappeared; as late as 1862 churchmen succeeded in having ice skating banned in Brooklyn; and of course the fight to legalize Sunday baseball took much longer.

In the South, ball playing was carried on, but not to the extent it was in the North. The pattern of Southern sport tended to be formed by the dominant planter group, whose influence far exceeded its number. The result was an inclination toward aristocratic pastimes like fox hunting. Yet ball play was not as completely foreign to that section as generally thought. A case in point is Moses Waddell's famous school in South Carolina, where students found relaxation in ball games from the stern classical curriculum.

Such simple, crude ball games as those described were played on a local, neighborhood basis and were admirably suited to the young, primarily rural America of the period. Few had great wealth or leisure. Playing sites were plentiful and convenient. Only the rudest preparation was necessary—laying "goals" or bases by driving sticks into the ground or placing flat rocks at approximate distances. Equipment requirements were minimum both in amount and cost. Any stout stick, wagon tongue, ax or rake handle made a capital bat; and a serviceable ball could be had by winding yarn around a buckshot or chunk of india rubber and then sewing on a leather cover, perhaps cut to size by the local shoemaker, to prevent unwinding. No other paraphernalia were needed. Availability of ample space, a negligible amount of inexpensive equipment, and the simple structure of the games made for popularity and wide participation. In short, the various ball games were adapted to their surroundings and in fact mirrored them.

Another feature of early nineteenth-century ball was the fact that it was overwhelmingly a participant's game. Relatively few watched; and the promoter who sold baseball games as entertainment was not to appear until a later day when American society became urbanized. This meager attendance at games and their noncommercial character are reflected in the paucity of detailed information and lack of descriptions of games in the press of the day. For example, even in 1843, an advertisement announcing the forthcoming publication of a "new and comprehensive" weekly sporting paper listed more than twenty sports it would cover, such as racing, hunting, shooting, fishing, rowing, pedestrianism, pugilism, "cricketing," skating, swimming, billiards, etc., but omitted any intent to report on ball playing.

The same applied to a leading theatrical and sports journal of the day, which contained lengthy indices of items pertaining to cricket during the 1840s, whereas baseball was disregarded. Furthermore, the absence of team play in any real or highly developed sense is to be noted; doubtless this was due to the fiercely individualistic atmosphere of a society in flux, which lacked any permanent stratification, and in which democracy was the byword. Sufficient sophistication for highly developed team play was lacking in America prior to the Civil War.

The simplicity, informality, and absence of organization in the game, plus the fact that it was not given headline attention in the contemporary press, enhanced the recreative values of ball playing, so that even the ascetic though progressive schoolteacher, William A. Alcott, confessed: "Our most common exercise was ball playing. In this, I was not very expert; but I believe I had all the healthful advantages which pertain to it, notwithstanding. It is really an excellent sport."

At the time this story was published in *The New Yorker*, 1937, Irwin Shaw was a socially conscious playwright and story writer who was fresh from his experience as a truck driver, factory worker, and semipro football player. In later years he became rich and famous as the author of such novels as *The Young Lions* and *Rich Man, Poor Man*.

IRWIN SHAW

No Jury Would Convict

"I come from Jersey City," the man in the green sweater was saying, "all the way from Jersey City, and I might of just as well stood home. You look at Brooklyn and you look at Jersey City and if you didn't look at the uniforms you'd never tell the difference."

Just then the Giants scored four runs and two men a few rows below stood up with grins on their faces and called to a friend behind us, "Johnny, Johnny! Did you see that, Johnny? You still here, Johnny? We thought you mighta left. What a team, Brooklyn!" They shook their heads in sardonic admiration, "What a team! You still here, Johnny?"

Johnny, wherever he was, didn't say anything. His two friends sat down, laughing.

The man in the green sweater took off his yellow straw hat and carefully wiped the sweatband with his handkerchief. "I been watching the Dodgers for twenty-three years," he said, "and I never seen anything like this." He put his hat on again, over his dark Greek face, the eyes deep and sad, never leaving the field where the Dodgers moved wearily in their green-trimmed uniforms. "Jersey City, Albany, and Brooklyn, that would make a good league. One helluva league. I would give Brooklyn twenty-five games headstart and let them fight it out. They would have a hard fight stayin' in the New York–Penn League. They would have to get three new pitchers. They're worse than Jersey City, I swear, worse . . ."

"Ah, now, listen," the man beside him said, "if that's the case why isn't Brooklyn in Jersey City and Jersey City in Brooklyn?"

"I don't know," the man in the green sweater said. "I honestly couldn't tell ye."

"They haven't got such a bad team."

"They ought to move them into the New York–Penn League. A major-league team . . ." He laughed sadly. "Look at that!" A man named Wilson was striking out for Brooklyn. "Look at Wilson. Why, he's pitiful. They walk two men to get at him in the International League. I bet Newark could spot them five runs and beat them every day. I'd give odds."

"You can't make a supposition like that," the man beside him protested. "They never play each other. It's not a fair supposition."

"Five runs, every day. If they didn't have those green caps they could play in a twilight league in Connecticut and nobody'd ever tell the difference, not in ten years. Look at that!" The Brooklyn shortstop fell down leaping at a grounder to his right. "No guts," the man from Jersey City said, "a major-league shortstop woulda had it and threw the man out. He fell to make a alibi."

"It was a hard-hit ball," his neighbor protested.

"Bartell woulda had it. He ain't no Bartell."

"He's got nine yards of tape on him," the man next to him said. "I saw with my own eyes in the dugout. He's a mass of cuts and bruises."

"That's Brooklyn. Always got tape all over them. They spend more money for tape than for players. Look at that."

One of the Giants hit a home run and three runs scored. The two men in front of us stood up with grins on their faces and called to their friend in back of us. "Still there, Johnny?" and sat down.

"For twenty-three years," the man in the green sweater said, "I been rootin' for this team. I'm gettin' tired of rootin' for a minor-league team in a major league. I would hate to see what would happen to those guys in Jersey City."

"I come to see them every day," his neighbor said stubbornly, "and they're a major-league team."

"Look at them," the man in the green sweater pointed his scorecard in accusation at the nine weary figures. "Take 'em one by one. Look at Wilson. Why, he's the worst ballplayer in the world. He's even worse than Smead Jolley."

He sat back triumphantly, having silenced his adversary for the moment.

He watched the play quietly for a few seconds, his Greek eyes bitter but resigned. "Why," he continued, "in Jersey City they put a catcher in to play center field instead of him. A catcher. I know Wilson."

"Wilson isn't the only one on the team," his neighbor said.

"All right. Cooney. What can Cooney do?"

"Cooney can field."

"All right, Cooney can field. But he has an air rifle for an arm. He can't reach second base in under seven bounces. Don't talk to me about Cooney."

"His arm's not so bad," the neighbor insisted.

"Not so bad? Why, Mac, if Cooney had an arm he'd be a pitcher."

"I never noticed anything wrong with his arm."

"Mac," the man in the green sweater said, "then you're the one man in the United States that don't know Cooney got a glass arm. The one man."

"How about Winsett?" his neighbor wanted to know.

Winsett was up at the plate by this time and the man in the green sweater watched him critically. "A cigar store Indian" he said finally. "Watch him swing."

"He hit sixty home runs the year before they brought him up," the Brooklyn fan said. "Cigar store Indians don't hit sixty home runs."

"I saw him," the man in the green sweater said, "when he was playin' in the International League. Do you know what he hit in the International League. . . . 250 . . . You know why? It's an outcurve league. The National League is also an outcurve league. He ought to be out somewhere playin' night baseball." At the top of his voice he called, "Come on, you cigar store Indian!"

Winsett hit a home run.

"This is a fine time to hit it," the man from Jersey City said, "they're behind seven runs and there's nobody on base and he hits a home run."

In the next inning a pitcher named Cantwell took up the bitter burden of pitching for Brooklyn. The face of the man in the green sweater lightened. "There's a pitcher," he said. "One of the best. Out in Jersey City they were goin' to give him a new automobile but he went to the Giants. Watch him!" he said as Cantwell disposed of the first two batters. "A prince of a fellow. A prince. Everybody likes him."

"He's been pitching lousy," his neighbor said, as Cantwell suddenly filled the bases.

"What do you expect?" the man from Jersey City said, anxiously watching the misery below. "He don't look like the Cantwell of Jersey City. Terry double-crossed him, he wanted to stay in Jersey City, he woulda got an automobile, but Terry took him and double-crossed him and shipped him to Brooklyn. How do you expect him to pitch? He broke his heart."

Cantwell struck out the third batter. The man in the green sweater stood up and applauded as the pitcher trudged into the dugout. "You bet your life he can pitch, the poor son of a gun, he's disgusted, the poor fella. That's it, Ben!" He sat down. "Wonderful pitcher, Ben, he's got a head."

"I never saw him strike out a man before," the Brooklyn fan said.

"There's very few of them makes a living out of strikeouts. Now if they only give Ben something to work on . . ."

Brooklyn scored three runs. Two men died on base when Wilson popped out.

"That Wilson," the man in the green sweater said, "they ought to trade him to the Salvation Army. He's the worst player in the world. Why, he's worse than Smead Jolley."

But he cheered lustily when Cantwell came through another inning unscored upon. "There's a pitcher," he said, "if I had a team, I'd buy him."

"You could buy him for the fare to Jersey City," a man in back said, "eleven cents."

"The only major leaguer on that ballclub!" the man in the green sweater said with finality. "If only those cheap bastards would buy a couple more like him, they'd have something. I'm not saying Brooklyn's bad as a town, because it's not, but they got office boys running the ballclub, office boys with snot in their ears. That cheap Grimes. I heard he used the ground keeper's truck to move his furniture in."

The Dodgers scored three more runs and the man in the green sweater was shouting triumphantly, the ancient Greek sorrow gone from his eyes for the first time in the entire afternoon. There was only one out and there was a man on third base and the Dodgers needed only one run to tie the score. Wilson was coming up to bat and the man in the green sweater groaned. "That's what happens when you have somebody like that on a team. He comes up at a time like this. That's always the way it happens. He's pitiful. In the International League they walk two batters to get at him."

But at the last moment somebody else batted for Wilson and struck out. "On low ones," the man in the green sweater said in pain, "a pinch hitter swinging at low ones."

Cantwell was to bat next.

"Let him stay up there!" the man from Jersey City shouted. "Let him win his own game." He turned to his public. "I would like to see old Ben smack one out and win the ballgame," he said, "and go right over to Terry and spit in his face."

But old Ben didn't get a chance. Grimes put a man called Spence in to bat for him and Spence popped out.

In the next inning the Brooklyn second baseman juggled a ball and another run scored. All hope fled from the dark Greek face. "Why is it," he asked, "that other teams don't do it?" He got up, preparing to leave. "A man on third and one out," he said, "and no score. They ought to shoot Grimes for that. No jury would convict. Ah," he said, moving down toward the exit gate, "I'm going to root for a winning team from now on. I've been rooting for a losing team long enough. I'm going to root for the Giants. You don't know," he said to the Brooklyn fan moving along with him, "you don't know the pleasure you get out of rooting for a winning team."

And he went back to Jersey City, leaving his heart in Brooklyn.

This article was written in September 1969, as the Mets were headed toward a miracle even greater than the Jets winning the Super Bowl and, for Met fans, at least comparable to Neil Armstrong's footprints on the moon. And yet here was Len Shecter wistfully longing for the bad old days, which he witnessed as a reporter and columnist for the *New York Post*. The article grew, the following year, into a fine little book called *Once Upon the Polo Grounds*.

LEONARD SHECTER

Bring Back the Real Mets!

It is not to be believed. This season, the Mets—the ever-loving New York Mets, for goodness sakes—have been involved in a pennant race. We were, none of us, ever going to be old enough to see this day. Our lot was to be forever enveloped in a cult of sweet misery, the kind enjoyed for so many years in Brooklyn when the Dodgers were "Dem Bums." The Mets played music to lose by, to love hopelessly by, to reminisce by. But there was never going to be that hot, thumping rhythm of a pennant race. Not for us. For our sons, perhaps, or their sons.

Except we had not counted on the swift pace of modern times, on the factor of dilution through additional expansion, of the knack eight years have of appearing to be a lifetime. So here we are, us Met fans, unexpectedly, shockingly, caught up in the final weeks' stampede. It is a beautiful thing, of course, and it makes tired blood surge once again. Winning has become a necessity rather than a surprise. Losing has become a disaster rather than a routine. It matters to us what the Chicago Cubs have done in the afternoon, and we get caught up in the pitching problems of the St. Louis Cardinals, and every once in a while we cast a terrified glance at the Pittsburgh Pirates.

It's exciting, exhilarating, fascinating. And yet, for some of us, a very few, there are days that will be better remembered. . . .

The kid's name was John Pappas. He was skinny, 5 foot 10 and not more than 150 pounds, and the sallow pallor of the city was on his face. He had a lot of black hair which he was wearing in a scraggly pompadour as he walked into the clubhouse of the New York Mets in St. Petersburg, Florida, that February morning in 1962, plunked down his little canvas bag with the cheap baseball shoes inside, and announced he was a pitcher and ready. The funny thing was, nobody laughed.

It couldn't happen now. A twenty-one-year-old unemployed furniture salesman from Queens who had never thrown a baseball for an organized team, he'd be seized, stuffed into a straitjacket, and whisked away to the nearest mental hospital. Then, at that time and place, however, he was handled gently. Who had ever told him, he was asked, that he could be a big leaguer? "I told myself," John Pappas said. "I'm not exactly a Herb Score, but I'm pretty fast." He stuck out his skinny, unimpressive chest.

The historical fact is that the Mets actually took a look. Johnny Murphy, then assistant to George Weiss, the club president, wasn't altogether happy about it. "He doesn't even *look* like an athlete," Murphy grumbled.

What matter? What did looks count against the kind of soaring hope that wrapped the Mets in silk and French perfume, as separate from reality as a lover's dream? For this was the springtime of a new team, the first expansion team in the National League in its first season. Oh, there was a Houston club out there someplace with the practical Paul Richards running it, who had, once the player draft to stock the teams had been completed, announced to the press: "Gentlemen, we've been had." The people around the Mets didn't feel that way. Nor the newspapermen who had pushed so hard to replace the National League Dodgers and Giants in New York. (This was so long ago there were still six newspapers in New York.) There was talk about the Mets finishing fifth, or even fourth or third. The dreams were sweet in those days.

Of course the Mets had to take a look at Pappas. Because there was always that chance that the devil had conspired to deliver Douglass (*The Year the Yankees Lost the Pennant*) Wallop's Shoeless Joe Hardy, and that the first time he threw a baseball, smoke would rise from the mitt and the catcher's hand would come out of it looking like a bag of peanuts. You don't fool around with the devil.

Murphy wouldn't let Pappas work out on the hallowed ground of the Mets' playing field. He took him down to some empty lot, and all the people covering the club went along, eyes shining, pulses pounding.

Then the skinny kid with all the hair started to warm up and it was all over.

He was no Shoeless Joe. He was no Herb Score. He couldn't even throw very hard. Indeed, he couldn't throw at all.

Too bad. But all it meant was a transference of hope to something else, to other people. It was a season for hope.

There was the hope, for example, that there really was an Elio Chacon. The Mets had shelled out $75,000 to the Cincinnati Reds for him and sent him a contract in Caracas, Venezuela, where, rumor had it, Chacon lived and played winter baseball. No reply. They sent him a letter raising their salary offer. No answer. A cable. No answer. Two more cables. Silence.

Finally, the Mets sent a cable to Sherman Jones, another of their new properties, who was playing on the same team. The cable asked Jones to get Chacon to contact the Mets.

Jones told him.

"He said O.K.," Jones was to recall. "That's all he ever said. That and yes and no, even when he talked Spanish."

In any case, the talk with Jones moved Chacon to send back his contract and ask for more money. The Mets came through, but again silence set in. Until, after training had started, this cable was received: "I AM WAITING PASSAGE. ELIO."

Murphy wasn't sure what this meant, but he arranged with an airline to deliver a ticket to Chacon's door. Acknowledgment was not forthcoming for more than a week. Then this: "I WILL REACHED MONDAY. SICK PARIENT, ELIO."

The airline told the Mets that Chacon was due at the Tampa airport at 10:57 of a Monday night, and when the time came, Lou Niss, the traveling secretary, was waiting. Chacon arrived 5 A.M. Tuesday.

"I asked him what happened to his plane," Niss said. "I still haven't been able to figure out what he said."

There was then a long press conference, the highlight of which went like this:

Q. During the World Series [between Cincinnati and the Yankees] you said you were going to get married. Did you?

A. I say only if we win the whole thing. [The Yankees won the Series.]

Q. What did you tell your girl friend?

A. I told her take it easy.

Q. Isn't she impatient?

A. No.

Q. Do you know what impatient means?

A. No.

It turned out he didn't know a lot about playing shortstop either, which is what the Mets needed him to do. Except the Mets were half a season finding out. They should have listened that spring to Jim Brosnan, the erudite Red pitcher. He was asked if Chacon could play shortstop. "Why should he?" Brosnan said. "He couldn't play second base."

The Mets always found things out too late.

It was a television commercial. The idea was that Casey Stengel, the marvelous manager of "the amazing Mets," as he had dubbed them before they owned even their first over-age ballplayer, had got into an argument with an umpire which so upset him he needed a Bromo-Seltzer to calm his stomach. It was a time when the Federal Communications Commission was attempting to crack down on people who endorsed products they really didn't use. So one of the flunkies from the advertising agency said to Stengel, "You use Bromo-Seltzer, don't you?"

"Why sure," Stengel said. "Only I never get sick, so I don't have to."

At any rate, the commercial was filmed, and most of the trouble came from Stengel overacting his bellyache. "That's a little too much," the director said.

"You mean you don't want me to die?" Stengel said. "I'm old enough."

And for the next weeks, whenever Stengel referred to the filming of the commercial, he said he did it for Alka-Seltzer.

On March 26, Jay Hook, mechanical engineer, pitcher, was kept in an exhibition ballgame against Baltimore until he had given up seventeen hits. The Mets lost, 18–8, which wasn't so bad. It was far from customary, however, to allow a young pitcher to take that kind of beating, and one can only put it down to one of Stengel's flashes of irascibility. Later, Hook was to go on to win the Mets' first league game, to stop their first long losing streak, and become the first Met pitcher to beat the Dodgers in New York. But on that March 26 he was upset enough to cry.

The situation reminded Richie Ashburn, the player who was one of the first to plug in on the sweet agony of the Met mystique, of a story. "It was in the minor leagues," he said. "I saw a team bat around three times on Warren Hacker. Now the manager goes out to take him out and he's mad. 'You can't take me out now,' Hacker says. 'I know I can get this guy out. I've got him out twice this inning.' "

Then there was Rod Kanehl. At twenty-eight, Kanehl had been in baseball eight years without playing in a major-league ballgame. Casey Stengel remembered him from a spring he'd spent with the Yankees, particularly a day in which a ball was hit over Kanehl's head and the outfield fence. Running after the ball, Kanehl went right on up and over the fence, picked it up, and climbed back onto the field. The old man was indelibly impressed, and when he saw Kanehl's name on a list of availables, he pointed a gnarled old finger and said, "I want him."

This was one of the areas in which Stengel and George Weiss were to have a running battle. One time, Stengel reported a conversation he had with Weiss about Kanehl. "Weiss says, 'I ain't seen him do anything in the field,' " Stengel rasped. "So I said, 'You're full of baloney, he can run the bases.' "

And not a great deal more, although before long he was to play every position for the Mets except pitcher and catcher, all of them with aplomb, none of them especially well. Right from the beginning, things happened to Kanehl that you put into threatening letters. The first thing he did was pull a muscle so badly that his leg took on the color of a tropical sunset and he couldn't walk for a week. The first time he got into a game—as a late-inning sub—the first ball hit to him went through his legs. And he pulled another muscle.

The next time he played—second base—he threw two double-play balls into the dirt, and when he was tried at third he was fooled on two pop fouls that dropped with sickening little thuds onto the ground behind him. (In fact, Kanehl never did learn to play second base, which he played a lot. What he couldn't do was make that flying double-play pivot. So he would plant himself on the bag and take the sliding runner's spikes in his shins. He made the DP, but he played three years with bleeding shins.)

It wasn't until late March, that first spring, that Rod Kanehl became a Met. It was against Sandy Koufax and the Dodgers. With runners on second and third in the ninth and the Mets down 3–1, Kanehl was called on to pinch-hit. This was a revolting development since Kanehl was sleeping off a terrible hangover in a corner of the dugout. When he walked out into the sun he decided that as punishment he had been struck blind.

Kanehl let the first pitch go by. "It was a good pitch," he was to say afterward, a crooked smile on his face, his dark eyes glinting with amusement. "A bummer. With hair on it. I mean it sounded like a good pitch. I didn't see it."

The next pitch was a curveball and it fooled Kanehl completely. He thought it was going to be a high fastball, started to swing, realized it was a curve as it headed down at him, and ducked away to save his life. The ball hit his bat anyway.

After that, the ball just naturally took itself down along the first-base line and Kanehl had a base hit. Two runs scored. Shocked, Koufax gave up a hit to Felix Mantilla, and the Mets won 4–3. That's how Rod Kanehl became a Met hero. Indeed, the very first Mets banner hung in the Polo Grounds, where the Mets played for their first two years, read:

WE LOVE THE METS
ROD KANEHL

When the time came that Kanehl no longer got so many lucky hits, this man who somehow represented the spirit of the team—a spirit of cheerful, willing, hilarious failure—was cut off without a backward glance. Nobody even thought to give him a job as coach. Yogi Berra got a job as coach. When you come right down to it, what the hell does Yogi Berra have to do with the Mets?

Amid all the optimistic enthusiasm that surrounded the Mets, the seventy-one-year-old Casey Stengel remained an island of sanity. Oh, he staged his little charades, picking two heavy-legged rookies named Dawes Hamilt and Bruce Fitzpatrick to trot out before visiting columnists as brilliant stars of the future. They were not, of course, and after the spring were never heard of again. But for one brief moment, Camelot. All over the country.

For the most part, though, Stengel said things like this:

"Most of our hitters are what? Putsie-downsies." He took a weak half swing, half bunt, to illustrate.

After the Mets had stirred the hearts of baseball fans all over by beating the Yankees in the ninth inning of their first spring encounter, Stengel remarked, "I'm glad we did good. It's good for the club. But we ain't so great. My pitcher didn't throw the ball over to first base so they got down and broke up two double plays. It was a good game, but we still did the same thing with men on base [not hit]. I don't know when they're going to learn."

Another time, a fan horned in on a Stengel press conference to say, "That Zimmer's the guts of your club, isn't he?"

Well, Don Zimmer was all right. He was one of those people it's supposed to be good to have around your club because he always tries so hard. Zimmer, it was true, had an intense look in his light eyes and when he walked on a baseball field he looked like a lion tamer going into the cage. In fact, though, his range around third base had become limited and his hitting soon proved illusory. Once the season started, he went 0 for 34 and was batting .080 when he was traded. Stengel must have known all the time, for what he said to the fan was, "Why, he's beyond that. He's much more. He's the perdotious quotient of the qualificatilus. He's the lower intestine."

And this one as the Mets finished spring training with a 12–15 record: "I'm mad as hell if I don't win. But I know if the other side put in their regulars I wouldna beaten them."

The day before the Mets were to play their first National League game, the lads were waiting for an elevator in the lobby of the Hotel Chase, in St. Louis, all dressed in their new team blazers which could only be described as Dodger blue. The elevator came. It was soon full. The boys in the back pushed. More got in. Altogether there were sixteen Mets in the elevator when it got stuck between floors. They were stuck for twenty minutes. "I knew it,"

Craig said in the elevator. "The first time in my life I'm going to open a season, I get stuck in an elevator. I'll probably be here for twenty-four hours."

"It wasn't so bad for the other guys," Hobie Landrith, the short catcher, said. "I'm not built high enough. I couldn't get any air down where I was."

This was taken to have been a portent of things to come with the Mets. It probably was, although it was far from the only one. A few days later, when the Mets opened at the Polo Grounds, Casey Stengel slammed the door of his newly built office. When he tried to get back into it, there was no key that fitted the lock. Workmen were summoned to disassemble the door frame.

A couple of other things happened that day. Brian Sullivan of the Metropolitan Opera and the St. Camillus Band rendered "The Star-Spangled Banner," but not together. And when the lineup was announced on the P.A. it was the wrong one, and then the Mets lost the game when Jim Marshall came off first base to take a throw he just couldn't wait to reach him and Richie Ashburn and Gus Bell let a ball drop between them in the outfield. It was also discovered after the game that Casey Stengel's undershorts were still emblazoned with the emblem of the New York Yankees.

The Mets lost their first nine games. There was no way of throwing stones at individual players. They all gave until it hurt. There was this game they lost to the Philadelphia Phillies, 11–9, for example. They lost it because Charlie Neal let two routine balls get by him at second base. They lost it because Landrith was guilty of two passed balls. They lost it because Frank ("Big Donkey") Thomas, who, it turned out, could hit home runs and was a whiz at helping stewardesses serve meals on airplanes, dropped an easy fly ball in left field. They lost it because of this kind of play:

In the second inning they were only three runs down. There were runners on first and third because Neal had let a line drive bounce off his glove. Tony Gonzales then hit a chopper back to the right side of the mound. Jim Marshall, the first baseman, came over for it. Craig Anderson, the pitcher, went after it and got it. He turned to throw it to first. Of course, no one was there. On the next play Zimmer couldn't find the handle on a little grounder and the Phillies had a five-run lead.

Stengel blamed Marshall. "Why should he go over there?" he grumbled. "He was out of place. No one knew where the hell he was."

Said Marshall: "Well, I don't know. I'm supposed to go for the ball until the pitcher calls me off. By the time he said anything, I was too far from the base to go back."

Then there was Neal. On a play like that, the second baseman ought to

come over and cover first. Neal just sort of stood there watching the play. And *that* was the Mets.

It is a distortion of history to believe, as some of the young Mets seem to now, that the old Mets were clowns who expected—even *wanted*—to lose. They lost, all right, and as Stengel once pointed out, "When you're losing, you commence to play stupid." But none of them *wanted* to lose.

This from Zimmer after the Mets had lost those first nine in a row: "It's got to get you down after a while. There ain't nobody looking to lose in this game no matter how lousy you are."

And when, after two seasons in which he had managed to lose forty six games—a record—Craig was finally traded, he sighed with great relief. "Losing," Craig said. "I never liked to lose. I never even got used to it."

It was a cold and miserable day at the Polo Grounds and the Mets were down 15–5 with two out in the ninth. A fan stood in the aisle in right field, his shoulders hunched against the cold, his hands deep in his coat pockets. He jiggled up and down for warmth and all the time he was rooting. "C'mon," he said, almost to himself. "C'mon, one more run, just one more run."

"Why one more run?" he was asked.

"That would make it six," he said. "Then you could say if they got any pitching they woulda won."

The fan turned back toward Don Zimmer, who was at the plate. "C'mon," he said. "Just one more."

Zimmer popped up to the catcher.

The fan shrugged his shoulders. "Ah well," he said. "I'll be back tomorrow. No use giving up now."

Then there was the couple who were arrested behind home plate one night for committing what, considering the location, was an act of extraordinary friendliness. "But, officer," the woman protested, "we're *married*."

One of the few rules Stengel put down for his players was that there would be no card playing. It was his belief that card playing led to gambling, gambling led to losing, and losing led to resentments. Shortly after Harry Chiti was obtained by the Mets, he went to Stengel during an airplane trip and asked for permission to start a gin-rummy game. Stengel said no. He suggested instead that if Chiti, a catcher, had nothing to do he might go over the opposition hitters. Chiti went to sleep.

The most interesting thing about Chiti is that he was obtained for "a player to be named later." When that player was finally named, it turned out to be Harry Chiti. Thus he was returned in payment for himself.

There is no other reason for his fame.

On May 9, the Mets picked up Marvelous Marv Throneberry from the Baltimore Orioles. George Weiss gleefully announced that he had managed to get Throneberry for cash, which was very hard to do. Throneberry was first called Marvelous when he was a young Yankee and it was believed, as it was about all young Yankees, that he was actually a marvelous ballplayer. He was something else.

When he came to the Mets he had a lifetime average of .238 and a reputation as a poor fielder. But as Weiss pointed out, "He has never had a chance to play regularly." The Mets gave him that chance. It revealed him.

Throneberry, twenty-nine at the time, looked much older. He was thickly built and his bald head was covered with freckles. He was from a small town in Tennessee, chewed tobacco, and had a country accent.

Although he occasionally hit the long ball, he also hit into a lot of double plays and often struck out at crucial moments. On the field he was a disaster. Very quickly, he was being booed by the generally gentle Polo Grounds fans. He had become the personification of ineptitude. His first reaction was the routine baseball-player one of savage anger. Slowly though, with the help of Richie Ashburn, whose locker was next to his in the clubhouse, he came to understand his special role. There was the rainy night, for example, after he had had one of his routinely terrible games. He sat in his underwear in front of his locker and allowed a leak in the ceiling of the decrepit old clubhouse to drip, drip, drip, directly onto his bald head.

"I deserve it," he said.

"Yes, you do," said Richie Ashburn.

Elio Chacon stopped a reporter near the batting cage in San Francisco one day. "Hey," he said, shyly. "You think we win today?"

The reporter, a gentle sort, said he was often disappointed, but he expected the Mets to win every day. Chacon nodded with satisfaction. "Well, we try every day," he said. "We try. That's muy important."

The Mets were beaten that day, twice, 11–4 and 10–3.

The Mets lost because of their pitching, hitting, fielding, and because they often had abysmal luck. They also lost because of umpires. That's what happens to bad teams. Pick a game at random in late July. The Mets were losing to St. Louis 6–4 in the ninth because they had made four errors, because of a two-out, bases-loaded, broken-bat blooper by the Cards' Ken Boyer, and because while Marvelous Marv was chasing Boyer in a rundown Stan Musial was able to score, laughing. Still, in the last of the ninth, the Mets had the tying runs on base when Choo Choo Coleman, the little catcher Stengel was trying (and failing) to build up into another Yogi Berra, was caught in a rundown between third and home. In the course of the rundown, Coleman was clearly tripped by catcher Jim Schaffer while he was not in possession of the ball. Instead of awarding Coleman home plate, umpire Mel Steiner called him out and the game was over.

When Ed Bouchee made an error on the field and then struck out with two runners on base, Marvelous Marv walked up to him, looking angry, and said, "What are you trying to do, steal my fans?"

On August 15, Al Jackson of the Mets held the Philadelphia Phillies to one run for fourteen innings. In the fifteenth, two runs scored when Tony Gonzales hit a sharp ground ball to first base. Although Marvelous Marv was there, when he put down his glove the ball just naturally jumped over it. Throneberry was not charged with an error. He had not, in fact, made an error in fifteen games.

He had a chance to make up for it all in the bottom of the fifteenth when he came up with runners on first and third. He struck out. "He ended up swinging on balls they was gonna walk him on," Stengel complained.

After the Mets had lost for the ninety-second time, Richie Ashburn said,

"They say it's easy to play on a loser. Hell it is. It's a lot easier to play on a winner. Seems to me I'm playing harder than I ever did before."

Marvelous Marv had a great September. He won several games with home runs and even started a couple of difficult and important first-to-second-to-first double plays. One day he helped beat the Dodgers with a home run and then made all three putouts in the ninth. Five kids came into the ballpark one night, each dressed in a white T-shirt with a black letter inked on. "M-A-R-V" they spelled out. The fifth wore a "!". When they climbed on top of the Mets dugout and did a dance, they were thrown out of the park. They bought their way back into the bleachers to see M-A-R-V!

Said Ashburn: "Throneberry is the people's choice. And you know why? He typifies the Mets. He's either great or terrible." He paused and turned to Throneberry. "But you better not get too good," he said. "Just drop a pop fly once in a while."

Said Throneberry: "Aw, I haven't dropped a pop fly in a week."

Throneberry did so well at the last that he received a $7,000 power boat for hitting an outfield sign more than anybody else. Ashburn received a $5,000 power boat after a vote by fans and newspapermen. Throneberry found out that since Ashburn's boat was a gift it was not taxable, but that since he had won his in a contest, his was. Said Throneberry, scratching his bald dome and looking exquisitely unhappy: "I don't understand it."

At the end of that first season, Ken McKenzie, a pitcher and the only Yale man on the club, told some of the thoughts he had about the events of the year. McKenzie: "When we started out this spring, I really thought we'd be all right, maybe even play .500 ball. I don't know what happened. *Something* happened, of course. You hear about clubs that win pennants. What happens is one guy picks up if another lets down. We've worked in reverse. We found a different way to lose every day.

"I don't think we were quite as bad as we looked. There was something this year that made every player a little worse than his potential. Our pitching, well, our pitching had a pattern. Error, base hit; error, base hit. When you're pitching good ball and there's an error behind you, you bend your back and make the pitches. This is exactly what we didn't do. We probably set a record for unearned runs. That's no alibi for the pitchers, not when he's giving up the runs after the error."

The Mets finished with a 40–120 record. They had had losing streaks of nine, eleven, thirteen, and seventeen. Said Stengel: "Strangers are hard to manage. It was like spring training all year. But I expected to win more games. I was very much shocked."

Said Throneberry: "You think the fish will come out of the water to boo me this winter?"

The Mets were not much different the next year. After the first game in 1963, Stengel stormed into his little Polo Grounds office, slammed his baseball cap down on his desk, and announced, "The attendance was robbed. We're still a fraud."

And not long after, Marvelous Marv Throneberry, playing right field, slipped and fell while chasing the first ball hit to him. He was able to hold the runner to two bases on the single and as he sat there on the wet grass, chagrin oozing from every pore, Duke Snider, now the center fielder, stood over him, hands on hips, and laughed and laughed. It was another good year.

There was never a team like the old Mets and there will never be another. It was put together by a chain of incredible coincidences: the mendacity of National League club owners who wanted to give up as few good players as possible in the expansion draft; the dogged if mistaken logic of George Weiss; the wildly improbable personality of Casey Stengel; the eccentrically shaped, decrepit, yet somehow intimate and friendly Polo Grounds, one of the last of the ballparks that made itself a factor in the playing of baseball games; the baseball-hungry fans, who could not be comfortable in the austere, cold Yankee Stadium, where triumph was cheap and tragedy nonexistent. To have been there when these coincidences collided with such shattering hilarity was to have been in a special place indeed.

Now it is all different. Casey Stengel is gone. The players, who try no harder than the old Mets, succeed more often and as a result are indistinguishable from baseball players all over. There is stuffiness in the front office. There is great concern about unimportant things. (The manager not long ago suggested to a newspaperman that he need not have blabbed in the public prints that the Mets scored their winning run on a bunt.) And, worst of all, when the Mets lose, there is nothing funny about it at all.

Do losers lose and winners win? Or are those who win, winners, and those who lose, losers? Character and destiny, chicken and egg. Riddles rampant on a field of green. Things as they are, things as they seem. Aristotle at the bat. Plato on the hill.

WILFRID SHEED

Notes on the Country Game

The 1980 World Series was supposed to feature the spoiled millionaires of Philadelphia vs. the enlightened millionaires of New York. I don't know what sort of millionaires they have in Kansas City—signals from the Sunbelt come in dimly on the Eastern Seaboard. But money and the modern ballplayer have been the talk all season, even when the lads fall to fighting over beanballs. (Nobody that rich wants to be hit in the head, goes the reasoning.)

Thus the Yankees put up with the bully-boy ravings of George Steinbrenner because they can't afford not to. New York is such a lucrative playground, in TV commercials alone, that Steinbrenner can chew out the help with impunity. Philadelphia apparently does not cast quite the same spell, so there the players chew out the manager instead. The question the World Series was *supposed* to answer was: Which is better for you, to chew or be chewed?

The Series we got did suggest that perhaps these are not baseball questions at all but messy fallout from the gossip culture. The Phillies were supposed to hate their manager so much that they might well lose four straight, or whatever it took, just to spite him. The Kansas City Royals, who, it seems, only mildly dislike their manager, should have cashed in on this quirk of brotherly love handsomely—everybody else has who's had the good luck to encounter the Phillies in October, by which time they must be a ball of seething hate.

Yet when the blather had cleared, one team had made sixty hits and the other fifty-nine; one team (a different one) had outscored the other 4.5 to 3.9 per game—which I believe comes close to the average score of all ballgames played anywhere since the beginning of time. In short, the verities triumphed over the froth of the press box. Baseball is so finely calibrated that the super teams win three out of five, and the dogs two out of five. It is not the least surprising to find two teams with exactly the same records after *160 games*. So a Series between *any* two big-league teams could be close. Yet in a World Series, these percentages fly out the window and everything is supposed to come down to character, as if ballplayers were prisoners of their nerves, like the rest of us.

The salient factor about this year's Series was that *neither* cast had been in one before. That took care of the stage-fright margin, or old Yankee edge. Maidenhood is everything in these matters. Yet while everyone else talked about money, the players themselves talked about character, as millionaires are wont to. The word must have a special meaning for them. Because as soon as a team begins to win, it *believes* it has character. Just let a couple of lucky hits fall in and the guys will say, "Yeah, we're that kind of team." The rhythm of streak and slump is so wild and unfathomable that the men riding it feel compelled to assert some kind of control over it. Contrariwise, in defeat the players "get down on themselves," search for scapegoats, question their own character. "We *proved* we had character," said the Phillies. Obviously. To win *is* to have character.

Morale also is more a function of winning than a cause of it: but it's a necessary function. It prolongs the streak from six wins to seven and picks up the junk game that could go either way, that magical third game in five.

There are some teams that sin against the Holy Ghost and reject the energy that victory brings. The Phillies were felt to be one of these, like the Red Sox. Pampered by country-club ownership, went the talk, they could not rise to the myth of team spirit, the sense that the Collective can somehow coordinate its private streaks and slumps to squeeze the extra game. Too rich, not hungry enough, injury-prone (injuries, strangely, are no excuse: character is supposed to thrive on them); teams like the Phillies are the pouting villains we need for our annual play-in-the-round.

Yet give one of them a hot hand—the Red Sox in '75, the Phillies last month— and you'll see who's pouty. Philadelphia did all the things rich brats are expressly supposed not to do. They came from behind four times in a row, counting the playoffs. Outfielder Bake McBride, the brat of brats, turned his orneriness into pure menace, treating the enemy as if they were his manager. Shortstop Larry Bowa, the team cynic, started seven double plays (a record) and cried with joy when it was all over. Pitcher Steve Carlton, who won't even talk to his friends, popped his fast ball so hard that the catcher's mitt sounded like a bat.

Perhaps the best symbol was third baseman Mike Schmidt because he seemed to personify defeat, almost to anticipate it, *without* being obnoxious, a more evolved mutant. Some dismal playoffs in the past had made him a loser in a Sartrean sense: i.e., *first* you lose, *then* you are a loser—you have defined yourself.

Yet suddenly he had his touch, and he seemed like a different man. And one realized how much one's concept of a team is a problem in perception, or propaganda. Because all the Phillies looked better in victory. For instance, the surliness in the clubhouse—was that really because they were counting their money, or was it because they just don't like reporters, the old-fashioned way? Being civilized to the press is often the only clue we have to these guys' personalities, and it isn't a bad one. But ballplayers from the outback can be unduly disturbed the first time they see themselves misquoted or laughed at in a big newspaper. A team, like an administration, is as lovable as its press corps makes it.

Baseball is pre-eminently the country game, because it takes up so much space, artificially transposed to the city where strangers boo you; the suspicious, uncommunicative rube has graced every clubhouse since Ring Lardner. In fact, you can probably find Steve Carlton himself somewhere in Lardner, right down to the hideous grimaces.

One of baseball's charming legends has Whitey Ford of New York City playing Henry Higgins to Mickey Mantle of Oklahoma and practically turning him into a boulevardier. Pete Rose struggles to perform the same task for the Phils, but it's tough work Higginsing half a squad. And of course the black styles of resentment practiced by McBride and Garry Maddox were undreamed of in Lardner, and will presumably have to be resolved outside the clubhouse.

As to those miserable objects, "today's kids," who allegedly can't stand discipline from an old-school manager—what about yesterday's kids, the Cleveland crybabies of 1940, or the Dodgers of '43, one of whom (Arky Vaughan) flung his uniform at Leo Durocher's feet? Ballplayers, rich or poor, have always been hard to handle—it is one of the few real tests of great managing—and a flinty-eyed brute like Rogers Hornsby had as little luck with it way back then as he would today.

On second thought, has anything changed as little as a major-league ballplayer, unless it be the game he plays? Babe Ruth holds a mirror to the 1920s, and the Gas House Gang might be said to reflect the Okie spirit of the 1930s.

But it's a weak reflection. You might have guessed from the hairdos in the 1960s that *something* was happening in America, but what?

You can't deduce much about an era from its ballplayers. Solitary men in a solitary game, they make their way one by one into the big leagues and out again, always slightly to the side of normal society. The team spirit they invoke so fervently is always ad hoc, always this gang this year. Their teammates, while they last, are closer than family, but they are always being ripped apart and replaced. No wonder some players are withdrawn and others full of empty good cheer. A barmaid in Lindells of Detroit told me that ballplayers were the stingiest and least friendly of all the athletes who traipsed through the place. Yet there are the Tug McGraws and Pete Roses who thrive on the change and uncertainty of the gypsy life, and who can briefly ignite the rest—as long as the rest are winning anyway.

Team spirit has little to do with the hard numbers of baseball, though it can quasi-mystically keep batting rallies going (or is it the rally itself that creates the spirit?). This Series came down to Willie Wilson's strikeouts and Willie Aikens's stone glove, and all the character in the world couldn't have done a thing about that. If Wilson never plays another Series, he will become another Mike Schmidt, a loser; if the wheel spins right, he will become Mr. October II. He will still be the same player, but he will look different. Which may be why athletes don't think much of fans.

Otherwise, chalk a small one up for the brat who chews, and file this away under "arrestingly average." Nineteen eighty was the year the percentages came back in the guise of melodrama: in other words, it was baseball at its finest.

The country game has its ugly moments, to be sure—the beanball bouts and mandatory melees that follow, or teammates duking it out in the locker room, or fans insulting/assaulting players in the parking lot. There have been on-field riots (see my own contribution to this volume), off-field tragedies (murders, suicides), and garden-variety vituperation aplenty. But nothing in recent memory has shocked and disgusted the baseball world like this explosion in the Texas Rangers' spring camp of 1977. Blackie Sherrod covered it for the *Dallas Times Herald*.

BLACKIE SHERROD

The Randle Incident

The sequence was all so incredibly swift, maybe four, five seconds at the most, and yet in afterthought, it hung there suspended in time, like slow motion or instant replay or the old newsreel films of the *Hindenburg* breaking apart reluctantly in dark Jersey skies.

There was the tableau of Frank Lucchesi and Lenny Randle talking, calmly it seemed to these witnessing eyeballs some 40 feet away—the Texas manager and his embittered player, once again debating Randle's past, present, and future with the Rangers. They stood maybe 18 inches apart, Lucchesi in his blue flowered shirt and gray slacks (he had not yet dressed for the game), Randle in his uniform, some 20 feet toward the Ranger dugout from the pregame batting cage.

There was no raising of voices, or even these jaded ears would have picked it up; no animation, no gestures, no jabbing of forefingers, no distending of neck veins. It seems to this memory that both men had their hands on hips, not belligerently but naturally as a couple guys on the street corner argue the respective talents of the Longhorns and Sooners. Three, four minutes the conversation continued while your eyewitness watched it idly, only vaguely curious at what appeared to be another review of Randle's discontent that he wasn't getting a full-scale chance at retaining his second-base job from the challenge of rookie Bump Wills.

(The debate surfaced angrily last week when Lucchesi exploded that he was "sick and tired of some punks making $80,000 moaning and groaning about their jobs." The word *punk* was the fuse.)

Lucchesi had walked on the Minnesota spring diamond, said hello to a few fans, walked away for a private chat with Jim Russo, the Baltimore superscout. (Trade talk?)

The forty-eight-year-old manager was en route back to the dugout tunnel to the locker room to get dressed when Randle approached. So the two men talked while Rangers took batting practice behind them, a cluster of players awaiting turns at the cage.

Suddenly with unbelievable quickness, Randle's right hand shot forth. No wild drawback nor windup, as a saloon brawler might use, but a straight strike from the body and here was Lucchesi falling slowly, turning to his right from the force, and there came a left with the same terrible rapidity. This was probably the blow that fractured Lucchesi's right cheekbone. Then another right and a left, all before the victim finally reached earth some 10 feet from where he was first struck. Your witness has seen the hand speed of Sugar Ray Robinson and the cobra strikes of Muhammad Ali, but the flurry of Randle's punches, all landing on the manager's face, must have broken all speed records.

After Lucchesi hit heavily on his right hip, his left arm curled above him in some helpless defense attempt, there were other Randle punches, maybe they landed, maybe not, before Bert Campaneris reacted from four strides away. He had frozen at first, probably as others stared in disbelief, but sprinted quickly to the scene, leaped astride the fallen Lucchesi and stretched his hands out, palms up, to fend off Randle. The furious player backed away, yelling, "Leave me alone!" while Jim Fregosi and others reached the dazed victim.

Then, while players carried Lucchesi to the dugout tunnel, his right eye already blue and puffing, blood trickling from his mouth, Randle preceded them to the dugout, pulled a bat from the rack and held it briefly, then dropped it and trotted to the outfield where he began to run wind sprints all alone. This was maybe the only positive move of the day, for who knows what player emotions might have followed. Ken Henderson, especially, had to be restrained when he saw Lucchesi, sitting propped against the tunnel wall while trainer Bill Zeigler tried to administer aid and judge the damage.

No witness could remember any similar baseball incident. Fights between players, surely, even spats between players and coaches, but never a player felling his manager. Eddie Robinson, the Ranger vice-president, arriving later, couldn't think of one. Sid Hudson, the veteran coach, shook his head. Burt Hawkins, the traveling secretary who watched Babe Ruth, also flunked.

So what prompted this unprecedented explosion? Randle, seemingly composed afterward, said Lucchesi had called him a "punk" again. Lucchesi, from his bed in Mercy Hospital, said this was a lie.

Was the Randle violent, savage action triggered by a remark in the apparent calm conversation? Was it a buildup of Randle emotions, of frustrations bred when he thought he was not being given enough chance to play?

A day earlier, Lenny had told Channel 4 interviewer Allan Stone, "I'm a volcano, getting ready to erupt."

"But," said Stone, "he was smiling when he said it."

If Randle's was a calculated action, would not a single punch have sufficed? What pushed him across the line into uncontrollable fury, an outburst that might end his baseball career forever? Probably no one will ever know.

In a corner of the dugout, by the bullpen telephone while Ranger players milled about in stunned aimlessness, a small white card glared from the wall. It was the lineup for Monday's game. The second line read: Randle, 2B.

Howard Ehmke was a draughthorse of a pitcher—not flashy, but dependable. At the close of the 1929 regular season, the books appeared to be closed on his career: won-lost record, 166–165. But in the World Series that year, Connie Mack gambled that the veteran had one more win left in him, and he did. Red Smith wrote this story on March 18, 1959, upon learning of Ehmke's death; so frequently did he find inspiration on the obituary page that he amassed enough elegiac columns to make for a collection of fond farewells, *To Absent Friends.* Walter W. Smith joined those friends before the book was completed; it was published with an additional farewell, by Dave Anderson.

RED SMITH

Howard Ehmke

Of all the stories Connie Mack used to tell at dinners, and he had a routine as fixed as any in vaudeville, his favorite concerned Howard Ehmke. It never varied by so much as a syllable in the telling. Late in the 1929 season, Connie would explain, it had become evident that nothing could stop the Athletics' drive to a pennant. Just before the last tour of the West, Connie called Ehmke into his tower office in Shibe Park in Philadelphia. Ehmke's days in the major leagues were ending. He sat on the bench almost all summer watching Lefty Grove, George Earnshaw, Rube Walberg, and others younger than he handling the chores on the mound. This was the scene as Connie described it:

" 'Howard,' I said, 'the time has come for us to part.'

"He looked at me. 'Mr. Mack,' he said, 'I have always wanted to pitch in a World Series.' He lifted his arm"—here Connie would raise his own thin right arm, fist clenched—" 'Mr. Mack,' he said, 'there is one great game left in this old arm.' That was what I wanted to hear. 'All right, Howard,' I told him. 'When we go west I want you to stay here. When the Cubs come in to play the Phillies, you watch them. Learn all you can about their hitters. Say nothing to anybody. You are my opening pitcher for the World Series.''

There was a sidelight which Connie omitted from his tale, but Al Simmons supplied it. When Ehmke started to warm up for the opener with the Cubs, Simmons snorted with consternation. "Are you going to pitch *him?*" he demanded incredulously.

"Is it all right with you, Al?" Connie asked.

Simmons gulped. "Oh, well—er, well, if you say so."

Skipping that bit, Connie would go on to tell how the Cubs lunged and stabbed at Ehmke's soft stuff. He would recall the strikeouts in order—Rogers Hornsby, Hack Wilson, Kiki Cuyler, Riggs Stephenson, Gabby Hartnett, Hornsby again, then Wilson—until the total reached thirteen for an all-time World Series record.

Connie attached a lot of importance to the secrecy surrounding his plan. He made it clear that in his opinion the element of surprise was a major factor in Ehmke's success. Chances are he never knew of a conversation which Ring Lardner repeated a year later.

Lardner was writing fiction and plays by 1929, but he had many friends in baseball after his years as a sportswriter. Joe McCarthy, the Cubs' manager, was one.

"I was chatting with Joe a little before the season ended," Lardner said. " 'I'm not afraid of Grove and Earnshaw,' he told me. 'We can hit speed. But they've got one guy over there I am afraid of. He's what I call a junk pitcher—but Joe used an indelicate expression. 'His name,' he told me, 'is Howard Ehmke, and he's the sucker we're going to see in this Series."

So maybe the Cubs' surprise wasn't quite so great as Connie liked to believe. He did enjoy telling the story, though, and today it all comes back because the morning paper reported the death of Howard Ehmke at sixty-five.

He was a big, handsome, light-haired man, head of a successful tarpaulin and awning firm in Philadelphia, and a pretty good horse player. He used to get to Miami every year during the Hialeah meeting and it was a pleasure to encounter him there, a quiet man of warmth and charm. This season he wasn't there.

Howard lived to see his strikeout record broken by Carl Erskine, pitching for Brooklyn against the Yankees. He wasn't in the stands when it happened, though. He and Mrs. Ehmke were taking a drive in suburban Philadelphia, listening with mild interest to the radio broadcast of the game.

At first it was just another game to Howard, but as Erskine turned back one Yankee after another, it took on a special interest. When Erskine got his ninth or tenth strikeout, Howard said, "Let's park and listen to the rest of this." He pulled off the road and cut the motor.

Another Yankee struck out. Then another. Now Erskine tied Ehmke's mark but the game wasn't over. Mrs. Ehmke was watching her husband. The fourteenth Yankee went down—it could have been Don Bollweg. Howard smiled quietly.

He said nothing as the game drew to an end. The record he had held for a quarter of a century was gone. He stepped on the starter. Nothing happened. The radio had drained his battery.

No greater love hath fan than this—and as with all things in baseball, there's precedent. James Whyte Davis of the original Knickerbockers, who began play on Hoboken's Elysian Fields in 1850, penned these burial instructions in his waning years: "All relations and immediate friends are well informed that I desire to be buried in my base-ball suit, and wrapped in the original flag of the old Knickerbockers of 1845, now festooned over my bureau. . . ." This, from *The Sporting News* of July 26, 1980, with a memorable last line.

THE SPORTING NEWS

Bury Me in My Old Cub Suit

Maniford (Hack) Harper of Washburn, Illinois, has lived and died with the Chicago Cubs for fifty-four years, and he's not planning to stop when he leaves this earthly vale.

Harper, sixty-five, has made a pact with a mortician to go to his grave in a Cubs uniform that he bought from his favorite team some years ago. The uniform and a bright blue cap with a red "C" on the front have been in mothballs, prepared for the day Hack is laid to rest.

"I'm going to be buried in the uniform because baseball is all I think about," said Harper. "It's my life. I don't care about cars or anything else, and I never have."

Harper's devotion to the Cubs began when he was in Shriners Hospital in Oak Park, Illinois, in 1926, at the age of eleven. Severely stricken with polio, he had been paralyzed on the right side of his body since he was seventeen months old.

He said that Cubs immortal Hack Wilson visited the hospital with some fellow players and walked up to him, tapped him on the shoulder, and said, "Stick it out, kid. Someday, you'll be able to walk."

From then on, Harper was a Cubs fan. People started calling him Hack, after the Cubs' slugger. At thirteen, he visited the tattoo parlor at a medicine show and had "CUBS" engraved on his left forearm in inch-high letters. For his high school graduation, he requested $25 to travel the 125 miles to Chicago to watch the Cubbies play for a week.

He has attended more than 1,500 games at Wrigley Field, and has collected 187 foul balls and had them autographed. He keeps them in a safe deposit box. For seven consecutive years, he traveled to Arizona to buy the first available spring-training ticket of the season—and still has the stubs to prove it.

"They're my whole life," said Harper. "Without the Cubs, I would be crazy."

Baseball analysis: Is less more? Wielding Occam's Razor, the parsimonious poet confounds the experts. From her 1971 volume, *More Poems to Solve.*

MAY SWENSON

Analysis of Baseball

It's about
the ball,
the bat,
and the mitt.
Ball hits
bat, or it
hits mitt.
Bat doesn't
hit ball, bat
meets it.
Ball bounces
off bat, flies
air, or thuds
ground (dud)
or it
fits mitt.

Bat waits
for ball

to mate.
Ball hates
to take bat's
bait. Ball
flirts, bat's
late, don't
keep the date.
Ball goes in
(thwack) to mitt,
and goes out
(thwack) back
to mitt.

Ball fits
mitt, but
not all
the time.
Sometimes
ball gets hit

(pow) when bat
meets it,
and sails
to a place
where mitt
has to quit
in disgrace.
That's about
the bases
loaded,
about 40,000
fans exploded.

It's about
the ball,
the bat,
the mitt,
the bases
and the fans.
It's done
on a diamond,
and for fun.
It's about
home, and it's
about run.

The obscure wish to be famous; the famous, to be obscure. Joe DiMaggio is a private man who plied a public trade and still does; like Garbo (and Steve Carlton), he has shielded himself from those who would use him, but this has had the paradoxical effect of making him all the more alluring to those he would repel. DiMaggio resisted the efforts of Gay Talese to interview him for *Esquire* in 1966, but the master of the profile got his man, as usual. Tom Wolfe has credited Talese with having created the "new journalism"—stylish reporting, employing the techniques of fiction—with his 1962 *Esquire* profile of another man of dignity, Joe Louis.

GAY TALESE

The Silent Season of a Hero

> *"I would like to take the great DiMaggio fishing,"* the old man said. *"They say his father was a fisherman. Maybe he was as poor as we are and would understand."*
> —Ernest Hemingway,
> The Old Man and the Sea

It was not quite spring, the silent season before the search for salmon, and the old fishermen of San Francisco were either painting their boats or repairing their nets along the pier or sitting in the sun talking quietly among themselves, watching the tourists come and go, and smiling, now, as a pretty girl paused to take their picture. She was about twenty-five, healthy and blue-eyed and wearing a red turtleneck sweater, and she had long, flowing blond hair that she brushed back a few times before clicking her camera. The fishermen, looking at her, made admiring comments but she did not understand because they spoke a Sicilian dialect; nor did she notice the tall gray-haired man in a dark suit who stood watching her from behind a big bay window on the second floor of DiMaggio's Restaurant that overlooks the pier.

He watched until she left, lost in the crowd of newly arrived tourists that had just come down the hill by cable car. Then he sat down again at the table in the restaurant, finishing his tea and lighting another cigarette, his fifth in the last half hour. It was eleven-thirty in the morning. None of the other tables was occupied, and the only sounds came from the bar, where a liquor salesman was laughing at something the headwaiter had said. But then the salesman, his briefcase under his arm, headed for the door, stopping briefly to peek into the dining room and call out, "See you later, Joe." Joe DiMaggio turned and waved at the salesman. Then the room was quiet again.

At fifty-one, DiMaggio was a most distinguished-looking man, aging as gracefully as he had played on the ballfield, impeccable in his tailoring, his nails manicured, his 6-foot 2-inch body seeming as lean and capable as when he posed for the portrait that hangs in the restaurant and shows him in Yankee Stadium swinging from the heels at a pitch thrown twenty years ago. His gray hair was thinning at the crown, but just barely, and his face was lined in the right places, and his expression, once as sad and haunted as a matador's, was more in repose these days, though, as now, tension had returned and he chain-smoked and occasionally paced the floor and looked out the window at the people below. In the crowd was a man he did not wish to see.

The man had met DiMaggio in New York. This week he had come to San Francisco and had telephoned several times but none of the calls had been returned because DiMaggio suspected that the man, who had said he was doing research on some vague sociological project, really wanted to delve into DiMaggio's private life and that of DiMaggio's former wife, Marilyn Monroe. DiMaggio would never tolerate this. The memory of her death is still very painful to him, and yet, because he keeps it to himself, some people are not sensitive to it. One night in a supper club a woman who had been drinking approached his table, and when he did not ask her to join him, she snapped:

"All right, I guess I'm *not* Marilyn Monroe."

He ignored her remark, but when she repeated it, he replied, barely controlling his anger, "No—I wish you were, but you're not."

The tone of his voice softened her, and she asked, "Am I saying something wrong?"

"You already have," he said. "Now will you please leave me alone?"

His friends on the wharf, understanding him as they do, are very careful when discussing him with strangers, knowing that should they inadvertently betray a confidence he will not denounce them but rather will never speak to them again; this comes from a sense of propriety not inconsistent in the man who also, after Marilyn Monroe's death, directed that fresh flowers be placed on her grave "forever."

Some of the old fishermen who have known DiMaggio all his life remember him as a small boy who helped clean his father's boat, and as a young man who sneaked away and used a broken oar as a bat on the sandlots nearby. His father, a small mustachioed man known as Zio Pepe, would become infuriated and call him *lagnuso* (lazy) *meschino* (good-for-nothing) but in 1936 Zio Pepe was among those who cheered when Joe DiMaggio returned to San Francisco after his first season with the New York Yankees and was carried along the wharf on the shoulders of the fishermen.

The fishermen also remember how, after his retirement in 1951, DiMaggio brought his second wife, Marilyn, to live near the wharf, and sometimes they would be seen early in the morning fishing off DiMaggio's boat, the *Yankee Clipper*, now docked quietly in the marina, and in the evening they would be sitting and talking on the pier. They had arguments, too, the fishermen knew, and one night Marilyn was seen running hysterically, crying as she ran, along the road away from the pier, with Joe following. But the fishermen pretended they did not see this; it was none of their affair. They knew that Joe wanted her to stay in San Francisco and avoid the sharks in Hollywood, but she was confused and torn then—"She was a child," they said—and even today DiMaggio loathes Los Angeles and many of the people in it. He no longer speaks to his onetime friend, Frank Sinatra, who had befriended Marilyn in her final years, and he also is cool to Dean Martin and Peter Lawford and Lawford's former wife, Pat, who once gave a party at which she introduced Marilyn Monroe to Robert Kennedy, and the two of them danced often that night, Joe heard, and he did not take it well. He was very possessive of her that year, his close friends say, because Marilyn and he had planned to remarry; but before they could she was dead, and DiMaggio banned the Lawfords and Sinatra and many Hollywood people from her funeral. When Marilyn Monroe's attorney complained that DiMaggio was keeping her friends away, DiMaggio answered coldly, "If it weren't for those friends persuading her to stay in Hollywood she would still be alive."

Joe DiMaggio now spends most of the year in San Francisco, and each day tourists, noticing the name on the restaurant, ask the men on the wharf if they ever see him. Oh yes, the men say, they see him nearly every day; they have not seen him yet this morning, they add, but he should be arriving shortly. So the tourists continue to walk along the piers past the crab vendors, under the circling sea gulls, past the fish 'n' chip stands, sometimes stopping to watch a large vessel steaming toward the Golden Gate Bridge which, to their dismay, is painted red. Then they visit the Wax Museum, where there is a life-size figure of DiMaggio in uniform, and walk across the street and spend a quarter to peer through the silver telescopes focused on the island of Alcatraz, which is no longer a Federal prison. Then they return to ask the men if DiMaggio has been seen. Not yet, the men say, although they notice his blue Impala parked in the lot next to the restaurant. Sometimes tourists will walk into the restaurant and have lunch and will see him sitting calmly in a corner signing autographs and being extremely gracious with everyone. At other times, as on this particular morning when the man from New York chose to visit, DiMaggio was tense and suspicious.

When the man entered the restaurant from the side steps leading to the dining room, he saw DiMaggio standing near the window, talking with an elderly maître d' named Charles Friscia. Not wanting to walk in and risk intrusion, the man asked one of DiMaggio's nephews to inform Joe of his presence. When DiMaggio got the message he quickly turned and left Friscia and disappeared through an exit leading down to the kitchen.

Astonished and confused, the visitor stood in the hall. A moment later Friscia appeared and the man asked, "Did Joe leave?"

"Joe who?" Friscia replied.

"Joe DiMaggio!"

"Haven't seen him," Friscia said.

"You haven't *seen* him! He was standing right next to you a second ago!"

"It wasn't me," Friscia said.

"You were standing next to him. I saw you. In the dining room."

"You must be mistaken," Friscia said, softly, seriously. "It wasn't me."

"You *must* be kidding," the man said, angrily, turning and leaving the restaurant. Before he could get to his car, however, DiMaggio's nephew came running after him and said, "Joe wants to see you."

He returned expecting to see DiMaggio waiting for him. Instead he was handed a telephone. The voice was powerful and deep and so tense that the quick sentences ran together.

"You are invading my rights, I did not ask you to come, I assume you have a lawyer, you must have a lawyer, get your lawyer!"

"I came as a friend," the man interrupted.

"That's beside the point," DiMaggio said. "I have my privacy, I do not want it violated, you'd better get a lawyer. . . ." Then, pausing, DiMaggio asked, "is my nephew there?"

He was not.

"Then wait where you are."

A moment later DiMaggio appeared, tall and red-faced, erect and beautifully dressed in his dark suit and white shirt with the gray silk tie and the gleaming silver cuff links. He moved with big steps toward the man and handed him an airmail envelope, unopened, that the man had written from New York.

"Here," DiMaggio said. "This is yours."

Then DiMaggio sat down at a small table. He said nothing, just lit a cigarette and waited, legs crossed, his head held high and back so as to reveal the intricate construction of his nose, a fine sharp tip above the big nostrils and tiny bones built out from the bridge, a great nose.

"Look," DiMaggio said, more calmly. "I do not interfere with other people's live. And I do not expect them to interfere with mine. There are things about my life, personal things, that I refuse to talk about. And even if you asked my brothers they would be unable to tell you about them because they do not know. There are things about me, so many things, that they simply do not know. . . ."

"I don't want to cause trouble," the man said. "I think you're a great man, and. . . ."

"I'm not great," DiMaggio cut in. "I'm not great," he repeated, softly. "I'm just a man trying to get along."

Then DiMaggio, as if realizing that he was intruding upon his own privacy, abruptly stood up. He looked at his watch.

"I'm late," he said, very formal again. "I'm ten minutes late. *You're* making me late."

The man left the restaurant. He crossed the street and wandered over to the pier, briefly watching the fishermen hauling their nets and talking in the sun, seeming very calm and contented. Then, after he had turned and was headed back toward the parking lot, a blue Impala stopped in front of him and Joe DiMaggio leaned out the window and asked, "Do you have a car?" His voice was very gentle.

"Yes," the man said.

"Oh," DiMaggio said. "I would have given you a ride."

Joe DiMaggio was not born in San Francisco but in Martinez, a small fishing village twenty-five miles northeast of the Golden Gate. Zio Pepe had settled there after leaving Isola delle Femmine, an islet off Palermo where the Di-Maggios had been fishermen for generations. But in 1915, hearing of the luckier waters off San Francisco's wharf, Zio Pepe left Martinez, packing his boat with furniture and family, including Joe who was one year old.

San Francisco was placid and picturesque when the DiMaggio's arrived, but there was a competitive undercurrent and struggle for power along the pier. At dawn the boats would sail out to where the bay meets the ocean and the sea is rough, and later the men would race back with their hauls, hoping to beat their fellow fishermen to shore and sell it while they could. Twenty or thirty boats would sometimes be trying to gain the channel shoreward at the same time, and a fisherman had to know every rock in the water, and later know every bargaining trick along the shore, because the dealers and restaurateurs would play one fisherman off against the other, keeping the prices down. Later the fishermen became wiser and organized, predetermining the maximum amount each fisherman would catch, but there were always some men who, like the fish, never learned, and so heads would sometimes be broken, nets slashed, gasoline poured onto their fish, flowers of warning placed outside their doors.

But these days were ending when Zio Pepe arrived, and he expected his five sons to succeed him as fishermen, and the first two, Tom and Michael, did; but a third, Vincent, wanted to sing. He sang with such magnificent power as a young man that he came to the attention of the great banker, A. P. Giannini, and there were plans to send him to Italy for tutoring and the opera. But there was hesitation around the DiMaggio household and Vince never went; instead he played ball with the San Francisco Seals and sportswriters misspelled his name.

It was DeMaggio until Joe, at Vince's recommendation, joined the team and became a sensation, being followed later by the youngest brother, Dominic, who was also outstanding. All three later played in the big leagues and some writers like to say that Joe was the best hitter, Dom the best fielder, Vince the best singer, and Casey Stengel once said: "Vince is the only player I ever saw who could strike out three times in one game and not be embarrassed. He'd walk into the clubhouse whistling. Everybody would be feeling sorry for him, but Vince always thought he was doing good."

After he retired from baseball Vince became a bartender, then a milkman, now a carpenter. He lives forty miles north of San Francisco in a house he partly built, has been happily married for thirty-four years, has four grand-children, has in the closet one of Joe's tailor-made suits that he has never had altered to fit, and when people ask if he envies Joe he always says, "No, maybe Joe would like to have what I have. He won't admit it, but he just might like to have what I have." The brother Vince most admired was Michael, "a big earthy man, a dreamer, a fisherman who wanted things but didn't want to take from Joe, or to work in the restaurant. He wanted a bigger boat, but wanted to earn it on his own. He never got it." In 1953, at the age of forty-four, Michael fell from his boat and drowned.

Since Zio Pepe's death at seventy-seven in 1949, Tom, at sixty-two the oldest brother—two of his four sisters are older—has become nominal head of the family and manages the restaurant that was opened in 1937 as Joe DiMaggio's Grotto. Later, Joe sold out his share, and now Tom is the co-owner of it with Dominic. Of all the brothers, Dominic, who was known as the "Little Professor" when he played with the Boston Red Sox, is the most successful in business. He lives in a fashionable Boston suburb with his wife and three children and is president of a firm that manufactures fiber-cushion materials and grossed more than $3,500,000 last year.

Joe DiMaggio lives with his widowed sister, Marie, in a tan stone house on a quiet residential street not far from Fisherman's Wharf. He bought the house almost thirty years ago for his parents, and after their death he lived there with Marilyn Monroe; now it is cared for by Marie, a slim and handsome dark-eyed woman who has an apartment on the second floor, Joe on the third. There are some baseball trophies and plaques in the small room off DiMaggio's bed-room, and on his dresser are photographs of Marilyn Monroe, and in the living room downstairs is a small painting of her that DiMaggio likes very much: it reveals only her face and shoulders and she is wearing a very wide-brimmed sun hat, and there is a soft sweet smile on her lips, an innocent curiosity about her that is the way he saw her and the way he wanted her to be seen by others— a simple girl, "a warm big-hearted girl," he once described her, "that everybody took advantage of."

The publicity photographs emphasizing her sex appeal often offended him, and a memorable moment for Billy Wilder, who directed her in *The Seven Year Itch*, occurred when he spotted DiMaggio in a large crowd of people gathered on Lexington Avenue in New York to watch a scene in which Marilyn, standing over a subway grating to cool herself, had her skirts blown high by a sudden wind below. "What the hell is going on here?" DiMaggio was overheard to have said in the crowd, and Wilder recalled, "I shall never forget the look of death on Joe's face."

He was then thirty-nine, she was twenty-seven. They had been married in January of that year, 1954, despite disharmony in temperament and time: he was tired of publicity, she was thriving on it; he was intolerant of tardiness, she was always late. During their honeymoon in Tokyo, an American general had introduced himself and asked if, as a patriotic gesture, she would visit the troops in Korea. She looked at Joe. "It's your honeymoon," he said, shrugging, "go ahead if you want to."

She appeared on ten occasions before 100,000 servicemen, and when she returned she said, "It was so wonderful, Joe. You never heard such cheering."

"Yes I have," he said.

Across from her portrait in the living room, on a coffee table in front of a sofa, is a sterling-silver humidor that was presented to him by his Yankee teammates at a time when he was the most talked-about man in America, and when Les Brown's band had recorded a hit that was heard day and night on the radio:

> . . . From Coast to Coast, that's all you hear
> Of Joe the One-Man Show
> He's glorified the horsehide sphere,

> Jolting Joe DiMaggio . . .
> Joe . . . Joe . . . DiMaggio . . . we want you on our side. . . .

The year was 1941, and it began for DiMaggio in the middle of May after the Yankees had lost four games in a row, seven of their last nine, and were in fourth place, five-and-a-half games behind the leading Cleveland Indians. On May 15th, DiMaggio hit only a first-inning single in a game that New York lost to Chicago, 13–1; he was barely hitting .300, and had greatly disappointed the crowds that had seen him finish with a .352 average the year before and .381 in 1939.

He got a hit in the next game, and the next, and the next. On May 24th, with the Yankees losing 6–5 to Boston, DiMaggio came up with runners on second and third and singled them home, winning the game, extending his streak to ten games. But it went largely unnoticed. Even DiMaggio was not conscious of it until it had reached twenty-nine games in mid-June. Then the newspapers began to dramatize it, the public became aroused, they sent him good-luck charms of every description, and DiMaggio kept hitting, and radio announcers would interrupt programs to announce the news, and then the song again: "Joe . . . Joe . . . DiMaggio . . . we want you on our side. . . ."

Sometimes DiMaggio would be hitless his first three times up, the tension would build, it would appear that the game would end without his getting another chance—but he always would, and then he would hit the ball against the left-field wall, or through the pitcher's legs, or between two leaping in-fielders. In the forty-first game, the first of a doubleheader in Washington, DiMaggio tied an American League record that George Sisler had set in 1922. But before the second game began a spectator sneaked onto the field and into the Yankees' dugout and stole DiMaggio's favorite bat. In the second game, using another of his bats, DiMaggio lined out twice and flied out. But in the seventh inning, borrowing one of his old bats that a teammate was using, he singled and broke Sisler's record, and he was only three games away from surpassing the major-league record of forty-four set in 1897 by Willie Keeler while playing for Baltimore when it was a National League franchise.

An appeal for the missing bat was made through the newspapers. A man from Newark admitted the crime and returned it with regrets. And on July 2, at Yankee Stadium, DiMaggio hit a home run into the left-field stands. The record was broken.

He also got hits in the next eleven games, but on July 17th in Cleveland, at a night game attended by 67,468, he failed against two pitchers, Al Smith and Jim Bagby, Jr., although Cleveland's hero was really its third baseman, Ken Keltner, who in the first inning lunged to his right to make a spectacular backhanded stop of a drive and, from the foul line behind third base, he threw

DiMaggio out. DiMaggio received a walk in the fourth inning. But in the seventh he again hit a hard shot at Keltner, who again stopped it and threw him out. DiMaggio hit sharply toward the shortstop in the eighth inning, the ball taking a bad hop, but Lou Boudreau speared it off his shoulder and threw to the second baseman to start a double play and DiMaggio's streak was stopped at fifty-six games. But the New York Yankees were on their way to winning the pennant by seventeen games, and the World Series too, and so in August, in a hotel suite in Washington, the players threw a surprise party for DiMaggio and toasted him with champagne and presented him with this Tiffany silver humidor that is now in San Francisco in his living room. . . .

Marie was in the kitchen making toast and tea when DiMaggio came down for breakfast; his gray hair was uncombed but, since he wears it short, it was not untidy. He said good-morning to Marie, sat down and yawned. He lit a cigarette. He wore a blue wool bathrobe over his pajamas. It was eight A.M. He had many things to do today and he seemed cheerful. He had a conference with the president of Continental Television, Inc., a large retail chain in California of which he is a partner and vice-president; later he had a golf date, and then a big banquet to attend, and, if that did not go on too long and he were not too tired afterward, he might have a date.

Picking up the morning paper, not rushing to the sports page, DiMaggio read the front-page news, the people-problems of '66: Kwame Nkrumah was overthrown in Ghana, students were burning their draft cards (DiMaggio shook his head), the flu epidemic was spreading through the whole state of California.

Then he flipped inside through the gossip columns, thankful they did not have him in there today—they had printed an item about his dating "an electrifying airline hostess" not long ago, and they also spotted him at dinner with Dori Lane, "the frantic frugger" in Whiskey à Go Go's glass cage—and then he turned to the sports page and read a story about how the injured Mickey Mantle may never regain his form.

It had all happened so quickly, the passing of Mantle, or so it seemed; he had succeeded DiMaggio as DiMaggio had succeeded Ruth, but now there was no great young power hitter coming up and the Yankee management, almost desperate, had talked Mantle out of retirement; and on September 18, 1965, they gave him a "day" in New York during which he received several thousand dollars' worth of gifts—an automobile, two quarter horses, free vacation trips to Rome, Nassau, Puerto Rico—and DiMaggio had flown to New York to make the introduction before 50,000: it had been a dramatic day, an almost holy day for the believers who had jammed the grandstands early to witness the canonization of a new stadium saint. Cardinal Spellman was on the committee, President Johnson sent a telegram, the day was officially proclaimed by the Mayor of New York, an orchestra assembled in center field in front of the trinity of monuments to Ruth, Gehrig, Huggins; and high in the grandstands, billowing in the breeze of early autumn, were white banners that read: "Don't Quit Mick," "We Love the Mick."

The banners had been held by hundreds of young boys whose dreams had been fulfilled so often by Mantle, but also seated in the grandstands were older men, paunchy and balding, in whose middle-aged minds DiMaggio was still vivid and invincible, and some of them remembered how one month before, during a pre-game exhibition at Old-timers' Day in Yankee Stadium, DiMaggio had hit a pitch into the left-field seats, and suddenly thousands of people had jumped wildly to their feet, joyously screaming—the great DiMaggio had returned, they were young again, it was yesterday.

But on this sunny September day at the Stadium, the feast day of Mickey Mantle, DiMaggio was not wearing No. 5 on his back nor a black cap to cover his graying hair; he was wearing a black suit and white shirt and blue tie, and he stood in one corner of the Yankees' dugout waiting to be introduced by Red Barber, who was standing near home plate behind a silver microphone. In the outfield Guy Lombardo's Royal Canadians were playing soothing soft music; and moving slowly back and forth over the sprawling green grass between the left-field bullpen and the infield were two carts driven by grounds keepers and containing dozens and dozens of large gifts for Mantle—a 6-foot, 100-pound Hebrew National salami, a Winchester rifle, a mink coat for Mrs. Mantle, a set of Wilson golf clubs, a Mercury 95-horse power outboard motor, a Necchi portable, a year's supply of Chunky Candy. DiMaggio smoked a cigarette, but cupped it in his hands as if not wanting to be caught in the act by teen-aged boys near enough to peek down into the dugout. Then, edging forward a step, DiMaggio poked his head out and looked up. He could see nothing above except the packed towering green grandstands that seemed a mile high and moving, and he could see no clouds or blue sky, only a sky of faces. Then the announcer called out his name—"*Joe DiMaggio!*"—and suddenly there was a blast of cheering that grew louder and louder, echoing and reechoing within the big steel canyon, and DiMaggio stomped out his cigarette and climbed up the dugout steps and onto the soft green grass, the noise resounding in his ears, he could almost feel the breeze, the breath of 50,000 lungs upon him, 100,000 eyes watching his every move and for the briefest instant as he walked he closed his eyes.

Then in his path he saw Mickey Mantle's mother, a smiling elderly woman wearing an orchid, and he gently reached out for her elbow, holding it as he led her toward the microphone next to the other dignitaries lined up on the infield. Then he stood, very erect and without expression, as the cheers softened and the Stadium settled down.

Mantle was still in the dugout, in uniform, standing with one leg on the top step, and lined on both sides of him were the other Yankees who, when the ceremony was over, would play the Detroit Tigers. Then into the dugout, smiling, came Senator Robert Kennedy, accompanied by two tall curly-haired young assistants with blue eyes, Fordham freckles. Jim Farley was the first on the field to notice the Senator, and Farley muttered, loud enough for others to hear, "Who the hell invited *him!*"

Toots Shor and some of the other committeemen standing near Farley looked into the dugout, and so did DiMaggio, his glance seeming cold, but he remaining silent. Kennedy walked up and down within the dugout shaking hands with the Yankees, but he did not walk onto the field.

"Senator," said the Yankees' manager, Johnny Keane, "why don't you sit down?" Kennedy quickly shook his head, smiled. He remained standing, and then one Yankee came over and asked about getting relatives out of Cuba, and Kennedy called over one of his aides to take down the details in a notebook.

On the infield the ceremony went on, Mantle's gifts continued to pile up— a Mobilette motor bike, a Sooner Schooner wagon barbecue, a year's supply of Chock Full O'Nuts coffee, a year's supply of Topps Chewing Gum—and the Yankee players watched, and Maris seemed glum.

"Hey, Rog," yelled a man with a tape recorder, Murray Olderman, "I want to do a thirty-second tape with you."

Maris swore angrily, shook his head.

"It'll only take a second," Olderman said.

"Why don't you ask Richardson? He's a better talker than me."

"Yes, but the fact that it comes from you . . ."

Maris swore again. But finally he went over and said in an interview that Mantle was the finest player of his era, a great competitor, a great hitter.

Fifteen minutes later, standing behind the microphone at home plate, DiMaggio was telling the crowd, "I'm proud to introduce the man who succeeded me in center field in 1951," and from every corner of the Stadium the cheering, whistling, clapping came down. Mantle stepped forward. He stood with his wife and children, posed for the photographers kneeling in front. Then he thanked the crowd in a short speech, and turning, shook hands with the dignitaries standing nearby. Among them now was Senator Kennedy, who had been spotted in the dugout five minutes before by Red Barber, and been called out and introduced. Kennedy posed with Mantle for a photographer, then shook hands with the Mantle children, and with Toots Shor and James Farley and others. DiMaggio saw him coming down the line and at the last second he backed away, casually, hardly anybody noticing it, and Kennedy seemed not to notice it either, just swept past shaking more hands. . . .

Finishing his tea, putting aside the newspaper, DiMaggio went upstairs to dress, and soon he was waving good-bye to Marie and driving toward his business appointment in downtown San Francisco with his partners in the retail television business. DiMaggio, while not a millionaire, has invested wisely and has always had, since his retirement from baseball, executive positions with big companies that have paid him well. He also was among the organizers of the Fisherman's National Bank of San Francisco last year, and, though it never came about, he demonstrated an acuteness that impressed those businessmen who had thought of him only in terms of baseball. He has had offers to manage big-league baseball teams but always has rejected them, saying, "I have enough trouble taking care of my own problems without taking on the responsibilities of twenty-five ballplayers."

So his only contact with baseball these days, excluding public appearances, is his unsalaried job as a batting coach each spring in Florida with the New York Yankees, a trip he would make once again on the following Sunday, three days away, if he could accomplish what for him is always the dreaded responsibility of packing, a task made no easier by the fact that he lately has fallen into the habit of keeping his clothes in two places—some hang in his closet at home, some hang in the back room of a saloon called Reno's.

Reno's is a dimly lit bar in the center of San Francisco. A portrait of DiMaggio swinging a bat hangs on the wall, in addition to portraits of other star athletes, and the clientele consists mainly of the sporting crowd and newspapermen, people who know DiMaggio quite well and around whom he speaks freely on a number of subjects and relaxes as he can in few other places. The owner of the bar is Reno Barsocchini, a broad-shouldered and handsome man of fifty-one with graying wavy hair who began as a fiddler in Dago Mary's tavern thirty-five years ago. He later became a bartender there and elsewhere, including DiMaggio's Restaurant, and now he is probably DiMaggio's closest friend. He was the best man at the DiMaggio-Monroe wedding in 1954, and when they separated nine months later in Los Angeles, Reno rushed down to help DiMaggio with the packing and drive him back to San Francisco. Reno will never forget the day.

Hundreds of people were gathered around the Beverly Hills home that DiMaggio and Marilyn had rented, and photographers were perched in the trees watching the windows, and others stood on the lawn and behind the rose bushes waiting to snap pictures of anybody who walked out of the house. The newspapers that day played all the puns—"Joe Fanned on Jealousy"; "Marilyn and Joe—Out at Home"—and the Hollywood columnists, to whom DiMaggio was never an idol, never a gracious host, recounted instances of incompatibility, and Oscar Levant said it all proved that no man could be a success in two national pastimes. When Reno Barsocchini arrived he had to push his way through the mob, then bang on the door for several minutes before being admitted. Marilyn Monroe was upstairs in bed, Joe DiMaggio was downstairs with his suitcases, tense and pale, his eyes bloodshot.

Reno took the suitcases and golf clubs out to DiMaggio's car, and then DiMaggio came out of the house, the reporters moving toward him, the lights flashing.

"Where are you going?" they yelled. "I'm driving to San Francisco," he said, walking quickly.

"Is that going to be your home?"

"That *is* my home and always has been."

"Are you coming back?"

DiMaggio turned for a moment, looking up at the house.

"No," he said, "I'll never be back."

Reno Barsocchini, except for a brief falling out over something he will not discuss, has been DiMaggio's trusted companion ever since, joining him whenever he can on the golf course or on the town, otherwise waiting for him in the bar with other middle-aged men. They may wait for hours sometimes, waiting and knowing that when he arrives he may wish to be alone; but it does not seem to matter, they are endlessly awed by him, moved by the mystique, he is a kind of male Garbo. They know that he can be warm and loyal if they are sensitive to his wishes, but they must never be late for an appointment to meet him. One man, unable to find a parking place, arrived a half-hour late once and DiMaggio did not talk to him again for three months. They know, too, when dining at night with DiMaggio, that he generally prefers male companions and occasionally one or two young women, but never wives; wives gossip, wives complain, wives are trouble, and men wishing to remain close to DiMaggio must keep their wives at home.

When DiMaggio strolls into Reno's bar the men wave and call out his name, and Reno Barsocchini smiles and announces, "Here's the Clipper!", the "Yankee Clipper" being a nickname from his baseball days.

"Hey, Clipper, Clipper," Reno had said two nights before, "where you been, Clipper? . . . Clipper, how 'bout a belt?"

DiMaggio refused the offer of a drink, ordering instead a pot of tea, which he prefers to all other beverages except before a date, when he will switch to vodka.

"Hey, Joe," a sportswriter asked, a man researching a magazine piece on golf, "why is it that a golfer, when he starts getting older, loses his putting touch first? Like Snead and Hogan, they can still hit a ball well off the tee, but on the greens they lose the strokes. . . ."

"It's the pressure of age," DiMaggio said, turning around on his bar stool. "With age you get jittery. It's true of golfers, it's true of any man when he gets into his fifties. He doesn't take chances like he used to. The younger golfer, on the greens, he'll stroke his putts better. The old man, he becomes hesitant. A little uncertain. Shaky. When it comes to taking chances the younger man, even when driving a car, will take chances that the older man won't."

"Speaking of chances," another man said, one of the group that had gathered around DiMaggio, "did you see that guy on crutches in here last night?"

"Yeah, had his leg in a cast," a third said. "Skiing."

"I would never ski," DiMaggio said. "Men who ski must be doing it to impress a broad. You see these men, some of them forty, fifty, getting onto skis. And later you see them all bandaged up, broken legs. . . ."

"But skiing's a very sexy sport, Joe. All the clothes, the tight pants, the fireplace in the ski lodge, the bear rug—Christ, nobody goes to ski. They just go out there to get it cold so they can warm it up. . . ."

"Maybe you're right," DiMaggio said. "I might be persuaded."

"Want a belt, Clipper?" Reno asked.

DiMaggio thought for a second, then said, "All right—first belt tonight."

Now it was noon, a warm sunny day. DiMaggio's business meeting with the television retailers had gone well; he had made a strong appeal to George Shahood, president of Continental Television, Inc., which has eight retail outlets in Northern California, to cut prices on color television sets and increase the sales volume, and Shahood had conceded it was worth a try. Then DiMaggio called Reno's bar to see if there were any messages, and now he was in Lefty O'Doul's car being driven along Fisherman's Wharf toward the Golden Gate

Bridge en route to a golf course thirty miles upstate. Lefty O'Doul was one of the great hitters in the National League in the early thirties, and later he managed the San Francisco Seals when DiMaggio was the shining star. Though O'Doul is now sixty-nine, eighteen years older than DiMaggio, he nevertheless possesses great energy and spirit, is a hard-drinking, boisterous man with a big belly and roving eye; and when DiMaggio, as they drove along the highway toward the golf club, noticed a lovely blond at the wheel of a car nearby and exclaimed, "Look at *that* tomato!" O'Doul's head suddenly spun around, he took his eyes off the road, and yelled, "Where, *where?*" O'Doul's golf game is less than what it was—he used to have a two-handicap—but he still shoots in the 80s, as does DiMaggio.

DiMaggio's drives range between 250 and 280 years when he doesn't sky them, and his putting is good, but he is distracted by a bad back that both pains him and hinders the fullness of his swing. On the first hole, waiting to tee off, DiMaggio sat back watching a foursome of college boys ahead swinging with such freedom. "Oh," he said with a sigh, "to have *their* backs."

DiMaggio and O'Doul were accompanied around the golf course by Ernie Nevers, the former football star, and two brothers who are in the hotel and movie-distribution business. They moved quickly up and down the green hills in electric golf carts, and DiMaggio's game was exceptionally good for the first nine holes. But then he seemed distracted, perhaps tired, perhaps even reacting to a conversation of a few minutes before. One of the movie men was praising the film *Boeing, Boeing,* starring Tony Curtis and Jerry Lewis, and the man asked DiMaggio if he had seen it.

"No," DiMaggio said. Then he added, swiftly, "I haven't seen a film in eight years."

DiMaggio hooked a few shots, was in the woods. He took a No. 9 iron and tried to chip out. But O'Doul interrupted DiMaggio's concentration to remind him to keep the face of the club closed. DiMaggio hit the ball. It caromed off the side of his club, went skipping like a rabbit through the high grass down toward a pond. DiMaggio rarely displays any emotion on a golf course, but now, without saying a word, he took his No. 9 iron and flung it into the air. The club landed in a tree and stayed up there.

"Well," O'Doul said, casually, "there goes *that* set of clubs."

DiMaggio walked to the tree. Fortunately the club had slipped to the lower branch and DiMaggio could stretch up on the cart and get it back.

"Every time I get advice," DiMaggio muttered to himself, shaking his head slowly and walking toward the pond, "I shank it."

Later, showered and dressed, DiMaggio and the others drove to a banquet about ten miles from the golf course. Somebody had said it was going to be an elegant dinner, but when they arrived they could see it was more like a

county fair; farmers were gathered outside a big barnlike building, a candidate
for sheriff was distributing leaflets at the front door, and a chorus of homely
ladies were inside singing *You Are My Sunshine.*

"How did we get sucked into this?" DiMaggio asked, talking out of the side
of his mouth, as they approached the building.

"O'Doul," one of the men said. "It's his fault. Damned O'Doul can't turn
anything down."

"Go to hell," O'Doul said.

Soon DiMaggio and O'Doul and Ernie Nevers were surrounded by the crowd,
and the woman who had been leading the chorus came rushing over and said,
"Oh, Mr. DiMaggio, it certainly is a pleasure having you."

"It's a pleasure being here, ma'am," he said, forcing a smile.

"It's too bad you didn't arrive a moment sooner, you'd have heard our singing."

"Oh, I heard it," he said, "and I enjoyed it very much."

"Good, good," she said. "And how are your brothers Dom and Vic?"

"Fine. Dom lives near Boston. Vince is in Pittsburgh."

"Why, *hello* there, Joe," interrupted a man with wine on his breath, patting
DiMaggio on the back, feeling his arm. "Who's gonna take it this year, Joe?"

"Well, I have no idea," DiMaggio said.

"What about the Giants?"

"Your guess is as good as mine."

"Well, you can't count the Dodgers out," the man said.

"You sure can't," DiMaggio said.

"Not with all that pitching."

"Pitching is certainly important," DiMaggio said.

Everywhere he goes the questions seem the same, as if he has some special
vision into the future of new heroes, and everywhere he goes, too, older men
grab his hand and feel his arm and predict that he could still go out there and
hit one, and the smile on DiMaggio's face is genuine. He tries hard to remain
as he was—he diets, he takes steam baths, he is careful; and flabby men in
the locker rooms of golf clubs sometimes steal peeks at him when he steps
out of the shower, observing the tight muscles across his chest, the flat stomach, the long sinewy legs. He has a young man's body, very pale and little hair;
his face is dark and lined, however, parched by the sun of several seasons. Still
he is always an impressive figure at banquets such as this—an *immortal*,
sportswriters called him, and that is how they have written about him and
others like him, rarely suggesting that such heroes might ever be prone to the
ills of mortal men, carousing, drinking, scheming; to suggest this would destroy
the myth, would disillusion small boys, would infuriate rich men who own
ballclubs and to whom baseball is a business dedicated to profit and in pursuit
of which they trade mediocre players' flesh as casually as boys trade players'

pictures on bubble-gum cards. And so the baseball hero must always act the part, must preserve the myth, and none does it better than DiMaggio, none is more patient when drunken old men grab an arm and ask, "Who's gonna take it this year, Joe?"

Two hours later, dinner and the speeches over, DiMaggio is slumped in O'Doul's car headed back to San Francisco. He edged himself up, however, when O'Doul pulled into a gas station in which a pretty red-haired girl sat on a stool, legs crossed, filing her fingernails. She was about twenty-two, wore a tight black skirt and tighter white blouse.

"Look at *that*," DiMaggio said.

"Yeah," O'Doul said.

O'Doul turned away when a young man approached, opened the gas tank, began wiping the windshield. The young man wore a greasy white uniform on the front of which was printed the name "Burt." DiMaggio kept looking at the girl, but she was not distracted from her fingernails. Then he looked at Burt, who did not recognize him. When the tank was full, O'Doul paid and drove off. Burt returned to his girl; DiMaggio slumped down in the front seat and did not open his eyes again until they'd arrived in San Francisco.

"Let's go see Reno," DiMaggio said.

"No, I gotta go see my old lady," O'Doul said. So he dropped DiMaggio off in front of the bar, and a moment later Reno's voice was announcing in the smoky room, "Hey, here's the Clipper!" The men waved and offered to buy him a drink. DiMaggio ordered a vodka and sat for an hour at the bar talking to a half dozen men around him. Then a blond girl who had been with friends at the other end of the bar came over, and somebody introduced her to DiMaggio. He bought her a drink, offered her a cigarette. Then he struck a match and held it. His hand was unsteady.

"Is that me that's shaking?" he asked.

"It must be," said the blond. "I'm calm."

Two nights later, having collected his clothes out of Reno's back room, DiMaggio boarded a jet; he slept crossways on three seats, then came down the steps as the sun began to rise in Miami. He claimed his luggage and golf clubs, put them into the trunk of a waiting automobile, and less than an hour later he was being driven into Fort Lauderdale, past palm-lined streets, toward the Yankee Clipper Hotel.

"All my life it seems I've been on the road traveling," he said, squinting through the windshield into the sun. "I never get a sense of being in any one place."

Arriving at the Yankee Clipper Hotel, DiMaggio checked into the largest suite. People rushed through the lobby to shake hands with him, to ask for his autograph, to say, "Joe, you look great." And early the next morning, and for the next thirty mornings, DiMaggio arrived punctually at the baseball park and wore his uniform with the famous No. 5, and the tourists seated in the sunny grandstands clapped when he first appeared on the field each time, and then they watched with nostalgia as he picked up a bat and played "pepper" with the younger Yankees, some of whom were not even born when, twenty-five years ago this summer, he hit in fifty-six straight games and became the most celebrated man in America.

But the younger spectators in the Fort Lauderdale park, and the sportswriters, too, were more interested in Mantle and Maris, and nearly every day there were news dispatches reporting how Mantle and Maris felt, what they did, what they said, even though they said and did very little except walk around the field frowning when photographers asked for another picture and when sportswriters asked how they felt.

After seven days of this, the big day arrived—Mantle and Maris would swing a bat—and a dozen sportswriters were gathered around the big batting cage that was situated beyond the left-field fence; it was completely enclosed in wire, meaning that no baseball could travel more than thirty or forty feet before being trapped in rope; still Mantle and Maris would be swinging, and this, in spring, makes news.

Mantle stepped in first. He wore black gloves to help prevent blisters. He hit right-handed against the pitching of a coach named Vern Benson, and soon Mantle was swinging hard, smashing line drives against the nets, going *ahhh ahhh* as he followed through with his mouth open.

Then Mantle, not wanting to overdo it on his first day, dropped his bat in the dirt and walked out of the batting cage. Roger Maris stepped in. He picked up Mantle's bat.

"This damn thing must be thirty-eight ounces," Maris said. He threw the bat down into the dirt, left the cage and walked toward the dugout on the other side of the field to get a lighter bat.

DiMaggio stood among the sportswriters behind the cage, then turned when Vern Benson, inside the cage, yelled, "Joe, wanna hit some?"

"No chance," DiMaggio said.

"Com'on, Joe," Benson said.

The reporters waited silently. Then DiMaggio walked slowly into the cage and picked up Mantle's bat. He took his position at the plate but obviously it was not the classic DiMaggio stance; he was holding the bat about two inches from the knob, his feet were not so far apart, and, when DiMaggio took a cut at Benson's first pitch, fouling it, there was none of that ferocious follow through, the blurred bat did not come whipping all the way around, the No. 5 was not stretched full across his broad back.

DiMaggio fouled Benson's second pitch, then he connected solidly with the third, the fourth, the fifth. He was just meeting the ball easily, however, not smashing it, and Benson called out, "I didn't know you were a choke hitter, Joe."

"I am now," DiMaggio said, getting ready for another pitch.

He hit three more squarely enough, and then he swung again and there was a hollow sound.

"Ohhh," DiMaggio yelled, dropping his bat, his fingers stung, "I was waiting for that one." He left the batting cage rubbing his hands together. The reporters watched him. Nobody said anything. Then DiMaggio said to one of them, not in anger nor in sadness, but merely as a simply stated fact, "There was a time when you couldn't get me out of there."

It is the anthologist's prerogative, I am told, to include one of his own best bits. Of all my baseball writing, this opening chapter of *Baseball's Ten Greatest Games*, published in 1981, may not be the best—others must answer to that—but it is my favorite. Come along now: the Tigers of Cobb and Crawford are about to do battle with the Athletics of Plank and Waddell, and the lines at the ticket booths are long.

JOHN THORN

September 30, 1907: You Are There

Game time is two o'clock, sixty minutes from now, but the 18,000 seats in Philadelphia's Columbia Park were filled hours ago and the gates have just been closed. You and I were fortunate to squeeze into the standing-room section roped off here on the center-field grass. A seat in the grandstand or bleachers would have been nicer, I know, but we mustn't complain: at least we gained admission, unlike the swarms of disgruntled fans milling outside the fences, and the thousands who risk their necks on the rooftops of houses which over-look this rickety wooden stadium.

Who would have imagined that a Monday date with the Detroit Tigers, perennial also-rans, could produce such a crush of humanity? Two years back, when the A's fought the Giants in the World Series, they didn't come close to filling up the park. But this summer the City of the Quakers has gone baseball mad as four teams—Chicago, Cleveland, Detroit, and Philadelphia— have played leapfrog with first place in the hottest pennant race of the young century. Now, though, with only one week left in the regular season, two of the teams have dropped off the chase—the White Sox, the "hitless wonders" who swept last year's World Series; and the Cleveland "Naps," as they are called in tribute to their star player-manager, Napoleon Lajoie.

Last Friday, when Connie Mack's Athletics took the field behind their Chippewa curveballer, Chief Bender, they were one-half game in front of the Tigers, who countered with their ace, Wild Bill Donovan. Though the A's cuffed him for thirteen hits, Donovan held on for a 5–4 victory. Rain washed out Saturday's contest, which was rescheduled for today as the second game of a doubleheader. What about yesterday, you ask? Sunday ball will not be legal in the state of Pennsylvania till 1934.

So it has come down to this: If the Tigers can take both ends of the twin bill, they will almost certainly capture the pennant. Even if they only get a split, they will still leave town in first place and will enjoy a scheduling edge over the A's: Detroit's last seven matches will be with the Washington Senators and St. Louis Browns, two weaklings, while the A's will have to contend with Mr. Lajoie's formidable Naps, in addition to the Senators.

The players are out on the field now, loosening up for the game. Warming up in foul territory for the A's is Jimmy Dygert, a chunky right-hander whose spitball has baffled the league this season. Do you recognize that tall, muscular guy over in left field, joking with the fans? He's Rube Waddell, the A's left-handed flamethrower, who leads the league in strikeouts every year. But don't expect to see him pitch today. He's been having a running feud with several of his teammates. Tired of Rube's antics off the field and lack of dedication on it, they have given him halfhearted support in recent outings. This bad blood may have cost the A's three or four games they ought to have won; today, Mack knows, is no time for less than all-out effort.

While we're on the subject of running feuds, look over there in the right-field corner, where young Ty Cobb is exercising by himself. Only twenty years old, he's on his way to the first of twelve batting titles, yet half the Tigers won't speak to him and several have fought him with their fists. Despite his slashing bat and his savage abandon on the base paths, young Tyrus came within a hairbreadth of being traded this spring. New manager Hughie Jennings, fed up with all the bickering on his team, arranged a deal with the New York Highlanders (later known as the Yankees) whereby Detroit would swap the greatest hitter of all time for a nondescript pitcher named Buffalo Bill Hogg. Only a last-minute hesitance kept Cobb from one day playing in the same outfield with Babe Ruth!

But enough talk of what might have been. It is nearly time to play ball. Hey, what's that commotion in the grandstand? The frustrated fans who were locked outside the park at one o'clock are now pouring over the right-field fence. The Keystone Cops rush toward the disturbance, but they don't have a chance. One gate-crasher they could nab, or ten, but not the hundreds who are scaling the wall. And look behind you—now they are cascading over the entire length of the outfield fence, thousands of them! The already crowded standing-room section begins to resemble a New York City subway car at rush hour.

As I was about to say before the ruckus started, Detroit will go with Donovan again. He's had two days' rest, all he really needs (a few weeks ago this work-horse beat Cleveland twice in two days). And besides, Philly is Bill's hometown. His family and friends are in the park, and Jennings wants to give him a chance to show off.

Donovan has been remarkable all year long. After closing the books on 1906 with 9–15 mark, his worst ever, the thirty-year-old hurler decided he didn't want to pitch anymore; he figured he was a pretty good hitter, and declared that from now on he'd play first base. Jennings knew better than to believe him. He let Donovan play a little first base in spring camp, but held him out of action once the season began. April passed and so did much of May with Donovan on the bench, begging to return to the mound. But Ee-Yah Hughie (a nickname he earned by his bloodcurdling shouts of "Ee-Yah!" to urge on his team) let Bill cool his heels on the sidelines until May 24, when he was finally permitted to pitch. His pent-up energies burst forth on the American League to the tune of twenty-five victories against only four defeats—and he might easily have gone 29–0, because his four losses came by scores of 1–0, 4–3, 4–2, and 4–1.

A roar rises from the crowd as Dygert strolls to the mound and the other A's take their positions: Ossie Schreck behind the plate, Home Run Harry Davis at first, Danny Murphy at second, Simon Nicholls at short, Hall-of-Famer Jimmy Collins at the hot corner; and an outfield of, left to right, Topsy Hartsel, Rube Oldring, and Socks Seybold. Defensively the A's are steady but not sensational. Except for Oldring and Nicholls, who are first-year starters, the other six fielders are "graybeards" over thirty, and three of them are on the steep part of their downhill slide—Collins, thirty-seven; Seybold, thirty-six; and Davis, thirty-four.

The avalanche of fence-vaulters continues even as Dygert sends his first pitch in to Davy Jones, Detroit's slap-hitting left-fielder. But as the Tigers go down in the first without a hit, the procession slows to a trickle and finally ends. There simply isn't a square inch of space left in which to put one more rooter.

Now the Tigers take their turn in the field. The battery is Donovan and Boss Schmidt, an ex-boxer whose fist shattered Cobb's nose last year; the inner ring consists of Claude Rossman at first, Germany Schaefer at the second sack, Charley O'Leary at short, and Rowdy Bill Coughlin at third; the outer circle shows Jones in left and Hall-of-Famers Sam Crawford and Cobb in center and right. Both offensively and defensively, the strength of this young club—not

a starter over thirty—resides in the outfield, though Rossman, too, is first-rate.

There is a buzz of anticipation in the air as Topsy Hartsel steps to the plate. And what's more, there are two brass bands, cowbells, cymbals, gongs, sirens, bugles, frying pans—all banging and clattering together to unnerve the Detroit fielders. Hartsel, a 5-foot 5-inch mighty mite, is an ideal leadoff man whose specialty is drawing the base on balls and letting the heavy hitters bring him around. This time, however, Hartsel rips a Donovan fastball for a single, and on the first pitch to Nicholls, he steals second. Connie Mack has identified the weak link in the Detroit defense—catcher Schmidt's erratic arm—and has exploited it immediately. Nicholls lays down a sacrifice bunt and Hartsel takes third. It's only the first frame, but the A's are playing for one run. Clearly Mack doesn't think he'll be getting many more off Wild Bill.

Now the managerial wheels are really spinning. Jennings moves his infield in, unwilling to concede the run on a hard-hit grounder; but Donovan spoils the strategy by walking Seybold. Now the shortstop and second baseman must pull back for a possible double-play ball. And Harry Davis complies, smacking one to the shortstop's left—but the ball kicks off O'Leary to second-baseman Schaefer, who picks it up and throws . . . too late. It's a hit. The run is in, Athletics occupy first and second, and there is still only one man down.

Danny Murphy follows with a bunt toward first which he beats out, loading the bases. Donovan has not exactly been bludgeoned, but he is being nibbled to death. Jimmy Collins lifts a fly to left, deep enough to score Seybold. Two down, but the A's will not let go of the Tiger tail yet. Oldring wallops a ball into the overflow crowd here in center field, a ground-rule double, and Davis comes home to make the count 3–0. The fans are giving a razzing to Donovan now, and his partisans, seated in the third-base deck, look awfully glum. At last Schreck is retired, and the A's take the field to an ovation.

Claude Rossman opens the Tiger second with a single to center. Coughlin then raps one to the mound but Dygert, in his haste to start the double play in motion, throws the ball into the dirt and both men are safe. Here's Schmidt, brandishing his big war club as he steps into the batter's box. He squares to bunt, and delicately lays one down to advance the runners. Just between you and me, I think Schmidt ought to have swung away. With the eighth- and ninth-place hitters to follow, and his team down 3–0, this was no time for Jennings to give up an out. Yes, second-guessing the manager is a bit unfair, but who can resist?

O'Leary, a little fellow with a very light stick, also knocks one back to Dygert, who once again sets sights on Rossman, now hung up between third and home. Back and forth Claude dances, trying to give O'Leary time to reach second base. Back and forth, back and forth in the rundown—until Dygert fires one to Schreck at close range that bounces off his chest protector. Rossman rushes past him to score. 3–1. Now Dygert's errant tosses in the field take their effect on the mound. He sends four wide ones to Donovan, loading the bases. Mr. Mack invites the rattled youngster to soothe his nerves with an early shower and in comes—Rube Waddell!

Connie Mack is a hunch player, and he's playing a big one now: First of all, that Waddell woke up sober this morning, and second, that his teammates would not throw away a pennant just to deny the Rube a win. As it turns out, Rube does not put his fielders to the test. Coming in with the bases loaded, he fans Davy Jones and Germany Schaefer with a combination of rising fastballs and explosive curves, then struts around the mound as the fans go wild. In later years Branch Rickey is to say that "when Waddell had control—and some sleep—he was unbeatable." Rube must have had a very tranquil Sunday night, for he fans Cobb and Rossman in the third and Schmidt and O'Leary in the fourth, making it six strikeout victims of the eight men he's faced.

While Waddell is making tabby cats of the Bengals, the A's resume their assault on Donovan. Socks Seybold opens the third with a double to right and chugs home on Davis's two-bagger to left. Murphy's bunt single then advances Davis to third, from where he scores on Oldring's force-out.

The 5–1 lead looks like money in the bank, and the A's even widen their margin in the fifth. Home Run Harry Davis, the league's four-base champ the last three years, leads off with his specialty, a booming drive over the scoreboard in right. Murphy is put down, but Jimmy Collins drives one against the scoreboard and into the crowd for an automatic double. Umpire Silk O'Laughlin jogs out to request return of the ball, as is the custom of the times, and the gentleman in the bowler hat who caught it assents.

Jennings has still given no sign to his bullpen—either he doesn't wish to embarrass Wild Bill in front of his folks; or he has given up on the contest and, with another game yet to play today, doesn't want to deplete his small staff. Whichever is the case, the A's are pleased to continue the shellacking. Oldring whacks a drive toward the corner in left. Davy Jones drifts back on the ball until he senses the crowd behind him, then, as is his habit, shies off; the catchable ball drops into the first row of standees for a run-scoring double.

The fifth inning ends without further ado as Donovan whiffs Schreck and Waddell. Loping toward the bench, Jones is intercepted at third base by a bunch of angry teammates; they threaten him with all sorts of mayhem if the game is lost, as now seems certain. Davy's faintheartedness has cost his team a run; however, one run doesn't look so very large when you're trailing 7–1.

But the complexion of the game changes radically in the top of the seventh, as shabby Philadelphia fielding enables the Tigers to tally four times on only one hit. Oldring muffs Donovan's lazy fly to open the door, and then Waddell experiences his first lapse of control, walking Jones. Schaefer follows with a perfect double-play grounder to Nicholls, but the kid kicks it.

Now the bases are loaded for Sam Crawford, the left-handed slugger who played alongside Waddell in the old Western League in 1899 and who, like the Rube, will be honored with a plaque in Cooperstown. So far today, Crawford has had no luck with Waddell; but this time Rube gets a pitch up in the strike zone where Sam likes it, and the ball goes sailing over Seybold's head for two bases and two runs.

Cobb, up next, has gone out weakly in his previous trips to the plate and does so once more; but Schaefer scores as Ty is thrown out at first. Crawford, who advanced to third on the play, himself comes in to score as Murphy scoops up Rossman's ground shot in the hole and fires to first in time. Coughlin, too, is put out, but the Tigers are now in striking distance at 7–5.

The A's get one back on their half of the inning on a single by Murphy, sacrifice by Collins, single by Oldring, and groundout by Schreck. Staggering through seven innings, Donovan has been walloped for fourteen hits, but Jennings will not take him out unless he asks out. And Wild Bill won't ask.

Fred Payne, who replaced Boss Schmidt behind the plate a few innings back, is retired to lead off the eighth. But O'Leary doubles and daringly steals third with Donovan at the bat. Wild Bill cannot bring him home, but Davy Jones does, with a single that cancels out the run he gave the A's in the fifth inning.

Well, here we are in the top of the ninth with the A's still up by a score of 8–6. Waddell has shown signs of weakening, but Mack will stick with him as the left-handed heart of the Tiger batting order—Crawford, Cobb, and Ross-man—comes up. (In 1907 there are not yet any relief specialists on the lines of a Bruce Sutter or Rich Gossage; and with pitching staffs that comprise five or at most six men, managers cannot play Captain Hook, yanking hurlers as they please.)

When Crawford loops a single over second base, the boisterous crowd falls into a moment's eerie silence—but erupts again as Cobb stands in for his turn. The Georgia Peach stirs up silent admiration for his skills and vocal hostility for his attacking, almost driven style of play. In a series with the Highlanders earlier this month he scored from first base on Rossman's sacrifice bunt! Like a man possessed, he circled the bases at full tilt while the stunned New Yorkers fumbled the ball around. Cobb doesn't play just to beat you; he wants to destroy you, and the A's rooters have taken particular delight in his futility at the plate today.

Waddell starts Cobb off with a fastball up and in, a tough pitch for Ty, who leans over the plate. He nonchalantly watches it go by. Waddell figures Cobb is looking for a ball out over the plate, perhaps one he can punch to the opposite field. So, Rube will say in later years, "I throws another for the inside corner and the second the ball leaves my hand I know I made a bum guess. This Cobb, who didn't seem to notice the first one, steps back like he had the catcher's sign, takes a toehold, and swings. I guess the ball's goin' yet."

Out it soars, over the right fielder, over the roped-in fans, and over the fence, coming to earth in the middle of 29th Street. A tie game! Connie Mack is so stunned he falls off the end of the A's bench, landing on a pile of bats. Cobb is not a home-run hitter—no one really is in this decade, not even Home Run Harry Davis, who will top the league with eight. And besides, the ball Cobb hit had been in play since the fifth inning and must have been pretty beat up. How could he have sent it so far? And did he steal the sign as Waddell suspected?

How he managed to wallop it so far no one can explain, but Cobb did know that he would get another fastball up and in. By casually letting the first pitch go by, he duped Waddell into thinking he was looking for a pitch away. Ty figured that Rube would try to cross him up and fire another in the identical spot. He was so confident he had pegged Rube's thoughts that as Waddell uncorked the pitch he jumped back off the plate and swung with everything he had in him.

Mack, scrambling to his feet, waves his scorecard frantically toward the bullpen. The great Eddie Plank, whom Mack had intended to hold out for the second game, comes running in as Waddell trudges slowly to the clubhouse. Mack's gamble on the Rube has proved a bust. Plank tosses in a few warm-up throws to Mike Powers, who has replaced Schreck, then sets down Rossman, Coughlin, and Payne in order.

Donovan blanks Philly in the ninth and tenth, and in the eleventh takes the mound to defend a lead. In the top of the inning Cobb had hit another long drive to right, this one landing in the overflow crowd, and Rossman had followed with a single to put Detroit up 9–8. But in the A's half, Nicholls doubles, Wild Bill wild-pitches him to third, and the run comes in on Davis's long fly.

The Tigers threaten in the twelfth, loading the bases with two outs, but Hartsel catches up with Crawford's drive down the left-field line. The A's also fail to score.

This game is nearly three hours old, a common enough duration today but quite uncommon at the turn of the century, when games were usually completed in ninety minutes or less. If someone doesn't win pretty soon, there won't be enough daylight to play the second game. With each passing moment, victory becomes more and more urgent for the A's. If the second game is not played today, no makeup will be scheduled.

Donovan and Plank breeze through the thirteenth. Though he must be weary from all the pitches he's thrown, Wild Bill is getting better as the contest wears on. In the early part of the game he seemed to have been throwing his "drop ball" (or sinker, as we know it) too hard, not giving it a chance to rotate and dip. Coming in straight as a string, it proved very hittable. But now as he tires, his arm-swing slows and he gets more "action" on the ball.

In the bottom of the fourteenth, Bill serves up a fastball to Harry Davis that the powerful first-sacker drives to deep center. Here comes Crawford racing back to the rope . . . he is leaning against the crowd to brace for the catch. But now a policeman runs in front of him, obscuring Sam's view with that comical high bobby's hat. The ball lands at Crawford's feet and bounds into the crowd!

Davis is perched at second base, believing he's hit a ground-rule double. But Jones and Cobb are racing out to center field to confront umpire O'Loughlin; they and Crawford believe interference should be called and the batter ruled out. The stadium is in an uproar. O'Loughlin, whose call it properly is, wavers and wavers, infuriating both the Tigers and the A's. At last he decides there *was* interference, and calls Davis out. But Silk's colleague, Tommy Connolly, who was behind the plate (only two umps work a game at this time), now offers *his* opinion—namely, that there was no interference and Davis should hold second base. Back and forth the players race between the umpires as the dispute rages. Even Connie Mack, known as a mild-mannered man for all his sixty-six years in baseball, uncharacteristically leaves the bench and harangues O'Loughlin long and loud.

Utter pandemonium erupts. The A's clear their bench and come galloping out to center field, followed in no time by the entire Tiger team. Nearly a thousand fans join them on the outfield grass, as do the police. Monte Cross, a fifteen-year veteran closing out his career as the A's backup shortstop, rushes into the mob with his fists doubled. He is promptly decked by Charley O'Leary.

Cross then dusts himself off and sets upon Claude Rossman, who gives back what he got and more. As Cross is being pummeled, to the rescue comes Waddell, freshly showered and in street clothes. Donovan grabs Waddell and tries to restrain him, but Rube will not be denied his fun, and tears loose. Donovan, however, is arrested by a cop who sees a chance to serve his hometown as never before.

Now Germany Schaefer approaches the policeman and sweetly points out to him, "My good man, you can't arrest Donovan. Why, the stands are filled with his Irish relatives. Pinch him, and they'll tear us apart."

"Perhaps I acted hastily," the cop concedes, releasing Donovan and collaring Rossman.

At last the warring factions are untangled and Rossman, too, is released. Seeking to reestablish their authority, the umpires declare Davis out because of the policeman's interference; they also banish both Rossman and Cross. Pitcher Ed Killian is recruited to replace Rossman at first base, and play resumes. The fans, who have slowly subsided in their anger, flare up anew as Danny Murphy singles. They know full well that Davis would have come in with the winning run on that hit.

As the autumn sky dims, the game winds on. It is plain now that there will be no second contest, and that the A's must win this one to regain first place. But they are unable to mount another threat; that wild fourteenth inning seems to have done them in. Plank continues to pitch masterfully; though he allows Cobb to reach third in the top of the seventeenth, he strands him there.

In the home half, young Eddie Collins pinch-hits for Oldring and singles, but does not score either. With the players scarcely able to see the ball and, by Cobb's description, "guess-hitting," at ten minutes to six the umpires call the game. It goes down in the record books as a tie.

But in fact the Tigers are the winners, for they retain their hold on first place. They go on to Washington, where in the opener they will come from behind to defeat a raw-boned rookie named Walter Johnson. While Detroit is sweeping the four-game set with the Senators, the A's will drop one to the Naps. Despite the final-week heroics of Jimmy Dygert, who will hurl three shutouts in four days, the Mackmen are dead.

Who were the heroes of this remarkable game? Cobb, certainly; his homer—one of only eleven the Tigers hit *all season long*—kept the game alive in the ninth and provided him with what he would always call his greatest day. For the A's, old Harry Davis, who drove in four runs, and young Rube Oldring, who drove in three. And Rube Waddell, who deserved a better fate.

And most of all, Bill Donovan, who allowed eight runs and fourteen hits through seven innings, and only one run and six hits over the next ten. Wild Bill threw well over two hundred pitches for the game in a display of stamina and heart the likes of which we will surely not see again.

John Updike is a jack of all literary trades—novelist, essayist, story writer, critic, poet—and, uniquely, their master as well. Baseball fans will remember his classic account of Ted Williams's final game, "Hub Fans Bid Kid Adieu," published in *The New Yorker* in 1960 and reprinted extensively since. Figuring that you've read that piece (if you haven't, you owe yourself), I turned to this lesser-known but beautiful effort—written when he was twenty-four—from Updike's first book, *The Carpentered Hen and Other Tame Creatures*.

JOHN UPDIKE

Tao in the Yankee Stadium Bleachers

Distance brings proportion. From here
the populated tiers
as much as players seem part of the show:
a constructed stage beast, three folds of Dante's rose,
or a Chinese military hat
cunningly chased with bodies.
"Falling from his chariot, a drunk man is unhurt
because his soul is intact. Not knowing his fall,
he is unastonished, he is invulnerable."
So, too, the "pure man"—"pure"
in the sense of undisturbed water.

"It is not necessary to seek out
a wasteland, swamp, or thicket."
The old men who saw Hans Wagner
scoop them up in lobster hands,
the opposing pitcher's pertinent hesitations,
the sky, this meadow, Mantle's thick baked neck,
the old men who in the changing rosters see

a personal mutability,
green slats, wet stone are all to me
as when an emperor commands
a performance with a gesture of his eyes.

"No king on his throne has the joy of the dead,"
the skull told Chuang-tzu.
The thought of death is peppermint to you
when games begin with patriotic song
and a democratic sun beats broadly down.
The Inner Journey seems unjudgeably long
when small boys purchase cups of ice
and, distant as a paradise,
experts, passionate and deft,
wait while Berra flies to left.

The Year the Yankees Lost the Pennant has suffered the sad fate of being swallowed up by *Damn Yankees*, the estimable Broadway musical and film which, of course, was based on the book. And Douglass Wallop's witty update of the Faust legend reads as well now as it did when it was new, in 1954. The setting for this excerpt: the 1958 pennant race is in its final day. The chronically awful Washington Senators—"first in war, first in peace, last in the American League," in Charlie Dryden's quip—are tied with the Yankees. They have soared from the nether regions of the standings since July, when Joe Hardy, the ultimate phenom, materialized out of thin air. Joe Hardy is in fact a middle-aged Senator fan named Joe Boyd who has sold his soul to the Devil, a Mr. Applegate. On this day Joe is waiting for something dreadful to happen because he now knows, as any sensible being would have recognized long ago, that the Devil is a Yankee fan.

DOUGLASS WALLOP

The Devil's Due

September 29, 1958, was a bright crisp day in the nation's capital. The wind had shifted during the night, and all over the city the flags were standing out to the southeast against a deep blue sky.

The flags were what Joe noticed first that morning when he rose and looked from the window of his hotel room. The flags: and then the taste of the autumnal air, a taste to stir the memory. For years it had been such weather as this that he had awaited through the long, humid Washington summers. In the past on such a day he would have stepped whistling from the house, grateful that the worst had finally ended, happy in his job.

It was ironic that such weather had been chosen for what surely would be the most miserable day of his life. Miserable not alone for his own sake, but for the misery he knew would come to an entire city; to an entire country, or surely that part of it lying west of the Hudson River.

Standing by the window, looking down at the street, seeing the people stream forth from the trolleys, walk briskly to their jobs, he winced with guilt. On the lips of these people, and those like them all over the city, there could be no conceivable topic but the game; in their hearts nothing less than confidence of victory. For why else would a team be lifted from the abyss and led so far if not intended for victory? Anything less would be cruelly incomprehensible. And it was he, Joe Hardy, the greedy and the gullible, who had led them within sight of the vision and who must stand helplessly by now while the vision was snatched away.

Team of destiny . . .

"Joe," said his waitress at breakfast, "I got ten dollars bet on you with my cousin in The Bronx, and I'm already counting the money."

Looking up from his eggs, he smiled, unable to reply.

After breakfast, he walked, and on every side he could feel the drama. It spoke from the newspaper headlines, from the makeshift scoreboards erected in shop windows; from the television sets assigned this day to the use of sidewalk viewers; and it spoke from the faces of the people themselves, from their greetings and snatches of conversation.

"It's Ransom gonna pitch."

"Ransom's only had two days' rest."

"It's still gonna be Ransom. That's what van Buren said."

There is a quality in the human soul, perverseness perhaps, that keeps hoping even when the cards are stacked, even when there is no hope. And for fleeting moments, feeling the drama, the excitement, Joe forgot Applegate; for fleeting moments he let himself feel the hope these people were feeling.

At other times, as he walked the familiar blocks near the hotel, blocks now transformed by the holiday atmosphere, he told himself that at least he had been able to give them this much. Today they were part of a setting, part of a drama, which all the world watched. He had given them pride of team; he had given them admiration for the fantastic feat the team had accomplished since July. He had given them . . .

But these thoughts gave him no comfort. They were specious, just as hope was self-torture.

He was dressing for the game, surrounded by guys alive with excitement, guys exchanging determined promises, guys with whom he would not be playing after today.

After today . . .

Hearing them was pain. And there was pain in watching Benny van Buren's attempt to maintain a crusty, taciturn, managerial air, when it was apparent that inside he was fluttering. For Mr. van Buren, like the fans, could not believe that a team so singled out by destiny could be left hanging in second place.

Now Mr. van Buren was opening a telegram, tacking it with others on the dressing-room bulletin board. Telegrams from well-wishers all over the globe, one from a fan in the Fiji Islands.

Mr. van Buren cleared his throat to speak. Standing near him was Mr. Welch, bundled now in his heavy winter overcoat since the change in weather, his eyes shining.

"Fellows," Mr. van Buren was saying, "first of all I wanna announce that it'll be Ransom going for us today, and we couldn't put the ball in better hands. . . ."

Sammy Ransom. Sammy of the gaunt, impassive visage . . . Sammy who would be pitching with only two days' rest . . . who, in the late innings, would lose the snap from his fireball and then would try to get by on heart alone . . . Sammy who had no way of knowing that heart stood for nothing with a slob named Applegate.

"And I also wanna say this," Mr. van Buren continued. "I hope we win today. I'm expecting to win. But whether we win or lose, I want to tell you guys that you've given me joy that seldom comes to a manager. You guys have played the greatest baseball I've ever seen in my life. . . ."

And when Mr. van Buren concluded, up jumped Rocky Pratt, a regenerated character by now, a man of team spirit, a man who never complained of headaches from excessive TV viewing. "Listen, Ben," he shouted, "all that stuff sounds fine, but there's just one thing wrong with it. We're not gonna lose. We're gonna win. Hey, you guys, who's thinking about losing?"

"Nobody," was the answering chorus.

"Then let's go out there and *win*," Pratt thundered.

An ovation rocked the park as the team took the field. It was a park this day jammed to the aisles. Even to its far reaches, there was not an empty seat . . . except . . .

Trotting out to his right-field post, Joe looked, and after the National Anthem was played, looked again. Two empty seats there were. Neither Applegate nor Lola was in the seat to which their season tickets entitled them. Applegate, so confident of the outcome that he disdained even to be a witness. And Lola . . . perhaps absent from heartbreak. But who could say about Lola?

The plate umpire signaled to play ball. Ransom peered in for his signal, wound up, let fire, and thus began a game that would live forever in the minds of men.

Pitching for the Yankees that day was Bix Kilgallen, a right-hander who already had twenty-three victories to his credit, and who, like Ransom, was a fireballer. But Kilgallen was not right that day; if Applegate was determined to exact the quintessence in cruelty, he could not be managing it more expertly, Joe thought. Even to the last he was dangling the bait.

For after the Yankees went out in order in the first, Joe came up in the Senators' half and rifled the second pitch on a line to deepest center. With his great speed, he beat the relay for an inside-the-park home run, and the score was 1–0. The ball park rocked with sound. The Yankees, although they still conducted themselves with the mien of champions, now looked not so tall in their uniforms, nor so lethal at bat.

And in the fourth, Joe, up again, lashed a towering drive over the scoreboard in right center. Although Joe's two homers were the only hits Kilgallen had yielded, he was yanked then in favor of Buttons Avery, the Yankees' venerable relief artist, famed for his control and his poise in the clutch.

Meanwhile Ransom, his fastball kicking like a live thing, was mowing down the champions with the precision of a machine-gunner. A single to left in the second, a scratch hit in the fifth, were all the Yankees could muster. In the sixth, his control momentarily gone, he walked the first two batters but steadied and came out of the frame unscathed.

And Joe, first man up in the seventh, doubled sharply to right center. A bunt and a long fly brought him around, and the score was 3–0.

Although the ballpark was still rocking, it was with sadness that Joe returned to the bench and sat watching while Sammy Ransom stroked the rabbit's foot Rocky Pratt had supplied for the occasion, the rabbit's foot he had been stroking between innings all through the game. How pitiably impotent was a rabbit's foot compared with what the Yankees had going for them today.

And yet, where was Applegate?

As Joe took the field for the eighth, it occurred to him there was nothing to prevent Applegate from occupying a seat in some other part of the stadium. A ruse of that sort would be completely in character, and he scanned the upper decks, looking for a flash of bright yellow sports shirt. There were these in plenty but no wearer, at least at such a distance, did he recognize as Applegate.

Nor did Applegate appear in the Senators' half of the eighth.

The ninth began, and although it was against his better judgment, Joe dared to hope.

The stands were hushed now, as tensely silent as they had been that day in Philadelphia before he had spoiled poor Bobby Schantz's no-hitter.

Only three outs away. Joe leaned forward as Ransom faced the first Yankee batter; Ransom, who had performed so gallantly. Three quick outs . . .

"Joe Hardy stinks out loud."

The rasping voice left no doubt. There sat Applegate in his accustomed seat.

"You stink, Hardy," he shouted.

Applegate, on his feet, brandishing a rolled score card, and holding his nose.

And then Joe could look no more because the first Yankee lined a ball over his head which he turned and chased to the base of the right-field wall, taking the carom neatly and whipping it into the infield in time to hold the hit to a double.

Applegate was fluttering his handkerchief in Joe's direction.

And Joe knew this was it.

The next batter singled sharply to center. The run scored, and it was now 3–1.

"How d'ya like that, Hardy?" Applegate was shouting. The partisan crowd was telling him to shut up and sit down but he took no notice. "That's the first one, Hardy," he bellowed. "And you ain't seen nothing yet."

And it was true. In quick succession, the next two Yankee batters pumped singles to left and center, scoring another run and putting men on first and third. It was now 3–2, and the gallant Ransom had had it. With slumped shoulders, he stood near the mound while a relief pitcher was called in from the bullpen.

"You lousy four-flusher, Hardy," Applegate was yelling.

The relief man was Bill Gregson, who had saved many a game for the team that summer. Van Buren could have made no better choice. Working craftily, Gregson got the first batter he faced on a long fly to left. That was out number one, but it also scored the runner from third, and the score now was tied at 3–3, with a man still on first. Shaving the corners too closely, Gregson walked the next man, but the one following went out on a pop-up behind second.

"Okay, Hardy," Applegate yelled. "This is it right here. This is the ballgame, old pal."

Not doubting it, Joe leaned forward. The runners led off. Gregson wound up, delivered. Ball one. Then strike one, and then . . .

The hit was a humpback, arching softly over the second baseman's head toward short right field and sinking fast. The Yankee runners were streaking down the base paths. And Joe Hardy was digging straight ahead, digging for the last notch of speed, diving with outstretched glove, and picking the ball off the grass tops, then falling hard to the ground, rolling over and over, but with his bare hand holding the ball aloft to prove it had been caught, and the roar that surged through the park was as much a roar of amazement as applause.

Picking himself up, Joe glanced at Applegate, who sat glumly back in his seat, and Joe realized that not even Applegate had expected him to catch that ball, realized it had been meant to fall safely, and that other hits would have followed, breaking the game wide open in favor of the Yankees, putting it beyond reach, and giving the Yankees their tenth consecutive pennant.

And as he trotted back to the bench, doffing his cap to the roar of the crowd, he realized something else. There was an acute pain in his right shoulder where he had hit the ground. And he felt suddenly winded, very tired. He, who had felt neither physical pain nor fatigue since the night of July 21st.

All's fair in love and war, Applegate had said. Applegate had not expected him to make that catch. Applegate was capable of playing it as dirty as the occasion demanded. . . .

He felt his stomach. It was still flat and hard.

The bench was silent, except for Mr. van Buren, who kept muttering over and over, as a man in a trance, "You saved it for us, Joe. That catch saved it for us. Can you win it for us now, Joe?"

Third up, Joe walked slowly over and selected a bat, then stooped at the edge of the dugout and watched while the first batter flied out to left.

One away. He advanced to the on-deck circle. *No, Ben, I don't think I can do it this time.* He looked up at the clear, blue sky beyond the left-field grandstand. *I've done it for you all season, but not this time. There's a guy sitting out there along the right-field line. I'm afraid he's too much for us, Ben.*

Two away.

Joe strode to the plate, and the sound that rose on the afternoon air was an appeal, a concerted plea from 30,000 fans, who seemed to sense that if the Senators didn't win it here and now with Hardy, the Yankees would wrap it up in the tenth, and second place would be a bitter reality.

Joe stepped in, set his spikes. *Even if I can't hit the one we need,* he thought, *it would be the greatest pleasure in the world to hit a hard one foul into the right-field boxes, maybe catch Applegate off guard.*

But that was trivial now.

He faced the pitcher.

The ball zipped in. Joe didn't offer. He was reminded of that first day in Detroit when he had faced Rocky Pratt. He had frozen then, and the feeling was the same now.

Strike two, and again he hadn't offered.

You've got no guts. And Applegate wins everything. He's made a monkey of you at every turn.

But his shoulder ached, and he felt very tired.

The Yankee pitcher curved one wide of the plate, tempting him. And it was now strike two, ball one.

The windup, and it was coming in, letter-high, near the outside corner, and with all his strength Joe swung, saw the ball start out on a line toward deep center field; and he was streaking for first, saw the ball clear the center fielder's head; and he was moving for second and the ball was rolling all the way to the center-field wall, the center fielder in pursuit; and he was digging for third and ahead of him he saw the third-base coach, flailing his arms, signaling him to go all the way.

And when it happened it was like a medicine ball, hard in the stomach. Joe faltered; then, clenching his fists, came on again, rounded third and headed for home, but now his temples pounded and his stomach quivered out ahead of him and his breath was coming in short, dry, harsh sobs, and the uniform was too tight, and his legs felt like wood. But he lumbered on down the third-base line, a third-base line that seemed unfamiliar now, and the figure of the Yankee catcher was like a giant in armor, standing there, blocking the plate. And Joe slid, reaching with his toe for a corner of the plate. And the ground came up hard to meet him, jolting his whole body. And the ball was jabbed hard against his thigh, like a hammer blow. He heard the umpire yell, "Safe!" and then he was rolling over and over, away from the plate, reaching for his cap, jamming it tight over his head, keeping his face to the ground, because he knew now that he was a middle-aged real-estate salesman named Joe Boyd.

He saw the Yankee catcher turn with a bellow of rage to confront the umpire; saw the whole Yankee infield and then the outfield, and then the bench rush for the umpire, bellowing as they came; and then the Senators were rushing up from their own bench. And keeping low to the ground, dodging among the swarming players, and moving at times animal-like on all fours, he reached the now-empty dugout and, still bent low, descended the steps leading to the dressing room. At the bottom he paused, and, mounting one step, peered cautiously over the coping.

The melee was furious. The Yankee catcher angrily dashed his cap to the ground. Yankee players confronted the umpire chest to chest, and then, running in from right field, came Applegate.

Snatching up the catcher's cap from the ground, he jammed it onto his own head and advanced menacingly on the beleaguered plate umpire. Jaw outthrust, he began to bark insults about the umpire's judgment, eyesight, ancestry, and sense of direction.

The umpire stood firm, arms folded, head held high, face inscrutable. For a few seconds he endured the tirade, then turned his back, but Applegate circled with him, jaw thrust even closer now, banging fist into palm.

Mr. van Buren stood aside from the fray, smiling, and as Joe watched he was joined by Mr. Welch, also smiling. Mr. van Buren draped an arm over the old man's shoulder, then bent slightly so that Mr. Welch could do likewise, and they stood, smiling, the manager and the owner of a pennant winner.

For the umpire, with a final nervous flick at the plate with his whiskbroom, was turning and heading off the field, still nagged by Applegate and the Yankees, but still imperiously adamant.

As they advanced, Joe ducked and fled into the dressing room; and although he knew his misery would be compounded now; although he knew he would be subjected to the rigors of hell without even the saving grace of youth and athletic prowess, even so the victory had been won, and he could not resist a glow of triumph. For this moment, at least, what did it matter that his personal punishment would be fearsome? Applegate, for once, had been foiled. The Senators had copped the pennant. The Yankees were finally a second-place team.

Nor could he resist a faint smile at the memory of Applegate's enraged countenance as he confronted the umpire. For the afternoon had proved an axiom long known to baseball men, and known now even to Applegate.

And this was that not even the devil could force an umpire to change his decision.

Philip Roth wrote earlier of how his baseball years prepared him for literature; here George Will reveals the roots of his conservatism: a misplaced trust. This piece, written in 1974, was collected in *The Pursuit of Happiness and Other Sobering Thoughts*. The Cubs' pursuit of a pennant since 1945 has driven more souls to drink than to temperance. Maybe by the time you read this the Cubs will have made it to the World Series and will have made a liberal of Mr. Will.

GEORGE F. WILL

The Chicago Cubs, Overdue

A reader demands to know how I contracted the infectious conservatism for which he plans to horsewhip me. So if you have tears, gentle reader, prepare to shed them now as I reveal how my gloomy temperament received its conservative warp from early and prolonged exposure to the Chicago Cubs.

The differences between conservatives and liberals are as much a matter of temperament as ideas. Liberals are temperamentally inclined to see the world as a harmonious carnival of sweetness and light, where goodwill prevails, good intentions are rewarded, the race is to the swift, and a benevolent Nature arranges a favorable balance of pleasure over pain. Conservatives (and Cub fans) know better.

Conservatives know the world is a dark and forbidding place where most new knowledge is false, most improvements are for the worse, the battle is not to the strong, nor riches to men of understanding, and an unscrupulous Providence consigns innocents to suffering. I learned this early.

Out in central Illinois, where men are men and I am native, in 1948, at age seven, I made a mad, fateful blunder. I fell ankle over elbows in love with the Cubs. Barely advanced beyond the bib-and-cradle stage, I plighted my troth to a baseball team destined to dash the cup of life's joy from my lips.

Spring, earth's renewal, a season of hope for the rest of mankind, became for me an experience comparable to being slapped around the mouth with a damp carp. Summer was like being bashed across the bridge of the nose with a crowbar—ninety times. My youth was like a long rainy Monday in Bayonne, New Jersey.

Each year the Cubs charged onto the field to challenge anew the theory that there are limits to the changes one can ring on pure incompetence. By mid-April, when other kids' teams were girding for Homeric battles at the top of the league, my heroes had wilted like salted slugs and begun their gadarene descent to the bottom. By September they had set a mark for ineptness at which others—but not next year's Cubs—would shoot in vain.

Every litter must have its runt, but my Cubs were almost all runts. Topps baseball bubble-gum cards always struggled to say something nice about each player. All they could say about the Cubs' infielder Eddie Miksis was that in 1951 he was tenth in the league in stolen bases, with eleven.

Like the boy who stood on the burning deck whence all but he had fled, I was loyal. And the downward trajectory of my life was set. An eight-year-old could not face these fires without being singed, unless he had the crust of an armadillo, and how many eight-year-olds do?

Of the sixteen teams that existed in 1949, all have since won league championships—all but the Cubs. And which of the old National League teams was first to finish in tenth place behind even the expansion teams? Don't ask. Since 1948 the Cubs have played more than 6,000 hours of losing baseball. My cruel addiction continued. In 1964 I chose to do three years of graduate study at Princeton because Princeton is midway between Philadelphia and New York—two National League cities. All I remember about my wedding day in 1967 is that the Cubs dropped a doubleheader.

Only a team named after baby bears would have a shortstop named Smalley—a right-handed hitter, if that is the word for a man who in his best year (1953) hit .249. From Roy Smalley I learned the truth about the word "overdue." A portrait of this columnist as a tad would show him with an ear pressed against a radio, listening to an announcer say, "The Cubs have the bases loaded. If Smalley gets on, the tying run will be on deck. And Smalley is overdue for a hit."

It was the most consoling word in the language, "overdue." It meant: in the long run, everything is going to be all right. No one is really a .222 hitter. We are all good hitters, all winners. It is just that some of us are, well, "overdue" for a hit, or whatever.

Unfortunately, my father is a right-handed logician who knows more than it is nice to know about the theory of probability. With a lot of help from Smalley, he convinced me that Smalley was not "overdue." Stan Musial batting

.249 was overdue for a hot streak. Smalley batting .249 was doing his best.

Smalley retired after eleven seasons with a lifetime average of .227. He was still overdue.

Now once again my trained senses tell me: spring is near. For most of the world hope, given up for dead, stirs in its winding linen. But I, like Figaro, laugh that I may not weep. Baseball season approaches. The weeds are about to reclaim the trellis of my life. For most fans, the saddest words of tongue or pen are: "Wait 'til next year." For us Cub fans, the saddest words are: "This is next year."

The heart has its reasons that the mind cannot refute, so I say:

Do not go gently into this season, Cub fans, rage, rage against the blasting of our hopes. Had I but world enough, and time, this slowness, Cubs, would be no crime. But I am almost halfway through my allotted three-score-and-ten and you, sirs, are overdue.

That's Mohandas Gandhi, not Jesse Gonder, and references in this piece to "the Mahatma" have nothing to do with Branch Rickey. A funny, funny sketch. By the way,
when Gandhi is introduced to Babe Ruth, the Sultan of Swat, he wonders where that
sultanate is. He should know. There is an Indian state of Swat, now a part of Pakistan,
that once had a Sultan, or Akhond, whose death in 1878 was reported by the *Times of
India* (Bombay) under the headline "The Akhond of Swat Is Dead." This report prompted
Edward Lear to write a poem, "The Akond of Swat," which was surely some sportswriter's inspiration for Ruth's "title." (Lear's ditty began like this: "Who, or why, or
which, or *what*, / Is the Akond of SWAT? / Is he tall or short, or dark or fair? / Does
he sit on a stool or a sofa or chair, / Or SQUAT, / The Akond of Swat?")

CHET WILLIAMSON

Gandhi at the Bat

History books and available newspaper files hold no record of the visit to America in
1933 made by Mohandas K. Gandhi. For reasons of a sensitive political nature that
have not yet come to light, all contemporary accounts of the visit were suppressed at
the request of President Roosevelt. Although Gandhi repeatedly appeared in public
during his three-month stay, the cloak of journalistic silence was seamless, and all that
remains of the great man's celebrated tour is this long-secreted glimpse of one of the
Mahatma's unexpected nonpolitical appearances, written by an anonymous press-box
denizen of the day.

Yankee Stadium is used to roaring crowds. But never did a crowd roar louder
than on yesterday afternoon, when a little brown man in a loincloth and wire-
rimmed specs put some wood on a Lefty Grove fastball and completely bam-
boozled Connie Mack's A's.

It all started when Mayor John P. O'Brien invited M. K. ("Mahatma") Gandhi
to see the Yanks play Philadelphia up at "The House That Ruth Built." Gandhi,
whose ballplaying experience was limited to a few wallops with a cricket bat,
jumped at the chance, and 12 noon saw the Mayor's party in the Yankee locker
room, where the Mahatma met the Bronx Bombers. A zippy exchange occurred

when the Mayor introduced the Lord of the Loincloth to the Bambino. "Mr. Gandhi," Hizzoner said, "I want you to meet Babe Ruth, the Sultan of Swat."

Gandhi's eyes sparkled behind his Moxie-bottle lenses, and he chuckled. "Swat," quoth he, "is a sultanate of which I am not aware. Is it by any chance near Maharashtra?"

"Say," laughed the Babe, laying a meaty hand on the frail brown shoulder, "you're all right, kiddo. I'll hit one out of the park for you today."

"No hitting, please," the Mahatma quipped.

In the Mayor's front-row private box, the little Indian turned down the offer of a hot dog and requested a box of Cracker Jack instead. The prize inside was a tin whistle, which he blew gleefully whenever the Bambino waddled up to bat.

The grinning guru enjoyed the game immensely—far more than the A's, who were down 3–1 by the fifth. Ruth, as promised, did smash a homer in the seventh, to Gandhi's delight. "Hey, Gunga Din!" Ruth cried jovially on his way to the Yankee dugout. "Know why my battin' reminds folks of India? 'Cause I can really Bangalore!"

"That is a very good one, Mr. Ruth!" cried the economy-size Asian.

By the top of the ninth, the Yanks had scored two more runs. After Mickey Cochrane whiffed on a Red Ruffing fastball, Gandhi remarked how difficult it must be to hit such a swiftly thrown missile and said, "I should like to try it very much."

"Are you serious?" Mayor O'Brien asked.

"If it would not be too much trouble. Perhaps after the exhibition is over," his visitor suggested.

There was no time to lose. O'Brien, displaying a panache that would have done credit to his predecessor, Jimmy Walker, leaped up and shouted to the umpire, who called a time-out. Managers McCarthy and Mack were beckoned to the Mayor's side, along with Bill Dinneen, the home-plate umpire, and soon all of Yankee Stadium heard an unprecedented announcement: "Ladies and gentlemen, regardless of the score, the Yankees will come to bat to finish the ninth inning."

The excited crowd soon learned that the reason for such a breach of tradition was a little brown pinch hitter shorter than his bat. When the pinstriped Bronx Bombers returned to their dugout after the last Philadelphia batter had been retired in the ninth, the Nabob of Nonviolence received a hasty batting lesson from Babe Ruth under the stands.

Lazzeri led off the bottom of the stanza, hitting a short chop to Bishop, who rifled to Foxx for the out. Then, after Crosetti fouled out to Cochrane, the stadium became hushed as the announcer intoned, "Pinch-hitting for Ruffing, Mohandas K. Gandhi."

The crowd erupted as the white-robed holy man, a fungo bat propped jauntily on his shoulder, strode to the plate, where he remarked to the crouching Mickey Cochrane, "It is a very big field, and a very small ball."

"C'mon, Moe!" Ruth called loudly to the dead-game bantam batter. "Show 'em the old pepper!"

"I will try, Mr. Baby!" Gandhi called back, and went into a batting stance unique in the annals of the great game—his sheet-draped posterior facing the catcher, and his bat held high over his head, as if to clobber the ball into submission. While Joe McCarthy called time, the Babe trotted out and politely corrected the little Indian's position in the box.

The time-out over, Grove threw a screaming fastball right over the plate. The bat stayed on Gandhi's shoulder. "Oh, my," he said as he turned and observed the ball firmly ensconced in Cochrane's glove. "That *was* speedy."

The second pitch was another dead-center fastball. The Mahatma swung, but found that the ball had been in the Mick's glove for a good three seconds before his swipe was completed. "Steerike two!" Dinneen barked.

The next pitch was high and outside, and the ump called it a ball before the petite pundit made a tentative swing at it. "Must I sit down now?" he asked.

"Nah, it's a ball," Dinneen replied. "I called it before you took your cut."

"Yes. I *know* that is a ball, and I did swing at it and did miss."

"No, no, a ball. Like a free pitch."

"Oh, I see."

"Wasn't in the strike zone."

"Yes, I see."

"So you get another swing."

"Yes."

"And if you miss you sit down."

"I just *did* miss."

"Play ball, Mister."

The next pitch was in the dirt. Gandhi did not swing. "Ball," Dinneen called.

"Yes, it is," the Mahatma agreed.

"Two and two."

"That is four."

"Two balls, two strikes."

"Is there not but one ball?"

"Two balls."

"Yes, I see."

"And two strikes."

"And if I miss I sit down."

Ruth's voice came booming from the Yankee dugout: "Swing early, Gandy baby!"

"When is early?"

"When I tell ya! I'll shout 'Now!' "

Grove started his windup. Just as his leg kicked up, the Bambino's cry of "Now!" filled the park.

The timing was perfect. Gandhi's molasses-in-January swing met the Grove fastball right over the plate. The ball shot downward, hit the turf, and arced gracefully into the air toward Grove. "Run, Peewee, run!" yelled Ruth, as the crowd went wild.

"Yes, yes!" cried Gandhi, who started down the first-base line in what can only be described as a dancing skip, using his bat as a walking stick. An astonished Grove booted the high bouncer, then scooped up the ball and flung it to Jimmie Foxx at first.

But Foxx, mesmerized by the sight of a sixty-three-year-old Indian in white robes advancing merrily before him and blowing mightily on a tin whistle, failed to descry the stitched orb, which struck the bill of his cap, knocking it off his head, and, slowed by its deed of déshabillé, rolled to a stop by the fence.

Gandhi paused only long enough to touch first and to pick up Jimmy's cap and return it to him. By the time the still gawking Foxx had perched it once more on his head, the vital vegetarian was halfway to second.

Right-fielder Coleman retrieved Foxx's missed ball and now relayed it to Max Bishop at second, but too late. The instant Bishop tossed the ball back to the embarrassed Grove, Gandhi was off again. Grove, panicking, overthrew third base, and by the time left-fielder Bob Johnson picked up the ball, deep in foul territory, the Tiny Terror of Tealand had rounded the hot corner and was scooting for home. Johnson hurled the ball on a true course to a stunned Cochrane. The ball hit the pocket of Cochrane's mitt and popped out like a muffin from a toaster.

Gandhi jumped on home plate with both sandaled feet, and the crowd exploded as Joe McCarthy, the entire Yankee squad, and even a beaming Connie Mack surged onto the field.

"I ran home," giggled Gandhi. "Does that mean that I hit a run home?"

"A home run, Gandy," said Ruth. "Ya sure did."

"Well, technically," said Umpire Dinneen, "it was a single and an overthrow and then—"

"Shaddup," growled a dozen voices at once.

"Looked like a homer to me, too," the ump corrected, but few heard him, for by that time the crowd was on the field, lifting to their shoulders a joyous Gandhi, whose tin whistle provided a thrilling trilling over the mob's acclaim.

Inside the locker room, Manager McCarthy offered Gandhi a permanent position on the team, but the Mahatma graciously refused, stating that he could only consider a diamond career with a different junior-circuit club.

"Which club would that be, kid?" said the puzzled Bambino.

"The Cleveland Indians, of course," twinkled the Mahatma.

An offer from the Cleveland front office arrived the next day, but India's top pinch hitter was already on a train headed for points west—and the history books.

George Brunet is not the only man to pitch in Organized Baseball in his late forties, but no other graybeard has ever hurled so many innings. In the majors, not Satchel Paige, Phil Niekro, Hoyt Wilhelm, or Jack Quinn. In the minors, not even Lefty George, who pitched over 100 innings at age fifty-seven, or Earl Caldwell, who at age forty-eight—with his son as his catcher—led his league in ERA. How to explain Brunet, the man with the golden arm? Must be something in the water.

STEVE WULF

Béisbol Is in His Blood

On the day he became eligible to collect his major-league pension, George Brunet of Aguila de Veracruz pitched a three-hitter to defeat León 3–0. Brunet's manager, a fellow by the name of Willie Davis, gave him a forty-fifth-birthday present by doubling in the first run and scoring the second. After the game the ballclub threw a surprise party for *El Viejo*, the Old Man. Brunet, genuinely surprised, blew out the candles and, with a tear in his eye, said to his friends, *"Muchas gracias. Nadie nunca a hecho esto para mi."* Nobody had ever done that for him. After twenty-eight years in professional baseball, thirty different uniforms and 4,719 innings, George Brunet was finally given a day, June 8, in Veracruz, Mexico.

Brunet's odyssey, surely the most arduous in the history of baseball, began in 1953 when he was a seventeen-year-old kid in Ahmeek, Michigan. Brunet was signed by Schoolboy Rowe and Muddy Ruel of the Detroit Tigers. If those names don't date him, just consider that Carl Yastrzemski, the present-day patriarch of the majors, was in the ninth grade. "They gave me $500," Brunet recalls. "I bought a dining-room set for my parents, a coat for my mother and a night on the town."

Brunet first reported to Shelby, North Carolina, in the Class D Tar Heel

League, but he had to pass through Alexandria, Virginia, Seminole, Oklahoma, Hot Springs, Arkansas, Seminole again, Abilene, Kansas, Crowley, Louisiana, and Columbia, Missouri, before reaching Kansas City and the big leagues in 1956.

"I remember my debut," he says. "We were ahead 4–2 in the fourth, but the Red Sox had the bases loaded. Bobby Shantz would normally come in, but for some reason George Susce, the pitching coach, told me to go. I remember riding out of the bullpen in a brand-new pink Lincoln Continental. I had no idea who was up, and now that I think about it, Hal Smith, the catcher, knew better than to tell me. The guy swings at my first fastball and misses, then fouls off another one, and I'm ahead 0–2 when it dawns on me that I'm pitching to Ted Williams. This is my idol. My legs start shaking. Somehow I get the ball up to the plate, and he hits a sharp grounder that Vic Power at first base turns into a double play. When I got back to the dugout and sat down, I literally cried out of relief. The next day Williams comes over to me before the game and says, 'Kid, if you keep that fastball down, you've got a long career ahead of you.' "

There are two points to that story: 1) Guys that George Brunet once played with are now worth big money in vintage bubble-gum cards, and 2) Ted Williams knew what he was talking about.

In the next eight seasons the well-traveled Brunet went down to Little Rock, back up to Kansas City, down to Buffalo, down to Little Rock again, out to Portland, Oregon, up to the Athletics once more, down to Louisville, up to Milwaukee, down to Vancouver, across to Hawaii, over to Oklahoma City, up to Houston, down to Oklahoma City again, up to Baltimore, down to Rochester, back to Oklahoma City, and finally, in 1964, up to Los Angeles.

From 1965 through 1968, Brunet was one of the leading left-handed pitchers in the league, averaging 226 innings a year with an ERA of 3.03. He began to bounce around again in 1969, when he was traded to the Seattle Pilots. In 1970 he pitched for the Washington Senators, managed by Ted Williams, and the Pittsburgh Pirates. In 1971 the St. Louis Cardinals used him for only nine innings. He went back to Hawaii for the rest of 1971 and all of 1972. While in Hawaii, he got an offer to pitch in Japan, but held out, waiting for a call from the Minnesota Twins. The call hasn't come, and Brunet never made it back to the big time. He left with a career won-lost record of 69–93 and a 3.62 ERA. His pension time, according to Brunet, comes to "thirteen years, three months and twenty days."

In his peripatetic career Brunet has pitched for a lot of peripatetic teams. He belonged to the Philadelphia Athletics for a short time before they moved to Kansas City, and later to Oakland. He pitched for the Milwaukee Braves before they were shifted to Atlanta, the Houston Colt 45s before they became the

Astros, the Los Angeles Angels before they adopted California, the Pilots before they turned into the Milwaukee Brewers, and the Senators before they were transformed into the Texas Rangers. Not only did these teams have identity crises, but they were also bad.

Brunet has survived because he has a great left arm. It is such a medical marvel, in fact, that he has had arm trouble just once. "That was back in 1958, a blood clot in my throwing arm," he says. "Kept me out for two weeks." Other pitchers have labored as long as Brunet, but almost all of them were relievers. Brunet has been a starter almost exclusively all this time. Performing in the Mexican League in the summer and the Mexican Pacific League in the winter, Brunet throws about 400 innings a year, although his statistics in the winter league aren't included in his official record. And he has made no concession to age. He is still a fastball and curveball pitcher, and he still challenges hitters, which is rare in the Mexican League, where nobody over 6 feet gets to see a fastball. When he pitched the three-hitter on his birthday, Brunet struck out Ivan Murrell, a former San Diego Padre and the Mexican League home run leader, three times. "He still goes after you," says Murrell. "He's better than a lot of guys in the majors right now."

Before a strike cut short the season by two months, Brunet had eight shutouts, which is only two short of the league record. But even if the strike forestalled Brunet's pursuit of the record, it didn't stop him from pitching. He merely joined Coatzacoalcos, one of the six teams that stayed together to play a new schedule.

Over the course of his career, Brunet has struck out 3,631 batters, which easily surpasses Walter Johnson's major-league lifetime record of 3,508. Even more amazing, Brunet has pitched all this time with nothing on under his uniform pants, which certainly makes him the greatest pitcher in baseball history never to wear a jockstrap and cup. "I just always felt more comfortable that way," he says. "Of course, getting out of the way of ground balls up the middle has cost me a few singles over the years."

His independent streak has always gotten Brunet in trouble. Perhaps the best measure of his arm is that it has persuaded so many teams to overlook the rest of him. "I was never a guy to hang around and kiss anyone's butt," he says. "I didn't have the right kind of personality for managers. If I didn't pitch as well as I did, I wouldn't have had any career at all."

Brunet mentions the spring of 1959, when he was going north with the A's as the fifth starter. A couple of nights before the A's broke camp, he and some of the boys were painting West Palm Beach, Florida, red. About 2 A.M. Brunet found himself directing traffic in front of the team's hotel. One of the cars he stopped contained Parke Carroll, the A's G.M., and Harry Craft, the manager. After Brunet showed up late for a team meeting the next day, George Selkirk, the farm director, called him in for a little chat. "George told me I really screwed up," Brunet recalls. "He said they were going to have to make an example of me and send me down." The A's did more than just send him down. Early the next season they traded him to the Braves.

In Milwaukee, Brunet found his role model, pitcher Bob Buhl. "One time we were pulling into a city," he says, "and Charlie Dressen [the manager] gets up in the front of the bus and says that anybody not in their room by midnight will be fined $500. Well, Buhl marches right up to Dressen, peels $500 off his bankroll, hands it to him, and walks off the bus. Now that's class."

Brunet even antagonized the one manager who gave him a chance, Bill Rigney. "I lost a lot of one-run games with the Angels," he says, "and Rigney used to say to me, 'I owe you a game,' every time he took me out. But one time I really got angry when he took me out, and we had words in the dugout. He knew enough to stop, but I just had to keep going. Finally, Rigney starts counting, '$100, $200, $300.' I didn't stop until he hit $700. Then I went in and tore the clubhouse apart. The next day I came in and wrote out a check for $700 to the Fred Hutchinson Cancer Fund."

Brunet was never much for running, either, which annoyed his pitching coaches and helped build his considerable girth. Nowadays Brunet looks a little like Yastrzemski gone to seed. In 1973 Hawaii manager Rocky Bridges gave him his walking papers because, he said, Brunet was out of shape. After a brief stop in Eugene, Oregon, Brunet was out of baseball. "I spent part of the year coaching some kids in a senior division league in Anaheim," he says. "We weren't far from the Angels' ballpark, so I could see the lights every night. One night I just looked at those lights and said, 'What the hell am I doing here?'"

So Brunet headed for Mexico, Poza Rica to be exact. He became one of the best pitchers in the league (62–55, 2.55 ERA) on one of the worst teams. In 1977—this should come as a chuckle to his former managers—Brunet even took over as the manager of Poza Rica. "It wasn't bad, but it got embarrassing losing every night," he says, explaining why he went back to pitching. On June 20 of that year, at the age of forty-two, he threw a no-hitter. He pitched in Poza Rica again in 1978, striking out 208 batters in 246 innings, and last year he was traded twice—to the expansion team in Coatzacoalcos and then to Mexico City. Overall, he won fourteen games and had a 3.13 ERA. Before the start of this season he was again traded, this time to a new team in Veracruz. Before the strike began on July 2, he was 11–10 with a 2.61 ERA.

Brunet says he's devoted to his three children back home in Anaheim, but he only gives them the three or four weeks between seasons. He is sensitive to the hardships of the Mexican ballplayer, who earns as little as $400 a month, yet as soon as the strike (over the formation of a players' association) was called, he found himself another team.

Brunet has adapted well to Mexican life. Most ballplayers from the States don't last more than a year or two, but Brunet is now in his eighth season. Each established club is allowed only three imports, while expansion teams get four, and former major leaguers like George Scott, Mike Kekich, Clarence Gaston, Mike Paul, and Bart Johnson have found their way south of the border. The Mexican League is Class AAA in designation, but it seems closer to Double A in performance. An American can make good money—Brunet earns about $3,500 a month—and it's a way to keep a career alive. That is, if you call this living.

For one thing, there's the travel. A short bus trip is six hours. Gaston recalls going from León to Tabasco in twenty-one hours—approximately the time it takes to travel from Philadelphia to Miami. Players can pass the hours by counting the crosses at the side of the road on hairpin turns. If the buses don't get to the players, Montezuma's revenge will. Almost nobody escapes. And sometimes the illness can be much worse. One Veracruz relief pitcher went on the disabled list this year with food poisoning.

Playing in the league can also be a frightening experience. The local police sometimes like to hang out in the dugout, wielding M-16s as if they were Louisville Sluggers. Brunet says he's had a gun pulled on him five or six times. "No big deal," he says. Sometimes the local fauna can be just as scary. Ballplayers say there is nothing quite like the sight of fans pelting each other and the field with live snakes.

The high emotional pitch also takes some getting used to. "If it weren't against the law, they really would kill the umpire," says Brunet. In a game between Veracruz and León, an argument with the umpire not only brought the León manager to home plate, but also coaches, players, a dwarf bat boy known as Spider, reporters, photographers, radio announcers and interested spectators. As usually occurs in the States, too, the umpire prevailed.

As for life outside the ballpark, well, sitting in front of an air conditioner is a major form of recreation. Mexico is, in the word of Veracruz centerfielder Victor M. Felix, "ccchhhottt." Last year Felix played for Tabasco, which didn't have a sauce named after it for nothing. Another favorite pastime among Mexican Leaguers is lighting up the local brand of smoke. Outfield grass refers to what the players have during batting practice, not what lies beyond the infield. Brunet prefers the more traditional methods of intoxication. He's slowed down some since his days in the majors, though. His pet Chihuahua, Nurci, keeps him in line. "She won't come near me when I'm drunk," he says.

There are times when Brunet finds himself caught between two worlds. "I'm still an outsider down here. But it's not easy going back to the States, either," he says. "When I do go back, I don't know what they're talking about. It's like I just heard about the Lindbergh baby." But Brunet's position has made him a sort of unofficial ambassador in the Mexican League. Americans are always coming to him for advice, and he's always willing to tell them what not to eat, where to have a good time, and whom to watch out for. "You've got to watch your glove at all times," he warns. "Even on the bench. You can never catch these kids. They just walk in, walk out, and the glove is gone."

Some of the children may be thieves, but they are also a big part of what's special about Mexican baseball. They hang over the dugouts and even sit on the benches. They've especially taken to Davis, whom they call "Wee-lee," as in "Wee-lee, *pelota*, Wee-lee, *pelota*." Davis doesn't know Spanish, and the children don't know English, but they communicate. As one Veracruz coach says, "*Béisbol* universal." Veracruz even has its own verison of the San Diego Chicken, the Aguila, a plump old man swathed in red-cotton feathers.

Veracruz is Mexico's largest port and oldest city, a working town that relies more on shipping than on tourism. Veracruz also has a baseball history: Josh Gibson, Monte Irvin, and Cool Papa Bell have played there. Several years ago the ballclub was sold and moved to Aguascalientes, but this year the team returned with Bobby Avila as the principal owner. Avila, the 1954 American League batting champion with Cleveland, is the former mayor of Veracruz. The club had been averaging 4,000 fans per game before the strike, thanks in no small part to Brunet and Davis.

In their four months together, Brunet and the forty-year-old Davis made quite a team. Davis's philosophy of running a ballclub can best be summed up by his belief that "if you step on people in this life, you're going to come back as a cockroach." Needless to say, he runs a loose ship, which suits Brunet just fine.

Davis brings special skills to the job. Twice during Brunet's birthday shutout he somehow conjured up double plays. He is so mesmerizing that he even has Brunet believing in reincarnation. George believes he can come back as a major-league reliever. Very soon.

"I know I can pitch two or three innings at a time up there," he says. "I know I can pitch better than what's his name, Burgermeyer [Tom Burgmeier, who, unbeknownst to Brunet, is having a fine season]. But somebody would have to ask me, and those days are gone. People up there must think I'm a fat old man who can barely get the ball up to the plate. Guys come down here and say, 'George, is that you? I thought that was your son pitching down here.'

"Maybe I'll go home in September and ask Jim Fregosi if I can work out with the Angels. All I ask is for someone to give me thirty pitches on the side and I'll show them what I can do. If I can't do it, fine. They can say, 'What is this piece of dog doo doing out here?' "

But Brunet hasn't been toiling all this time just for another shot in the major leagues. "To be honest with you, it's the only thing I know," he says. "Nobody's going to take a forty-five-year-old man and train him for a new career. Besides,

I can't think of anything that has made me happier than pitching. Still, I wish I had a dollar for every batter I ever faced." That, George, would come to more than $20,000.

If and when Brunet gives it up, he has a standing offer to be a fishing guide from Jerry Crider, a former White Sox pitcher who runs a hunting and fishing lodge on the coast of Mexico. Brunet would especially like that, because of what happened thirty years ago when the whole thing started.

"It was on my fifteenth birthday," he recalls. "I was going fishing when it began to rain, so I headed back. I wandered over to one of the games they played in Ahmeek. They needed a pitcher, so they asked me. Most of those guys were a lot older than I was, and I had on my fishing boots with the hobs on them. But damn if I didn't go out there and throw a no-hitter. Hell, this is easy, I thought. Little did I know."

Baseball is a backward-looking game. We believe the good old days—when we, along with our idols, were the boys of summer—to have been played in the Garden of Eden. Change can only be for the worse. As Lardner mourned the passing of the dead-ball style of play, succeeding generations waxed nostalgic over their departed sluggers. But as Jonathan Yardley notes in this passage from his 1977 biography, *Ring*, Lardner's disillusionment with baseball proceeded from more than the jackrabbit ball; the snake had entered the garden in the form of Arnold Rothstein, and such favorites as Eddie Cicotte and Joe Jackson had been among the eight who fell.

JONATHAN YARDLEY

Frank Chance's Diamond

They were in many respects really just big overgrown boys, and Ring loved the ones who were natural, without pretense, hard players on the field and genial companions off it. Utterly without pretensions himself, he naturally gravitated to those players who shared his unaffected ease. The longer he covered baseball regularly, the more he concentrated on the game itself, and the more he tended to focus his attention—and his admiration—on those men who played it as he believed it should be played.

In that regard, it is important to emphasize that although the form of the game and its rules have changed remarkably little over the years, baseball before the introduction in 1920 of what Ring called "Br'er Rabbit Ball" was markedly different in style and execution. A couple of statistics make the point plainly enough: In 1911 home runs were hit at an average of .41 per game for *both* teams; a half-century later, in 1961, the figure was 1.90, an increase of more than four and a half times. By the same token, in 1911 triples were hit at a rate of 1.07 per game; in 1961 the figure was .53, a decrease of almost exactly one half.

The home run is the hallmark of the power game, the triple of the speed game. The home run symbolizes a game dominated by brute force, one in which victory can be won by the proverbial "single swing of the bat." The triple, by contrast, is emblematic of a game in which more complex skills dominate: the skill of the batter in placing hits and his speed in covering the bases, as well as the skill of the fielder in holding the runner to as few bases as possible. Objective students of baseball would say that both the power game and the speed game have their merits, and that the balance between the two that has evolved since 1961—the biggest home-run year in baseball history, and one of the least interesting seasons artistically—has produced a "better" game than ever before. But Ring in this respect was no objective student at all. He had been brought up on "dead-ball" baseball, and he simply would not accept any other kind as a legitimate form of the game. By the same token, the standards of excellence he came to believe in were shaped by the dead-ball game, and they remained his standards despite the ways in which baseball changed.

Though it would be three more years before he would express his understanding of baseball excellence with absolute clarity, Ring gave a strong indication of the direction in which he was moving in a piece written for the Chicago *Examiner* in August 1912. He was discussing the White Sox, who were having an indifferent year, and he went to some lengths to single out a player who had gotten little attention:

> Morris Rath, Jimmy Callahan's second baseman, appears to be doomed to go through his baseball career without recognition as a star, and this despite the fact that he is one of the steadiest ball players in the American League.
>
> Rath is referred to by his mates as the brains of the White Sox infield. This title was given him by Matty McIntyre in a spirit of kidding, and yet it is anything but undeserved. Morris is probably no smarter than either of the Sox third basemen, Lord and Zeider, and he is usually so quiet that his headwork goes unnoticed. He seldom is guilty of a foolish play, and his "noodle" is so well thought of by the manager that he is often entrusted with the job of signing for waste pitches, and throws with runners on.
>
> In the International League last season Rath hit well over .300. In fact, his figure was closer to .400. His extra base clouts were few and far between and his record of stolen bases was nothing to boast of. At present, he is a few points below .300, but he has the happy habit of reaching first base oftener than any one else on the team. He is a hard man to pitch to, a man who seldom swings at bad balls.
>
> Rath is shy of bodily strength and ability to steal his way around the paths. Otherwise, he is a mighty good ball player and a man who can be depended on to hold up his end, offensively and defensively.

Everything Ring most admired, and not just in ballplayers, is suggested there. It happens that Rath turned out to be not the ballplayer Ring thought him to be—he played only three more seasons, and those with mixed results—but he helped Ring locate the essence of what he admired. That was: reliability, hard work, "brains," self-improvement, fulfillment of one's abilities whatever their limits, selflessness. Three years later Ring elaborated on the point in four baseball articles he wrote for *American Magazine.* In effect, he used the four articles to identify his own baseball heroes and to explain why they were heroic. The pieces are written in a strained effort at idiomatic language that is now difficult to read without wincing, but it is worth the effort to gain an understanding of what Ring was saying.

The first piece was a tribute to the Boston Braves of 1914, the "Miracle Braves" who had been led by their manager, George Stallings, from last place in late July to the National League championship and then a shocking World Series victory over the redoubtable Philadelphia Athletics. Ring had sentimental reasons for admiring the Braves—he had covered them for the Boston *American* in 1911 (the year he and Ellis married), when they were hopeless losers known as the Rustlers—but there was no sentimentalism in his assessment of their success. They won, he made clear, because Stallings had goaded them to play at or above their best, and the players were willing to make the effort:

> I say the Braves won by hustlin' and fightin' rather than because they was a aggregation o' world-beaters. . . . A club that cops in spite of a few weaknesses has did more than a club that cops because they's no other club in their class. . . . The kind o' men that can do their best in a pinch is the kind that's most valuable in baseball or anywhere else. They're worth more than the guys that's got all the ability in the world but can't find it when they want it.

Ring, who knew better than anyone else that his own talents were limited, held in the highest respect those people "that can do their best."

The second article was called "Some Team" and was Ring's "line o' dope," his personal all-star team. Its members were: Nap Rucker of Brooklyn and Willie Mitchell of Cleveland, left-handed pitchers; Walter Johnson of Washington, Grover Cleveland Alexander of the Philadelphia Phillies, Christy Mathewson of the New York Giants, and Eddie Cicotte of the White Sox, right-handed pitchers; Jimmy Archer of the Cubs and Ray Schalk of the White Sox, catchers; Jake Daubert of Brooklyn, first base; Eddie Collins of the Philadelphia Athletics, second base; Rabbit Maranville of the Boston Braves, shortstop; Frank Baker of the Athletics, third base; Ty Cobb of Detroit, Tris Speaker of the Boston Red Sox, and Joe Jackson of the White Sox, outfielders. As Ring acknowledged, a few of the selections were surprising, notably that of Nap Rucker, but his reasons for choosing Rucker were revealing: ". . . I'm choosin' him because he ain't no flash in the pan, as they say. He's been pitchin' long

enough to show that he ain't no accident, and he ain't nowheres near through.
. . . Rucker knows what he's out there for. He ain't like a lot o' these pitchers
that leaves their brains on the bench." To the reliability for which he had cited
Morris Rath, Ring wrote: "They ain't a smarter pitcher in baseball and they's
nobody that's a better all-round ballplayer, no pitcher, I mean." Still another
requirement, then, was added: versatility, the ability to contribute to one's
team in more than one way.*

The last two pieces were about Ty Cobb and Christy Mathewson, the individual players Ring most admired. That these were the two he chose was
vivid testimony to his refusal to let a player's personality color his evaluation
of his performance. Cobb probably was the most hated man ever to play major-
league baseball. He was a racist, a bully, and a psychopath. He drew no distinction between teammates and opponents; he fought them all, and all of
them detested him. Mathewson, on the other hand, was such an upright, kind,
and selfless individual that some skeptics wondered if he was for real. He was
a graduate of Bucknell, he looked like a combination of Dink Stover and Frank
Merriwell, and according to Hugh Fullerton, he "specializes in chess and when
on the circuit spends his evenings at chess clubs playing the local champions."

All of which made absolutely no difference to Ring. He did make a halfhearted effort to portray Cobb as a decent fellow, but what really mattered to
him was Cobb the ballplayer. When Cobb came into the league in 1905, Ring
wrote, "he runs bases like a fool" and "he couldn't hit a left-hander very good."
Despite these lapses he was a fine, indeed an extraordinary, player, but that
wasn't good enough for him:

> That was when he first come up here. But Ty ain't the guy that's goin' to stay
> fooled all the time. When he wises up that somebody's got somethin' on him, he
> don't sleep nor do nothin' till he figures out a way to get even. . . . He seen he
> couldn't hit the curve when it was breakin', so he stood way back in the box and
> waited till it'd broke. Then he nailed it. . . .

Cobb was widely accused by jealous fellow players of being "lucky" (as if
he had any control over that), but Ring felt that "he makes his own luck" by
heady play. Cobb could do his best in a pinch, and so could Mathewson:

> They's a flock o' pitchers that knows a batter's weakness and works accordin'.
> But they ain't nobody else in the world that can stick a ball as near where they
> want to stick it as he can. . . . I s'pose when he broke in he didn't have no more

* There is a sad footnote to "Some Team." One of the men Ring considered but did not select
was Ray Chapman, the young shortstop for the Indians. "Chapman at Cleveland's goin' to be
good," Ring wrote, "if he don't have no more accidents." Five years later Chapman was killed by
a beanball.

control than the rest o' these here collegers. But the diff'rence between they and him was that he seen what a good thing it was to have, and went out and got it.

One thing Matty had little of, however, was luck. For all his brilliance, for all his 367 victories and his stunning 2.13 lifetime earned-run average, he lost some of the most heartbreaking games in some of the most brutal circumstances. Worst of them all was the final game of the 1912 World Series, when his Giant teammate, Fred Snodgrass, made the famous error that led to two unearned Red Sox runs and a crushing loss. Ring was there, and he filed this report:

BOSTON, MASS., Oct. 16—Just after Steve Yerkes had crossed the plate with the run that gave Boston's Red Sox the world's championship in the tenth inning of the deciding game of the greatest series ever played for the big title, while the thousands, made temporarily crazy by a triumph entirely unexpected, yelled, screamed, stamped their feet, smashed hats and hugged one another, there was seen one of the saddest sights in the history of a sport that is a strange and wonderful mixture of joy and gloom. It was the spectacle of a man, old as baseball players are reckoned, walking from the middle of the field to the New York players' bench with bowed head and drooping shoulders, with tears streaming from his eyes, a man on whom his team's fortune had been staked and lost, and a man who would have proven his clear title to the trust reposed in him if his mates had stood by him in the supreme test. The man was Christy Mathewson.

Beaten, 3 to 2, by a club he would have conquered if he had been given the support deserved by his wonderful pitching, Matty tonight is greater in the eyes of New York's public than ever before. Even the joy-mad population of Boston confesses that his should have been the victory and his the praise.

No, Ring didn't let his admiration for Mathewson influence his appreciation for the pitcher's courage, or vice versa, but he did have a special feeling for this great man who had such bad luck. In the fall of 1925 Mathewson died of tuberculosis—the same disease that contributed to Ring's death eight years later—and Ring, despite his normal dislike for such assignments, agreed to be publicity chairman of the Christy Mathewson Memorial Foundation, which was raising funds for a gymnasium and memorial rotunda at Bucknell, and a cross at Saranac Lake, where he died.

Ring may have been thinking about Matty when he wrote, in a 1930 piece on "Br'er Rabbit Ball," that "I have always been a fellow who liked to see efficiency rewarded. If a pitcher pitched a swell game, I wanted to see him win it. So it kind of sickens me to watch a typical pastime of today in which a good pitcher, after an hour and fifty minutes of deserved mastery of his opponents, can suddenly be made to look like a bum by four or five great sluggers who couldn't have held a job as bat boy on the Niles High School scrubs." From the day of its introduction, the lively ball preyed on Ring's mind: it had ruined *his* game. Once, in the late twenties, he dropped into the press box at the Polo Grounds and watched a few innings. When he got up to leave, a reporter pointed to the batter, Chuck Klein, and said, "There's a fellow can hit 'em." Ring replied, "Swings good, but how far do you think he'd hit 'em with the old ball?" In the summer of 1932, when illness forced John McGraw to retire, Ring wrote him a nostalgic letter:

> . . . Baseball hasn't meant much to me since the introduction of the TNT ball that robbed the game of the features I used to like best—features that gave you and Bill Carrigan and Fielder Jones and other really intelligent managers a deserved advantage, and smart ball players like Cobb and Jim Sheckard a chance to do things.
>
> You and Bill Gleason and Eddie Collins were among the few men left who personified what I enjoyed in "the national pastime."

What must be stressed, however, because so often exactly the opposite is claimed, is that Ring had not given up on baseball per se. He made his changed attitude quite clear in a column written in 1921: "I got a letter the other day asking why didn't I write about baseball no more and I usen't to write about nothing else, you might say. Well friends, may as well admit that I have kind of lose interest in the old game, or rather it ain't the old game which I have lose interest in it, but it is the game which the magnates has fixed up to please the public with their usual good judgment."

Ring wanted baseball to be what it had been—or what he remembered it as being—when he was young. The game he remembered was clean, honorable, ordered, subtle, intricate, beautiful, somehow *natural*. The game he saw for the last dozen years of his life was, he thought, corrupt, obvious, tainted, graceless, *unnatural* because it did not always appropriately reward the diligent and the lazy. In some measure he was right, in some measure he was merely nostalgic and even sentimental. Yet it is not pure coincidence that the Black Sox Scandal occurred in 1919, that the jackrabbit ball was introduced in 1920. Baseball was not the only American institution that was corrupted in the wake of world war and the beginning of that disastrous experiment in institutionalized morality, Prohibition. It's just that of the institutions that were corrupted, this was the one Ring knew best. It had been too large a part of his life for him to part with it without grief.

THE ARMCHAIR
BOOK OF BASEBALL II

Edited by John Thorn
Illustrations by Bernie Fuchs

Foreword by A. Bartlett Giamatti

To Susan

CONTENTS

Foreword

Baseball grew with the country, its origins and first examples Ante-Bellum, its growth and first golden age coterminous with Reconstruction and the period through the First World War. Baseball grew in the surge toward fraternalism, fraternal societies, sodalities, associations, and aggregations that followed the fratricide of the Civil War. Baseball also showed who had won the war and where the country was building, which was in the industrial cities of the North. It was and is a conservative game, remembering its origins or even making up origins (as in the myth that Abner Doubleday invented the game in 1839 in Cooperstown, New York). In a fashion typically American, baseball carried a lore at variance with its behavior; it promoted its self-image as a green game while it became a business. That gap in baseball between first promise and eventual execution is with us to this day, as it is with us in so many other ways.

Genteel in its American origins, proletarian in its development, egalitarian in its demands and appeal, effortless in its adaptation to nature, raucous, hard-nosed, and glamorous as a profession, expanding with the country like fingers unfolding from a fist, image of a lost past, evergreen reminder of America's best promises, baseball fitted and still fits America. It fits so well because it embodies the interplay of individual and group that we so love and because it conserves our longing for the rule of law while licensing our resentment of lawgivers.

In *Democracy In America*, Alexis de Tocqueville implicitly characterizes the American capacity to invest any principle with the character of religious belief when he shrewdly says, "The Americans have combated by free institutions the tendency of equality to keep men asunder and they have subdued it." He leads us to an understanding of our American moral hunger for egalitarian collectivity, which impels us as individuals to aggregate and then to invest the aggregation with numinous meaning, over and over again, as if for the first time every time. This American capacity for religious awe, especially when applied to our social and political institutions, at first enchants and then appalls those from other cultures. They find it difficult to comprehend how so many different institutions can be laden with significance akin to religious value merely in order to expunge class and other distinctions and to promote and protect egalitarian diversity.

If such a characterization may be at least suggested by a sympathetic French observer in the 1830s, what can we learn of ourselves from an observer who did not visit and leave, but who left and visited? In 1877, Henry James published *The American*. The hero is Christopher Newman and we meet him in the Louvre. The year is 1868. The confrontation between the new American man and the Old World, urban and aesthetic in its values, is initially less striking than the contraries embodied in Newman himself. "His eye," says James, ". . . was full of contradictory suggestions: and though it was by no means the glowing orb of romance you could find it in almost anything you looked for. Frigid yet friendly, frank yet cautious, shrewd yet credulous, positive yet sceptical, confident yet shy, extremely intelligent and extremely good-humoured, there was something vaguely defiant in its concessions and something profoundly reassuring in its reserves."

In this eye, this Ego Americanus, there are contraries more complex and tensions more clear than in the generalizing characteristics of Tocqueville. But our French visitor wrote in the 1830s, when institutional coherence promised to subdue the centripetal force of equality. James writes in the 1870s. By then the promise of a more perfect Union had been broken by a savage Civil War. Now America would, once again, be compelled to compose or recompose herself in the aftermath of division and upheaval; once again, free institutions, baseball now among them, would have to play the role of subduing the tendency equals have to be asunder. Now there was no escaping the gap between America's promises and her execution of them. Post–Civil War America was complex in darker and subtler ways than Tocqueville could have foreseen. The matter of race would now forever claim the American conscience, if not its consciousness. That compound whose mix forms the American character—of moral energy and pragmatic efficiency, optimism and guile, admiration for the maverick and love of the underdog, and respect for law—would be forever flecked with race-anxiety.

Law—defined as a complex of formal rules, agreed-upon boundaries, authoritative arbiters, custom, and a set of symmetrical opportunities and demands—is enshrined in baseball. Indeed, the layout of the field shows baseball's essential passion for and reliance on precise proportions and clearly defined limits, all the better to give shape to energy and provide an arena for equality and expression. The pitcher's mound is comprised of a pitcher's rubber, 24 inches by 6 inches, elevated in the middle of an 18-foot circle; the rubber is 60 feet 6 inches from home plate; the four base paths are 90 feet long; the distance from first base to third, and home plate to second base, is 127 feet 3⅜ inches; the pitcher's rubber is the center of a circle, described by the arc of the grass behind the infield from foul line to foul line, whose radius is 95 feet; from home plate to backstop, and swinging in an arc, is 60 feet. On this square tipped like a diamond containing circles and contained in circles, built on multiples of three, nine players play nine innings, with three outs to a side, each out possibly composed of three strikes. Four balls, four bases break (or is it underscore?) the game's reliance on "threes" to distribute an odd equality, all the numerology and symmetry tending to configure a game unbounded by that which bounds most sports, and adjudicates in many, Time.

The game comes from an America where the availability of sun defined the time for work or play—nothing else. Virtually all our other sports reflect the time clock, either in their formal structure or their definition of a winner. Baseball views time as daylight and daylight as an endlessly renewable natural resource; it may put a premium on speed, of throw or foot, but it is unhurried. Daytime, like the water and forests, like the land itself, was assumed to be ever available. When it was not, the work of playing ceased. Until, that is, the lights in stadiums brought day to night and let the day worker watch (or engage in) play in the false sun of the arc light.

The point is, symmetrical surfaces, deep arithmetical patterns, and a vast, stable body of rules ensure competitive balance in the game and show forth a country devoted to the ideals of equality of treatment and opportunity; a country whose deepest dream is of a divinely proportioned and peopled (the "threes" come from somewhere) green garden enclosure; above all, a country whose basic assertion is that law, in all its mutually agreed-upon manifestations, will govern—not nature inexorable, for all she is respected, and not humankind's whims, for all that the game belongs to the people. Baseball's essential rules for place and for play were established, by my reckoning, with almost no exceptions of consequence, by 1895. By today, the diamond and the rules for play have the character of Platonic ideas, of preexistent immutabilities that encourage activity, contain energy, and like any set of transcendent ideals, do not change. The image of the place for play, varied in reality, now often domed or carpeted, lit up at night, but unchanged in our mind's eye, is a shared image across America. In the lore of a society whose mobility has always been one of its distinguishing features, the baseball field is an image of home.

What is baseball, and indeed so much of the American experience, about but looking for home? *Nostos*, the desire to return home, gives us a nation of immigrants always migrating in search of home; gives us the American desire to start over in the great green garden, Eden or Canaan, of the New World; gives us the concept of a settled home base and, thus, the distance to frontiers;

gives us a belief in individual assertion that finds its fulfillment in aggregation, a grouping with the like-minded and similarly driven; gives us our sentimental awe of old ways; gives us the game where the runner runs counterclockwise for home plate.

The hunger for home makes the green geometry of the baseball field more than simply a metaphor for the American experience and character. The baseball field and the game that sanctifies boundaries, rules, and law, and appreciates cunning, theft, and guile; that exalts energy, opportunism, and execution, while paying lip service to management, strategy, and long-range planning, is finally closer to an embodiment of American life than to the mere sporting image of it.

In this splendid volume, the reader will find diverse perspectives, from different eras of our game's, and country's, history. Ample material out of which to construct one's own view of the role baseball plays in the life of a person or of a people. Ample material to assemble a vision of the ongoing pleasure of the game as it renews itself with every pitch, every game, every season. Baseball is best played in the sun, on grass; but it can also, like literature, be played in the head. And there it lasts longest, and never loses its abiding innocence. There, the gap between promise and performance disappears.

A. BARTLETT GIAMATTI
President of the National League
of Professional Baseball Clubs

Introduction

As good as baseball is at its very considerable best—say, games six and seven of the 1986 World Series—for me it is even better in the recollection. To know something of the game's past rounds out the perception of its present, connecting the two in ways that are often trivial, occasionally profound, always satisfying. The 1986 World Series opened with a 1–0 shutout of the New York Mets by Boston Red Sox left-hander Bruce Hurst. A reading of tea leaves, or chicken entrails, or whatever it is oracles read these days, would have revealed the following: the last time a Red Sox team won a World Series was 1918, when another Red Sox left-hander won the opener with a 1–0 shutout. Whose shutout was it? Ruth's—an anagram of Hurst. Oracles not being what they used to be (to the determinedly nostalgic, what is?), the 1986 Red Sox did not win the Series in six games as their 1918 forebears did. But they were only one strike away. . . .

Baseball is a backward-looking game, in which every action on the field resonates against plays imprinted—in the mind's eye and in the record books—long ago. Baseball's undertow of history is powerful, drawing fans and players to the statistics, to old-timers' games, and to Cooperstown, summer after summer. What other sport has so rich and vibrant a past, so copious an accounting, so honored an alumni? Only cricket may be mentioned in the same breath.

"Only connect," advised E. M. Forster in *A Passage to India*. His prescription pertained not to the national sport of England and India but to humankind, increasingly solitary in its progress through this century. In America, where culture, class, ideology, and religion fail to unite us, baseball is the tie that binds, connecting fathers with sons across the inarticulate void of generations, connecting the immigrant with America, connecting the man with the vitality of his boyhood and the boy with the prospect of his manhood.

Baseball's hold, as strong as an embrace, as casual as a pat on the back, binds this book as it binds our people. From Walt Whitman's report of a rugged game played before the Civil War to Neal Karlen's look at the drug-ravaged careers of the 1986 San Jose Bees, from the paean to the box score by Damon Runyon to the rigorous statistical analysis by Bill James, this collection of writings celebrates the game that is more than a game.

The kind response to the first *Armchair Book of Baseball*—which I introduced by complaining that "I could more easily have gathered a book three times this size"—has permitted the publication of a second, every bit the equal of its dad. The general principles of selection are the same two that prevailed first time around: to bring together the best writing that, when collected, would present a panoramic view of the game; and to select only one piece by any one writer, thus denying the temptation to reprint *The Glory of Their Times* in its entirety. (I have violated the second guideline, sort of, by including one bit by Peter Golenbock flying solo and another in which he ghosted for Sparky Lyle, and by including two wraith-writer jobs by Ed Linn.) I have also sought to avoid frequently anthologized pieces, so you will not have the pleasure of reading again a portion of Ring Lardner's *You Know Me Al* or James Thurber's harbinger of Eddie Gaedel, "You Could Look It Up." Oh, well . . . perhaps in *The Armchair Book of Baseball III*.

I wish to thank artist Bernie Fuchs; editors Marta Goldstein and Elizabeth Rapoport of Scribners; designer Alan Benjamin; and, as usual, friend and collaborator David Reuther. For bibliographic help, Tom Heitz, John Blomquist, and Bill Deane of the National Baseball Hall of Fame; for general aid and bonhomie, the Society for American Baseball Research; for leads to specific pieces, Jim Carothers, Ralph Graber, and Bill Felber. And for nothing specific but everything that counts, Susan, Jed, and Isaac.

JOHN THORN
Saugerties, New York

How did Ty Cobb get to be that way? Paranoid, obsessive, bigoted, sensitive, cruel, he was as complicated a bundle as ever stepped onto a ball field. The shaping of this compelling personality began in the cotton country of northeastern Georgia. Charles C. Alexander's fine 1984 biography opens in that region called The Narrows, where William Herschel Cobb, a twenty-year-old schoolteacher, married twelve-year-old Amanda Chitwood. Tyrus was born in 1886, and the itinerant family eventually settled in the small town of Royston. There his father became, successively, the mayor, newspaper editor, and state senator. The Cobbs were accomplished, respected, and proud—until August 1905, when a shotgun blast stained the family honor and strained young Ty's faith in humanity.

CHARLES C. ALEXANDER

"Don't Come Home a Failure"

Convinced that education was the key to both social progress and personal advancement, W. H. Cobb kept after his children to get as much as they could from the schooling available at Royston and then look forward to college. He had particularly high hopes for Tyrus, obviously an intelligent boy who might very well become a lawyer or a physician. Yet while he did capably in arithmetic and grammar and even won a couple of prizes in school oratory contests, the boy would not apply himself the way he should, seemed distracted by too many things outside school.

Tyrus Cobb also gave signs of being stubborn, high-strung, and quick-tempered. In the fifth grade he beat up a fat boy for missing a word in the class spelling bee and thereby giving victory to the girls' team. Not that young Cobb was normally so scrupulous in his own spelling. It was just that the kid had flubbed the boys' chance to win because he hadn't worked hard enough. Joe Cunningham, who lived next door to Tyrus and was his best boyhood friend, sensed that there was something in him that made him different from the other town boys. "You saw it the moment you set eyes on him," Cunningham said many years later. "He just seemed to think quicker and run faster. He was always driving and pushing, even in grade school."

Besides spelling bees, that drive and push found expression in footraces, rock throwing, tree climbing, and various other demonstrations of boyish physical prowess. Once young Cobb insisted on walking a tightrope stretched across

the street in the center of town. Clearly, he was something of a showoff, but he was also a born competitor, obsessed with winning. "I . . . saw no point in losing if I could win" was the simple way, as an old man, he expressed what he had felt even as a boy.

Eventually it was baseball that became the main outlet for the boy's competitive energies. As was true in small towns throughout the country, the principal manifestation of Royston's collective existence took place at local baseball games. From the 1890s up to the 1920s baseball was far and away the most popular form of athletic competiton in America, and going to baseball games was one of the leading forms of entertainment and recreation. On Saturday afternoons all summer, a big percentage of the white townspeople and even some local blacks (carefully kept off to one side) turned out to see the local aggregation compete against some nearby community's team. They called it town or semipro baseball, because sometimes the team members split a few dollars contributed by their followers. Although such baseball was the source of most of the talent that eventually made it into the major leagues, the older boys and younger men who played for the town teams knew how remote the possibility was that any of them would ever be "discovered" by a professional scout. Mostly they played for the fun of it.

Royston went in for baseball in a bigger way than most places its size. Besides the Royston Reds in their flaming flannels, there was also an organized team for younger boys called the Rompers. A right-handed thrower and left-handed batter, Tyrus played for the Rompers until he was about fourteen. One Saturday the Reds found themselves without a shortstop for a game with Commerce. Pressed into service, the frail-looking boy handled eight chances without an error and, by holding his hands apart so he could get better leverage on the big bat he had to swing, managed to slap three hits through and over the infield.

Soon after that Bob McCreary, who managed and caught for the Reds, clerked in the local bank, and was the son of one of the town's physicians, talked Tyrus's father into letting the boy go with the team to Elberton, some 20 miles south on a spur of the Southern Railroad, in the heart of the peach country. As a brother in the Masonic Order, McCreary promised Professor Cobb that he would look out for Tyrus, make sure he behaved himself. At Elberton, Tyrus again got three hits, the last one driving in the winning run. Later on that summer, playing center field, he saved a win over Harmony Grove with a diving catch. For that the Royston people showered the field with coins, and Tyrus picked up $10 or $11, the first money he ever made playing baseball. And he experienced what it was like to be cheered by a crowd. "Once an athlete feels the peculiar thrill that goes with victory and public praise," he said sixty years later in reminiscing about those early exploits, "he's bewitched. He can never get away from it."

By that time Tyrus had already angered his father by trying to trade some of the professor's books for a new baseball glove he had seen at the local dry-goods store. After the Harmony Grove game, though, he no longer had to make do with the old ragged glove he had sewn together himself. He also ordered pamphlets on "how to sprint" and practiced making quick starts for the next base. Baseball had become the focus of his life, and in the summer he played anywhere and as much as he could when he was not having to sit in Baptist Sunday school, work the fields on his father's farm, or listlessly tend to chores around the house in town.

He even played in North Carolina during warm-weather visits to his relatives there. Although the Cobb children evidently saw little of their Chitwood kin, they made regular trips by train up to see their Cobb grandparents. Tyrus grew very close to his "Granddad Johnny," a feisty, imaginative little man who captivated him with tales of bear hunting in the mountains and also taught him the finer points of 'coon and 'possum hunting. His grandmother healed his cuts, scrapes, and bites and kept his digestive track cleaned out with an array of mountain remedies, and his Aunt Norah often drove him in her buggy into Murphy or Andrews so he could find some boys to get up a ball game. Tyrus seems to have had his happiest boyhood times with the North Carolina Cobbs, going there not only in summertime but sometimes during the mid-winter school recess, as well.

He was there early in January 1902 when he received a letter from his father. In later years he would carry that letter on his person and eventually have it printed. Writing under the letterhead of the Franklin County Board of Education and signing himself "Yours affectionately, W. H. Cobb," his father commented on the 2 inches of snow that had just fallen at Royston. He was glad that Tyrus was up in "that picturesque and romantic country" where there was "solitude enough to give nature a chance to be heard in the soul." To see "God's handiwork among those everlasting hills," to hear "the grand oratorios of the winds" and "the rush of her living leaping waters"—all that was a vital part of the education he wanted his son to have. To be truly educated was not just to "master the printed page"; it was also "to catch the message of star, rock, flower, bird, painting and symphony," to have "eyes that really see" and "ears that really hear and an imagination that can construct the perfect from fragment." "Be good and dutiful," he went on, "conquer your anger and wild passions. . . ." Be guided by "the better angel of your nature," not "the demon that lurks in all human blood and [is] ready and anxious and restless to arise and to reign."

"My overwhelming need was to prove myself as a man," wrote Tyrus Cobb many years later about his feelings in his adolescence. Clearly, proving himself meant winning and keeping the approval of the imposing man he called not "Pa" or "Papa" but "Father." For all his rhapsodizings about the education of the soul through contact with nature, W. H. Cobb expected his ball-playing son to master lots of printed pages. Yet the boy simply could not share the ambitions his father had for him. Tyrus was supposed to go to college and eventually enter law or medicine. He might even attend the U.S. Military Academy and embark on a career as an army officer. But he had to settle down and apply himself, even though the boy was convinced that he "could never match my celebrated father for brains." It was not easy being Professor Cobb's son. Too much was expected of him at school and in the town. Both his scholarship and his conduct were supposed to be exemplary—and neither was. "I felt guilty," he remembered, "that some great, vaulting ambition hadn't seized me beyond handling hard hoppers and line drives."

Tyrus dutifully went with his father to Carnesville, the county seat, so he could meet Col. W. R. Little, one of the area's foremost lawyers, and browse in the colonel's law library. But he found the reading to be "dry as hell" and decided right then that the law was not for him. Maybe medicine. He began accompanying Dr. Moss on his travels around the southern part of the county. On one occasion he assisted Moss in removing a bullet from a young black whom a white boy had shot in the stomach. Tyrus administered the chloroform and, at Moss's direction, felt around inside the youth to see if he could find the bullet. When he found nothing, Moss declared that the slug must have missed the intestine and sewed the patient up. Somehow he survived. Tyrus, his hand covered with gore, had discovered that the sight of blood and exposed tissue hardly bothered him at all. Conceivably he could become a surgeon. But try as he might, he simply could not work up much enthusiasm for a life in medicine.

About that time Tyrus had occasion to see plenty of his own blood when he accidentally shot himself in the left shoulder with his .22 rifle. After he got the bleeding stopped, W. H. Cobb jumped on a train with his son and took him the 75 miles into Atlanta to see a battery of physicians presumed to be more knowledgeable than the country doctors at home. Although they lacked X-ray equipment, the Atlanta doctors were able to determine that the bullet had apparently bounced off Tyrus's clavicle without breaking any bone and then lodged somewhere in the vicinity. Unable to locate the bullet, they sewed up the boy's shoulder and wished him well. The wound healed nicely, and the small slug remained inside Tyrus Cobb's shoulder for the rest of his life.

Being shot seems to have interfered not at all with young Cobb's ripening baseball career. Armed with his own bats, made, with help from Joe Cunningham, of prime ash in the same toolshed where Joe's father built coffins for local deceased citizens, Tyrus became the star player on the Royston Reds. Having grown to about 5 feet 10 inches and 150 wiry-muscled pounds by the time he was sixteen or seventeen, he played both infield and outfield, ran the bases with abandon, and hit whistling line drives. In March 1902 a trip into Atlanta and out to Piedmont Park, where the American League Cleveland Broncos were doing their spring training, heightened his baseball passions. Befriended by Bill Bradley, Cleveland's hard-hitting third baseman, Tyrus took pictures of the players with his little box camera and generally reveled in his first encounter with real professional ballplayers, and big leaguers at that.

Back home, as he later put it, "my father held me down, withholding acceptance of me as the man I yearned to be." School no longer held much interest for the youth, and inasmuch as Professor Cobb thought baseball a waste of time, Tyrus could find no way to please this man who awed, intimidated, and frustrated him but whom he nonetheless loved deeply. No doubt W. H. Cobb also loved his son, but he seems to have been the kind of person who carefully guarded his emotions and, even with his own wife and children, found it hard to show affection. Sparse with his praise, he was quick and sharp with his criticism. It seemed to Tyrus that try as he might, "I couldn't reach him."

In the spring of 1903 the youth finally did reach his father, for maybe the only time in his life. He threw himself into putting in the cotton crop, plowing and seeding from dawn to nightfall, sweating alongside the black hired hand. As the tender plants began to grow, he discovered a new warmth and intimacy with his father, who started talking with him about their crop, about work mules, about the competition American cotton producers were increasingly meeting from foreign-grown cotton, about whether they should sell or wait for prices to rise. Tyrus was so enthused by it all that he got a job with a local cotton factory and learned how the cotton was ginned, baled, graded, and moved to market. Everything he learned he discussed with his father, who was pleased that at least his son showed a good head for business. Tyrus Cobb would later think back on 1903 as "a great year in my life," the time when "Professor Cobb 'bought' me as his son. . . ."

Yet despite the new closeness with his son, W. H. Cobb had not changed his mind about the folly of baseball. Tyrus felt guilty about taking a few dollars for playing for a team over in South Carolina, because if word got around that he'd played for money, he would be ineligible for college athletics—if he went to college. For Tyrus that was still an open question. Early in 1904, however, he took a step that was bound to decide the issue once and for all. Despite the surge of love he had for his father, "I still felt that I was being held in some sort of bondage. So I decided I would become a ballplayer and get away."

A local athlete named Van Bagwell had had a tryout in 1903 with Nashville in the Southern League but had not made the team. That winter he told young Cobb that he believed Tyrus had the talent to make it in professional ball. That helped the boy get up his courage secretly to write letters to each of the teams in the South Atlantic ("Sally") League, which had just been formed over the winter as a Class C circuit with franchises in six cities in Georgia, South Carolina, and Florida. He included a little information about himself and asked for a tryout. One reply came back, from Con Strouthers, manager and part owner of the Augusta Tourists, saying that Cobb could come to spring training if he wished but that he would have to pay his own expenses. A couple of days later a contract arrived specifying a salary of $50 a month—if Tyrus made the team.

Dazzled as he was by the contract and the prospect of a professional career, Tyrus dreaded having to tell his father that he was leaving and that he needed money for traveling and living expenses until he got his first check. First he revealed his plans to his mother. Amanda Cobb—a kindly enough mother, it seems, but not a major factor in the boy's life—told him to go ahead if he had to and kept the matter to herself. Tyrus waited to confront his father until the night before he had to report at Augusta. Professor Cobb, whose hopes for the boy had swelled over the past year, responded with a stern lecture that went on for hours. Tyrus, he argued, was at a critical point in his life; what he did now might determine his whole future. He stood a good chance to end up "a mere muscle worker." Baseball was filled with no-accounts who drank and gambled and ran after lewd women. The boy could not argue, only keep saying, "I just have to go."

At last the man gave up, opened his rolltop desk, and sat down to write out six checks for $15 each, which he gave his son with the admonition for him to "get it out of your system." Early the next morning Tyrus Cobb, age seventeen, stepped aboard a Southern Railroad car for the journey south to Augusta. Although the trip was only about 85 miles by rail, it took nearly all day, because Tyrus had to change trains at Elberton and again just across the Savannah River at Calhoun Falls, South Carolina. It was late afternoon by the time he got into Augusta on the Charleston and Western North Carolina.

Augusta, Georgia, in 1904 was a thriving little city of something more than

40,000 inhabitants. Proud of its wide downtown streets, its new trolley line, and its attractive neighborhoods, Augusta was an important nexus of the cotton trade and increasingly noted for textile and iron and steel manufacture. Besides Atlanta, it was the biggest place Cobb had ever been.

The next day Cobb donned his red Royston uniform and took the field at neat little Warren Park, home of the new Tourists. He amazed and amused manager Strouthers and the other players by cutting in front of fielders for ground balls and flies to the outfield, making wild dashes from base to base, and generally going against the accepted procedures of the workouts and intrasquad games. He stood around hoping somebody would let him up to the plate for a few swings, but rarely did the other men, nearly all older than he was and most of them with professional experience, give him a chance to hit. When the Augusta team played the Detroit Tigers of the American League, also training at Augusta, Cobb watched from the bench. Nor did he get into any of the other exhibition games.

When the season started, all the Augusta infield positions were occupied by veterans. Strouthers's first baseman was being stubborn about signing his contract, so the manager had to shift his center fielder to first. Inasmuch as there were only fourteen or fifteen men still with the team, Strouthers had no choice but to put the young recruit from Royston in center field on opening day, April 26, 1904, at Warren Park against Columbia. Hitting in seventh place in the lineup, Cobb responded with a single and double in four times up against a pitcher named George Engel and scored two runs. Engel helped himself out with a home run, and Columbia won the game 8–7.

It was an impressive debut, or so Cobb thought. As it turned out, it was a moment of glory and nothing more. After he went hitless the next day, Strouthers called him into his office and told him that his first baseman had just signed, his center field could go back to his position, and he could no longer use Cobb. What the boy had dreaded but had not let himself believe could happen had happened. Now he faced the prospect of going back home to his disapproving father and acknowledging that he had been right, that baseball wasn't really a practicable career, only something he'd had to get out of his system.

Confused and depressed, Cobb wandered back to the little hotel where he had a room. There Thad Hayes, a pitcher from Alabama who had also just got his release, told him about a semipro team over at Anniston, Alabama, being managed by Hayes's friend. That team needed a pitcher and maybe an outfielder, as well; Cobb should come along with him to Anniston.

Released outright by Augusta, the boy was thus a free agent who could play wherever he wished. Still, he felt compelled to talk over the matter with his father. At the local telephone office he was astonished and overjoyed when W. H. Cobb told him to take the job at Anniston. But whatever happened, "Don't come home a failure." "In giving me his blessing, his sanction of my quest for success in my hour of defeat, my father put more determination in me than he ever knew. I had the shivers when I hung up." So Cobb described his feelings when he recalled that moment more than a half a century later.

Cobb and Hayes used most of the little money they had left in getting to their new team. Anniston, a smoky mill town in northeastern Alabama, was a member of a loosely organized outfit called the Tennessee-Alabama League. The league was not officially recognized by professional baseball's ruling National Commission and thus was not part of what was called Organized Baseball. Yet even as an "outlaw league," it was considerably above the level of competition Cobb had known with the Royston Reds.

Playing two or three times a week in towns around northern Alabama and southern Tennessee, Cobb soon was the league's leading batter, according to the rough statistics the various teams kept. Although he may not have been greatly affected by Baptist Sunday school back in Royston, he did intend to live rigorously by one Biblical injunction: put not thy light under a bushel. Playing for Anniston was fun, and at $65 a month plus free room and board, he was doing a lot better financially than if he had managed to stay with Augusta. Sooner or later, though, he had to get back into Organized Baseball.

Grantland Rice, the sports editor of the Atlanta *Journal*, began receiving regular communications from Alabama attesting to the sensational exploits of the young outfielder Cobb. Written in a variety of cursive styles and signed with names like "Jones," "Brown," and "Smith," the letters and postcards continued to come until Rice finally wrote in his column that "over in Alabama there's a young fellow named Cobb who seems to be showing an unusual amount of talent." Not until many years later, when Cobb told him about it, did Rice learn that it was really Cobb who had sent all those notices touting his ballplaying talents. Nor did Cobb himself learn until after his father's death that W. H. Cobb had clipped Rice's column and carried it around to show his friends in Royston and Atlanta.

After about three months with Anniston, Cobb received a telegram from the Augusta club inviting him to rejoin the team. By that time the Tennessee-Alabama League was about ready to collapse, anyway. In Augusta, Con Strouthers had sold his interest in the club and resigned as manager, giving way to catcher Andy Roth. Cobb first made sure that Strouthers, for whom he had vowed never to play again, was really gone, then hustled back to the Tourists. He reappeared in the lineup on August 9, again against Columbia. His return to the Sally League proved less than triumphal. Playing all the outfield positions at one time or another, Cobb appeared in thirty-five games during the remainder of the season and finished with an uninspiring .237 batting average, thirty-third among some fifty to fifty-five regular players in a league that had only one .300 hitter.

Back in Royston for the off-season, Cobb could bask in the adulation of his friends. His father remained unimpressed even when Cobb banked the $200 he had saved and showed no signs of having lost his virtue during the summer away from home. Again it was necessary for him to work hard at the Cobb farm, this time sowing the winter wheat crop, before his father warmed up **and was again willing to offer praise for something he had done.**

Otherwise, Cobb tramped the woods, sometimes hunting but mostly just staying outdoors as much as he could, and wondered about his future. It was just possible that he might not be good enough to go very far in baseball. He gave some thought to enrolling at the University of Georgia to start the long years of study that would lead to his becoming a surgeon. That would please his father. Over the winter, though, he got an inquiry from Andy Roth about whether he planned to play for Augusta again in 1905. The eighteen-year-old veteran of less than a third of a season in Organized Baseball wrote back saying that he had to have $90 a month. Remarkably, Roth and President John B. Carter agreed to Cobb's terms, and the youth prepared to give baseball another try.

Cobb had grown another inch and put on a few more pounds since the previous spring, and he was faster than ever. More determined, too. In 1905 the Detroit Tigers again trained at Augusta, having agreed with the Augusta owners to return in exchange for first claim on whatever players Detroit liked on the local team. When Bill Armour, the new manager of the Tigers, showed up at Warren Park for the first time, second baseman Herman "Germany" Schaefer greeted him with an account of the wild antics of a kid on the Augusta team named Cobb. According to Schaefer, Cobb wanted to steal a base on every pitch, tried to take two bases on singles, even tried to go from first to third base on bunts. "He's the craziest ballplayer I ever saw," said Schaefer.

Yet the Tigers soon began to take the kid seriously. In the two exhibition games Augusta played with Detroit, Cobb rapped a single off Bill Donovan, one of the Tigers' aces, another off Jesse Stovall, and a single and triple off Eddie Cicotte, a Detroit semipro star the Tigers had signed and subsequently decided to leave with Augusta.

Cobb started the season as the leadoff hitter and regular left fielder for Augusta. His hitting was mediocre in the early going, and his erratic base running and outfield play dismayed his manager. He also got on Roth's nerves by complaining that the team lacked discipline, that it was, in the baseball parlance of the day, a "joy club." Cobb himself soon "fell into the spirit of things. I was fast losing my ambition to go higher in the game." At one point Roth wanted to sell his troublesome young outfielder to Charleston for a token $25, but the owners thought otherwise, and Cobb stayed.

By mid-July the Tourists had lost fifteen of their last twenty games and were drifting in fourth place in the six-team league. Not that they lacked talent. Besides Cobb, the Augusta roster included three other future major leaguers: Cicotte, who pitched two no-hit games that year; Nap Rucker from Crabapple, Georgia, who roomed with Cobb on the road and pitched a no-hitter of his own; and infield Clyde Engle. But it was not a good ball club. Roth finally turned over the team to outfielder and team captain George Leidy, although Roth stayed on as first-string catcher.

Soon after Liedy took over, Cobb, in a game at Savannah with his team leading 2–0, took his position in the outfield eating a bag of popcorn or peanuts. (Accounts vary.) As he munched away, a fly ball soared in his direction. Trying to hold on to his snack at the same time that he pursued the ball, Cobb missed making the catch, and a run scored. Although Augusta went on to win the game, Manager Leidy was not amused by Cobb's gaffe. What followed that night was a scene that might well have been lifted from one of the period's books of boys' fiction, wherein a well-meaning but irresponsible lad is straightened out by the wise counsel of an older man—father, minister, employer, or whatever. In this case it was George Leidy.

A journeyman minor leaguer whose main ambition now was to have a few successful years as manager, Leidy asked Cobb to ride with him on the trolley line out to a local amusement park. As they rode and later as they strolled around the park, Leidy talked quietly but earnestly, telling Cobb that he had to stop fooling around, that he had a lot of ability and a great future in baseball if he worked hard to make the most of his talents. He went on to describe life in the big leagues—traveling in comfortable Pullman cars, staying in fine hotels in big cities, eating good food, wearing expensive clothes, gaining fame and success. On other nights, as well—while they ate together, took in vaudeville shows, or just sat on hotel porches—Leidy continued to boost Cobb's confidence and determination. Completely won over, Cobb promised henceforth to become the best ballplayer he could possible be.

In the mornings at the ballpark Leidy worked with Cobb, teaching him the intricacies of the hit-and-run, the delayed steal, hitting to the opposite field, and above all, the art of bunting. Hour after hour Leidy threw to him and Cobb bunted at an old sweater placed to either side of home plate. He worked on sacrifice bunts, on drag bunts, on faking bunts and slapping the ball past third basemen. And in the games in the afternoons, Leidy let Cobb do what he wanted at bat and on the base paths, confident that with what he had learned, the kid would usually do the right thing.

Within a short time Cobb had become the outstanding player in the Sally League. His team continued to flounder, but at the end of July the baseball tabloid *Sporting Life* could report that "Cyrus Cobb" was the first in the league that season to make 100 base hits. The club's owners raised his salary to $125 a month. Meanwhile, scouts from Detroit and other big-league teams, as well as Indianapolis of the American Association, turned up regularly at Augusta's games. Henry "Heinie" Youngman from the Tigers sat on the bench with Cobb one day and questioned him about his background. The Macon first baseman told him he had heard Cobb was about to go up. Now it seemed only a matter of time until Cobb could notify his father that he had made it into the big time and was on his way to the kind of rewards and recognition his father had envisioned for him in more traditional endeavors. For a few days during a home stand he happily hosted his seventeen-year-old brother, Paul, a good semipro ballplayer himself, who had come to watch Cobb in action.

Early on the morning of August 9, 1905—"the blackest of days," he later termed it—Cobb received a telegram in Augusta from Royston. His father had been killed in some kind of shooting accident. Cobb agonized through the slow, zigzag train trip back to Royston. Tired, bewildered, desolated, he arrived to hear a story of unbelievable horror. His mother, they told him, had shot his father.

What he probably was not told—at least not to his face—was that for some time it had been common gossip in Royston that Professor Cobb's pretty wife had taken a lover. The gossip must eventually have got around to W. H. Cobb. On Tuesday evening, August 8, he had told his wife he was going out to the farm for a couple of days, hitched his horse to his buggy, and left the house. Paul and Florence were staying with friends. Later that night Amanda Cobb went upstairs to the room over the front porch she shared with her husband, locked the windows (even though the temperature had been in the nineties that day and it was still warm and humid), and went to bed. A little later W. H. Cobb was seen alone on foot in town. Shortly after midnight Amanda Cobb was awakened by a noise on the porch roof. A figure she could not make out was struggling to raise one of the windows to her bedroom. Grabbing the loaded double-barreled shotgun that always stood in a corner of the room, she pointed it toward the window and fired once. After what witnesses later described as a considerable interval, she fired again. Approaching the shattered window, she peered into the darkness to find her husband lying in a widening pool of blood.

At the Cunningham house next door, Joe Cunningham heard the blasts and ran over to see what had happened. There he found, as he described it to his daughter many years later, "the worst thing I ever saw." Although Professor Cobb was still breathing, he had a gaping hole in his abdomen, and one of the shotgun blasts had literally blown his brains out. The young man ran to get Dr. H. F. McCreary, who pronounced W. H. Cobb dead at 1:30 A.M. He found a revolver in Cobb's coat pocket.

The next day a coroner's jury heard Amanda Cobb give her account of the shooting and others testify about what they had heard and seen. By the end of the day the coroner's jury had ordered Amanda Cobb's arrest on a charge of voluntary manslaughter. W. H. Cobb's funeral was held on August 11 at the Cobb house, where people crowded in and overflowed the front yard and into the street. He was buried at the local cemetery in a coffin built by Joe Cunningham's father, with the professor's Masonic brothers officiating at the gravesite. The day after that the county sheriff arrested Amanda Cobb, and the local justice of the peace set her bond at $7,000. She was quickly able to post the 10 percent of the bond necessary to keep herself from having to spend any time in jail. By the end of the month a grand jury sitting at Carnesville had returned an indictment against her. Her trial was to take place that fall.

Tyrus Cobb left no account of what he felt and did in Royston during that dreadful time. He did spend four days after the funeral with his mother, brother, and sister. That he was able to get himself together in fairly short order and resume his baseball duties suggests a great deal about the young man's will, concentration, and above all, his continuing drive to confirm his father's trust. Now, though, it was also a matter of upholding the family's reputation at a time when scandal and suspicion hung over it. The best way to do that was to achieve such success as a ballplayer that people would have to respect the Cobb name and especially his father's memory.

Cobb rejoined his team on Wednesday, August 16, at Augusta, where the previous week the local newspaper had tactfully reported his father's death. Against the Charleston Sea Gulls he made two hits in the first game of a doubleheader but went hitless in the second game. By that time George Leidy was out as manager of the Tourists, and Andy Roth was in again. Whoever managed Augusta no longer much concerned Cobb, though, because three days after he got back, he received formal notification from Charles D. Carr, now club president, that he had been sold to the Detroit Tigers and was to report to that team by the end of the month.

By August the second-division Tigers were plagued by an accumulation of disabling injuries and down to three outfields, one of whom, the veteran Duff Cooley, was hobbling on one good leg. Club Secretary Frank J. Navin and Manager Bill Armour had to pick up somebody to help the team finish out the season, and the club's finances would not permit the purchase of a player from the upper minor leagues. So Augusta, at the bottom of the minors and where Detroit already had an option to buy whichever player it wanted, was the logical place to turn. Good reports had reached Detroit on infielder Clyde Engle, who could also help out in the outfield. But Bill Byron, a native Detroiter umpiring in the Sally League (en route to a notable career in the National League), told Heinie Youngman that Cobb had greater promise. In Detroit, Bill Donovan, whom Cobb had impressed in spring training, told Armour basically the same thing. So for $700—the price agreed to in the spring for the player Detroit chose, plus $200 thrown in because he was being taken before the season was over—Cobb, still four months short of his nineteenth birthday, became a big leaguer. "I only thought," he later said, "Father won't know it."

Cobb played his last game for Augusta on August 25 before a fine Friday crowd of about 1,400, against league-leading Macon. His solid hitting and dashing style on the bases and afield had captivated the local "bugs," as baseball fans were called in those days; and when he came to bat in the bottom of the first inning, a group of them met him at home plate with a bouquet of flowers and a gold watch. He stammered his thanks, shook hands all around, waved to the crowd, finally got into the batter's box, and struck out. Subsequently, he singled twice, stole a base, and threw out a runner as the Tourists took another defeat, 5–0. Cobb's final-game performance gave him more than forty stolen bases (third in the league) and, with the Sally League season ending in a few days, ensured him the batting championship at .326. Taking chances in the field, however, had been costly. His thirteen errors gave him the lowest fielding average among outfielders appearing in more than a hundred games.

As would often be the case in his baseball career, Cobb both won the admiration of the paying customers and left a sour taste in the mouths of the club management. Just before he left Augusta, he groused to local sportswriters that he should have got part of his purchase price and that in fact he'd been ill treated all season, being kept at the bottom of the salary scale on the team. Whether or not his complaints were justified, one could well understand his ill temper. Although his big-league adventure awaited him in Detroit, he still had to go by Royston on his way north and, however briefly, again be a part of the mess at home.

Cobb was on his way to Detroit in earnest by Saturday night, the twenty-sixth, traveling at the Augusta club's expense. The trip of some 700 miles should have taken about thirty hours, but Cobb missed his connections in Atlanta and Cincinnati. Exhausted and bedraggled, he finally arrived about 10:30 P.M. on Tuesday after being en route from Augusta for something like four days. Carrying his Augusta uniform roll, a small grip, his little Spalding fielder's glove, and three bats in a cloth bag, he alighted from the train at the Michigan Central terminal in Detroit and looked around at "what for me was an unknown land." Nobody was there to meet him. Hiring a horse-drawn cab, he had the driver take him to a cheap hotel that turned out to contain a burlesque house, as well, near the Tiger ballpark. There he paid $10 in advance for a week's worth of room and board.

Meanwhile, notices about his purchase had appeared on the sports pages of the Detroit papers, giving sketchy facts about his background and indicating that his arrival was imminent. On August 27 the Detroit *Free Press* printed a photograph of Cobb in street clothes. It showed a thin-faced young man with a slightly hooked nose, somewhat jugged ears, small but intense blue-gray eyes, and a full head of finely textured, reddish-blond hair parted in the middle. Three days later Joe S. Jackson, chief baseball writer for the *Free Press*, remarked that all those on the Detroit team who had observed Cobb in the spring had been impressed by his speed and that Bill Byron thought he was one of the fastest men leaving the batter's box he'd ever seen. Noting that Cobb had led the Sally League in hitting, Jackson added, "He won't pile up anything like that in this league. . . . If he gets away with a .275 mark, he will be satisfying everybody." That same day Tyrus Raymond Cobb played in his first game in the major leagues. There would be 3,032 more.

After winning 103 games in 1980, his first (and only, it was to transpire) season as skipper of the Yankees, Dick Howser was eased out of the job in a highly uneasy news conference. Dave Anderson reported the "execution" with restraint and craft: "I've always been a believer in letting people hang themselves with their own words," he later wrote. Howser went on to manage the Kansas City Royals to the World Championship, and George Steinbrenner went on to further executions—at this writing George has since fired seven more Yankee managers.

DAVE ANDERSON

Sandwiches at an Execution

Near the door of George Steinbrenner's office in Yankee Stadium yesterday, there were two trays of bite-sized roast beef, turkey, and ham sandwiches, each with a toothpick in it. As soon as fourteen invited newsmen entered his office for the execution of Dick Howser as manager and the transfer of Gene Michael from general manager to dugout manager, the Yankees' principal owner looked around.

"Anybody want any sandwiches?" he asked. "We've got a lot of sandwiches here."

Gene Michael had piled four little roast beef sandwiches on a small plastic plate, and he had a cup of coffee. But as he sat against the far wall, under a huge Yankee top-hat insignia and several enlarged photos of memorable Yankee Stadium moments, he was the only one eating when Dick Howser suddenly appeared and walked quickly to a chair in front of the table with the sandwiches.

"Nobody wants a sandwich?" George Steinbrenner asked. "Nobody wants a drink?"

One of the newsmen ordered a glass of white wine from the bartender, but that was all. Then there was a momentary silence as George Steinbrenner, husky in a soft-blue shirt with a navy-blue-and-green-striped tie, sat at a big tan vinyl chair behind his shiny round desk. On the desk was a gold numeral one, maybe several inches high, and a small sign announcing, "Lead, Follow or Get the Hell Out of the Way," and a miniature brass ship's telegraph.

"During the season it's always pointed to full speed ahead," he would explain later. "But in the off-season it's on standby."

To the owner's right, about 10 feet away, Dick Howser sat stiffly. His legs crossed, he was wearing a beige shirt, a brown tie, brown pants, and brown cowboy boots. He was staring out away from George Steinbrenner, staring blankly at the white draperies that had been drawn across the huge window that overlooks the grassy geometry of the field where Dick Howser no longer would work. Most of the time he had his left index finger up against his left cheek, as if to keep from having to look at the Yankee owner, who now was discussing the managerial situation that had been simmering for several weeks.

"Dick has decided," George Steinbrenner began, "that he will not be returning to the Yankees as manager."

Dick has decided. That would be the premise of George Steinbrenner's explanation. Dick has decided. Ostensibly he suddenly decided to go into real estate development in Tallahassee, Florida, and be the supervisor of Yankee scouts in the Southeast after having been the manager for the Yankee team that won 103 games last season, after having been in baseball virtually all his life as a major-league infielder, major-league coach, college coach, and major-league manager of baseball's most famous franchise.

But baseball's most famous franchise also has baseball's most demanding owner. When the Yankees were swept in three games by the Kansas City Royals in the American League championship series, George Steinbrenner steamed. And now Dick Houser is in real estate and is a Yankee scouting supervisor.

"At no time," George Steinbrenner said yesterday, "did I lay down rules or commandments that Dick would have to live by if he returned as manager. The door was open for him to return, but he chose to accept this business opportunity. It took so long because he wanted to make sure he was doing the right thing."

All the while Dick Howser stared at the drawn draperies.

"But could Dick," somebody asked George Steinbrenner, "still be the manager if he wanted to be?"

"Yes."

"Dick, why don't you want to be here?"

"I have to be cautious here," Dick Howser said, staring straight ahead. "But the other thing popped up."

"Were you satisfied that you could have returned without conditions?"

"I'd rather not comment on that," Dick Howser said.

"If you had won the World Series instead of being eliminated in the playoffs," he was asked, "would you have taken this real-estate opportunity?"

"That's hard to say."

"Were you fired, Dick?"

"I'm not going to comment on that," the former manager said.

"I didn't fire the man," the owner said.

Maybe not, but it is reasonable to believe that George Steinbrenner suggested that Dick Howser look for employment elsewhere. That way George Steinbrenner could put Gene Michael, whom he considers a more combative manager, in the dugout. Perhaps to soothe his conscience, he disclosed yesterday that Dick Howser could be paid his reported $100,000 salary for each of the remaining two years on his three-year contract.

"I feel morally and contractually obligated to Dick and his wife, Nancy," the owner said. "I took him out of Florida State, where he was the baseball coach and where he could have stayed for life. If it hasn't worked out, maybe it's my fault."

If it hasn't worked out. Until then it had been "Dick had decided." But perhaps on a slip of the tongue it was "if it hasn't worked out." Anybody who knew George Steinbrenner knew that all along. And anybody who knew Dick Howser knew that, if given a choice, he would not decide to go into real-estate development rather than be the Yankees' manager.

But still George Steinbrenner persisted.

"I think it's safe to say," he said at one point yesterday, "that Dick Howser wants to be a Florida resident year round, right, Dick?"

Dick Howser didn't even answer that one.

Say this for Dick Howser—instead of going along with George Steinbrenner's party line yesterday, he declined to comment. By not answering questions, he answered them. Anybody could see that. And anybody could see through George Steinbrenner's scheme.

"What advice," Dick Howser was being asked now, "would you give Gene Michael?"

"To have a strong stomach," Dick Howser replied, smiling thinly, "and a nice contract."

Minutes later, the execution was over. Dick Howser got up quickly and walked out of the room without a smile. Behind his round desk, George Steinbrenner looked around.

"Nobody ate any sandwiches," the Yankee owner said.

This beautiful and now famous essay is the culmination of Angell's first baseball book, *The Summer Game* (1972). At the beginning of his baseball assignment for the *New Yorker*, Angell saw that he could not beat the beat reporters at their own game and so "would have to find some other aspect of the game to study," he wrote in the foreword to *The Summer Game*. "My main job, as I conceived it, was to continue to try to give the feel of things—to explain baseball as it happened to me, at a distance and in retrospect. And this was the real luck, for how could I have guessed then that baseball, of all team sports anywhere, should turn out to be so complex, so rich and various in structure and aesthetics and emotion, as to convince me, after ten years as a writer and forty years as a fan, that I have not yet come close to its heart?" Oh yes he has.

ROGER ANGELL

The Interior Stadium

Sports are too much with us. Late and soon, sitting and watching—mostly watching on television—we lay waste our powers of identification and enthusiasm and, in time, attention as more and more closing rallies and crucial putts and late field goals and final play-offs and sudden deaths and world records and world championships unreel themselves ceaselessly before our half-lidded eyes. Professional leagues expand like bubble gum, ever larger and thinner, and the extended sporting seasons, now bunching and overlapping at the ends, conclude in exhaustion and the wrong weather. So, too, goes the secondary business of sports—the news or nonnews off the fields. Sports announcers (ex-halfbacks in Mod hairdos) bring us another live, exclusive interview in depth with the twitchy coach of some as yet undefeated basketball team or with a weeping (for joy) fourteen-year-old champion female backstroker, and the sports pages, now almost the largest single part of the newspaper, brim with salary disputes, medical bulletins, franchise maneuverings, All-Star ballots, drug scandals, close-up biogs, after-dinner tributes, union tactics, weekend wrap-ups, wire-service polls, draft-choice trades, clubhouse gossip, and the latest odds. The American obsession with sports is not a new phenomenon, of course, except in its current dimensions, its excessive excessiveness. What *is* new, and what must at times unsettle even the most devout and unselective fan, is a curious sense of loss. In the midst of all these successive spectacles and instant replays and endless reportings and recapitulations, we seem to have forgotten what we came for. More and more, each sport resembles all sports;

the flavor, the special joys of place and season, the unique displays of courage and strength and style that once isolated each game and fixed it in our affections, have disappeared somewhere in the noise and crush.

Of all sports, none has been so buffeted about by this unselective proliferation, so maligned by contemporary cant, or so indifferently defended, as baseball. Yet the game somehow remains the same, obdurately unaltered and comparable only with itself. Baseball has one saving grace that distinguishes it—for me, at any rate—from every other sport. Because of its pace, and thus the perfectly observed balance, both physical and psychological, between opposing forces, its clean lines can be restored in retrospect. This inner game—baseball in the mind—has no season, but it is best played in the winter, without the distraction of other baseball news. At first, it is a game of recollections, recapturings, and visions. Figures and occasions return, enormous sounds rise and swell, and the interior stadium fills with light and yields up the sight of a young ballplayer—some hero perfectly memorized—just completing his own unique swing and now racing toward first. See the way he runs? Yes, that's him! Unmistakable, he leans in, still following the distant flight of the ball with his eyes, and takes his big turn at the base. Yet this is only the beginning, for baseball in the mind is not a mere returning. In time, this easy summoning up of restored players, winning hits, and famous rallies gives way to reconsiderations and reflections about the sport itself. By thinking about baseball like this—by playing it over, keeping it warm in a cold season—we begin to make discoveries. With luck, we may even penetrate some of its mysteries. One of those mysteries is its vividness—the absolutely distinct inner vision we retain of that hitter, that eager base runner, of however long ago. My father was talking the other day about some of the ballplayers he remembered. He grew up in Cleveland, and the Indians were his team. Still are. "We had Nap Lajoie at second," he said. "You've heard of him. A great big broad-shouldered fellow but a beautiful fielder. He was a rough customer. If he didn't like an umpire's call, he'd give him a faceful of tobacco juice. The shortstop was Terry Turner—a smaller man, and blond. I can still see Lajoie picking up a grounder and wheeling and floating the ball over to Turner. Oh, he was quick on his feet! In right field we had Elmer Flick, now in the Hall of Fame. I liked the center fielder, too. His name was Harry Bay, and he wasn't a heavy hitter, but he was very fast and covered a lot of ground. They said he could circle the bases in twelve seconds flat. I saw him get a home run inside the park—the ball hit on the infield and went right past the second baseman and out to the wall, and Bay beat the relay. I remember Addie Joss, our great right-hander. Tall, and an elegant pitcher. I once saw him pitch a perfect game. He died young."

My father has been a fan all his life, and he has pretty well seen them all. He has told me about the famous last game of the 1912 World Series, in Boston, and seeing Fred Snodgrass drop that fly ball in the tenth inning, when the Red Sox scored twice and beat the Giants. I looked up Harry Bay and those other Indians in the *Baseball Encyclopedia*, and I think my father must have seen that inside-the-park homer in the summer of 1904. Lajoie batted .376 that year, and Addie Joss led the American League with an earned run average of 1.59, but the Indians finished in fourth place. 1904. . . . Sixty-seven years have gone by, yet Nap Lajoie is in plain view, and the ball still floats over to Terry Turner. Well, my father is eighty-one now, and old men are great rememberers of the distant past. But I am fifty, and I can also bring things back: Lefty Gomez, skinny necked and frighteningly wild, pitching his first game at Yankee Stadium, against the White Sox and Red Faber in 1930. Old John McGraw, in a business suit and a white fedora, sitting lumpily in a dark corner of the dugout at the Polo Grounds and glowering out at the field. Babe Ruth, wearing a new, bright yellow glove, trotting out to right field—a swollen ballet dancer, with those delicate, almost feminine feet and ankles. Ruth at the plate, uppercutting and missing, staggering with the force of his swing. Ruth and Gehrig hitting back-to-back homers. Gehrig, in the summer of 1933, running bases with a bad leg in a key game against the Senators; hobbling, he rounds third, closely followed by young Dixie Walker, then a Yankee. The throw comes in to the plate, and the Washington catcher—it must have been Luke Sewell—tags out the sliding Gehrig and, in the same motion, the sliding Dixie Walker. A double play at the plate. The Yankees lost the game; the Senators go on to a pennant. And, back across the river again, Carl Hubbell. My own great pitcher, a southpaw, tall and elegant. Hub pitching: the loose motion; two slow, formal bows from the waist, glove and hands held almost in front of his face as he pivots, the long right leg (in long, peculiar pants) striding; and the ball, angling oddly, shooting past the batter. Hubbell walks gravely back to the bench, his pitching arm, as always, turned the wrong way round, with the palm out. Screwballer.

Any fan, as I say, can play this private game, extending it to extraordinary varieties and possibilities in his mind. Ruth bats against Sandy Koufax or Sam McDowell. . . . Hubbell pitches to Ted Williams, and the Kid, grinding the bat in his fists, twitches and blocks his hips with the pitch; he holds off but still follows the ball, leaning over and studying it like some curator as it leaps in just under his hands. Why this vividness, even from an imaginary confrontation? I have watched many other sports, and I have followed some—football, hockey, tennis—with eagerness, but none of them yields these permanent interior pictures, these ancient and precise excitements. Baseball, I must conclude, is intensely remembered because only baseball is so intensely watched. The game forces intensity upon us. In the ballpark, scattered across an immense green, each player is isolated in our attention, utterly visible. Watch that fielder just below us. Little seems to be expected of him. He waits in easy composure, his hands on his knees; when the ball at last soars or bounces out to him, he seizes it and dispatches it with swift, haughty ease. It all looks easy, slow, and, above all, safe. Yet we know better, for what is certain in baseball is that someone, perhaps several people, will fail. They will be searched out, caught in the open, and defeated, and there will be no confusion about it or sharing of the blame. This is sure to happen, because what baseball requires of its athletes, of course, is nothing less than perfection, and perfection cannot be eased or divided. Every movement of every game, from first pitch to last out, is measured and recorded against an absolute standard, and thus each success is also a failure. Credit that strikeout to the pitcher but also count it against the batter's average; mark this run unearned, because the left fielder bobbled the ball for an instant and a runner moved up. Yet, faced with this sudden and repeated presence of danger, the big-league player defends himself with such courage and skill that the illusion of safety is sustained. Tension is screwed tighter and tighter as the certain downfall is postponed again and again, so that when disaster does come—a half-topped infield hit, a walk on a close three-and-two call, a low drive up the middle that just eludes the diving short-stop—we rise and cry out. It is a spontaneous, inevitable, irresistible reaction.

Televised baseball, I must add, does not seem capable of transmitting this emotion. Most baseball is seen on the tube now, and it is presented faithfully and with great technical skill. But the medium is irrevocably two-dimensional; even with several cameras, television cannot bring us the essential distances of the game—the simultaneous flight of a batted ball and its pursuit by the racing, straining outfielders, the swift convergence of runner and ball at a base. Foreshortened on our screen, the players on the field appear to be squashed together, almost touching each other, and, watching them, we lose the sense of their separateness and lonesome waiting.

This is a difficult game. It is so demanding that the best teams and the weakest teams can meet on almost even terms, with no assurance about the result of any one game. In March 1962, in St. Petersburg, the World Champion Yankees played for the first time against the newborn New York Mets—one of the worst teams of all time—in a game that each badly wanted to win; the winner, to nobody's real surprise, was the Mets. In 1970, the World Champion Orioles won 108 games and lost 54; the lowest cellar team, the White Sox, won 56 games and lost 106. This looks like an enormous disparity, but what it truly means is that the Orioles managed to win two out of every three games they played, while the White Sox won one out of every three. That third game made the difference—and a kind of difference that can be appreciated when one notes that the winning margin given up by the White Sox to all their opponents during the season averaged 1.1 runs per game. Team form is harder to establish in baseball than in any other sport, and the 162-game season not uncommonly comes down to October with two or three teams locked together at the top of the standings on the final weekend. Each inning of baseball's slow, searching time span, each game of its long season is essential to the disclosure of its truth.

Form is the imposition of a regular pattern upon varying and unpredictable circumstances, but the patterns of baseball, for all the game's tautness and neatness, are never regular. Who can predict the winner and shape of today's game? Will it be a brisk, neat two-hour shutout? A languid, error-filled 12–3 laugher? A riveting three-hour, fourteen-inning deadlock? What other sport produces these manic swings? For the players, too, form often undergoes ter-rible reversals; in no other sport is a champion athlete so often humiliated or a journeyman so easily exalted. The surprise, the upset, the total turnabout of expectations and reputations—these are delightful commonplaces of baseball. Al Gionfriddo, a part-time Dodger outfielder, stole second base in the ninth inning of the fourth game of the 1947 World Series to help set up Lavagetto's game-winning double (and the only Dodger hit of the game) off the Yankees' Bill Bevens. Two days later, Gionfriddo robbed Joe DiMaggio with a famous game-saving catch of a 415-foot drive in deepest left field at Yankee Stadium. Gionfriddo never made it back to the big leagues after that season. Another irregular, the Mets' Al Weis, homered in the fifth and last game of the 1969 World Series, tying up the game that the Mets won in the next inning; it was Weis's third homer of the year and his first ever at Shea Stadium. And so forth. Who remembers the second game of the 1956 World Series—an appallingly bad afternoon of baseball in which the Yankees' starter, Don Larsen, was yanked after giving up a single and four walks in less than two innings? It was Larsen's *next* start, the fifth game, when he pitched his perfect game.

There is always a heavy splash of luck in these reversals. Luck, indeed, plays an almost predictable part in the game; we have all seen the enormous enemy clout into the bleachers that just hooks foul at the last instant and the half-checked swing that produces a game-winning blooper over second. Everyone complains about baseball luck, but I think it adds something to the game that is nearly essential. Without it, such a rigorous and unforgiving pastime would be almost too painful to enjoy.

No one, it becomes clear, can conquer this impossible and unpredictable game. Yet every player tries, and now and again—very rarely—we see a man who seems to have met all the demands, challenged all the implacable averages, spurned the mere luck. He has defied baseball, even altered it, and for a time at least the game is truly his. One thinks of Willie Mays, in the best of his youth, batting at the Polo Grounds, his whole body seeming to leap at the ball as he swings in an explosion of exuberance. Or Mays in center field, playing in so close that he appears at times to be watching the game from over the second baseman's shoulder, and then that same joyful leap as he takes off after a long, deep drive and runs it down, running so hard and so far that the ball itself seems to stop in the air and wait for him. One thinks of Jackie Robinson in a close game—any close game—playing the infield and glaring in at the enemy hitter, hating him and daring him, refusing to be beaten. And Sandy Koufax pitching in the last summers before he was disabled, in that time when he pitched a no-hitter every year for four years. Kicking swiftly, hiding the ball until the last instant, Koufax throws in a blur of motion, coming over the top, and the fastball, appearing suddenly in the strike zone, sometimes jumps up so immoderately that his catcher has to take it with his glove shooting upward, like an infielder stabbing at a bad-hop grounder. I remember some batter taking a strike like that and then stepping out of the box and staring back at the pitcher with a look of utter incredulity—as if Koufax had just thrown an Easter egg past him.

Joe DiMaggio batting sometimes gave the same impression—the suggestion that the old rules and dimensions of baseball no longer applied to him and that the game had at last grown unfairly easy. I saw DiMaggio once during his famous hitting streak in 1941; I'm not sure of the other team or the pitcher—perhaps it was the Tigers and Bobo Newsom—but I'm sure of DiMaggio pulling a line shot to left that collided preposterously with the bag at third base and ricocheted halfway out to center field. That record of hitting safely in fifty-six straight games seems as secure as any in baseball, but it does not awe me as much as the fact that DiMadge's old teammates claim they *never* saw him commit an error of judgment in a ball game. Thirteen years and never a wrong throw, a cutoff man missed, an extra base passed up. Well, there was one time when he stretched a single against the Red Sox and was called out at second, but the umpire is said to have admitted later that he blew the call.

And one more for the pantheon: Carl Yastrzemski. To be precise, Yaz in September of the 1967 season, as his team, the Red Sox, fought and clawed against the White Sox and the Twins and the Tigers in the last two weeks of the closest and most vivid pennant race of our time. The presiding memory of that late summer is of Yastrzemski approaching the plate, once again in a situation where all hope rests on him, and settling himself in the batter's box—touching his helmet, tugging at his belt, and just touching the tip of the bat to the ground, in precisely the same set of gestures—and then, in a storm of noise and pleading, swinging violently and perfectly . . . and hitting. In the last two weeks of that season, Yaz batted .522—twenty-three hits for forty-four appearances: four doubles, five home runs, sixteen runs batted in (RBIs). In the final two games, against the Twins, both of which the Red Sox *had* to win for the pennant, he went seven for eight, won the first game with a homer, and saved the second with a brilliant, rally-killing throw to second base from deep left field. (He cooled off a little in the World Series, batting only .400 for seven games and hitting three homers.) Since then, the game and the averages have caught up with Yastrzemski, and he has never again approached that kind of performance. But then, of course, neither has anyone else.

Only baseball, with its statistics and isolated fragments of time, permits so precise a reconstruction from box score and memory. Take another date—October 7, 1968, at Detroit, the fifth game of the World Series. The fans are here, and an immense noise—a cheerful, 53,634-man vociferosity—utterly fills the green, steep, high-walled box of Tiger Stadium. This is a good baseball town, and the cries have an anxious edge, for the Tigers are facing almost sure extinction. They trail the Cardinals by three games to one, and never for a moment have they looked the equal of these defending World Champions. Denny McLain, the Tigers' thirty-one-game winner, was humiliated in the opener by the Cardinals' Bob Gibson, who set an all-time Series record by striking out seventeen Detroit batters. The Tigers came back the next day, winning rather easily behind their capable left-hander Mickey Lolich, but the Cardinals demolished them in the next two games, scoring a total of seventeen runs and again brushing McLain aside; Gibson has now struck out twenty-seven Tigers, and he will be ready to pitch again in the Series if needed. Even more disheartening is Lou Brock, the Cards' left fielder, who has already lashed out eight hits in the first four games and has stolen seven bases in eight tries; Bill Freehan, the Tigers' catcher, has a sore arm. And here, in the very top of the first, Brock leads off against Lolich and doubles to left; a moment later, Curt Flood singles, and Orlando Cepeda homers into the left-field stands. The Tigers are down 3–0, and the fans are wholly stilled.

In the third inning, Brock leads off with another hit—a single—and there is a bitter overtone to the hometown cheers when Freehan, on a pitchout, at last throws him out, stealing, at second. There is no way for anyone to know, of course, that this is a profound omen; Brock has done his last damage to the Tigers in this Series. Now it is the fourth, and hope and shouting return. Mickey Stanley leads off the Detroit half with a triple that lands, 2 inches fair, in the right-field corner. He scores on a fly. Willie Horton also triples. With two out, Jim Northrup smashes a hard grounder directly at the Cardinal second baseman, Javier, and at the last instant the ball strikes something on the infield and leaps up and over Javier's head, and Horton scores. Luck! Luck twice over, if you remember how close Stanley's drive came to falling foul. But never mind; it's 3–2 now, and a game again.

But Brock is up, leading off once again, and an instant later he has driven a Lolich pitch off the left-field wall for a double. Now Javier singles to left, and Brock streaks around third base toward home. Bill Freehan braces himself in front of the plate, waiting for the throw; he has had a miserable Series, going hitless in fourteen at bats so far and undergoing those repeated humiliations by the man who is now racing at him full speed—the man who must surely be counted, along with Gibson, as the Series hero. The throw comes in chest high on the fly from Willie Horton in left; ball and base runner arrive together; Brock does not slide. Brock does not slide, and his left foot, just descending on the plate, is banged away as he collides with Freehan. Umpire Doug Harvey shoots up his fist: out! It is a great play. Nothing has changed, the score is still 3–2, but everything has changed; something has shifted irrevocably in this game.

In the seventh inning, with one out and the Tigers still one run shy, Tiger manager Mayo Smith allows Lolich to bat for himself. Mickey Lolich has hit .114 for the season, and Smith has a pinch hitter on the bench named Gates Brown, who hit .370. But Lolich got two hits in his other Series start, including the first homer of his ten years in baseball. Mayo, sensing something that he will not be able to defend later if he is wrong, lets Lolich bat for himself, and Mickey pops a foolish little fly to right that falls in for a single. Now there is another single. A walk loads the bases, and Al Kaline comes to the plate. The noise in the stadium is insupportable. Kaline singles, and the Tigers go ahead by a run. Norm Cash drives in another. The Tigers win this searching, turned-about, lucky, marvelous game by 5–3.

Two days later, back in St. Louis, form shows its other face as the Tigers rack up ten runs in the third inning and win by 13–1. McLain at last has his Series win. So it is Lolich against Gibson in the finale, of course. Nothing happens. Inning after inning goes by, zeros accumulate on the scoreboard, and anxiety and silence lengthen like shadows. In the sixth, Lou Brock singles. Daring Lolich, daring the Tiger infielders' nerves, openly forcing his luck, hoping perhaps to settle these enormous tensions and difficulties with one more act of bravado, he takes an excessive lead off first, draws the throw from Lolich, breaks for second, and is erased, just barely, by Cash's throw. A bit later, Curt Flood singles, and, weirdly, he, too, is picked off first and caught in a rundown. Still no score. Gibson and Lolich, both exhausted, pitch on. With two out in the seventh, Cash singles for the Tigers' second hit of the day. Horton is safe on a slow bouncer that *just* gets through the left side of the infield. Jim Northrup hits the next pitch deep and high but straight at Flood, who is the best center fielder in the National League. Flood starts in and then halts, stopping so quickly that his spikes churn up a green flap of turf; he turns and races back madly, but the ball sails over his head for a triple. Disaster. Suddenly, irreversibly, it has happened. Two runs are in, Freehan doubles in another, and, two innings later, the Tigers are Champions of the World.

I think I will always remember those two games—the fifth and the seventh—perfectly. And I remember something else about the 1968 Series when it was over—a feeling that almost everyone seemed to share: that Bob Gibson had not lost that last game and the Cardinals had not lost the Series. Certainly no one wanted to say that the Tigers had not won it, but there seemed to be something more that remained to be said. It was something about the levels and demands of the sport we had seen—as if the baseball itself had somehow surpassed the players and the results. It was the baseball that won.

Always, it seems, there is something more to be discovered about this game. Sit quietly in the upper stand and look at the field. Half close your eyes against the sun so that the players recede a little and watch the movements of baseball. The pitcher, immobile on the mound, holds the inert white ball, his little lump of physics. Now, with abrupt gestures, he gives it enormous speed and direction, converting it suddenly into a line, a moving line. The batter, wielding a plane, attempts to intercept the line and acutely alter it, but he fails; the ball, a line again, is redrawn to the pitcher, in the center of this square, the diamond. Again the pitcher studies his task—the projection of his next line through the smallest possible segment of an invisible seven-sided solid (the strike zone has depth as well as height and width) 60 feet and 6 inches away; again the batter considers his even more difficult proposition, which is to reverse this imminent white speck, to redirect its energy not in a soft parabola or a series of diminishing squiggles but into a beautiful and dangerous new force, of perfect straightness and immense distance. In time, these and other lines are drawn on the field; the batter and the fielders are also transformed into fluidity, moving and converging, and we see now that all movement in baseball is a convergence toward fixed points—the pitched ball toward the plate, the thrown ball toward the right angles of the bases, the batted ball toward the as yet undrawn but already visible point of congruence with either the ground or a glove. Simultaneously, the fielders hasten toward that same point of meeting with the ball, and both the base runner and the ball, now redirected, toward their encounter at the base. From our perch, we can sometimes see three or four or more such geometries appearing at the same instant on the green board below us and, mathematicians that we are, can sense their solution even before they are fully drawn. It is neat, it is pretty, it is satisfying. Scientists speak of the profoundly moving aesthetic beauty of mathematics, and perhaps the baseball field is one of the few places where the rest of us can glimpse this mystery.

The last dimension is time. Within the ballpark, time moves differently, marked by no clock except the events of the game. This is the unique, unchangeable feature of baseball and perhaps explains why this sport, for all the enormous changes it has undergone in the past decade or two, remains somehow rustic, unviolent, and introspective. Baseball's time is seamless and invisible, a bubble within which players move at exactly the same pace and rhythms as all their predecessors. This is the way the game was played in our youth and in our fathers' youth, and even back then—back in the country days—there must have been the same feeling that time could be stopped. Since baseball time is measured only in outs, all you have to do is succeed utterly; keep hitting, keep the rally alive, and you have defeated time. You remain forever young. Sitting in the stands, we sense this, if only dimly. The players below us—Mays, DiMaggio, Ruth, Snodgrass—swim and blur in memory, the ball floats over to Terry Turner, and the end of this game may never come.

Much of baseball's appeal is its apparent permanence, its resistance to the change that swirls about the rest of society. But even though the game seems to stop time and time seems to have forgotten baseball (it really isn't all that much different from the game played in 1893), change has indeed stealthily worked its mischief. Marty Appel was not asleep at the typewriter, however, and adds these updates: first "compensation player," Joel Skinner, going from Pittsburgh to Chicago for the loss of White Sox free agent Ed Farmer; first to turn down a million-dollar annual contract, Johnny Bench, who chose to retire after the 1983 season; and first teams to use computers extensively to chart the opposition, the White Sox and A's of 1983.

MARTY APPEL

Noting the Milestones

Ralph Darwin Miller of Cincinnati died on May 8, 1973, at the age of 100 years, 54 days. Few if any baseball people noted the death other than to observe that Ralph had pitched for Brooklyn and Baltimore in 1898 and 1899 with a 6–16 record.

What should have been noted was the passing of two milestones—Miller was the last nineteenth-century major leaguer and also the only major leaguer (out of some 12,000) to live to see his 100th birthday.

It's not surprising, of course, that these things should have passed unnoticed. So much happens each day in baseball, so many statistical milestones are approached or reached, that it becomes an impossible task to properly log everything.

For example, when Hank Aaron retired after the 1976 season, did anyone note that he was the last player to arrive in the majors from the old Negro Leagues? He had played in the Negro American League in 1952.

And what honor awaits Tony Perez or Bert Campaneris? One of them (or perhaps Luis Tiant with a recall) will be the last Cuban player in the majors, signed before such immigration was halted. *

Has anyone noted that Tug McGraw is the last major leaguer still active to have played for Casey Stengel?

Again, history sails before us all the time, but we don't always have the

---

* It turned out to be Perez, in 1986.

wisdom to jot it down. Some of the achievements in baseball's modern, or post–World War II, era have been in the appearance of the game, such as tight uniforms, instant replays, or batting helmets, while others have been individual achievements.

Ron Blomberg was baseball's first official designated hitter, stepping up to the plate for the New York Yankees in Fenway Park on April 6, 1973. But in 1978 Blomberg became the first player with a guaranteed, multiyear contract to be released and paid in full when the White Sox made such a decision. They were not the first club to have to make such a difficult financial choice.

The game-winning RBI became an official baseball statistic in 1980, and the very first one was recorded by Cincinnati's George Foster on April 9. He was an appropriate choice for the distinction, having led the National League in RBIs three times.

The "save rule" for relief pitchers became an official baseball statistic in 1969, and the first save was recorded by Los Angeles's Bill Singer on April 7 against the Reds.

The first player in the major leagues born in the 1950s was John Mayberry (born February 18, 1950), who debuted with Houston in 1968. The first player born in the 1960s was Tim Conroy (born April 3, 1960), who pitched for Oakland in 1978.

The last Brooklyn Dodger to remain active in the majors was Don Drysdale, who retired in 1969, twelve years after the club's final year in Brooklyn. The last New York Giant was Willie Mays, who concluded his career with the 1973 New York Mets.

The World Series itself has of course been full of subtle "firsts" and milestones in modern times, many unnoticed or unappreciated at the time.

For example, if you accept the fact that the Dodgers left behind many loyal New York (and Brooklyn) fans when they and the Giants moved West in 1958, one can review the yearly World Series between 1949 and 1966 to find that New Yorkers had a "stake" in the Series for eighteen consecutive years, between the Yankees, Giants, and Dodgers. It was uninterrupted until the St. Louis-Boston Series of 1967.

The Dodgers pennant in 1959 brought about the first World Series games on the West Coast, but it wasn't until 1974 (Los Angeles vs. Oakland) that the entire Series was played in the Pacific Time Zone.

The first World Series game to be played on artificial turf was in 1970 at Cincinnati; the first all-artificial turf Series was last year's Kansas City-Philadelphia one.

The Royals-Phillies matchup also produced the first Series in which both managers were rookies and the first in modern times in which both teams were seeking a first World Championship.

The Royals were the first American League expansion team to make it to the World Series, but the New York Mets of the National League got there first—in 1969, and again in 1973, winning it all in '69 against Baltimore.

When Ken Brett pitched for Boston in the 1967 World Series, he became the first teenager to take the mound in the Fall Classic in history, being only nineteen at the time. The first teenager to appear at a position other than pitcher goes all the way back to Fred Lindstrom of the Giants, who hadn't yet reached his nineteenth birthday in 1924.

Did you know that it wasn't until 1947 that anyone hit a pinch-hit homer in a World Series game? It was the Yankees' Yogi Berra, hitting for Sherm Lollar who accomplished it. And a year later, 1948, marked the last appearance to date of a playing manager in a World Series, when Lou Boudreau led the Cleveland Indians against the Braves.

The first World Series in which six umpires were used came in 1947 and gave the National League's George Magerkurth and the American League's Jim Boyer the distinction of being the first "foul-line" umpires in history.

Eddie Mathews, with the 1968 Tigers, was the last Boston Brave, while Phil Niekro, still active with Atlanta, is the last remaining Milwaukee Brave. Boston moved to Milwaukee in 1953, and Milwaukee moved to Atlanta in 1966.

The last St. Louis Brown was pitcher Don Larsen, whose major league career ended in 1967, fourteen years after the Browns moved to Baltimore to become the Orioles. The last Philadelphia Athletic was fancy-fielding Vic Power, who retired following the 1965 season, eleven years after Philadelphia moved to Kansas City. There is one remaining Kansas City Athletic in the majors— Reggie Jackson.

The "old" Washington Senators moved to Minnesota in 1961, and Jim Kaat, still pitching in 1981, was with them. The "new Senators," who existed from 1961 to 1971, had five still-active major leaguers in 1981—Toby Harrah, Del Unser, Len Randle, Jeff Burroughs, Larry Bittner, and Bill Fahey. (All are gone.)

The Seattle Pilots played for only one season—1969—before moving to Milwaukee. The last Seattle Pilot still playing in 1981 was Oakland infielder Fred Stanley, although Lou Piniella of the Yankees spent spring training of 1969 with the Pilots.

Two modern clubs underwent name changes in the 1960s. The Los Angeles Angels adopted California, and the last of the L.A. Angels was Jim Fregosi, who retired in 1978 to manage his old club. And who will be the last man to have worn the uniform of the Houston Colt .45s, prior to their becoming the Astros? Will it be Rusty Staub, Joe Morgan, or Jerry Grote, all active in 1981?

Ballparks have certainly undergone changes over the years, most dramatically with the introduction of indoor baseball through the construction of the Astrodome in Houston, which opened in 1965. That brought about the need for the first artificial turf, and a year later it was installed in the Astrodome following lengthy tests. Chem Strand, a division of Monsanto, designed the product, and it lasted twelve seasons before a new carpet was necessary.

It was Riverfront Stadium in Cincinnati that introduced cutout sliding areas around the bases on June 30, 1970, rather than a full dirt infield.

Dodger Stadium, opened in 1962, was the first to have different-colored seats in each section and the first to have an organist excite the crowd with a call of "CHARGE!" Dodger fans also brought a relaxed, casual style of dress to the ballpark, following an era when suit, tie, and hat were the norm for male fans.

Shea Stadium in New York was the first to do away with light towers in favor of rows of lights along the roof of the upper deck. The year was 1964.

The Giants, at Candlestick Park, were the first to have a so-called dugout at field level rather than dug out below the ground. It was Riverfront Stadium that first measured fence distances in meters and the Kingdome in Seattle that took it one better, measuring the distances in fathoms, in keeping with its nautical theme.

The first message board in a stadium was built by the Yankees in 1959 in the old Yankee Stadium, a simple board eight lines high, eight spaces wide. A year later, Bill Veeck introduced his exploding scoreboard in Comiskey Park, Chicago.

The Astrodome, in 1965, brought animation in lights to scoreboard art, opening the gates for complex message boards. The first instant-replay boards in baseball came along in 1976, in the new Yankee Stadium and in ol' Fenway Park.

The sight of banners parading through the stands were popularized by the "New Breed" of fans in New York's Polo Grounds, when the Mets played there in 1962–63.

Players used to leave their gloves on the field when they were at bat—even in fair territory—but that was outlawed in 1953. Many clubs used to have a dirt path between home plate and the pitcher's mound, but by the early 1950s, that had been eliminated for good, mostly for aesthetics.

The introduction of new teams in the 1960s and 1970s created the opportunity to recognize "firsts," such as the first player to belong to each team's major-league roster. The honorees, not necessarily products of the selection draft, were:

Los Angeles Angels—Eli Grba
Washington Senators—John Gabler
New York Mets—Hobie Landrith
Houston Colt 45s—Ed Bressoud
San Diego Padres—Ollie Brown
Seattle Pilots—Marv Staehle
Kansas City Royals—Roger Nelson
Montreal Expos—Manny Mota
Seattle Mariners—Dave Johnson
Toronto Blue Jays—Phil Roof

Charles O. Finley's Kansas City Athletics brought some changes to baseball style in the 1960s. First came the green-and-gold uniforms of 1963, ending the exclusivity of white at home, gray on the road. In 1965, the manager (Mel McGaha) and his coaches wore white caps to distinguish them from the players. In 1967 came white shoes for the entire team. And to proper color coordinate it all, of course, came green shin guards and chest protectors for the A's catchers.

Tight uniforms originated in 1960, when Willie Mays of the Giants had a tailor go to work on his. That started a trend still in use today, although, interestingly, the 1981 Texas Rangers loosened theirs up a bit to accommodate the high temperatures in Arlington.

The orlon-wool-blend uniforms, better known as "flannels," became history in 1973 when the Yankees and Giants, the last holdouts, moved to knit material. The first to don the new look was the Pittsburgh Pirates, on the day they moved into Three Rivers Stadium—July 16, 1970. And it was the Pirates—in 1976–who introduced and retained the old-fashioned square baseball caps.

Names on the uniform backs date back to 1960, when the White Sox introduced them, with the Z in Kluszewski backwards to guarantee photo coverage. Bill Veeck was running the White Sox.

Fans have always had a high interest in uniform numbers, so the wearing of 00 by Paul Dade of Cleveland in 1977 should get a place in history, as well as the 0 by Al Oliver of Texas the following year. And while Carlton Fisk's 72 is one of the highest numbers worn in many years, it's not a record. Bill Voiselle wore 96 during his National League pitching career of 1942–50.

And how about the last pitcher to wear a single-digit number? It was Dooley Womack of the Oakland A's in 1970, who wore number 3.

Even umpires have looked different with the passage of time. American League umpires went to gray pants in 1967 and two years later were permitted to work without ties and jackets on unusually hot days. In 1971, they received red blazers, but by 1980 the leagues standardized, and once again the "men in blue" were truly in blue.

Soon we will witness the last umpire to wear an outside chest protector, and it will be either Bill Haller, Marty Springstead, Russ Goetz, George Maloney, or Bill Kunkel, the last American League umpires employing them.[*]

Johnny Bench altered the catcher's chest protector by having one made that fastened at the neck and waist rather than forming a strap down the back. Steve Yaeger of Los Angeles introduced the flap on the mask to protect the neck after he'd been hit by a flying bat. The year of his gift to baseball equipment was 1977.

In 1958, Baltimore manager Paul Richards designed an oversize catcher's mitt for Gus Triandos to work with knuckleball pitcher Hoyt Wilhelm, a concept still used today. A six-fingered fielder's glove was used by third baseman Ken Boyer of St. Louis in 1962.

"Hawk" Harrelson brought a lot of cosmetic changes to baseball. He popularized the use of a batting glove in 1964 following a day of golf and resulting raw hands. (The glove was first introduced by golf pro Danny Lawler in 1949, when he gave one to Bobby Thomson, but it was in vogue only for batting practice and spring training before Harrelson.)

The Hawk also popularized wrist bands, lamp black under the eyes, and high

---

[*] It turned out to be Jerry Neudecker, in 1985.

stirrups, although San Francisco's Tito Fuentes was pulling the sock high around the same time.

Long hair seemed to become popular with Harrelson while other players were still in crew cuts. Reggie Jackson brought mustaches and beards into vogue with Oakland in 1972. After he grew his mustache, Charlie Finley offered any teammate who grew one a $300 bonus. By the '72 World Series—which the scruffy-looking A's won—nineteen of their twenty-five players had them.

Joe Pepitone used a hair dryer in 1968 amid much publicity, but eight years later, when the new Yankee Stadium opened, every locker had an electrical outlet to accommodate one.

Branch Rickey's own company, American Baseball Cap, brought helmets into use. Phil Rizzuto was the first player to wear one, dating back to 1951, but the following year, on September 15, the entire Pittsburgh Pirate team wore them both at bat and in the field.

The last player to wear only a hard liner in his regular cap was Boston's Bob Montgomery, who retired in 1979. Now every player wears the helmet, most of them with earflaps.

It was Brooks Robinson who first wore the earflap for added protection, and Brooks also had half the bill of his helmet removed for greater visibility.

Even bats have changed in appearance. In 1969, Frank Torre of Adirondack suggested that a 1-inch stripe be painted around the center of the bat so that his company's product might be better identified. In 1975, Hillerich and Bradsby, makers of Louisville Sluggers, turned out a black bat for Pat Kelly of the White Sox, duplicating a style used by Rogers Hornsby and others in the 1920s and 1930s. In 1981, Pete Rose used a rose-colored bat made by Mizuno, and Dave Winfield used a blue bat made by Adirondack, but both limited use to batting practice.

The cup-ended or hollowed-out bats were first introduced in Japan and admired there by Lou Brock. Jose Cardenal of the 1976 Cubs was the first American player to have his Louisville Sluggers so designed, feeling that it put more weight into the "meat" of the bat.

The "tape-measure home run" was born on April 17, 1953, when Mickey Mantle powered one 565 feet in Washington and Yankee public relations director Red Patterson actually borrowed a tape measure to count it off.

The baseballs themselves were made of horsehide until 1974, when Spalding switched to the more available cowhide, and in 1976, the Rawlings name first appeared on major-league baseballs.

Bat Day, the most popular of baseball's gift days, was originated by Rudie Schaffer, Bill Veeck's deputy in Chicago.

Old-Timers' Days were made annual events in 1947 by the New York Yankees' Larry McPhail.

The weighted "doughnut" used by hitters in the on-deck circle was invented in 1968 by Elston Howard, then with the Red Sox.

The last playing manager was Don Kessinger of the White Sox in 1979.

The first night All-Star Game was played in July 11, 1967 in Anaheim. The first Championship Series was played in 1969 after four divisions were created for baseball.

Instant Replay, now so commonly accepted, was first used at a local level, when WPIX-TV in New York replayed the ruin of a no-hitter on July 17, 1959, with announcer Mel Allen asking director Jack Murphy to run the tape right there rather than wait for the postgame show. It showed Ralph Terry's no-hitter go down the drain as a base hit by Chicago's Jim McAhany fell in front of Norm Siebern in the ninth inning.

The first color telecast was on August 11, 1951, with Brooklyn hosting Boston for a doubleheader in Ebbets Field, carried by NBC.

The first woman baseball announcer on a regular basis was Mary Shane with the 1977 White Sox.

The first black player was, of course, Hall of Famer Jackie Robinson, who broke in with Brooklyn in 1947.* There are other firsts worth noting along the way, as well—the first black coach, Jim Gilliam of Los Angeles in 1965, for example. The first black umpire was the American League's Emmett Ashford in 1966. The first black manager was Cleveland's Frank Robinson in 1975. The first black general manager was Atlanta's Bill Lucas in 1977.

An all-black lineup appeared for the Pittsburgh Pirates on September 1, 1971, with Al Oliver at first, Rennie Stennett at second, Jackie Hernandez at short, Dave Cash at third, an outfield of Willie Stargell, Gene Clines, and Roberto Clemente, Manny Sanguillen catching, and Dock Ellis pitching.

The Baltimore Orioles introduced a base sweeper named Linda Warehime in 1969, and Oakland introduced ball girls down the foul lines in 1971.

Players like to make "curtain calls" after dramatic home runs these days, but that all started in 1961 after two of the most dramatic home runs in baseball history—Roger Maris's sixtieth and sixty-first, both at Yankee Stadium. On both occasions, teammates forced the shy Maris to step out of the dugout to acknowledge the fans' cheers.

The first $100,000 "bonus baby" was pitcher Paul Pettit, who signed with the Pirates in 1950 and who wound up with one major-league victory.

The first free-agent draft was conducted in June 1965, and Rick Monday, taken by the Kansas City Athletics, was the first player selected. The first player selected in the first reentry draft (1976) was Reggie Jackson (by Montreal), but the first to sign out of that draft was Bill Campbell with Boston.

The first player to exercise the "10 and 5 Rule," stopping his own trade thanks to length of service with one club, was Ron Santo of the Cubs.

We'll probably see the first computer in a dugout before long or the first team to play in T-shirts and no caps or the first stadium to bring relief pitchers in by helicopter, as we head for the twenty-first century. But let's all vow to pay just a bit more attention to the "historic happenings," as they occur, lest they get lost in the dust of the ever-changing scene of baseball's history.

* In this century, that is. See the essay "Out at Home," below, by Jerry Malloy.

Joe DiMaggio as Ponce DeLeon? With a Mister Coffee as the Fountain of Youth? Why not—baseball makes the old young with its magical mix of echo and revelation. The cryogenic power of nostalgia freeze-dries both idyll and idol, perhaps unfairly: maybe DiMaggio doesn't like being trapped in Baker's 1936, or his own. This charming piece ran in the New York *Times* on December 1, 1984.

RUSSELL BAKER

Idylls of the Kid

Joe DiMaggio is seventy. His birthday was last Sunday. The papers made nothing of it and I would not have been aware of it if we hadn't seen him Tuesday night doing his Mister Coffee commercial on television. "Joe DiMaggio is old," Harry said.

"Joe DiMaggio can never be old," I said. This is true in a very important unfactual sense. Joe DiMaggio inhabits a world in which I am always eleven years old. In it I always wear corduroy knickers and brown knee-length stockings held up by rubber bands and move around on roller skates. There is a Philco radio in the parlor. Inside is the voice of Franklin D. Roosevelt.

"That hair is gray," Harry said.

"Joe looks terrific, Harry."

He did, too. The commercial he was doing, of course, was in color. That was all wrong. Joe DiMaggio looks truly natural only in black and white. This is because when I see him he is always nineteen or twenty or some age like that, much older than I on my roller skates but not really old as Carl Hubbell, say, is old.

Hubbell pitches for the New York Giants. So we are talking, obviously, about the age of black and white, and neither Hubbell, who seems old but oh so magically unbeatable with his fabulous screwball, nor DiMaggio, who seems young and gawky, can exist in the age of color.

I see them always where they belong, motionless yet mysteriously and beautifully fluid in grainy black-and-white newspaper pictures on the sports pages of the *Journal American* and the *Daily Mirror*, the papers built for kids, with plenty of comics, full coverage of the electrocutions at Sing Sing, and great action still photos of great achievers, the old great Hubbell, the young great DiMaggio.

"Harry," I said, "Joe DiMaggio cannot be seen authentically on color television. Or on television at all, for that matter. No wonder you think he's old. Did you ever see DiMaggio play on television?"

I certainly never did. A few times I may have seen him swing the bat in one of the grainy black-and-white newsreels accompanying the double-feature bill at the Capitol or Horn movie theaters. This is probably why I often associate Joe DiMaggio with skating up to the Horn to see a Charlie Chan and a Laurel and Hardy.

"Snap out of it," Harry said. "Nobody has seen a Charlie Chan and a Laurel and Hardy on a double bill since Mussolini was in his prime."

"And those were the real Charlie Chans starring Warner Oland," I said, "not the decadent later Charlie Chans with Sidney Toler."

"The truth is," said Harry, "that you, just like me, never saw DiMaggio play anywhere except in a newsreel, so don't give me that malarkey about Joe's gracefulness being too pure to be appreciated by today's ignorant TV audiences."

Harry is a good man, but there is no poetry in him. He is a believer in facts. It has never occurred to him that there might be a wide chasm between fact and truth. The truth of this particular matter is that I can see DiMaggio play whenever the mood is on me.

This is something I owe to radio. By turning on the Philco, besides getting the voice of Franklin D. Roosevelt, I can often get sounds from the Yankee Stadium, sounds with power to create pictures inside my head more spectacular than television can possibly convey.

When I am eleven years old, in corduroy knickers, skimming down Washington Avenue on roller skates, these radio sounds show me Joe DiMaggio loping across a beautiful field of grass in the faraway, exotic Bronx, to haul in the white ball whirling out of the sky. Then I can see Joe stepping into the batter's box, wearing those loose billowing knickers real ballplayers all wore until television spurred them to vanity and vanity drove them to skin-tight double knits, like so many cruising sex objects.

"Harry," I said, "I hope Joe retires before television corrupts the baseball uniform. I'd hate to see him prancing around the diamond like some common, run-of-the-mill uniformed sex object."

The conversation had become pointless, since Harry had gone home in some disgust, leaving me, as he had said at the door, free to "skate up to the Horn and catch the new Mister Moto movie starring Peter Lorre on a double bill with Randolph Scott driving the cattle to Abilene."

Aside from having no poetry in him, Harry also has a weakness for ham-handed sarcasm, but I let it pass and, since my lumbago had me almost prostrate, went early to bed. Next morning Harry, the eternal fact man, phoned early.

"I looked it up. DiMaggio turned seventy on November 25," he said. In corduroy knickers, on roller skates, I said, "Harry, do you think we'll ever make enough money to go to Yankee Stadium sometime and see a game?"

If a tree falls in a forest where there is no one to hear it, does it make a noise? This hoary philosophical gambit is recalled by the analysis of baseball through new statistics, or sabermetrics (Bill James's term in recognition of the Society for American Baseball Research, or SABR). Reliever Firpo Marberry didn't know he set a record with his fifteen saves in 1924, because saves weren't invented until 1960—but he saved those games all the same. This article from SABR's *The National Pastime* measures the production of clutch batters on weak-hitting teams. (You can't drive in base runners who aren't on base.) The results are surprising, especially to Mr. Colbert.

BOB CARROLL

Nate Colbert's Unknown RBI Record

Nate Colbert set a single-season RBI record in 1972; hardly anyone noticed. Even today—ten years after the fact—few fans and fewer record books are aware of the big right-handed slugger's accomplishment. In fact, if it hadn't been for his performance on August 1 of that year—the best single day ever enjoyed by a major-league hitter—he might not be remembered at all.

Some of Colbert's obscurity may be blamed on the season. Nineteen seventy-two was not the happiest of baseball years. It began with Gil Hodges's fatal heart attack at spring training and ended with Roberto Clemente's tragic death in an airplane crash. In between, a player walkout shortened the season by thirteen days.

Another strike against Colbert was his team. The '72 San Diego Padres weren't quite the worst club in the National League—the Phillies were .001 lower—but it was hard to get excited about anything that happened on a 58–95 team sporting a .227 team batting average. Unless you had a cousin on the roster, you probably wouldn't even read the Padres' box scores.

A third strike on Colbert was his habit of missing third strikes. He could hit home runs and keep his batting average higher than his weight, but he also fanned more often than Scarlett O'Hara during a Georgia July. On average, he struck out every fourth time he went to bat. Among ten-year men, only Dave Kingman has been easier prey.

All in all, Nate was the wrong player on the wrong team in the wrong year to be making his mark on history.

His record doesn't reveal itself by a cursory glance at his batting stats for 1972: a .250 average, with 38 home runs and 111 RBIs. Forget the 127 strikeouts and it's a good year. But great? Record setting?

Take a look at San Diego's team batting. During the whole season, the Padres managed a mere 488 runs. Why, it seemed like the 1927 Yankees had that many by Memorial Day!

Now put the figures together. Colbert batted in 22.75 percent of his team's runs! Think of it this way: each batter makes up 11.1 percent of his team's lineup; Colbert did the work of two and then some. No major-league batter has ever done more for his team.

"How Nate ever knocked in 111 runs that otherwise dismal season has puzzled the experts ever since," says Padre statistician Mil Chipp. "He usually batted behind Derrel Thomas, Dave Roberts, and Jerry Morales. And none of them were that adept at getting on base. Thomas's on-base percentage (OBP) in 1972 was 29 percent, Roberts's was 28 percent and Morales's 31 percent." Colbert himself led the team with his modest 34 percent OBP.

It was no contest in RBIs. Chipp points out: "The only Padre players 'close' to Nate . . . were Leron Lee (47) and Clarence Gaston (44). They were light-years away."

There is a certain element of controversy involved in any RBI record: is it the man or the opportunity? Ever since the ribbie was dreamed up, some fans have opposed it as a measure of individual achievement. At the end of the 1880 National League season, according to Preston D. Orem's *Baseball (1845–1881) from the Newspaper Accounts*:

> The Chicago *Tribune* proudly presented the "Runs Batted In" record of the Chicago players for the season, showing Anson and Kelly in the lead. Readers were unimpressed. Objections were that the men who led off, Dalrymple and Gore, did not have the same opportunities to knock in runs. The paper actually wound up almost apologizing for the computation.

Ernie Lanigan, patron saint of ribbies, in his 1922 *Baseball Cyclopedia*, observed:

> As far back as 1879 a Buffalo paper used to include the runs batted in in the summary of the box score of the home game. Henry Chadwick urged the adoption of this feature in the middle '80s and by 1891 carried his point so that the National League scorers were instructed to report this data. They reported it grudgingly and finally were told they wouldn't have to report it.

Lanigan took up the ribbie torch in 1907 for the New York *Press*, working up the figures annually. At last, on the request of the Baseball Writers' Association of America (BBWAA), the major leagues added RBIs to their 1920 averages.

Yet, even more than a hundred years after RBIs were introduced, many fans view the stat skeptically. If a man singles, goes the argument, he has performed an individual act. But, to get a ribbie on that same single, he must have a teammate in scoring position. Colbert's 111 is an excellent total, but how many more might he have driven home in 1972 had he played for heavy-hitting Pittsburgh? For the record, Pirate first baseman Willie Stargell drove in 112.

Looking at the *percentage* of a team's runs driven in somewhat circumvents the anti-RBI argument. In theory, at least, a player on a light-hitting team with fewer opportunities to drive in runs can show his mettle by knocking in a high percentage. Conversely, a player with a group of bombers clustered around him in the batting order must drive in a much higher number to achieve the same percentage.

When Hack Wilson set the major-league record with 190 ribbies in 1930 (soon to be revised upward, to 191 or 192), his team scored another 803. His percentage was 19.04. Lou Gehrig's American League mark of 184 accounted for "only" 17.24 percent of the '31 Yankees' 1,067 runs. The accompanying chart shows all those players since 1900 who have knocked in 150 or more runs in a season, along with their teams' runs and their percentages. It comes as no surprise that all the 150-plus boys played on teams that scored a ton. Colbert's Padres scored an ounce, but his percentage was three points better than the highest of the big RBI guys.

As a matter of fact, only eight men in major-league history—from 1876 on— have topped the 20 percent mark. More men have hit .400.

The first hitter to achieve the improbable 20 was, not surprisingly, Babe Ruth. What is indeed surprising is that the Babe did it before he became a Yankee. In 1919, his last season in Boston, he drove in 114 runs—a 20.13 clip— for the fifth-place Red Sox. Although he topped that RBI *total* eleven times in a Yankee uniform, he never again drove in so high a proportion. (Note: some sources credit Ruth with only 112 RBIs in 1919, a 19.8 percent.)

It took sixteen years before another player reached 20 percent. Then the Braves' Wally Berger chased home teammates at 22.61 (130 out of 575). Despite Berger's efforts, the Braves won only thirty-eight games and came in dead last on a stretcher. But Wally's mark stood as the record until Colbert's big year.

Swish Nicholson drove the Cubs up to fifth place in 1943 with his 20.25 percent (128 out of 632). The Cubbies were back in fifth place in 1959 when Hall of Famer Ernie Banks made the "20 Club" with 21.25 (143 out of 673). That performance earned Banks his second consecutive MVP Award. Interestingly, he's the only 20-percenter to be so honored by the BBWAA.

Jim Gentile became the fifth member of the society in 1961. His 20.41 percent (141 out of 691) was a big factor in lifting the Orioles into third place, but it went virtually unnoticed in the excitement over Roger Maris's asterisk pursuit. Maris was also crowned the RBI "leader" on the basis of one more ribbie than Gentile, but his percentage was only 17.17 (142 out of 827).

Big Frank Howard belongs in the 20-percenter Hall of Fame—he topped the magic mark *twice*. In 1968 with Washington, he knocked in 106 runs (out of

Top Single-Season Run Producers					
Players	Team-Lg-Year			RBIs*	Team Runs*	Pct. of Team Runs
Hack Wilson	Chi	N	1930	190	998	19.04
Lou Gehrig	NY	A	1931	184	1067	17.24
Hank Greenberg	Det	A	1937	183	935	19.57
Lou Gehrig	NY	A	1937	175	975	17.95
Jimmie Foxx	Bos	A	1938	175	902	19.40
Lou Gehrig	NY	A	1930	174	1062	16.38
Babe Ruth	NY	A	1921	171	948	18.04
Chuck Klein	Phi	N	1930	170	944	18.01
Hank Greenberg	Det	A	1935	170	919	18.50
Jimmie Foxx	Phi	A	1932	169	981	17.23
Joe DiMaggio	NY	A	1937	167	979	17.06
Sam Thompson	Det	N	1887	166	969	17.13
Sam Thompson	Phi	N	1895	165	1068	15.45
Al Simmons	Phi	A	1930	165	951	17.35
Lou Gehrig	NY	A	1934	165	842	19.60
Babe Ruth	NY	A	1927	164	975	16.82
Babe Ruth	NY	A	1931	163	1067	15.28
Jimmie Foxx	Phi	A	1933	163	875	18.63
Hal Trosky	Cle	A	1936	162	921	17.59
Hack Wilson	Chi	N	1929	159	982	16.19
Lou Gehrig	NY	A	1937	159	979	16.24
Vern Stephens	Bos	A	1949	159	896	17.75
Ted Williams	Bos	A	1949	159	896	17.75
Al Simmons	Phi	A	1929	157	901	17.43
Jimmie Foxx	Phi	A	1930	156	951	16.40
Ken Williams	StL	A	1922	155	867	17.88
Joe DiMaggio	NY	A	1948	155	857	18.09
Babe Ruth	NY	A	1929	154	899	17.13
Joe Medwick	StL	N	1937	154	789	19.52
Babe Ruth	NY	A	1930	153	1062	14.41
Tommy Davis	LA	N	1962	153	842	18.17
Rogers Hornsby	StL	N	1922	152	863	17.61
Lou Gehrig	NY	A	1936	152	1065	14.27
Mel Ott	NY	N	1929	151	897	16.83
Lou Gehrig	NY	A	1932	151	1002	15.07
Al Simmons	Phi	A	1932	151	981	15.39
Hank Greenberg	Det	A	1940	150	888	16.89

* RBI and Team Runs figures courtesy of David Neft.

Players	Team-Lg-Year			RBIs*	Team Runs*	Pct. of Team Runs
The "20-Percent Club"						
Nate Colbert	SD	N	1972	111	488	22.75
Wally Berger	Bos	N	1935	130	575	22.61
Ernie Banks	Chi	N	1959	143	673	21.25
Jim Gentile	Bal	A	1961	141	691	20.41
Bill Buckner	Chi	N	1981	75	370	20.27
Bill Nicholson	Chi	N	1943	128	632	20.25
Frank Howard	Was	A	1968	106	524	20.23
Babe Ruth	Bos	A	1919	114	565	20.18
Frank Howard	Was	A	1970	126	626	20.13

* RBI and Team Runs figures courtesy of David Neft.

524) for a 20.23 percent. Two years later, he reached 20.13 (on 126 out of 626). Unfortunately, Washington finished last both years, but without Frank's bat they would have finished in Guam.

Another two years went by before Colbert set the record. Since then only one player has been able to break the 20 barrier, Bill Buckner with 20.27 percent for the Cubs in last year's [1981] strike-shortened season. Buckner's accomplishment is interesting in that it came on only seventy-five RBIs.

Most of the 20 percenters played on second-division teams not only in their big years but for the majority of their careers; most of them might also be characterized as underrated. The relationship is not coincidental.

The key to Nate Colbert's record occurred on August 1, 1972 in Atlanta, where the Padres met the Braves in a twilight doubleheader. Colbert was among the league leaders in home runs and RBIs, but a slump had plunged his batting average toward .200. He'd also been forced to miss a couple of games the previous week when he'd injured a knee in a collision at home plate.

On the plane from Houston, Padre manager Don Zimmer asked Nate if he'd prefer to sit out another day or two. The big slugger insisted it didn't matter how he felt. He wanted to play in the Braves' cozy park, and he was determined "someone was going to pay" for his recent slump.

Before all the Atlanta fans had even found their seats for the opener, Nate put San Diego in front in the first inning with a three-run homer off Ron Schueler. In the third frame he contributed to a four-run Padre outburst by singling home a teammate. Another single and a bases-empty homer off Mike McQueen in the seventh gave him four-for-five and five ribbies in the 9–0 Padre win.

The second game was even better. Tom Kelley opened for the Braves, and he was as wild as a *Penthouse* party. He walked Colbert in the first inning, and Nate came around to score. Pat Jarvis replaced Kelley in the second inning just in time to face Colbert with the bases loaded. Nate promptly cleared them with his third homer of the evening.

A two-run blast off Jim Hardin in the seventh made the score 9–1. But the shell-shocked Braves fought back to make it 9–7 going into the final inning. Colbert was due up fourth. Cecil Upshaw retired the first two Padres, but Larry Stahl got a ground single to right. And up came Colbert.

The sidearming Upshaw had always given him trouble, so Nate decided to just try to meet the ball for a hit. Upshaw threw a high fastball for the first pitch. Colbert met it. Home run.

"I was shocked when I hit it," Colbert recalled. "I couldn't believe it when I saw it go over the fence. It was unreal! When I rounded second base, Umpire Bruce Froemming said to me: 'I don't believe this.' I told him: 'I don't, either.' "

The next day, it took the New York *Times* three paragraphs just to explain the records Colbert had broken or tied:

> The 13 runs batted in erased the major league record of 11 for a double-header, which had been shared by three American League batters, Earl Averill of the Cleveland Indians (1930), Jim Tabor of the Boston Red Sox (1939) and Boog Powell of the Baltimore Orioles (1966). The National League record of 10 was established in 1947 by Enos Slaughter of the St. Louis Cardinals.
>
> The 6-foot-1½-inch 200-pound Colbert also broke the National League record of 12 runs batted in in two consecutive games by Jim Bottomley of St. Louis in 1924. The major league mark is 15, established in 1925 by Tony Lazerri of the New York Yankees.
>
> The five home runs in a double-header by Colbert equaled the major league mark set by Stan Musial of the Cardinals in 1954 and also broke Musial's record of 22 total bases in a twin bill.

Yet when 1972 ended and Colbert had racked up a record even more impressive than any of these, not a newspaper in the land gave it so much as an agate line.

Call it Catch-22.75.

The short, happy life of the Inter-American League (IAL): two and a half months in 1979, with far-flung franchises from Miami to Maracaibo and more former big leaguers than you could shake a maraca at; the league's official song could have been "Yes, We Have No Mañanas." Although nearly forgotten, the IAL should be remembered as a forerunner of the intercontinental baseball that is surely to come and for its champion, the Miami Amigos, which supplied the Mets' Davey Johnson with his managerial baptism.

BILL COLSON

The Over-the-Hill League

With their tongues planted firmly in their cheeks, the players were touting the game as the Cuban Death Match. Facing each other were forty-two-year-old Mike Cuellar and thirty-four-year-old Oscar Zamora. Cuellar, the masterful screwballer, was a three-time twenty-game winner for the Orioles a while back and in 1969 shared the American League Cy Young Award. The less renowned Zamora played for the Astros as recently as last season. He now has a thriving shoe business in Miami and finds time to pitch only every eighth day or so.

This Latin showdown didn't occur in an Old-Timers' Game in Baltimore or on a dusty diamond in San Juan but in Miami, where the Amigos were opening their second home stand of the year against the San Juan Boricuas. And who in the world are the Amigos and the Boricuas? Well, they are none other than the first- and fourth-place teams, respectively, in the fledgling Inter-American League. The Inter-American is different from other minor leagues not only because it is peopled largely by players with familiar and semifamiliar names but also because it has clubs in Panama City, Panama; Santo Domingo, Dominican Republic; and Caracas and Maracaibo, Venezuela, as well as in Miami and San Juan.

On this night a predominantly Latin crowd of 3,152—the Amigos' largest turnout of the season—came to see the new show in town, and they weren't disappointed. After giving up two runs in the first inning, Zamora settled down and beat San Juan on six hits, two of them by Bobby Tolan, late of the Cards, Reds, Padres, Phils, Pirates, and Nankai Hawks. Inspired by their cheerleaders, the Hot and Juicy Wendy's Girls, the Amigos shelled Cuellar in the fifth when first baseman Brock Pemberton, who played for the Mets in '75, hit a grand-slam home run. The loss was the first in five decisions for Cuellar, who has been pitching with a pulled hamstring since his third start.

Many of the Cuban expatriates in the crowd had seen Cuellar pitch for the Havana Sugar Kings in 1957 and '58, and the game had the same festive atmosphere that characterizes games in Cuba. The spectators beat out Latin rhythms on conga drums and cowbells and reacted vociferously to events both on and off the field. When a shapely young woman in hot pants and halter top left her seat, she got a rousing round of applause. Her return was greeted by a standing ovation that stopped the game.

Unfortunately, customs and immigration officials aren't as thrilled by the goings-on in the Inter-American League. When the Boricuas left Caracas for Miami, the authorities kept Cuellar from boarding the team's flight, and he barely made it to the game on time. Nobody knows exactly what the holdup was except that it concerned visas, which are a persistent problem for the Cuban-born players in the league. Miami backup catcher Jorge Curbelo hasn't made it into Venezuela in two tries. In addition, a few members of the Santo Domingo Azucareros failed to show for a game in Puerto Rico, reportedly because of visa difficulties. Visas aren't the Azucareros' only problems; the club's discombobulated management didn't send box scores to the league until the season was six weeks old.

Immigration and front-office foul-ups are just a few of the IAL's many growing pains. After only six weeks of the season, two owners, two general managers, and one manager have been replaced, and the Boricuas have moved some of their games from San Juan to various sites in the interior of the Commonwealth because they were drawing only about 200 fans a game. In fact, attendance has been poor everywhere except Caracas, where the Metropolitanos are attracting nearly 7,400 a game, 2,400 more than any other Triple A team and 3,500 more than the Oakland A's.

Traveling has also been rough, even by minor-league standards. In most places, the hotels and clubhouses have been decidedly second-rate, and the Amigos have yet to take a flight that wasn't at least an hour late. Because of the vagaries of Caribbean air travel, they have started one game at 10:00 P.M., had another suspended in the eighth inning, and had to fly to a third in two shifts, with the second group not arriving until minutes before game time.

Such troubles are not wholly unexpected considering that the infant IAL was hastily put together over the winter. It is the brainchild of Bobby Maduro, who owned the Sugar Kings in pre-Castro Cuba and from 1967 to '78 was Bowie Kuhn's assistant for inter-American baseball. To get the new league under way, Maduro had to overcome strong opposition from the Caribbean winter leagues, which view the Inter-American as a competitor for Latin players' services and Latin fans' affections, and from several major-league owners, who felt they had a corner on baseball talent in the Caribbean.

Unlike teams in Triple A leagues based solely in the United States and

Canada, those in the IAL are not affiliated with big-league organizations. As a result, Inter-American rosters are composed almost entirely of players who have been released or overlooked by major-league teams. And that's precisely what Maduro wanted.

"This league was desperately needed," he says, "and I wrote a letter to the commissioner ten years ago telling him so. When I started in baseball, there were fifty-six minor leagues. Now there are only eighteen. Today, if you're not good enough to make it to the majors in three years, you're eliminated from consideration."

Miami Manager—and sometime player—Dave Johnson, a three-time Gold Glove winner with Baltimore and a .262 lifetime hitter, sees a need for a league that welcomes older players.

"The system isn't conducive to breeding talent anymore," he says. "The real problem is that, as a rule, scouts and minor-league managers are incompetent judges of ability. Usually they were .220 hitters who couldn't get jobs outside of baseball.

"You can't imagine the number of talented players these guys have hurt or overlooked. The Yankees were using the best pitcher in baseball, Ron Guidry, as a reliever in the minors. Also, with expansion and the rush to get kids into the majors came the elimination from Triple A ball of the veteran player. Instead of being a tough educational step to the big leagues, Triple A has become nothing more than glorified Double A. Owners didn't really appreciate the value of having young prospects playing against veterans."

Veterans are one thing the IAL has plenty of. The league boasts such golden oldies as thirty-eight-year-old Cesar Tovar, thirty-five-year-old Dave May, thirty-five-year-old Clarence (Cito) Gaston, and thirty-six-year-old Adolfo Phillips. And most of them can still play. According to Santo Domingo manager Mike Kekich, who is best remembered for his spouse swap with Fritz Peterson when both pitched for the Yankees, "They're now reaching their outer limits"—that is, they are still good enough to be major leaguers but in another year or two will be over the hill.

The Amigos, whose average age is 27.5, have thirteen players with big-league experience, twice as many as any other club except Santo Domingo, which has eight. Among the better known are pitchers Bob Reynolds (Montreal, St. Louis, Milwaukee, Baltimore, Detroit, Cleveland), Mike Wallace (Phillies, Yankees, Cardinals, Rangers), and Hank Webb (Mets); designated hitter Hal Breeden (Cubs, Expos), who is in a slump—"I just went 0 for Puerto Rico"; and outfielder Danny (the Sundown Kid) Thomas, who won the Triple Crown in the Eastern League in 1976. He also hit .276 in thirty-two games that season for the Brewers but was released because, as a member of the World Wide Church of God, he was forbidden to play from sundown Friday until sundown Saturday.

Whether they have been up to the big leagues or only as far as Double A, all of these players know this is probably their final shot at getting another serious look by the majors.

"Baseball has said we're dead," says Wallace, who was 6–0 pitching out of the Yankee bull pen in 1974 and never had a losing record in four seasons in the majors. "We're all trying to prove them wrong. Ninety-five percent of us have eaten the pink slip. It's almost like a bond among us. Even the trainer has been released. My only hope was to come down here and win twenty, and even that may not be sufficent."

Wallace, now 6–1, may well get twenty wins the way the Amigos are playing. Because their front office got organized earlier than the other teams' and because Miami is the only IAL club based in the United States, the Amigos had an advantage when it came to signing players. Consequently, they have a 28–8 record and a 7½-game lead. When the players and managers are asked to assess the IAL, they invariably tell you that, on balance, the quality of the league's play is somewhere between Triple A and Double A but that the Amigos are in a class by themselves. "We are probably the best Triple A club in existence," says Johnson.

Miami has a team batting average of .296 and a team ERA of 2.45. The Amigos' best batters are outfielders Jim Tyrone (.357), who was hitting over .300 for Oakland in 1977 when Charlie Finley benched him, and Leon Brown (.346), who hit over .300 in three of his four years in Triple A and was with the Mets for most of the 1976 season. Miami also has a twenty-six-year-old reliever from Nicaragua named Porfirio Altamirano, who may throw as hard as anyone in the majors. This is his first year of pro ball, and he has a 0.91 ERA. Each of these players, says Johnson, could help a major-league club right now.

For the time being, they must be content with playing in what they have nicknamed the Mañana League. "Every time you need something in one of those countries, you always hear *mañana, mañana*," says Wallace, reviving a shopworn stereotype. Although the players don't like to admit it, it is they who make this the Mañana League, because without it, there would be no *mañana* for most of them.

By the time this model of a spot report appeared, the Philadelphia Phillies had rolled up a record of misery unmatched in the National League: since their inception in 1883, no world championships and only two pennants, plus a collapse of epic proportion in the closing weeks of 1964 as they lost ten games in a row and with them the flag. As recounted below, their collapse of October 7, 1977, was a comparative jewel of compactness, requiring only ten minutes. The phutile Phils were only one out away from taking a two-games-to-one lead in the League Championship Series, and then, with incredible swiftness, the Astroturf was swept out from under their feet.

BILL CONLIN

The Ten-Minute Collapse

Dusty Baker hit a tough chopper to third, and Mike Schmidt pounced on the wicked short hop like a jaguar running down a rabbit.

That was one out in the top of the ninth, seven straight ground balls thrown by Gene Garber. And 63,719 fans were on their feet, a shrieking chorus that all afternoon had roared with the blood lust of a Roman Coliseum mob rooting for the lion.

Rick Monday bounced out to Teddy Sizemore. The Vet throng was chanting "DEEEFENSE." Eight straight ground balls by Geno. Game three was history. One more out, Geno, baby, and this was a 5–3 Phillies' victory. The Dodgers had coughed up two eighth-inning runs to go with three the crowd and plate umpire Harry Wendelstedt had bled from starter Burt Hooton in the second.

The Dodgers were down to their suspect bench. Ancient Vic Davalillo hauled his well-traveled bones to the plate, more wrinkles on his leather face than there are base hits left in his bat.

On deck was Manny Mota, thirty-nine years old, one final straw for Tommy Lasorda to clutch at should Davalillo reach first base.

Thus began the shortest, most devastating nightmare in the history of a town steeped in an athletic tradition of flood, fire, and famine, a town where some seasons even down seemed like a long way up.

A funeral dirge would be appropriate at this point, Beethoven's *Eroica*, perhaps, or a few choruses from *Lohengrin*.

You thought the *Titanic* went down fast!

The 1964 Collapse took ten games. This one took ten minutes. It was like watching the shambles of 1964 compressed into an elapsed-time film sequence.

With two outs, the Phillies met the enemy, and it was them.

Davalillo legged out a superb bunt to Sizemore, as if that is the normal play for a thirty-nine-year-old man with just forty-eight at bats after the Dodgers picked him up for late-season insurance.

"If he had hollered, 'Hey, I'm gonna lay one down,' we still couldn't have stopped it," First Baseman Richie Hebner said after the incredible 6–5 loss. "It was just a perfect bunt, a great play on Vic's part."

Mota came up swinging for a home run. He hit one in the final regular-season game last Sunday, hadn't hit one before that since the 1972 season.

He fouled a pitch back, then fell behind 0 and 2 with a swing so lusty it almost dislodged his batting helmet.

"Two strikes I am trying to just protect the plate," Mota said over the joyous babble of the winner's clubhouse. "I'm not a power hitter; I try to hit line drives. He threw me an inside slider."

Mota jumped on the pitch like a Santo Domingo street urchin putting the touch on a well-heeled gringo tourist. "Thank you, *señor*, may God bless you for this gift."

The fly ball carried, driving Greg Luzinski back toward the bull-pen fence in left. There was enough controversy in this schizophrenic game to keep a Warren Commission busy for weeks, and this was one chapter.

Luzinksi leaped at the fence. The ball lodged briefly in the webbing of his glove, then jarred loose, hit the fence, and nestled back into Bull's grasp. Wouldn't it have been a much easier play for fleet-footed Jerry Martin, often Luzinski's defensive caddy?

"He was the third batter up in the ninth," Danny Ozark said, wearing the dazed look of a train-wreck survivor. "I wanted him in the lineup in case the game was tied."

Davalillo was being held at third when Luzinski threw to second. The ball skidded through Sizemore's legs. Davalillo scored, and Mota huffed to third on the second baseman's error.

The inning reached a ten on the Richter Scale of natural disasters when Davey Lopes roped a one-hop shot off the heel of Schmidt's glove, off his knee, deflecting to Larry Bowa at shortstop. Bowa made a brilliant pickup and gunned a strike to Hebner. First-base umpire Bruce Froemming double-clutched, then spread his hands palm down. Hebner shrieked and stamped. Ozark erupted from the dugout. The veins in Bowa's neck bulged like telephone cables.

"If he had called the play right, both me and Hebner would have been thrown out," Ozark seethed in his office after a calm performance in the mass interview room. "He didn't know what the bleep to call it, so he called it safe. He was stunned by Bowa's throw, as far as I'm concerned. He just anticipated Bowa couldn't make the throw. He's got his hands stuffed in his pockets half the bleeping time."

For the second time in the tense war, the unwavering eye of the TV replay cameras would show Lopes out by a narrow margin, just as they proved from two angles that Steve Garvey never touched the plate on Bob Boone's superb block in the second.

Garber unfurled a pickoff move that skidded past Hebner, and Lopes jetted to second. "It was a sinker that exploded," Hebner said. "I should have got more body in front of it."

The Phillies fiery Götterdämmerung was complete when Bill Russell bounced a single up the middle.

Mike Garman, sixth Los Angeles pitcher on an afternoon of baffling selection by Lasorda, retired Bowa and Schmidt, then drilled Luzinski with a high, tight fastball.

Hebner bounced Garman's first pitch to Steve Garvey, and the crowd stood in a collective silence reserved for the demise of a great matador in a jammed Plaza de Toros.

Death had come to the executioners. The Phillies had met the enemy, and it was them.

These profiles of Dickey Pearce and George Wright, the two great shortstops of base-ball's Pleistocene era, were part of a fascinating series on "The Fifty Greatest Ball Players in History" that ran in the *New York Evening Journal* in 1911–12. What makes these profiles so interesting today is that the author, veteran sportswriter Sam Crane, was himself a major-league second baseman who formed a keystone tandem with Pearce back in 1877 and frequently opposed Wright. The latter was one of the first men installed in the Hall of Fame, while Pearce has an outstanding claim to induction, inasmuch as he was the first to play shortstop *as an infielder*—not restricting his scope to short fly balls and relaying throws from the outfield, as was the practice in the 1840s and early '50s.

SAM CRANE

The Men Who Invented Shortstop

In the days of the old games between the Mutuals of New York and the Atlantics of Brooklyn in the late sixties and early seventies, when the fans of those days were even more partisan than now when the Giants and Superbas cross bats, there was one player who was more feared by the New Yorkers than any other on the Atlantic team, and that was Dickey Pearce.

The little fellow was not bigger than a good-sized cruller, the only food product at the time that seemed to be available by fair means or foul in those days, but little, fat, pudgy Dickey Pearce was about the whole show in the Atlantic team and did more, possibly, in his own way to win games for the famous old Atlantic club than any other player on the old team.

At any rate, every lover of baseball in Brooklyn thought so at the time, and it is a matter of baseball history over in the neighborhood of the Union Grounds and Capitoline Grounds that Dickey Pearce's short, pudgy legs brought in more tallies for the Atlantics than all the slugging sprinters there were on the team.

And why? Simply because Dickey knew how to get on first base.

He was not a slugger like many of his fellow players, but he had so studied the science of batting as it was in vogue at the time that his "fair foul" hits often counted much more than the home-run wallop of his bigger and stronger teammates.

Dickey Pearce was the originator of the present bunt. And that was the hit that transformed batting in his day. It was not known as the bunt at that time, and Dickey himself had no idea that he was making baseball history. But he had the baseball instinct, and that was that a player had to get on first base before he became a factor in the run getting. He appreciated the fact that unless he could reach first there was no possibility of his spikes denting the plate.

When Dickey first began to play baseball, the score was kept by cutting notches on a pine stick and every notch meant a tally. A fence rail instead of a pine stick did just as well, and the fence rail in Dickey's day was the official press box. Anyhow, what those notches figured up meant the road to victory for his side, and no player was more frequent than little Dickey in crossing over the plate and shouting gleefully, "Tally Pearce one."

Dickey played on the many open lots around Brooklyn for many years before he got his first chance on a real team. He was considered too small.

But like all little men, Dickey was cocky. He saw the big fellows play, and as he peeked through the knotholes in the fences of the Union and Capitoline grounds for two innings and then "flashed" his ten pennies to get into the enclosure when the gates were opened to the kids after the second inning, as was the custom at the time, Dickey came to the conclusion that he could play as well as any of the stars. But how to "mingle" was the great question.

The first start he got was to carry water to the players, and when he got that job, he was the envy of all of his fellows.

Finally he was allowed to carry the bat of one of his idols, and from that advancement he was allowed to chase balls in the outfield while the "big fellows" were at practice. Then on one long-to-be-remembered day he was asked to bat against one of the pitchers, who was out alone for practice, and he made a base hit. The pitcher took notice of him and told his captain there was a promising youngster that would bear watching.

The regular nine was shy of one player one day in a "match," and Dickey was selected to take his place. The ambitious youngster was put in at right field, a position at the time that was considered only fit for the "scrubs." Any old player could play right field. But my bold Dickey was there with both feet—not in fielding, possibly, for nothing came his way—but at bat the youngster was in his element. He was a hard man to pitch to, as all midgets have been, since, from Davy Force to Billy Keeler, and Dickey showed up some of the regular members in getting to first and getting around the bases.

That accidental chance to play made Dickey Pearce. He was put on the regular team and placed at shortstop, for the reason that he was considered to be too short-legged to cover ground in the outfield. It was a fortunate selection, for Dickey took to shortstop like a duck to water, and in the first game he played in that position, he showed such ability that none of the old-timers on the team had a chance to beat him out of the job. And none did after that for years and years. Dickey Pearce's name at shortstop for the Atlantics was stereotyped, and the scorecards always had his name in that position as long as he played baseball with that club, and that was for many years.

In fact, Pearce was a close rival of the great and only George Wright for the supremacy in the position.

Against the Mutuals in the games the Atlantics played with their New York opponents, and when partisanship was at the highest pitch, Dickey Pearce was always a star. When he went to bat, it was more than two to one that the little bit of a "sawed-off" would get his first.

Dickey Pearce's first chance to shine as a star of national reputation was when he played with the Atlantics against the Red Stockings of Cincinnati when the latter famous team lost its first game after an uninterrupted string of victories for a season and a half. In that great and historical game, Pearce's work, both as shortstop and at the bat, was the feature of the victor's game.

In the eleventh inning it was Dickey Pearce who started the rally that enabled the Atlantics to win out 8–7.

Pearce was the first player to work the "fair foul," a ball that was hit by chopping down at the ball, making it hit on fair ground and then bounding off into foul ground. It is a hit that is foul now under the present rules, but in those days there was no rule that prevented it from being perfectly fair. I have seen both Dickey Pearce and Ross Barnes get three bases by working this foxy bit of batting.

I have heard of home runs being made on the same hit, but I never saw it done, and I doubt if Dickey ever did, simply because I do not imagine that his short legs could ever carry him the distance, but many is the game little Dickey sewed up by the shrewd stab.

There were lots of objections and protests made in those days on that hit, but no rules could be found to prevent it, and until the rules were altered, Dickey always was high up in the existing batting records.

Pearce, by reason of that "fair foul," has been credited with originating the now famous bunt, but as Dickey worked it the hit was never intended to be worked as we understand it now.

I am inclined to give John M. Ward the credit of discovering the bunt as now played. But that is a story for a future article.

Dickey Pearce made such a big reputation with the Atlantics that he was in demand by the best clubs in the country, and finally he cast his fortunes with the old Mutuals, of New York, his old rivals. Over in Brooklyn he was considered somewhat of a renegade at the time, but that was the dawn of professionalism that had been more or less under disguise at the time, but Dickey's fine work with the crack New York team enabled him to retain his reputation and popularity, and he was a star until he was obliged to quit on account of age bedimming his former grand abilities.

Dickey kept in touch with the game for a long time after he got out of active participation in it as a player. He still continued to retain his popularity with players young and old, by whom he was considered an oracle.

When the Players' League was formed, in 1890, Dickey was given the position of grounds keeper of the Brotherhood Grounds (the present Polo Grounds) and helped Buck Ewing to lay out the field. And as Dickey laid it out then, it stands today. Of course grounds keeper Murphy has made improvements since, with all the money that since has come into the local club's coffers, but still, Pearce has to be given the credit for putting the field in the condition that allowed of the present model field of the country.

Dickey did not die overburdened with wealth, but he was well cared for until he passed away, a little over a year ago. He had a daughter who became prominent on the stage, and she saw that he wanted for nothing in his declining years.

The last time I saw Dickey Pearce was at one of the "old-timers' " reunions at Paddock's Island in Boston Harbor, three years ago, and the veteran was there, the recipient of all the love and respect that was his due. It was veneration, because we all appreciated what he had done for baseball.

As honest as the day.

Baseball was bettered by Dickey Pearce's connection with it.

There have been many great shortstops, but for all-round ability there has been none who ever played the position who has been able to force George Wright from the top-notch rung of the ladder of fame.

The game has gone along for over forty years, too, since George first blossomed out as a star, and I have in mind when I give him this lofty record all of those grand players who have shone so brilliantly in the past and present.

There have been shortstops and shortstops. The Dickey Pearces, Davy Forces, Bob Fergusons, Jack Glasscocks, Ed Williamsons, Herman Longs, Jack Nelsons, Johnny Wards, and other old-time luminants, who have come and gone, leaving reputations and records a mile long.

The Tinkers, Doolans, Elberfelds, McBrides, Brashes, Bridwells, Barrys, and Turners of the present are also all in my mind, who are thought by the fans of today to be preeminent. I have known them all and have seen them all play, but to George Wright I give the credit of being the best ever.

It is difficult to make the admirers of the "speed boys" of today think that any of the old-time ball players could approach the players of the present for stops, ground covering, and throwing, but while I acknowledge that there are more fast players today, still there were individuals in the earlier days of the sport who excelled the best who are now exploiting the game.

The game is faster now and has progressed simply because there are more speedy players now than in the past.

George Wright is a brother of Harry Wright, that noble old veteran around whom my first article on famous ballplayers was written. The fame of the Wright brothers was countrywide forty years ago, and George was the real player of the two. George's reputation as the greatest player of his time has not been dimmed in the least.

He was born in upper New York City, Yorkville, in the fifties, and with his elder brother, Henry, naturally took to baseball after learning the rudiments of cricket, taught him by his father, Sam Wright, the old professional cricketer.

Baseball was born in George Wright. He was consequently a natural ballplayer. He first came into prominence in the national game with the Unions, of Morrisania, with which club he played shortstop, the position he always occupied afterward in his long and brilliant baseball career. I do not remember that he ever played any other position. It therefore became second nature to him, and the many, many plays he was called on to perform that brought victory after victory to his teams year after year at critical stages were from intuition, although at times they often took on the look of being uncanny.

George Wright was probably as quick thinking a player as ever wore a uniform. His wits were always about him. He was invariably upon his mental tiptoes, and whenever he would pull off one of those grand, unexpected plays that were so dazzlingly surprising as to dumfound his opponents, his prominent teeth would gleam and glisten in an array of white molars that would put our own Teddy Roosevelt and his famed dentistry establishment far in the shadow.

In a game between the Boston Red Stockings and Philadelphia Athletics in 1873, when the Quakers had three men on base and none out, George caught a fly ball in his cap, tossed the ball to the pitcher, thereby putting the ball in play again, according to the rules of that time, and a triple play resulted, but it was not allowed.

But it was in such critical times that George showed his great nerve and quick thinking abilities. He was always ready to grasp a point of play and never hesitated, no matter how many chances there were to take by missing the anticipated point.

From New York George went to Cincinnati in 1868 and joined the Cincinnati Red Stockings, of which his brother Harry was manager. George was the all-around star of that famous bunch of champions. He led the club in batting and run getting, and these departments of play at that time were of the most importance.

In the fifty-seven games the Red Stockings played George took part in fifty-two. He made 339 runs, 59 of which were homers. His batting average was .518, showing that he made a fraction over a base hit every two times he was at bat.

Wonder if Ty Cobb could have done any better with the underhand pitching in vogue in those days?

George went to Boston in 1871 with his brother, Harry, as manager, and in the Hub George more than lived up to the reputation he had made in Cincinnati. He was the star of the Boston Red Stockings until 1879, when he went to Providence to manage the Providence Grays, the team that won the championship that year, although by a very close call. That wound up his active career on the diamond.

In 1874 George was a member of the Boston club that accompanied the Athletics to England, and while the introduction of baseball to our English cousins was not a pronounced success, still the ballplayers taught the Britishers some few points about their own game—cricket. It was always eighteen ballplayers against eleven cricketers, but the Americans were never defeated at the English game, and George Wright was the crack batter of the American eighteen.

George was the first shortstop to play a deep field. He played forty years ago just as far back of the line as the players in the same position do today. It was George's strong throwing arm and deadly accuracy that allowed of his playing so deep, and he of course saw the advantage there was to be gained in covering ground by playing deep. He was the first to grasp that idea.

George Wright was about 5 feet 10 inches tall and weighed about 160 in his prime. I remember him; he had a thick crop of dark curly hair, a small mustache and a dab on either cheek for a bluff at "siders." He was slightly bowlegged, and I never knew a bowlegged ballplayer who was not a crackerjack—à la Hans Wagner.

George Wright is a millionaire, having gained wealth and prominence in the sporting-goods business in Boston. He started in a small way in 1872, the year after he went to Boston to play ball.

George is one of the Hub's most respected citizens and still keeps in touch with the national game that he has done so much to build up. He is the proud father of Beals Wright, the champion tennis player.

A new literary theory: it is sometimes noted that Casey Stengel's gift of gab was Joycean, but might not Joyce's stream-of-consciousness technique—the Molly Bloom soliloquy, for instance—have been inspired by the Ol' Perfesser? After all, both of these giants hit the big leagues at about the same time, found glory in the early 1920s, and were widely vilified and misunderstood in the following decade. Oh, well; never mind. Here, from Bob Creamer's splendid biography of "a man that's been up and down," in Stengel's marvelous phrase, is a portrait of the artist as an old man.

ROBERT W. CREAMER

Do Not Go Gentle: Talking, Talking, Talking

Stengel lived for ten years after his retirement from the Mets—ten years and a month, to be exact. He was out of baseball. The Mets made him a vice-president, gave him a nebulous assignment as overseer of scouting in California, invited him to spring training and to club affairs and continued to pay him, but after fifty-six years it was finally over. He was no longer a factor in the game.

He kept as close to it as he could. He went to the World Series in Los Angeles in 1965, barely two months after his operation, looking natty in a yellow shirt and a blue tie, "just in case they want me on television." He flew back to New York in midwinter for the baseball writers' dinner, and in the spring of 1966 he showed up with Edna at St. Petersburg to watch the Mets in training.

Dressed in a red-checked sport jacket and a red tie and swinging his crooked black cane, he talked in St. Petersburg about the Mets and many other things and joked about the cane. "I don't really need this," he said, "but I have to limp or I can't get into the Hall of Fame." There is a rule that says a man must be out of baseball for at least five years before he is eligible for election to the Hall of Fame. It's a foolish provision, put into effect because baseball is afraid of its own sentimentality; it worries that it might elect someone impulsively who really doesn't belong, disregarding the fact that there is a bull penful of men who were elected to Cooperstown *after* the waiting period who don't belong there, either. After his retirement from the Mets the seventy-five-year-old Stengel faced five years of waiting before he could even be considered for

election. However, the Baseball Writers Association of America, which conducts the Hall of Fame elections, consulted feverishly but secretly and agreed to waive the rule in Stengel's case. An unpublicized ballot was taken, and Casey was voted in, not long before he reached St. Petersburg that spring, although he didn't know about it yet.

On March 8, a few days after he had arrived in Florida, the Mets asked Casey to come out to the spring-training field to take part in a ceremony. The sportswriters were giving a plaque to George Weiss, he was told, and they wanted Casey to make the presentation. They told him to bring Edna along, too. It was a coldish morning for Florida, with a little of what Jimmy Cannon called "New York" in the wind. Stengel, wielding his cane, limped onto the field and walked with surprising quickness toward the clubhouse. He had on street clothes but wore a Mets baseball cap. As he reached the clubhouse, he was surrounded by writers and photographers, and he saw TV cameras, and he began to suspect something. The commissioner of baseball, Gen. William Eckert, was on the field, and so was Ford Frick, Eckert's predecessor and a member of the Hall of Fame committee.

Casey looked around, wondering. Someone gave Edna a bouquet of flowers; and someone else guided Casey toward a microphone where Frick stood, waiting to speak. Casey leaned over to Edna and said, "I gotta find out what I'm doing here."

The Met players stopped practicing and gathered around. The small crowd of spectators who had come to watch practice crowded closer to the chain-link fence that kept them off the field. Frick began to speak. He explained the eligibility rule and the fact that it had been waived and said a special vote had been held and Stengel had been elected to Cooperstown.

Casey, holding his cap in his hand, bowed his head quickly, then waved his cap, and everyone applauded. Edna kissed him. Casey was grinning, his wrinkled face beaming, looking, as Cannon wrote, very young. He stepped to the microphone.

"Edna," he said, "I appreciate that kiss."

He spoke for a few minutes, saying, among other things, "It's a terrific thing to get in it while you're still alive." After the little ceremony ended, he went over to the fence beyond third base to talk to the spectators gathered there, most of them elderly.

"They just put me in the Hall of Fame," he said. He mentioned a formal breakfast he had been to that morning, saying, "I got one leg and a cane, and I thought they was giving me a doughnut at the breakfast, which is pretty good because they get fifteen, twenty cents for a doughnut now, but they give me the full course, very good. I walked over thirty feet without the cane on a carpet to make the speech at the breakfast. But a coach walks ninety feet and there ain't no carpet, so I can't be a coach." The crowd laughed and applauded, and Casey acknowledged the applause by bending over halfway to the ground in a long, low bow, sweeping his cap across the ground.

A Met official asked him if he could walk over and talk to the spectators in the little grandstand beyond home plate. "I can't make the same speech," he said, but he limped over and spoke for a while there and then sat down on the team bench, still holding his black cane. He said, "Being in the Hall of Fame is an amazing thing. I didn't expect it to be so quick." He paused, then said, "It's bigger than I thought it was. This Hall of Fame thing is bigger than anything I ever saw."

For the rest of his life, whenever Stengel signed an autograph, he'd add the Hall of Fame to his signature. Even his letters were signed that way. When Ira Berkow wrote Casey outlining a book they might do together, Casey replied: "Dear Ira: Your conversation's; and the fact you were the working writer were inthused with the Ideas was great but frankly do not care for the great amount of work for myself. Sorry but am not interested. Have to many proposition's otherwise for the coming season. Fact cannot disclose my Future affair's. Good luck. Casey Stengel, N.Y. Mets & Hall of Famer."

That summer he and Edna went to Cooperstown for his formal induction to the Hall of Fame. Ted Williams had been elected at the same time as Casey, and the two were honored together. Williams, often an arrogant and difficult man when he was playing, made one of the best speeches ever heard at Cooperstown, a sensitive, intelligent expression of what baseball meant to him, what it had done for him and what it could still do for others.

Stengel followed, and while for once in his life he was unable to top another speaker, he was fine, too. He said, "I want to thank everybody. I want to thank some of the owners who were amazing to me and those big presidents of the leagues who were so kind to me when I was obnoxious." He thanked his parents, and he thanked George Weiss, "who would find out whenever I was discharged and would reemploy me." Casting back over his half century in baseball, he encapsulated his career in one brief sentence: "I chased the balls that Babe Ruth hit."

Stengel returned to Cooperstown faithfully every year after that for the Hall of Fame ceremonies, a pilgrimage that took considerable effort for an old man: from Glendale through Los Angeles to the airport; a flight across the country to New York City; another flight on a smaller airline to an airport in central New York state; a forty-mile drive from the airport over country roads to the little village of Cooperstown. He'd almost always arrive a couple of days early so that he could move around town, visiting and talking with people, savoring the atmosphere of baseball, his hawklike walk and garrulous face, as Kevin Cunningham called it, recognized everywhere.

His energy and drive remained high, even into his eighties. He and Edna would fly East each spring to the Mets' training camp in Florida. He'd return to New York every summer for the Mets' Old-Timers' Day. He'd attend Dodger games in Chavez Ravine and Angel games in Anaheim. He dedicated a baseball field in Glendale that was named for him and said, "I feel greatly honored to have a ballpark named after me, especially since I've been thrown out of so many."

He'd go to the World Series. He'd fly to New York in January for the baseball writers' dinner there, and he'd go to other cities for dinners, luncheons, gatherings of almost any sort. He spoke at all of them. At them, before them, and after them. He never flagged. At one dinner, after talking glowingly about the Mets, he grabbed a broom that chanced to be near the speakers' table and marched off the dais chanting, "Metsies! Metsies! Metsies!" Asked not long before he died who was the best manager he ever saw, he said, "*I* was the best manager I ever saw, and I tell people that to shut 'em up and also because I believe it."

Early in 1973, a month or so after Roberto Clemente of the Pirates was killed in a plane crash off Puerto Rico, Stengel went all the way to Manchester, New Hampshire, for a sports dinner. He spoke at the dinner, as did Curt Gowdy, the broadcaster, who delivered an eloquent tribute to Clemente. After the dinner, broadcaster Ken Meyer of WBZ in Boston took Casey aside for a taped interview. It turned out to be a classic Stengel performance.

What follows is a nearly exact transcription of that half-hour interview, with bracketed annotations here and there that try to explain some of the things Stengel was talking about. He was eighty-two years old, he was 3,000 miles from home, he had attended several banquets and luncheons on his journey, and on this day he had been talking, almost without stopping, for hours. He talked over breakfast, talked through lunch, talked with small groups of friends and admirers over predinner drinks. During the banquet he talked with the people sitting on either side of him on the dais. He had made his customary rambling speech in his heavy, growling voice, seemingly without taking a breath, charming and confusing his listeners, most of whom laughed automatically, not really knowing what they were laughing at.

Now, late at night, the banquet over, the long day done, he sits in a small room and talks on. Rather, he flows on, a Mississippi of words, overwhelming, unceasing. Meyer begins the interview by asking Stengel about Clemente and about the 1960 World Series when Clemente and the Pirates defeated Stengel and the Yankees.

"What," asks Meyer, "do you remember about that Series and Clemente?"

That's the petcock that opens the flows. Stengel starts talking, his voice hurrying, one sentence running into the next without pause:

"Well, I tell ya, it's an amazing Series. I thought I was going to win the Series easy when I went to Pittsburgh, and I was very, uh, uh—I blame myself on the whole Series. I mean for the Yankees losing. Now here's the reason why I make that statement was because I thought Ford was so good, and I thought that my pitching staff was a little better than what they had in, uh, Pittsburgh, and they had—the idea was I never pitch Ford in the first game in the World Series, and that's why I'm blamin' myself in the Series in the long run. When Ford did pitch the second game [*actually the third game*] he was never scored on. He wasn't scored on in the second game he pitched, so the blunder I made not stopping, *starting* him in the first game was because in the last of the World Series I went to pitch Ford and Ford says, 'Why, I can't loosen up my arm.' Now if I'da pitched him in the first game, he'da been in better shape to go in the last game when I blow the Series. [*If Ford had started the first game, he probably would have pitched the fifth game instead of the sixth, which would have given him sufficient rest to come back as a relief pitcher in the seventh game.*]

"Therefore was on carelessness, and as good as the club was [*Pittsburgh*], I didn't think that they was gonna have much of a chance. But I found out the longer I played in that Series, Clemente commenced being alive again. In other words, I mean he was a right fielder and a right fielder—he's like Kaline. He plays right field and a man that's a right fielder—uh, I was played many outfield positions. [*This preoccupation with right field and right fielders is caused by the slip Casey makes when he says Clemente "commenced being alive again." He is talking about Clemente in the 1960 World Series, but the player's recent death intrudes, and Casey is momentarily flustered. He gets back on the track by taking a fix on right field: Clemente was a right fielder; so was Al Kaline; so, too, was Stengel for part of his career.*] He has to throw to second base. You run a ball out, and you run hard, and he's facin' throwin' to second, he's facin' throwin' to first, and there, facin' there, but when you get to first base and you go to third [*on a ball hit to right*] just thinkin' a man that hits the ball down the right-field line the right fielder *has to turn around to throw to third*. He's out of position, where a left-handed man on the foul line is *in* position to throw to second, to throw to third on the hit-and-run plays from first to third. [*A right-handed-throwing right fielder fielding a ball near the foul line has to turn his body in order to throw to second or third base, whereas a left-hander does not.*] And in his *hitting.* [*Stengel suddenly recalls Clemente's hitting, mentions it, and then drops it.*] In turning around, a left-handed man, you'd think he'd be better out in right field, but he [*Clemente*] displayed, he and Kaline, that it's an amazing thing how a right-handed thrower could be that great as they were in the outfield.

"So then—Clemente then got *better.* [*Better than what? It's not clear, but it's a compliment.*] Now when it comes to hitting, you'd—he's so *quick* with the *wrists* and, you know, with the bat. Every time we went to pitch different to him, we were supposed to throw at him, back of him, you know, or move him back from home plate, and then when we'd pitch the ball over the plate, why he could hit down on the ball, and he rubbed the balls out [*hyperbole: Clemente wore the imprint off the ball*], which they said the effort he put into his work is like Gowdy said [*at the banquet*]. The effort he puts into his work all through the Series showed up, and it showed up there that he beat out three of those balls on me in the infield and if he hadn't I woulda finally won the last Series. Except that I, uh, pitchin' Ford the second game insteada the first game I never got to pitch Ford in the third game [*a third time*] of the Series and he wasn't scored on in two games. Now he's an outstanding player [*Clemente again*]; he can do everything, and it's like Kaline did, and I studied outfielding so much I can't understand how a man where I can play the best or in center field why a man what's right-handed shouldn't be in left field because a left-handed man in left field and he's out of position so half the time himself, yessir?" [*Stengelese at its most indecipherable. I don't know what he means by "where I can play the best or in center field," although I suspect DiMaggio and Mantle are stirring in his subconscious. The inanity of the passage seems suddenly to weigh upon him, and he returns the lead to the interviewer with an abrupt "Yessir?"*]

Meyer says, "All right, you mentioned Ford, and it seems a logical question. Why did you choose to pitch Art Ditmar in the first game instead of Ford? What caused the change?"

"Well," Stengel says, "I told ya because they pitched their best pitcher. Who was their best pitcher? It's the man that lived out in Idaho, and he was, uh, was that, uh, wonderful pitcher. [*Vernon Law. Casey can't remember his name, but he remembers that Law was from Idaho.*] He pitched in the spots [*was used in the tough games*]. He's been a coach and so on and so forth. [*Law became a coach after his playing career ended.*] He was a terrific pitcher, and I figured why pitch Ford against him? I know Ford is good, and I thought I was gonna beat 'em the Series, anyway, and we did; we had fourteen to nothing and sixteen to two [*the Yankees won three games overwhelming, 12–0, 10–0, and 16–3; the Pirates won their four games by margins of one, one, two, and three runs*], but they commenced then. They had Virdon in center field, he commenced makin' good catches, and then I had Shantz that had a crippled arm and when the ball went through and hit Kubek in the jaw, see? [*Casey is talking now about the seventh game of the 1960 World Series, the loss of which still galls him more than ten years later.*] The main thing about that was there was just a double play, and my pitcher had to go out on the next thing, because we had a secret on the bench and he said, 'I am gonna pitch for ya but my arm is sore.' So every time he warmed up he'd give me a signal to go without changin'. I'd warm a man up every inning [*Ralph Terry said Casey had him warm up five times during that game*], but he pitched five innings until that play that happened to Kubek, in which he missed the ball on the double play. Then he told me, he says, 'I can't pitch anymore, my arm is sore.' I mean, he said it was hurting *more*. Each inning I made him go out and warm up. The pitcher. So he was—Shantz was all right while he was in there. [*Sore-armed Bobby Shantz pitched five innings of excellent relief in the seventh game of the 1960 Series until that potential double-play ball took a bad bounce and hit Tony Kubek in the throat, but each inning as he warmed up he'd glance at Casey on the bench and signal whether or not he could go on. Finally, after the abortive double play, Stengel took him out.*] Then I took him out, and there wasn't anybody that I picked was right. [*Jim Coates gave up a three-run home run, and Terry the game-winning homer.*] And then I asked Ford to go in, and Ford said, 'Well, I said I can't loosen up.' And that's true 'cause he pitched the day before, and I shoulda pitched him the first game and I'da had him to relieve in the last game."

Meyer abandons the question of why Stengel picked Ditmar to start and says, "Another guy that was paid tribute to and who was lost during 1972 was a guy you also played in World Series competition with five or six times: Jackie Robinson [*who had died a few months before, in October 1972*]. What reflections and memories do you have about a great athlete like this?"

"Well," says Stengel, "I think he was a great athlete. I think he was one of the best football men that ever played. So was other men out there, like Tipton [*Eric Tipton, a Duke University football star who was a major-league outfielder from 1939 to 1945*]. Both of them were amazing in the same things in the same league in the Pacific Coast. [*Tipton played against Southern California in the 1939 Rose Bowl, and Robinson was a halfback for UCLA at the same time, so Casey seems at least mildly justified in lumping them in the same league. On the other hand, he may also be thinking of Kenny Washington, a great black running back who played football with Robinson at UCLA.*] And Robi'son at first was great. But as I ask ya now, ya have Satchel Paige here [*Paige was another guest at the banquet*], and I think later he might say a few words for ya. Because I watched Satchel Paige play twelve years before Robi'son started. And when Robi'son played against us and when he hit the ball as he did to the infield, it was because no left-hander had ever completed a game in the Dodger stadium at Ebbets Field, and when I put in the relief pitcher that I put in, why, that's when they popped the ball up the—to the—catcher because a relief pitcher did not start a game he just relieved. Which the relief for me was left-handed as it made Robi'son pop the ball up like he did. [*The popup Robinson hit in the 1952 World Series off left-hander Bob Kuzava; Stengel starts to gloat a little but thinks better of it and switches to compliments.*] Robi'son was a very good base runner and stealer. He was sensational stealing. [*But he cannot go on praising this man he disliked so.*] And, aaah, he was not the greatest fielder in my position. [*He means "opinion" and he gets flustered again.*] I know four or five men and where everybody said he was, he was in for the Brooklyn club at that time, but when they played with the Monarchs in Kansas City—that was one of the many colored teams I ever saw—I thought that they had four or five men that were outstanding in their play." [*He gets off the subject by ending the last sentence with an abrupt downward intonation and waits for the next question.*]

Meyer says, "All right. After ten pennants in twelve seasons, et cetera, you came back [*to the majors*] with the Mets. What induced you to come back and start over with an expansion ball club?"

"Well," Stengel says, "I, uh, I was turned loose by the Boston club one year and I said, 'Why not lay out in the, uh, and see if you wanna go back into baseball?' [*Casey gets a little mixed up here between 1937, the year after he was fired by Brooklyn, and 1944, the year after he was fired by Boston.*] And at that time I was offered an opportunity to go to two clubs [*that was 1944*] and while I went out I was in the oil business [*that was 1937*]. I looked up and I was given a chance to go with the Boston Braves [*after 1937*]. So I said, 'Well, I laid out one year [*1937*] and got a job, so this time [*1961, after being fired by the Yankees*] I laid out another year and that statement of yours [*earlier, off microphone, Meyer had asked him about the job offer he had received from the Detroit Tigers*], that's true. Mr. Fetzer [*John Fetzer, the Detroit owner*] came to see me himself and two of the—well, I guess they had two of the men who run the higher office [*the Detroit front office*] also called on me and asked if I would consider allowing my name to be used after, I think, they got rid of—Scheffling, wasn't it? *No!* They *hired* Scheffling [*Bob Scheffing, who became the Detroit manager in 1961*] when I told them Scheffling, uh, would be hired [*Casey recommended Scheffing*] and they said Scheffling instead of hiring three or four men that they had in view. I did [*recommended Scheffing, apparently*]. I still laid out a year. And then they [*the Continental League?*] offered me the opportunity so that Branch Rickey came and offered me a chance to go, uh, uh, if I would go, uh, in with the college team before they decided on expansion [*I think Casey means "Continental," not "college"*], which two teams not to use, or what teams to use. Why, he gave me a chance that I coulda gone with a club if he got in charge of it for an expansion, see? I mean, I coulda gone with him [*Rickey? Fetzer?*] but insteada that I had, uh, had, uh, Mrs. Payshon [*Joan Whitney Payson*] and, uh, Mr. Grant [*M. Donald Grant*] called me on the phone out on the Coast twice and offered me a chance if I would go, and I said, no, I was gonna maybe lay out for the rest of the year. But insteada doin' that Mr. Weiss was down at a racetrack, or in the winter he was in New Orlins, and he was also down in Florida, and he talked to him [*Grant talked to Weiss*] and he says [*Weiss says*], 'I myself will take a position over here with the Mets.' So they made him president of the Mets at that time and allowed him to get in touch with me, and then he convinced me after a period that I would go. Well, I was known in Brooklyn and I played with the Giants in '21, '22, and '23, when we played against Ruth and the Yankees, and I had a feeling out there that everybody knew me, see? More so than I would say to pick some other team. And when they decided they would start in the expansion league out in New York that's why I accepted the task. When Weiss took the job, he convinced me that I could go there and do the best I could, and they've been very nice to me up there. Of course, we were what you could call a complete flop" [*voice lifting gently at the end*].

Meyer says, "But in 1949 you were not a complete flop. Your first year with the Yankees, seventy-four injuries, and you still won yourself a pennant. You were like a magical wizard. How did you do it?"

"Well," says Stengel, "I believe it was platooning like the latest thing they asked me [*at the banquet*], and I never talked about it tonight [*pause, as though wondering why he hadn't talked about it*] was why is it now that I hope for you to have pinch hitters. I was a platoon manager, and McGraw platooned me, so if he platooned me I found out he was right, because he win three pennants [*during the three years Casey was with the Giants*]. And I felt when I started in baseball that they were not the same [*the two players being platooned?*]. They got twenty-four clubs [*there were twenty-four big-league teams in 1973*] and they can't fill the rosters. And I say right now with twenty-four clubs, as good as their training and their schools are to educate players, they're not whatcha want [*said almost sadly*]. In other words there still is too many holes to fill or some man gets sick or gets injured on ya and, uh, uh, it's, uh, it—[*he's forgotten the question and can't find his way back to it*]. To me they *have* to have platooning, and that gives an old man a job. Or if you owned a ball club for fourteen million or twelve million or ten million, how would you like to go along and say, 'I won't pinch-hit?' [*Stengel is objecting to players who object to platooning, who don't want to sit on the bench to be used as pinch hitters.*] Now, like I would say, 'The National League and you wouldn't pinch-hit?' Well, let me give you a good tip about it. What if you're in last place and you got new pinch hitters there and you turned them loose? Or what do ya, what if, how many men can hit good that are *pitchers*? Like today they honored Wood out there. [*Joe Wood, the famous old Boston Red Sox pitcher, who was honored at the banquet, was an excellent hitter, but Casey doesn't dwell on that and goes off on a tangent.*] I saw that man play, Wood. He's eighty-four years old and I'm eighty-two, and I watched him and I saw him today, you know, talked to him. I went out with my father to see him [*Wood was a Kansas City boy*]; now think of that, though it's true. I, when I was seventeen years old and he was nineteen, and he was pitching when he was seventeen, so I was fifteen when I went out and saw him. I said, 'Oh my goodness.' I'm thinkin' then of maybe going in semipro ball. Later I worked up in the big league and, uh, so on and so forth [*Casey is trying to recall something*] and it's like—Waite Hoyt! Waite Hoyt come out [*to Ebbets Field for a tryout as a pitcher when Stengel was a player*] with, his mother made his trousers. And he pitched battin' practice when I was in a slump in the big league, and I got mad. Waite Hoyt is—I'm eighty-two, Waite Hoyt now must be seventy-one years of age, and when I saw him out there, fourteen or fifteen, I was mad that the ball club made me—give me him for batting practice, a young kid in town [*Hoyt was a schoolboy sensation*] that the pitcher brought up. But now that he's seventy and he been into Europe, been in a World Series. He shut out—in '21 he pitched for the Yankees and shut us out, twice, when I was with the Yankee ball—I mean the Giant ball club. Later on in life, just think, I went over to Europe and Asia with him. China, so forth. And he was an outstanding pitcher then [*when he was fourteen*] but he didn't *look* that way then, see? Now, now I'm seventy [*a slip of the tongue*], and I saw him in two of these meetings in the Hall of Fame, and he's, uh, just think, he's seventy years old! Retired. I'm eighty-two [*correcting himself*]. But when I was twenty-four and that guy was only fourteen years old—now when they brought him out to the park I thought I'd *kill* him, you know, when he was just—threw the ball up to the plate and the pitcher brought him out. We didn't have many men, and I was disappointed [*that I had to bat against a kid*]. But then in '21 in the World Series I saw what he could do. Then he got better different times. He was a fellow that took care of himself, changed his methods of living. [*Hoyt, a heavy drinker, stopped and became a success in Cincinnati as a play-by-play announcer.*] He was a young, wonderful kid, and a terrific kid, and a handsome kid. And he always went on the air, and he worked for, always, somebody that was on radio. And he was such a handsome kid he ought to a been working *television* when he started because he was, uh, uh, had, had beautiful looks and there's, uh, and he, uh, without going on very far, important to the team and a very good speaker. [*Stengel is trying to remember what he was talking about before he got off on the subject of Waite Hoyt. He can't regain the thread, and so he finishes talking about Hoyt in a confidential tone.*] He laughs when he tells the jokes but they say you shouldn't do it, but he enjoys his own jokes, and I guess [*chuckles*] that's why he laughs at them."

Meyer, going back to the topic Casey forgot, asks firmly, "How about your '49 club?"

"It was a very *good* club," Stengel says, welcoming the topic back, "and I had the best man on the club was, who? Joe DiMaggio. He's worked up to be. When I took over the ball club, they commenced losing some of their best players. Now I commenced then, and I had Rizzuto at shortshop, and that's terrific. Now at second base we had four or five men, that I would say during the year which one would you play? I like Coleman for a double play [*Jerry Coleman*]. Beautiful, wonderful fellow, great. Could throw straight overhand, and if it was an ordinary first baseman, he [*Coleman*] never threw bad, because he threw overhanded. If he threw sidearm, the ball would sink and sink into the ground. So he became a good double-play man. And I had Rizzuto, who was perfect there [*at shortstop*]. Then later on I had, uh, naturally I had Martin that I brought up [*Billy Martin, who joined the Yankees in Casey's second year as manager*]. And they had to fight it out. [*Martin and Coleman were both second basemen.*] Each one went away to the war and save me [*from picking one over the other*]. Like when Martin went into the service for a year, why I had McDougald to play for me [*Gil McDougald*], and a very awkward man, a wonderful man. And now he's coaching now, I guess it's—is it Fordham he's coaching, or New York University? *Fordham*, yeah, and he's gonna be, I bet he'll be a splendid coach. 'Cause his wife writes me very good letters. Every Christmas she writes they have four or five kids, and she writes what the four or five kids do almost every day of the year. And that's a terrific thing. We don't have any children. And I liked him and I liked her. We went to Europe [*he means a trip the Yankees made to the Orient after the 1955 season*], and she quit halfway over. I mean the Orient. She quit halfway on the trip because she was too excited and not having those children at home without her, see? So she left the club and went back there after a short trip over in the Orient. [*Mrs. McDougald went as far as Japan and then returned home.*] Then he became better than he looked. [*Not after his wife left; Casey means McDougald looked awkward when he arrived in the majors but proved to be a far better player than he appeared to be.*] And he always hit. And they used to say to me, 'Why do you play that man with that silly stance?' [*McDougald had an odd batter's stance.*] And I said, 'Al Simmons did it that way,' and Al Simmons [*now in the Hall of Fame*] did put his foot in the bucket, or bent over, you know? And this boy here [*McDougald*] with men on base was a terrific hitter, and he hurt his back the last year he played for me and he didn't tell me, or they shoulda told me [*the doctors?*]. And I played him then at third again [*McDougald was a third baseman, later became a second baseman and then a shortstop before ending up on third again*], but if he'da been better—with a bad back you can't play third base because you gotta dip too quick, see? And when you're playin' shortstop even— Amazing after Rizzuto went into television, he was amazing playing shortstop. [*McDougald, before he hurt his back, took over at shortstop when Rizzuto was released. Actually, he became the regular shortstop when Rizzuto was still with the team.*]

"And then he could, and I put him in there [*at shortstop*] without buying another shortstop [*to replace Rizzuto*] because for this reason: he said I could play it if I played a month. But he had a wonderful way of studying. He could *surmise* you're gonna hit it to your right or to your left when he played short. And he played deep and got rid of the ball quick. So he did an outstanding job where I could have blown, with the ball club being weak at short.

"I was so successful [*self-directed sarcasm*] after I found DiMaggio played for me. To think: there's a man played in a ballpark that wasn't fitted for him. He played in a park that wasn't built for him. [*Yankee Stadium with its enormous left field works against right-handed batters like DiMaggio.*] Williams [*Ted*] played in a park where he hit to right field [*Fenway Park with its long right field, where the left-handed Williams had a problem similar to DiMaggio's in Yankee Stadium*] and—he should have—a right-hand man hits to left field and it looks like a bandbox [*Fenway, with its short left field*]. I used to say, well, uh, there with, uh. [*A vague thought has distracted him; it's that Joe's brother, Dominic, a fine player and a right-handed batter, played for the Red Sox in Fenway without becoming a great hitter, and Stengel doesn't*] *want to criticize him, especially to a Boston broadcaster.*] I had to say with DiMadge that if DiMadge had played in Boston—I don't mean that his brother wasn't great—but he should have played for us [*Williams, that is, not Dominic*] and somebody should've had DiMaggio there [*Fenway*] for years and he musta— he would've had an *outstanding* career, I imagine, of just tapping that ball and playing with it against that fence and—but he was terrific on my ball club. When I came up to the big leagues he was so good that I found out I never had to watch the outfield [*that is, signal the outfielders where to play*], because DiMaggio, wherever he went—if he went to the left center, ya didn't have to yell at the right fielder or the left fielder. They shifted automatically. They were positive his judgment was right, and it was, too, and it saved me, too. Many a tight place where the ball was hit where this man was lodged out there in the proper position."

"Casey—" Meyer begins.

"I'd like," Stengel says, "the best pitchers. I'd like ya to ask about them sometime."

"Go ahead," Meyer says.

"Well, I tell ya why I liked the best pitchers. I—I never—the first pitcher I got there then I got stuck on was Reynolds. [*Allie Reynolds, who with Vic Raschi and Ed Lopat formed the big three of Stengel's pitching staff through his early pennant-winning years.*] Because I put him in and he could strike out [*opposing batters*] and then I put him in one game to relieve and, my goodness, he got 'em out, and [*chuckles*] I had six pitchers back there. And the best part about pitching in that pitching staff was this. He [*Reynolds*] could start and he could relieve, and when I had the Quiz Kids—we were playing them. [*The young Philadelphia Phillies, whom the Yankees played in the 1950 World Series, were nicknamed the Whiz Kids, but Casey got that name mixed up with the name of a popular radio quiz show of the late 1930s and early 1940s that featured precocious youngsters called the Quiz Kids.*] I had Ford pitch [*in the World Series against the Phils*] and people that never knew how to write a World Series with both ball clubs came from all over the United States just to get in on free tickets and write and never had sports editors. [*Casey sweepingly indicts the sportswriters who criticized his strategy in the 1950 Series.*] They wondered why I took Ford out in the seventh inning [*it was the ninth*], and it was true they hit some balls hard off Reynolds [*who relieved Ford*], and I know that he [*Ford*] always said, 'Well, that old man knows,' that I'm hired by the club when he [*Ford*] was in the Eastern League. Now the trouble with that [*the press criticism*] was this. That I went and put in Reynolds—when Reynolds went in there, they [*the Phillies*] put in a couple of their boys, sure they hit him, and they just *got* to make a *b-e-e-g* foul, you know? And *foul* and *foul*, and they were out. [*Casey has confused Reynolds's relief of Ford in the last game of the 1950 World Series—when he came in with two out in the ninth and struck out pinch hitter Stan Lopata, a power hitter who did hit a hard foul—with Reynolds's relief of Raschi in the last game of the 1953 World Series, when he took over after the seventh inning, was hit hard but won the game and, as in 1950, the Series.*]

"So," Casey goes on, "when I went in [*the clubhouse*] they quizzed me and said, 'Why'd you take that Quiz Kid out?' [*meaning Ford, who was only twenty-two*]. And they'd been writing the Quiz Kwids [*sic*] with the Philadelphia players, but that was *wrong*. The Quiz Kid was *Reynolds*, and he was the oldest fella I had on the club [*delivered in an ingenuous Mark Twain "There you are" tone*].

"So he became a two-way man. Reynolds. Berra was catchin' good, too, then and we had a terrific thing with, uh, with, uh, I'd say Raschi. He was, uh, he was, I thought Raschi was the best pitcher I had on the team for nine innings [*meaning as a starting pitcher, in contrast to Reynolds, who could start and relieve*]. Now I tell ya why. Every time he pitched in the seventh, eighth, and ninth he'd almost *die* out there, tryin' to throw a ball hard. He knew that he *tried* to put more on that ball now. If I'm *tired* [*great emphasis on "die" and "tried" and "tired," so that you hear the effort, hear the weariness*], my arm will have too many baseballs being called balls. That guy in the eighth and ninth inning he'd give me, he'd give me, I mean he was almost a sure bet, and Berra admits that now, too. Boy, he was the best on the club in the eighth or ninth inning. But if I relieved with him, you'd be surprised. I was shocked. He couldn't do it.

"Now, Joe Page. Joe Page was what you'd call, well, they called him the fireman. Go up to Boston and they'd say, they got 'em now, they got the Yankees done. And I'd just call him in from the bull pen, and when he went around there, they'd start in fainting in the stands. They'd say, 'Oh my God, putting in that fireman.' And he did a tremendous job. He had guts. I believe in platooning pitchers now, too. And now they want to know why you can't pitch nine innings. Like Satchel Paige. I watched him pitch, but he had to pitch every day where he went. And I watched him when he had to rub it [*his arm, not the baseball*]. And you take now how scientifically they can hurt your arm, you know, at the elbow, or guys that work— Well, we used to have to drive automobiles with a clutch. You'd get sore joints. [*From shifting gears?*] Like a hinge bad on a door, you can't close it. Nowadays the best thing that I saw in the great Case's opinion was, I think, is a—everybody has a doctor [*every team*]. Now the doctor don't mean very much—they do it for spring training. [*The doctor comes to Florida for a vacation.*] And here every club now has an outstanding doctor. It's wonderful, but they just do— I guess when they go and say— [*Casey decides not to go on criticizing doctors.*] Well, with my experience, football, baseball, basketball, they got ways of handling fellas."

"Casey," says Meyer, ending the interview, "I'm going to use another word from your own vocabulary and that's 'amazing.' That's what you've been for these last twenty-five minutes. Thanks so very, very much."

"Yes, it's very good," Casey says, not ending the interview. "I wanted just to ask you another question about some of the players that I had I told you about when I changed to those other clubs. I had people come around and say, 'Well why don't ya?' [?] I used to have an interest in minor leagues and each time I had an interest was—it was to take young fellas and start 'em out. I believe in young fellas. I believe right now in young fellas. I believe right now that it's almost impossible to have some of the men not fail with the rapid thing of seeing a man's weakness. It used to be they [*young players*] didn't believe ya when you're watchin' the ball come across the plate. They [*the coaches*] would say, 'I'm tellin' ya this and you stand there. Do this, see? Look right at home plate. *Now* if you don't hit the ball you understand?' All right. Say, 'Well, you leaned in.' They say, 'Naw, I didn't.' Then if you show them that quick replay now do they get it? 'Well, uh,' they say, 'I swore I did not.' [*A strong protesting "Naw, I didn't," a meek embarrassed "I swore I did not."*]

"Well," says Casey, "the pitcher watches the ball, and that's the reason why you lose what any other teacher would tell ya. And that's why if you lean in, there's six guys like Paige and he's watchin' ya, and if you lean in he goes around once more and he throw in here. How can you lean in and pull back and the distance is sixty feet? And that's why he [*Paige*] became great. I saw him when he could throw like lightning, and I asked him myself. Men interview him at times, you know. And semipro games. And he was great. And you know what he used to do? He used to go in under the hot shower and put the hot shower on him, you know? And this was his rub, because they never had the trainer. And then he'd pitch the next day because he was so well known in the small towns. Yeah, he did a big job.

"All right! [*Now he's finishing the interview.*] It was very nice to do it. Nice to see ya here. I hope sometimes I can meetcha around. Very much enjoyed it, and I think I'll do better next time.

"If you wanta know this here year and know what I'm doin' at any time, I've had five or six offers to do this and that, you call me in Glendale, California, and I'll give you all the answers. And that's what I do now with the Mets. And they ask me. Well, I'm workin' for a woman [*Mrs. Payson*], and they ask me, 'Well, what do you do for 'em?' And I said, 'Well, I'm very careful now that I don't disturb 'em, as they're doin' well without me.' I tell you what, I saw rapid advancement, rapid advancement. If you've got somebody and he says, 'Well, he's stupid, and he's laid up.' Half of the men that we used to get, they came in there and they— I mean they were good enough, but they *slowed* up for you. They had injury in their lives. Maybe trouble with—eye trouble. Maybe they'd say, 'I cannot see with one eye.' Maybe they had to say, 'Well, I tell you what; I can't pitch anymore, but I can pitch three innings.' But Satchel Paige even said tonight he was going to spring training. He wouldn't pitch Friday and Saturday, too. He never was a relief pitcher [*not in the Negro Leagues, but Paige was a relief pitcher in the American League*]."

"Casey," says Meyer, "thanks again."

"You bet." Casey snaps it off vigorously. "I'll, uh, I'll go, uh, I'll have you in mind, and anytime something comes up, ask me what. I told you about the pinch hitter and about the old man. The old man gets to play now, and if he plays— If you own the ball club and you get the receipts, most of it, you better do well at home. You play half your games at home, and if you don't have a pinch hitter at home and your club is green, why you better have to play those home games in— The older man gets to play two or three years longer in baseball where the young man in pinch-hitting doesn't do great, *but* if the pitcher knew, I'm gonna throw the ball over the plate, the young man goes up, says, 'I'm gonna kill that pitcher.' And then he hits at bad pitches. But the old fella gets hit with the ball or makes you nibble on it.

"Thank you very much. I'm glad you give me that interview, and someday if you're in a pinch call me up and I'll have a better answer."

And that did end the interview.

Alphabetical fortuity brings us, in close marching order, four of the more compelling figures of the game's early days: Pearce and Wright, just before, Candy Cummings and Jim Devlin to follow. But now some background on Mr. Cummings's perfidious pitch. Historians dispute whether this 120-pound pony deserves more credit as pioneer or publicist, but he is certainly a historical figure to reckon with. Others may have established competing claims of authorship, more or less convincing (those of Fred Goldsmith, Phonnie Martin, Bobby Mathews, Tommy Bond, and Jim White), but Candy's claim still seems the best, and he rode it—and in this 1908 reminiscence, wrote it—into immortality.

CANDY CUMMINGS

How I Pitched the First Curve

I have been asked how I first got the idea of making a ball curve. I will now explain. It is such a simple matter, though, that there is not much explanation.

In the summer of 1863 a number of boys and myself were amusing ourselves by throwing clam shells (the hard-shell variety) and watching them sail along through the air, turning now to the right and now to the left. We became interested in the mechanics of it and experimented for an hour or more.

All of a sudden it came to me that it would be a good joke on the boys if I could make a baseball curve the same way. We had been playing "three old cat" and town ball, and I had been doing the pitching. The joke seemed so good that I made a firm decision that I would try to play it.

I set to work on my theory and practiced every spare moment that I had out of school. I had no one to help me and had to fight it out alone. Time after time I would throw the ball, doubling up into all manner of positions, for I thought that my pose had something to do with it; and then I tried holding the ball in different shapes. Sometimes I thought I had it, and then maybe again in twenty-five tries I could not get the slightest curve. My visionary successes were just enough to tantalize me. Month after month I kept pegging away at my theory.

In 1864 I went to Fulton, New York, to a boarding school and remained there a year and a half. All that time I kept experimenting with my curve ball. My boyfriends began to laugh at me and to throw jokes at my theory of making a ball go sideways. I fear that some of them thought it was so preposterous that it was no joke and that I should be carefully watched over.

I don't know what made me stick at it. The great wonder to me now is that I did not give up in disgust, for I had not one single word of encouragement in all that time, while my attempts were a standing joke among my friends.

After graduating, I went back to my home in Brooklyn, New York, and joined the "Star Juniors," an amateur team. We were very successful. I was solicited to join as a junior member the Excelsior club, and I accepted the proposition.

In 1867 I, with the Excelsior club, went to Boston, where we played the Lowells, the Tri-Mountains, and Harvard clubs. During these games I kept trying to make the ball curve. It was during the Harvard game that I became fully convinced that I had succeeded in doing what all these years I had been striving to do. The batters were missing a lot of balls; I began to watch the flight of the ball through the air and distinctly saw it curve.

A surge of joy flooded over me that I shall never forget. I felt like shouting out that I had made a ball curve; I wanted to tell everybody; it was too good to keep to myself.

But I said not a word and saw many a batter at that game throw down his stick in disgust. Every time I was successful, I could scarcely keep from dancing from pure joy. The secret was mine.

There was trouble, though, for I could not make it curve when I wanted to. I would grasp it the same, but the ball seemed to do just as it pleased. It would curve, all right, but it was very erratic in its choice of places to do so. But still it curved!

The baseball came to have a new meaning to me; it almost seemed to have life.

It took time and hard work for me to master it, but I kept on pegging away until I had fairly good control.

In those days the pitcher's box was 6 feet by 4, and the ball could be thrown from any part of it; one foot could be at the forward edge of the box, while the other could be stretched back as far as the pitcher liked; but both feet had to be on the ground until the ball was delivered. It is surprising how much speed could be generated under those rules.

It was customary to swing the arm perpendicularly and to deliver the ball at the height of the knee. I still threw this way but brought in wrist action.

I found that the wind had a whole lot to do with the ball curving. With a wind against me I could get all kinds of a curve, but the trouble lay in the fact that the ball was apt not to break until it was past the batter. This was a sore trouble; but I learned not to try to curve a ball very much when the wind was unfavorable.

I have often been asked to give my theory of why a ball curves. Here it is: I give the ball a sharp twist with the middle finger, which causes it to revolve with a swift rotary motion. The air also, for a limited space around it begins to revolve, making a great swirl, until there is enough pressure to force the ball out of true line. When I first began practicing this new legerdemain, the pitchers were not the only ones who were fooled by the ball. The umpire also suffered. I would throw the ball straight at the batter; he would jump back, and then the umpire would call a ball. On this I lost, but when I started the spheroid toward the center of the plate, he would call it a strike. When it got to the batter, it was too far out, and the batter would not even swing. Then there would be a clash between the umpire and the batter.

But my idlest dreams of what a curved ball would do as I dreamed of them that afternoon while throwing clam shells have been filled more than a hundred times. At that time I thought of it only as a good way to fool the boys, its real practical significance never entering my mind.

I get a great deal of pleasure now in my old age out of going to games and watching the curves, thinking that it was through my blind efforts that all this was made possible.

The final weeks of the 1877 National League season witnessed a mysterious collapse of the Louisville club, permitting Boston to take the pennant rather handily. The suspicious Louisville directors soon caught on that four of their players had sold out to gamblers. Among these was star pitcher Jim Devlin, who had hurled every one of the club's 129 games over the previous two years. Distraught over his banishment by the league that winter, impoverished and penitent, the poor soul begged help from Boston manager Harry Wright and league president William Hulbert. His poignant letter to Wright is reproduced below, and the wrenching scene in Hulbert's office is described by one-time pitching ace and sporting goods magnate Albert Spalding, whose office adjoined Hulbert's.

JIM DEVLIN

"I Am Honest, Harry"

Phila   Feb 24th 1878
Mr Harry Wright
*   Dear Sir*
as I am Deprived from Playing this year I thought I woed [would] write you to see if you Coed [could] do anything for me in the way of looking after your ground or anything in the way of work   I Dont Know what I am to do   I have tried hard to get work of any Kind   But I Canot get it   do you Know of anyway that you think I Coed [could] get to Play again   I Can asure you Harry that I was not Treated right and if Ever I Can see you to tell you the Case you will say I am not to Blame   I am living from hand to mouth all winter   I have not got a Stich of Clothing or has my wife and child   You Dont Know how I am Situated for I Know if you did you woed [would] do Something for me   I am honest Harry   you need not Be afraid   the Louisville People made me what I am to day   a Begger   I trust you will not Say any-thing to anyone about the Contents of this to any one   if you Can do me this favor By letting me take Care of the ground or anything of that Kind   I Beg of you to do it   and god will reward you if I Dont   or let me Know if you have any Ide [idea] of how I Coed [could] get Back   I am Dumb Harry   I dont Know how to go about it   So I Trust you will answear this and do all you Can for me   So I will Close by Sending you & Geo and all the Boys my verry Best wishes   hoping to hear from you Soon   I am yours Trouly
*   James A Devlin*
*   No 908   Atherton St*
*   Phila   Pa*

Spalding writes:

His lips gave utterance to such a plea for mercy as might have come from one condemned to the gallows. . . . It was a scene of heartrending tragedy. Devlin was in tears, Hulbert was in tears . . . I heard Devlin's plea to have the stigma removed from his name. I heard him entreat, not on his own account—he acknowledged himself unworthy of consideration—but for the sake of his wife and child. . . . I saw the president's hand steal into his pocket as if seeking to conceal his intended act from the other hand. I saw him take a $50 bill and press it into the palm of the prostrate player. And then I heard him say, as he fairly writhed with the pain his own words caused him, "That's what I think of you, personally; but, damn you, Devlin, you are dishonest; you have sold a game, and I can't trust you. Now go; and let me never see your face again; for your act will not be condoned so long as I live."

An archetypal figure of legend and literature is the wise fool, who accepts the world's mockery and, secure in his special relationship with higher powers, keeps his counsel. In the early days of baseball, when superstition was more widespread than today, managers sought a competitive edge by taking on as mascots a range of misfits, from dwarfs and hunchbacks to dingbats like Charles Victor (Victory) Faust, whose luck rubbed off on John McGraw's Giants from 1911 through 1913. The aptly named Faust makes an appearance in *Ragtime*, the 1975 novel that also presented such historical figures as J. P. Morgan and Henry Ford and brought fame to its author. Here a father feels his grip on his family slipping away as an outsider, Coalhouse Walker, holds the reins. Enter baseball.

E. L. DOCTOROW

Family

It was clear the crisis was driving the spirit from their lives. Father had always felt secretly that as a family they were touched by an extra light. He felt it going now. He felt stupid and plodding, available simply to have done to him what circumstances would do. Coalhouse ruled. Yet he had been to the Arctic, to Africa, to the Philippines. He had traveled out West. Did that mean only that more and more of the world resisted his intelligence? He sat in his study. Everyone he thought about, even Grandfather, he saw in terms of his own failed concern. He had treated Grandfather with the arrogant courtesy one gives to the senile even before the condition had set in. From Younger Brother he was completely estranged. Toward his wife he felt drastically slipped in her estimation, an explorer in body only, the spirit trapped in his own father's prejudices. He was beginning to look like him, too, going dry and juiceless in everything, with a mad glint showing in the corner of his eye. Why did that have to be?

He condemned himself most for the neglect of his son. He never talked to the boy or offered his companionship. He had always relied on his presence in the child's life as a model for emulation. How smug that was, how stupid, as the tactic of a man who had acted in his life to distinguish himself from his own father. He looked for the boy and found him on the floor of his room reading in the evening paper an account of the successful play of the New York baseball nine under the masterful coaching of John J. McGraw. Would you like to see that team? he said. The boy looked up, startled. I was just thinking of

it, he said. Father went to Mother's room. Tomorrow, he announced, I am taking the boy to see a game of baseball. He said this with such resolve in its rightness that she was checked in her response, which was to condemn him for an idiot, and when he left the room, she could only wonder that she had had that thought in the first place, so separated from any feeling of love.

* * *

The next afternoon, when father and son left the house, two reporters followed them part of the way on their brisk walk to the railroad station on Quaker Ridge Road. We're going to the Giants baseball game, Father advised them. That's all I will say. Who's pitching? one of the reporters asked. Rube Marquard, the boy said. He's won his last three chances.

Just as they reached Quaker Ridge, a train pulled in. This was the New York Westchester and Boston railway. It did not go anywhere near Boston, nor did it provide service all the way to New York. But it gave a smooth ride to the Bronx and left them with a trolley connection, the 155th Street crosstown, which went over the Harlem River to the Polo Grounds at Coogan's Bluff.

It was a fine afternoon. Large white clouds moved briskly under a clear blue sky. As the trolley came across the bridge, they could see on the bluff overlooking the wooden stands several huge trees that, lacking leaves even in this season, supported derbied figures of men who preferred not to pay to enter the park but to watch the game festooned in the branches like black flowers swaying in the wind. Father caught some of the boy's excitement. He was immensely pleased to be out of New Rochelle. When they reached the park, crowds were streaming down the stairs from the El, cabs were pulling up and discharging their passengers, newsboys were hawking programs of the game, and there was a raucous energy everywhere in the street. Horns blew. The overhead tracks of the El left the street mottled with sun. Father bought the expensive fifty-cent admission, then paid extra for a box, and they entered the park and took their seats behind first base in the lower of the two decks where the sun would for an inning or two cause them to shade their eyes.

The Giants were dressed in their baggy white uniforms with black pinstripes. The manager, McGraw, wore a heavy black cardigan over his barreled trunk with the letters "NY" emblazoned on the left sleeve. He was short and pugnacious. Like his team, he wore socks with thick horizontal stripes and the small flat cap with a peak and button on the crown. The opponents of the afternoon were the Boston Braves, whose dark blue flannels were buttoned to the neck with the collar turned up. A brisk wind blew the dirt of the field. The game began, and almost immediately Father regretted the seats he had chosen. The players' every ragging curse could be heard clearly by his son. The team at bat shouted obscene taunts at the opposing pitcher. McGraw himself, the paternal figure and commander of his team, stood at third base, unleashing the most constant and creative string of vile epithets of anyone. His strident caw could be heard throughout the park. The crowd seemed to match him in its passions. The game was close, with first one team, then the other, assuming the lead. A runner sliding into second base upended the Giant second baseman, who rose howling, limping in circles and bleeding profusely through his stocking. Both teams came running from their dugouts, and the game was stopped for some minutes while everyone fought and rolled in the dirt and the crowd yelled its encouragement. An inning or two after the fight the Giant pitcher Marquard seemed to lose his control and threw the ball so that it hit the Boston batsman. This fellow rose from the ground and ran out toward Marquard, waving his bat. Again the dugouts emptied, and players wrestled with each other and threw their roundhouse punches and beat clouds of dust into the air. The audience this time participated by throwing soda-pop bottles onto the field. Father consulted his program. On the Giant side were Merkle, Doyle, Meyers, Snodgrass, and Herzog, among others. The Boston team boasted a player named Rabbit Maranville, a shortstop who he noted roamed his position bent over with his hands at the end of his long arms grazing the grass in a manner that would more properly be called simian. There was a first baseman named Butch Schmidt and others with the names Cocrehan, Moran, Hess, Rudolph, which led inevitably to the conclusion that professional baseball was played by immigrants. When play was resumed, he studied each batsman: indeed, they seemed to be clearly from the mills and farms, rude-featured, jug-eared men, sunburned and ham-handed, cheeks bulging with tobacco chew, their intelligence completely absorbed in the effort of the game. The players in the field wore outsized flapping leather gloves that made them look like half-dressed clowns. The dry dust of the diamond was blotched with expectorant. Woe to the campaigns of the Anti-Spitting League in the example of these men. On the Boston side the boy who picked up the bats and replaced them in the dugout was, upon second look, a midget, in a team uniform like the rest but proportionately minute. His shouts and taunts were piped in soprano. Most of the players who came to bat first touched him on the head, a gesture he seemed to invite, so that Father realized it was a kind of good-luck ritual. On the Giant side was no midget but a strange skinny man whose uniform was ill fitting, who had weak eyes that did not align properly, and who seemed to shadow the game in a lethargic pantomime of his own solitude, pitching imaginary balls more or less in time to the real pitches. He looked like a dirt eater. He waved his arm in complete circles, as a windmill turns. Father began to watch the game less than he did this unfortunate creature, obviously a team pet, like the Boston midget. During dull moments of the game the crowd yelled to him and applauded his antics. Sure enough, he was listed in the program as mascot. His name was Charles Victor Faust. He was clearly a fool who, for imagining himself one of the players, was kept on the team roster for their amusement.

Father remembered the baseball at Harvard twenty years before, when the players addressed each other as Mister and played their game avidly, but as sportsmen, in sensible uniforms before audiences of collegians who rarely numbered more than a hundred. He was disturbed by his nostalgia. He'd always thought of himself as progressive. He believed in the perfectibility of the republic. He thought, for instance, there was no reason the Negro could not with proper guidance carry every burden of human achievement. He did not believe in aristocracy except of the individual effort and vision. He felt his father's loss of fortune had the advantage of saving him from the uncritical adoption of the prejudices of his class. But the air in this ballpark open under the sky smelled like the back room of a saloon. Cigar smoke filled the stadium and, lit by the oblique rays of the afternoon sun, indicated the voluminous cavern of air in which he sat pressed upon as if by a foul universe, with the breathless wind of a 10,000-throated chorus in his ears shouting its praise and abuse.

Out in center field, behind the unroofed or bleacher seats, a great display board indicated the number of outs and the inning and the hits and runs made. A man went along a scaffold and hung the appropriate marked shingles that summarized the action. Father sank into his chair. As the afternoon wore on, he entertained the illusion that what he saw was not baseball but an elaborate representation of his own problems, accounted, for his secret understanding, in the coded clarity of numbers that could be seen from a distance.

He turned to his son. What is it you like about this game, he said. The boy did not remove his gaze from the diamond. The same thing happens over and over, he said. The pitcher throws the ball so as to fool the batter into thinking he can hit it. But sometimes the batter does hit it, the father said. Then the pitcher is the one who is fooled, the boy said. At this moment the Boston hurler, Hub Perdue, threw a pitch that the New York batter, Red Jack Murray, swung at. The ball soared into the air in a high, narrow arc and seemed then to stop in its trajectory. With a start Father realized it was coming directly at them. The boy jumped up and held out his hands, and there was a cheer behind them as he stood with the leather-covered spheroid resting in his palms. For one instant everyone in the park looked in their direction. Then the fool with the weak eyes who imagined he was a player on the team came up to the fence in front of them and stared at the boy, his arms and hands twitching in his baggy flannel shirt. His hat was absurdly small for his abnormally large head. The boy held out the ball to him, and gently, with a smile almost sane, he accepted it.

An interesting note is that this poor fellow, Charles Victor Faust, was actually called upon to pitch one inning in a game toward the end of this same season when the Giants had already won the pennant and were in a carefree mood. For a moment his delusion that he was a big leaguer fused with reality. Soon thereafter the players became bored with him, and he was no longer regarded as a good-luck charm by Manager McGraw. His uniform was confiscated, and he was unceremoniously sent on his way. He was remanded to an insane asylum and some months later died there.

At the end of the ball game a great anxiety came over Father. He felt it had been stupid to leave his wife alone. But as they left the park, borne by the streaming crowd, he realized his son had taken his hand. He felt an uplift of his spirit. On the open trolley he put his arm around the boy's shoulders. Arriving in New Rochelle, they walked briskly from the train station, and when they came in the door, they gave a loud hello! and for the first time in days Father felt like himself. . . .

"Nice guys finish last," Leo Durocher once said when asked why he wasn't a nice guy like Billy Meyer of Pittsburgh. These immortal words became the title for his tough and splendid autobiography, written with Ed Linn. Leo managed for twenty-four years and finished last only once, the year he took control of a basket-case Chicago Cub franchise; the following year, he brought the Cubs in third. It's hard to be neutral about Leo the man or Leo the manager, but it's impossible to make light of his record: he may have claimed only three pennants in a career that spanned 1939 to 1973, but in the history of baseball only five men won more games. This nasty episode took place in 1971.

LEO DUROCHER with ED LINN

The Santo Explosion

It was one of Santo's slumps that led, indirectly, to the worst argument I ever saw in a clubhouse. The only thing that didn't fly was fists, and for a while there it was a very near thing. And it wasn't Santo's fault. I have nobody to blame but myself. As a bow to the modern ballplayer, I had formed the habit of holding open meetings. "Okay, boys," I'd say after I had spoken my piece. "Now we'll forget that I'm the manager, and let's hear what's on your mind." Keep asking for it, buddy, and you're going to get it.

The real culprits were Milt Pappas and Joe Pepitone, a pair of renegades we had picked up during the previous season. Pappas I will never forgive. All I did for Pappas was save his life after he had done everything but crawl on his knees to me. He started on me in Acapulco in the winter of 1969 while my wife and I were sitting in a restaurant. Pappas was a great friend of our traveling secretary, Blake Cullen, and he came over to our table to say hello. "Goddam, get me, Leo," he said. "I want to pitch for you."

Now, Milt could pitch, but he had a reputation everywhere he had ever been of being one of the great clubhouse lawyers of our time. That's why Baltimore, his original club, had let him go; it was, from everything I heard, why Cincinnati had let him go; and it was probably why he no longer felt he had a glowing future in Atlanta. That didn't bother me at all. I always felt that I could handle the renegades.

I didn't think Atlanta was going to give him up that easily, though, and I told him so.

The following summer he wooed me. Early in the season we played three games in Atlanta, and he came to me three different times. The first two times he came over while I was on the field watching batting practice to let me know Atlanta wasn't using him and he definitely could be had. Just what I needed. To begin with, there's an antifraternization rule. You're not supposed to even talk to a player in the other uniform, let alone be talking about making a deal for him. The last day, I was told that he was waiting for me at the bus outside our clubhouse. "Get him out of there," I yelled.

Same thing when Atlanta came to Chicago a week later. And all the time he kept telling Blake Cullen how much he would like to be with the Cubs, and Blake would come to me and ask whether I thought Pappas could help us.

There was no question that he could help us. We needed another starting pitcher bad, and you only had to look at the box scores to see that Pappas was right in feeling that his future did not lay in Atlanta. So I talked to John Holland about him. John wasn't crazy about the idea, but—lucky me—I finally was able to talk him into it.

The guy could pitch, all right. But he always wanted to spit the bit out; that was the other part of his reputation. He'd give you a great six, seven innings, and if he had a one-run lead, he was through. If he won it, fine, he got credit for the win. If you lost, he was off the hook. If he was a run behind, it was a different story; he'd really be bearing down. The time that tore it, he was pitching against Cincinnati after he had been with us about a month, and he was pitching just great. (A couple of weeks earlier he had shut the Reds out, the only time they were shut out all year.) This time, I made the mistake of sending Joe Becker, my pitching coach, over to ask him how he felt, "Aahh,

I'm all in," Milt said. "I'd get a new pitcher in there." I took him out. My fault.

Cincinnati tied the game in the eighth and beat us in the ninth. If that wasn't bad enough, he threw a temper tantrum in the clubhouse when he heard the score had been tied. My coaches came to me in a body to tell me that I should never do that with Pappas. "I know," I said. "I wanted to be sure."

I sat everybody down, and I said, "I want to apologize to the rest of the team. I screwed up today." And then I turned to Pappas and told him he was never going to do that to me again. "You're going to start, and you're staying in there until I take you out, and nobody's going to ask you. Quit looking over your shoulder at me. I blame myself, because I should know better."

From that day on, he never got to talk to me. He'd come into the dugout looking for me, and wherever he went, I'd go the other way. He'd look into the dugout from the mound, and I'd put my head down. It didn't matter what he said to the coaches. They were under instructions never to relay any of his complaints to me. I made him stay nine. *Pitch*, I'd say to myself. *You ain't going to get out of there today; you're pitching too good. They're going to get a couple of men on, and somebody's going to get a base hit before I take you out now. Tired or not, you're pitching too good.* The same year we had the blowup, he won more games for me, seventeen, than he had ever won before in his life. And pitched more innings.

But he was always agitating. He became the player representative when Randy Hundley quit, a job nobody else wanted and Milt always loved. He had also been the player rep at Baltimore, Cincinnati, and Atlanta. Worst thing that could have happened. Once he was the player representative, he was holding meetings all the time. Practically overnight, all harmony disappeared from the Chicago clubhouse.

And it wasn't that the players looked on him with any particular affection, either. There was one time during a road trip that we were going from someplace or other to Cincinnati. We had been playing horribly, and since the first day in Cincinnati was open, I had Blake Cullen reroute us to Chicago. And not to give the players a day with their loved ones! "We're going to work out at Wrigley Field," I told them, "and everybody is to be there."

Milt Pappas didn't show up. His wife called up to say he was sick. As soon as the other guys saw he wasn't there, they just stood around on the field hollering, "Where is Pappas? Where is Pappas?" I was so mad about it myself that I sent everybody back into the clubhouse and told them they could go home. "See you tomorrow in Cincinnati." That was our workout. That was what we had made the trip to Chicago for.

Milt showed up about three days later with a note from his family doctor.

Pepitone was another kettle of fish entirely. I knew exactly what I was getting when I got him. A couple of days before Ernie Banks went on the disabled list, Pepitone had left Houston, wailing that he couldn't stand (1) Harry Walker, the manager; (2) Spec Richardson, the general manager; (3) anybody else who tried to tell him what he had to do. "I can't stand a million rules," Peppy had said—and a beautiful example was the awful thing they were trying to do to Peppy in Houston. They had actually tried to assign him a roommate on the road, like everybody else. Pepitone had gone home to his hairstyling salon in Brooklyn to brood about man's inhumanity to man, and he was nothing if not available.

He didn't come cheap, either. Although it was announced as a straight sale, it wasn't. We had to agree to give up a minor-league player at the end of the season, and the player was going to be Roger Metzger, who we really hated to lose.

It was a calculated risk we were willing to take because we were fighting for the division title, and Peppy was another guy who could play. He was a good hitter, he could run, he had a good arm. He knew how to play ball. He was the best first baseman we had, and he was also the best outfielder. He could do everything. It was just a question of how much of it he was willing to give you on any particular day.

It was a crime, watching a guy like that wasting all that talent. Because basically Peppy was a lovable guy. He could charm the birds out of the trees. No matter how mad you might be when you started to talk to him, you'd go away thinking, He's his own worst enemy, poor fellow. Too bad. Which, I guess, was exactly what Peppy, poor fellow, wanted you to go away thinking. Training rules? Forget it. No training rules where Joe Pepitone was concerned. What were you going to do, fine him? He was in debt up to his eyeballs when he came to us. He always owed the club half of his year's salary before the year started. Gratitude? You're kidding. His attitude, like most of them, was "I'm entitled to it."

A shining example of the new breed. Mod all the way.

I came into the office one day, and right outside my door there's a Harley-Davidson motorcycle. I called Yosh to find out whose it was. Listen, it didn't have to be Peppy's. We had another nut there, Ray Newman, who used to ride to the park from the Executive House, 10 or 12 miles away, on his bicycle. That was my left-handed relief pitcher. One day he ran it right into a bus and almost killed himself. Had to get rid of the bicycle. Him, too, while we were at it.

Peppy couldn't understand why I would object to having a motorcycle in the clubhouse. It seemed reasonable enough to him. "Every time I try to get on it out on the parking lot, the kids bother me."

We tried to put him on a budget. See you later, pal. He'd go into Cincinnati and visit Dino's, a fancy haberdashery, and the next thing you knew, you'd walk into the clubhouse, and he'd be putting on a fashion show.

"Joe, who's paying for this?"

"They took a check."

If you're thinking that Pepitone was sent to me in just retribution and that somewhere the ghosts of Sidney Weil and Branch Rickey were laughing uproariously, I have to admit that the same thought occasionally crossed my own mind.

If you have picked up the impression somewhere along the line that Joey Amalfitano is very important to me, you are absolutely right. Joe came to me in the spring of 1954 as an eighteen-year-old bonus boy who had just been signed by the New York Giants. Just what I didn't need, an untried kid I had to keep on the roster. But he hustled all the time, was very bright, and he got 120 percent out of his talent. After I left the Giants, he was sent down to the minors, but I always stayed in contact with him and used whatever influence I had to get him back there. He lived with his parents in Long Beach, California, in the off-season, helping with the family fishing fleet. He is a good son, and he is highly religious. Or wouldn't you say that a man who has got up with the dawn a minimum of four times a week all his life to take communion is highly religious?

I will never forget one Sunday in Mexico when I took Joe and a couple of other people to the bullfights in Acapulco. It was a little after seven at night, and we had barely started to drive back to the Racquet Club when Joe said, "Let me out."

"Let me out for what?" I yelped. "We've got five miles to go yet. How are you going to get back?"

He'd take a cab.

"Wait a minute, where are you going?"

To church.

"What church? Where's there a church?"

Up in the hills, he said. There was an open-air church up there that had a seven-thirty evening mass. "I'll walk up."

Don't you know, we went up with him in the burning heat? Worst-looking church you ever saw in your life. All open air. Kids running in and out. Mosquitoes everywhere.

But Joey wasn't going to miss mass.

By a stroke of luck, Joey was playing for the Cubs when I got there. Right away, I made him one of my coaches. If I hadn't, we probably never would have got Jim Hickman, who also had a role to play in the explosion.

We were making a deal with Los Angeles for Phil Regan, the relief pitcher I needed, and as the deal was worked out, we agreed to send a pitcher from our minor-league club in Tacoma to their minor-league team in Spokane. To even it off, Bavasi was going to send someone from Spokane to Tacoma. He gave us a list of four players we could choose from, and Hickman, who had been one of the original members of the New York Mets, was on it. "Grab him," Joey said. "He always hit well in Wrigley Field." A year later he was up with us, and in 1970, the guy who had been one of four names thrown into a minor-league deal won the All-Star Game for the National League with a hit in the thirteenth inning. What a year he had for us! He played the outfield for us, he played first base in a pinch, and when he wasn't starting, he was hitting home runs as a pinch hitter. He hit 32 home runs and knocked in 115 runs. He won game after game for us to keep us in the pennant race.

A very quiet, soft-spoken young man from Hennings, Tennessee. "My hillbilly," I called him. During spring training the following year, he was sitting morosely at a table in the Pink Pony, having a drink and doing his best, in his polite way, to get rid of some girl who was bothering him. Yosh came over to where Lynne and I were sitting. "Better go over and talk to Hickman."

I went over to the table and told the girl to get lost. "Jim, what's your problem, buddy? Anything I can do? Anything you want to tell me about?"

"Well," he said. "I don't want to bother you. You've been so good to me."

I finally got him to tell me. He had asked for $46,000, because that was what he thought he deserved, and all Holland had wanted to give him was $40,000. "I wanted to play for you," he said, "and I don't like to hold out, so I signed for the forty thousand." He just didn't like to get into a big fight over money, it went against him, but that didn't mean he didn't feel he was being cheated.

I said, "I wish you'd have told me about it, Jim. I wish I'd have known about it before you signed." I didn't know if I could do him any good now that the contract was signed, I told him, but I sure as hell was going to try.

I bided my time until Holland was in a particularly good mood, and then I said, "You know we've got a very unhappy player on this club." I sketched in the background for him very quickly. "Couple of thousand one way or the other doesn't make any difference, but there's a six-thousand-dollar difference here. It's entirely up to you, John. But he's been a hell of a guy on the club. Cost us nothing and done a great job since he came here. Very popular with the fans. Drew people in the park. I think he's an outstanding player on our club. I hate to see him unhappy."

"What are you asking me to do?"

"That's an unfair question, John," I said, laughing it up a little. "I'll just leave it up to you."

"Send him in to see me," John sighed.

I sent him in, and Holland gave him the $46,000.

And Jim Hickman never forgot it.

Now you have the main cast of characters. Pappas, Pepitone, Amalfitano, and Hickman. And Santo.

The whole thing started, really, when we arrived in Atlanta late at night on the last stop of a road trip before returning to Chicago. Santo got on the elevator with me, just the two of us, and asked if he could talk to me in private. When we got to my suite, it developed that he wanted to talk about the Day they were giving him the second Sunday after we got back. "I never wanted a Day to begin with," he said. "And now I'm going so lousy that the fans are going to be on me. I just wish you'd talk to Holland about calling it off."

No way, Holland told me. Too much had already been done. It was a hell of a time for him to be asking that it be called off, John said, especially since it had been Ron himself who had asked for it. *Ron had asked for it!* Yeah, while they had been negotiating his contract, Ron had argued that since Banks and Williams had been given a Day, he was entitled to one, too. Now in fairness to Ron, I want to add very quickly that Ron was a diabetic, something he had kept entirely to himself up to then. The principal beneficiary of Santo Day, as the plans were worked out, was to be not Ron himself but the Diabetic Association. In fairness to myself, I should say that I didn't know this—I'm not sure anybody outside of the front office knew it—until it came out during the actual ceremonies. I hadn't even known there was going to be a Day until Ron told me about it in my suite in Atlanta.

In the course of that same talk, Ron had also asked if it would be all right with me if he didn't take batting practice. Just, you know, to see if it might help him shake his slump. Sure, Ron. Good idea. Might be just the thing. He had done pretty well for two days, too. And then he had gone into an even worse slump. When I called the meeting on August 23, we had been home for three days, and Ron had not had a base hit in twelve times at bat. And he still wasn't taking batting practice.

To complete the background, we were still very much in the pennant race: 4½ games behind Pittsburgh with thirty-seven games left to play. We had lost two straight to Houston, though, the last loss coming when Doug Rader doubled off Pappas on an 0–2 pitch, the unforgivable sin for a pitcher.

That was one of the things I brought up in the course of the meeting. We weren't hustling, I told them. We weren't bearing down. We were slipping back into the sloppy, uncaring ways that had beaten us for three straight years now. I said, "The guy in left field, Number twenty-six, I write his name in the lineup every day and forget about him. He's out there taking batting practice. He's out there early fielding and throwing." I said, "I got a guy over here, Beckert, busting his rear end. He's having a super year. Challenging Clemente for the batting title. He's out there every day. He works on his hitting, he works on his fielding. He works on all his weaknesses. He made himself into a hell of a player."

But there were some of them, I said, who didn't seem to care. "I'm out there watching the workout, Ronnie, and you're not even there during batting practice. You're coming out late."

"Well, in my case," Ronnie said, "I don't care to hit some days."

"Well, that's what I'm trying to say, Ronnie. Maybe if you came out there and practiced, you wouldn't get into these slumps you get into periodically."

And that's where Ronnie started to blow up. He was different from Beckert, he said. I had given him permission not to take batting practice, and now I was jumping all over him. "You say we're all the same to you, and we're not all the same. It doesn't matter what I do, you're right on my ass. . . ."

Well, this wasn't what I wanted at all. "Wait a minute," I said. "The only thing I'm trying to tell you is that you got to go on the field and practice. If nothing else, the fans come out early to see you, and you don't hit, you're not even there, and they're disappointed."

It might have ended right there except that Pappas had to open his mouth. "The whole trouble in this locker room," he said, "is that you don't know how to handle us."

I had to sit there for ten minutes and listen to Milt Pappas lecture me on the proper way to handle ballplayers, something Milt Pappas knew all about from never having managed.

"Listen, Pappas," I said, when he was finished. "I brought you here from Atlanta. I've given you the ball. I don't know what you've got to complain about. You've been winning more games the way I've been handling you than you ever won in your life."

Pepitone's locker was right next to Pappas's, which was a mistake right there. "I want to say something," Peppy said. "You know, I played for the Yankees with some very good clubs, and Ralph Houk is just a super guy. He lets you play. The trouble with this club is if a guy makes a mistake on the field you talk about him on the bench. Houk never did that."

He held the floor for about ten minutes, too, telling me what a great manager Ralph Houk was, what a super guy. The only thing he didn't tell me was why Houk had finally thrown up his super hands and practically given him away. At the end, Peppy yelled at the top of his voice, "Hell, I can take it. Hell, I've been down that road before. But Ronnie can't take it. You got to rub Ronnie. You got to pat him."

"Are you through?" I asked him. Yes, he was through. "Okay, now I'm going to speak. Nobody wanted you, Pepitone. We took a chance and brought you here. Who in the hell sets any rules for you? You can come and go as you please. Do you mean to tell me that when you screw up in the ballgame I don't have the right to criticize you? Who the hell are *you*?" Now Joe started to pipe up again, and I had to remind him that I had asked him whether he had finished. "I'm going to do the talking now," I said.

Oh, no, I wasn't. Santo was yelling again. They had got him all worked up, and as emotional as Ronnie is, he was accusing me of all kind of things. And he wasn't alone. I had lost control of the meeting; it was out of hand. They had me backed against the wall, and when my back is against the wall, I hit back. "Wait a minute," I said. "Let me ask you something, Ronnie. Isn't it true that you came to my room in Atlanta to talk to me about calling off this Day that's coming up Sunday?"

Yes, it was.

"Didn't I tell you we couldn't do that, Ron?"

Yes, I had.

"Isn't it also true that you had a problem signing a contract this year and wanted a stipulation that the Cubs would have a Day for you because they gave one to Billy Williams and Ernie Banks? You told me you never wanted the Day, and that was an erroneous statement on your part, wasn't it?"

The room was absolutely quiet. "That's a lie!" Ron screamed, and took a leap across the room at me. I thought he was going to belt me one, that's how mad he was. If he had, there would have been a fight for sure, and I'd have probably been killed. He didn't swing at me, though. He just stood nose to nose with me and kept yelling.

"Do you want me to get Mr. Holland down here to clear that up, Ron?" I finally asked.

Yeah, why didn't I just get Mr. Holland down and clear it up?

I went over and picked up the phone. "John, we got a bit of a problem. I think you should come down here."

To keep things cooled down while we were waiting, I went up to my office to get some cigarettes. The office was up a little flight of stairs and through the equipment room. I'd hardly got there before I heard a racket. Santo had started after me. My guess is that he wanted to ask me to call Holland back or, possibly, to intercept Holland before he got to the locker room. There's no way of knowing. Some of the other players had grabbed him at the top of the steps, and I could hear Milt Pappas yelling, "Let him go. Let him do what he has to do. Let him go get him."

And Jim Hickman, who had just got out of the hospital, was yelling back, "Why don't you sit down, Pappas, and shut up. Just for once in your life, shut up!"

Holland was there within the minute. Without saying a word to him, I took him back down the steps into the dressing room. "I just want you to answer one question for me," I told him. "Yes or no. Isn't it true that the idea for this Day for Santo was brought up by Ron?" I put him on the spot, no question about it. "Didn't it enter into your discussion when you were trying to sign his contract? That's all. Just yes or no."

"Well, yes," he said. "In a way he did. When he signed his contract."

Santo blew up again. A lie. It was a goddam lie!

And poor John said, "Well, it seems to me that it did enter into your conversation that you desired to have a Day, Ron. It was so long ago that you probably don't remember. It was brought up casually, but you did bring it up. Not that you're not deserving of it, Ron."

Ron let out a scream. "Ooooohhh, my God! Ohhh, Jesus Christ." And then he was back at me. "I heard about you, but I didn't want to believe it."

Now Pepitone piped up again. "That's the most horseshit thing I've ever seen. You see what you've done! You've destroyed him. What kind of a manager are you?"

And Pappas is right in there agreeing with him. My heavenly twins. Look what I had done. I had destroyed Ron Santo.

Holland was trying to quiet them down. But I was burning. "Wait a minute," I yelled. "Let me say something." I told them I was sorry this had all come about. "I didn't know there was this much hatred for me on this ball club. So I've got a solution to the whole thing. *I'll see you later!*" I turned to Holland. "You can take the uniform and shove it up your ass. Just get yourself another manager."

I was stalking through the equipment room, with my shirt already off, when I thought of something else and came running back down the stairs. "One more thing," I said. "And all I need is a yes or no on this, too, John. Is there a player on this club that I didn't fight with you and Mr. Wrigley to get more money? Every player on this club. Didn't I always fight with you when you asked me? More money, more money, more money. Fighting for the player when I should have been on the executive side?"

"That's right. You were in the middle of it, always fighting for the player."

"Yeah," I said. "I think we've all done pretty well since I been here." I went back upstairs, took off the uniform, and went into the shower.

What was happening down in the clubhouse while I was showering I heard about later. Holland talked to the players and told them if they let me walk out of there under these conditions they were going to go down in history with the Cleveland Crybabies, who had petitioned the front office to fire their manager, Ossie Vitt, for being so mean to them. Well, that had happened in 1940, before most of our players had been born. Holland had to explain to them how the Cleveland players had become the laughingstock of the whole country.

After Holland was through, Jim Hickman said, "We've gotten this far with him, we can't let him go. He's helped us all, and we need him."

When some of the others, who had previously been silent, began to express the same sentiments, Pappas jumped up and yelled, "Let's take a vote on it."

Holland didn't say a word. It was Joey Amalfitano who jumped up on the equipment trunk and took over. Addressing himself specifically to Santo, Pappas, and Pepitone, he said, "I'm asking each one of you, has anybody ever told you three guys what to do in your careers? You think you're going to tell that man what to do? Leo's a personality all to himself. He's been here before you, and he'll be here after you're gone. This isn't a guy that walked off the street. He knows what he's doing. And you think you're going to change him? Mr. Holland can't even change him. If you think we got a chance to win the pennant without him, you're crazier than I think you are."

With nobody saying a word, Joey looked straight at Santo. "You want him to come back, Ron?"

And Santo said, "Yeah."

"Then get your ass up there with me." Which is strong language for Joey Amalfitano.

I had taken my shower and put on my street clothes when Amalfitano came in with Santo. The first thing he said to me was that Ron hadn't meant it. "What you said, Leo, I don't think you should have said. And the names you called him, Ron, you shouldn't have said, either. Now if you're two adults, like I think you are, you got to apologize to each other and shake hands."

"Ronnie," I said, "I haven't got a thing in the world against you." As we shook hands, Ronnie, who was just emotionally drained, threw his arms around me. "I didn't mean to say the things I said, Leo," he said. "You know how I get. How hot-tempered . . ." I had a cigarette in my hand, and I was shaking so bad I could hardly hold it. "Ronnie," I said, "I'm not mad at you. Hell, you got a right to your feelings. You had a right to pop off. It was an open meeting. So did I. Forget it. But those other two bastards . . ." I was never going to forgive them.

And I wasn't going to put the uniform back on, either.

"No, no," Joey said. "You've preached all your life you can't stand a quitter. And you're going to quit? You're just going to walk out of here and leave us by ourself?"

"I've had enough, Joe. I'm tired."

"Bullshit!" It was a swearing day for Joey.

Nothing he could say was going to change my mind. I was through. After Joe and Santo had left, Peanuts Lowrey, my other coach, came in to plead with me. And then, to my surprise, Ernie Banks, who was a player-coach by then, came up. "Please, Leo," he said. "Don't quit. We want you here. We need you. Don't go doing something you might regret."

"Well, I think I've had enough, Ernie. I've had enough of this."

While all this was going on, Jim Hickman had taken charge in the clubhouse. He started by telling Pappas and Pepitone what ungrateful bastards they were, and then he ate the rest of them out for the way they had turned on me. I guess it was the longest speech my hillbilly ever made in his life. There were three or four of them who never spoke to Jim Hickman again. What really surprised me when I heard about it was that J. C. Martin, my reserver catcher, and Chris Cannizzaro, who had just joined the team, were supporting him. "I've been around for a long time," Martin told them, "and this is the worst thing I've ever seen."

As for John Holland, he had come up to my office right behind Ernie Banks. Same plea. Same answer. "All right, then," he said. "If you won't do it for me, do it for Mr. Wrigley." After everything Mr. Wrigley had done for me, there was nothing I could say to that. And John knew it. I looked at my watch; the game was starting in seven minutes. I put the uniform back on and walked through the locker room as if nothing had happened. We won, 6–3. Santo had two doubles and a single and knocked in three runs.

The story broke all over the papers the next day. Which was to be expected. Everything that happened in the locker room was always all over the papers the next day. Dick Dozer of the *Tribune* told me straight out, "I don't care whether I ever go into your clubhouse or not, Leo. I don't have to. Ten minutes after the door opens, I know every word that was spoken in there."

So what else was new? Every writer who covered the Cubs had his private source among the players. Sometimes their information was even accurate.

The controversy continued to swirl around our heads for more than a week. Durocher was through again. You can't fire twenty-five players, but you can fire the manager. When Mr. Wrigley finally let it be known that he was standing solidly behind me, he did it, with his customary flair for the unusual, not by calling a press conference but by taking out a paid advertisement in all of the Chicago papers.

What follows are some selected excerpts from that advertisement:

Many people seem to have forgotten, but I have not, that after many years of successful seasons . . . the Cubs went into the doldrums and for a quarter of a century were perennial dwellers of the second division in spite of everything we could think of to try. . . .

We figured out what we thought was needed to make a lot of potential talent into a contending team, and we settled on Leo Durocher, who had the baseball knowledge to build a contender and win pennants, and also knowing that he had been a controversial figure wherever he went, particularly with the press because he just never was cut out to be a diplomat. He accepted the job at less than he was making because he considered it to be a challenge, and Leo thrives on challenges. . . .

In his first year we ended in the cellar, but from then on came steadily up, knocking on the door for the top. . . .

Each near miss has caused more and more criticism, and this year there has been a constant campaign to dump Durocher that has even affected the players. . . .

All this preamble is to say that after careful consideration and consultation with my baseball people, Leo is the team manager and the "Dump Durocher Clique" might as well give up. He is running the team, and if some of the players do not like it and lie down on the job, during the off season we will see what we can do to find them happier homes.

(signed) Phil Wrigley

P.S. If only we could find more team players like Ernie Banks.

I have my own P.S. I kept handing Milt Pappas the ball. I never will forgive him. Pepitone? Ahhh, Pepitone. Peppy is like me. He has made a career of being forgiven.

He had this little bar, called Peppy's Thing, only a block from where I lived. (The bar went under like everything else. I heard that Santo lost some money on it, too.) I dropped in one morning a couple of weeks later, just as I had been in the habit of doing earlier. Yosh and a couple of the other players were there, and so Peppy called me in back so that he could tell me how sorry he was. "I wish I had a knife," he said, "so I could cut my tongue out."

Peppy's always sorry. Ten seconds after I walked up the steps that day, he was buttonholing my coaches to tell them that he was sorry. In the newspaper stories the next day, Joe Pepitone was my greatest defender. He didn't get around to apologizing directly, of course, until after Wrigley's ad had appeared.

But if he was conning me, he did a magnificient job at it. Over the winter, Bill Wrigley wanted to know whether I'd give Peppy a two-year contract if I was the owner of the club. It was another way, you understand, of helping him to work out his debts by giving him a guaranteed income over a period of time. Work out his debts? The combined resources of the Bank of England and the Bank of America couldn't get him out.

After everything that had happened, I went to bat for him again. Yeah, he had the talent. Yeah, he could do it all. "Yeah," I said. "I would."

They did.

He appreciated it so much that he came down to Scottsdale for spring training with this eighteen-year-old girl he was living with. As soon as Holland heard about it, he ordered me to tell Pepitone to get her out of there. "We can't stand that kind of thing! Can't have that on this club!"

Peppy was already half into his salary by then, and we hadn't got out of Scottsdale. "If she leaves," he told me, "I leave."

I said, "That's probably the way it's going to be. Because I was told by Mr. Holland to tell you."

Immediately, he changed his tune. "Leo, I got this girl down here with me because I'm in love with her. I'm so much in love with her I'm home with her every night. If she wasn't here, I'd be out with some broad tonight. And every night I'd be out with some broad."

Which did make sense. Isn't it better that I'm going home every night instead of chasing around? Isn't that what you want from me? Stability. You've got to admit that it made better sense.

Guys like that always make sense. Once that kind of guy sees he can get around you, he'll con you right out of your shoes.

It was out of my hands, I told him. She had to leave. "But," I said, taking the first step backward, "if you want to talk to John, go ahead. I won't stand in your way."

I guess he gave John the same treatment, because when he came out, he was able to hand me the glad news that John was leaving it entirely up to me. "You're the boss, Leo. Whatever you say."

And *again* I let him. I let him keep the broad down there, and it was wrong. Wrong, wrong, wrong . . .

Right to the end. Leo the Lamb. I'm tough to play for, huh? If you couldn't play for me, you couldn't play for anybody.

Pepitone? He lasted about a month into the season, and then we traded him to Atlanta for a minor-league first baseman. A couple of months later, he was playing in Japan. The last I heard he wasn't happy there, either. The Japanese people were very inconsiderate. They insisted upon speaking Japanese.

Give Peppy a couple of hours with the emperor and the country will go bilingual.

When fans talk about phenoms and flashes in the pan, the names that crop up include Hurricane Hazle, Gene Bearden, and Bobo Holloman. When the talk turns to unquestioned stardom cruelly nipped in the bud, they think of Addie Joss, Ray Chapman, Herb Score—and Tony Conigliaro. Others have fallen victim to the beanball, among them Mickey Cochrane, Joe Medwick, Frank Chance, and Dickie Thon; but only Tony C. accomplished so much so young—56 homers before his twentieth birthday, 160 before his twenty-fifth, despite missing a year and a half. Then, as if the failing eyesight and flattened career weren't enough, he suffered a major heart attack at age thirty-seven. The late Ray Fitzgerald, a Boston institution, felt for him.

RAY FITZGERALD

Tony C, as in Courage, Comebacks, Coronary

January 12, 1982—Tony Conigliaro, fighting for his life at Massachusetts General after suffering a serious heart attack last Saturday, was the No. 1 maker of headlines during his short career with the Red Sox. Not even Carl Yastrzemski had as much flair for the dramatic as this former St. Mary's of Lynn All-Scholastic.

Whether it was for hitting a game-winning home run or dating glamorous Hollywood actress Mamie Van Doren or writhing at home plate in agony or making a courageous comeback or calling a press conference at three in the morning to announce his retirement, Tony C. had no peer as a sports newsmaker in Boston.

From the time the teenaged Conigliaro put on such a batting show at Scottsdale, Arizona, in the spring of 1964 that the Red Sox promoted him from Class D to the starting lineup on Opening Day to his final futile days of trying to see a baseball well enough to hit it in 1975, he was one of a kind.

Conigliaro's latest adversity has brought back a bunch of memories for a Red Sox baseball writer—me—who was new to the beat during Tony's years on the team. Some of those years were thrilling, some poignant, and a couple still bring a lump to the throat.

The days and years and games run into one another, but I especially remember two particularly dramatic home runs. On a warm June night in 1967, with the White Sox ahead, 1–0, in the bottom of the eleventh, Conigliaro hit a two-out, three-and-two pitch over the Fenway screen. Sometimes I have trouble remembering my middle name, but almost fifteen years later I *know* without looking it up that a right-handed Chicago pitcher named John Buzhardt gave up the homer.

In 1969, in a grueling night game that seemed as though it might last forever, Conigliaro slammed a home run to deep left-center field in Chicago off Joel Horlen to beat the White Sox again, this time by 7–6.

Conigliaro had the perfect Fenway Park stroke. Many a left fielder watched helplessly as a lazy Conigliaro fly ball—a poke that would have been an easy out in every other American league park—barely made the net. But he could hit prodigious homers, too. If he had been a major leaguer until he was thirty-six, and thus had played for seventeen seasons, there is little doubt he would have hit at least 500 home runs.

He was a fearless hitter and never backed away from a fast ball. Once, when sidearmer Fred Lasher of Detroit hit Conigliaro on the leg with a pitch, Tony dropped his bat, raced to the mound, and attempted to nail the pitcher with a karate kick.

But the very characteristic that made him a great hitter was the one that shortened his career on that hot August night when a Jack Hamilton fastball crashed into the side of Conigliaro's face. A smoke bomb thrown on the field had held up the game for several minutes, and I've always felt the delay might have taken away some of Conigliaro's concentration.

He was out the rest of that season and all of 1968 and then made two dramatic comebacks. He tried pitching in the Instructional League early in 1969, but that didn't work out, so he went to spring training determined to make it again as a hitter. For a while his swings were so bad that it was painful to watch him in the batting cage.

But gradually the stroke returned and with it the confidence, and I remember him saying one day after getting a couple of line-drive hits in an exhibition game at Sarasota that he no longer doubted his ability to hit big-league pitching again.

In his first regular-season game back, on April 9 in Baltimore, Conigliaro hit a tenth-inning homer with a man on base that put the Red Sox ahead. He returned to Fenway Park a few days later and got the most prolonged ovation this side of Bobby Orr.

In 1970 Conigliaro hit thirty-six homers, an amazing total for someone who had been considered all done two seasons previously. He was traded to California that winter, and in 1971 his vision began to deteriorate again. And one night, after he'd struck out several times in an extra-inning game, he called a press conference to announce his retirement.

Four seasons later he came back one more time with the Red Sox. After another tumultuous ovation on Opening Day in Fenway, he singled to right in his first at bat after being away almost four years.

However, although he had a few key hits early in the season, he had been away too long. He went to the minors in Pawtucket in an attempt to recapture the graceful swing, but this time he couldn't do it.

Conigliaro, Hollywood handsome, with soft Italian eyes and a quick smile, was often controversial and might not always have been the easiest player to manage. But nobody could ever accuse him of giving less than his best on the field.

Tony C. was a headline maker who had more talent in his line of work than most of us are given in ours, but he was seldom at the head of the line when good luck was being handed out.

He could use what fate owes him right now.

G. H. Fleming, professor of English literature and specialist in Victoriana, has created a genre of baseball books patterned after Akira Kurosawa's film masterpiece *Rashomon*. Fleming's first book-length collage was *The Unforgettable Season*, a kaleidoscopic newspaper reconstruction of the unparalleled events in the National League of 1908; then came *The Dizziest Season*, a similar approach to the 1934 National League race; and finally *Murderers' Row*, a look at how the Yankees tore up the American League in 1927. Here Fleming focuses on the central play in the 1908 season, the most famous and costly blunder in baseball history: Fred Merkle's "bonehead play" that cost the New York Giants the pennant.

G. H. FLEMING

The Merkle Blunder

On *September 23, 1908, as I wrote in* The Unforgettable Season, *"the Giants and Cubs played the most celebrated, most widely discussed, most controversial contest in the history of American sports. The game was declared a 1 to 1 tie." This was, of course, the game of the "Merkle blunder." As Kurosawa's film masterpiece* Rashomon *beautifully illustrated, the same event may be seen in different ways by different people; and so it was with what took place at the Polo Grounds on that momentous day. What is the truth, and what is illusion? You be the judge. As in* The Unforgettable Season, *everything below is presented exactly as it appeared in the original accounts of 1908.*

Monday, September 21

Here is something for the fans to consider. Suppose Fred Tenney should be crippled. That would be a calamity, wouldn't it? Yes, it would in one way, but it wouldn't keep the Giants from winning the pennant. There is a young fellow on the bench named Fred Merkle who can fill that job better than nine-tenths of the first basemen in the league. He is crying for a chance to work, but with Tenney playing like a youngster just out of college, it would be silly to take him out of the game.

BOZEMAN BULGER, Chicago *Tribune*

Wednesday, September 23

There were rumors afloat last night to the effect that Mr. Tenney had injured his back and might not play today.

Chicago Tribune

"Take nothing for granted" is the motto that hangs over the desk of President Pulliam. Evidently McCormick has never seen it. When he cracked a grounder to center in the fifth inning of the second game [of a doubleheader which the Giants lost to the Cubs] he loafed a little, thinking it a sure hit. Evers went over for a fine stop, and his throw just nailed McCormick. It should have been an infield hit.

New York Globe

Thursday, September 24

Censurable stupidity on the part of Merkle yesterday placed the Giants' chances of winning the pennant in jeopardy. His unusual conduct in the final inning perhaps deprived New York of a victory that would have been unquestionable had he not committed a breach in baseball play that resulted in Umpire O'Day calling the game a tie.

With the game tied in the ninth inning and two outs and New York having a runner, McCormick, on third base waiting for an opportunity to score and Merkle on first, looking for a similar chance, Bridwell hit into center field, a fair ball sufficient to win the game had Merkle gone on his way down the base path while McCormick was scoring. But instead of going to second base, Merkle ran toward the clubhouse, evidently thinking his share in the game had ended when Bridwell hit the ball into safe territory.

Manager Chance quickly grasped the situation and directed the ball be thrown to second base, which would force out Merkle.

Manager Chance ran to second base, and the ball was thrown there, but immediately Pitcher McGinnity interfered in the play, and a scramble of players ensued, in which, it is said, McGinnity obtained the ball and threw it into the crowd before Chance could complete a force play on Merkle, who was far from the baseline. Merkle said he had touched second base, and the Chicago players were equally positive he had not done so.

Chance then appealed to Umpire O'Day for a decision. The crowd, thinking the Giants had won, swarmed on the playing field in such a confusion that none of the fans seemed able to grasp the situation, but finally their attitude toward O'Day became so offensive that the police ran into the crowd and protected the umpire.

Umpire O'Day finally decided the run did not count, and inasmuch as the spectators had gained such large numbers on the field the game could not be resumed, O'Day declared the game a tie. Although both Umpires, O'Day and Emslie, it is claimed, say they did not see the play at second base, Umpire O'Day's action was based upon the presumption that a force play was made on Merkle.

The singular ending of the game aroused intense interest throughout the city, and everywhere it was the chief topic of discussion.

New York *Times*

Hofman threw the ball to Evers, but before the latter could step on second base, McGinnity, who had been on the coaching line and was on his way to the clubhouse, took a hand and grabbed the ball away from Evers. Evers and Tinker then grabbed McGinnity and wrestled with him, trying to get the ball. They weren't successful, for the next minute the ball was sailing over toward the left-field bleachers. Some Chicago player rescued it and brought it in. Merkle in the meantime had been trying to go back to second base before the ball could be brought there, and two or three Chicagoans were hanging on to him, trying to keep him from the bag.

There were excited cranks surging around the grouped and tussling players and many more swarming around the umpires, on their way to the exit beneath the stand. The Chicago players chased the umpires to find out what ruling had been made, and the cranks gathered around both, jostling, elbowing, and rubbering. The police jumped in quickly and scattered the crowds right and left as the umpires slowly made their way to the exit, the players following at their heels. The umpires made their escape finally, and then a crowd tagged on to the heels of Captain Chance and other Cubs who had been in the wrangling and turmoil. The police blocked off the crowd as the players moved across the field.

Everywhere in the stands and on the field spectators were all at sea as to what had happened and as to the status of the game. The cops were too active for anything in the way of violence to break loose. It was the general impression, too, that New York had won, and there was a feeling of satisfaction over that. Herzog, who had made the first run for the Giants, was carried off the field on the shoulders of a shouting string of admirers.

Charles Murphy, president of the Chicago club, came down from his box in the upper stand to find out what the umpire's decision had been. When O'Day was asked how the game stood, he replied: "Emslie says he didn't see the play at second base, and it's no game, I suppose."

New York *Sun*

When Bridwell slammed his hit in the ninth, Merkle, instead of starting promptly for the second bag, made a move toward the clubhouse. Warned by the yells of Little Johnnie Evers, the boy orator, who was entreating Hofman to chuck the ball to the infield, Merkle changed his course and waddled toward second base. The crowd, at this time, was surging out onto the field, and exactly what happened no man can say. But this much is certain: Hofman threw the ball to the infield; it bounced off Evers's back, rolled toward King, and was finally corraled by Joe McGinnity. When three or four frantic Cubs tried to tear the ball from Joseph's grasp, it disappeared from the scene and plays no further part in the interesting narrative.

Merkle, when he had touched second base, wanted to stay and see the fight out as Frank Chance, Evers, Steinfeldt, and a few other invaders were making frantic protests to Emslie and O'Day, but Mathewson dragged him away, and they went on a run to the clubhouse.

The writer wishes to assure the fans that neither Emslie nor O'Day saw the play at second base, and neither Emslie nor O'Day knows whether Merkle went to second base ahead of or behind the ball. As a matter of fact, the ball never got there.

The moment that both umpires started for their little coop and the crowd started for the El and surface cars, members of the visiting club rushed toward Emslie and shouted, "Merkle hasn't touched second base." Emslie kept on going, remarking in reply, "I didn't see any such play." O'Day also hurried to the shelter of the stand, though Chance tried nobly to get within slugging distance and the gathering thousands from stands and bleachers began to threaten the impetuous Chicago leader in rather ugly fashion.

Hank O'Day and Robert Emslie stayed in that little coop for many moments, talking it over. Emslie, seeing that he has a wig, was the judge, and Hank was the attorney. Many and learned were the arguments going back and forth, because neither of the worthy arbitrators had seen the play, and they were to make up in talk what they lacked in vision. When they finally came out of the gloom and were braced by a gathering of baseball scribes, Emslie declined to be interviewed, and O'Day muttered something about "no game."

WILLIAM F. KIRK, New York *American*

Never was a victory more cleanly won. The Giants and Cubs gave one of the most brilliant exhibitions of baseball in the history of the game, and all the way the Giants had just that shade of superiority that wins games and pennants. First of all, credit must go to Mathewson, who outpitched Pfiester, the southpaw who has bothered the Giants all season, but there was brilliant work all around, and McGraw's men fully justified the confidence of the crowd that went up to the Polo Grounds sure that New York would hold the lead so splendidly earned.

No matter what the ultimate decision as to the game may be, and that decision may determine the ownership of the pennant, yesterday's was a glorious victory.

New York was without the services of Tenney, who has a bad leg, and Merkle, who was to acquire notoriety soon enough, took his place. He played well, but Mathewson dominated the struggle and pitched a game that he has never surpassed in his wonderful career.

New York *Tribune*

The facts gleaned from active participants and survivors are these: Hofman fielded Bridwell's knock and threw to Evers for a force play on the absent Merkle. But McGinnity cut in and grabbed the ball before it reached the eager Trojan [Evers, who came from Troy, New York]. Three Cubs landed on the Iron Man from as many directions at the same time and jolted the ball from his cruel grasp. It rolled among the spectators who had swarmed upon the diamond like an army of starving potato bugs.

At this thrilling juncture "Kid" Kroh, the demon southpaw, swarmed upon the human potato bugs and knocked six of them galley-west. The triumphant Kroh passed the ball to Steinfeldt after cleaning up the gang that had it. Tinker wedged in, and the ball was conveyed to Evers for the force-out of Merkle. . . .

Some say Merkle eventually touched second base, but not until he had been forced out by Hofman to McGinnity to six potato bugs to "Kid" Kroh to some more Cubs and the shrieking, triumphant Mr. Evers, the well-known Troy shoe dealer. There have been some complicated plays in baseball, but we do not recall one like this in a career of years of monkeying with the national pastime.

Peerless Leader Chance ran at O'Day to find out what Hank had to say, but the sparrow cops, specials, 200 cops, and Pinks—slang for Pinkertons—thought Chance was going to bite Hank on the ankle. Half a hundred men in uniform surrounded the Peerless Leader, and thousands of bugs surrounded them. Bill Marshall [the utility player usually known as Doc], who is an expert on bacteria, and Del Howard rushed in to help the Peerless Leader. Another squad of cops had O'Day in tow some yards away.

Hank didn't know Chance wanted to converse with him, and they couldn't get together, anyhow. Finally the cops got O'Day into a coop under the stand and tried to slam the door in the face of the Peerless Leader. He jammed his robust frame in the opening and defied the sparrow chasers. Chance later got to O'Day, who said Emslie, working on the bases, did not see the second-base play because of the crowd, but Hank informed Chance that McCormick's run didn't count.

Still later, Hank submitted gracefully to an interview by war scribes. He said Merkle was forced at second and the game ended in a tie. None of the Giants remained to make public statements. Part of the crowd lifted a player in white to their shoulders and bore him to the clubhouse. The Giant thus honored was not Mr. Merkle. He left long before the trouble started.

CHARLES DRYDEN, Chicago *Tribune*

Merkle lost his head. He started for the clubhouse but only took a few steps when Matty, waiting his turn at bat, yelled to him. Chance was watching Merkle and frantically called to Hofman to field the ball to second. Hofman was also in the air and began to hunt for the ball. Evers ran down the field, waving his arms and legs at Hofman like a guy gone daffy.

The crowd, thinking the game was won, poured over the stands in a surging mass that swept some of the players off their feet.

Just then Chance and Steinfeldt got to second on the run, and those two, with Evers, surrounded McGinnity and began to wrestle with him for possession of the ball. Seeing he was outnumbered and getting wise to why they wanted the ball, Joe threw it into the left-field bleachers.

Where that ball is now no one knows, except perhaps the fan who captured it and has it in a frame over his pillow.

One thing is certain: it never got to second. Merkle got to second. He started late, but he got there. The ball never did.

Chance tore after Emslie, but the crowd blocked his way, not really knowing why they did it but blocking him all the same.

Chance fought like a real bear, and a grizzly at that, to get to the umpires. He's a husky guy, that Chance, and from the way he almost got through, he'd do well on a football team. But you can't buck a line of thousands, and Chance was stalled. He had his lungs with him, however, and did some yelling. This was partly drowned by the yells of the crowd, which had become a mob.

It began to look ugly. Chance was packed in the center of a push that didn't even give him elbow room. And O'Day was in a like predicament.

The near cops were spectators on the outside fringe of affairs. Then the real blue boys got busy. They formed a flying wedge and got to the center of the maelstrom. It took a few pokes with their nightsticks to do it, but when did a cop hide his stick when it was handy?

They rescued Chance, and the umpires were locked up behind the grandstand for safekeeping until such time as the crowd could be scattered to their homes.

GYM BAGLEY, New York *Evening Mail*

The Cubs are right, under every rule of baseball law and common sense, and entitled to win their protest. Rules are rules, and clubs having boneheaded mutts on the base paths deserve only to be penalized.

All honor to Hank O'Day. There has been much roasting of Hank, both on account of the exactly similar Pittsburgh affair some weeks ago [on September 4] and because he seemed to be handing the lemons to the Cubs in all close decisions. But Hank has shown the genuine goods and has put himself on record as an honest umpire and a game man—all honor and praise to Hank O'Day!

W. A. PHELON, Chicago Journal

It is high time that the league took a decided stand on the rules that are not specific enough for the controversial play of yesterday. It has long been an unwritten baseball law that as soon as a home player crossed the plate with a run that breaks a tie after the eighth inning the game is over that instant. A batter runs out his hit, and that is all. If a batter singles and scores a runner from second base, it is necessary for him to touch only first base.

If a game does not end when the winning run scores, then, pray, why does not a batter who makes a long hit get full credit for it? If it is a three-bagger and a man scores from third, why does not the batter get as many bases as he can take? If a ball is lifted into the bleachers, thereby scoring a runner ahead of the batter, no credit is given for a home run. [Since 1920, a ball thus hit has been ruled a home run.] Then why should base runners be compelled to run around the sack after the winning run has been scored?

If the National League throws out the game on such a technicality, the organization does not deserve any more of the splendid patronage it has had in this city. When games are played in an office with technicalities by politicians of the game, it is time for Ping-Pong to be chosen for the great American game.

SID MERCER, New York Globe

"When I saw Merkle leave the base path," declares Christy Mathewson, "I ran after him and brought him back to second base so as to make our lead unquestionable. He was on second base after McGinnity tossed away the ball, following his tussle with the Chicago players. Maybe Evers got the ball and touched the base afterward. If he did, it didn't prove anything. I can state positively that no force play was made before Merkle got to the base. He wanted to stick there when he saw the scrapping on the diamond, but I pulled him away, and we went to the clubhouse." [A myth later developed, and continues to receive support in print, that because Mathewson, unable to tell a lie, informed National League President Pulliam that Merkle had not touched second base, Pulliam ruled the game a tie.]

New York Globe

Friday, September 25

Following a sleepless night of agony throughout the length and breadth of Manhattan, haggard bugs waited all morning for President Pulliam's decision on the riotous windup of Wednesday's game. War scribes from far and near assembled in Pulliam's outer office, where he conversed on general topics in his usual affable manner. Then he retired to the inner sanctum and sent out a neatly typewritten ruling, which in effect ruled the game a 1–1 tie.

Barring himself within the inner precincts, Mr. Pulliam declined to see anybody; nor would he come forth to reveal the future. Questions sent in by scribes came back in the original state—unanswered. Nothing was said about playing off the tie game, as provided by the league constitution, which says such games shall be played. As this is the last day the game could be played, the Giants are subject to a fine. It rests with the home club to arrange such matters, but McGraw announced last night the contest would not be played over.

Umpires O'Day and Emslie were present in Pulliam's office when the decision was rendered. Secretary Williams of the Cubs notified these officials the Chicago team would be at the Polo Grounds at 1:30 today [September 24], the regular hour for starting doubleheaders. Hank and Bob were dumb as clams. All they did was do a looking, listening part.

Thinking the Giants might assemble on the field at 1:30 and attempt to put something over, the Cubs swallowed a quick lunch and hiked to the scene of combat. A dozen Giants were there in uniform, with a crowd pouring in, but the locals made no effort to line up in battle array. At 1:30 the Peerless Leader put a complete team on the field, with Coakley pitching and Kling behind the bat. Tom Needham kindly stood at the plate with a pestle in his hand while Coakley pitched four balls. There were no umpires to tell Needham whether he struck out or got a pass.

The bugs howled derision, but Chance had made his little play and will claim the game by forfeit.

CHARLES DRYDEN, Chicago Tribune

I have never seen local lovers of the game so fairly boiling over with anger as they were yesterday when President Pulliam's decision was announced. Eddie Tolcott voiced the opinion of all true lovers of the game when he said to me yesterday: "There was never a more hideous outrage committed. It is a slur on the great national game, the sport we all love and admire above all others for its heretofore absolute cleanliness and absence of all taints of dishonesty or unfairness.

"That the foundation of the sport should be undermined by such a contemptible trick is shameful. If the Cubs win the pennant by that one game they stole from the Giants, the streamer would amount to nothing but a dirty, dishonored dishrag. The Cubs' title to the championship would be discredited, and the name Champions would be an empty honor. It is simply a disgrace that any gentleman connected with the national game should stoop to such unsportsmanlike methods as I understand President Murphy has. If the Giants are robbed of their fair victory, I shall be ashamed to say I was ever connected with baseball."

SAM CRANE, New York Evening Journal

One of the remarkable things in this baseball race is the attitude of Mr. Fan and all his family and friends toward the late disaster at the Polo Grounds.

Truly, John McGraw should feel grateful for the sympathy of almost the entire baseball world in the controversy over that memorable battle with the Cubs.

For doing what is right, Umpire Hank O'Day and President Pulliam are being condemned all over the country, while Frank Chance and his Cubs are everywhere being branded as poor sportsmen because, forsooth, they acted with intelligence and took advantage of the rules to gain an edge in a race that is so close that every fraction counts.

The game of baseball takes nothing for granted. Because the play happened to be a final one does not make it excusable to slur the rule. It is just as much a crime against the baseball code to fail to complete a play at the end of a game as in the middle. Merkle was asleep and worked his little dab of gray matter very poorly. He paid the penalty of thoughtlessness, just as he must have paid the penalty had he been caught asleep off base.

Frank Chance was a man on his job. He saw the mistake and took advantage of it, and for this he deserves not condemnation but praise for his watchfulness and thoughtfulness.

As a matter of fact, the Giants deserved not merely to have the game declared a tie but to forfeit it. McGinnity's effort to stop the play by throwing away the ball is distinctly interference, the penalty for which is loss of the battle. And if you probe that cautious mind of John J. McGraw, you will probably find him secretly satisfied that no worse result followed the indiscretions of Merkle and McGinnity.

JOHN E. WRAY, St. Louis *Post-Dispatch*

Saturday, October 10

During the last few days many veteran ballplayers have come to the front and spoken in behalf of Fred Merkle, the young Giant who has been unmercifully roasted by many fans for his alleged failure to touch second base at the finish of the memorable September 23 contest. Seasoned ballplayers like Joe Kelley, Bill Dahlen, Billy Gilbert, Willie Keeler, Frank Bowerman, and Manager Billy Murray of the Philadelphia Club are among them. They call attention to the fact that ever since the rule was adopted under which a game ends when the team last at bat scores the winning run, players have run for the clubhouse as soon as the runner crossed the plate, without advancing to the next base.

New York *World*

How good was Roger Maris? During his playing days the largely antagonistic New York press portrayed him as a home-run-hitting automaton, in the current manner of Dave Kingman and Ron Kittle. In the wake of his recent death, many observers now cite his superb right-field play, his astute baserunning, seven World Series appearances in a nine-year span, and his winning character; some have gone so far as to suggest him for the Hall of Fame. The view from this corner is that Maris was a solid player, a ballplayer's ballplayer who for three years, 1960–62, was as good as anyone. And if the Yankees hadn't wrecked his body, as detailed in this passage from Peter Golenbock's *Dynasty*, he might have gone on to merit a plaque in Cooperstown, after all.

PETER GOLENBOCK

Roger Maris

With the pennant race virtually over, everyone concentrated on the Mantle-Maris home-run derby. In every park where the Yankees played, attendance records were set as people flocked to see whether Mantle and/or Maris would break Babe Ruth's single-season home-run record.

At Yankee Stadium the booing of Mantle had ceased. It was as though the Yankee faithful were apologizing to him for the harsh treatment he had been receiving all those years, and to make up for any past hurts, the Stadium fans were making a concerted effort to understand his temperament, overlook his imperfections, and shower him with huzzahs of love. In one game in which Houk had kept Mickey on the bench because of his sore arm, he went into the game for defensive purposes and received a standing ovation. A few nights later when he hit his fifty-second home run, the Stadium crowd rose as one and applauded and stomped wildly as he trotted slowly around the bases. Mantle was deeply moved. The applause did not stop until after he had crossed home plate and returned to the dugout.

On September 10 Mickey hit his fifty-third home run. It was a long home run in the first inning against Jim Perry. His arm was aching, and his legs pained him chronically—but still he played. The home-run derby had caught him up in something that didn't permit rest.

Then a head cold further deteriorated his physical condition, and on September 11, just before the Yankees left for a long road trip, Yankee announcer Mel Allen, worried about Mantle, took him to his personal physician for a

penicillin shot. For the next week Mantle's physical condition did not improve, but Mickey kept playing. His home-run total stayed at fifty-three, while Maris hit his fifty-seventh home run against Frank Lary of the Tigers on September 16. On September 17 Bill Skowron made an error to send a game into extra innings, thus giving Maris two extra at bats. In the twelfth Maris hit his fifty-eighth home run off Terry Fox to win the game.

The next day Mantle arrived at the ballpark drawn and sweating badly. He had a temperature of 103 degrees and was developing an infection and rash where he had been given the penicillin shot. There were only three games remaining before the Yankees played their 154th ball game of the season, Commissioner Frick's Midnight Hour to break Ruth's record. Mantle could not play anymore. He was too weak. His challenge to the Babe was over.

Now only Maris remained, and the mounting pressure on the young right fielder was choking him in a viselike stranglehold. The publicity was increasing in quantum jumps. Reporters hounded his every footstep, recording what he was eating at every meal and following him to the movies. "The only time

I'm by myself is when I'm taking a crap," Maris said. Life was becoming increasingly more unpleasant for the man in the goldfish bowl.

Before and after every game the reporters and cameramen were lined up three deep in front of Maris's cubicle. One afternoon Maris listened to and answered a series of questions cabled to New York from a wire service in Tokyo. From halfway around the globe they were asking the same questions he had been answering for the last two months. "No wonder I'm going nuts," Maris said when he was finished. Writers who never covered sports before were covering Maris, and some of their questions bordered on the absurd. He was getting questions like "How does it feel to be hitting so many home runs?" and "Does all of this make you excited?" and "Do you still sleep well at night?" There were also questions like "What's a .260 hitter like you doing hitting so many home runs?"—to which Maris answered, "You've got to be a fucking idiot." That Roger was hitting .260 was discussed often. "Would you rather hit sixty home runs or bat .300?" he was asked. "No comment," Roger said. Obviously if it meant more to him to hit .300, he would have cut down on his swing and tried to hit .300. The reporter persisted. "Well, which would you?" he was asked. "What would you rather do?" Roger asked him. "I'd rather hit .300," the reporter said. Maris exhaled. "You do what you want, and I'll do what I want."

Away from the ballpark anyone who saw Maris on the street or in a restaurant wanted his autograph. He was not afforded five minutes of peace and quiet. "Some people want autographs on demand no matter what you're doing," Maris said. "They think they have a right to order me around. It's just a matter of courtesy." Maris shook his head. Too often there was no courtesy.

Only on the field was he afforded refuge from reporters, photographers, and autograph seekers. On the diamond, however, some of the fans, seeing that Roger was a man with a temper who reacted adversely to criticism, constantly reminded him that they thought Mickey Mantle should be the one breaking Ruth's record. Others reminded him that they thought that Ruth's record never should be broken at all. At the Stadium he took a frightful booing, and though the people applauding far outnumbered those booing, the ferocity of the minority made a strong impact on Maris. He was not used to being booed, but it was especially weird, since he was being booed for doing something extraordinary. "Give me the Kansas City fans anytime," Maris said. "There's no place that can compare with the people there." While at Kansas City, Roger during one streak was 6 for 110. Never once was he booed. But Roger's criticism of the New York fans didn't make him any more popular.

On the road Maris was the target of vicious verbal abuse and bottle throwing. After a doubleheader in Detroit during which Roger spent the entire day dodging garbage thrown at him from the right-field stands, he was so upset that he hid from reporters in the trainer's room for forty minutes after the game. "It's pretty tough to have to listen to it all through two games and then come in and have to answer a lot of questions I've answered a hundred times." Most of the reporters were not very sympathetic. Maris was causing them to miss their deadlines. The next day in the New York papers Maris was labeled a boor, a crybaby, and worse.

On September 19 the Yankees flew to Baltimore for a series with the Orioles. Maris needed three home runs in three games to break the record within Frick's deadline. Baltimore was the hardest park in the league in which to hit a home run. The day before, Hurricane Esther had skirted the city, and a powerful wind was still blowing in from right field as the Yankees and Orioles prepared to play a Sunday doubleheader. Before the games Maris as usual was surrounded by reporters. "My daughter, Susan," Maris said, "is four, and she's getting to an age where she wants her daddy home. She can't understand why the other kids her age have their daddys home and hers isn't. That's what I'm thinking about. Everybody thinks all I have on my mind are home runs." One reporter wanted to know if it was true the Yankees were having him trailed by private detectives. He denied it. The rumor was not allowed to die, though. In gossip columns Maris's name was appearing alongside names of renowned starlets, making him even less receptive to writers of the press. "How can they write shit like that?" he kept asking.

The Yankees split the doubleheader. Maris did not hit a home run. Steve Barber, a left-hander, was sharp in the first game. Skinny Brown and Hoyt Wilhelm, two knuckleball pitchers, stopped him in the second.

One more game to go. The 154th of the season. Maris needed two home runs to tie the record, three to break it. The pressure was causing Maris excruciating inner pain. Maris was a stoic individual, but he was human, though few accepted his frailties. Before the game Roger was sitting silently in front of his locker. It was very early. Most of the reporters had not yet arrived to stampede him. Maris's face was haggard; his eyes were red. Shaking, Maris walked from his locker. He went into manager Ralph Houk's office. Tears began streaming down his face. The shakes became worse. "I need help," Roger said to Houk. "I need help. I can't stand it anymore. All those goddam questions. I'm at the end of my rope. I just can't take it anymore." He buried his head in his hands. Houk was surprised at the intensity of Maris's distress, but the Yankee manager was able to convince his hitting star that with just a little more patience the season would be over. When the two men finished talking, Maris was once more in complete control and before the game answered the questions of reporters with outward calm. Only the constant tapping on the floor with his spiked shoes indicated this game was any more important than any other.

Baltimore manager Paul Richards didn't want Maris to break the record against his club. To stop Maris, he pitched another of his fast, young arms, twenty-two-year-old right-handed flamethrower Milt Pappas. Pappas had a further advantage. With Mantle still out, he could pitch around Maris.

Maris, batting in the first inning, hit a long fly ball to right field. There was a gasp, then a groan. Maris had gotten a little too far under it and flied out to

Oriole right fielder Earl Robinson. In the third, when Maris batted again, he said to Oriole catcher Gus Triandos, "If you don't think my ass is tight, you're crazy." Pappas threw, and Maris hit a rising line drive far above the outstretched glove of the second baseman that quickly rose until it landed out of reach in the Baltimore bleachers. It was Maris's fifty-ninth home run, tying Ruth for the second most ever hit in a 154-game season. Hank Greenberg and Jimmy Foxx each had hit fifty-eight home runs in a season.

In the ninth inning, with the Yankees safely ahead and one inning from winning another pennant, Maris again batted. There were two outs. Facing him was Hoyt Wilhelm, the toughest relief pitcher in the history of baseball, a knuckleball pitcher with more wins, more saves, more innings pitched, more strikeouts, and the lowest earned run average of any reliefer ever. It was said that trying to hit Wilhelm's knuckler was like trying to swat a fly in midair with a pencil. The ball darted so erratically that neither Wilhelm nor the catcher ever knew where or how it would break, one reason catcher Gus Triandos led the league in passed balls year after year. In the 112 innings Wilhelm had pitched this year to this game, he had allowed but five home runs.

Wilhelm, a quiet man, was more than willing to throw Maris a fastball or two to give him a chance, but Richards, the crusty manager, told Wilhelm, "If you throw him anything but knuckleballs, it will cost you $5,000." Obviously too dear a price to pay for being a nice guy. On Maris's final chance for immortality, Wilhelm threw Maris knuckleballs. The first one hit his bat and glanced off foul. It was deadly silent in the Baltimore ballpark. In homes across the country all activity ceased while Maris batted. The second pitch was again a flutter ball, and again Maris took a half swing at the elusive, darting pitch. This time, however, the ball hit the bat, and while Roger stood in the batter's box, the ball bounded 10 feet down the first-base line, in fair territory. Wilhelm ran over to field the ball, and it was easy for him to tag Maris, who had barely left the plate. The chase to catch the Babe as defined by Ford Frick was over.

There was a noisy Yankee clubhouse after the game. The Yankees had won the game 4–2, clinching the pennant. The players were celebrating with champagne. Everyone was drenched with the bubbly—except Maris. The players knew that he did not engage in that sort of hijinks. They respected him for it and left him alone. Reporters surrounded him admiringly. His eyes were strange, wild and crazy. He was breathing strenuously, trying to catch his breath. "I tried," he said. He took several more swallows of air. "I tried." Everyone could feel the deep respect for Maris in that clubhouse. The other players shook his hand and congratulated him for his effort. They gazed at him in awe. "I felt," one reporter said, "like I was in church."

Despite Frick's ruling, there were still nine games left in the season for Maris to hit more home runs, nine more games of answering endless questions, nine more games of pressure. When Maris talked, his right leg jiggled nervously. In the fourth game of the Baltimore series he went oh for four and after the game discovered his blond hair was falling out in clumps. Bald spots were appearing on the back of his head. He was frightened, and he ran to Dr. Gaynor, the team physician, to find out why. It was the result of nervous tension.

With five games left in the season, on September 26 the Yankees returned to the Stadium for two games against Baltimore and three against the Red Sox. Everyone was still interested in Maris, but the tension had lifted perceptibly after the 154th game. In game 158 versus Baltimore, against twenty-two-year-old Jack Fisher, another Baby Bird with great promise, Maris swung at a curveball that Fisher threw a little too high. After Maris swung, he remained at the plate, leaning on his bat, watching the flight of the ball. The vocal crowd of less than 20,000 people, many of whom were packed into the lower right-field stands where Maris hit most of his home runs, rose, baseball gloves ready to retrieve the souvenir, and when the ball fell into the upper-deck stands, the crowd sent up a deafening roar. Maris nonchalantly tossed the bat away and circled the bases in a jog, savoring the moment. The Oriole right fielder retrieved the ball after it bounced back onto the field and tossed it back in as the Yankees waited for Maris to return to the dugout. When Maris crossed the plate and disappeared into the dugout, every Yankee walked over to him to shake his hand. The crowd continued to cheer, and it would not to stop until Maris reappeared to take a bow, something he was extremely reluctant to do. "I didn't know what to do," Roger said, "I never was in a spot like that." His teammates knew what to do. They pushed him back out onto the field where Maris doffed his cap and waved to the appreciative fans. Maris was even with the Babe. Fisher, who had given up Ted Williams's final home run the day Ted retired, was philosophical. "I'm out there to win," Fisher said. "It doesn't matter to me whether it's Maris's sixtieth or someone else's first. I don't care who hits home runs as long as I win." Fisher lost 3–2.

The next day, exhausted and harried, Maris took the day off. He sat on the bench and watched the game. Mantle, his infection worse, stayed home.

Maris played in games 160 and 161 and was shut out. Again most of the fans who came sat in the three decks of right-field box seats, trying to capitalize on a $5,000 reward offered for home-run number 61. It was like "Let's Make a Deal" where Monte Hall innocently asks, "Who wants to win some money?" and everyone in the audience shouts, "Me, me, me, me, me."

That left game 162. There was tension, because it was Maris's final opportunity, but at this game much of the attraction was of instant riches for the person who caught the ball.

Only one run was scored in the ball game. The Boston pitcher, twenty-four-year-old Tracy Stallard, a fastball-pitching rookie, threw his finest game of the year, a slick five-hitter. One of those hits came in the fourth inning. Maris, waiting patiently in the batter's box, took an outside fastball and a curve inside as the fans booed Stallard loudly. Maris banged his spikes with the end of his bat and set himself again. The pitchers in the Yankee bull pen were all peering in from their right-field vantage point, hoping Maris would hit the ball to them. Before the game Maris had told them, "If you catch it, don't give it to me. Take the five thousand dollars." With the count 2 and 0, Stallard threw a fastball out over the plate. Roger swung smoothly, and a joyous roar followed the crack of the ball on bat as the ball rose high and carried over the head of right fielder Lu Clinton, backed against the stands. It fell into the lower-right-field stands for a home run, the sixty-first home run of the season for Maris. When the ball descended, the rush of fans to catch it was frenzied. "Holy cow!" yelled Yankee announcer Phil Rizzuto. "Look at the fight for that ball!" Even when the lucky fan caught it, others punched him and tried to take it away from him. He was ultimately rescued by the Stadium police.

Maris circled the bases, as usual not showing any emotion, but in the stands, apart from the fighting for the ball, the rest of the fans were screaming in absolute ecstasy, so pleased that Maris had overcome the forbidding odds against him over the excruciatingly drawn out season. As Maris rounded third, a young fan jumped out of the lower stands and raced to shake his hand. Maris shook it, as he did the hand of third-base coach Frank Crosetti. After Maris crossed the plate, the entire Yankee team was waiting for him. When they returned to the dugout, Maris's teammates would not let him in. While the crowd continued its wild, spontaneous cheering, the players kept pushing Maris back on the field, where he sheepishly waved his cap. Four times he tried to reenter the dugout. Four times he was rebuffed. Even when he was finally allowed back in, the cheering continued. It was a magic moment in baseball history.

Stallard, who each time he batted received an ovation for having the guts to pitch to Maris when he could have more safely walked him, was not upset by the home run. "I have nothing to be ashamed of," Stallard said. "He hit sixty others, didn't he?" Maris's home run was the Yankees' 240th of the season, a new record. Previously the record was 221 set by the 1947 Giants and 1956 Reds. The home run also gave Maris the RBI crown as he finished the year with 142, one more than Baltimore first baseman Jim Gentile.

The Yankees won the pennant by eight games over a strong Detroit team. Whitey Ford finished the year with a remarkable 25–4. Ralph Terry finished second in winning percentage to Ford with a 16–3 record. Bill Stafford, losing many close games and not getting credit for a number of other excellent performances, finished 14–9, and Jim Coates and rookie Rollie Sheldon both finished 11–5. Luis Arroyo completed one of the finest relief performances in baseball history with a 15–5 record and twenty-nine saves.

At the bat there was never a team with as much power throughout the entire batting order. Richardson and Kubek were not power hitters, but they were adept at getting on base, to be driven in by the others. Behind them were Maris, who finished with 61 home runs and 142 RBIs, Mantle with 54 home runs and 128 RBIs, first-baseman Bill Skowron, injury-free for most of the season, finishing with 28 home runs and 89 RBIs. Yogi Berra hit 22 home runs, Ellie Howard hit 21, and the third-string catcher, John Blanchard, also hit 21. Clete Boyer, the third baseman, had 11. It was a year for home runs, as opposing players were hitting them, too. Gentile hit 46. Harmon Killebrew hit 46. Rocky Colavito hit 45, and Norm Cash, 41. It was an exciting year, a year in which

Roger Maris, complete with asterisk, became the Home-Run King of baseball.

Before the advent of television and of the "new journalism," an athlete to be idolized needed only to be proficient on the field. The guy could have been the meanest, nastiest son of a bitch since Simon Legree, but if he could hit consistently with men on base or pitch with lightning speed, he was a hero, and how he treated his fellow man was quite irrelevant.

By 1961, however, television made Roger Maris visible and instantly recognizable even to those people who didn't know a stolen base from a stolen car. To the fan, the personality of the athlete had become as important as his statistics, and Maris's isolationist philosophy served to make him look both belligerent and nasty. In truth, toward most people he was neither of these. To most he was an honest, outspoken, unsophisticated man who was kind and considerate to his friends and warm and loving to his family. To those who infringed upon his privacy, especially to newspaper reporters who dogged his every step during his home-run chase, he was irritable, unfriendly, and distant. As a result, the reporters wrote what they observed: that Maris was irritable, unfriendly, and distant. Thus the fans who read the papers saw Maris in this light, and when they came to the ballpark, they believed that to boo Maris was to boo a Snidely Whiplash in pinstripes, a man who would tie Little Nell to the railroad tracks and watch the train run over her. This image of Maris made the equally closemouthed Mickey Mantle in comparison look like Dudley Dooright, the man who would ride in and save Little Nell. Neither characterization was accurate, but the fans saw these two men this way, and to this day their respective images have remained.

Maris's problems with the press and the fans really began the day in December 1959 when it was announced that George Weiss had obtained him from the Kansas City Athletics. To most players, going to the Yankees was an honor and a privilege. It was a chance for World Series loot. To Maris, a devout family man, it meant being separated from his wife and children, since he didn't want to uproot them from their Kansas City home.

When the trade was announced, the New York reporters immediately called Maris for a comment. They expected to hear how thrilled he was to be coming to New York. Instead, Maris said that he liked it in Kansas City and didn't want to leave. "I know that financially I can do much better in New York," he said. "Therefore I will go." It was not a diplomatic answer, but it was honest, consistent with his basic philosophies of life: "To thine own self be true" and "Don't bullshit me." It was his strict adherence to his own principles that caused Maris to be labeled a malcontent and a troublemaker.

In 1953, when Roger signed with the Cleveland Indians, the club wanted him to start at Daytona Beach, Florida, in Class D. Maris insisted on playing for Fargo, a Class C team in his hometown, where he could play in front of friends and be with his girl. The Indians said no. Roger refused to accept no for an answer and said that he wouldn't play. He'd go out and work for a living. Roger got his way, played at Fargo, and hit .325. This stubbornness nevertheless began his reputation as a troublemaker. Maris, however, felt he knew what was best for Maris and figured that what was best for him was also going to be best for whoever was paying his salary.

In 1954 Cleveland wanted Maris to spend another year at Fargo. This time Roger demanded to be promoted. He was, to Keokuk in Class B, where he hit .315 with thirty-two home runs and twenty-five stolen bases. In '55 he was promoted to Tulsa in Class AA. Early in the season, after Maris overthrew third base from right field and cost the team a game, the Tulsa manager, Dutch Meyer, ordered a special practice for Maris. Meyer hit fly balls to right field, and the embarrassed and enraged youngster practiced his throwing to third. After a number of long throws, Maris, steaming at what he felt to be an unjust humiliation, tucked his glove under his arm and walked off the field while Meyer stood at home plate with his fungo bat, screaming, "Get back out there." Maris resolutely continued to the dugout and into the locker room.

"I'll never take abuse from anybody, big or small, important or unimportant, if I think it's undeserved," Maris said. "You've got to have enough pride to stand up for yourself." Maris was immediately demoted to Reading. Meyer was fired shortly thereafter.

In 1956 Maris starred for Reading, where Yankee general manager George Weiss first noticed the youngster, and in 1957 he starred at Indianapolis, the top minor-league team in the Cleveland organization. Weiss followed Maris's progress.

In 1957 he finally was brought up to the Indians. Weiss told Kansas City A's owner Arnold Johnson that if he could trade for Maris, the Yankees would trade the A's for him and then make an offer Johnson would not be able to refuse. Weiss knew that Cleveland general manager Frank Lane would never trade Maris to the Yankees. Injuries and another Maris feud made it possible for Johnson to acquire Maris in mid-1958. Weiss, true to his word, acquired Maris from the A's in the winter of 1959. It is said that when Weiss acquired Bob Turley and Don Larsen in the winter of 1954, he set the rest of the American League back five years. When he acquired Maris in the winter of 1959, he set it back another five years.

The Yankees in 1959 had finished a dismal third. In 1960 Maris helped return the franchise to its winning tradition. In 1960 he hit thirty-nine home runs, in '61 he hit sixty-one to break Babe Ruth's record, in '62 he hit thirty-three, and in '63, though he was out half the season with injuries, he still managed to hit twenty-three home runs. In 1964 Maris hit twenty-six home runs, and then in '65 he broke his hand and played sparingly as the Yankees plummeted. For five years Roger Maris was one of the great home-run hitters in the game, and teamed with Mantle, they were the most fearsome one-two punch since Ruth and Gehrig.

Casey Stengel, who managed him in 1960, didn't completely understand the closemouthed Maris. "That's Maris," Casey said. "You tell him something, and he'll stare at you for a week before answering," but Casey nevertheless appreciated his excellence as a complete ballplayer. "I give the man a point for speed," Casey said. "I do this," he said with unassailable logic, "because Maris can run fast. Then I can give him a point because he can slide fast. I give him another point because he can bunt. I also give him a point because he can field. He is very good around the fences—sometimes on top of the fences. Next I give him a point because he can throw. A right fielder has to be a thrower or he's not a right fielder. So I add up my points," Casey concluded, "and I've got five for him before I even come to his hitting. I would say this is a good man."

Maris was far better than a good man. Back-to-back in 1960 and 1961 he won the Most Valuable Player award in the American League. In '61 he won the Hickok Belt for the best professional athlete of the year. He was named the Top Catholic Athlete of the Year. He won the Sultan of Swat award, the Bill Corum award from the New York City B'nai B'rith. What he never won was a sympathetic press. At banquets he was criticized for mumbling "thanks" and sitting down. The Yankees kept getting letters complaining that he didn't speak. It was reported that the Yankees tried to explain to Maris the value of public speaking and that they even wrote a speech for him. "I'm no speaker," Maris protested.

When spring training of 1962 began, Maris figured that the pressures the media placed on him would cease. He was wrong. From the start of spring training there was a new set of standard questions, the most prevalent one being "Will you hit sixty-two home runs in 1962?" Maris became angry whenever someone asked him that. "This was the first time in thirty-four years that someone hit sixty home runs. Anybody who expects me to do it again must have rocks in his head," he replied.

In March his worst public-relations problems began when a reporter from the Fort Lauderdale *News* wrote that when one youngster asked Maris for an autograph, Maris wrote an *X* on the ball. It was a malicious, false accusation, making Maris appear cruel to children. Maris was livid. He had made an *X*, but Maris, who liked kids, was only making a joke and afterward signed a personal inscription and his signature. Maris vowed not to talk to any reporters from the local Florida papers. The next day a Miami reporter asked Maris, "How do you think you'll do this season?" "No comment," growled Maris. "How much do you weigh?" "No comment," Maris answered. "Do you think we should sign a nuclear-disarmament treaty with the Russians?" "No fucking comment," Maris growled. Maris then explained that his new policy was not to give interviews. "Let 'em write what they want," said Roger. "Ted Williams was right. Go your way and let the writers go theirs."

A few days later, the day after St. Patrick's Day, Oscar Fraley, the author of the "The Untouchables," the TV show starring Robert Stack as Eliot Ness, wrote an article for UPI about Maris that was prominently displayed at the top of the Fort Lauderdale sports page. Fraley had never met Maris or even talked to him, but he knew he didn't like him, anyway. Fraley criticized Maris for his refusal to be courteous with newspapermen and submit to interviews. "If either of my two sons has a hero," Fraley concluded in his article, "I hope it's a modest fellow named John Glenn, who went for the circuit when it really counted. Because guys like Maris bat a round zero with me."

When the fighting-mad Maris finally caught up with Fraley, Roger called him every name in the book, publicly, to his face. "If you weren't so old," Maris told him, "I'd knock you right on your ass." He stormed into the clubhouse. Following behind him was Jimmy Cannon, the highly respected journalist from the New York *Journal-American*. "Can I talk to you?" Cannon asked the shaken Maris. "Not now," Maris said. "Later." Cannon shot back, "Go fuck yourself."

Two days later Cannon began a two-part series. The headlines of the two columns read: "Maris—'The Whiner'—a Threat to Yank Pennant" and "Maris Envies Mantle's Prestige Among Yankees." It was another distorted piece by an irate journalist who should have controlled his temper and been more objective. "The community of baseball feels Mantle is a great player," Cannon wrote. "They consider Maris a thrilling freak who batted .269 . . . but his reputation is demolished when they compare him to Mantle. This apparently irritates Maris, who gives the impression that he inhabits a league filled with enemies. Obviously Maris considers Mantle a competitor instead of a partner on a team."

By this time Maris was ready to pack his bag and go home. His character had suffered such assassination that if he had discovered a cure for cancer he still would have been thought of as an arrogant and aloof scientist. "Rude Roger," some writers were calling him in the papers. Cannon continued to call him the Whiner.

There was yet another ugly scene. A photographer asked Maris to pose with New York Mets coach Rogers Hornsby, one of the game's great hitters. Maris, still seething at the beating he was taking, did not want to pose. During the 1961 season Hornsby had said that there was only one thing Maris could do as well as Babe Ruth, and that was run. In his agitated state, Maris saw Hornsby as another critic who had been taking potshots at him. The headlines in the papers the next day read, "Hornsby Calls Maris 'Little Punk Ball Player!' " "I've posed with some real major leaguers, not bush leaguers like he is," Hornsby said.

Before the end of spring training Roger was so agitated that he didn't know his friends from his enemies. He even offended the elderly Dan Daniel of the *World-Telegram*, one of Maris's strongest supporters. "Maris will have to learn to laugh, even while bleeding internally," Daniel wrote. "If he continues to be the Angry Man, may the Lord have mercy on him. The customers won't."

And the customers didn't. When Roger did not hit sixty-two home runs in 1962, he was booed. When he responded to the booing by giving the finger to the fans, the booing increased. By the end of 1962 Maris had hit thirty-three home runs, an excellent total for anyone else but unsatisfactory to the fans. The booing upset the Yankee management. If Manager Houk had not insisted that Maris remain with the Yankees, General Manager Roy Hamey would have traded him at the end of '62. The booing continued. He was a marked man.

"Some kids feel they're big shots if they boo me," Maris said. "I don't have to explain why I don't like certain fans. Would you like it if someone threw a beer can at you? How 'bout if someone threw a bottle at you?

"What the hell," Maris said philosophically, "as long as I stay in New York, it's going to keep on. They're on my back, and they're never going to get off. There's no use letting it bug me." Maris was right. They never did get off his back, even after he helped lead the Yankees to five straight pennants. The booing did, however, bug him.

The writers never got off his back, either. It was never written that Maris was surly because he was bitter. "Charm is not his strong suit," wrote writer Charles McCabe. "He is said to feel he should be paid to smile. And maybe even breathe. It is believed that in his sleep he intones the stirring shibboleth of the professional athlete, 'What's in it for me?' He is a redneck. He ain't bright. He's about as lovable as a tarantula. And he ain't even hitting .300 these days." "What would the New York writers say," said Maris, "if they knew my uncle was Adolph Eichmann?"

His teammates, traveling with him every day, felt that Maris was a straightforward, no-nonsense person. They admired him for his courage, marveled at his sixty-one home runs in the face of intense pressure, and respected him for what he was: the best right fielder in the American League. Around his teammates Maris did not have to pick and choose every word. He had a cutting, Billy Martin type of humor, so that when Ellie Howard got on the bus, Martin would say, "Ellie, get in the back," and everyone would laugh. "Hey, Mick," Maris would say, "I'm not talking to you today. I'm jealous of you." Roger, contrary to what McCabe wrote, was not a dumb guy. He was, in fact, quite articulate around his friends—only around his friends. He had been burned too often to trust any strangers.

In 1964 Maris's hitting was the key factor in the Yankees' winning the pennant, his last great Yankee hurrah. In June 1965 Maris, playing despite a pulled hamstring muscle, tried to score from second base on a base hit. When he slid home, he dislocated two fingers on his right hand when they caught on the spikes of umpire Bill Haller, who had been standing too close to the plate. Several days later, batting against Washington, he felt something pop in the palm of his right hand while swinging the bat. There was no official diagnosis of what had happened to him, but throughout the season the Yankee bulletins kept saying Maris was almost ready to play. When the season ended, Maris had not played one inning after the June injury. The hand was so badly injured he was unable to turn a doorknob with it. It was broken. Maris played again in 1966 but was only a shadow of his old self. The fans still booed him, the press still picked on him, and his performance suffered terribly. He hit .233 with thirteen home runs and only drove in forty-three runs. The Yankees finished last. In December 1966 Yankee general manager Lee MacPhail traded Maris to the St. Louis Cardinals for Cardinal third baseman Charlie Smith, the ex-Met, White Sox, Phillie, and Dodger who never hit too well and wasn't much of a fielder, either. It was the final insult from the Yankees. Roger Maris for Charlie Smith. When Maris led the Cardinals to pennants in 1967 and 1968 it was Maris who had the last laugh. In his first time at bat in a Cardinal uniform Maris hit a double and went flying into second. The Cardinal fans gave him a standing ovation. He was made. He was promised a beer distributorship by Gussie Busch, the Budweiser beer baron who owns the Cardinals. In 1968 he retired to his Gainesville, Florida, home to run that beer distributorship.

I was aware of Maris's antipathy toward the media when I wrote him a letter asking him if I could talk to him. When he didn't write back, I assumed that he wished to continue his anonymity. Then, while driving through the Southeast, on a hunch I detoured through Gainesville, Florida, hoping to find him working at his beer distributorship, located near the Gainesville airport. When I arrived, he wasn't there, and I waited two hours for him. All the employees, including his brother, said that they did not know where he was or how he could be reached. The only evidence that Roger Maris was associated with the operation was a Sultan of Swat trophy, awarded for his home-run hitting, and a Most Valuable Player Award, tarnished mementos that sat alone, unexplained, on the bottom shelf of a drab brown glass-enclosed case, the silver bowls uncared-for symbols of an uncherished past.

After waiting fruitlessly, I went to visit with Bill Skowron in Dunnellon, Florida, about 75 miles south of Gainesville. Skowron and Maris were close friends, and Bill generously offered to call Roger and ask him if he would have breakfast with us. "I'd love to see you, Moose," Maris said, "but leave the other guy home." After writing Maris another letter, I gave up.

Months later, when I was arranging to see Clete Boyer in Atlanta, I called Clete to tell him when I was coming. Clete said, "I got a buddy of mine down here with me. Roger Maris."

"Will he talk with me?" I asked.

"I don't know," Clete said. "You'll have to see."

We met at Boyer's nightclub, the Golden Glove, where a live band was playing very loud rock music in the darkly lit, low-ceilinged bar. Boyer, Maris, and I sat down at a table, ordered drinks, and made small talk for a minute or two. Clete then excused himself to go to the bar and talk business. I was left alone at the table with Maris, who hasn't changed much since his playing days. He still looked like the son of Odin, a sandy-haired Viking with piercing eyes and broad shoulders. I told him about some of his Yankee teammates I had seen, but I didn't come right out and ask him if he would talk. I didn't want to ask, because if he said no, it would have spoiled everyone's evening. Maris and I sat over our drinks, minutes of deadly silence hanging heavily while the blaring of the raw rock music was drowning out coherent thought. I was groping for a comfortable topic when Roger looked up from his drink. "This noise is really brutal," he said. "Let's go out into the parking lot. We can talk there." He got up to go. I followed.

The air outside was fresh, and though the music was still audible, it was no longer piercing. I sat on one of the parked autos while Maris stood alongside, sipping his drink. Seeing my tape recorder, Roger nodded toward the music. "You'll get some good background music." He smiled. Already I was saying to myself, *Is this the Roger Maris who kicks dogs and hates children?*

"I guess," I said, choosing my words carefully, "the thing I want to ask you about most is that after 1961, when you hit all those home runs, your relationship with the Yankees deteriorated. You had problems with newspapermen, the fans were really lousy, and it was just a bad thing." Now I had to phrase the question properly. "What are your feelings today about all the things that happened to you in New York?" I asked.

Maris sipped his drink. "Actually," he said, "I don't really feel that bad about it. It's something that happened, something that I had no control over. It was the writers' control. Sure, things could have been handled a lot differently by the Yankees. But they weren't. And it was just something that . . ." He paused and shrugged his shoulders. "Who knows how they happened or why they happened? It's stuff that's gone behind me, and really, it hasn't bothered me a lick." He paused again. "It would have been a lot nicer had it been the other way around, but . . ." A shrug.

"It almost seemed that everyone was holding this tremendous feat that you had performed against you," I said.

"Well," Maris said, "you might call it that. I guess I came along and did something that evidently was sacred, something that nobody was supposed to do. Especially me."

"Did this feeling against you affect your play?" I asked.

"There's no question about it," Maris said. "You don't go out there and play one hundred and sixty-two ball games and have people on your back continuously day in and day out and not have it affect your play. It took a lot away from the game as far as I personally was concerned. Naturally you're trying to do your best, but when all the elements are somewhat against you, I don't really feel that I got the best out of me."

"You were under a great deal of pressure," I said.

"Well, like I said before, and I'll say again, as far as playing the ball game, there was no pressure. Playing was probably the easiest part of it. Well, mentally it got pretty strong, the press before and after the ball games, the continuous questions, continuously trying to be on your guard because there were a certain few looking for you to maybe make a slip. I'm not trying to knock anybody, you understand, but when you're trying to answer one question, someone else butts in with another thing, and another guy comes in on half of what you said, and they misinterpret, and through all the continuous questions being fired at you, the pressure was quite strong. Mentally it was tough. I needed time off, and in the last week I took a day off."

"In the spring of the next year, the spring of '62, it was one incident after another."

"Yeah," Roger said. "There were a lot of things I didn't understand. There are a lot of things I won't ever understand. But," he said, again shrugging, "these things happen. They have happened to other ballplayers before me, a certain few. But like I say, unfortunately I was one of those few who had that type of publicity, and you just somewhat have to live with it. The Fraley article, for instance," he said. "After I read that, I was burning, and I just didn't want to talk with anyone. And Jimmy Cannon came over and asked me if he could talk to me, and I said, 'Jimmy, not right now. I'm not in the mood to talk with anyone.' And we were close friends, I thought. Every morning we had breakfast together. And Jimmy said to me, 'If that's the way you feel, the hell with you.' And that was the end of our friendship." There was a look of hurt and disappointment on Roger's face. "I really thought our friendship was worth more than that," Roger said. "To me it's all over and done with, what happened with the Yankees, and the people I got to know, I let them judge me for themselves. I just let it go at that."

"Any number of your teammates," I said, "told me that there was one season when you had a broken wrist, and the doctor didn't even tell you it was broken."

"It was a broken hand," Roger said. "Someone was told not to tell me; I can't say it was the doctor."

"Ralph Houk certainly must have known that the X rays showed it to be broken," I said.

"Well, I'm sure Ralph knew about it," Maris said. "It's sort of a peculiar thing. I didn't feel that I was just the ordinary run-of-the-mill ballplayer, and to break a hand in May and not find out about it until a week before the season was over in September . . . you know? And it just sort of seems strange, because the whole time they kept saying it was a day-to-day proposition. I felt personally that there were a few people who made me look like I didn't *want* to play, that I was just there to draw a salary. And I really didn't think that was too right, either.

"Once I broke the hand in '65, though," he said, "really, it was all over for me, because even today I don't have the gripping strength in two fingers of my right hand. I would swing the bat and have that hand slip right out there.

"It was sort of a disappointing thing," he continued, "because the ball club had taken X rays. We took X rays in Washington. We took them in Minneapolis. We took them in New York, and there was never any mention of a break. At first it started out I could go out in the field and take infield, throw the baseball. Then the ball club every four or five days asked me to take batting practice, so I'd go ahead and try a few swings, and it didn't work, and it got to the point where I couldn't even throw a baseball, 'cause I couldn't hold the baseball in my hand. And yet they were asking me to continuously take the batting practice. Now I'm not going to knock Mr. Houk. I'm not going to knock anybody. Everybody's going to draw their own conclusions. There are just a lot of things that I don't understand, and I never will. A lot of things. I just don't want to get into knocking Ralph. I've got my own personal feelings. I feel that a lot of things could have been handled a lot differently than they were, and naturally I was quite disappointed in the way they were handled. I can turn around and say something in my defense, and that means nothing.

So you end up sitting back and saying, 'Let it quiet down.' I was more interested in just having things quiet down than continuously bringing up things from the past."

"There reached a point," I said, "near the end of your Yankee career you told Lee MacPhail you weren't going to play in New York anymore."

"No," Roger said. "I really didn't say it that way. I said that I was not going to play anymore. Anywhere. I had plans to retire after the '66 season, and I told Ralph Houk that. I told Ralph that in July of '66, and when I came to the end of the season, rather than announce I was not going to play the following year, Ralph told me to wait till spring training before I announced it to make sure of what I was doing. So I said okay, and I went home after the season ended. Lee MacPhail called me up one day and asked me if I had changed my mind. I said, 'No, I haven't.' But just detecting the way he was talking, I thought he had something in mind, and I said, 'Lee, if you have any intentions of trading me, let me know now, and I'll announce my retirement.' He said, 'No, we have no intentions of trading you.' I said, 'Then let's just do it the way Ralph wanted to do it, wait till spring training, but I'm still not going to play.' And he said, 'Okay.' And a few days later I was traded. So I personally thought that they could have respected me a little bit by letting me retire if I wanted to retire instead of doing things the way they did them. If I wanted to retire, I think I should have had that much courtesy from the ball club. But when this came up the way it did, I had voiced to only a couple of people that I was retiring, and the writers would have made me look bad again. They'd say, 'Well, he's not going to play because he was traded away from the Yankees.' They would have jumped on me like it was a big news story. So I finally agreed to go ahead and play the year." Roger ultimately played two more years, an integral number of the 1967 and '68 pennant-winning Cardinals.

"Will you ever come back to New York?" I asked. "You never come back to the Old-Timers' Games."

"Oh," Maris said, "one day I'll come back. When, I don't know. Right now I just don't have the desire to do a lot of those things. Like this year I had many people writing letters to me, asking me to come back to the Old-Timers' Games in New York, and from what I understand, the ball club put out the word through the announcers that the reason I'm not coming back to New York for the Old-Timers' Game is because I'm afraid the people are going to boo me." Roger smiled and shook his head. "I've been booed by the best of them for many years," he said. "The ball club is trying to push off, 'Well, bad ole Roger again, he's not going to come out because the poor boy is afraid of boos.' That's not the case. I have had other reasons why I have not wanted to go up there. The ball club knows what they are. Ralph Houk knows what they are. Lee MacPhail knows what they are."

"But aren't Ralph and Lee gone?" I asked.

Roger grimaced slightly and nodded, but his silent response indicated that though the two men were not Yankee executives any longer, the wounds they caused him still remained. There was something heroic in Maris's stoicism, in his insistence in not verbally retaliating against the men who helped sully his image.

"You've got to understand me," Maris said. "I've never believed in knocking people. Never. It's not my nature. I really don't even care to get into those kinds of things, 'cause all you do is reopen wounds. Right now Roger Maris is in Podunk. Nobody knows he's around. You know? Half of us haven't heard of him in the last five years, and it's beautiful. I really hate to reopen old wounds. No news is good news. This is basically what it amounts to."

Clete Boyer joined us in the parking lot, and following him was an older woman, tottering slightly, and in her hand was a Polaroid camera. "Can I take your picture?" she asked Boyer, a hometown Atlanta favorite. "Why, sure you can," Clete said graciously. "Roger Maris is here, too. You can get both of us together." The lady didn't register any surprise or delight that Clete's friend Maris was there, too. "You know who Roger is, don't you?" Clete asked the woman.

"No, ah don't," she said.

Roger, posing with Boyer, smiled. "That's just the way I like it."

This is the opening of *The Celebrant*, a novel little noted upon its publication in 1983 but one that has since steadily risen in stature. Greenberg's agreeably archaic style combines with an evident appetite for the game—he gets the baseball *right*, as no contemporary novelist has except perhaps Mark Harris—to produce what is, in this editor's opinion, the most satisfying of all baseball novels. In the following passage, Greenberg fillets that curious phenomenon of hero worship and exposes its cannibalistic core: the hope and dream of the fan for merged identity and transference of powers.

ERIC ROLFE GREENBERG

Hero

Our family came to New York in the winter of '89, and in the spring I saw my first game of baseball. I was eight. My mother's brother, a jeweler, had preceded us across the Atlantic; Uncle Sid's family was small—only four children—but the crowding was awful, and in April my father thought to find a place of our own across the river in Brooklyn. He inquired of a German-speaking landlord near Prospect Park, who asked if there were children; my father answered "nine," the German nodded, and the two men shook hands. The following Sunday we stacked all we owned onto a rented dray and, daunted by the spectacular height of the new bridge, crossed the river by ferry. We returned before nightfall, much abashed. The German had understood my father to say he had no children, and when he arrived with nine, the door was slammed in his face.

I missed this famous encounter. I'd run off to the park after my older brother Eli and discovered there clay diamonds cut into an immense field of grass, an expanse so generous that half a dozen ball games were under way at once, some so distant that they appeared contests between toy miniatures. But toy players could hardly have amazed me more than these—adults! grown men playing games!—and many in uniforms complete with gaudy striped stockings. Far away a bat struck a ball; seconds later I heard the sound. This phenomenon was a great excitement, and I ran back and forth, altering the time lapse until I was nearly trampled by an outfielder in furious pursuit of a fly ball. I dodged as he sprang, and as he stretched out in full flight, the side of his shoe caught

my cheek. I reeled and fell down. The ball bounded on, and the man who'd kicked me spat dirt from his mouth, looked up, and said, "Well, *shit!*"—the first words ever spoken to me on a ball field.

The family stayed in Manhattan. We found the game everywhere, in every imaginable variation. There were large lots along both rivers that allowed the full exercise, and each street and alley had its own rules and exceptions. First by imitation, then by practice, we learned the game and the ways of the boys who played it, the angle of their caps, the intonations of their curses and encouragements. Our accents disappeared; our strides became quick and confident. My left-handedness, regarded by my parents as a devil's curse, turned to my advantage in the pitcher's box. I threw a submarine ball, my knuckles grazing the dirt as I released it. "Get those knuckles dirty, Jackie!" my infielders would shout—Jackie, not Yakov.

The new fashion of overhand pitching soon threatened my eminence. When the National League legalized the pitch, the neighborhood clubs followed suit; I tried the style but had trouble keeping the ball low, and it's the high pitch that's hit a distance. Our team enlisted a big fellow who could throw the overhand pitch with mustard, and to counter his advantage, I attempted to learn the curve. It was accounted a disreputable pitch, the refuge of a trickster who had not the honest strength to power the ball over the plate. I found it difficult, for my fingers were too short to give the ball sufficient spin. Soon I was in the outfield, not liking the change; pitching is the core of the game. Vowing to master the curve, I threw to Eli for an hour every evening in the narrow alley behind our tenement. The youngsters on the block would come out and carry on as if I were pitching for the Giants against the Orioles for the Temple Cup: "Keeler's up, Jackie; watch it now! Ball one—come on, put it over! The curve, the curve! Oh, he hit it! Base hit! Now Jennings—better bear down, Jackie! McGraw's on deck!"

Finally, at fifteen, I made the curveball work. I threw it as hard as the fast one, and it broke just as it reached the plate, a small break but a sharp one, straight down. It was a ground-ball pitch, and it kept my infielders busy. In tandem with the big fellow I won a good many ball games and achieved something of a neighborhood celebrity.

At the close of the '97 season the league sponsored an awards dinner at a restaurant on Grand Street, and there I shook hands with a major-league player. His name was Jack Warner. I'd watched him play shortstop for an uptown semiprofessional club, marveling at his size and power, but he lacked speed, and the professional leagues had made him first an outfielder, then a catcher. His face showed the marks of that ignoble position. At the dinner, his eyes never leaving the page, he delivered a speech analogizing baseball and life. Practice, dedication, clean living, and fair play—these guaranteed success on and off the field. We froze in a handshake while a photographer immortalized the moment, and then I took a silver cup from him. He turned to the organizer of the event and asked for his fee.

In the spring I was asked to a professional tryout at Manhattan Field, far uptown. Men with leather faces and tobacco-stained teeth examined me microscopically and stood in at bat as I pitched. A week later a letter arrived, the first I'd ever received, offering a contract with the Altoona club of the New York–Pennsylvania League.

My parents wouldn't hear of it.

Prizefighters, jockeys, ballplayers: these were professional athletes. Most celebrated were the fighters at the championship level; heavyweight Corbett could get a room at most hotels, and it was said that the better people of San Francisco welcomed him to their salons. The exemplary Gentleman Jim thus crossed once-impregnable barriers, but the gulf between his status and that of the journeyman was vast. Club fighters were neighborhood heroes, yet the unspoken assumption was that they fought because they were unfit to do anything else; a man did not opt for the ring, he was condemned to it. Most jockeys were black, apprenticed to trainers or breeders; one thought of them as one thought of the horses they rode. Some professional ballplayers were locally bred, but an increasing number were itinerants from distant farmlands who lived out of cardboard suitcases in back-street boardinghouses. Annually they jumped from league to league and team to team for the sake of a few dollars' increase in salary. To bankers and landlords and shopkeepers they were suspect, disreputable; to a man with daughters they were dangerous. An underclass supported them. Ballpark crowds were mean and roistering.

I was seventeen and done with school; I'd stayed at it longer than most. All the pressure of a family's traditions, hopes, and plans pressed down upon me. I was the fifth son; the first had driven teams to put the second through college, and the third, Eli, sold my Uncle Sid's jewelry to see the fourth through his studies. I was obliged to provide for young Sam's higher education. I argued that I could do this on a ballplayer's salary, $20 a month, but though my parents came to believe that I'd actually be paid to play ball, the issue went far deeper than money. We had not crossed the ocean to find disgraceful employment.

I had not the wherewithal to resist my parents. Rather than be dead to them—for my father threatened to turn his back to me and say a kaddish for my soul—I put away the contract and assumed Eli's position at Uncle Sid's jewelry store, while Eli packed a case of samples and sought markets in faraway cities. I was no sales clerk, nor as proficient as my cousins in working the precious metals and stones, but I did show a flair for design. Should a customer find nothing on display to his liking, I'd inquire what he had in mind and quickly sketch a model; often enough, a sale would result. Once I turned this trick to delight a trio of sisters who were shopping for an anniversary present for their parents. When the piece was done, I delivered it to their home, far uptown in Turtle Bay—and what a home, a mansion with fantastic wrought-iron fencing at the doors and windows and an interior elegance that to my mind quite belied the small mezuzah posted at the entry. That Jews could achieve such grandeur was well nigh unbelievable.

The next week the youngest of the daughters returned to the shop to thank me and to order another piece. She was merry; she kept me so long at the sketch pad with her suggestions and alterations that Uncle Sid had to bustle us out of the store at closing time. I escorted her home by trolley and learned her name—Edith—while she learned of me everything I could babble in an hour. When our club played in Central Park the following Sunday, she was there with her sisters; they carried matching parasols that spun prettily in their gloved hands. I pitched well that day, breaking off the curveball time after time. Afterward we shared lemonade in the Ramble.

The next day I could hardly lift my arm. The curveball was proving too great a strain. I needed a week between turns, and soon that wasn't enough. In the end I was back in the outfield, where the dream of Altoona and the big leagues faded. Playing less, I found time for afternoons with Edith; often I had to choose between her company at a concert or museum and Eli's for a ball game. Once my brother had offered to escort all three Sonnheim girls to the Polo Grounds; the suggestion scandalized Edith's father, who coldly opined that baseball had ceased to be a gentleman's game after the Civil War, when it had been taken over by professional athletes. Might as well recommend a tour of the Tenderloin!

In deep summer, with Edith at her family's lodge on Lake George, I was ever at the ballpark—the new Polo Grounds, where the Giants were declining from their glory years of the early nineties, or more frequently the Atlantic Avenue park in Brooklyn to watch the Superbas, stocked with Baltimore veterans, driving to the championships of '99 and 1900. Eli would introduce me to his sporting friends as his "expert" and make a great show of consulting me in whispers before placing a bet. It seemed he required a wager to excite his interest, whereas for me the game was all.

As the spring of 1901 turned toward summer, Eli urged me to join him on his annual "big swing" west to the Mississippi, north to Chicago, and east along the Lakes. "Sport, we'll eat a steak and see a ball game in every city!" he swore. Uncle Sid accepted Eli's contention that my designs would be improved with a better knowledge of our markets, and Edith was away. I bought a suitcase—leather, not cardboard—and packed for my first excursion beyond the Hudson. Our first calls were in Philadelphia, where the steaks weren't much to speak of and the ball game worse. The National League club was on the road, and we decided to test the infant American League, which had no New York franchise. The great attraction was Napoleon Lajoie, whose batting average for the Americans was a hundred points above what he'd hit for Philadelphia's Nationals the year before. His outrageous success seemed proof of the new league's inferiority. Nap was one of several former collegians courted for the club by Philadelphia's gaunt manager, Connie Mack; another was Plank, who pitched that day and easily beat the Milwaukee entry. Lajoie had three hits and scored twice.

We caught up with the Philadelphia Nationals in Pittsburgh. They missed Lajoie; the home club beat them authoritatively to move further ahead in the race. In Cincinnati dwelt a cadet branch of the family, and we stayed nearly a week. A second cousin, whose face was a startling female approximation of my brother Sam's, took me on an outing along the river and somehow contrived a rainstorm, a sheltering toolshed, and a blanket, but she could not contrive a different face, and the matter came to nothing. To my joy, the Cincinnati Red Stockings arrived for the latter part of our visit, and with them our own wonderful Brooklyn club, Ned Hanlon and his boys, the defending World Champions. But the club was fading, the old Baltimore heroes further past their prime, and we sensed there would be no pennant flying over Atlantic Park at year's end.

On a Saturday morning in mid-July we stepped off the westbound train into the heat of St. Louis and proceeded to the Chase Hotel. My brother always put up at the best hotels, signing as "E. Kapp." The name Kapinski would not be welcome on those registers. As I unpacked, he searched out sheaves of the hotel's stationery and addressed invitations to the buyers of the town, requesting the honor of their presence at our "suite" on the Monday following. That done, he summoned an assistant manager to lay plans for breakfast, mid-morning, and luncheon service: oysters and champagne, deviled eggs, a variety of sausage to suit the Swiss and Germans among our clientele. (Later Eli would cadge some kosher delicacies for our coreligionists, some of whom would first set foot in the Chase at our invitation.) He would welcome them all; he would tell the latest tales and gags; he would profess that, had he a choice, he would visit them at their offices, but to carry his samples on the dangerous streets was to court dire attack; he would show his wares and write his orders. In such ways did Eli advance the family business as it increasingly turned from retailing to manufacture. A middle-range market was emerging between the jeweler's private customer and the mail-order public, and the avenue to it was the department store. Our product line was priced below the artisan's custom work and above the COD merchandise that Eli accurately described as cheap junk. His job was to secure outlets against the efforts of dozens of direct competitors, and he shared the rails with a gaggle of salesmen hawking hardware or hose or outrageous feathered wraps; together they were inventing the business of the new century. Not all stayed at the grand hotels, but my brother would have put up at the Chase (or Boston's St. James or Baltimore's Belvedere) had his suitcase carried sandstone or cement.

Yet for all this show, his delight was to invite guests to the local ballpark. He'd staked this out as his personal form of business entertainment, leaving the burlesques and bawdy houses to his fellows of the selling trade. Here professional calculation matched his personal inclination. For himself, Eli Kapinski of New York, no fancy out-of-town attraction could rival those of home, but a major-league ball game in any city carried a sort of guarantee. For his clients—what a disarming suggestion! An afternoon at the ballpark, so refreshing, so American!

Shortly before three o'clock on a cauterizing Monday we rented a hack, collected three buyers who'd breakfasted with us that morning, and set out for League Park. St. Louis in July was the hottest place on the circuit, the hottest place God ever made a city. Our guests blamed the heat for the team's sorry record in the National League; they'd never finished above fifth place. I pointed out that the city's entry had won four championships in the old American Association in the eighties. "Mildest summers on record," I was assured. This season their club had known early success, but now, beset by slump and injury, they were losing ground to Pittsburgh. Still the fans prayed for a cool summer and came to League Park in record number; more than 20,000, an unprecedented gathering, had encircled the field for the previous game of the current series with the New York Giants.

In the matter of rooting, a boy's first team is his team forever. I'd seen my first big-league game below Coogan's Bluff ten years before, and whatever Brooklyn's current success, the Giants were the club of my heart, their championships my own. But seven years' famine had followed the feast, and a dozen managers had come and gone under the club's owner, Tammany politico Andrew Freedman. A great war was waged between Freedman and my own idol, Amos Rusie, the huge right-hander who'd won thirty-six games in glorious '94. Rusie refused to sign a contract in '96, came back to win forty-eight games for a lesser club in '97 and '98, and then held out for two full seasons rather than throw another pitch for Freedman. He called the owner a liar, a chiseler, a welcher, and a cheat; Freedman called Rusie a Republican. They were both right. Without Rusie or any other player of great regard, the Giants finished last in 1900. They'd replaced most of their infield and half their mound staff, but their current fifth-place standing owed largely to the advent of a talented collegiate pitcher of their own, a right-hander who was scheduled to throw for New York.

Play had just begun when we arrived at League Park. We watched from the outfield as the Giants mounted an early attack. Sudhoff, the elfin St. Louis pitcher, began badly: a walk, a base hit, and then a drive that skipped under the right fielder's glove and rolled to our feet. The tallest of our clients, a thin man with merry eyes, kicked the ball back toward the fielder. Far away, in the middle of the diamond, the umpire threw up his hands and shouted, "Hold! Three bases!" Two Giants scored, and we moved with haste to the grandstand, a single-tiered wooden structure that rose along both foul lines. Having paid a quarter a head to enter the park grounds, we were now charged as much again to gain the grandstand and needed fifty cents more for box seats beneath the low, shading roof. But an attendant at the box-seat turnstile swore there was no room for us in the shade, and when Eli protested, he scolded us with Irish vigor: "You want to come out early these days, we're winning now, don't you know!" Finally we found room behind third base for three on one grandstand bench and for two more directly behind. The thin client and a bearded one flanked Eli, while the stoutest squeezed in next to me. We doffed our jackets and loosened our collars. The Giants had scored no more, and the teams had changed sides. Little Jess Burkett stood in for St. Louis, hands high on the bat, feet spread wide. Behind him, Patsy Donovan, who doubled as manager, picked at the tape around the handle of his bat. The sun burned down, the cries of the crowd floated in the humid air, and the umpire pointed a finger at the New York pitcher and bid him throw.

This pitcher was big—gigantic, compared to Wee Willie Sudhoff—yet his motion matched Sudhoff's for balance and ease until he pushed off the pitcher's slab with his right foot and drove at the plate with startling power. His follow-through ended in a light skip, and he finished on his toes, his feet well apart, his hands at the ready for a fielding play. I heard the umpire's call but didn't know if Burkett had swung and missed or taken the strike, for my eyes hadn't left the pitcher. He took the catcher's return throw and regained the hill in three strides. His broad shoulders and back tapered to a narrow waist; he wore his belt low on his hips, and his legs appeared taut and powerful beneath the billowing knickers of his uniform. A strong, muscular neck provided a solid trunk for a large head, and his cap was tipped rather far back on his forehead, revealing a handsome face and an edge of thick light brown hair. He bent for his sign, rolled into his motion, and threw; this time I followed the ball and saw Burkett top it foul.

The fat man moved against me, reaching for his kerchief. "Who's your pitcher?" he asked.

"It's Mathewson," I said. "Christy Mathewson."

"That's Mathewson? Big kid!"

"He is that. He's bigger than Rusie, that's for sure."

"Throws hard."

"Yes, he does."

"He's winning for you, isn't he?"

"Eleven games, best on the club."

"Not bad for new corn."

"Actually, he pitched a few last year," I said.

"Win any?"

"No. As a matter of fact, he lost two in relief. Then he went back to school."

Another fastball: Burkett's swing was late, and the ball bounced to first base. Ganzel gloved it and tossed underhand to Mathewson, who caught it in full stride and kicked the base for an out.

"He got over there in a hurry, too," the fat man observed.

"Hey, sport, take this and bring back some wieners and beer for us all, won't you?" said Eli, pushing a silver dollar into my hand. He winked and clapped my arm. "Hurry back, now; I'm going to need your advice."

I struggled to the aisle and headed along the walkway that divided the grandstand benches from the box seats. As I reached the ramp, I paused to watch Donovan at bat. His red face was lined with a manager's web of worry. Patsy fought off the pitches with short, choppy swings, hitting several foul before earning a base on balls. Ganzel met him at first, and they exchanged a greeting. Ganzel was ancient, nearly forty, and Donovan beside him looked as old. I scanned the Giants in the field: Strang and Hickman, on either side of second base, were no striplings, and Davis, New York's playing manager at third, was older yet. They were all past thirty in the outfield. The catcher was Jack Warner, he of the awards dinner years before; already he was a veteran of years. Schriver, ready at the bat for St. Louis—enough to say that they called Schriver "Old Pop." At the center stood Mathewson, young as an April morning in that sweltering July, and I, small in the crowd at the top of the ramp, turned and walked down into the shadow beneath the grandstand.

The vendors at their sizzling grills cursed loudly as fat spattered on their aprons. All about, sports in checkered vests argued, passed money, and wrote betting slips. Every inning, sometimes every pitch, was worth a wager. With my dollar I bought five pigs-in-a-blanket and as many bottles of beer and pocketed two bits in change. I worked my way back up the ramp with some difficulty. Near our seats the fans came to my rescue, passing the food hand over hand to Eli with the efficiency of a fire brigade. I couldn't resist an urge to toss the quarter to my brother, who snared it backhanded. The section resounded with cheers, and the ballplayers on the field turned at the commotion.

"Still two–nothing, sport. Donovan was caught trying to steal. Hey, here we go again!" Eli cried as a base hit began the Giant second. But their game was all sock-and-run; after Strang's single, Warner flied out.

"They don't believe in the bunt, do they?" said the fat man.

"They won't win till they learn how," said Eli. "You've got to be able to lay it down, right, sport?"

"Here's Mathewson," I said. "He'll be bunting."

Eli looked at me. "A dollar says he brings off the sacrifice. All around?"

The clients accepted the wager. Sudhoff pitched, and Mathewson pushed the ball onto the grass and ran to first with the sprightly grace of a smaller man. He was narrowly out.

"He can bunt," the thin man conceded.

"Double or nothing that they score," said Eli.

Sudhoff walked a man, and the next nailed the first pitch on a low line over second base. Two Giants crossed home.

"Double or nothing they score again!" said Eli. I pushed my knee into his back, but he looked over his shoulder and winked. The three buyers took the bet and cheered when a fly ball ended the inning and wiped out their debts. Mathewson walked slowly to the pitcher's mound, dug at the slab with his toe, smoothed the dust, and worked into his warm-ups. Again his size and youth impressed. The bearded man beside Eli studied him.

"Mathewson, his name is?"

"College kid," said Eli. "Connie Mack signed him for Philly, but he jumped to New York."

"Where's he from?"

"Pennyslvania," said Eli at the same time that I said, "Bucknell College."

"Imagine a college man playing ball for a living!"

I mentioned Lajoie and Plank, whom we'd seen in Philadelphia, but the bearded man snorted that the new league would sign anyone, and while he knew Lajoie had played in a college uniform, he doubted the boy had ever seen the inside of a classroom. Nor had Mathewson, he'd wager.

The fat man turned to me. "But you said he went back to school after last season!"

"Quit the team in September to do it," I said.

"You've seen him before?"

No, I explained; in recent seasons the more talented Brooklyn club had caught my fancy, and I hadn't been among the few at the Polo Grounds when the rookie threw his first big-league pitches that summer or won his first victories in the spring. What I knew of Mathewson came from notes in the newspapers: his age, a year greater than my own, and his home, the farming country of the Susquehanna Valley; his fame as a Bucknell footballer. I knew he'd pitched in professional leagues in New England and Virginia and that while he'd put his name to a major-league contract with Connie Mack, he'd never worn a Philadelphia uniform. Instead, he'd come to New York, and now, in his first full year, he had a third of the club's victories. If his skills were the test, he belonged in the National League, but like the bearded client, I wondered why a true collegian would choose the life of a professional ball-player.

The second inning ended quickly, and while Sudhoff hit his stride in the third, Eli began to orchestrate wagers with every batter. If I thought the proposition doubtful, I'd signal by pressing my knee into his back, but he ignored my advice as often as he accepted it, and I came to understand that a deeper game was in progress. Eli was selling jewelry, and it wouldn't do to take too much of his clients' money. Each time he won, he offered double or nothing on the next bet; at best he would finish little better than even, and at worst, far worse. I engaged in chatter with the partisans around us when the Giants batted or gazed over the Midwestern crowd dotted with wide-brimmed western hats among the standard derbies and occasional boater. Far down the right-field line was the only uncrowded grandstand section; there the coloreds sat in overalls and yellow straw hats. When St. Louis batted, I studied Mathewson. He could throw hard and with excellent control, shading the edges of the strike zone, mixing his fastball with a curve that seemed somehow erratic. Sometimes it fell an astonishing measure, while other times—what did it do? Certainly it behaved differently from the drop, but from our location I couldn't track the pitch. When St. Louis came to bat in the fifth inning, I excused myself and threaded my way to a spot close behind home plate. Now I could see the inner game, the fierce battle between pitcher and batter where power and control sought mastery over instinct and guess.

Mathewson began against Padden with a pitch that came in hard at belt level and dropped abruptly and dramatically, a superb overhand curve, and one that had wrenched my arm when I'd tried it. The second pitch was a fastball on the outside part of the plate, a second strike. Now another breaking ball, but so unlike the first, slower and breaking in reverse, in the nature of a left-hander's curve; I'd never seen a right-hander throw one. Nor had Padden, who swung late and was lucky to tip it foul. Padden stepped out of the box and shook his head like a man who'd just seen a rabbit leap out of his own hat. He took his stance a bit closer to the plate, leaning over to guard the outside corner. Then, in an instant, he was on his back in the dirt; comically, the bat landed on his head. Mathewson's fastball had reclaimed that disputed inside territory. Padden dusted off his knickers and took his stance farther off the plate. Mathewson stretched and threw another reserve curve, and Padden missed it badly. Strike three.

Mathewson worked through the St. Louis lineup just so. Always the first pitch was a strike, and usually the second; then a teasing pitch down low or that strange fading curve thrown where no batter could hit it squarely, if at all. His rhythm and motion were balletic: a high kick, a swing of the hips, a stride forward, and finally the explosive release of the ball. There was intelligence as well as power behind the pitches: he had a four-run lead and found it to his purpose to walk Kruger with two out in the fifth and then retire the light-hitting Ryan and to pass the dangerous Burkett in the sixth in favor of facing Donovan, who grounded out. When I rejoined Eli in the seventh inning, Mathewson had allowed three base runners but no hits.

"Think they'll get to him, sport?"

I'd never witnessed a no-hit game. I'd come close to pitching one four years before, as close as the eighth inning, but a swinging bunt that squiggled up the first-base line had foiled me, and in my disappointment I'd been racked for three runs. "He's doing pretty much what he wants," I said.

"A dollar says he gets by Schriver," Eli offered; the odds were heavily against a no-hitter, and betting with Mathewson seemed the safest way to protect the clients. Old Pop took a fastball for a strike, and the crowd booed. Its cries had taken on the anger of the heat and the temper of frustration. The fat man ground his cigar beneath his patent-leather boot and muttered something about Schriver; the club missed its injured sluggers. Mathewson pitched, and Pop grounded weakly to Strang at second base. One out in the seventh.

"Double or nothing, all around?"

Now Padden again, and the first pitch a high strike, the second higher yet— but Padden had no wish to wait for another curve and swung, lifting a fly to center field, where Van Haltren had hardly to move to glove it. Two outs now.

"Double or nothing?"

"It's a bet."

"What happens on a walk?" I asked.

"Do you think he'll pass him, sport?"

"He'll be careful with Wallace. It's his pattern."

Eli nodded. "I say he'll get him out. Double or nothing on an out." Mathewson's fastball flashed, and Wallace took it and jawed loudly at the umpire's strike call. Now that strange breaking pitch, and Wallace bounced it to third; he was out by two steps at first. The Giants came off the field as the crowd booed all the more, at Wallace, at the umpire, at the summer's merciless heat, at the cast of impending defeat.

The fat man tapped Eli on the shoulder. "It's four dollars now, right?"

"Two," said Eli.

"Four."

"No, the bet on Schriver brought us even."

"We were even before then. It's four."

"Well, if you insist," said Eli, laughing.

The Giants went down swiftly in the eighth, but New York's efforts at bat hardly mattered now; we wanted Mathewson pitching. In the St. Louis half he began with a strikeout, and the buyer's debts to Eli doubled to $8 apiece. The total was nearly a month's salary to me. Next was Ryan, hardly a threat; after taking two strikes, he chased a high fastball and lifted it to the center fielder's range. Van Haltren loped easily across the grass and reached out to cradle it, but the web of his glove seemed to fail him, and the ball dropped at his feet.

Twenty thousand roared, but the fat man shook his head. "An error," he said.

"It's all the same," said Eli, attempting a mournful expression. "We're even."

"No, as far as I'm concerned, it's an out."

"The man's on second base," said Eli.

"But the bet is on a no-hit game, isn't it? The pitcher against the hitter. The man should have been retired. Now, double or nothing?"

It seemed it was a matter of integrity, for which the fat man had a reputation; when Eli made to forgive the debts of the men flanking him, they proved no less upright than their colleague. They could play the inner game as well as my brother, for what might be lost in money was more than made in future favor. Word spread from the press benches that "error" was indeed the official call; the no-hitter was intact. Eli shifted ground: why not call the play "no bet"? The compromise was accepted, and the balance among the men reverted to $8 apiece.

While the party debated, I studied Mathewson. He showed no annoyance in the wake of the misplay. His team still led by four runs, the inning was late, and the weak-hitting Nichols was at bat, with pitcher Sudhoff to follow. Mathewson set, glanced at the base runner, and threw. Nichols's bunt was a surprise; the score, the inning, the pitcher on deck, all argued against it. Catcher Warner was slow to move after the ball, but Mathewson was upon it instantly, the ball in his glove, then in his hand, then at first base. Two outs, and $16 due to Eli from each of his clients.

"Double or nothing?"

Sudhoff, the little pitcher, hit the ball sharply, but Mathewson snatched it out of the air, and the inning was over. At the Giant bench Mathewson greeted center fielder Van Haltren with a forgiving slap on the rump. He was far more cheerful than Eli, a man due $96 of easy money. When Mathewson batted in the Giant ninth, he was applauded by the home fans, and I cheered. Mathewson tugged at the bill of his cap in acknowledgment. "Imagine, a college kid!" said the bearded client. Most of the crowd had conceded the game, and many would prefer a defeat of special regard to a spoiling single in the home ninth. For myself, I wanted three clean outs and a glorious end; our clients' purses were of no matter.

"Double or nothing?"

Burkett led off. Mathewson started with a fastball; for the hundredth time he took Warner's return throw and climbed the mound. On the right knee of his knickers was a round smudge of red clay, the emblem of a hundred strides and a hundred pitches launched. He bent, stretched, and pitched again, a fastball in on Burkett's hands; it ticked the bat and sailed past Warner, who walked slowly in the heat to retrieve it.

"Oh, college boy! Oh, you college boy!"

Mathewson stood on the hill, waiting for the catcher to return to position, his left leg slightly bent, his weight on the right. He gloved Warner's toss and bent for his sign, the ball resting in the pocket of his small brown glove. He seemed as fresh as when he had begun, and quite still: no heaving breath, no sleeve drawn across his face to clear the summer sweat. All question left me. This was Mathewson's place and moment; my whole being was with him. Burkett would not deny him, nor Donovan next or old Pop Schriver, that dark moving figure on the St. Louis bench.

"So young!" muttered the bearded man.

And I was old, I thought. I was older than Mathewson, older than Schriver, older than any of them in uniform. My youth had ended on a ragged lot by the Hudson when the curve ball had beaten my arm and my spirit—no, when I'd folded the contract into a drawer and reported for work at Uncle Sid's shop. I was on the road, yes, but as an old man, hawking samples in old men's hotels, learning how I might bet to keep old men happy. I watched Mathewson, and he became my youth; it was my fastball burning by Burkett, it was my curve that little Jess lifted to the outfield, and after the ball came back and around the infield, I felt it was my glove closing around it, my arm that launched the fastball at Donovan's knees and the next that cut the black of the plate on the outside. My youth made him chase a breaking ball in the dirt, and there were two outs; here was Old Pop, and I had the game and the no-hitter in my hand.

Curveball: Schriver lets it pass for a strike.

The other, fading curve: Schriver, off balance, swings and ticks the ball foul. Ganzel picks it up barehanded and throws it to me. Schriver is nervous; I see his hands moving on the bat, his heel twisting in the dirt.

I waste a pitch high, ball one. I take Warner's toss, wrap the ball in my glove, jam the package under my arm, reach for the resin, dust my hand. There is a lone, incomprehensible cry from the grandstand, then silence. I turn, I bend, I look for Warner's sign. I toe the slab. I stretch. I throw.

Ground ball.

I reach; it is past me—but Strang is there, he takes it on a high bounce, he waits for Ganzel, old Ganzel, to set himself at first, he snaps a sidearm throw, and the ball disappears into Ganzel's mitt.

The crowd's hoarse voice rises in the heat, the Giant bench empties, the fielders race to the mound, and the team leaps to touch and embrace—

Mathewson.

Those who know Zane Grey only for *Riders of the Purple Sage* and other purple-prose shoot-'em-ups may be surprised to learn of his connection with the national pastime. Not only did he publish three baseball books (including *The Redheaded Outfield*, in which this story appears), but he also was a star outfielder for the University of Pennsylvania, in 1896 making a spectacular catch that enabled the Quakers to defeat the New York Giants in an exhibition game. Moreover, he went on to play four seasons in the bush leagues (brother Reddy was a cup-of-coffee major leaguer) before finding his true vocation.

ZANE GREY

Old Well-Well

He bought a ticket at the twenty-five-cent window and, edging his huge bulk through the turnstile, laboriously followed the noisy crowd toward the bleachers. I could not have been mistaken. He was Old Well-Well, famous from Boston to Baltimore as the greatest baseball fan in the East. His singular yell had pealed into the ears of 500,000 worshipers of the national game and would never be forgotten.

At sight of him I recalled a friend's baseball talk. "You remember Old Well-Well? He's all in—dying, poor old fellow! It seems young Burt, whom the Phillies are trying out this spring, is Old Well-Well's nephew and protégé. Used to play on the Murray Hill team—a speedy youngster. When the Philadelphia team was here last, Manager Crestline announced his intention to play Burt in center field. Old Well-Well was too ill to see the lad get his tryout. He was heartbroken and said, 'If I could only see one more game!' "

The recollection of this random baseball gossip and the fact that Philadelphia was scheduled to play New York that very day gave me a sudden desire to see the game with Old Well-Well. I did not know him, but where on earth were introductions as superfluous as in the bleachers? It was a very easy matter to catch up with him. He walked slowly, leaning hard on a cane, and his wide shoulders sagged as he puffed along. I was about to make some pleasant remark concerning the prospects of a fine game when the sight of his face shocked me and I drew back. If ever I had seen shadow of pain and shade of death, they hovered darkly around Old Well-Well.

No one accompanied him; no one seemed to recognize him. The majority of that merry crowd of boys and men would have jumped up wild with pleasure to hear his well-remembered yell. Not much longer than a year before, I had seen ten thousand fans rise as one man and roar a greeting to him that shook the stands. So I was confronted by a situation strikingly calculated to rouse my curiosity and sympathy.

He found an end seat on a row at about the middle of the right-field bleachers, and I chose one across the aisle and somewhat behind him. No players were yet in sight. The stands were filling up, and streams of men were filing into the aisles of the bleachers and piling over the benches. Old Well-Well settled himself comfortably in his seat and gazed about him with animation. There had come a change to his massive features. The hard lines had softened, the patches of gray were no longer visible; his cheeks were ruddy; something akin to a smile shone on his face as he looked around, missing no detail of the familiar scene.

During the practice of the home team Old Well-Well sat still with his big hands on his knees; but when the gong rang for the Phillies, he grew restless, squirming in his seat and half rose several times. I divined the importuning of his old habit to greet his team with the yell that had made him famous. I expected him to get up; I waited for it. Gradually, however, he became quiet as a man governed by severe self-restraint and directed his attention to the Philadelphia center fielder.

At a glance I saw that the player was new to me and answered the newspaper description of young Burt. What a lively-looking athlete! He was tall, lithe, yet sturdy. He did not need to chase more than two fly balls to win me. His graceful, fast style reminded me of the great Curt Welch. Old Well-Well's face wore a rapt expression. I discovered myself hoping Burt would make good; wishing he would rip the boards off the fence; praying he would break up the game.

It was Saturday, and by the time the gong sounded for the game to begin, the grandstand and bleachers were packed. The scene was glittering, colorful, a delight to the eye. Around the circle of bright faces rippled a low, merry murmur. The umpire, grotesquely padded in front by his chest protector, announced the batteries, dusted the plate, and, throwing out a white ball, sang the open sesame of the game: "Play!"

Then Old Well-Well arose as if pushed from his seat by some strong propelling force. It had been his wont always when play was ordered or in a moment of silent suspense or a lull in the applause or a dramatic pause when hearts beat high and lips were mute to bawl out over the listening, waiting multitude his terrific blast: "Well-Well-Well!"

Twice he opened his mouth, gurgled and choked, and then resumed his seat with a very red, agitated face; something had deterred him from his purpose, or he had been physically incapable of yelling.

The game opened with White's sharp bounder to the infield. Wesley had three strikes called on him, and Kelly fouled out to third base. The Phillies did no better, being retired in one, two, three order. The second inning was short, and no tallies were chalked up. Brain hit safely in the third and went to second on a sacrifice. The bleachers began to stamp and cheer. He reached third on an infield hit that the Philadelphia shortstop knocked down but could not cover in time to catch either runner. The cheer in the grandstand was drowned by the roar in the bleachers. Brain scored on a fly ball to left. A double along the right foul line brought the second runner home. Following that, the next batter went out on strikes.

In the Philadelphia half of the inning young Burt was the first man up. He stood left-handed at the plate and looked formidable. Duveen, the wary old pitcher for New York, to whom this new player was an unknown quantity, eyed his easy position as if reckoning on a possible weakness. Then he took his swing and threw the ball. Burt never moved a muscle, and the umpire called strike. The next was a ball, the next a strike; still Burt had not moved.

"Somebody wake him up!" yelled a wag in the bleachers. "He's from Slumbertown, all right, all right!" shouted another.

Duveen sent up another ball, high and swift. Burt hit straight over the first baseman, a line drive that struck the front of the right-field bleachers.

"Peacherino!" howled a fan.

Here the promise of Burt's speed was fulfilled. Run! He was fleet as a deer. He cut through first like the wind, settled to a driving stride, rounded second, and by a good, long slide beat the throw in to third. The crowd, which went to games to see long hits and daring runs, gave him a generous hand clapping.

Old Well-Well appeared on the verge of apoplexy. His ruddy face turned purple, then black; he rose in his seat; he gave vent to smothered gasps; then he straightened up and clutched his hands into his knees.

Burt scored his run on a hit to deep short, an infielder's choice, with the chances against retiring a runner at the plate. Philadelphia could not tally again that inning. New York blanked in the first of the next. For their opponents, an error, a close decision at second favoring the runner, and a single to right tied the score. Bell of New York got a clean hit in the opening of the fifth. With no one out and chances for a run, the impatient fans let loose. Four subway trains in collision would not have equaled the yell and stamp in the bleachers. Maloney was next to bat, and he essayed a bunt. This the fans derided with hoots and hisses. No team work, no inside ball for them.

"Hit it out!" yelled a hundred in unison.

"Home run!" screamed a worshiper of long hits.

As if actuated by the sentiments of his admirers, Maloney lined the ball over short. It looked good for a double; it certainly would advance Bell to third, maybe home. But no one calculated on Burt. His fleetness enabled him to head the bounding ball. He picked it up cleanly and, checking his headlong run, threw toward third base. Bell was halfway there. The ball shot straight and low with terrific force and beat the runner to the bag.

"What a great arm!" I exclaimed, deep in my throat. "It's the lad's day! He can't be stopped."

The keen newsboy sitting below us broke the amazed silence in the bleachers.

"Wot d'ye tink o' that?"

Old Well-Well writhed in his seat. To him it was a one-man game, as it had come to be for me. I thrilled with him; I gloried in the making good of his protégé; it got to be an effort on my part to look at the old man, so keenly did his emotion communicate itself to me.

The game went on, a close, exciting, brilliantly fought battle. Both pitchers were at their best. The batters batted out long flies, low liners, and sharp grounders; the fielders fielded these difficult chances without misplay. Opportunities came for runs, but no runs were scored for several innings. Hopes were raised to the highest pitch, only to be dashed astonishingly away. The crowd in the grandstand swayed to every pitched ball; the bleachers tossed like surf in a storm.

To start the eighth, Stranathan of New York tripled along the left foul line. Thunder burst from the fans and rolled swellingly around the field. Before the hoarse yelling, the shrill hooting, the hollow stamping, had ceased, Stranathan made home on an infield hit. Then bedlam broke loose. It calmed down quickly, for the fans sensed trouble between Binghamton, who had been thrown out in the play, and the umpire, who was waving him back to the bench.

"You dizzy-eyed old woman, you can't see straight!" called Binghamton.

The umpire's reply was lost, but it was evident that the offending player had been ordered out of the grounds.

Binghamton swaggered along the bleachers while the umpire slowly returned to his post. The fans took exception to the player's objection and were not slow in expressing it. Various witty encomiums, not to be misunderstood, attested to the bleachers' love of fair play and their disgust at a player's getting himself put out of the game at a critical stage.

The game proceeded. A second batter had been thrown out. Then two hits in succession looked good for another run. White, the next batter, sent a single over second base. Burt scooped the ball on the first bounce and let drive for the plate. It was another extraordinary throw. Whether ball or runner reached home base first was most difficult to decide. The umpire made his sweeping wave of hand, and the breathless crowd caught his decision.

"Out!"

In action and sound the circle of bleachers resembled a long curved beach with a mounting breaker thundering turbulently high.

"Rob-b-ber-r!" bawled the outraged fans, betraying their marvelous inconsistency.

Old Well-Well breathed hard. Again the wrestling of his body signified an inward strife. I began to feel sure that the man was in a mingled torment of joy and pain, that he fought the maddening desire to yell because he knew he had not the strength to stand it. Surely, in the years of his long following of baseball he had never had the incentive to express himself in his peculiar way that rioted him now. Surely before the game ended he would split the winds with his wonderful yell.

Duveen's only base on balls, with the help of a bunt, a steal, and a scratch hit, resulted in a run for Philadelphia, again tying the score. How the fans raged at Fuller for failing to field the lucky scratch.

"We had the game on ice!" one cried.

"Get him a basket!"

New York men got on bases in the ninth and made strenuous efforts to cross the plate, but it was not to be. Philadelphia opened up with two scorching hits and then a double steal. Burt came up with runners on second and third. Half the crowd cheered in fair appreciation of the way fate was starring the ambitious young outfielder; the other half, dyed-in-the-wool home-team fans, bent forward in a waiting, silent gloom of fear. Burt knocked the dirt out of his spikes and faced Duveen. The second ball pitched he met fairly, and it rang like a bell.

No one in the stands saw where it went. But they heard the crack, saw the New York shortstop stagger and then pounce forward to pick up the ball and speed it toward the plate. The catcher was quick to tag the incoming runner, and then snap the ball to first base, completing a double play.

When the crowd fully grasped this, which was after an instant of bewilderment, a hoarse crashing roar rolled out across the field to bellow back in loud echo from Coogan's Bluff. The grandstand resembled a colored cornfield waving in a violent wind; the bleachers lost all semblance of anything. Frenzied, flinging action—wild chaos, shrieking cries—manifested sheer insanity of joy.

When the noise subsided, one fan, evidently a little longer winded than his comrades, cried out hysterically, "O-h! I don't care what becomes of me—now-w!"

Score tied, three to three, game must go ten innings—that was the shibboleth; that was the overmastering truth. The game did go ten innings—eleven—twelve, every one marked by masterly pitching, full of magnificent catches, stops, and throws, replete with reckless baserunning and slides like flashes in the dust. But they were unproductive of runs. Three to three! Thirteen innings!

"Unlucky thirteenth," wailed a superstitious fan.

I had got down to plugging, and, for the first time, not for my home team. I wanted Philadelphia to win, because Burt was on the team. With Old Well-Well sitting there so rigid in his seat, so obsessed by the playing of the lad, I turned traitor to New York.

White cut a high twisting bounder inside the third base, and before the ball could be returned, he stood safely on second. The fans howled with what husky voice they had left. The second hitter batted a tremendously high fly toward center field. Burt wheeled with the crack of the ball and raced for the ropes. Onward the ball soared like a sailing swallow; the fleet fielder ran with his back to the stands. What an age that ball stayed in the air! Then it lost its speed, gracefully curved, and began to fall. Burt lunged forward and upward; the ball lit in his hands and stuck there as he plunged over the ropes into the crowd. White had leisurely trotted halfway to third; he saw the catch, ran back to touch second, and then easily made third on the throw-in. The applause that greeted Burt proved the splendid spirit of the game. Bell placed a safe little hit over short, scoring White. Heaving, bobbing bleachers—wild, broken, roar on roar!

Score 4–3—only one half inning left for Philadelphia to play—how the fans rooted for another run! A swift double play, however, ended the inning.

Philadelphia's first hitter had three strikes called on him.

"Asleep at the switch!" yelled a delighted fan.

The next batter went out on a weak pop-up fly to second.

"Nothin' to it!"

"Oh, I hate to take this money!"

"All-l o-over!"

Two men at least of all that vast assemblage had not given up victory for Philadelphia. I had not dared to look at Old Well-Well for a long while. I dreaded the next portentous moment. I felt deep within me something like clairvoyant force, an intangible belief fostered by hope.

Magoon, the slugger of the Phillies, slugged one against the left-field bleachers, but being heavy and slow, he could not get beyond second base. Cless swung with all his might at the first pitched ball, and instead of hitting it a mile, as he had tried, he scratched a mean, slow, teasing grounder down the third-base line. It was as safe as if it had been shot out of a cannon. Magoon went to third.

The crowd suddenly awoke to ominous possibilities; sharp commands came from the players' bench. The Philadelphia team was howling and hopping on the sidelines and had to be put down by the umpire.

An inbreathing silence fell upon stands and field, quiet, like a lull before a storm.

When I saw young Burt start for the plate and realized it was his turn at bat, I jumped as if I had been shot. Putting my hand on Old Well-Well's shoulder, I whispered, "Burt's at bat. He'll break up this game! I know he's going to lose one!"

The old fellow did not feel my touch; he did not hear my voice; he was gazing toward the field with an expression on his face to which no human speech could render justice. He knew what was coming. It could not be denied him in that moment.

How confidently young Burt stood up to the plate! None except a natural hitter could have had his position. He might have been Wagner for all he showed of the tight suspense of that crisis. Yet there was a tense, alert poise to his head and shoulders that proved he was alive to his opportunity.

Duveen plainly showed he was tired. Twice he shook his head to his catcher, as if he did not want to pitch a certain kind of ball. He had to use extra motion to get his old speed, and he delivered a high, straight ball that Burt fouled over the grandstand. The second ball met a similar fate. All the time the crowd maintained that strange waiting silence. The umpire threw out a glistening white ball, which Duveen rubbed in the dust and spat upon. Then he wound himself up into a knot, slowly unwound, and, swinging with effort, threw for the plate.

Burt's lithe shoulders swung powerfully. The meeting of ball and bat fairly cracked. The low driving hit lined over second a rising, glittering streak and went far beyond the center fielder.

Bleachers and stands uttered one short cry, almost a groan, and then stared at the speeding runners. For an instant, approaching doom could not have been more dreaded. Magoon scored. Cless was rounding second when the ball lit. If Burt was running swiftly when he turned first, he had only got started, for then his long sprinter's stride lengthened and quickened. At second he was flying; beyond second he seemed to merge into a gray flitting shadow.

I gripped my seat, strangling the uproar within me. Where was the applause? The fans were silent, choked as I was, but from a different cause. Cless crossed the plate with the score that defeated New York; still the tension never laxed until Burt beat the ball home in as beautiful a run as ever thrilled an audience.

In the bleak dead pause of amazed disappointment Old Well-Well lifted his hulking figure and loomed, towered over the bleachers. His wide shoulders spread, his broad chest expanded, his breath whistled as he drew it in. One fleeting instant his transfigured face shone with a glorious light. Then, as he threw back his head and opened his lips, his face turned purple, the muscles of his cheeks and jaw rippled and strung, the veins on his forehead swelled into bulging ridges. Even the back of his neck grew red.

"Well! Well! Well!"

Earsplitting stentorian blast! For a moment I was deafened. But I heard the echo ringing from the cliff, a pealing clarion call, beautiful and wonderful, winding away in hollow reverberation, then breaking out anew from building to building in clear concatenation.

A sea of faces whirled in the direction of that long-unheard yell. Burt had stopped, statuelike, as if stricken in his tracks; then he came running, darting among the spectators who had leaped the fence.

Old Well-Well stood a moment with slow glance lingering on the tumult of emptying bleachers, on the moving, mingling colors in the grandstand, across the green field to the gray-clad players. He staggered forward and fell.

Before I could move, a noisy crowd swarmed about him, some solicitous, many facetious. Young Burt leaped the fence and forced his way into the circle. Then they were carrying the old man down to the field and toward the clubhouse.

I waited until the bleachers and field were empty. When I finally went out, there was a crowd at the gate surrounding an ambulance. I caught a glimpse of Old Well-Well. He lay white and still, but his eyes were open, smiling intently. Young Burt hung over him with a pale and agitated face. Then a bell clanged, and the ambulance clattered away.

This scientific look at the game's tradition of chicanery comes from an intriguing collection entitled *Newton at the Bat*. When did cheating first rear its ugly head on a diamond? Probably at Hoboken's Elysian Fields, where Alexander Cartwright and his Knickerbocker comrades cavorted in the 1840s. However, the first documented instance of rule skirting was Jim Creighton's adding an underhanded wrist snap to his underhand pitching delivery, violating the rule that obtained in 1859 or so. The torch of deceit passed to King Kelly, John McGraw, Clark Griffith, on up through such moundsmen as Russ Ford, Lew Burdette, and Gaylord Perry. All were honored in their generation and were the glory of their crimes.

STEPHEN S. HALL

Baseball's Dirty Tricks

"The tradition of professional baseball has been agreeably free of charity," Heywood Broun noted back in 1923. "The rule is 'Do anything you can get away with.'"

Sixty years later, it may be added, charity still does not begin at home . . . or at first or on the pitcher's mound. Whether it is increasing friction at the grip of a moving object (i.e., using pine tar on the handle of a bat) or creating an aerodynamic irregularity on a moving sphere (i.e., throwing a scuffed-up or cut baseball), all players are amateur practitioners of applied physics when it comes to the tricks of the trade.

Batters, of course, believe they have the toughest job in the game. A variation of a millimeter or two at the point where bat meets ball can make the difference between a Rod Carew and a Rod Kanehl. A batter facing an 85-mile-per-hour fastball on its 56-foot journey from pitcher's hand to home plate has only about forty-five-hundredths of a second to decide if and when to swing.

That is also about how long the chalk lines of the batter's box remain intact at the beginning of the game. With the boundaries blurred, some batters stand farther from the mound, gaining perhaps 3 inches of patience. Those 3 inches translate into an extra two-thousandths of a second to look over the pitch. Two milliseconds.

To a few, that advantage is too slight to matter, and they step, figuratively, even farther over the line. Players have been known to drill a half-inch-diameter hole down from the fat end of the bat—anywhere from 8 to 14 inches—and cap it or fill it with cork. Some feel that if cork is stuffed into the core, the bat might transfer energy to the ball better—and also not sound too hollow if a suspecting umpire or opposing catcher decided to tap it on the ground. But the people at Hillerich and Bradsby, makers of the "Louisville Slugger" bat, say corking a bat doesn't do anything except make it more likely to break.

"They're wrong; I can guarantee you that," counters former Detroit Tiger first baseman Norm Cash. Thoroughly unrepentant, Cash admits using a corked bat en route to winning the 1961 American League batting title with a .361 average (along with 41 home runs and 132 RBIs). Cash, like most ballplayers a self-confessed nonphysicist, explains the advantage of corked bats with a layman's simplicity and clarity: "The faster you can swing the bat, the more you can hit the ball."

Cash has the law on his side in this case—Newtonian laws of motion, to be exact. "It's the same principle as when an ice skater wants to go into a spin and pulls the body in to spin faster," explains Peter Brancazio, a professor of physics at Brooklyn College. "The greater the distance of the mass from the axis of rotation, the harder it is to rotate." Top-heavy bats are harder to turn around. And bat speed, both hitters and physicists agree, is more important than mass when it comes to making good contact with the ball.

The trend in major-league baseball is toward lighter bats with thin handles and thick barrels—the type preferred by Rod Carew of the California Angels. It is also a nightmare for manufacturers, because thin-handled bats break easily. "The problem," says Rex Bradley of Hillerich and Bradsby, "is that the good Lord doesn't make timber that good." Yet the Carew-style bat is a step closer to the ideal baseball bat, which in fact would be a golf club—at least in an ideal world in which the ball was stationary. The head of a golf club, like the "sweet spot" of a bat (about 4 inches down from the end of the barrel), is where the best contact is made; the thin shaft is just there to move the head through the air. Likewise with Carew's thin handle.

There are also tales of bats with flattened sides (Nellie Fox reputedly used one), bats whose hollowed innards were filled with a free-floating dollop of mercury, bats fortified around the midsection with tacks, and even a bat stuffed like sausage with Super Balls. (Such a bat reportedly broke open on American Leaguer Graig Nettles in 1974.) According to Paul Kirkpatrick, a retired Stanford physicist, "That's going in the wrong direction. The harder the material, the more energy will be returned to the ball after a collision. If you put a bat in a vise and bang on it, it won't vibrate long; it absorbs the force. But a steel bar will ring a few seconds because very little of the collision is absorbed. If a bat were made entirely of cork, the only thing it would be good for is bunting."

A perfectly legal but vanishing tradition is the old clubhouse soup bone. Players used to expend considerable elbow grease rubbing the "sweet spot" of their bats on a soup bone to harden the surface. (Today's practitioners use soda-pop bottles.)

"Yeah, I used to bone 'em," says former slugger Frank Howard. "I'd spend two hours boning 'em and rubbing 'em, and then the first time up, I'd hit one off the end or on the handle and break the damn bat."

"You could do things with bats years ago that you can't do anymore," adds former Yankee shortstop Tony Kubek, now an announcer for NBC Sports. "We used to take an ice pick and carve out the dark grain, which was the softer part of the wood. Then you'd put pine tar in the grooves, let it harden, and resand it." This supposedly gave the bat a harder surface and put more sock into a swing, although even Kubek concedes that the main advantage may have been psychological.

Rex Bradley recalls hearing of cases where the grooves in a bat were carved out but never filled in—"like scoring on a golf club," he says. The idea is that a grooved bat, like a grooved golf club, imparts backspin when it makes contact with the bottom of the ball. Others maintain that the direction of the bat at impact is much more important in generating backspin than grooves in the bat. But there seems to be no question that backspin helps a fly ball. "I imagine it could add twenty to thirty feet to a three-hundred-fifty-foot hit," says Brancazio, and that could easily be the difference between a long out and a home run.

To take away that advantage, of course, the home team could always toss its supply of baseballs into the freezer. This is exactly what the good-pitch, no-hit Chicago White Sox used to do—according to Tony Kubek and others—when the Yankees and other hard-hitting teams came to town in the late 1950s. A frozen ball shows no spunk: The all-important coefficient of restitution—the ability of an object (such as a baseball) to rebound after a collision with another hard object (such as a bat)—goes down with temperature. This is because the core of each baseball is a combination of cork and rubber and rubber becomes less bouncy when the temperature is lowered.

Talk of resilience and spunk invariably provokes discussion of the ball's liveliness. There is quite a lively discussion going on right now, in fact, between Rawlings, which manufactures all major-league baseballs, and MacGregor Sporting Goods, which would like to. Like many corporate discussions these days, this one is taking place in court. In an antitrust suit against Rawlings, MacGregor charges, among other things, that the Rawlings ball fails to meet major-league specifications. Major-league baseballs, for example, are supposed to weigh between 5 and 5¼ ounces and have a coefficient of restitution of between .514 and .578 (this determined after a collision when the ball is traveling about 58 miles per hour). For a softball traveling at 55 miles per hour, by contrast, the coefficient of restitution is .400, while for a Super Ball it is .850.

MacGregor hired Richard Brandt, a physicist at New York University, to test about fifty Rawlings baseballs. He found that 20 percent of the balls had coefficients of restitution higher than the .578 limit—in one case as high as .607. Brandt adds, "The balls are supposed to have a circumference between nine and nine and one quarter inches, but almost half of the balls were too small." Both these factors individually contribute to a livelier baseball, and in combination they can make "a significant difference," according to Brandt. "If you compare today's baseballs with ones from the past, the old ones were twenty-five to thirty percent less lively. What that means is that if you went back to 1927, when Babe Ruth hit sixty home runs, and you used the modern ball, Ruth would have hit eighty home runs."

Rawlings maintains that Brandt uses an unorthodox method of measuring the coefficient of restitution, hitting the balls with a flat metal plate instead of shooting them out of an air cannon. Brandt responds that "any freshman physics student could tell you that the results will be the same." Brandt, in fact, tested the baseballs both ways and says the results were exactly the same.

Until they hear otherwise, Brandt's findings give pitchers one more reason to justify their time-tested mischief. In a sport where Hall of Famer Whitey Ford once admitted to throwing a doctored pitch in an Old-Timers' Game, it is obvious that choirboys and winners don't sit on the same bench. Baseball outlawed the spitball in 1920, but it is the sport's version of the 55-mile-an-hour speed limit: It has been estimated that one-third to one-half of all pitchers in the majors throw doctored balls.

And a pitcher doesn't have to go to his mouth to make the ball dance. Any irregularity in the cowhide surface—whether it is cut, scuffed, shined, or freighted with mud—changes the pattern of airflow around the baseball as it makes its journey to the plate. All that's needed is to make one side rougher than the other, and this can be accomplished by making one side smoother than usual.

"In the [1982] World Series we saw something that is technically legal: Bruce Sutter (the St. Louis relief pitcher) rubbing the ball on his pants," says Tony Kubek. "Well, that's what we used to call a 'shiner'—a dry spitball." Others, according to one American League veteran, will use the less legal sandpaper—often on the official label, where it is more difficult for umpires to pick up. A scuff ball is thrown somewhat like a whiffle ball: the pitcher puts the rough side away from the way he wants it to break. For example, to make the pitch curve right, the scuff is put on the left and thrown overhand.

There may be a tiny consolation in all this for hitters who face scuff balls and other ballistic indignities: if they make good contact, the ball may actually travel a bit farther. The boundary layer of a scuffed ball experiences turbulence, and this in turn reduces the size of the wake behind the ball, thus reducing drag. In short, a roughed-up ball is aerodynamically more efficient than a perfect sphere. "Is that right?" asked a wide-eyed Detroit slugger Darrell Evans when Brancazio passed on the good news. "Usually we try to get the scuffed ones out of the game, but . . ."

This is an excerpt from the 1953 novel *The Southpaw, by Henry W. Wiggen; Punctuation Freely Inserted and Spelling Greatly Improved by Mark Harris.* "Author" Wiggen, rookie pitcher of the New York Mammoths, anticipated by several years such real-life pitcher-authors as Jim Brosnan, Jim Bouton, Pat Jordan, and Sparky Lyle. Nature imitates Art.

MARK HARRIS

Henry Wiggen Goes Up

It is now 3 A.M. in the morning, and I am disgusted. It is a very cold winter night out, and I have got a fire in the fireplace.

I begun this book last October, and it is now January, and I doubt that I am halfway through. I will give 1 word of advice to any sap with the itch to write a book—do not begin it in the first place.

I got 12 chapters wrote on this blasted thing and it was not easy. My hand does not grip a pencil so good, for it is rather large, and I went and bought a couple big fat pencils called an Eagle number 4 from Fred Levine that does not make my hand so tired. Fred is still rather cool to me.

After I got through the 12 chapters I bumped into Aaron yesterday morning, and he said, "Well, Henry, I do not see much of you anymore. Ain't you afraid of putting on weight staying indoors like that?"

"I have wrote 12 chapters," I said, "and lost 12 pounds at the least."

"I admire your get up and go," he said.

"Get up and go hell," said I. "It is the sit down and stay that gets books wrote," and he got a great laugh out of that.

Well, like a fool I stood there gassing with him, and the next thing I knowed I promised him that if him and Pop dropped over tonight—that is, *last* night— I would read the works out loud. Then I went back and polished up number 12 a bit, and in the evening me and Holly slung sandwiches and coffee together, and about 7 Pop and Aaron come. I begun to read out loud, starting with chapter 1 and following through in order, though here and there I skipped over parts that seemed too personal to mention. I did not read the pages concerning me and Thedabara that night, nor the pages concerning me and Holly. Holly knows it's there, though, and says okay, and Thedabara will never know the difference because I doubt that she ever looked at a book since Perkinsville High and ain't likely to take up the habit now. I left out the swear words, too, for Pop's sake. He gets all red when you swear around him around women.

Every so often they would laugh, and then again they would sit so still it was like if it would of been a book it would of been 1 of those that you can't lay it down. Sometimes when they laughed they would laugh in the wrong spot, though.

After number 6 Holly called the halt for food, and we all drifted in the kitchen, and afterwards I begun to read out loud again, burping most of the way through 7, and when I got through with number 12 I said that was all I done to date.

Nobody said a word. They all just sat there, and I said, "Do not be bashful. Say anything you want, pulling no punches," for to my mind it was all very good. I damn near broke my hand doing it. Finally Holly was the first to speak, and she said, "The first 11 chapters is just about right, but number 12 is too long."

Now, if that was not a dirty crack! Of all the chapters number 12 was the 1 I was proudest of, for it run 73 pages on both sides of the paper, and I done it in less then a week. If that is not some kind of a record I will be mighty surprised.

"Yes," said Aaron, "I think number 12 is too long."

"Have you ever wrote a book?" said I to him.

"No," said he.

"Well, then," said I, "why are you so quick to run down what another writer did?"

"That is not the proper attitude on your part, Henry," he said, "for we are gathered here for the purpose of being helpful. I agree with Holly that number 12 is too long. But we must take it apart and see *why* it is too long and how we might cut it down and aim it to the point."

"Well, then," said I, "half of it is wrote on yellow paper and half on white. Leave us throw out all the yellow," and I took all the yellow and tore it in 2. However, I tore it so as to be able to paste it up again, for I will be damned if I will write 73 pages front and back and take a week doing it and bust my hand besides and then just heave it out.

"No," said he, "that is not the way to go about it."

"Very well," said I, "then we might just as well forget the whole thing and skip number 12 and start in on number 13."

"In my opinion," said Aaron, "all that is wrong with the chapter is that it has got too much material that does not belong. It is up to us to try to decide what is good and what is too much."

And then it all begun, and the sum and total was this:

First off, I had wrote 9 pages front and back covering the time from when we broke camp at Aqua Clara to the time we arrived in Queen City in the Four-State Mountain League AA. I give an excellent picture of all the cities we went through, all the games, and the view that you got coming down off the slope of the mountains into Q. C., and then I told a good bit about the type of a place Q. C. is and the Blue Castle Hotel, which was the headquarters of the club when we was at home. "That is too much space to give to things of such little importance," said Aaron.

"That is a lot of rubbage," said I. "If you have got the sense to think back on chapter 11 you will remember that it run 9 pages front and back between the time Sid Goldman hit the home run, about 3 o'clock, until midnight. That is 9 pages covering 9 hours, while this is 9 pages covering 3 *weeks*, so it seems to me that you are the slightest bit cockeyed in your calculations."

"But the things that happened in number 11," said he, "was important things concerning important people such as the remarks of Mr. Moors. I actually think that the whole exhibition trip could be knocked off in 1 page." Well, I finally agreed.

Then I done 9 pages front and back about Mike Mulrooney, telling about his family which I met in Q. C. and his whole life history. Part of it I copied out of a book called "Forty-One Diamond Immortals," but mostly it was my own writing. I give him a great build-up, for he is 1 of the grandest men that ever lived. That is what nobody liked. Holly said, "About 1 dozen times you said Mike Mulrooney is 1 of the grandest men that ever lived. That is not saying anything."

"The hell it ain't," said I, "for if you knowed Mike you would say the same."

"I do not say that Mike is not all you say," said she, "but you must tell us why."

"Because he *is*," said I. "Because he does not wish to run the whole show but just live an easy going life and not worry you ragged about setting the whole world on fire. Because if you make a mistake he will not eat you out in front of all the rest nor give you the icy glare every time he runs into you in the hotel. He will stand by you and not go about talking behind your back. He will treat you all the same, no matter if you are on the way up or the way down, for he takes the attitude that if you are not the greatest ballplayer in the world still and all you are a human being. He is not a frog," said I, "that goes about kissing the ass of every writer and every club official and everybody else that he thinks can do him any good. Mike says if they do not like the way he runs his club in Q. C. he will go back to his ranch in Last Chance, Colorado, but he will never stoop down to where his head is lower than his shoulders for the purpose of getting a brown nose."

"Excellent, excellent," said Holly, and up she jumped. "You have told us more about Mr. Mulrooney right there then you done in the 9 pages of Chapter 12 concerned with him."

"Rats," I said.

Then Pop throwed in. "Here is what they mean," said he. "It is like a baseball game. If you was to pitch a ball game and win it by a score of 1–0 would you tell me how it went inning by inning, every foul ball and every little detail along the way? No, the main thing is how was the run scored and what particular scrapes you was in."

"Very well," said I, "out goes the 9 pages on Mike."

"Then there is the description of all the cities of the league," said Aaron.

I done 16 pages front and back on the different towns of the Four-State Mountain League, and I thought I done a fine job, and Aaron said, "Yes, you done a fine job. Yet it is like your pa says. It is not to the point. You do not need to tell us about the cities, for we know all about them. I have never seen a 1 of them, yet I know what they are like. They are like Perkinsville. They are all the same."

"They are all different," said I. "In some you have got the mountains, and in others you have not, and in 1 place you will have a fine and modern ball park while elsewhere it will be an old park."

"But they are talking about building a new 1," said he.

"Why yes," said I. "Naturally."

"And in every town you was in you walked about on the main street," said he, "and then you got tired and went back and laid in the hotel. You and Coker and Canada and Perry."

"Yes," said I. "You guessed it."

"You said to 1 another, "This is a dull town and there is nothing to do until game time," and you laid on your bed in your shorts, and you talked about everything, baseball mostly, and you told each other over and over again your whole life history."

"Why, yes," said I.

"In Salt Lake you went and seen the big tabernacle, for that was where everyone told you to go. In Denver you went and seen the capitol with the big gold dome on top, and you also took a trip through the mint, for that was where everybody told you you must go in Denver. In all the cities you admired such places as these, though as a matter of fact you thought they was rather a bore. So after awhile you went over and laid in the park, and you fed the squirrels and birds and looked at the girls, and after awhile even *that* become a bore. There was the railroad station and the hotel, and each was the same as the next and it got so you could not hardly tell them 1 from the other."

"Yes," said I, "that is about the way it was. Yet they was all different."

"No," said he. "No, they were not. For they was all about like Perkinsville. There was a Legion club in Wichita, and you hung at the Legion club, and they made a big fuss over you. Maybe they even give you a dinner."

"They did not," said I. "It was the Chamber of Commerce of Queen City that give me the dinner."

"They sung songs to you," said he. "They sung For He Is a Jolly Good Fellow, For He Is a Jolly Good Fellow, and they give you a wrist watch."

"They give me a traveling bag," I said.

"With your name in silver," said he.

"With my name in silver," I said.

"They are all the same," said he. "There is no need to have so many pages concerning the cities."

I give in. Out they went.

There was a long letter waiting at the hotel when I hit Q. C. the second summer from Thedabara Brown, broke in Sacramento and wishing she could see me in Q. C. I copied it down, 5 pages front and back, and nobody could see the sense in putting it in. "There will be nothing left," I said. "You are blasting away my chapter until there is nothing left but air. It was 2 whole summers. You cannot skip over 2 whole summers in a couple pages."

"I am after the high spot," said Aaron. "Never mind the mail of little Miss Brown. What was the very biggest thing about the 2 summers at Q. C.?"

"I guess," said I, "the big thing is that I shook off my greenness and got myself ready for the big-time."

"Ah," said Aaron, "now we are getting somewheres."

"If so," said I, "we are getting there in reverse gear. It took up 4 days of my time to write the 39 pages that you have just throwed out like it was so much wrapping off a load of fish. It took me 1 whole afternoon alone to put my hands on the letter from Thedabara Brown and then copy it down, plus a whole morning copying out the material on Mike Mulrooney from "Forty-One Diamond Immortals," holding the book in 1 hand and writing it all down with the other. That is how you do everything—backwards and in reverse." I would not of stood for it, but we had another break for coffee and sandwiches, and Pop said he thought they was right in connection with Chapter 12.

"You take that business with Lindon Burke," said he. "That is too much on that."

I had give 12 pages to Lindon. He is a fine fellow. In July of the first summer Mike got a telegram from New York, asking for Lindon right away. The Mammoths was flagging at the time, and Dutch was of the opinion that they needed a righthander for relief, maybe for a starter, though it was my opinion then and still is that the Mammoths have always had *too goddam many* righthanders. Nonetheless we was all glad for Lindon. We had a big celebration before he went. We was in Denver, and we beat Denver that night, and Lindon's train was not until morning, and we stood him a dinner at Boggio's. We all made speeches. I wrote down what I could remember of each 1, for each and every 1 was a dandy. Then I copied down the menu, for I swiped 1. It was signed by everybody who was there that night. The last speech of all was that of Mike Mulrooney, and after he finished he give Lindon the present we bought, consisting of a silver bracelet with his name. Then we all started in to sing, "Stand up, stand up, stand up and show us your ugly face," and he stood up and begun to speak. But he could not speak, for he was bawling, and the tears was racing down his cheek. Then Mike got back up, and he was laughing, and he said, "Lindon need not make no speech. Instead of that, he must win the first game he gets to pitch up there in the big-time, for after all he is a pitcher and not an after-dinner speaker." Lindon shook his head, meaning he would do it, and sure enough he done it, beating Washington the first full game he pitched, and that night we got a wire saying "I done it, and I am thinking of all you boys," signed Lindon Burke.

"Very well," said I to Pop, "I will trim that down."

"You could also chop out the amusement park," said he.

I done 8 pages concerning 1 afternoon me and Perry and Coker and Canada went to Mountaineer Park in Q. C. For a dime you could throw 3 baseballs at wooden bottles stood up on a barrel, and if you knocked them all off you got a prize. "If I cannot knock them bottles off," said I to the boys, "I will turn in my suit and go home and pump gas," and I got up close, and I throwed, and I will be damned but I could not knock them off.

Then Perry give the man a dime. He did not get up close but went off to the side a bit, and he bent down like he was fielding a ground ball, and then, still in the bending position, he flipped in with that little snap throw a good second baseman knows how to make, and he clubbed the bottle dead center, and off they all went. The man give him a prize, consisting of a raggedy doll.

Then I said to the man, "Give me 3 more, and here is your dime," and I took the balls, and I said, "How far is it from that barrel to this here counter?" meaning the place you was to throw from.

"About 6 feet," said the man.

"Well then," said I, "I will pace off 54 more and make it an even 60," and back I went. There was people passing back and forth up and down the midway, and I said, "Out of the way, folks, unless you wish to be beaned," and the people lined up to see what was going on. I throwed from the 60 feet, which is the regular pitching distance, and I tagged the center bottle on the nose, and off they all went, and Canada collected my raggedy doll and I come down and flipped the man a dozen dimes or more and went back to the 60 feet. About 2 throws in 3 I turned the trick. There was a quite a big crowd gathered around, and the bigger the crowd the hotter I am, and Perry and Canada and Coker gathered up my prizes. I must of spent 4 dollars in dimes, and we had about 50 dolls and wind-up toys and candy canes and balloons and circus masks and glass jugs and a little red fire engine and a bowl of goldfish, and I give it all away to the kids except a couple candy canes that It ate myself. It warmed me good. That night I shut out Omaha.

"Why," said I to Pop, "it was a good time and ought to be in."

"Son," said he, "as long as you are doing it you might as well do it in a straight line. Aaron and Holly have read many books and know how they ought to be wrote."

"They do not know center field from the water fountain," I said. "They make me dizzy. What is the sense of writing a chapter for them to tell me chuck it out the door?"

"Now," said Aaron, "we was saying that the big thing about the 2 summers in Q. C. was that you shook off your greenness and was getting ready to go up to the big-time." He never forgets what he was saying. He will meet you and pick up the conversation he was snarled up in 3 weeks before, after you had forgot all about it.

"Right," said I.

"Just what is left?" said he.

I shuffled through the pages, and there was nothing left but 14 pages front and back regarding Coker and Canada and Perry. We was the closest of buddies in Q. C. If someone was to come looking for 1 all they need do is find the other 3. We was either in Perry and my room or Coker and Canada's, or else the coffee shop, or else we was somewheres out on the town, whatever town it may be, walking along and seeing the sights.

The only other place we could be was at the park, and we always went there together, and we had our lockers 1 next to the other, and we would dress and then go out on the field together. If it was not my day to work I might take a turn at first base during the infield drill, for squarehead Flynn would leave me do so. He is a prince of a fellow but still with Q. C. He will be there till he is old and gray.

When I worked it was a pleasure to have that infield behind me. Ground balls was sure outs. Then, too, Coker and Perry was a grease of lightning on double plays, and Canada down at third had no little hand in double plays himself. They set a record for the Mountain League in that department the first summer, and they busted their own record the summer after.

After the ball games, in the clubhouse, the 4 of us sung together in the shower. I wrote out all the songs we sung, such as "I Love You As I Never Loved Before," "Some Enchanted Evening," "Going to Wash That Man Right Out of My Hair," "The Good Old Summertime," "Sweet Adeline," "Down by the Old Mill Stream," "Meet Me In St. Louis," "Goodnight, Irene," "White Christmas," "God Bless America," "A Bicycle Built for 2," "Old Black Joe," "My Old Kentucky Home," and some songs that Coker sung back in the coal mines of West Virginia, and it took up 7 pages front and back. That was a good deal of work.

Nonetheless Aaron said it had no place in the book. "For God's sake," said I, "they was the best infield the Mountain League ever seen and if it was up to you they would be slid over without hardly a mention."

"Just exactly what *is* a double play?" said Holly.

I leaned forwards and put my head down on my arms.

"Go ahead and tell her, Hank," said Pop, and I lifted up my head and begun to explain.

"The most usual type is when you have a man on first," I said. "Then the batter hits a ground ball to the infield, and the infielder scoops it up and tosses to second. That gives you a force on 1 man. Then the second baseman or the shortstop, whichever took the throw, he rifles it down to first base. If it gets to first base ahead of the runner you have worked the play. You have got 2 men out on the 1 pitch."

"That does not sound hard," said Aaron.

"It is a beautiful play when done right," said I. "It is harder than it sounds. The average ballplayer can get from home plate to first base in 3 seconds. A fast man can do it in less. So you have got 3 seconds to field the ball clean, fire it to second, make the play there, keep clear of the runner, pivot and throw to first. That is a lot of work to do in 3 seconds. The shortstop and the second baseman have got to be like a fine machine, working together to the split of a second. They have got to know each other like a book. It is like they was 1 and the same man, not 2 different men. That is how Perry and Coker works, like they was 1 and the same man. It is beautiful. Then, too, it is a great help to any pitcher. It saves wear and tear on him. A good double play combination around second base will save you many a ball game. It can win a pennant for you or lose it."

"All this brings us to the very point of the whole discussion," said Aaron.

"I must say it is about time," said I, "for it is now 2 o'clock in the morning and we have jawed away at this thing for 7 hours. There is nothing left."

"There is still the main point left," said Aaron. "You have jammed it all in 1 sentence, but it is the main point," and he picked up 1 half of the last page that I had tore in 2, and he read what I had wrote. He read: "Well, the outcome was that I went up to the Mammoths in September of the second summer, and I pitched 1 inning in relief against Boston."

"You might just as well throw that out, too," said I, "for you cannot have a chapter that has got only 1 sentence in it."

"Yet that is the big point," said he, "for that is what you were aiming at from the time you first took a baseball in your hand. The rest of the chapter is full of dead matter that leads you nowheres."

"I will not write it over," said I. "I should of never begun it. It is chapter 12 and that is a bad number for me and always was."

"That is up to you," said he. "If you wish to leave number 12 out of your book it is your right to do so. However, it seems to me that whatever chapter follows 11 ought to be about when you was sent up to the Mammoths."

"Tomorrow," I said. "I will do it tomorrow. I thank you all for your wonderful goddam help."

Aaron and Pop went home, and I was tired, and yet I could not calm down and sleep. I lit the fire in the fireplace and shaved a new point on an Eagle #4. I thought I would write a few minutes and then turn in. Yet when you get to writing you run on and on, and it is hard to stop, and I have wrote 14 more pages front and back and *still* not got into the main point, which is when I went up to the Mammoths. I will do it tomorrow—that is, tonight. It is now daylight and I must first get some sack.

Well, the outcome was that I went up to the Mammoths in September of the second summer, and I pitched 1 inning in relief against Boston.

The word come on a hot afternoon. Me and Perry was laying on our beds in our room in the Blue Castle Hotel in Queen City in the Four-State Mountain

League when in come Coker and Canada in their shorts and bare feet. Canada said it was so hot he had took 4 showers since noon. Coker said you would never know what hot was until some summer's day you was down in a coal mine in West Virginia, and then you would know.

"I will tell you what hot is," said Perry. "If you was ever to be in the Ford Rouge plant of a summer's day you would know what hot is. When I lay me down here and I think it is hot I say to myself be thankful you are laying here in your under drawers with this pitcher of ice water in your hand and be glad you are not back in the Ford plant." He took a drink from the pitcher, and he passed it to me, and I drunk and I give it to Canada. "I only hope I can save my money and never go back to the factory," said Perry.

Just then in come Mike Mulrooney, manager of the Queen City Cowboys and 1 of the grandest men you will ever meet. He taught me more baseball then any man before or since. Pop set me up and Mike put the finish on. When I went to Q. C. the summer before I was a fair enough country ballplayer, and when I come away I was big-time, and Mike said, "Well boys, leave us phone down and have them send up some steam heat." This give us all a big laugh, for Mike was always ready with a joke. He flopped down in a chair and begun to fan himself with the newspaper. We sat, and we waited for him to say what he come to say, for Mike seldom come just for the visit. He always come for a purpose. Maybe he would come to tell of a fault he seen in 1 of us, or he would come and wise us up on some trouble another fellow was having. He might say, "Now boys, I want you to help me out with Squarehead Flynn," meaning Squarehead Flynn the first baseman. "I do not think it is kind to Flynn to call him by the name of Squarehead, so if you boys will just call him Flynn or Bob it will be a big favor to me." We done it when we remembered, though "Squarehead" seemed to fit perfect. But if Mike Mulrooney was to ask it you could never refuse. Still and all he never jumped right into the business of his visit, and we always waited, and he would talk about the weather or last night's ball game or some old-time remembrance, and on this day he said, "I do not call this hot. Nowadays the ballplayer has got things better. It is cool at night, and we play so much at night nowadays, and the trains and the hotels is air-condition. I will tell you what I call hot. I remember double-headers in St. Louis when it was 110 in the shade."

"What would you say is the hottest city of all?" said Canada.

"St. Louis," said Mike. "Washington is close. All of them is hot. I remember hot days everywhere. Yet I was always a good hot weather ballplayer."

"The hotter it is the better Pop likes it," said I.

"I have played ball in cold and snow in Boston and wet and dry and thunder and lightning. I once played ball in the flood in Cincinnati. But the worst of all is heat," said Mike. "However, I did not drop in for story hour. The reason I come is because I just heard from Dutch." He took a wire out of his pocket and handed it to me. It was the wire I was waiting 20 years to see. It said:

R. DVA 165 SER PD WUX NEW YORK 12 1158A
MICHAEL J. MULROONEY
        BLUE CASTLE HOTEL
                        QUEEN CITY
    SHIP ME WIGGEN FASTEST

                    DUTCH

I have got the wire yet, and I could not believe my eyes, and the other boys come around behind me and looked, and Canada give a whoop and shot out the room and spread the news around. I sat froze to my bed, and the first 1 I saw was Pop in my mind, and I said, "I must send a wire to Pop."

"I have sent 1," said Mike.

"I better get moving," I said, and I begun to cram things in my bags.

Mike laughed. "Do not be in such a hurry, Hank. I have got your plane reservations for 11 tonight," and I sat back down, and Mike said, "I hope it is the right thing."

"I am ready," said I.

"Yes, you are ready," said he. "But you have still got many things to learn." He fussed and fidgeted, and finally he said, "I will tell you the truth, for you will hear nothing but lies from now on. You are a natural ballplayer. You have won 21 games this year. You are a regular horse for work. Yet you have got things to learn. When you get up to the Mammoths there will be 1 man that will be no end of help to you."

"That is Sad Sam Yale," said I.

"No," said he, "it is not Sam. Do not listen to a single word said by Sam Yale. Do not play cards with him. Do not drink with him. Do not lend him money nor borrow any. If you see him with a woman put that woman down in your book as a tramp, for if she is not a tramp at the start Sad Sam will make her 1. Everything that Yale touches will turn to shit. Except only 1 thing, and that is a baseball. When he is pitching you must glue your eyes to him and never take them off. You must learn to watch him and never listen to him, and you will learn much about baseball and much about life."

"Then who is the man that will help me?" said I.

"That is Red Traphagen," said he, meaning the Mammoth catcher. "When he says something that has got to do with playing baseball you must hang on his every word like it was the word of God. He is the smartest ballplayer in baseball today. If he did not have so much respect for his own personal self-respect he would be in line to be a manager. But he will not brown-nose. On the ball field he will talk only about baseball, and you must listen. If you can remember to do it write it down afterwards and study it once in a while. But when you are off the field do not pay him no more mind then if he was a pillar or a post. He is all full of chatter and nonsense. He does not believe in God." Mike was quite religious himself and went almost every Sunday. I did not know if I believed in God or not. I rather suppose I did not, but I said nothing.

I said, "It is sad to me to hear what you say of Sad Sam Yale."

"Yes," said he, "it is sad. It is always sad when a great ballplayer goes wrong as a man. I am not telling you these things out of anything personal. I am telling them to you because I want you to be a great and immortal ballplayer. You have all the makings. You learn fast and never forget. But never listen to Sam nor the men that is his pals. If they was once good in their heart they are good no longer, for Sam Yale has did them in. Steer clear of Knuckles Johnson and Goose Williams and Swanee Wilks." Mike grabbed the water pitcher and took a swig, and then he took some ice from the tray and dumped it in the pitcher and sloshed it around. "There is nothing more to tell," said he. "Remember that the parks will be bigger than in the Mountain League. But do not let this make you over-confident. Do not relax too much at first. When you are in trouble rely on your curve and forget the fast 1. Do not forget that the boys you will be throwing against will be hitting harder than any you have ever faced. Remember that you will be throwing against the very best ballplayers in the world. True, some of the best ballplayers in the world will be on your side, too.

"Henry, I will tell you the damn truth. The damn truth is that I can tell you no more about baseball. You are already a fine young pitcher. When you are up there you will be playing the same game you been playing all your life. The ball will be the same, and the bases will be the same 90 feet apart, and there will be 9 men to a side, and the game is still decided by who scores the most runs. The main thing is not half so much the other teams but your own men that you will be playing with and traveling with and be close to every hour of the day from February to October. I have told you what I know about the men. The rest I do not know so well. They are young men. Let me see," and he leaned back and begun to reel off the men on his fingers. "The Carucci brothers, they are Roman Catholics of the Italian race, and good boys, and they stick together. I do not know them, nor I do not know Lucky Judkins, for he is young and new. Scotty Burns and Sunny Jim Trotter is the rest of the outfielders. They do not mix in with the rest. They stay to theirselves and sometimes I think this is best.

"Ugly Jones and Gene Park are steady hands. You can depend on them. I do not know Goldman or Gonzalez. Gonzalez does not speak the language, and he is just as well off. They are the kind of young men that Dutch is trying to build a club around. That is your infield, for the rest will be cut loose." Mike looked at Coker and Perry and Canada. "Here is the rest of your infielders right there in their underwear if they show up good in Aqua Clara in the spring. That is a secret amongst us 5, but it is the straight dope from Dutch.

"Red Traphagen will catch about 135 games a year. I have spoke about him and Goose. Bruce Pearson is your other catcher. He was big-time when I sent him up, but he does not get enough work. This has knocked his spirits all to hell.

"The pitching is young. If the pitching comes through you will have a winner up there in New York in the next year or 2. It all depends. Sam and Knuckles and Horse Byrd is your only veterans. Carroll I do not know. Castetter was sent down today, and he will never go back up. That leaves Sterling and Gil Willowbrook and Macy, plus Lindon Burke and yourself. Tell Lindon that if he gives himself 10 seconds between pitches he will help his control." Mike kept looking off in the distance, like he was in a dream. There was more he had on his mind to say, and we knowed it, and we waited, and he did not say it. I always wonder what it was, and I wonder to this day. Yet he said nothing but only rose and said, "I will see you boys at the park tonight," meaning Coker and Canada and Perry.

"I will be there, too," said I, "for my plane does not leave till 11."

Mike laughed, and he said, "There is no need, but it is up to you." Then he left, and we begun to dress for supper.

I got in uniform that night and worked out. The crowd give me a fine hand when I come on the field, for they had by now read it in the paper, and I tipped my hat and played pepper with some of the boys. Then I moved down to first base and took a hand in the drill and kept pretty loose.

After the drill I ducked back through the dugout and into the clubhouse, and I was alone. I showered and dressed, feeling sad. I cleaned out my locker. The 4 of us had lockers together, 1 right after the other, and I stuck a note in their lockers, and it said, "I will see you in Aqua Clara in the spring, and we will be in the Series next October. Good luck. Your friend, HENRY WIGGEN."

Then out I went, catching a cab on Rocky Mountain Avenue. We heard about 2 innings along the way, the Cowboys pasting the hell out of Denver. Perry hit a home run with 2 on in the third. The cabbie asked me if I had ever saw the Cowboys play. He said it was the best club they had in Q. C. in quite some years. I said I had saw them play once or twice and thought particularly high of that fellow by the name of Wiggen. He told me that Wiggen was signed on by the Mammoths and had went off that very day to New York by air. "What is your line of work?" said he to me.

"I am a heaver in the horsehide plant," said I. That was a joke that me and Coker and Perry and Canada played on people. We would run into some people in a restaurant or a bowling alley or somewheres and get to talking, and they would say, "What do you boys do?" Then Coker would speak up. "We work in the horsehide plant," he would say. "This here is Henry, and he is a heaver, and this here is Perry, and he is a scooper. I work alongside of Perry. This here is Canada, and he works the far throw."

They would say, "What is the far throw?"

"Why," said Coker, "everybody knows what a far throw is. Only a particularly pinheaded person would not know."

"Oh," they would say. "A *far* throw. I did not hear you right at first."

The cabbie said, "You are a what in a what?"

"A heaver in the horsehide plant," said I. "Sometimes I am a swatter, but mostly I am a heaver."

"Where is that?" said he, "for I seem to forget."

"Why, it is over there near the ball park. Do you mean to say you are a cabbie and do not know where the horsehide plant is?" said I.

"Oh," said he, "the *horse*hide plant. Why do you not speak up when you speak?"

At the airport I picked up my tickets and weighed my bags through and bought some insurance out of a machine, 50,000 dollars made out to the New York Mammoths. What a simple soul! Then I read some magazines while they dillied and dallied until finally they left us on the plane. The last I heard we beat Denver 15–3, but I could not get the details, and I have never been back to Q. C. since.

It took me about 10 minutes to get past the clubhouse guard. Naturally they post a guard there, for you have got any number of these kids that in the course of a year tries to worm through and tell Dutch Schnell what a great ballplayer they are. The guard gripped me like I was some sort of a crook and led me in the clubhouse. We seen Sid Goldman sitting on a bench putting laces in his shoes, and he looked up, and at first he did not recognize me, and I said, "Sid, why do you not tell this fellow just who I am?"

The cop said, "Do you know this boy?" and Sid squinted at me and said, "Yes, he is the new pitcher," and the cop left go of my arm. Sid stretched out his hand. "I hit a home run off you 1 time in Aqua Clara," he said, and he give me a smile.

"And last spring I struck you out twice in Jacksonville," I said, for we had played a couple exhibitions there. Q. C. and the Mammoths, and we shook hands and he said, "Boy, if you will pull us out of this slump you are my friend for life."

The Mammoths at the time was 6 games behind Brooklyn, which was in second, and only 2 games ahead of Cleveland, with Washington behind Cleveland, about 1½ games. There was the danger of falling back to fourth and maybe out of the first division money altogether. They had give up all idea of climbing higher. What they wanted now was to fight off Cleveland.

"Well," said I, "you have just shook hands with the best lefthander this town has ever saw," and he laughed, and just then Dutch Schnell come up behind me, and he said, "If you are 1 half so good as you say you are I will be 1 happy old man." Then he took me down the line and give me the locker Bub Castetter had before he was sent down. Dutch tore off Castetter's name and said they would put up mine, and I said he might as well paint it with paint that would last forever, for I had a mind to stay up in the big time for 20 or 25 years, and he said he was highly encouraged by my remarks, and he turned and walked back through the door to his office.

The boys begun to gather. Sid introduced me to them as they come in, and some of them shook my hand and chatted, and some of them shook it but never said a word. The gloom hung heavy. The 1 who spoke the most was George Gonzalez, and he blabbered away for 2 minutes in Spanish, and I never understood a word, and I said, "Do you remember when I struck you out on

3 pitches at Aqua Clara?'' and he said, "Up yours, up yours," which is the only 2 words of English that he seems to know. It was the only time anybody in the clubhouse laughed all day. Me and Lindon Burke dressed side by side, and he asked me how everybody was back in Q. C., and I told him they was all fine and running away with the flag, and somebody said, "It is nice to hear that somewheres there is a Mammoth club that is winning a flag."

"Buck up your courage," said I, "for the tide is changing now that I am here."

"Shut up," said the voice.

"No, sir," said I. "I will not shut up."

But just then Lindon nudged me with his elbow, and he said, "You had best shut up."

In come Bradley Lord with a suit over his arm, and he brung it down to me. It smelled all fresh and clean like it just been took out of the moth balls, and I looked at the number on the shirt, and it said "48" and I said, "I cannot wear such a shirt."

"Why not?" said he.

"Because of the number," said I. "I cannot wear no number that has got 12 in it."

"That is ridiculous," said he.

Then the same voice come again, and it said, "Bradley Lord, God damn you, go back and get that boy a shirt with a number like he likes it or I will break your f——ing back between my 2 f——ing hands." The boys all call him Bradley Lord, for nobody likes him well enough to call him Bradley, and yet nobody would ever call him Mr. Lord, and then I knowed whose voice it was. It was Sad Sam Yale's, for I could tell by the way he said it—"God damn you"— which was the first thing he ever said to me at Aqua Clara that time. His voice was like thunder, and it rolled like thunder rolling in across the mountains, and you could feel it in your belly, for it made you shiver and shake, and Bradley Lord scampered off and come back with a different shirt, number 44, and he said real soft, "Is that a better number?"

"Yes it is," said I, and I took it, and away went Bradley Lord. I shouted out, "Thank you, Sam."

"F—— you too," said he.

Cleveland was in town, finishing up on a 3-game series. We had beat them the first day, and they beat us the next, which was the day before I come, and the day I come they not only beat us but massacred us as well, winning 9–1 and drawing up to 1 game behind. The scoreboard showed Washington beating Chicago, and that made us feel no better, and the clubhouse afterward was quieter than hell.

Generally the Mammoth clubhouse will be full of writers. But when we hit the slump that year Dutch give the order not to let a single 1 of them donkeys in. You cannot blame him. They are like the plague. There is not a 1 of them that has got the guts and gumption to get out there and play ball theirselves, yet they know just exactly how the game should be played. They will get the fatigue from climbing 6 steps, yet they know how Perry Simpson should steal a base. They will get a cramp in their arm from writing a few words down on paper, yet if a ballplayer pitches 7 innings and poops out they are as libel as not to decide he is a quitter. They tell Dutch how to manage the club, and if he does right they will crow in their column for 2 weeks, saying it was all their idea to begin with. They are like fans. Red says the only difference between the writers and the fans is that the fans have at least got the honesty to pay their own way in the park.

Yet ballplayers read the papers day and night, mostly buying "The News" in New York. Red Traphagen will buy "The Star-Press," but I can't see it. I only buy it on Sunday when they run the pitching records and batting averages.

Cleveland lost the day after to Boston, Boston turning the trick again the following night whilst we was taking 2 in a row from Chicago. That give us our 3-game edge again and things begun to be more tolerable around the clubhouse. I got to know some of the boys, and half the club was my personal friends before the week was out. The west went back west, and Brooklyn moved in at the Stadium beginning on a Sunday, and a hot 1, with Sad Sam slated to work. There was a good crowd, for Brooklyn always draws well against the Mammoths, besides which they was still hopeful of overtaking Boston, which they finally done 2 days before the end, as you know. I was down in the bullpen as usual but I did not throw a ball all afternoon, just sitting and watching while Sam turned in a neat job. We scored 3 in the third and 2 in the fifth and that was enough. 5–0.

We still had the 3-game edge on Cleveland when Boston come in in the middle of the week with the flag hot in their nose and dumped us 2 straight, and we lost ground. Things was back to where the clubhouse was like a museum, so silent and still, the boys watching their third-place money about to float away, and maybe fourth as well, and I dared not speak above a whisper, for the tension was so high it was like you was sitting on thin ice and the least little rustle would crack it and down you would go in the drink.

Friday Dutch pitched Sam, hoping to beat Boston and hang on, Sam grumbling from overwork, but he had it that day, and the guts to go with it. I was in the bullpen again. He got in trouble in the fifth, and I got up and took off my jacket and begun to throw down to Bruce, and then he pulled out of his trouble and I sat down again. Then he was in trouble in the sixth, and then out of it again, and in the eighth Boston had 2 on and 2 down when a young kid name of Hillhouse, now no longer with Boston, hitting for the pitcher, clubbed a drive into right-center that Pasquale Carucci went halfway up the fence and pulled down or it would of went for a triple at least. It was 1 of the finest fielding gems that I ever seen, and I am lucky to have had the chance. Pasquale got a great hand from the crowd. It was still 0–0 and anybody's ball game.

In the last of the eighth Gene Park and Red Traphagen singled, and Dutch played the gamble and lifted Sam and sent Swanee Wilks up to hit. I knowed my turn had come, for there was only me and Lindon in the bullpen, and Dutch would not send a righthander in against Boston if he could help it at a time like now.

I warmed up hard. I was really throwing, and Swanee lined a single into right, and Gene scored, and I knowed it was now my ball game to win or lose for Sam, and when the signal come from the dugout Lindon said to me, "You will do it, boy," and I started across the field. Pasquale Carucci, on his way out to right, he give me a slap on the rump, and then it come over the speaker. I will never forget it: *"Your attention please. Now pitching for New York. Wiggen. Number forty-four. Now pitching for New York."*

Down around second base Gene Park give me a cluck-cluck with his mouth, meaning good luck, and Sid Goldman and George Gonzalez was waiting at the hill with Red and Dutch, and they said words to me, though I forget them, and then Red went down behind the plate and I throwed a few, and Dutch headed back for the dugout and Sid and George back to their spots, and Ugly come in from short and said something and then turned and went back, and then I was alone.

I remember. I remember I seen Sad Sam standing at the dugout door, and I seen Dutch on the bench with his legs crossed, and I seen the club all leaned forward with their elbow on their knees like they do, waiting and waiting to see if I was a man or just another boy, and down in the coaching boxes the Boston coaches was roaring insults out my way, saying did I happen to know I was now in the big-time and did I not know this and that, usually things of a rather low-down nature, and Red called down from behind the plate, "Give me what I call for and we will be back in the showers in 5 minutes," and I said to myself, "I will try. Yet at this particular moment I am not sure that I could hit the side of a barn with a basketball." I looked down at the ball in my hand, and it did not seem like my hand a-tall but like the hand of a stranger attached to my wrist, and the arm was not mine and I did not believe I could trust it. I wished I was anywhere but where I was, maybe down in Borelli's in Perkinsville, relaxed, *listening* to this ball game. And then I thought of Borelli's, and it flashed like a vision through my brain that probably this very minute Pop was down in Borelli's, and there was a silence amongst the men, and the barbers was standing with razors in mid-air, and I could just see old Borelli running out in the street and setting up the cry.

Then I wound and pumped and throwed. It was a ball, slightly wide, and just about then a cheer went up, and I did not know why. For an instant I thought Dutch was lifting me, and I looked around, puzzled, and Ugly Jones laughed and pointed to the scoreboard, and I looked, and it showed 5 runs in the second inning for St. Louis at Cleveland, and I knowed that if we won now we would be breathing easier again.

The batter was Black. I remembered the knee-high curve Sad Sam had throwed when me and Pop come down that day for the Opener, and Black had connected by sheer luck, and Red called for that kind of a pitch now, and it cut the corner, as clean a strike as you ever seen, and Hunt Glidden, the umpire, called it a ball, and I stormed down towards the plate and made a few remarks about how it was my belief umpires ought to be pensioned off once they went blind, and Glidden said to me, "You have throwed 2 pitches in the big time and already you are a hot head. Now get back out there and pitch," and I offered a few further bits of advice about the knack of being an umpire, and he turned his back. George shouted down from third, "Up yours, up yours," and Ugly and Gene come in and give Glidden a piece of their mind, and Dutch come up off the bench and told Glidden several things more or less harsh in tone. It seemed to bring the club to life, I think it was the first time in several days that it showed any life, and I went back out and throwed the same pitch again, and this time it was a strike and no mistake.

Then it was a fast ball, letter high, and Black never seen it, and the count was 2 and 2. Then I struck him out with the screw.

The crowd give me a good hand, and they give the razzberry to Granby, the next Boston batter, for he was not popular in New York since 1 time he spiked Ugly Jones in a play at second. He tried to cross me up by bunting down the third base line. I seen him shift when the ball left my hand, and I went down fast, and Red yelled "Wiggen, Wiggen," meaning for George to get out of the way, and I fielded it clean and whirled and fired to Sid Goldman at first, and Granby was out by a full step.

Now I was relaxed. It was like I was always up there, like I was there all my life, with the Mammoths, and I went back to the hill and scrubbed around with my toeplate, and I fingered the resin bag, and I looked up at the scoreboard and out at the fielders, and I was no more nervous then if I was back in the Legion League in Perkinsville.

Fielding stepped in. Casey Sharpe, the Boston clean-up man, was kneeling in the on-deck circle. "Get on," shouted he to Fielding, "and I will drive you home," and then he shouted something out at me that I will not repeat, and I shouted down to him, "Go back to the dugout, Casey, for number 3 is at the plate." Fielding must of liked those shoulder balls I throwed him, for he went after 2. He did not have the good fortune to get wood on them, however, and then Red called for the screw, and Fielding got a slice of it, and he skied it up behind third base. Ugly and George both went for the ball, and Ugly called "George" and George took it on the lope, a very easy play, and that was the ball game.

You would of almost thought we clinched the pennant. The clubhouse was downright cheerful. We got a later score on Cleveland, and Cleveland was losing, and Dutch come by, and he said to me, "Good work," and then he went back in his office. That was the game we needed, and we knowed it.

Patricia Moors was all smiles. Bradley Lord give us the warning, and she come through on the way to the office. She stopped near the door, and she said, "Sam Yale, nice game," and he told her he thought so himself, considering that he was more overworked then a nigger, and she said, "Where is Pasquale Carucci?" and he come forward, and she said, "That was a fine catch. I never saw DiMaggio make a better 1," DiMaggio being Pasquale's hero since he was a kid, and Pasquale said "Thank you, ma'am," and then she looked around some more, and her eyes lit on me, and mine on her.

"1-2-3 they come up and 1-2-3 they went down," I said, and she laughed, and when she laughed all the diamonds jiggled on her ears, and she brushed back her hair with 1 arm, and I think there was about 4 pounds of bracelets on the arm, and she stood looking at me.

"You set them down fine," she said.

"I rather thought the same," said I.

And still she stood there and looked at me, and I at her. "The trouble with you," she said, "is that you do not have enough confidence in yourself," and she laughed and turned and went off towards the office, and I watched her go, and a fine sight it was.

That day we dressed slow, me and Lindon, and in the days after. We made the last tour of the eastern clubs, and I worked just about every day down in the bullpens, yet Dutch did not use me. He said he would pitch me the last game, which was Sunday in Boston, and we beat them Friday and Saturday and knocked them out of the top spot, Brooklyn taking 2 from Washington in Brooklyn, and then it rained on Sunday and I never got the chance. I guess nobody give a damn but me, the race already settled, Brooklyn, Boston, New York and Cleveland finishing 1-2-3-4.

We had a meeting in the hotel that afternoon, and the boys voted shares of the third-place money. They voted me 100 dollars, which was good enough pay for 1 inning of work, and then we broke up, and it was sad because you knowed there was some amongst us that had played their last games in the big time. Next year they would be on their way down, down and down to nowheres.

Yet I was happy, for I was on the way up, and I said to Lindon, "I guess we are sitting on top of the world, away up in the clouds, and the gate is open and the music is playing," and Lindon said the same.

This first-person recollection is from one of the outstanding books of oral history that appeared in the mid-1970s: John B. Holway's *Voices from the Great Black Baseball Leagues*. That book, along with Robert Peterson's *Only the Ball Was White*, sparked a new interest in black baseball that predated Jackie Robinson and led to further study of those dimly documented days. Perhaps the most neglected of the "invisible men" playing professional baseball in the shadow of the major leagues was Hilton Smith, Satchel Paige's other—and some would dare to say better—half.

JOHN B. HOLWAY

Hilton Smith Remembers

Hilton Smith was the invisible man of black baseball. For years he toiled behind the glare of an almost blinding star known to the world as Satchel Paige, but who in reality was a hyphenated pitcher named Paige-Smith. After Satchel had pitched three innings to draw a crowd (and incidentally earn his 15 percent of the gate), Hilton Smith would trudge in from the bull pen and finish the game. And there are many black hitters who declare that of the two, when Smith appeared, the hits became even tougher to collect.

Ironically, Smith had been the star on the Monarchs before Paige arrived. Indeed, even for a while afterward Smith continued to be the ace of the staff. In 1941 Paige-Smith went barnstorming against Bob Feller and Ken Heintzelman of the white big leagues, and, wrote Bob Burnes, sports editor of the St. Louis Globe-Democrat, "Smith showed the best speed and sharpest curve of the quartet."

Even the New York Yankees learned to respect Smith. He beat them in Caracas, Venezuela, in the spring of 1947, and while most U.S. papers ignored the game, John Drebinger of the New York Times didn't. "For the first five innings," he reported, "the Bombers ran into quite a Tartar in Hilton Smith, a right-hander, who gave up only one hit, a single to Phil Rizzuto, and two passes."

I met Smith in 1969 in his handsome brick house on a terraced lot in one of Kansas City's best black neighborhoods. Although somewhat heavier than in his playing days, he does not look a bit like the grandfather he is. He talks in a high-pitched, rapid voice about the particular burden he carried for years as Satchel Paige's other half.

Hilton Smith Speaks . . .

I played twelve years with the Kansas City Monarchs, 1937–48, and I won twenty games or more every year. Not counting exhibitions, I won 161 league games and lost 22, but most people have never heard of me. They've only heard of Satchel Paige. That's because I was Satchel's relief.

Every Sunday I'd start, then Monday night come on in relief, start on Wednesday and maybe Friday, according to how Satchel was feeling. It was my turn to relieve him in all big games. He'd go two or three innings; if there was a big crowd and we had to win it, I'd go in there and save it. Then the next day I'd look in the paper and the headline would say: "Satchel and Monarchs Win Again."

I just took my baseball serious; I just went out there to do a job. But Satchel was an attraction; he could produce, and he'd clown a lot. I guess it really hurt me. I tried to get away, but there wasn't anything I could do about it.

Now Satchel never did pitch much here in Kansas City. Oh, no, he never did a lot of pitching here. But ooh, when he left here, my goodness, they'd eat him up all those other places, because he was an attraction, but these people here, they never did. He never was able to produce here. Some little old team would be able to hit on him, like Memphis and a lot of the teams like that. I remember '41 we opened up here against Memphis, and they got to him in about the second inning, and I relieved him. I shut them out the rest of the game, and we went on and beat them. So they never did book him in here hardly, I mean advertise him as a star pitcher. He played with us all those years, but he didn't do too much pitching here. I pitched all Sunday games.

Satchel was a great pitcher, I don't take anything away from him. I'd like to have seen him in his early age, back in '29 and the early thirties. Good God, he could throw that ball! And perfect control; he never walked anybody. He could throw it. But he hurt his arm in '37, and it didn't come back until '41. His arm was sore all those years, and he played with the Monarchs' "small team," while I was with the "big team." In '39 he came and played us over in Kansas City, and I shut him out 9–0. We just wore Satchel out. So I was the star.

But in '41 Satchel suddenly got his arm back, and that was the worst break I got. I guess in '42 Satchel was as great a pitcher as you want to see. He had a good curveball, and he always had that good fastball, and in '42 he just had everything on the ball. That's when he hit his peak.

I actually hit my peak, too, in '41. I was to the place then that I could just do anything, I felt that good. I thought I could go out there and get *anybody* out. I won twenty-five games and lost one that year. A semipro team in Dayton, Ohio, beat me, 1–0, after I had relieved Satchel. We struck out eighteen between

us; they got one hit off Satchel and none off me but beat me on an error. It was the only game I lost that year.

In 1941 I pitched one game against Bob Feller's All-Stars. Walker Cooper was catching. Johnny Hopp was at first base—he had a good year that year, hit about .300; oooh, that guy could hit! The outfield was Ival Goodman, Stan Musial, and somebody else. They hit Satchel pretty hard in the first four innings, and I came in and relieved him in the fifth. I held them, struck out six of them in five innings, didn't give but one hit, but they beat us 4–3. Bobby Feller pitched three innings, and Kenny Heintzelman of Philadelphia pitched the last six. He really broke off some jugs that day, because I doubled with nobody out and didn't score. It would have been the tying run, but the guy struck out all the rest of them.

One of my greatest thrills was beating Dizzy Dean in Wrigley Field, Chicago, in 1942. We had a turnout of 30,000 people that day. Yeah, boy, you're talking about some good baseball, there was some that day. You remember big old Zeke Bonura, used to play with the White Sox? He played first base. Buddy Lewis of Washington played third and Cecil Travis short. All of them were major-league ballplayers who were in the service, and they came up for that game. Dizzy Dean pitched the first three innings. We "carried" Dizzy; because he wasn't too good, we kind of carried him along. I beat him 3–1. Satchel pitched the first five innings for us and came out with the score 1–1. He had struck out three, walked one, gave up two hits and one run. I struck out three, didn't walk anybody, gave up one hit and no runs. Big Joe Greene, our catcher, got a hit with two men on around the seventh inning, and I held 'em. In the ninth Travis came up with one on. Barney Serrell, our shortstop, said, "Make him hit it on the ground," and that's just what it was, a double play, and the ball game was over.

Jackie Robinson used to tell me, "Hilton, you're going under the same thing with Satchel that I went under with Kenny Washington at UCLA." See, at UCLA Jackie had to play second to Kenny. Kenny was a great football player; we all heard about him, but I never heard about Jackie until I went to the Coast in 1942.

In fact, I'm the one who signed Jackie to a Monarchs' contract. I had met him in '42 when Red Ruffing had a team in the service out there on the Coast. Jackie asked me about getting him a job, so I wrote to Mr. Wilkinson, the owner of the Monarchs, and he wired back to keep in touch with Jackie, so I did. In 1944 he got out of the service and joined the Monarchs.

Actually, Jackie didn't look that good. He was a little old to be a major-league rookie—twenty-seven—but there weren't any good young ballplayers then. Jackie's arm was weak at shortstop; Willie Wells was better than Jackie at that position. But the Dodgers picked him on account of he'd played college baseball; he'd played with white boys before.

I was born in 1912 in Giddens, Texas, a little town between Austin and Houston. Rube Foster came from about 25 miles from my house, a little town right above me.

I patterned myself after my uncles. I had two uncles that my mother would let me play with. They were powerful good ballplayers. I guess I inherited my ability from them. They were good, but they played out in the country there, played for fun. I just loved it, and that was what started me off. I just made myself, didn't have a teacher. I kept picking up and looking and learning as I went up.

I started out playing with my dad, who was a schoolteacher. I played for my dad's team when I was in the tenth grade. I guess I was about fifteen. During the summertime I played with older boys—they were all grown men. I pitched against the town high school team and shut them out 2–0.

Austin had a team, the Austin Senators, a semipro team that played Houston and all the towns down there. They had a pitcher named Willie Owens who had played with Birmingham in the Negro Leagues. In 1931, when I was nineteen, I went down and pitched against him one Saturday and beat 'em, I just beat 'em good. He went back to Austin and said, "My goodness, there's a little kid there, he's something else." So when the Chicago American Giants came down there to play Austin the next weekend, Austin came down and got me to pitch for them. I beat 'em 5–4 in eleven innings.

So Austin picked me up to play in Mexico. Mexico had an awful good ball club; they were good enough to play the major leaguers when they went down there that fall. Ramon Bragana was there pitching. They had Chili Gomez, who had been there and played with Washington. I'm telling you, we had a lot of trouble beating those guys. Well, we started another boy, and they ran him out. Then I went in and relieved him and got them out. So they started me Sunday again. The manager told me just to go out there and throw hard. But my arm was so sore—I wasn't nothing but a kid, and I hadn't been pitching that much baseball—I couldn't get anybody out. I don't think I got anybody out the first inning.

Next Thursday they started me again. The manager said, "Listen, I want you to go out there and try to get by the first inning." I said, "Yes, sir." I asked him, "Can I throw some curveballs today?" He said, "Yeah, I guess so."

I beat 'em 5–1, and I hit in all five runs. I struck out so many of them, they didn't think I was the same pitcher.

Monroe, Louisiana, had a real good Negro team then. They were champions of the Southern Conference, had beaten everybody. They had Red Parnell out of Houston; a little old guy name of Ducky Davenport; and Barney Morris and Goose Curry out of Memphis pitching. They had a tremendous ball club. They came to Austin and played us two games. They were talking about they heard of this little schoolboy up there and said, "Well, we came up here to work him over." But we had a great big ballpark, and I beat 'em 2–1. They couldn't believe it. They said, "Well, this big old park, no wonder you won. When you come to Monroe"—Monroe had a small park—"we'll hit so many home runs off you . . ." So I went to Monroe the following Sunday and beat 'em 4–2.

Monroe picked me up to play with them and carried me to Pittsburgh. That was the first time I saw Satchel Paige. I played with Monroe for the next three years. I had a great year in '32; won thirty-one games, didn't lose a ball game.

When the Pittsburgh Crawfords came down to Monroe to play us, I opened up against them. With Josh and them it was one of the best teams of all time: Oscar Charleston, Pee Wee Stephens, Ted Page, Double-Duty Radcliffe. I led them, 2–0, in about the sixth inning, when Boojum Wilson came up and got a hit. Then Josh Gibson hit a home run off me to tie the game 2–2. I came out the next inning. I was only twenty years old then. I was nervous, I'd never faced those kind of ballplayers before.

I pitched against the American Giants in '33. They beat the Crawfords out that year, beat Satchel and them. Yep, they won the championship and came to New Orleans. Chicago had Mule Suttles, Willie Wells, Jack Marshall, Alex Radcliff; outfield was one of the best outfields I ever saw—major league or anybody else: Steel-Arm Davis, Turkey Stearns, and Nat Rogers. They were a *tremendous* ball club.

We beat them three out of five ball games. Sure did, 'cause I remember now. They beat us the first ball game, Sunday—I think it was about 5–1. They stayed over till Saturday, and Bill Foster pitched against me—I'm strictly a rookie now—and I beat him 6–1. We came back and beat 'em again Sunday, 3–2, in twelve innings. George Giles tripled with a man on base and beat 'em. Bill Foster came back Monday and beat us—that guy pitched three ball games in a week's time. Then I beat Cornelius. I think they got four hits, and all the hits were the infield variety; they never hit the ball out of the infield. And it was just natural stuff; I didn't know how to pitch to those guys. Curveball and fastball were all I threw.

I went to Bismarck, North Dakota, in 1935. The league broke up down South, and Monroe went on a tour all around the Midwest. We weren't making any money, just touring around, but we were playing good ball, beating just everybody we met. I didn't know what it was to lose a ball game; I hadn't lost a ball game. We got into Bismarck the fifth of July—I never will forget that. A guy named Churchill was mayor of the city and had a ball club. Barney Morris, who played with Monroe, had gone to Bismarck earlier that spring. Satchel was pitching for them, too. They were getting ready to go to this Wichita semipro tournament, and they needed another pitcher. Churchill asked me about staying, and I said I didn't know. He offered me $125 a month. I wasn't making a quarter, but I told him no, I didn't want to, so he said, "How about $150?" I told him okay.

I didn't lose a ball game with Bismarck the whole year, but I didn't pitch much. I played right field on that club most of the time and batted third or fourth.

When we went to Wichita, to the semipro tournament, we didn't lose a ball game. I pitched the first game and shut somebody out 2–0; I don't remember who it was. I played outfield the rest of the games and hit fourth. Satchel and Chet Brewer did all the pitching.

The next year, when I went back to Bismarck, Satchel had gone East, so I did all the pitching down there in Wichita. I won four games, and all four of them were shutouts. Last time I saw the records on that, about six years ago, my record was still holding. I had more shutouts than any pitcher who had ever been in the tournament. I don't know if anyone's broken it or not. Satchel had the strikeout record.

Actually I didn't really learn how to pitch until I came to the Monarchs that fall. I just had natural stuff before that. I learned by having such guys for teachers as Frank Duncan, Bullet Rogan, and Andy Cooper.

Rogan. . . . He played with us in '38, and then he was through. He was a guy who, if you didn't know him, you'd think he was kind of a snob like, but he was a nice guy, and he used to get on you if you didn't do your job. He was umpiring, and I'd be pitching, and right after the ball game he'd come out and he'd tell me, "You've got a lot of stuff, but why'd you do such and such a thing?" I'd say, "Well, I don't know." He'd say, "Well, from now on, you *know*." I'd answer, "Okay, I'll do it." Next time he was umpiring and I got in the ball game, he'd say, "Un-huh, I see you're picking up."

Andy Cooper was a smart manager, and he was a great teacher—great teacher! A student of baseball. He would take me aside and just sit there and talk to me, and I'd watch how he'd pitch. And my owner, Wilkinson, would talk to me. He was a doll, that guy. He had played a little semipro ball himself, and he really knew baseball. He said, "Look, you've got everything, but use your wrist a little more, see if you can't get a little more hop on your ball." I took him at his word, and sure enough it worked.

So I'd watch and observe and listen.

The first ball game I pitched in this park out here in Kansas City was a no-hitter. I beat the Chicago American Giants 4–0. Nobody got on first base—I mean a perfect game. The Giants had Sug Cornelius pitching, Larry Brown catching, Alex Radcliff. They were *hard* to beat.

I didn't lose many games that year. I probably lost three the whole season.

The Monarchs used to play Texas League teams all the time. We played Oklahoma City when they were in the Texas League in '37. They had a good team, too; they had finished way up in that league, Double A baseball. We wanted to find out how good we were. Shoot, I pitched two ball games against them, and they haven't scored yet. I beat 'em Friday night, and we played 'em two games Sunday. We beat them the first ball game, and the second game they kind of started hitting our pitching, and Cooper brought me in there. A boy named Clay Touchstone—he was a great pitcher—I had beat him. He said, "What is this, the World Series, you bring that man back in here! Doggone, let us win *something!*" But I beat them. We beat them three straight. But we wanted to prove a point, see. We didn't have a chance to play in those leagues. We wanted to prove a point that we were good enough to.

We played the major leaguers about seven games that fall, too, and I pitched three of them. I pitched eighteen innings in all, and they never got a score off me. They had Johnny Mize on first, Lonnie Fry on second. Outfield had Ivy Goodman, Vince DiMaggio, and Gus Suhr. Pitchers were Mace Brown, Lou Fette—he won twenty games that year—Mike Ryba and Bob Feller.

I pitched three innings in Rock Island in relief and didn't give up any hits or runs. Bob Feller started for them, and we beat 'em, but I don't think we scored on Bob that day; he only pitched three innings. Lou Fette came on next, and we beat him. Next day I pitched six innings and didn't give up any runs. And then I beat Fette in a nine-inning game. I shut them out 10–0 in Oklahoma City.

Mize didn't get a hit off me the whole series. He was hitting everybody else, but he didn't hit me. How could that man hit that ball standing way back from the plate? I kept a-looking at him. I guess I had a curveball as good as anybody's in baseball at that time. My fastball ran; it just jumped. I bet I only struck him out twice that whole series, but he would hit the ball weakly back to me. I just kept it on the outside; the curveball would break in, and the umpire would call it. He'd try to pull it, and he never was able to pull it.

In 1937 I was on Martin Dihigo's team in Cuba. Josh was down there with Havana. Early Wynn was playing with Springfield in Triple A ball, and he only won one game down there that year. And he was going to the majors the next year! He could not win down there. Boy, it was tough.

That was 1937. In '37, '38, and '39 I had tremendous years. I could pitch and hit, both. Andy Cooper'd pinch-hit me for his fourth-place hitters just as quick. Several years I hit over .400 pinch-hitting, outfield, first base, and pitching.

I was pitching about four times a week, because we were playing six or seven games a week, and we only carried about four pitchers. Maybe sometimes we'd have five; that was the most. We didn't know what it was to relieve. When you went out there, you didn't look at the bull pen; you were expected to go the whole route.

They knew I wasn't wild; they knew I threw strikes. We didn't hardly walk anyone. The curve, we'd just slice it off, pfffft. And everybody threw hard. Good curveballs, and that live fastball moved. Today you see a lot of these guys' fastballs, just straight. But our fastballs *moved*. We had to have two curveballs, a big one and a small one. Now they call it a slider, but those guys were throwing it years and years back. It kind of just darted over the corner like that. Good control.

We were tremendous rivals with the Washington Homestead Grays. Tremendous rivals. A lot of those guys could have got in the majors, they were such good ballplayers. And gentlemen—Buck Leonard and them were such nice guys. We'd set and talk and jolly one another. My goodness! I pitched against them one night in New Orleans in 1939. They had Leonard, Josh, and all of them, and I struck out so many that night ol' Josh came up to me, said, "Say, fellow, look, you doctoring the ball or something?" I said, "Here it is; look at it."

Up until '42 I had more trouble with Josh than I did any other ballplayer. Gibson had those great big old muscle arms, weighed about 205, 6 foot 1. He would swing flatfooted, wouldn't stride. The first time I faced him, he hit a home run off me. But in '42 I didn't have any trouble with him at all. No, from then on I really began to get him out.

I learned how to get Buck Leonard out, too. I'd slow the ball up on him, screwball him, and slow curveballs. He'd ground out—oh, he'd get hits sometimes, but I mean I could get him out.

In 1942 I remember we played the Homestead Grays in Washington. Boston had played a day game against the Senators that day and drew 3,000; we played the Grays that night and drew 28,000. That's the year we beat the Grays four straight for the Negro World Championship.

We had a tremendous ball club that year. A lot of the boys had jumped to Mexico, and they all came back in '42. We had Joe Greene catching, John O'Neil first base, Jesse Williams short, Newt Allen second. Outfield we had Ted Strong, Willard Brown, and a boy named Bill Simms—he was a ballplayer never got much publicity, but he could do anything; he could hit, oooh, he could hit. Ted Strong was just as good a ballplayer as there was in baseball, but he kind of laid on the bottle. That got him in his late years.

We had a tremendous pitching staff in '42. We had Satchel, Jack Matchett, a boy named Connie Johnson, who played in the majors. And Lefty LaMarque and a boy named Booker McDaniels. Nobody hardly beat us. That particular year, '42, I don't think I lost maybe one or two ball games the entire year.

This kid Connie Johnson was awful good, too. He had hurt his arm when he went in the majors. I'd like to have seen *him* go in there before he hurt his arm. You talking about Satchel and me—Johnson and I would team up and beat anybody. I remember Baltimore came here with Campanella and all those good ballplayers. I beat them 3–1. He came back the second game and beat them 3–1. I mean we didn't lose—he and I didn't lose. Johnson—ooh, that guy could throw that ball. He wasn't but about nineteen or twenty years old. He hurt his arm in '42. He went into the service and came back. His arm came back to him, but nothing like it had been.

That '42 World Series. We opened up against the Grays in Washington. I think Satchel pitched the first game, and Jack Matchett relieved him. I started the second game; Satchel relieved me. We changed around. He said, "Hilton, you've been relieving me all this year. Let me relieve you; just see what we can do." I pitched five innings; he pitched four. When I left, the score was 5–0. They scored four runs off Satchel, and we beat 'em, 8–4. Then we went over to New York. Satchel started, and Matchett relieved him, and we beat 'em, 9–3. Then we went to Philadelphia and beat 'em 9–5, and I beat 'em the last ball game in Portsmouth, Virginia; I think it was 14–2. We just silenced them, just whipped 'em. I mean we killed their pitchers, and they didn't do anything with our pitching.

My arm went dead in 1943. I hurt it, and I played first base and outfield for two years. In '44 I began working back into shape, so I went out on the Coast that fall and played baseball against Bob Lemon, who's right down here as manager of Kansas City now. They had a good ball club. All those guys were in the service. They had an All-Star Game, and I beat them that evening.

Biz Mackey caught me. Oooh, my goodness, I didn't know he was such a catcher! I think I struck out fifteen of those guys. That guy was a marvelous catcher! I just—ooh, I just was on *edge*, and it looked like all my stuff was just working. Had the hitters looking like they didn't know what to do. Mackey told me, "I don't see how in the world you *ever* lose a ball game."

My arm came back in 1945 or '46, and in 1946 we played Newark for the Negro World Championship. They had Larry Doby and Monte Irvin, and I beat them two games. I beat them in Chicago, 5–1, and I beat them in New York, 2–1. No, that's wrong, I didn't beat them, I had them 1–0 going into the sixth inning, and Satchel came in. We had a guy from the Coast named Hamilton to replace Jackie Robinson—a good hitter, a good-looking boy. A big boy from Newark slid into second on the double play and broke his leg. Hamilton just laid there, and before we could resume play, it was almost an hour. So I cooled off, got stiff, and walked a man, and Satchel came in and relieved me. They tied it up, but he went on and beat them 2–1.

Monte Irvin played shortstop for Newark, and he looked awful good. Yeah, he was a *good* ballplayer. There's one guy I was really pulling for when he went to the majors.

But Doby didn't look too good. Three straight times I struck him out in Chicago, and he started jawing with the umpire. I asked him, "Doby, why do you want to jump on the umpire?" And he said, "Man, do you see my owner sitting up there in the stands? I've got to look good for her."

Roy Campanella didn't show me anything, either. Campanella and I were very good friends. I used to pitch against old Campy when he was seventeen years old. I'd strike him out all the time. In the All-Star Game one year I struck that boy out two times.

Campanella came down to the Polo Grounds one night when we were playing Newark in the World Series and asked me what did I think about playing with the Dodgers. He said the front office had told him to talk to me. He asked how old I was, and I told him thirty-four. Actually, they were wondering about Jackie [Robinson]. Jackie was around twenty-seven when he went up there, and they were debating whether he was too old. They knew he had to make it within one year, because if he didn't, he would be too old.

I figured I was too old at thirty-four. See, we were getting a pretty good salary, and we were afraid to go down to the minors and take a pay cut. With the Monarchs I was making $800 a month, and I felt like $400 would have been the best I could have got in Triple A baseball. Don Newcombe went down to the minors from Newark and stayed for three years, and I don't think he was getting over $250 a month.

Had it been opened up—had there been some other team beside the Dodgers—I probably would have taken a chance. I knew the Dodgers were pretty well loaded and I'd have to sit around in the minors and they'd be slow about bringing me up, and at my age that was too much. I wouldn't have minded going down to the minors for one year, then come back up. But at that particular time I felt I was too old to have a comeback with the Monarchs if I didn't make it with the Dodgers right away. Campanella said, "Well, think it over and let me know." But I couldn't see going down there for them.

That fall I went with Satchel to play against Bob Feller's big-league All-Stars. I remember they had Sam Chapman, Jeff Heath, and Charlie Keller in the outfield; Mickey Vernon, who won the batting championship, was on first; Phil Rizzuto and Kenny Keltner in the infield; pitching was Feller, Bob Lemon, Johnny Sain, Dutch Leonard, and Spud Chandler. I never *saw* so many good pitchers. Boy! Bob Feller said, "I wish I had this ball club all year to play with!" They had a powerhouse. Man!

We played fifteen or sixteen games, and I relieved in two and pitched two complete games. I broke even with them. They beat me 6–3, and I beat Feller 3–2. I gave up four or five hits. Vernon gave me the most trouble; he got two doubles.

What messed us up was Jackie Robinson had an All-Star team that fall—Monte Irvin went with him, and that left us with no outfielders. We had a pickup outfield—and Sam Jethroe had to catch when Quincy Trouppe got hurt. That really weakened our ball club defensively; we picked up a boy named Gene Benson to play center field. Artie Wilson played short, Hank Thompson played second, Buck O'Neill first. Catching, Quincy Trouppe started off; then he got his finger hurt.

We started off in Pittsburgh and went to Youngstown, played in Cleveland, Cincinnati, Chicago—just overflow crowds. We really lost a lot of money in Chicago. We had 30-some thousand there and thought we'd get ten or fifteen. They weren't expecting so many people, and Bob Feller himself had to go and try to help the ticket taker. They just rushed us. The policemen were taking up tickets and taking up money. My goodness. I don't know how much money we lost. Everywhere we went, just overflow crowds. They really poured out to see us that year. And we played some great baseball.

Hank Thompson just wore out that Bob Feller on that tour. I mean he just wore him out! He hit a home run and a double in Wichita, another home run off him somewhere else. Hit a home run in New York, because we beat Bob Feller 4–0 in New York. We had around 40,000 people, and our cut was $300 that day, each player.

Bob Feller's people made around $6,000 apiece for that trip. Ken Keltner said, "Hilton, my goodness!" I think his salary was $12,000 that year, and he cleared $6,000 for that trip.

But that was the end of it. They broke it up after that; the commissioner stopped it. Stan Musial was supposed to be on that club from the start, but that's the year St. Louis played Boston in the World Series in those little bandboxes they had for parks. Musial got in the World Series instead of coming with us, and he must have made a little over $2,000 for winning the Series. My goodness, he raised all kind of heck about it. Some of those players said, "The heck with the World Series when we can make this kind of money here." And that was the end of it.

I guess one of my greatest thrills was pitching against the New York Yankees in 1947—March 17—in Caracas, Venezuela. That was the first time I pitched against a whole major-league ball club. And they had quite a club, too, believe you me. Dr. [Bobby] Brown was about as good a hitter as I've seen. Boy! He was playing third base. Rizzuto was at shortstop, Stirnweiss was playing second, first base was Tommy Henrich and Nick Etten. Outfield was Keller, big Cliff Mapes, Johnny Lindell, and Yogi Berra. I think Ralph Houk was catching. Pitching they had Allie Reynolds. They had quite a ball club. I pitched six innings, didn't give up any runs, and gave up one hit, to Rizzuto. We won 4–3.

So I pitched against enough major leaguers to see if I was on the level. You know, naturally if you never compete with those people, you're always in doubt in your mind whether you're good enough to play against them. But I played against them enough, and they never did hit me. So I feel that had I had a chance, I could have pitched in the big leagues.

All our source of guys being developed was through the Negro League. Yeah, they were taking them, and I don't think any of the clubs got much out of it— Doby, Irvin, Newcombe, Campanella, Ernie Banks. And they were great attractions. You could see it in '46, the first year Jackie went to Montreal. Then in '47 Negro baseball began to go back. All the people started to go Brooklynites; everybody who had never known anything about baseball. Even if we were playing here in Kansas City, everybody wanted to go over to St. Louis to see Jackie. So our league really began to go down, down, down.

It looked like it was dead, so I played in Fulda, Minnesota, in '49, and in '50 I went out to Armco-Sheffield Steel here in Kansas City. They had a ball club, and they wanted me to manage it. So I said, "Well, maybe I better get on out of here." So I gave it up. I could have pitched a little more. But I'd seen so many ballplayers that just kept a-hanging around when they were over the hill, so I'd always made up my mind when I got to the place where I was going down, I'd just give it up. I'm a supervisor with Armco now. I'm lucky; I got a real good job.

A young girl asked me one day, "Did you ever play ball? I've heard my father and a lot of them talk about you. How did you get started?" and one thing and another. I told her, and she said, "Funny, there's no literature or anything. We would like to read about some of the older ballplayers so we'd know something about them." I said, "Well, maybe eventually there will be a book or something." She said, "If you ever run across one, let us know."

It was a rough life—ride, ride, ride, and ride. I remember many a day, ride a bus, get out and get you a little bit to eat, go to the ballpark, go out there and pitch nine innings, play a doubleheader, play outfield the second game. But I enjoyed baseball; I really did. It was spoiling me. I loved it, and it was sweet. We had some great moments. I enjoyed every bit of it.

Here's the thing of it: I know we were playing better ball than some of the lower teams in the big leagues. The only difference was, they had a better bench, more people sitting on the bench. See, if we had one shortstop, we had one shortstop, and our guys just played day in and day out. The majors had more replacements, more pitchers and reserves. Just man-for-man, we were tremendous. We'd put our ball club on the field and something's got to give; those guys could hit that ball, I don't care who was pitching. And we had pitchers could get anybody out and could throw the ball over the plate.

I look at these eighteen- and nineteen-year-old kids today—wild, can't get the ball over to save their lives. They have good coaches who talk to 'em, tell 'em things, but one thing, I don't think they have that desire to want to play, to *want* to develop, to want to learn. They just take it for granted: "Oh, I can go out and play golf." A lot of them quit. All this opportunity they've got. But we played because we loved it. I didn't care if I never got a dime, I just loved it that well. I just used to eat and sleep baseball. And I always had a desire.

I enjoyed baseball; I really did. I tell those kids, "You wouldn't believe I made my living for thirteen or fourteen years at baseball." They say, "You did!" I say, "Yeah, that's the only job I had. And here you all are just monkeying around here." See, I always wanted to win, and it's hard, you know—I just can't hardly take it the way these kids play ball. I always wanted to win, and I gave it my best.

I'd pick Buck Leonard as the best first baseman I ever saw. Martin Dihigo at second. Willie Wells shortstop. At third base I'd pick Kenny Keltner of Cleveland. In the outfield I'd put Sam Chapman, and Charlie Keller of the Yankees. Catcher of course is Josh Gibson. Pitching staff? I'd have to go with Lon Warneke of the Cubs. Ooh, that boy could *pitch!* And Bobby Feller, of course, and Bob Lemon, and Raymond Brown of the Homestead Grays. And yeah, oh, yeah, I'd put Satchel in there, too.

From the marvelously titled *Baseball When the Grass Was Real*, the first of Don Honig's four oral histories, comes this flavorful reminiscence of baseball in the storm-tossed 1940s. Max Lanier's major-league career actually began in 1938 and ran through 1953, and today fans may know him principally as the father of Astros' manager Hal Lanier, but Max was a fine southpaw with a colorful *curriculum vitae*. Read on.

DONALD HONIG

Max Lanier Remembers

Looking back on it all, I can tell you that it happened too quick. It doesn't seem like it could be that long ago. Time really flies. I know when I signed that first contract, it looked as big as this room.

I was pitching a high school game, down home in North Carolina. I won it 2–0. When I came out of the ballpark later, this guy was standing there waiting for me.

"Hi, Max," he said.

"Hi yourself," I said. I didn't know who he was.

"Can I give you a ride back to the school?" he asked.

"Well, I don't know you," I said.

He pulled out his identification and showed it to me. Frank Rickey, Branch's brother. Representing the St. Louis Cardinals.

"You interested in playing pro ball?" he asked.

"Yes, indeed," I said. That was one of my dreams. I was already playing semipro ball while I was still in high school. We had a pretty good semipro club there in Denton, North Carolina. This was around 1934.

Frank Rickey signed me to a contract when I was sixteen years old. My family wasn't too enthused about the idea. You see, I'd been offered a scholarship by Duke University, and my parents wanted me to accept it, but I turned it down to play pro ball.

I signed right out of high school, with a Class B club. I stayed there a week and then they wanted to send me to a D club, Huntington, West Virginia, for $70

a month. I didn't go for that, and I quit and came home. That was my first money dispute with the Cardinals. It didn't take long, did it? One week.

I started playing semipro ball again, in Ashbury, North Carolina. In 1936 I won sixteen straight games. That's against no losses. One day I walk out of the ballpark, and there's Frank Rickey standing there.

"Back again, are you?" I asked.

"How would you like to go to Columbus in the American Association?" he asked.

"Why should I?" I asked.

"It would be a great opportunity for you," he said. "That's Triple A ball."

"I might consider it," I said. "Under one condition—that you guarantee I'll be on the ball club the whole year."

I guess you talk that way when you've got a 16–0 record, no matter who you've won them against.

"How do you know you can pitch in Triple A?" he asked.

"I think I can," I said, "because we've got a lot of ballplayers right here who are that good, and I'm doing all right against them."

He went along with it. I was talking tough, but to tell you the truth, you couldn't afford to bargain too much with the Cardinals back then, because they had so many ballplayers. They were way ahead of everybody else in that respect. At one time they had about thirty farm clubs. And they kept us hungry. That was Branch Rickey's philosophy: a hungry ballplayer was a better ballplayer. I'll tell you one thing about him: he could tell you how much he paid you for each pitch, not how many games you won or lost.

The competition was murder. When I was coming up, they had, just in left-hand pitchers, fellows like Howie Pollet, Al Brazle, Harry Brecheen, Ernie White, Preacher Roe. That was pretty stiff competition. Why, Preacher Roe couldn't even make the club!

I got lucky at Columbus and won ten and lost four. The next year I went up to the Cardinals. Frisch was managing then. He was tough on young ballplayers. I didn't appreciate it then, but I did later. He'd find faults no matter what you did, but if you paid attention to him, you'd find yourself learning something. He was a good baseball man and a full-fledged character at the same time. I remember one time Paul Waner was wearing us out with line drives. Finally Frisch stood up in disgust and yelled, "Who on this ball club can get that Waner out?" Max Macon was sitting on the bench—this was before he went to the Dodgers. Well, Max liked to pop off a little, anyway, and he said, "I can get him out." Frisch was delighted to hear that. He clapped his hands and said, "Atta boy. Get down there and warm up." Waner comes up again. Frisch brings in Macon. The first pitch Waner hits a line drive and breaks Macon's little finger. Frisch couldn't help but lie down on the bench and laugh himself silly.

Pepper Martin was on that ball club. I'd say he was the most colorful ballplayer I ever saw. He was a real fun lover. He'd come into the clubhouse and tie your uniform into knots or nail your shoes to the floor. Sometimes during a game you'd be out there pitching, and he'd walk over from third base to talk to you and slap a wad of chewing gum onto your wrist.

One day, I think it was in Chicago, he pulled a beauty. He was great at throwing paper sacks full of water out the window. Well, there was a mezzanine in the lobby of this hotel, with a staircase leading up to it from the ground floor. Pepper got himself a paper sack full of water and hung around by the mezzanine window with a newspaper in his hand. He was waiting for Frisch. When Frisch came along, Pepper dropped his water bomb right on Frank's head, then tore back down the stairs, threw himself into a big chair, crossed his legs, and opened the newspaper and looked as though he'd been sitting there all day.

Frisch came storming in, wringing wet. He ran up to Pepper and said, "Damn you, if I wasn't seeing you sitting there, I'd swear it was you that did it!"

Pepper brought his paper down, looked at him as innocent as a baby, and said, "Did what, Frank?"

Another time, we lost a doubleheader in the Polo Grounds. That's pretty rough going when you lose two. You don't hear a voice in the clubhouse, much less see anybody smile. So we trudged into the clubhouse, and it's like a tomb. Buzzy Wares, our first-base coach, goes to light up a cigar. Well, Pepper had switched matches on him, and the matches were loaded. Buzzy strikes a match, and it explodes. Buzzy exploded right along with it.

"Damn you guys!" he yells. "Lose a doubleheader and you're still pulling pranks."

He went and got another book of matches. But Pepper had loaded the cigar, too. Everybody's sitting there watching Buzzy light it. When twenty-five guys are sitting stone still, watching you light your cigar, you ought to suspect something. But I guess Buzzy was too mad to take notice. Boy, he took notice a second later. The damn thing blew up in his face, and he had tobacco in his eyes, his ears, his nose. Twenty-five guys turned around and looked into their lockers, their shoulders shaking. You wouldn't want to be caught laughing then, would you?

Pepper kept you loose, all right.

Joe Medwick was in his heyday when I joined the ball club. So was Johnny Mize, one of the greater left-hand hitters. He and Medwick were as good a pair of hitters as I've seen. Of course, after Joe took that beaning, he seemed to lose some of his edge. That was in 1940, at Ebbets Field, soon after he'd been traded over to the Dodgers. I've heard stories that there was some bad blood, that we were throwing at him, but I never believed it.

I was rooming with the fellow that hit him, Bob Bowman, and I didn't know of any reason for Bob to be throwing at him. Here's what I think happened. Charley Dressen was coaching third for Brooklyn, and he always tried to call the pitches. He was skilled at that, but sometimes he called them wrong. Bowman was wrapping his curveball, and then he wrapped a fastball the same way, and it faked Dressen. Medwick stepped right into it, thinking it was going to be the curve. I think that's what happened. And Joe got hit hard.

Bowman was upset about it, I know. He never showed up in the room that night. He was supposed to be in at twelve, and he didn't come in. I thought, gosh, maybe something's happened to him. I didn't want to call the manager, because there was the chance Bob might be out having a couple of drinks, and I didn't want to get him in dutch. So I called Pepper, and he told me that they'd sent Bowman on to Boston. They wanted to get him out of town because they were afraid some of those very rabid Dodger fans might try something the next day. But I wished somebody had told me about it.

We had some pretty good throwing contests with the Dodgers in '41 and '42. Guys like Whitlow Wyatt and Mort Cooper would come close to you when they wanted. Of course, we never threw to hit anybody, but we'd brush them back. We had some great battles with the Dodgers.

Somebody would start throwing close, or there would be some jockeying from the dugout, and that would start it off. Durocher was a great one for that. You could hear him in the dugout: "Stick it in his ear. Knock him down." Stuff like that. You never knew when he meant it. You take that kind of thing, some mean pitchers, a great rivalry, and put it in the middle of a tense pennant race, and you're going to have some fun out there.

I remember this one time Marty Marion was taking a throw at second and Medwick slid into him pretty high. I guess Marty didn't like spikes up in his face, so he just flipped Joe. The next thing you knew, the whole gang was out there. I was pitching that day. Dixie Walker ran right by me and made a diving tackle into Kurowski, and then Jimmy Brown and me went after Walker. Oh, it was a great one. Players rolling and scrambling and wrestling all over the grass. Nobody got hurt. Nobody ever gets hurt in those things. Safest place to be in a baseball fight is right in the middle of it.

Another time, in St. Louis, in 1942, I saw Stan Musial get mad. It was the only time I ever saw Musial really get mad. Les Webber was pitching for the Dodgers, and he threw four pitches behind Musial's head. That's the worst place to throw, because a guy's instinct is to jerk back from a close pitch.

Musial was steaming. The whole ball club was steaming. You just knew something was going to happen. Walker Cooper was the next hitter. He hit a ground ball, and when he went across first, he jarred Augie Galan. Augie was playing first that game. Mickey Owen was backing up the play, and he didn't like what Cooper had done. What does Mickey do but jump right up on Cooper's back. Mickey was a scrapper, but he wasn't too big, and Cooper was like an ox. I remember looking at that sight and thinking, *What in the world is he doing up on Cooper's back, how's he going to get off, and what's going to happen when he does get off?*

Well, Cooper, he was so strong, he just threw Mickey right over on the ground and held him there. Next thing you knew, we were all out there again.

I had particularly good luck against the Dodgers. One of the reasons, I think, was Durocher. He'd sit in that dugout and holler at me and get me mad. He thought he was going to upset me, but the madder I got, the better I could pitch.

I believe there was more pressure in '42 than in '41. We were 10½ games behind the Dodgers in August. Then we went on the road and won something like twenty-three out of twenty-six ball games. Finally we got within two games of the Dodgers and went into Ebbets Field. Mort Cooper pitched the opener, and he beat Whitlow Wyatt a close game. That put us just one back.

I was scheduled for the next day, but I'd been having a little trouble with my elbow. Billy Southworth came up to me in the clubhouse.

"Max," he said, "I believe I'll pitch Beazley today and let you rest that elbow."

"No, sir," I said. "I've beaten them four times already, and I think I can beat them once more."

He thought about it for a moment, then handed me the ball.

I beat Max Macon 2–1 that day. Kurowski hit a home run in the second inning with one on, and then they got one run in the second inning. And that was it.

I can tell you who was the last hitter I faced. Billy Herman. One of the best. I threw him a fastball, and he took it. Well, I knew Billy—when he takes a pitch, he's looking for something else. So I wasted my curve and threw him another fastball for a strike. He was a guess hitter, and I figured he was guessing on the curve. So I threw him another fastball, right down the middle, and he took it for strike three. And we were tied with the Dodgers for first place.

We went on from there to Boston. Naturally you're not supposed to look at the scoreboard, and naturally you do. We were behind late in the game, and when we saw the Dodgers had lost, we went and came up with a big inning and won the game. We took over first place, and from then on they never caught us.

We played the Yankees in the Series that year. The Yankees had been in a lot of World Series, and they were a little bit cocky, though any ball club that had won as many pennants as they had had a right to be. I think we were kind of nervous in the first game. They beat us 7–4, but something happened in that game that took away our nervousness and gave us confidence. We were behind 7–0 going into the last of the ninth. We scored four runs and had the tying run at the plate. Musial was the hitter, and he flied out to deep right.

Well, that rally made us feel better, even though we lost the game. It showed we could throw a scare into the Yankees. And then we did more than scare them. We beat them four straight. I think that was one of the biggest World Series upsets ever.

I'll tell you, beating the Yankees in '42 will always be the highlight for me, more so than winning in '44 against the Browns, even though I beat them in the sixth game for the championship.

I went into the service in 1945 and missed most of that year. I came back in '46. I reported to the club in St. Pete. I was rarin' to go, but I hadn't signed my contract yet, so they wouldn't let me work out. The reason I hadn't signed was that old bugaboo, money. I'd won seventeen in 1944, plus the big game in the Series. I was making $10,000 and was holding out for more.

Eddie Dyer was the manager then, and he was anxious for me to start working out. I was hanging around the clubhouse, waiting to get the thing settled. Eddie saw me there.

"Come into my office," he said.

I followed him into the office, and he closed the door.

"I'm going to call Mr. Breadon in St. Louis," he said.

"Think it'll do any good?" I asked.

"I don't know," he said. "We can try. You get on the other phone."

So I listened to the conversation.

"Mr. Breadon," Eddie said, "this boy is worth more money than what you've offered him."

"Do you think so?" Breadon asked.

"Yes, I do think so," Eddie said.

"Well," Breadon said, "I'll give him five hundred more. He can take it or go home."

So I had to take it. I wasn't satisfied, but I took it. I felt I'd been dealt with unfairly, but there wasn't much I could do about it.

When the season started, it seemed I couldn't do anything wrong. In the first month I had six starts, six complete games, six wins. I was pitching great ball, but I still wasn't entirely happy, because of the way I'd been treated by Breadon.

One night I was leaving the ballpark in Philadelphia, and a couple of guys approached me. One of them was Bernardo Pasquel. He was the brother of Jorge Pasquel, a multimillionaire Mexican who owned a league in Mexico.

They were offering a lot of money to big leaguers who were willing to jump. Some guys, like Mickey Owen and Sal Maglie, had already gone.

That first conversation didn't amount to much, but he said he would contact me in New York, which was our next stop. I didn't say much to him one way or the other at that time.

When we got into New York, I found out that Lou Klein, our second baseman, and Fred Martin, a pitcher, had already agreed to go to Mexico. They started talking to me about going with them. Then Pasquel contacted me, and we all met at the Roosevelt Hotel. I was a little hesitant; after all, it was quite a big move to be contemplating. But I'll tell you something. I'd had some trouble with my elbow the last few games. Nobody knew about it but me. I wasn't letting on to anybody, but I was getting concerned. I knew if that elbow went, I'd be in trouble. I'd be nowhere then. You know what a pitcher with a bad elbow is worth.

So I began to get receptive. Pasquel's first offer wasn't good enough, but finally he made me the right offer. I got a bonus of $25,000 to sign and $20,000 a year for five years. I couldn't turn it down. I said, shucks, I'll pitch the rest of my life for the Cardinals and come out with nothing. I think the highest-paid guy on the ball club at that time was $14,000, and I'm talking about a ball club that had won three out of the last four pennants and had a lot of top stars on it.

After the meeting I went back with Klein and Martin to the Hotel New Yorker, where the Cardinals were staying. After thinking it over, I let Pasquel know the next day. We didn't tell anybody, not the Cardinals, not anybody. We went to St. Louis and from there drove to Mexico City.

I thought I was making the right move at the time. Remember, I'd just received this shabby treatment from Breadon. In the long run, though, I think that whole business probably didn't help us as much as it did some of the rest of the players, because I do know the Cardinals started paying more money.

When I got down there, Jorge Pasquel told me just to run and work out for a couple of days to get used to the high altitude. But my third day there I got into a ball game. It was the damnedest thing. I was sitting on the bench, watching the game. In the ninth inning the other team got the bases loaded with nobody out. All of a sudden the game stops. I look around to see what's happening, and Jorge Pasquel is coming out of his box. He walks across the field and comes to our dugout and says to Mickey Owen, who was managing the team, "I want Max to go in." Mickey didn't say anything; he just looked over at me and shrugged, as if to say, "It's his money."

So they stopped the game long enough for me to warm up. And I went out there and threw nine pitches and struck the side out. Pasquel came into the clubhouse after the game and patted me on the back and said, "Max, I won this game, didn't I?"

Pasquel owned the whole league, you see. They said he was worth something like $70 million. He used to sit up in his box during the game and eat off silver trays.

Conditions down there weren't too good. Half the time you couldn't play, you were so sick. You know, problems with the water. Mexico City was the only place where you didn't have to boil the drinking water; they had artesian wells there. And I got to where I was eating out of cans most of the time; I was afraid to eat the food.

I couldn't believe there was that much difference between two countries that were so close together. The conditions in the smaller cities were terrible. Tampico. San Luis Potosí. Puebla. Gosh, that Tampico was hot. I'd be so tired after pitching a game there that I couldn't talk above a whisper. There was no air conditioning, for one thing. Didn't even have screens in the windows. They had these overhead fans with the big black blades that used to go around and around very slowly and not do a damn thing.

Sometimes we traveled by plane, sometimes by bus. Those bus rides through the mountains were hell. They'd drive on either side of the road, didn't make any difference. The one that had the loudest horn had the right-of-way, I'll tell you.

The whole thing didn't last very long. I stayed in Mexico about a year and a half. We found out later why the Pasquel brothers were after the big leaguers to come down there. At that time Alemán was running for president, and I think there was some family relationship between him and Jorge Pasquel. Now the people in Mexico loved baseball. It was worked out so Alemán got the credit for us coming down there. They figured he'd get some votes out of it. And he did get elected. So I think the whole thing was strictly a political deal. After the election Pasquel started cutting everybody. He cut me from $20,000 a year to $10,000. That's when we started jumping back to the States.

Of course, everybody who went to Mexico was suspended from the big leagues for five years. I thought that was a little stiff. Heck, we didn't go down there to hurt anybody. We just didn't think we were making enough money.

After I got back, this was in '48, I formed an All-Star team, and we went on the road and played about eighty ball games against college and semipro teams. We played all over, Kansas, Iowa, Nebraska, Wisconsin, Indiana, Louisiana. But do you know, we got to where we couldn't get a ball game. I'm not especially against Happy Chandler—I suppose he had his job to do—but he tried to stop us from playing. We knew we couldn't play in professional ball-parks against professional ballplayers, but he shouldn't have tried to stop us from playing against colleges and semipro clubs. But he did.

We were supposed to be suspended for five years, but in '48 we started a lawsuit against baseball, and that's how we got back. We had them by the tail then because the suspension was illegal.

I went up to Drummondville, Canada, in '49 and was playing ball there. Around the end of June I got a phone call from Fred Saigh, who now owned the Cardinals.

"You've been reinstated," he said. "You ready to come back?"

"Sure," I said. "If the price is right."

"Look," he said, "you did the club an injustice when you went to Mexico, and we can't give you any more money."

"You don't have any reason to say that," I told him, "because you didn't even own the ball club then. You can forget about it if you think I'm going to come back for the same amount of money I was getting before I left. I'm making more money here in Drummondville than you're offering me."

Eddie Dyer got on the phone then.

"Max," he said, "we sure would like to have you back. We think we can win the pennant, and the fellows would like to have you back."

"Eddie," I said, "if you were managing in the minor leagues, making more money than the major leagues offered, what would you do?"

"I'd probably stay where I was," he said.

"Well," I said, "those are exactly my circumstances right now."

Saigh called me back the next day.

"We'll double your salary," he said. "And we'll give you expense money if you can get to St. Louis by the Fourth of July."

Well, that sounded just great to me. As a matter of fact, I was there on the second of July.

I pitched for the Cardinals for a few more years and then in '52 was traded to the Giants. The next year I went back to St. Louis, but this time it was with the Browns. Bill Veeck owned the ball club, and what a great guy he was. Veeck was a generous and good-natured man and a real hell raiser when he wanted to be. Of course, we didn't have a very good ball club, but that didn't seem to dampen his spirits any. One time we'd lost eight straight, and he decided to give a party, to loosen us up.

This was in Cleveland, at the Aviation Room in the Carter Hotel. It was a pretty fancy place, decorated with a lot of airplane stuff, and had a big, glass-framed picture of Eddie Rickenbacker on the wall. Veeck told the whole ball club to be there, every man. He hired a piano player, and he had plenty of food and drink laid out. It was a great time; we were singing songs and laughing and telling stories. You'd have thought we had just won the World Series instead of riding an eight-game losing streak.

Around one o'clock in the morning a few of us started getting ready to leave. But Veeck got by the door and said, "Nobody can leave until I say they can leave." Then he started opening champagne and squirting it at everybody. Vic Wertz and myself, we caught him and poured a bottle of it right down his back. He was laughing so hard we could hardly hold him. Then there was one bottle of scotch left, and Veeck grabbed it and threw it at Eddie Rickenbacker's picture and smashed the glass frame into a thousand pieces.

It was a great party. Cost him $1,850, Veeck said. We went out the next day, nice and loose, and lost our ninth straight.

The land of baseball is one: a man may be lonely though in a crowd, but no one is alone at a ball game. In the poet's words, "That each of us was a player for a moment": this is the satisfying feeling of unity, of connection, that each of us craves.

ROLFE HUMPHRIES

Night Game

Only bores are bored,—wrote William Saroyan—
And I was a bore, and so I went to the ball game;
But there was a pest who insisted on going with me.
I thought I could shake him if I bought one ticket,
But he must have come in on a pass. I couldn't see him,
But I knew he was there, back of third, in the row behind me,
His knees in my back, and his breath coming over my shoulder,
The loud-mouthed fool, the sickly nervous ego,
Repeating his silly questions, like a child
Or a girl at the first game ever. *Shut up,* I told him,
For Christ's sweet sake, shut up, and watch the ball game.
He didn't want to, but finally subsided,
And my attention found an outward focus,
Visible, pure, objective, inning by inning,
A well-played game, with no particular features,—
Feldman pitched well, and Ott hit a couple of homers.

And after the ninth, with the crowd in the bleachers thinning,
And the lights in the grandstand dimming out behind us,
And a full moon hung before us, over the clubhouse,
I drifted out with the crowd across the diamond,
Over the infield brown and the smooth green outfield,

So wonderful underfoot, so right, so perfect,
That each of us was a player for a moment,
The men my age, and the soldiers and the sailors,
Their girls, and the running kids, and the plodding old men,
Taking it easy, the same unhurried tempo,
In the mellow light and air, in the mild cool weather,
Moving together, moving out together.
Oh, this is good, I felt, to be part of this movement,
This mood, this music, part of the human race,
Alike and different, after the game is over,
Streaming away to the exit, and underground.

Here is Bill James at his considerable best: asking the questions few have thought to ask and fewer still to pursue the answers. James does all the tedious spadework to get to the bottom of things, not just rearranging the terrain and shouting, "Eureka!"

BILL JAMES

A History of Platooning

Who invented platooning? Where does it come from? When did it become common? What was said about it when it began? Who was the first manager to platoon extensively?

One of the things I had wanted to do with this book was to answer those questions. Platooning existed prior to 1910 but was rare; by 1920 it was common. It is curious that baseball has, really, not even a myth to explain the origins of platooning; its beginnings are not shrouded in a haze but blanketed in utter darkness. This is atypical for baseball, for as historian David Voight has pointed out, baseball men love myths of creativity and have spun birth-in-a-thunderclap legends about the inception of almost everything connected with the game. Of platooning, though, one sees only an occasional suggestion that "some say it was John McGraw" who first realized that a left-handed batter might have an advantage against a right-handed pitcher, and vice versa.

It was not John McGraw who first realized this. For one thing, there is the matter of switch-hitting. The fact that one would switch-hit, bat right-handed against a left-hander and left-handed against a right-hander, implies clearly a recognition of the platoon advantage. The first man to switch-hit—and thus, in one sense, the inventor of platooning—was Bob "Death to Flying Things" Ferguson, whom we have encountered several times in the early history of the game. Ferguson played in the major leagues from the time they were organized (1871; he was twenty-six then and a well-known "amateur" player) until 1884;

he was switch-hitting before McGraw was born. Ferguson was more noted as a glove man and manager, but he did hit .351 in 1878.

His experiment with switch-hitting was not widely imitated at first, in part perhaps because nobody wanted to be like Bob Ferguson, but in the 1880s it became the fashion, and there were quite a number of switch-hitters. Will White, the bespectacled pitcher, was a switch-hitter (1877–86). The first outstanding switch-hitter was Tommy Tucker (1887–99), who won the American Association batting title in 1889 with a .372 mark. After him there were a bunch of them. There were at least four outstanding switch-hitters in the 1890s. John Montgmery Ward experimented with switch-hitting in 1888, plus, of course, you have the famous switch-pitcher, Tony Mullane. Actually, according to Al Kermisch, at least three right-handed pitchers of the 1880s pitched a few innings left-handed—Mullane, Larry Corcoran, and Icebox Chamberlain.

So the platoon advantage was something they were thinking about, but when did they start platooning? In *The Glory of Their Times*, Al Bridwell (a left-handed batter) was discussing the play on which Merkle failed to touch second in 1908:

> I stepped back into the box. Jack Pfiester was pitching for the Cubs, a left-hander. We didn't platoon in those days. The fact that Pfiester was a lefty and I was too didn't bother anybody. I was supposed to be able to hit left-handed pitching just as well as right-handed.

Let us use 1908, then, as the back boundary of platooning; it started sometime after then.

The boundary of platooning on the other end is 1920, when the strategy had its first big vogue. I have heard a number of baseball people say in the last few years that Casey Stengel was the first man to platoon extensively. This is completely false; Tris Speaker platooned at four positions in 1921, and platoon arrangements at two or three positions were quite common at that time. A few years later platooning fell out of favor and was not widely used for many years until Stengel revived it—but by no stretch of the imagination did he initiate it or even raise it to new levels.

If platooning was being done at three and four positions in 1920, then it must have begun sometime before 1920, but when? Jim Baker and I attempted to answer this question by "walking it backward," starting at 1920. Pardon me; I intend to describe that process here in some detail. In the 1920 World Series, both managers used platoon arrangements. In Game One, with Marquard (a left-hander) starting, Tris Speaker started Joe Evans in left field, George Burns at first base, and Smokey Joe Wood in right field, all right-handed batters; when a right-hander (Al Mamaux) relieved Rube, the left-handed hitting Charlie Jamieson pinch-hit for Evans, and left-handers Doc Johnston and Elmer Smith came into the game to play first base and right field. Speaker continued to make strict platoon moves with these six players throughout the series, in which Brooklyn split its innings almost equally between left-handed and right-handed pitchers. For his part, Brooklyn's Wilbert Robinson used the right-handed Bernie Neis in right field against the Duster Mails, the only left-hander to pitch for Cleveland, but Tommy Griffith (a left-handed hitter) against all the other pitchers.

What about 1919? In the 1919 World Series, Cincinnati's manager used Bill Rariden as catcher against Chicago's two left-handed pitchers (Williams and Kerr) but used Ivy Wingo against the right-handers. That's a platoon arrangement. For his part, Kid Gleason of the White Sox used Nemo Leibold in right field against Cincinnati's right-handers and Shano Collins against the left-handers.

In short, platooning is strong in 1919; it's easy to find. In the 1918 World Series—I'm using World Series because the box scores are available—the Cubs did not platoon themselves and started left-handers in all six games, so Boston didn't platoon, either. In the 1917 Series, the White Sox again used the Leibold/Collins platoon arrangement in right field—sort of. All five of Leibold's at bats in the Series did come against right-handed pitching, but Collins played all of the time against left-handers and half of the time against right-handers.

For his part, John McGraw did not have an option to platoon in that Series, and that could be significant. Chicago had basically a five-man pitching staff, with two right-handers and three left-handers, but the two right-handers (Faber and Cicotte) did all the pitching in the World Series. If you look at the Giants' lineup, it's basically a right-handed-hitting lineup—so that may imply that Pants Rowland, in 1917, was selecting his starters with recognition of the platoon advantage.

In 1916 Boston platooned Tilly Walker in center field with Chick Shorten. Brooklyn platooned Casey Stengel in right field with Jimmy Johnston. In 1915 Philadelphia (National League) used only one left-hander in the Series, Eppa Rixey, who was brought into the game in the third inning. When Rixey entered, the Red Sox made a response move, bringing Del Gainor off the bench to play first base instead of Hoblitzell. A trip to the microfilm room at the library to find some more box scores confirms that this was, indeed, a platoon arrangement. However, Philadelphia did not platoon; they used exactly the same lineup to face the left-handed Dutch Leonard in Game Three that they had used the first two games.

It's growing weaker; we're down to one team and one position here. The 1914 Series is the same cities—Philadelphia against Boston—but a switch of leagues. This is the Braves against the Athletics. Philadelphia started a right-hander in Game One and a left-hander in Game Two; Boston made two response moves, starting the right-handers Les Mann and Ted Cather in place of the left-handers Joe Connolly and Herbie Moran. In Games Three and Four, the A's went back to right-handers, and the Miracle Man, George Stallings, went back to Moran and Connolly. When a left-hander relieved in Game Four, Mann came back in, but Moran stayed in right field, as Stallings played to preserve the lead. Connie Mack did not platoon in the Series.

Two things about this, I would later decide, were significant. Number one, it was the first time that a manager had platooned at two positions in a World Series. And number two, it was the first time that a National League manager had platooned in the World Series—and quite possibly the first time that a National League manager had platooned, period.

Let's continue to walk it back. In the 1913 World Series (Connie Mack vs. John McGraw), neither team made any platoon changes, although both teams used both left-handed and right-handed pitching. In the 1912 World Series (Jake Stahl vs. John McGraw), neither team made any platoon changes. In the 1911 World Series (Mack vs. McGraw again), neither team made any platoon changes. Significantly, Connie Mack used a left-handed catcher and a right-handed catcher all year, but did not use them in a platoon arrangement, choosing instead to rotate them on some other basis. He started the left-handed Lapp against the left-handed Marquard in one game and the right-handed Thomas against the right-handed Mathewson in another.

Christy Mathewson put his name on a book written during that 1911 World Series, the book *Pitching in a Pinch*. On page 44 of that book, he says that Josh Devore "has improved greatly against all left-handers . . . so much so that McGraw leaves him in the game now when a southpaw pitches, instead of placing Beals Becker in left field as he used to." This would be evidence of early platooning on the part of John McGraw, except for one thing. Beals Becker was also a left-handed batter. In taking Devore out against a left-hander, McGraw was not platooning, but reacting to a weakness on the part of the player—a weakness that many other players must have had before 1910.

With platoon combinations in the World Series drying up, I started looking for evidence of platooning in the rest of the league. If a manager platoons at a position and sticks with it, this is fairly easy to recognize in the statistics; you'll have a left-handed batter with 60–80 percent of the at bats (50–70 percent in our own time), and a right-handed batter who plays the same position with 20–40 percent of a full season's at bats. The problem, of course, is that with platooning in an embryonic state, you're not going to get that kind of commitment to it; a manager might platoon a man in left field for a few weeks, then play him regularly for a month at third base to cover an injury, then bench him entirely, or any number of other options. You can recognize possible platoon combinations, but you have to get into the box scores to know for sure whether they were or were not.

Jim Baker and I spent a good many hours checking out those possible platoon combinations. We found no evidence that any National League manager was platooning prior to 1914. This certainly does not mean that there isn't, anywhere between 1876 and 1914, any platoon combination in that league; there may well be. We didn't find it. With platoon combinations stopping sharply before 1914, it seemed appropriate to look more closely at what happened that year.

The account of the 1914 World Series in the *Reach Guide* runs to many thousands of words but makes only two brief references to this matter. The first occurs in the discussion of Game Two, the second in the discussion of Game Four:

> In accordance with his season-long policy, Manager Stallings shifted his outfield to meet southpaw pitching, and Mann and Cathers acquitted themselves creditably. . . .
> When Pennock relieved Shawkey, Manager Stallings followed his season custom and substituted right-handed Mann for left-handed Connolly in the sixth inning but allowed Moran to remain in the game when his turn at bat arrived in the seventh inning.

Stallings's handling of his outfield that year deserves an essay in itself. He used eleven outfielders in 1914, several of them interesting people but none of them terrific ballplayers, giving each of those at least two weeks in the outfield to impress him. It is not strictly true that he alternated on a left/right basis all season; for one thing, the right-handed-hitting Mann had 389 at bats, and if you count the number of left-handed pitchers in the National League in 1914, you quickly realize that that ain't right. At one point in the season Boston went about three weeks without seeing a left-hander. But he did platoon when he saw a left-hander; one of the people he platooned with, incidentally, was Josh Devore.

Anyway, that is not this essay. For this essay, the key point is that Stallings was "The Miracle Man," the media hero of the 1914 season. As best you can tell, he deserved to be; what he did that season is like winning the pennant by coming up with a handful of Hurricane Hazles. His cleanup hitter for much of the season was Rabbit Maranville; Maranville led the team in RBIs, too. The *Reach Guide* gave him a two-page spread: Boston's Miracle Man. So what you have here is a manager who is (1) following a new and experimental policy, (2) having remarkable results, and (3) receiving extensive praise. Although no one that I can find cited his platooning as the key to his accomplishment, it is a fact that the popularity of the strategy grew rapidly, as we have seen, after 1914. For example, the other Boston manager, Bill Carrigan, who was not platooning in 1914, began platooning in 1915.

George Stallings was a smart man. He graduated from the Virginia Military Institute in 1886 at the age of seventeen; whether or not that is unusual I don't know. He then began to study medicine, but Harry Wright, then managing the Phillies, saw him catching a game and offered him a contract. He went to spring training with the Phillies in 1887, but Wright cut him. Ten years later, Stallings was managing the Phillies. He was the bright guy who buried the wire into the third-base coach's box.

But he did not, as best I can ascertain, invent platooning. He apparently imported it to the National League from the American. In 1911, Hughie Jennings, manager of Detroit, platooned in left field—not all year, but most of it—with Davy Jones and Delos Drake. Jones, also interviewed in *The Glory of*

Their Times, makes no reference to this. But it happened, and for a time I thought this would stand as the first identifiable case of platooning. Note the distinction; we are down now to trying to find the first, isolated instance of platooning.

I missed one for a while because I was looking for left/right combinations. But because we knew that Hughie Jennings was platooning in 1911, I thought I'd better look a little more carefully at his earlier teams, particularly his pennant-winning teams of 1907–09. In the 1909 World Series, I noticed that Boss Schmidt, a switch-hitter, did not play in one game, the one game that a left-hander had started. In the 1908 World Series, again, there was one game that Schmidt had not played and one game that a left-hander (Jack Pfiester, the man who just weeks earlier had surrendered the single to Al Bridwell, providing the back boundary for platooning) had started for the opposition. They were, again, the same game. In the 1907 Series there was, again, one game started by a lefty—and again, it was the one game in the series that Schmidt did not play.

The three Series games that Schmidt missed were started by Freddie Payne, Ira Thomas, and Oscar Stanage—all three of them right-handers. Though Schmidt was listed as a switch-hitter, he was, in effect, a left-handed platoon player. The microfilm quickly confirmed this.

Schmidt was, obviously, a left-handed hitter who couldn't hit left-handed pitching, and tried to switch-hit in desperation. But unlike McGraw, who replaced Devore with another left-hander, McGraw's old teammate Jennings had evolved a series of platoon combinations—Schmidt and Payne, then Schmidt and Thomas, then Schmidt and Stanage. It is interesting to note that Thomas, as a platoon player in 1908, hit .307. He was traded to Philadelphia after that season, and in Philadelphia, not platooning, he hit .223.

These were the only platoon combinations I found that Jennings was using; I never found any instances of his generalizing the principle and platooning at another position. In the time that he was using this arrangement in Detroit, one of his rivals was the New York Highlanders, who were lifted briefly out of the basement and into the pennant race during a period in which they were, quite by coincidence, I'm sure, managed by George Stallings. Stallings had a bad New York club in the pennant race in 1910, and it is during that period that I find the first instance of platooning on any team other than Detroit. The Miracle Man experimented for a time with platooning Charlie Hemphill and Bert Daniels in center field.

It seems, in short, to have been Stallings who first formulated the idea of platooning as a weapon rather than as a possible response to a player's weakness.

I wish that we could let it rest there, because that makes a creditable story. Hughie Jennings was a famous and successful (1) ballplayer and (2) manager. He was a lawyer, an educated man, but also a part of the Old Orioles with McGraw and Wee Willie, a running mate and later a coach of little Napoleon. That's a good story—the lawyer/manager thought up the idea of platooning sometime while he was playing, implemented it when he became a manager in 1907, and immediately won a pennant with it. This spread the idea at least as far as George Stallings, and Stallings's success attracted the attention of others, and platooning became popular. That makes perfect sense; if Hughie Jennings didn't invent platooning, he should have.

It makes sense, and it fits. If you were to draw a schematic of baseball history and you were to say, "Where *should* platooning begin?" you would come up with the answer that an American League team should have begun platooning at the catcher's position sometime about 1905.

Platooning should have begun at the catcher's spot, obviously, because that was the one spot at which few teams (very few teams) used regular players prior to 1920; almost every baseball team from 1876 to 1920 consists of a pitching staff, seven regulars and two or three catchers. (Sometimes the seven regulars change in a season, but rarely would any manager alternate.) Platooning should have begun about 1905 because (1) we know it was common by 1920 and (2) it would have been very difficult to platoon prior to 1900.

There are two reasons why it would have been difficult to platoon prior to 1900. Number one, the rosters were too small. The National League teams in the 1890s used a varying number of people, but seventeen is about the median, and with the game under severe economic pressure, the crunch was to reduce it even lower. When baseball became popular again after the turn of the century, the rosters swelled rapidly in size, reaching twenty-five by the end of the decade. That makes it a lot easier to platoon.

Number two, there weren't enough left-handers. Of the fifty-two National League pitchers listed in the 1900 *Spalding Guide* (1899 season), only nine were left-handed. My guess is that that ratio represented a big increase from the earlier part of the decade. Let me ask you: if you were playing with a sixteen-man roster, in a twelve-team league with only nine left-handed pitchers in it, do you think you would platoon?

Platooning should have started in the American League, because that's where the left-handers were. For some reason, or probably no reason, the American League from 1901 through 1915 had many more left-handed pitchers than the National; a spot check of 1905 shows that American League left-handers accounted for 316 decisions, 26 percent of the league total; National League left-handers accounted for only 178 decisions, 15 percent of the total. You can start considering platooning at 26 percent; it's very difficult to do at 15 percent.

It's a good story, and it fits, but it isn't exactly true. We had walked it back now to 1907, before the Bridwell line, and I was ready to declare that the start of it. But I felt compelled to check out the rest of Boss Schmidt's career, and guess what. Jennings did not invent a platoon arrangement. He inherited it.

Schmidt came to the majors in 1906. I had Jim check out a forty-eight game sample of the Tiger's schedule for 1906. Here's what he found:

Schmidt started:	19 games
Against left-handers	1
Against right-handers	18
John Warner started:	17 games
Against left-handers	5
Against right-handers	12
Freddie Payne started:	12 games
Against left-handers	10
Against right-handers	2

John Warner was a left-handed batter—and that's a platoon arrangement; the Tigers started the catcher who would give them the platoon edge (considering Schmidt a left-hander) in forty of the forty-eight games.

Well, what about 1905?

No major-league team was platooning in 1905, at any position. I state this with some confidence, as we made a real effort to nail it down.

What I did is, I developed the idea of a "platoon scan." To make a platoon scan, you divide a team's starts into games against right-handed starters and games against left-handed starters. Then you go through that team's box scores, game by game, and you count the number of left-handed batters (or right-handed batters) in the lineup. If they have three left-handed batters in the lineup against a right-handed pitcher, you write down a "3" under "Right." Boston's platoon scan for one twenty-two-game sample in 1905 looks like this:

	Right	Left
Boston	3322223333333	432222233

Using this method, if a team is platooning, it very quickly becomes obvious, even if there is some shifting around in the lineup that might tend to disguise it. Full-scale platooning would look like this:

	Right	Left
Boston	3322223333333	321111122

While the inconsistent, spotty platooning that you might otherwise miss would look something like this:

	Right	Left
Boston	3322223333333	312211231

If they're *really* platooning, the average of the "Right" column and the average of the "Left" column will differ by 1.00 (or 2.00 if platooning at two positions). But even if they're just kind of experimenting, a separation of .40 or .50 should appear quickly.

We took samples of at least fifty games for every American League team in 1905, and quite simply, there was no platooning in that league. We didn't do the platoon scans in the National League, but we did do a thorough job of checking out player usage patterns that could have resulted from platooning, and I am 99 percent certain that no National League team was platooning in 1905.

It makes a terrible story, you see. The first known platoon arrangement was operated by some guy named Bill Armour, who nobody knows anything about, who thought it up and implemented it in his fifth and final season as a major-league manager, had a poor year, and was fired?

I don't know that. I know this: no one was platooning in the major leagues in 1905, and Bill Armour was platooning in 1906. I still get the feeling, somehow, that somebody did platoon, sort of, sometime in the nineteenth century. It would have been awkward as hell, but they could have done it. I fully expect some other baseball researcher to take an interest in this subject and find an earlier platoon arrangement.

The other thing that we didn't find was the discussion of the issue. What I had expected to find, somewhere in this process of walking it backward—and what I still know must exist, somewhere—is a whole bunch of essays by journalists of the period discussing the issue, talking about who started it and what the idea is and who else is doing it and where's it all going to end. It's a funny business, doing this kind of research. One time Baker and I were talking about general managers over lunch, and we got to wondering who the first general manager was. We decided it was our job to find out that kind of stuff, so we got up and went back to the office and decided to dig into it. The first book I picked up was the 1928 *Reach Guide*, and I flipped to page 23, and it said, "William Evans, famous American League umpire, [was] chosen general manager of the [Cleveland] club. This is a new office in a ball club." So we found the answer to that question, I swear, inside of twenty seconds after specifically setting out to look for it.

Well, this time we weren't lucky. We never could find that article saying that "Alfred Smartguy has a new strategy this year of playing his left-handed hitters against right-handed pitchers." We could never find Fred Lieb telling us what he thought about the idea in the New York *Press*, with Grantland Rice answering the next day in the *Tribune* and Damon Runyon the third day in the *American*. Maybe that's why platooning has no myth of creativity, like everything else; it just sort of snuck up on everybody, and it was fifteen years old before anybody realized it was here to stay.

Well, let's go forward with it. Tris Speaker, like Jennings, inherited a platoon arrangement and improved upon it. In mid-season, 1919, he took over a Cleveland team that was platooning at two positions. He extended that arrangement to three positions in 1920 and occasionally to four positions in 1921, as discussed before, making him the first manager to use extensive platooning.

As platooning grew, John McGraw was never ahead of the pack at any time; he was not the first man to platoon or the first to platoon at two positions or three or four or anything. He was never the last one to adapt, either, but so

---

A CAPSULE HISTORY OF PLATOONING

(For those of you who are too "busy" to read the whole thing)

1871—First professional league opens with Bob Ferguson, the first switch-hitter.

1889—Tommy Tucker, first outstanding switch-hitter, wins American Association bat title at .372.

1906—First known platoon arrangement, involving Detroit catchers Boss Schmidt, John Warner, and Freddie Payne.

1914—First known National League platoon arrangement; first platooning at more than one position helps Boston win World Series title.

1920—First extensive platooning, by Tris Speaker in Cleveland.

1930—Platooning falls into disfavor.

1949—Platooning revived by Casey Stengel's success in New York.

1968—Earl Weaver hired by Baltimore, adds batter/pitcher record keeping and evolves personal style in platooning.

---

far as I can tell, he never used a strict platoon arrangement. He used more of a platoon recognition in alternating players.

As the American League had more left-handed pitching, platooning, as it developed, was always more of an American League thing. The American League champions platooned at at least one position every year between 1915 and 1925, with the possible exception of 1922. The major proponent of platooning in the National League in this period was Bill McKechnie, who had extremely good success with platoon combinations at Pittsburgh, including his 1925 combinations of George Grantham (.326) and Stuffy McInnis (.368) at first base and Earl Smith (.313) and Johnny Gooch (.298) behind the plate.

After about 1930, platooning fell into some disfavor. Even McKechnie, who had been so successful with it at Pittsburgh, abandoned the practice, though there were always a few who kept a candle burning for it. Casey Stengel, a player when platooning was in its heyday, was one of those—and if you look at his records as a player, it isn't hard to understand why. As a platoon player in 1922 and 1923, Stengel hit .368 and .339, the lower figure being fifty-five points above his career average.

Casey would eventually breathe new life into platooning. One reason for this was that he took some criticism for platooning through much of his career and he became defensive about it; he spoke about it as "my platooning," particularly after his platooning was vindicated in New York. For those of us in my generation, Stengel stands at the border of our memory, and only records exist before him. But through those records you can walk platooning backward a long, long way before 1949.

Pat Jordan was a pitching prodigy whose glorious big-league career seemed assured: he threw four consecutive no-hitters in Little League; he starred in high school; he was a bonus baby of the Milwaukee Braves in 1959; and then he was nothing. Of course, Jordan soon saw that life is more than baseball and became a fine writer. *A False Spring* is an anomaly in baseball writing: it is a book about failure and the self-knowledge that failure sometimes brings; and in that is its success.

PAT JORDAN

A False Spring

I see myself daily as I was then, framed in a photograph on the desk in my attic room. The picture was taken on June 27, 1959, at County Stadium in Milwaukee, Wisconsin, a few minutes before the Milwaukee Braves were to take the field against the Chicago Cubs, to whom they would lose that day 7–1.

I am standing midway between the first-base line and the home team's dugout. To my back I see the stadium's half-filled bleachers. I am wearing a Braves' uniform. Although the photograph is black and white, I see all the colors. My cap has a navy crown, a white M, and a red bill. My flannel uniform is the color of cream. It is trimmed—shirt and pants—with a half-inch-wide tricolored stripe of black-and-red-and-black satin. The word "Braves" is scripted in red and outlined in black at a slight upward angle across the front of the shirt. The script is underlined by a black-and-gold tomahawk. Below the tom-ahawk, in the left-hand corner of the shirt, is "24" in large block numerals, also red and outlined in black. Unseen in the photograph but clearly in my mind's eye is the small gold patch stitched onto the shirt-sleeve below my left shoulder. It is the face of an Indian of indeterminate tribe, the face contorted by a war cry no less menacing for being inaudible.

To my right is Whitlow Wyatt, the Braves' fifty-two-year-old pitching coach. Wyatt is smiling at me. My gaze, however, is directed to my left toward Warren Spahn, the Braves' great left-handed pitcher. Both Spahn and I are perspiring. We have just finished running wind sprints in the outfield and are apparently on the way to the clubhouse to change our shirts when we stop to pose for this photograph. . . . For whom? For some faceless fan leaning over the dugout roof, imploring, "Please!" whose good fortune it was to catch us in an obliging mood? So we stop, strike a pose, so casual, and wait for the camera's click. To pass this moment, as he has innumerable others like it, Spahn, hands on hips, turns to me with some bit of small talk, a phrase, meaningless, meant only to fill the instant. And I listen. Nonchalantly, hands on hips also, I listen to Spahn. To Spahnie. To Spahnie, who is talking to me, so much younger and yet with my amused smile looking so at ease—today amazed at how truly at ease I do appear, at how naturally I did fit, in that uniform, between those men, with Spahn, Spahnie and I, the best of friends, I, too, having done this small thing so often, having struck this obliging pose for so many fans, waiting only for the camera's click before tossing off a remark at which Spahnie and I would laugh on the way into the clubhouse to change our shirts.

I was eighteen years old that day, and the photograph had been arranged by the publicity department of the Milwaukee Braves, with whom I had just signed my first professional baseball contract. Of all the major-league uniforms I wore that summer—and I wore many—none was so gaudy and none so impressive as the uniform of the Braves. That was one reason I signed with them rather than with one of the other fifteen major-league teams that had also offered me a contract. There were other reasons. The Braves had agreed to pay for my college education, to pay me a salary of $500 per month during each baseball season, and to deposit in my savings account every June 27 for the next four years a certified check for $8,750. All told, my bonus amounted to more than $45,000, distributed over a four-year period. It was one of the largest bonuses— if not *the* largest—any young player received from the Braves in 1959. For my part, I promised to leave Milwaukee the following morning on a flight to McCook, Nebraska, where I would begin my professional career as a pitcher with the McCook Braves of the Class D Nebraska State League.

I pitched in the minor leagues for three years, at towns like McCook, Davenport, Waycross, Eau Claire, and Palatka, before I was given my unconditional release by those same Milwaukee Braves. I never did pitch a game in Milwaukee County Stadium, nor did I ever again speak to Warren Spahn. I did, however, keep the cash.

As I write this, confronted on my desk by that reminder of unfulfilled promise, thirteen years have elapsed since I posed with Warren Spahn and ten years since my last professional game. I was married the year I left baseball (the phrase I always use) and now have five children. I also returned to college and graduated in 1965 with a bachelor of arts degree in English. I taught English at a parochial all-girls high school for five years (the only male in a world of nuns and teenyboppers) and finally turned to writing. I have had little to do with baseball since my release by the Braves. Except for an abortive comeback attempt at twenty-two (at twenty-two?), I have not pitched a game.

That "comeback" was a disaster. It had been urged on me by my brother, George, a lawyer, thirteen years older than I, who had had so much to do with my career, with my having had a career, that he could never reconcile himself to my having lost it. Years after I left baseball, he still kept on the wall of his law office that photograph of me at County Stadium. It was a constant embarrassment to me. Yet he never tired of explaining to his clients who that young player next to Spahn was or what his promise had once been. I think he did this from a sense of loyalty to me, a brotherly duty not to abandon, and also because he remembered me only as I had been before that publicity shot. He never saw me pitch in the minor leagues, especially that last year, and so never saw the roots of my failure, a failure that has always bewildered him. George remembered me only as I had been in high school, when there was little I could not do on a pitcher's mound. Or in Little League, when my successes, which he shared, were close to total. In those days I often pitched to him on the sidewalk in front of our house. Our parents sat on the front porch and watched. They applauded my efforts. After a fastball that cracked in his catcher's mitt, my brother would yank his hand out of the glove and shake it fiercely as if to shake off the hot pain. And they would applaud. My brother, tall, gangling, wearing a white button-down shirt, the sleeves rolled up past his elbows, would grimace in both mock and very real pain as he shook his burning hand. How I responded to that gesture!

One day when George couldn't "work with me," as he used to call it, I badgered my father into catching me. I was eleven, I think, and already threw quite hard. My father, a lefty, had never been much of an athlete. He had been an orphan, and in his teens he turned to gambling for his satisfactions, and in later years for his livelihood. His interest in sports was less fervid than that of the rest of us. My mother was passionately devoted to Joe DiMaggio, and George and I were just as passionately devoted to my pitching, which we thought of even then as potentially a career. For my father, sports were never something to be played, but something to lay 9–5 on. He was in his early forties then, and although he'd ceased to gamble full-time, he was still a betting man. And occasionally he would deal cards in a late-night poker game. He was an excellent dealer and was paid handsomely for his efforts. It was in the hands, he said. His fingers were small and soft and plump; my mother said they were like the link sausages she threw in the spaghetti sauce. But how they flashed when dealing cards! He used only his left hand. His fingers were pressed together in the shape of a trowel. They supported the deck. He dealt with a flick of his wrist, his thumb shooting cards around the table with such speed and precision one listened for clicks.

My father began to catch me with reluctance. He had to wear the catcher's mitt—meant for one's left hand—on his right hand. His little finger fit into the glove's fat thumb, which stuck out ridiculously. He grumbled as I threw. His mind was on the card game at which he would deal later that evening at a local Italian athletic club. "Fellow athletes," my mother used to say, and we'd all laugh. All except my father. He took his sport seriously, too. To impress him, I cut loose with a fastball without telling him. Startled, he caught it on the middle finger of his left hand, the one without the glove. The finger split open, and blood spurted out, spotting his shirt and pants. For just a second he looked at his finger in disbelief. Then he ran bellowing into the house. I was too terrified to follow. When I finally did get up the courage to go inside, I found him sitting at the kitchen table, his hand wrapped in a blood-soaked handkerchief. He was trying to deal a poker hand to my white-faced mother. With a glance she warned me to silence. The cards slipped in his bleeding hand. They began to spill, slide down his wrist. He tried to pin them to his side with his elbow. They scattered across the floor. He glared at them. Cursed their ancestry. Snatched them up with his good hand and tried to deal again.

Years later we would laugh at that scene—my mother and I terrified, my father dealing, the cards spilling, curses and blood-stained kings. It became one of those anecdotes for which families invent a significance that eluded them but in retrospect grows to mythical proportions. The point became—my speed! I threw *that* hard! Hard enough, at eleven, to break a grown man's finger, pink and vulnerable as it might have been. It seems, even then, we were attuned to such small evidences of my destiny. My parents, brother, and I always had more than a premonition that my talent was something beyond the ordinary. It was a gift, we knew, and so it must be cultivated with the greatest care. For instance, my mother never asked me to do chores on a day I was to pitch, while my father spent all his spare money on the best equipment for me. (At eleven I had a $30 glove and $27 kangaroo-skin baseball spikes.) George, a struggling lawyer then, spent most of his lunch hours working out with me at the park near home. He would catch me for about twenty minutes, then make me run wind sprints from home plate to first base and back again. All the while I ran, he would remind me in long monologues just how badly I wanted a baseball career and how hard I must work at it. This way, the entire family shared in the development of my talent. From the very first I was aware that this talent I possessed must be treated with reverence, because it was only partly mine, and partly my family's. My talent united my family in a way we have never been since I lost it.

When I was twelve years old and in my final season of Little League baseball, my name appeared regularly in headlines in the sports section of the Bridgeport, Connecticut, *Post-Telegram*. The stories varied only slightly. Another no-hitter. More strikeouts. My third consecutive no-hitter. My fourth. And so it went. A season of six games in which I allowed two hits and struck out 110 of the 116 batters retired when I was on the mound. I had been almost perfect. Just two hits all year. And in my last two games every single out made was, in fact, a strikeout (thirty-six in a row, since Little League games last only six innings), with scarcely a walk, an error, or a foul ball in between. After the fourth consecutive no-hitter, my parents were called by a reporter for Ripley's *Believe It Or Not*. He wanted to verify certain facts. Possibly I would appear in one of their columns, he said. Where, I wondered? Alongside some Zulu tribesman who could fit an entire watermelon, lengthwise, in his mouth?

One night we received a call from Dick Young, the sportswriter for the New York *Daily News*. He interviewed my parents and me over the telephone. A few days later he wrote a column about me. In August the New York Yankees, with whom we were all enamored, invited my parents and me to appear on Mel Allen's television show prior to a Yankee–Red Sox doubleheader. We arrived at the Stadium properly awed—my mother wearing a corsage and my father and I dressed uncomfortably in suits and ties. We were treated royally. Pinstripes everywhere. Pictures of Ruth and Gehrig and DiMaggio. My mother swooned. Yankee executives hovered over me, smiling. "So this is our little pitcher? Does he want to be a Yankee when he grows up?"

Needless to say, I did not think of myself as "a little pitcher." Nor did I think I had to "grow up" before I could pitch for the New York Yankees. I was ready then, and to prove it I had brought my glove in a brown paper bag. I expected Mel Allen to turn to me in mid-interview and say, "Well, Pat, why don't you throw a few? Show the fans your stuff." And I would step on to the field and proceed to astonish all the viewers and fans, but most importantly, the Yankees, with my blazing fastball. What an embarrassment it would be for Vic Raschi! How he would envy me, throwing in my suit and tie with more speed than he ever dreamed of having!

We sat in box seats along the third-base line. Television cameras were aimed at us from the field. The signal was given. Mel Allen, turning to his right, asked my parents a question. His lips peeled apart like an open wound. My father fidgeted; my mother touched her corsage. One of them answered. More questions. Nervous smiles. Quick glances at the cameras and then back to Mel Allen. I sat at the end of the row, farthest away. I could barely hear. It did not matter. I just sat there waiting, my heart pounding, the brown bag at my feet. And when it was almost over and I knew it was too late for me to throw, Mel Allen leaned across my parents and asked me a question. I was so disheartened I couldn't answer. He repeated it. I mumbled something, and he returned to my parents. I sat there, glaring across the field at Vic Raschi, warming up with his pathetic fastball.

My brother remembered this. The no-hitters, the headlines, Dick Young, Mel Allen. He remembered it all so well that when I told him what I'd written about that day at Yankee Stadium, he said, "But you forgot Casey Stengel! Remember what he said when he found out about the strikeouts?" I didn't remember. "He said, 'I guess your fellas don't need no gloves when you pitch.' "

What I had been is still clear to my brother. It is a picture whose lines have been redrawn so often, retracing identical successes year after year, that it has become etched in his memory. He never saw those lines erased during my years in the minor leagues and then somehow redrawn, without his knowledge, until what they defined when I was released by the Braves in 1962 was something unrecognizable to him. That was why he urged me to make a comeback so soon after I had left baseball. He would not accept the fact that I had lost it all in only four years. It would take only a little practice, he said. We could work out on his lunch hour. He would have me throwing like my old self again. That was the phrase he used: throwing like my old self. Then, when I was ready, he would pick some Sunday afternoon and some team in the Senior City League and would inform the newspapers and the scouts he knew that I would pitch that day. And after the game, after I had struck out thirteen or fourteen batters, the scouts would be only too eager to sign me again. "Maybe even another bonus," my brother said, only half kidding. "But smaller, naturally."

The high school field where we threw was always deserted at noon. I would arrive first, to claim the field, then wait for George. I passed those agonizing minutes pacing from the pitcher's mound and back again, praying that no one else would show up, would intrude on this routine, our ritual, wishing my brother would hurry so we could get it over with and I could flee. He would then pull up in his new air-conditioned car. A successful lawyer now, approaching forty, with a touch of gray in his wiry hair, which he still wore in a crew cut. He had fleshed out a lot and was no longer gangling. Still, he was 6 feet 4 inches tall and very sturdy looking. Unbreakable is the word that perhaps best described him, still describes him. He played sports mechanically, as if by memory but not instinct. He moved stiffly, his back a poker that seemed incapable of bending. *He* seemed incapable of bending, of ever breaking— as I had in the minor leagues. (His argument for my attempting this comeback was brief: "You aren't going to quit, are you?") He wore dark-rimmed glasses and a snazzy bow tie. He would take off his jacket, some Scottish plaid from the racks of J. Press in New Haven, and fold it neatly over a bench. Then he would roll up the sleeves of his shirt. Very carefully, fold after even fold, past his elbows, that same white button-down shirt, the gesture suddenly calming me, reassuring me. Then we would begin throwing as we had so many times before.

But my comeback did not work out as my brother had planned. I have never again thrown like my old self. And on the day I finally took the mound in the same semipro league in which five years before I had struck out batters at will, I was unable to retire a single man. The fans loved it. They laughed and hooted each time my poor catcher (some high school boy I have never seen again) scrambled back to the screen to retrieve another of my wild pitches. I wore my Braves' uniform that day, a further affront to those fans, many of whom had seen me pitch before and who had been burdened too long with my past successes. I left the game in the first inning. So many runs were scored, so many batters walked or hit, so many wild pitches bounced in front of the plate or flung over my catcher's up-stabbing mitt, that I have retained only fragments from that day. Jagged little pieces . . . the shouts of "has-been," "washed-up," "always a bum." The look of pity on my catcher's face as he walked out to reassure me for the tenth time. A look he is not easy with at his age. And I, feeling bad for him, too. He senses that something is eluding him besides my fastballs. The fans *so* vicious at this meaningless game? It frightens him. This exorcising of private devils. He crouches for another pitch. I begin my windup, rear back, and catch him shooting a look over his shoulder at the fans. The ball rattles the home-plate screen. The runner on third trots home and with a little jump lands on the plate with both feet. I sigh, exhausted, feeling empty. Truly empty. Without insides. Filled only with air. Floating above things for a change. Not caring now. Untouchable. Not a bad feeling. Nice, really. New to me. At ease now, I wait for the ball. Look around. Catch sight of my brother. All else dissolves—fans, players, noise, heat, exhaustion, time—is gone. I see only him. Standing beneath a tree along the first-base line. Wearing dark glasses. Watching and not seeing. He clenches his fist, makes a short, pistonlike punch into an invisible gut. Mine! He still believes! Amazing! It doesn't matter if I don't believe. He does. In spite of me, it can still be done. Merely by an act of his will. Another punch. But the niceness remains. I shrug.

I think often about that day. And about the others, too, the good ones. Baseball was such an experience in my life that ten years later I have still not shaken it, will probably never shake it. I still think of myself not as a writer who once pitched but as a pitcher who happens to be writing just now. It's as if I decided at some point in my life, or possibly *it* was decided, that of all the things in my life only that one experience would most accurately define me. It hardly matters whether this is a fact or a private delusion. It matters only that I devoted so great a chunk of my life to baseball that I believe it's true. I believe that that experience affected the design of my life to a degree nothing else ever will. Yet it never seemed to end properly, neatly, all those bits and pieces finally forming some harmonious design. It just stopped, unfinished in my memory, fragmented, so many pieces missing. Over the years I have begun sorting and resorting those bits and pieces—delicately, at first—finding every now and then a new one to further flesh out that design, finally discovering the pieces had always been there and that what had been missing was in me. This book, then, is an attempt not to relive that experience but to resee it, once and for all, as it truly was, somehow frozen in time, unfragmented, waiting only for me to develop the perception needed to see it whole.

The bird dogs came first. They appeared one spring day in my sophomore year of high school, drawn by the odor of fresh talent and sweet young grass. I knew about bird dogs even then, at fifteen, and had been waiting impatiently for them to appear. It was a sign. On that day baseball ceased to be just a game for me; it also became my career.

They were called bird dogs because they sniffed out talent, although the name does not do justice to the men. They were kindly, stooped old men in plaid shirts and string ties. They had once owned taverns or hardware stores and in their youth had possibly played ball with Kiki Cuyler or Georgie Cutshaw. Now, retired, they measured out their weekday afternoons at a succession of high school baseball games. They were always easy to spot, even from the pitcher's mound, since few adults ever bothered to attend the meaningless games my coach let me pitch as a sophomore; and because they always stood behind the home-plate screen, as if they were ill at ease unless viewing life through a maze of wire triangles. Their job was to unearth talent for the major-league team with which they were affiliated. It was a loose affiliation, really. In most cases it consisted simply of their friendship with some organization's full-time scout. Most bird dogs never got paid a cent for their efforts, although occasionally one might be slipped $100 if his discovery reached the major leagues. But they were so old (in their seventies and eighties) and the gestation period of a professional ballplayer so long (often more than six years in the minor leagues) that few bird dogs lived long enough to see their judgments confirmed. That wasn't the reason they spent the time and effort, anyway. They did it to pass the time, for one thing, and because they loved the game. But most of all they did it because they appreciated talent. Just discovering it and watching it develop was satisfaction enough for these old men.

One day in my sophomore year at Fairfield Prep, a Jesuit-run high school in Fairfield, Connecticut, I struck out nineteen apprentice plumbers, bricklayers, and carpenters from nearby Bullard-Havens Technical High School. That night, Johnny Barron, an aged Cincinnati bird dog, telephoned our house. He spoke first with my father and then my mother, as if, like some Victorian suitor, he was seeking permission to court me—which, in a way, he was. Finally, I took the receiver with trembling hands. His voice surprised me. It was ragged and halting, yet somehow at ease, as if we were old friends. And in his mind we were old friends since he'd just seen me pitch.

Johnny did most of the talking that night. He took much for granted. He detailed my strengths and weaknesses (weaknesses?) with a familiarity that would have annoyed me were it not for the warmth in his voice. He said of my fastball, "And when you do make the big leagues, it'll be your fastball that takes you there. It's a beautiful fastball!" It was a strange word to use, I thought, one reserved for a painting or statue or some other work of art. He was a strange man, too. He took such delight in just talking to me that it embarrassed me, even though I'd been aware from the first that my talent, with which I was so familar as to be no longer awed by it (just as I was no longer awed by my ability to walk), was to others so extraordinary as to inspire a respect that approached adoration. Its presence could lead a dignified old man like Johnny Barron to lose his composure when merely talking to its possessor, a fifteen-year-old boy. However, the fact that this respect was for the talent, not its possessor, escaped me then.

Johnny concluded his talk a little breathlessly, saying, "I wish we could sign you now. But we can't until you graduate high school. By that time most of the other clubs will be bidding a lot of money for you. I'll be out of the picture then. Our scouts and front-office people will have taken over. But I hope you'll remember me, that I was the first to appreciate your gift. It will mean a lot to me." Although I was not sure what he wanted or why, I promised, and he hung up satisfied. I seldom pitched a game that year without spotting him behind the backstop. Often I would not feel comfortable on the mound until spotting him and would spend long moments rubbing up a baseball until I did. Strangely enough, I never talked to Johnny again, although he often spoke with my parents during the games I pitched. When I did sign a professional baseball contract in 1959, it was with the Braves, however, not the Reds. But I kept my promise and had the local newspaper insert a small paragraph near the bottom of the article that told of my signing. The paragraph mentioned how John Barron, Sr., of Haddon Street, Bridgeport, Connecticut, had been the first bird dog to notice me.

I pitched four one-hitters in my sophomore year of high school, and the following year my reputation as a major-league prospect was firmly established. The bird dogs, like Johnny, were gone by then. They had been replaced by full-time scouts who moved in quickly, like carpetbaggers, to take advantage of the friendships cultivated by the bird dogs. The scouts were younger men, in their fifties usually, and their appreciation of talent was more professional than aesthetic. They were not unkind men, although they were certainly not so lovable as the bird dogs. But maybe when I caught my first whiff of that bonus money I was not so lovable, either, and perhaps it was a good thing that bird dogs like Johnny Barron could not see me then.

When my brother, George, was twelve years old, my father took him along on a gambling foray into Canada. In Montreal my father won $10,000 in an all-night poker game. The game broke up after dawn, and my father went directly to a bank where he exchanged the large bills for singles, which he stuffed into an old valise. He returned to the hotel as my brother was waking. He made him sit up in bed and put his hands over his eyes. Then he emptied the contents of the valise over his head. The bills fluttered about my brother like falling leaves. They both began to laugh idiotically and to toss the bills into the air until the room was littered with them. For the rest of the day, while my father slept, my brother counted and stacked the bills. And he played with them daily over the next few weeks, although each day their number diminished until finally none were left. Then he and my father returned to Connecticut. If George and I inherited any legacy from our father, who in a lifetime of gambling let over a million dollars slip through his fingers, it was this ironic disregard for money. Money was never something one saved in our home (there were no piggy banks), nor was it something one learned the value of (no stern lectures on lost dimes). Nor was it an evil. It was simply something one needed a minimum of in order to live. Any amount beyond that should be acquired as effortlessly as possible and consumed just as effortlessly. My father was a master at both, although his mastery of the former was surpassed by the latter. My brother and I still cherish this legacy, however, and it has greatly affected our lives. Yet during 1958 and 1959 the anticipation of a large amount of money became our common obsession in a way it never has before or since.

It began during my junior year of high school. I had won twelve consecutive games over a two-year period and had averaged almost two strikeouts per inning. I'd been equally successful pitching in the Senior City League, a nearby semiprofessional circuit filled with ex-minor leaguers in their twenties and thirties. In my first appearance with them, at the age of fifteen, I pitched a one-hit shutout. But beyond such achievements and my obvious physical talent, I had the look of a finished pitcher. I was big for my age. At sixteen I stood six feet tall and weighed 175 pounds. My pitching delivery, so painstakingly cultivated by my brother, was smooth and natural and all of a piece, unlike other young pitchers whose deliveries are composed of distinct and conscious stages. My mannerisms on the mound were those of a professional. My brother had taught me how to shake off a catcher's sign with a flick of my glove; how to landscape the dirt on the mound with my spikes; how to hold a runner to first base with the barest of peeks over my left shoulder; and how to receive my catcher's return throw with such a disdainful snap of the glove that the batter could not help but feel my contempt for him. My brother and I left no detail unperfected. We discussed the proper way for a pitcher to wear his uniform, and we decided that a fastball pitcher, like myself, should let his pants' legs fall well below his knee before fastening them. Only infielders and pitchers without "stuff" wore their pants' legs fastened at the knees. "Besides," my brother said, "it'll make you look taller in the eyes of the scouts."

I'd been able to master these peripheral details because for ten years I'd done little else but pitch. I had never really liked the rest of the game, for it was filled with too much dead time. Only the pitcher, isolated on a small rise, seemed constantly in motion. He was the catalyst about whom the fans, the players, and the game itself revolved. I liked this feeling of power, of being the center of the action, of controlling things. When not pitching, I had no desire to play shortstop or left field or even take my turn at bat. I was solely a pitcher— and in my mind's eye I am still one today. I often go to the small park near home and, when the field is deserted, take the mound and begin to pitch baseballs into the screen behind home plate. It relaxes me. The pump, the kick, the follow through. No longer the center of the action, no longer controlling things, feeling often powerless, I take comfort only in the act as it has finally become for me, divorced from all externals. I am at home with it because it was the first thing in my life that I could do well and others couldn't. At eight, this discovery was my first hint that I was a distinct and separate entity with potentials and abilities entirely my own. I stood out, both in my own eyes and to those around me. Because I owed my first distinctness to this talent, I mistook it for the only distinctness I would ever have. I *was* my talent. Its loss would be a loss of self. So I played to it. I polished it at the expense of everything else. And I could do it so well, naturally, almost without effort, that it became increasingly easy for me to neglect any other potential whose luster would have demanded a strenuous effort.

But at sixteen I knew none of this. I knew only that I loved to pitch. And it was this strong affection for my talent as much as the talent itself that drew the dozen or so major-league scouts to each game I pitched as a high school junior. Unlike the bird dogs, who had appeared alone and inconspicuously, the full-time scouts entered the park in garrulous clusters. They carried aluminum deck chairs in one hand and fat little black notebooks in the other. They were always deeply tanned from their recent spring training with "the big club" in

Florida or Arizona, while we in New England were not even pink from our faint and fleeting spring sun. They dressed with the flamboyance of traveling men who seem always to be anticipating warmer climates. They wore bright Banlon jerseys and golf sweaters and gold slacks and black-and-white loafers with tiny tassels and, even on the most sunless of days, dark glasses. And yet, despite this flamboyance, their clothes were in a way quite nondescript, of indefinable origin, a wardrobe of brand names that could have been pieced together anywhere across the country. Those Haggar slacks might have been picked up in a Sears Roebuck in Stockton, California, on the hot, dusty day they saw that farm boy strike out seventeen, or at a J. C. Penney's in Fayetteville, North Carolina, on the muggy evening they watched that good Nigra boy hit four home runs. The scouts' origins were as indefinable as their clothes'. Those men had been worn thin by years of travel, then rewoven with remnants from all their stops so that even a native New Yorker might now chew tobacco and speak with faint threads of a southern drawl.

The scouts unfolded their deck chairs in the grass behind the home-plate screen and watched the game with what seemed to be barely passing interest. They talked mostly among themselves. Their conversation seldom touched on what was happening before their eyes. They paused only infrequently to pull out a stopwatch and time a runner to first base or maybe to ask a neighbor about that last putout, which they then recorded in the notebooks they had to turn in to the front office as proof they were doing their job. But these pauses were merely interruptions in their perpetual talk about good restaurants nearby where they would meet after this, their third game of the afternoon; or about too much bourbon consumed last night in a motel room in Naugatuck, Connecticut, and how they couldn't handle it like they used to, or women, either, for that matter, and they'd all laugh; or finally about that good Polack boy they'd given a $40,000 bonus a few years ago and was now hitting .227 in the Three I League but still was saving their hide with the front office by showing a little power, and thank God for small blessings. Their conversation touched rarely on the progress and doings of "the big club" for which they worked—that world, although in the same universe, was just too many light-years removed from their own, from this moment and the high school game they were only half watching. Inevitably, during the course of these games, their talk drifted to mutual friends in baseball, old friends who were doing well financially or physically, or maybe not so well, who were actually broke, or maybe sick, or dying even of the Big C, or worse than that, who were out of baseball. There was nothing worse than being out of baseball for men who'd spent their lives in it. It was like being out of the mainstream of all that really mattered in life, the good life. And it was so unnecessary, stupid even, to be out of baseball. There was always a place for those who kept their noses clean. "Don't ever make enemies," they were taught on becoming professionals. "You never know who you might be playing for someday." The scouts had listened and survived. They had played for fifteen years in the minor leagues and never moved higher than the Sally League. And when they got hurt one day and kept on playing for the good of the organization and in so doing had sacrificed their careers (a smart sacrifice really, for by then they had no careers), they were rewarded on their fortieth birthday with a job as manager of Mayfield, Texas, in the Kitty League. And at fifty, when they could no longer take the pressure of the six-hour bus rides from Mayfield to Corpus Christi, which had begun to get to their kidneys, they were rewarded further with a job of full-time scout for the Eastern Seaboard, or maybe the West Coast or the Southwest Territory. They breathed easily now, a little more easily, anyway. As long as they didn't do anything foolish, they would never be out of baseball. They would never have to join that "lunch-bucket brigade" that they feared and that they joked about as they watched from their deck chairs behind the home-plate screen.

But it wasn't all the good life for the scouts. There were hazards. And in those days before the advent of the free-agent draft, they could be treacherous.* It was easy for the bird dogs. They simply pointed to the talent. It was the scouts who had to then bring it down on the wing. They needed good reflexes and strong insides and a quick mind and plenty of endurance, even at their age. Without these qualities, too much talent might escape them, and they'd find themselves out of baseball, just as they might if they got trigger-happy and bagged too many $100,000 bonus babies who never made it past the Three I League. And always there was the competition squatting right there beside them, eating and drinking and laughing with them, but nevertheless scheming against them, just as they, too, were scheming. It was a risky business, and that's what appealed to them. It was exciting; it kept them young. To do it well they had to retain at least remnants of those physical attibutes that had meant so much to them in their playing days. They had been physical men in their youth, and their values and pleasures had remained physical beyond middle age. As long as they remained in baseball, no matter how peripherally, they would never completely lose that physicality, would never grow too old to

---

* The free-agent draft was initiated by the major leagues in 1965. Prior to it, all amateur players were free to sign with any club of their choice the moment their high school class was graduated. By the 1950s, when baseball, like most sports, had become a vastly more lucrative business than ever before (thanks primarily to television), major-league teams began offering large sums of money to untried youngsters in order to outbid their rivals for his services. The result was a bidding war that reached its peak when Rick Reichardt, a Madison, Wisconsin, teenager, was given a $175,000 bonus by the California Angels. The free-agent draft eliminated such excesses by eliminating the open market on players. It made all free agents susceptible to two major-league drafts, one held in June and the other in January. If a player was drafted by a club in one phase, he was unable to sign with any club but that one for six months. Then, if still unsigned, he was returned to the draft pool and could be drafted by a new club in the next phase. The process repeated itself until a player either signed with a club that drafted him; enrolled in a four-year college, in which case he could not be drafted until his class was graduated or he had turned twenty-one; or was no longer drafted. At no point, however, was a player free to bargain with or sign with any club other than the one that owned his current draft rights. Players could no longer auction themselves off to the highest bidder, so bonus demands plummeted. Now, in order to sign a draft choice, a major-league club had only to make its offer tempting enough to convince a player it would be foolish to waste six months hoping he might be drafted by a new club that would offer him more money. In fact, usually when a player was redrafted, he was offered less money than before.

function in the only way that had ever mattered. Even approaching sixty, it would still be possible for them to consume large quantities of bourbon or have an occasional woman in their motel room, while other men their age were going on errands for their wives or tending an orange tree in the backyard of their home in St. Petersburg, Florida.

But the competition *was* fierce. The scouts needed all the weapons they could carry. Money was the most powerful. If they were sufficiently impressed with a prospect, they simply offered him more money than anyone else. Few prospects could refuse. But such offers were rare and a little too risky for most scouts, who treated bonus money as if it were fished dollar by dollar from their own pockets. It was safer for them to equal a rival's offer and then bring up other weapons. A scout for the Yankees, for instance, might inform a prospect, some thickly muscled outfielder from Sioux City, that Mickey Mantle's legs were starting to go. The Yankees would need someone soon to carry on that pin-striped tradition of great outfielders that began with Babe Ruth and continued through DiMaggio and Mantle. If the prospect still wavered, the scout had only to point to those World Championship pennants flying above Yankee Stadium. There was a great deal of money to be made playing for the Yankees in New York, money that no ballplayer, no matter how talented, would ever see in Pittsburgh.

That may have been true once, a scout for the Milwaukee Braves might say to that same prospect, but don't forget, the Braves defeated the Yankees in the 1957 World Series and were forging a new and more powerful dynasty of their own. Ah, yes, a scout for the lowly Washington Senators might say, the Yankees and Braves are powerful teams. They have extensive farm systems loaded with much talent. The Senators, however, have finished in last place three years running, and their farm system is a mere skeleton of most clubs' and sorely lacking in talent. Of course, this means that a young prospect signing with the Senators would move rapidly through their system to the major leagues, whereas he might languish unnoticed in the more corpulent systems of the Yankees and Braves. That's all very nice, a scout for the recently transplanted Dodgers might respond, but what happens when a ball game is over? A ballplayer has to live in the city in which he plays. After a strenuous day at the ballpark he needs to fall back on a life-style conducive to relaxation. Such a life-style can be found only on the Coast. The West Coast. L.A. And that scout would spin tales of eager starlets and perpetual sunshine that few boys from Sioux City ever dreamed existed, except between the covers of *Playboy*, and which few could resist. But some did. And if a scout could not bring down a prospect with money or such arguments, he brought him down with the force of his own personality. Or what purported to be a personality. Most scouts had discovered early in their careers that they possessed certain attributes useful in capturing young talent. And so they traded on them, just as in their playing days they had traded on their hustle, which for a while had obscured their inability to hit. They traded so heavily on these attributes that eventually they became vivid parts of themselves, which, like their clothes, drew one's attention but revealed nothing of the man.

With each new success my junior year, the scouts lavished more and more attention on my parents, my brother, and myself until there was barely a moment when their presence was not felt. On a night before I was to pitch, for instance, a scout would telephone our home. Once he had identified himself as a scout, he would be turned over to my brother, to whom we had entrusted my career. (I was not allowed to talk to scouts.) While he gave directions to the ballpark or accepted or refused a dinner invitation, I would be upstairs sleeping, trying to sleep, anyway, actually just lying perfectly still, catching bits of the conversation below—the names of famous men like Paul Richards or George Weiss, who were making a special trip from New York or Baltimore to see me pitch.

In school the next day as I daydreamed through my classes, strange men in bright clothes wandered the corridors in search of my classroom or waited for me in the school parking lot when I went outside to eat lunch. Those same men reappeared later in the afternoon as I warmed up far down the left-field foul line. At first I could distinguish them only as middle-age men carrying deck chairs and black notebooks, but as the year progressed and I saw the same faces game after game, I began to distinguish one scout from another. I never really got to know them personally, except for one or two, and so I remember them only vaguely as possessors of a certain eccentricity. And yet, to this day, I *see* them quite clearly, as in snapshots that have been perfectly preserved. I retain a memory filled with such snapshots taken at various moments as I paused on the mound between pitches.

Has there ever been a more motley crew of ballplayers? Not even the Miami Amigos or Santo Domingo Azucareros (see Bill Colson's piece on the Inter-American League) had more "hope junkies." Steve Howe, Mike Norris, Ken Reitz, Derrel Thomas—why would these exiles from the Show play for peanuts in the Class A California League with a team that had no major-league affiliation? Easy: no one else would have them, and the dream of return still gripped them. Ex-dopers, head cases, rebels, but overridingly, ballplayers and human beings—presenting the 1986 San Diego Bees, in a fine portrait from *Rolling Stone*.

NEAL KARLEN

Bad-Nose Bees

The Rebel Cave

It's three in the morning in the subterranean cement training room below the San Jose Bees ballpark. The 10-by-20 windowless bunker is as musty and cluttered as Bruce Wayne's Bat Cave. Though the airless cell with the low ceiling is the size of a Bowery flop, the three professional athletes who actually live here call it the Stadium Hilton.

The Hilton sports no bathroom, so Ken Reitz is outside peeing in the dark beneath the grandstand. Down below, Mike "Stash" Bigusiak and Darryl Cias are half out of their uniforms, lounging on their greasy mattresses and trying to forget the last three days on the road. It's been a long night. Earlier in the evening the Bees were two-hit by the Fresno Giants, a collection of peach-faced, cocky teenagers wearing the sparkling uniforms of a bush-league team with major-league connections. After the game, the unshowered Bees were treated to a fifteen-minute dinner at a roadside Burger King. Then it was back on the bus for a rickety four-hour ride home, up California's desolate Central Valley and over the Pacheco Pass road, a suicide run to the South Bay.

Such is life for the lowliest team in the lowly California League. You ride a bus with a million miles under the hood, hang your one uniform on a locker-room hook, sleep in cheap motels, draw $11 a day meal money, and pay for whatever pleasure you can find on the road. Average California League salary: $750 a month.

It sure ain't the Show. That's what baseball players call the major leagues. When you're part of the Show's cast, you ride first-class on chartered airplanes, sleep in fancy big-city hotels, play ball in air-conditioned domed stadiums, and have your pick of some of the finest groupies in the country. Average Show salary: $431,521 a year.

Team captain and third baseman Ken Reitz, catcher Darryl Cias, and six other San Jose Bees have already played the Show, many in starring roles. But somewhere along the line, most were labeled—incurable drug addict, head case, or rebel—and banished, probably forever, from the major. They all want back.

But on this late San Jose night, the bunker beneath the third-base line will have to do. The denizens have redecorated the place: rug remnants lifted from the dumpster of nearby Carpet City, U.S.A. now line the bare cement floor. There's a refrigerator, a beer sign, and three broken bleacher seats for guests. Cias, a devoted painter who bears a striking resemblance to Jimmy Buffett, has recently finished a huge, madly grinning portrait of a green-faced Charles Manson on the inside door. "I am *not* a fan of the man," says the laid-back twenty-nine-year-old. "I painted Charles Manson as a conversation piece."

Cias's winding road through Organized Baseball began hours after his high-school prom. That was when the Oakland A's signed the promising catcher for $15,000. He made slow but steady progress through the minors, finally getting called up at the beginning of the 1983 season. He batted a solid .333 with the A's, then headed to South America, where he starred in winter ball. He thought he was a shoo-in to start for Oakland in 1984.

Over the winter, however, the team had hired a new general manager, Karl Kuehl. A strict disciplinarian who liked to lecture his troops on the psychology of victory, Kuehl apparently couldn't come to terms with Cias's Gomer Pyle attitude toward the diamond wars. "He was a real Nazi," remembers Cias. "He believed that you couldn't have fun and work at the same time. To me the game was always fun. I played because I loved the game."

After the first few games of spring training, Kuehl told Cias he was sending him back to the minors. Cias, convinced he could catch for someone else in the majors, asked for his outright release. The A's refused; Cias asked louder. The A's finally relented, and Cias suddenly found himself unemployable. "Anytime a new team wants to sign you," he explains, "they call your last team and ask why you were released. Now if the general manager is any kind of human being, he says, 'There just wasn't any room on the team.' But Kuehl said, 'Cias is a problem; he doesn't want to work.' That was a lie—Karl Kuehl is the only guy in my entire life I didn't get along with."

Kuehl, still with the A's, pish-poshes the notion that personality played any part in the decision to get rid of Cias. "We *like* people who have fun," he insists. "Darryl was a good guy to have on a ball club—he kept guys loose and had a positive attitude. It's unfortunate when you run into a numbers problem. With younger guys moving up, sometimes you just have to make room. No major-league ball club is going to let someone go who they feel can help them."

Kuehl professes disbelief when he learns Cias thinks he personally blackballed the catcher. "Oh my God, not at all!" he says. "You know, at one point a couple months after Darryl left, we had some injuries, and our manager wanted to have him back. We tried to reach him—and no one knew where to find him."

Meanwhile, Stash Bigusiak, who has been listening to Cias lament from his mattress, chuckles, shakes his head, and flips on the Hilton's battered black-and-white TV. Footage of bombed-out buildings from the U.S. raid on Libya flashes on the screen. "Shit," he says, shaking his head again. "And we think we've got problems."

Unlike Cias, Stash never even made it to the Show. Signed three months after his high school graduation for $25,000, he made good progress through the Los Angeles Dodgers organization. But in 1976, shortly after he was named minor-league player of the month for his work with the Clinton, Iowa, farm club, Stash's career screeched to a halt. He says his manager, Bob Hartsfield, called him a "dumb Polack." Stash then told the skipper he would deck him if he repeated the slur. The manager said it again. Moments later, says Stash, the manager was on the floor, and Stash was out of baseball. "I was a punk," says Stash. "That's one of the bad things about baseball—it takes young, immature kids and puts them in the limelight. And ten years later you end up like this." (Hartsfield, now a scout with the Houston Astros, says the incident never took place. "Forget it," he scoffs. "I never had any problems with Mike. He just couldn't throw the ball real hard. He couldn't get anybody out.")

Stash spent the next decade away from baseball. For the past two years he'd been working as a gumshoe for an Atlanta, Georgia, detective agency. But even while videotaping adulterous couples from behind motel hedges, he couldn't forget his aborted career. When his girlfriend, a producer for the Cable News Network, gave him his walking papers, he signed with the Bees and headed West. Though he now spends a lot of time trashing his ex-girlfriend's memory, he keeps two framed snapshots of her prominently displayed in the Hilton. "She'll be back," he says as he adjusts the TV's coat-hanger aerial, "just as soon as I hit the Show."

Ken Reitz has finished his predawn piss under the grandstand and returns to the Hilton wearing only his underwear, black-and-white checked tennis shoes, and sunglasses. Cias holds up a clipping he's been handed and laughs. "Hey, Reitzy," says the catcher, "we were just reading about you. In The New York TIMES!!" Reitz, thirty-five, yawns, pulls out a slimy mattress from the closet, and lies down. Cias reads aloud:

"Dateline St. Louis, April 23, 1979. 'The St. Louis Cardinals third baseman, Ken Reitz, said today that his temper had cost him $1,250. The penalty stemmed from an incident that occurred April 11 during a ten-hour rain delay at Lambert Airport here while the team was waiting to fly to Pittsburgh. Reitz said the amount represented damages he and two teammates caused to a Trans World Airlines waiting room, plus a fine of undisclosed amount. . . .'"

"We were sitting in this airport VIP lounge for *ten hours*," Reitz says. He laughs, takes off his shades, and settles back on the mattress. "Everybody was loaded—the players, the sportswriters, everybody. Keith Hernandez and I started to play football. I went out for a pass and crashed through a plate-glass partition. Then everybody went wild. I started throwing chairs, and some phones got ripped out of the wall."

"A twelve hundred and fifty dollar fine," marvels Cias.

Reitz folds his arms behind his head and stares at the concrete ceiling. "Twelve hundred and fifty dollars, shit," he says with a laugh. "I made *two million dollars* playing baseball, and I don't know where a *fucking cent* is." Cias stares dumbfounded and says, "Reitzy, you're laughing. How the hell can you laugh?" Stash barks, "What else is he supposed to do?" Reitz yawns, turns out the light, and giggles, "Yeah, what else am I supposed to do?" Cias returns the giggle. "Christ, Reitzy, you know I used to have a picture of you from the cover of the *Sporting News* on my wall?"

Reitzy is already asleep.

Most of the Bees dispersed that night as soon as the bus wheezed to a wee-hour halt in front of San Jose Municipal Stadium. Hank Wada—a Zen master, former star catcher with the Nishetetsu Lions, and the Bees' acupuncturist and pitching coach—mysteriously vaporized from the parking lot like Kane in *Kung Fu*. Meanwhile, the five Japanese youngsters on the squad headed home to their boardinghouse across the railroad tracks from the stadium. Outfielder Mickey Yamano probably had gotten the most out of the torturous trip back from Fresno. Before he boarded the bus, he had known only two American phrases: "thank you" and "hamburger." Now, after a midnight tutorial offered by team captain Reitzy, Mickey could hum "Jingle Bells" and say "cow," "six-pack," "Hulk Hogan," and "blow job."

A few Bees near the bus tried to round up a proper quorum for an after-hours booze jaunt. "Hey, Howser," one yelled to the most notorious Bee of all. "You want to go drinking?" But infamous wild man Steve Howe, the 1980 National League Rookie of the Year, passed. Someone told Howe what L.A. sportswriters—the very men who'd hounded him out of their town in 1985 after portraying him as John Belushi in a jockstrap—were calling his new team. "The Bad-*Nose* Bees?" laughed the rowdy, personable Howe. "I've got a *great* nose. The son of a bitch could suck an egg through a garden hose." But not tonight, not this year, no more.

Steve Howe is on a mission. And although he has not turned into a wimp—it was *his* idea to paint the team bus black with a huge logo reading EAT ME—Howe has informed everyone that he has taken a vow of sobriety worthy of a Hank Wada disciple. He, too, headed into the dark alone, back to the San Jose Hotel where he lives under an assumed name.

The Blackball

The Encyclopedia of Baseball gives no clue as to why so many ballplayers with big-league talent are spending their summers playing ball for the barrel-bottom Bees. The team's lineup of ex-big-league stars, each still in what should be his prime, is impressive: besides Reitz, Cias, and Howe, there is pitcher Mike Norris, thirty-one, who won twenty-two games and was runner-up for the Cy Young Award with the Oakland A's in 1980; and Daryl Sconiers, twenty-six, a power-hitting first baseman who was knighted by the California Angels as Rod Carew's heir apparent. Then there is Derrel Thomas, who in fifteen respectable years in the majors set the all-time record for most nicknames denoting a walking time bomb. Thomas's monikers include Hot Dog, Minute Man, Farmer John, and Junkyard Dog.

Somewhere along the line, each of these Bees blew a promising major-league career and was banished from the Show. For Howe, Norris, Thomas, and Reitz it was drugs. Reitz, a twelve-year major-league veteran who holds the single-season record for fewest errors committed by a third baseman, said he was so hooked on pills that by the time the Pittsburgh Pirates cut him, "I was functionally psychotic." Reitz's number came up on a Chicago expressway a few years back. Convinced a stranger was lurking in his backseat, Reitz pulled over, took out a shotgun, and blew his car to bits.

Substance abuse among baseball players is a tradition older than the seventh-inning stretch. Ever since the *Sporting News* reported in the 1880s that St. Louis Browns outfielder Curt Welch habitually hid cases of beer behind the billboards lining Sportsman's Park, it has been common knowledge that baseball players enjoyed getting high before, after, and sometimes *during* games. In 1903, a Cincinnati newspaper went so far as to publish the following advice to the city's constantly besotted Reds: "Whenever a ball looks like this—ooo—take a chance on the middle one."

Later, Babe Ruth, Mickey Mantle, and many of the innocently cast Brooklyn Dodger "Boys of Summer" did much of their best work either plastered or hung over. Pete Rose admitted he used to enjoy an occasional pregame upper; pitcher Dock Ellis even said he was tripping on acid when he threw a no-hitter for the Pittsburgh Pirates in 1970.

Still, the game retained its squeaky-clean image. For the public, baseball players were working-class heroes who, like most of their fans, were paid little money for a lot of work and who suffered at the hands of their employers. Sportswriters, paid as poorly as the players, served the players as friends and propagandists. Even well-paid superstars were treated with kid gloves, and their images remained as shiny and vacuous as a smile on a Wheaties box. Hence, Ty Cobb was not even fined when he was accused in the 1920s of fixing a game years earlier. Hence, when Babe Ruth allegedly came down with a vicious dose of the clap that caused him to miss part of the 1925 season, the press reported that the Bambino had simply eaten too many hot dogs and come down with "the bellyache heard around the world."

The first real dent in the public's one-dimensional perception of ballplayers came with the publication in 1970 of *Ball Four*, pitcher Jim Bouton's locker-room journal of life in the big leagues. Though the book seems quaint by today's tell-all standards, it created a scandal. Here, for the first time, were players as they really were—painfully human. They drank, they fought, and they whored.

The next blow came in 1976 when baseball's reserve clause was lifted and players were allowed to market themselves to the highest bidder. During the next ten years, fans watched as average salaries went up almost 900 percent and their favorite players heedlessly shuttled from team to team. At the same time, a new breed of sportswriter emerged. Unwilling to act as sycophants for the game, they increasingly portrayed both owners and players as they often were: greedy and stupid. In other words, as people.

In the past, the owners burnished the game's image by pridefully booting out chance screwups. Except, that is, when the jugheads turned out to be superstars who filled the owners' stadiums and bankbooks. No longer. With the public calling for the heads of its former heroes, not even stars like Mike Norris and Steve Howe could keep messing up. "Knowing what I know now," says Howe with a sigh, "I would never have come forward [with my addictions]. I would have kept my mouth shut and not said a word to anybody." Howe's statistics were great even when he was addicted—and he realizes that if he had not gone public with his problems, he would have saved a couple of the strikes that baseball allows its premier players.

The Rebel Leader

Last spring, thirty-year-old Harry Steve found himself in the role of president, general manager, and field boss of the sorry San Jose Bees. Harry, a slight, chain-smoking man in an almost constant state of agitation, had already been running the club for two years as a salaried employee. But when the team's owner, businessman Peter Kern, refused to raise his $1,000-a-month salary, Harry came up with an offer that even Kern couldn't turn down. Harry would run the team for free, keep any profits the never-before-profitable Bees made, and pay for any losses out of his own pocket. Kern agreed, and Harry got what he had always dreamed of, his own baseball team. Never mind the fact that he was broke and there was virtually no way the Bees could make any money.

Harry Steve's gamble was insane. Of the 150 teams that compose the country's eleven minor leagues, only three have no affiliation with a major-league organization and, as a result, get no free players or financial help. Without that big-league umbilical, an independent club is doomed to suck, both on the field and at the cash register. All the good young players are already owned by major-league teams with minor-league affiliates, and it's almost impossible to turn a profit solely on gate receipts.

As fate would have it, the team Harry got for free was one of those doomed independents. For the last three years, the San Jose Bees have finished last in the California League, averaging a dismal 752 fans a game. The Bees were so bad that no one ever complained when the San Jose *Mercury News* barely mentioned the team.

Harry's first move upon arriving in San Jose was to try and lure a major-league team to associate itself with his team. No one would touch the dreck franchise or the unorthodox general manager. The only deal Harry could strike was with the Seibu Lions of Japan's Pacific League. That's how he came by Hank Wada and his five samurai.

Finally, at the end of his wits and bankbook, Harry got an idea. Instead of making do with young, talentless minor-league castoffs, he would try using genuine major-league athletes branded as untouchables by the men who run the Show. He would hire every talented dope fiend or head case who had been thrown a blackball by the majors. He would pay them peanuts, win some games, draw some fans, and maybe make some money; in return, the pariahs would get another shot at showing the world they had learned their lesson. So Harry got out a phone book and tracked down the twenty-eight-year-old host of a radio show called "Steve Howe's Rock and Roll Revue" in Whitefish, Montana.

The Rebel Reliever

In 1980, Steve Howe brought his 95-mile-per-hour fastball to the Los Angeles Dodgers. In his first year, Howe became the ace of the Dodgers relief staff, winning seven games and saving seventeen more. He finished with a 2.65 earned run average and was named National League Rookie of the Year. In the next two years, he won or saved dozens, had a minuscule ERA, and was named to the National League All-Star Team. The Dodgers won the World Championship, and Howe won a World Series game.

Howe, drawing an $800,000-a-year salary, was quickly buttered up as the toast of baseball-crazed L.A., whose sycophants rate personal access to Dodger stars on a par with lunch at Spago with Quincy Jones. Steve Howe, a twenty-two-year-old son of an auto worker from Pontiac, Michigan, wandered unaware into the dangerous sludge of Hollywood hangers-on. To put it mildly, he began to party.

At the end of the 1982 season, he publicly announced he was a cocaine addict and checked into an Arizona clinic for five and a half weeks. He went in again the following May, at which time the Dodgers fined Howe one month's salary—$53,867. He briefly fell off the wagon in September and told management of his problem. They suspended him for the entire 1984 season. Manager Tommy Lasorda's advice to Howe: "You sleep with dogs, you're going to wake up with fleas."

"It was brutal in L.A.," he now says. "I found out one thing—the difference between real people and phony people. Everyone wanted something from me. I was fun at first—and then I got in trouble." After he came forward with his addiction, the local press began hounding him. "Baseball is a great part of my life, but it was tedious to go to the park. I reached the point where I didn't want to pick up the newspaper because I was afraid of what someone was writing about me."

Determined to get out of Los Angeles, Howe asked for his release and last year signed with the Minnesota Twins. Eager to please his new bosses, Howe rushed himself back from arm surgery. His fastball still hummed, but his elbow ached. Not wanting to let down his teammates, he took the pitching mound secretly stoned on painkillers. "Needless to say," says Howe, "I wasn't too effective. I was taking three hundred to eight hundred milligrams of Darvocet, and I never knew whether to throw a slider or go to sleep."

At the end of last season, Howe went back to Montana to prepare for the coming year. He fielded phone calls from several other major-league teams interested in his still-hopping fastball, and it looked as if the Twins might re-sign him. He headed down to spring training in Florida, confident that a number of teams would be bidding for his arm. But when he got there, no one would even let him throw batting practice. Word was out—newly installed, hard-guy commissioner Peter Ueberroth was not happy with Howe's past or the fact that his name had come up, along with those of several other major leaguers, at last year's heavily publicized trial of a Pittsburgh cocaine dealer. With Ueberroth frowning, no team dared touch Steve Howe. After it became obvious that no one was going to sign him, he went back to Montana and a part-time job as a DJ for a local radio station. And then Harry called. Howe doesn't mind that he isn't living the life of a Show star. "First-class is in the mind," he says. "If you're happy, you can have fun in the desert. And I'm finally happy."

The deal with the Bees was simple. Howe would get about $2,000 a month, a chance to play, and a constant supply of urinalysis bottles to fill. If and when Howe's contract was purchased by a major-league team, Harry would get al-most 50 percent of the buy-out action. In today's bull market for relief pitchers who can throw 95-mph fastballs, Harry could make a few hundred thousand dollars.

Steve Howe also brought Harry Steve's team much-needed publicity. As soon as word got out that he was negotiating with Howe, it seemed that every outcast ex-big leaguer in the country was calling San Jose. Harry is quick to point out that he wasn't on any moral crusade. "As long as they're ready to play," he said, "I don't care what they do. I'm not going to be a baby-sitter— these guys know this is their last chance around." The players didn't care that Harry was refusing the role of Mother Teresa. "Shit," says Reitz, "he was the only one in all of baseball willing to give me a fourth second chance."

While all the other teams in the league sported spiffy pro-model warm-up jerseys, Harry printed up T-shirts for his players that read THE BAD NEWS BEES. The team—which hadn't had new uniforms in several seasons—got freshly minted on-field apparel. "I bought them on credit," says Harry. "Buy now, worry later, I figured. The creditors will get their money; maybe not on time, but they'll get it."

Opening Day

The team was a mess. Harry couldn't afford to send the Bees to Arizona for spring training, and there was barely enough time to get the new guys fitted for uniforms, let alone *practice*. Then there was a slight problem with Derrel Thomas. Upon arriving in San Jose, Thomas decided that he, not Harry, should be the manager. Secretly gathering the players, Thomas outlined a bizarre plan for a dugout coup. The Bees said no; when Harry caught wind of the plot, he fired Thomas. The Junkyard Dog cleaned out his locker in five minutes and was last seen speeding his sports car up Highway 101.

And then there was the erratic behavior of Mike Norris. "When I was a kid," Norris told a reporter while he was still with the A's, "I used to scribble on pieces of paper that I was going to be the greatest pitcher ever." Five years ago, that seemed possible. But with the good life came the bad. Since his 1981 All-Star year, Norris has reportedly been in two drug-treatment centers and was recently placed in a two-year counseling program as a result of his 1985 arrest for possession of cocaine. Last winter, he spent four days in a Dominican Republic jail cell for allegedly carrying marijuana into the country. Even though the charges were later dropped, they didn't help Norris's growing reputation as a player who had blown his shot at greatness.

This spring, Roger Angell devoted his annual *New Yorker* baseball preview to the topic of drugs in baseball. The best baseball writer ever wrote:

> Anyone who has been involved with the sports world can easily bring to mind a particular athlete whose shining, wonderfully promising career was cut down by drug addiction. (For me, this will always be Mike Norris, the angular and elegant right-handed pitcher . . . with the A's. . . . I can still see the unique little flourish of his trailing leg as he finished his delivery, and his comical, hot-dog mannerisms on the mound, and recall the charm and intelligence of his interviews. . . .)

Norris arrived in camp with a permawear grin and a Willie Mays "sayhey-heyhey" for anyone in earshot. After casing out his new teammates, Norris opined, "I feel like I'm at an AA meeting," But he quickly announced that he would not be one to judge. "I'm in the Fun Hall of Fame"—he giggled—"and now I gotta start acting like a member of society, not like Jimi Hendrix." Unbothered by references to his several convictions for cocaine possession, Norris says he was so confident of his willpower that he recently tested himself with a visit to his favorite Oakland dealer. The dealer laid out ten grams of coke and invited Norris to sample. Instead of inhaling, Norris says, he blew the coke over the entire room. "I can still see the stuff floating through the air," he says with a laugh.

The reason he's with the San Jose Bees? "There's an unspoken law in the majors about not hiring me," Norris snaps. "There's got to be. I'm too good to be here. Except, I guess, that I fucked myself and *put* myself here." But he has no intention of showing up his fellow Bees. "I've got a Jaguar and a Mercedes sitting pretty in my garage. But I ain't going to be big-leaguing my teammates." There was another reason for Norris keeping his automobiles where they were— the California Department of Motor Vehicles had suspended his license.

Norris misses several practices his first week. His excuses include missed rides and command performances with the IRS and DMV. Harry is worried but not surprised. "I knew who Mike Norris was before I signed him. He is just someone who is very irresponsible in his personal life. But he is sincere, he means well, and he has a good heart." Does Norris plan to be around for the season opener? "Heyheyhey," says Norris, "I'll be there."

Opening Day finally arrives at San Jose Municipal Stadium; Steve Howe warms up on the sidelines. The stands are overflowing with 4,911 fans, lured by the appeal of Harry Steve's geek show. He has gone all out for the opener, investing $51 in rock tapes that boom over the stadium's scratchy public-address system. A local grocery clerk sings "The Star-Spangled Banner," and John Novak, an almost totally deaf, one-legged, seventy-one-year-old retired railroad baggage handler, throws out the first ball. ("They could have gotten a president," Novak told reporters, "but they chose me.") Finally, and to loud cheers, Steve Howe takes the mound.

Howe blows the first Salinas Spur away on three straight major-league strikes. Several beefy major-league scouts are in the stands, chomping cigars and taking careful notes. Howe goes on to toy with the Spurs for five innings, giving up only one hit and no walks. "Most of these guys have no idea what it means to be set up by a major-league pitcher," he later says gleefully. "They're just out there hacking."

The Bees lose their next two games at home and head to Fresno for the season's first road trip. "I'm not worried," says Harry, "because there's *no* way this team is not going to be in first place at the end of the season. We just haven't had any practice." Harry is exicted about Fresno; he has scheduled Norris to start and has told several scouts to show up—with their checkbooks.

The Bees' team bus pulls up in front of the Tropicana Inn, an ugly motel splayed on the ugliest concrete strip in Fresno, which was ranked two years ago as the worst American city in which to live. Across the street, loitering in the parking lot of a furniture-rental store, are four of what must surely be the fattest hookers in the Central Valley. "All the teams stay at the Tropicana," says Fern, who says her *real* job is working the legalized chicken ranches of Nevada. On most game days, however, she can be found right here, bird-dogging the Tropicana.

Norris is not on the bus ride from the motel to the Fresno stadium. He shows up minutes before game time in a dented green Buick, nicknamed Bess, owned and driven by his pal Ken Foster, a journeyman bush-league outfielder. "Hey-heyhey," yells Norris, several pairs of cleats slung over his shoulder. Norris explained later that Bess had stalled on the way to Fresno. "I was sitting out there with the cows, thinking, *They ain't never going to believe this one*. I thought I'd miss this game and Mike Norris's days with the Bees would be history." Harry decides to hold Norris out until the team gets back to San Jose.

The first game is a fiasco. Some 1,500 fans have shown up for the Fresno Giants' Opening Day; the rain starts twelve seconds after the national anthem. The showers intensify, the Bees and Giants boot half a dozen balls in the mud and the umpire doesn't stop the game. By the seventh inning the deluge has whittled the paid audience to 23, including 8 bare-chested drunks doing a mambo in the aisles. It starts to hail, and the leader of the pack wanders behind the backstop and quiets the stadium by waving his arms. "Hey, Howe," the young drunk screams toward the Bees' dugout 15 feet away, "you're a douche bag! A real douche bag! Yeah, a real fucking douche bag!" With that, he dumps a beer over his head. In the dugout, Howe and Harry listen impassively, both with cigarettes cupped in their hands. The Bees lose 6–4.

Back at the motel, Captain Reitz hosts a midnight party in his motel room. Nine players jam inside with cases of beer; Reitzy turns on the tube and blasts MTV. "Springsteen, you like Springsteen?" he asks the Japanese players. Three nod their heads, jump from the bed, and air-guitar an accompaniment to a blasting "Born in the U.S.A." Harry observes it all, silently sucking up ciggies. At two-thirty, the party breaks up.

The Bees lose the next night, getting only two hits and making six errors. After the game, the team moves right from the dugout to the waiting team bus that will take them back to San Jose. Everyone, that is, except Mike Norris and Ken Foster, who have sped off in Foster's green bomber. Five minutes later, the bus pulls up to a Burger King at the edge of Fresno. Across the street, in the parking lot of Rep's House of Ribs, are the four hookers from outside the Tropicana. "Come on," yells Fern from across the road, "we'll do you right here. Twenty-five bucks." Howe walks across the road, and the girls begin preening. When the pitcher comes within 10 feet, he makes a wide veer to the left. He trundles off into the dark, returning with a pack of cigarettes. "I'm amazed," says Harry Steve, "by how many women want to drop their drawers for Steve Howe. Just because he's Steve Howe!"

Munching fries, the team quietly reboards the bus for the midnight ride back to San Jose. The silence is shattered as soon as the bus hits the highway. Reitz, sipping from a flask of vodka, decides it's time to introduce the Japanese kids to the sing-along. As the bus careens through the pitch-dark flatlands, he leads the team in boisterous choruses of "New York, New York" and "We Are the World." The smiling Japanese join in, mouthing "heyheyhey" for lyrics.

Howe says this team has the best spirit of any he's ever been on. "You have to be close. This is our last chance," he says. Even Harry allows a tad of sentiment to creep in. "I never went into this as a moral thing," he says. "I did it to win ball games and make some money. But once I got to know these guys, I took a real personal interest. I'd like to see these guys beat the system and forget about their pasts and go on from here. This rebel image is great. Some of those major-league teams that were laughing when we signed Howe will begin standing in line when they see how he can still pitch. Now there's a part of me, the adventurous part, that says I never want a development deal."

An hour out of Fresno a burning car is spotted on the side of the road. It is green, a bomber, and empty. "Bess!" shout several players. A mile on, two black men in baseball uniforms are standing on the side of the road with their thumbs out. In this part of California it is not safe to be a black man hitchhiking on the highway at midnight. Even if they are carrying baseball bats.

The bus pulls over, and Howe runs out the door to welcome Norris and Foster with high fives. Norris, delighted, wanders back to the bus with a mock-arthritic Fred Sanford waddle. "I am *so* happy to see you guys," he yells. "I was about to call up a bitch and tell her to get her ass down to this fucking exit." Harry is silent, barely listening to explanations about the broken radiator that led to Bess's cremation.

In the back of the bus muted conversations are held regarding the fates of the team's stars. All agree, Ueberroth allowing, that Howe should be up in the majors within weeks—his fastball is popping, his head is centered. But no one is betting on Norris. "He's lost thirty pounds," ventures one. "His strength is all gone. He looks like Kunta Kinte."

As the bus throttles through the darkness, Jim Bolt, an innocent-looking first-year infielder, excitedly quizzes seatmate Daryl Sconiers. "So what's it like up in the Show?" he whispers. "I hear there are guys whose whole job is to keep track of your luggage." Sconiers, veteran of three full major-league seasons, nods. "Your luggage. Your plane ticket. Your check. All you have to do is play." The bus rumbles on, over the Pacheco Pass, home.

The Bad News Bees

Two nights later, Norris and Foster are two hours late to the San Jose ballfield. More car problems, they say. Harry shakes his head, looks in their eyes, and fires them both. All three chat for a few seconds, then shake hands. Norris and Foster clean out their lockers and hand back the last pro-baseball jerseys they will probably ever wear. Both know there are no more Harry Steves in Organized Baseball, but there are smiles on their faces as they head to the parking lot and Foster's new old car. At last sight, they were burning rubber toward Oakland.

"I knew this wasn't going to be some fantasy where this all worked out perfect," Harry later told reporters. Howe reflected pragmatically: "The public doesn't care if your car broke down. They just see you're late. I'm at the ballpark an hour before I'm supposed to be because of that. I'm not going to let anything get in the way of me getting back to the majors. Too much money to be made."

Finally playing together as a team, the Bees catch fire in the coming weeks. They win seven out of eight and pull from last place to within three games of the league lead. Howe is magnificent, clocking in with another win, some saves, a 1.97 ERA, and only three walks in thirty-two innings. More important, he passes four drug tests—three administered by Harry and one by the California League under the auspices of Peter Ueberroth's office. (That the league subjected Howe to a test is not unusual—under order from Ueberroth, all minor-league players are now subject to random urinalysis.) With Howe's fastball humming and his specimens clean, the cigar-chomping scouts in the stands are replaced by major-league executives with buffed nails. When it comes down to actually signing someone like Steve Howe, the big boys who sign the checks make the final call.

In mid-May, the Fresno Giants pull into town. Howe is scheduled to pitch the last game of the series. In attendance, he and Harry know, will be Al Rosen, president of the San Francisco Giants, and Pat Gillick, vice-president of the Toronto Blue Jays. Two hours before game time, John Johnson, president of the National Association, which governs minor-league baseball, calls Harry with news that he has been informed by Ueberroth's office that there is a "discrepancy" in a fifth drug test administered to Howe thirteen days before. Refusing to say exactly what that discrepancy is, the California League temporarily suspends its best pitcher.

Harry Steve is infuriated. "*Thirteen* days to get drug-test results?" he mutters. "Shit, I could test him myself in a day. There was a mistake." He ignores the suspension—something that is just not *done* in Organized Baseball—and goes with his scheduled pitcher. Howe throws five strong innings and is put on the ineligible list the next day by Johnson. "I know I'm going to get fined and suspended myself," says Harry, "but it just wasn't fair." A week later, California League president Joe Gagliardi announces Harry's penalty: a two-week suspension and a $500 fine.

Howe, banned from even suiting up, says, "It's like what was said in *North Dallas Forty*—we say it's a game, and the owners say it's a business. So we say it's a business, and they say it's a game. The owners' attitude is 'We say it, you believe it, or you're gone.' I'll be back. Count on it."

With Howe gone, the team sputters, falling back into last place. Harry, who has been keeping in touch with Norris, gives him a call and asks him to come back. He says he re-signed the erratic player "because we were into a losing streak and had some pitchers that weren't doing the job. I know he can pitch in our league. Hopefully he can win games for us."

Meanwhile, the residents of the Stadium Hilton ponder their future. Reitz, batting only .231 a month into the season, realizes he will probably never play back in the Show. But he has some other plans. He recalls his time in the drug hospital, after he got straight, when he stayed on as a counselor. Staying up all night with violent runaway teenagers tripping on angel dust, he got a new idea. "I realized how much I liked working with young people," he says. "It made me think I could be a good coach. But first I have to prove to people that I'm not insane."

Cias, batting a strong .306, spouts nothing but hope. "I have something to prove to myself," he says. "I can still play. I don't want to be one of those sour guys who quits and then years later tells everybody how he could have played major-league baseball." Cias is willing to bide his time; until he gets the call, he will busy himself airbrushing billboards out in the Bees' outfield. "You should see what I'm going to do to the TraveLodge sign," he says.

There is a void, however, down in the Stadium Hilton. A couple of weeks into the season Harry made a painful decision regarding Mike Bigusiak. "He stunk," says Harry. "He just plain stunk." So Stash is now gone for good from the Stadium Hilton, and he is sorely missed by his cave mates. Upon getting fired, he took away the few things he brought to San Jose—his cleats, his glove, and the two framed pictures of the woman who he was sure would be back "just as soon as I hit the Show."

Heading south on 101, Stash passed near Monterey, home of John Steinbeck's Cannery Row. Like the Stadium Hilton, like Harry Steve's gamble, like the unknown futures of Steve Howe, Derrel Thomas, and Mike Norris, Cannery Row, wrote Steinbeck, "is a poem, a stink, a grating noise, a quality of light, a tone, a habit, a nostalgia, a dream." Like those who tried one last time at San Jose Municipal Stadium, "its inhabitants are, as the man once said, 'whores, pimps, gamblers, and sons of bitches,' by which he meant Everybody."

Lake Wobegon, Minnesota (1418 alt., 942 pop.) sits plunk in the middle of the author's imagination and, by now, square in the heart of America. This excerpt is taken from *Lake Wobegon Days*.

GARRISON KEILLOR

Old Hard Hands

It took me a long time to learn to read. I was wrong about so many words. *Cat, can't. Tough, through, thought. Shinola.* It was like reading a cloud of mosquitoes. Donna, in the seat behind, whispered right answers to me, and I learned to be a good guesser, but I didn't read well until Mrs. Meiers took me in hand.

One winter day she took me aside after recess and said she'd like me to stay after school and read to her. "You have such a nice voice," she said, "and I don't get to hear you read in school as much as I'd like."

No one had told me before that I had a nice voice. She told me many times over the next few months what a *wonderful* voice I had as I sat in a chair by her desk reading to her as she marked work sheets. "The little duck was so happy. He ran to the barn and shouted. 'Come! Look! The ice is gone from the pond!' Finally it was spring."

"Oh, you read that so well. Read it again," she said. When Bill the janitor came in to mop, she said, "Listen to this. Doesn't this boy have a good voice?" He sat down, and I read to them both. "The little duck climbed to the top of the big rock and looked down at the clear blue water. 'Now I am going to fly,' he said to himself. He waggled his wings and counted to three. 'One, two, three.' And he jumped and—" I read in my clear blue voice. "I think you're right," Bill said. "I think he has a very good voice. I wouldn't mind sitting here all day and listening to him."

One word I liked was *popular*. It sounded good, it felt good to say, it made lights come on in my mouth. I drew a rebus: a bottle of Nu-Grape + U + a Lazy Ike. *Pop-u-lure*. It didn't occur in our reading book, where little children did the right thing, although their friends scoffed at them, and where despised animals wandered alone and redeemed themselves through pure goodness and eventually triumphed to become Top Dog, the Duck of Ducks, the Grand Turtlissimo, the Greatest Pig of Them All, which, though thrilling, didn't appeal to me so much as plain *popular*. "The popular boy came out the door, and everybody smiled and laughed. They were so glad to see him. They all crowded around him to see what he wanted to do."

Morning and afternoon, school recessed and we took to the playground; everyone burst out the door except me. Mrs. Meiers said, "Don't run! Walk!" I always walked. I was in no hurry, I knew what was out there. The girls played in front. Little girls played tag and stoopball, hopscotch, skipped rope; big girls sat under the pine tree and whispered. Some girls went to the swings. Boys went out back and played baseball, except for some odd boys who lay around in the shade and fooled with jackknives and talked dirty. I could go in the shade or stand by the backstop and wait to be chosen. Daryl and David always chose up sides and always chose the same people first, the popular ones. "Let somebody else be captain!" Jim said once. "How come you always get to choose?" They just smiled. They were captains; that was all there was to it. After the popular ones got picked, we stood in a bunch looking down at the dirt, waiting to see if our rating had changed. They took their sweet time choosing us; we had plenty of time to study our shoes. Mine were Keds, black, though white ones were more popular. Mother said black wouldn't show dirt. She didn't know how the wrong shoes could mark a person and raise questions in other people's minds. "Why do you wear black tennis shoes?" Daryl asked me once. He had me there. I didn't know. I guessed I was just that sort of person, whether I wanted to be or not. Maybe not showing dirt was not the real reason, the real reason was something else too terrible to know, which she would tell me someday. "I have something to tell you, son." She would say it. "No! No!" "Yes, I'm afraid it's true." "So that's why—" "Yes. I'm sorry I couldn't tell you before. I thought I should wait." "But can't I—" "No, I'm afraid not. We just have to make the best of it."

Nine boys to a side, four already chosen, ten positions left, and the captains look us over. They chose the popular ones fast ("Brian!" "Bill!" "Duke!" "John!" "Bob!" "Paul!" "Jim!" "Lance!"), and now the choice is hard, because we're all so much the same: *not so hot*—and then they are down to their last grudging choices, a slow kid for catcher and someone to stick out in right field where nobody hits it, except maybe two guys, and when they come to bat, the captain sends the poor right fielder to left, a long, ignominious walk. They choose the last ones two at a time, "You and you," because it makes no difference, and the remaining kids, the scrubs, the excess, they deal for as handicaps. ("If I take him, then you gotta take *him*.") Sometimes I go as high as sixth, usually lower. Just once I'd like Daryl to pick me first. "Him! I want him! The skinny kid with the glasses and the black shoes! You! Come on!" But I've never been chosen with any enthusiasm.

I think that if Wally ("Old Hard Hands") Bunsen were here, things would be different for me; he and I would be close friends. He was a true champion, a man among men, known for his kindness as well as athletic prowess. He saved a boy from drowning once, and another time he brought a crippled kid to the ball game to see him hit a double off Carl Hubbell. That was in the season he spent with the Chicago Cubs.

Born, Lake Wobegon, August 1, 1910. Died, Lake Wobegon, June 11, 1936. I know those dates by heart. The year 1933 he was with the Cubs and batted .348 from April to July and then came home. He died while batting for the Lake Wobegon Volunteers (who later became the Whippets), versus Albany, bottom of the seventh inning, with men on first and third (later known as "The Dead Man's Spread"). He batted left, threw right, was 6 feet 2 inches and weighed 181 pounds. His golden hair was parted down the middle, and he wore a gold ring on his right hand. The little finger of his right hand was cut off in a corn picker, 1931. The little white house next door to the Dieners' was his house; he slept on the back porch, even in winter, and his dog's name was Buddy. His parents' names were Clara and Oscar. He was smart as a whip, and if he hadn't played ball, he would have been an inventor. He made a gasoline-powered sled, an automatic apple corer, and an electric water fountain for his mom's rock garden.

Two pictures of him hang in the Sidetrack Tap: one in his Cubs uniform, his bat cocked, and the other with Jack Dempsey, who is kissing him on the cheek, a great tribute when you think about it. What sort of man would the Heavyweight Champion of the World kiss? A man's man, of course. I wasn't allowed in the Sidetrack as a boy, but I went in—just to have a look at the pictures, and they were permanently imprinted in my mind, and from his wonderful grin I began to imagine him as a personal friend.

Wally Krebsbach: "He had wings on his feet and a whip for an arm. He ran, he threw, he came to bat, and it was all play to him. He just laughed out there, it was so natural to him. A beautiful ballplayer. God gave him the talent, and he had no trouble with it. The outfield was his home, and any ball hit near him just naturally belonged in his hand. He came to bat and had no trouble in his mind; he was meant to hit."

His trouble with the Cubs lay in his glove. Growing up in Lake Wobegon, being poor, he learned to play without one, and by the time he could afford to have it, he was such an excellent bare-handed fielder he didn't bother with a glove. Thus the nickname "Old Hard Hands." His palms were like leather. In 1931, a Cubs scout went to look at a prospect in Duluth, and the hotel clerk said "Dobbins? Hell, you ought to see a guy in this little town near St. Cloud; he could put Dobbins in his back pocket." So the scout came to town, in his gabardine suit with a bottle of rye in his valise, and took one look at Wally shag flies and waved $500 in his face as if he were trying to wake him up. "One thing, kid, you gotta get a glove," he said. Wally was about to leave for spring training the next January, but his father got sick, so he stayed until he recovered, which wasn't until May, and the year after that he went to Florida and put on the uniform.

"Dear Folks," he wrote. "Arrived this morning and went straight to the park for practice. The grass is brown, and the ground is hard as cement, but guess it will do. Tried on so many gloves and none felt just right, so just picked the smallest one and hoped for the best. Ran for an hour and felt better, then lunch. Food here is all fried. Felt queasy after but swung the bat okay and then came back to the hotel, which is small but clean. The others went to a movie. Miss you all."

He begged the Cubs to let him play bare-handed, but they said it was against the rules. "You will get accustomed to it," they said. He was so good in every department, they figured it would be easy for him to learn this one little thing. A man who stood at the plate so relaxed and easy, then cocked his hip, lifted his foot, and the next you saw was him trotting slowly toward first—a man who if he did have to leg it cruised on the base paths so deceptively fast, the center fielder trotted in and picked up Wally's single and went to lob it to the cutoff man and saw Wally ambling into second—a man whose eye in the field was so keen, he was momentarily distracted by a pigeon gliding into the grandstand or a shooting star—a man whom people would have paid just to watch him throw a ball home, so hard it hummed, so true the catcher never moved his feet—surely a man so talented could learn to wear a glove on his left hand and catch with it.

"He could've, but his heart wasn't in it," says Wally Krebsbach. "It didn't feel right to him. It threw him off balance. It took the fun out of the game. He actually got headaches from it. And then he dropped a couple, and that made him ashamed, and then he came home. They offered him more money, but he just laughed. It wasn't worth it to him.

"If they'd let him play the way he wanted to, bare-handed, he would've been the greatest they ever saw, but they wouldn't, so he came home.

"He wasn't the same. He looked forty. His hand shook. Then he had a run of bad luck. His dad passed away. That was hard on him. And then his girl told him she didn't love him anymore—that took all the spirit out of him. Nobody could cheer him up after that. He told me—he said, 'Buddy, she says to me, she says, "My daddy says you're nothing but a ballplayer and you'll never hold down a regular job, but that doesn't matter to me. I could love you, anyway." She says, "It's your hands being so hard. I just can't get used to it." Can you believe that, Buddy?' he says. He couldn't believe it. He said, 'A man is *supposed* to have hard hands, ain't he? Who has soft hands? Nobody but fruitcakes and bank clerks.' He was broken up over her for weeks.

"And then he got the idea from the way people talked that he'd been a failure, that if he was any good he'd be in Chicago. And that just killed him. He knew it wasn't true; it was that they thought it that killed him. He knew how good he was; he didn't have to prove it by going someplace else. A man is just *good*; he can be good anywhere. This was his own family who looked down on him, though, so it tore him apart. Clarence's dad, that's Wally's brother, he gave him a hard time about quitting the team and embarrassing the family, as if he had any right to talk about it. Well, Wally didn't have a job; he was living off what he'd earned from the Cubs, and he was lying around in that sleeping porch, thinking too much, just living from Sunday to Sunday for the Volunteers games. One Saturday night he comes down here and asks for a drink. My old man was bartending; he says no. So Wally left. Where he found it I don't know, but he found enough to last him all night, because when he came to the game next day, he was suited up, and that was about all. He looked like death on toast.

"He never should have played. Dutch and me, we argued with Henneman to send him home, but there was naturally a big crowd to see him play, so play he did. I never saw a man sweat so much. His eyes bugged out. He flopped on the bench and almost passed out. Then he dropped one in the top of the seventh. It wasn't important, we were up by six runs, there were two outs, we said, 'Shake it off,' but it bothered him so that when he come up to bat, he was set to kill one. And instead it killed him.

"It was the bottom of the seventh, Roy on first and me on third, no outs, a count of two-and-two, and he stepped out of the box and looked down toward me, but he wasn't looking *at* me, because his eyes wouldn't focus. He was clearing his throat, and I thought he was choking, so I called time and ran in, but he wasn't choking; he was crying. He says, 'I'm no good.' I said, 'You're the best. You're the best there ever was.' And then I went back to the bag."

Wally stops. He can't finish the story. He shuts his eyes, and tears squeeze out from his eyelids and fall down his poor old face. Up and down the bar, old guys look away and touch their eyes. The alarm clock ticks by the cash register, and you can hear the electric clock hum in the Cold Spring beer sign. The big fan above the door hums. Everything else stops at the Sidetrack when he comes to the point in the story everybody has heard him tell so often.

The rest is: Wally Bunsen swung at the next pitch, an inside fastball across the letters, and fouled it off into his own head and fell across home plate and died. They said he never knew what hit him. Some of his family said that was what comforted them in this terrible tragedy, that he hadn't had to suffer, but of course he had suffered a great deal more than they knew.

When I thought of him, I imagined him as my best friend and him and me taking off to go fishing together. I even practiced what we would say. He'd say, "Nothing beats fishing." And I'd say, "*You're* not just talking."

Nearly seven decades later, the Black Sox Scandal retains its strong, strange hold on the imagination. Novelists have reveled in the ripe characters and mock-profound implications of the "fix." The sordid tale becomes baseball's equivalent of the Fall, with Shoeless Joe Jackson cast as the fig-leafed Adam, Arnold Rothstein as the serpent, and Chick Gandil as—think about it—Eve. Abe Attell might even be the worm in the apple; and Judge Landis, Moses the deliverer. . . . One could go on. But casting a cold eye on the actual events, Byzantine though they were, turns up no martyrs, no heroes: not Jackson, not Eddie Cicotte, not even Buck Weaver. He who would know the true story, or as near as we can get it, must put the novels aside and first read Lardner's *Remember the Black Sox?*, written in 1938. Here, the lowdown on the legendary 1919 World Series.

JOHN LARDNER

Remember the Black Sox?

The first of October 1919 was the Fourth of July all over again in Cincinnati. Most of the big stores were closed for the day. Flags draped the business section of town, and newsboys yelled themselves hoarse. Senator Warren Gamaliel Harding and party had the bridal suite at the Sinton Hotel. Barney Oldfield held court at the Gibson.

Tickets? You could still get a block of three for a hundred bucks from that operative over there in the corner of the lobby, if you liked to do business with Sitting Bull on a strictly Custer basis. The face value of a block was $16.50— first, second, and sixth games, Cincinnati at home.

Everybody who was anybody would be at the ball game that afternoon. Anybody who was everybody would do the best he could. They were setting up direct-wire connection, follow it play-by-play on the scoreboard, getcher official lineup here, getcher autograph picture of Eddie Roush!

Big-league baseball had boomed in its first season after the World War. Every year the magnates cleared their throats and said, "Baseball, the national pastime, has enjoyed a banner year," and this time, in the autumn of 1919, they never spoke a truer word. The fever was soaring. Lotteries or pools, selling tickets on total scores for the week, had done a million-dollar business from Oregon to Virginia since May. Batting averages were familiar to the country, and players heroic, as they never had been before.

And now, at the end of the bobtailed—140 games—but lively season, the fans were sitting down, unglutted, to a World Series that was a World Series.

Or, rather, to an exhibition of skill and science by the greatest ball club of all time, complete with human foils. For the White Sox, of Chicago, were like John L. Sullivan in the days when the Strong Boy toured the country offering $100 to the local volunteer who could go three rounds with him.

Cincinnati, the critics said, would last five rounds anyway—the series was five games out of nine. The Reds were simply the survivors of a National League dogfight. But the Sox . . .

Take the testimony of an expert witness, Edward Trowbridge Collins.

"They were the best," says Eddie, their captain and second baseman. "There never was a ball club like that one, in more ways than one. I hate to say it, but they were better than the Athletics I played with from 1910 through 1914.

"Offensively, from top to bottom, there wasn't a breather for an opposing pitcher in the lineup; and when it came to pitchers, Cicotte, Williams, Kerr, and Faber were tops as pitchers in the American League at the time—all on one club."

Shano Collins or Nemo Liebold in right field; your witness, Eddie Collins, the peer of Lejoie, Hornsby, and Gehringer, second base; Buck Weaver, natural ballplayer of natural ballplayers, third base; Shoeless Joe Jackson, forerunner of Ruth , left field; Hap Felsch, great thrower and dangerous hitter, center field; Chick Gandil, a slick genius, first base; Swede Risberg, sure-handed fielder and tidy batsman, shortstop; Ray Schalk, the fastest and smartest catcher of his generation, behind the plate; and Cicotte, Williams, Kerr.

The Reds were just a pretty good team, and their best friends did not claim more for them at the time. The Redlegs who survive today—Greasy Neale, for one, whose brain, working on the sideline of the Yale Bowl every fall, can be

heard to purr like a dynamo as far away as Bridgeport—will not contradict you when you classify them as the short-enders of the century. On paper, they were 5 to 1.

But October first brought high carnival to Cincinnati just the same. Thirty-one thousand squeezed into the grandstand and bleachers, and hundreds of thousands stood outside by the scoreboards.

This was the first postwar World Series, the crowning glory of baseball's renaissance, and it was Shineball Eddie Cicotte pitching for the White Sox—the greatest right-hander, next to Walter Johnson, in the game.

Cicotte's second pitch of the day hit the batter, Maurice Rath, Red second baseman, in the small of the back. It wasn't the first pitch, as generally believed. The first was a called strike.

In the last half of the fourth inning, Cicotte took the mound with the score 1–1 and looked nervously around at his fielders. Something about his manner had been puzzling the inmates of the press box from the start, from the time he hit Rath. Now they muttered, "What the hell?" Those men behind Eddie Cicotte could field their positions in their sleep.

Then boff! boff! boff! A run was in, and there were Reds on second and third. Dutch Ruether, Cincinnati pitcher, came to the plate. He whaled a terrific triple between Felsch and Jackson.

A few minutes later, five Red runs were in, and Cicotte was out. Kid Gleason, tough, gray little manager of the White Sox, was on the playing field, yanking his arms around, crazy with rage and grief.

The Reds won the ball game 9–1, as the Sox batsmen, each a sharpshooter, waved gently at Ruether's delivery.

Cincinnati went solidly nuts that night. But some of the folks from out of town—ballplayers who watched from the grandstand, certain Chicago baseball writers, and a small percentage of Chicago fans—were mumbling and shaking their heads. This wasn't any part of the ball club they'd been seeing.

Something Rotten in Denmark

Kid Gleason went into conference that night with his employer, the Old Roman, Charles A. Comiskey. And up in a double room at the Sinton Hotel, where the telephone rang every sixty seconds, a fellow called Bennett, from Des Moines, became very irritable.

"This thing is beginning to smell," he said to his roommate, a fellow from New York. "The dogs in the street know it."

If, by dogs in the street, Mr. Bennett meant smart gamblers, he was absolutely correct. But the country at large didn't know for another twelve months that the fix was in—the biggest, sloppiest, crudest fix of a sporting event that ever was known to man. It was a makeshift job; compounded in equal parts of bluff and welsh and cold gall, with no contributor or agent-contributor knowing what the man next to him was up to, and very seldom bothering to find out.

The series was fixed on the strength of a fake telegram, with the help of a pair of go-betweens who lost their shirts on it. Three quarters of the bounty money was withheld from the players who threw the series. Arnold Rothstein, widely accused of being the Judas-in-chief of the stratagem, could sit back and deny the charge blandly and securely, because, after coming up and telling him what they were going to do and insuring him a handsome betting profit, the fixers went through with the thing without him.

It was a haphazard business, all right, comical in some of its aspects, but it nearly wrecked baseball for all eternity. Those who followed its unraveling in 1920 remember that it touched off a rash of scandal rumors that spread across the face of the game like measles. A hundred players and half a dozen ball clubs were involved in stories of sister plots. Baseball was said to be crooked as sin from top to bottom.

And people didn't take their baseball lightly in those days. They threw themselves wholeheartedly into the game when the war ended, so much so that the sudden pull-up, the revelation of crookedness, was a real and ugly shock. It got under their skins. You heard of no lynchings, but Buck Herzog, the old Giant infielder, on an exhibition tour of the West in the late fall of 1920, was slashed with a knife by an unidentified fan who yelled: "That's for you, you crooked such-and-such!"

Buck's name had been mentioned by error in a newspaper rumor of a minor unpleasantness in New York that John J. McGraw had ironed out ruthlessly a few years before. Buck was innocent as a newborn pigeon, but rumors were rumors, and the national temper was high.

"Too high," says Mr. Herzog, looking back. "I never want to see the like again."

It's a fact that some of the White Sox, after the scandal hearings, were unwilling to leave the courtroom for fear of mobs.

Well, that was the business that nearly forestalled the careers of Joe Di-Maggio, Jerome H. Dean, Carl Hubbell, Lou Gehrig, Mickey Cochrane, William (Terrible) Terry, and Paul Waner. The public came within a whisker's width of never seeing another box score, never heckling another umpire, never warming another hot stove. It was close—too close for comfort. And though the baseball magnates of 1938 like to think of 1919 as a tightly sealed chapter, and though the Hall of Fame at Cooperstown is closed, actually if not officially, to Joe Jackson, Buck Weaver, and Eddie Cicotte—well, we're wallowing in baseball luxury now. We can afford to look back at the abyss after eighteen years of hard, steady climbing.

To a loosely knit group of technicians on the fringe of baseball, the news of the scandal, when it broke, was no complete surprise. It took the country by storm, but Jack Doyle remembers that there were rumors of something off-key several days before the series began, which means a full year before the story became public property.

"You couldn't miss it, if you were doing important betting," says Mr. Doyle, Broadway's price maker. "The thing had an odor. I saw smart guys take even money on the Sox who should have been asking five to one. Those Sox, may they rest in peace, should have been the shortest-priced favorites that ever started a World Series."

The series was scheduled to open on the first of October. On September twenty-ninth, in Boston, well-known professionals began to grab all the 4-to-1 money they could lay their hands on, and backed the price down to even money. Similar movements started simultaneously in Pittsburgh, New York, St. Louis, Des Moines, and Philadelphia. The Red wave seemed senseless, but Nat Evans and Nick the Greek were not senseless fellows when it came to laying their funds on the line. Nor were Rachel Brown and Sport Sullivan and Joe Gedeon.

The fix had been clumsy. It's small wonder that sharp-eared characters like Nicholas Dandolos were "wised up and kicking the market to hell," in the subsequent bitter words of Abe Attell. They were even wised up in Wall Street, where bets of $1,000 were placed on Cincinnati at even money.

The series began with Cicotte's strange defeat. It grew stranger. In the second game, Lefty Claude Williams—"the best pitcher in this league," said Gleason— yielded three walks and two hits in the fourth inning, for three runs. The Reds picked up another run in the sixth. The final score was 4–2.

In the Bag

"The game was given to Cincinnati on a platter," said Gleason. It was a thing any manager might say under the circumstances, and when Wee Dickie Kerr, former bantamweight prize-fighter, shut out the Reds in the third game, the fans of Chicago took heart. But the small-time professionals of the city were going around hotel lobbies with sheaves of folding money in their hands, offering 5 to 2 on Cincinnati, begging to be covered. The market was dead, for the moment.

Eddie Cicotte's second start, in the fourth game of the series, produced an eerie development. Cicotte, a good fielding pitcher, managed to turn in two errors before three men were out. For one, he made an atrociously bad throw to Chick Gandil on first. The other came after Pat Duncan, young Red out-fielder, had reached second. Larry Kopf singled into Joe Jackson's territory. Joe's great arm rifled the ball ahead of the runner, toward home. Cicotte made the technically proper play—when he saw that Duncan was not going to try to score, he intercepted the throw, apparently to make sure that Kopf would not try to take two bases while the ball was going all the way to the plate. But instead of completing the interception, Cicotte's gloved hand batted the ball to the grandstand. Duncan scored. Then Kopf did, too, on Greasy Neale's double off Cicotte. The Sox supporters were not alone in expressing their chagrin over Cicotte's performance when the Reds won, 2–0.

"In all his life he never pulled two like that before," said Gleason to reporters.

On October seventh, trailing by four games to one, the Sox rallied behind a failing Kerr and won the hard way, in the tenth inning, on hits by Weaver and Gandil. Cincinnati businessmen lost $60,000 in bets that day.

The Sox won again behind Cicotte, next afternoon.

And then, on October ninth, with Chicago fans yelling for a stretch finish, and the Reds seemingly on the run, the greatest ball team on earth collapsed like a parasol. The generous Williams gave up three runs before two were out in the first inning. In Chicago's half of the first in this game, with Liebold and Eddie Collins on base, and no one out, Weaver and Felsch went down in order, on two swinging strikeouts. And the mighty Jackson finished the inning by fouling out.

"If they'd shut their eyes, they couldn't 'a' done it," said Kid Gleason. The Kid seemed to have aged ten years in nine days. The furrows in his face were deeper, and his feet moved with a drag.

Rumors soared like kites in the breeze off Lake Michigan on October tenth, the day after the series ended. They were rumors strong enough to demand public attention. Charles A. Comiskey offered a reward of $20,000 for "a single clue" to evidence that his "boys" had been to the tank. No clues were forthcoming, and the rumors subsided. Chicago did not know that Commy was hiring private detectives to carry on the investigation undercover, or that the paychecks of eight White Sox players were held up—Jackson, Cicotte, Williams, Gandil, Felsch, Weaver, Risberg, and the utility infielder and pinch hitter, Fred McMullin.

Christy Mathewson spoke of the rumors at the time. He said it was ridiculous to question the honesty of the series. To be sure, Matty was a National League booster and the recently retired manager of the Cincinnati club (1918), and talk of a fix was hard for him to stomach.

The Hard Way to Deception

His arguments were irrefutable:

1. Too many players would have to be approached and bribed. One man can't throw a series.

2. A manager can't throw a series. The team will hustle in spite of him.

3. A pitcher can't do it. He would be yanked at the first sign of weakness.

4. You can't fix several players on one club and be sure your secret is safe.

5. No player would want to risk everything—his career, his future, his income—for a bundle of quick cash.

"And besides," said Matty, summing up, "it's just unthinkable, generally."

It was unthinkable, all right, and the way they worked it, it was grotesque. The dizziest wonder of all is that the whole house of marked cards did not topple about the ears of Sleepy Bill Burns and Billy Maharg and Abe Attell and Bennett, of Des Moines, and the boys on the field, long before Jake Daubert planted his shoe on first base for the final put-out of the series.

Before we examine the gamblers and their methods, though, let's have a look at the boys on the field. Unthinkable, said Matty. But this was a ball club unique in baseball history. Eddie Collins tells you it was the greatest club of all time and the greatest trouble club.

"That's what made its greatness so hard to understand," Eddie says. "As a rule, the chief requirement for a great team is harmony and cooperation on and off the field. That was an important thing about Connie Mack's teams. The White Sox? They were night and day to the Athletics. They seethed with discord and bitterness. Time after time they were close to open fighting with fists among themselves. And still they won going away."

It was a team of cliques, conspiracies, headaches, and fights. Collins and Chick Gandil, playing side by side in the infield, hadn't been on speaking terms since 1917, following a queer episode in which Gandil raised a pool among the players to reward the members of another club which had helped them win the pennant. Ray Schalk, the catcher, spoke to only three of the pitchers between games, Faber, Kerr, and Lowdermilk.

Gandil was known around the league as a gambler and a troublemaker. Cicotte used to say, "Chick was raised with low characters. He ain't got no ethics." Ethics or not, Chick had a strong influence over Cicotte and the happy-go-lucky Jackson.

Was the ball club underpaid? That's the excuse which many critics give for what happened in 1919. Commy was a powerful, upright man, a baseball pioneer, but his best friends could not call him a lavish spender—not with the hired help. The salaries of the "takers," or Black Sox, excepting McMullin, the utility man, ranged from $5,000 to $10,000. Jackson got a little more, $12,000. And they were the stars of the team—some of them the stars of all baseball.

This was before a fellow named Ruth revolutionized the game and nudged the wage scale upward with the blows of his mighty bat. Few ballplayers had five-figure incomes prior to 1920. But Commy's scale was lower than most, and his players were better than any. It's not hard to understand that the prospect of making the equivalent of a year's salary—"all in one whack, all green," as Jackson said—would dazzle the boys.

Throwing a ball game—"It's easy," said Cicotte later. "Gee, how easy! And you can make it look good." There was a lot of talk like that in the summer of 1919, among some of the players, especially in the later months, when it became obvious that the Sox were a shoo-in for the pennant. The talk was mostly in hotel rooms. One of the hotels was the Ansonia, in New York. They were talking there one day, Gandil and Cicotte, and a couple of outsiders were with them—a former ballplayer and a former fighter.

Sleepy Bill Burns had pitched here and there in both major leagues, with the White Sox and the Reds among other clubs. He moved from team to team, not sticking long with any. Bill had a habit of going to sleep on the bench, which won him his nickname. He was a guy who had been around. He admitted it.

Treason From Within

Billy Maharg, from Philadelphia, was an old-time lightweight who had fought some of the good ones, including Freddie Welsh.

Gandil and Cicotte and Burns and Maharg sat talking in the hotel room, with the door shut and the window open and a hot breeze and the smell of asphalt sifting in. Presently Burns and Maharg went away. A couple of days later, Sleepy Bill went out to the racetrack. They were running at Jamaica then.

"Where's Rothstein?" he asked of a fellow he knew.

"Over on the rail."

Bill went over. Arnold Rothstein, the "real-estate operator" and sportsman, a pale-faced pouter pigeon of a man, said, "Hello."

"The series can be fixed," said Bill. "It's ripe. But it'll take financing. They'd want a hundred grand."

Rothstein shook his head.

"They'll do business," urged Burns. "It's strictly an investment."

"No, not me," said Rothstein. "It's not the money. It's the details. It's too risky. It can't be done."

Burns took "no" for an answer. At least, he swears up and down that he did, and Rothstein's intimates of the time swear he did, and while one man's oath is another man's succotash, the thing is altogether logical. For Rothstein had his ear to the ground. He knew the mood and temper of some of the White Sox. One way or another, he thought, the fix would be in, and there was no sense in tying up money that could otherwise be bet.

This thought occurred later to other minds, to the mortification of the White Sox who threw the series. The bankrolling of the scheme—the payoff—was a department which gripped the interest of almost nobody.

Rothstein used to say, in the years that followed, that he never made a nickel betting on the series of 1919, but people close to him put the figure now at closer to $60,000.

It was Abe Attell who next tuned in on the eloquence of Sleepy Bill Burns. Bill was eloquent still, but a trifle discouraged, and even shocked, by the nearsighted reluctance of business leaders to invest in a sure-fire scheme. Bill was like Fulton, peddling his steamboat. It seemed to him sometimes that he had been born too soon. These were backward times.

But Abe Attell gave him hope. Abe was another fellow who had been around. One of the greatest small fighters of all time—former featherweight champion of the world, a miracle of speed, skill, and science—he had taken to living by his wits when he left the ring. Abe's wits were in first-class condition. "I think maybe Rothstein has changed his mind," he said.

That was good enough for Burns.

It was at the Sinton, a couple of days before the series began, and not until then, that Attell showed Burns, Maharg, and Gandil "proof" that Rothstein was financing the deal. The proof was a telegram signed with Rothstein's name.

It was all the proof that Gandil, now ringmaster of the players' side of the circus and chief go-between, ever saw. Would the boys be paid off? Chick didn't know, and he didn't much care. He had money. He was betting it.

An Open Secret

And so, it seemed to Attell and Bennett, was everybody else. Bennett, Des Moines gambler, was working with Abe, digging up money and getting it down at the best odds possible, but the best odds were none too good by the morning of October first. It was most annoying. Those thieves in Boston, New York, Pittsburgh, St. Louis, and elsewhere were butchering the price. Even dumb ballplayers around the leagues were on the line for Cincinnati and getting rich.

"Kind of an open secret, eh, pal?" said Mr. Attell.

"It smells," grumbled Mr. Bennett.

"Well, keep punching," said Abe. "Get it down."

The ballplayers, tipped off by Gandil that the promised fee was $100,000, to be paid in installments of $20,000 after each of the five losing games and split among them, were getting restless and uneasy in their hotel rooms and around the clubhouse. Cicotte's nerves were close to breaking.

"You can't bluff me," he told Burns, Maharg, and Gandil. "I got to have $10,000, and have it now."

He got it after the first game, which he lost. But he and the rest of the boys were drifting around in a heavy mist.

"We didn't know nothin'," says Joe Jackson. "Not a thing."

Burns and Maharg, calling at Attell's room on the morning of the second game, got $10,000 for Cicotte, and no more. Eddie said later that he found the money half hidden under his pillow—two or three $1,000 bills and several hundreds in the pile.

A total of $25,000 was paid up, divided among three players. The rest say they never touched a dime, and the facts seem to bear them out. The payoff department, as noted above, was not popular with any of the gamblers involved in the deal. It was office work, drudgery, giving no scope to the soaring qualities of the intellect.

And out on the ball field, the Sox went blindly through their paces. They were cutting their own throats on the strength of a fake telegram, and they were doing a thorough job. The fix of the series was a hit-or-miss business by the gamblers, who seemed to be making up the plot as they went along, but the players' work was well done.

Cicotte lobbed the ball to the plate "so you could read the trademark on it." Williams, "the best control pitcher in the league," gave out passes like a drunken press agent. Risberg's foot missed the bag by twelve inches on an easy double-play ball. Felsch played his position for Neale as though Greasy, a long hitter, were a crippled schoolgirl.

"It's too terrible to watch," shuddered Gleason, on the bench.

But the lighthearted Joe Jackson, now confused and shaken, could not pass up all that appetizing Cincinnati pitching. Joe was the leading batsman of the series, with .375. He hit the only home run. And when he walked to the plate, he carried his lucky hairpins with him. Hairpins were always lucky for Joe. He took them along up there even when he knew that Lady Luck had gone to Cain's Warehouse for the duration of the series.

Burns and Maharg were moaning in close harmony with the players. Thinking that the third game was also in the bag for Cincinnati, they had lost all their funds betting against Dickie Kerr. And they felt they had reason enough to do so.

"If we can't win for Cicotte and Williams," Gandil had said a few days before, "we're not gonna win for no busher."

The sixth game, won by Chicago the hard way, was a betting counterstroke. Cincinnati businessmen, supporting their home team heavily by now, were milked at odds which favored the Reds. On the last game, when the White Sox seemed to be coming back, a group of Texas oil men admitted later that they were taken for $82,000. Gambling experts all over the country were sitting in on the game by then, and business was good.

The series ended, and the boys went home to hunt, fish, and loaf—and to grumble and chew their nails, for there was trouble about the delivery of those series paychecks, and friends in Chicago wrote some of them that Commy's detectives were up to their noses in hot scents.

As the winter wore on, Gandil made a fuss—for publication—about his next season's salary, and dropped quietly from the club. When the scandal broke, the following September, Chick was in a hospital in Lufkin, Texas, having his appendix removed. He lost this spare part the same day, September twenty-eighth, that Eddie Cicotte lost his nerve and talked to the grand jury of Cook County.

The White Sox, racked by internecine strife, nobody talking to anybody, were still a good enough ball club at the time to be fighting with Cleveland for the pennant—one game behind, three games to go. Comiskey, with his world breaking about him, sent seven copies of one telegram to seven men:

> You and each of you are hereby notified of your indefinite suspension as a member of the Chicago American League baseball club.
>
> Your suspension is brought about by information which has just come to me directly involving each of you in the baseball scandal now being investigated by the present Grand Jury of Cook County resulting from the world series of 1919.
>
> If you are innocent of all wrongdoing, you and each of you will be reinstated; if you are guilty, you will be retired from organized baseball for the rest of your lives if I can accomplish it.
>
> Until there is a finality to this investigation, it is due the public that I take this action, even though it cost Chicago the pennant.

Actually, the information had not "just come" to Commy. It was all in his hands when the scandal suddenly went off in scattered pops, like a string of firecrackers. The grand jury had subpoenaed Bill Burns, Abe Attell, Arnold Rothstein, and others on September twenty-fourth. Billy Maharg had told his side of the case to Jimmy Isaminger, Philadelphia's alert baseball writer, and the story was circulated nationally. There was nothing for Commy to do but break up his ball club, and, in fairness to him, it should be said that he did a thorough and relentless job of it. Offers from Colonel Jake Ruppert and other club owners of "your choice of players" were rejected with thanks. Cleveland clinched the pennant.

Shoeless Joe's Exit Line

In a queer set of semiformal talks with the grand jury, Cicotte, Jackson, Williams, and Felsch told their stories. The shock hit the baseball public between the eyes, but the hearing fathered two phrases which promptly became paid-up members of the American language. There is nothing bogus about the origin of these phrases; just a little juggling. Three local writers and a news-service man were on hand when a kid stepped out of a group of kids and said to Jackson, just leaving the confessional:

"It ain't true, is it, Joe?"

"Yes, boys, I'm afraid it is," said Shoeless Joseph.

The authenticity of this incident seems pretty well established by the fact that four different men mentioned it in four different stories within three hours of the time that Jackson left the hearing. The capsule, cross-section version of the kid's remark was, "Say it ain't true, Joe," and if he didn't actually put it that way, he leaves himself open to a charge of untidy rhetoric.

As for Cicotte, Eddie "did it for the wife and kiddies" three times in the presence of the court stenographer, who took his words down in shorthand.

The grand jury and prosecuting staff of Cook County were seriously seeking indictments for conspiracy against the eight Sox. The magnates weren't. Not when they thought it over. They would handle this thing in their own way. They did.

There is a Napoleonic bee in the bonnet of nearly every baseball magnate, owing, probably, to the fact that he has the power of buy-and-sell over his employees; the power—it has been called unconstitutional—of auctioneering in terms of men, of blacklisting and suspending without hearing, of writing and signing contracts which guarantee the rights of the owner, but not the chattel.

It would prick the vanity of many a club owner today to see his affairs—baseball affairs—settled in a court of law. Commy and his colleagues wanted to keep this thing in the lodge. They had their own way of dealing with it—more effective and ruthless, when you consider the facts, than any judgment a criminal court could pass.

The trial of the eight Sox, in July and August 1921, was a little on the hollow side. The signed confessions taken by the grand jury the year before had "disappeared"—certain of the magnates advancing the theory, which would have been funnier in dialect, that Rothstein had made a secret trip to Chicago and bribed an aide of the district attorney's to burn them.

These confessions were the backbone of the case for conspiracy, although Sleepy Bill Burns testified for twelve hours, and went to sleep in the box before he had finished. The night of the acquittal, the Sox held a celebration party at an Italian restaurant near the Loop. The jurors held a celebration party in the same restaurant the same night. There was no prearrangement about this joint revel, and though their private rooms adjoined, the two parties kept sternly to themselves.

Then the magnates went to work. Kid Gleason had taken the stand in defense of his players in the "kangaroo" court, but when the state acquitted them the Kid turned cold as steel. He had little vitality left in his small, tough body after 1910, but all there was of it he directed against the men who had sold him out. He never spoke to one of them again.

The retrial of the Black Sox by baseball's own tribunal was a star-chamber affair. The decision was foregone, and the action swift. The eight men—Gandil, Cicotte, Jackson, Felsch, Weaver, Risberg, Williams, and McMullin—were barred from the game for life. This meant organized baseball, which meant everything but the frayed fringes of the professional game—semipro ball, sandlot ball, twilight-league ball. Within a few months, most of the outlaws were skimming those fringes for what they could find.

Where Are They Now?

The boys, all of them, pleaded their innocence for years afterward, to anyone who would listen. Eddie Cicotte came back from the semipro honky-tonk to Detroit, to argue his case on street corners. Joe Jackson buttonholed patrons in his barbecue hutch in South Carolina. Hap Felsch harangued the customers at his Milwaukee beer parlor.

It's obvious today that some of them, fix or no fix, were never paid money to throw a game. That all of them are serving life sentences without trial. That, with one or two exceptions, none of them belongs in the same league with Arnold, Tarquin, Cesare Borgia, or Guy Fawkes.

Where are they now? Shoeless Joe keeps his clippings and talks his baseball in his West Greenville, South Carolina, liquor store. Joe is a hero among the textile workers of the community. He says he gets more fan mail now than when he was in the big leagues. The scandal drove him from baseball before he piled up much money at it. But the publicity the scandal gave him has enabled him to parlay a successful barbecue stand into a prospering liquor store. He manages a successful semipro team.

Cicotte went into the automobile industry in Detroit and stayed there. He is a paymaster.

Up till recently, Gandil was playing Sunday ball in Shreveport and minding his own business.

Happy Felsch has been selling bottled conviviality across the bar in Milwaukee for fifteen years. Hap steadfastly refused to handle the hard stuff, though, until repeal.

Buck Weaver's home address is Chicago, and he dabbles in softball, and spends his winters on the Coast, where major-league scouts still take his tips occasionally on promising ballplayers. Some years ago, 10,000 Chicagoans signed a petition for Buck's reinstatement. No answer.

Horsehide Exile

Risberg, now a San Franciscan and a part-time fruit picker in Southern California, plays semipro games now and then. Williams, a Missourian born, was last heard of in Springfield, where he tried his hand at a softball league. The mysterious Fred McMullin used to live in Pasadena—no forwarding address.

If they never did anything else, the outlawed Sox—black or white, take your pick—were responsible for the presence of that snow-haloed, hawk-faced gentleman who hangs over the edge of his field box at the World Series, chewing the brim of his hat. Judge Kenesaw Mountain Landis once fined the Standard Oil Company $29,000,000, a tidy assessment. When the scandals broke in 1920, there was a cry for a high commissioner to replace the three-man commission at the head of baseball, and the judge was elected, and if you hear eight strong voices joined some evening in the strains of We Made Him What He is Today, those are the outlaws serenading Judge Landis.

There's another matter which calls the Sox of 1919 to mind these days. Up in Cooperstown, New York, where Abner Doubleday experimented with balls and bats some nine-and-ninety years ago, there is a Hall of Fame.

The names of great ballplayers have been or will be inscribed there—Ruth, Cobb, Wagner, Johnson, Mathewson, Speaker, Young, Lajoie, and Alexander. Which of the Black Sox, on playing merit alone, deserve mention in the same breath? Well, Jackson, Weaver, and Cicotte, by general agreement among the people, especially the ballplayers, who saw them in action. There is no ruling which says that the baseball writers cannot vote the Sox to the Hall, if they feel in their hearts that they belong there. There never will be a ruling until some outlaw collects enough votes to qualify him for the holy tablets, and the magnates hope very earnestly that no such emergency will arise.

The Spalding Guide, the voice of the magnate, said editorially in 1921:

> The gambler has done his worst again. He is the respecter of no game. He would as quickly buy the youth in the lot as the professional in the arena, if he could. He has tried both. He will try again. The honest ballplayer need have no fear of any gambler. There are thousands and thousands of honest ballplayers. There is another small group—they were ballplayers once—to be immured in the Chamber of Oblivion. There let them rest.

That seems to be official.

The lot of the official scorer is not a happy one. If he has any sense of personal integrity, he will call 'em as he sees 'em. If he has any sense of self-preservation and job security, he will, now and then, tilt the table homeward—preserving no-hitters, boosting the averages of batting-title contenders, sustaining errorless streaks. But controversies and scandals of a historic magnitude are few: the six bunt "hits" allowed Nap Lajoie on the final day of the 1911 season; the dubious hit that denied Howard Ehmke a double no-hitter; and the questionable third and final .400 season by Ty Cobb. Fred Lieb began as an official scorer in the year he first covered baseball, 1911. Sixty-six years and millions of words later he told his story in a captivating memoir, *Baseball as I Have Known It*.

FRED LIEB

"Hits Are My Bread and Butter"

In my first year in the press box and my first year at official scoring, Frank Farrell, president of the Highlanders, called me up and said, "What does a player have to do to get an error in our park?" I said, "Make an error." And he said, "Then why don't you put some errors in our box scores? Yesterday Jack Knight made two errors that you scored as hits for Ty Cobb."

"Well," I said, "about those hits, I thought one of them was too hot to handle. The other one was hit to deep short, Knight had a long throw, and maybe the throw pulled Chase a little off the bag, but I thought Cobb had it beaten, anyway. So I marked them both hits."

"Listen," Farrell retorted, "when my players make errors, I want you to give errors. I pay Jack Knight forty-five hundred dollars a year [supposedly a lot of money in 1911] for playing shortstop, and when he makes errors, I want you to give 'em to him."

That telephone conversation I will let stand as a fair measure of this not untypical franchise owner of the period. I knew enough about the relations between Farrell and Knight to know that Farrell was looking for statistical support to help him knock down Knight's salary when contract time came around. The statistical game can be played by owners as well as by players.

Criticism for a scoring decision can also come from parties with no financial interest in it. I once drew about my head the unleashed sarcasm of Bill Hanna, then of the New York *Sun-Herald*. It was in 1919, and I was substituting as official scorer for Bill Farnsworth. It involved a not-hit game pitched by a

Cleveland pitcher, Ray Caldwell, a former Yankee. It happened that my wife and Mrs. Caldwell were very friendly, and the Caldwells and Liebs frequently visited each other's houses. But this had nothing to do with my judgment of the play that gave Ray his no-hitter. In the middle of the game Frank Baker, Yankee third baseman, hit a smash toward right field. Bill Wambsganss, the Cleveland second baseman, who would make an unassisted triple play in the World Series in 1920, was playing Baker deep in the hole, on the grass. As I saw the play, Wamby made a good play to knock it down but then cuffed it around enough to let the slow Baker beat his throw. I thought this added up to an error, I so scored it and didn't give any further thought to it. The next morning Hanna started his story of the game in this manner: "A no-hit game was credited to Slim Caldwell at the Polo Grounds yesterday. It was so scored by the official scorer, but I will insist till my dying day that it was not an error but a hit for Frank Baker."

Bob Shawkey, who pitched thirteen years for the Yankees, also reproved me for that scoring decision. "I think you took a hit away from Bake yesterday," he told me through the screen before the next day's game. I laughed. "Bob, I think it's funny for a pitcher to be grousing at my scoring another pitcher with a no-hitter. And Caldwell was your pitching teammate here until last year." Then I closed the door on him by telling him what is the essential truth about any "score" a scorer makes: "It was my judgment that it was an error; that's the way I scored it, and that's the way it goes into the official records."

Most controversies over a scoring decision burn themselves out quickly, but a decision I made in August 1922 had repercussions for several months and kept popping up years later. It is the story behind Cobb's .401 batting average in 1922. In brief, a hit I scored for Cobb—and I wasn't even the official scorer—made it possible for Cobb to hit .400 for the third time. Without that hit he would have finished at .399.

A bit of background is necessary to understand the tangle. First, a man named Irwin Howe, who was the American League statistician, also ran a baseball statistics bureau and sold unofficial hitting, pitching, and fielding records to a lot of newspapers. Now, Howe took his figures day by day from the AP box scores, and I was scorer for the AP, but not the official scorer.

On the day of this particular play it had started to rain, and I moved back into the stands from the uncovered press box. But Jack Kieran, then of the *Tribune* and that year the official scorer, stayed at his post despite the rain. When Cobb came to the plate on the disputed play, it was raining fairly hard, and the infield was getting gooey. Cobb hit a grounder toward Everett Scott, the Yankee shortstop. It rolled close to the ground, and in going over a soggy field, a ball picks up a lot of wet soil. Scott had just a little trouble handling the muddy ball, and he didn't get Cobb by a full step. Considering the condition of the field and Cobb's speed, I gave it a hit. I wasn't near Kieran and gave no further thought about it. Neither did Kieran, who sent in an official score for the game, showing Scott had made an error.

Meanwhile, Howe, using my AP score, fed "hit" into his computations, and at the end of the season Howe's unofficial statistics showed Cobb at .401 (his third season batting over .400), and the official figures in due course showed him at .3995. Now if the difference had been between Cobb's hitting .348 and .346, Howe would have thought no more about it. It was very common for unofficial and official averages to vary a point or two. But here the question was whether this immortal had or had not again hit the magic .400 figure. If Howe had just given out his 1922 official American League averages—with Cobb hitting .401—without comment, I feel no one would have challenged. Neither the public, nor the baseball writers knew anything about the August incident. However, perhaps from a sense of guilt, Howe sent out a brief explanation along with the figures to explain Cobb's .401 average. It went: "I noted that the averages reached from my official scoring sheets had Cobb hitting .3995. With the unofficial averages giving him .401, I felt how can we deprive this great player of a third .400 average over a fraction of a point?

"It was then that I compared Cobb's official sheets with the unofficial figures we had in the office, game for game, until we reached the August game in the New York Polo Grounds in which Kieran had scored as an error for Scott and Fred Lieb's Associated Press showed a hit for Cobb. I took into consideration Lieb's long experience as a scorer. Since Kieran was scoring officially for the first year, I felt I was justified in using Fred Lieb's score."

In the meantime, Ban Johnson, American League president, got into the act. Ban was a stickler for supporting his umpires, and now he stood behind his designated statistician, Howe, 100 percent. Johnson and I exchanged some vitriolic telegrams, which appeared in the national press. He said he always had regarded me as a competent scorer, and he was dismayed that in the Cobb case I did not have the guts to stand up for my score. My reply was that my scoring was not an issue. I was standing up for a principle, that the official scorer is official. The fat was now in the fire. In no time at all the situation was splashed across the sports pages, and the fans for the most part were on Cobb's side. The New York writers, I'm happy to say, argued that the official scorer should have the final decision, and there wasn't any point in having official scorers if they'd throw out one of his decisions just to give a man a .400 batting average.

So the case came up at our Baseball Writers Association meeting the following winter. I was in an awkward position, as I was both national president and chairman of the New York chapter. Speaking as chairman in behalf of John Kieran, who felt concerned that his score had been tossed out and mine accepted, I told the members that I felt the same way: Kieran was the official scorer, and if the situation had been reversed and my official score had been tossed out, I'd have been incensed.

Some of the chapters, particularly Detroit and Philadelphia, were strongly in favor of Cobb. After I had made my statement, several writers asked, "Don't you like Cobb? Are you penalizing him for something he may have done in New York or to you? Why would you deprive Cobb of a .400 average for a fraction?" There were other chapters that stood behind Kieran loyally. They were bascially defending the official scoring system and trying to make other writers see that their turn at official scoring could come to them sometime and also that to change something for Cobb opened the door to protests by some Joe Blow backed by a few friends.

When it came time to vote, two of the chapters, Brooklyn and Washington, decided to abstain. Then by a narrow 5–4 vote, the association upheld Kieran's official score. Furthermore, it added a statement to the resolution to the effect that the 1923 *Baseball Guides* should be instructed to carry an asterisk after the .401 figure, the footnote reading, "Not recognized by the Baseball Writers Association."

John Kieran was not at all satisfied with the decision and I fully understand why. He had been supported at the end, when the vote was taken, by only five of the eleven chapters—a minority—counting the abstainers as nonsupporters. They had let an "unofficial" hit carry the day. They had undercut the official scoring system. It took some years before the kettle stopped simmering in the association over this one. And as an aftermath of the controversy, the Baseball Writers Association changed its bylaws so that no one could hold the position of national president and chapter chairman at the same time.

The next year, in 1923, I became more personally involved in a different kind of controversy with Cobb. It happened this way: the managers of the teams playing each day always gave the evening papers the starting lineups about ten minutes before game time, which then was 3:30. This enabled the writers to telegraph them downtown and catch one of the early editions. We were consistently having trouble getting the lineup of the Detroit Tigers when they came to town. Cobb by this time was player-manager. Somebody complained to Jack Lenz, the announcer. Jack blamed Cobb: "Cobb doesn't give us his lineup until just the minute the game starts." (In those days, before public address systems, an announcer with a big cheerleader's megaphone would read off the lineups, facing the stands from behind home plate.) We persuaded Lenz to complain to Cobb, whose response was "Why should I give a damn about those twenty-five- and thirty-dollar-a-week sons of bitches?"

The next day in the *Evening Telegram* I took a whack at Cobb for his high-handedness toward the press and wrote that he had done pretty well over the years and that a lot of us "twenty-five- and thirty-dollar-a-week" boys had probably given him a lot of doubtful hits. I had in mind the two I had given him in 1911 that Frank Farrell had complained to me about.

The next day Cobb sent the Tigers' trainer up to the press stand with a message: "Mr. Cobb wants to see you after the game." So when I saw Cobb, he began, "I don't like what you wrote about me yesterday; that wasn't very nice." I said, "Well, I don't like the way you acted when Lenz asked you to send the lineups a little earlier." We got to jawing at each other, and he said, "Do you believe that stupid SOB over me?" I said, "I have no reason to think that Jack would lie." Cobb said, "Well, we may have to have this out man-to-man." I well knew Cobb's reliance on fisticuffs to settle arguments, so grinning weakly, I said, "You probably weigh one hundred eighty-five, and I weigh one hundred sixty-five, and you're in shape and I'm not, so I guess I'm not in your class."

Oddly enough, my lack of interest in a fight didn't rouse him further, and he soon calmed down. Out of this came a good friendship between us. I remember especially an all-day conversation with him in 1931 as I stopped over in San Francisco after my arrival from Japan at the end of a tour with an All-Star team. Cobb, then in retirement, was living in the suburb of Atherton. Ty was on a talking jag that day—he had an old acquaintance to talk baseball with and wouldn't let me go. During the evening he pumped me about his chances of getting the general manager's position with the Philadelphia Phillies; he thought he could put some guts into the team and get it out of its rut in the second division. I remember recommending that he buy the Phillies, a franchise he could have picked up for perhaps $300,000 at the time. But Ty, perhaps the prudent investor, wasn't interested in financial control or ownership. Nor did he want another job as field manager. He wanted front-office managerial control, a salary commensurate with his baseball name, and a return to baseball. As it turned out, he never did get back inside.

Equal in importance, in the realm of baseball statistics, to my scoring the hit that ultimately gave Ty Cobb his .401 batting average in 1922 was the decision I made against Howard Ehmke of the Red Sox the next year. This was, in retrospect, perhaps the saddest decision I ever made, for it prevented Ehmke from becoming the first pitcher ever to throw two successive no-hitters. (Johnny Vander Meer of Cincinnati would do it for the first and only time in 1938.) Ehmke was then with the last-place Red Sox of 1923, and the Yankees were winning an easy pennant, their third in a row. Ehmke had had a great season: he would wind up winning twenty games with a bad ball club. It was in September, on what I believe was the last swing around the East for the eastern teams. The first batter for the Yankees was Whitey Witt, a fast little leadoff man who got a good jump from the plate and was quick getting down the line. So he hit a chopper down the third-base line to Howard Shanks, a former outfielder who was playing third. The ball took an odd hop, and Shanks muffled it against his chest. By the time he was ready to throw, he saw there was no chance to get Witt, and so he didn't throw. Considering all these things—the ball took a strange hop and Witt was the fastest man, I think, in the American League at that time in getting down to first base—I decided it was a hit, however scratchy. There was no murmuring over my "score" in the press box at the time.

Strange as it may seem, that was not only the only Yankee hit that day but Witt was the only Yankee to reach first base. After that, Ehmke retired twenty-seven men in order. As early as the sixth inning some of the Boston writers said, "Don't you think you ought to change that, Fred? This man has a chance to be the first two-no-hit man." "No," I said, "I scored it a hit then, and it's a hit in the early edition of my paper, and it's a hit in my score book."

As the innings progressed and Ehmke went one-two-three, one-two-three, the pressure on me became heavier, and even the New York writers, Boyd of the *Evening World* especially, said, "Oh, Fred, you *must* change that!"

I said, "No, it's a one-hit game in my book, and it's going to stay that way." So it went in as a one-hitter. Of course, it *was* a doubtful call on my part, and if it had happened later in the game I just might have scored it as an error for Shanks. My obstinacy about not changing my score stemmed from a talk I had in 1912 with Tom Lynch, president of the National League, best known as "king of the umpires." The day before our talk, Jeff Tesreau of the New York Giants had been given a no-hitter by the official scorer in Philadelphia under pressure after the game from Sid Mercer. Mercer was backed up by the Giants first baseman, Fred Merkle, who told the scorer that the one hit charged against Tesreau was really his (Merkle's) error. The scorer let himself be swayed and between games of a doubleheader reversed himself. Lynch was angry at such scoring and told me never, never change a scoring decision once I had made it. "Be like an umpire," he said. "He can't be influenced by anyone to change a decision he made in the second inning. Whether right or wrong, it was his honest judgment. As a scorer, hold your ground the same way. I don't like no-hitters that are scored in the clubhouse."

My ruling against Ehmke caused quite a rumpus, for the game was taken to the American League headquarters, and the editor of *Baseball Magazine* had four hundred signatures on a petition sent to Ban Johnson, American League president, protesting this scoring decision. The umpire, Tom Connally, was asked about the play, and he said, "If that wasn't an error, I never saw one." That made me feel even worse. So there was quite an aftermath to it.

In the year after I had been Yankee official scorer, Ossie Vitt, then second baseman for the Detroit Tigers, came to the chicken screen in front of the press box and said, "How many hits did I get yesterday?" I looked in my score book and said, "Two." And he said, "Well, I made three." And I said, "Well, my score book says that you had two, and the other time you got on base by an error by Ward, our second baseman." Vitt said, "I got *three!*" Then I said, "What I say doesn't count, anyway, because I'm not the official scorer." Vitt said, "Sam Crawford says you are." I said, "Well, I'm not."

So Vitt went back to the bench, and his teammate Sam Crawford repeated I was the official scorer. "You are the official scorer." Vitt then shouted, "And I want you to know that when I make hits I want you to give them to me. *Hits are my bread and butter!*" Vitt's phrase made a good title for a *Saturday Evening Post* article I wrote a few years later. But it took a while for the players to understand I was no longer robbing them of hits as official scorer.

In 1920, as a nonvoting member of the Rules Committee of organized baseball (serving on behalf of the Baseball Writers Association), I introduced a rule whereby a batter knocking the ball out of the park in the bottom of the ninth inning or in a succeeding extra inning would receive credit for a home run, even after the winning run was scored. The batter would also be credited with all the runs that crossed the plate on the hit, exactly as he would be if he had hit the home run in the first or eighth inning.

Up to that time if the score was, say, 1–1 in the bottom of the ninth (or tenth or eleventh) inning and a batter hit a ball into the bleachers with a man on third, the batter received credit for only a single on the theory that the game ended when the man on third scored and it took only a single to bring him in. Furthermore, the home-run hitter in this case received credit for only 1 RBI.

My suggestion was hotly criticized by Hank O'Day, a veteran umpire who was one of three representatives of the National League on the committee. Hank insisted vociferously to the last that no run could be scored after the winning run had crossed the plate. This particular rule he regarded as sacred and untouchable. Hank also charged me with trying to get more home runs for Babe Ruth, whom the Yankees had bought from Boston a few weeks earlier.

In the final vote, however, my measure won, 5–1, with Hank still beating his fist on the table and shouting, "I'm telling you, it is illegal. You can't score runs after a game is over!" By now my amendment has been in the rules for over half a century, and hundreds of players have me to thank for additional home runs and RBIs credited to them under such last-inning circumstances.

In 1977 Sparky Lyle was the top reliever in baseball and led the New York Yankees to the World Championship. In 1978 Goose Gossage came over from the National League, and Lyle went to long relief, or in Graig Nettles's memorable phrase, "from Cy Young to Sayonara." He also went the way of Henry Wiggen, from pitcher to author, keeping a log of the tumultuous 1978 season. Shaping it with the considerable aid of Peter Golenbock, Lyle created *The Bronx Zoo*, probably the biggest-selling baseball book ever. This passage ends just before the firing of Billy Martin (who said of Reggie Jackson and George Steinbrenner, "One's a born liar, the other's convicted") and the Yankees' incredible climb to the pennant under Bob Lemon.

SPARKY LYLE with PETER GOLENBOCK

The Bronx Zoo

Tuesday, July 11   Lake George, New York

I'm really glad I didn't go to the All-Star Game. Mary and I have been camping out in the woods, and we're having a wonderful time away from the madness. Goose went to the game, Billy brought him in, and he ended up getting his ass kicked and losing the game. Just like what happened to me last year.

You can pitch during the regular season and not have your good stuff and get by, but in the All-Star Game you have no chance. I don't care who goes out there. If you have the good stuff, you'll be all right. But if you don't when you're facing one tremendous hitter after another, boy, it's very scary. Goose still hasn't gotten sharp, and he didn't have a prayer out there in San Diego this evening.

I remember my first All-Star Game. It was in '73, and I was very happy to have made that team, because I never dreamed I'd get a chance to play in one. I thought I should have been named after some of the years I had had before that, but I wasn't, so I really hadn't counted on ever playing in one. Managers rarely pick relief pitchers, anyhow. Ordinarily they use starters in relief. The game was in Kansas City, and I remember pitching to Willie Mays, who had announced that it would be his last year. I struck him out on three pitches.

The writers asked me if I felt bad striking Willie Mays out in his last All-Star Game. I said, "Hell, no. Why should I feel bad?" They said, "It was his last All-Star Game." I said, "I don't know what you're getting at, but I felt real good about striking him out. Real good. I'm sorry I didn't get the chance to strike him out twice."

I went to the All-Star Game three times, in '73 and the last two years, but I don't want to go again. The All-Star Game is a popularity contest, a matter of being in the right place at the right time. Take Mark Belanger, for instance. He played for years before he got into an All-Star Game, and he's been the top fielding shortstop every year. He plays as well as anybody, but the fans don't even look at him. The ballplayers should pick the players. We play against the guys. We know who's hitting the best and who's having the best years. Some of the best guys sometimes don't even get on the ballot because they're rookies or they got traded, and another guy who's on the ballot, he may be having a lousy year, but he's going to get votes. It's so ridiculous.

Graig hurt his toe in our last game against Boston and, as a result, missed the last couple of games before the All-Star break. Graig had been elected to be the starting third baseman for the American League in the All-Star Game, but the Yankee management called him up and told him he couldn't go, which made him mad as hell. They said it was for his own good, which made him even madder. The game was played in San Diego, Graig's hometown, and he wanted to play in front of his family and friends. Jeez. How could they do that to him after the way he's played for the New York Yankees?

Graig has been jerked around more than anyone on this team. He had a contract problem last year, which they could have taken care of in a matter of minutes, but no, they had to mess with his mind for three-quarters of a season before straightening it out. The front office gave him a lot of grief about his contract, and they didn't give a damn about him. You know, the old "You play third base and shut your goddam mouth" sort of thing. It's unbelievable what George did to him.

When Graig signed a contract in July 1976, George and Graig agreed that Graig would get some deferred compensation. Graig asked George the best way to do it, and George set it up in such a way that Graig would be able to take the money anytime he wanted. The only problem with that was that the IRS doesn't see it as deferred compensation if you can take it anytime you want. George had given him the worst possible advice.

What made things complicated was that in August the owners and players agreed to a new contract, one that gave the players the right no longer to be bound to the reserve clause after a certain number of years, and when Graig discovered last spring that he had tax problems, when he went to George and asked him to change the contract to get him a better tax break on his deferred compensation, George refused to do it. George was afraid to change it because he didn't want Graig under a new contract. When Graig got mad, as he had every right to be, and walked out of camp, George made him look bad in the press. George came out with this: "If Graig realizes he made a mistake by leaving this team and he learns from it, I'm willing to sit down and help him. But he has to stand up like a man and admit he made a mistake." The next day Graig handed in a printed statement saying he was sorry.

And now all of a sudden the tide has turned where they need him. They're afraid he's going to hurt himself worse by playing in the All-Star Game, so now it's "For your own good, Graig, we feel . . ." They're acting real concerned. And what really pissed him off was that they weren't concerned about him as a person at all. All they cared about was a void that they might not be able to fill. It just proves one more time how management dicks you around, dicks you around until they need you, and all of a sudden they turn around and look you in the eye and act real sincere and expect you to believe them and buy what they say. It's like a guy sticking you in the back with a knife and then turning around and putting a bandage on and fixing you up. Graig just said, "Go screw yourself. I'm playing."

The only way Graig got to play was that the day before the game Reggie called and said he had a temperature, and they put Graig on in Reggie's place.

The second half of the season began today, and before the game George held a meeting. I knew he wouldn't be able to go through an entire season without jumping in. He couldn't stand it. He's done everything he could to stay in the background, but he can no longer stand by and watch this crap. It's not his nature. I will say this for him: when he makes up his mind to do something, he'll do it come hell or high water. He'll get a lot of flack for this after his promise not to interfere, but he won't give a damn. That's what makes him so interesting.

You can usually tell when George holds a meeting. When it's Billy's meeting, it's "Meeting in five minutes." When George holds a meeting, it's "The guys better get over here. We're having a meeting." This afternoon George was in Billy's office, and Billy came out and started to say, "Will you gather round here, please," and right in the middle of the sentence, we heard, "Can I have your attention? Can I have your attention?" It was George. He said, "We've done it your way for the first half of the season, and it didn't work, and now we're going to do it my way. I still believe we can win the pennant, but we're going to have to try harder. I've had a talk with Billy, and there are going to be some changes made, and if you don't like them, come and see me and I'll try to accommodate you."

He said, "There are going to be some changes made in the lineup; some players aren't going to play as much, but there's no sense in getting mad. This is the way it's going to be. It's my ball club. I sign the checks, and I'll do what I want."

Under George's lineup, Thurman will play right field, rookie Mike Heath will catch, Reggie will DH, and Gary Thomasson will be in left. George is also bringing in Clyde King to help coach the pitchers. Lou and Roy end up on the bench, or Lou may end up DHing against lefties, which means that Reggie's the DH against righties and nothing else.

It wasn't one of those "Rah rah, you have to have balls" meetings that George likes. It was short and sweet. Still, you can shuffle the guys around all you want, and you still can't play Randolph and Dent, 'cause they're out, and you can't start Messersmith or Clay or Cat or Gullett, 'cause they're out. We have exactly three starters left: Guidry, Dirt, and Figgie, and Figgie's forearm has been hurting. That leaves Beattie and this kid Rajsich. They're good prospects. Plus, nobody's going to make any trades with us, 'cause Rosen refuses to trade unless it's a steal for the Yankees. I do not mind telling you that we are in a shitload of trouble.

After George left the clubhouse, Billy finished the meeting. He told us we are going to get a list of dos and don'ts, and he brought up the tie thing again. He said he was now going to enforce the tie rule. It's going to be $25 for the first time, and it escalates up. I just can't see bringing this up time and again. Just fine me and get it over with. Saying, "We're going to do this, we're going to do that," that's half the trouble. They set down rules, and when we break them, nothing's said. Everybody's guilty of not wearing ties, not just one or two guys. But not wearing ties isn't why we're not winning.

After the meeting was over, Mickey Rivers was talking about George's moves. He feels they're horseshit. "He shouldn't be screwing around with a team that won the World Championship," he said. "It ain't right to panic. All Steinbrenner has to do is wait until the hurting guys get healthy. Then we would have started to win. There isn't any need for this crap." Mickey's right about George, but George doesn't have the patience to wait for the guys to get well. He wants to start winning now.

To me the worst part of George's shuffling the lineup is with Thurman in right field, they have to alternate Thomasson and Lou in left. I don't agree with that, because I don't give a damn who's pitching, when Lou gets hot, he can hit anybody. All they're going to do now is screw up Lou's stroke. And I don't know why Thurman's not catching anymore, unless his legs are hurting so much he can't catch. I'd rather see him behind the plate, Thomasson in left and Lou in right, with Reggie DHing. That's our best ball club. Thomasson's good. He's an aggressive ballplayer. He wants to play. He's hit a couple of home runs that have helped us, and he's a steady outfielder. One game he slid into the fence and caught the ball to save the game. That's what we need. A couple of more plays like that could turn this club right around. It happened last year. We came from behind a couple of times, and it fired up the whole team, and there we were, playing good all of a sudden. Right now, we're far from that. It's going to be a long, hard road. Today Garcia made an error that let in two unearned runs, and we lost to the White Sox, 6–1. Fortunately, the Red Sox also lost. We're eleven games out, and we're going to have to play better ball to have a chance at catching the Sox.

Friday, July 14   New York

Gid's arm finally may be tired. He gave up six runs in the nine innings he pitched, but he didn't lose because Cliff hit a pinch-hit home run in the bottom of the ninth inning to tie it. Goose won it in relief in the eleventh when Graig drove Reggie home with a single. Willie Randolph played his first game since mid-June, and it was great to see him back. It's nice to win every once in a while when you're playing poorly.

There haven't been many funny things happening. It's been very quiet. I didn't think I would ever see this on the ball club, but it has a lot to do with what Billy's going through. He looks awful, and he hasn't slept much, and George is giving him a rough time 'cause we're so far back, and nobody wants to intimidate him any more than he has been already. Billy doesn't like us to carry on, especially after we lose, so we haven't been. Not that anybody really feels like carrying on. We're getting tired of losing. This may sound like the players want to keep Billy, and I believe they do. After you play for him awhile, off and on you hate him and like him, but that's his way of sparking a ball club. Some of the guys have been saying, "Maybe they should fire him," but when they start to talk about who would replace him, they say, "Christ, keep the man."

I saw Catfish today for the first time in a couple of weeks. He's been through so much this year, and a lot of people think he may be finished. He even might think that. If he does, he's not going to hang on. He'll just say, "Screw it. See ya." He has too much pride to hang on.

As a last resort Cat was put under anesthesia, and the Yankee orthopedist, Dr. Maurice Cowen, stretched his pitching arm back farther than Cat could have by himself. By doing this, Dr. Cowen broke the adhesions in his arm that were causing him pain and keeping him from throwing naturally. What's hard for me to understand is how they know just the right amount to bend the son of a bitch. Do they bend it this far? or this far? or this far? How do you know that when you wake up your arm won't fall off?

Saturday, July 15   New York

George has been saying all along that he would call me up to his office when he was ready to talk about my contract, and today he made the call. I told Mary, "If he offers me close to what I want, I'll sign." I'm not the type of guy who harps on something and fights and then at the very end, when the other guy makes an offer, says to himself, "Well, hell, if he'll give me this much, I'll try and get a little bit more." When I arrived at George's office, he said he would give me $200,000 a year for the next three years, and it's their option whether they want to pick me up for the 1981 season. I agreed to that because if I can't pitch by 1981, what the hell, nobody's going to want me, anyway.

It's a fair offer, and I'm satisfied. I really hadn't been expecting anything like that from George. I had learned to cope with my depression over the money and was at peace with myself. I had lost my fire and had quit trying to piss George off. I just accepted what was as what was. If he had called me and said tough shit again, I probably wouldn't have said a thing. I might very well have said, "Okay, screw it," and been satisfied with my $135,000 a year.

Figgie made his first start since July 3 and gave up eight runs in four innings. Dennis Leonard beat us 8–2. In the second, Figgie had Pete LaCock 0 and 2, and threw him a curve. It was the same sort of thing that happened with Ron Fairly. LaCock hit it out, and the Royals had a 5–0 lead. Me and Kammeyer mopped up.

For the second game in a row Billy had Reggi DHing and batting sixth. The way he's been hitting, he's lucky he isn't lower in the order. We're a better team when Reggie's not playing the outfield, and we're a better team when he's not hitting in the number-four spot, because he strikes out too much. Billy has known this all along. Unfortunately for Billy, George puts pressure on Billy to bat Reggie fourth and play him in right. When Reggie's in a slump like he is now, he strikes out a hell of a lot with runners on base. We lost a lot of games 'cause of that this year, and as long as he does this, I guess we're going to lose a lot more. And what makes it bad is that when he strikes out, he doesn't put any pressure at all on the opposing pitcher. The pitcher just throws the ball anywhere. That's all, just throw it up there, 'cause he's not going to touch it. With men on base, it's important to put pressure on that pitcher, to make him throw a wild pitch or make him pitch in and out, up and down to tire him out. If they would put someone who doesn't strike out a lot in there, you're gonna have a different ball game. Some of those runners would score.

Billy batted Munson third, Chambliss fourth, and Nettles fifth. It's a smart move on Billy's part.

Sunday, July 16   New York

We were losing 3–1 with the bases loaded. Lou Piniella got up against Larry Gura, and he hit a ball 430 feet—where it was caught by Amos Otis in the deepest part of Death Valley. Lou couldn't believe it! He thought he had a home run for sure, that he had won the ball game, and all he ended up with was a long out. After the game he was moaning and groaning about Yankee Stadium. Piniella was saying, "To hit a home run here you need help from Superman, Batman, Robin, Spiderman, Wonder Woman, Godzilla, King Kong," and he kept naming more and more comic-book characters. We've lost eight out of ten, Boston is thirteen games in front, and the way things are going, we'll be watching the play-offs this fall on Channel 4.

Gura, who's now 7–2 for Kansas City, played for the Yankees, but one morning last spring Billy saw him and Rich Coggins in their whites going to play tennis. Billy, who calls tennis a pussy game, went right up a tree.

You have to understand, Billy was seeing this guy who hadn't been pitching well going out to play tennis. Billy said to himself, *What the hell is he playing tennis for when he isn't pitching worth a crap? Swinging that racket can't be doing his pitching any good. No wonder he's horseshit.* Gura, on the other hand, is thinking, *I'm keeping in shape playing tennis.* They're looking at it from different standpoints. But the manager, of course, is going to win out. Billy said, "I'll get rid of them fuckers." And that's just what he did.

Reggie didn't play tonight. Gura's a lefty, and Billy benched Reggie in favor of right-handed Cliff Johnson, who is making the situation worse by going 0 for 4 every time he plays. These days when Reggie plays, it's only to DH, which I know he doesn't like. Even so, Reggie hasn't said very much. He told reporters, "I'm not talking anymore." Who knows what's lurking in the heart of Mr. October? I'm sure we'll find out soon.

On the surface it seems that Billy's sitting Reggie down against lefties is bad on Billy's part, and yet Billy isn't treating Reggie any different from the way he treats anyone else. A number of guys like Piniella, Thomasson, and Roy White were even hitting the ball and found themselves sitting. Spencer was one of the hottest hitters on the team for a little while, and all of a sudden he stopped playing. When you're struggling like we are, you have to try things, and Reggie hasn't been swinging the bat very well, and that's the reason Billy takes him out. Not for any other reason.

It's hard to tell what's running through Reggie's mind. Billy has finally been allowed to keep Reggie out of the outfield because he hurts us too much out there, but any time a manager does that to a ballplayer, especially a ballplayer with an ego as big as Reggie's, the ballplayer is going to go into a tizzy. No ballplayer likes to be told he sucks, even if he knows it's true, and what makes it worse is that because it's New York, the Yankees, the team of controversy, Reggie Jackson, Billy Martin, George Steinbrenner, it gets magnified way out of proportion, and everyone makes a big deal out of it. The writers are now going to run over to Reggie and ask him provocative questions like "Is Billy deliberately showing you up?" or "Do you think you're good enough to play right field?"; questions like that, and Reggie's going to say something bitchy, and then the writers will go back to Billy, and after the writers get finished with them, there's going to be some shit flying.

Billy didn't want Reggie on the Yankees. Billy wanted Joe Rudi, a right-handed batter who hits in the clutch and who's an excellent defensive out-fielder. Rudi, however, isn't very colorful, and he isn't a draw. Reggie, with his big mouth and his big swing, puts people in the park. Plus he's a home-run hitter, and he makes a good play in the field every once in a while. George knew this and spent almost $3 million to sign him. What George didn't know was that this guy is a real piece of work.

After George signed him, when he told the papers, "I didn't come to New York to become a star. I brought my star with me," right then I knew. I said to myself, *This guy is going to be trouble.* He's always telling everybody how great he is, and you never know whether he believes the stuff he says or not. This spring he told a TV reporter how important it was that people respect him. Then he said, "But to be respected, you have to be godly." Godly? Is he kidding? I respect plenty of people, but not one of them looks like the pope, or Charlton Heston even.

Reggie's a mystery to me. He's a very intelligent guy. I've watched him on TV when he announces for ABC's Superstar competition during the off-season. He ad-libs, jokes around, uses the right words, and you can see that Reggie's a really smart person. If you listened to Reggie, you'd think he was the only intelligent guy on the whole Yankee team. That's what Reggie says—over and over. He told that to Carlos May once. May didn't give a damn what his IQ was and told him so. Reggie said, "You can't even spell IQ." Another time Reggie was giving Mickey Rivers the same jive. "My IQ is 160," he told Mickey. Mickey looked at Reggie and said, "Out of what, Buck, a thousand?" Cracked everybody up. Reggie's always trying to show Mickey how much smarter he is. One day he asked Mickey, "What am I doing arguing with someone who can't read or write?" Mickey replied, "You oughta stop reading and writing and start hitting."

Another thing I noticed about him. When Reggie was taking so much heat after his article in *Sport* magazine, he told a reporter, "The guys don't like me 'cause I'm black." The guys didn't like him 'cause he came to our team, and he wasn't here three months when he attacked Thurman in a magazine article and told everybody how great he was. Then we got pissed, and he said it was because he's black! Why did he have to say a thing like that?

Reggie isn't one personality. He's several. Some days he's real happy and friendly and nice, and other days he's nasty and surly and always growling at everybody. Then on other days he sits by himself and doesn't talk.

Reggie doesn't usually talk much with the other players, anyway. Mostly it's with the press. We get to read the bull he says in the papers the next day. I don't pay attention to anything the guy says, never, and I'll tell you why. We were in Oakland for a game, and after it was over, Reggie was being interviewed on the radio. Radios were on in the clubhouse, and we could hear what he was saying. Reggie's talking away, and he says, "You can't believe most of what the New York writers are saying about this team." Well, the New York writers are listening to him say this, and when he comes back to the clubhouse, they are pissed. They ask him exactly what he meant by that. Reggie for a few seconds didn't know what to say, and then he said, "You guys heard that? If I knew you were listening, I wouldn't have said it."

When Reggie started playing with the Yankees last year, Billy discovered that Reggie wasn't nearly as good as Reggie thought or said he was. Billy started batting Reggie fifth instead of fourth, where he was used to batting, and George went crazy. George ordered Billy to bat him third or fourth. Billy told the press, "It's no big deal. Reggie's just not used to playing the way other people want him to." But it was a big deal, because Reggie's George's boy, and for the two years Reggie's been here, Billy rarely can play Reggie the way he wants to, which is frustrating for Billy, 'cause he feels a team should do everything it can to win, regardless of whose feelings get hurt.

Billy almost got fired last year over Reggie. We were getting our ass kicked by Boston, and George was on Billy's back because we weren't in first place, and in the middle of the game Jim Rice hits a pop fly to right field. The ball fell in, and Reggie trotted after it like it didn't matter at all, and he took forever to throw it back in. Billy walked out to the mound to take out the pitcher, Mike Torrez, and as I was walking in from the bull pen to relieve him, Billy also sent Paul Blair out to right to replace Reggie, who had without a doubt loafed after that ball. Billy was so angry he wanted to embarrass Reggie. If you lose, Billy always wants you to go down fighting, and Billy had been pissed off because even though Reggie had been winning some games for us, he was costing us a lot of ball games with his fielding.

Let's face it, Reggie's a bad outfielder. He has good speed to get to the ball, but the catching part is shaky. Before the game, Billy had wanted Reggie to shag fly balls during batting practice, but Reggie had refused. See, if Reggie had done that, I don't think Billy would have been as angry as he was. And Billy's taking Reggie out of the game embarrassed him in front of all the people in the park and all the people watching on national television, which really hurt Reggie a lot. Reggie hates to be embarrassed, especially in front of 50 million people. So when Reggie came in to the dugout, Reggie said, "What did I do? What did I do?" Billy said, "You know what you did." Reggie said, "You have to be crazy to show me up in front of all those people," and then Reggie made the mistake of calling Billy an old man.

When Reggie said that, something in Billy snapped. Billy hates to be embarrassed as much as Reggie does, and when he said that, Billy went for his throat. Ellie, Howser, and Yogi had to wrestle him to the bench to keep him from reaching Reggie. Reggie was yelling at Billy, "You better start liking me," as if to say, "If one of us is going to go, it isn't going to be me."

George had not been at the game. He was at a funeral someplace, and he had watched the game on TV, and he saw the whole thing. A couple of days later he decided to fire Billy for losing his temper, but when Milt Richman of UPI leaked the story, the reaction of the fans was so hostile, George changed his mind.

When I heard that Billy was going to get fired, I went to him and told him, "I want you to know something. If you get fired because of this incident, I'm going home. I'm going to pack my bags and go back to New York for the rest of the road trip, and I'll show up when the team gets back." What I would have been saying was, if you fire Billy over an incident like that, where Reggie was loafing and Billy was punishing him for it, then you might as well have made Reggie the manager. "I can't see the manager taking the consequences when he's right," I told Billy. Not so much that it was Reggie and Billy. If it had been any manager and player, I would have felt the same way.

Monday, July 17   New York

Before the game tonight Reggie met with George for more than an hour, and they must have discussed Reggie's bitch that Billy's been batting him low in the order and has been DHing him—against righties—because tonight Paul Splittorff, who's a lefty and a good one, started for Kansas City and Reggie played. Splittorff had been the opposing pitcher when Billy benched Reggie in the final game of the play-offs last year. Tonight against Splittorff, Reggie DHed and batted fourth in the lineup. Reggie ripped Billy about that before the game. He told the reporters, "One day I won't play. The next day I'm the cleanup hitter." The way he's been hitting, he's lucky he's ever the cleanup hitter.

Billy really burned my ass tonight, too. Billy told me I was going to pitch the sixth and seventh innings and then he was going to bring Goose in. In other words, it was Long-Man Lyle again. It didn't matter how well I pitched. He wasn't going to leave me in there. Billy keeps telling me he understands how I feel about going into games early, and yet it keeps happening again and again. So tonight Catfish made his first start since May, and he pitched well. He left with a 5–3 lead after five innings and a third. Billy sent me in, and I got out of the inning, and I shut them out in the sixth, too. I walked in from the mound, went into the dugout, and said, "That's it, my two innings," and I left. I walked up the runway to the clubhouse to get dressed. When Fowler came after me to pitch the seventh, I told him, "I'm not a long man, and you're not going to put me in that job. Two innings are two innings, and now the other guy can take over." I showered, dressed, and went home.

He's made me the long man, and now, when I go out there to pitch, I can see Goose behind me in the bull pen warming up. If I give up one or two hits, the manager's walking out to the mound to take me out. Leave me out there, for Christ's sake. I'll get out of it. I got in it, I'll get out of it. But Billy doesn't do that anymore. With Goose back there, he doesn't feel he has to.

After I left the park, I was driving home in my van, listening to the game on the radio. Goose had given up two runs in the top of the ninth to tie it, and in the bottom of the tenth Thurman leads off with a single. Phil Rizzuto then starts talking about Reggie bunting. The first time Reggie tried to bunt, I thought, *That's good. Reggie's trying to move the runner over.* After he fouled off another bunt for strike two, I said, *Well, hell, at least he tried. Now he'll have to hit away.* But when he bunted with two strikes and struck out, I thought, *Holy shit. I can't believe this. There is going to be hell to pay.* Just listening to the radio and knowing how the game is played, I knew Reggie wasn't bunting to move the runner. He was bunting to get back at Billy.

I don't know. But I didn't feel it was entirely my fault that we lost. Thurman dropped a fly ball in right to help load the bases in the eleventh. With two outs, Goose went to 3 and 2 on Willie Wilson, and on the next pitch Heath and Goose both started walking off the mound, knowing it was strike three. Umpire Marty Springstead, however, called it a ball, the winning run came in, and Goose got so mad he got thrown out of the game. Kammeyer came in, gave up a two-run single to Patek and another run to make it 9–5, and when we scored two in the bottom of the eleventh, it was too little too late.

Tuesday, July 18   New York

It's too bad Reggie and Billy had to clash, but the way both of them are, that's something that's going to go on forever. Neither one of them is going to let a dead dog die. No way, and neither one of them is gonna get any good out of it.

I can see why Billy got so goddam mad at Reggie. Reggie was telling everybody, "I bunted because I thought that was the best thing to do since I wasn't swinging the bat so good." To me that's a weak excuse for doing what he did. He got himself into trouble he didn't count on, and now he's trying to get himself out of it. When a manager gives a sign and the third-base coach tells you, "Reggie, swing away. Don't bunt," and he bunts, anyway, you might as well not have a manager.

And what gets me is that Reggie can make a statement like "I bunted because I thought it was right to bunt" and the reporters accept it. They don't give it a second thought that "Hey, wait a second. Is this guy bullshitting us or putting us on?" They don't force him into a corner. Why doesn't Steve Jacobson ask him the type of question he asks everyone else, where you have to give an answer: "You mean to tell us, Reggie, you honestly weren't mad at Billy? You expect us to believe you really were interested in moving the runner over?" But they don't do that 'cause why should they? This way they go over to Billy and tell him what Reggie says, and it gives Billy an opportunity to call Reggie a liar, and they go back to Reggie and tell Reggie what Billy says, and Reggie says something nasty back, and it is on.

The Yankees have announced that Reggie has been suspended for five games, which is right. Mickey Rivers, though, was angry that he was suspended. Mickey thought they should have just fined him and let him play. "We need a big bat in the lineup right now," Mickey said. But Reggie's been 2 for 16 since the All-Star break.

We needed the day off today, but Boston won again and is sixty-one and twenty-eight, fourteen games in front of us. Forget this season. The rest of the year is just playing out the string.

When Jackie Robinson opened the 1947 season with the Brooklyn Dodgers, most base-ball fans and writers believed that he was the first black to play in the major leagues. (Robinson himself believed that at the time.) He was the third. (Who were the first two? Read on.) For a few years in the 1880s, with slavery dead and Jim Crow not yet ascendant, a spirit of racial tolerance prevailed in America that permitted black and white to rub shoulders without strife. Many black players performed at all levels of Organized Baseball into the 1890s, but the color bar that Jackie Robinson broke was erected in the International League in 1887. How and why it happened makes com-pelling reading; from *The National Pastime.*

JERRY MALLOY

Out at Home

Baseball is the very symbol, the outward and visible expression of the drive and push and rush and struggle of the raging, tearing, booming nineteenth century.

MARK TWAIN

. . . social inequality . . . means that in all the relations that exist between man and man he is to be measured and taken not according to his natural fitness and qualification, but [by] that blind and relentless rule which accords certain pursuits and certain privileges to origin or birth.

MOSES F. WALKER

It was a dramatic and prophetic performance by Jackie Robinson. The twenty-seven-year-old black second baseman opened the 1946 International League season by leading the Montreal Royals to a 14–1 victory over Jersey City. In five trips to the plate, he had four hits (including a home run) and four RBIs; he scored four runs, stole two bases, and rattled a pitcher into balking him home with a taunting *danse macabre* off third. Branch Rickey's protégé had punched a hole through Organized Baseball's color barrier with the flair and talent that would eventually take him into the Hall of Fame. The color line that Jackie Robinson shattered, though unwritten, was very real indeed. Baseball's exclu-sion of the black man was so unremittingly thorough for such a long time that most of the press and public then, as now, thought that Robinson was making

the first appearance of a man of his race in the history of Organized Baseball.

Actually, he represented a return of the Negro ballplayer not merely to Organized Baseball but to the International League, as well. At least eight elderly citizens would have been aware of this. Frederick Ely, Jud Smith, James Fields, Tom Lynch, Frank Olin, "Chief" Zimmer, Pat Gillman, and George Bausewine may have noted with interest Robinson's initiation, for all of these men had been active players on teams that opened another International League season, that of 1887. And in that year they played with or against eight black players on six different teams.

The 1887 season was not the first in which Negroes played in the International League, nor would it be the last. But until Jackie Robinson stepped up to the plate on April 18, 1946, it was the most significant. For 1887 was a watershed year for both the International League and Organized Baseball, as it marked the origin of the color line. As the season opened, the black player had plenty of reasons to hope that he would be able to ply his trade in an atmosphere of relative tolerance; by the middle of the season, however, he would watch helplessly as the International League drew up a written color ban designed to deprive him of his livelihood; and by the time the league held its off-season meetings, it became obvious that Jim Crow was closing in on a total victory.

Yet before baseball became the victim of its own prejudice, there was a period of uncertainty and fluidity, however brief, during which it seemed by no means inevitable that men would be denied access to Organized Baseball due solely to skin pigmentation. It was not an interlude of total racial harmony, but a degree of toleration obtained that would become unimaginable in just a few short years. This is the story of a handful of black baseball players who, in the span of a single season, playing in a prestigious league, witnessed the abrupt conversion of hope and optimism into defeat and despair. These men, in the most direct and personal manner, would realize that the black American baseball player soon would be ruled "out at home."

I

The International League is the oldest minor league in Organized Baseball. Founded in 1884 as the "Eastern" League, it would be realigned and renamed frequently during its early period. The league was not immune to the shifting sands of financial support that plagued both minor and major leagues (not to mention individual franchises) during the nineteenth century. In 1887 the league took the risk of adding Newark and Jersey City to a circuit that was otherwise clustered in upstate New York and southern Ontario. This arrangement proved to be financially unworkable. Transportation costs alone would doom the experiment after one season. The New Jersey franchises were simply too far away from Binghamton, Buffalo, Oswego, Rochester, Syracuse, and Utica in New York, and Hamilton and Toronto in Ontario.

But, of course, no one knew this when the 1887 season opened. Fans in

Newark were particularly excited, because their "Little Giants" were a new team and an instant contender. A large measure of their eager anticipation was due to the unprecedented "colored battery" signed by the team. The pitcher was George Stovey, and the catcher was Moses Fleetwood Walker.

"Fleet" Walker was born in Mt. Pleasant, Ohio, on the route of the Underground Railroad, on October 7, 1857. The son of a physician, he was raised in nearby Steubenville. At the age of twenty he entered the college preparatory program of Oberlin College, the first school in the United States to adopt an official admissions policy of nondiscrimination by sex, race, or creed. He was enrolled as a freshman in 1878 and attended Oberlin for the next three years. He was a good but not outstanding student in a rigorous liberal arts program. Walker also attended the University of Michigan for two years, although probably more for his athletic than his scholastic attainments. He did not obtain a degree from either institution, but his educational background was extremely sophisticated for a nineteenth-century professional baseball player of whatever ethnic origin.

While at Oberlin, Walker attracted the attention of William Voltz, former sportswriter for the Cleveland *Plain Dealer*, who had been enlisted to form a professional baseball team to be based in Toledo. Walker was the second player signed by the team, which entered the Northwestern League in 1883. Toledo captured the league championship in its first year.

The following year Toledo was invited to join the American Association, a major-league rival of the more established National League. Walker was one of the few players to be retained as Toledo made the jump to the big league. Thus did Moses Fleetwood Walker become the first black to play major-league baseball, sixty-four years before Jackie Robinson. Walker played in forty-two games that season, batting .263 in 152 at bats. His brother, Welday Wilberforce Walker, who was two years younger than Fleet, also played outfield in five games, filling in for injured players. Welday was 4 for 18 at the plate.

While at Toledo, Fleet Walker was the batterymate of Hank O'Day, who later became a famous umpire, and Tony Mullane, who could pitch with either hand and became the winningest pitcher, with 285 victories, outside the Hall of Fame. G. L. Mercereau, the team's batboy, many years later recalled the sight of Walker catching barehanded, as was common in those days, with his fingers split open and bleeding. Catchers would welcome swelling in their hands to provide a cushion against the pain.

The color of Walker's skin occasionally provoked another, more lasting kind of pain. The Toledo *Blade*, on May 5, 1884, reported that Walker was "hissed . . . and insulted . . . because he was colored," causing him to commit five errors in a game in Louisville. Late in the season the team traveled to Richmond, Virginia, where manager Charley Morton received a letter threatening bloodshed, according to Lee Allen, by "seventy-five determined men [who] have sworn to mob Walker if he comes on the ground in a suit." The letter, which Morton released to the press, was signed by four men who were "determined" not to sign their real names. Confrontation was avoided, for Walker had been released by the team due to his injuries before the trip to Richmond.

Such incidents, however, stand out because they were so exceptional. Robert Peterson, in *Only the Ball Was White*, points out that Walker was favorably received in cities such as Baltimore and Washington. As was the case throughout the catcher's career, the press was supportive of him and consistently reported his popularity among fans. Upon his release, the *Blade* described him as "a conscientious player [who] was very popular with Toledo audiences," and *Sporting Life*'s Toledo correspondent stated that "by his fine, gentlemanly deportment, he made hosts of friends who will regret to learn that he is no longer a member of the club."

Walker started the 1885 season with Cleveland in the Western League, but the league folded in June. He played the remainder of 1885 and all of 1886 for the Waterbury, Connecticut, team in the Eastern League. While at Waterbury, he was referred to as "the people's choice" and was briefly managed by Charley Hackett, who later moved on to Newark. When Newark was accepted into the International League in 1887, Hackett signed Walker to play for him.

So in 1887 Walker was beginning his fifth season in integrated professional baseball. Tall, lean, and handsome, the thirty-year-old catcher was an established veteran noted for his steady, dependable play and admired, literally, as a gentleman and a scholar. Later in the season, when the Hamilton *Spectator* printed a disparaging item about "the coon catcher of the Newarks," the *Sporting News* ran a typical response in defense of Walker: "It is a pretty small paper that will publish a paragraph of that kind about a member of a visiting club, and the man who wrote it is without doubt Walker's inferior in education, refinement, and manliness."

One of the reasons that Charley Hackett was so pleased to have signed Walker was that his catcher would assist in the development of one of his new pitchers, a Negro named George Washington Stovey. A 165-pound southpaw, Stovey had pitched for Jersey City in the Eastern League in 1886. Sol White, in his *History of Colored Base Ball*, stated that Stovey "struck out twenty-two of the Bridgeport [Connecticut] Eastern League team in 1886 and lost his game." The *Sporting News* that year called Stovey "a good one, and if the team would support him they would make a far better showing. His manner of covering first from the box is wonderful."

A dispute arose between the Jersey City and Newark clubs prior to the 1887 season concerning the rights to sign Stovey. One of the directors of the Jersey City team tried to use his leverage as the owner of Newark's Wright Street grounds to force Newark into surrendering Stovey. But as the *Sporting Life* Newark correspondent wrote, ". . . on sober second thought I presume he came to the conclusion that it was far better that the [Jersey City] club should lose Stovey than that he should lose the rent of the grounds."

A new rule for 1887, which would exist only that one season, provided that walks were to be counted as hits. One of the criticisms of the rule was that in an era in which one of the pitching statistics kept was the opposition's batting average, a pitcher might be tempted to hit a batter rather than be charged with a "hit" by walking him. George Stovey, with his blazing fastball, his volatile temper, and his inability to keep either under strict control, was the type of pitcher these skeptics had in mind. He brought to the mound a wicked glare that intimidated hitters.

During the preseason contract dispute, Jersey City's manager, Pat Powers, acknowledged Stovey's talents, yet added:

> Personally, I do not care for Stovey. I consider him one of the greatest pitchers in the country, but in many respects I think I have more desirable men. He is headstrong and obstinate, and, consequently, hard to manage. Were I alone concerned I would probably let Newark have him, but the directors of the Jersey City Club are not so peaceably disposed.

Newark planned to mute Stovey's "headstrong obstinance" with the easy-going stability of Fleet Walker. That the strategy did not always work is indicated by an account in the Newark *Daily Journal* of a July game against Hamilton:

> That Newark won the game [14–10] is a wonder, for Stovey was very wild at times, [and] Walker had several passed balls. . . . Whether it was that he did not think he was being properly supported, or did not like the umpire's decisions on balls and strikes, the deponent saith not, but Stovey several times displayed his temper in the box and fired the ball at the plate regardless of what was to become of everything that stood before him. Walker got tired of the business after a while, and showed it plainly by his manner. Stovey should remember that the spectators do not like to see such exhibitions of temper, and it is hoped that he will not offend again.

Either despite or because of his surly disposition, George Stovey had a great season in 1887. His thirty-five wins is a single-season record that still stands in the International League. George Stovey was well on his way to establishing his reputation as the greatest Negro pitcher of the nineteenth century.

The promotional value of having the only all-Negro battery in Organized Baseball was not lost on the press. Newspapers employed various euphemisms of the day for "Negro" to refer to Newark's "colored," "Cuban," "Spanish," "mulatto," "African," and even "Arabian" battery. *Sporting Life* wrote:

> There is not a club in the country who tries so hard to cater to all nationalities as does the Newark club. There is the great African battery, Stovey and Walker; the Irish battery, Hughes and Derby; and the German battery, Miller and Cantz.

The Newark correspondent for *Sporting Life* asked, "By the way, what do you think of our 'storm battery,' Stovey and Walker? Verily they are dark horses and ought to be a drawing card. No rainchecks given when they play." Later he wrote that "Our 'Spanish beauties,' Stovey and Walker, will make the biggest kind of drawing card." Drawing card they may have been, but Stovey and Walker were signed by Newark not for promotional gimmickry but because they were talented athletes who could help their team win.

Nor were other teams reluctant to improve themselves by hiring black players. In Oswego, manager Wesley Curry made a widely publicized, though unsuccessful, attempt to sign second baseman George Williams, captain of the Cuban Giants. Had Curry succeeded, Williams would not have been the first, nor the best, black second baseman in the league. For Buffalo had retained the services of Frank Grant, the greatest black baseball player of the nineteenth century.

Frank Grant was beginning the second of a record three consecutive years on the same integrated baseball team. Born in 1867, he began his career in his hometown of Pittsfield, Massachusetts, then moved on to Plattsburg, New York. In 1886 he entered Organized Baseball, playing for Meriden, Connecticut, in the Eastern League until the team folded in July. Thereupon he and two white teammates signed with the Buffalo Bisons, where he led the team in hitting. By the age of twenty Grant was already known as "the Black Dunlap," a singularly flattering sobriquet referring to Fred "Sure Shot" Dunlap, the first player to sign for $10,000 a season and acknowledged as the greatest second baseman of his era. Sol White called Frank Grant simply "the greatest ballplayer of his age," without reference to race.

In 1887, Grant would lead the International League in hitting with a .366 average. Press accounts abound with comments about his fielding skill, especially his extraordinary range. After a series of preseason exhibition games against Pittsburgh's National League team, "Hustling Horace" Phillips, the Pittsburgh manager, complained about Buffalo's use of Grant as a "star." The Rochester *Union* quoted Phillips as saying that "this accounts for the amount of ground [Grant] is allowed to cover . . . and no attention is paid to such a thing as running all over another man's territory." Criticizing an infielder for this excessive range smacks of praising with faint damns. Grant's talent and flamboyance made him popular not only in Buffalo but also throughout the International League.

In 1890 Grant would play his last season on an integrated team for Harrisburg, Pennsylvania, of the Eastern International League. His arrival was delayed by several weeks due to a court battle with another team over the rights to his services. The Harrisburg *Patriot* described Grant's long-awaited appearance:

> Long before it was time for the game to begin, it was whispered around the crowd that Grant would arrive on the 3:20 train and play third base. Everybody was anxious to see him come and there was a general stretch of necks toward the new bridge, all being eager to get a sight at the most famous colored ball player in the business. At 3:45 o'clock an open carriage was seen coming over the bridge with two men in it. Jim Russ's famous trotter was drawing it at a 2:20 speed, and as it approached nearer, the face of Grant was recognized as being one of the men. "There he comes" went through the crowd like magnetism, and three cheers went up. Grant was soon in the players' dressing room and in five minutes he

appeared on the diamond in a Harrisburg uniform. A great shout went up from the immense crowd to receive him, in recognition of which he politely raised his cap.

Fred Dunlap should have been proud had he ever been called "the White Grant." Yet Grant in his later years passed into such obscurity that no one knew where or when he died. (Last year an obituary in the New York *Age* was located, revealing that Grant had died in New York on June 5, 1937.)

Meanwhile, in Binghamton, Bud Fowler, who had spent the winter working in a local barbershop, was preparing for the 1887 season. At age thirty-three, Fowler was the elder statesman of Negro ballplayers. In 1872, only one year after the founding of the first professional baseball league, Bud Fowler was playing professionally for a white team in New Castle, Pennsylvania. Lee Allen, while historian of baseball's Hall of Fame, discovered that Fowler, whose real name was John Jackson, was born in Cooperstown, New York, in about 1854, the son of itinerant hops pickers. Thus, Fowler was the greatest baseball player to be born at the future site of the Hall of Fame.

As was the case with many minor-league players of his time, Fowler's career took him hopscotching across the country. In 1884 and 1885 he played for teams in Stillwater, Minnesota; Keokuk, Iowa; and Pueblo, Colorado. He played the entire 1886 season in Topeka, Kansas, in the Western League, where he hit .309. A Negro newspaper in Chicago, the *Observer*, proudly described Fowler as "the best second baseman in the Western League."

Binghamton signed Fowler for 1887. The *Sportsman's Referee* wrote that Fowler ". . . has two joints where an ordinary person has one. Fowler is a great ballplayer." According to *Sporting Life*'s Binghamton correspondent:

Fowler is a dandy in every respect. Some say that Fowler is a colored man, but we account for his dark complexion by the fact that . . . in chasing after balls [he] has become tanned from constant and careless exposure to the sun. This theory has the essential features of a chestnut, as it bears resemblance to Buffalo's claim that Grant is of Spanish descent.

Fowler's career in the International League would be brief. The financially troubled Bings would release him in July to cut their payroll. But during this half season, a friendly rivalry existed between Fowler and Grant. Not so friendly were some of the tactics used by opposing baserunners and pitchers. In 1889, an unidentified International League player told the *Sporting News*:

While I myself am prejudiced against playing in a team with a colored player, still I could not help pitying some of the poor black fellows that played in the International League. Fowler used to play second base with the lower part of his legs encased in wooden guards. He knew that about every player that came down to second base on a steal had it in for him and would, if possible, throw the spikes into him. He was a good player, but left the base every time there was a close play in order to get away from the spikes.

I have seen him muff balls intentionally, so that he would not have to try to touch runners, fearing that they might injure him. Grant was the same way. Why, the runners chased him off second base. They went down so often trying to break his legs or injure them that he gave up his infield position the latter part of last season [i.e., 1888] and played right field. This is not all.

About half the pitchers try their best to hit these colored players when [they are] at the bat. . . . One of the International League pitchers pitched for Grant's head all the time. He never put a ball over the plate but sent them in straight and true right at Grant. Do what he would he could not hit the Buffalo man, and he [Grant] trotted down to first on called balls all the time.

Fowler's ambitions in baseball extended beyond his career as a player. As early as 1885, while in between teams, he considered playing for and managing the Orions, a Negro team in Philadelphia. Early in July 1887, just prior to his being released by Binghamton, the sporting press reported that Fowler planned to organize a team of blacks who would tour the South and Far West during the winter between 1887 and 1888. "The strongest colored team that has ever appeared in the field," according to *Sporting Life*, would consist of Stovey and Walker of Newark; Grant of Buffalo; five members of the Cuban Giants; and Fowler, who would play and manage. This tour, however, never materialized.

But this was not the only capitalistic venture for Fowler in 1887. The entrepreneurial drive that would lead White to describe him as "the celebrated promoter of colored ball clubs and the sage of baseball" led him to investigate another ill-fated venture: the National Colored Base Ball League.

II

In 1886 an attempt had been made to form the Southern League of Colored Base Ballists, centered in Jacksonville, Florida. Little is known about this circuit, since it was so short-lived and received no national and very little local press coverage. Late in 1886, though, Walter S. Brown of Pittsburgh announced his plan of forming the National Colored Base Ball League. It, too, would have a brief existence. But unlike its southern predecessor, Brown's Colored League received wide publicity.

The November 18, 1886, issue of *Sporting Life* announced that Brown already had lined up five teams. Despite the decision of the Cuban Giants not to join the league, Brown called an organizational meeting at Eureka Hall in Pittsburgh on December 9, 1886. Delegates from Boston, Philadelphia, Washington, Baltimore, Pittsburgh, and Louisville attended. Representatives from Chicago and Cincinnati also were present as prospective investors, Cincinnati being represented by Bud Fowler.

Final details were ironed out at a meeting at the Douglass Institute in Baltimore in March 1887. The eight-team league consisted of the Keystones of Pittsburgh, Browns of Cincinnati, Capitol Citys of Washington, Resolutes of Boston, Falls City of Louisville, Lord Baltimores of Baltimore, Gorhams of

New York, and Pythians of Philadelphia. (The Pythians had been the first black nine to play a white team in history, beating the City Items 27–17 on September 18, 1869.) Reach Sporting Goods agreed to provide gold medals for batting and fielding leaders in exchange for the league's use of the Reach ball. Players' salaries would range from $10 to $75 per month. In recognition of its questionable financial position, the league set up an "experimental" season, with a short schedule and many open dates.

"Experimental" or not, the Colored League received the protection of the National Agreement, which was the structure of Organized Baseball law that divided up markets and gave teams the exclusive right to players' contracts. *Sporting Life* doubted that the league would benefit from this protection, "as there is little probability of a wholesale raid upon its ranks even should it live the season out—a highly improbable contingency." Participation in the National Agreement was more a matter of prestige than of practical benefit. Under the headline "Do They Need Protection?" *Sporting Life* wrote:

> The progress of the Colored League will be watched with considerable interest. There have been prominent colored baseball clubs throughout the country for many years past, but this is their initiative year in launching forth on a league scale by forming a league . . . representing . . . leading cities of the country. The League will attempt to secure the protection of the National Agreement. This can only be done with the consent of all the National Agreement clubs in whose territories the colored clubs are located. This consent should be obtainable, as these clubs can in no sense be considered rivals to the white clubs nor are they likely to hurt the latter in the least financially. Still the League can get along without protection. The value of the latter to the white clubs lies in that it guarantees a club undisturbed possession of its players. There is not likely to be much of a scramble for colored players. Only two [sic] such players are now employed in professional white clubs, and the number is not likely to be ever materially increased owing to the high standard of play required and to the popular prejudice against any considerable mixture of races.

Despite the gloomy—and accurate—forecasts, the Colored League opened its season with much fanfare at Recreation Park in Pittsburgh on May 6, 1887. Following "a grand street parade and a brass band concert," about 1,200 spectators watched the visiting Gorhams of New York defeat the Keystones, 11–8.

Although Walter Brown did not officially acknowledge the demise of the Colored League for three more weeks, it was obvious within a matter of days that the circuit was in deep trouble. The Resolutes of Boston traveled to Louisville to play the Falls City club on May 8. While in Louisville, the Boston franchise collapsed, stranding its players. The league quickly dwindled to three teams, then expired. Weeks later, Boston's players were still marooned in Louisville. "At last accounts," reported the *Sporting News*, "most of the Colored Leaguers were working their way home doing little turns in barbershops and waiting on table in hotels." One of the vagabonds was Sol White, then nineteen years old, who had played for the Keystones of Pittsburgh. He made his way to Wheeling, West Virginia, where he completed the season playing for that city's entry in the Ohio State League. (Three other blacks in that league besides White were Welday Walker, catcher N. Higgins, and another catcher, Richard Johnson.) Twenty years later he wrote:

> The [Colored] League, on the whole, was without substantial backing and consequently did not last a week. But the short time of its existence served to bring out the fact that colored ballplayers of ability were numerous.

Although independent black teams would enjoy varying degrees of success throughout the years, thirty-three seasons would pass before Andrew "Rube" Foster would achieve Walter Brown's ambitious dream of 1887: a stable all-Negro professional baseball league.

III

The International League season was getting under way. In preseason exhibitions against major-league teams, Grant's play was frequently described as "brilliant." *Sporting Life* cited the "brilliant work of Grant," his "number of difficult one-handed catches," and his "special fielding displays" in successive games in April. Even in an 18–4 loss to Philadelphia, "Grant, the colored second baseman, was the lion of the afternoon. His exhibition was unusually brilliant."

Stovey got off to a shaky start, as Newark lost to Brooklyn 12–4 in the team's exhibition opener. "Walker was clever—exceedingly clever behind the bat," wrote the Newark *Daily Journal*, "yet threw wildly several times." A few days later, though, Newark's "colored battery" performed magnificently in a 3–2 loss at the Polo Grounds to the New York Giants, the favorite National League team of the Newark fans (hence the nickname "Little Giants"). Stovey was "remarkably effective," and Walker threw out the Giants' John Montgomery Ward at second base, "something that but few catchers have been able to accomplish." The play of Stovey and Walker impressed the New York sportswriters as well as New York Giants' Captain Ward and manager Jim Mutrie, who, according to White, "made an offer to buy the release of the 'Spanish battery,' but [Newark] Manager Hackett informed him they were not on sale."

Stovey and Walker were becoming very popular. The Binghamton *Leader* had this to say about the big southpaw:

> Well, they put Stovey in the box again yesterday. You recollect Stovey, of course—the brunette fellow with the sinister fin and the demonic delivery. Well, he pitched yesterday, and, as of yore, he teased the Bingos. He has such a knack of tossing up balls that appear as large as an alderman's opinion of himself, but you cannot hit 'em with a cellar door. There's no use in talking, but that Stovey can do funny things with a ball. Once, we noticed, he aimed a ball right at a Bing's commissary department, and when the Bingo spilled himself on the glebe to give that ball the

right of way, it just turned a sharp corner and careened over the dish to the tune of "one strike." What's the use of bucking against a fellow that can throw at the flag-staff amd make it curve into the water pail?

Walker, too, impressed fans and writers with his defensive skill and base-running. In a game against Buffalo, "Walker was like a fence behind the home-plate. . . . [T]here might have been a river ten feet behind him and not a ball would have gone into it." Waxing poetic, one scribe wrote:

> There is a catcher named Walker
> Who behind the bat is a corker,
> He throws to a base
> With ease and with grace,
> And steals 'round the bags like a stalker.

Who were the other black ballplayers in the International League? Oswego, unsuccessful in signing George Williams away from the Cuban Giants, added Randolph Jackson, a second baseman from Ilion, New York, to their roster after a recommendation from Bud Fowler. (Ilion is near Cooperstown; Fowler's real name was John Jackson—coincidence?) He played his first game on May 28. In a 5–4 loss to Newark he "played a remarkable game and hit for a double and a single, besides making the finest catch ever made on the grounds," wrote *Sporting Life*. Jackson played only three more games before the Oswego franchise folded on May 31, 1887.

Binghamton, which already had Bud Fowler, added a black pitcher named Renfroe (whose first name is unknown). Renfroe had pitched for the Memphis team in the Southern League of Colored Base Ballists in 1886, where "he won every game he pitched but one, averaging twelve strikeouts a game for nine games. In his first game against Chattanooga he struck out the first nine men who came to bat," wrote the Memphis *Appeal*; "he has great speed and a very deceptive down-shoot." Renfroe pitched his first game for Binghamton on May 30, a 14–9 victory over Utica, before several thousand fans.

"How far will this mania for engaging colored players go?" asked *Sporting Life*. "At the present rate of progress the International League may ere many moons change its title to 'Colored League.'" During the last few days in May, seven blacks were playing in the league: Walker and Stovey for Newark, Fowler and Renfroe for Binghamton, Grant for Buffalo, Jackson for Owsego, and one player not yet mentioned: Robert Higgins. For his story, we back up and consider the state of the Syracuse Stars.

IV

The 1887 season opened with Syracuse in a state of disarray. Off the field, ownership was reorganized after a lengthy and costly court battle in which the Stars were held liable for injuries suffered by a fan, John A. Cole, when he fell from a grandstand in 1886. Another fall that disturbed management was that of its team's standing, from first in 1885 to a dismal sixth in 1886. Determined to infuse new talent into the club, Syracuse signed seven players from the defunct Southern League after the 1886 season. Although these players were talented, the move appeared to be backfiring when, even before the season began, reports began circulating that the Southern League men had formed a "clique" to foist their opinions on management. The directors wanted to sign as manager Charley Hackett, who, as we have seen, subsequently signed with Newark. But the clique insisted that they would play for Syracuse only if Jim Gifford, who had hired them, was named manager. The directors felt that Gifford was too lax, yet acquiesced to the players' demand.

By the end of April, the Toronto *World* was reporting:

> Already we hear talk of "cliqueism" in the Syracuse Club, and if there be any truth to the bushel of statements that team is certain to be doomed before the season is well under way. Their ability to play a winning game is unquestioned, but if the clique exists the club will lose when losing is the policy of the party element.

Another off-season acquisition for the Stars was a catcher named Dick Male, from Zanesville, Ohio. Soon after he was signed in November 1886, rumors surfaced that "Male" was actually a black named Dick Johnson. Male mounted his own public relations campaign to quell these rumors. The Syracuse correspondent to *Sporting Life* wrote:

> Much has been said of late about Male, one of our catchers, being a colored man, whose correct name is said to be Johnson. I have seen a photo of Male, and he is not a colored man by a large majority. If he is, he has sent some other fellow's picture.

The *Sporting News'* Syracuse writer informed his readers that "Male . . . writes that the man calling him a Negro is himself a black liar."

Male's performance proved less that satisfactory, and he was released by Syracuse shortly after a 20–3 drubbing at the hands of Pittsburgh in a preseason game, in which Male played right field, caught, and allowed three passed balls. Early in May he signed with Zanesville of the Ohio State League, where he once again became a black catcher named Johnson.

As the season began, the alarming specter of selective support by the Southern League players became increasingly apparent. They would do their best for deaf-mute pitcher Ed Dundon, who was a fellow refugee, but would go through the motions when Doug Crothers or Con Murphy pitched for the Stars. Jim Gifford, the Stars' manager, not equal to the task of controlling his team, resigned on May 17. He was replaced by "Ice Water" Joe Simmons, who had managed Walker at Waterbury in 1886.

Simmons began his regime at Syracuse by signing a nineteen-year-old left-handed black pitcher named Robert Higgins. Like Renfroe, Higgins was from Memphis, and it was reported that manager Sneed of Memphis "would have signed him long ago . . . but for the prejudice down there against colored men." Besides his talents as a pitcher, Higgins was so fast on the base paths that *Sporting Life* claimed that he had even greater speed than Mike Slattery of Toronto, who himself was fast enough to steal 112 bases in 1887, an International League record to this day.

On May 23, two days after he signed with the Stars, Higgins pitched well in an exhibition game at Lockport, New York, winning 16–5. On May 25 the Stars made their first trip of the season to Toronto, where in the presence of 1,000 fans, Higgins pitched in his first International League game. The Toronto *World* accurately summed up the game with its simple headline: "DISGRACEFUL BASEBALL." The Star team "distinguished itself by a most disgusting exhibition." In a blatant attempt to make Higgins look bad, the Stars lost 28–8. "Marr, Bittman, and Beard . . . seemed to want the Toronto team to knock Higgins out of the box, and time and again they fielded so badly that the home team were enabled to secure many hits after the side should have been retired. In several instances these players carried out their plans in the most glaring manner. Fumbles and muffs of easy fly balls were frequent occurrences, but Higgins retained control of his temper and smiled at every move of the clique. . . . Marr, Bittman, Beard, and Jantzen played like schoolboys." Of Toronto's twenty-eight runs, twenty-one were unearned. Higgins's catcher, Jantzen, had three passed balls, three wild throws, and three strikeouts, incurring his manager's wrath to the degree that he was fined $50 and suspended. (On June 3 Jantzen was reinstated, only to be released on July 7.) The *Sporting News* reported the game prominently under the headlines "THE SYRACUSE PLOTTERS; The Star Team Broken Up by a Multitude of Cliques; The Southern Boys Refuse to Support the Colored Pitcher." The group of Southern League players was called the "Ku-Klux coterie" by the Syracuse correspondent, who hoped that player Harry Jacoby would dissociate himself from the group. "If it is true that he is a member of the Star Ku Klux Klan to kill off Higgins, the negro, he has made a mistake. His friends did not expect it. . . ."

According to the Newark *Daily Journal*, "Members of the Syracuse team make no secret of their boycott against Higgins. . . . They succeeded in running Male out of the club, and they will do the same with Higgins." Yet when the club returned to Syracuse, Higgins pitched his first game at Star Park on May 31, beating Oswego 11–4. *Sporting Life* assured its readers that "the Syracuse Stars supported [Higgins] in fine style."

But Bob Higgins had not yet forded the troubled waters of integrated baseball. On the afternoon of Saturday, June 4, in a game featuring opposing Negro pitchers, Syracuse and Higgins defeated Binghamton and Renfroe 10–4 before 1,500 fans at Star Park. Syracuse pilot Joe Simmons instructed his players to report the next morning to P.S. Ryder's gallery to have the team portrait taken. Two players did not comply, left fielder Henry Simon and pitcher Doug Crothers. The Syracuse correspondent for the *Sporting News* reported:

The manager surmised at once that there was "a nigger in the fence" and that those players had not reported because the colored pitcher, Higgins, was to be included in the club portrait. He went over to see Crothers and found that he was right. Crothers would not sit in a group for his picture with Higgins.

After an angry exchange, Simmons informed Crothers that he would be suspended for the remainder of the season. The volatile Crothers accused Simmons of leaving debts in every city he had managed, then punched him. The manager and his pitcher were quickly separated.

There may have been an economic motive that fanned the flames of Crothers' temper, which was explosive even under the best of circumstances: he was having a disappointing season when Simmons hired a rival and potential replacement for him. According to the *Sporting News'* man in Syracuse, Crothers was not above contriving to hinder the performance of another pitcher, Dundon, by getting him liquored up on the night before he was scheduled to pitch.

Crothers, who was from St. Louis, later explained his refusal to sit in the team portrait:

I don't know as people in the North can appreciate my feelings on the subject. I am a Southerner by birth, and I tell you I would have my heart cut out before I would consent to have my picture in the group. I could tell you a very sad story of injuries done my family, but it is personal history. My father would have kicked me out of the house had I allowed my picture to be taken in that group.

Crothers's suspension lasted only until June 18, when he apologized to his manager and was reinstated. In the meantime, he had earned $25 per game pitching for "amateur" clubs. On July 2, he was released by Syracuse. Before the season ended, he played for Hamilton of the International League, and in Eau Claire, Wisconsin, all the while threatening to sue the Syracuse directors for $125.

Harry Simon, a native of Utica, New York, was not punished in any way for his failure to appear for the team portrait; of course, he did not compound his insubordination by punching his manager. The Toronto *World* was cynical, yet plausible, in commenting that Simon "is such a valuable player, his offense [against Higgins] seems to have been overlooked." The sporting press emphasized that Crothers was punished for his failure to pose with Higgins more than his fisticuffs with Simmons.

Thus in a period of ten days did Bob Higgins become the unwilling focus of attention in the national press, as the International League grappled with the question of race. Neither of these incidents—the attempt to discredit him with intentionally bad play nor the reluctance of white players to be photographed with a black teammate—was unprecedented. The day before the Stars' appointment with the photographer, the Toronto *World* reported that in 1886 the Buffalo players refused to have their team photographed because of the presence of Frank Grant, which made it seem unlikely that the Bisons would have a team portrait taken in 1887. (Nonetheless, they did.) That Canadian paper, ever vigilant lest the presence of black ballplayers besmirch the game, also reported, ominously, that "the recent trouble among the Buffalo players originated from their dislike to [sic] Grant, the colored player. It is said that the latter's effective use of a club alone saved him from a drubbing at the hands of other members of the team."

Binghamton did not make a smooth, serene transition into integrated base-ball. Renfroe took a tough 7–6 eleven-inning loss at the hands of Syracuse on June 2, eight days after Higgins's 28–8 loss to Toronto. "The Bings did not support Renfroe yesterday," said the Binghamton *Daily Leader*, "and many think the shabby work was intentional."

On July 7, Fowler and Renfroe were released. In recognition of his consid-erable talent, Fowler was released only upon the condition that he would not sign with any other team in the International League. Fowler joined the Cuban Giants briefly, by August was manager of the (Negro) Gorham Club of New York, and he finished the season playing in Montpelier, Vermont.

On August 8, the Newark *Daily Journal* reported, "The players of the Bing-hamton base ball club were . . . fined $50 each by the directors because six weeks ago they refused to go on the field unless Fowler, the colored second baseman, was removed." In view of the fact that two weeks after these fines were imposed the Binghamton franchise folded, it may be that the club's investors were motivated less by a tender regard for a social justice than by a desire to cut their financial losses.

According to the Oswego *Palladium*, even an International League umpire fanned the flames of prejudice:

It is said that [Billy] Hoover, the umpire, stated in Binghamton that he would always decide against a team employing a colored player, on a close point. Why not dispense with Mr. Hoover's services if this is true? It would be a good thing for Oswego if we had a few players like Fowler and Grant.

There were incidents that indicated support for a color-blind policy in base-ball. For example:

A citizen of Rochester has published a card in the *Union and Advertiser* of that city, in which he rebukes the Rochester *Sunday Herald* for abusing Stovey on account of his color. He says: "The young man simply discharged his duty to his club in whitewashing the Rochesters if he could. Such comments certainly do not help the home team; neither are they creditable to a paper published in a Christian community. So far as I know, Mr. Stovey has been a gentleman in his club and should be treated with the same respect as other players."

But the accumulation of events both on and off the field drew national attention to the International League's growing controversy over the black players. The forces lining up against the blacks were formidable and deter-mined, and the most vociferous opposition to integrated baseball came from

Toronto, where in a game with Buffalo on July 27, "the crowd confined itself to blowing their horns and shouting, 'Kill the nigger.'" The Toronto *World*, under the headline "The Colored Ball Players Distasteful," declared:

> The *World*'s statement of the existence of a clique in the Syracuse team to "boycott" Higgins, the colored pitcher, is certain to create considerable talk, if it does not amount to more, in baseball circles. A number of colored players are now in the International League, and to put it mildly, their presence is distasteful to the other players. . . . So far none of the clubs, with the exception of Syracuse, have openly shown their dislike to play with these men, but the feeling is known to exist and may unexpectedly come to the front. The chief reason given for McGlone's* refusal to sign with Buffalo this season is that he objected to playing with Grant.

A few weeks later the *World* averred, in a statement reprinted in *Sporting Life*:

> There is a feeling, and a rather strong one, too, that an effort be made to exclude colored players from the International League. Their presence on the teams has not been productive of satisfactory results, and good players as some of them have shown themselves, it would seem advisable to take action of some kind, looking either to their nonengagement or compelling the other element to play with them.

Action was about to be taken.

V

July 14, 1887, would be a day that Tommy Daly would never forget. Three thousand fans went to Newark's Wright Street grounds to watch an exhibition game between the Little Giants and the most glamorous team in baseball: Adrian D. (Cap) Anson's Chicago White Stockings. Daly, who was from Newark, was in his first season with the White Stockings, forerunners of today's Cubs. Before the game he was presented with gifts from his admirers in Newark. George Stovey would remember the day, too. And for Moses Fleetwood Walker, there may have been a sense of déjà vu—for Walker had crossed paths with Anson before.

Anson, who was the first white child born among the Pottawattomie Indians in Marshalltown, Iowa, played for Rockford and the Philadelphia Athletics in all five years of the National Association and twenty-two seasons for Chicago in the National League, hitting over .300 in all but two. He also managed the Sox for nineteen years. From 1880 through 1886, Anson's White Stockings finished first five times and second once. Outspoken, gruff, truculent, and

---

* John McGlone's scruples in this regard apparently were malleable enough to respond to changes in his career fortunes. In September 1888 he signed with Syracuse, thereby acquiring two black teammates—Fleet Walker and Bob Higgins.

haughty, Anson gained the respect, if not the esteem, of his players as well as opponents and fans throughout the nation. Cigars and candy were named after him, and little boys would treasure their Anson-model baseball bats as their most prized possessions. He was a brilliant tactician with a flair for the dramatic. In 1888, for example, he commemorated the opening of the Republican national convention in Chicago by suiting up his players in black swallow-tailed coats.

In addition to becoming the first player to get 3,000 hits, Anson was the first to write his autobiography. *A Ball Player's Career*, published in 1900, does not explicitly delineate Anson's views on race relations. It does, however, devote several pages to his stormy relationship with the White Stockings' mascot, Clarence Duval, who despite Anson's vehement objections was allowed to take part in the round-the-world tour following the 1888 season. Anson referred to Duval as "a little darkey," a "coon," and a "no-account nigger."

In 1883, when Walker was playing for Toledo, Anson brought his White Stockings into town for an exhibition. Anson threatened to pull his team off the field unless Walker was removed. But Toledo's manager, Charley Morton, refused to comply with Anson's demand, and Walker was allowed to play right field. Years later *Sporting Life* would write (mistaking Walker's position):

> The joke of the affair was that up to the time Anson made his "bluff" the Toledo people had no intention of catching Walker, who was laid up with a sore hand, but when Anson said he wouldn't play with Walker, the Toledo people made up their minds that Walker would catch or there wouldn't be any game.

But by 1887 times had changed, and there was no backing Anson down. The Newark press had publicized that Anson's White Stockings would face Newark's black Stovey. But on the day of the game it was Hughes and Cantz who formed the Little Giants' battery. "Three thousand souls were made glad," glowed the *Daily Journal* after Newark's surprise 9–4 victory, "while nine were made sad." The *Evening News* attributed Stovey's absence to illness, but the Toronto *World* got it right in reporting that "Hackett intended putting Stovey in the box against the Chicagos, but Anson objected to his playing on account of his color."

On the same day that Anson succeeded in removing the "colored battery," the directors of the International League met in Buffalo to transfer the ailing Utica franchise to Wilkes-Barre, Pennsylvania. It must have pleased Anson to read in the next day's Newark *Daily Journal*:

THE COLOR LINE DRAWN IN BASEBALL.

The International League directors held a secret meeting at the Genesee House yesterday, and the question of colored players was freely discussed. Several representatives declared that many of the best players in the league are anxious to leave on account of the colored element, and the board finally directed Secretary White to approve of no more contracts with colored men.

Whether or not there was a direct connection between Anson's opposition to playing against Stovey and Walker and, on the same day, the International League's decision to draw the color line is lost in history. For example, was the league responding to threats by Anson not to play lucrative exhibitions with teams of any league that permitted Negro players? Interestingly, of the six teams that voted to install a color barrier—Binghamton, Hamilton, Jersey City, Rochester, Toronto, and Utica—none had a black player; the four teams voting against it—Buffalo, Oswego, Newark, and Syracuse—each had at least one.

In 1907, Sol White excoriated Anson for possessing "all the venom of a hate which would be worthy of a Tillman or a Vardaman* of the present day. . . ."

> Just why Adrian C. Anson . . . was so strongly opposed to colored players on white teams cannot be explained. His repugnant feeling, shown at every opportunity, toward colored ballplayers, was a source of comment throughout every league in the country, and his opposition, with his great popularity and power in baseball circles, hastened the exclusion of the black man from the white leagues.

Subsequent historians have followed Sol White's lead and portrayed Anson as the *meistersinger* of a chorus of racism who, virtually unaided, disqualified an entire race from baseball. Scapegoats are convenient, but Robert Peterson undoubtedly is correct:

> Whatever its origin, Anson's animus toward Negroes was strong and obvious. But that he had the power and popularity to force Negroes out of organized baseball almost single-handedly, as White suggests, is to credit him with more influence than he had, or for that matter, than he needed.

The International League's written color line was not the first one drawn. In 1867 the National Association of Base Ball Players, the loosely organized body that regulated amateur baseball, prohibited its members from accepting blacks. The officers candidly explained their reason:

> If colored clubs were admitted, there would be in all probability some division of feeling, whereas, by excluding them no injury could result to anybody and the possibility of any rupture being created on political grounds would be avoided.

This 1867 ban shows that even if blacks were not playing baseball then, there were ample indications that they would be soon. But the NABBP would soon disappear, as baseball's rapidly growing popularity fostered profession-

---

* Sen. Benjamin R. ("Pitchfork Ben") Tillman, of South Carolina, and Gov. James K. Vardaman, of Mississippi, were two of the most prominent white supremacists of their time.

alism. Also, its measure was preventive rather than corrective: it was not intended to disqualify players who previously had been sanctioned. And since it applied only to amateurs, it was not intended to deprive anyone of his livelihood.

Press response to the International League's color line generally was sympathetic to the Negroes—especially in cities with teams that had employed black players. The Newark *Call* wrote:

> If anywhere in this world the social barriers are broken down it is on the ball field. There many men of low birth and poor breeding are the idols of the rich and cultured; the best man is he who plays best. Even men of churlish dispositions and coarse hues are tolerated on the field. In view of these facts the objection to colored men is ridiculous. If social distinctions are to be made, half the players in the country will be shut out. Better make character and personal habits the test. Weed out the toughs and intemperate men first, and then it may be in order to draw the color line.

The Rochester *Post-Express* printed a shrewd and sympathetic analysis by an unidentified "old ball player, who happens to be an Irishman and a Democrat":

> We will have to stop proceedings of that kind. The fellows who want to proscribe the Negro only want a little encouragement in order to establish class distinctions between people of the white race. The blacks have so much prejudice to overcome that I sympathize with them and believe in frowning down every attempt by a public body to increase the burdens the colored people now carry. It is not possible to combat by law the prejudice against colored men, but it is possible to cultivate a healthy public opinion that will effectively prevent any such manifestation of provincialism as that of the ball association. If a negro can play better ball than a white man, I say let him have credit for his ability. Genuine Democrats must stamp on the color line in order to be consistent.

"We think," wrote the Binghamton *Daily Leader*, "the International League made a monkey of itself when it undertook to draw the color line"; and later the editor wondered "if the International League proposes to exclude colored people from attendance at the games." Welday Walker used a similar line of reasoning in March 1888. Having read an incorrect report that the Tri-State League, formerly the Ohio State League, of which Welday Walker was a member, had prohibited the signing of Negroes, he wrote a letter to league president W. H. McDermitt. Denouncing any color line as "a disgrace to the present age," he argued that if Negroes were to be barred as players, then they should also be denied access to the stands.

The sporting press stated its admiration for the talents of the black players who would be excluded. "Grant, Stovey, Walker, and Higgins," wrote *Sporting Life*, "all are good players and behave like gentlemen, and it is a pity that the line should have been drawn against them." That paper's Syracuse correspondent wrote "Dod gast the measly rules that deprives a club of as good a man as Bob Higgins. . . ." Said the Newark *Daily Journal*, "It is safe to say that Moses F. Walker is mentally and morally the equal of any director who voted for the resolution."

Color line or no color line, the season wore on. Buffalo and Newark remained in contention until late in the season. Newark fell victim to injuries, including one to Fleet Walker. Grant's play deteriorated, although he finished the year leading the league in hitting. Toronto, which overcame internal strife of its own, came from the back of the pack, winning twenty-two of its last twenty-six games; they may have been aided by manager Charley Cushman's innovative device of having his infielders wear gloves on their left hands. On September 17, Toronto swept a doubleheader from Newark at home before 8,000 fans to take first place. One week later they clinched their first International League title. To commemorate the triumphant season, the Canadian Pacific Railway shipped a 160-foot-tall pine, "the second tallest in America," across the continent. Atop this pole would fly the 1887 International League pennant.

Before the season ended, there was one further flare-up of racial prejudice that received national attention. On Sunday, September 11, Chris Von der Ahe, owner of the St. Louis Browns, canceled an exhibition game that was scheduled for that day in West Farms, New York, against the Cuban Giants. Led by its colorful and eccentric owner and its multitalented manager-first baseman, Charles Comiskey, the Browns were the Chicago White Stockings of the American Association. At ten o'clock in the morning Von der Ahe notified a crowd of 7,000 disappointed fans that his team was too crippled by injuries to compete. The real reason, though, was a letter Von der Ahe had received the night before, signed by all but two of his players (Comiskey was one of the two):

> Dear Sir: We, the undersigned members of the St. Louis Base Ball Club, do not agree to play against negroes tomorrow. We will cheerfully play against white people at any time, and think by refusing to play, we are only doing what is right, taking everything into consideration and the shape the team is in at present.

The Cuban Giants played, instead, a team from Danbury, New York, as Cuban Giant manager Jim Bright angrily threatened to sue the Browns. Von der Ahe tried to mollify Bright with a promise to reschedule the exhibition, a promise that would be unfulfilled. The Browns' owner singled out his star third baseman, Arlie Latham, for a $100 fine. Von der Ahe did not object to his players' racial prejudice. In fact, he was critical of them not for their clearly stated motive for refusing to play but for their perceived lack of sincerity in pursuing their objective:

> The failure to play the game with the Cuban Giants cost me $1,000. If it was a question of principle with any of my players, I would not say a word, but it isn't.

Two or three of them had made arrangements to spend Sunday in Philadelphia, and this scheme was devised so that they would not be disappointed.

VI

There was considerable speculation throughout the off-season that the International League would rescind its color line or at least modify it to allow each club one Negro. At a meeting at the Rossin House in Toronto on November 16, 1887, the league dissolved itself and reorganized under the title International Association. Buffalo and Syracuse, anxious to retain Grant and Higgins, led the fight to eliminate the color line. Syracuse was particularly forceful in its leadership. The Stars' representatives at the Toronto meeting "received a letter of thanks from the colored citizens of [Syracuse] for their efforts in behalf of the colored players," reported *Sporting Life*. A week earlier, under the headline "Rough on the Colored Players," it had declared:

> At the meeting of the new International Association, the matter of rescinding the rule forbidding the employment of colored players was forgotten. This is unfortunate, as the Syracuse delegation had Buffalo, London, and Hamilton, making four in favor and two [i.e., Rochester and Toronto] against it.

While the subject of the color line was not included in the minutes of the proceedings, the issue apparently was not quite "forgotten." An informal agreement among the owners provided a cautious retreat. By the end of the month, Grant was signed by Buffalo, and Higgins was retained by Syracuse for 1888. Fleet Walker, who was working in a Newark factory crating sewing machines for the export trade, remained uncommitted on an offer by Worcester, as he waited "until he finds whether colored players are wanted in the International League [sic]. He is very much a gentleman and is unwilling to force himself in where he is not wanted." His doubts assuaged, he signed, by the end of November, with Syracuse, where, in 1888, he would once again join a black pitcher. The Syracuse directors had fired manager Joe Simmons and replaced him with Charley Hackett. Thus, Walker would be playing for his third team with Hackett as manager. He looked forward to the next season, exercising his throwing arm by tossing a claw hammer in the air and catching it.

After a meeting in Buffalo in January 1888, *Sporting Life* summarized the International Association's ambivalent position on the question of black players:

> At the recent International Association meeting there was some informal talk regarding the right of clubs to sign colored players, and the general understanding seemed to be that no city should be allowed more than one colored man. Syracuse has signed two whom she will undoubtedly be allowed to keep. Buffalo has signed Grant, but outside of these men there will probably be no colored men in the league.

Frank Grant would have a typical season in Buffalo in 1888, where he was moved to the outfield to avoid spike wounds. For the third straight year his batting average (.346) was the highest on the team. Bob Higgins, the agent and victim of too much history, would, according to *Sporting Life*, "give up his $200 a month, and return to his barbershop in Memphis, Tennessee," despite compiling a 20–7 record.

Fleet Walker, catching seventy-six games and stealing thirty bases, became a member of a second championship team, the first since Toledo in 1883. But his season was blighted by a third distasteful encounter with Anson. In an exhibition game at Syracuse on September 27, 1888, Walker was not permitted to play against the White Stockings. Anson's policy of refusing to allow blacks on the same field with him had become so well-known and accepted that the incident was not even reported in the white press. The Indianapolis *World* noted the incident, which by now apparently was of interest only to black readers.

Fowler, Grant, and Stovey played many more seasons, some with integrated teams, some on all-Negro teams in white leagues in organized baseball, some on independent Negro teams. Fowler and Grant stayed one step ahead of the color line as it proceeded westward.

Fleet Walker continued to play for Syracuse in 1889, where he would be the last black in the International League until Jackie Robinson. Walker's career as a professional ballplayer ended in the relative obscurity of Terre Haute, Indiana (1890), and Oconto, Wisconsin (1891).

In the spring of 1891 Walker was accused of murdering a convicted burglar by the name of Patrick Murphy outside a bar in Syracuse. When he was found not guilty, "immediately a shout of approval, accompanied by clapping of hands and stamping of feet, rose from the spectators," according to *Sporting Life*. His baseball career over, he returned to Ohio and embarked on various careers. He owned or operated the Cadiz, Ohio, opera house and several motion picture houses, during which time he claimed several inventions in the motion picture industry. He was also the editor of a newspaper, the *Equator*, with the assistance of his brother Welday.

In 1908 he published a forty-seven-page booklet entitled *Our Home Colony; A Treatise on the Past, Present and Future of the Negro Race in America*. According to the former catcher, "The only practical and permanent solution of the present and future race troubles in the United States is entire separation by emigration of the Negro from America." Following the example of Liberia, "the Negro race can find superior advantages, and better opportunities . . . among people of their own race, for developing the innate powers of mind and body. . . ." The achievement of racial equality "is contrary to everything in the nature of man, and [it is] almost criminal to attempt to harmonize these two diverse peoples while living under the same government." The past forty years, he wrote, have shown "that instead of improving we are experiencing the development of a real caste spirit in the United States."

Fleet Walker died of pneumonia in Cleveland at age sixty-six on May 11,

1924, and was buried in Union Cemetery in Steubenville, Ohio. His brother Welday died in Steubenville thirteen years later at the age of seventy-seven.

VII

In *The Strange Career of Jim Crow*, historian C. Vann Woodward identifies the late 1880s as a "twilight zone that lies between living memory and written history," when "for a time old and new rubbed shoulders—and so did black and white—in a manner that differed significantly from Jim Crow of the future or slavery of the past." He continued:

> . . . a great deal of variety and inconsistency prevailed in race relations from state to state and within a state. It was a time of experiment, testing, and uncertainty— quite different from the time of repression and rigid uniformity that was to come toward the end of the century. Alternatives were still open and real choices had to be made.

Sol White and his contemporaries lived through such a transition period, and he identified the turning point at 1887. Twenty years later he noted the deterioration of the black ballplayer's situation. Although White could hope that one day the black would be able to "walk hand-in-hand with the opposite race in the greatest of all American games—base ball," he was not optimistic:

> As it is, the field for the colored professional is limited to a very narrow scope in the base ball world. When he looks into the future he sees no place for him. . . . Consequently he loses interest. He knows that, so far shall I go, and no farther, and, as it is with the profession, so it is with his ability.

The "strange careers" of Moses Walker, George Stovey, Frank Grant, Bud Fowler, Robert Higgins, Sol White, et al., provide a microcosmic view of the development of race relations in the society at large, as outlined by Woodward. The events of 1887 offer further evidence of the old saw that sport does not develop character—it reveals it.

He caught his first major-league game at the age of seventeen and his last at the age of thirty-seven. He played for four decades, with four teams, and put mind over batter for at least four hundred pitchers. Today he is a rising star of television broadcasting as the urbane voice of the Mets and ABC's Monday Night Baseball. And as if all that weren't enough, he even writes well. Presenting James Timothy McCarver and what are laughably termed the tools of ignorance.

TIM McCARVER

How a Catcher Calls a Game

If I had ever had a doubt that catching was my calling, it was wiped away during the 1973 season, when I made an attempt at playing first base. Joe Torre was the third baseman on that Cardinals team (with catchers at the corners and one behind home plate, I'm amazed we didn't win it all that year), and he warned me right away about the dangers of first base.

"Your biggest problem," Torre said, "will be to keep your mind in the game. You're going to find it wandering and wandering and wandering."

Sure enough, I'm looking in the stands, I'm looking everywhere, I don't know what to do with myself. All you have to worry about at first base is catching a ball if it's hit to you on a line—what a bore. I wanted to be back in the action, where every pitch is racing through your mind.

For too long catchers have been measured in baseball along the same lines as the rest of the players. And not just by the fans, either. When I argued contract, the front office would judge me by comparing my numbers from year to year. "Well, the guy is a .275 hitter," they'd say, "and maybe we'll add ten extra points on to that because of the grueling position behind the plate." But that's all. It didn't matter if I caught 150 games or handled the league's best pitching staff, because they didn't understand that stuff—and they weren't going to deal with it, either.

What they were really doing was getting their priorities backward. They'd look at a guy as a hitter who caught instead of as a catcher who hit. As a matter of fact, on August 5, 1967, I was hitting .355 and leading the league ("You can

look it up," as Casey said), and I ended the season as the runner-up to Orlando Cepeda for the MVP Award. Well, the next year I hit .253, but we won the pennant by nine games. The pitching staff had a record thirty shutouts, and I felt I made more of a winning contribution that year than in any of my previous five. But even so, I didn't get a raise.

Montreal's Gary Carter is going through the same thing right now. Gary was criticized after last season because his numbers were declining. But when Gary first came up, he was very easy to read behind the plate. A lot of catchers have a tendency to call pitches that they can't hit, so Gary would fall behind with the breaking ball by calling for it too often and too early and then he'd be forced to come in with the 2 and 1 or 3 and 1 fastball. He couldn't come in with more breaking balls when he was behind on the hitter, and as a result they were all sitting back and waiting for the fastball. (A guy like Rusty Staub, who may be the best hitter I've ever seen at working a guy into a hole where he has to throw him one pitch, can eat up a catcher like that.) Today, though, Carter is more valuable to his team than he ever was because he is no longer an easy catcher to read. He has learned to keep the ball off of the fat part of the bat—and that is the catcher's ultimate task.

People just don't take these things into consideration when they talk about a catcher's value to a team. They don't understand that contrary to the axiom that you hit off of, or read, the pitcher, the game's best hitters hit off of the catcher. The catcher is out there every day, not every four days, and very few pitchers want to constantly shake off their catcher. So, if you can get into the mind of a catcher, you can be a better hitter. The common talk about catching will inevitably revolve around a guy's arm or how many passed balls he's allowed, not in what situations the guy calls for certain pitches or his success in getting a pitcher to hit certain locations or his ability to communicate successfully with a staff. These hidden elements are the backbone of a baseball game but are rarely discussed. They will be now.

Calling Pitches
(Or, Is That Finger Tentative?)

Dave Cash, the former Phillies second baseman, used to tell me that he couldn't wait until he could call a game from second base someday. Talk about megalomania; the guy actually thought he could do a better job *from second base* than I was doing from behind the plate. Well, that's just indicative of how much a catcher is second-guessed. And what this has done is make many catchers tentative. They're more afraid of failure than excited by success.

How can you tell if a catcher is not giving the signs with conviction? Usually, if he is too deliberate behind the plate. Now, there's a difference between deliberate and tentative (Carlton Fisk is the most deliberate catcher in the game; he prefers to work slowly), but if a catcher gets down into a crouch and then gets back up, he's not sure what to call.

The Padres' Terry Kennedy seems to be a guy who's caught in the middle, thinking much too long about the perfect pitch. You see, he's an example of a guy who has been second-guessed instead of instructed in the proper technique. Who knows what the perfect pitch is? It hasn't been thrown. These guys should let their instincts take over and just fire that signal down there. The point is, if you're tentative, you're going to get a tentative fastball or a doubt-ridden curveball, to coin a phrase. And sometimes the way a pitcher goes about throwing a pitch is more important than the particular pitch. The Astros' Alan Ashby is a guy who doesn't get much credit, but he certainly isn't tentative. The Braves' Bruce Benedict and the Dodgers' Mike Scioscia are guys who also seem secure behind the plate.

Once you understand the importance of getting that finger down with conviction, there are some rules to remember as you call for the first pitch. Generally speaking, it's much easier to work a good hitter than it is a poor hitter. Poor hitters have no idea what you're going to throw to begin with, so why try to outthink them? You go after them with stuff, rather than with pitch selection. But there's beauty in working a good hitter. There's really no formula for doing it; there's feel. What can your pitcher do? Can he get the breaking ball over behind on the count?

Pitchers *definitely* should start more hitters off with breaking balls. That doesn't mean you're going away from the fastball. On the contrary. It means you're keeping the fastball fresh. By throwing the fastball all the time, you're making your best pitch, in effect, your worst pitch. So how do you keep the fastball fresh? By calling things your pitcher doesn't ordinarily throw. As an example, if a left-handed hitter is facing the Pirates' Kent Tekulve—and his fastball away is certainly his best pitch—you have to find a way to keep that as his best pitch. One way is to get ahead and then use the fast ball in, off the plate, to move the hitter back. This will give the outside of the plate back to Tekulve.

To be successful, a pitcher has to be able to throw a breaking ball for a strike when he's behind on the count, because a batter ahead on the count will sit on one pitch, usually the fastball. So if a catcher can call for that breaking ball, the percentages go down dramatically that the pitch will be met with damaging results. (Remember, though, we're talking about fastball pitchers. If a guy like the Giants' Mike Krukow, who may throw 70 percent breaking balls, is pitching, a hitter will be more inclined to sit on the breaking ball behind in the count.)

Now, let's set up a confrontation. We'll put a great thinker up at the plate, like the Mets' Keith Hernandez, and match him against the Reds' hard-throwing right-hander Mario Soto. On the first two pitches, Hernandez has guessed fastball and seen two sliders, one of which was called a strike. On an even count a pitcher has got to come in with the pitch that he can get over best. To me, Soto's got the best straight change-up in baseball, so on a 1 and 1 or 2 and 2 count, I might just call for three in a row (*this* time, and three straight fastballs the next time—every at bat is different with a thinker up there). But a lot depends on where you came from, too. If you came from 2 and 0 to run the count to 2 and 2, the hitter's thinking defensively. If you came from 0 and 2 to 2 and 2, the hitter's on the offensive. With each ball a pitcher throws when he's ahead in the count, the hitter fills up the hole a little bit; he's not as deep in trouble as he was, and he's not protecting the outside part of the plate as much as he's looking for a pitch on the inside part of the plate—fertile ground for a good hitter.

If Hernandez has waited me out and worked out a walk, the strategy shifts. With Soto pitching, a man on first base and a left-handed batter at the plate, I'm much less inclined to go to the off-speed pitch. A hitter is more likely to pull an off-speed pitch, and with the second baseman cheating toward second for the double play and the first baseman holding the runner on, there's a big hole over there—and the good hitters shoot for that hole. So the better the hitter, the less inclined I am to call for the off-speed stuff.

So, I've now called for two fastballs to the Mets' next hitter, Darryl Strawberry. If both pitches were strikes, what *must* be done now is to call for a pitch out of the strike zone. It continually amazes me that pitchers are not patient enough to make a hitter swing at a bad ball with the count at 0 and 2. A 1 and 2 pitch is different. That is the count, more than any other count, where you want to polish a guy off. But on 0 and 2, why throw a strike? Bob Gibson was impatient that way, as are most strikeout power pitchers: they just don't want to finesse hitters. So what if a hitter bloops a flair over the shortstop after you've jammed him? You've done all that you can do.

But sometimes that's just not enough. I remember a situation back in 1963 when Ron Taylor was pitching for the Cardinals in a 2–1 game at Wrigley Field. There were two men out in the ninth, a runner at second and pinch-hitter Ken Aspromonte at the plate when our manager, John Keane, decided to take a walk to the mound. When a manager comes to the mound in that situation, what he immediately does is plant the seed of doubt in your mind. And that's what Keane did on this day. He comes out for a conference and says, "You know, we've had good luck with this guy when he hits the ball hard."

Now I'm young at the time, but not that young. I just can't put together what he's saying. "When we make good pitches on this guy," Keane goes on, "he has a tendency to get jammed and slap a flair for a hit."

"What are you talking about, Johnny?" I said. "What you're saying makes no sense. Are we supposed to try and get him to hit the ball hard?"

Sure enough, on the first pitch Taylor jams Aspromonte, who hits a flair to left center to tie the game. In the eleventh inning Aspromonte wins the game with a flair to right center. It was the most incredible thing, but the incident taught me a valuable lesson. And that is: if you think long enough about a guy doing a certain thing, eventually he'll do it. It all goes back to conviction; you've got to believe in what you're doing, and you can't let anyone—including the manager—flip-flop your thinking. As Jim Kaat used to say, "If you think long, you think wrong."

Communication
(Or, How to Be a Pitcher's Friend)

I think the first thing I learned in the big leagues was never to hang out with a pitcher, because for them every four days was either a wake or New Year's Eve. It can kill you.

Honestly, I don't think there was ever a good pitcher I didn't have a disagreement with. When Bob Gibson was on the mound and Johnny Keane demanded that I go out there and talk to him, I dreaded it.

"God dammit, go out there and slow him down," Keane would say.

"He doesn't want me out there," I'd answer.

"Well, I'm running this club, and I don't give a damn what he wants."

So I'd just sort of go out there about halfway to the mound and stand there, trying to appease everybody.

But Gibby was this snarling, raging competitor, and he wanted me nowhere near him. "Keep your ass away from me while I'm working," he'd scream. "I like to work fast, and I don't want any help from you. You just put those goddam fingers down as fast as you can, and if I don't like it, I'll shake them off."

The great pitchers tend to be like that, though, and a catcher has to be something of a diplomat. The key ingredient in communicating with a pitcher is to get him to trust you. You can't walk out to the mound and tell a guy, "What you have to do is throw strikes," or "Don't give him anything good to hit, but don't walk him." What's he going to say? "Okay, sure"? It's incredible how many times a pitcher will hear that and how many meetings on the mound are just pure rubbish as a result. And the more often you go out there—like Mike Scioscia of the Dodgers does—the less effective your advice will be. So what you have to do is work on his confidence. "Here's what you're going to do tonight, and you will do it because I have caught you a lot of times and I have confidence in you."

Once a pitcher trusts you, you've cleared a big hurdle. You've taken the heat off him, and now that he doesn't have to worry about making the decisions, he can concentrate on pitching. A pitcher has enough trouble trying to do what you want him to do out there without having to worry about pitch selection.

Of course, there's a lot of anger (overt and otherwise) that exists in a pitcher-catcher relationship. And a catcher's job is to cut away all of the other crap and make sure you get down to the issues. You have to keep a pitcher honest and aware of his limitations, for the more honest the pitcher, the better the chance for the outcome. Sometimes it takes going toe-to-toe to make it work. I remember in spring training of 1965 I had a little confrontation with Steve Carlton. Lefty was twenty at the time, and the Cardinals were world champions. I had never caught Carlton before this game, and he had kind of a lackluster performance. Not terrible, mind you (two runs in three innings), just kind of typical for the first outing of the spring. Anyway, after the game I'm showering, and Carlton comes over to me with this kind of "you dummy" look on his face and says rather flippantly, "You're going to have to call for more breaking balls behind in the count."

I said, "What? First of all, how many pitches have I ever called for you? Are you basing this on three innings? You're going to start telling me what I'm supposed to do when we don't even know each other?"

We got involved in a very heated conversation, and I backed Steve against the wall to the point where he was swallowing a lot, if you know what I mean. We were both sorry later, of course, but incidents like this one took place for about the first four years that we knew each other. It is only once a pitcher trusts you, that you can deal with him in a two-way relationship.

Once you've established a relationship with a pitcher, there are times you'll find that he needs you. Not during a six-game winning streak, when he's on top of the world (in fact, you may need to be intentionally aloof toward the guy to bring him back down to earth), but when he's going bad. That's when pitchers start groping and taking advice from everybody. "Hey, my mailman told me I'm not coming over the top with my curveball; what do you think?" These are the times when you have to comfort the guy, get him to turn the page. Steve Carlton has always been able to put a home-run ball out of his mind immediately, and that's a vital trait for a successful pitcher. What a catcher must do is help him work on it.

I first realized that I had reached the point of ultimate trust with Lefty during the 1973 season. He had been traded to Philadelphia the year before, and we were playing the Phils out in St. Louis. Steve was knocked out of the box early and was in the midst of a bad streak. He phoned me in the Cards' dugout during the game and asked me to meet him under the stands. He wasn't getting good pop on his fastball, he explained—it was flat and just gliding in. I told him I thought he was dropping his hand down and pushing the ball. That was the only technical point I could help him with that day, but I knew that I had gained his trust, even though now we were on different clubs.

Location
(Or, Stay in Your Lanes)

When Steve Carlton and Fernando Valenzuela pitch, they help illustrate a staggering epidemic in baseball today. Major-league hitters simply do not know the strike zone. Look at the Pirates when they were going good—Dave Parker, forty walks a year, Willie Stargell maybe fifty. The best-kept secret in all of baseball is Steve Garvey's poor pitch selection; two years ago, in 625 at bats, he walked just twenty times, ten times intentionally.

Carlton and Valenzuela illustrate this point so well because their out pitches (Carlton's slider and Valenzuela's screwball) are rarely strikes. They simply give the illusion of being strikes, and by the time the hitter realizes that, he's already decided to swing. When those two guys are pitching, I'd bet that close to 90 percent of their strikeouts come on pitches out of the strike zone. So when you're talking about location, the first point to remember is that the illusion of a strike can do as much damage to a hitter as will a strike.

Carlton, in fact, concentrates on location before every start. He sits in the training room, closes his eyes, and concentrates on the lanes of the plate. His idea is to divide the plate into three sections, the outside width of the ball, the inside width of the ball, and the fat part of the plate. Gibson taught Lefty a lot about this. Gibson used to say, "The plate's seventeen inches; the middle twelve belong to the hitter; the inside and outside two and a half are mine. If I hit my spots, he's not going to hit it."

Before Gibson would pitch, he'd concentrate on the fertile lanes: "Inside and outside," he'd say. "The more I think about them, the more I'll hit them. There's no such thing as the middle twelve; it just doesn't exist." That's all he'd think about, and before long he had eliminated the idea of bad pitches, because all he was thinking about were the channels.

Now that your pitcher is thinking about his lanes, you get him ready to work the hitter inside and out. How many times have you heard someone say that a pitcher just has to keep the ball down to be successful? Well, that one statement shows how many baseball people continue to say what their predecessors have said without giving it any thought. Carlton never mentioned the lane from the knees to the letters. There's no lane there, and you can be dangerously close to the middle of the plate where the fat part of the bat lies. The lanes where you get a guy out are those two to three inches inside and outside. (Of course, sinkerball pitchers like Tekulve or the Angels' Doug Corbett must keep the ball down to be successful, but they're different animals—they rotate the plate so that their lane is the low road.)

Once you've made the decision to pitch in and out, there are no hard-and-fast rules dealing with where you can be most effective. (Remember, it is not the pitch itself that is most important, but how you got there.) But Gibson used to say, "If you make a mistake away, it's a single; if you make a mistake inside, it's a home run."

A catcher, knowing that his pitcher is set to work the hitter in and out, will move his target accordingly. (Pittsburgh's Tony Peña, who, by the way, I feel is the best defensive catcher in baseball because of his uncanny ability to get to balls in the dirt, gets a lot of attention for getting into his crouch with one leg sticking straight out. It's wonderful that he can do that, but technically it's not correct because he should be working both sides of the plate.) However, he must be careful not to set that target up too early, because a lot of guys peek. What a catcher has to do is give the pitcher the signal, watch him go into his windup and then, while the hitter's waiting for the pitch and too intent to notice, move either to the inside or the outside part of the plate by the time the pitcher releases the ball.

If you're seated outside, the umpire is inclined to give you that outside pitch. While the catcher is off the plate, the umpire has moved with him—he's working the slot between the batter and the catcher—and the pitcher has hit the mitt perfectly. Even though the pitch may not be a strike, it's too close to take, so the umpire will ram his arm up there for a strike.

Catchers are a smart breed, of course, so once a hitter figures out that you're setting up outside, you occasionally decoy. Hitters are attuned to where a catcher is sitting by the pounding on the glove, so a lot of times a catcher will go boom, boom, boom inside; and then bang, the pitch is made, and he's sitting on the outside with the ball in his mitt.

Playing Catch
(Or, Putting It All Together)

When I've tried to put together all the do's and don'ts of pitch selection and location, I've found that Steve Carlton puts it best. What you must do is ignore the batter, Carlton says, and think of the pitcher and catcher as having an elevated game of catch.

What any pitcher who hopes to succeed in the major leagues must learn is to throw through the batter and to the catcher. Too many young pitchers may be overly impressed with the way a big-league hitter puts his jock on. They throw to him and not through him. It's the same when a catcher throws the ball down to second base. If he throws *to* second base, his ball is more likely to go into the dirt than if he's throwing to the outfield grass (with the shortstop or second baseman cutting it off before it gets there). That's what you call throwing through the bag, and a catcher must have his pitcher do the same thing when a hitter is in the box.

It's always been a great frustration of mine that the hidden aspects of a catcher's performance have never been adequately explained. I've tried to do that in this story, and hopefully I've shed some light on the subject. At the very least, the next time you see a manager take a slow walk to the mound, you'll be able to guess what he's talking about. He'll probably be telling his pitcher to keep the ball down (and warning him not to give the batter anything good to hit—but not to walk him). And you'll know exactly what the pitcher will answer. Thanks very much for the advice, but I'm pitching to my catcher, and we're going to work in and out. And by the way, we think you're making far too many trips to the mound.

If it hadn't been for the intrusion of Messrs. Malloy and McCarver, we could have moved neatly from the Bronx Zoo to Yazoo, the Mississippi city that raised Willie Morris. This chapter from his autobiographical *North Toward Home* is about growing up with baseball, about recreation and re-creation, and about a memorable bit of oneupmanship.

WILLIE MORRIS

The Phantom

Like Mark Twain and his comrades growing up a century before in another village on the other side of the Mississippi, my friends and I had but one sustaining ambition in the 1940s. Theirs in Hannibal was to be steamboatmen; ours in Yazoo was to be major-league baseball players. In the summers we thought and talked of little else. We memorized batting averages, fielding averages, slugging averages; we knew the roster of the Cardinals and the Red Sox better than their own managers must have known them, and to hear the broadcasts from all the big-city ballparks with their memorable names—the Polo Grounds, Wrigley Field, Fenway Park, Yankee Stadium—was to set our imagination churning for the glory and riches those faraway places would one day bring us. One of our friends went to St. Louis on his vacation to see the Cards, and when he returned with the autographs of Stan Musial, Red Schoendienst, Country Slaughter, Marty Marion, Joe Garagiola, and a dozen others, we could hardly keep down our envy. I hated that boy for a month and secretly wished him dead, not only because he took on new airs but because I wanted those scraps of paper with their magic characters. I wished also that my own family was wealthy enough to take me to a big-league town for two weeks, but to a bigger place even than St. Louis: Chicago, maybe, with not one but two teams, or best of all, to New York, with three. I had bought a baseball cap in Jackson, a real one from the Brooklyn Dodgers, and a Jackie Robinson Louisville Slugger, and one day when I could not even locate any of the others for catch or for baseball talk, I sat on a curb on Grand Avenue with the most dreadful feelings of being caught forever by time—trapped there always in my scrawny and helpless condition. *I'm ready, I'm ready,* I kept thinking to myself, but that remote future when I would wear a cap like that and be a hero for a grandstand full of people seemed so far away I knew it would never come. I must have been the most dejected looking child you ever saw, sitting hunched up on the curb and dreaming of glory in the mythical cities of the North. I felt worse when a carload of high school boys halted right in front of where I sat and they started reciting what they always did when they saw me alone and daydreaming: *Wee Willie Winkie walks through the town, upstairs and downstairs in his nightgown.* Then one of them said, "Winkie, you *gettin'* much?" "You bastards!" I shouted, and they drove off, laughing like wild men.

Almost every afternoon when the heat was not unbearable, my father and I would go out to the old baseball field behind the armory to hit flies. I would stand far out in center field, and he would station himself with a fungo at home plate, hitting me one high fly, or Texas Leaguer, or line drive after another, sometimes for an hour or more without stopping. My dog would get out there in the outfield with me and retrieve the inconsequential dribblers or the ones that went too far. I was light and speedy and could make the most fantastic catches, turning completely around and forgetting the ball sometimes to head for the spot where it would descend or tumbling head-on for a diving catch. The smell of that new-cut grass was the finest of all smells, and I could run forever and never get tired. It was a dreamy, suspended state, those late afternoons, thinking of nothing but outfield flies as the world drifted lazily by on Jackson Avenue. I learned to judge what a ball would do by instinct, heading the way it went as if I owned it, and I knew in my heart I could make the big time. Then, after all that exertion, my father would shout, "I'm whupped!" and we would quit for the day.

When I was twelve I became a part-time sportswriter for the Yazoo *Herald,* whose courtly proprietors allowed me unusual independence. I wrote up an occasional high school or Legion game in a florid prose, filled with phrases like "two-ply blow" and "circuit ringer." My mentor was the sports editor of the Memphis *Commercial Appeal,* whose name was Walter Stewart, a man who could invest the most humdrum athletic contest with the elements of Shakespearean tragedy. I learned whole paragraphs of his by heart and used some of his expressions for my reports on games between Yazoo and Satartia, or the other teams. That summer, when I was twelve, having never seen a baseball game higher than the Jackson Senators of Class B, my father finally relented and took me to Memphis to see the Chicks, who were Double A. It was the farthest I had ever been from home and the largest city I had ever seen; I walked around in a state of joyousness, admiring the crowds and the big park high above the River, and best of all, the grand old lobby of the Chisca Hotel.

Staying with us at the Chisca were the Nashville Vols, who were there for a big series with the Chicks. I stayed close to the lobby to get a glimpse of them; when I discovered they spent all day, up until the very moment they left for the ballpark, playing the pinball machine, I stationed myself there, too. Their names were Tookie Gilbert, Smokey Burgess, Chuck Workman, and Bobo Hollomon, the latter being the one who got as far as the St. Louis Browns, pitched a no-hitter in his first major-league game, and failed to win another before being shipped down forever to obscurity; one afternoon my father and I ran into them outside the hotel on the way to the game and gave them a ride in our taxi. I could have been fit for tying, especially when Smokey Burgess tousled my hair and asked me if I batted right or left, but when I listened to them as they grumbled about having to get out to the ballpark so early and complained about the season having two more damned months to go and about how ramshackle their team bus was, I was too disillusioned even to tell my friends when I got home.

Because back home, even among the adults, baseball was all-meaning; it was the link with the outside. A place known around town simply as the Store, down near the train depot, was the principal center of this ferment. The Store had sawdust on the floor and long shreds of flypaper hanging from the ceiling. Its most familiar staples were Rexall supplies, oysters on the half shell, legal beer, and illegal whiskey, the latter served up, Mississippi bootlegger style, by the bottle from a hidden shelf and costing not merely the price of the whiskey but the investment in gas required to go to Louisiana to fetch it. There was a long counter in the back. On one side of it, the white workingmen congregated after hours every afternoon to compare the day's scores and talk batting averages, and on the other side, also talking baseball, were the Negroes, juxtaposed in a face-to-face arrangement with the whites. The scores were chalked up on a blackboard hanging on a red-and-purple wall, and the conversations were carried on in fast, galloping shouts from one end of the room to the other. An intelligent white boy of twelve was even permitted, in that atmosphere of heady freedom, before anyone knew the name of Justice Warren or had heard much of the U.S. Supreme Court, a quasi-public position favoring the Dodgers, who had Jackie Robinson, Roy Campanella, and Don Newcombe—not to mention, so it was rumored, God knows how many Chinese and mulattoes being groomed in the minor leagues. I remember my father turned to some friends at the Store one day and observed, "Well, you can say what you want to about that nigger Robinson, but he's got *guts*," and to a man the others nodded, a little reluctantly, but in agreement nonetheless. And one of them said he had read somewhere that Pee Wee Reese, a white southern boy, was the best friend Robinson had on the team, which proved they had chosen the right one to watch after him.

There were two firehouses in town, and on hot afternoons the firemen at both establishments sat outdoors in their shirt-sleeves, with the baseball broadcast turned up as loud as it would go. On his day off work my father, who had left Cities Service and was now a bookkeeper for the wholesale grocery, usually started with Firehouse No. 1 for the first few innings and then hit No. 2 before ending up at the Store for the postgame conversations.

I decided not to try out for the American Legion Junior Baseball team that summer. Legion baseball was an important thing for country boys in those parts, but I was too young and skinny, and I had heard that the coach, a dirt farmer known as Gentleman Joe, made his protégées lie flat in the infield while he walked on their stomachs; he also forced them to take 3-mile runs through the streets of town, talked them into going to church, and persuaded them to give up Coca-Colas. A couple of summers later, when I did go out for the team, I found out that Gentleman Joe did in fact insist on these soul-strengthening rituals; because of them, we won the Mississippi State Championship, and the merchants in town took up a collection and sent us all the way to St. Louis to see the Cards play the Phillies. My main concern that earlier summer, however, lay in the more academic aspects of the game. I knew more about baseball, its technology and its ethos, than all the firemen and Store experts put together. Having read most of its literature, I could give a sizable lecture on the infield-fly rule alone, which only a thin minority of the townspeople knew existed. Gentleman Joe was held in some esteem for his strategical sense, yet he was the only man I ever knew who could call for a sacrifice bunt with two men out and not have a bad conscience about it. I remember one dismaying moment that came to me while I was watching a country semipro game. The home team had runners on first and third with one out when the batter hit a ground ball to the first baseman, who stepped on first and then threw to second. The shortstop, covering second, stepped on the base but made no attempt to tag the runner. The man on third had crossed the plate, of course, but the umpire, who was not very familiar with the subtleties of the rules, signaled a double play. Sitting in the grandstand, I knew that it was not a double play at all and that the run had scored, but when I went down, out of my Christian duty, to tell the manager of the local team that he had just been done out of a run, he told me I was crazy. This was the kind of brainpower I was up against.

That summer the local radio station, the one where we broadcast our Methodist programs, started a baseball quiz program. A razor-blade company offered free blades, and the station chipped in a dollar, all of which went to the first listener to telephone with the right answer to the day's baseball question. If there was no winner, the next day's pot would go up a dollar. At the end of the month they had to close down the program because I was winning all the money. It got so easy, in fact, that I stopped phoning in the answers some afternoons so that the pot could build up and make my winnings more spectacular. I netted about $25 and a ten-year supply of double-edged, smooth-contact razor blades before they gave up. One day, when the jackpot was a mere $2, the announcer tried to confuse me. "Babe Ruth," he said, "hit sixty home runs in 1927 to set the major-league record. What man had the next-highest total?" I telephoned and said, "George Herman Ruth. He hit fifty-nine in another season." My adversary, who had developed an acute dislike of me, said that was not the correct answer. He said it should have been *Babe* Ruth.

This incident angered me, and I won for the next four days, just for the hell of it.

On Sunday afternoons we sometimes drove out of town and along hot, dusty roads to baseball fields that were little more than parched red clearings, the outfield sloping out of the woods and ending in some tortuous gully filled with yellowed paper, old socks, and vintage cow shit. One of the backwoods teams had a fastball pitcher named Eckert, who didn't have any teeth, and a fifty-year-old left-handed catcher named Smith. Since there were no catcher's mitts made for left-handers, Smith had to wear a mitt on his throwing hand. In his simian posture he would catch the ball and toss it lightly into the air and then whip his mitt off and catch the ball in his bare left hand before throwing it back. It was a wonderfully lazy way to spend those Sunday afternoons—my father and my friends and I sitting in the grass behind the chicken-wire back-stop with eight or ten dozen farmers, watching the wrong-handed catcher go through his contorted gyrations and listening at the same time to our portable radio, which brought us the rising inflections of a baseball announcer called the Old Scotchman. The sounds of the two games, our own and the one being broadcast from Brooklyn or Chicago, merged and rolled across the bumpy outfield and the gully into the woods; it was a combination that seemed perfectly natural to everyone there.

I can see the town now on some hot, still weekday afternoon in midsummer: ten thousand souls and nothing doing. Even the red water truck was a diversion, coming slowly up Grand Avenue with its sprinklers on full force, the water making sizzling steam clouds on the pavement while half-naked Negro children followed the truck up the street and played in the torrent until they got soaking wet. Over on Broadway, where the old men sat drowsily in straw chairs on the pavement near the Bon-Ton Café, whittling to make the time pass, you could laze around on the sidewalks—barefoot, if your feet were tough enough to stand the scalding concrete—watching the big cars with out-of-state plates whip by, the driver hardly knowing and certainly not caring what place this was. Way up that fantastic hill, Broadway seemed to end in a seething mist—little heat mirages that shimmered off the asphalt; on the main street itself there would be only a handful of cars parked here and there, and the merchants and the lawyers sat in the shade under their broad awnings, talking slowly, aimlessly, in the cryptic summer way. The one o'clock whistle at the sawmill would send out its loud bellow, reverberating up the streets to the bend in the Yazoo River, hardly making a ripple in the heavy somnolence.

But by two o'clock almost every radio in town was tuned in to the Old Scotchman. His rhetoric dominated the place. It hovered in the branches of the trees, bounced off the hills, and came out of the darkened stores; the merchants and the old men cocked their ears to him, and even from the big cars that sped by, their tires making lapping sounds in the softened highway, you could hear his voice, being carried past you out into the delta.

The Old Scotchman's real name was Gordon McLendon, and he described the big-league games for the Liberty Broadcasting System, which had outlets mainly in the South and the Southwest. He had a deep, rich voice, and I think he was the best rhetorician, outside of Bilbo and Nye Bevan, I have ever heard. Under his handling a baseball game took on a life of its own. As in the prose of the *Commercial Appeal*'s Walter Stewart, his games were rare and remarkable entities; casual pop flies had the flow of history behind them, double plays resembled the stark clashes of old armies, and home runs deserved acknowledgment on earthen urns. Later, when I came across Thomas Wolfe, I felt I had heard him before, from Shibe Park, Crosley Field, or Yankee Stadium.

One afternoon I was sitting around my house listening to the Old Scotchman, admiring the vivacity of a man who said he was a contemporary of Connie Mack. (I learned later that he was twenty-nine.) That day he was doing the Dodgers and the Giants from the Polo Grounds. The game, as I recall, was in the fourth inning, and the Giants were ahead by about 4–1. It was a boring game, however, and I began experimenting with my father's shortwave radio, an impressive mechanism a couple of feet wide, which had an aerial that almost touched the ceiling and the name of every major city in the world on its dial. It was by far the best radio I had ever seen; there was not another one like it in town. I switched the dial to shortwave and began picking up African drum music, French jazz, Australian weather reports, and a lecture from the British Broadcasting Company on the people who wrote poems for Queen Elizabeth. Then a curious thing happened. I came across a baseball game—the Giants and the Dodgers, from the Polo Grounds. After a couple of minutes I discovered that the game was in the eighth inning. I turned back to the local station, but here the Giants and Dodgers were still in the fourth. I turned again to the shortwave broadcast and listened to the last inning, a humdrum affair that ended with Carl Furillo popping out to shortstop, Gil Hodges grounding out second to first, and Roy Campanella lining out to center. Then I went back to the Old Scotchman and listened to the rest of the game. In the top of the ninth, an hour or so later, a ghostly thing occurred; to my astonishment and titillation, the game ended with Furillo popping out to short, Hodges grounding out second to first, and Campanella lining out to center.

I kept this unusual discovery to myself, and the next day, an hour before the Old Scotchman began his play-by-play of the second game of the series, I dialed the shortwave frequency, and, sure enough, they were doing the Giants and the Dodgers again. I learned that I was listening to the Armed Forces Radio Service, which broadcast games played in New York. As the game progressed, I began jotting down notes on the action. When the first four innings were over, I turned to the local station just in time to get the Old Scotchman for the first batter. The Old Scotchman's account of the game matched the shortwave's almost perfectly. The Scotchman's, in fact, struck me as being considerably more poetic than the one I had heard first. But I did not doubt him, since I could hear the roar of the crowd, the crack of the bat, and the Scotchman's precise description of foul balls that fell into the crowd, the gestures of the base coaches, and the expression on the face of a small boy who was eating a lemon popsicle in a box seat behind first base. I decided that the broadcast was being delayed somewhere along the line, maybe because we were so far from New York.

That was my first thought, but after a close comparison of the two broadcasts for the rest of the game, I sensed that something more sinister was taking place. For one thing, the Old Scotchman's description of the count on a batter, though it jibed 90 percent of the time, did not always match. For another, the Scotchman's crowd, compared with the other, kept up an ungodly noise. When Robinson stole second on shortwave, he did it without drawing a throw and without sliding, while for Mississippians the feat was performed in a cloud of angry, petulant dust. A foul ball that went over the grandstand and out of the park for shortwave listeners in Alaska, France, and the Argentine produced for the firemen, bootleggers, farmers, and myself a primitive scramble that ended with a feeble old lady catching the ball on the first bounce to the roar of an assembly that would have outnumbered Grant's at Old Cold Harbor. But the most revealing development came after the Scotchman's game was over. After the usual summaries, he mentioned that the game had been "re-created." I had never taken notice of that particular word before, because I lost interest once a game was over. I went to the dictionary, and under "re-create" I found, "To invest with fresh vigor and strength; to refresh, invigorate (nature, strength, a person or thing)." The Old Scotchman most assuredly invested a game with fresh vigor and strength, but this told me nothing. My deepest suspicions were confirmed, however, when I found the second definition of the word—"To create anew."

So there it was. I was happy to have fathomed the mystery, as perhaps no one else in the whole town had done. The Old Scotchman, for all his wondrous expressions, was not only several innings behind every game he described but was no doubt sitting in some air-conditioned studio in the hinterland, where he got the happenings of the game by news ticker; sound effects accounted for the crack of the bat and the crowd noises. Instead of being disappointed in the Scotchman, I was all the more pleased by his genius, for he made pristine facts more actual than actuality, a valuable lesson when the day finally came that I started reading literature. I must add, however, that this appreciation did not obscure the realization that I had at my disposal a weapon of unimaginable dimensions.

Next day I was at the shortwave again, but I learned with much disappointment that the game being broadcast on shortwave was not the one the Scotchman had chosen to describe. I tried every afternoon after that and discovered that I would have to wait until the Old Scotchman decided to do a game out of New York before I could match his game with the one described live on shortwave. Sometimes, I learned later, these coincidences did not occur for days; during an important Dodger or Yankee series, however, his game and that of the Armed Forces Radio Service often coincided for two or three days running. I was happy, therefore, to find, on an afternoon a few days later, that both the shortwave and the Scotchman were carrying the Yankees and the Indians.

I settled myself at the shortwave with notebook and pencil and took down every pitch. This I did for four full innings, and then I turned back to the town station, where the Old Scotchman was just beginning the first inning. I checked the first batter to make sure the accounts jibed. Then, armed with my notebook, I ran down the street to the corner grocery, a minor outpost of baseball intellection, presided over by my young Negro friend Bozo, a knowledgeable student of the game, the same one who kept my dog in bologna. I found Bozo behind the meat counter, with the Scotchman's account going full blast. I arrived at the interim between the top and bottom of the first inning.

"Who's pitchin' for the Yankees, Bozo?" I asked.

"They're pitchin' Allie Reynolds," Bozo said. "Old Scotchman says Reynolds really got the stuff today. He just set 'em down one, two, three."

The Scotchman, meanwhile, was describing the way the pennants were flapping in the breeze. Phil Rizzuto, he reported, was stepping to the plate.

"Bo," I said, trying to sound cut-and-dried, "you know what I think? I think Rizzuto's gonna take a couple of fast called strikes, then foul one down the left-field line, and then line out straight to Boudreau at short."

"Yeah?" Bozo said. He scatched his head and leaned lazily across the counter.

I went up front to buy something and then came back. The count worked to nothing and two on Rizzuto—a couple of fast called strikes and a foul down the left side. "This one," I said to Bozo, "he lines straight to Boudreau at short."

The Old Scotchman, pausing dramatically between words as was his custom, said, "Here's the windup on nothing and two. Here's the pitch on its way— There's a hard line drive! But Lou Boudreau's there at shortstop, and he's got it. Phil hit that one on the nose, but Boudreau was right there."

Bozo looked over at me, his eyes bigger than they were. "How'd you know that?" he asked.

Ignoring this query, I made my second prediction. "Bozo," I said, "Tommy Henrich's gonna hit the first pitch up against the right-field wall and slide in with a double."

"How come you think so?"

"Because I can predict anything that's gonna happen in baseball in the next ten years," I said. "I can tell you anything."

The Old Scotchman was describing Henrich at the plate. "Here comes the first pitch. Henrich swings, there's a hard smash into right field! . . . This one may be out of here! It's going, going— No! It's off the wall in right center. Henrich's rounding first, on his way to second. Here's the relay from Doby . . . Henrich slides in safely with a double!" The Yankee crowd sent up an awesome roar in the background.

"Say, how'd you know that?" Bozo asked. "How'd you know he was gonna wind up at second?"

"I just can tell. I got extravision," I said. On the radio, far in the background, the public-address system announced Yogi Berra. "Like Berra right now. You know what? He's gonna hit a one–one pitch down the right-field line—"

"How come you know?" Bozo said. He was getting mad.

"Just a second," I said. "I'm gettin' static." I stood dead still, put my hands up against my temples and opened my eyes wide. "Now it's comin' through clear. Yeah, Yogi's gonna hit a one–one pitch down the right-field line, and it's gonna be fair by about three or four feet—I can't say exactly—and Henrich's gonna score from second, but the throw is gonna get Yogi at second by a mile."

This time Bozo was silent, listening to the Scotchman, who described the ball and the strike, then said: "Henrich takes the lead off second. Benton looks over, stretches, delivers. Yogi swings." (There was the bat crack.) "There's a line drive down the right side! It's barely inside the foul line. It may go for extra bases! Henrich's rounding third and coming in with a run. Berra's moving toward second. Here comes the throw! . . . And they *get* him! They get Yogi easily on the slide at second!"

Before Bozo could say anything else, I reached in my pocket for my notes. "I've just written down here what I think's gonna happen in the first four innings," I said. "Like DiMag. See, he's gonna pop up to Mickey Vernon at first on a one–nothing pitch in just a minute. But don't you worry. He's gonna hit a three-hundred-eighty-foot homer in the fourth with nobody on base on a full count. You just follow these notes and you'll see I can predict anything that's gonna happen in the next ten years." I handed him the paper, turned around, and left the store just as DiMaggio, on a one–nothing pitch, popped up to Vernon at first.

Then I went back home and took more notes from the shortwave. The Yanks clobbered the Indians in the late innings and won easily. On the local station, however, the Old Scotchman was in the top of the fifth inning. At this juncture I went to the telephone and called Firehouse No. 1.

"Hello," a voice answered. It was the fire chief.

"Hello, Chief, can you tell me the score?" I said. Calling the firehouse for baseball information was a common practice.

"The Yanks are ahead five to two."

"This is the Phantom you're talkin' with," I said.

"Who?"

"The Phantom. Listen carefully, Chief. Reynolds is gonna open this next inning with a pop-up to Doby. Then Rizutto will single to left on a one–one count. Henrich's gonna force him at second on a two-and-one pitch but make it to first. Berra's gonna double to right on a nothing-and-one pitch, and Henrich's goin' to third. DiMaggio's gonna foul a couple off and then double down the left-field line, and both Henrich and Yogi are gonna score. Brown's gonna pop out to third to end the inning."

"Aw, go to hell," the chief said, and hung up.

This was precisely what happened, of course. I phoned No. 1 again after the inning.

"Hello."

"Hi. This is the Phantom again."

"Say, how'd you know that?"

"Stick with me," I said ominously, "and I'll feed you predictions. I can predict anything that's gonna happen anywhere in the next ten years." After a pause I added, "Beware of fire real soon," for good measure, and hung up.

I left my house and hurried back to the corner grocery. When I got there, the entire meat counter was surrounded by friends of Bozo's, about a dozen of them. They were gathered around my notes, talking passionately and shouting. Bozo saw me standing by the bread counter. "There he is! That's the one!" he declared. His colleagues turned and stared at me in undisguised awe. They parted respectfully as I strolled over to the meat counter and ordered a dime's worth of bologna for my dog.

A couple of questions were directed at me from the group, but I replied, "I'm sorry for what happened in the fourth. I predicted DiMag was gonna hit a full-count pitch for that homer. It came out he hit it on two and two. There was too much static in the air between here and New York."

"Too much *static*?" one of them asked.

"Yeah. Sometimes the static confuses my extravision. But I'll be back to-morrow if everything's okay, and I'll try not to make any more big mistakes."

"Big mistakes!" one of them shouted, and the crowd laughed admiringly, parting once more as I turned and left the store. I wouldn't have been at all surprised if they had tried to touch the hem of my shirt.

That day was only the beginning of my brief season of triumph. A schoolmate of mine offered me $5, for instance, to tell him how I had known that Johnny Mize was going to hit a two-run homer to break up one particularly close game for the Giants. One afternoon, on the basis of a lopsided first four innings, I had an older friend sneak into the Store and place a bet, which netted me $14.50. I felt so bad about it I tithed $1.45 in church the following Sunday. At Bozo's grocery store I was a full-scale oracle. To the firemen I remained the Phantom, and firefighting reached a peak of efficiency that month, simply because the firemen knew what was going to happen in the late innings and did not need to tarry when an alarm came.

One afternoon my father was at home listening to the Old Scotchman with a couple of out-of-town salesmen from Greenwood. They were sitting in the front room, and I had already managed to get the first three or four innings of the Cardinals and the Giants on paper before they arrived. The Old Scotchman was in the top of the first when I walked in and said hello. The men were talking business and listening to the game at the same time.

"I'm gonna make a prediction," I said. They stopped talking and looked at me. "I predict Musial's gonna take a ball and a strike and then hit a double to right field, scoring Schoendienst from second, but Marty Marion's gonna get tagged out at the plate."

"You're mighty smart," one of the men said. He suddenly sat up straight when the Old Scotchman reported, "Here's the windup and the pitch coming in. . . . Musial *swings!*" (bat crack, crowd roar). "He drives one into right field! This one's going up against the boards! . . . Schoendienst rounds third. He's coming on in to score! Marion dashes around third, legs churning. His cap falls off, but here he *comes!* Here's the toss to the plate. He's nabbed at home. He is *out* at the plate! Musial holds at second with a run-producing double."

Before I could parry the inevitable questions, my father caught me by the elbow and hustled me into a back room. "How'd you know that?" he asked.

"I was just guessin'," I said. "It was nothin' but luck."

He stopped for a moment, and then a new expression showed on his face. "Have *you* been callin' the firehouse?" he asked.

"Yeah, I guess a few times."

"Now, you tell me how you found out about all that. I mean it."

When I told you about the shortwave, I was afraid he might be mad, but on the contrary; he laughed uproariously. "Do you remember these next few innings?" he asked.

"I got it all written down," I said, and reached in my pocket for the notes. He took the notes and told me to go away. From the yard, a few minutes later, I heard him predicting the next inning to the salesmen.

A couple of days later, I phoned No. 1 again. "This is the Phantom," I said. "With two out, Branca's gonna hit Stinky Stanky with a fastball, and then Alvin Dark's gonna send him home with a triple."

"Yeah, we know it," the fireman said in a bored boice. "We're listenin' to a shortwave, too. You think you're somethin', don't you? You're Ray Morris's boy."

I knew everything was up. The next day, as a sort of final gesture, I took some more notes to the corner grocery in the third or fourth inning. Some of the old crowd was there, but the atmosphere was grim. They looked at me coldly. "Oh, man," Bozo said, "*we* know the Old Scotchman ain't at that game. He's four or five innings behind. He's makin' all that stuff up." The others grumbled and turned away. I slipped quietly out the door.

My period as a seer was over, but I went on listening to the shortwave broadcasts out of New York a few days more. Then, a little to my surprise, I went back to the Old Scotchman, and in time I found that the firemen, the bootleggers, and the few dirt farmers who had shortwave sets all did the same. From then on, accurate, up-to-the-minute baseball news was in disrepute there. I believe we all went back to the Scotchman not merely out of loyalty but because, in our great isolation, he touched our need for a great and unmitigated eloquence.

Joe's American Legion Junior team actually amounted to an All-Star squad from all the country towns surrounding ours; it was easier to make the high school team first. On Tuesday and Friday afternoons we would ride in our red-and-black bus through the heavy green woods to the small crossroads towns to play the locals. The crowds would sometimes be in a foul frame of mind, especially if the farmers had got hold of the corn gourd early in the day. Since we were the "city boys," with our pictures in the Yazoo *Herald* every now and again, we were particularly ripe for all that boondocks venom. The farmers would stand around the field shouting obscenities at the "slickers," sometimes loosening up their lungs with a vicious organized whoop that sounded like a cross between a rebel yell and a redneck preacher exorcizing the devil and all his family. More often than not, to compound the injury, we got beat. Yet far from being gracious in victory, those sons of dirt farmers rubbed our noses in our own catastrophes, taunting us with threats to whip us all over again in the outfield pasture, while their elders stood around in a group as our coach chased us into the bus and shouted, "You ain't such hot stuff, slickers!" or "Go on back to town now, boys, and get your *photos* took some more." One afternoon when I ruined the no-hitter the best pitcher in the county had going (he later made Double A), with a broken-bat fluke into right field in the eighth inning, I thought those farmers might slice me in pieces and feed me to the boll weevils. "You proud of that little skinny hit?" one of them shouted at me, standing with his nose next to mine, and his companion picked up the broken bat that had done the evil deed and splintered it apart against a tree trunk. When we beat the same team two or three weeks later on our home field, I ran into their shortstop and catcher, two tough hard-noses, on Main Street the following Saturday. They sidled right up to me and waited there glowering, breathing in my face and not saying a word for a while. We stood nostril to nostril until one of them said, "You think you're somethin', don't you, bastid? Beat us at home with your crooked umpires. Next time you come see us we'll whup you till the shit turns green." And they did.

The next summer, when I made the Legion team, I finally came under the tutelage of Gentleman Joe, a hard taskmaster of the old school despite his unfamiliarity with "stragety," as he called it. Gentleman Joe would always have us pray before a game and sometimes between innings when the going got rough. He was a big one for church and began to remind me more and more of my old fourth-grade teacher. But his pep talks, back behind the shabby old grandstand of our playing field, drew on such pent-up emotions, being so full of Scriptures and things of God's earth, that I suspected we were being enlisted not to play baseball but to fight in the Army of the Lord.

That was the team that won the Mississippi championship, beating almost everybody without much trouble. Before the final game for the championship in Greenwood, with 4,000 people waiting in the stands, Gentleman Joe delivered the best speech of all. "*Gentlemen*," he said, using that staple designation that earned him his nickname, "I'm just a simple farmer. Fifteen acres is all I got, and two mules, a cow, and a lot of mouths to feed." He paused between his words, and his eyes watered over. "I've neglected my little crop because of this team, and the weevils gave me trouble last year, and they're doin' it again now. I ain't had enough rain, and I don't plan to get much more. The corn looks so brown, if it got another shade browner, it'd flake right off. But almost every afternoon you'd find me in my pickup on the way to town to teach you gentlemen the game of baseball. You're fine Christian gentlemen who don't come no finer. But I saw you gettin' a little lazy yestiddy, showin' off some to all them cute little delta girls in the bleachers. We didn't come way up here to show off; we come up here to *win!*" Then, his pale blue eyes flashing fire, half whispering and half shouting, he said: "Gentlemen, I want us to pray, and then . . . I want you to go out there on that field and win this Miss'ippi championship! You'll be proud of it for the rest of your lives. You'll remember it when you're ole men. You'll think about it when you're dyin' and your teeth are all gone. You'll be able to tell your grandchildren about this day. Go out there, gentlemen and *win this ball game for your coach!*" After we prayed and headed for that field like a pack of wild animals, the third baseman and I shouted in unison, and we meant it: "Boys, let's get out and win for our *coach!*" That fall they gave us shiny blue jackets, with "Miss. State Champions" written on the back; I was so happy with that jacket I almost wore it out. And when my old dog Skip died of a heart attack trying to outflank a flea that had plagued him since the Roosevelt administration, looking at me with his sad black eyes and expiring in a sigh as old as death, that is what I wrapped him in before I took him in my arms and put him in the ground.

Two or three years later, when we were past the age for Legion competition, I had my last confrontation with baseball. The owner of the tire store organized a semipro team, made up of college and high school players from around the state. There was a popular tire that year called the "Screaming Eagle," and thus we were the Yazoo "Screaming Eagles," the pride of the delta. Out of a roster of fourteen, one made it to the major leagues, one to a Triple A league, and two to Double A. That team won the Deep South Championship, and at the national tournament in Wichita beat the U.S. Navy and ended up close to the top.

The state league we played in, making $25 or $30 apiece a game, was composed of both delta and hill-country towns, and we played to big Saturday night crowds who had heard about the Screaming Eagles, under lights so faulty that it was difficult to see a ball coming at you in the outfield. Insects bigger than fifty-cent pieces caromed off the bulbs and zoomed around us in our isolated stations in the field, and the ground was full of holes, ruts, and countless other hazards. Playing center field one night in one of the hill towns, I went back to examine a sloping red mound of earth that served as the outfield fence; I discovered a strand of barbed wire 8 or 10 feet long, an old garbage can full of broken beer bottles, and a narrow hole, partially covered with Johnson grass, that looked as if it might be the home for the local rattlers. The most indigenous field of all was near a little delta town called Silver City. It was built right on a cotton field and was owned by the two young heirs to the plantation on which it sat, one of whom later made it all the way to the New York Yankees. The grandstand would seat close to 2,000 people, but the lights were so bad you had to exert all your finer perceptions to discriminate between the bugs and the balls; this took genius and tested one's natural instincts. It was here, in the state finals, that a sinking line drive came toward me in right field, with the bases loaded and two out in the first inning; I lost track of that ball the moment it came out of the infield. A second later I felt a sharp blow on my kneecap, and then I saw the ball bouncing 30 feet away over by the bleachers. "*Get* it, boy! Stomp on it! Piss on it!" the enemy bleacher section shouted gleefully, and by the time I could retrieve it, three runs had scored. Between innings our pitcher, who soon would be pitching in the major leagues for the Pittsburgh Pirates, looked at me wordlessly but with a vicious and despairing contempt. Right then, with the world before me, I promised myself that if I ever made it to those mythical cities of the North, the ones I had dreamed about in my Brooklyn cap, it would have to be with a different set of credentials.

This 1898 newspaper clipping turned up in a dusty scrapbook kept by turn-of-the-century star Cy Seymour. It is a strange story, to be sure, but replete with unexpected pleasures: the refreshingly matter-of-fact (if, to modern sensibilities, brutal) attitude toward disability; the post-playing-career whereabouts of Hugh "One Arm" Daily (here spelled Daly), previously unknown; and the stunningly offhand solution to one of the game's most perplexing mysteries—the origin of the epithet "yannigan," reserved for scrub or second-rate players.

NEW YORK *WORLD*

Armless, Legless Baseball Pitchers

Herbert Van Cleef, of Trenton, N.J., is the baseball wonder of the age. He is a legless pitcher and has as many curves, shoots, drops, snake twisters, and raise curves as even "Si" Seymour, of the Giants, can untangle from his celebrated left "whip."

There have been one-legged catchers, one-armed twirlers, and wooden-headed players galore during the long history of the national game, but Van Cleef tops all the baseball freaks who ever came down the pike.

The most famous cripple who ever played the game was Hugh Daly, better known to patrons of the sport fifteen years or so ago, when he was in his prime, as "One Arm Daly," and "Fin Daly." Daly's left arm was cut off just below the elbow, and when he was pitching, the stump was covered with several layers of chamois skin, topped with hard leather. Daly was a very prominent professional player for many years. He pitched for the Cleveland League Club and many other prominent clubs in both the National League and American Association. He is best remembered by New Yorkers as a pitcher for the old Metropolitans in 1882. He was a star player of that famous band known as "Mutrie's Indians."

Although having just but one hand, Daly was a fair batter and made in his career many long hits. He was one of the wildest Indians of the Mutrie "push." He was a great poker player and could shuffle cards as deftly as the best, and when playing the "paper" with his fellow players, seldom got up from the table without having most of their salaries in his pockets.

"Tom" Deasley was "Fin's" catcher and they were a great pair when they did the battery work. "Tom" was about as crazy as they make 'em—"nutty" his associate players said, but "Tom" was as good and game a catcher as ever donned a mask and could handle Daly's terrific speed and curves to the "Queen's taste." The two were the best of friends, and yet they were continually squabbling during a game, only to "blow the froth" amicably together when the game was over.

One incident that happened during a game in Baltimore that the writer witnessed will serve to illustrate the peculiar eccentricities of the pair. Daly's stump was somewhat tender, although well protected, and he was never over anxious to face a hot hit or hard throw. Deasley knew this weakness of his partner and, when not feeling in the best of humor, would throw the ball back to Daly on a line and hard. In this particular game the two had some unusually hot words, and "Tom," to get even, threw several swift balls back to his pitcher. "Arch them, 'Tommy,' arch them!" shouted Daly, but Deasley paid no attention to this plaintive appeal, but continued to send them back on a line. At last Daly held up his finger and, motioning to Deasley, said: "Come here, 'Tommy.' I want to show you a new sign."

The two met midway between the plate and the pitcher's box, and as Deasley leaned forward to hear the instructions, Daly, with a terrific uppercut, landed the stump on the point of Deasley's jaw. Poor "Tom" got the cleanest knockout of his career. The game was played out after "Tom" had been revived, but he "arched" them during the balance of the contest.

Deasley is now in some asylum in Philadelphia, having "gone nutty for fair," and Daly is back at his old business as a scene shifter in a Baltimore theater.

Another cripple who was famous as a ballplayer was "Con" Yannigan, who made a big reputation around Hartford, Connecticut, several years ago. He was a first baseman and had a cork leg. Yannigan was brought out by "Steve" Brady, of the "Old Mets." "Steve" considered him one of the best first basemen he ever saw. A great play of his was to block off base runners with his game leg. Opposing players could sharpen their spikes to a razor edge, but "Con" didn't scare for a cent.

"Charlie" Bennett, the great catcher of the Detroit and Boston champion teams, has both of his legs off, as the result of a railroad accident, but has done no catching since.

So that Van Cleef is, without doubt, the star wonder of the age as a baseball pitcher. He lost his legs in a railroad accident two years ago. Before that unfortunate occurrence Van Cleef was a pitcher of merit. He was captain of a local team in Trenton and acknowledged to be its best player. In fact, he had professional aspirations and no doubt would have become a league player. "Mike" Tiernan, who is a native of Trenton, knew Van Cleef well and had promised to push him forward.

The accident to Van Cleef did not dampen his ardor or enthusiasm as a ballplayer. Just as soon as he had recovered from his injuries, he attended a game. It was between his old team and another local club for the city championship. His team was defeated by reason of the poor work of the pitcher. This was gall and wormwood to Van Cleef. He immediately issued a challenge for a return game, saying he would pitch for his side the next time—and would win, too. He was laughed at and derided, but when the second game came off, Van Cleef was there and in uniform ready to pitch. He was not on his old legs, however, but in a small carriage pushed by his brother.

As the game progressed, it was seen that Van Cleef had retained all of his old curves and speed, and he also worked several new tricks on his opponents. He never pitched a better game, even when he was whole, and his side won, as he said it would. His reputation has become national.

Van Cleef will make his first appearance in this vicinity this afternoon at Standard Park, Fair View, Hudson County, New Jersey. He will pitch for the Standard Athletics against the second team of the Englewood Field Club. Standard Park is 9 miles from the city, on the line of the Northern Railroad of New Jersey. The game is for the benefit of the legless pitcher, and his pluck and gameness are surely entitled to recognition.

The Dean of American Sportswriters was a mere tad when the first three of these Casey sequels were published in *Base-Ball Ballads* (1910). The first he wrote in 1906 and published the following year under the pseudonym James Wilson; the second, Rice declared, was rivaled for pathos only by Goldsmith's *Deserted Village*; the third is a delightful parody of Eugene Field's "The Man Who Worked with Dana on the Noo York Sun"; and the fourth was written years later in amazed response to a letter to the newspaper editor inquiring what exactly *was* "Casey at the Bat." There are many sequels to Ernest Lawrence Thayer's classic original, first published in the San Francisco *Examiner* on June 3, 1888. These include such implausible efforts as "Mrs. Casey at the Bat," "Casey's Daughter at the Bat," and even "Casey—Forty Years Later"!

GRANTLAND RICE

That Man from Mudville

CASEY'S REVENGE

There were saddened hearts in Mudville for a week or even more;
There were muttered oaths and curses—every fan in town was sore.
"Just think," said one, "how soft it looked with Casey at the bat,
And then to think he'd go and spring a bush-league trick like that!"

All his past fame was forgotten—he was now a hopeless "shine."
They called him "Strike-Out Casey," from the mayor down the line;
And as he came to bat each day his bosom heaved a sigh,
While a look of hopeless fury shone in mighty Casey's eye.

He pondered in the days gone by that he had been their king,
That when he strolled up to the plate they made the welkin ring;
But now his nerve had vanished, for when he heard them hoot
He "fanned" or "popped out" daily, like some minor-league recruit.

He soon began to sulk and loaf, his batting eye went lame;
No home runs on the scorecard now were chalked against his name;
The fans without exception gave the manager no peace,
For one and all kept clamoring for Casey's quick release.

The Mudville squad began to slump, the team was in the air;
Their playing went from bad to worse—nobody seemed to care.
"Back to the woods with Casey!" was the cry from Rooters' Row.
"Get someone who can hit the ball and let that big dub go!"

The lane is long, someone has said, that never turns again,
And Fate, though fickle, often gives another chance to men;
And Casey smiled; his rugged face no longer wore a frown—
The pitcher who had started all the trouble came to town.

All Mudville had assembled—ten thousand fans had come
To see the twirler who had put big Casey on the bum;
And when he stepped into the box, the multitude went wild;
He doffed his cap in proud disdain, but Casey only smiled.

"Play ball!" the umpire's voice rang out, and then the game began.
But in that throng of thousands there was not a single fan
Who thought that Mudville had a chance, and with the setting sun
Their hopes sank low—the rival team was leading "four to one."

The last half of the ninth came round, with no change in the score;
But when the first man up hit safe, the crowd began to roar;
The din increased, the echo of ten thousand shouts was heard
When the pitcher hit the second and gave "four balls" to the third.

Three men on base—nobody out—three runs to tie the game!
A triple meant the highest niche in Mudville's hall of fame;
But here the rally ended, and the gloom was deep as night,
When the fourth one "fouled to catcher" and the fifth "flew out to right."

A dismal groan in chorus came; a scowl was on each face
When Casey walked up, bat in hand, and slowly took his place;
His bloodshot eyes in fury gleamed, his teeth were clenched in hate;
He gave his cap a vicious hook and pounded on the plate.

But fame is fleeting as the wind, and glory fades away;
There were no wild and woolly cheers, no glad acclaim this day;
They hissed and groaned and hooted as they clamored: "Strike him out!"
But Casey gave no outward sign that he had heard this shout.

The pitcher smiled and cut one loose—across the plate it sped;
Another hiss, another groan. "Strike one!" the umpire said.
Zip! Like a shot the second curve broke just below the knee.
"Strike two!" the umpire roared aloud; but Casey made no plea.

No roasting for the umpire now—his was an easy lot;
But here the pitcher whirled again—was that a rifle shot?
A whack, a crack, and out through the space the leather pellet flew,
A blot against the distant sky, a speck against the blue.

Above the fence in center field in rapid whirling flight
The sphere sailed on—the blot grew dim and then was lost to sight.
Ten thousand hats were thrown in air, ten thousand threw a fit,
But no one ever found the ball that mighty Casey hit.

Oh, somewhere in this favored land dark clouds may hide the sun,
And somewhere bands no longer play and children have no fun!
And somewhere over blighted lives there hangs a heavy pall,
But Mudville hearts are happy now, *for Casey hit the ball.*

L'envoi

There is no sequel to this plot—except in Mudville's square
The bronze bust of a patriot—arms crossed—is planted there.
His cap is cocked above one eye—and from his rugged face
The sneer still curls above the crowd—across the marketplace.

And underneath, in solid bronze, these words are graved in flame—
"Here is a man who rose and fell—and rose again to fame—
He blew a big one in the pinch—but facing jeering throngs
He came through Hell to scramble back—and prove a champ belongs."

MUDVILLE'S FATE

I wandered back to Mudville, Tom, where you and I were boys
And where we drew in days gone by our fill of childish joys;
Alas! the town's deserted now, and only rank weeds grow
Where mighty Casey fanned the air just twenty years ago.

Remember Billy Woodson's place, where, in the evening's shade,
The bunch would gather and discuss the home runs Casey made?
Dog fennel now grows thick around that "joint" we used to know,
Before old Casey whiffed the breeze some twenty years ago.

The grandstand, too, has been torn down; no bleachers met my gaze
Where you and I were wont to sit in happy bygone days;
The peanuts which we fumbled there have sprouted in a row
Where mighty Casey swung in vain just twenty years ago.

O how we used to cheer him, Tom, each time he came to bat!
And how we held our breath in awe when on the plate he spat;
And when he landed on the ball, how loud we yelped! But O
How loud we cursed when he struck out some twenty years ago!

The diamond is a corn patch now; the outfield's overgrown
With pumpkin vines and weedy plots; the rooters all have flown—
They couldn't bear to live on there, for nothing was the same
Where they had been so happy once before that fatal game.

The village band disbanded soon; the mayor, too, resigned.
The council even jumped its graft and in seclusion pined;
The marshal caught the next train out, and those we used to know
Began to leave in flocks and droves some twenty years ago.

For after Casey fanned that day the citizens all left,
And one by one they sought new lands, heartbroken and bereft;
The joyous shout no more rang out of children at their play;
The village blacksmith closed his shop; the druggist moved away.

Alas for Mudville's vanished pomp when mighty Casey reigned!
Her grandeur has departed now; her glory's long since waned.
Her place upon the map is lost, and no one seems to care
A whit about the old town now since Casey biffed the air.

THE MAN WHO PLAYED WITH ANSON
ON THE OLD CHICAGO TEAM

Thar showed up out in Mudville in the spring of '83
A feller evidently just recoverin' from a spree.
He said his name was Casey, and he wuz a sight to view
As he walked into the ballpark and inquired for work to do.
Thar wuzn't any openin', for you should understand
That wuz the time when Mudville had a bunch of stars on hand;
But the stranger lingered, tellin' Mickey Nolan and the rest
What an all-fired battin' av'rage he possessed when at his best,
Till finally he stated, quite by chance, as it would seem,
That he had played with Anson on the old Chicago team.

Wal, that was quite another thing; we owned that any cuss
Who'd played with old Pop Anson must be good enough for us;
So we took Casey at his word and signed him while we could,
Well knowin' if we didn't that some other ball club would,
For Kankakee wuz lookin' round for people that could play,
And Pikeville wouldn't overlook this feller any day;
And we give him quite a contract, tho' it made the others swear,
Sayin' we had done 'em dirty and it wuzn't on the square;
But we laid back and cackled, for the pennant warn't no dream
With the man who'd played with Anson on the old Chicago team.

It made our eyeballs nigh pop out and pop back in again
To hear that Casey tellin' of old Anson and his men;
Why home runs wuz so common that nobody waved a hat,
With Williamson, King Kelly, or Fred Pfeffer at the bat;
A man who didn't hit above .500 couldn't stick
With that old bunch, for Anson would release him mighty quick;
They handled ground balls with their teeth and often shut their eyes

While in the act of pullin' down the longest, hardest flies;
And after all the "fannin' bees" each night we used to dream
Of the man who played with Anson on the old Chicago team.

But somehow this feller Casey never felt like goin' in;
He spent his time at Wilson's shakin' poker dice for gin.
Whenever he wuz needed he wuz always sure to shirk,
Remarkin' he would have to wait before he started work.
If any other gent had loafed the way he used to do,
We'd have fined him fifty dollars every day, and benched him too;
But you see the fans respected him and backed him to the last
On account of his connections with the diamond in the past,
For no one felt like knockin' or handin' out a call
To the man who'd played on Anson's team, the greatest of 'em all.

Wal, finally the climax came—the big test of the year—
And the fans wuz there in bunches from the country far and near,
Especially attracted by the statement made that day
That, having rounded into shape, big Casey wuz to play.
The other nine wuz lookin' kinder worried and upset,
And they wouldn't even listen to an even-money bet.
We kidded 'em and joshed 'em, but no wagerin' wuz done,
Till at last they placed a thousand at the odds of ten to one;
But even at these odds it looked an easy-money scheme,
With the man who'd played with Anson on the old Chicago team.

But Casey never drew a chance to shine in any way;
They handed him a base on balls without the least delay;
The pitcher didn't seem to care to put one over straight
While the man who'd played with Anson was a-standin' at the plate.
He only had one fly in left, which bounded off his head
(It seems the sun was shinin' in his countenance, he said);
And so the people waited in much anger and suspense
For Casey's opportunity to drive one through the fence;
And it came—O yes—it landed with a nauseating rap
For the man who'd played with Anson and referred to him as "Cap."

Old Mudville was a run behind when that last inning came;
The bases full and two wuz out—a hit would win the game.
"He's got to put it over now," each rooter waved his hat,
And shouted in delirium as Casey stepped to bat.
The first two inshoots jumped across the center of the plate,
As Mr. Anson's college chum found out a bit too late;
The next looked good and Casey swung—there came a mighty crack—
But the noise originated from the spine in Casey's back.
In reaching for that outshoot he had wrenched the spinal beam
Of the man who played with Anson on the old Chicago team.

That night we wired Anson to discover if he knew
A man by name of Casey, as we felt we ought to do;
And when the answer came next day it stirred up quite a fuss:
"Yes, I remember Casey well—he carried bats for us."

We hunted for him quite a spell, but he had gone away,
Else the daisies would be bloomin' over his remains today.
But if you land in Mudville on the lookout for some fun,
Don't ever mention Casey's name unless you wear a gun.

HE NEVER HEARD OF CASEY!

I knew a cove who'd never heard of Washington and Lee,
Of Caesar and Napoleon from the ancient jamboree,
But, bli'me, there are queerer things than anything like that,
For here's a cove who never heard of "Casey at the Bat"!

He never heard of Mudville and its wild and eerie call,
"When Flynn let drive a single, to the wonderment of all,"
Nor the stormy roar of welcome that "recoiled upon the flat
As Casey, mighty Casey, was advancing to the bat."

"There was ease in Casey's manner," from the Ernest Thayer style,
"There was pride in Casey's bearing," and his tanned face wore a smile,
And when they thundered "Attaboy!" of course he tipped his hat,
But here's a cove who never heard of "Casey at the Bat"!

"Who is Casey?" Can you beat it? Can a thing like this be true?
Is there one who's missed the drama that ripped Mudville through and through?
Is there a fan with soul so dead he never felt the sway
Of these famous lines by Thayer in the good old Thayer way?

"Ten thousand eyes were on him as he rubbed his hands with dirt;
Five thousand tongues applauded as he wiped them on his shirt;
Then while the writhing pitcher ground the ball into his hip,
Defiance gleamed in Casey's eye, a sneer curled Casey's lip."

The drama grew in force and flame, and berserk went the mob,
With Casey representing more than Hornsby, Ruth, or Cobb;
And as the pitcher cut one loose as if fired from a gat—
Say, here's a guy who never heard of "Casey at the Bat"!

"The sneer is gone from Casey's lip, his teeth are clenched in hate;
He pounds with cruel violence his bat upon the plate."
And as the pitcher shot one through to meet the final test,
There's one low and benighted fan who never heard the rest.

Ten million never heard of Keats, or Shelley, Burns, or Poe;
But they know "the air was shattered by the force of Casey's blow";

They never heard of Shakespeare, nor of Dickens, like as not,
But they know the somber drama from old Mudville's haunted lot.

He never heard of Casey! Am I dreaming? Is it true?
Is fame but windblown ashes when the summer day is through?
Does greatness fade so quickly and is grandeur doomed to die
That bloomed in early morning, ere the dusk rides down the sky?

Is there nothing left immortal in this somber vale called Earth?
Is there nothing that's enduring in its guarding shell of worth?
Is everything forgotten as the new age stumbles on
And the things that we once cherished make their way to helengon?

Is drifting life but dust and dreams to fade within a flash,
Where one forgets the drama of the Master and the Ash?
Where one has missed the saga with its misty flow of tears,
Upon that day of tragedy beyond the tramping years?

"Oh! Somewhere in this favored land the sun is shining bright;
The band is playing somewhere, and somewhere hearts are light;
And somewhere men are laughing, and somewhere children shout,
But there is no joy in Mudville—mighty Casey has struck out!"

Rise, De Wolf Hopper, in your wrath, and cut the blighter down!
Although Wang may be forgotten in the passing of renown,
There's a graver crime committed which should take you to the mat,
For here's a cove who never heard of "Casey at the Bat"!

I had an epic written which I thought would never die,
Where they'd build a statue for me with its head against the sky;
I said "This will live forever"—but I've canned it in the vat,
For here's a guy who never heard of "Casey at the Bat"!

In 1969 the city of Duddy Kravitz became major league, with the expansion of the senior circuit into Montreal (and San Diego). But Montreal and Quebec had long ago shown themselves to be big league in heart with their welcome of black players in first the Provincial League and then the International League, with the Royals. Now if only the Big O could be completed and the team name changed (who remembers the 1967 Exposition, anyway?), there would be no more complaints about this lovely city being bush league.

MORDECAI RICHLER

Up from the Minors in Montreal

Pronouncing on Montreal, my Montreal, Casey Stengel once said, "Well, you see they have these polar bears up there, and lots of fellows trip over them trying to run the bases, and they're never much good anymore except for hockey or hunting deer."

Alas, we have no polar bears up here, but kids can usually heave snowballs at the outfielders at the opening game of the season, and should the World Series ever dare venture this far north, it is conceivable that a game could be called because of a blizzard. Something else. In April, the loudest cheers in the ballpark tend to come when nothing of any consequence seems to have happened on the field, understandably baffling the players on visiting teams. These cheers spring from fans who sit huddled with transistor radios clapped to their ears and signify that something of importance has happened, albeit out of town, where either Guy Lafleur or Pierre Mondou has just scored in a Stanley Cup play-off game.

Baseball remains a popular game here in spite of the Expos, but hockey is the way of life.

Montreal, it must be understood, is a city unlike any other in Canada. Or, come to think of it, the National League. On the average, 8 feet of snow is dumped on us each winter and, whatever the weather, we can usually count on three bank robberies a day here.

This is the city of wonders that gave you Expo in 1967, the baseball Expos a couple of years later, and, in 1976, the Olympic Games, its legacy, among other amazing artifacts, a stadium that can seat or intern, as some have it, 60,000 baseball fans. I speak of the monstrous Big O, where our inept Expos disport themselves in summer, their endearing idea of loading the bases being to have two of their runners on second. Hello, hello. Their notion of striking fear into the heart of the opposition being to confront them with muscle, namely one of their pinch-hitting behemoths coming off the bench: group average, .135.

Major-league baseball, like the Olympics and the Big O itself, was brought to this long-suffering city through the machinations of our very own Artful Dodger, Mayor Jean Drapeau.

Bringing us the Games, he assured Montrealers that it would be as difficult for the Olympics to cost us money as it would be for a man to have a baby. He estimated the total cost of all facilities at $62.2 million but, what with inflation and unfavorable winds, his calculations fell somewhat short of the mark. Counting stationery and long-distance calls, the final cost was $1.2 billion. Never mind. To this day our ebullient mayor doesn't allow that the Games were run at a loss. Rather, as he has put it to the rest of us, there has been a gap between costs and revenue. And, considering the spiffy facilities we have been left with, it would be churlish of us to complain.

Ah, the Big O. The largest, coldest slab of poured concrete in Canada. In a city where we endure seven punishing months of winter and spring comes and goes in an afternoon, it is Drapeau's triumph to have provided us with a partially roofed-over $520 million stadium, where the sun never shines on the fans. Tim Burke, one of the liveliest sportswriters in town, once said to me, "You know, there are lots of summer afternoons when I feel like taking in a ball game, but I think, hell, who wants to sit out there in the dark."

"Shivering in the dark" might be more accurate, watching the boys lose line drives in the seams of the artificial turf.

"The outfield," another wag remarked, "looks just like the kind of thing my aunt used to wear."

Furthermore, come Cap Day or Bat Night ours is the only park in the National League that fills a social office, letting the poor know where to get off, which is to say, the scruffy kids in the bleachers are beyond the pale. They don't qualify.

It's a shame, because the Expos, admittedly major league in name only, came to a town rich in baseball history, and, to begin with, we were all charged with hope. In their opening game, on April 9, 1969, the Expos took the Mets 11–10 at Shea Stadium, collecting three homers and five doubles. Five days later, the 29,184 fans who turned up for the home opener were electrified by an announcement over the public address system. "When the Expos play a doubleheader," we were informed, "the second game will go the full nine innings, not seven."

Those of us old enough to remember baseball's glory here, the Montreal Royals of the old International League, nodded our heads, impressed. This was the big time. "Montreal," said Warren Giles, president of the National League, "is a growing and vibrant city." Yessirree. And we hollered and stamped our feet as our champions took to the field under the grim gaze of manager Gene Mauch, who had the look of a marine drill sergeant.

I still have that incomparably bubbly Opening Day program. *Votre première équipe des ligues majeures.* Vol. 1, No. 1. *Publié par Club de Baseball Montréal Ltée.* "The Expos believe they landed a real prize when they snatched Gary Sutherland from the Philadelphia Phillies. Big things are expected from John Bateman, the former Houston Astros' fine receiver. Bob Bailey impressed everybody with his tremendous hustle. Ty Cline is a two-way player. 'In the field,' said Larry Shepard, manager of the Pittsburgh Pirates, 'Don Bosch can be compared with none other than Willie Mays.' Larry Jaster has youth on his side. This may be the year Don Shaw comes into his own. Angel Hermoso is one of the fine young Expo prospects the scouts have hung a 'can't miss' label on. On a given day, Mike Wegener, only twenty-two, can throw with the best. Don Hahn was a standout performer during spring training. Bob Reynolds's main forte is a blistering fastball. Expansion could be 'just what the doctor ordered' for Coco Laboy."

To be fair, the original Expos included Rusty Staub, sweet Mack Jones, and Bill Stoneman, a surprisingly effective player who pitched two no-hitters before his arm gave out. Manny Mota, another original draft choice, was one of the first to be sent packing by a management that was to become celebrated for its lame-headed dealings, its most spectacular blunder being a trade that sent Ken Singleton and Mike Torrez to Baltimore for a sore-armed Dave McNally and a totally ineffective Rich Coggins. It should also be noted that the Expos did take their home opener, defeating the Cardinals 8–7, and that tiny Parc Jarry, where they were to play, futile in their fashion, for another eight years, was a charming, intimate stadium with the potential to become another Fenway Park.

Opening day, I recognized many of the plump faces in the box seats on the first-base line. Among them were some of the nervy kids who used to skip school with me on weekday afternoons to sit in the left-field bleachers of Delormier Downs, cheering on the Royals and earning nickels fetching hot dogs for strangers. Gone were the AZA windbreakers, the bubble gum, the scuffed running shoes, the pale, wintry faces. These men came bronzed to the ballpark from their Florida condominiums. Now they wore foulards and navy blue blazers with brass buttons; they carried Hudson's Bay blankets in plastic cases for their bejeweled wives; and they sucked on Monte Cristos, mindful not to spill ashes on their Gucci sandals. Above all, they radiated pleasure in their own accomplishments and the occasion. And why not? This was an event, and there they were, inside, looking out at last, right on the first-base line. Look at me. "Give it some soul, Mack," one of them shouted.

An article in that memorable Opening Day program noted that while the province of Quebec had never been known as a hotbed of major-league talent, we had nevertheless produced a few ballplayers, among them pitchers Claude Raymond and Ron Piché, and that three more native sons, Roland Gladu, Jean-

Pierre Roy, and Stan Bréard, had once played for another ball club here, the Montreal Royals.

Oh, I remember the Royals, yes indeed, and if they played in a Montreal that was not yet growing and vibrant, it was certainly a place to be cherished.

Beta Dodd, "The Girl in Cellophane," was stripping at the Gayety, supported by 23 Kuddling Kuties. Cantor Moishe Oysher, the Master Singer of his People, was appearing at His Majesty's. The Johnny Holmes Band, playing at Victoria Hall, featured Oscar Peterson; and a sign in the corner cigar-and-soda warned Ziggy Halprin, Yossel Hoffman, and me that

LOOSE TALK COSTS LIVES!
Keep It Under
Your
STETSON

I first became aware of the Royals in 1943. Our country was already seventy-six years old, I was merely twelve, and we were both at war.

MAY U BOAT SINKINGS EXCEED REPLACEMENTS;
KING DECORATES 625 CANADIANS ON BIRTHDAY

Many of our older brothers and cousins were serving overseas. Others on the street were delighted to discover they suffered from flat feet or, failing that, arranged to have an eardrum punctured by a specialist in such matters.

R.A.F. HITS HARD AT COLOGNE AND HAMBURG
2,000 Tons of Bombs
Rain on Rhine City

On the home front, sacrifices were called for. On St. Urbain Street, where we served, collecting salvage, we had to give up American comic books for the duration. Good-bye, Superman, so long, Captain Marvel. Instead, we were obliged to make do with shoddy Canadian imitations printed in black and white. And such was the shortage of ballplayers that the one-armed outfielder, Pete Gray, got to play for the Three Rivers club on his way to the Browns, and French Canadians, torn from the local sandlots, actually took to the field for our very own Royals: Bréard, Gladu, Roy.

Even in fabled Westmount, where the very rich were rooted, things weren't the same anymore. H.R., emporium to the privileged, enjoined Westmount to "take another step in further aid of the Government's all out effort to defeat aggression!"

HOLT RENFREW ANNOUNCE THAT BEGINNING
JUNE FIRST <u>NO DELIVERIES</u> OF MERCHANDISE
WILL BE MADE ON <u>WEDNESDAYS</u>

This forethought will help H.R. to save many gallons of gasoline . . . and many a tire . . . for use by the government. Moreover, will it not thrill you to think that the nondelivery of your dress on Wednesday will aid in the delivery of a "block-buster" over the Ruhr . . . Naples . . . Berlin . . . and many other places of enemy entrenchment?

Our parents feared Hitler and his panzers, but Ziggy, Yossel, and I were in terror of Branch Rickey and his scouts.

Nineteen thirty-nine was not only the date we had gone to war; it was also the year the management of the Royals signed a contract with Mr. Rickey, making them the No. 1 farm club of the Brooklyn Dodgers. This dealt us young players of tremendous promise, but again and again, come the Dodgers' late-summer pennant drive, the best of the bunch were harvested by the parent team. Before we had even reached the age of puberty, Ziggy, Yossel, and I had learned to love with caution. If after the first death there is no other, an arguable notion, I do remember that each time one of our heroes abandoned us for Ebbets Field, it stung us badly. We hated Mr. Rickey for his voracious appetite. "There has been no mention officially that the Dodgers will be taking Flowers," Lloyd MacGowan wrote in the *Star* on a typical day, "but Rickey was in Buffalo to watch the team yesterday. The Dodgers can't take Flowers without sending down a flinger, but chances are the replacement for the burly lefty will hardly be adequate."

The International League, as we knew it in the forties, its halcyon years, was Triple A and comprised of eight teams: Montreal, Toronto, Syracuse, Jersey City, Newark, Rochester, Baltimore and Buffalo. Newark was the number-one farm team of the Yankees and Jersey City filled the same office for the Giants. But Organized Baseball had actually come to Montreal in 1898, the Royals then fielding a team in the old Eastern League, taking the pennant in their inaugural year. In those days the Royals played in Atwater Park, which could seat 12,000, and from all accounts was a fine and intimate stadium, much like Parc Jarry. During the twenty-one years the Royals played there, they offered Montreal, as sportswriter Marc Thibault recently wrote, *"du baseball parfois excitant, plus souvent qu'autrement, assez détestable,"* the problem being the troubled management's need to sell off their most accomplished players for ready cash. Be that as it may, in 1914, long before we were to endure major league baseball in name only here, George Herman Ruth came to Atwater Park to pitch for the Baltimore Orioles. Two years later, the team folded, a casualty of World War I, and another eleven years passed before the Royals were re-suscitated.

It was 1928 when George Tweedy "Miracle Man" Stallings bought the then-defunct Syracuse franchise and built Delormier Downs, a stadium with a 22,000 capacity, at the corner of Ontario and Delormier streets. An overflow crowd of 22,500, including Judge Kenesaw Mountain Landis, was at the opening game, which the Royals won, defeating the fearsome Reading Keystones 7–4. Twelve months later Stallings died. In 1929, not a vintage year for the stock market, the Royals finished fourth. Two years later, Delormier Stadium, like just about everybody, was in deep trouble. There were tax arrears and a heavy bank debt to be settled. The original sponsors resigned.

In the autumn of 1931 a new company was formed by a triumvirate that included a man who had made millions in gas stations, the rambunctious, poker-playing J. Charles-Emile Trudeau, father of our present prime minister. Another associate of the newly formed club, Frank "Shag" Shaughnessy, cunningly introduced the play-off system in 1933 and two years later became the club's general manager. In 1935, fielding a team that included Fresco Thompson, Jimmy Ripple, and Del Bissonette, the Royals won their first pennant since 1898. However, they finished poorly in '37 and '38, and, the following year, Mr. Rickey surfaced, sending in Burleigh Grimes to look after his interests.

Redemption was at hand.

Bruno Betzel came in to manage the team in 1944, the year the nefarious Branch Rickey bought the Royals outright, building it into the most profitable club in all of minor-league baseball, its fans loyal but understandably resentful of the head office's appetite, praying that this summer the Dodgers wouldn't falter in the stretch, sending down for fresh bats, strong arms, just when we needed them most.

The Royals finished first in 1945, and in '46 and '48 they won both the pennant and the Little World Series. They were to win the pennant again in '51 and '52, under Clay Hopper, and the Little World Series in '53, when they were managed by Walter Alston. The Royals fielded their greatest team in 1948, the summer young Duke Snider played here, appearing in seventy-seven games before he was snatched by Mr. Rickey. Others on that memorable team included Don Newcombe, Al Gionfriddo, Jimmy Bloodworth, Bobby Morgan, and Chuck Connors. The legendary Jackie Robinson and Roy Campanella had already come and gone.

Sam Jethroe was here in 1949, and two years later Junior Gilliam was at third, and George Shuba hit twenty home runs. In 1952, our star pitcher was southpaw Tommy Lasorda, the self-styled Bob Feller of the International League. Lasorda pitched his last game for the Royals on July 4, 1960, against Rochester, which seemed to be hitting him at will. Reminiscing recently, Lasorda recalled, "I knew I was in trouble when I saw our manager's foot on the top of the dugout step. If the next guy gets on base, I'm going to be out of there. I turned my back to the hitter and looked up toward the sky. Lord, I said, this is my last game. Get me out of this jam. I make the next pitch, and the guy at the plate hits the damnedest line drive you ever saw. Our third baseman, George Risley, gets the tips of his fingers on it but can't hang on. The ball bloops over his hand, and our shortstop, Jerry Snyder, grabs it. He fires it to Harry Shewman at second base, who relays it to Jimmy Korada at first. Triple play."

A year later the Royals were dissolved, and in 1971 the Delormier Stadium was razed to make way for the Pierre Dupuy School.

* * *

On weekday afternoons kids were admitted free into the left-field bleachers, and by the third inning the more intrepid had worked their way down as far as the first-base line. Ziggy, Yossel, and I would sit out there in the sun, cracking peanuts, nudging each other if a ball struck the Miss Sweet Caporal sign, hitting the young lady you-know-where. Another diversion was a porthole in the outfield wall. If a batter hit a ball through it, he was entitled to a two-year supply of Pal Blades. Heaven.

Sunday afternoons the Royals usually played to capacity crowds, but come the Little World Series, fans lined up on the roof of the adjoining Grover Knit-To-Fit Building, and temporary stands were set up and roped off in center field. Consequently, as my cousin Seymour, who used to sit there, liked to boast, "If I get hit on the head, it's a ground-rule home run." After the game, we would spill out of the stadium to find streetcars lined up for a half mile, waiting to take us home.

In 1945, the Royals acquired one of ours, their first Jewish player, Kermit Kitman, a William and Mary scholarship boy. Our loyalty to the team was redoubled. Kitman was a center fielder and an Opening Day story in *La Presse* declared, "*Trois des meilleurs porte-couleurs du Montréal depuis l'ouverture de la saison ont été ses joueurs de champ: Gladu, Kitman, et Yeager. Kitman a exécuté un catch sensationnel encore hier après-midi sur le long coup de Tores à la 8e manche. On les verra tous trois à l'oeuvre cet après-midi contre le Jersey-City lors du programme double de la 'Victoire' au stade de la rue Delormier.*"

In his very first time at bat in that opening game against the Skeeters, Kitman belted a homer, something he would not manage again until August. Alas, in the later innings he also got doubled off second. After the game, when he ventured into a barbershop at the corner of St. Catherine and St. Urbain, a man in another chair studied him intently. "Aren't you Kermit Kitman?" he asked.

"Yeah," he allowed, grinning, remembering his homer.

"You son of a bitch, you got doubled off second; it cost me five hundred bucks."

Leadoff hitter for the Royals, Kitman was entitled to lower berth one on all their road trips. Only twenty-two years old but a college boy, he was paid somewhat better than most: $650 monthly for six months of the year. And if the Royals went all the way, winning the Little World Series, he could earn another $1,800. On the road, his hotel bill was paid, and he and the other players were each allowed three bucks a day meal money.

There was yet another sea change in the summer of 1946. After scouting what were then called the Negro Leagues for more than a year, Mr. Rickey brought the first black player into Organized Baseball. So that spring the Royals could not train in the regular park in Daytona, which was segregated, but had to train in Kelly Field instead.

Actually, Jackie Robinson had been signed on October 23, 1945, in the offices of the Royals at Delormier Stadium, club president Hector Racine saying, "Robinson is a good ballplayer and comes highly recommended by the Brooklyn Dodgers. We paid him a good bonus to sign with our club."

The bonus was $3,500, and Robinson's salary was $600 monthly.

"One afternoon in Daytona," Kermit Kitman told me, "I was leadoff hitter and quickly singled. Robinson came up next, laying down a sacrifice bunt and running to first. Stanky, covering the sack, tagged him hard and jock high. Robinson went down, taking a fist in the balls. He was mad as hell, you could see that, but Rickey had warned him, no fights. He got up, dusted himself off, and said nothing. After the game, when he was resting, Stanky came over to apologize. He had been testing his temper, under orders from Rickey."

Kitman, a good glove man, was an inadequate hitter. Brooklyn born, he never got to play there. Following the 1946 season, he was offered a place on the roster of another team in the Dodger farm system but elected to quit the game instead.

The 1946 season opened for the Royals on April 18, with a game in Jersey City. The AP dispatch for that day, printed in the Montreal *Gazette*, ran:

> The first man of his race to play in modern organized baseball smashed a three-run homer that carried 333 feet and added three singles to the Royals' winning 14–1 margin over Jersey City. Just to make it a full day's work, Robinson stole two bases, scored four times and batted in three runs. He was also charged with an error.

Robinson led the International League in hitting that year with a .349 average. He hit 3 home runs, batted in 66 runs, stole 40 bases, scored 113 runs, and fielded .985 at his second-base position. And, furthermore, Montreal adored him, as no other ballplayer who has been here before or since. No sooner did Robinson reach first base, on a hit or a walk, than the fans roared with joy and hope, our hearts going out to him as he danced up and down the base path, taunting the opposing pitcher with his astonishing speed.

We won the pennant that year and met the Louisville Colonels, another Dodger farm club, in the Little World Series. The series opened in Louisville, where Robinson endured a constant run of racial insults from the Colonels' dugout and was held to a mere single in two games. Montreal evened the series at home and returned to Delormier Downs for the seventh and deciding game. "When they won it," Dick Bacon recently wrote, recalling that game in the 200th anniversary issue of the *Gazette*, "Jackie was accorded an emotional send-off unseen before or since in this city.

"First they serenaded him in true French Canadien spirit with '*Il a gagné ses Epaulettes*' and then clamored for his reappearance on the field.

"When he finally came out for a curtain call, the fans mobbed him. They hugged him, kissed him, cried, cheered, and pulled and tore at his uniform while parading him around the infield on their shoulders.

"With tears streaming down his face, Robinson finally begged off in order to shower, dress, and catch a plane to the States. But the riot of joy wasn't over yet.

"When he emerged from the clubhouse, he had to bull his way through the waiting crowd outside the stadium. The thousands of fans chased him down Ontario Street for several blocks before he was rescued by a passing motorist and driven to his hotel.

"As one southern reporter from Louisville, Kentucky, was to write afterward:

" 'It's probably the first time a white mob of rioters ever chased a Negro down the streets in love rather than hate.' "

That was a long time ago.

I don't know whatever became of Red Durrett. Marvin Rackley, of whom Mr. Rickey once said, "I can see him in a World Series, running and hitting," has also disappeared. Roland Gladu, who got to play twenty-one games with the old Boston Braves, failed to sign the major-league skies with his ability. Robinson died in 1972, and last season a plaque to his memory was installed in the chilly Big O. Jean-Pierre Roy now does the French-language broadcasts for the Expos, and a graying but still impressive Duke Snider is also back, doing the color commentary for Expo games on CBC-TV, trying his best to be kind to an uninspired bunch without compromising himself.

The Expos have yet to play .500 ball or, since Mack Jones's brief sojourn here, come up with a player that the fans can warm to. But there is hope. Next year, or maybe five years from now, the Big O will be completed. The retractable roof will be set in place. And, in this city of endless winter and short hot summers, it will be possible to watch baseball played under a roof, on artificial grass, in an air-conditioned, possibly even centrally heated, concrete tomb.

Progress.

Before the advent of free agency, the ironclad reserve clause made the baseball player a chattel, to be bought and sold regardless of his wishes and denied access to any potential employer but his current one. When it came time to negotiate a salary, the owner's ultimate bargaining position was to say, "Play for me at the wage I offer or play for no one"; the only leverage the player had was to (1) jump his contract and hook on with a rival league—which in this century was only briefly a real option, (2) hold out and hope to pressure management, or (3) play for no one. Edd Roush, a hardheaded and independent man, on separate occasions did all three. This is a chapter from the incomparable *The Glory of Their Times*.

LAWRENCE S. RITTER

Edd Roush Remembers

"Who is he, anyhow, an actor?"

"No."

"A dentist?"

". . . No, he's a gambler." Gatsby hesitated, then added coolly: *"He's the man who fixed the World Series back in 1919."*

"Fixed the World Series?" I repeated.

The idea staggered me. I remembered, of course, that the World Series had been fixed in 1919, but if I had thought of it at all I would have thought of it as a thing that merely happened, *the end of some inevitable chain. It never occurred to me that one man could start to play with the faith of fifty million people—with the single-mindedness of a burglar blowing a safe.*

"How did he happen to do that?" I asked after a minute.

"He just saw the opportunity."

"Why isn't he in jail?"

"They can't get him, old sport. He's a smart man."

F. Scott Fitzgerald, The Great Gatsby

Yes, I knew at the time that some finagling was going on. At least that's what I'd heard. Rumors were flying all over the place that gamblers had got to the Chicago White Sox, that they'd agreed to throw the World Series. But nobody knew anything for sure until Eddie Cicotte spilled the beans a year later.

We beat them in the first two games 9–1 and 4–2, and it was after the second game that I first got wind of it. We played those first two games in Cincinnati, and the next day we were to play in Chicago. So the evening after the second game we were all gathered at the hotel in Cincinnati, standing around waiting for cabs to take us to the train station, when this fellow came over to me. I didn't know who he was, but I'd seen him around before.

"Roush," he says, "I want to tell you something. Did you hear about the squabble the White Sox got into after the game this afternoon?" And he told me some story about Ray Schalk accusing Lefty Williams of throwing the game, and something about some of the White Sox beating up a gambler for not giving them the money he'd promised them.

"They didn't get the payoff," he said, "so from here on they're going to try to win."

I didn't know whether this guy made it all up or not. But it did start me thinking. Later on in the Series the same guy came over to me again.

"Roush," he says, "you remember what I told you about gamblers getting to the White Sox? Well, now they've also got to some of the players on your own ball club."

That's all he said. Wouldn't tell me any more. I didn't say anything to anybody until we were getting dressed in the clubhouse the next day. Then I got hold of the manager, Pat Moran, just before the pregame meeting.

"Before you start this meeting, Pat," I said, "there's something I want to talk to you about."

"Okay," he says, "what is it?"

"I've been told that gamblers have got to some of the players on this club," I said. "Maybe it's true, and maybe it isn't. I don't know. But you sure better

do some finding out. I'll be damned if I'm going to knock myself out trying to win this Series if somebody else is trying to throw the game."

Pat got all excited and called Jake Daubert over, who was the team captain. It was all news to both of them. So at the meeting, after we'd gone over the White Sox lineup, Moran looked at Hod Eller, who was going to pitch for us that day.

"Hod," he said, "I've been hearing rumors about sellouts. Not about you, not about anybody in particular, just rumors. I want to ask you a straight question, and I want a straight answer."

"Shoot," says Hod.

"Has anybody offered you anything to throw this game?"

"Yep," Hod said. Lord, you could have heard a pin drop.

"After breakfast this morning a guy got on the elevator with me and got off at the same floor I did. He showed me five thousand-dollar bills and said they were mine if I'd lose the game today."

"What did you say?" Moran asked him.

"I said if he didn't get damn far away from me real quick he wouldn't know what hit him. And the same went if I ever saw him again."

Moran looked at Eller a long time. Finally, he said, "Okay, you're pitching. But one wrong move and you're out of the game."

Evidently there weren't any wrong moves. Because ol' Hod went out there and pitched a swell game. He won two of the games in that Series.

I don't know whether the whole truth of what went on there among the White Sox will ever come out. Even today nobody really knows exactly what took place. Whatever it was, though, it was a dirty rotten shame. One thing that's always overlooked in the whole mess is that we could have beat them no matter what the circumstances!

Sure, the 1919 White Sox were good. But the 1919 Cincinnati Reds were *better*. I'll believe that till my dying day. I don't care how good Chicago's Joe Jackson and Buck Weaver and Eddie Cicotte were. *We* had Heinie Groh, Jake Daubert, Greasy Neale, Rube Bressler, Larry Kopf, myself, and the best pitching staff in both leagues. We were a very underrated ball club.

I played center field for that Cincinnati club for eleven straight years, 1916 through 1926. I came to Cincinnati from the Giants in the middle of 1916, along with Christy Mathewson and Bill McKechnie.

Of course I started playing ball long before that, around 1909 or so, right here in Oakland City, Indiana. In those days every little town had an amateur club, and so did Oakland City. Never will forget it. I was only about sixteen at the time. Oakland City had a game scheduled with a neighboring town this day, and one of Oakland City's outfielders hadn't shown up. Everybody was standing around right on the main street of town—only a small town, you know—wondering what to do, when one of the town officials says, "Why not put that Roush kid in?"

I was kind of a shy kid, and I backed away. But the manager says, "Well, that's just what we'll do if he don't show up in five more minutes."

We waited for five minutes, and the outfielder never did show, so they gave me a uniform and put me in right field. Turned out I got a couple of hits that day, and I became Oakland City's regular right fielder for the rest of the season.

The next year, of course, I was right in the middle of it. We reorganized the team—the Oakland City Walk-Overs, that's what we called ourselves—and had a pretty good club. In those days, you know, I used to throw with *either* hand. I'm a natural lefty, see, but when I was a kid, I never could find a lefty's glove. So I just used a regular glove and learned to throw righty. Batted lefty but got so I could throw with my right arm almost as well as with my left.

The year after that we got in quite a hassle. That would be 1911. Seems as though some of the Oakland City boys were getting $5 a game, and I wasn't one of them. So I started raising Cain about this under-the-table business and treating some different than others.

Wound up we had such an argument that I quit the hometown club and went over and played with the Princeton team. Princeton is the closest town to Oakland City, about 12 miles due west. And don't think that didn't cause quite a ruckus. Especially when Princeton came over to play Oakland City *at* Oakland City, with me in the Princeton outfield. A fair amount of hard feelings were stirred up, to say the least. I think there are still one or two around here never have forgiven me to this very day.

I played with Princeton about a year and a half, and then a fellow connected with the Evansville club in the Kitty League asked me would I like to play for them in professional baseball. Well, Evansville's only about 30 miles from Oakland City, almost due south, and the idea of getting paid for playing ball sounded real good to me. And Dad thought it was terrific. He'd played semipro ball himself, when he was young. William C. Roush was his name. A darn good ballplayer, too. So I signed with Evansville and finished the 1912 season with them.

I bought a lefty's glove when I started playing with Evansville, figuring I might as well go back to the natural throw. From then on I always threw left-handed, 'cause it didn't carry quite so well when I threw with my right. Wasn't really a natural throw.

After that, things moved quick. Evansville sold me to the Chicago White Sox—of all teams, considering what happened later—in the middle of the following season. I stayed with them a month—Cicotte was there then, and Buck Weaver and Ray Schalk—and then they optioned me to Lincoln, Nebraska, in the Western League.

The next year the Indianapolis club in the new Federal League got in touch with me and offered me $225 a month, almost twice what I was getting at Lincoln. So I jumped to the Federal League for the next couple of years. That Federal League wasn't a bad league. Too bad it only lasted two years. Ran into a lot of financial troubles and folded in December of 1915. Of course, it was an outlaw league, you know, raiding the other leagues for its players. The established leagues threatened that anybody who jumped to the Feds would never be allowed back in organized ball, but once the Feds broke up, they were glad to get us.

We had some good players there the two years the Federal League lived. A lot of old-timers jumped over, like Three-Fingered Brown, Chief Bender, Eddie Plank, Davy Jones, Joe Tinker, Jimmy Delahanty, Al Bridwell, and Charlie Carr, the old Indianapolis first baseman. They didn't care if Organized Ball never took them back, 'cause they were near the end of the trail, anyway.

But there were also a lot of younger players, like Benny Kauff, Bill McKechnie, and myself. All three of us were sold to the New York Giants when the Federal League collapsed, and that's where we reported in the spring of 1916.

Me, I didn't like New York. I'm a small-town boy. I like the Midwest. Well, it wasn't *exactly* that. Not entirely, anyway. It was really McGraw I didn't like. John J. McGraw. I just didn't enjoy playing for him, that's all. If you made a bad play, he'd cuss you out, yell at you, call you all sorts of names. That didn't go with me. So I was glad as I could be when he traded me to Cincinnati in the middle of the '16 season. I couldn't have been happier.

McGraw traded Mathewson, McKechnie, and me to Cincinnati for Wade Killefer and Buck Herzog, who had been the Cincinnati manager. Matty was to replace Herzog as the new manager. I still remember the trip the three of us made as we left the Giants and took the train to join the Reds. McKechnie and I were sitting back on the observation car, talking about how happy we were to be traded. Matty came out and sat down and listened, but he didn't say anything.

Finally I turned to him and said, "Well, Matty, aren't you glad to be getting away from McGraw?"

"I'll tell you something, Roush," he said. "You and Mac have only been on the Giants a couple of months. It's just another ball club to you fellows. But I was with that team for sixteen years. That's a mighty long time. To me, the Giants are 'home.' And leaving them like this, I feel the same as when I leave home in the spring of the year.

"Of course, I realize I'm through as a pitcher. But I appreciate McGraw making a place for me in baseball and getting me this managing job. He's doing me a favor, and I thanked him for it. And by the way, the last thing he said to me was that if I put you in center field, I'd have a great ballplayer. So starting tomorrow you're my center fielder."

Well, we got to Cincinnati, and sure enough, right off Matty puts me in center field. Greasy Neale was the right fielder. It was his first year with the Reds, too, but he'd been there since the start of the season and, of course, I was a newcomer. The first game I played there, about three or four fly balls came out that could have been taken by either the center fielder or the right fielder. If I thought I should take it, I'd holler three times: "I got it, I got it, I got it." I'd holler while I was running for it, see.

But Greasy never said a word. Sometimes he'd take it, and sometimes he wouldn't. But in either case he never said a thing. We went along that way for about three weeks. What I finally did was watch *both* him and the ball. If it looked to me like I could catch the ball and get out of his way, I'd holler and take it. But if it looked like it was going to be a tie, I'd just cut behind him and let him take it. He still never hollered and didn't have too much else to say to me, either. So I didn't have too much to say to him.

You see, I could watch both him and the ball at the same time because I didn't really have to watch the ball. As soon as a ball was hit, I could tell where it was going to go, and I'd just take off and not look at it anymore till I got there. So I'd take a quick glance at him while I was running.

Finally, one day Greasy came over and sat down beside me on the bench. "I want to end this, Roush," he says to me. "I guess you know I've been trying to run you down ever since you got here. I wanted that center-field job for myself, and I didn't like it when Matty put you out there. But you can go get a ball better than I ever could. I want to shake hands and call it off. From now on, I'll holler."

And from then on Greasy and I got along just fine. Grew to be two of the best friends ever. In fact, I made a lot of good friends those years I played in Cincinnati, still my close friends to this day. I think that Cincinnati club from 1916 to 1926 was one of the nicest bunch of fellows ever gathered together.

We even had Jim Thorpe there one year, you know. By thunder, there was a man could outrun a deer. Beat anything I ever saw. I used to be pretty fast myself. Stole close to 300 bases in the Big Leagues. And I had a real long stride, for the simple reason that in the outfield if you don't take a long stride your head bobs up and down too much and makes it hard to follow the flight of the ball. But Jim Thorpe would take only two strides to my three. I'd run just as hard as I could, and he'd keep up with me just trotting along.

One day I asked him, "Jim, anybody in those Olympic Games ever make you really run your best?"

"I never yet saw the man I couldn't look back at," he says to me. I believed him.

Well, sir, I really hit my own stride those years in Cincinnati. Led the league in batting twice, hit over .350 three years in a row—'21, '22, and '23—and generally had a ball. The lowest I ever hit while I was there was .321 in 1919, and that was good enough to lead the league that year. We won the pennant and the World Series in 1919 and finished either first, second, or third in seven of the eleven years I was there. Good teams—very much underrated. Like I say, *better* than the 1919 White Sox.

Of course, I hit very different from the way they hit today. I used a 48-ounce bat, heaviest anyone ever used. It was a shorter bat, with a big handle, and I tried to hit to all fields. Didn't swing my head off, just snapped at the ball. Until 1921, you know, they had a dead ball. Well, the only way you could get a home run was if the outfielder tripped and fell down. The ball wasn't wrapped tight, and lots of times it'd get mashed on one side. I've caught many a ball in the outfield that was mashed flat on one side. Come bouncing out there like a jumping bean. They wouldn't throw it out of the game, though. Only used about three or four balls in a whole game. Now they use sixty or seventy.

Another thing that's different now is the ballparks. Now they have smooth infields and outfields that aren't full of rocks, and they keep them nice. Back in the old days there were parks weren't much better than a cow pasture. Spring training was the worst. Some of those parks they'd want you to play exhibition games in had outfields like sand dunes, and others were hard as a cement sidewalk. The hell with that! I wouldn't go to spring training, that's all.

I used to hold out every year until the week before the season opened. That's the only time they ever had any trouble with me, contract time. Why should I go down there and fuss around in spring training? Twist an ankle or break a leg. I did my *own* spring training, hunting quail and rabbits around Oakland City.

After eleven years with the Reds, they traded me to the Giants for George Kelly. That was after the 1926 season. Well, I figured that was it. I was around thirty-four, and I wasn't about to start taking abuse from McGraw that late in life. However, I figured I had one chance: maybe I could get McGraw to trade me.

So in January of '27, when the Giants sent me a contract for $19,000, same as I'd been getting in Cincinnati, I sent it right back and wrote them I wouldn't play in New York. A couple of weeks later another one arrived, calling for $20,000. I figured they hadn't gotten the point. So I wrote a letter telling them I wouldn't play with the Giants for *any* kind of money. And wouldn't you know it, two weeks after that another contract arrived, calling for $21,000. I didn't even bother to send that one back.

Since they didn't seem to get the point the way I was doing it, I finally wrote and said I wanted $30,000. I figured that would sink in and they'd get the idea. Send me to another club.

Well, spring training started—and ended—and the team began to move up north, playing exhibition games along the way. I was still busy hunting quail right here around Oakland City. Then one day I got a call from McGraw. Would I meet him in Chattanooga next week? After thinking it over, I decided I might as well.

I arrived at the hotel in Chattanooga at eight o'clock on a Thursday morning, and when I registered, the clerk said to me, "Mr. McGraw left a message for you to come up to his room as soon as you arrive."

Well, it was eight o'clock, and I hadn't had any breakfast. So I went into the dining room and ordered a good meal. About nine o'clock a bellboy comes over and says, "Mr. McGraw would like to see you in room 305."

"All right," I says, "tell him I'll be there."

About that time the ballplayers started to drift in, so I visited with them awhile. One of them gave me a good cigar, so I sat down in a comfortable chair in the lobby and talked to some of the boys while I enjoyed it. About eleven o'clock one of the coaches came over. "McGraw wants to know why you're not up there yet?"

Finally, by about twelve-thirty or so, after I'd finished visiting with the ballplayers, completed a detailed reading of three newspapers, and had a haircut and a shoeshine, I decided to go upstairs and see Mr. John J. McGraw.

"What the devil's the matter with you, Roush?" he says. "Don't you want to play ball for me?"

"Hell, no," I said. "I don't want to play ball for you. Haven't you figured that out by now?"

"Why not?"

" 'Cause I don't like the way you treat your players, that's why. First time you call me a damn so-and-so, somebody's going to get hurt."

"Listen, we'll get along fine. Don't you worry," he says.

"Yeah. I've heard that one before."

"Sit down," he says, "and listen to me. You know this game as well as I do. You play your own game and I'll never say anything to you."

"That's another one I've heard before."

"Well," he says, "it's the truth."

"The first time something happens out there and you start on me," I said, "I'm taking off for Oakland City, Indiana. Why don't we stop all this horsing around and you just send me to another ball club?"

"I won't do it," he says. "I've been trying to get you back ever since I traded you away a long time ago. Now you're either going to play for me or you're not going to play ball at all. I'm sure not going to let you go a second time."

"Okay," I said, "if that's the way you feel about it. If you give me my salary, I'll try it. But I still say I'll be back in Oakland City, Indiana, in ten days."

"How much do you want?"

"Twenty-five thousand dollars."

"I can't pay it."

Well, I took my hat and started for the door. "Where do you think you're going?" he says.

"Back to Oakland City, Indiana. Why?"

"Now hold on," he says. "Come back and sit down. I'll tell you what I'll do. I'll give you a three-year contract for seventy thousand."

"All right," I said, "I'll take it."

I signed the contract, went out to the ballpark, got into a uniform, and played six innings that afternoon. Got two hits out of three times up, too.

I played that three-year contract out, and after that I quit and finally did come back to Oakland City, Indiana. McGraw kept to his word and never bothered me. But it wasn't like playing in Cincinnati. I missed my teammates, and I missed the Cincinnati fans.

I've read where as far as the Cincinnati fans are concerned I'm the most popular player ever wore a Reds' uniform. I don't know about that. It's not for me to say. But—assuming it's true—I'll tell you one thing: the feeling is mutual.

I have included this essay only to demonstrate how an always entertaining and otherwise enlightened writer can overcome a glaring perceptual disability and achieve national standing as a pundit. Mr. Rooney might benefit from reading George Will's contribution to this volume.

ANDY ROONEY

Real Men Don't Wear Knickers

David Fisher has made me mad . . . not angry, mad. Angry isn't a strong enough word for what I am at David Fisher.

David Fisher, who writes baseball books, wrote an article saying the Super Bowl is only important because it means the baseball spring training season is four weeks away.

The time has come for football fans to face baseball fans . . . face-to-face. We might as well come out with it. The taste and mentality of the average baseball fan—and there is no more average group of people anywhere—is best expressed in the old song:

"Buy me some peanuts and Cracker Jack
  I don't care if I never get back."

Baseball is a pleasant little game, but to compare it to football is to compare tiddlywinks with chess. Baseball is known as "the national pastime," and that's fitting. It appeals to people on whose hands time hangs heavy. (I can't help noting here that our last several presidents have been calling the winners' locker room after the Super Bowl in place of throwing out the first ball on opening day of baseball.)

Fisher, referring to football, asks, "What kind of ball game is it that allows most of the players to go through an entire season without ever touching the ball?"

Football is not handball, Mr. Fisher. The game's tactility involves people touching people and moving them from one place to the other or to the ground.

Football is a game that employs every physical and mental attribute known to man and a few known to woman.

It would be interesting if the National Football League and major-league baseball could organize an off-season contest between all the players in both sports that would allow us to compare the IQ of all baseball players with that of all football players. Or perhaps it could be limited to the coaches and managers. Any game in which Billy Martin is hired to tell the players what to do because he's smarter than they are must have a lot of dumb players.

Baseball fans are often Democrats who voted for Ronald Reagan. They are people whose idea of a good time is to sit out in the hot sun, drinking warm beer from a paper cup while watching grown men in baggy knickers try to hit a ball with a stick. A player who hits the ball three out of every ten times he tries is said to be "hitting .300." He's hitting .300 what? I suppose it doesn't sound like enough to say a player is "hitting thirty percent."

Fisher notes that Phil Niekro, a pitcher, will be playing the game again this year at age forty-seven. It's nice for Niekro, and I approve of being nice to the elderly, my peer group, but if a man forty-seven years old can still play the game at the highest level, it cannot be a very demanding game. There is no other sport in which that happens. If it were possible, Muhammad Ali would still be heavyweight boxing champion at forty-four; Joe Namath would still be the Jets quarterback at forty-two; and Swaps would be running in the Derby again this year.

The two baseball leagues have different rules. One of them lets a tenth player try to hit the pitched ball in place of one of the regular players. He's called "the DH," meaning "designated hitter." Last year the designated hitter for Seattle, Gorman Thomas, came to bat 484 times and missed the ball 380 times. It seems to me he's more like a DM, designated misser.

What they call a baseball "glove" bears about as much relationship to a human hand as snowshoes bear to a man's feet. It's not a glove; it's a leather basket. Of course they can catch a ball that comes anywhere near them with it.

I do not hate baseball fans. Pity I feel, yes, but not hate. Quite the contrary. I believe the federal government should make every effort to see that baseball fans are accorded equal rights with the more fortunate among us. It's not their fault that they got in with a bad crowd when they were young.

The novel that supplies this exciting passage won the 1984 Edgar Allan Poe Award for best first mystery. The struggling Providence Jewels have a killer in the clubhouse. Relief pitcher Rudy Furth has been found dead in the whirlpool, leaving whispers about underworld entanglements and violently lovesick groupies. Center fielder Harvey Blissberg, playing private eye, has figured out that Rudy—at the behest of Frances, his mob-connected lover—was dumping games that pitcher Bobby Wagner started. Here Blissberg confronts Wagner in the locker room and tells him a thing or two he knows about Frances.

R. D. ROSEN

Strike Three, You're Dead

". . . She's smart, Wags. She knows you're a streak pitcher. Most of those streaks have been winning ones, but she knew that—when was it, Wags, three years ago?—she knew that even when you went something like twenty and thirteen that season, eight of those losses were in a row. She realized that you only knew how to win, not how to lose. She knew that if she got Rudy to throw a few games, you might do the rest of the damage yourself. That was one of the reasons your old manager didn't like you, wasn't it? You didn't bounce back when you lost.

"And Rudy was only a decent relief pitcher, so he could come in and throw a few pitches just fast enough to cost you the game, and no one would ever think he was in the tank. But Frances didn't know when to stop. She gave you a chance to prove you were a little smarter than she gave you credit for. She threw Rudy in the tank once too often, and you smelled it."

Harvey watched the minute hand on the clock over Bobby's shoulder twitch from 5:29 to 5:30.

"What do you care about any of it?" Bobby said evenly. "He was a punk, Professor. He was trash. Why didn't you leave it alone? What did it matter to you?"

"It mattered."

"I never did anything to him."

"That's not how it works."

"He screwed with my career. He screwed with the biggest thing I've got."

"Frances did, not Rudy. Frances did it to you."

"And you were about to screw me even more, Professor." Bobby came two steps closer and stopped, 6 feet away.

Harvey pushed away from the desk in his chair. "I didn't know what I was going to find. I was just looking."

"I wish I could help you, Professor."

"Don't be a fool. Put that bat down."

"He hit me first." Bobby's voice was unnervingly soft. "He wouldn't tell me. Then I found the money, and I couldn't believe it. It was sitting in his pocket, and he still wouldn't admit anything. He just sat in the whirlpool with that shit-eating grin and said he always carried a lot of cash. You get that, Professor? He always carried around a few big bills like that. That's when it got serious." He tapped the head of Harvey's bat against the indoor-outdoor carpeting. "He got out of the whirlpool and shoved me."

"Put the bat down, Wags."

"I didn't have the bat with me then." Bobby appeared almost hypnotized. "Just wanted to talk it out. Then he came at me, and we mixed it up, and he shoved me against the bat rack and—"

"It's going to be all right, Wags." Harvey felt his heart pounding in his neck.

Bobby came forward another step. "It's too late," he said. "It's much too late. I thought you'd understand about the rat. That was strike one." He now held the bat in front of him horizontally, one hand on each end. "Then I left you a message in Yankee Stadium. Why didn't you pay attention? Strike two, Professor."

He slid the hand that was on the head of the bat down to join the other on the handle. "Now this." He looked down at the thick book of statistics on Felix's desk. "Now you know too much. And you know what they say. Strike three you're dead."

"Goddam it, you—"

Bobby swung the bat back over his head like an ax and brought it down.

Harvey grabbed the statistics book just in time and held it up with both hands in front of his face, twisting his head as far to the side as he could. The force of the bat flattened the book against his shoulder and carried Bobby's body forward on top of Harvey.

Before Bobby could recover his balance, Harvey speared him in the groin with an outstretched leg, leaped from the chair, and dashed for Felix's door. He ran across the locker room toward the runway that led to the dugout.

The metal door swung outward, and Harvey jumped down the three cement steps to the runway. Ahead of him, a square of morning light showed the dugout and a section of the left-field stands against pink sky.

Bobby came down the steps after him. For an instant, Harvey thought about running up onto the field, but it was Bobby's running shoes against his penny loafers, Bobby's bat against his bare hands. Halfway down the runway, Harvey took a left and pushed open the door to the unused network of tunnels that ran under the stands. He kicked off his loafers in stride and took off into the darkness.

The floor of the tunnel was damp, and Harvey's socks were soaked through within a few steps. The tunnel was about 6 feet wide, dark green walls with rashes of rust, but then the light from the runway faded, and Harvey was running in total darkness. Behind him, Wagner's shoes slapped soddenly, too infrequently to be a run.

"Take your time, Professor. There's nowhere to go." The voice surrounded him.

Harvey slowed, lowering his feet into the cool puddles on the cold concrete. He reached out with his right hand, felt for the oily wall, and followed its gentle curve. They were behind home plate somewhere, and the tunnel followed the contour of the stands. He had never been in the catacombs. He knew there were connecting tunnels but couldn't be sure they weren't dead ends. The main tunnel had to feed out somewhere, probably near the visitors' clubhouse under the stands on the third-base line. That still wouldn't do him any good; the door to the clubhouse would be locked from the outside. He had been stupid not to run onto the field when he had the chance; there, at least, he could have seen what his chances were.

With his left hand, he reached out for the other wall, hoping to find an alcove, a doorway, anything. The tunnel wasn't narrow enough for him to feel both walls at the same time. For all he knew, he had already missed a connecting tunnel. Maybe he could crouch down against one side of the tunnel and hope that Wagner would walk right past him. Then he could run back to the clubhouse and out to the street.

His foot came down on a piece of paper.

"There you are," Wagner's voice said close behind him, and Harvey broke into a run again, dragging a hand along the wall.

"He was just a punk, Professor. He never belonged in the big leagues." The voice was soft and deep as it reverberated down the passage. "Your roomie was a nothing."

After every two slaps of Wagner's feet came a harder noise, the bat tapping against the concrete.

Abruptly, there was no wall at Harvey's right hand. He moved quickly into the opening and saw a hairline of light ahead. After 10 or 12 yards, he found a doorknob that turned, but not easily; it felt as if it would squeak if he twisted it too far. He leaned against the corner of the passageway and caught his breath in a series of silent heaves. He heard Wagner walk past the opening, his bat clicking.

The door probably connected the catacombs to the near end of the visitors' dugout. In that case, the central tunnel would have to end soon, where it met the runway that ran from the far end of the dugout to the clubhouse. Seventy, maybe 80 feet. Wagner would know shortly that he had lost Harvey.

Wagner's footfalls suddenly became faster and louder. Harvey turned the doorknob and pulled on the heavy door. It let out a thin screech. Light flooded the passageway. Harvey found himself where he had expected, at the end of the dugout between the end of the bench and the water cooler against the wall. Just below eye level was Rankle Park's grass. The sky was as soft as tissue, infused with pink over the stands.

Harvey leaped onto the end of the bench by the door and pressed himself against the back wall of the dugout. Wagner appeared suddenly, carelessly, in the doorway. He took a step toward the dugout steps, where he stopped, like a man whose peripheral vision was burdened. He turned and raised the bat. Harvey jumped off the bench and grabbed the shaft of the bat with both hands and brought his knee up into Wagner's gut. Wagner vomited air and doubled over. When he straightened up, Harvey had the bat and was standing on the grass at the lip of the dugout.

"You tried to kill me, you bastard." Harvey, panting, held the bat over his head.

Below him, Wagner clasped his hands over his stomach. His black hair was matted in wild curls on his forehead. "What happens now, Professor?" he said between gasps.

"Just go home."

"There's nothing in it for me."

"There's nothing in it for you here."

"There's you, Professor."

"The bat's mine now," Harvey said, but Wagner had seen the ball bag near his feet. It was the size of a bowling-ball bag, made of canvas, and it was filled with baseballs for batting practice. The Yankees must have left it in the dugout after Saturday's game. Wagner picked it up in his left hand, reached in for a baseball with his right, and started up the steps.

"I used to be pretty good at this," Wagner said, squeezing the ball.

Harvey retreated a few steps, waving his bat. "You're crazy, Wags," he screamed. "I'll hurt you if I—have to."

"You just had your chance."

Harvey backpedaled on the grass in foul territory. "I'll hurt you."

"No, you won't." Wagner bounced the baseball lightly in his right hand. "I'll take this bag of balls against your bat."

Harvey turned and ran toward the infield. From a distance of 60 feet, 6 inches, any major-league pitcher could nail a target the size of a human head; Bobby Wagner could put it right in your ear. There were two ways to go after a batter. If you only wanted to scare him, you aimed the ball directly at his head, because he would instinctively fall away from the pitch. But if you really wanted to hurt him, you would throw your best fastball a foot or so behind his head, and he would fall back into it. As Harvey ran, he saw it happening again and again— the batter involuntarily throwing himself, as if magnetized, into the path of a perfectly aimed beanball. If the batter was lucky enough to get his batting helmet between his cranium and the ball, he'd be able to get up and play ball again. If he wasn't, it was a most unnpleasant way to end a baseball career.

Harvey was not wearing a batting helmet. Of course, he was a moving target. But then, he only had 30 feet on Wagner, and Wagner had a bagful of baseballs. Harvey bobbed and weaved as he ran to give Wagner less to throw at.

He was about to look to see where Wagner was when the first ball combed his hair above his left ear. He heard it sizzle as it flew by and rolled out to right field. Now he looked back and saw Wagner 40 feet behind him, running, dipping into the bag for another ball. Harvey veered right. Wagner had to stop to throw again, and by the time he released the ball, Harvey was 60 feet away, near second base.

The ball struck him in the meat of his deltoid behind his left shoulder, and his entire arm went numb. He stumbled forward, managing to keep his balance, and switched the bat to his right hand. He cut to his right, toward the Jewels' dugout along the first-base line. It gave Wagner the angle on him, but he had to chance it now; his best hope was to make the dugout, then the runway, the clubhouse, the street, his car. The electric tingling in his left arm was going away, and it hurt like a bitch; as he ran, he carried it dead at his side. The 90 feet between second base and the foul line had never been so endless. As he tore across the infield, he could see Wagner winding up out of his right eye.

He turned his head, and the ball was coming at it, bearing down, a 95-mile-an-hour Bobby Wagner rising fastball. For a split second that went on too long, Harvey felt transfixed, almost attracted to the ball. He had seen the pitch countless times before, under better circumstances, when Wagner was with Baltimore—the red seams reduced to streaks in the blur of the backspin, less than half a second from mound to plate, the ball taking off in the last 20 feet.

This time the ball was rising toward his head. In that split second, Harvey felt that he and the ball were fated to meet. That was the thing about a good beanball, not a brushback pitch but one meant to change your idea of batting forever: it seemed to pursue you.

Harvey fell forward onto the damp infield grass, and the ball whistled furiously over him. It caromed off the top concrete edge of the dugout and bounced ineffectually into right. He clambered to his feet. There were still 40 feet between him and the dugout. He couldn't find enough traction in his socks, and the dugout was not getting any closer.

He was 10 feet from the top step of the dugout when the back of his right thigh exploded in pain. His leg gave, and he crumpled to the ground. He heard Wagner breathing coarsely behind him. Harvey tried to get up, but the feeling had gone out of his leg, and he fell back on his seat.

Wagner had caught him just above the back of the knee, and as Harvey clutched his leg in pain, he wondered why Bobby had not simply gone for his head again; it would have been quicker. He was just toying with him now.

Wagner walked slowly toward him off the mound, the ball bag dangling from his left hand. His right hand was caressing another baseball. He came in short heavy strides, looking right at Harvey, and stopped past the first-base line, 20 feet away. The two of them were surrounded by 37,000 empty seats. Harvey did not even try to get up. He still had the bat, though, and from a sitting position, he wound up awkwardly and heaved it at Wagner. It missed him by 3 feet and skidded along the grass.

The pitcher looked at him. "Nice try, Professor."

"Please," Harvey said.

"It wouldn't take much from here, would it?" Wagner said. "What do you think—one pitch, maybe two?"

"Please," Harvey said again.

"They'd never know it was me."

"Of course they would," Harvey panted. "I've told Linderman everything I know. I've told Mickey. Don't be stupid." Propelling himself with one hand, he inched helplessly away from Wagner. "If you kill me, it'll be murder. It's only manslaughter now. You didn't mean to kill Rudy. Anyway, it was the whirlpool that finished him, not you. He provoked you, didn't he? It's manslaughter, but if you kill me, they'll really put you away."

Wagner looked down at him, chewing his gum. Harvey couldn't tell if he even heard what he was saying. Wagner kept turning the ball over in his hand, like a madman mindlessly practicing his tic.

"You made one mistake," Harvey called out. "Are you listening? You made one mistake. Frances has been making mistakes all summer. Rudy, too. Compared to them, I'd say you look like a prince. Go home. Go home and it's between you and me. It won't do you any good if they know you even came after me, so just go home. You've got to trust me, Wags. I never saw you this morning. You're going to be all right."

Wagner lifted his right hand and wiped his brow with the back of it.

"Go home," Harvey pleaded.

Wagner dragged his forearm across his face, and it made Harvey think of the famous photo of him, after he had no-hit Kansas City in 1978. Bobby was on his stool in front of his locker at Memorial Stadium in Baltimore, his uniform drenched with beer poured over him by jubilant teammates; he had his arm over his face, and he was weeping with joy.

Now his arm fell away, and there was no expression at all. "You're through, Professor," he said.

Harvey felt his bowels begin to loosen.

Wagner put the ball bag at his feet and cocked his arm.

There was a kind of mechanical fluttering noise and then a great whooshing sound. Harvey looked up.

The entire system of sprinklers set into Rankle Park's outfield turf had gone on. Twelve jets of water rose simultaneously into the air behind Wagner and began twirling slowly in the morning sunlight.

Wagner turned for an instant, and when he did, Harvey scrambled the 10 feet to the dugout and dropped onto the wooden duckboards.

Three hundred fifty feet away, a maintenance door in the left-field fence opened, and a member of the grounds crew, a tiny figure pushing a wheelbarrow, came out. He spotted Wagner, put the wheelbarrow down, placed his hands on his hips, and yelled, "Hey! You!" at the top of his voice.

Wagner looked at the baseball in his right hand as if it were the first one he had ever seen, fixed Harvey with his eyes, then looked over his shoulder at the figure with the wheelbarrow.

He walked in toward the dugout another 10 feet, until he could see Harvey cowering on his knees on the dugout floor. He stopped and threw the ball as hard as he could up into the upper deck along the first-base line.

Harvey listened to it rattle briefly among the wooden seats.

Then Wagner went past Harvey into the dugout runway and was gone.

A boy wrestles with his insecurities and wonders, *What does it mean to be a man?* *What does a man do?* (Lots of us old boys continue to wonder about this, as well.) It is easy to get lost in the wide world with its thickets of ambivalence; the imperatives in baseball, on the other hand, are few and unequivocal—either you do or you don't—and, as in center field, one stands always in the clear. When real life overwhelms, thinking about baseball is particularly a comfort. From *Portnoy's Complaint.*

PHILIP ROTH

Center Field

So I ran all right, out of the hospital and up to the playground and right out to center field, the position I play for a softball team that wears silky blue-and-gold jackets with the name of the club scrawled in big white felt letters from one shoulder to the other: S E A B E E S, A.C. Thank God for the Seabees A.C.! Thank God for center field! Doctor, you can't imagine how truly glorious it is out there, so alone in all that space. . . . Do you know baseball at all? Because center field is like some observation post, a kind of control tower, where you are able to see everything and everyone, to understand what's happening the instant it happens, not only by the sound of the struck bat but by the spark of movement that goes through the infielders in the first second that the ball comes flying at them; and once it gets beyond them, "It's mine," you call, "it's mine," and then after it you go. For in center field, if you can get to it, it *is* yours. Oh, how unlike my home it is to be in center field, where no one will appropriate unto himself anything that I say is *mine!*

Unfortunately, I was too anxious a hitter to make the high school team—I swung and missed at bad pitches so often during the tryouts for the freshman squad that eventually the ironical coach took me aside and said, "Sonny, are you sure you don't wear glasses?" and then sent me on my way. But did I have form! Did I have style! And in my playground softball league, where the ball came in just a little slower and a little bigger, I am the star I dreamed I might become for the whole school. Of course, still in my ardent desire to excel I too frequently swing and miss, but when I connect, it goes great distances,

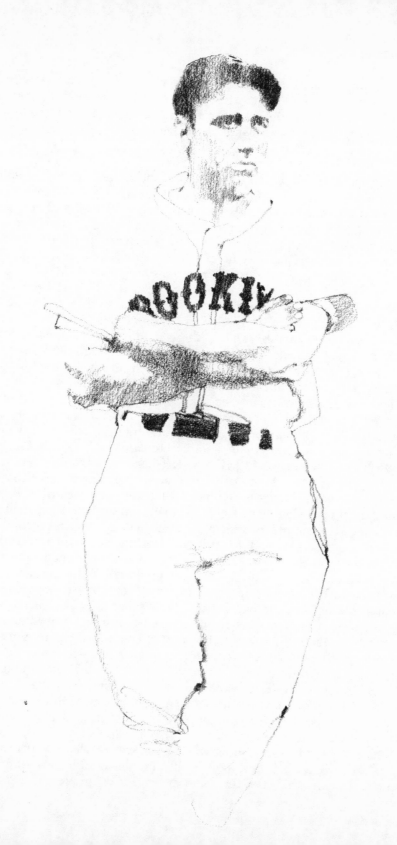

Doctor, it flies over fences and is called a home run. Oh, and there is really nothing in life, nothing at all, that quite compares with that pleasure of round- ing second base at a nice slow clip, because there's just no hurry anymore, because that ball you've hit has just gone sailing out of sight. . . . And I could field, too, and the farther I had to run, the better. "I got it! I got it! I got it!" and tear in toward second, to trap in the webbing of my glove—and barely an inch off the ground—a ball driven hard and low and right down the middle, a base hit, someone thought. . . . Or back I go, "*I* got it, *I* got it—" back easily and gracefully toward that wire fence, moving practically in slow motion, and then that delicious DiMaggio sensation of grabbing it like something heaven- sent over one shoulder. . . . Or running! turning! leaping! like little Al Gion- friddo—a baseball player, Doctor, who once did a very great thing. . . . Or just standing nice and calm—nothing trembling, everything serene—standing there in the sunshine (as though in the middle of an empty field or passing the time on the street corner), standing without a care in the world in the sunshine, like my king of kings, the Lord my God, the Duke Himself (Snider, Doctor, the name may come up again), standing there as loose and as easy, as happy as I will ever be, just waiting by myself under a high fly ball (*a towering fly ball*, I hear Red Barber say as he watches from behind his microphone—hit out toward Portnoy; *Alex under it, under it*), just waiting there for the ball to fall into the glove I raise to it, and yup, there it is, *plock*, the third out of the inning (*and Alex gathers it in for out number three, and, folks, here's old C.D. for P. Lorillard and Company*), and then in one motion, while old Connie brings us a message from Old Golds, I start in toward the bench, holding the ball now with the five fingers of my bare left hand, and when I get to the infield—having come down hard with one foot on the bag at second base—I shoot it gently, with just a flick of the wrist, at the opposing team's shortstop as he comes trotting out onto the field, and still without breaking stride, go loping in all the way, shoulders shifting, head hanging, a touch pigeon-toed, my knees coming slowly up and down in an altogether brilliant imitation of the Duke. Oh, the unruffled nonchalance of that game! There's not a movement that I don't know still down in the tissue of my muscles and the joints between my bones. How to bend over to pick up my glove and how to toss it away, how to test the weight of the bat, how to hold it and carry it and swing it around in the on-deck circle, how to raise that bat above my head and flex and loosen my shoulders and my neck before stepping in and planting my two feet exactly where my two feet belong in the batter's box—and how, when I take a called strike (which I have a tendency to do, it balances off nicely swinging at bad pitches), to step out and express, if only through a slight poking with the bat at the ground, just the right amount of exasperation with the powers that be . . . yes, every little detail so thoroughly studied and mastered, that it is simply beyond the realm of possibility for any situation to arise in which I do not know how to move, or where to move, or what to say or leave unsaid. . . . And it's true, is it not?—incredible, but apparently true—there are people who feel in life the ease, the self-assurance, the simple and essential affiliation with what is going on, that I used to feel as the center fielder for the Seabees? Because it wasn't, you see, that one was the best center fielder imaginable, only that one knew exactly, and down to the smallest particular, how a center fielder should conduct himself. And there are people like that walking the streets of the U.S. of A.? I ask you, why can't I be one! Why can't I exist now as I existed for the Seabees out there in center field! Oh, to be a center fielder, a center fielder—and nothing more!

This backhand paean to the box score appeared in the New York *American* on September 17, 1920. How much of the doubleheader's detail can you fill in? And don't you wish that today's box score, though improved by adding the "pitching box," had retained the individual fielding totals and the pinch hitters' lines?

DAMON RUNYON

The Soul of Wit

The Sporting Ed. says, "Cut 'er short!
There's not much space to-day for sport.

"Between the ads,
Between the news.
All excess words I must refuse."

So short it is.
Quite short you see.
Two ball games at the old P. G.

The Pirates won.
The Giants won.
Scores: Three to one, and four to none.

The Sporting Ed. says:
"That'll do."
The box scores tell the rest to you.

FIRST GAME.

PITTSBURGH	ab	r	h	o	a	e
Bigbee, lf	4	1	1	2	0	0
Cutshaw, 2b	2	0	0	2	1	0
S'thworth, rf	4	2	3	3	0	0
Nicholson, cf	4	0	1	3	0	0
Whitted, 3b	4	0	3	2	3	0
Grimm, 1b	3	0	0	9	0	0
McKechnie, ss	4	0	0	3	3	1
Schmidt, c	2	0	0	3	1	0
Hamilton, p	3	0	0	0	0	0
Totals	30	3	8a	26	8	1

a Kelly out: hit by batted ball.

NEW YORK	ab	r	h	o	a	e
Burns, lf	4	0	1	1	0	0
Bancroft, ss	4	0	0	0	2	1
Young, rf	3	0	0	4	1	0
Frisch, 3b	3	1	1	1	3	0
Kelly, 1b	3	0	1	15	3	0
King, cf	3	0	0	3	0	0
Grimes, 2b	3	0	1	1	4	0
Snyder, c	3	0	0	1	3	0
Barnes, p	2	0	0	1	2	0
bGriffin	1	0	0	0	0	0
Douglas, p	0	0	0	0	1	0
Totals	29	1	4	27	19	1

b Batted for Barnes in eighth inning.

Pittsburgh	0	0	0	0	0	2	0	0	1—3
New York	0	0	0	0	0	0	1	0	0—1

Two-base hit—Whitted. Stolen bases—Frisch. Kelly. Sacrifices—Young. Grimm. Cutshaw. Left on bases—Pittsburgh, 4: New York, 4. Bases on balls—Off Barnes, 3: off Hamilton, 2. Hits—Off Barnes, 3 in 8 innings: off Douglas, 3 in running. Struck out—By Hamilton, 3. Losing pitcher—Barnes. Umpires—O'Day and Quigley. Time—One hour and forty-five minutes.

SECOND GAME.

PITTSBURGH	ab	r	h	o	a	e
Bigbee, lf	3	0	0	0	1	0
Cutshaw, 2b	3	0	0	3	4	0
S'thworth, rf	3	0	1	3	0	0
Nicholson, cf	3	0	0	4	0	0
Whitted, 3b, 1b	3	0	0	2	2	0
Grimm, 1b	2	0	0	8	1	0
aCarey	1	0	0	0	0	0
Trainor, ss	0	0	0	0	0	0
M'K'ie, ss, 3b	3	0	0	2	1	0
Schmidt, c	3	0	0	1	1	0
Ponder, p	2	0	0	1	2	0
bBarbare	1	0	0	0	0	0
Totals	27	0	1	24	12	0

a Batted for Grimm in eighth inning.
b Batted for Ponder in ninth inning.

NEW YORK	ab	r	h	o	a	e
Burns, lf	3	1	0	3	0	0
Bancroft, ss	4	0	0	2	2	0
Young, rf	4	1	1	4	0	0
Frisch, 3b	3	0	0	0	0	0
Kelly, 1b	4	1	2	6	1	0
King, cf	3	1	1	1	0	0
Doyle, 2b	3	0	1	2	2	0
Smith, c	3	0	1	7	1	0
Nehf, p	3	0	1	2	0	0
Totals	30	4	7	27	6	0

Pittsburgh	0	0	0	0	0	0	0	0	0—0
New York	1	1	0	0	0	0	1	1	0—4

Two-base hit—Kelly. Home runs—King. Young. Stolen bases—Burns. Nehf. Left on bases—Pittsburgh, 1: New York, 4. Bases on balls—Off Nehf, 1: off Ponder, 3. Struck out—Ry Nehf, 7: by Ponder, 1. Umpires—Quigley and O'Day. Time of game—One hour and thirty minutes.

The play's the thing. Here are three contributions from the Bard, or in his manner, beginning with some gleanings from the plays by Henry Chadwick in 1868, then A. Donald Douglas's 1912 parody of Hamlet's soliloquy, and concluding with a witty, contemporary piece by Louis Phillips, published in a 1985 issue of the *Saturday Review*. Shakespeare's other recognized contributions to baseball's dramatic literature are *The Comedy of Errors*, *A Midsummer Night's Dream*, and, of course, *The Speed Merchant of Venice*.

WILLIAM SHAKESPEARE (& friends)

Bard at the Bat

Old Billy, ye play writer, must have been ball player once. Read what he says:

"You base (foot) ballplayers."—*Lear*.
"Why, these balls bound."—*Merry Wives*.
"Now, let's have a catch."—*Twelfth Night*.
"I will run no base."—*Merry Wives*.
"And so I shall catch the fly."—*Henry V*.
"Hector shall have a great catch."—*Troilus and Cressida*.
"More like to run the base."—*Cymbeline*.
"As swift in motion as a ball."—*Romeo and Juliet*.
"Ne'er leave striking in the field."—*Henry IV*.
"After he scores."—*All's Well*.
"Ajax goes up and down the field."—*Troilus and Cressida*.
"Have you scored me?"—*Othello*.
"He proved best man i' the field."—*Coriolanus*.
"The word is pitch and pay."—*Henry V*.
"However men do catch."—*King John*.
"What foul play had we?"—*Tempest*.
"Unprovided of a pair of bases."—*Titus Andronicus*.
"No other books but the score."—*Henry VI*.
"These nine men in buckram."—*Henry VI*.
"His confounded base."—*Henry VI*.

"I will fear to catch."—*Timon.*
"What works, my countrymen, in hand? Where go you with *bats* and clubs?"
—*Coriolanus.*
"Let us see you in the field."—*Troilus and Cressida.*
"The very way to catch them."—*Coriolanus.*

THE BATTER'S SOLILOQUY

By A. Donald Douglas

(In the ninth inning, with a man on third, two gone,
and the score 2–2)

To wait, or not to wait,—that is the question:
Whether 'tis nobler in this game to suffer
The taunts and yells of the outrageous fans,
Or to dodge the curves and drops of an erratic pitcher,
And, by my coolness 'scape them? To wait—to walk,—
No more; and by a walk to say we stroll
To first, and then be daring like Ty Cobb,
And work the Double Steal,—'tis a consummation
Devoutly to be wished. To walk—to steal,—
To steal. Perchance to score. Ay, there's the rub;—
For in that Double Steal what chance may come
When we have rattled the opposing pitcher,
Must give us runs: there's the respect
That makes a walk of so long life;
For who would bear the yells and taunts of fans,
The umpire's wrong, the bleachers' contumely,
The pangs of disprized hope, the game's delay,
The insolence of gamins, and the spurns
That one must take from the unknowing
When he himself his fame might make,
By a 2-bagger? Who would roastings bear,
To grunt and swear under a weary game,
But that the dread of something after it,
The Minor Leagues, from whose ranks
No old-time star returns, startles the mind;
And makes us rather bear those ills we have
Than fly to others whence we ne'er return?
These bleachers do make cowards of us all;
And thus the fumble of a hard-hit grounder,
Is yelled at by the bleacher mob,
And thus in places of great chance and moment,
We all make bonehead plays that lose the game.

SHAKESPEARE MAKES BASEBALL'S GREATEST PLAYS

By Louis Phillips

At one time, Shakespeare owned part interest in a ball club—the Stratford Variorums—and this team once played a series of exhibition games against a team consisting of America's all-time great players. The night of the season opener, Shakespeare and his sister invited me to attend the game with them. We were unfortunately late in arriving at the ballpark, so Shakespeare hurried me to my seat:

SHAKESPEARE: "But, sirrah, make haste, Percy is already in the field." *(Henry IV, IV, ii, 74–75)*

It took me a moment to realize that Shakespeare was referring to his center fielder—Joe Percy. Falstaff, the manager of the Variorums, came onto the field to change pitchers. Falstaff wanted a fresh hurler to face Ruth.

ME: Tell me, who's your catcher?

SHAKESPEARE: "Passion, I see, is catching." *(Julius Caesar, III, i, 283)*

ME: Number 38. Yogi Passion, catcher. This is a strange lineup.

SHAKESPEARE: "Now name the rest of the players." *(A Midsummer Night's Dream, I, ii, 39)*

ME: We have Hector Richmond in right field, Joe Percy in center, Jory Richmond in left, Al Richmond at third, Ajax Richmond at second, Laertes Richmond at first, Titus Richmond at short. . . .

SHAKESPEARE: "I think there be six Richmonds in the field." *(Richard III, V, iv, 11)*

Claudius let fly with a fast ball. Ruth hit a towering fly to right.

SHAKESPEARE: "Hector shall have a great catch." *(Troilus and Cressida, II, i, 99–100)*

HECTOR *(to himself, in right field)*: "I'll catch it ere it come to ground." *(Macbeth, III, v, 25)*

Alas, Hector did not catch it. He overran the ball, scoring Mantle from second.

SHAKESPEARE: "That's monstrous. O that that were out!" *(Two Gentlemen of Verona, III, i, 365–66)*

Claudius was replaced by a young pitcher named Aumerle (related to Rudy York). A great home-run hitter took his place in the batter's box.

SHAKESPEARE: "Here Aaron is; and what with Aaron now?" *(Titus Andronicus, IV, ii, 54)*

ME: A home run, I should guess.

SHAKESPEARE: "Strike him, Aumerle." *(Richard II, V, ii, 85)*

Hank pounded a hard grounder to the first baseman. Ruth broke for third.

SHAKESPEARE: "Come, for the third, Laertes, you do but dally." *(Hamlet, V, ii, 297)*

Laertes fired a perfect strike to the third baseman. Ruth hit the dirt.

SHAKESPEARE: "The fool slides. . . ." (*Troilus and Cressida*, III, iii, 215)
ME: That was a great throw from Laertes!

Ruth leaped to his feet and began to argue the call. Bill Martin, manager of the All-Stars, stormed out of the dugout.

SHAKESPEARE'S SISTER: Be calm, brother. Let the umpire decide the question.
SHAKESPEARE: "There is three umpires in the matter I understand." (*The Merry Wives of Windsor*, I, i, 137)
ME: The Babe was safe!
SHAKESPEARE:"Out, dog, out, cur!" (*A Midsummer Night's Dream*, III, ii, 65)
ME: Safe! Al missed the tag!
SHAKESPEARE: "Out, I say!" (*Macbeth*, V, i, 35)

Martin was finally ejected from the game. Al Simmons stepped to the plate.

ME: He's going to hit it.
SHAKESPEARE *(taunting the batter)*: "Thou canst not hit it, hit it, hit it. Thou canst not hit it, my good man." (*Love's Labor's Lost*, IV, i, 125–26)

The pitch was thrown. Simmons swung, missed, and missed again. Edwin Snider was annnounced as the next batter. He hit a pop fly to Percy.

ME: It's an easy out. . . . Percy's under it.
SHAKESPEARE: "No doubt but he hath got a quiet catch." (*Taming of the Shrew*, II, i, 331)

The lead of the American All-Stars held up. Nonetheless, Shakespeare had completely fallen under the spell of baseball. As he and I and his sister left the stadium he turned to me and said:

I'll make a journey twice as far t'enjoy a second night of such
sweet shortness." (*Cymbeline*, II, iv, 43–44)

In addition to the standard scholarly histories of baseball by Harold Seymour and David Voigt, there are many anecdotal chronicles of the sport; of these, none is more entertaining and erudite than Robert Smith's *Baseball*, first issued in 1947 and then again in substantially different form in 1970. Fred Dunlap, The Only Nolan, Joe Start, Silver Flint, Deacon McGuire, Toad Ramsey—although these names may be unfamiliar to today's fans, they were heroes in their day.

ROBERT SMITH

Of Kings and Commoners

In the 1880s a man who was best at his trade would be called King, or sometimes he would be "The Only." Baseball's greatest King and the only one who wore the title to his grave was Mike Kelly. Everybody in the land has heard of Kelly, for he is as famous as Casey—the legendary figure who batted for Mudville in the poem by Ernest Thayer. Some used to say that Casey himself was modeled after Kelly, but this was not a fact. There was only one Kelly, and no figure in fact or fiction ever approached him. He was the Kelly who used to slide and whose name on that account has become a catchword in the tongue, still used by men and women who never knew the fellow who made it famous.

"Slide, Kelly, slide!" the fans in Boston used to sing.

"Slide, Kelly, on your belly!

"Slide, Kelly, slide!"

Although Mike Kelly was not the first to slide in order to avoid a tag, he was the most earnest practitioner of this dodge, and he invented ways of sliding to base that few of his contemporaries ever dared to try. He not only slid on his belly; he slid on his backside, and he slid on his thighs. He would fall away from a base in his slide and then reach out to grab it as he coasted by. Or he would ride in on the seat of his pants with his two feet flicking so that the man with the ball did not know where to put the tag. Or, in the days before they had remembered to make a rule about runners passing each other on the base paths, he might get the man running ahead of him to stop suddenly in front of home plate, legs aspraddle, to let Kelly slide in between the man's feet to tag the plate and score a run.

To get on base to do his sliding, Mike of course had to hit the ball. And for a time he was one of the games' mightiest hitters. But he learned his trade slowly and for a time did not seem at all sure to make it.

Michael J. Kelly was born in Troy, New York, then known as Lansingburgh, before the Civil War began. His father, still only a few years out of Ireland, enlisted in the Union Army when the war started, then reenlisted when the war was over and brought his family down to live in Washington, D.C., where he was stationed. Baseball was important in Washington in those days, for it was the era of the Nationals and of George Wright and the many others appointed to government jobs so they might play the "noble game" for the glory of the capital city. Young Mike, in school, where he was the fastest runner to be found, grew up on stories of the great games the mighty Nationals played all over the land. But in his school it was not the grown-up game that was played but "burn ball," one of the oldest versions of baseball, in which runners could be put out by "burning" their shrinking hides with a hard-thrown ball when they wandered off the base. To stay alive on the baselines in that game, a youngster had to be particularly agile, and none was more agile than Mike.

But the New York game, as played by the Nationals, still was real baseball to Mike and to those of his mates who were best at it. So Mike joined the Keystones, a club of juniors, to play New York ball. At that time Mike's private hero was Old Reliable Joe Start (he never dropped a throw), the husky first baseman of the New York Mutuals; when Mike grew old enough to raise a mustache of his own, he grew one just like Joe's. When ill health forced the elder Kelly out of the army, the family moved to Paterson, New Jersey, where Mike organized a baseball club of his own and insisted it be named the Keystones. In this collection of scrawny young Irishmen, not one of whom could brag of scratch enough to buy a whole uniform, Mike was the best—the hardest thrower, the fastest runner, the most reliable batsman. Among the dozen youngsters on the club, there was just one baseball cap—an authentic, multicolored, hard-billed cap almost exactly like the one Joe Start wore. It had cost fifteen cents. Mike had no fifteen cents to buy it with, but he insisted he would not play for the club in match games if he could not wear the cap. So when the Keystones took the field, there was no mistaking Kelly—the only one with a baseball hat on. And when the game began, there was no missing him, either—the boy who moved the fastest, hit the ball the farthest, and was having the most fun.

Mike Kelly liked to catch, because the catcher, facing the whole club, really ran the team, got into all the action, and took the most punishment. The club had a strong-arm pitcher named Nolan, who, by the time Mike had become King Kelly, was himself known the baseball world over as The Only Nolan. Eddie Nolan at that time was a railroad fireman, building his shoulder muscles by firing hungry freight engines along the Hudson River. Mike Kelly was working in a Paterson mill for three dollars a week.

The Nolan-Kelly battery made the Keystones invincible for three years; then Eddie began to play the game for money and moved away. Young Mike stayed on, still playing for fun and earning his income now by bringing the New York papers into Paterson at dawn. This job meant getting up at four in the morning, but it gave Mike every bright afternoon to play ball. By the time he was eighteen, Mike had become a semiprofessional ballplayer. In the wintertime, he undertook to learn to be a silk weaver, for it was a rare baseball job in that day (1876) that could offer a man enough to live on the year around. Mike quickly found he was no weaver, nor did he ever have any stomach for the twelve-hour day the mills offered—it being acknowledged even by the nation's advanced thinkers that a shorter workday would simply mean disaster for the laboring man. Mike decided he was never meant to be a laboring man, so he took a full-time job in the spring with the professional baseball club at Port Jervis, New York, but a buggy ride from home.

From Port Jervis, where he quickly proved himself the class of the lineup, young Mike advanced to the Cincinnati Buckeyes of the National League—a revival of the team that had died when the Red Stockings were born. Whether it was homesickness or curveball pitching, no one now can say, but Mike started off the 1879 season in Cincinnati in a sorry state indeed. In his first twenty-one times at bat he reached first but once, and that time through a fielding error. His baseball career might have ended right then, and history would have had to seek another slider, for the manager of the Buckeyes—Cal McVey, once the star of the Atlantics—had sent for a new ballplayer to haul his team out of the slump. To make room for him, Cal told himself, he would drop either Kelly or Dickerson, an outfielder who had been too ill to play regularly but who still was batting better than Kelly. When young Mike got wind of this, he took off like a man possessed. The very next day, in four times at bat, he hit two doubles, a triple, and a home run. In the next game against mighty Chicago, Kelly batted in every one of Cincinnati's runs and beat the White Stockings—and saved his place in the major leagues.

There was no World Series in the fall then, but ballplayers often stretched the season, and kept the paydays coming, by joining one of the many barnstorming teams to show big-time baseball to the Far West. Most famous of the great barnstorming clubs of that era was the Hop Bitters team of Rochester, New York, wearing the name of a patent medicine. The Bitters, a minor-league outfit, were the equal of many a big-league club and listed a number of famous players on their roster. But Kelly, in California, playing with a club made up chiefly of Cincinnati and Buffalo men, punched the Hop Bitters club full of holes. Adrian Anson, then the "captain"—that is, manager—of the Chicago club was so impressed with Kelly that he undertook at once to sign him for the White Stockings. It took the two of them—the dour Anson and the merry Mike—more than a week to settle a difference of $100 in the salary offer. But they decided on a figure finally, and Mike moved to Chicago, where he soon became the most famous baseball player in the world.

Mike was sometimes referred to as a "big fellow," and indeed, at the top of his fame, he did seem to stand out beyond all the players on his club. His uniform was always a bit more flamboyant than the other players', with letters on it that stood out almost an inch from the shirtfront. His shoulders were broad, his eyes agleam, his mustache flourishing, his hair neat and luxuriant. But at his best he weighed only 170 pounds, and he stood a scant 6 feet off the ground. Cap Anson himself was a bigger and broader man. But no one else cut quite the figure that Kelly did, in the press, on the field, or along the street.

A he-man in that day was a "hearty" man who could ingest abnormal quantities of food and drink. Mike Kelly loved whiskey and good roast beef with the ardor of a medieval friar, but Cap Anson, who believed in severe conditioning of his ballplayers, let no man on his squad load himself with lard. By the time he was ready to open the season with Kelly, Mike was greyhound lean, faster than ever in the field and on base, sharp-eyed at bat, and quick as a spider behind the plate. His great deeds on the ball field grew into legends, until some were exaggerated beyond belief. It was said he never tagged third base on his way home and sometimes went from first to third by way of the pitcher's box. No doubt he did frequently cut a base when the lone umpire was watching a play in the other direction. At least once he scored from second base without getting close enough to third to reach it with a pole. But much of his improvisation did not break the rules. It simply took advantage of loopholes the rule makers had left.

There was a rule that allowed a substitute to enter a game "on notice to the umpire." Kelly, learned in these careless phrasings, once leaped from the bench (where he might have been left to heal a hangover), shouted to the umpire, "Kelly now catching," and put away a foul ball the regular catcher could not have reached. The umpire would not allow the out, even after Kelly showed him the rule. After that they changed the rule.

Kelly performed most of his wildest feats in exhibition games, where he played for applause or strove to excite or anger the spectators. In one such game, when the ball he had hit became lost in the outfield brush, Kelly added suspense to the proceedings by leaving the baselines to run a solemn circle around each outfielder before he ran home. At a game in St. Louis, where the cheap seats were often crammed with denizens of the Kerry Patch—the Irish ghetto—Kelly, playing the outfield, invited the fans behind him to join in a chorus of "The Battle of Boyne Water"—an Orangeman's song calculated to curdle the whiskey of any true son of the sacred soil.

Still no one ever held a grudge against Kelly, who was the "King" to fans and "Kell" to his teammates. There was never an ounce of malice in the man, and there was a hogshead full of kindness and generosity in his heart. The opponents he beat, the umpires he taunted or hornswoggled, the fans he sometimes enraged, all finally adored him and begrudged him not a penny of the sudden wealth his fame brought him.

Eventually, Kelly was sold to Boston—sent away from Chicago "because of a woman," it was whispered. The price the Boston Beaneaters paid for him was $10,000—enough in those days to buy a ballpark. Promptly Kelly was named "The $10,000 Beauty," after a stage lady who used that title in her promotion. And the Boston Irish swarmed to make him welcome. His fans even chipped in one day to buy him a spanking pair of grays and a gig to go with them, so that the King of the Diamond could ride out on Washington Street in style, in gloves and gleaming top hat and needle-toed button shoes.

Like many a latter-day baseball king, Kelly thought money was made to spend, and he never laid by a nickel. Friends, acquaintances, even unhappy strangers who needed a fiver, could count on Kell to produce it. The little old lady who sold flowers in the street could unload her entire store of blossoms on old Mike. Although his salary ($2,000 dollars for playing ball and $3,000 for "use of his picture") was thought large enough to support a prince and was supplemented by money he took in for reciting "Casey at the Bat" on the vaudeville stage, Kelly was always a week or two ahead of the paymaster.

His play in Boston began to flag a little. On days when he had time to take aboard a proper helping of whiskey before the game began, he might circle unsteadily beneath an easy fly ball and then miss it altogether. Secure in the love the fans felt for him, Kelly never let such lapses fret him. "By God, I made it hit me glove," he would exult, and put it from his mind. It was not long, however, before even the most devoted fans grew tired of seeing precious ball games go home with the other side just because Mike Kelly had a drop taken. The Boston club shipped Mike to New York one day "on loan." Mike, in the big city, cut an even wider swath, and the loan was very quickly repaid, with hardly any thanks.

It was downhill after that for Kelly. He played awhile in Allentown and was dismayed when the fans not only failed to laugh at his antics but even hissed and booed at his failures in the field. *Ah, well*, he consoled himself, *they still love old Kell in the theater.* But now the audiences no longer laughed at the way he imitated De Wolf Hopper. Kelly tried running a saloon, too, along with Honest John Kelly, the umpire. But all this seemed to mean was that for a while he got his drink wholesale. When he was thirty-seven years old, he took a boat to Boston to fill a vaudeville engagement there, and on the boat he came down with pneumonia, as so many big, hearty men were prone to do. He was carried off on a stretcher and put to bed in his hotel, where he seemed to be getting better. Then suddenly his temperature shot up again, and he was rushed to the Boston Emergency Hospital, where he breathed his last under an oxygen tent.

Then finally the baseball world mourned him and remembered the way he had been at his best—so devil-may-care, so fast on his feet, so quick to slide, to slide, to slide.

Adrian Constantine Anson was very nearly the opposite of Mike Kelly in nature, yet nearly as widely known to fame in his day and every bit as fearsome a foe. Anson was dour and given to self-discipline, whereas Kelly was gay and a stranger to restraint. Anson was taller and heavier than Mike, a mightier man at bat but a leader rather than a member of a team, and a cross-grained, self-sufficient fellow as bitter in his prejudices as he was indomitable in his convictions. Anson played big-league baseball for more than twenty seasons, from 1871, when he was just turned twenty, to 1897, when he was past forty-six. He played every position on the diamond, including pitcher, but for the greater part of his career he was first baseman and captain of the Chicago White Stockings, who eventually became the Cubs. At the start of his career he was known as "Baby" Anson, or the "Marshalltown Infant." (He had been the first white child born in Marshalltown, Iowa.) Long before he was finished, he was known as "Pop," from being so much older than anybody else on the field. For a time after he left the Chicago club, they were known as the "Orphans," because they had lost their Pop.

Anson was known in his day as "an inveterate coacher," a coacher being one who was given, of course, to coaching. But coaching, in the seventies and eighties, as has been noted earlier, did not mean giving instructions or advice. It meant bellowing encouragement and derision at friend or foe. Some people came to the park as much to hear Anson yell as to watch him hit. He yelled at everyone. Standing near third base, towering over the enemy baseman, he would roar an invitation to the batter: "Knock the ball down here! This is the weak spot!"

Umpires, naturally, felt the rough side of Anson's tongue. He even scared one umpire—poor Dickey Pearce—into reversing a decision and ordering back to the plate a man who had just been awarded first base for being hit with the ball.

Teammates, too, could expect a public hazing by Anson if they booted a ground ball or let a fly elude them. But most treasured by true Anson fans were the orations that Cap would often deliver when he found umpires, foes, and fans all conspiring against him. Then he would turn to face the stands, and in a voice calculated to start rocks to rolling on a distant hill, he would berate the people who were hooting at him, belittle the city that housed them, and warn them of the humiliations his club would hang about their ignorant necks.

Anson was a homely man, not given to dandified dress. His nose was off center, and his ears were not mates. In his earlier days, according to the mode, he let his mustache grow and even waxed the ends a little. But his size and the obviously oak-hard condition of his body impressed all who faced him. And the voice that would have silenced the Bull of Bashan demanded attention and obedience. When he had delivered one of his orations to the enraptured stands, he would pound his great hands together like two wooden hammers and bellow:

"Come on, fellows! Play the game!"

And the game would be played.

Anson was one of the great batters of baseball. He swung a heavy stick and could hit the ball hard and far. But he always taught his players to choke up a little on the bat, the better to control it. This was known as "stopping it down" in that day and was a habit sometimes decried by those who thought a real man should try to break the ball in two whenever it came his way. Anson himself had no use for bunting, which he ridiculed as "the baby act." But he was one of the first to teach the advantage of keeping control of the bat in order to "hit the ball where it was pitched" instead of trying to lay into it with all one's power, to pull it into the batter's favorite field.

For himself, Anson always cradled the bat loosely in his arms at the plate, as if he were not certain how he might take hold of it. He did not cut the air with the bat or pound the plate, nor did he, as some of the ostentatious batters of that era did, stand with the bat "charged"—rifle style—toward the pitcher. Like Ty Cobb, a fiery batsman of a later day, Anson kept his hands well apart on the bat handle so he could choke up, or swing a long bat, depending on the pitch. The ball Cap Anson hit was the dead ball, not wound so tightly as the modern ball and without the cork center. Still, even with the pitcher only fifty feet away, big Cap set records that no modern hero would be ashamed of.

In 1884, Cap Anson hit five home runs in two days. When he completed his playing career, he was still batting better than .300. His fielding, however, was stodgy, and today he would be called dead on his feet around the base. He never felt that it was his part to scamper up the baseline to field a ground ball. Rather, he left that to his miraculous second baseman, the great Fred Pfeffer, who owned the biggest mustache in the game. Fred, having to cover all the ground between first and second base, often could stop a ground ball only by flinging himself full length on the turf, while Big Anse stood watching him from a few feet away. Then Fred, having stopped the ball, would have to flip it to Anson while lying facedown or on his side. But if he got it anywhere near the big man, that was enough, for Anson seemed able to stretch himself 5 yards in any direction, while still keeping a toe on the bag. Chicago fans used to scream with delight to see Anson reach high, high into the air and pluck a wild throw with his tiny glove.

Anson's real pride, however, was his ability to find good ballplayers almost everywhere he looked. While he led the Chicago forces, they owned many of baseball's greatest names—not only Kelly and Pfeffer but John Clarkson, Anson's best pitcher, and Silver Flint, the white-haired catcher who was sometimes known as The Only Flint. If Spalding, seeing a chance to trade off a star to advantage, approached Anson to test the captain's feeling about it, Anson never chewed the matter over for more than a minute. Even when Spalding, with some trepidation, brought the news to big Anse that Mike Kelly might be traded, Anson snapped his answer immediately:

"Sure! Trade anybody!"

There were always new ballplayers to be brought in and developed, and Anson was confident he could find them, as he had found Kelly out on the Coast with a bunch of barnstormers. Sometimes he could turn a fairly good ballplayer into a star just by seeing to it that the man kept his weight down and his reflexes sharp. He was one of the few managers in that far-off day who did not feel it was good for a player to fill himself chock full at the dining table. He gave his men gymnastics to do every day and laid down training rules designed to keep them out of the saloons and put them into their beds at a decent hour. Nor did he ever ease up on himself. He never drank strong liquor. He checked his weight as jealously as a jockey. His own pregame fare was a bowl of bread and milk. He sought his lone bed soon after the sun was gone. And he saved his money.

Like many another he-man of his day, Anson felt there was something two-fisted about exhibiting scorn for Negroes. He helped create the "unwritten rule" that barred black men from big-league baseball for sixty years and still keeps them from becoming managers. In Anson's days there were several ballplayers of African descent who performed in the major leagues without once threatening the ruin of the state. The first to enter the majors was Moses Fleetwood Walker, who, with his brother Welday, had starred in baseball at Oberlin College. Fleet Walker became a catcher with the Toledo Club of the American Association (a major league in the 1800s), where he teamed with ambidextrous Tony Mullane to help the likely lad from Cork win thirty-five games in a season. (Brother Welday played in the outfield at Toledo.) But here and there throughout the circuit, Walker met men who refused to share the diamond with any man so lost to good manners as to wear black skin. And crude Cap Anson, one day at Newark, where Fleet Walker and another black athlete, George Stovey, played minor-league ball, indignantly demanded that the Newark management "get those niggers off the field!" This request, hastily honored by the Newark bosses, set a style that was followed in organized baseball until 1945, when Branch Rickey hired Jack Roosevelt Robinson to play for Montreal.

There was another "King" in professional baseball besides King Kell, but the title never stuck to him as it did to big Mike, perhaps because it did not fit quite so alliteratively—or perhaps because Fred Dunlap, the King of Second Basemen, never cut quite the figure Mike did either off the field or on. Still there were numberless ball kranks in that day who would not have swapped you a Dunlap for three Mike Kellys.

The nickname that did stick to Dunlap was Sure-Shot, for Fred was noted for the sharpshooting accuracy with which he could fire the ball from any angle into the first baseman's glove. Fred, who played second base for Cleveland and St. Louis, was also the strongest man in professional baseball and the most fearless. More than one amateur bully who tried to misuse Fred Dunlap carried home a set of bruises that lasted him a month.

Fred was only 5 feet 8, small enough for a drunk to pick on. But he had been an athlete all his life and never let himself grow soft. He had spent his entire youth playing ball, from the time he was ten, when his parents had died. The elderly couple that took him in required only that little Fred fetch a growler of beer every morning in return for his board and keep. After that he was free to attend school or play baseball as he chose. Fred chose baseball and never learned to read or write until he was past eighteen, when someone helped him to spell out his name so he could sign papers.

Little Fred learned to run like a rabbit, not from fear but from eagerness to get from base to base or to run down a baseball and get into the game. His hands were really too small for a ballplayer, being dainty as a girl's. But endless practice made him adept as a monkey at grabbing a sizzling ground ball in either hand and firing it off from the very spot he seized it. His whistling throws, which seemed to clear the grass by no more than half a foot, never seemed to lose an inch of altitude in flight and almost never missed the mark by more than an inch or two. It was King Kell who, after watching Fred fire the ball to base, gave him the name of "Sure-Shot." Kell also agreed that Fred could outdress him, for Fred delighted to spend his money on clothing—as do so many poor boys who have known the humiliation of hand-me-downs. Fred was also, despite his short stature, an impressive and graceful figure off the diamond. He cultivated refined manners, wore spotless linen, and knew how to behave at a polite dinner table, even though he could never have read the menu.

What he did know most of was baseball. An alert, fast-thinking man who had studied the game since he began to play it as a tiny boy on a Philadelphia vacant lot, he seemed always able to stay a play or two ahead of the enemy. While team baseball in Fred's day was at its very beginning, with the great stars often scorning to move out of their positions and with basemen frequently anchored to the base, Fred moved about the diamond as George Wright had done and as Charlie Comiskey was beginning to do—backing up throws, trying for balls that technically "belonged" to another fielder, and diving for ground balls that no one seemed to have a prayer of reaching. Lying flat on the ground, Fred could still uncork a throw that would sting the palm of the first baseman and hit right in the center of the glove. If Fred found it difficult to get his right arm free for a throw, he could throw just as hard and just as accurately with his left, for he wore no glove on either.

Fred was also as fierce a slider as King Kell was. He handled himself on the baselines without fear or hesitation and would hurl his small, hard body into a base with such desperation that he would sometimes scare the baseman half out of his pants. He was sometimes called on to pitch and was ready to play any other position, too, as he had often had to do on the Philadelphia meadows to fit himself into a lineup.

In 1884, when players, outraged by the new "reserve rule," which bound them for life to the club that signed them, decided to join the new Union Association, Fred Dunlap became manager of the St. Louis club in that league. He was then twenty-five years old, lean, hard, and brown as an Indian from his constant being outdoors. He had the nose of an Indian, too, and deep brown eyes. But he weighed only 160 pounds, and despite his fierce and dignified demeanor, he did not scare Curt Welch of the rival St. Louis Browns. One day Welch, having talked himself into a froth of anger at the upstart "Onions," who were trying to take the bread out of his mouth, swaggered into the Union park and "called out" Fred Dunlap. Fred calmly went to meet the rugged Welch and within three minutes had beaten the big man so badly that Curt had to have help to get home.

Fred's inability to sign his first contract (with the Philadelphia Acmes), the humiliation of having to make an X where his signature should have gone, was what prompted him to learn to write his name. When it came time to sign the biggest contract of his life—the $6,000 contract with the St. Louis Maroons of the Union Association—Fred was able to write Fred Dunlap on the proper line even though he could not read a word of what preceded it.

After the Union Association folded up, Fred returned to the National League as manager of the St. Louis Browns, then was reduced to the ranks for his next few seasons with St. Louis and Detroit. In 1887 he starred in the great traveling World Series between Detroit and St. Louis, when the two teams played fifteen games in Pittsburgh, Brooklyn, New York, Philadelphia, Washington, Boston, Baltimore, and Chicago as well as in the two home cities. For his work in this series Fred pocketed a few hundred dollars extra. But Fred was never hard up while he was playing ball and never dropped money at the racetracks and saloons, as Mike Kelly did.

Fred's greatest playing days were spent in Cleveland, from 1880 to 1883. Here he belonged to the combination acknowledged the greatest of his era— Big Bill Phillips at first, Dunlap at second, Jack Glasscock, the King of Short-stops, next, and tough Mike Muldoon at third base. After his terms at St. Louis and Detroit, Fred went back to managing in Pittsburgh but lasted only one full season. He played a few games for Pittsburgh in 1890 and one for New York. He ended his career the next season, with Washington. He was said to have laid up $100,000 and had nothing to worry him for the rest of his life, having gone into the building business, where fortune seemed assured. But eleven years later a Philadelphia policeman, in the local morgue, saw a body that looked like Fred Dunlap's. He persuaded Lave Cross of the Philadelphia Athletics to come view the body, and Lave confirmed that this was the man he had often faced on the diamond, the King of All the Second Basemen, penniless, dead, alone, and destined now for Potter's Field.

If a man were not named King, he might instead be called The Only to indicate that there was none other like him on the globe. In the 1880s there were two "Onlys," but one was awarded the name when he played with the original—when Silver Flint was set to catching the fiery fastball of The Only Nolan, Flint became The Only Flint. But Nolan became Only because he was the only one of his kind—a pitcher who threw thirty games one season in which he did not allow the enemy a run. Indeed, his average "earned run" allowance in 1877 was half a run per game, in seventy-six complete games. He won sixty-four of these games, for an average of .941. When fans called him The Only then, no one in baseball disputed the title.

Eddie Nolan had played ball with Mike Kelly's Keystones in Paterson, New Jersey, where Nolan had a job firing freight engines for the Lackawanna Rail-road. Eddie developed such strength in his shoulders on the job that he seemed able to throw fastballs forever. But he also had a startling curve, in that day when a curveball of any degree would cause men to marvel. Eddie's curve was labeled an "inshoot," for it broke sharply toward a right-handed batter. Actually it was probably the natural hop that an overhand fastball often shows when it is thrown with great strength. And there were no pitchers of that day any stronger than Eddie Nolan. Eddie pitched from the 50-foot distance, so many a batter caught no more than the briefest glimpse of Eddie's fastball.

Only or not, Nolan's big-league career was brief. He started with the minor-league club in Columbus, Ohio, when he was eighteen years old. When he defeated the mighty Indianapolis club, allowing only four hits and striking out twelve, the Indianapolis owner, W. B. Pettit, promptly hired Eddie away from Columbus by offering him one of the top salaries of the day—$2,500 a year, there being at that time no reserve rule to keep a club from luring a player away.

During Eddie's first year at Indianapolis, the club belonged to a loose sort of league called the "League Alliance," which had no set schedule and no real organization. Two big-league clubs did belong to the Alliance—the New York Mutuals and the Philadelphia Athletics, both expelled from the new National League for failing to complete their schedules. So Eddie Nolan faced opposition as strong as any other pitcher in the game. His record, however, not having been made in an organized league, has no official standing.

Next year, The Only Nolan pitched in the National League, but his record did not approach that of his first season. He began, apparently, to look upon the wine when it was red and in other ways do despite unto the lords of baseball; suddenly he found himself expelled from the league for failure to show up for a game—and presumably for giving his boss a short answer when he was questioned about it. Eddie was out of the game for a whole season until the Indianapolis fans raised such a howl that he was reinstated and assigned to the Cleveland club. But he never again showed the skill and strength that had made him the only one of his kind. To this day, however, no one has matched him. There has never been an earned run average posted that even approached Nolan's. Even in the old days, when pitchers might work several times a week, no other pitcher ever pitched seventy-six games and lost only four of them. Eddie Nolan, therefore, brief as was his fame and deep as it has been buried, still remains The Only.

Charles Radbourne might himself have been named The King or The Only because he was certainly *sui generis* and for a time topped all the pitchers in the game. But instead Radbourne was named for his willingness to show up for work when lesser men might have kept to their beds. He was known as the Old Hoss. And true to his name, he could be hitched to the wagon, any wagon, any day, and would plug along until he dropped. Nor did he, until he had been cruelly put upon, ever offer his employer any trouble over the wage he was awarded. Radbourne first earned his fame as a hitter, and he might have built himself a longer career and earned greater fame had he not been so given to homesickness. He would work all day and all night if need be, but he didn't want to be taken too far from the barn.

Radbourne, born in Rochester, New York, was moved to Bloomington, Illinois, while a baby. As a teenager he was living in Danville, Illinois, and became a brakemen on the Indiana, Bloomington and Western Railroad. In his off time he played baseball, like practically every healthy young man of his day, except that he was better at it than most. He played in exhibition games in the area, sometimes took a short trip with one of the traveling professional clubs, and once even pretended to be a college boy to pitch for Illinois Wesleyan against a team of pros. (That episode gave rise to a story that he was "a college graduate." Actually, he never went beyond the seventh grade.) Finally, at the age of twenty-four, he was talked into joining the Peoria Reds, as right fielder and a full-time pro. His salary was just about what he had been earning on the railroad—$55 a month. After one season, however, big Charlie decided that was all the professional baseball he wanted. It kept him away from home too blamed long.

That winter one of early baseball's ablest promoters, Ted Sullivan, at that time manager of the Dubuque Rabbits of the Northwestern League, woke Radbourne up late one chilly night to offer him a grand cure for homesickness—a salary of $75 a month plus room and board to come play for Dubuque.

Rad's career as pitcher began with Dubuque. The Rabbits being about the only team in the league strong enough to deal with a club mightier than the Bloomer Girls, the Northwestern League folded early, and Ted Sullivan took his Rabbits for a run around the small towns of the Midwest. In town after town, before crowds of farmers who might have traveled half a day to see him, big Rad showed off his pitching skills. It was soon offered as gospel among the kranks of that area that this big-shouldered sharpster from back in Illinois was throwing a "crooked baseball." How else could he make it hop this way and that on its flight to the plate? And how could it be that the strongest lads in the farm country could do no more than feebly trickle Rad's pitches along the ground?

But inasmuch as Rad seemed able to pull the same tricks even with the home club's baseball, a few of the shrewder observers in the grain belt concluded that Rad was perpetrating an optical illusion or using some form of hypnotic suggestion. And to assure themselves that such deeds were really being done, villagers and farmers by the hundreds hastened out to the local ball lot when the Rabbits came to town. And Ted Sullivan let Rad work every day.

While Rad was not really hypnotizing anyone, he was studying the art of pitching as few had done before him. He was forever trying out new deliveries. But his best, according to Sullivan, was his underhand fastball that hopped upward as it neared the batter. He could throw a reverse curve like the modern screwball, and he invented a pitch he called a "spitter," although he used no spit on it. Apparently it was some type of knuckle or fingertip ball—the "dry spitter" of the early twentieth century—for it had a way of dropping like a stoned duck just before it reached the batter. "It would," said contemporary batters, "come straight at you, then change its route all of a sudden." It was this "slow ball" that became Rad's most famous weapon and the one that made simple folk wonder if Rad were not in league with the devil.

Although Rad pitched into the era when overhand pitching was allowed, he always threw the ball underhand. This helped him get through his toughest season, when he won the pennant for the Providence Grays, for there was many a morning that year when Rad could not raise his poor arm high enough to brush his hair.

Providence had two pitchers that season (1884), and each was in his own way a difficult man. Rad was moody, perhaps still given to spells of longing for his own little home in Danville. The other pitcher, Charles Sweeney, supposed to be the speediest pitcher in baseball at that time, was nervous and quick to violent wrath. (He ended his days in San Quentin prison, convicted of homicide.) Rad and Sweeney, instead of pulling loyally together like one Old Hoss beside another, pulled in opposite directions. Sweeney liked to brag, and Rad liked to put Sweeney down. After Sweeney struck out nineteen batters in a game against Boston and commented on the record once or twice, Rad expressed irritation. Then, after Hugh Daily, Chicago's one-armed pitcher, also struck out nineteen Boston batters, Rad gave Sweeney a loud hoss laugh. Why, even a *cripple* could fan that bunch! Sweeney might have put a mark or two on Rad's shining countenance had not Manager Frank Bancroft halted the row while it was still nothing but bad words. Rad told the manager what he thought of his interference, and he was rewarded with a five-day suspension. (Nowadays, a pitcher with a five-day suspension might not miss a turn. Rad probably would have missed two or three.)

Providence had to get another "change" pitcher at once, to keep in right field in case Sweeney ever tired. They brought in Cyclone Joe Miller from the Chicago Unions. Sweeney, in his next game, built up a fat lead over Philadelphia so Bancroft decided to take a look at Cyclone Joe in action. He instructed Sweeney to change places with the right fielder. To Sweeney this was a public humiliation, and he damned the whole notion to hell, then walked off the diamond, never to come back. (He took a train to Boston to join the outlaw "Onions"—the St. Louis club in the Union Association.) Bancroft then had to lift Rad's suspension and had to beseech Rad to carry most of the burden for the remainder of the season.

Would he do it? *Could* he? Rad, no sorehead, promptly agreed. He thereupon won eighteen ball games in a row, lost one to Jimmy Galvin of Buffalo, then won eight more. Some days, to get his sore arm working, he would have to start warming up gently two or three hours before taking the mound. But the Old Hoss never halted and never complained. With Rad doing most of the work, Providence won the pennant. Rad promptly had offers from nearly every team in the "outlaw" league. But he accepted a small advance in salary to stay with Providence.

Eventually, however, Radbourne learned that loyalty worked only one way in Organized Baseball. He joined Boston in 1886, where he earned a salary (the league maximum) of $4,500 and was paid an under-the-table bonus. He won twenty-seven games for Boston the first year and twenty-four the second year. In 1888 he fell off to seven victories and in 1889 was handed a salary cut. He won nineteen games that year, but the next season, along with almost all the other stars of the game, he joined the Brotherhood Strike and played for the Boston Club in the Players' League, winning twenty-seven games.

Next year, back in the National League, the Old Hoss began to crack. It was said that the livelier ball used in the Players League had ruined his arm. But before many years were out symptoms of advanced syphilis showed up in the sturdy frame, so it seems fair to assume that physical deterioration had already set in as his baseball career ended. Rad retired to Bloomington, where he opened a combination poolroom and café, which drew patronage from many fans who came to goggle at the baseball greats who would appear from time to time to shake the hand of the mighty Old Hoss. In 1895, Rad lost part of his face and one eye in a hunting accident, and he never left home again. Two years later he died, at the age of forty-two.

Radbourne was not by any means the only professional ballplayer who ever drank strong waters and stayed out late at night. Drinking, cursing, and dalliance were just as popular among athletes of the 1880s as they are with the paid performers of today. But there were always some who eschewed such behavior or took such small helpings as to be practically doing without. Such straitlaced examples to the young were usually nicknamed "Deacon," although sometimes, if they were given to particularly gracious behavior, they might be dubbed "Lady"—a name that in that less sophisticated era suggested no perversion and was accepted as all in fun.

The most famous Deacon of all was Deacon McGuire, who stayed in professional baseball so long there were kranks grown to manhood who could not recall when the Deacon had not been playing for money. The Deacon's given name was James, and he started his working life as an iron molder in Michigan. Because he had hands about twice the size of a normal man's, he took easily to baseball and became a catcher in the barehand days when a man who took on that job knew full well he was inviting two hands full of broken fingers, an almost certain broken nose, a mouth half bereft of teeth, and possibly a vagrant eye, as well. But the Deacon was tougher than bull beef, and he never quailed before a pitcher in all his career, which lasted from 1884 until 1912.

When he started out, he was the battery mate of a fast and tricky pitcher named Charles Busted Baldwin, who was called "Lady" Baldwin because of his gentlemanly ways. Lady threw a "snake ball" that tantalized the batters of the day with its sudden deviations from the expected path. But it never fazed Deacon McGuire, who took every pitch in his oak-hard hands, snagged all the foul tips he could reach and refused to let finger fractures keep him from the game. The Deacon could get away from the iron foundry only on Saturday afternoons and Sundays, so Lady Baldwin became a weekend pitcher, there being no one else in that part of southern Michigan who could hold Lady's fastball.

It was said of Deacon McGuire, even before he had become a major-league catcher, that he "could catch a cannonball." No one ever tested the accuracy of that claim, but it seems certain that if any *had* sent a cannonball the

Deacon's way, he'd have stabbed for it with one hand or the other. Both hands were equally battered when Deacon was still a youth, and by the time he was permitted to wear protective equipment behind the bat, his hands looked like two ancient cypress roots torn out of a swamp.

After playing for Terre Haute and Toledo, Deacon McGuire entered big-league baseball with Detroit, where he teamed with Wild Bill Donovan, the original wild man, who could aim for the strike zone and put the ball over the grandstand. Once the Deacon signaled to Donovan for a pitchout, and Donovan, firing full strength, very nearly pitched the ball out of the park. McGuire leaped for the ball, just took a small piece of it with his longest finger, and had the finger bent straight back by the force of the throw. The flesh was stripped right off the bone, neat as a filet of flounder. Bald Bob Emslie, umpiring behind the plate, took one look at the finger and fell in a faint. But the Deacon remained erect, had the finger attended to, and was catching again before the end of the week. "We were short of catchers," he explained.

By that time, the Deacon was using a catcher's glove with a little padding in it, but his meat hand had been nearest the ball. In semipro ball in southern Michigan and while at Terre Haute, Deacon used only the thin fingerless gloves permitted. (Sometimes they were flesh colored to hide the catcher's shame.) At Toledo, Deacon caught the pitches of Hank O'Day, who earned his greatest fame as an umpire. O'Day was even faster than Lady Baldwin, so McGuire would usually tuck a piece of beefsteak under the skin of the tight glove on his left hand. After the game it was not always easy to see where steak stopped and McGuire began.

In 1895, Deacon McGuire, while playing with Washington, caught every inning of every game his club played—all 133 of them. And in that season, there being no foul-strike rule to shorten a batter's stay at the plate, an inning might last partway to forever.

Deacon went on to play on the clubs that won pennants for Charlie Ebbets of Brooklyn, a thrifty gentleman in the true clubowner tradition, who awarded his club a $4,000 bonus ($160 each) for taking the 1899 flag and then, when they won the championship again in 1900, blessed each man with a pair of cuff links. The Deacon after that played again for Detroit, then came to New York to catch for the American League club from 1904 to 1906. He was sitting on the bench in 1904 on the day Happy Jack Chesbro flung that famous wild pitch that lost the pennant to the Puritans (later the Red Sox) from Boston. Had the Deacon been on the job, he might just possibly have brought that ball down and have been with another pennant winner. But he had no fault to find with Red Kleinow, the catcher who could not reach the ball even though some of Happy Jack's partisans insisted afterward the pitch should have been called "passed ball by the catcher."

"There wasn't a chance of stopping that spitter," said McGuire. "It might as well have gone over the top of the grandstand."

(In the next inning, McGuire went to bat for Chesbro and received a base on balls, but he did not score.)

Three years later, McGuire himself was in Boston, managing the club now called the Red Sox. In 1909, 1910, and 1911 he managed the Cleveland club and in 1912 returned to Detroit as a coach. That year, while the club was playing in Philadelphia, all the regulars went on strike to protest the suspension and fine of Ty Cobb, who had climbed into the stands in New York one day to punch a fan who had been screaming insults at him. To protect the franchise, manager Hughey Jennings had to hire a bunch of new ballplayers from among the local semipros. Deacon McGuire went behind the plate to catch his last big league game. He made one hit, scored one run, and was charged with two errors. Detroit lost 24–2. Deacon Jim at that time was fifty years old.

Old Hoss Radbourne's slow pitch that dropped dead before it reached the batter was improved upon by many practitioners of that era and those who came after. None ever labored on this project more effectively than did an unreformed bricklayer named Thomas "Toad" Ramsey, who was "discovered" pitching (at the age of sixteen) in a vacant lot beside a firehouse in Indianapolis. His discoverer was a man named Jack Kerins, who ran a baseball team for one John T. Brush, president of the When Clothing Company. (Brush eventually became owner of the New York Giants.) Kerins saw young Toad striking out boys of all sizes, and he signed him on as a relief pitcher for the semipro club known as the "Whens." Despite his youth and despite the fact that he stood flatfooted in the pitching box and cranked his left arm twice around like a windmill before letting the ball go, Toad Ramsey soon became the best-known and the ablest left-handed pitcher in the land. Because his career was short, his name did not live long in baseball annals and his accomplishments will never be misremembered at Cooperstown. In his day, however, he was a greater marvel to most men than the electric trolley car.

Toad almost moved right into the major leagues at seventeen, because Indianapolis was awarded an American Association franchise the year after Toad joined the Whens and Kerins was made manager of the big-league club. But when Kerins asked if he could bring along his young pitcher, who had led the Municipal League the previous season, the owner said no. A major-league ball club, the owner decided, was no place for a teenaged boy. He was probably right, but it is doubtful if Toad's morals were nourished with quite the care they required, even with the club he did join—Chattanooga of the Southern League. Toad led that league in strikeouts and was sold next season to Louisville of the American Association, a big league at that time. In 1886, after one uncertain season with Louisville, Toad began to strike out everyone in sight. In an exhibition game against Detroit, a team that carried the heaviest hitters of the day—Dan Brouthers, Deacon White, Hardy Richardson, and Larry Twitchell—Toad Ramsey struck out thirteen, including all the four sluggers. When he faced Pittsburgh, he struck out twelve, and two days later he beat Cincinnati with fourteen strikeouts. He next took on the St. Louis Browns, the top club in the game. He struck out sixteen of them in ten innings. Altogether that season he had 499 strikeouts and twice fanned seventeen. His sixteen-strikeout game against St. Louis had spread his fame through the nation, and he continued to earn headlines all summer.

Toad Ramsey, just twenty-two years old that year, also pitched a no-hit no-run game against Baltimore in July, although the records do not give him credit for it. He struck out seventeen in that game and did not even grant the Baltimores a long fly. There were no hits listed in the Baltimore *Sun* boxscore next day, and the writer acknowledged that it was the "greatest game ever seen in Baltimore," with not a single hit by the home club. Since that day, however, someone has tucked a base hit in after Baltimore center fielder O'Connell's name.

Two days later, Toad faced Baltimore again and in twelve innings struck out seventeen. He granted one hit this time and had the home fans howling with laughter at the manner in which the locals flailed in vain at young Ramsey's "drop ball."

Next season, Toad might have really pitched himself into the Hall of Fame except that the professional thinkers of the game decided to see how baseball would work if the batter were allowed four strikes. This rule made the hill a whole lot steeper for Toad. But he won ball games and struck out batters all the same. On June 21, 1887, he struck out seventeen Cleveland batters, granting each one of them four strikes, just as the book said he should. A week later he struck out sixteen St. Louis batters. Altogether he pitched sixty-five games that season and won thirty-seven of them, with a total of 355 strikeouts.

How did he do it? It was all an accident. Or at least his trick pitch that caused men to disbelieve their eyes came about as a result of a stupid accident that befell him when he was a bricklayer's apprentice and should have been in school. Somebody dropped a hod of bricks or some such trifle on young Tom's left hand and cut the tendon in his middle finger so he could not flex it. As a result, he could merely perch this finger atop the ball and so threw a natural knuckleball. He practiced the pitch faithfully as a boy, and when he had become a professional, he could drop four out of five pitches right on the plate—and often did so to win side bets.

Some years later a young man christened Mordecai Peter Centennial Brown (he having been born in 1876) suffered a similar accident. He lost the better part of his right index finger in a corn chopper and so could not grip a baseball tight. As a result, he, too, threw a ball to which the thumb imparted most of the spin and which would drop, or seem to, with extreme suddenness as it reached the plate. But Brown did not become a pitcher right away, perhaps feeling that his handicap prevented him. In amateur ball he was always an infielder. When he joined the St. Louis club in the National League in 1903, he was throwing a wide curve that dropped very quickly away from the batter. But he did not use his pitch with full effect until he came to the Chicago Cubs in 1904. Then he ran off eight winning seasons in a row and pitched the club to a pennant in 1908. Whether his pitch was any more mystifying or any better controlled than Toad Ramsey's is a question. But he had far better control of his appetites.

Poor Toad Ramsey, sulking because the thrifty Louisville manager would not reward his winning thirty-seven games by offering him a small raise in salary, took to sharing his sorrow with whatever bartender would listen. In 1888, he was seldom in condition to play baseball, and he won only eight games out of forty-one that he tried. In 1889 Toad gave his full attention to drinking and for three solid weeks during the baseball season was not even able to find the ballpark. After this he was sold to the St. Louis Browns. There Toad took the pledge—even though the club owner, Chris Von der Ahe, self-styled "greatest feller in baseball," had taken up baseball as a means of promoting the sale of beer. In 1890, while most of baseball's big stars were playing in the Players League, Toad remained among the scabs and won twenty-six games. But Von der Ahe thought Toad should win every game—just he as decided, after seeing a right-field home run, that all balls should be hit to right field—and he scolded his loyal employee for losing occasionally. Toad lost his temper and promptly his job, as well. He completed his playing career by wandering from club to club in the South, and he resumed his drinking career at the same time. He wound up with the Admirals of Indianapolis, back home again, broke and without control of his magic pitch. In one game against Lebanon, Toad issued fourteen walks.

After that Toad did some umpiring, organized a minor league so he could find a pitching job (with Kokomo), learned he was unable to find the plate even in Kokomo, and so went back to bricklaying. Mordecai Brown, whom Toad might have matched, wound up in the Hall of Fame. Toad has been forgotten.

The composer of "The Washington Post March" was born in that city in 1854 and grew up among such future big-timers as Paul Hines, Charley Snyder, and Joe Gerhardt. John Philip Sousa was not only a baseball fan but also a baseball player, pitching for a team composed of members of his own traveling band. This bit is excerpted from an article the "March King" published in *Baseball Magazine* as "The Greatest Game in the World."

JOHN PHILIP SOUSA

Balls and Batons Forever

I played ball off and on from my sixth year until about my forty-fifth. The last game I played, probably the grand finale of my diamond career, was with a nine composed of members of my band. In the report of the game, my forty years of off-and-on service was dismissed by the following criticism of a reporter:

> It has long been apparent to those who have watched Sousa leading his band that if he ever got into a pitcher's box he would be too swift for the eye to follow. The only trouble was that the March King had no control over the ball when he started to wrap himself up and you could not tell whether the ball was coming out in the direction of the batsman or the center fielder.

And this scathing criticism simply because, in one inning, I gave four men bases on balls and forced in a run! Ye gods and little fishes, but I was sore on that reporter! Handing out such a line of talk to a man who had been in the game for almost forty years! But I knew that there must be something wrong, and I decided to quit the game.

In my band we have had a ball team for many years. Playing at the Exposition in Paris in 1900, on our natal day, the Fourth of July, our team played the nine of the American Guards on the Bagatelle Field in Paris. What could have been more appropriate for two American organizations in a foreign land to do on the glorious Fourth?

Last June, a year ago, at Willow Grove, Philadelphia, our band played the Marine Corps nine, my old colleagues, for I was for twelve years bandmaster of the U.S. Marine Corps. The following is the account of a baseball reporter of that, to us, great event:

If Connie Mack could have witnessed the game of baseball yesterday morning he would have been tempted to make John Philip Sousa an offer. The March King proved a wonder in the pitcher's box, and although he lasted but one inning, he retired Lieutenant O'Leary's colts in one, two, three order; then Mr. Sousa retired to the coaching line, where he gave an imitation of Arlie Latham that caused the spectators to howl with delight. When Umpire Schlotterbeck said "play ball," the versatile athlete musician, composer and author cast an eagle eye over the field, noted that his men were all in place and ready to come in on the first beat; then he spat on the new ball, threw his right leg around in front of the left, raised his arm above his head, lunged forward, and the umpire said "Strike one!" Suffice it to say Hopkins fanned. It was a surprise for the Marines. They had been looking for something easy, and no one imagined that any man could write a march to

King Edward VII and twirl the sphere for a strike out on big Hopkins, the slugger, all in the same season.

The following is from *Musical America*, 1907:

To the baseball player who must stand in the sizzling sun hurling a baseball as nearly as he may over a home base, the swinging of a baton by the conductor of an orchestra seems lazy work, and he might be surprised to learn that when John Philip Sousa wants to rest, it is in the pitcher's box that he seeks diversion. For it's true, no matter how astonishing it may seem, that the composer of the worldwide-known marches and exceedingly tuneful operas is really a pronounced baseball fan; not one whose fandom merely leads him to a seat in the bleachers or grand stand to yell at plays or misplays, but one who is a captain of a ball team of his own, who is a pitcher of no mean skill, who strikes 'em out with the best of them, and whose players in one campaign won eleven out of thirteen games played. . . .

Jules Tygiel is professor of history at San Francisco State University and commissioner of the Pacific Ghost League (a computerized "Rotisserie League" of considerable sophistication and bonhomie). There is ease in Tygiel's manner, whether in the groves of academe or the green fields of the mind. His 1983 book, *Baseball's Great Experiment: Jackie Robinson and His Legacy*, is a masterful blend of these twin devotions. Jackie Robinson's entrance into Organized Baseball has been documented often, though never better than in Tygiel's book; here are the less well known stories of Sam Jethroe, Luke Easter, Bob Thurman, Ray Dandridge, Chuck Harmon, and Piper Davis.

JULES TYGIEL

"The Only Thing I Wanted to Do Was Hit the Major Leagues"

I was explaining the "situation" to Luke shortly after he joined our team. I told him that a few fans might not like him because of his race, that he must overlook their boos. But Luke explained the whole thing to me when he said, "Mister Starr, everybody likes me when I hit that ball!"

San Diego Padres president William Starr, 1949

I

Luscious Easter was a figure of Bunyanesque proportions. His massive 6-foot 4-inch frame radiated awesome strength, yet he charmed people with his gentle manner and humor. Easter's tastes in fashion included "racy pinstripe suits" and a diamond ring that resembled "the headlight of the Santa Fe Chief." His age was indeterminate; his background shrouded in mystery. The records list his birth date as August 4, 1921, but Luke referred to that as his "baseball birthday" and hinted that he might be five, or perhaps ten, years older. Despite his advanced age, Easter had not appeared in the Negro Leagues until 1947, when he materialized on the Homestead Grays as the power-hitting replacement for the late Josh Gibson.

Upon arrival in the Pacific Coast League two years later, Easter remained a relative unknown. Bill Veeck made a special excursion to Puerto Rico to sign

the giant slugger during the winter and offered his services to the San Diego Padres. Veeck advised Padres President William Starr that his latest discovery "could hit the ball as hard and as far as Babe Ruth." "I thought he was kidding me," admitted the incredulous Starr. In the Padres first six games Easter pounded two prodigious home runs and two blistering line-drive triples. Starr and the baseball fans of the western slope knew that Veeck had not exaggerated.

The arrival of Luke Easter in the Pacific Coast League in 1949 heralded the advent of widespread minor-league integration. During the next few years Easter and other black athletes introduced interracial baseball to cities and towns throughout the nation, enduring regional variations of prejudice and discrimination while struggling to advance to the major leagues. To younger players the lower classifications represented the gateway to stardom. But for many Negro League veterans, trapped by the persistent racism of the newly integrated sport, the minor leagues at mid-century marked the final frustration of a lifetime of exclusion.

Easter was not the first black player in the Pacific Coast League. In 1948 the Padres had fielded John Ritchey, a promising young catcher who batted .300 as a part-time performer. Ritchey's debut had elicited minimal reaction in the West. The following season, the Padres signed a working agreement with the Cleveland Indians, who assigned Easter and shortstop Artie Wilson to join Ritchey on the roster.

Easter quickly captured the imagination of Coast League personnel and fans. In his first fifteen games the black first baseman batted .436 with 5 home runs and 23 runs batted in. Observers hailed him as the "greatest natural hitter the Coast League has seen since Ted Williams." "I've seen a lot of powerful hitters in my time," reflected Sacramento Manager Del Baker, "but for sheer ability to knock the ball great distances, I've never seen anybody better than Easter." Manager Fred Haney of Hollywood agreed. "I wish they'd get him out of here before he kills every infielder in the Coast League," exclaimed Haney.

The prowess of the massive black athlete became legend on the West Coast. Scouts marveled at Easter's "amazing fielding" and his speed, labeling him "the fastest big man in baesball." Writers compared his batting and drawing power to Babe Ruth. As early as March 23, the *Sporting News* reported, "fans are coming here from miles away to see him bust the apple." In a four-week tour of Oakland, San Francisco, Los Angeles, and Hollywood, the Padres attracted 240,000 customers, setting new records in Los Angeles and San Francisco. In the latter city, an estimated 1,000 fans stood atop automobiles to gaze over stadium walls at the conquering hero. When Easter came to bat, both blacks and whites in the crowd rose to their feet, tossing hats and seat cushions in the air when he hit safely. "When he takes his turn at batting practice," described sportswriter Frank Finch, noting the unusually early crowd arrival, "the other players, the sportswriters, the goober salesmen and fans rivet their eyes on the batting cage to watch Luke powder the ball."

Easter's tape-measure home runs combined with his status as one of the few blacks in the Pacific Coast League to make him the frequent target of brushback pitches. A month into the season, League President Clarence Rowland, in response to complaints about close pitches directed at Easter, issued a memorandum cautioning against the use of the beanball. Easter seemed unperturbed. Against Portland in April pitchers "low bridged" him twice. The first time up Easter hit the next pitch for a home run, and the second time he "lashed a savage drive" right back at the pitcher.

Remarkably, Easter performed his spectacular feats while playing with a painful injury. During spring training Easter had broken his kneecap in a collision. Although surgery was required to repair the damage, doctors advised Easter that he could continue to play without incurring irreparable harm. Easter was determined to complete the season, but by late June the pain had become unbearable. On July 1 Easter's career with the Padres came to an end. He had played in eighty games and batted .363 with 25 home runs and 92 runs-batted-in. To the chagrin of Coast League owners, attendance dropped to pre-Easter levels after his departure. Owners estimated that Easter's injury cost them $200,000 in gate receipts.

Luke Easter was the most spectacular of the wave of black athletes who entered Organized Baseball in 1949. With major-league teams signing non-whites in greater numbers, blacks appeared in every Class AAA and Class A minor league in 1949. (Both AA circuits, the Texas League and the Southern Association, were in the Jim Crow belt.) Major- and minor-league organizations, finally convinced that integration had become a reality, found the cream of the Negro Leagues at their disposal. They purchased many aging stars and young prospects from that dying institution. Generally underestimating the quality of play in the Negro Leagues, baseball officials placed most of the new recruits in classifications far beneath the players' talents. As a result, blacks compiled astounding statistics in the early years of integration.

In the Pacific Coast League, "prompted by the record-breaking box-office draw of Luke Easter," several clubs entered the hunt for black talent. In late May, Commissioner Chandler voided Artie Wilson's contract with the Cleveland Indians, who released him from their San Diego franchise. The Oakland Oaks quickly signed the shortstop, and the spindly, spray-hitting Wilson immediately established himself as the outstanding infielder in the Pacific Coast League. Wilson won the league batting championship with a .349 average, also pacing the league in hits and stolen bases. The Portland Beavers and Los Angeles also added blacks to their rosters during the 1949 campaign. Within two years every Pacific Coast League club fielded blacks.

Integration proceeded more slowly but no less successfully in the American Association. Roy Campanella had broken the league color line in 1948. At the start of the 1949 season, young Jim Pendleton, a fleet shortstop for the St. Paul Dodgers, was the sole black in the Association. His isolation ended on June 5 when the New York Giants assigned Negro League veterans Dave Barnhill, a pitcher, and Ray Dandridge, an infielder, to their Minneapolis Millers franchise. Barnhill met with indifferent success; Dandridge became the sensation of the American Association.

When he signed with the Giants, Dandridge stated that he was twenty-nine years old. He admits now that he actually was thirty-six. Many believe that even that figure stretches the truth. He had begun his playing career in 1933 with the Detroit Stars. One year later, he joined the Newark Eagles, where he played third base in the "black million-dollar infield" alongside shortstop Willie Wells, second baseman Dick Seay, and first baseman Mule Suttles. Roy Campanella called it the greatest infield alignment he ever saw. In 1940 millionaire Jorge Pasquel lured Dandridge to the Mexican League, lavishing favors and bonuses on his star infielder for the next eight years. Mexican fans, recalls Dandridge, treated him like a king. While Jackie Robinson broke the color line in 1947, Dandridge was serving as player-manager of the Alamendares club in the Mexican League.

Those who witnessed this short, stocky, strikingly bowlegged athlete in action agree that he may well have been the premier third baseman in baseball annals. Historian Richard Crepeau, who watched an almost-forty-year-old Dandridge in the twilight of his career, calls him the greatest performer at the hot corner that he ever observed. Sam Lacy asserts that Dandridge's "quick hands would give the efforts of Billy Cox and Brooks Robinson the aspect of a replay in slow motion." Plus, adds Lacy, "he could hit far better than either of them." Monte Irvin concurs. "There's never been a third baseman who could play better than Dandridge. I don't care who it was—Brooks Robinson, Graig Nettles, Pie Traynor—nobody." Yet in 1949 even the most knowledgeable of white baseball fans had never heard of Ray Dandridge.

Dandridge arrived in Minneapolis hoping that his play in the highest minor leagues would earn him an opportunity in the majors despite his advanced age. On June 5 he debuted against Warren McDermott, a young fastballing strikeout artist. "You know what he did to me," Dandridge states rather than asks. "I had to eat dirt. He throwed at my head." The veteran rookie was undaunted. "I didn't pay it no mind. So I get back up. Next one, he came down the groove with it, and I hit it right by his head, dead centerfield." Dandridge did not reach base on that play, robbed by an outstanding infield stop. The following night he began a twenty-eight-game hitting streak. He complemented his batting with the acrobatic fielding that had made him a legend among Negro and Mexican League patrons. Local reporters dubbed him "Old Bandy Legs the Dandy" and the "Black Honus Wagner." Minneapolis fans idolized him. Dandridge completed the season with a .364 batting average, just two points shy of the league lead. "Ol' Man Dandridge" finished second in the American Association balloting for Rookie of the Year.

The third Triple A minor league, the International League, had featured black players on the Montreal team since 1946. In 1949 league President Frank Shaughnessy boasted before the season, "We will have the most colorful league of all time." Both the Jersey City franchise, affiliated with the Giants, and the Yankee farm team at Newark added blacks to their rosters. On all three clubs blacks approached the high standards set by Easter, Wilson, and Dandridge.

At Montreal the Dodger farm club, which had already treated Canadian fans to Robinson, Campanella, and Newcombe, offered Dan Bankhead and Sam Jethroe. Reporters labeled Bankhead, working his way back to the major leagues, "the wild man of the International League." Nonetheless, he posted a 20–6 record while leading the circuit in strikeouts and walks. Jethroe, nicknamed "The Jet" and "Mercury Man," emerged as the foremost gate attraction in the league. He batted .326 and scored 151 runs. His 89 stolen bases established a new league record.

The Little Giants of Jersey City featured three black players: Monte Irvin, Hank Thompson, and pitcher Ford Smith. While Smith experienced a disappointing season, both Irvin and Thompson won promotion to the Giants in July. Irvin, the thirty-year-old former Newark Eagle, whom many had deemed the most likely prospect to break the color line before World War II, amply demonstrated his still-considerable talents. In 63 games with the Little Giants, he batted .373 and drove in 52 runs. (In 1950 the parent club again asked Irvin to start the season at Jersey City. In 18 games he batted .510 and drove in 33 runs, earning him the appellation of "Mr. Murder, Inc." and a hurried call to the Polo Grounds.)

The Yankees had less success with their initial signees. Angel Marquez and Frank Austin began the season with the Newark Bears, and both played well. In May, when Chandler awarded Marquez's contract to the Indians, however, the Yankees also sold Austin, leaving their top farm team with no black players. The Bears, struggling at the box office, remained all white until late July, when the Yankees purchased outfielder Bob Thurman and catcher Earl Taborn from the Kansas City Monarchs. Thurman was the more impressive prospect of the two. The *Courier* described him as a "home run hitter deluxe," who, despite his powerful six-foot one-inch, 210-pound frame, had "tootsies lined with mercury." The *Courier* added that Thurman, a former pitcher, "could throw with the best of them."

Thurman immediately lived up to his advance billing. In his first game he hit two singles and then powered "one of the longest homers ever seen at the [Newark] ballpark." Thurman hit two more home runs in his first week of play, including a grand slam. Like Easter, his former Negro League teammate, Thurman astounded spectators with the sheer distance of his drives. All of his home runs traveled over 400 feet, and at least one exceeded 500 feet. After a month with Newark, Thurman was batting .371, though a hand injury dropped his average to .317 at the season's end.

At times, the black players in Triple-A baseball in 1949 appeared so unstoppable that rival managers devised unique strategies to thwart them. In the Pacific Coast League, where Artie Wilson's opposite-field swinging produced 211 hits, San Francisco Manager Lefty O'Doul applied a "reverse shift," bringing his center fielder in to play shortstop and placing all of his fielders except the first baseman to the left of second base. The strategy failed to significantly deter Wilson. At Buffalo, Manager Paul Richards defied conventional baseball logic and intentionally walked the pitcher when there were two outs and nobody on base to pitch to leadoff hitter Sam Jethroe. "If we get the pitcher out," explained Richards, "we have Jethroe leading off. . . . [If] he gets on base, he's going to steal second and very possibly third." On the other hand, argued Richards, if he walked the pitcher, even if Jethroe reached base, "He can't hurt us with his speed because he's got the pitcher in front of him."

The black influx was not confined to the Triple A level. Throughout the minor leagues in the North and West blacks appeared for the first time with comparable results. At Wilkes-Barre, Harry "Suitcase" Simpson established himself as "one of the greatest sluggers" ever to perform in the Class A Eastern League, clouting "the longest drives hit in three of the loop's parks." His teammate Roy Welmaker, a veteran Negro League pitcher, registered twenty-two victories. Wilkes-Barre attendance increased dramatically. In the New England League, George Crowe batted .365 and drove in over 100 runs.

Needless to say, not all the black players active in 1949 attained these levels of performance. Many were given brief tryouts and then released; others displayed routine abilities. Nonetheless, given the relatively small numbers of black players in Organized Baseball, a high proportion produced not just good seasons but spectacular ones. At the same time, the black standard-bearers in the majors continued their outstanding examples. Robinson, Doby, Campanella, and Newcombe all appeared in the All-Star Game. Robinson enjoyed his finest season as a professional. He batted .342 and won the National League Most Valuable Player Award, leading the Dodgers to the pennant. Newcombe became the Rookie of the Year. Paige, alone among the five black major leaguers who played an entire season, fared poorly, registering only four wins in eleven decisions.

In the age of Jim Crow common stereotypes had depicted black ballplayers as road-show clowns, far inferior to their white counterparts. The high standards established by baseball's racial pioneers created a new, no less stereotypical, image of the black athlete. "They have an inborn advantage in natural speed and strength," concluded Boston Brave scout Jack Zeller, "and when they also possess high intelligence, they are better athletes, as a class, than whites." The black ballplayer loomed as a "mercury-footed" daring base runner, like Robinson, Jethroe, and Wilson; the author of gargantuan home runs, like Doby, Easter, and Thurman; a pitcher of blazing speed, tinged with a touch of wildness, like Newcombe and Bankhead. Americans readily assimilated the new image of blacks. As "natural" athletes, blacks depended on brawn and reflex rather than brain or reason; as entertainers, they entered a domain in which they were already accepted. But these exacting standards raised the expectations for all blacks who entered baseball in the 1950s. Lesser performances provoked a chorus of boos and provided baseball executives with a rationale for keeping above-average, though not exceptional, black players in the minor leagues.

II

"I am a man of substance, of flesh and bone, fiber and liquids—and I might even be said to possess a mind," lamented the black protagonist in Ralph

Ellison's novel *Invisible Man*. "I am invisible, understand, simply because people refuse to see me." Ellison's portrayal of black America won the National Book Award in 1952. That same year, eighteen-year-old John Roseboro began his professional baseball career in the Dodger farm system. For the next several seasons Roseboro played in cities like Pueblo, Colorado, Sheboygan, Wisconsin, and Danville, Illinois—a pioneer on a frontier that few realized existed, an invisible man in baesball's vast minor-league domain.

Most Americans perceived racial prejudice as a southern problem, but hostility to blacks knew no regional boundaries. The introduction of black minor-league athletes was an unwelcomed occurrence in many communities, particularly those in which few blacks resided or in which *de facto* segregation prevailed. "There isn't a Nigger in Sheboygan," Roseboro wrote his parents during his first season. "Send your clippers to me. The peckers don't know how to cut a nigger's hair." In most towns, Roseboro and his black teammates lived in run-down boardinghouses separate from their white colleagues. Restaurants often refused them service. In Salt Lake City, aware that most eating places would not welcome them, the black players on the Pueblo Dodgers tried a small Chinese restaurant. The waiters ignored them until, following a long wait, the Chinese owner asked them to leave. At rustic minor-league ball parks, fans taunted Roseboro with cries of "Sambo," "Chocolate drop," and "Snowball."

The Dodgers, states Roseboro, "have always been a first-class organization." The team that had broken the color line, it remained throughout the 1950s more sensitive to the problems of black players than other clubs. Nonetheless, they offered little in the way of advice or assistance to the young black prospects in the farm system. "At the same time when they signed blacks and Latins," asserts Roseboro, "they should have made sure they would be welcome. If the black Dodgers weren't welcome in a motel, hotel, or theater, the white Dodgers should have fought for their rights and walked out." Instead, Roseboro discovered that "the Dodgers didn't care if I had race troubles to go with my growing-up troubles and playing troubles."

"You ache with the need to convince yourself that you do exist in the real world," asserted Ellison's invisible man. Recalling the indignities of his minor-league career, Roseboro relates, "I'm sorry I didn't have the guts to do anything about it. . . . But what could I have done? Gotten locked up for disturbing the peace? I didn't know what to do about bigotry."

Throughout the nation black athletes re-created Roseboro's experiences amidst the indifference of baseball officials. Minor-league intermediaries rarely, if ever, relayed reports of race relations, and afraid to jeopardize their careers, the players themselves rarely complained. Major-league executives remained blissfully unaware of conditions in their farm systems, an ignorance born of insensitivity and unfamiliarity rather than malice.

The reception accorded black athletes varied from region to region and city to city. Blacks who played in the Northern League in Wisconsin and Minnesota have fond memories of towns like Eau Claire and St. Cloud. Other areas were far less appealing. Piper Davis, the former player-manager of the Birmingham Black Barons, entered organized baseball in 1950. During the next eight years he appeared in four different minor leagues. As a barnstormer in the Negro Leagues and as a basketball player with the Harlem Globetrotters, Davis had traveled extensively throughout the United States. When young players would ask him about conditions in the South, Davis would reply, "They love me in the South. They tell me where I can go. They got signs up that say, 'Negroes here and whites here.' " In the North, on the other hand, Davis explained, "You don't know where you can eat. You go into a restaurant in the lower part of Illinois and Indiana, the waitress pass you up ninety miles an hour. And finally you come up and say, 'Can we get some service?' They say, 'We don't serve Negroes.' " Black players, alleged Davis, were refused service more in the West than in the South.

Other athletes agreed with Davis's tongue-in-cheek observations. Pitcher Dave Hoskins, who later became the first black in the Texas League, experienced the harshest treatment of his career with Grand Rapids of the Central League. Former major leaguer Leon Wagner contends that "conditions in southern Illinois were worse than I ran into in Tennessee." Syracuse, New York, ranked as one of the worst spots for blacks in the International League. Davis reports that in Pacific Coast League cities, where the large wartime and postwar migration of blacks had unleashed widespread racist sentiments, "I learned more names than I thought we had."

Fans routinely hurled racial insults at black athletes, with certain spectators reappearing regularly to taunt them. Bob Thurman recalls an old man in Baltimore who always called him an "African Bohemian." An Oakland fan would sit behind the dugout with a bottle of Jim Beam, and when an opposing black player would appear, he would howl at Davis, "Hey, Piper, here comes your cousin." Artie Wilson had a personal heckler in Sacramento who "called me all kinds of names." Most players rarely responded outwardly. "Every time I would hear a racial remark, I'd look straight ahead, and I'd just ignore it," says Davis. "I played mad a lot," laughs Thurman. "But I didn't let on. I was burning right in there, but I'd just take it out on the ball."

Local displeasure at the appearance of black players also manifested itself outside of the ballparks. Piper Davis attended spring training in Oakland in 1951 and stayed with the local Oaks at the California Hotel. When the season began, the team stopped paying for players' housing, and his welcome evaporated. Returning from his first road trip, Davis discovered that the hotel had not reserved a room for him. Teammate Hank Behrman arranged to have a rollaway bed placed in his room to temporarily accommodate Davis. "Checkout time was two o'clock Monday," recalls Davis. "I made it my business to be right over there at two o'clock for checkout. No room. Tuesday, no room." On Wednesday hotel officials assigned Davis a room on the mezzanine right next to the elevator. "Looked like the elevator was in the room, it was so close," says Davis. When the team left for its next road trip, Davis attempted to reserve lodgings for his return. The clerk informed him that the hotel would no longer accommodate him. In many cities black players regularly faced this type of treatment as they learned the limits of racial acceptance.

Minor-league teams exacerbated this situation with their own segregation policies. Ball clubs rarely assigned blacks and whites as roommates. Where a team fielded more than one black, they always lived together. Where a solitary black appeared, he would normally have his own quarters. Only on rare occasions did teams violate this rule. In 1947, when Don Newcombe returned for a second season at Nashua without Roy Campanella, he roomed with his new catcher, Gus Gallipeau. At Olean in the Pony League, Chuck Harmon shared his lodgings with white teammate Paul Owens, who later became the general manager of the Philadelphia Phillies. In 1949 when shortstop Artie Wilson reported to Oakland, he relates, "I was supposed to room by myself, but I had one who chose to room with me, so I had no trouble at all." The "one" was Wilson's double-play partner, Billy Martin.

These examples represent the exceptions. Throughout the 1950s and well into the next decade, most teams took precautions against interracial accommodations. "I played on four different Triple A teams by myself, and that was rough," recalls Bob Thurman. "I'd go to the movies by myself." Teammates rarely invited the genial Thurman to accompany them socially. An invitation by a new teammate on the San Francisco Seals to go to a movie so shocked Thurman, he "almost fainted." At the night's end, the two players returned to the hotel with "two blondes." Four days later the Seals traded away the white player. Thurman sorely felt the absence of social companionship. "If you had a bad day, you didn't have anybody to talk to. You'd talk to yourself," he remembers. "You had to be like a steel man to take being alone."

Despite the absence of social contact and friendships, Thurman and most blacks who played in the 1950s have few complaints about their teammates. "I never had any trouble with any players," says Thurman, "because I respected the players and they always respected me." Wilson describes his white colleagues as "super." Piper Davis recalls only one instance of conflict with his teammates. After he swung at a pitch and fell off balance, he heard a voice from the dugout call, "Get up, Uncle Remus." Davis sat down next to the culprit when he returned to the dugout and in his firm, quiet way let it be known that he would not tolerate future remarks. No further taunts reached Davis.

The racial tension inherent in the early years of integration notwithstanding, fights between black and white teammates proved rare. In 1949 in the Eastern League, pitcher Roy Welmaker and his white catcher squared off on the field following the catcher's refusal to support Welmaker's protests on close pitches. The pair exchanged several blows before teammates separated them. The following year, white pitcher Marino Pieretti and black shortstop Frank Austin of the Portland Beavers battled after a batting-practice dispute. "It wasn't a racial fight; it was just a baseball fight," concluded reporters, none of whom wrote of the incident until several decades later. Other minor flare-ups doubtless occurred, but contrary to the fears of integration opponents, little overt friction ever surfaced among blacks and whites involuntarily united on the same squad.

Nonetheless, every season after 1947 witnessed incidents of interracial conflict on the diamond. During the International League play-offs in 1948, "they came close to fighting the Civil War all over again," claimed Dink Carroll. Syracuse catcher Stan West attacked Montreal hurler Don Newcombe after the latter had brushed him back at the plate. Newcombe, not usually known for his even temper, ducked West's charge and refused to fight. "Had he tangled with West," reported Carroll, "there might have been a race riot in the stands that would have made a tornado look like a zephyr." The next season, Luis Angel Marquez engaged in two altercations with white players in the Pacific Coast League.

These episodes, and others like them, were typical of baseball battles; despite enraged tempers, minimal combat ensued. The first true racial donnybrook occurred in Oakland in 1952. San Francisco Seals pitcher Bill Boemler regularly aimed fastballs at Piper Davis and Ray Noble, the Oaks' two black stars. In mid-July he hit Davis on the elbow, sidelining him for a week. On July 27 Boemler twice forced Davis to sprawl in the dirt. Davis responded with a two-base hit. On the next play, he attempted to score with Boemler covering home plate. "I said, 'Here's my chance,'" recalls Davis, "and I bowled him over." According to accounts of the game, Boemler attempted to tag Davis with a "vicious blow in the face." Davis "tore into the pitcher with both fists." Teammates and black and white fans soon joined the pair. Noble, according to a sportswriter, "knocked down San Francisco players as though they were ten pins." And Davis states, "Noble was hitting everything white coming towards him." One reporter described the battle as "one of the most slam-bang baseball fights ever witnessed." Several days later, a San Francisco-based "Group of 19" threatened violent retaliation against Davis and Noble when the pair appeared at Seals Stadium. The Oaks turned the matter over to the local police and FBI, and both men played as scheduled. They encountered no difficulties.

The Coast League free-for-all constituted a rare event. It was triggered, however, by the most common weapon of antiblack hostility, the beanball. During the 1949 season when blacks first appeared in the minor leagues in significant numbers, a near epidemic of beanings resulted. Beanballs hospitalized one out of four black nonpitchers in Triple A baseball in 1949. In June, Hank Thompson had to be carried off the field and hospitalized after being hit in the head by a pitch. Two weeks later Jim Pendleton in the American Association was rushed to the hospital, the victim of a Lew Burdette fastball. On July 26 an "errant" pitch knocked infielder Parnell Woods, recently acquired by the Oakland Oaks, unconscious, and attendants removed him on a stretcher. "As soon as you walked up there, you'd get knocked down," recalls Thurman of his first year in Organized Baseball.

The inordinate number of black victims did not decline as integration progressed. The 1951 season began with the beaning of Portland shortstop Frank

Austin on March 31. Six weeks later Bob Boyd of Sacramento received X rays at the hospital, after a pitch struck him in the head. In the Western League "errant" pitches found Denver second baseman Curt Roberts four times in one day. Roberts established a Western League record when pitchers struck him for the fifteenth time that season. The following year a beaning hospitalized the unfortunate Roberts.

That so many black players required hospitalization indicates that these were not always routine "brushback" pitches calculated to intimidate the batters but included "beanballs" designed to injure them. Throughout the early years of baseball integration and even beyond, black players, particularly those pioneering in a new league, faced greater dangers than the average performer. Where a black pitcher also appeared, the potential of retaliation offered a modicum of protection. On occasion, blacks would protest and fight back. But most players accepted this harassment as part of the game. "I was knocked down in the Negro Leagues so much," asserts Thurman, "this didn't bother me." In one instance, Thurman shouted out to his opponent, "You got guts enough to knock me down, show the fans you got guts enough to throw some strikes now." Thurman hit the next pitch for a home run. "Boy, did I ever suck him in," he laughs. "Man, that thing is still going out!"

If a player hoped to ascend to the major leagues, he ignored the physical and verbal taunts tossed before him. "You just go out there and try to work harder and you end up having guys that are calling you names come up and shake your hand," says Chuck Harmon philosophically. "That meant more to me than wanting to punch them in the mouth."

Harmon's minor-league record reveals the success of his policy. During three seasons with Olean in the Pony League, Harmon batted .351, .374, and .375. Promoted to higher classifications, Harmon remained a .300 hitter. Nor was Harmon an exceptional case. Despite the adversity that confronted them and their relatively small numbers, blacks appeared regularly among the league leaders wherever they played. In 1952 and 1953 five blacks finished among the top-ten American Association hitters. In the Pacific Coast League, Bob Boyd, Piper Davis, and Artie Wilson finished in the top three spots in batting in 1952. The following season, black hitters won the batting championship in both the American Association and the Pacific Coast League, while for the second straight year, a black was named the Most Valuable Player in the International League. Blacks duplicated these performances at many lower levels, as well.

Jackie Robinson had endured his pioneering ordeal amidst considerable fanfare and publicity. In the aftermath of his accomplishment, scores of other blacks performed in the unexposed corners of the United States, re-creating his trials and triumphs. Their remarkable achievements and contributions to the cause of racial equality rarely received acknowledgment. But at a time when segregation remained an unyielding American reality, they, like Robinson, carved out and affirmed the black man's niche in the national pastime.

III

For Negro League veterans the minor leagues marked the final stepping-stone on a prolonged odyssey. Their careers had encompassed the Jim Crow circuits, the interracial barnstorming tours, and the international flavor of Caribbean baseball. Finally allowed into Organized Baseball, many hoped for one last opportunity to play in the major leagues. In most cases, however, baseball officials continued to deny them. Philadelphia Athletics General Manager Art Ehlers confessed in 1953 that many Negro League players should have advanced rapidly in previous years. "The majors were reluctant," stated Ehlers, "and the men who were ready became overage and lost their opportunity." While minor-league spectators thrilled to the exploits of Ray Dandridge, Piper Davis, Artie Wilson, and others, these great talents remained unknown to baseball's broader audience.

Among the greatest mysteries of the early 1950s were the ages of the Negro League players flooding into the higher minor leagues. To enhance their possibilities for advancement, blacks routinely lied about their age, shearing off anywhere from two to ten years. Sug Cornelius recalls truthfully telling scouts who approached him that he was thirty-nine years old. "Then I read in the paper . . . out in San Diego, about eight or nine guys I had played with were playing," says Cornelius. "They were all twenty-six, twenty-eight years old. I could have kicked myself. I should have told him I was younger." Many players did just that. Pitcher Roy Welmaker walked into the Cleveland training camp in 1949 claiming to be twenty-seven. He won twenty-two games for the Class A Wilkes-Barre team that season and the Indians promoted him to San Diego in 1950. Welmaker won eight of his first ten Pacific Coast League decisions and was hailed as "the best lefty to come down the pike in many moons." But Welmaker "admitted he would never again see his thirty-sixth birthday," and the Cleveland management proclaimed him too old for a trial in the majors.

The assumption that black players were older than the years they claimed sometimes worked to their detriment. "Why, my Pappy isn't that old," exclaimed Dan Bankhead in response to rumors that he was thirty-nine. When Buzz Clarkson reported for a brief stint with the Boston Braves in 1952, a reporter described him as "a comparatively ancient colored shortstop," whose "indeterminable" age "was the only thing against him." Sam Jethroe charges that suspicions that he was older than his thirty-one years in 1953 may have shortened his major-league career.

The major-league antipathy for aging players doomed most of the surviving stars of the Jim Crow era to the Triple A arena. Only a handful played in the majors for any prolonged period of time. Satchel Paige fared better than most. Cleveland released Paige after he won only four games in 1949. It was not coincidental that Bill Veeck, Paige's patron, had relinquished control of the club. In 1951 Veeck purchased the hapless St. Louis Browns, and he immediately returned Paige to the spotlight. At least forty-three years of age, Paige established himself as one of the outstanding relief pitchers in baseball during the next three seasons. In 1952, pitching for a team that won only sixty-four games, the great hurler won twelve games and saved ten more. Veeck sold the Browns after the 1953 season. The new owners proclaimed a youth movement and dropped Paige.

The indefatigable Paige spent two years on the barnstorming circuit before Veeck, operating the Triple A Miami Marlins, beckoned again. Paige literally descended from the heavens on opening day, deposited by a helicopter. Marlin Manager Don Osborne believed Paige's appearance was another Veeck publicity stunt, but the "old man" hurled a four-hit shutout in his first start. Used primarily as a relief pitcher, Paige posted an 11-4 record with 16 saves and a remarkable 1.86 earned run average. "He stood out on the mound, and you could hear his stomach growl," recalls John Roseboro. "With all his windups and deliveries and soft stuff, it was a thrill just to bat against him." Paige remained in the International League for three years. In his final season, he won 10, lost 10, and boasted a 2.96 earned run average.

Luke Easter's Organized Baseball career paralleled that of Paige. At the close of the 1949 season the Indians rushed Easter to Cleveland, amidst much fanfare, to help in their abortive pennant drive. Easter, overweight and still recuperating from his operation, batted only .222 with no home runs. The disappointed Indian fans made Easter "the most booed player in the history of Cleveland Stadium." The *Sporting News* quickly pointed out, "There was no racial connotation. He was expected to hit and he didn't." In the spring of 1950 Easter started the season slowly, evoking more jeers. In mid-May he finally uncoiled his power. At the season's end he had belted 28 home runs and driven in 107 runs. Over his first three seasons with the Indians, Easter averaged 29 home runs and 100 RBIs. Nearing the age of forty and continually plagued by knee and ankle injuries, he appeared in only sixty-eight games in 1953. The following year, Easter returned to the minors.

Easter's playing career had not ended. For the next decade he reigned as the toast of the International League, appearing first with the Buffalo Bisons and later for the Rochester Red Wings. As the years passed, Easter could barely run, and his defensive range grew more limited, but he remained a dangerous hitter, ever capable of launching one of his prodigious projectiles. As late as 1957, Easter hit forty home runs. At Rochester, fans greeted his appearances with cries of "Luuuuuke, Luuuuuke, Luuuuuke" and waited through one-sided defeats in hopes that he might pinch-hit. He became the most popular player in the league, particularly among the younger fans. "In the early 1960's," writes sports columnist Bob Matthews, who grew up in Rochester, "I was convinced Luke Easter was the greatest man alive." It was not until 1964, at the age of forty-three or perhaps forty-eight or maybe fifty-three, that Luke took his last swing as a Red Wing.

Several other Negro League stars also had relatively brief careers in the major leagues. Sam Jethroe won the Rookie of the Year Award in 1950 as a Boston Brave, but failing eyesight, poor defense, and an influx of younger black players on the Braves banished him to the International League in 1953. After wandering through the Triple A maze for five years, Bob Thurman finally won promotion to the Cincinnati Reds in 1954. Already thirty-three years old, Thurman seved primarily as a pinch hitter for five seasons, slugging 16 home runs in only 190 at bats in 1957. Pitcher Connie Johnson also amassed a five-year major-league career despite a belated start while in his mid-thirties.

Baseball players refer to a brief tenure in the major leagues as "a cup of coffee." Artie Wilson received his "cup" of big-league life with the New York Giants in 1951. The former Black Baron shortstop had batted .348 and .312 in his two seasons in the Pacific Coast League. In spring training he earned a place on the Giants with a .480 batting average. But Wilson engaged in little regular-season action, registering only twenty-two at bats. "I was a rookie," he explains, "and a rookie does not get to break in with a[n infield] combination like Eddie Stanky and Alvin Dark." In late May the Giants had to make room for another rookie—Wilson's former Black Baron teammmate, twenty-year-old Willie Mays. Wilson was dispatched to Minneapolis where he performed briefly before his former owners in Oakland requested his return to boost lagging ticket sales. He remained in the Pacific Coast League for the rest of his career. A consistent .300 hitter, Wilson never again received a major-league offer.

Quincy Trouppe also received a brief taste of life in the big leagues. A powerfully built catcher who prided himself on his defensive skills and general knowledge of baseball, Trouppe had been a player-manager on several Negro and Mexican League clubs. At the age of thirty-nine, he received an opportunity to play for the Cleveland Indians in 1952. "I guess no one who has ever broken into Organized Baseball could have felt any better than I did when I inked my name to that new Cleveland contract," writes Trouppe in his autobiography. But in two and a half months in the majors Trouppe batted only ten times. In June, Cleveland assigned him to Indianapolis. "The terrible disappointment nearly choked me," states Trouppe. He protested his demotion but was advised, "You don't have a record to go on." The veteran catcher "thought about all the highs and lows that went into putting together twenty-two years of playing ball on two different continents and on islands in between." Yet, according to Organized Baseball logic, he had no record. Trouppe reported to Indianapolis in the American Association, where he hit six home runs in his first two weeks, but the Indians never recalled him. At the season's end, Trouppe retired.

Although denied the full measure of fame and achievement that they deserved, players like Trouppe and Wilson at least had the satisfaction of playing in the major leagues. Other black stars, like Piper Davis and Ray Dandridge, were not as fortunate.

There is little doubt that Lorenzo "Piper" Davis possessed major-league abilities. "If he'd had a chance when he was young," asserts Clyde Sukeforth, who scouted Davis for the Dodgers, "he'd have been outstanding." The versatile line-drive-hitting Davis performed ably at all positions. In 1945 the Dodgers considered him in their initial search for black players. In 1947 the St. Louis Browns took out an option on his services. But when the Browns released Hank Thompson and Willard Brown, they also allowed the option on Davis to expire.

Three years later, the Boston Red Sox made their initial foray into the black player market when they purchased Davis from the Birmingham Black Barons. The Red Sox paid Barons' owner Tom Hayes $7,500, with the promise to double that figure if Davis remained in the Boston organization past May 15. Davis, the player-manager of the Barons, claimed to be twenty-nine years old, cutting two years off his real age. Red Sox General Manager Joe Cronin told reporters that he had obtained the "sleeper" of the season in the "twenty-six-year-old" Davis. "He's a fine kid," boasted Cronin. "I'm going to try him out with the Scranton, Pennsylvania, club. If he makes good, I'm going to waste no time in moving him on to Boston." Scranton, although only in the Class A Eastern League, was Boston's highest affiliate above the Jim Crow region.

Davis reported to the Red Sox training camp in Cocoa, Florida, in the spring of 1950. On the first day of practice, he recalls, "I took the routine exercises, got ready to throw. I patted that ball around for a minute or more, but it felt like fifteen. Nobody spoke to me." Another player finally offered to toss the ball with Davis. Local custom forbade Davis from dressing, living, or eating with his teammates. "I lived in the city with one of the waiters," remembers Davis. "I'd eat in the waiters' quarters. The team ate out in the dining room. I had to dress in the visitors' clubhouse." Davis did not start in the first exhibition game, but in the late innings he emerged from the dugout as a pinch hitter. "Well, I'll be damned," he heard a fan exclaim. "Boston done got a nigger." "That's one of the times I said my prayers in baseball," Davis relates. "I said, 'Lord let me hit this ball, please,' and I hit a screaming shot. If I'm not mistaken, I hit it over the boards."

The Scranton farm team played several exhibition games in southern towns, but Red Sox officials dispatched Davis directly to Pennsylvania rather than challenge the Jim Crow laws. The veteran Negro League performer rejoined the club at the start of the regular season and proceeded to batter Class A pitching. On May 13, two days before Boston was required to pay the second half of Davis's purchase price to the Black Barons, he led the team in batting, with a .333 average, home runs, runs batted in, and stolen bases. When the Scranton general manager summoned Davis to his office, the athlete anticipated a promotion to the Red Sox Triple A farm club at Louisville. Instead, the general manager informed him that the Red Sox had released him for "economical reasons."

The action infuriated Scranton field manager Jack Burns. Burns assured Davis that he had played no role in the decision. The manager escorted Davis to the locker room and advised him, "You just take anything in here you want." Davis declined the offer. "I just took my cap, because I knew they wouldn't want my cap, anyway. They gave me my own brush and comb. They had all the combs up on the shelf. They gave me my own private brush and comb."

The Scranton club did not even offer Davis a train ticket to return to Birmingham. Ironically, at Union Station in Washington, D.C., where law required all blacks to detrain and relocate to the blacks-only cars, Davis suddenly found himself face-to-face with Joe Cronin. Cronin awkwardly repeated the tale of "economic woe" that led to Davis's dismissal before the two men went to their respective Jim Crow seats. Cronin later sent Davis first-class transportation and meal money to pay for his trip home.

Davis never accepted the Red Sox explanation of "economical conditions." "I knew that was a joke," he asserts, "because [Red Sox owner] Tom Yawkey's one of the richest men in the East." Indeed, the financial fortunes of the Red Sox had reached a new peak. The club had shown a profit in four of its previous five seasons, and the value of its assets had tripled during that period. In 1949 Boston attendance had surged to a record 1.6 million, a figure that would not be topped for eighteen years. Red Sox officials asserted that "at thirty-three, the Negro first baseman was not considered a major league prospect." In the eyes of the Boston management, Davis, really thirty-one, had aged seven years in a few months. Four seasons passed before Yawkey's Red Sox signed another black player; not until 1959 did a black man even don a Boston uniform in spring training.

In 1951 Davis joined the Oakland Oaks. For the next six years he delighted the Pacific Coast League fans as a utility infielder-outfielder, twice batting over .300. In 1956, ten years after the Dodgers had declined to sign him, Davis was traded to the Brooklyn farm team in Hollywood. The following season the Dodgers assigned him to their AA franchise at Fort Worth. "In the Texas League," recalls Davis, "I couldn't eat with [the team] anywhere and stay with them, either. I couldn't even play in Shreveport." When the team arrived at a restaurant to eat, Davis waited in the bus until they brought him food. On one occasion, when they forgot to bring him a meal, Davis advised his manager to ignore it. "I'm not worth waiting for, anyway," he exclaimed bitterly. The following season, the Dodgers sent him a new contract, but Davis returned it unsigned. A retired athlete at thirty-eight years of age, Davis had never played in a major-league game.

Like Piper Davis, Ray Dandridge deserved a chance to perform at baseball's highest levels. A perennial All-Star in the Negro and Mexican leagues, Dandridge compiled three consecutive outstanding seasons with the Giants' top farm club at Minneapolis. At third base, reported the *Sporting News*, "He astounded veteran observers with his plays. . . . The bowlegged Dandridge moves like a cat." After batting .364 in 1949, he won the Most Valuable Player Award in the American Association in 1950, hitting .311 and leading his team to the pennant. In 1951 he continued to harass Triple A pitchers with a .324 average, while pacing all third basemen in fielding. In May, Dandridge watched Willie Mays, his young black roommate, ascend to the Giants, but the great black veteran remained behind.

"My biggest point in life was that I wanted to put my foot in major-league ball," Dandridge asserts. Several stars on the Giants called for this elevation. Monte Irvin recalls that he and Hank Thompson urged Manager Leo Durocher to promote Dandridge. White pitcher Sal Maglie, who had befriended the third baseman while both played in Mexico, snarled, "Why the hell don't you bring that son of a bitch out of Minneapolis?" Durocher and the Giant front office steadfastly refused.

Ironically, the Giants were a pioneer club in baseball integration and seemed less conscious of a racial quota system than other teams of that era. Chub Feeney, then a Giant executive and now the president of the National League, explains, "Ray was considered several times, and the strange thing about it was that [owner] Horace [Stoneham] loved him. Called him 'Dandy Dandridge.' " Age, not race, blocked Dandridge's chances according to Feeney. "Ray was probably in his early forties, and by that time we had Henry Thompson and then Bobby Thomson at third base. There just never came a time when there was a real need." In retrospect, Feeney admits, "Probably we could have brought him up at the end of the season or something . . . if we'd recognized the fact that he had felt that need."

Dandridge believes that his immense popularity in Minneapolis provided another reason for the failure of the Giants to promote him. Stoneham, he says, told him that the organization wanted him there because of his drawing power. Dandridge charges that the Giants turned down offers from other teams in order to keep him in the Twin Cities. Years later he rebuffed Stoneham at an Old-Timers' Game. "I said, 'Horace, I don't even want to talk to you,' " he heatedly recalls. " 'You had the chance to sell my contract. You had the chance to bring me up, and you wouldn't do it. The only thing I wanted to do was hit the major leagues. . . . You could have called me up for even one week! I could have said I hit the major leagues.' "

"I loved baseball and everything in it. My life has been nothing but baseball," Dandridge told a reunion of Negro League players in 1980. His audience remembered him as perhaps the finest third baseman to ever play the game. Most other baseball fans do not know him at all. Long the victim of racism, in the end Dandridge fell victim to the universal experience of aging and the insensitivity characteristic of the newly integrated national pastime. For Ray Dandridge, Piper Davis, and countless others who ended their obscure, yet sparkling careers in the minor leagues, the demise of segregation occurred too late.

Bob Uecker's lifetime batting average through six major league seasons was .200; he never hit a triple or stole a base. When asked his secret for catching the knuckleball, he replied, "It's easy—I just wait for it to stop rolling, then I pick it up." Like Joe Garagiola before him, Uecker shrewdly transformed a mediocre career (yes, mediocre, not terrible) into a running joke and himself into a national celebrity. The Milwaukee-born catcher went into play-by-play broadcasting for the Brewers, funny beer commercials, stand-up comedy, and, inevitably, autobiography. Here is Uecker's last hurrah, with the 1966 Phillies.

BOB UECKER

Catcher in the Wry

The Phillies, like the Cardinals, were a team trying to regroup. No manager had survived more adversity than Gene Mauch. His first team had established a major-league record by losing twenty-three straight games in 1961. Near the end of the streak, they came off a road trip to find a large crowd waiting for them at the airport in Philadelphia. They figured, obviously, it was a lynch mob. A pitcher named Frank Sullivan called out, "Leave the plane in single file. That way they can't get us with one burst."

But the fans came to welcome them home again, to cheer, to give them support. There is no way to know what makes a Phillies fan tick. They rallied behind Gene Mauch, and in time he gave them a contender, only to see the Phillies blow a ten-game lead in the nightmare season of 1964. The next year they were never a factor, and now Mauch had decided to retool the club.

I felt at home with the Phillies when I reported to camp at Clearwater in March. The roster included such cashews as Richie Allen, who liked everything about a ballpark except getting there; Bo Belinsky, the flamboyant left-hander who thought he had been Rudolph Valentino in a prior life; and John Boozer, a pitcher whose idea of fun was to eat bugs and worms and watch people gag. He did a better job in the clubhouse than D-Con. He would be talking to a writer, and one of the players would hand him a live worm or a beetle. Some of the reactions were terrific.

Belinsky reported to camp two days late, explaining that he had been trapped by a snowstorm in Texas on the drive from California. Those Texas snowstorms can be murder.

In addition to the ex-Cardinal trio, Mauch had traded for Phil Linz, an infielder the Yankees had fired for playing the harmonica on the team bus after a loss, and Jackie Brandt, who once watched part of an All-Star Game while sitting in the dugout in the nude.

The Phillies had a terrific roster. I don't mean in talent but in names, the kind that headline writers loved, like Wine and Boozer, and the kind that just had a certain ring, like Ferguson Jenkins, Cookie Rojas, and Clay Dalrymple.

I had been brought in to back up Dalrymple, a seven-year vet and an underrated fellow, whose .213 average in 1965 was well below his form. Clay hit from the left side, which meant that once again I would have a chance to start against the left-handers. It was hard to tell if I had made any progress. I had been traded to my third team in three years. The Phillies issued me uniform No. 10. I had worn 9 in St. Louis and 8 in Milwaukee. Was this progress?

When the players talked about the best and the brightest managers, the name of Gene Mauch often came up. He was quick-tempered, but he did not give up on people easily. His career as a player had been similar to mine. He was a shortstop who always seemed to line up behind someone better, such as Phil Rizzuto, with the Yankees, or Pee Wee Reese, with the Dodgers.

Frustrated, still a kid, Mauch once confronted his manager, Casey Stengel, in the dining room of a hotel where the Yankees stayed. "Dammit, Casey," he blurted, "I've got to play."

Stengel looked up from his soup and nodded. "Go talk to Mr. Rizzuto," the old man said. "If it's okay with him, it's okay with me."

Mauch was the most intense manager I ever knew. He would sit on the bench with his arms folded, and his eyes never stopped moving. He didn't miss a thing. They used to tell a story about when Mauch was playing for the Red Sox and on the way to the airport the team bus got stuck under an overpass. The driver and the team got out to study the problem. Finally, Mauch said, "Let the air out of the tires and fill them up on the other side." And so they did.

I was in the lineup on Opening Day, 1966, caught Chris Short, and drove in a run with a single as we beat the Reds and Joe Nuxhall, 3–1. Then a really uncharacteristic thing happened. I hit home runs on consecutive days at the end of April. In my first six games I had produced four hits, half of them homers, and driven in six runs. A curious start, it was worth three stars and a full, hand-lettered page in the scrapbook:

TWO HOMERS
IN TWO
DAYS!

BIG UKE
IS STARTING TO
FIND THE RANGE

ONLY 505 CAREER
HOMERS BEHIND
MAYS & OTT!!

Ah, yes, the future stretched ahead as smooth and inviting as the Pennsylvania Turnpike. When I connected for my third homer on Memorial Day, against the Mets, Mark wrote a story for the school paper at Drury and mailed a copy to Bob Howsam. The Cardinals were in the process of sending Mahaffey and Johnson to the minors. The trade was looking rather one-sided for the Phillies.

The story went like this:

Bob Howsam has finally, publicly, admitted in May that he was completely wrong in October. The story we got then was that we were trading White, Groat, and Uecker for Johnson, Corrales, and Mahaffey because we (the Cardinals) were fully committed to our youth movement.

Well, it doesn't look too good for smiling Bob. How can you say you're in a youth movement and trade a thirty-one-year-old slugger like White and then keep a broken-down, thirty-seven-year-old pitcher named Curt Simmons, who only pitches against the Phillies and can't beat them?

With his homer, double, and three runs batted in on Memorial Day, and his two singles two days later, Uecker raised his average to a lusty .266. With three homers . . . he seems likely to get a new career high in every hitting department, and last year had been his best. He's hitting better than either Bill White or Dick Groat, the men he was traded with, and that ought to make him the big man in the deal. The key man in the deal!

Howsam, you're an idiot.

With aplomb, Howsam wrote back:

Dear Mr. Stillwell,

Thank you for sending along the article which appeared at Drury.

It's nice to know, too, that you have remained Cardinal fans.

We hope you and your Fan Club will have the opportunity to visit the new Busch Memorial Stadium and see the Cardinals play. I think you'll enjoy it.

> Kindest regards,
> Bob Howsam
> General Manager

The first time the teams met in 1966, the Phillies edged the Cards 5–3. Bill White singled home our first two runs. I singled to open the winning rally and scored the tie-breaking run on a bases-loaded walk to Groat, who had two hits. It's true, hitting well is the best revenge.

On June 3 I slugged my fourth homer of the year, equaling the total for my entire big-league career. The blow was off an ex-teammate, Ray Sadecki, then pitching for the Giants. By the All-Star break I had raised my total to six, the same number as John Callison, a guy who was usually good for twenty-five to thirty a season.

I would have felt great except that everybody around the Phillies kept wondering what was wrong with Callison. Four teams figured to stay in the pennant race most of the way, the Dodgers, Giants, Pirates, and the Phillies. We needed a big year from Callison. In fact, we needed a big year from everybody.

The point should be made right here that it can be harmful for a fellow who doesn't hit homers to suddenly start banging a few. It is like a guy who discovers girls late in life and thinks he can catch up all at once. And the next thing you know, you are in a jar at the Harvard Medical School.

But sooner or later you have to try. You see a Richie Allen twitch a muscle, and the ball flies off the bat and lands 500 feet away. And you think, *Is there any reason I can't do that?* The next thing you know, your hands are down at the end of the bat, and all your weight is on your heels.

In a way, those homers, hitting in the .270s, and getting four (4) votes for the All-Star Game may have been my undoing. Up to then my theories had stood the test of time, like milk of magnesia: (1) The more I played, the closer I was to getting shipped out, and (2) the better I performed, the more they expected.

If I had been content to just hit .200 every year, all singles, and throw out a runner now and then, I might have played as long as Gaylord Perry. Your body doesn't wear out very fast when you catch a game every four or five days.

On July 17 I tagged my seventh homer in what turned out to be a fifteen-inning win over the first-place Giants. On the Phillies, only Allen and Bill White had more, even though a total of twelve players had started more games.

I had no personal goals in mind, which was just as well, because I did not hit another homer during the rest of the season.

Harry Grabiner was the penurious Charles Comiskey's general manager with the White Sox, the bearer of ill tidings come contract time and thus the object of considerable ill will from players such as Joe Jackson and Eddie Cicotte. But Harry was a solid and competent company man, and when Bill Veeck bought the Cleveland Indians, he brought him over from Chicago to help keep the franchise solvent. In 1948 the long-dormant Indians were the surprise of baseball, giving Harry Grabiner his first winner since the Black Sox of 1919. From *Veeck—as in Wreck*.

BILL VEECK with ED LINN

An Epitaph for Harry Grabiner

One of the great joys of our quick success at Cleveland was watching the fun Harry Grabiner was having. After all the years of scrimping at Chicago, Harry was showing them all how he could operate when he had a chance to go first-class. As a man, he had always traveled first-class. Harry had a wonderful family. His daughter was June Travis, a Hollywood actress of some note before her marriage. His wife, Dottie, was a woman of such beauty that if you placed her and June side by side you could not tell which was the mother and which the daughter.

Reserved as Harry normally was, he was a wild and uninhibited rooter. During the course of a game he would keep jumping out of the office to run to the top of the stairs and cheer our boys through every rally. Harry was a hitter. Early in our association I learned to stay away from those stairs during my tours around the park, because Harry could pound you black and blue. In Cleveland, he was finally getting a chance to root home a winner.

He was a tremendous asset in running the business end of the club, because he was always practical. When it came to paying $100,000 for a Zoldak, he'd say, "Great." But he would suggest some alternative that would serve the same purpose at about half the price.

I have said before that Harry was an honorable man. Let me give another example. I had dealt with Harry quite a bit in Milwaukee, in both the buying and selling of players, and out of our old friendship in Chicago we always leveled with each other. I had a forty-year-old pitcher named Earl Caldwell whom I had bought from the Texas League, a sidearm, almost underhanded pitcher who had been up with the Athletics fourteen years earlier and had later put in time with the Browns. By the time he reached us, he was a fussy old guy who always wore rubbers and carried an umbrella. The rest of the players called him "Grandmother."

When I got Caldwell, I promised him I'd do my best to get him another shot at the majors, a promise I made to almost all my players. Although he had only a middling sort of year, I called Harry and told him I thought Caldwell might be able to help the White Sox in relief. Harry didn't want him. The next year, though, Caldwell had a pretty good season. I was operating the club out of the Corona hospital as the year ended, and this time I told Harry I was sure Caldwell would help him.

"But he's nine hundred years old," Harry said. "I wouldn't have any idea what to offer you for him and—I don't have to tell you—I don't have any money to fool around with."

I said, "Harry, pay me five thousand dollars, then pay me what he's worth to you after you have him. If you don't think he's worth anything, send him back on June 15 and I'll give back the five thousand dollars, and at least I've got him into the majors again like I promised."

Caldwell surprised even me. He pitched brilliantly for the White Sox from the start, far better than he had ever pitched before in his life. In the middle of May, Harry sent us $10,000. I immediately called to thank him and to let him know I was very well pleased with the price. Caldwell continued to pitch well, and in mid-August another $10,000 arrived.

That was the kind of fellow Harry was. He had agreed to pay me what the man was worth to him, and he was scrupulous about keeping his word. To my immense delight, Grandmother Caldwell was an even better pitcher for Harry the next year, far and away the best relief pitcher in the American League.

Now let's go back to Cleveland. Before the 1948 season we had set an attendance goal of 2 million people. As the season progressed, it became increasingly evident that we were going to roll right over our goal and go on to smash all records. Harry had a paper schedule of our home games on which he kept track of the attendance. He had three columns of figures. In the first column were the figures he had projected at the beginning of the year to show the attendance we would have to have, game by game, in order to reach our 2 million goal. In the second column, he would write down the actual attendance of each game as the season progressed. In the third column, he kept adjusting his original projection, game by game, to show what he now estimated our final figures would be, based upon our advance, our position in the race, and the constantly rising enthusiasm. It was all pretty complicated.

Harry and I shared the same office, and it became a sort of ritual for him to stop off at the desk every day to fill in the previous day's attendance and perhaps make a new projection. He kept the schedule in the inside pocket of his jacket, folded in three parts, and by the time we entered our last home stand of the season, it had been folded and unfolded so often that it had come completely apart. Harry would have to hold the frazzled, dirty pieces together on my desk while he ran down the attendance column, adding in his head, as always, because with his machinelike mind he never bothered to make a footing and write down a total.

We had been home on that last home stand for about a week when Harry stopped by at about five o'clock to go through the usual routine. He was in marvelous spirits. Our attendance was already half a million over his original estimate, and, more important, we had started the winning streak that was to carry us back into first place. I was sitting at the desk, as usual. Harry, as usual, seated himself on the very edge of the desk itself, leaning down over the tattered schedule. All things as usual. In a minute or two we would each get up and go our separate ways. I would step out into the stadium and begin to mix with the early customers. Harry would go up to the press room to sip his usual cup of tea and act as host to the writers.

And all of a sudden I heard him say, "I can't add. I can't add."

I looked up, startled. In his eyes, I could see . . . what? No, not fear, but a sort of dull shock. For Harry not to be able to add was like me not being able to talk.

"Harry," I said, "what's the matter?"

"I can't add." The same incomprehension. The same dull shock.

"You're just tired," I said automatically. I was frightened to death. "You're tired, Harry," I said. "Come on over to the couch and sit down."

But he reached out for my hand, and in that same quiet voice he said, "I can't think. Bill, hold my hand. I can't think."

I knew at that moment that it was something serious, something more than a stroke. Harry Grabiner was spilled there across my desk, grabbing on to my hand, the three sections of his schedule spread out around him, broken and awry. And Harry Grabiner was saying that he couldn't think. Harry Grabiner. I knew this was it, that it was over, that from one second to the next he had died there on my desk. No question about it. No question.

While we were waiting for the doctor, I brought Harry over to the couch and held him in my arms like a frightened child. The moment anyone came into the office, he would huddle closer to me in terror and whimper, "Don't let him get near me, Bill. Don't let him get near me." The only other person he wasn't afraid of was Ada Ireland, our telephone operator.

The doctor took one look at him and told me there was nothing he could do. "I could open his head, look in, and sew it back up," he told me. "All that would do would make him die a little sooner. I know what I'd see without cutting him open."

I left Harry huddled in Ada's arms and went out front to put in a rush call to a psychiatrist I knew quite well. A last, forlorn hope. I introduced him to Harry not as a psychiatrist but as a friend who had dropped in to say hello. He didn't have to ask Harry more than three or four questions before he knew it was out of his field. "Something inside his head has been eaten away," he told me. "His mind is about gone."

I had called June immediately, and she had quickly flown in from Chicago with her husband, Fred Friedlob. Harry was taken back to Allegan, where, through some hidden reservoir of strength and will, he held on until we won that play-off game in Boston. He wanted so badly to win that pennant, his first pennant after all those years. He walked around outside the house all during the game, listening to the radio broadcast, and the moment it was over and we had won, he walked back into the house and collapsed.

Harry had always wanted to show them that he was a good operator.

"East is East and West is West," wrote Kipling, "and never the twain shall meet"—not even in that shared obsession, baseball/*besuboru*. Baseball in Japan goes back to 1873, when a visiting American professor taught the rudiments of the game to his students at what is now the University of Tokyo. American major leaguers toured the land of the rising sun repeatedly, beginning in 1913, and by 1936 Japan had formed its own professional baseball league. American imports first appeared in 1951 and have been an important, yet controversial, part of the Japanese game for much of the postwar era. Whiting, who lives in Japan, is the author of *The Chrysanthemum and the Bat: Baseball Samurai Style*.

ROBERT WHITING

You've Gotta Have "Wa"

"I don't know what it is they play here," grumbled former California Angel Clyde Wright after his first season as a Tokyo Giant. "All I know is, it ain't baseball." Wright had learned what many expatriates in the Land of the Rising Sun had known for years: baseball, Japanese style, is not the same game that's played in the United States. Since adopting the sport, the Japanese have changed it around to incorporate the values of samurai discipline, respect for authority, and devotion to the group. The result is a uniquely Japanese game, one that offers perhaps the clearest expression among all sports of Japan's national character.

Like the American game, the Nippon version is played with a bat and ball. The same rule book is also used, but that's where resemblance between the two ends. Training, for example, is nearly a religion in Japan. Baseball players in the United States start spring training in March and take no more than five or six weeks to prepare for the season. They spend three to four hours on the field each day and then head for the nearest golf course or swimming pool.

Japanese teams begin training in the freezing cold of mid-January. Each day they're on the field for a numbing eight hours, and then it's off to the dormitory for an evening of strategy sessions and still more workouts indoors. Players run 10 miles every day, and one team, the Taiyo Whales, periodically performs the "Death Climb," twenty sprints up and down the 275 steps of a nearby Shinto shrine.

That's only the beginning. The average Japanese game is more like a board meeting at Mitsubishi than an athletic event. As each new situation arises, there is so much discussion on the field among the manager, coaches, and players that most games last three hours.

Unlike their counterparts in the States, losing managers in Japan are seldom fired outright. Instead, they go through an elaborate, time-consuming ritual designed to save face all around. It culminates with a public apology by the deposed skipper, his resignation, and, often, an all-expenses-paid trip to the United States for him to "study baseball."

Such phenomena are the tip of the iceberg. Below the waterline are the concept and practice of group harmony, or *wa*. It is this concept that most dramatically differentiates Japanese baseball from the American game.

The United States is a land where the stubborn individualist is honored and where "doing your own thing" is a motto of contemporary society. In Japan, *kojinshugi*, the term for individualism, is almost a dirty word. In place of "doing your own thing," the Japanese have a proverb: "The nail that sticks up shall be hammered down." It is practically a national design.

In Japan, holdouts are rare. A player takes what the club gives him, and that's that. Demanding more money is *kojinshugi* at its worst, because it shows the player has put his own interests before those of the team. Katsuya Nomura, the Nankai Hawk catcher who has hit 652 home runs in his career, said, upon quietly accepting a minuscule raise after winning yet another of his numerous home-run titles, "If I had asked for more money, the other players would have thought I was greedy."

The U.S. player lives by the rule: "*I know what's best for me.*" In Japan, the only ones who know what's best are the manager and coaches. They have the virtues Orientals most respect going for them—age and experience, hence, knowledge. Their word is law. In the interest of team harmony they demand that everyone do everything the same way. Superstar Sadaharu Oh must endure the same pregame grind as the lowliest first-year player. At thirty-eight Shin-ichi Eto, a three-time batting champion and a ten-year All-Star, found that forty minutes of jogging and wind sprints before each game left him exhausted by game time. He asked to be allowed to train at his own pace. "You've been a great player, Eto-*san*," he was told, "but there are no exceptions on this club. You'll do things according to the rules." Eto lost weight, his batting average dropped, he spent the second half of the season on the bench and then reluctantly announced his retirement. Irrational? Perhaps, but any games lost because Eto was dog tired were not as important as the example he set.

In the pressure-cooker world of U.S. pro sports, temper outbursts are considered acceptable and at times even regarded as a salutary show of spirit. Unreleased frustrations, the reasoning goes, might negatively affect a player's concentration. Japanese players are expected to follow Sadaharu Oh's example. "When he strikes out," says an admirer, "he breaks into a smile and trots back to the bench." Oh has been known to be glum during a batting slump, but temper tantrums—along with practical joking, bickering, complaining, and other norms of American clubhouse life—are viewed in Japan as unwelcome incursions into the team's collective peace of mind. They offend the finer sensitivities of the Japanese, and as many American players have learned the hard way, Japanese sensitivities *are* finer.

Michio Arito was the captain of the Lotte Orions, a ten-year veteran and the team's longtime batting mainstay. Because of a badly bruised hand he had been able to play only by taking a lot of painkillers, and before a crucial game that would, as it turned out, mean the pennant for the Orions, the manager decided to replace him with a healthier player. When Arito heard he'd been benched, he yelled, threw his glove, and slammed his bat against the bench. Next day, at the Orions' victory party, Arito was summoned forth to atone for his sins. After bowing deeply to all, he said, "I am sorry for my childish actions yesterday. I have upset our team spirit, and I deeply apologize."

Jim Lefebvre, a former Los Angeles Dodger infielder who spent five years in Japan, can still not quite believe what he saw there. "It's incredible," he says. "These guys are together almost all the time from January to October. They live together, eat together, play baseball together. I've never seen one fight, one argument. In the States, there's always somebody who mouths off and starts trouble."

If you ask a Japanese manager what he considers the most important ingredient of a winning team, he would most likely answer, *"Wa."* If you ask him how to knock a team's *wa* awry, he'd probably say, "Hire an American."

Former American major leaguers have been an active part of Japanese baseball for eighteen years. The somewhat lower level of play in Japan has given these *gaijin* (outsiders) a temporary reprieve from the athletic scrap heap. And although the Japanese have paid the *gaijin* high salaries, they have not been elated with the overall experience of having them on their teams.

Money is a particular sore point. Foreigners make two to three times as much as Japanese players of similar ability. This, combined with the free Western-style house and the other perks that the *gaijin* seem to view as inalienable rights, sets them too far above their teammates. And more than one American player has brought in an agent to negotiate his contract. That is considered to be in very bad taste. A contract discussion is regarded as a "family affair," with the official team interpreter, despite his obvious bias, acting as a go-between.

Avarice is only part of it, however. Deportment is the rest. Although few Americans hold a Japanese batting or pitching record, many have established standards in the area of bad conduct. For example, the amiable former Dodger Norm Larker set the Japan single-season high for smashed batting helmets with eight. Joe Stanka, a six-foot five-inch 220-pound behemoth, was ejected from games a record four times in his seven-year stay in Japan. Ken Aspromonte, who later managed the Cleveland Indians, was the first man in the history of Japanese baseball to be fined by his manager for "conduct unbecoming a ballplayer."

Aspromonte pulled off this feat during a sojourn with the Chunichi Dragons of Nagoya back in 1965. Furious after being called out on strikes, Aspromonte stormed back to the bench, kicked over chairs and launched the inevitable attack on the water cooler. He was just doing what comes naturally to many American players, but Dragon Manager Michio Nishizawa did not enjoy the show. He yanked Aspromonte out of the game and suspended him. An incredulous Aspromonte was fined $200 and required to visit Nishizawa's home and issue a formal apology to get back in his manager's good graces.

Other Americans have followed in Aspromonte's footsteps. Ex-Giant Daryl Spencer was one of the more memorable. Like most former major leaguers, Spencer insisted on following his own training routine, and it was considerably easier than everyone else's. One night, as he was lackadaisically going through his pregame workout, his manager on the Hankyu Braves, Yukio Nishimoto, decided something had to be done.

"You don't look sharp, Spencer-*san*," he said. "You need a rest."

"What do you mean I need a rest?" Spencer growled. "Who's leading this team in home runs, anyway?"

"I don't think you can hit this pitcher," Nishimoto said.

"I can't hit him? I'm batting .340 against that guy!"

"Not tonight. That's my feeling. You're out."

That was too much for Spencer to take. He was in the dressing room changing into street clothes when he heard his name announced in the starting lineup. Nishimoto had put Spencer down as the third batter, but only because he was planning to "fool" the opposition by inserting a pinch hitter in the first inning.

Now Spencer was smoldering. When the game began and he heard the name of the second batter over the loudspeaker, he decided to get even. Clad in a pair of shorts and shower clogs, he headed for the dugout. Grabbing a bat and smirking in the direction of Nishimoto, he strode out to the on-deck circle to take a few practice swings.

Spencer's entrance delighted the fans and his picture was in all the papers the next day. Nishimoto was not amused. He ordered Spencer off the field and slapped him with a suspension and a $200 fine. Spencer paid up, later reporting with a wide grin, "It was worth every penny."

In 1972, John Miller became the first American to be released solely for his misconduct. Miller, who played briefly for the Yankees and Dodgers, arrived in Japan in 1970 and soon became the most dangerous batter on the Chunichi Dragons. He was a battler. A U.S. coach once said, "Miller is the kind of guy I'd want on my team. He'll fight you with everything he has. He doesn't know how to quit."

However, Miller wasn't the kind of guy the Japanese wanted. He was seldom on time for practice. If a workout was scheduled for 2:00 P.M., Miller would arrive at 2:10. This was more serious than it sounds, because his teammates would invariably be raring to go by 1:50.

"He always had some excuse," says a team official. "One day it would be because the traffic was heavy. Another day, he'd missed the train. He never once said he was sorry."

When reprimanded for being late, Miller responded in a most un-Oriental way. "Japanese customs are too military. I do good in the games, don't I? What else matters?"

Miller's hot temper sealed his fate as a Dragon. The coup de grace came in the twelfth inning of a big game. Miller had been slumping, and he had a bad game. He had been up four times without a hit. The fifth time, with the score tied, he was removed for a pinch hitter.

Miller blew his top. "You didn't have to take me out," he railed at his manager. "I've had it. I don't want to play for you anymore. I don't care if this team wins or not."

To Americans it would have been a fairly routine example of blowing off steam. To the Japanese, however, Miller might just as well have slit his throat. Although he later apologized and finished the year as the team leader in home runs, he was released at the end of the season. A second American on the team, Barton Shirley, who batted .190, was kept. He wasn't a battler.

Willie Kirkland, who had played for the Giants and Indians, was a happy-go-lucky sort who liked to tease his teammates. One day Kirkland was bemusedly watching an aging infielder who had recently been elevated to player-coach straining through a batting drill. "Hey, man, you're a coach now," Kirkland yelled playfully. "You don't have to practice anymore."

The player-coach took Kirland's jest as a comment on his declining usefulness, and he launched a roundhouse right that barely missed. It took half a dozen men to restrain him.

"I was just joking," Kirkland protested. "He was making fun of me," the unappeased coach retorted.

Kirkland left Japan with at least one enemy and considerable doubts about the Japanese sense of humor.

The Japanese didn't find Richie Scheinblum a barrel of laughs, either. A noted clubhouse wit in the United States, Scheinblum spent his two years as a Hiroshima Carp baiting the umpires. Shane, as he was known on the club's official roster, was frequently agitated by the plate umpire's idea of Scheinblum's strike zone. It was considerably larger than the one Shane had in mind.

Scheinblum searched for a Japanese phrase to convey his sentiments to the men in blue, something that would really get under their collective skins. A Japanese friend came to the rescue, and soon Scheinblum was saying, "You lousy Korean," to arbiters who crossed him.

There is as much love lost between Koreans and Japanese as, say, between William Buckley and Gore Vidal. To the umpires, Scheinblum's taunts were intolerable. To stop him, they imposed a stiff fine each time he uttered the dreaded epithet. When Scheinblum finally departed Japan for the last time, no cries of "Come back, Shane!" were heard—at least not from the umpires.

It wasn't until Clyde Wright came along that rules of behavior for foreigners were finally codified. Wright, a pitcher of some note with the California Angels, made his first Japanese appearance, with the Yomiuri Giants, in 1976. A self-described "farm boy" from eastern Tennessee, Wright was regarded by those who knew him in America as a tough-as-nails competitor who didn't believe in hiding his feelings.

The Giants are something of a national institution in Japan. They are the oldest team, the winningest (twelve pennants in the past fifteen years), and by a million miles the most popular. Their games, all of which are nationally televised, get high ratings, and one out of two Japanese will tell you he is a Giant fan.

Their manager, Shigeo Nagashima, is the most beloved sports figure in the land. As a player he won a Central League-record six batting titles and was personally responsible for the most exciting moment in Japanese baseball history, a game-winning (or *sayonara*) home run in the only professional game Emperor Hirohito has ever attended. Sadaharu Oh plays for the Giants.

The Giants are the self-appointed custodians of national virtue. Popular belief has it that their players are neater, better mannered, more disciplined, and more respectful than those of other clubs. Their *wa* is in better tune. In early 1977, when one writer, a former Giant player turned magazine reporter, suggested otherwise in print, he was forever banned from the team clubhouse. Among his blasphemous relevations were: (1) some Giant players did not like other players on the team; (2) a few players thought Nagashima could be a better manager; (3) some younger Giants did not especially care for the Saturday night 10:00 P.M. curfew at the team dormitory; (4) some Giant wives objected to the season-long "energy-conserving" rule forbidding them to have sexual relations with their husbands before "important" games. Tame material as far as exposés go, but to the *shoguns* of Yomiuri, the Giant name had been desecrated, and someone had to pay.

Wright also faced the difficulty of being a foreigner on a team that traditionally liked to consider itself pure-blooded—Oh's Chinese ancestry and the few closet Koreans on the Giants notwithstanding. Wright was only the second non-Oriental *gaijin* to play for the team, and the sight of a fair-skinned American in a Giant uniform was a bit unsettling to the multitudes. Wright soon gave them reason to be even more unnerved. In the sixth inning of an early-season game, with the score tied 1–1, Wright allowed the first two batters to get on base. Nagashima walked out on the field to take him out of the game. Few American managers would have removed him so abruptly. It was Nagashima's feeling, however, that Wright was getting weak, and that was that.

When Wright realized what was happening, he blew a gasket. To the horror of 50,000 fans at Tokyo's Korakuen Stadium and a Saturday night TV audience of millions, he brushed aside Nagashima's request for the ball and stalked off the mound, an angry scowl on his face. Halfway to the bench, he threw the ball against the dugout wall, cursed, and disappeared into the clubhouse.

Once inside, he kicked over a trash can, ripped off his uniform, shredded it, and flung it into the team bath. Amid a rapid-fire discharge of obscenities, he said something that the official team interpreter was able to understand: "Stupidest damn baseball I've ever seen. If this is the way the Giants treat their foreign ballplayers, I'm going. I've had it."

Nothing like this had ever happened on the Giants. Other teams had problems but not the proud *Kyojin*. No one had ever shown this much disrespect for Nagashima. Crazy Wright, as he was instantly renamed by the press, became headline news in the sports dailies the next day. Letters, telegrams, and phone calls poured into the Yomiuri offices. Outrageous! Inexcusable! Unforgivable! Wright should be sold. Released. Deported. Shot. Drawn and quartered. And not necessarily in that order.

Only Nagashima kept his cool. First, he patiently explained to his American pitcher that what he had done was not "stupid" baseball but simply the Japanese way of playing the game. It's a group effort. Then the manager faced the angry masses. There would be no disciplinary action. He was glad that Wright cared so much about winning. And he wished that some of his Japanese players would show as much fight.

Such benevolent words from the prince of Japanese baseball dissipated much of the public's antagonism toward Crazy Wright. It did not, however, pacify the front office. Management was not as eager as Nagashima-*san* to let Western ways penetrate their organization. They issued a set of ten rules of etiquette that Wright and every other American player the Giants might henceforth deem worthy of their uniform would be obliged to obey.

The Japanese press quickly gave it a name: The *Gaijin* Ten Commandments. This is how they went:

1. Obey all orders issued by the manager.
2. Do not criticize the strategy of the manager.
3. Take good care of your uniform.
4. Do not scream and yell in the dugout or destroy objects in the clubhouse.
5. Do not reveal team secrets to other foreign players.
6. Do not severely tease your teammates.
7. In the event of injury, follow the treatment prescribed by the team.
8. Be on time.
9. Do not return home during the season.
10. Do not disturb the harmony of the team.

Willie Davis, then a practicing Buddhist, thought it would be different for him. Davis was perhaps the best all-round American player ever to come to Japan. He was a seventeen-year veteran of the major leagues and a former captain of the Los Angeles Dodgers. He had been an All-Star; he could run like a deer and hit and field with a grace and skill that few American big leaguers, let alone Japanese, possessed. Even at thirty-seven, Davis could have continued to play in the United States—in fact, he has been a pinch hitter for the Angels this season—but when the chance to go to Japan came in 1977, he took it. Not for the money ($100,000), he insisted, but "for the good of baseball."

Davis was a product of his times, of America's "quest for meaning." While others were exploring the wonders of Transactional Analysis, est, and the like, Davis was a devout member of the *Soka Gakkai*, the Nichiren Buddhist sect that had America chanting. Because Japan was the birthplace of the *Soka Gakkai*, Davis assumed he would be right at home. It was a misguided assumption.

The religion's sacred chant, *namu Myoho renge-kyo*, was an important part of Davis's daily life. He did it faithfully, because it brought him inner peace. When he joined the Dragons, he naturally continued this practice—in the morning, at night, in his room, in the team bath, and on the team bus. When not intoning the chant himself, he would play tapes of it on a portable cassette recorder.

Davis reasoned that the chanting would be music to his teammates' ears. Instead, it drove them nuts. They complained: there was no peace and quiet on the team; they couldn't sleep. The incantatory chant that supposedly would bring inner harmony to anyone who regularly intoned it was rapidly eroding the Dragons' collective *wa*

What particularly annoyed the Japanese players was Davis's locker-room chanting. Before each game, he would pull out his beads, and off he'd go. *"Namu Myoho renge-kyo, namu Myoho renge-kyo, namu Myoho renge-kyo."*

"He'd pray that he'd do well, that the team would win, and that nobody would get hurt," his manager, a Japanese-Hawaiian named Wally Yonamine, says, "but it gave the others the feeling they were at a Buddhist funeral."

When the game began, Davis was a ball of fire—at least during the first half of the season. He was by far the most feared Dragon hitter, and on the base paths he displayed a flair the Japanese had never seen before. Nonetheless, the team was in last place. Key players were injured, and the pitching was subpar. Team *wa* was out of whack, and many Dragons blamed their American Buddhist for it.

It was more than the chanting, which Davis soon modified to please his teammates. There was, for example, the matter of his personal attire. Davis liked his Dragon training suit so much he had half a dozen made in different colors. He wore them in public, agitating club executives, who felt Davis was tarnishing the team's dignified image.

Davis would sometimes practice in stocking feet, and he once appeared for a workout with his comely wife, who was wearing hot pants and who jogged with him on the field. "It's so . . . so unprofessional," one sportswriter observed. "Davis is destroying our team's spirit in training," grumbled a player. "We can't concentrate on what we're doing."

Several players complained that Davis had special privileges. They referred to him as "Davis, the King," and as "Davis, our precious black *gaijin*."

Yonamine was caught in the middle. "I'd try to tell them not to worry about it," he says. "Forget about how much money a man makes or how little he practices. What he does in the game is all that counts." Few Dragons were willing to accept that piece of American advice.

Davis's biggest liability was his gregariousness. "People didn't understand him," says a team official. "He was loud. He'd get excited. He'd yell a lot and wave his arms. It was all in English, and people didn't have the faintest idea what he was saying, but it looked as though he was arguing."

Once he reproached a teammate for not attempting to score on a play that Davis had initiated. "Why didn't you try for home?" Davis shouted. That was the wrong thing to do, because the player was not only the team captain but also a playing *coach*. In Japan, a player does not yell at a coach, much less question his judgment.

In August 1977, when Davis had 25 home runs and a .306 batting average, he broke a wrist in a collision with the outfield fence. It put him out for the year. The Dragons immediately went on a winning streak. During the last two months of the season they had the best record in the league and missed finishing second by a hair.

"It's our pitching," Yonamine insisted. But if you listened to Dragon supporters and students of Japanese baseball, it was all because the team *wa* had been restored.

"I knew Willie as well as anyone,," says Lefebvre, a teammate of Davis's on the Dodgers. "He had his quirks, but then we all do. He was named captain, and you're not chosen captain of a team like the Dodgers if you're a troublemaker. If you can't get along with Willie, you don't belong on a baseball team."

The Dragon front office apparently felt that it was Davis who didn't belong on a baseball team—at least not theirs. They traded him, and at the start of the following season the most exciting player ever to wear a Chunichi Dragon uniform was laboring in the backwaters of Fukuoka, contemplating the infinite and subtle mysteries of *wa* in between playing for the lowly Crown Lighter Lions.

Of course, not every American who comes to Japan wreaks havoc on his new team. There have been some, notably Felix Millan, Clete Boyer, and George Altman, who did their best to please their Japanese hosts. In turn, the Japanese liked them, describing their demeanor as being *majime*. It means serious, sober, earnest, steady, honest, faithful. They did everything that was asked of them. They kept their mouths shut, their feelings to themselves.

Some, like Boyer, paid a substantial price for the goodwill they engendered. The former Yankee fielding whiz had three reasonably good seasons for the Taiyo Whales, but in his fourth year, when he began to reach the end as a player, he ran smack up against the cultural wall.

Boyer decided that he needed to be used more sparingly, and he asked the club to rest him every third game. "I hit in the first two, but then I get tired," he explained. "I'd do a better job with an extra day off."

The team trainer argued that what Boyer needed was not more rest but more training. Because he was older, the trainer reasoned, Boyer would have to work harder to keep up with the others. The team owner, after considering the probable reaction of the fans to an $80,000-a-year *gaijin* sitting on the bench a third of the time, agreed with the trainer. Boyer reluctantly acquiesced. In an effort to keep his energy level up, he took massive vitamin injections and worked very hard. Still, he finished the season hitting .230 and then retired to coaching. His goodwill, of course, remained intact.

Lefebvre, too, obeyed all the rules, yet he ended up incurring the largest fine in Japanese baseball history. His manager on the Lotte Orions, Masaichi Kaneda, Japan's only 400-game winner and the "God of Pitching," had personally recruited and signed Lefebvre—to a multiyear contract worth $100,000 a year—and had predicted that Lefebvre would win the Triple Crown. Lefebvre hit only .265 with 29 home runs his first season. Hampered by a leg injury, he fared even worse in succeeding years.

Kaneda was so embarrassed that he resorted to open ridicule of his "star" in an effort to regain lost face. Once, after Lefebvre had committed a particularly damaging error, Kaneda apologized to the other players for the American's "poor play." Another time, after a similar misplay, Kaneda temporarily relegated his *gaijin* to a farm team.

Lefebvre tried logic in appealing to Kaneda. "Look, you won four hundred games, right?" he said. "That makes you the winningest pitcher in Japanese history, right?"

"Right," Kaneda proudly replied.

"You also lost 250 games, didn't you?"

"Yes."

"Then that also makes you the losingest pitcher in Japanese history."

"Yes, but . . ."

"But what? Don't you see? Even the greatest in the game have bad times. Give me a break, will you?"

But Kaneda kept up the pressure. And the unhappy Lefebvre endured it until his fifth season. After being summarily removed from the lineup in the middle of an important game, Lefebvre finally lost control. Walking back to the bench, he threw his glove at the dugout wall, producing a rather loud *whack*.

Kaneda, sitting nearby, assumed that Lefebvre had thrown the glove at him. He sprang to his feet and raised his fists. "You want to fight me?" he yelled. Lefebvre, who saw his playing career rapidly coming to an end, anyway, stepped forward to meet the challenge. Coaches intervened, but after the game Kaneda levied a $10,000 fine against his American "troublemaker" and suspended him.

"It was a big game, and I wanted to stay in it," says Lefebvre, "but what made me even madder was the way Kaneda took me out. He waited until I'd finished my infield warm-ups; then he came and waved me out. That's embarrassing. But I certainly wasn't trying to throw the glove at him. It missed him by *five* feet."

Kaneda wasn't interested in Lefebvre's version of the incident. If he had misunderstood his *gaijin*'s intentions, perhaps others on the team had, as well. What would they think if it appeared that the "God of Pitching" tolerated that sort of behavior?

Refused a private audience with Kaneda, Lefebvre took his case to the public. He called a press conference. Yes, he had lost his temper. That he regretted. But, no, he was not guilty as charged. A standard fine of 50,000 yen (about $250) he could understand. But there was no way he would pay the outrageous sum of $10,000. There was no way he *could* pay it. Kaneda was just getting back at him for his failure to win the Triple Crown. Or Kaneda was making him the scapegoat for everything else that was wrong on the team. Or perhaps Kaneda was simply taking this opportunity to demonstrate his skills as a "*gaijin* tamer." Whatever the reason, Lefebvre wasn't going to take it all lying down.

When Kaneda heard that he was being openly opposed, he called his own press conference and vowed that Lefebvre would "never, ever, again wear the uniform of the Lotte Orions."

Lefebvre was in limbo for weeks while the coaching staff and management covertly worked to find a solution. At one stage they suggested secretly dropping the fine but making an announcement that Lefebvre had paid it. As long as Kaneda, and his public, didn't know the truth, they concluded, Kaneda's ego and image would suffer no damage. Lefebvre refused. He had his own ego and his own image to worry about. He appealed to a highly placed baseball official in the United States, whom he refuses to identify. The official made a call to Kaneda, and the next day the fine was quietly dropped. Lefebvre was allowed to put his uniform back on.

In the eighteen years since Don Newcombe and Larry Doby became the first ex-major leaguers to play in Japan, not a season has passed without a controversial incident involving a *gaijin* player. Last year's "villain," for example, was a former San Diego reserve infielder named John Sipin, who twice during the season took exception to deliveries apparently aimed at his person and engaged the offending pitcher in hand-to-hand combat. After the second melee Sipin was hit with a three-day suspension, fined 100,000 yen ($500), and castigated by the press for his "barbaric" behavior. One sports-page editorial likened his conduct to that of a *yakuza* (Japanese gangster), while another called Sipin a throwback to the days of the U.S. military occupation when, to hear some Japanese tell it, American GIs regularly roamed the streets, beating up on the local citizenry.

"If Sipin doesn't want to get hit by the ball," said one commentator, "he should jump out of the way. There is no place for fighting on the field." In the face of such reasoning, Sipin had no recourse but to acknowledge his sins and promise to mend his ways.

Japanese team officials have understandably grown weary of the perennial conflicts wrought by their foreign imports and in recent years have tried to be more selective in signing Americans. Character investigations have become a standard part of the recruiting process, and more and more managers are going for those quiet, even-tempered types who keep their feelings to themselves and fit into the Japanese system. The 1979 crop of twenty-four *gaijin* (there is a limit of two per team) is the most agreeable, mildest-mannered group of foreign players ever to play in Japan. It includes Wayne Garrett, Felix Millan, Lee Stanton, and Carlos May, as well as a number of unknowns who never quite made it in the majors. There is even an American manager, Don Blasingame. Collectively they are so subdued that one American player's wife says, "This is the best-behaved bunch of ballplayers I've ever been around, either here or in the States. I just can't believe it."

Garrett, a former Met, is so obliging that he agreed to get up at 7:30 and join his teammates in their daily "morning walk." Stanton, late of the Angels and Mariners, amicably allowed the Hanshin Tiger batting coach to change his batting style. May, an ex-White Sox and Yankee, is so low-key that some fans can't believe he's American.

Millan, a former Brave and Met, has been the quintessence of propriety. When he arrived last spring for his second year as a Taiyo Whale, he politely refused an offer to let him train as he wished and instead endured all the rigors of a Japanese preseason camp with his teammates. When he was benched on Opening Day, he sat quietly in the dugout, a shy smile on his face, intently watching the action. When he got his chance to play a week later, he went 4-for-4, won his spot back, and of late has been leading the league with a .354 average.

Davey Hilton, a former Padre, is setting new highs in cross-cultural "understanding." Last year's Central League All-Star second baseman and a hero of the Japan Series, he undertook an off-season weight-training program and arrived in camp this season a proud 20 pounds heavier. He was immediately accused by his suspicious manager of loafing during the winter, reprimanded for being "overweight," and told to reduce. A few days later he developed a sore arm and asked permisison to ease up in fielding practice. He was coldly informed that no one got special treatment and was cautioned not to let his American head get too big for his Japanese cap. To top things off, after getting only two hits in his first three games of the season, he was benched and was ordered to take extra batting practice and to alter his batting stance. Through it all Hilton remained calm. "This is Japan," he told himself. "They do things differently here." Predictably, his average began to climb. By mid-season he was over .300, out of the doghouse, and on his way to becoming an All-Star again.

Japanese observers are somewhat baffled by this outbreak of civility. One reporter speculated, "It must be the sagging dollar, the recession in the U.S. Americans have it good here, and they're afraid of losing what they have." American players, who pay both Japanese and U.S. income taxes and who wince at such Japanese prices as $50 for a steak dinner, attribute their good manners to other factors: adaptability and a new awareness of cultural differences.

Whatever the reason, the new tranquillity is certainly producing results. Americans are having their best year. Twelve of them are batting better than .300, and the affable Chuck Manuel, an ex-Minnesota sub, is leading the Pacific League in home runs despite having been sidelined for fifty-eight days with a broken jaw.

Of course, a Reggie Jackson might look down his nose at the accomplishments of Manuel and his confreres—given the smaller parks and the slightly inferior level of play in Japan. But with his stormy background it is doubtful that Jackson-*san*, in spite of his considerable abilities, will ever be invited to come over and prove he can do better.

America's poet expounded on America's game in this little-known June 18, 1858, editorial from the Brooklyn *Daily Times*. (For calling it to my attention, thanks to Jim Carothers.) But these were not Whitman's only published words on the national pastime: in the 1855 edition of *Leaves of Grass* appears the line "Upon the race-course, or enjoying picnics or a good game of base-ball"; and in the Brooklyn *Eagle* of July 23, 1846 (only one month after the Knickerbockers' first match game!), he wrote: "In our sun-down perambulations, of late, through the outer parts of Brooklyn, we have observed several parties of youngsters playing 'base,' a certain game of ball." By the way, in the box score you'll note a heading "H.L."—this signifies "Hands Lost," or outs made at bat or on the base paths; you'll also note Pierce at shortstop for the Atlantics—this is Dickey Pearce, profiled earlier in this volume by Sam Crane.

WALT WHITMAN

On Baseball, 1858

Base Ball

The game played yesterday afternoon between the Atlantic and Putnam Clubs, on the grounds of the latter club, was one of the finest and most exciting games we ever witnessed. The Atlantics beat their opponents by four runs, but the general opinion was that the defeat was as much the result of accident as of superior playing.

On the fourth innings the Putnams made several very loose plays and allowed their opponents to score nine runs, and those careless plays were sufficient to lose them the game. On every other innings, they played carefully and well, as the score will show. They were also particularly unfortunate in having three of their men injured in the course of the game. Mr. Master, their catcher, being disabled from occupying his position on the fifth innings, was compelled to take the first base and his place taken by Mr. Burr, who in his turn was disabled on the seventh innings and his place supplied by Mr. McKinstry, the fielder, Mr. Burr taking the third base. Mr. Jackson was injured on the eighth innings so much as to be compelled to discontinue playing, and Mr. Ketcham was substituted in his stead, so that at one time no less than three men on the Putnam side were so seriously injured as to be unable to run their bases. Notwithstanding these accidents, however, the score is highly creditable to the Putnams (always excepting the fourth innings), and we doubt if any other club can show a better one in a contest with such opponents. The Atlantics, as usual, played splendidly and maintained their reputation as the *Champion Club*. Messrs. M. O'Brien, P. O'Brien, Boerum, Pierce, and Oliver of that club cannot easily be surpassed in their respective positions. Messrs. Master, Gesner, and McKinstry, of the Putnam Club, also deserve special commendation.

The score is as follows:

ATLANTIC			PUTNAM		
	H.L.	Runs		H.L.	Runs
Price, 1st base	3	3	Burr, field	2	2
M. O'Brien, ptchr.	4	2	Meserole, field	4	2
Boerum, catchr.	3	2	Dakin, ptchr.	5	0
Mann, 3d base	3	2	Kelly, 1st base	5	0
P. O'Brien, field	2	2	Gillespie, 3d base	2	2
Pierce, short	4	0	Gesner, 2d base	2	2
Oliver, 2d base	4	2	Master, catchr.	3	1
Hamilton, field	1	3	Jackson, field	2	2
Ireland, field	3	1	McKinstry, short	2	2
		17			13

RUNS EACH INNINGS

Atlantics:—1st, 1; 2d, 1; 3d, 1; 4th, 9; 5th, 2; 6th, 1; 7th, 1; 8th, 0; 9th, 1 = 17.
Putnam:—1st, 0; 2d, 0; 3d, 2; 4th, 0; 5th, 1; 6th, 2; 7th, 6; 8th, 2; 9th, 0 = 13.
[June 18, 1858]

This good-humored grab bag of baseball bits reflects the serious interest of a serious fan and the love of a conservative man for a conservative game. A football fan (Andy Rooney, say) might accuse baseball of being old-fashioned; a baseball fan would heartily concur, adding that archaism in the defense of virtue is no vice. Sidelight: I now know that I am not the only father to have rendered "Take Me Out to the Ball Game" *sotto voce* at my children's bedtime.

GEORGE F. WILL

Don't Beep in My Outfield

It has been said that baseball is to the United States what revolutions are to Latin America, a safety valve for letting off steam. I think baseball is more serious than any Latin American revolution. But, then, I am a serious fan.

How serious? I like *Sports Illustrated*'s baseball issue even more than its swimming-suit issue. I would sell my soul for the thrill of hearing a manager say of me what Joe DiMaggio's manager said when asked if DiMaggio could bunt. The manager said he didn't know and "I'll never find out, either." The last words my four-year-old daughter hears at night are ". . . at the old ball game." (On the "as the twig is bent" principle, my parenting involves the use of "take me out to the ball game" as a lullaby.) I have one son who even knows the names of the first-base coaches. That is like knowing the name of the secretary of commerce. I have told my other son that if he can hit a slider when he is sixteen he can quit school. I believe in incentives, and Rogers Hornsby, who said: "Don't read, it'll hurt your eyes." So much for my credentials, okay? Now, listen up. The Japanese have gone too far.

Gadget

I am not talking, as everyone else is, about how crummy the Japanese are being about American exports. I am talking about a Japanese export, another electronic gadget. It is a sonar system that beeps to warn an outfielder chasing a fly ball that he is approaching the fence. My objection is not that the technology is Japanese. My nationalism stops short of that of the Cub pitcher who, when asked if he threw spitballs or otherwise violated the rule against doctoring the ball with foreign substances, replied: "I don't put any foreign substance on the baseball. Everything I use on it is from the good ole U.S.A." My objection to talking fences is not patriotic but aesthetic.

The thought of beeping fences intrudes jarringly on April, a month of buds and box scores. The philosopher in us is consoled by the thought that, although ours is an age of dizzying flux, baseball retains a healthy Luddite hostility to modernity. But already some degenerate teams are using infernal machines, rather than honest manual labor with a fungo bat, to propel balls for fielding practice. And now beeping fences? If this insensate lust for high-tech baseball does not abate, baseball will become as bad as—this is harsh, but it must be said—football.

That football fans have coarse characters and frayed moral fibers cannot be a matter of mere chance. The explanation has something to do with a fact noted here before: football combines two grim features of American life, violence and committee meetings (huddles). It also has something to do with football's lunatic fascination with technology. The coaches stalk the sidelines wired up like astronauts so they can talk to the assistant coaches with whom they have spent the previous six days doing computer analysis of game films. The NFL is even considering "helmet radios" so that quarterbacks calling plays at the line of scrimmage can be heard clearly by receivers.

Baseball's emphasis in not on machinery, it is on mind, although some players modestly deny this. Bill Lee, Red Sox pitcher, said: "When cerebral processes enter into sports, you start screwing up. It's like the Constitution, which says separate church and state. You have to separate mind and body." Rot. Baseball's emphasis on mind accounts for its fine sense of moral nuance, as in the batter who, after being brushed back by a pitch, said: "They shouldn't throw at me. I'm the father of five or six kids." Mind, in the form of mastery of facts, is also required of baseball fans.

Martin Nolan, who edits the editorial page of the Boston *Globe* but is not otherwise dangerous, is a typical fan. The highlight of his life was when he walked into a saloon and answered that day's question: name the only player active when Ruth hit his last home run and Aaron hit his first (Phil Cavaretta). Heinie Groh boasted that he held the record among non-Yankee, non-switch-hitting third basemen for playing in the most World Series with the largest number of different teams. Ah, but somewhere out in this broad land there is a young right-handed non-switch-hitting third baseman with visions of the glory that will be his when he breaks Groh's record. As baseball folks say (stop me if you've heard this), records are made to be broken. Or, as Yogi Berra wired Johnny Bench when Bench broke Yogi's career record for home runs by a catcher, "I always thought the record would stand until it was broken."

Cash

One baseball scholar whose mind may have snapped assures me that Harry Chiti, who was a catcher, sort of, holds this record: he is the only player ever traded for himself. Detroit traded him to the Mets for cash and a player to be named later. The Mets looked him over and designated him the player to be named later. Chiti was, of course, an ex-Cub. Before the Cubs attained their current grandeur, Cubness was the subject of a quiz compiled by a sadist and sent to masochists like me: (1) What Cub slugger dislocated his shoulder carrying his suitcase down to the hotel lobby? (2) Why was it bad that Cub pitcher Bill Hands recorded fourteen straight strikeouts? (3) What Cub batter holds the major-league record for leaving the most runners stranded on base in a nine-inning game? (4) What Cub right fielder, trying to throw a runner out at the plate, beaned the bat boy? (5) Cub catcher Cuno Barragon hit a homer in his first major league at bat. How many did he hit in his career? (6) The Cubs once set a major-league record by scoring five times in the bottom of the eleventh inning. Who won? (7) The Cubs once blew a 13–2 lead and lost on a home run. Who hit it? (8) The Cubs scored twenty-two runs and lost on a home run. Who hit it? You could look it up. But you only need to look below.

Last week baseball posed, for this fan and other Tories, a metaphysical puzzle. It expanded the league championship series from best-of-five to best-of-seven games. This puts in conflict two principles that are moral absolutes. One is: the more baseball the better. The other is: everywhere, but especially in baseball, change is deplorable. Well, some absolutes are more absolute than others, and the former principle is absoluter.

Answers: 1. Dave Kingman. 2. He did it as a batter. 3. Glen Beckert. 12. 4. Mike Vail. 5. One. 6. The Mets, who scored six in the top of the inning. 7 and 8. Mike Schmidt.

Ted Williams's relations with the press—notably the hometown reporters, and most notable among these, Dave Egan—ranged from rancid to rabid. So when he made his farewell speech to Fenway fans on September 26, 1960 (prior to the game, which he capped with a home run in his final at bat), he couldn't resist one last jab: "Despite the fact of the disagreeable things that have been said of me—and I can't help thinking about it—by the knights of the keyboard out there [tilting his head up toward the press box], baseball has been the most wonderful thing in my life." And Williams was the most wonderful hitter anyone under the age of fifty ever saw. In this opening section of his autobiography, *My Turn at Bat*, he gets a lesson in press relations from the world's greatest athlete.

TED WILLIAMS

Jousting with the Knights of the Keyboard

I'm glad it's over. Before anything else, understand that I am glad it's over. I'm so grateful for baseball—and so grateful I'm the hell out of it as a player. This business of managing the Washington Senators might yet prove a terrible mistake, but it's a new course, and I'm excited about it. I certainly do not have a youth wish. I mean, I wouldn't go back to being eighteen or nineteen years old, knowing what was in store, the sourness and the bitterness, knowing how I thought the weight of the damn world was always on my neck, grinding on me. I wouldn't go back to that for anything. I wouldn't *want* to go back. I've got problems now. I've always been a problem guy. I'll always have problems. But I'm grateful that part of my life is over.

I wanted to be the greatest hitter who ever lived. A man has to have goals—for a day, for a lifetime—and that was mine, to have people say, "There goes Ted Williams, the greatest hitter who ever lived." Certainly nobody ever worked harder at it. It was the center of my heart, hitting a baseball. Eddie Collins used to say I lived for my next turn at bat, and that's the way it was. If there was ever a man born to be a hitter, it was me. As a kid, I wished it on every falling star: please, let me be the hitter I want to be.

I remember the first time I saw Carl Yastrzemski, a youngster in the Red Sox batting cage a few years ago, and how much he reminded me of myself at that age—I mean he positively *quivered* waiting for the next pitch. And I have to think there was nobody who had any more opportunity than I did, along with the God-given physical attributes and the intense desire. Almost always the first at the ballpark, almost always the last to leave. I'm talking about from a kid on. I have to laugh now at my last five or six years in Boston, how I just wanted to get in and get out, to beat the crowds, to get it over with.

I should have had more fun in baseball than any player who ever lived. I played in what I think was baseball's best-played era, the years just before World War II, and then the real booming years, 1946 through the early '50s. We were always fighting for a pennant; we played before the biggest crowds. I won batting championships and home-run championships and Most Valuable Player Awards, and when it was all over, I made the Hall of Fame. I had people around who encouraged me—a real hitter's manager like Joe Cronin, who would sit around the clubhouse for hours talking hitting, and I always loved that, and Joe McCarthy, who in my mind was the best of managers.

I played before the greatest fans in baseball, the Boston fans, and I know what you're going to say about *that*: Old Teddy Ball Game loved those fans, all right. He spat at them and made terrible gestures and threw a bat that conked a nice old lady on the head one day, and he never tipped his hat to their cheers. And you would be right. But there came a time when I knew, I *knew*, they were for me and how much it meant to me, and I will get into that later. As for tipping my hat, I did my first year but never afterward. I couldn't, not if I played another twenty years. I just couldn't. I was fed up for good with that part of the act.

Certainly baseball doesn't owe me anything, a not too well educated, not particularly smart guy who played probably the only game in which he could excel. And *to* excel, to participate, to see things, to have a few material things, I'm grateful for all that. I think at the same time I've taken a lot of undue abuse. My twenty-two years in baseball were enjoyable, but many times they were unhappy, too. They were unhappy because I was in a shell an awful lot. I felt a lot of people didn't like me. I did things I was ashamed of, and sorry for, and yet know in my heart I would do again under the circumstances, because that was me. I felt—I *know*—I was not treated fairly by the press, and I'm not going to go soft on that now. And I'm not going to say the Boston management did not deserve part of the blame for those bad relations, because it did, especially when I was a young player, when I needed and should have had some protection, some common meeting ground to head these things off before they got worse, which they always did.

Oh, I hated that Boston press. I've outlived the ones who were really vicious, who wrote some of the meanest, most slanderous things you can imagine. I can *still* remember the things they wrote, and they still make me mad: how I was always trying to get somebody's job—the manager's, the general manager's, the guy's in the radio booth—and I never coveted another man's job in my life. Or how I didn't hit in the clutch and yet drove in more runs per time at bat than anybody who ever played this game except Babe Ruth and got on base more times per at bat than anybody, *including* Babe Ruth. I was a draft dodger. I wasn't a "team" man. I was "jealous." I "alienated" the players from the press. I didn't hit to left field. I took too many bases on balls. I did this, I did that. And so on. And so unfair.

I remember the time I broke my elbow in 1950. I'd had one of my best years in 1949. I batted .343, I hit 43 home runs, I drove in 159 runs, I was voted Most Valuable Player in the league, and gee, we missed winning the pennant on the very last day. I had started 1950 like it was going to be an even better year for me. I felt great. Then in the All-Star Game, first inning, Ralph Kiner hit one deep into left center in Comiskey Park. I ran a long way and caught it and crashed the fence with my elbow. I didn't know then how serious it was. The elbow swelled up, and there was pain, but I played seven more innings and even got a single in the fifth inning to put the American League ahead, 4–3. Later they X rayed and found that I had broken thirteen little chips off the head of the radius, and they were talking about taking out the whole thing, which would have finished me for good, but they managed to make a repair.

This *has* to be the greatest disappointment of my career, because as time went on and my arm never completely came around, I knew I would never again be the hitter I was. It was two months before I played again. I could barely straighten the elbow. To this day I have trouble with it. But the Red Sox were anxious for me to get started because we were hot in the pennant race. I went back into the lineup. It was a mistake, because I wasn't ready. For two weeks I hit like an old woman. I was miserable. I wanted to play, but I wasn't doing the club any good. We lost in the last week to the Yankees, and do you know what they wrote in Boston? They wrote, "The Red Sox do better without Williams." That's the kind of writers they were.

There's no doubt, of course, that things got started and grew worse partly because of my temperament, because of my emotional, explosive nature. I have never been regarded especially as a man with great patience. Certainly as a young player I had none at all with myself. I was impetuous; I was tempestuous. I blew up. Not acting but *reacting*. I'd get so damned mad, throw bats, kick the columns in the dugout so that sparks flew, tear out the plumbing, knock out the lights, damn near kill myself. *Scream*. I'd scream out of my own frustration.

There was the time in Minneapolis. I've still got the scars on my wrist. It was 1938, the year before I went up to the Red Sox, and to appreciate how intense I was, you have to remember that it was a year any nineteen-year-old kid ballplayer would love to have had. I led the American Association in everything—runs, average, RBIs, homers, everything. I had a wonderful manager, Donie Bush, who put up with me. The town was mine, and I loved it.

Anyway, Lloyd Brown was pitching for St. Paul, a tough little pitcher with a good curve. I got him to 3 and 1 in the first inning, bases loaded, short right-field fence. Now he has to come in with the fastball. He does. Right there. Perfect. If I'd gotten that much more bat on the ball, it would have gone 440 feet, but I hit just under it and popped it up, and the St. Paul first baseman reached over the boxes and made a hell of a play. Boy, I'm mad now.

I go back to the bench, this little wooden bench, little cracker-box dugout in Minneapolis, and I'm so mad I don't know what to do. I sit down, and here's this big water cooler right there next to me. About half full of water. And I just can't contain myself. *Whoomph, kerr-rash.* I hit it with my fist. They must have thought a cannon had gone off in the dugout. It just exploded. Blood's flying, glass, everything. Well, I was lucky I didn't cut my hand off. There was one cut that went pretty deep and just missed a nerve. You don't have to cut very much there to do real damage. I could have ended my career before it started. As it was, it wasn't even bad enough to take me out of the game. But that shows you how intense I was.

I was never able to be dispassionate, to ignore the things people said or wrote or implied. It just wasn't in me. In my heart I don't believe I am any more sensitive to criticism than a lot of athletes, but I am certainly in the upper bracket of sensitivity, maybe the top 3 percent. In a crowd of cheers I could always pick out the solitary boo. I don't mean to say that criticism affected my hitting, because the boos always seemed to have the reverse effect. My last real outstanding season was in 1957, when, as an old man pushing forty, I hit .388. I spent the season being mad at the world for one reason or another. I don't think I said two words to the Boston writers all year. That hardly made life pleasant.

I read recently where Joe DiMaggio said that he felt the Yankees always tried to win without him. There had never been anything written like that; he just sensed it. So Joe's got to be a sensitive guy, too. And there he was in New York with the grandest press support in the world—because the Yankees won.

And there I was in Boston, where there must be more newspapers per capita than any place in the world, with writers vying for stories, all trying to outdo the others, all trying to get a headline, all digging into places where they had no business being. They—one of them—sent a private detective to San Diego in 1942 to find out if I really did support my mother. They went out into the street to take a "public opinion" poll on my parental qualifications in 1948 when I happened to be in Florida fishing when my daughter Bobby Jo was born—*prematurely.* That type of thing.

Well, I had been a fresh kid. I did a lot of yakking, partly to hide a rather large inferiority complex. When somebody asked a question, I answered it. Never very coy, never very diplomatic. As a result, I would get myself in a wringer. I'd say to myself, Damn, I wish I hadn't said that, or said it that *way,* and sure as hell when I pick up the paper it's even worse than I thought.

There were people, friends of mine, even writers in other cities who I liked, always telling me to try harder, and I'll tell you a story. I was demonstrating fly casting at the Sportsman's Show in New York one year, something I still do, because if I didn't make it as the greatest hitter, I'm not far from being the greatest fly caster. This was one year Jim Thorpe was on the program. Right off I was carried away with Thorpe. He looked the part of the big Indian—not the big, *big* Indian but a *big* Indian. Boy, just one look and you knew he had it. He was about sixty-five then, and I was so impressed with how quiet and

attentive he was, how he would listen to people. Here's Jim Thorpe, all-time all-time, and he'd listen to anybody. He'd smile and he'd laugh and he'd listen.

Well, Thorpe had played some in the big leagues, and somebody told him, "Look, you can help Williams. He's getting into trouble with the press, charging around like he does, and you can give him some advice. He looks up to you." So about the sixth day of the show, Thorpe took me aside for a heart-to-heart on how I should try to get along with the press.

He said, "You know, they can make it awful miserable for you, but they can make it easier for you, too. It's better to get along with 'em." He kept going on in this real easy way, and then we started talking about hitting.

I said, "How long did you play in the big leagues, Jim?"

"Oh, five-six years."

"How good a hitter were you?"

"I was a pretty good hitter. Everybody said I couldn't hit the curveball, but I hit .327 one year."

I can see I'm getting him stirred up a little bit now.

He says, "The writers were always saying I couldn't hit the curve, and not only that, one of them wrote one day, 'And Thorpe isn't very good for the team, either.'" I could see this bothered Thorpe an awful lot.

"You know," he says, "I thought about this a long time, that I wasn't a team player. And one day this writer comes into the clubhouse. I went right over to him and told him, 'I don't think that was a very fair article. I'm hitting .323. I must be hitting *something*, if I can't hit a curveball. But the thing that really hurts me is you say I'm not a team man. I'm a little upset with that.'"

Well, if you ever met Jim Thorpe, you would realize that if he was upset a little bit, he was *upset*. So he says to this writer, "What do you think you would do if somebody wrote something like that about you?"

And Thorpe said the writer answered, "Well, I guess I'd punch him in the nose."

Thorpe smiled that big Indian smile and says, "So I punched him in the nose, and down he went." We both laughed like hell.

This beautiful passage is from a letter the novelist sent to baseball writer Arthur Mann on February 16, 1938, only seven months before his death and two weeks after Mann had taken him to the annual New York dinner of the Baseball Writers Association of America. There Wolfe—who at that time was developing the character of ballplayer Nebraska Crane for his novels *The Web and the Rock* and *You Can't Go Home Again*—sat star-struck, gazing at the likes of Ruth, Wagner, Foxx, and Gehrig. Baseball and the weather of our lives—a fitting conclusion to this *Armchair Book of Baseball*.

THOMAS WOLFE

The Sound of the Ball, the Smell of Old Dry Wood

I cannot tell you how much I enjoyed the Baseball Writers' dinner and how much I think I got out of it. Not that I learned so much, but I think there was a big value in verification—in seeing the animal at first hand and in communication with his fellows. The point is, one of the characters in this immense long book that I am writing is a baseball player,* and I realize from past observation how easy it is for a writer to go wrong when writing about a professional athlete: the sporting writer, or the writer of baseball fiction, does it best of all, I think, because they put him in a certain limited setting—on the field or on the bench or at the training camp. My problem is a different one: I think I may have told you that one reason I have always loved baseball so much is that it has been not merely "the great national game" but really a part of the whole weather of our lives, of the thing that is our own, of the whole fabric, the million memories of America. For example, in the memory of almost every one of us, is there anything that can evoke spring—the first fine days of April—better than the sound of the ball smacking into the pocket of the big mitt, the sound of the bat as it hits the horsehide: for me, at any rate, and I am being literal and not rhetorical—almost everything I know about

---

* Nebraska Crane.

spring is in it—the first leaf, the jonquil, the maple tree, the smell of grass upon your hands and knees, the coming into flower of April. And is there anything that can tell more about an American summer than, say, the smell of the wooden bleachers in a small-town baseball park, that resinous, sultry, and exciting smell of old dry wood.

Book I

The editor wishes to acknowledge the following for permission to include the selections listed:

The Associated Press, "Ticket Taker Talks Technique," by Bill Doyle, copyright © 1979 The Associated Press. Reprinted with permission. Atheneum Publishers, Red Smith, excerpted from "Howard Ehmke" in *To Absent Friends*. Copyright © 1982 Atheneum Publishers, Inc. (First appeared in New York Herald Tribune, March 19, 1959). Reprinted with the permission of Atheneum Publishers, Inc. *The Atlantic Monthly*, "Pitchers and Catchers" by Moe Berg, copyright © 1941 by Moe Berg. Reprinted by permission of Samuel Berg, M.D. "A Study in Suet" from *The Hot Stove League* by Lee Allen. First published by A. S. Barnes, 1955. *Dallas Times Herald*, "The Randle Incident" by Blackie Sherrod, copyright © 1977 *Dallas Times Herald*. Delacorte Press, "No Jury Would Convict" from *Short Stories: Five Decades* by Irwin Shaw. Copyright © 1937, 1938, 1939, 1940, 1941, 1942, 1943, 1944, 1945, 1946, 1947, 1949, 1950, 1952, 1953, 1954, 1955, 1956, 1957, 1958, 1961, 1962, 1963, 1964, 1967, 1968, 1969, 1971, 1973, 1977, 1978 by Irwin Shaw. Originally published in the *New Yorker*. Reprinted by permission of Delacorte Press. Doubleday and Company, Inc., "Mr. October" from *How Life Imitates the World Series* by Thomas Boswell. Copyright © 1982 by the Washington Post Writer's Group. Reprinted by permission of Doubleday and Company, Inc. Harper and Row, Publishers, Inc., "Gallery of Buffs" from *Who Struck John?* by Jimmy Cannon. Copyright © 1956 by Jimmy Cannon. Reprinted by permission of Harper and Row, Publishers, Inc.; "Carl and Jimmy" from *The Boys of Summer* by Roger Kahn. Copyright © 1971, 1972 by Roger Kahn. Reprinted by permission of Harper and Row, Publishers, Inc.; "The Chicago Cubs, Overdue" from *The Pursuit of Happiness, And Other Sobering Thoughts* by George F. Will. Copyright © 1978 by The Washington Post Company. Reprinted by permission of Harper and Row, Publishers, Inc. Holt, Rinehart and Winston, "Richards Vidmer Remembers" from *No Cheering in the Press Box* by Jerome Holtzman, copyright © 1974 by Jerome Holtzman. Reprinted with the permission of Holt, Rinehart and Winston. Houghton, Mifflin, "Shoeless Joe Jackson Comes to Iowa" from the novel *Shoeless Joe* by W. P. Kinsella, Houghton, Mifflin, New York, 1982. Originally published as a short story by Oberon Press, Ottawa, 1980. Copyright © W. P. Kinsella 1980. *Inside Sports*, "An American Tragedy" by Ira Berkow and Murray Olderman, copyright © 1980 by Ira Berkow. Alfred A. Knopf, "Tao in the Yankee Stadium Bleachers." Copyright © 1954 by John Updike. Reprinted from *The Carpentered Hen and Other Creatures* by John Updike, by permission of Alfred A. Knopf, Inc. Little, Brown and Company, "Beans" from *Blue Highways* by William Least Heat Moon. Copyright © 1982 by William Least Heat Moon. By permission of Little, Brown and Company in association with the Atlantic Monthly Press; "Pick-up Game" from *Pride of the Bimbos* by John Sayles. Copyright © 1975 by John Sayles. By permission of Little, Brown and Company in association with the Atlantic Monthly Press; "Analysis of Baseball" from *New and Selected Things Taking Place* by May Swenson. Copyright © 1971 by May Swenson. Reprinted by permission of Little, Brown and Company in association with the Atlantic Monthly Press. Los Angeles Times Syndicate, "Did Babe Herman Triple into a Triple Play?" (*Baseball Digest*) by Jim Murray, copyright © 1973, Los Angeles Times Syndicate. Reprinted with permission. Four Winds Press, an imprint of Macmillan Publishing Company, "September 30, 1907—You Are There" from *Baseball's Ten Greatest Games* by John Thorn. Copyright © 1981 by John Thorn. Reprinted with the permission of Macmillan Publishing Company. McGraw-Hill Book Company, "Josh" from *Only The Ball Was White* by Robert Peterson, copyright © 1970 by Robert Peterson. Reprinted with the permission of McGraw-Hill Book Company. *The Nation*, "Notes on the Country Game" by Wilfred Sheed. Copyright © 1980 The Nation. Reprinted with the permission of The Nation. National Lampoon, "George Brett's Vanished and Restored Homer" by Glenn Eichler. National Lampoon May 1984. *The National Pastime*, "Ladies and Gentlemen, Presenting Marty McHale" by Lawrence Ritter. Reprinted from *The National Pastime*, volume 1, number 1. Copyright © 1982 The Society for American Baseball Research, Inc. *National Review*, "Baseball and the Meaning of Life" by Donald Hall. Copyright © 1981 by National Review, Inc., 150 East 35th Street, New York, N.Y. 10016. Reprinted with permission. New Directions Publishing Corporation, "Cobb Would Have Caught It" from *In the Rose of Time* by Robert Fitzgerald. Copyright © 1943 by Robert Fitzgerald. Reprinted by permission of New Directions Publishing Corporation. The New Republic, Inc., "Baseball? Boingball," by Eugene J. McCarthy. Reprinted by permission of *The New Republic*, copyright © 1982, The New Republic, Inc. New Yorker, "Gandhi at the Bat" by Chet Williamson. Copyright © 1983 by the New Yorker Magazine, Inc.; reprinted by permission of the author and the author's agent, James Allen. *The New York Times*, "Yankees Toss Game Away in Thirteenth," anonymous. Copyright © 1912 by The New York Times Company; "Love Me, Love My Bear" by Russell Baker. Copyright © 1981 by The New York Times Company; "Aaron Hits 715th, Passes Babe Ruth" by Joe Durso. Copyright © 1974 by The New York Times Company; "Was There Ever a Guy Like Ruth?" by John Kieren. Copyright © 1927 by The New York Times Company; "Lines Composed in Exaltation Over the North Atlantic" by James Michener. Copyright © 1980 by The New York Times Company; "My Baseball Years" by Philip Roth. Copyright © 1973 by The New York Times Company; "Out of Left Field" by William Safire. Copyright © 1981 by The New York Times Company; "Bring Back the Real Mets!" by Leonard Shecter. Copyright © 1969 by The New York Times Company. Reprinted by permission. W. W. Norton and Company, "The Devil's Due" reprinted from *The Year the Yankees Lost the Pennant* by Douglass Wallop by permission of W. W. Norton and Company, Inc. Copyright © 1954 by John Douglass Wallop. Copyright renewed 1982 by John Douglass Wallop. The Philadelphia Inquirer, "La Vie En Rose" by Pete Rose from *The Philadelphia Inquirer*, August 12, 1981. Copyright © 1981 The Philadelphia Inquirer. Reprinted with permission. Pinnacle Books, "Name Calling," reprinted by permission of Pinnacle Books, Inc., from *The Baseball Book of Lists* by Phil Pepe and Zander Hollander. Copyright © 1983 by Associated Features Inc. Random House, Inc., "JHWH" from *The Universal Baseball Association, Inc.* by Robert Coover. Copyright © 1968 by Robert Coover. Reprinted by permission of Random House, Inc.; "What Does It Take" from *The Bill James Abstract* by Bill James. Copyright © 1982 by Bill James. Reprinted by permission of Random House, a division of Random House, Inc.; "Frank Chance's Diamond" from *Ring—A Biography of Ring Lardner* by Jonathan Yardley. Copyright © 1977 Jonathan Yardley. Reprinted by permission of Random House, Inc. Scribner's Sons, Ring Lardner, "A Busher's Letters Home" from *You Know Me Al.* Copyright © 1916 Charles Scribner's Sons, copyright renewed 1944 Ellis A. Lardner. Reprinted with permission of Charles Scribner's Sons. "How Baseball Began" by Harold Seymour, Ph.D., from *The New-York*

Book II

The editor wishes to acknowledge the following for permission to include the selections listed:

"Don't Come Home a Failure," from *Ty Cobb*, by Charles C. Alexander, copyright © 1984 by Charles C. Alexander, reprinted by permission of Oxford University Press, Inc.; "The Food on the Table at the Execution" (retitled "Sandwiches at an Execution"), by Dave Anderson, copyright © 1980 by The New York Times Company, reprinted by permission of the New York *Times*; "The Interior Stadium," from *The Summer Game*, by Roger Angell, copyright © 1971 by Roger Angell, originally published in *The New Yorker*, reprinted by permission of Viking Penguin, Inc.; "Noting the Milestones," by Martin E. Appel, copyright © 1987 by Martin E. Appel, reprinted by permission of the author; "Idylls of the Kid," by Russell Baker, copyright © 1984 by The New York Times Company, reprinted by permission of the New York *Times*; "Nate Colbert's Unknown RBI Record," by Bob Carroll, from *The National Pastime*, copyright © 1982 by the Society for American Baseball Research, reprinted by permission of the publisher; "The Over-the-Hill League," by Bill Colson, *Sports Illustrated*, June 4, 1979, copyright © 1979 by Time, Inc., all rights reserved, reprinted by the permission of *Sports Illustrated*; "The Ten-Minute Collapse," by Bill Conlin, copyright © 1977 by Philadelphia Newspapers, Inc., reprinted by permission of the Philadelphia *Daily News*; "The Men Who Invented Shortstop," by Sam Crane, from the New York *Evening Journal*, 1911–1912; "Do Not Go Gentle: Talking, Talking, Talking," from *Stengel: His Life and Times*, by Robert W. Creamer, copyright © 1984 by Robert W. Creamer, reprinted by permission of Simon & Schuster, Inc.; "How I Pitched the First Curve," by Candy Cummings, from *Baseball Magazine*, September 1908; "I Am Honest, Harry," by Jim Devlin, manuscript excerpt from the Albert G. Spalding Collection, New York Public Library, also taken from *America's National Game*, copyright © 1911 by American Sport Publishing Company; "Family," from *Ragtime*, by E. L. Doctorow, copyright © 1974, 1975 by E. L. Doctorow, reprinted by permission of Random House, Inc.; "The Santo Explosion," from *Nice Guys Finish Last*, by Leo Durocher with Ed Linn, copyright © 1975 by Leo Durocher and Ed Linn, reprinted by permission of Simon & Schuster, Inc.; "Tony C, as in Courage, Comebacks, Coronary," by Ray Fitzgerald, copyright © 1982 by Globe Newspaper Co., reprinted by permission of the Boston *Globe*; "The Merkle Blunder," by G. H. Fleming, from *The National Pastime*, copyright © 1982 by the Society for American Baseball Research, reprinted by permission of the publisher; "Roger Maris," from *Dynasty*, by Peter Golenbock, copyright © 1975 by Peter Golenbock, reprinted by permission of the author; "Hero," from *The Celebrant*, by Eric Rolfe Greenberg, copyright © 1983 by Eric Rolfe Greenberg, reprinted by permission of Dodd, Mead & Company, Inc.; "Old Well-Well," by Zane Grey, from *The Red-headed Outfield and Other Stories*, copyright © 1915 by McClure Newspaper Syndicate; "Baseball's Dirty Tricks," by Stephen S. Hall, originally published in *Science '83 Magazine*, copyright © 1984 American Association for the Advancement of Science, reprinted in *Newton at the Bat*, Schrier, Allman, eds., Charles Scribner's Sons, 1984; "Henry Wiggen Goes Up," from *The Southpaw*, by Mark Harris, copyright © 1953 by Mark Harris, reprinted by permission of the author; "Hilton Smith Remembers," from *Voices of the Great Black Baseball Leagues*, by John B. Holway, copyright © 1975 by John B. Holway, reprinted by permission of Dodd, Mead & Company, Inc.; "Max Lanier Remembers," from *Baseball When the Grass Was Real*, by Donald Honig, copyright © 1975 by Donald Honig, reprinted by permission of the author and his agents, Raines & Raines; "Night Game," from *Collected Poems* by Rolfe Humphries, copyright © 1956 by Indiana University Press, reprinted by permission of the publisher; "A History of Platooning," from *The Bill James Historical Baseball Abstract*, by Bill James, copyright © 1986 by Bill James, reprinted by permission of Villard Books, a Division of Random House, Inc.; "A False Spring," from *A False Spring*, by Pat Jordan, copyright © 1973, 1974, 1975 by Pat Jordan, reprinted by permission of Dodd, Mead & Company, Inc.; "Bad-Nose Bees," by Neal Karlen, *Rolling Stone*, July 17–31, 1986, copyright © 1986 by Straight Arrow Publishers, Inc., all rights reserved, reprinted by permission; "Old Hard Hands," from *Lake Wobegon Days*, by Garrison Keillor, copyright © 1985 by Garrison Keillor, reprinted by permission of Viking Penguin, Inc.; "Remember the Black Sox?," by John Lardner, April 30, 1938, *The Saturday Evening Post*, reprinted with permission of *The Saturday Evening Post*; "Hits Are My Bread and Butter," from *Baseball as I Have Known It*, by Frederick G. Lieb, copyright © 1977 by Frederick G. Lieb, reprinted by permission of The Putnam Publishing Group; "The Bronx Zoo," from *The Bronx Zoo*, by Sparky Lyle and Peter Golenbock, copyright © 1979 by Albert "Sparky" Lyle and Peter Golenbock, reprinted by permission of Crown Publishers, Inc.; "Out at Home," by Jerry Malloy, from *The National Pastime*, copyright © 1982 by the Society for American Baseball Research, reprinted by permission of the publisher; "How a Catcher Calls